WISDEN

ON THE ASHES

WISDEN

ON THE ASHES

THE AUTHORITATIVE STORY OF CRICKET'S GREATEST RIVALRY

EDITED BY
Steven Lynch

FOREWORD BY
Sir Alec Bedser

First published in the UK in 2009 by
John Wisden & Co
An imprint of A & C Black Publishers Ltd
36 Soho Square, London W1D 3QY
www.wisden.com
www.acblack.com

"Wisden" and its woodcut device are registered trademarks of John Wisden & Co

ISBN 978 14081 0983 0

Images on pages viii, 200, 207, 241, 253, 269, 303, 317, 356, 367, 380, 408, 431, 457, 490, 559,
and 582 courtesy of Getty Images. Image on page 21 courtesy of Rupert Peploe.
All other images reproduced from the editor's private collection.

A CIP catalogue record for this book is available from the British Library.

This book is produced using paper that is made from wood grown in managed, sustainable
forests. It is natural, renewable and recyclable. The logging and manufacturing processes
conform to the environmental regulations of the country of origin.

Typeset in Minion by Palimpsest Book Production Ltd, Grangemouth, Stirlingshire
Printed in the UK by CPI William Clowes Beccles NR34 7TL

Contents

Acknowledgements

"Remember that any book always involves about twice as much work as you first think," Matthew Engel, the former *Wisden* editor told me when I agreed to try to condense the story of 316 England–Australia Test matches into one volume of reasonably sensible length. His wise words hit home forcibly about halfway through the task, as another 10,000-word tour review loomed out of the yellow pages of history. But, by wielding the computer equivalent of the red pen with Zorro like abandon (and largely ignoring my father Brian, visiting from Australia, for which I apologise), *Wisden*'s story of the Ashes did eventually fit between these reassuringly yellow covers. That it does so owes much to my colleagues Christopher Lane, Scyld Berry, Hugh Chevallier and Harriet Monkhouse of Wisden, not least for tolerating my temporary absence from an even smaller and fatter yellow book; to Charlotte Atyeo and Nicky Thompson of A&C Black, and their design team; the typesetters at Palimpsest; and, last but certainly not least, my wife Karina, who put up with my rare appearances outside the office and still supplied tea and cake, while our son Daniel also tried to help, in between trying to eat the cake. Thanks are also due to the many *Wisden* contributors over the years whose work is reprinted here, and to Sir Alec Bedser for providing such a thoughtful Foreword. Perhaps the biggest round of applause, though, should go to the successive generations of English and Australian cricketers who have made the Ashes what they are – the most famous rivalry in international sport.

Most of the illustrations are from Getty Images, with some from the editor's private collection. The photograph of the Hon. Ivo Bligh was kindly provided by his great-grandson, Rupert Peploe. The Records section was compiled by Philip Bailey.

STEVEN LYNCH

Dates to the right of the headings – often following the name of the writer – when shown refer to the edition of Wisden *in which the extract first appeared. For example, the 2005 Ashes series was covered in* Wisden 2006.

Alec Bedser: 104 wickets in 21 Ashes Tests.

Foreword

S ir Alec Bedser played in five Ashes series, playing 21 Tests and taking 104 Australian wickets. He is the only English bowler to have taken 30 or more wickets in Ashes series at home and away. After retiring as a player, he was an England selector for 13 Ashes series (plus one in which the Ashes were not at stake, and the two one-off Centenary Tests). He was also the manager for the 1974–75 and 1979–80 tours of Australia, after being the assistant manager in 1962–63.

It is a great pleasure to be asked to write this foreword, as I have had a long associa-tion with both the Ashes and *Wisden*. Indeed the Ashes has been a significant factor throughout much of my life, while *Wisden* has recorded and reported on my entire cricket career.

One of the greatest honours in my career was being selected as one of *Wisden*'s Five Cricketers of the Year in 1947. In 2007, at the dinner to launch that year's *Wisden*, I was honoured to be presented with a special leatherbound copy of the 1947 almanack to mark the 60th anniversary of my being named. As I write this foreword, my great friend and ex-Surrey and England colleague Arthur McIntyre, who was born less than two months before me in 1918, is the only Wisden Cricketer of the Year still alive who is older than me.

I think my earliest Ashes-related memory is seeing the *Evening News* when Don Bradman scored 334 at Headingley in 1930. It was unusual to have big photos in the papers in those days, let alone a cricket one, but I remember half of the front page was taken up by a photo of The Don. I had just had my 12th birthday the previous week, and seeing Bradman on the front page made a big impression on me.

Six years later I remember listening to bits of Alan McGilvray's radio commentaries of the 1936–37 Ashes series in Australia. By that time my twin brother Eric and I were set on a cricket career with Surrey, and like any young cricketer I wanted to play for England against Australia. When Australia toured in 1938 I was busy playing for Surrey's Second Eleven, so I didn't get to see any of the Tests. However, I only just missed out, as we arrived back at The Oval at the end of a West Country tour just a few hours after the final Test finished. I remember looking at the pitch which, after four days' play, was as perfect a strip as I ever saw. Hutton had made a world-record score of 364 and England had declared on 903 for 7. The groundsman, Bosser Martin, had predicted that they would get a thousand on his pitch so I remember him being upset that Wally Hammond had declared!

Eric and I made our Surrey debuts in 1939, but our careers were almost immedi-ately put on hold as we joined the RAF when war broke out. I played a little cricket in the early part of the war, including some matches at Lord's against the Australian forces, who included the great and inimitable Keith Miller. But after serving in Italy and France I arrived back at The Oval for the beginning of the 1946 season having not played at all for two years. After only ten games I made my England debut against India at Lord's. It was a dream start as I took 11 wickets in each of my first two Tests, and ended the season being selected for the winter tour of Australia.

I was one of only four men under the age of 30 on that tour, which we ended up losing 3–0. But other than the result, the whole thing was an amazing experience. We travelled there on Ministry of War transport – the *Stirling Castle* troop ship. The voyage was particularly memorable because the passengers were made up of 17 England cricketers and some 600 war brides! But our trip home was even more special, because we returned by flying boat, stopping off at numerous exotic places such as Singapore (where we stayed at the famous Raffles Hotel) and Cairo (where we landed on the Nile).

At the end of that 1946–47 series I began a remarkable run of four Ashes Tests in which I dismissed Bradman six times. In the Fourth Test I managed to bowl him for nought, which I followed up by dismissing him again in the second innings of the last Test, and then again in both innings of the first two Tests in the 1948 series (including another duck). Although we rarely spoke to each other on those tours (he didn't socialise much in his playing days), we became very close friends later, and Eric and I visited Don and his wife Jessie in Adelaide on countless occasions during the next five decades.

In 1953 we had a very strong team which famously won back the Ashes 19 years after losing them. I took 39 wickets in the five-match series, and looking back I think my career high point was at Trent Bridge in the First Test when I had match figures of 14 for 99. My last England tour as a player was to Australia in 1954–55. Unfortunately I got shingles on the way out, which laid me low for the entire tour. I played in the First Test, but was below my best and it proved to be my last in the Ashes. So it was from various pavilions that I watched Frank Tyson terrorise the Aussies while we retained the Ashes. I played my last Test for England the following summer, and I finally retired from first-class cricket at end of the 1960 season; Eric followed me into retirement a year later.

In 1961 I watched the whole of the Ashes series while writing for the *Daily Mail*. I particularly remember watching Fred Trueman's 11 wickets at Headingley, which included a spell of five for none. That series was the start of many years of watching Ashes Tests. I was assistant manager to the Duke of Norfolk on the 1962–63 tour, and was a selector right up to 1985. I was manager of the 1974–75 tour when the Australians unleashed Jeff Thomson, who terrorised our team much as Tyson had done theirs 20 years earlier. Thomson had a wonderful action, and I think he may even have been a touch quicker than Frank.

During my long stint as a selector I was chairman for eight series against Australia, as well as two one-off matches, one of which was the Centenary Test at Melbourne in March 1977. Not only was that a marvellous game (with the result almost unbelievably being the same as in the first-ever Test which it was celebrating), but it was probably the most enjoyable match I ever attended as a spectator. This was because every former Ashes player from both countries was invited as the Australian Board's guest, and it was wonderful to meet up with so many old friends. Little did we know that behind the scenes Kerry Packer was recruiting players for his breakaway "cricket circus".

Our captain in the Centenary Test, Tony Greig, turned out to be Packer's right-hand man, so the following summer we appointed Mike Brearley as captain for the 1977 Ashes, which we won 3–0. That series was notable for the return of Geoff Boycott from self-imposed exile, and the debut of a young all-rounder named Ian Botham. By 1981 Botham had become a giant of Test cricket and was England captain. But after a poor start to that summer's Ashes series, we replaced him as captain and reappointed Brearley. He seemed to inspire Botham, whose performances in the next three Tests made his legend and retained the Ashes. I never thought I would again see such euphoria about cricket as there was that summer – but I was wrong. I was present at The Oval in 2005 when England won back the Ashes after a thrilling series, and it was great to see cricket celebrated across the country.

My Ashes experiences have led to lifelong friendships with numerous Australians as well as England team-mates. I have already mentioned my close friendship with Bradman, but I also treasure my friendships with many other Aussies as well. Indeed I was thrilled when four of them (Arthur Morris, Neil Harvey, Alan Davidson and Ken Archer) flew over to England in July 2008 to attend my 90th birthday party. It was a long way for them to come, but I hope they enjoyed meeting up and sharing memories as much as I did.

As I said at the beginning, the Ashes have been a major part of my life, but I think they have been a special part of many of other lives too, not just those privileged to have taken part but also the millions who have been entertained. Cricket is fortunate to have an international contest which is the envy of all sports. The history of the Ashes is the most eventful sporting story of all, and there can be no better way to read about it than through the original words of *Wisden* which make up this splendid anthology.

ALEC BEDSER
Woking, December 2008

Introduction

"It's the Ashes!" shouted the commentator Brian Johnston on TV as England swept to victory at The Oval in 1953. His excitement probably gave a few people at the BBC heart failure, in an era when the continuity announcers still wore bow-ties, but he summed up the feelings of a nation which had beaten Australia at last after 19 long years. It was much the same in 2005, when one country rejoiced (and another growled and licked its wounds) after the most absorbing Test series of them all.

Just mention "The Ashes" to a follower of cricket and he or she is likely to drift off into a type of reverie, remembering past battles, be it 2005 or 1981 or even the Bodyline series of 1932–33, the one to which almost any devotee would ask to be transported if the Tardis magically materialised outside their door. England and Australia have done battle for the tiny little urn for well over 100 years, each having periods of dominance and each (usually England, admittedly) having periods of despair when another victory seemed about as close as landing a man on Mars.

England v Australia Test series are an ongoing soap opera, with regular instalments (now standardised at every two years or so, but it was even more frequent than that in the 1880s). The cast is refreshed every time, with old favourites being gently pushed aside by new heroes. At the time of writing it seems certain that the likes of Shane Warne, Marcus Trescothick and Glenn McGrath won't appear in the 2009 series, providing opportunities for newcomers to the pantheon. Stuart Broad? Mitchell Johnson? Ryan Sidebottom? Brad Haddin? Sooner or later, no doubt, one or more of them will carve their name in Ashes history.

The rivalry is genuine and intense, but by and large friendly, with the odd exception like Bodyline, which threatened not only to derail cricket relationships but diplomatic ones, too. The main reason for this, I believe, is the underlying comradeship of the people of England and Australia. Behind all the teasing and name-calling is a long affinity and a long friendship (even the term "Pommie bastard" is affectionate, or so my Antipodean friends assure me). Some of the early reports in *Wisden* bang on about the "Mother Country", and refer to Australia and the Australians as "the Colonies" and "Colonials". I don't think this is meant disparagingly, although it might read like that now: it was just the way people spoke and wrote at the time. Remember that Australia didn't become a separate country until 1901: until then it was a series of colonies, if fiercely proud ones. Cricket's part in uniting Australia was an important one – and the desire of Australians to beat the "Mother Country" and show that they could stand on their own feet was important, too.

The first *Wisden* almanack appeared in 1864, so it was reasonably well established by the time what has been accepted as the first Test match was played between England

and Australia at Melbourne in 1877, not that it was advertised as such. *Wisden* took a while to recognise that these games were more important than Gentlemen v Players, or Eton v Harrow, but almost from the start the almanack included detailed accounts of what eventually became known as Test matches. And that is what we have collected together here: all the *Wisden* match reports from Test matches between England and Australia – edited versions of all 316 of them from 1876–77 to 2006–07 – together with extracts from the tour reviews, relevant Editor's Notes, Cricketer of the Year essays and other Ashes-related articles. For the sake of completeness we have featured all the Tests, including the dozen or so in which the Ashes were not at stake.

There might just be some surprises along the way. I didn't know before starting this collection that another spoof obituary appeared in the press two days before the famous "Ashes" notice in the *Sporting Times* in 1882. And I hadn't realised that the credit for resurrecting the legend of the Ashes, which had been almost forgotten after the original brouhaha in 1882–83, was down to Pelham Warner, a man more commonly associated these days with his rather hapless performance as England's co-manager in the Bodyline series. There's also the Ashes Test in which they got through 15 substandard balls in the first two innings, the one where Australia declared at 32 for 7 (and won), two matches England won after following on, the series when Australia came back from 2–0 down to win 3–2, and arguably the most famous Editor's Note of all – when Sydney Pardon observed that England's selection for the 1909 Oval Test "touched the confines of lunacy".

The other aspect that leaps out from the pages is a cavalcade of cricket's greatest names. W. G. Grace pops up early on ("a capital innings from Dr Grace" was a leitmotif of early *Wisden*s), then the limelight shifts to Victor Trumper, to S. F. Barnes, to Warwick Armstrong, to Walter Hammond... and then to Don Bradman.

Bradman's achievements still boggle the mind more than 60 years after he retired. No one has ever reeled off big scores so consistently, or dominated to the same extent. It's arguable that no one has dominated any sport in the way The Don did cricket: his Test batting average of a boundary short of 100 is more than 50% better than anyone else's (60.97 is the next-best for a complete career of a decent number of innings). Those who say that Bradman had it easy because of friendly wickets, helpful laws and unscientific field-placings overlook the fact that the other fine batsmen of Bradman's time slot into what we still consider the benchmarks of a pretty good Test batsman (an average of more than 40) or a great one (more than 50). Hammond, England's pre-eminent batsman of Bradman's era, averaged 58.45, and Jack Hobbs 56.94. Bill Ponsford, the Australian who made two first-class 400s, averaged 48.22 in Tests.

Only Bradman, too, has had a whole strategy invented just to curb him. Bodyline – the practice of stacking the leg-side field with catchers and then bouncing the ball fast at the batsman's body and head – restricted Bradman to an average of "only" 56.57, and England won the Ashes easily (4–1), so it might be said to have worked, although the fuss it caused meant it was a victory achieved at considerable cost. *Wisden*'s coverage of the controversy shows up the time-lag in communications in the 1930s, compared to our instant satellite gratification. These days everyone would have seen for themselves exactly what the tactics were, and had them explained by a chorus line of former Test players. But in 1933 *Wisden*'s editor Stewart Caine was still sure "that English bowlers, to dispose of their opponents, would of themselves pursue such methods or that Jardine would acquiesce in such a course is inconceivable". He did, however, admit that the matches had to be "described largely from cabled reports and hearsay evidence", a handicap we don't have nowadays when sometimes – as with Dennis Lillee and Jeff Thomson in 1974–75 – the bowling has looked to be more Bodyline-ish even than what Harold Larwood and Bill Voce served up in 1932–33. *Wisden* had caught up by 1934, when the new editor Sydney Southerton wrote a balanced and defining article condemning Bodyline.

Don Bradman remained the focal point of the Ashes story until his retirement in 1948. Soon after that came Johnston's outburst at The Oval, when England beat a Don-less Australia to win back the Ashes, starting a brief period of dominance that included Jim Laker's astonishing 19-wicket haul at Old Trafford in 1956. And the Ashes survived the colourless 1960s and lived through the colourful '70s, saw off the challenge of World Series Cricket, and established itself once again as cricket's marquee series in 1981, with another epic rubber, this one dominated by Ian Botham.

Botham, now a knight of the realm as well as a blunt TV commentator, was a central figure in 1985 and 1986–87, too, before his mate Allan Border ushered in a period of Aussie supremacy in 1989. Border, Mark Taylor and Steve Waugh presided over eight successive series victories, which was either amazing or appalling, depending on which hemisphere you came from. By 2005, though, what people in England and Australia craved was an exciting series, to rekindle the Ashes. The essence of a decent rivalry is that both sides are in contention and that the matches are close, and successive series which were over by about halfway did not fit the bill. All but the most one-eyed of Australian fans wanted a good battle. And what transpired was better than anyone can have expected: *Wisden* had no hesitation in dubbing the 2005 Ashes the Greatest Test Series of all, and devoted a special section to it. But pride comes before a fall, they say, and the 2006–07 rematch – the last series covered in this book – was a contender for Worst Series. Good or bad, it all goes into the Ashes melting pot.

Collating all the material for this book has been a pleasure – and sometimes a bit of a pain. Some of the early reports were too long, while others were too short or almost non-existent: in 1885 the Editor apologised for not carrying much information on the previous year's Ashes series, pointing out that full details had been printed in another book, "whereas no other annual has appeared... in which so much space is devoted to the leading Counties, the Universities, the Gentlemen of Philadelphia and the MCC." The 2005 Editor fortunately chose not to follow this lead. Early on, it seems, time was – literally – of the essence: many reports carried exhaustive details of exactly when Dr Grace went in, or when Ulyett or Mr Murdoch or Briggs was out. For the sake of space – and readers' attention spans – I had to remove some of this sort of thing, and also usually cut out details of who had been left out of a particular Test squad, unless it seemed of particular importance.

I tried wherever possible not to tinker with the wording of the pieces, preferring to retain the period feel of the language, but I have occasionally inserted the odd comma into pieces where they originally seem to have been mysteriously banned. The major changes have been in the length of some of the articles, especially the tour reviews, which have grown and grown over the years and these days often weigh in at around 5,000 words – too long for a work like this. I have tried to shorten them sympathetically, leaving in details of the important figures of each series. The same goes for match reports. If anyone feels deprived, or wishes to find out more about a specific tour, the unexpurgated reports and articles can be found in the Archive section of our website, www.wisden.com.   STEVEN LYNCH

Early Days:
1876-77 to 1882

It should be borne in mind that the early encounters between sides representing England and Australia were more business ventures than international sporting contests. The very first tour of Australia by an English cricket team, in 1861–62, had only taken place because the sponsors, Spiers & Pond, had no luck tempting Charles Dickens to come out for a lecture tour. Most of these pioneering trips were done for profit, rather than the good of the game (It's tempting to bracket them alongside the modern-day ICL, IPL, EPL and every other sort of L).

The other important factor to remember is that few of the early tours involved really representative sides. For example, the England side in what has come to be accepted as the very first Test of all, at Melbourne in March 1877, was some way from being the best XI the country could have mustered, not least because it was an all-professional outfit – which meant no amateurs like W. G. Grace, by far the leading player of the time. But that match has claimed its place in cricket history for two main reasons: it was the first time sides representing England and Australia had met on level terms – i.e. 11 a side – and the fact that Australia won upset the accepted order of things.

The Englishmen demanded a return fixture, which they won, and the ball was well and truly set in motion. Another side, this time with the odd amateur (but still Grace-less), toured in 1878–79, lost again, and also ran into crowd trouble. Around this time Australian sides started making regular visits to what *Wisden* tended to call the "Mother Country", and because of the limited player-base (cricket was then largely centred on Melbourne and Sydney) the teams tended to be nearer to full-strength. Again their trips were profit-making exercises (the players usually signed up for a share in any surplus).

Back in the Mother Country herself, little attention was paid to the efforts of the touring teams that went to Australia. Partly this was because of the difficulty in gaining information in those far-off days: it wasn't terribly exciting to find out in your morning paper that England had won in Ballarat or Broken Hill three weeks previously. *Wisden* didn't attempt to report the overseas matches properly until 1884: the almanack's first detailed account of that inaugural Test in 1877 was printed 99 years later. Insularity played a part, too: when the "Colonials" came to Britain they were usually soundly beaten when something approaching the best available England side was put out, as happened at The Oval in 1880 in what is now accepted as the first Test match on English soil.

All this changed in 1882 when, also at The Oval, the Australians pulled off a nail-biting victory, by just seven runs, over the might of the whole of England (Grace and all). Fred Spofforth, Australia's "Demon" bowler – the spiritual fore-runner of Gregory, McDonald,

Grimmett, O'Reilly, Lindwall, Miller, Lillee, Thomson, Warne and McGrath – took 14 wickets, and suddenly England could no longer take success against Australia for granted.

It hurt. The English press could hardly believe it, and one young journalist, Reginald Brooks, was moved to place a mock obituary in the *Sporting Times*: "In Affectionate Remembrance of English Cricket, which died at The Oval on 29th August, 1882, Deeply lamented by a large circle of sorrowing friends and acquaintances. R.I.P. N.B. – The body will be cremated and the ashes taken to Australia."

That's how it all began: a semi-private joke in a sporting paper. Little acorns, and all that. Actually Brooks is rather fortunate to be remembered as the man who sparked off all the fuss, as two days before his announcement, the weekly newspaper *Cricket* included something very similar: "Sacred to the memory of England's supremacy in the cricket field, which expired on the 29th day of August, at The Oval. Its end was Peate" (the last part referred to the last man out, Yorkshireman Ted Peate).

Fortuitously for the infant legend, an England team was planning to tour Australia that very winter, and someone leapt on the bandwagon to announce that the Honourable Ivo Bligh, the Surrey player who was going to lead the latest adventure, was going Down Under to recapture those ashes.

Young Mr Brooks couldn't possibly have imagined what he had started.   S. L.

AUSTRALIA V ENGLAND 1876–77
1877

James Lillywhite's team left England on September 21, 1876. They steamed away from Southampton on calm water and under a sunny summer-like sky, roars of good hearty English cheers from shore wishing them "God Speed". The compiler of this book hopes they have had a pleasant voyage out; wishes them a successful career in Australia, and trusts they will have a safe return home to Old England.

First Test
At Melbourne, March 15, 16, 17, 19, 1877. Australia won by 45 runs.   Gordon Ross, 1976

Having cheerily farewelled James Lillywhite's team in 1877, the following year Wisden gave only the briefest of mentions to the results: "This team played 23 matches; won 11; lost four; and eight were drawn." The omission was rectified some 99 years later, when an article looking forward to the centenary of Test cricket included reports of the 1876–77 Tests:

It was warm and sunny in Melbourne on March 15, 1877, when Charles Bannerman took guard and prepared to receive the first ball from Alfred Shaw in what has come to be universally regarded as the first Test match. Bannerman did not commit his name to history purely because he scored the first run: he happened to make 165. Both sides were very much below full strength. W. G. Grace was missing to begin with, while spite of being the home side Australia had considerable difficulty in their selection. Evans, Allen and Spofforth (three bowlers who had caused the England players some problems) all declined to play, the latter stating categorically that the absence of Murdoch to keep wicket was his reason for refusing to take part.

Bannerman's was a truly remarkable performance. He scored 165 before retiring hurt after receiving a blow on the hand; the next-highest score by an Australian was 18 – by Garrett, the No. 9. Due to Bannerman's superhuman effort, Australia reached 245; a collection was taken to mark Bannerman's feat and it raised one pound a run. When England batted Jupp, who opened, hit 63, Charlwood 36, and Hill, coming in at No. 9, an unbeaten 35. England were all out for 196, but they swiftly struck back. Shaw and Ulyett, who had had a comparatively quiet time in the first innings, bowled magnificently, and the Australian innings was soon in some disarray from which it was never able completely to recover. Shaw and Ulyett had taken the first nine wickets to fall, until Lillywhite bowled the last man in. Australia were all out for 104; England thus needed 154 to win and were favourites to get them, but they were shattered by the bowling of Kendall, who had taken only one wicket in the first innings; this time he took seven, to finish with an aggregate of eight for 109. England's first four batsmen totalled 79 between them, but the other seven contributed only 24.

There was great jubilation in Australia, but also a few uncomplimentary remarks addressed to the England cricketers. *The Australasian* wrote that this was the weakest side by a long way that had ever played in the Colonies, notwithstanding the presence among them of Shaw, who was termed the premier bowler of England. It added: "If Ulyett, Emmett and Hill are fair specimens of the best fast bowling in England, all we can say is, either they have not been in their proper form in this Colony or British bowling has sadly deteriorated." *Scores and Biographies* had this to say: "The defeat of England must candidly be attributed to fatigue, owing principally to the distance they had to travel to each match, to sickness, and to high living. England were never fresh in any of their engagements, and, of course, had not near their best XI."

But what were the facts? Well, the party had landed from its New Zealand trip only the day before the match began. The date had been fixed to allow a few days after landing, but the ship was delayed *en voyage,* and the accommodation had been so poor that some of the party had been obliged to sleep on deck. They were in no shape for a serious game of cricket, least of all Armitage, who had something of a nightmare match. In bowling to Bannerman, he tossed one ball wide over the batsman's head – a delivery which brought forth the remark that the Australians could not reach Armitage's bowling with a clothes prop! The next ball he rolled along the ground; worse still, Armitage dropped Bannerman at mid-off, off Shaw, before he had reached double figures. All in all, for the players of England, it was an unhappy match. And it was the first time that an Australian side confined to 11 players had defeated any XI from England.

Toss: Australia. **Australia 245** (C. Bannerman 165*) **and 104** (A. Shaw 5-38);
England 196 (H. Jupp 63, W. E. Midwinter 5-78) **and 108** (T. K. Kendall 7-55).

Second Test

At Melbourne, March 31, April 2, 3, 4, 1877. England won by four wickets.   Gordon Ross, 1976

So nettled were the English party that they were anxious to arrange another match on level terms and this was done. This time, Spofforth sank his differences and was in the Australian team, and with his presence in their side the local public predicted a second victory. But England won by four wickets, due principally to the splendid batting of Ulyett, who scored 52 in the first innings and 63 in the next. This time the Australian public accused England of kidding in the first match in order to obtain another game and another gate. On a previous occasion when Spofforth and Evans had bowled the side out for 35, and in the next innings Armitage scored 38, a critic asked: "How can they be playing square, when they make only 35 one day between all of them, and on another day one man makes more than the whole of the team put together?"

Australia again won the toss, but their early batsmen wilted in the face of a fine piece of fast bowling by Hill, who took the first four wickets, including the valuable prize of Bannerman – who had been strongly backed by the great gambling community to score a lot more runs – bowled him for 19. Midwinter was top-scorer with 31 as Australia were all out for 122. Spofforth, apparently, held the view that only Murdoch was able to take his bowling effectively. It seems that Blackham lost little time in proving to Spofforth how wrong he was. In his third over, a fast delivery lifted and Blackham, standing up, stumped Shaw brilliantly. As Kendall had previously bowled Jupp for a duck, England were four for two and remarks were already being made about the poor quality of the English side in derisory terms.

Throughout cricket's long and enduring history, the inherent steel-like toughness of Yorkshiremen has driven back many a foe in adversity, and here, Yorkshire won a match for England. The scores of the five Yorkshiremen were 49, 52, 48, 49 and 21. The scores of the other six players were 0, 1, 14, 7, 2, 0. They carried England to score of 261 and a lead of 139. The "Demon" Spofforth had taken three for 67.

Australia batted consistently right down the card in their second innings – Gregory, the captain and No. 10, top-scoring with 43. England's attempt to score the 121 required for victory began calamitously. They were nine for three and half the side were out for 76, but Ulyett stood in the breach once again with a magnificent 63. Hill struck the winning blow. England were home, but even this victory did not alter the view of the Australian public that this was a weak England side. But they had a very high regard for the batting capabilities of Ulyett, and they thought there were one or two average batsmen, but they rated Kendall ahead of any of the England fast bowlers. "We would counsel whoever may enter into future speculations for importing an England XI," advised one writer, "to bear in mind the great improvement of Colonial cricket, and not to imagine that anything will do for Australia."

Toss: Australia. **Australia 122** (A. Hill 4-27) **and 259** (J. Lillywhite 4-70, J. Southerton 4-46); **England 261** (G. Ulyett 52, T. K. Kendall 4-82) **and 122-6** (G. Ulyett 63).

AUSTRALIA V ENGLAND 1878-79

The visit of Lord Harris's team to Australia in our memorably severe winter of 1878–79 originated in an invitation from the Melbourne Club to The Gentlemen of England. That invitation was addressed to Mr I. D. Walker, who, however, was then in India; consequently the correspondence on his behalf was undertaken by that gentleman's brothers, Mr V. E. Walker and Mr R. D. Walker. The visit was arranged, with the proviso of taking out two professionals if it was found impossible to get together a fairly representative team wholly composed of gentlemen. That proviso it was found necessary to act upon. Morley was asked, but declined to go; and the two professionals selected were George Ulyett and Thomas Emmett. The long illness, and subsequent death, of the brother of Mr I. D. Walker prevented that gentleman becoming one of the team. Lord Harris kindly undertook the management.

The main body of this little cricketing army of England's – strong in batsmen and fieldsmen, but weak in slow bowling and wicket-keeping – left Southampton in the P&O SS *Australia* on October 17, 1878. On the midnight of Monday, December 2, they were met at the bay by the Adelaide reception committee, and three gentlemen from Melbourne – representatives of the Melbourne Cricket Club, whose guests the Englishmen were. A four-in-hand drag took them to Adelaide that night, and on the following morning the Mayor of Adelaide gave them a most hearty welcome.

A private Assembly Ball in honour of the Englishmen was held in the Town Hall on December 11, at which Lady Jervois, His Excellency the Governor Sir William Jervois, and about 300 other ladies and gentlemen were present. The team had almost daily practice up to the 12th, on which day they got into full cricketing harness, and commenced their first match.

Only Test

At Melbourne, January 2, 3, 4, 1879. Australia won by ten wickets.

The ground was largely attended, 7,000 being present before the day was out. His Excellency the Governor and Lady Bowen were among the company who filled every place of vantage for witnessing the match. Lord Harris won choice, and, after due thought, chose his side should bat, but his decision had hardly been given when rain fell freely for a short period. Mr Lucas and Ulyett commenced the batting; and unfortunately the second ball Ulyett played on before a run was scored. With the score at six Mr Webbe was bowled; at ten Mr Lucas was bowled; and at 14 Mr Hornby was bowled.

Lord Harris stayed well, but when Mr Royle had made three singles, Spofforth's bowling captured three wickets with three successive balls – the victims being Mr Royle, Mr Mackinnon and Emmett, seven wickets being then down for 26 runs. Mr Absolom was next in; he forthwith played his old, old game of knocking the ball all over the ground, and with Lord Harris, increased the score to 89, when Garrett bowled his lordship for 33 – a good innings. Mr Absolom continued hitting hard for the honour of the old land, until a capital catch at long field by A. Bannerman closed his score for 52, and England's innings for 113, Spofforth's bowling having taken six wickets for 48 runs.

Charles Bannerman and Murdoch began the Australian batting to the bowling of Ulyett and Emmett. Bannerman was out for 15; and when 37 had been scored Horan was had at wicket. Then A. Bannerman and Spofforth got together; Bannerman was missed by Mr Hone at wicket before he had made a run, and Ulyett missed both batsmen, so they stayed together until time was called, the score then standing at 93. (One of the team wrote home: "I have seen more mistakes in Melbourne than I expected to see in the time we were out. I can only account for it in the strong light here, the sky being so deep a blue that it dazzles our eyes, and you cannot judge a catch at all.")

Next day at noon the match was resumed, and when Spofforth had increased his score by four he was had by cover point. Garrett made 26, and was out at 131. And at 158 one of Mr Hornby's grubs bowled Allan. Boyle helped A. Bannerman to make up the 200, the hoisting of which numbers elicited loud cheers, but shortly after Mr Royle caught out Mr Boyle for 28, mainly made by five fours. When there was but one wicket to fall A. Bannerman played the ball on, and so was out for 73, the largest score hit in the match. Emmett bowled 59 overs for 68 runs, seven wides and seven wickets.

The Englishmen's second innings was commenced by Mr Lucas and Ulyett. They had made 26 when Mr Lucas was out from a capital catch by Boyle. Four wickets were down for 34; but Lord Harris and Mr Royle stayed a bit; just prior to time Lord Harris was caught for 36 – another good hit of batting, and the top score of that innings.

On the third day the English innings was resumed by Mr Mackinnon and Mr Absolom; neither stayed, but Emmett and Mr Schultz did, the latter making 20, Emmett taking his bat out for 24; and so the score was hit to 160, and the one-innings defeat averted by these two batsmen.

Toss: England. **England 113** (C. A. Absolom 52, F. R. Spofforth 6-48) **and 160** (F. R. Spofforth 7-62); **Australia 256** (A. C. Bannerman 73, T. Emmett 7-68) **and 19-0**.

AUSTRALIA V ENGLAND 1880

Wisden *did not carry a full review of Australia's 1880 tour of England – the practice of summing up tours in that way did not start until 1884. However, there is a brief report of the solitary Test played – the first one on English soil, at The Oval. It was prefaced by an apologetic note from "the compiler", regretting the pressure of space prevented him from including a longer report of "this famous contest".*

For the first time, England took on Australia with a fully representative side. W. G. Grace, the biggest name in 19th-century cricket, scored 152 of England's imposing 420, then Nottinghamshire's fast left-armer Fred Morley took 5 for 56 as Australia were shot out for 149. They did better in the follow-on – skipper Billy Murdoch made 153 not out – but England were left with a smallish target. Although both of W. G.'s brothers made ducks in their only Test (Fred Grace died later that year), England won by five wickets.

In all, the Australians played 37 matches, winning 21, losing four and drawing 12. Apart from the Test, their only first-class defeat came at the hands of Nottinghamshire.

Only Test
At The Oval, September 6, 7, 8, 1880. England won by five wickets.

The compiler much regrets that the limited space allotted to the Australians' matches precludes the possibility of giving a lengthened account of this famous contest. He must therefore rest content to put on record the following facts anent the match:

That in the history of the game no contest has created such worldwide interest; that the attendances on the first and second days were the largest ever seen at a cricket match; that 20,814 persons passed through the turnstiles on Monday, 19,863 on the Tuesday, and

3,751 on the Wednesday; that fine weather favoured the match from start to finish; that the wickets were faultless; that Mr Murdoch's magnificent innings of 153 not out was made without a chance, and contained one five, 18 fours, three threes, 13 twos and 41 singles; that Mr W. G. Grace's equally grand innings was made with only one hard chance, and comprised 12 fours, ten threes, 14 twos, and 46 singles; that superb batting was also shown by Mr Lucas, Lord Harris, Mr McDonnell, and Mr Steel; that the fielding and wicket-keeping on both sides was splendid; that a marvellous change in the aspect of the game was effected on the last day; that universal regret was felt at the unavoidable absence of Mr Spofforth; and that England won the match by five wickets.

Toss: England. **England 420** (W. G. Grace 152, A. P. Lucas 55, Lord Harris 52) **and 57-5**;
Australia 149 (F. Morley 5-56) **and 327** (W. L. Murdoch 153*).

AUSTRALIA v ENGLAND 1881–82

In 1881–82 three prominent English professionals – James Lillywhite, Arthur Shrewsbury and Alfred Shaw, who captained the side – arranged the most ambitious cricket tour to that date, including 30 matches in America, Australia and New Zealand. Wisden records that the team arrived in Sydney by the steamship Australia, which made the fastest trip on record from San Francisco.

There were four matches against a full Australian side, and these have come to be regarded as Test matches. The fact that this was a privately arranged trip probably explains the absence of a proper tour report in Wisden, although there are reports of the individual Tests played by what the Almanack calls "Shaw's XI". Australia won two of the matches, and two were drawn. It was a strongish England side, although none of the leading amateur players of the day, such as W. G. Grace, were there. The side did include Billy Midwinter, who had played for Australia in the first Test of all, and remains the only player to appear on both sides in England–Australia Tests.

The Australian stars were Tom Horan and Percy McDonnell, who both made centuries, and "Joey" Palmer, who took 24 wickets in the four Tests, including 11 for 165 in the second one (which Australia won), the first to be played at Sydney. For England, George Ulyett hit 149 in the fourth match – but in vain, as rain washed out the final day's play.

In all the Englishmen played 18 matches in Australia, winning eight and losing three, seven in New Zealand and five in America. Billy Bates and Edmund Peate both took 30 wickets in the first-class matches, while George Ulyett topped the batting averages with 549 runs at 39.21.

First Test
At Melbourne, December 31, 1881, January 2, 3, 4, 1882. Drawn.

The departure of the steamer which was to take Shaw's team to New Zealand was delayed by the steamship authorities from the morning of January 4 till 3.45 in the afternoon in the hope that this very important match might be concluded. But all to no purpose, as the heavy scoring all round necessitated the game being drawn when the Australians had scored 127 out of 283 required to win. The Englishmen had the advantage of batting first on a splendid wicket, an advantage which was increased when the weather became uncertain after the opening day. Altogether no fewer than 1,049 runs were scored for the loss of 33 wickets, giving an average of 31.26 runs per wicket. Ulyett, Selby and Bates played splendidly for England, but in some cases the visitors' scores would not have been so large had the Australian fielding been as good as usual. Horan was by far the highest scorer for the Colonists, and the merit of his splendid innings was enhanced by the fact that it was made without a chance against the best professional bowlers of the old country. The result of the match was a fairly even draw, the home team wanting 156 to win, with seven wickets to fall.

Toss: England. **England 294** (G. Ulyett 87, J. Selby 55, W. Bates 58)
and 308 (J. Selby 70, W. H. Scotton 50*, W. H. Cooper 6-120); **Australia 320** (T. P. Horan 124) **and 127-3.**

Second Test
At Sydney, February 17, 18, 20, 21, 1882. Australia won by five wickets.

Spofforth and A. C. Bannerman were absent from the home team, but it was nevertheless a very strong one. The Englishmen batted first, but Palmer bowled splendidly throughout, and as the fielding of the Colonists was almost perfection, Shaw's XI were out for the very modest total of 133. On Massie and Blackham going in, the former gave a chance at slip before a run was scored, which was not accepted, and for this mistake the Englishmen paid dearly, as no fewer than 79 runs were put on before Massie was caught.

Resuming next morning in the presence of fully 16,000 spectators, but in less favourable weather, the other nine wickets fell for the addition of 111 runs. On the Monday Ulyett and Barlow offered a most determined resistance to the Colonial bowling, as it was not until 122 had been totalled that a separation was effected, Ulyett being the first to leave for a capital but somewhat lucky innings. Soon after Barlow was caught for an admirable 62, made without a mistake, and with the exception of Shaw and Shrewsbury none of the rest stayed long, and the total, though good, was not so large as might have been expected.

In going in for the 169 they required to win, the Colonists lost two wickets before stumps were drawn, the score then standing at 35. The following morning Murdoch gave two chances before he was dismissed by a brilliant catch, and two other wickets also fell; so the Australians won the match by five wickets.

During the game Murdoch was presented with a splendid gold watch, and gold Maltese cross, in recognition of his great innings of 321 for New South Wales against Victoria. Barlow and Ulyett afterwards received each a Maltese cross set with diamonds for their fine batting, and Blackham was presented with a service of plate for his fielding.

Toss: England. **England 133** (G. E. Palmer 7-68) **and 232** (R. G. Barlow 62, G. Ulyett 67,
G. E. Palmer 4-97, T. W. Garrett 4-62); **Australia 197** (W. Bates 4-52) **and 169-5.**

Third Test
At Sydney, March 3, 4, 6, 7, 1882. Australia won by six wickets.

The Englishmen batted first, and after four of their best wickets had been taken for a few runs Shrewsbury played up splendidly, and was the principal means of the score being a good one. His batting was described as being absolutely free from fault. The commencement of the Colonists' innings did not point to the prospect of a large score, as when time was up on the opening day the three best batsmen were out, and the score only 24. Rain put a stop to the game early on the second day; the overnight not-outs were still in, Bannerman with 59 and McDonnell with 72, the total being 146. On the Monday the wicket was dead, but in spite of that Bannerman added 11 to his score, and McDonnell no fewer than 73, although not one of the other five batsmen could succeed in getting into double figures. McDonnell's batting was extremely brilliant, but he was thrice let off. Bannerman played in capital style, and the two batsmen put on 191 runs while they were together. Both sides found the wicket difficult when going in for the second innings. Shrewsbury batted capitally again and received assistance from Ulyett and Pilling, but when the second venture was over the Australians had only 64 to get to win; but Peate bowled magnificently, and before the requisite number were knocked off, four of the best batsmen among the Colonists were dismissed.

Toss: England. **England 188** (A. Shrewsbury 82, G. E. Palmer 5-46) **and 134** (G. E. Palmer 4-44, T. W. Garrett 6-78); **Australia 262** (A. C. Bannerman 70, P. S. McDonnell 147, E. Peate 5-43) **and 64-4**.

Fourth Test
At Melbourne, March 10, 11, 13, 14, 1882. Drawn.

Bonnor and Jones were left out of the Colonists' team while Spofforth occupied a place in the XI, but "The Demon" was the least effective of all the trundlers in the match. The hitting was very severe all round, but particularly in the second innings of the Englishmen, when 220 runs were scored from the bat off 98 overs. Shaw won the toss and his team went in first, remaining at the wickets all day, and losing eight wickets for 282 runs. The feature of the innings, and of the match, was the grand batting of Ulyett, who went in first and was ninth out, having made 149 out of 239, without giving a chance until he had scored 132, and that was his only mistake. It is the highest innings yet made by an Englishman against Spofforth's bowling. Ulyett followed up his splendid performance by scoring 64 in brilliant style in the second innings, and he was backed up by Barlow, Selby, and Bates, who all played first-class cricket. Murdoch exhibited his best form while scoring his 85, and McDonnell batted in dashing style for his 52. When stumps were finally drawn, and with them the match, the Englishmen had a great advantage, as they were 243 runs ahead with eight wickets to fall.

Toss: England. **England 309** (G. Ulyett 149, T. W. Garrett 5-80) **and 234-2** (G. Ulyett 64, R. G. Barlow 56, W. Bates 52*); **Australia 300** (W. L. Murdoch 85, P. S. McDonnell 52, W. E. Midwinter 4-81).

AUSTRALIA V ENGLAND 1882

Again, Wisden *did not carry a full review of Australia's 1882 tour of England – the practice of summing up tours like that began with the next visit, in 1884. However, there is a long report of the solitary Test played – the epic encounter at The Oval that Australia won by seven runs and which spawned the legend of the Ashes.*

Although the report is little more than a catalogue of dismissals, it does convey some of the "intense excitement" which surrounded the climax of the match, in which England, set only 85 to win, subsided from 51 for two to 77 all out and defeat. As the tension mounted, one spectator died of a heart attack, while another reputedly chewed through the handle of his umbrella.

After the match Reginald Shirley Brooks, a young journalist, placed a mock obituary in the Sporting Times, *lamenting the death of English cricket and announcing that the body would be cremated and the ashes taken to Australia. Sport's greatest rivalry thus grew out of what was little more than a jolly jape: English newspapers started saying that the next England tour of Australia, scheduled for the following winter, would be a quest to recapture the Ashes. From tiny acorns. . .*

In Affectionate Remembrance
OF
ENGLISH CRICKET,
WHICH DIED AT THE OVAL
ON
29th AUGUST, 1882,
Deeply lamented by a large circle of sorrowing
friends and acquaintances.

R. I. P.

N.B.—*The body will be cremated and the
ashes taken to Australia.*

How it all began: the spoof obituary in the *Sporting Times* after Australia won at The Oval in 1882.

Only Test

At The Oval, August 28, 29, 1882. Australia won by seven runs.

The compiler proceeds to give a short account of the contest, leaving the reader to attribute the Australian victory to the fact that the Colonists won the toss and thereby had the best of the cricket; to the fact that the English had to play the last innings; to the brilliant batting of Massie; to the superb bowling of Spofforth; to the nervousness of some of the England side; to the glorious uncertainty of the noble game; or to whatever he or she thinks the true reason.

Monday: Murdoch beat Hornby in the toss. Massie was clean-bowled by a yorker on the leg stump at six. At 21 Murdoch played a ball from Peate on to his wicket, and, after adding a single, Bonnor was clean-bowled middle stump. Then, at 26, Bannerman was splendidly caught by Grace at point, left hand, low down, having been in an hour and five minutes for nine runs. Horan was bowled, leg stump, at 30. Blackham joined Giffen, and, with the total unchanged, was bowled second ball. Garrett was the new batsman, and a double change of bowling was found necessary before the newcomer was well caught at long-off just after luncheon. At 59 Blackham skyed a ball and was caught, and Spofforth, the last man, joined Jones. The "Demon" hit a four, and then Jones was caught at third man, the innings closing for 63. At 3.30 Grace and Barlow started the first innings of England. Spofforth bowled Grace at 13, and Barlow was caught at forward point for 18. The score was raised to 50 after half-an-hour's play, but at 56 Ulyett ran out to drive Spofforth and was easily stumped. At 59 Lucas was snapped at the wicket, and one run later Studd was bowled with a bailer without scoring, and half the wickets were down for 60. Read joined Lyttelton, and just when the score reached the total of the Australian innings the latter was caught at the wicket. Eight wickets were down for 96 when Hornby came in. Read made a cut for three and Hornby scored a single, bringing up the 100. With only one run added, however, Hornby's leg stump fell, and the innings closed about five minutes before the call of time.

Tuesday: Massie and Bannerman commenced the Australians' second innings at 12.10, the Colonists being 38 to the bad. Thirty went up after about 28 minutes' play. At 12.45 the balance was knocked off. Barnes relieved Studd at 47, and from his first ball Lucas badly missed Massie at long-off, the batsman then having made 38. It was not until the score reached 66 that loud applause greeted the dismissal of the great hitter, bowled leg stump by Steel. Massie had made 55 out of 66 in 55 minutes, and his hits consisted of nine fours, two threes, three twos, and seven singles. Bonnor took the vacant wicket, but at 70 his middle stump was knocked clean out of the ground, and Murdoch came in, but immediately lost Bannerman, caught at extra mid-off, with the total unchanged. Horan joined Murdoch, and the bowling was changed, with the result that the incomer was easily caught. Giffen, who took his place, was out in the same way. When the score had been hit up to 99 rain fell, and luncheon was taken.

Resuming at 2.45, after another shower, Blackham was well caught at the wicket without any addition to the score. At 114 Jones was run out in a way which gave great dissatisfaction to Murdoch and other Australians. Murdoch played a ball to leg, for which Lyttelton ran. The ball was returned, and Jones, having completed the first run, and thinking wrongly, but very naturally, that the ball was dead, went out of his ground. Grace put his wicket down, and the umpire gave him out. Several of the team spoke angrily of Grace's action, but the compiler was informed that after the excitement had cooled down a prominent member of the Australian XI admitted that he should have done the same thing. There was a good deal of truth in what a gentleman in the pavilion remarked, amidst some laughter, that "Jones ought to thank the champion for teaching him something". Spofforth partnered Murdoch, but was bowled middle stump at 117. Garrett came in, and very shortly after, a very smart piece of fielding on the part of Hornby, Studd and Lyttelton caused Murdoch to be run out at 122 for a very careful and good innings of 29. Boyle was last man in, but failed to score, and the tenth wicket fell at the same total.

England, wanting 85 runs to win, commenced their second innings at 3.45. Spofforth bowled Hornby's off stump at 15, made in about as many minutes. Barlow joined Grace, but was bowled first ball at the same total. Ulyett came in, and some brilliant hitting by both batsmen brought the score to 51, when a very fine catch at the wicket dismissed Ulyett. Thirty-four runs were then wanted, with seven wickets to fall. Lucas joined Grace, but when the latter had scored a two he was easily taken at mid-off. The game was slow for a time, and 12 successive maiden overs were bowled, both batsmen playing

England v Australia 1882   Only Test
At The Oval, August 28, 29. Result: Australia won by seven runs.

AUSTRALIA	First innings		Second innings
A. C. Bannerman c Grace b Peate	9	– c Studd b Barnes	13
H. H. Massie b Ulyett	1	– b Steel	55
*W. L. Murdoch b Peate	13	– (4) run out	29
G. J. Bonnor b Barlow	1	– (3) b Ulyett	2
T. P. Horan b Barlow	3	– c Grace b Peate	2
G. Giffen b Peate	2	– c Grace b Peate	0
†J. M. Blackham c Grace b Barlow	17	– c Lyttelton b Peate	7
T. W. Garrett c Read b Peate	10	– (10) not out	2
H. F. Boyle b Barlow	2	– (11) b Steel	0
S. P. Jones c Barnes b Barlow	0	– (8) run out	6
F. R. Spofforth not out	4	– (9) b Peate	0
B 1	1	B 6	6

1-6 2-21 3-22 4-26 5-30 6-30   63   1-66 2-70 3-70 4-79 5-79 6-99   122
7-48 8-53 9-59 10-63   7-114 8-117 9-122 10-122

First innings – Peate 38–24–31–4; Ulyett 9–5–11–1; Barlow 31–22–19–5; Steel 2–1–1–0.
Second innings – Peate 21–9–40–4; Ulyett 6–2–10–1; Barlow 13–5–27–0; Steel 7–0–15–2;
Barnes 12–5–15–1; Studd 4–1–9–0.

ENGLAND	First innings		Second innings
R. G. Barlow c Bannerman b Spofforth	11	– (3) b Spofforth	0
W. G. Grace b Spofforth	4	– (1) c Bannerman b Boyle	32
G. Ulyett st Blackham b Spofforth	26	– (4) c Blackham b Spofforth	11
A. P. Lucas c Blackham b Boyle	9	– (5) b Spofforth	5
†Hon. A. Lyttelton c Blackham b Spofforth	2	– (6) b Spofforth	12
C. T. Studd b Spofforth	0	– (10) not out	0
J. M. Read not out	19	– (8) b Spofforth	0
W. Barnes b Boyle	5	– (9) c Murdoch b Boyle	2
A. G. Steel b Garrett	14	– (7) c and b Spofforth	0
*A. N. Hornby b Spofforth	2	– (2) b Spofforth	9
E. Peate c Boyle b Spofforth	0	– b Boyle	2
B 6, l-b 2, n-b 1	9	B 3, n-b 1	4

1-13 2-18 3-57 4-59 5-60 6-63   101   1-15 2-15 3-51 4-53 5-66 6-70   77
7-70 8-96 9-101 10-101   7-70 8-75 9-75 10-77

First innings – Spofforth 36.3–18–46–7; Garrett 16–7–22–1; Boyle 19–7–24–2.
Second innings – Spofforth 28–15–44–7; Garrett 7–2–10–0; Boyle 20–11–19–3.

Toss won by Australia   UMPIRES L. Greenwood and R. Thomas

carefully and coolly. Lyttelton scored a single, and then four maiden overs were followed by the dismissal of that batsman – bowled, the score being 66. Only 19 runs were then wanted to win, and there were five wickets to fall. Steel came in, and when Lucas had scored a four, Steel was easily caught and bowled. Read joined Lucas, but amid intense excitement he was clean-bowled without a run being added. Barnes took Read's place and scored a two, and three byes made the total 75, or ten to win. After being in a long time for five Lucas played the next ball into his wicket, and directly Studd joined Barnes the latter was easily caught off his glove without the total being altered. Peate, the last man, came in, but after hitting Boyle to square leg for two he was bowled, and Australia had defeated England by seven runs.

The Birth (and Rebirth) of the Ashes: 1882-83 to 1912

After Australia's nerve-shredding victory at The Oval in 1882, which led to the spoof obituary notice lamenting the "death of English cricket... the body will be cremated and the Ashes taken to Australia", it so happened that a group of English players were embarking on a tour of Australia that same winter. The Honourable Ivo Bligh, the captain, made what may have been a throwaway remark about recapturing those Ashes, and the idea took root, especially among the amateurs in his team, many of whom had been Bligh's Varsity contemporaries.

Bligh's team did win their series, 2-1, against the men who had lowered England's colours. Confusingly, a fourth match was then played against a combined Australian side, which included two players who had not been in England, so the records suggest a 2-2 draw - but Bligh's "quest for the Ashes" centred on the first three games against Billy Murdoch's men. During one of the other tour games, in up-country Victoria, a group of "Melbourne ladies" decided to embody the nascent legend into tangible form, and made a small trophy which they presented to Bligh (one of the group, Florence Morphy, later married Bligh, who eventually succeeded as Lord Darnley). Bligh was presented with a small terracotta urn containing some ashes - no one is sure now whether this was the remains of a stump, a bail, a ball or even a woman's veil - which remained in his possession until he died.

Until Bligh's death the urn remained a family heirloom, and after this tour what was really something of a private joke faded. References to the Ashes are few and far between during the remainder of the 19th century, although the Australian all-rounder George Giffen does include two chapters on "Fights for the Ashes" in an 1899 book, and the legend might have been forgotten altogether had it not been for Pelham Warner, a great servant of cricket who captained England, did much sterling work behind the scenes at Lord's where a stand is named after him, and also founded *The Cricketer* magazine in 1921.

Warner was appointed captain of the England team which toured Australia in 1903-04 - the first to be directly organised by MCC rather than privately raised. It was only two years after the previous venture, in which Australia had won the last four Tests after being clobbered in the first one. *Wisden*'s reports of that series are perfunctory, possibly suggesting a lack of interest, and possibly as a means of drumming up enthusiasm Warner resurrected the notion of a noble crusade to recapture the Ashes, a concept which caught the imagination of the Australian press. Warner's original idea might also have been fuelled by the fact that Bligh's wife, who had helped create the trophy in the first place, happened to be sailing to Australia on the *Orontes* with the MCC team. Later, Warner called his tour account *How We Recovered The Ashes*. The first mention of the Ashes in

Wisden came in 1905, in an entertaining article by B. J. T. Bosanquet – the inventor of the googly and the architect of success in the decisive Fourth Test – which augmented the almanack's coverage of this 1903–04 tour.

The fact that the Ashes could be said to have been in abeyance for around 20 years did not discourage cricket contact between England and Australia. The 1880s and 1890s were the busiest time for exchanges between the two countries: both "Black Jack" Blackham, a legendary wicket-keeper, and the diminutive batsman Sid Gregory made eight separate Test-playing tours of England. Other legendary names lit up the matches: even W. G. Grace, who had declined numerous invitations, finally led a tour, under the generous patronage of Lord Sheffield, in 1891–92. Grace played on against Australia until 1899, when he was almost 51, by which time new heroes had emerged – the exotic Indian prince Ranjitsinhji and his soulmate C. B. Fry for England, and talented Australians such as Clem Hill and Victor Trumper. This era, and the first decade of the 20th century, has become known as cricket's "Golden Age", a romantic notion which I suspect must have been helped by the trend for brilliant eye-catching amateur batsmen to dominate the poor put-upon professional bowlers.

It was a golden time for Ashes cricket, too. The 1899 season, in which Trumper trumpeted his genius, featured the first five-Test series in England, a development with which *Wisden* took issue as it detracted from the other tour games. A wet 1902 season still included two of the most exciting Tests of them all, and at home in 1907–08 Australia won the First Test by two wickets, then England took the second by one, winning it with an overthrow when a fielder missed a chance to run out A. Fielder (Arthur, the Kent fast bowler and England's last man) and bring about Test cricket's first tie.

This golden period ended violently, with the outbreak of the Great War in 1914, two years after the experiment of a Triangular Tournament in England, with England and Australia being joined by South Africa (a wet summer, and the fact that the Australian side was weakened after a dispute with their board, rather ruined the idea, which has never been tried again). But the era finished with England–Australia Tests in good shape. Both countries' cricket was now centrally organised, which meant the teams were usually fully representative. The sides were also reasonably well matched: the Ashes, now established as the prize for winning, changed hands three times between 1903–04 and 1911–12.

The Ashes, however, were still not a proper trophy. The little urn was just a treasured keepsake in Cobham Hall, Lord Darnley's home in Kent. For a time it stood on a mantelpiece in one of the rooms: one story has a chambermaid knocking it over and replacing the mysterious contents with ashes from the grate. It was not until after Bligh's death in 1927 that the urn was bequeathed to MCC for safe keeping. It was put on display in the Long Room, then moved to the Lord's Museum when that was set up in 1953. Apart from occasional trips outside – notably a nationwide tour of Australia alongside the 2006–07 series – the physical manifestation of the Ashes has stayed there ever since, regardless of which country actually holds them.

Debate continues about whether the Ashes should physically move to Australia after they win them. I happen to think that they should – the suggestion that they are too fragile to move was shown up by that 2006–07 jaunt, and the argument that they are not really a proper trophy is contradicted by more than 100 years of fierce cricketing competition between England and Australia for "ownership" of the urn.   S. L.

AUSTRALIA V ENGLAND 1882–83

The Honourable Ivo Bligh set sail in autumn 1882 with a mission: to bring back the Ashes of English cricket, which had been said to have been cremated (and taken to Australia) after England's surprise defeat at The Oval in September. Bligh's side, which was a mixture of professionals and amateurs, beat Billy Murdoch's 1882 tourists 2–1 in a three-match series and so succeeded in their quest.

Confusingly, after three matches against a team drawn exclusively from those who toured England in 1882, there was one further representative match, in which two players who had not been on that tour (Edwin Evans and the nomadic Billy Midwinter) were chosen for Australia. That match – which was played on four separate pitches at Sydney – went narrowly to the home side.

There was a certain amount of press interest in the Ashes idea in Australia, but in England talk of it was largely confined to the touring team. Wisden, at any rate, seems to have decided not to recognise the phenomenon just yet. Again there was no modern-style tour review, and no mention anywhere of the new trophy.

First Test

At Melbourne, December 30, 1882, January 1, 2, 1883. Australia won by nine wickets.

A large number of catches were missed in this match, and the Englishmen were by far the greatest sinners in this respect. In the first innings of the home team, Bannerman, McDonnell and Bonnor might all have been dismissed for comparatively few runs had the chances been accepted. So great was the interest manifested in this contest that the attendance was the greatest known at any three-day match in Australia. The winning of the toss was a distinct gain to Murdoch's men, as they were thus enabled to bat on the opening day, while the visitors were compelled to play the whole of both innings on a wicket which the heavy showers of Sunday had seriously affected.

With the total five Bannerman narrowly escaped being run out, and without any addition Massie was finely caught and bowled. Soon after Murdoch came in, Bannerman was missed at slip by Barnes. Both batsmen played with the greatest of care, and carried the score to 81, when a yorker dismissed Murdoch, and Horan was caught. At 96 Bannerman was cleverly stumped, and Giffen, his successor, nearly shared a similar fate. His partner, McDonnell, however, was the first to leave, clean-bowled, after being twice missed. Bonnor joined Giffen and at once commenced to hit tremendously hard. He gave a possible chance to Barlow at the boundary when he made seven, and drove the next ball clear of the spectators into the pavilion reserve for five *[until 1910 the ball had to be hit clean out of the ground for a six – Ed.]*, and an over later scored another five, the ball going into the ladies' enclosure. Giffen was stumped at 190. Bonnor scored another five and then had a life at the hands of Read. After that some steady play brought the total to 232, when Bonnor made his fourth five, a terrific hit which would have gone over the outer fence for six had the ball not struck a tree.

Heavy showers on the Sunday and again early on Monday had considerably affected the wicket to the disadvantage of the batsmen, and the sun shining out with great power just before the game was resumed caused it to play treacherously. After giving a couple of somewhat hard chances Spofforth was caught at 287, and at the same total Garrett was dismissed. With four runs added the innings terminated, Bonnor being caught in the slips. The Englishmen commenced batting at 1.05, their start being a most disastrous one. With only two singles scored Palmer bowled the captain, and at seven Leslie was caught, over half an hour being consumed in scoring those seven runs.

Luncheon was then taken and, directly after, C. T. Studd was bowled: three wickets were down for only eight runs. With an addition of 12 Barlow was missed, and at 36 he was stumped. Steel, who had batted in capital form, was clean-bowled at 45, and half the wickets were down. Read and Bates, by good cricket, then raised the score to 96, when the former played on. Four runs were added and then rain caused a brief adjournment. On resumption Bates was caught without any addition, and at 117 G. B. Studd was unfortunately run out.

Man with a mission: The Hon. Ivo Bligh set off to recapture the Ashes in 1882–83.

There were then only two wickets to fall, but those two wickets gave considerable trouble. Barnes had not been seen to greater advantage in any of the previous matches, and Tylecote batted with pluck and determination. Tylecote was bowled at 156, having been missed by Bonnor just before. Being 114 to the bad the visitors had to follow on, and in the short time left for play that day they made 11 runs, with no wicket down.

The wicket was not improved by the showers which fell on Monday night, but the weather was fine though dull when play was resumed. Barlow and Tylecote, the overnight not-outs, continued to bat in excellent form, and it was not till after three appeals to the umpires had been answered in their favour, and the total had reached 64, that the latter played a ball on to his wicket. Barlow was soon bowled, but on Steel joining C. T. Studd another good stand was made. The total was advanced to 105 before the former, who had been missed by Giffen, was bowled.

Bligh was bowled at 108; Steel's well-played innings was brought to a close at 132; and Leslie, who was unwell, hit his wicket at 150. Then three wickets all fell at 164, Read being bowled and G. B. Studd and Bates caught. The Australians were set the task of scoring 56 to win. Massie was caught before a run was made, but Bannerman and Murdoch hit off the required number.

Toss: Australia. **Australia 291** (G. J. Bonnor 85) **and 58-1;**
England 177 (G. E. Palmer 7-65) **and 169** (G. Giffen 4-38).

Second Test

At Melbourne, January 19, 20, 22, 1883. England won by an innings and 27 runs.

The splendid bowling of Bates was the chief factor in the reverse the home team experienced, though the defeat would undoubtedly have been less severe had the easy chance Bates gave before he had scored been accepted. The eighth wicket would have then fallen at 199, whereas the mistake allowed him to compile 55, and, with Read, to carry the total to 287. Bates's wonderful analysis in the first innings was even better than it reads, as four of the runs debited to him were the result of an overthrow. His great services in the match were rewarded by a collection of £31 after the game.

Bligh won the toss, and on a splendid wicket, C. T. Studd and Barlow faced Spofforth and Palmer. At 28 Studd was bowled middle stump by Palmer, and at 35 Barlow's wicket fell to the same bowler. Though Leslie and Steel were both suffering from the enervating influences of the Australian climate, they succeeded in making a long stand, though batting with less vigour than usual. The score was 106 before the two were parted by a splendid piece of fielding. Leslie played a ball hard to the off and started for a run. The ball went to Spofforth who, standing forward cover-point, very smartly threw down the wicket, and Leslie was run out for an almost faultless 54, his only mistake being a hard return to Palmer when he had made 48. Read filled the vacancy, but at 131 lost Steel, easily caught for a well-played 39, made without a chance. Barnes joined Read, and but for a very bad throw-in by Horan, would have been run out before he had made many runs. This let-off resulted in 64 being added – Barnes was bowled at 195. With only four more runs added Tylecote was bowled, and Bligh fell to a shooter. Bates received a great piece of good luck directly he came in. He gave a very hot return to Giffen which was not accepted, and was then badly missed by Horan, two mistakes for which the Australians paid dearly. When play was adjourned for the day the score was 248 for seven wickets.

On Saturday, a separation was not effected until 39 more runs had been added to the overnight total, Barnes being then caught for an exceedingly well-played innings, despite the chances he gave at the commencement. The score stood at 287 when he was dismissed, he and Read having put on 88. The innings was then quickly finished off. Read was caught and bowled for a masterly 75, with only one chance, and that a hard one, when he had 64.

After luncheon Massie was clean-bowled at 56 for a brilliant 43, and when Murdoch joined Bannerman the play became so exceedingly slow that half an hour was consumed in scoring ten runs. Bannerman was clean-bowled at 72, and at 75 Horan was finely caught – right-handed very high up. Then Bates accomplished the hat-trick, dismissing McDonnell, Giffen, and Bonnor with successive balls. Blackham was bowled at 85, and Garrett shared the same fate at 104. With an addition of ten runs a yorker got rid of Palmer, and without any increase Spofforth was bowled and the innings terminated for 114, Murdoch carrying his bat for 19, the result of a two-and-a-half-hour stay. Being in a minority of 180 the Australians had to follow their innings. When 21 runs had been scored Murdoch was bowled, and seven runs were added before the call of time.

On Monday, Blackham was clean-bowled before any addition had been made. Bonnor at once commenced to hit grandly. The first 26 runs scored were all made by him, and included in the 34 he contributed before he was finely caught by Morley were three hits out of the ground for five each. Bannerman was caught at 72, and Horan and McDonnell carried the score rapidly to 93, when another good catch by Morley got rid of Horan, and half the wickets were disposed of. Luncheon was then taken with the total at 122, and upon resumption ten runs were added and then Giffen was caught. Garrett was then caught at 139, and Palmer at 153. The Englishmen thus gained a decisive victory.

Toss: England. **England 294** (C. F. H. Leslie 54, W. W. Read 75, W. Bates 55, G. E. Palmer 5-103, G. Giffen 4-89); **Australia 114** (W. Bates 7-28) **and 153** (W. Bates 7-74).

Third Test

At Sydney, January 26, 27, 29, 30, 1883. England won by 69 runs.

The first match having resulted in a win for the Australian XI, and the second in a victory for the Englishmen, the third contest was invested with extraordinary interest, and on the opening day the attendance was the largest ever witnessed on the Moore Park ground, it being computed that from 20,000 to 23,000 spectators were present.

The Hon. Ivo Bligh again beat Murdoch in the toss. Barlow and C. T. Studd, by excellent cricket, carried the total to 41, when the latter was finely caught at the wicket. With three runs added, Leslie was bowled by a fast yorker, making room for Steel. From the last ball bowled before luncheon Barlow was well caught, the total then standing at 67. At 76 Barnes was caught at the wicket, and then Read and Tylecote offered so prolonged a resistance that 115 were put on before Tylecote was run out for 66, the highest score he made during the tour, which was described as "a most brilliant display of safe all-round hitting, without giving a possible chance to anyone in the field". Bates partnered Read, and the total was quickly hit up to 223, when an easy catch at square leg got rid of the Reigate amateur after a "fine, vigorous, all-round display".

Showers fell during the night, and on Saturday the wicket was a trifle dead and the sky cloudy and threatening more rain. These circumstances, however, apparently in no way militated against the success of Bannerman and Giffen, who ran up the capital total of 76 for the first wicket, Giffen being the first to leave after a good innings of 41. Murdoch succeeded him, and when he had been badly missed by Leslie when he had scored five, and Bannerman had had a life at the hands of Morley when he had made 39, the two batsmen brought up the hundred. Then rain caused a cessation of play from 3.15 to 5.15. On the sloppy wicket 33 more runs were scored in three-quarters of an hour, during which time Bannerman was again missed, this time by Barnes. At the call of time the total was 133 for one wicket, Bannerman being not out 68.

During Saturday night and Sunday, rain fell heavily with but little intermission, and when the game was continued on the Monday the ground was exceedingly dead and heavy. With seven added Murdoch was lbw, and McDonnell, who succeeded him, clean-bowled at the same total. Bannerman and Horan put on 36, and then Bannerman was caught off Morley when within six of a century. Despite the chances he gave, his 94 was a grand innings, his off-driving and cutting being frequently brilliant. Massie was caught at point without increasing the score. Bonnor followed, but was splendidly caught before he had scored a run, and six wickets were down for 178. Horan fell to a one-handed catch at mid-off, and Garrett was caught in the slips. Palmer stayed with Blackham while 22 runs were added, was then caught, and the innings terminated.

When the wicket used by the visitors had been rolled C. T. Studd and Leslie commenced the second innings. Leslie was clean-bowled at 13, but Barlow helped take the score to 45, when Studd shared the fate of Leslie for a freely hit 25. Steel was lbw at 55, but Barlow and Read brought the total to 87. Then Read was bowled, having given a possible chance early in his innings. At 94 Barlow was sent back for a carefully compiled 24, and at the same total Barnes was lbw. Morley kept his wicket up for a time but was eventually bowled without scoring, and the innings closed for 153, the English captain carrying his bat for 17. Murdoch's team was set the task of scoring 123 to win, and in the little time left for play Morley bowled four overs and Barlow three, without a run being scored or a wicket lost.

On Tuesday the game was resumed in splendid weather. Giffen was bowled at 11, and Bannerman caught at point at 12. Murdoch was caught at 18, and without any runs being added, McDonnell fell to a splendid catch at point. Horan was run out at 30 and Massie was caught at 33. Blackham hit with great vigour. He lost Bonnor at 59, and Spofforth at 72, and then played a ball onto his wicket at 80. Garrett, the last man, came in, and when two leg-byes and a wide had been scored, Barlow bowled him, and the innings terminated for 83, the Englishmen thus winning the match by 69 runs.

Toss: England. **England 247** (W. W. Read 66, E. F. S. Tylecote 66, F. R. Spofforth 4-73) **and 123** (F. R. Spofforth 7-44); **Australia 218** (A. C. Bannerman 94, F. Morley 4-47) **and 83** (R. G. Barlow 7-40).

Fourth Test
At Sydney, February 17, 19, 20, 21, 1883. Australia won by four wickets.

The XI selected to represent the full strength of the Colonies included nine members of the team which visited the old country in the summer of 1882 under the command of Murdoch, and was completed with the addition of Midwinter and Evans. The interest in the contest was intense, and one authority states that 55,000 attended the match. The game was not concluded until ten to six on the fourth day, and it was so splendidly contested that up until four o'clock or later neither side could claim advantage.

Each XI contained a lame man. Giffen had an injured leg, but with Murdoch to run for him, contrived to play two good and useful innings, and was allowed a substitute in the field. Morley's injured side, however, seriously handicapped the visitors, as he was practically useless as a bowler after sending down a few overs, and of little service in the field. Mistakes in the field were many in number, and had chances been accepted, Steel would have been nought instead of 135 not out, and Bannerman seven in place of 63. Bonnor was credited with three lives in his first innings before he had made 17. But notwithstanding these errors, the fielding on both sides was often brilliant, and nothing was finer than the display of G. B. Studd. Of the batsmen none deserves warmer praise than Blackham, who played a faultless first innings of 57 when runs were badly wanted, and to whose good and resolute batting on the fourth day the Colonists owed their victory. Each innings was played on a fresh wicket.

For the third time in succession fortune favoured Bligh in the toss. Barlow was caught at point at 13, and Leslie fell to a catch in the slips, with the total at 37. Steel filled the vacancy, and before he had scored played one from Boyle which dropped within an inch of Murdoch's hands. At the luncheon interval the score stood at 48. On resumption Steel gave a chance to the wicket-keeper before he had added to his score, and the two batsmen then made a long stand: 73 runs were put on at a rapid rate, and then C. T. Studd after starting for a run was unable to get back before Midwinter threw down the wicket. His 48 was described as "a finished exhibition of cricket without the shadow of a chance being given". Steel was badly missed by Bonnor in the slips, and the score was then taken to 150 before Read was caught. With 180 on the board rain caused a short adjournment. On resuming

What all the fuss is about: the tiny Ashes urn, with its velvet bag.

Bates was out to a splendid running catch by Bonnor at long-on. Steel then scored a single and brought 200 up, and his individual score to 100. A chance of a run-out followed, but the ball was returned to the wrong wicket and Steel escaped. By fast scoring the total reached 236 when Bligh was clean-bowled for 19. G. B. Studd came in and runs were put on at a great pace till a very fine piece of fielding by Bannerman resulted in Studd being run out. At this point play ceased for the day, the score being 263 for nine wickets, Steel not out 135.

On Monday the fourth ball of the first over proved fatal to Morley. Steel was loudly cheered for his very fine innings, which included 16 fours. He gave four chances while scoring his first 45, but his last 90 runs were made in his best form and without a mistake. His was the highest score he contributed during his visit to the Antipodes, and throughout his stay at the wickets his batting was of the most vigorous description. Bonnor and Bannerman went in for Australia, and when only three runs had been made the former gave a chance to Steel at long-on which was not accepted. At 31 Bannerman was caught in the slips, and Bonnor was again missed by Steel. At 34 Murdoch was clean-bowled, and Horan caught with the total at 39. Giffen came next, and as his leg was injured on the opening day, he had Murdoch to run for him. When Bonnor had made 24, he had a third life at the hands of Steel, and shortly after luncheon was taken, the score at 58. On resumption of play Bonnor had a narrow escape at point, and then the score was rapidly hit up to 100, when Giffen was finely caught for an excellent innings of 27, made under difficulties. Midwinter was clean-bowled at 128. Before 150 went up Bonnor gave another chance to Steel – a difficult one – and at 157 the players adjourned for refreshments. On resuming only three runs were added before Bonnor was caught for an exceedingly lucky innings of 87, and Palmer was easily taken at point. Seven wickets were then down for 164, and a follow-on seemed not improbable, but on Evans joining Blackham a resolute stand was made. Runs were put on at a rapid rate, Blackham doing most of the scoring, and it was not until 220 had been totalled that he was clean-bowled for one of the best and most dashing innings he has played. When Boyle, the last man, came in, 42 runs were wanted to bring the sides on even terms. When 27 of this number had been hit off, stumps were drawn for the day.

On the third day Boyle added nine and Evans two, and the former was then caught at mid-off. The second innings of the Englishmen was commenced at 12.45. With the total at 43, luncheon was taken. With 54 on the board C. T. Studd was caught at short leg for a finely played 31. When Leslie had scored a single Barlow was caught in the slips for a patient innings of 20, and at 77 Horan clean-bowled Leslie with his first ball. Read scored seven and then played on, and Tylecote was clean-bowled without scoring, the fourth wicket falling at 99 and the fifth at 100. Bates having joined Steel, 12 runs were added and then the latter was clean-bowled for a good and carefully compiled 21. Bligh helped Bates put on 26 and was then caught at point, and seven wickets were down for 137. Barnes followed and a capital stand was made, 41 runs being added to the score before the Notts professional was caught and bowled for 20. The visitors' second innings closed for 197.

On Wednesday, the fourth day, the Colonists went in a second time, wanting 199 runs to win. Bannerman and Murdoch began, and the former was missed at the wicket when he had made seven. Murdoch exhibited extreme care, and 113 balls were bowled before he scored a run. At luncheon no wicket had fallen, the total being 39. On resuming, five runs were added and then Murdoch was caught in the slips from a lofty hit. Bonnor took his place, but was caught at 51, and without any addition Horan was caught and bowled. With Murdoch to run for him, Giffen filled the vacancy, and a long stand was then made without a chance being given. At 107 a parting was at last effected, Bannerman being caught at point for a splendid 63, made at a much more rapid rate than usual with him. Blackham came in and batted in the same resolute way as in the first innings, the English bowling being fairly mastered. At 147, Giffen gave a difficult chance to Steel which was not accepted, but in stepping out to the same bowler was smartly stumped for a capital 32, the score then standing at 162 for five wickets. With two runs added Evans hit a ball over the bowler's head and was caught, and when Midwinter joined Blackham the requisite runs were hit off, and the Australians won the great match of the tour by four wickets.

Toss: England. **England 263** (A. G. Steel 135*) **and 197; Australia 262** (G. J. Bonnor 87, J. M. Blackham 57) **and 199-6** (A. C. Bannerman 63, J. M. Blackham 58*).

ENGLAND V AUSTRALIA 1884

The programme of the fourth Australian team consisted of 32 matches, 18 of which were won, seven drawn and seven lost. Scott and Cooper were the only members of the team who had not visited England before, and while the former proved an emphatic success, the latter was a decided failure. Scott secured the third place in the batting list with an average of 22.27, but the seven wickets taken by Cooper cost 46.3 runs each.

Murdoch quite maintained his splendid form with an average 30.28 against 30.31 in 1882. McDonnell's rose from 17.16 to 23.29, and Giffen's from 18.9 to 21.2. Bannerman's fell from 22.8 to 19.11, and Bonnor's from 20.15 to 19.6. Blackham batted up to his reputation, and Midwinter secured an average of 19.2. Spofforth, whose wonderful bowling was the feature of the tour, took 216 wickets at an average of 12.50. Palmer and Boyle were more expensive than in 1882, but Giffen bowled with greater success than before.

First Test

At Manchester, July 10, 11, 12, 1884. Drawn.

This was the first of three matches arranged to be played between the Australians and the full strength of England *[and the first Test at Old Trafford – Ed.]*. Owing to unfavourable weather the wicket was unfit for cricket on the Thursday, and play was consequently confined to the Friday and Saturday. The result was a draw in favour of the Australians, England being 93 runs on with a wicket to fall in their second innings. Shrewsbury and Lucas played admirable cricket in both innings. Grace exhibited great skill and judgment in scoring his 31, and O'Brien made runs at a time they were badly wanted. Grace was one hour and a quarter scoring his 31, and Lucas was at the wickets two hours for his 24. The Australians hit with more vigour and confidence than their opponents, and McDonnell, Murdoch and Midwinter contributed capital innings.

Toss: England. **England 95** (F. R. Spofforth 4-42, H. F. Boyle 6-42)
and 180-9 (G. E. Palmer 4-47); **Australia 182**.

Second Test

At Lord's, July 21, 22, 23, 1884. England won by an innings and five runs.

England won this match *[the first Test ever played at Lord's – Ed.]* by an innings, and the main elements of this success were the magnificent batting of A. G. Steel and the bowling of Ulyett. The Australians batted first, and despite a capital innings of 63 by Giffen they lost nine wickets for 160 runs. Then Scott proved how well he merited a place in the team. He was admirably supported by Boyle, and before parting was effected 69 runs were put on for the last wicket. Scott played cool, confident, skilful cricket, and his 75 included ten fours, five threes, and six twos. The chief hits in Giffen's excellent 63 were four fours, three threes and ten twos. Boyle made his runs in plucky determined style. When time was called on the opening day England had lost three wickets for 90 runs, so the match then stood in a fairly even position. Lucas batted finely for his 28, and Shrewsbury's 27 was also a good innings.

Next morning Steel commenced his remarkable innings. At 120 Ulyett was bowled by a yorker for a good 32, and at 135 Harris was clean-bowled. Barlow then came to Steel's aid and a complete mastery was obtained over the bowling, 98 being put on before Barlow was caught in the slips for an invaluable 38. Just previous to Read's dismissal Steel had completed his hundred, and he was now joined by Lyttelton.

Another long stand was made, 76 runs being put on before Lyttelton was bowled for a capital innings of 31. Only three runs were added, and Steel's magnificent innings came to a close. Steel had been at the wickets while 261 runs had been scored, and a hard chance to Boyle when he had made 48 was the only blemish on his innings. His 148 consisted of 13 fours, four threes, 18 twos, and 48 singles, and was the highest score made against the Australians during the season. Peate and Christopherson put on 28 runs for the last wicket, and before play ceased that day the Australians had lost four wickets in their second innings for 73 runs.

On the last day Scott made a gallant effort to save the innings defeat, but without avail. He was highest scorer in both innings of the Australians, and his total of 105 (for once out) was a very fine performance. Ulyett's bowling figures speak for themselves, but he was undoubtedly helped by the ground.

Toss: Australia. **Australia 229** (G. Giffen 63, H. J. H. Scott 75, E. Peate 6-85) **and 145** (G. Ulyett 7-36); **England 379** (A. G. Steel 148, G. E. Palmer 6-111).

Third Test

At The Oval, August 11, 12, 13, 1884. Drawn.

The third and last of the three great matches arranged to be played against the full strength of England resulted in a draw, England wanting 120 runs to avert a single-innings defeat, with eight wickets to go down. The fact that three individual scores of over 100 runs were scored on the first day rendered the match unique in the annals of the game. When stumps were drawn, the score stood at 363 for two wickets, Murdoch having scored 145, and Scott 101, the pair having added 205.

Bannerman was out with the score at 15, and McDonnell at 158, but 205 more runs were added that day without further loss. On the Tuesday Scott was caught at the wicket after adding a single to his overnight score, but Murdoch was not dismissed until he had compiled 211, being the sixth batsman out with the total at 494. The remainder of the innings was alone remarkable for the success which attended Lyttelton's lobs. He went on for the second time when six wickets were down for 532, and took the last four wickets in eight overs for only eight runs.

McDonnell's very brilliantly hit 103 included 14 fours, and was made while 158 runs were scored. Scott was batting three hours and a half for his 102, out of 207 put on while he was in, and he gave one real chance in his splendid innings, and that was when he had made 60. Murdoch's magnificent innings of 211 consisted of 24 fours, nine threes, 22 twos, and 44 singles, and the celebrated batsman was at the wickets a little over eight hours, while 479 runs were scored. He gave three chances, all off Ulyett's bowling, when his individual score reached 46, 171, and 205 respectively.

The only innings on the England side calling for special notice were those played by Scotton and Read. They became partners when eight wickets had fallen for 181, of which number Scotton had scored 53, 21 of them having been made on the previous evening. They were not separated until they had put on 151 for the ninth wicket. Scotton was the first to leave, having been at the wickets five hours and three-quarters, while 332 runs were made. He never gave the slightest chance, and it is not too much to say that his splendid display of defensive cricket was the cause of England saving the match.

Read's 117 was a superb display of hard and rapid hitting, his hits being 20 fours, one three, 12 twos, and ten singles. One difficult chance to Spofforth was the only blemish in his innings.

Toss: Australia. **Australia 551** (P. S. McDonnell 103, W. L. Murdoch 211, H. J. H. Scott 102, Hon. A. Lyttelton 4-19); **England 346** (W. H. Scotton 90, W. W. Read 117, G. E. Palmer 4-90) **and 85-2.**

Australia v England 1884–85

The eighth team of English cricketers who visited the Australian Colonies – the second band of professionals who went out under the management of Shaw, Shrewsbury, and Lillywhite – left Plymouth in the SS *Orient* on Friday, September 18, 1884. On October 7 the cricketers reached Aden, and the same day sailed for Port Adelaide, where they arrived early on the morning of Wednesday, October 29.

At Adelaide they were met by the leading members of the South Australian Cricket Association, who conducted them to the city, where the Mayor accorded them an official reception, remarking that he was sure their visit would be a very pleasant one. Similar kindly greetings were extended to them wherever they went, but from the moment the members of Murdoch's team landed from the *Mirzapore*, it became evident they were animated by a feeling of bitter hostility towards Shaw and his party. As a commencement, the Victoria contingent of the team declined to play for their Colony against the Englishmen, urging as an excuse their want of practice, while it afterwards transpired that Murdoch's XI had endeavoured to arrange a match with New South Wales on the same days as those fixed for the contest. Next, Murdoch and A. Bannerman refused to take part for New South Wales against the tourists, and after a meeting between Shaw's team and Murdoch's at Adelaide, each side receiving £450, the climax of the quarrel was reached when Murdoch's men declined to play for Combined Australia against the Englishmen on New Year's Day.

This unpatriotic conduct was severely condemned by the public and press of Australia, as the following will show: "At a luncheon given at Adelaide the Attorney-General of South Australia [the Hon. C. C. Kingston] said that he could not let the occasion pass, as a lover of the game for itself, without referring to the conduct of the Australian XI, who appeared to sink everything for monetary considerations. If the cricketing public of Australia were to allow the game to be sacrificed for money it would be a national calamity from a cricket point of view. [Applause.]

Peace was partially restored towards the close of the tour, and in the last three matches against representative XIs, A. C. Bannerman was opposed to the English team on each occasion, Bonnor and Giffen appeared in two matches, and Scott, Palmer, McDonnell and Blackham each played once. Spofforth, it must be stated, was not in accord with the other members of the Australian team. He did not arrive until some time after all the others had landed, and was always favourably disposed towards the Englishmen, playing against them whenever circumstances permitted.

First Test

At Adelaide, December 12, 13, 15, 16, 1884. England won by eight wickets.

This was the first occasion on which England and Australia had met on even terms on the Adelaide Oval, and the contest resulted in an easy victory for the tourists by eight wickets, the Colonists, however, batting one short in their second innings, owing to an accident to Bannerman on the second day. Briggs was far from well, but otherwise there was nothing amiss with any of the Englishmen. On the other hand the Australian captain had to deplore the loss of Spofforth, who was unable to take his place in the team through the death of a relative, and of Midwinter, forbidden to play in consequence of an attack of congestion of the lungs; while Giffen, owing to rheumatism, was almost unfit for cricket.

The main features of the match were the splendid batting of McDonnell and Barnes, the fine hitting of Ulyett, and the wonderful defence and patience of Scotton. Palmer for Australia, and Peel and Bates for England, were the most successful bowlers. Both weather and wicket were perfection on the opening day.

Murdoch won the toss, and both Bannerman and McDonnell batted in characteristic form, for when Bannerman was given out lbw at 33 for a couple of singles his partner had 30 to his credit. Murdoch succeeded, but when he had scored five he skyed a ball to short leg, which the wicket-keeper secured. At 56 luncheon was taken, McDonnell having 47. Upon resuming, both batsmen scored freely, and aided by indifferent fielding, took the score to 95 before Scott was clean-bowled for 19 after twice escaping being run out. The association of McDonnell and Blackham resulted in the score being exactly doubled, as it was not until 190 was telegraphed that the former pulled a ball into his wicket. His 124 was an exhibition of most brilliant cricket. He gave a chance to Barnes at long-off, and should have been run out later on. When Giffen came in, Blackham did nearly all the scoring, and the excellent total of 224 for four wickets was reached. Then an extraordinary collapse took place, and the remaining batsmen were got rid of for only 19 runs.

The first innings of the English team began at 12.15 on the second day, but when 11 only had been made Shrewsbury pulled a ball on to his wicket before he had scored. Before 20 had been totalled Bannerman had his forefinger split nearly the whole length in endeavouring to stop a tremendous hit from Ulyett's bat, and was unable to take any further part in the match. A sharp shower stopped play for a quarter of an hour shortly before luncheon. After 40 minutes' interval the game resumed and Ulyett scored rapidly. The 100 went up at three o'clock, but with seven runs added Ulyett was caught at mid-off for a very finely hit innings of 68, out of 96 added during his stay. Barnes joined Scotton, and both men played very carefully for a time. At length Barnes began to hit freely, and at the call of time Scotton had made 71 and Barnes 86, and the total had reached within ten runs of their opponents' score, with eight wickets still to go down.

Heavy rain had fallen between cessation of play on the Saturday and its resumption on the Monday, and when Scotton and Barnes went in on the third day they found the wicket greatly in favour of the bowlers. Both batsmen, however, played admirable cricket, and it was not until the total had been augmented by 49 runs, and the partnership had realised no fewer than 175, that Scotton was stumped for a most patient and valuable 82. He was at the wickets six hours. Bates was caught at 306 from a tremendous hit to long-on and the remaining wickets were secured without much trouble. Flowers' 15 included a terrifically hit off-drive from Boyle, and the decision of lbw, which sent him back, gave great dissatisfaction to the Englishmen. Read followed, but at 334 lost Barnes – clean-bowled with a yorker. Barnes had been at the wickets nearly five hours, and his 134 was described as "a grand exhibition of first-class cricket".

The last two wickets added 20, and Murdoch's XI began their second innings 126 to the bad. At 28 a fast yorker sent Blackham back. Murdoch was clean-bowled, middle stump, at 56, and then McDonnell and Giffen made the stand of the innings. Both batsmen scored at a great pace, but when the total reached 125 an appeal for leg-before to Giffen was answered in his favour. The ball going to leg, McDonnell ran down to Giffen, who would not move, and the former was easily run out. At the close the total was 152 for four wickets, or 26 runs on.

More heavy rain soaked the wicket on Monday night, and when the Colonials resumed their innings on Tuesday the ball bumped very much, and the innings was quickly finished off for the addition of only 39, Bannerman's finger being too severely damaged to permit his going in again. On the Englishmen commencing the task of making 66 to win, Flowers was out at eight, and Scotton at 14, both falling to splendid catches by Scott. Then, on a rapidly improving wicket, Shrewsbury and Barnes hit off the required runs, and at 1.20 the English team had won the match.

Toss: Australia. **Australia 243** (P. S. McDonnell 124, J. M. Blackham 66, W. Bates 5-31)
and 191 (P. S. McDonnell 83, R. Peel 5-51); **England 369** (W. H. Scotton 82, G. Ulyett 68, W. Barnes 134, G. E. Palmer 5-81) **and 67-2**.

Second Test

At Melbourne, January 1, 2, 3, 5, 1885. England won by ten wickets.

This match *[in which the Australian side showed 11 changes to the previous game, after a dispute over payments – Ed.]* was commenced, continued, and ended in perfect cricketing weather, albeit the heat was intense on the third day. The match was exceedingly well attended, upwards of 10,000 spectators being present on the first day, and about 6,000 on the second and third days.

Being successful in the toss Shrewsbury decided his side should bat first, and went in with Scotton as usual. Scotton was not at home with the left-hander, Bruce, who twice nearly succeeded in bowling him, and at 28 sent him back with the fast ball. Barnes came in, and a long stand was made. Despite numerous changes of bowling the partnership added no fewer than 116 runs before a separation was effected through Barnes pulling a rather wide ball into his wicket, his innings of 58 being made by sterling cricket. Shrewsbury was caught at short slip from a full pitch at 161, his score of 72 being made in his best form, and without a mistake. Bates should have been caught when he had made five, and with the total at 191 pulled a wide ball into his wicket. Flowers was caught at point, and at 204 the sixth wicket fell, Read being bowled off his legs, while the next ball clean-bowled Ulyett. A long score now appeared improbable, but with Briggs and Attewell together runs came freely till the latter was caught over the bowler's head at 259. Of the 44 runs added before Peel was bowled, Briggs made no fewer than 39. Stumps were then drawn, the total 303 for nine wickets.

Next morning Briggs and Hunter defied all the efforts of the bowlers for exactly an hour, and added 98 before the little Lancashire professional Briggs fell to one of the finest catches at deep square leg ever witnessed on the ground, Horan securing the ball just as he fell flat on his back. Briggs was enthusiastically cheered for his superb innings of 121, which contained only ten singles. He gave a couple of difficult chances – the first when he had made 104, and the second when he had 117, but these were the only blemishes in his splendid innings. Hunter's invaluable not-out innings of 39 contained a grand straight-drive for five, the ball going clean over the ladies' pavilion.

At 2.15 Morris and Jones opened the batting for Australia. From the last ball of the first over Morris was out lbw, and with the total at 46 Jones was similarly dismissed. Then Horan and Trumble kept together for a long time. Five bowlers were tried, but the score reached 124 before Horan fell to point for a carefully and well-played 63, after giving a chance to Barnes when he had made 30. Before play ceased for the day with the total at 151 for three wickets, Trumble was lucky in being twice missed.

On the third day the overnight not-outs were not parted until 190 went up, Trumble being then well caught and bowled by Barnes for an excellent 59, despite the chances given. Pope, Marr, and Musgrove were very quickly disposed of, the seventh wicket falling at 203. Jarvis then received valuable assistance from Worrall, the two putting on runs faster than any other pair on the Australian side. Both played capital cricket, and there appeared a chance of the follow-on being saved, but at last Jarvis was well caught from a lofty hit by Briggs. His masterly innings of 82 was devoid of the slightest blemish. The innings closed for 279. Being 122 to the bad the Colonists had to follow their innings. Bruce scored 20 of the first 29, and then Ulyett clean-bowled Jones. Horan followed, and just before time was called, fell a victim to the wicket-keeper. The score was then 66 for two, and 56 runs were still wanted to save a single-innings reverse.

Nothing approaching a long stand was made on the last day. Trumble was for the second time in the match caught and bowled by Barnes, the total standing at 86. Marr was caught and bowled at 95, and then Jarvis, who had been at wickets three-quarters of an hour for ten, was given out lbw. Six runs were still wanted to save a one-innings defeat when Robertson, the last man, joined Morris. Eleven were scored before Barnes clean-bowled Robertson, so the Englishmen had to go in again.

Toss: England. **England 401** (A. Shrewsbury 72, W. Barnes 58, J. Briggs 121, S. P. Jones 4-47) **and 7-0**;
Australia 279 (T. P. Horan 63, J. W. Trumble 59, A. H. Jarvis 82) **and 126** (W. Barnes 6-31).

Third Test

At Sydney, February 20, 21, 23, 24, 1885. Australia won by six runs.

The Australian XI on this occasion included four members of Murdoch's team – Bannerman, Scott, Bonnor and Spofforth – and of the remaining seven, five had been members of representative teams visiting the Old Country. Evans and Trumble completed one of the strongest combinations the Australian Colonies could produce, and after playing 25 matches without a single reverse, the tourists sustained a narrow defeat, after one of the finest contests ever witnessed at Sydney.

Barnes did not bowl a single over during the match, and in commenting on the long stand made by Garrett and Evans, the correspondent of the *Sporting Life* said:

"Garrett was missed at slip at 106, and then with Evans added 80 for the last wicket; but somehow the English bowlers could not bowl a bit, and Barnes, the wicket being made for him, was actually not tried." Barnes proved himself to be the most destructive bowler in the first-class matches of the tour, and it is therefore to be hoped that the following extract from an Australian paper does *not* give the true reason for the non-appearance of Barnes the bowler: "It should be stated that owing to some unpleasantness between Shrewsbury and Barnes, the latter refused to bowl when asked to do so. Everyone is aware that the first thing a cricketer has to do is to obey the captain, and therefore there is no excuse for Barnes. In the report on the second day's play adverse comment was passed on Shrewsbury for not putting Barnes on when Garrett and Evans made their stand. It appears that Shrewsbury did ask Barnes, and that the latter refused, as he did again in the second innings. It is to be regretted that a cricketer of Barnes' experience and skill should so far forget himself and his side as to let personal pique affect the result of a contest."

The fierce storm which raged during the luncheon interval was the cause of the attendance on the opening day being limited to 2,000, but on Saturday there were 10,000 present. On Monday the spectators estimated to number 6,000, while not less than 4,000 were present to witness the exciting finish on the fourth day.

Massie beat Shrewsbury for choice of innings, and sent in Jones and Bannerman to face Peel and Attewell. Bannerman gave a hard chance to slip at 20. At two o'clock a terrific storm of lightning, thunder and hail burst over the ground. In an incredibly short time it had the appearance of a field of snow, and then, the hail quickly melting, the ground became a sheet of water. It was scarcely expected that play could be resumed that day, but the water was soon absorbed, and at quarter-past four Jones and Bannerman continued their innings, the wicket of course being in a sloppy condition. At 45 Jones was stumped, and a run later Bannerman was caught at short leg. Horan was caught at the wicket, and Scott well taken at slip. Two wickets fell at 83, Bonnor being caught at slip and Jarvis clean-bowled first ball. Trumble was caught in the long field at 92, then Garrett and Spofforth played out time, the score being 97 for eight wickets.

On Saturday Garrett and Evans made a splendid stand for the last wicket. Five bowlers were tried, but to no purpose: at lunch-time the two batsmen were still together, and the total 175. After the interval Ulyett succeeded in getting Evans caught, no fewer than 80 runs having been put on for the last wicket. The new wicket having been rolled, Shrewsbury and Scotton opened for the Englishmen. The first five overs were maidens, and then 20 soon appeared. At 31 Shrewsbury was caught and bowled by Spofforth. Other misfortunes quickly followed, as at 33 Ulyett was clean-bowled with a yorker, and the first ball Barnes received bounded from the wicket-keeper's legs, and the batsman had to retire, stumped. The later batsmen gave little trouble and England were all out for 133.

Bannerman and Bonnor began the second innings of Australia on the third day. The score was slowly hit to 28 and then Bannerman gave a couple of chances which were not accepted. Bonnor, having made 29 out of 37, was bowled by a yorker, and then Horan and Bannerman took the total to 56, when lunch was taken. Upon resuming Bannerman was caught at point, having been at the wickets an hour and a half for 16 runs. When 110 had been posted Horan made a grand square-leg hit off Flowers, the ball pitching into the pavilion reserve. Bates bowled Horan off his thigh for 36, made in his best form. Half the wickets were now down for 119. Massie and Trumble carried the score to 151, when the former was then clean-bowled by a breakback. Jarvis was caught and bowled after making a couple, and then Trumble, who had played exceedingly well, was taken at long-on for 32. A splendid one-handed catch at mid-off dismissed Spofforth and brought the innings to a conclusion for 165 just after five o'clock. The Englishmen wanted 214 to win. Only 14 were scored when one of Spofforth's fastest deliveries clean-bowled Scotton, and when Ulyett had made four he was thrown out by Bannerman in trying a short run. Shrewsbury and Barnes then kept their wickets intact until the call of time, the score being 29 for two.

Before a run was scored on the last day Barnes was caught at the wicket, but Shrewsbury and Bates put on 30 before the former was clean-bowled by Spofforth, who dismissed Briggs in the same way a couple of runs later. Half the wickets were now down for 61, and an easy victory for the Colonials seemed assured. Bates and Flowers took the score to 92, when Bates fell a victim to the wicket-keeper for a fine and free 31, which included two fours and a grand hit to long-on, off Spofforth, clean over the fence for five. Flowers and Read then made the splendid stand which completely altered the aspect of the game. The bowling was repeatedly changed, but both batsmen played with ease and confidence and scored with great freedom. Spofforth came in for severe punishment, but when only 20 runs were wanted, he had his revenge by clean-bowling Read. The only really bad stroke Read made was off the first ball he received from Spofforth, but he gave no chances, and his innings of 56 included no fewer than nine fours.

Flowers and Read had put on 102 runs for the seventh wicket. Attewell came in, but was run out with the total unchanged, and only five were added before Peel was caught at the wicket. When Hunter, the last man, went in only 15 were wanted and the excitement round the ground was intense. By twos and singles the total was hit up to 207, when Spofforth took the ball, and from his first delivery Flowers was caught at point from a rising ball, and the touring team suffered their first defeat, by seven runs.

Toss: Australia. **Australia 181** (T. W. Garrett 51*, W. Attewell 4-53, W. Flowers 5-46) **and 165** (W. Bates 5-24); **England 133** (F. R. Spofforth 4-54, T. P. Horan 6-40) **and 207** (W. Flowers 56, J. M. Read 56, F. R. Spofforth 6-90).

Fourth Test

At Sydney, March 14, 16, 17, 1885. Australia won by eight wickets.

The very close finish in the previous match caused an extraordinary amount of interest to be taken in this contest, and there could not have been fewer than 12,000 spectators on the opening day, while 6,000 was the estimated number on each of the other days. The Australian team was differently constituted, Palmer, McDonnell, Giffen and Blackham taking the places of Scott, Massie, Jarvis and Evans. These changes, as the result proved, greatly added to the bowling strength of the team without weakening its batting powers to any appreciable extent. The successful bowling of Giffen in the first innings, and of Palmer in the second, went, perhaps, as far towards achieving victory as the magnificent hitting of Bonnor. On the first day 11 wickets fell for 280 runs; on the second day only seven were dismissed for an aggregate of 297; while on the third day, after a night's heavy rain, 14 wickets were captured for a total of only 116 runs.

Shrewsbury won choice of innings, and took Ulyett with him to the wickets. Spofforth had not arrived, so bowling was entrusted to Giffen and Palmer. When Ulyett had made ten he pulled a ball into his wicket, and simultaneously with his dismissal Spofforth appeared on the field, and when Shrewsbury hit Palmer for a couple of fours that bowler gave way to Spofforth. Shrewsbury batted in fine free form, and Scotton played a strictly defensive game as usual. At luncheon the score was 50, and upon resuming Scotton was caught at the wicket for four. Barnes and Shrewsbury raised the total to 76, when the English captain was clean-bowled for a capital innings of 40. Barnes and Bates scored with great freedom, and a short time only elapsed before the century was hoisted. Giffen at last succeeded in clean-bowling Barnes with a break-back at 159, the outgoing batsman's 50 having been made in his best form. Jones bowled for Trumble, and after some time made a magnificent catch from his own bowling, which sent Bates back for a splendidly hit 60.

With Read and Flowers together the 200 was soon telegraphed. At 219 Flowers was clean-bowled, and Briggs, after making a three from the first ball he received, was well caught at point from the second. Giffen bowled Attewell after he had scored a single, and Read gave a chance of stumping. Later on, with his score on 37, he was caught from a no-ball of Spofforth's, and with the total 252 was clean-bowled by Giffen for a very freely hit innings of 47. Hunter scored 13, including two fours in succession from Spofforth, but in trying a third he was clean bowled, and brought the innings to a conclusion for 269. Only ten minutes remained for play, so Garrett and Palmer were deputed to open. Ulyett sent down the first over, and the last ball – a fast yorker – clean-bowled Palmer. When the total reached 11 for one wicket play ceased for the day.

Only four runs were added next morning before Peel bowled Trumble off his legs. McDonnell, having scored 20 out of 25, was caught at extra cover-point at 40. No other wicket was obtained before luncheon, at which time the score had reached 80. Bannerman gave a difficult chance to Scotton, which was also missed, and then Horan was well caught at slip off Ulyett at 119. Bonnor came in next, and Bannerman had another life at the hands of Scotton – a very easy one this time. Off Flowers' second ball Bannerman was caught at point for 51, seven wickets then being down for 134.

At this point the prospects of a follow-on appeared very probable, but upon Jones joining Bonnor a magnificent stand was made, and the aspect of the game underwent a complete change. Bonnor started in very indifferent form, but afterwards hit with the utmost brilliancy. After a short period of slow play Bonnor hit Barnes to the pavilion for four, and drove the next ball over the boundary for five. From this time to the close the bowling was punished with the utmost severity, and eventually Bonnor saved the follow-on. At length Barnes went on again, and from his first ball Bonnor was easily caught at third man with the total at 288. Bonnor's magnificent 128 included four fives, and 14 fours. He and Jones put on 154 for the eighth wicket. It was not to be expected that so long an innings should be played without chances being given, and Bonnor's fine contribution was not without blemishes. Though narrowly escaping being bowled several times, he gave no real chances in the field until he had made 81, when Peel misjudged a bad hit. With his score 98 he might have been caught by Barnes at slip, and later on was missed by Read at long-on. At the call of time the total stood at 308 for eight.

Heavy rain having fallen from a little after midnight until nine o'clock on the morning of the third day, the wicket was altogether in the favour of the bowlers when the game resumed at noon. The last two Australian wickets only added one run, Jones being immediately run out for a fine defensive innings of 40, while Spofforth fell to a capital catch at third man after scoring a single. The Englishmen commenced their second innings in a minority of 40 runs, Shrewsbury and Ulyett again being the first pair. They were opposed by Spofforth and Palmer, and no change of bowling was found necessary during the innings. Ulyett was caught at cover-point after making a couple, and Scotton fell to mid-off without having troubled the scorers. A fine catch at long-on got rid of Shrewsbury, and Bates was given out caught at the wicket, the fourth wicket falling with the score at 20. Read was caught at short leg, then Barnes and Flowers kept their wickets intact until lunch-time, when the total had reached 42.

Upon resumption Flowers was caught at third man at 46, and then 20 runs were added before Briggs, in attempting a fourth run for a bye, was run out. Barnes was caught at short mid-on from a bumper, Peel caught and bowled by Spofforth, and Hunter clean-bowled, the innings closing for the poor total of 77. The Australians had therefore only 38 runs to make, but these were not obtained without the loss of two good wickets, McDonnell being caught at third man, and Bannerman clean-bowled. Horan and Jones then hit off the required runs.

Toss: England. **England 269** (W. Barnes 50, W. Bates 64, G. Giffen 7-117) **and 77** (F. R. Spofforth 5-30, G. E. Palmer 4-32); **Australia 309** (A. C. Bannerman 51, G. J. Bonnor 128, W. Barnes 4-61) **and 38-2**.

Fifth Test

At Melbourne, March 21, 23, 24, 25, 1885. England won by an innings and 98 runs.

Although the home XI won choice of innings, and, as the Australian captain admitted, had in no marked manner anything the worst of luck, they suffered a crushing defeat. There were about 8,000 spectators present on the opening day, but the attendance fell to less than a quarter of that on the following days.

Horan won the toss. Peel and Ulyett started the bowling, and from the latter's second ball Bruce should have been taken at the wicket, but Hunter dropped the catch. In Ulyett's next over, Bruce was very lucky in escaping being run out, and at 21 he was easily caught for 15. Bannerman was caught at third man, and Horan at once given out lbw. Jones came in, but at 34 was also given out lbw, and without a run added Giffen was bowled. Jarvis and Walters carried the total to 45, when the latter was bowled off his leg, and six wickets were down. Luncheon was then taken.

Nine wickets were down for 99 when Spofforth joined Trumble. The great bowler immediately began to hit in most vigorous fashion, and runs were put on at a rapid rate. Attewell relieved Barnes who had been hit for a five by Spofforth, the ball clearing the pavilion gate. A ringing cheer accompanied the hoisting of 150, but at 163 Attewell sent down a short-pitched fast one which clean-bowled Spofforth for a rattling 50, Trumble carrying his bat for a good defensive innings of 34. The wicket having been rolled Barnes and Scotton opened the batting. When stumps were drawn no wicket had fallen, and the total had reached 44.

On the second day for a considerable time runs were put on at a very slow rate, the first 16 occupying 40 minutes. At 60 Bruce clean-bowled Scotton, and at 96 Giffen clean-bowled Read. Ulyett scored a single from Giffen and then played the first ball he received from Spofforth hard on his leg, from whence it rolled into the wicket and disturbed the bails. Luncheon was then taken, the score being 97 for three wickets. At 136 Bruce bowled for Spofforth. This change met with success, as at 141 Barnes was caught off Bruce for a finely played 74. Bates came in, and though unwell, punished the bowling severely. About this time several chances were given but not accepted. Shrewsbury should have been caught by McShane off Spofforth, while Bates was missed four times – at long-off by Horan, at third man by Jones, at point by Bruce, and in the long field by McShane. Bates scored his first 33 runs while Shrewsbury made six, and as soon as the 200 went up illness compelled him to retire, his individual score then being 54. At 256, Spofforth, who changed ends, bowled Flowers off his legs. At the call of time Shrewsbury had made 54, the total being 270 for five wickets.

On the third day, the total had reached 324, and the partnership yielded 68, before Briggs was caught at short slip for a vigorous and excellent 43. Attewell was caught at mid-off with the total unchanged, and then Bates resumed his innings. He had not, however, sufficiently recovered to hit in his usual vigorous form, and after adding seven runs was caught at long-on. At lunch-time Shrewsbury had made 86, and the total stood at 347, which was afterwards raised to 386 before Giffen clean-bowled Hunter for 18, the last wicket having increased the score to the extent of 49 runs. Shrewsbury carried his bat for 105 out of 289 scored while he was in, and his fine innings – the highest he had made in Australia – was only marred by the one chance to McShane.

Garrett and Bannerman commenced Australia's second innings at three o'clock. Bannerman was nearly bowled first ball, and should have been caught before he had scored. It mattered little, however, as he was taken at long slip after making a couple. A fast ball from Ulyett bowled Garrett, and Giffen was caught at short leg. When 50 was posted Attewell relieved Ulyett, and bowled Horan at 60. Jones was clean-bowled at the same total. Trumble was given out lbw at 91. Walters, who followed, was brilliantly caught at mid-off by Attewell at 100, and then Bruce and Jarvis played out time.

By previous arrangement the match was not continued until 2.15 on the last day. The Australians, with three wickets to fall, required 118 to save a single-innings defeat, and the very slight chance they had of accomplishing so heavy a task was rendered hopeless by a heavy fall of rain in the early morning, which gave the bowlers a great advantage. Only a single was scored before Jarvis was caught at mid-on, and with a couple added Spofforth was caught at long-on. Bruce and McShane put on 17 runs, and then the former was caught at short slip for a very meritorious innings of 35, bringing the match to a conclusion, and giving the Englishmen victory by an innings.

Toss: Australia. **Australia 163** (F. R. Spofforth 50, G. Ulyett 4-52) **and 125;**
England 386 (W. Barnes 74, A. Shrewsbury 105*, W. Bates 61).

ENGLAND V AUSTRALIA 1886

The fifth tour of Australian cricketers in England was emphatically a failure, whether we regard it as an event of itself, or compare it with previous visits of the teams of the colonies. Perhaps if the XI under Mr Scott had been making a new experiment – had been breaking fresh ground – we should have found much to admire, and very little to find fault with, and should have satisfied ourselves, with something like smug conceit, that our rivals from the South had done very well, and, indeed, were quite as powerful as there had been any reason to expect. But history cannot go backwards, and there can be no room for doubt that, satisfactory as the 1886 Australian tour may have been to the pride of Englishmen, the tour was a feeble and spiritless thing. We saw on too many occasions a mere playing-out of time, and on one or two days a failure of nerve and an exhibition of weakness which those who had looked upon the Australians at their best – as we saw them in 1882 – found it difficult to believe possible.

The causes of the non-success were the limited amount of high-class batting, the partial failure of Spofforth's bowling, the uncertainty of the fielding, a lack of enthusiasm and cohesion in the team, and the absence of the necessary amount of authority and experience on the part of the captain. W. L. Murdoch may not have exhibited all the qualities which go to make up that rare and valuable being, an ideal captain – but he certainly had a larger experience and a stronger will than the gentleman who, with the best of intentions, and the greatest sincerity of purpose, led the team of 1886.

Moreover (and this is a very important factor in the case) our own professional batting and bowling had greatly improved since the previous visit, and the Australians were meeting men who bowled more after their own fashion, and who batted with a determination and fertility of resource which at the most they could only hope to equal. Our Gentlemen were probably a class below their predecessors of a few years back, but we still had in Mr Grace and Mr Read batsmen who were equal to the greatest emergencies.

Giffen was emphatically the success of the tour, and the fact that he came out first in both batting and bowling speaks volumes for his excellence. Indeed it would be impossible at the present day to name his superior as an all-round cricketer.

First Test

At Manchester, July 5, 6, 7, 1886. England won by four wickets.

The first of the three great contests between England and Australia had been looked forward to with an immense amount of interest, and the composition of the English team had caused a good deal of controversy. In the original team Mr Hornby was to have been captain, and Barnes was selected; but owing to an injury to his leg the popular Lancashire captain had to stand out, while Barnes was prevented from playing by a strain in his side. Barlow and Briggs were the two men chosen to fill the vacancies.

Fully 10,000 witnessed the first day's play, which was good and interesting throughout. The weather, although dull and overcast in the morning, turned out beautifully fine, and the wicket afforded the bowlers very little assistance. Having the good fortune to win the toss the Australians at the start fared remarkably well. Jones played superb cricket, and Jarvis hit with great brilliancy for 45. The score was 181 when the fifth wicket fell, and there seemed every prospect of a long total, but afterwards came such a collapse that the last five wickets went down for 24 runs. Jones, who went in first, was lbw for a faultless 87. Out of 204 runs from the bat, Jones, Jarvis, Trumble, and Scott made no fewer than 177. The fielding was exceedingly smart and accurate, and Pilling kept wicket to perfection.

A little less than an hour remained when the Englishmen commenced their innings, and the score was only nine when Mr Grace was very cleverly caught at slip. Shrewsbury was let off from a sharp chance in the same position from the first ball he received, but afterwards batted well, and he and Scotton were together at the call of time, when the score stood at 36 for one wicket.

On the second day the interest was thoroughly sustained throughout. The Australians bowled and fielded admirably, and the Englishmen, who scarcely seemed to play in their best form, scored with difficulty. Shrewsbury, after making 31, was bowled by a yorker, and Scotton, after exhibiting great patience, was caught at point at 80. Mr Read batted in splendid style for 51 and was out to a very good catch at third man at 131. At the luncheon interval the score was 140 for five, and afterwards Ulyett and Briggs were speedily disposed of, the total, with seven men out, being only 160. Then, when it seemed most probable that the Australians would lead on the first innings, Lohmann and Barlow made an invaluable stand, and quite altered the aspect of affairs. When he scored only a single, however, Lohmann was badly missed by Palmer at long-on, and for this mistake the Australians had to pay very dearly. Lohmann hit with great nerve and judgment, while Barlow played his usual sound and steady game. The score was up to 206 before Lohmann was bowled, 46 having been added. In the end the total reached 223, or 18 runs to the good, Barlow taking out his bat for an invaluable 38.

With an hour and 20 minutes remaining, the Australians went in again, and though Jones and Scott put on 37 for the first wicket, matters went so badly with the Colonists afterwards that before the close four wickets had fallen for 55. Giffen and Jarvis were both out to Barlow, and Bonnor, who exhibited very bad judgment, was caught from a very tame stroke on the off side within five minutes of time. The second day's play left the Australians 36 runs to the good, with six wickets to fall in their second innings.

On the concluding day the Australians thoroughly kept up their reputation for playing an uphill game, and though they were defeated at the finish, they made a splendid fight of it, and the interest in the match never for a moment ceased. Thanks mainly to the capital batting of Scott, and the plucky hitting of Garrett and Spofforth, the total reached 123. As the Englishmen were only left with 106 runs to get, it looked as if they would gain a very easy victory, but so disastrous was the start that perhaps the three best batsmen in England – Grace, Read, and Shrewsbury – were dismissed for only 24. It must be stated, however, that the wicket was beginning to crumble a little, and was by no means so easy as it had been on either of the previous days.

The Australians now began to realise that they had a chance, and bowled and fielded with remarkable keenness. It was at this point that Barlow joined Scotton, and the two batsmen, displaying most praiseworthy care and judgment, wore down the splendid bowling, and again turned the scale in favour of England. The partnership altogether lasted an hour, and yielded 41 runs, the score being thus 65 when the fourth wicket fell. Later on, Mr Steel played in moderate form, but he was missed from an easy chance by Bonnor at short slip, and had this come off the Englishmen would probably have had to fight very hard for their victory. At 90 Barlow's long and extremely good innings of 30 was ended by a clever catch close in, and when the game was a tie Ulyett hit out recklessly, and was caught in the long field. Briggs made the winning stroke at 20 minutes to six, and the English were left winners of a remarkable match. Special praise must be awarded to Barlow, who took seven wickets for 44 in the second innings, made three catches, and scored 68 runs in the match for once out.

Toss: Australia. **Australia 205** (S. P. Jones 87, G. Ulyett 4-46) **and 123** (R. G. Barlow 7-44);
England 223 (W. W. Read 51, F. R. Spofforth 4-82) **and 107-6**.

Second Test
At Lord's, July 19, 20, 21, 1886. England won by an innings and 106 runs.

The meeting of England and Australia at Lord's is by almost common consent reckoned to be the most important match of a Colonial tour, and the immense superiority of the best XI in England over Australia was clearly and unmistakably proved.

The first day's play was greatly interfered with by rain. However, some remarkable batting was shown by the Englishmen, who had the good fortune to win the toss. At first the wicket was in splendid condition, but the rain which fell between 25 minutes past 12 and a quarter to two altered its character, and for the greater part of the time that Shrewsbury and Scotton were together the bowlers had a distinct advantage. Despite the unfavourable circumstances, between 12,000 and 13,000 persons visited the ground. Mr Grace was caught at the wicket when the score was 27, and after that Scotton and Shrewsbury, by some wonderful defence, wore down the bowling, and took the total up to 77 before Scotton was clean-bowled by Garrett. Throughout the remainder of the day Shrewsbury played one of his very finest innings, meeting all the bowling with ease and confidence, and scarcely ever seeming in difficulties.

On the second day the weather was much more favourable, and the cricket proceeded without interruption. There was an immense crowd, with 15,663 paying for admission. Barnes was not dismissed until the score had reached 280, the famous Nottingham pair having added no fewer than 161 runs. Later on Ulyett hit freely for 19, and ultimately the innings closed for 353. Shrewsbury, who had gone in first wicket down with the score at 27, was the last man out, and too much praise cannot be afforded him for his most extraordinary performance. He was at the wickets for six hours and 50 minutes, and though he gave a couple of difficult chances, there was scarcely any fault to be found with his batting. It should be stated that the wicket on this morning was rapidly improving, but Shrewsbury had thoroughly mastered all the varying conditions. His 164, with 16 fours, was the largest score ever made against Australian bowling in England.

The Australians had always had such a reputation for playing an uphill game that many expected great things from them, more especially as when they went in the wicket afforded bowlers little assistance. As it turned out, however, the batting was of a most disappointing character, and though Scott and Jones put on 45 for the first wicket, the whole side were out for the poor total of 121. The chief cause of this remarkable breakdown was the superb bowling of Briggs, who was put on as first change and took five wickets at a cost of only 29 runs. The English fielding could scarcely have been improved upon. Going in a second time against the formidable majority of 232, the Australians lost one wicket for 12 runs before the call of time.

As the weather remained fine on the third day, and the wicket became, if anything, rather easier, there were still many who believed in the ability of the Australians to make the game a draw, and at one time it seemed quite likely that they would, for Palmer, Trumble and Jones all batted with extreme caution. When the score was 76 for two, however, Briggs was put on at the Pavilion end in place of Steel, a change which proved to be the turning-point of the innings. From this end Briggs bowled with even greater success than he had met with on the previous day from the Nursery wicket, and one after another the batsmen went down before him. At a quarter-past three the whole side were out for 126, and the Australians thus suffered a most crushing defeat. Briggs, who was immensely cheered all round the ground, took six wickets at a cost of only 45 runs, so that in the whole match he obtained 11 wickets for 74.

Toss: England. **England 353** (A. Shrewsbury 164, W. Barnes 58, F. R. Spofforth 4-73);
Australia 121 (J. Briggs 5-29) **and 126** (J. Briggs 6-45).

Third Test

At The Oval, August 12, 13, 14, 1886. England won by an innings and 217 runs.

The third and last meeting had been robbed of a large amount of its interest by the poor form shown by the Australians, who had suffered defeat on each of the two previous occasions. Nevertheless there was a large company on the opening day, 11,360 persons passing through the turnstiles. As the team which gained so decisive a victory at Lord's had worked well together, it was a fitting compliment to play identically the same England XI in this third match.

For the second time the Englishmen won the toss, and once more they took full advantage: the Australians were engaged for the whole day in getting down two wickets. However, the batting was not of high quality. Although Mr Grace made his highest innings against Australian bowling, it was pretty generally admitted that his cricket was more faulty than usual. He gave an easy chance to Scott at short slip when he had made six, at 23 he hit a ball very hard back to Giffen, a possible chance to that bowler's left hand; when he had 60 he might perhaps have been caught in the long field, had Bruce started earlier for the ball, and at 93 McIlwraith had a difficult one-handed chance at slip. Moreover, just before getting out, when his total was 169 he hit a ball straight back to Garrett, who failed to hold it. Still, these blemishes notwith-standing, the innings was a very fine one. He made the enormous proportion of 170 out of 216 during his stay, and his figures were 22 fours, four threes, 17 twos and 36 singles.

In an hour and 52 minutes before luncheon Mr Grace made 40 runs, and in two hours and 38 minutes afterwards he made 130. This marked difference in the rate of scoring was accounted for to a large extent by the state of the wicket, which was by no means perfect up to the interval, but which improved steadily as the afternoon wore on. Scotton batted with extraordinary patience even for him, and contented himself by keeping up his wicket while Mr Grace hit. The two put on 170 before they were parted. Scotton's 34 – an innings of immense value – occupied no less than three hours and three-quarters, and at one period he was an hour and seven minutes without making a single run. After the dismissal of Scotton and Mr Grace some beautiful cricket was played by Shrewsbury and Mr Read. When time was called, the score was 279 with only two wickets down.

On the Friday there was another immense attendance, 9,786 paying for admission. Again everything went in favour of the Englishmen, and at the close the Australians found themselves in a hopeless position, wanting no fewer than 358 to avert a single-innings defeat, and having ten wickets to fall. It must be stated, however, that the English team had all the best of the luck, for the rain which fell in London on the Thursday evening seriously damaged the ground, and the Australians had to play the cream of the English bowling on a wicket on which run-getting was a matter of great difficulty.

The English innings lasted until ten minutes to four in the afternoon, the total ultimately reaching 434. It was generally thought that, as the Englishmen were in such a position that they could not lose, some of the batsmen threw their wickets away. Shrewsbury only added two to his overnight score, and after his departure Barnes, Mr Steel, Barlow, and Ulyett were dismissed in rapid succession, seven wickets being down for 320. Then came a most brilliant display of cricket on the part of Mr Read and Briggs, who hit at a tremendous pace, and at one time made 56 in half an hour. Briggs was at last well caught at slip at 410 for a very dashing 53. When it seemed almost certain that Mr Read would reach his hundred he was out to a well-judged catch in the long field. Out of 202 runs scored while he was at the wickets, he made 94 by perfect cricket. He hardly gave a fair chance, and seldom seemed in the least difficulty with the bowling. He was batting for about three hours and a half.

The batting of the Australians proved to be of the most disappointing description. The innings opened at ten minutes past four, and just before six the whole side were out for the wretchedly poor total of 68. Being assisted by the condition of the ground, Lohmann and Briggs bowled magnificently and carried all before them, only two men on the Australian side – Palmer and Trumble – showing the least ability to contend against them. The English fielding was exceptionally brilliant, and the catch with which Briggs dismissed Blackham deserves a special word of praise. Following their innings against the enormous majority of 366, the Australians scored eight runs without the loss of a wicket before the call of time.

The cricket on the concluding day needs but brief description. The Australians could not hope to avert defeat, and though Giffen and Palmer batted well, the total in the end only reached 149. The only chance of saving the game was to stop in the whole of the day. Even with the ground in the best of condition this would have been a task to tax the powers of any XI, but with the wicket still assisting the bowlers it was practically out of the question. Lohmann and Briggs again proved by far the most successful bowlers, and in the whole match Lohmann obtained 12 wickets for 104 runs, while Briggs secured six for 58. All ideas as to the ability of the 1886 Australian XI to meet the full strength of England were totally dispelled by this crushing defeat. In fairness to the Colonials it must be stated that, at The Oval at any rate, they had all the worst of the wicket; but they played throughout with a lack of the life and energy that have usually characterised Australian cricket.

Toss: England. **England 434** (W. G. Grace 170, W. W. Read 94, J. Briggs 53, F. R. Spofforth 4-65);
Australia 68 (G. A. Lohmann 7-36) **and 149** (G. A. Lohmann 5-68).

Australia v England 1886–87

The team taken out to Australia in the autumn of 1886 was one of the strongest that ever left England for the Colonies. The team took part in 29 matches, of which ten were of first-class importance. It is understood that the tour did not yield much profit, but the cricket shown was very fine indeed, not a single defeat being sustained on a hard wicket. An accident at Sydney prevented Barnes playing after the end of January, and the loss of his batting and bowling made a great difference to the XI.

Turner, the New South Wales bowler, met with extraordinary success, and, though the wickets gave him great assistance, it would be impossible to say too much in his praise. The Englishmen thought that not even Spofforth, in his best day, was more difficult on slow grounds, the ball breaking back at such a pace as to beat even Shrewsbury's defence.

First Test

At Sydney, January 28, 29, 31, 1887. England won by 13 runs.

The great match and also the most conspicuous triumph of the tour, the Englishmen winning by 13 runs after being dismissed in their first innings for a total of 45. When stumps were drawn on the Saturday they did not seem to have even a remote chance of success, being only some 20-odd runs to the good with three wickets to fall in their second innings. On the Monday, however, they played up in splendid style, and gained a victory that might fairly be compared to the seven-run win of Australia over England at The Oval in 1882. Briggs, Flowers, and Sherwin batted so well that Australia had to go in with 111 to get. With the wicket in very fair order this seemed an easy task, and defeat was not thought of, but Barnes bowled so finely, and was so ably supported by Lohmann, that the total only reached 97. Barring one mistake the English fielding was magnificent. Except that Giffen was still too ill to appear, the Australian team was almost a representative one, though Palmer and Horan should have been played in preference to Midwinter and McShane.

Toss: Australia. **England 45** (C. T. B. Turner 6-15, J. J. Ferris 4-27) **and 184** (J. J. Ferris 5-76); **Australia 119 and 97** (W. Barnes 6-28).

Second Test

At Sydney, February 25, 26, 28, March 1, 1887. England won by 71 runs.

The Australian team was very far indeed from a representative one, the only Victorian player on the side being Midwinter. Jones, however, was the only prominent Sydney man who was away. Having the best of the play all through, the Englishmen won by 71 runs. Lohmann's fine bowling in the first innings, and Barlow's batting being the main elements of success. Turner and Ferris bowled admirably for the Australians, but their exertions were not sufficient to avert defeat.

Toss: England. **England 151** (J. J. Ferris 5-71, C. T. B. Turner 5-41) **and 154** (C. T. B. Turner 4-52,
J. J. Ferris 4-69); **Australia 84** (G. A. Lohmann 8-35) **and 150** (W. Bates 4-26).

AUSTRALIA V ENGLAND 1887–88

Two English teams visited Australia in the season of 1887–88, but it is certain that such
a piece of folly will never be perpetrated again. Having regard to the fact that 11-a-side
matches are only practicable at Melbourne, Sydney, and Adelaide, it was clear from the
first that two combinations would not be able to pay their way, and, though we do not
know the exact result of Shaw, Shrewsbury, and Lillywhite's venture, the Melbourne
Club frankly admitted a heavy loss over Mr Vernon's team.

It would serve no purpose now to go into the cause of the blunder, for a blunder
in every way it undoubtedly was. The Melbourne authorities averred that it was well
known their intention of bringing out an English team had only been postponed from
the previous year, while the Sydney people, who supported Shaw and Shrewsbury,
declared that for all they knew, when they asked Shrewsbury and his friends to get up
an XI for the centenary celebration in New South Wales, the Melbourne Club's project
had been abandoned. Wherever the blame lay, the effect was to throw a damper on the
visits of English cricketers to the Colonies.

It is satisfactory to think, however, that, apart from financial considerations,
both tours were completely successful, the cricket shown being in every way creditable to the Englishmen. Mr Vernon's team only lost one match, and in that they
played an innings of over 300, while Shaw and Shrewsbury's side suffered but two
defeats. For one special occasion the two teams joined forces, and decisively beat
Combined Australia.

The record of Mr Vernon's combination was indeed a brilliant one when we take
into consideration that the death of his father compelled Lord Hawke to return to
England, and that Bates's services were lost through a painful accident to his eye – an
accident which kept him out of all first-class cricket in England in 1888, and from which,
it is feared, he can never wholly recover. He was injured while practising on the Melbourne
Ground, a ball hit from a neighbouring net striking him with frightful force.

Shaw and Shrewsbury's team also team played in a style that did high credit to
English cricket. They only lost two matches, both against New South Wales; and the
batting of Shrewsbury and the bowling of Lohmann and Briggs may rank among the
best achievements of our players in the Colonies.

Only Test
At Sydney, February 10, 11, 13, 14, 15, 1888. England won by 126 runs.

In this match the two English teams joined forces and put a combined XI into the
field. The Colonial side, which included seven of the players who afterwards went to
England, was very strong, but George Giffen's absence prevented it from being quite
representative. Horan and Bruce, too, would have been better than some who were
playing. The match was played on a ground that was much damaged by rain, and

the Englishmen, having the upper hand throughout, won handsomely. Towards this brilliant and gratifying result the splendid bowling of Peel and Lohmann mainly contributed, the two taking 18 wickets between them. Shrewsbury's fine play in the first innings and Maurice Read's hitting in the second also demand recognition. Not since the visit of George Parr's team in 1863–64 had English cricket been so represented on an Australian ground.

Toss: Australia. **England 113** (C. T. B. Turner 5-44, J. J. Ferris 4-60) **and 137** (C. T. B. Turner 7-43); **Australia 42** (G. A. Lohmann 5-17, R. Peel 5-18) **and 82** (G. A. Lohmann 4-35, R. Peel 4-40).

ENGLAND V AUSTRALIA 1888

The chief interest of spectators during the tour of the sixth Australian team in England centred on Turner and Ferris. The mighty Spofforth, the greatest bowler we had ever seen, was with the team no more; there was neither Giffen nor Palmer. The Australians of 1888 were for all practical purposes a new XI trusting to two young bowlers. The choice of captain had fallen upon Percy McDonnell, and it is difficult to see who else could have been selected. It was at once seen that Turner and Ferris were bowlers of high capacity and considerable resource, that their action was free from tricks of any kind, and that they both were, like all Australians we have ever seen, scrupulously and irreproachably fair. Bonnor, who had been here since 1886, joined the team on its arrival.

Jones, the best batsman, fell ill during the tour. A period of anxiety for the manager ensued. No risk was run, no danger was incurred, no steps were taken to which the strictest purist in morals could have objected; but, acting under full medical authority and sanction, the secret of the highly contagious nature of Jones's illness [smallpox – Ed.] was strictly and faithfully kept, and only one or two members of the team itself and three or four persons outside it knew until months afterwards, when all danger was past and the unlucky young fellow was about again, what a narrow escape the ship had had from foundering before the voyage was a quarter over.

We do not wish to make much capital out of this victory of the old country in the international contests. The Australians themselves would freely admit that this team were not equal, or anything like equal, to the best contemporary XI of England. Of course the beating we had at Lord's is a recorded fact and will be remembered against us, but it was in no sense a defeat upon our merits, and not one Englishman in a thousand will feel it as belonging to the same category as our overthrow at The Oval in 1882.

McDonnell came out at the top of the batting, but Bonnor displayed his inequalities of form, playing a giant's game one day and a lawn-tennis game the next. Trott amply and fully justified his selection by scoring the highly creditable total of 1,212 runs. Worrall is a batsman of the rural or bucolic type. He must be a descendant of that village wonder who hit "bloomin' 'ard, bloomin' 'igh, and bloomin' often." But Worrall is degenerate. He certainly hits hard and high – and seldom.

Blackham's wicket-keeping was excellent all through the summer, his form on many occasions being considered equal to that of his best days. As this was Blackham's sixth tour, higher praise is impossible.

GREAT BOWLERS OF THE YEAR – C. T. B. TURNER

Charles Thomas Byas Turner was born in Bathurst, in New South Wales, on November 16, 1862. He stands about 5ft 9in, and bowls right-hand, above medium pace, with a beautifully easy delivery, his hand not being very high at the moment the ball quits it. He has a fine break from the off, and bowls a wonderful yorker, but the great thing about him is that he makes the ball rise from the pitch faster perhaps than any bowler we have seen. He first appeared in Bathurst in December 1881, when against Shaw's team he took 17 wickets for 69. After that he steadily played club cricket until November 1886, when he met with surprising success against Shaw and Shrewsbury's team, taking six for 20 and seven for 34 in the first match, and eight wickets for 80 on a good wicket a month later. These performances were eclipsed by what he did in January 1887, when he took the wickets of Barnes, Barlow, Gunn, Briggs, Scotton, and Flowers for 15 runs. He had the largest share in winning NSW the third match with Shaw's team, as he took eight wickets in the first innings for 32 runs, and six for 27 in the second.

First Test

At Lord's, July 16, 17, 1888. Australia won by 61 runs.

Although it was seen that the Australians were by no means equal on their merits to the best team in England, there was a considerable amount of anxiety as to the result of the first of the three great Test matches. In dry weather and on a hard wicket, confidence in the strength of English batting would have been almost unlimited, but the weather for weeks had been so bad, and the Australian bowling had proved so destructive, that many quite dispassionate judges thought the game would be so fluky that victory would depend almost entirely upon success in the toss.

Our batting had probably become stronger so far as the professionals were concerned, but it certainly had not maintained its position among amateurs, there being many good Gentlemen batsmen, but no new ones who had any claim to be chosen in a strictly representative XI. On the other hand, our bowling was probably stronger than ever, while the fielding of the selected team left nothing to be desired.

McDonnell, having won the toss, went in with Bannerman to commence a match about which everyone's nerves were in a high state of tension, and at a time when all concerned, from batsmen, bowlers, and umpires down to the merest spectators, felt the importance of the issue, and how much was at stake. We ought, however, to say that to the best of our knowledge there was little or no betting of any consequence, and certainly, with all the eagerness and keenness of feeling, there was no bitterness or acrimony on either side.

The Australians played with great courage and spirit, and achieved a performance for which they were fully entitled and for which they received a large amount of credit. They played quite the right game, hitting out pluckily, and never attempting to show correct cricket. The Englishmen started well enough, getting rid of Bannerman and Trott for three runs, but then Bonnor and McDonnell were both missed. The total was only 82 when the ninth wicket fell, and, though this was not a bad score under the conditions, it was not good enough to look like winning. Ferris, the last man, joined Edwards, who should have been run out, and then this pair, by some invaluable and fearless hitting, put on 30 before they were separated. The Englishmen went in in a bad light, and lost Abel, Barnes and Lohmann for 18 before stumps were drawn.

On Tuesday morning W. G. Grace did not add to the ten he had made overnight. Wicket after wicket fell until eight were out for 37, and it looked quite possible that England would have to follow on. Briggs and Peel averted this disaster, but the whole side were out for 53, or 63 to the bad. The English bowling and fielding during the second innings of Australia were superb, and the ground was altogether against batsmen, so that it was no wonder they were out for 60. Indeed, but for Ferris's capital hitting the total would not nearly have reached that number. But it was clear England was at a great disadvantage, and that the 124 wanted to win would be more than could be made. Mr Grace began really well, and 29 runs were made before the first wicket fell. At 34, however, the champion was out, and from that time Turner and Ferris carried everything before them.

Toss: Australia. **Australia 116** (R. Peel 4-36) **and 60** (G. A. Lohmann 4-33, R. Peel 4-14); **England 53** (C. T. B. Turner 5-27) **and 62** (C. T. B. Turner 5-36, J. J. Ferris 5-26).

Great Bowlers of the Year – J. J. Ferris

John James Ferris was born in Sydney, on May 21, 1867. He is a little below medium height, and sturdily built; bowls left-hand, rather above medium pace, with a very high delivery. His chief break is from leg, but every now and then he sends in a good ball which comes with his arm. He was first associated with the Belvedere Club, of which H. Moses was captain, and played in the Inter-Colonial match in 1886, when he took ten wickets, six in one innings and four in the other. This success was followed up by another still greater, for, in the return match between the two Colonies, he took nine wickets at an average cost of five runs, and largely helped to win the game. He bowled conspicuously well against Shaw's team in 1886-87, and the admirable way in which he shared the work with Turner led to his being selected for the recent tour in England. Ferris, like Turner and McDonnell, is in a bank at Sydney.

Second Test

At The Oval, August 13, 14, 1888. England won by an innings and 137 runs.

This game it was, more than any other, which took from the Australians their chances of rivalling the fame of the team that came over six years before. If they could have beaten England twice out of three times, the tour would have been regarded in Australia, with a great deal of justice, as a triumph.

The Australians again won the toss, and went in first on a splendid wicket with everything in favour of long scoring. Yet by lunch-time on the first day the match was practically over, and at half-past three the Australians were all out for 80. McDonnell was out in Peel's first over. Briggs knocked down Trott's off stump in his first over, and in his next clean-bowled Bonnor. Edwards and Bannerman played very slow cricket indeed, and the score was up to 40 when, in Barnes's first over, Bannerman was out to a grand one-handed catch by Lohmann in the slips. Seven wickets were down for 50 when the luncheon bell rang, and afterwards the last three wickets put on 30 runs.

The Englishmen went in shortly before four o'clock, and for a few minutes there was a good deal of anxiety. Grace was easily caught at third man and Ulyett caught at the wicket, two men being out with only six runs on the scoreboard. Directly after this, however, runs came fast, and, thanks chiefly to Abel and Barnes, the score was 185 for five when play ceased for the day.

On Tuesday Abel increased his score to 70, an innings without a fault, which included nine fours as its principal hits. Sugg played very fluky cricket indeed, and Peel was ninth out at 259 for a capital 24. Eventually, the last man Wood played a defensive game while Lohmann gave the spectators a display of brilliant, fast and dashing hitting which has not often been surpassed. He made 62 runs in 55 minutes without a chance or even a bad hit, and yet so freely and vigorously did he score from all the bowlers that his figures included only one single, while there were no fewer than ten fours. This last wicket put on 58 runs, and gave the Englishmen an overwhelming advantage.

The Australians began their second innings with McDonnell scoring 32 out of 34. After his departure the result was only a question of time. The bowling and fielding were exceedingly good, and Wood at the wicket surpassed himself. Although there were one or two mistakes they were not serious, and the Australians were all out for 100, thus being beaten in a single innings with no fewer than 137 runs to spare.

Peel bowled remarkably well, but the feature of the innings was the bowling of Barnes, who in 29 overs took five wickets for 32 runs – a splendid performance with the ground still in excellent condition. The crowd followed the game with great attention, and applauded heartily the few good things that the Australians did, while they naturally and very properly rewarded with the cheers so dear to public men the magnificent all-round cricket of the winners. We have praised the Colonial team for what they did at Lord's, but the confidence and the abounding energy were this time on the side of England, and it was worth going miles to see how freely and with what skill our representatives acquitted themselves. With McDonnell, Turner, and Blackham taking three of our men's places, what a wonderful XI of the World could have been formed.

Toss: Australia. **Australia 80** (J. Briggs 5-25) **and 100** (W. Barnes 5-32, R. Peel 4-49); **England 317** (R. Abel 70, W. Barnes 62, G. A. Lohmann 62*, C. T. B. Turner 6-112).

GREAT BOWLERS OF THE YEAR – JOHNNY BRIGGS   1889

Johnny Briggs was born at Sutton-in-Ashfield, Nottinghamshire, on October 3, 1862. He played in the Colts' match at Old Trafford in 1879, and appeared for Lancashire that year. He bowls left-hand, and bats right. For several seasons Briggs was known as a very useful batsman, and a wonderful field at cover point; in fact since Mr Royle gave up important cricket there has been no fieldsman equal in celebrity to the popular young Lancastrian. Though he was a useful county bowler his immense ability was not known until the Test match at Lord's in 1886, when he was put on as first change and took five wickets for 29 runs. Australia had to follow on, and in their second innings Briggs was again successful: altogether in the match he took 11 wickets for 74. From that day down to the present he has been justly regarded as one of the most able and destructive bowlers in the country.

Third Test

At Manchester, August 30, 31, 1888. England won by an innings and 21 runs.

Although most people had made up their minds as to the relative merits of England and Australia, this match was important as being the rubber game, and interest was heightened when it was seen that the wet weather had come back again, and, therefore, probably the batting of England was less to be depended upon. There had been a great deal of rain just before the contest, and the ground was very soft when play commenced, so that when the Englishmen won the toss, they obtained a great advantage.

The ground could scarcely get better, while it was almost sure to be exceedingly difficult as it dried. This is what really happened, and, after the Englishmen had made a good score under the existing conditions, the Australians were helpless against Peel, with Lohmann and Briggs to help him. Turner at once began to do wonders, as he bowled Abel before a run had been scored, and clean-bowled Ulyett with the first ball he had at him. Walter Read and W. G. Grace then hit freely until at 58 Read was out to a good ball. After this nearly everybody made runs, the champion's 30 being the highest, and the best innings in the match. Mr Grace was out to a wonderful catch at long-on; Bonnor with the sun in his eyes could not judge the ball properly, but got to it just on the boundary, and made the catch with his right hand high up in the air. Sugg played capital cricket, and so did Barnes; while afterwards, Briggs and Pilling, getting together when nine wickets were down, put on 36 for the last wicket and took the total to 172. The finish of the first day's play saw the Australian score at 32 for two wickets, McDonnell and Bannerman being out.

On the Friday play started at a quarter past 11, and at five minutes to two the game was over. There was a lot of sunshine, and every minute made the ground more difficult. The best batting in the Australian first innings was that of Lyons, who hit hard and well, and, with Blackham, put on 36 runs. Peel's bowling was certainly the feature of the innings. He was on all through, and he took seven wickets. He was backed up by some superb fielding. The Colonial team had a minority of 91 against them, and they started at 20 minutes to one o'clock. This innings was one of the most remarkable ever seen in a big match, even allowing that the wicket, bad as it had been before, was now very much worse.

Bannerman was caught at forward point from the first ball, and before a run had been scored McDonnell, in hitting out at Lohmann, was clean-bowled. There was a leg-bye, and then Bonnor placed a ball easily into Grace's hands, standing in quite close at forward point and taking the ball without any fuss at all. With three men out for a single run, the excitement was tremendous. The score was only seven when Abel and Lohmann cleverly ran Trott out, and, with the total unaltered, the fifth and sixth wickets fell, Lohmann bowling Blackham and Woods at consecutive balls. This start was certainly one of the features of the season. After two runs had been scored, Lyons gave Walter Read at point an easy catch, which was dropped.

The batsmen, after these mistakes, played up with a lot of energy and determination, hitting very hard and scoring fast. They put on 48 in half an hour, before Turner was bowled for a capital 26. Edwards fell to a magnificent left-hand catch by Grace, close to the ground at forward point, and then just before lunch Lyons was bowled, and the last wicket fell, England winning in a single innings. Lyons's 32 was an excellent display, and his hits on such a wicket and against such bowling deserve a lot of praise.

Peel's bowling was again very successful, but this time Lohmann and Briggs had a considerable share in the wickets. However, Peel's performance in the match – 11 for 68 – was altogether admirable. The Australians undoubtedly had the worst of the luck, but England, brilliantly led by W. G. Grace, played a grand game. Notwithstanding the threatening weather on the opening day, 8,080 spectators paid admission at the gates, while on Friday there was a good crowd present in the morning, and it is not too much to say that several thousands more were prepared to go up to the ground in the afternoon from Manchester and the surrounding towns, where the news of the collapse of the Colonial batting created a great deal of excitement. This result gave England the rubber, and was received with extreme satisfaction throughout the country.

Toss: England. **England** 172 (C. T. B. Turner 5-86); **Australia 81** (R. Peel 7-31) **and 70** (R. Peel 4-37).

Great Bowlers of the Year – George Lohmann

George Alfred Lohmann was born at Kensington on June 5, 1865, and first played for Surrey in 1884. He is by general consent one of the best bowlers and most accomplished all-round cricketers ever seen, and he fairly challenged comparison with Turner by what he did during 1888. Lohmann and Turner are, indeed, very much alike. They bowl with remarkable skill and judgment; their batting and fielding are invaluable to their side, and they both have that peculiar electrical quality of rising to a great occasion. It has often enough been said of cricketers of proved skill, when they have failed, that the match has been too big for them, but certainly no match was ever too big for George Lohmann or Charles Turner.

England v Australia 1890

From whatever point of view it is looked at, the seventh tour of Australian cricketers in England can only be regarded as a failure. Though disappointed of the services of Giffen, Moses, and one or two others they would have wished to include, the promoters set out with every confidence of a successful trip, and it certainly did not enter their minds that their campaign would leave them with more defeats than victories. Such, however, was the case, the record standing at 38 matches played, 13 won, 16 lost and nine drawn.

As soon as it was seen that the players were not bearing out the hopes entertained of them, a good deal was said and written about the non-representative character of the team, but it is well to bear in mind that the team included no fewer than nine players who would have had excellent claims to be chosen in absolutely the best XI of

Australia – Murdoch, Blackham, Turner, Ferris, Jones, Lyons, Trott, Barrett and Trumble.

The one serious mistake was the selection of K. E. Burn. The Tasmanian player had on many occasions – notably against Mr Vernon's English XI in 1887–88 – proved himself a capable batsman, but it was as a wicket-keeper that he was chosen, and only when he had accepted the terms offered him and joined the ship at Adelaide was the discovery made that he had never kept wicket in his life. How this ludicrous blunder arose we are quite unable to say, but fortunately for the team the consequences were less serious than they might have been. Blackham, despite the length of his career and the enormous amount of work he has gone through, proved to be in marvellous form, and fairly equalled his exploits of 1880 and 1882.

Pioneer keeper: "Black Jack" Blackham made eight tours of England.

Naturally a good deal of the interest centred on W. L. Murdoch, who had returned to the game after an absence of about five years, and, as in 1880, 1882 and 1884, was captain of the side. It was rather a risky experiment for the greatest of all Australian batsmen to come back after such a long interval, but the result proved that he had not misjudged his powers. It would be an exaggeration to say that he added anything to the laurels he had gained during his previous trips, but inasmuch as he scored the largest aggregate of runs and came out with the best average, it would be equally wrong to say that he failed. Where Murdoch struck us as having fallen off was in his power of playing on defective wickets. Certainly when the ground was affected by rain he was far less successful than in the earlier part of his career. This may perhaps be accounted for by the fact that he is no longer quite so quick on his legs as he once was.

GREAT WICKET-KEEPERS – J. M. BLACKHAM

John McCarthy Blackham, born on May 11, 1855, does not need any very lengthy notice, his name being a household word with all who take any interest in the game of cricket. By general consent – and speaking for ourselves we entirely agree with the popular verdict – he is the greatest wicket-keeper the world has yet seen. His reputation dates from the appearance on English cricket grounds of the first Australian team in 1878. So fine was the form he showed when keeping to Spofforth, Garrett, Boyle and Allan, that by all English experts his pre-eminent ability was at once admitted, no one being found to question his greatness. Since that first trip Blackham has been a frequent visitor, it being indeed his unique distinction to have been a member of every team that has visited us from the Australian Colonies. During one or two of the later tours he fell a little below his best standard, as it was quite natural he should have done after so many years of hard work; but the season of 1890 found him, in his 36th year, in unimpaired possession of his powers. No one, to our thinking, has ever taken the ball quite so close to the wicket as Blackham, and he was one of the first wicket-keepers who regularly dispensed with a long-stop to fast bowling. In his own style Blackham is remarkable, and many have been the occasions during his various tours in this country on which he has made runs at a pinch, after more orthodox players have failed.

First Test

At Lord's, July 21, 22, 23, 1890. England won by seven wickets.

This was emphatically the great match of the tour. No other game was looked forward to so eagerly and to the result of no other game was so much importance attached. The result was a victory for England, but we may state emphatically that scarcely any one of their 38 engagements reflected so much credit on the Australians as this encounter. No side could well have given a better display of bowling and fielding, or striven harder to beat opponents manifestly superior to themselves.

The England XI, if not quite the best in the country, still formed a splendid combination, and the batting can best be judged from the fact that the three last men on the order were Lohmann, Mr MacGregor and Attewell. It was a great compliment to Mr MacGregor to select him as wicket-keeper, but no one disputed that the distinction had been fairly earned by his achievements for Cambridge. It may be said at once that, though he missed one or two difficult chances, he kept wicket magnificently all through, fairly dividing honours with Blackham. In the whole course of the game neither wicket-keeper gave away a single bye.

An immense amount of rain had fallen in London on the Thursday and Friday before the match, but the ground recovered itself far more rapidly than anyone expected, and the wicket – rather slow to begin with – got steadily better and better as the game went on, and was at its best on the concluding day. The Australians, who won the toss, were batting on the Monday from just after 12 o'clock till a quarter to four, for a total of 132. The one feature of the innings was the amazing hitting of Lyons, who in three-quarters of an hour scored 55 out of 66 before being bowled by a yorker. His innings included eight fours.

When England went in the cricket was of the most sensational character, Grace, Shrewsbury, W. W. Read and Gunn – unquestionably the four best bats on the side – being all got rid of for 20 runs. With things looking very black indeed, Maurice Read and Ulyett then, in the course of an hour and a half, against superb bowling and fielding, put on 72. The stand they made, coming when it did, was invaluable, and it would be difficult to praise them beyond their deserts. At the close of play the score was 108 for five wickets, and on Tuesday the innings finished for a total of 173, or 41 runs to the good. The innings lasted four hours and a quarter, and not a single chance was missed. Ulyett's 74 was a splendid display, only marred by a little unsteadiness towards the close. Lyons bowled with great success on a wicket that was considerably firmer and faster than on the previous day.

Going in for the second time at 20 minutes to two, the Australians were batting all the rest of the afternoon, and at the drawing of stumps had made 168 for nine wickets. Lyons again hit brilliantly, scoring 33 in 25 minutes, but the feature of the day was the wonderful defence of Barrett. On the third morning the Australian innings closed for 176, Barrett, who had gone in first, taking out his bat for 67. He was at the wickets for four hours and 40 minutes. England had 136 to get to win, and with the wicket in capital order there was not much doubt about the task being accomplished. Shrewsbury was out at 27, but Grace and Gunn took the score to 101 and thus practically decided the match. Towards the finish Grace hit magnificently, and his not-out innings of 75 was entirely worthy of his reputation.

Toss: Australia. **Australia 132** (J. J. Lyons 55, W. Attewell 4-42) **and 176** (J. E. Barrett 67*); **England 173** (G. Ulyett 74, J. J. Lyons 5-30) **and 137-3** (W. G. Grace 75*).

Second Test

At The Oval, August 11, 12, 1890. England won by two wickets.

The Surrey committee, through no fault of their own, were unable to secure the England team they would have wished to put into the field, a variety of circumstances occurring to thwart them. Yorkshire retained Ulyett and Peel to play against Middlesex at Bradford, Mr Stoddart preferred to assist the latter county, while Briggs and Attewell were suffering from injuries. Under the circumstances the Surrey executive did the best they could, giving places to three cricketers who had never before had the distinction of representing England against Australia. Mr Cranston had been scoring so well all summer that no one could say he was unworthy of the honour conferred on him, while the only objection to Martin and Sharpe was that for all their fine bowling their presence on the side clearly took away from the batting strength.

The Colonial players had sustained so many defeats that it was unreasonable to expect the same amount of interest that had been excited in previous years by the meeting with England at The Oval, but when the ground was saturated, good judges, remembering what Turner and Ferris are capable of on a damaged wicket, confidently predicted a capital game, and their anticipations were more than realised. The opening day's play was just what might have been expected after the great amount of rain that had fallen. The ball beat the bat all through the afternoon, and 22 wickets went down for an aggregate score of only 197.

The Australians, who won the toss, and of course took first innings, were batting nearly two hours and a half for a total of 92. This could only be pronounced a poor performance, for several showers had fallen during the morning, and the wicket was by no means so difficult as it afterwards became. A very fine display of batting was given by Trott, who stayed at the wickets an hour and 20 minutes for 39. He was out at last in a curious way, a ball that he played on to his pad running up his arm and being caught wide on the leg side by the wicket-keeper. Martin bowled wonderfully well on his first appearance for England, taking six wickets at a cost of 50 runs. Lohmann, who was inclined to pitch short, probably found the ground too slow for him. England started very badly, Grace being easily caught at slip from the first ball he received, Shrewsbury at the end of half an hour being finely taken at point at ten, and Mr W. W. Read being bowled at 16. If Gunn when two had been caught at slip by Trumble – the ball going right past his hands to the boundary – the four best batsmen would have been out for 19. As it was, Gunn and Mr Cranston carried the score to 55 when the amateur foolishly started for a short run and lost his wicket.

With 70 on the board for four wickets, England looked to have much the best of the game, but on Charlton taking the ball from Turner at 77, the batting broke down completely, the innings being finished off for 100, or only eight runs to the good. With the ground in a very difficult state, the Australians lost Barrett and Ferris in their second innings for five runs, and the second day they stayed in till 25 minutes to two, the last wicket falling for 102, which left England 95 to get. Trott again played much the best cricket on his side and Lyons hit vigorously for 21.

Under ordinary circumstances England's task would have been an easy one, but with the wicket as it was it was impossible to feel over-confident. Mr Grace ought for the second time in the match to have been caught from the first ball that he received, but Trott at point dropped a ball cut straight into his hands. Despite this lucky let-off, however, the four best England wickets fell for 32, the interest then reaching a very acute point. With 63 wanted, Mr Cranston was joined by Maurice Read, and they made a splendid effort for their side. If, however, with the total at 63 and his own score at 17 Read had been caught by Murdoch at mid-on, the Australians would in all probability have won. As it was, the score had been taken to 83 – only 12 to win with six wickets to fall – when Read was caught at long-on for an invaluable 35. On his dismissal there came a collapse that recalled the great match in 1882, Mr Cranston, Lohmann and Barnes being dismissed in such quick succession that with eight men out two runs were still wanted to win.

Amid indescribable excitement Sharpe became Mr MacGregor's partner, and five maiden overs were bowled in succession, Sharpe being beaten time after time by balls from Ferris that broke back and missed the wicket. Then at last the Surrey player hit a ball to cover point, but Barrett, who had a chance of running out either batsman, over-threw the ball in his anxiety, and a wonderful match ended in a victory for England.

Toss: Australia. **Australia 92** (F. Martin 6-50) **and 102** (F. Martin 6-52);
England 100 (J. J. Ferris 4-25) **and 95-8** (J. J. Ferris 5-49).

Third Test
At Manchester, August 25, 26, 27, 1890. Abandoned.

The third match was to have been played at Old Trafford, but owing to the persistent bad weather the game had to be abandoned without a ball being bowled. Play was postponed from the first day to the second, and from the second to the third, but it was never found practicable to make a start.

AUSTRALIA v ENGLAND 1891–92

The tour undertaken by Lord Sheffield's team was in one respect unique. Never before in the history of visits paid by English cricketers to Australia or by Australian cricketers to the mother country had the enterprise been undertaken by a single individual.

Inasmuch as two of the three Test matches against Combined Australia ended in defeat, the tour was in one sense a disappointment, but this was only the fortune of war. Moreover, our defeats had one very beneficial effect, the double triumph of the Australians restoring the game to its old place in the affections of the Colonial public.

Apart from the fact of two of the big matches having been lost, the tour was a great success, Lord Sheffield's action in arranging the trip, and the manner in which he carried it out, earning unstinted praise. It was understood that the expenses considerably exceeded the receipts, but this was largely due to the liberal scale on which everything was done. That Lord Sheffield was well satisfied with his own reception in Australia was best proved by the fact that he presented a handsome trophy to be competed for by the different Colonies.

Beyond everything else the tour was remarkable for the reappearance in Australia, after an interval of 18 years, of Mr W. G. Grace. When the most famous of all cricketers visited the Colonies in 1873 he was at the very height of his powers, and not a few of his warmest admirers regarded it as rather a hazardous venture on his part to go out again at so late a period of his career. Events proved, however, that Mr Grace's confidence in himself was not misplaced. He came out at the head of the batting averages. When we remember that he was in his 44th year, and that his position as the finest batsman in the world had been established at a time when all the other members of the team were children, this feat must be pronounced nothing less than astonishing. His only big score was 159 not out against Victoria, but he played most consistently all through the tour, and rarely failed to make runs.

Speaking generally, the side did not quite come up to expectations, the chief fault being a want of steadiness in the batting. On the part of most of the men there was too strong a tendency to force the hitting, and the presence of either Shrewsbury or Gunn [who declined the terms offered – Ed.] would have been invaluable. Still, at times some fine batting was shown, Abel's innings of 132 not out at Sydney and Mr Stoddart's 134 at Adelaide being probably equal in quality to anything they have done at home. Lohmann, without being up to his best standard as a bowler, did splendid all-round work, his fielding at cover-slip gaining unbounded admiration from all Colonial critics.

First Test

At Melbourne, January 1, 2, 4, 5, 6, 1892. Australia won by 54 runs.

This match excited an extraordinary amount of interest. It lasted into the fifth day, and, after a struggle which by general consent had rarely or never been surpassed in the Colonies, was won by the Australians. The Englishmen lost the game on the Tuesday afternoon, when they went in for the last innings with 213 runs wanted to win. With the wicket still in good order they entertained little doubt of accomplishing their task, and when Grace and Stoddart had hit up 60 runs without being separated, Australia's chance seemed very remote. However, then Grace was caught at mid-off and Stoddart bowled in trying to pull a long-hop. Then came such a collapse that before the drawing of stumps there were seven wickets down. On Wednesday morning the remaining players did their best, but the innings was all over for 158.

In the early stages some fine cricket was shown on both sides. Bruce batted most brilliantly and Bannerman, though his play was intolerably slow to look at, also rendered invaluable service to Australia. His two innings of 45 and 41 lasted respectively three hours and a quarter and four hours. W. G. Grace's 50 was a capital display, and Bean, in getting the same number, showed better cricket than on any other occasion during the tour. The Australians worked very hard to win and fully deserved their victory.

Turner and Trott bowled admirably in the last innings, but the most sensational piece of bowling was that of McLeod, who, in the Englishmen's first innings, got rid of Abel, Grace and Stoddart in two overs.

Toss: Australia. **Australia 240** (W. Bruce 57, J. W. Sharpe 6-84) **and 236** (J. J. Lyons 51); **England 264** (W. G. Grace 50, G. Bean 50, R. W. McLeod 5-53) **and 158** (C. T. B. Turner 5-51).

Second Test

At Sydney, January 29, 30, February 1, 2, 3, 1892. Australia won by 72 runs.

The second of the three big matches produced one of the finest performances in the history of Australian cricket, a performance, indeed, fully comparable to the seven-run victory at The Oval in 1882. The Australians proved victorious, and it can safely be said that the records of first-class cricket furnish few instances of a finer uphill game.

Up to the end of the second day everything went in favour of the Englishmen. Thanks to Lohmann's bowling and Abel's batting, they gained indeed so commanding an advantage that the match seemed as good as over. The close of an innings on each side had left them with a lead of 162, and the Australians, on going in for the second time, lost Trott's wicket for a single run. Abel's superb innings of 132 not out lasted five hours and 25 minutes, and contained 11 fours. Only once before had anyone taken his bat right through the innings in an England and Australia match, the previous instance being Dr Barrett's performance at Lord's in 1890.

On Monday, the third day, there came an extraordinary change in the cricket, Lyons, Bannerman, and George Giffen batting with such success that it took the Englishmen all the afternoon to obtain two wickets, the total meanwhile being increased from one to 263. Lyons certainly gave one chance to Abel at slip when he had made 49, and we believe he offered another to the same fieldsman, but otherwise his 134 – which included 16 fours – was a magnificent innings. On the fourth day the weather was unsettled and rain considerably affected the wicket. Everything went wrong with the Englishmen, who made several bad mistakes in the field. The Australians' innings closed for 391, and the Englishmen, wanting 230 to win, had to go in when the ground was in a very treacherous state. Abel, Bean and Grace were got rid of for 11 runs, and only a downfall of rain prevented further disasters.

The following morning the wicket rolled out much better than anyone could have expected, and the Englishmen still had a chance, Australia's bowling being weakened by the absence of McLeod, who had been called home by the death of his brother. Giffen and Turner, however, bowled wonderfully well, and despite the very fine batting of Stoddart, the innings was finished off for 156, Australia winning by 72 runs and so gaining the rubber. Bannerman's innings of 91 had much to do with the victory. Invaluable as it was, however, it would in a match of less interest have thoroughly tired out the spectators. He was actually at the wicket seven hours and 28 minutes. Out of

204 balls bowled at him by Attewell he only scored from five. At the finish of the game, there was a scene of almost indescribable enthusiasm.

Toss: Australia. **Australia 144** (G. A. Lohmann 8-58) **and 391** (A. C. Bannerman 91, J. J. Lyons 134, W. Bruce 72, J. Briggs 4-69); **England 307** (R. Abel 132*, G. Giffen 4-88) **and 156** (A. E. Stoddart 69, C. T. B. Turner 4-46, G. Giffen 6-72).

BATSMAN OF THE YEAR – A. E. STODDART

Mr Andrew Ernest Stoddart was born at South Shields on March 11, 1863. The county of Durham can thus boast one of the most brilliant exponents of cricket and rugby football the world has yet seen. Famous cricketers as a rule take to the game very early in life, but Stoddart is a notable exception, for he did not go in seriously for cricket till 1885, when he became associated with the Hampstead Club. That August, he played his first match for Middlesex. A few days later he made it clear that they had found a prize, an innings of 79 at Trent Bridge leaving no doubt as to the exceptional nature of his powers. The highest score he has made in a first-class match was 215 not out for Middlesex against Lancashire at Old Trafford in 1891, and one of his finest perform-ances was in the Centenary match at Lord's in 1887, when he scored 151 for England against the MCC, putting on 266 for the first wicket with Arthur Shrewsbury. To him moreover belongs the honour of having made the highest individual score on record – 485, for Hampstead against the Stoics in August 1886. At the present day there are few batsmen as good as Stoddart, and certainly none more attractive to look at. He continually gets runs under conditions that find most batsmen at fault, his play both on slow and fiery wickets being quite exceptional. Stoddart paid his first visit to Australia as a member of Mr G. F. Vernon's team in the autumn of 1887. In the autumn of 1891 he went to the Colonies again with Lord Sheffield's team.

Third Test
At Adelaide, March 24, 25, 26, 28, 1892. England won by an innings and 230 runs.

As some compensation for their defeats at Melbourne and Sydney, the Englishmen won in a single innings. It was a brilliant victory, but inasmuch as they batted on a perfect wicket, and the Australians had to go in when the pitch had been ruined by rain, it cannot be pretended that the result represented with any accuracy the merits of the two XIs. In justice to the English team, however, it should be mentioned that before the rain came on they had scored 490 for nine wickets. This being the case, it is not unreason-able to suppose that even had the weather remained fine, the game would still have ended in their favour. Stoddart's batting and Briggs's bowling were the features of the game. In scoring 134 Stoddart was at the wickets three hours and 50 minutes, his hits including two fives and 15 fours. He gave three chances, but not one of them was easy, and from first to last he played in his best form. Grace's 58 was quite faultless, and the only mistake in Peel's admirable 83 – which lasted three hours – was a hard return to Giffen when he had made 60. Briggs took six wickets in each innings.

Toss: England. **England 499** (W. G. Grace 58, A. E. Stoddart 134, J. M. Read 57, R. Peel 83);
Australia 100 (J. Briggs 6-49) **and 169** (J. Briggs 6-87).

ENGLAND V AUSTRALIA 1893

Had the eighth Australian team come to England with no more preliminary flourish than attended the visits of 1888 and 1890, their record would not have been regarded as at all unsatisfactory. They came, however, as an absolutely representative side, every player except H. Moses having been available for selection, and had of necessity to bear comparison with the great XIs of 1882 and 1884 – teams which, so far at least as this country is concerned, showed Australian cricket at its highest point of development. Judged from this high standard, it cannot be said that the band of players who toured here last summer came up to the sanguine expectations formed of them.

It is more upon their drawn matches that the claims to distinction of this team will rest. Though they had no chance of victory, and would in all likelihood, with the ground as it was, have suffered defeat, they played a very creditable game against England at Lord's; and at Manchester they did still better. Still, in the only Test match brought to a definite conclusion, the Australians suffered defeat in a single innings.

Scarcely any previous XI from the Colonies included a larger number of dependable run-getters. Great hopes were built on Giffen and Bruce, whose absence from England in 1888 and 1890 prevented those teams being regarded as really representative of Australian cricket. When, in the third match, Giffen made 180 against Gloucestershire, it seemed as if he were going to play right up to his Australian form, but on the whole, he was a long way from sustaining his reputation as the best of present-day Australian batsmen. The fact of his having to do so much bowling no doubt told considerably against him as a batsman. As a matter of fact he never seemed really comfortable against some of the exceptionally fast bowlers he had to meet, and in ten of the 12 innings in which they were opposed, Richardson got him out.

Most remarkable, however, was the success of Harry Graham. Taking everything into consideration and remembering especially how short had been his experience of first-class cricket in the Colonies, we are inclined to think that no Australian batsman during his first tour in England has played so well. By scoring 219 at Derby Graham had the distinction of the highest innings of the tour, but his greatest triumph was gained at Lord's, when he made 107 against England. Blessed with any amount of confidence, he showed himself capable of getting runs under all sorts of conditions. His value to the side was much enhanced by his exceptional excellence in the long field.

Blackham captained with zeal, but we doubt if by temperament he is quite fitted for so anxious and onerous a position. We are afraid we must add that his wicket-keeping began to show the effects of time and hard work. The fielding of the team was very uneven – at times brilliant, but on some occasions inexcusably faulty.

First Test
At Lord's, July 17, 18, 19, 1893. Drawn.

Despite the moderate record which the Australians had obtained, the first of the representative matches proved quite as attractive as ever, and there was a great gathering at the ground. On a fast wicket the success of England would have been generally anticipated, but so much rain had fallen that the wicket was necessarily very treacherous, and on Monday morning it was known that owing to an injured finger W. G. Grace for the first time since matches between England and Australia had been played in this country would not do battle for the old country. Stoddart captained the England team, and winning the toss was placed in a very awkward position, for with the sun shining and the ground soft, it was obvious that the wicket must improve as time wore on, the question remaining whether he would be justified in putting the other side in.

Few people expected a total of 150, and the performance of the Englishmen in staying at the wickets until after half-past five and scoring 334 was really wonderful. They had a good deal of luck, three or four catches being dropped, but at the same time it was an extraordinary achievement to make so many runs. The honours of the day were divided between Shrewsbury and Jackson, each of whom in a strangely different style was seen to remarkable advantage. Shrewsbury was four hours and ten minutes making 106, Jackson only an hour and three-quarters in scoring 91.

Shrewsbury's batting was marked by extreme patience, unfailing judgment, and a mastery over the difficulties of the ground, of which probably no other batsman would have been capable. A far greater surprise was the success of Jackson. Everyone felt the Cambridge captain had done sufficiently good work to entitle him to a place in the team, but few indeed could have anticipated that he would triumph so completely over the conditions. He went in when Stoddart and Gunn had been disposed of for 31, but far from being over-anxious from the first played with the utmost confidence, driving everything over-pitched with great power, whilst the way he pulled short-pitched balls to square leg was quite a liberal education. After making 50, he ought to have been caught at mid-on, and he gave two other chances, but his display was one of which any batsman might well have been proud. Jackson hit 13 fours, and Shrewsbury nine. In all they put on 137, and after five wickets had fallen, Flowers assisted Shrewsbury to put on 80 more. Before play ceased the Australians lost Lyons and Giffen for 33.

Cricket on the second day was carried on under far more favourable conditions, the ground having practically recovered from the rain and the bowlers getting very little assistance. The play was naturally very keen on both sides, and the Australians had to work so hard for their runs that only 38 were obtained in the first hour against the admirable bowling of Lockwood. Half the wickets were down for 75, but then came Gregory and Graham's partnership which completely altered the aspect of the match. These two young cricketers began by making a series of short runs, and obviously upset the fieldsmen by the fearless and rapid manner in which they travelled between the wickets. Very soon, too, the bowlers became anxious, and almost before the spectators could realise it runs were coming at a great pace. So admirably did the two bat that at lunch-time 120 had been added without further loss, and in all the total had reached 217 before Gregory was dismissed. At 264 Graham's splendid, though by no means faultless, innings was ended by a catch at the wicket. Out of 189 added during his stay, he had made 107, hitting a five and 12 fours. The innings then came to a speedy conclusion, and, although Stoddart was not seen at his best against the bowling of Turner and McLeod, Gunn and Shrewsbury raised the score to 113 before the close.

The two Notts men next morning played a sterling game, running no risks but making good use of such opportunities as presented themselves. In all their partnership produced 152 runs, and but for the rain which interrupted play Shrewsbury would probably have had the unique distinction of scoring two separate hundreds. As it was he was bowled just after play was resumed. Later Wainwright forced the game to good purpose, and at lunch-time the score was up to 234 for eight wickets. A drizzling rain prevented play being resumed, and shortly afterwards it was announced that England had closed their innings. Preparations were made for the Australians, who had 300 to get to win in three hours and three-quarters, to commence their innings. No play, however, was possible, and the game had to be left drawn.

Toss: England. **England 334** (A. Shrewsbury 106, Hon. F. S. Jackson 91, C. T. B. Turner 6-67)
and 234-8 dec.(A. Shrewsbury 81, W. Gunn 77, G. Giffen 5-43);
Australia 269 (S. E. Gregory 57, H. Graham 107, W. H. Lockwood 6-101).

CRICKETER OF THE YEAR – THE HON. F. S. JACKSON   1894

F. Stanley Jackson, whose batting was one of the best features of the 1893 season, was born on November 21, 1870. In the autumn of 1889 Jackson went up to Cambridge, and the following spring quickly made himself certain of his Blue. By 1891, though it was clear he was an all-round cricketer of more than ordinary ability, he had done nothing in first-class company to foreshadow what he has since accomplished. The season of 1892 left him in a far higher position than he had occupied before, but had it been necessary to put the full strength of England into the field, no one would have thought of giving him a place. All the more remarkable, therefore, was his extraordinary development last season as a batsman. His first big match at Cambridge showed he was in splendid form, and he went on playing with such conspicuous success that when it became known that MCC had chosen him for England in the First Test against Australia, satisfaction was expressed on all hands. How abundantly he justified his selection: no one who was so fortunate as to be at Lord's will ever forget the batting shown by him and Arthur Shrewsbury. Taking into account the importance of the occasion and the condition of the ground, it was some of the most wonderful cricket of the year. Mr Jackson followed up by scoring 103 at The Oval. He has great confidence and splendid hitting power, and on his form of last season is perhaps the best forcing player on the on side now before the public. His Cambridge career is over, but it is to be hoped that Yorkshire may for some time to come enjoy the advantage of his services.

Second Test
At The Oval, August 14, 15, 16, 1893. England won by an innings and 43 runs.

The game, the only one of the three Test matches brought to a definite issue, proved a great triumph for English cricket, the Australians being beaten by an innings. The proceeds of the match were set apart for the benefit of the popular Surrey batsman

Maurice Read, and although the end was reached early on the third day, a sum of £1,200 was, we understand, realised from the gate receipts and the subscription lists.

Again the Englishmen won the toss, but whereas at Lord's they derived no benefit therefrom, it was a distinct advantage at Kennington Oval. They made splendid use of their opportunity, batting so well on the capital wicket that at the close of the first day they had obtained 378 runs for the loss of only half their wickets. Another admirable commencement was made by Grace and Stoddart, who, beginning shortly after midday, were still together at luncheon, when the score had been carried to 134 – Stoddart 71, Grace 63. Afterwards the total was raised to 151, and then the partnership came to an end. Stoddart was first dismissed, his innings of 83, although marred by a considerable number of more or less easy chances, including some very fine hits. It may be mentioned that during the first hour the ball now and then got up in an awkward style. Before another run had been added Grace was out for a really admirable innings of 68, in making which the famous batsman had displayed some of his highest skill.

Shrewsbury and Gunn put on 49 at a fair pace before Gunn was bowled, middle wicket, and though Ward did not commence too well, he and Shrewsbury gradually wore down the bowling. In all 103 runs were added before Shrewsbury's fine innings was brought to a close. Ward left soon afterwards, the latter portion of his 55 being characterised by real excellence. Three-quarters of an hour remained, and Jackson and Walter Read knocked the bowling about so freely that 67 more runs were put on before the call of time.

There was another tremendous gathering on the second day, and the success which attended the efforts of the Englishmen was naturally keenly appreciated. Jackson and Read headed the best total previously made by England against Australia – 434 in 1886 at The Oval – and in all put on 131 for the sixth wicket, the total being up to 442 when Read was out for a creditable 52. The last few batsmen did little with Giffen, and when Mold came in Jackson still wanted a single to complete his hundred. There was a most exciting over bowled by Giffen to Jackson, the batsman being in sad difficulties with one or two balls, but at length he lifted one right on to the covered seats, and so achieved the great distinction of making a hundred against Australia. He was directly afterwards run out for a grandly hit innings of 103, which included 13 fours.

The English innings extended over seven hours, and amounted to the huge score of 483. There was an extraordinary breakdown in the batting of the Australians, for after Bannerman and Lyons had put on 30 for the first wicket, seven batsmen were dismissed for an addition of 29 runs. In all the innings occupied only an hour and 40 minutes, the last wicket falling for 91 – a wretchedly poor score, considering that the wicket was fast and true, even allowing for the particularly skilful bowling of Lockwood and Briggs. The Australians followed on, 392 in arrears, and a very different display of batting was given. Bruce went in first with Bannerman, and the play was so free that 54 runs were made in little more than half an hour. Afterwards Giffen and Bannerman, by fine cricket, not only sent up the hundred but raised the score to 126 before Bannerman was out, while at the drawing of stumps 158 had been made for the loss of two wickets.

For some time on Wednesday, although the Australians were in a desperate position, there seemed no slight possibility that they would give the Englishmen a lot of trouble. Indeed, the total reached 340 with only six men out, but then the batting broke down so completely that the innings closed for the addition of nine more runs, and England were left with a single-innings victory. Trott and Graham played a great game, and added 106 for the fifth wicket. Trott, indeed, showed really superb cricket, and probably his 92 was the finest exhibition he has ever given in England. His innings included 17 fours.

Toss: England. **England 483** (W. G. Grace 68, A. E. Stoddart 83, A. Shrewsbury 66, A. Ward 55, W. W. Read 52, Hon. F. S. Jackson 103, G. Giffen 7-128); **Australia 91** (W. H. Lockwood 4-37, J. Briggs 5-34) **and 349** (A. C. Bannerman 55, G. Giffen 53, G. H. S. Trott 92, J. Briggs 5-114, W. H. Lockwood 4-96).

CRICKETER OF THE YEAR – GEORGE GIFFEN   1894

George Giffen, who by general consent has for some time past been regarded as the greatest all-round cricketer yet produced by the Australian Colonies, was born in Adelaide on November 27, 1859, and first came to England in 1882. He was then a young player of comparatively little experience, but though his doings during that memorable tour were by no means exceptional, good judges were almost unanimous in predicting for him a brilliant career. He came again to England in 1884, and it was clear that his powers had considerably developed. Then on his third visit to this country, with the disappointing team that came over in 1886, he met with brilliant success, coming out at the top of the averages both in batting and bowling. He scored 1,454 runs and took 162 wickets.

Meanwhile his performances in Australia were more remarkable than ever, and each succeeding winter we read of his making phenomenal scores for South Australia, and in the same matches taking a very large proportion of the wickets. He did not as a batsman do very much against Lord Sheffield's team in 1891–92, but so enormous was his reputation that when it became known that he was coming to this country for the fourth time in 1893, the English public naturally expected great things. It would be flattery to pretend, however, that his play came up to anticipation. He bowled very well indeed – better on hard wickets than any other member of the side – but apart from a couple of long innings his batting fell far below his Australian standard. It cannot be said, therefore, that his fourth visit to England added to his reputation. Of course he did a lot of good work, but he did not prove the tower of strength that his friends in South Australia had expected. Still, whatever his shortcomings in 1893, his record during the last ten years in Australia is sufficient to stamp him one of the world's greatest all-round players.

Third Test
At Old Trafford, August 24, 25, 26, 1893. Drawn.

When the fixtures were made in the previous December it was distinctly agreed that all the counties should give up whatever men were required for the three Test matches, but unfortunately the arrangement was not adhered to, and in this, the last match of the rubber, F. S. Jackson and the other Yorkshiremen, who might have been included in the England team, were all playing against Sussex at Brighton. Furthermore, Lockwood, owing to a strained leg, could not play, but for all that the side pitted against the Australians was a very powerful one.

There was a surprisingly moderate attendance to witness the opening day, in which the Australians, after totalling 204, got two English wickets down for 54. At the start, Lyons hit out freely, but when he left, Bannerman and Giffen played very cautiously. Four of the best men were out for 73, but then came an invaluable stand by Bruce and Graham, the former playing the most stylish cricket of the day. They added 56 in three-quarters of an hour, and afterwards Trumble and Bruce put on 64 more. Bruce was seventh out at 174 for a grand 68. The innings was then quickly finished off, Richardson showing a very gratifying result for his labours. There was a most disheartening commencement to England's innings, Grace running out Stoddart before a run had been made. This disaster had a very prejudicial effect upon the batting, which was afterwards marked by extreme care rather than attractiveness. Shrewsbury and Grace looked like playing out time, but shortly before the close Shrewsbury was caught at deep square leg.

Next day there was a tremendously keen struggle. Up to lunch-time the cricket was perhaps open to the charge of dullness, but afterwards it became brilliant and exciting, the skilful batting of the Englishmen finding its counterpart in the smart fielding and steady bowling of the Colonials. Grace and Gunn began well, carrying the score to 73 before Grace was bowled off his pads, but then came a particularly stern fight. Giffen and Turner pitched very short to Gunn, who ran no risks, and it took him and Ward three-quarters of an hour to add 20. Read, too, stayed for some time, but just when he appeared likely to score well, he was out to a good ball, and half the wickets were down for 112. Brockwell remained with Gunn, and at lunch-time the score was 145 for six. So far nearly two hours and a half had been occupied in making 91 runs, but afterwards the game underwent a remarkable change, 98 being obtained in an hour and a half.

Briggs did little, but Gunn hit out in grand form, and the crowd became quite enthusiastic when there seemed a prospect of the Australians' score being headed. Before this was achieved, however, MacGregor was out, but Richardson rendered Gunn valuable assistance, helping to put on 42. Mold, who came in before Gunn had reached his hundred, succeeded in keeping up his wicket until he had achieved that great feat. The innings came to an end immediately afterwards, Gunn carrying out his bat for 102, a really grand innings, lasting four hours and ten minutes. The arrears were cleared off without loss, Lyons making 33 out of 56 in 35 minutes, and when play ceased the score was 93 for three.

On the Saturday the weather was not so favourable, but the wicket lasted very well. The Australians had four men out for 99, but then Bruce joined Bannerman and hit so brilliantly that 54 runs were obtained in 40 minutes. Just afterwards Bannerman was very badly missed at slip at 50, but there were eight wickets down for 182. Then there was a distinct chance of the Englishmen winning, but Turner and Blackham batted with great pluck, and before the innings closed a victory for England was practically impossible. Bannerman deserved great praise for his 60, in making which he was at the wickets three hours and 55 minutes.

England had 198 runs to get to win, and only two hours and a quarter remained.

Grace and Stoddart made no attempt to hit off the runs. Together they put on 78 for the first wicket, and within half an hour of the close the hundred went up with only one man out. At the finish England had six wickets to fall and wanted 80 to win, the draw being rather in favour of the old country.

Toss: Australia. **Australia 204** (W. Bruce 68, T. Richardson 5-49, J. Briggs 4-81) **and 236** (A. C. Bannerman 60, T. Richardson 5-107); **England 243** (W. Gunn 102*, G. Giffen 4-113) **and 118-4**.

AUSTRALIA v ENGLAND 1894-95

It is perfectly safe to say that since the visit of George Parr's XI in 1863–64 no tour of English cricketers in Australia has been from every point of view more brilliantly successful than that of Mr Stoddart's team. The players returned home loaded with honours and delighted with their trip. They had abundant reasons for satisfaction, inasmuch as in the contests with Australia they had won the rubber by three matches to two.

To these Test games everything else in the tour was subordinated. Never, probably, have five matches excited more widespread interest. They drew such crowds of people to the Australian grounds that the Melbourne Club and the trustees of the Sydney Ground, under whose joint auspices the tour was undertaken, divided between them a profit of about £7,000. In England the interest was greater than had ever been felt in matches played away from our own shores, the enterprise of the *Pall Mall Gazette*, in arranging when the big matches were in progress for long cable messages, keeping lovers of the game in closer touch with cricket in Australia than they had ever been before. It so happened that after England had been victorious at Sydney and Melbourne the Australians won at Adelaide and Sydney, the rubber thus depending on the fifth and last match. This conquering game was won by Mr Stoddart's team, a wonderful display of batting by Brown and Ward in the last stage of the contest giving them the victory. The excitement in London when the result came to hand could scarcely have been greater if the match had been played at Lord's or The Oval.

This was undoubtedly a fine side, though in the absence of Mr W. G. Grace, Mr F. S. Jackson, Gunn and one or two others, it could not be said to fully represent England. This being the case, the triumphant result was all the more gratifying. Lockwood, who ought to have been the best all-round man, failed disastrously both as bowler and batsman. Brockwell, too, though not altogether unsuccessful, was very far indeed from keeping up the reputation he had established in England in 1894.

As a set-off against all these shortcomings, however, Mr Stoddart himself, Mr MacLaren, Brown and Ward batted superbly; and Richardson, Peel and Briggs did capital work with the ball. Indeed, it was Richardson's wonderful bowling that first made victory probable in the last Test match. In the interest of his side Mr Stoddart played a safer and more cautious game than he has ever adopted in England, and as the reward of his self-denying patience had the satisfaction of being at the top of the batting. His highest and best innings was 173 against Australia at Melbourne.

The First Test was in some respects the most extraordinary in the history of the game. The Australians lost by ten runs, after a first innings of 586, and the aggregate score of 1,514 runs was without precedent in first-class cricket. Only a night's rain when Australia had the match in hand gave the Englishmen a chance of victory, but all the same it was a wonderful win, Peel's bowling on the saturated pitch being unplayable. Mr Stoddart managed his team all through the tour with unfailing tact, and gained greater popularity than any previous English captain in the Colonies.

Young Batsman of the Season – A. C. MacLaren · 1895

Mr A. C. MacLaren, who was born on December 1, 1871, came prominently before the public while still very young, appearing for Harrow against Eton at Lord's in 1887, when less than 16 years of age. So great was his natural aptitude, however, and so carefully had he been coached, that even then he was, as far as his physical means permitted, a finished batsman. On the strength of his fine batting for Harrow, he was tried for Lancashire, and in his first county match – against Sussex at Brighton, in August 1890 – he played a splendid innings of 108. Other players have got into three figures in their first county engagement, but we question if the feat had ever been done before by a batsman coming straight from a public-school XI. Since he left school his powers have ripened less quickly than might have been expected, but he is now unquestionably in the front rank of English batsmen. His style is perhaps not quite so pretty to look at as in his schooldays, but he has great resources, being able to play with almost equal success, according to circumstances, a cautious or a brilliant game. Over and above his batting, he is an exceptionally good field, standing generally in the slips or at mid-off.

First Test

At Sydney, December 14, 15, 17, 18, 19, 20, 1894. England won by ten runs.

This was probably the most sensational match ever played in either Australia or England. Going in first, the Australians made a poor start, losing three wickets – all bowled down by Richardson – for 21 runs. Iredale and Giffen, however, put on 171 for the fourth wicket, and Giffen and Gregory 139 for the fifth. Giffen's splendidly played 161 lasted a little over four hours and a quarter. At the close of the first day the score stood at 346 for five, and in the end the total reached 586, Gregory and Blackham scoring 154 together for the ninth wicket. In recognition of his wonderful innings of 201 a collection was made for Gregory, the sum subscribed on the ground amounting to £103.

In face of a score of 586 the Englishmen had a dismal prospect, but they set to work with the utmost resolution and kept the Australians in the field from Saturday afternoon till the following Wednesday. Still, though they ran up totals of 325 and 437 – Ward taking the chief honours in each innings – they only set Australia 177 to get. At the close of the fifth day 113 had been scored for two wickets, and the match looked all over. Drenching rain in the night, however, followed by bright sunshine, completely altered the condition of the ground, and Peel – well backed up by Briggs – proved so irresistible that the Englishmen gained an astonishing victory by ten runs.

Australia v England 1894–95   First Test

At Sydney, December 14, 15, 17, 18, 19, 20, 1894. Result: England won by ten runs.

AUSTRALIA

	First innings		Second innings
J. J. Lyons b Richardson	1	– b Richardson	25
G. H. S. Trott b Richardson	12	– c Gay b Peel	8
G. Giffen c Ford b Brockwell	161	– lbw b Briggs	41
J. Darling b Richardson	0	– c Brockwell b Peel	53
F. A. Iredale c Stoddart b Ford	81	– (6) c and b Briggs	5
S. E. Gregory c Peel b Stoddart	201	– (5) c Gay b Peel	16
J. C. Reedman c Ford b Peel	17	– st Gay b Peel	4
C. E. McLeod b Richardson	15	– not out	2
C. T. B. Turner c Gay b Peel	1	– c Briggs b Peel	2
*†J. M. Blackham b Richardson	74	– (11) c and b Peel	2
E. Jones not out	11	– (10) c MacLaren b Briggs	1
B 8, l-b 3, w 1	12	B 2, l-b 1, n-b 4	7

1-10 2-21 3-21 4-192 5-331 6-379   586   1-26 2-45 3-130 4-135 5-147 6-158   166
7-400 8-409 9-563 10-586   7-159 8-161 9-162 10-166

First innings – Richardson 55.3–13–181–5; Peel 53–14–140–2; Briggs 25–4–96–0; Brockwell 22–7–78–1; Ford 11–2–47–1; Stoddart 3–0–31–1; Lockwood 3–2–1–0.
Second innings – Richardson 11–3–27–1; Peel 30–9–67–6; Lockwood 16–3–40–0; Briggs 11–2–25–3.

ENGLAND

	First innings		Second innings (following on)
A. C. MacLaren c Reedman b Turner	4	– b Giffen	20
A. Ward c Iredale b Turner	75	– b Giffen	117
*A. E. Stoddart c Jones b Giffen	12	– c Giffen b Turner	36
J. T. Brown run out	22	– c Jones b Giffen	53
W. Brockwell c Blackham b Jones	49	– b Jones	37
R. Peel c Gregory b Giffen	4	– b Giffen	17
F. G. J. Ford st Blackham b Giffen	30	– c and b McLeod	48
J. Briggs b Giffen	57	– b McLeod	42
W. H. Lockwood c Giffen b Trott	18	– b Trott	29
†L. H. Gay c Gregory b Reedman	33	– b Trott	4
T. Richardson not out	0	– not out	12
B 17, l-b 3, w 1	21	B 14, l-b 8	22

1-14 2-43 3-78 4-149 5-155 6-211   325   1-44 2-115 3-217 4-245 5-290 6-296   437
7-211 8-252 9-325 10-325   7-385 8-398 9-420 10-437

First innings – Jones 19–7–44–1; Turner 44–16–89–2; Giffen 43–17–75–4; Trott 15–4–59–1; McLeod 14–2–25–0; Reedman 3.3–1–12–1; Lyons 2–2–0–0.
Second innings – Jones 19–0–57–1; Turner 35–14–78–1; Giffen 75–25–164–4; Trott 12.4–2–22–2; McLeod 30–6–67–2; Reedman 6–1–12–0; Lyons 2–0–12–0; Iredale 2–1–3–0.

Toss won by Australia   UMPIRES C. Bannerman and J. Phillips

Second Test

At Melbourne, December 29, 31, 1894, January 1, 2, 3, 1895. England won by 94 runs.

The second of the Test matches resulted in a well-earned win for the Englishmen. On the opening day the wicket was in a very bad state from the recent rain, and Giffen put England in. His policy proved a wise one, the innings being finished off in two hours for 75. The wicket had considerably improved when Australia went in, but Richardson bowled so finely that before the end of the afternoon they were all out for 123, or only 48 to the good. A dry Sunday allowed the ground to recover, and the Englishmen in their second innings batted under the most favourable conditions. It was not until the fourth day was well advanced that they were got rid of, the total reaching 475. Mr Stoddart, risking nothing, played a great game for his side, his 173 lasting five hours and 20 minutes. Australia wanted 428 to win, and when on the fourth day 190 went up with only one wicket down, the chances seemed against the Englishmen. Brockwell's bowling, however, brought about a sudden change, and with several batsmen failing, the score for nine wickets was only 268. It then seemed as though the match would soon be over, but Iredale and Turner added 60 runs together and played out time. On the fifth morning, the end came in the second over, Iredale being bowled by Peel.

Toss: Australia. **England** 75 (C. T. B. Turner 5-32) **and** 475 (A. E. Stoddart 173, R. Peel 53, G. Giffen 6-155); **Australia** 123 (T. Richardson 5-57) **and** 333 (G. H. S. Trott 95, W. Bruce 54, F. A. Iredale 68, R. Peel 4-77).

Third Test

At Adelaide, January 11, 12, 14, 15, 1895. Australia won by 382 runs.

On no occasion during the tour were the Englishmen so completely outplayed on a hard wicket as in the third of the five Test matches. In face of a modest score of 238, they only just escaped following on, and in the end were beaten by 382 runs, their only excuse being that the intense heat at Adelaide robbed them of sleep and put them completely off their form. The all-round cricket of Albert Trott and a splendid innings of 140 by Iredale were the features of the match. Iredale was at the wicket for four hours, and in addition to scoring 110 runs without being out, Trott had the remarkable analysis in the second innings of eight wickets for 43 runs *[by the end of 2008 still the best figures of any bowler on Test debut – Ed.]*.

Toss: Australia. **Australia** 238 (G. Giffen 58, T. Richardson 5-75) **and** 411 (W. Bruce 80, F. A. Iredale 140, A. E. Trott 72*, R. Peel 4-96); **England** 124 (G. Giffen 5-76, S. T. Callaway 5-37) **and** 143 (A. E. Trott 8-43).

Fourth Test

At Sydney, February 1, 2, 4, 1895. Australia won by an innings and 147 runs.

The Fourth Test resulted in a win for Australia by an innings. Recent rain had so much affected the ground that Mr Stoddart, on winning the toss, put the Australians in. Up to a certain point his policy was quite successful, six wickets falling for 51, but some wonderful hitting by Graham, combined with several blunders in the field, entirely altered the situation. Albert Trott, as at Adelaide, hit very finely, and the innings which had opened so badly did not close till the total had reached 284. Owing to wretched weather play was impossible on the second day, and whatever chance the Englishmen might have had was destroyed. On the Monday, on a terribly difficult wicket, they were helpless against Turner and Giffen, and suffered an overwhelming defeat.

Toss: England. **Australia 284** (H. Graham 105, A. E. Trott 85*, J. Briggs 4-65);
England 65 and 72 (G. Giffen 5-26, C. T. B. Turner 4-33).

Fifth Test
At Melbourne, March 1, 2, 4, 5, 6, 1895. England won by six wickets.

As was only natural, with the record standing at two victories each, the fifth and last of the Test matches excited enormous interest. Indeed, it may be questioned whether any previous game in the Colonies had ever aroused such intense and widespread excitement. Numbers of people journeyed thousands of miles in order to be in Melbourne on the all-important occasion. The Australians, after anxious deliberations as to the constitution of their team, decided to leave out Turner and play Lyons. For this they were severely blamed after the match; but the fact should be borne in mind that Turner during the season had met with little or no success on hard wickets. Mr Stoddart's team gained a brilliant and remarkable victory for England. It was only, however, after a desperate and protracted struggle that this result was arrived at, the game lasting well into the fifth day.

From first to last the match was played on a perfectly true wicket, which gave no advantage to one side over the other. The Australians, who had the good fortune to win the toss, led off in splendid style, scoring on the opening day 282 runs for four wickets. Darling and Gregory, not out with 72 and 70 respectively, were soon got rid of on the second morning, but the total reached 414. In face of this big score the Englishmen made 385, MacLaren and Peel playing very finely and putting on 162 for the fifth wicket. The Australians opened their second innings well, but on the fourth day, when a dust storm caused considerable discomfort both to players and spectators, Richardson bowled superbly, and they were all out for 267. This left Mr Stoddart's team 297 to get to win, and it was anybody's match.

At the close the score stood at 28 for one, and to the dismay of the Englishmen, Mr Stoddart was lbw first ball next morning. The position was desperate, but at this point Ward and Brown made the stand which, if they are never to do anything more, will suffice to keep their names famous. By wonderful batting – Ward's patient defence being scarcely less remarkable than Brown's brilliant hitting – they put on 210, their partnership practically ensuring the success of their side. After the fourth wicket had fallen, the end soon came, MacLaren and Peel being in at the finish. Though the spectators were greatly disappointed, they cheered the Englishmen most heartily.

Australia v England 1894–95

Fifth Test

At Melbourne, March 1, 2, 4, 5, 6, 1895. Result: England won by six wickets.

AUSTRALIA	First innings		Second innings	
G. H. S. Trott b Briggs		42	– b Peel	42
W. Bruce c MacLaren b Peel		22	– c and b Peel	11
*G. Giffen b Peel		57	– b Richardson	51
F. A. Iredale b Richardson		8	– b Richardson	18
S. E. Gregory c Philipson b Richardson		70	– b Richardson	30
J. Darling c Ford b Peel		74	– b Peel	50
J. J. Lyons c Philipson b Lockwood		55	– b Briggs	15
H. Graham b Richardson		6	– lbw b Richardson	10
A. E. Trott c Lockwood b Peel		10	– b Richardson	0
†A. H. Jarvis not out		34	– not out	14
T. R. McKibbin c Peel b Briggs		23	– c Philipson b Richardson	13
B 3, l-b 10		13	B 5, l-b 6, n-b 2	13

1-40 2-101 3-126 4-142 5-284 6-286   **414**   1-32 2-75 3-125 4-148 5-179 6-200   **267**
7-304 8-335 9-367 10-414   7-219 8-219 9-248 10-267

First innings – Richardson 42–7–138–3; Peel 48–13–114–4; Lockwood 27–7–72–1; Briggs 23.4–5–46–2; Brockwell 6–1–22–0; Ford 2–0–9–0.
Second innings – Richardson 45.2–7–104–6; Peel 46–16–89–3; Lockwood 16–7–24–0; Briggs 16–3–37–1.

ENGLAND	First innings		Second innings	
A. Ward b McKibbin		32	– (2) b G. H. S. Trott	93
W. Brockwell st Jarvis b G. H. S. Trott		5	– (1) c and b Giffen	5
*A. E. Stoddart st Jarvis b G. H. S. Trott		68	– lbw b G. H. S. Trott	11
J. T. Brown b A. E. Trott		30	– c Giffen b McKibbin	140
A. C. MacLaren hit wicket b G. H. S. Trott		120	– not out	20
R. Peel c Gregory b Giffen		73	– not out	15
W. H. Lockwood c G. H. S. Trott b Giffen		5		
F. G. J. Ford c A. E. Trott b Giffen		11		
J. Briggs c G. H. S. Trott b Giffen		0		
†H. Philipson not out		10		
T. Richardson lbw b G. H. S. Trott		11		
B 8, l-b 8, w 4		20	B 6, l-b 5, w 2, n-b 1	14

1-6 2-110 3-112 4-166 5-328 6-342   **385**   1-5 2-28 3-238 4-278   **(4 wkts) 298**
7-364 8-364 9-366 10-385

First innings – Giffen 45–13–130–4; G. H. S. Trott 24–5–71–4; A. E. Trott 30–4–84–1; McKibbin 29–6–73–1; Bruce 5–1–7–0.
Second innings – G. H. S. Trott 20–1–63–2; Giffen 31–4–106–1; A. E. Trott 19–2–56–0; McKibbin 14–2–47–1; Bruce 3–1–10–0; Lyons 1–0–2–0.

Toss won by Australia   UMPIRES T. Flynn and J. Phillips

ENGLAND V AUSTRALIA 1896

Though they did not succeed in winning the rubber, the team of 1896 recovered for Australian cricket an amount of prestige such as had not been enjoyed since the great tours of 1882 and 1884. When the players set sail some critics were far from hopeful as to their prospects, but the results were sufficient to prove that even the best experts may at times go astray in their judgment.

To a very large extent the improvement was, we think, due to the change in the leadership. Trott was by no means anxious for the post, but almost from the first match it was clear that he was in every way fitted for it. Blessed with a temper that nothing could ruffle, he was always master both of himself and his team. More than that his judgment in changing the bowling was rarely or never at fault.

Allowing for their natural disappointment at losing the rubber with England, the Australians have abundant reason to congratulate themselves. They had the satisfaction of beating England at Manchester and in not one of their matches with the counties did they suffer defeat, rivalling the famous team of 1882.

When the best XI went into the field, the only thing really lacking was a fearless hitter of the type of Massie, Lyons, or the late Percy McDonnell. It was urged that the batting was apt to become monotonous, many of the batsmen playing with far more steadiness than is necessary on perfect wickets. The charge was well founded, the batting on many occasions being uniformly careful in character. The explanation of this is very simple. Of the 14 players who made up the team, only five had been to England before, and the others had only played at home, where big matches are fought out to a definite issue. Time being a matter of no importance, batsmen get into the habit of risking nothing, and the result is that their careful methods often beget tedious cricket.

There was not a bowler of quite the same class as Spofforth, Palmer, Turner and Ferris, no batsman to compare with W. L. Murdoch as we knew him in 1882 and 1884, and Kelly, though a highly competent wicket-keeper, did not come within measurable distance of Blackham. Still the side played so well together and maintained such a high standard of skill at all points as to form a truly formidable combination.

Hill, the youngest member of the team, had some failures, but for all that his first trip to England was a brilliant success, and we shall no doubt see him again. He is a left-handed batsman of an entirely different style to Darling, lacking that player's driving powers, and getting most of his runs on the leg side.

The surprising point was the bowling. It is no exaggeration to say that nine out of ten English cricketers thought it would be the weak point, and that for its sustained excellence no one was quite prepared. There was of course Giffen, but, for all his skill and knowledge, there was no reason to suppose he would be more effective at 37 than in his younger days. But Jones's tremendous pace made him from the start very effective; Giffen showed no falling-off; and Trumble, for the first time in three visits to England, was able to inspire our batsmen with a feeling of apprehension. At first, it is true, McKibbin was a failure, but once he ran into form he did great things, the amount of work he got on the ball on the wet wickets in August being almost incredible.

There is one thing left to be said and that unfortunately is not of a pleasant nature. Up to last season one of the special virtues of Australian bowling was its unimpeachable fairness. Despite the evil example set by many English throwers, team after team came over without a bowler to whose delivery exception could have been taken, but unhappily things are no longer as they once were. We have not the least hesitation in saying that a fast bowler with the action of Jones, or a slow bowler with a delivery so open to question as McKibbin, would have found no place in the earlier XIs that came to England. Jones's bowling is, to our mind, radically unfair, as we cannot conceive a ball being fairly bowled at the pace of an express train with a bent arm. As was only natural in the case of a slow bowler McKibbin's action was less talked about, but there can be little doubt that he continually threw his off-break.

First Test

At Lord's, June 22, 23, 24, 1896. England won by six wickets.

The first of the three Test matches proved an enormous attraction. On the opening day no fewer than 25,414 people paid for admission. The full attendance was estimated at nearly 30,000, but while this great crowd was in itself a compliment to the Australians it had a grave disadvantage. The field of play was seriously encroached upon, and a good many of the people saw very little of the cricket. Under the circumstances it would hardly be fair to criticise the conduct of those present, but there was certainly an absence of the quiet and decorum usually characteristic of Lord's.

For two days the match was favoured with delightful weather, but the condition changed on the third morning. The match was the most sensational of the whole tour, fortunes changing in a fashion that was quite bewildering. Trott had the good fortune to win the toss, and when his side went in on a perfect wicket a score of at least 250 was confidently expected. To the amazement of everyone, the Australians failed in a fashion that has seldom been seen on a dry true pitch, being all got rid of by Richardson and Lohmann in an hour and a quarter for 53. The Surrey bowlers did wonders, but lack of nerve must have been largely answerable for such an astounding collapse.

England went in soon after half-past one, and when time was called had scored 286 for eight. This was a very fair performance, but at one time something much bigger seemed in prospect, 250 being on the board with only four men out. It must be admitted that the bowlers were far from fortunate in the support they received, Abel being palpably missed in the slips when nine, and W. G. Grace let off at long-on at 51. Abel, apart from his one chance, played a splendid innings. He hit 13 fours, and was at the wickets three hours. Jackson, who in brilliant style scored 44 out of 69, palpably gave away his innings. The encroachment of the crowd prevented Darling catching him and, at once, he gave the fieldsman a second opportunity.

The attendance on the second day was only half as large, a great many evidently thinking the match as good as over. Those who stayed away missed some of the finest cricket of the whole season. England's innings was quickly finished off for 292, and then the Australians, with a balance of 239 against them, went in again. The early play suggested a repetition of Monday's breakdown, Darling and Eady being got rid of for three runs. Giffen and Trott, however, stayed together at a critical time and carried the score to 62. Then Gregory and Trott resisted the bowling for nearly two hours and three-quarters, putting on no fewer than 221 runs. So far as could be seen, neither gave a chance, but the English players were positive that Trott, when 61, was caught by Hayward in the slips. Gregory hit 17 fours in his 103, and Trott struck 24 fours in his

143. When Gregory left the Australians were 44 ahead with six wickets to fall, and England's position was certainly an anxious one. Richardson and Hearne, however, bowled in splendid form, and the innings ended for 347, the last six wickets having gone down for 64.

England wanted only 109 to win, and at the close they had scored 16 for the loss of Abel's wicket. Had the ground remained firm and dry, the finish would no doubt have been uneventful, but rain quite altered the condition of the pitch, and the Englishmen had a vastly more difficult task than expected. Thanks chiefly to Brown and Stoddart, they hit off the runs for the loss of four wickets, but it might have gone desperately hard with them if the Australians had accepted all the chances offered. Kelly, standing back to Jones's bowling, was especially at fault.

Toss: Australia. **Australia 53** (T. Richardson 6-39) **and 347** (G. H. S. Trott 143, S. E. Gregory 103, T. Richardson 5-134, J. T. Hearne 5-76); **England 292** (W. G. Grace 66, R. Abel 94) **and 111-4**.

CRICKETER OF THE YEAR – K. S. RANJITSINHJI

1897

Kumar Shri Ranjitsinhji, the young batsman who has in the course of four seasons risen to the highest point of success and popular favour, was born on September 10, 1872. It was in 1892 that the English public first heard his name, and there is little doubt that he ought that year to have been included in the Cambridge XI. The authorities perhaps found it hard to believe that an Indian could be a first-rate cricketer. However, Ranjitsinhji's opportunity came in 1893 when, in his last year at the university, he gained a place in the XI. For the immense advance he showed in 1895, it is safe to say that very few people were prepared. In the first-class averages he ran a desperately close race with A. C. MacLaren and W. G. Grace, scoring 1,775 runs with the splendid average of 49. Then last season he scored more runs in first-class matches than had ever been obtained by any batsman in one season, beating Mr Grace's remarkable aggregate of 2,739 in 1871. As a batsman Ranjitsinhji is himself alone, being quite individual and distinctive in his style of play. He can scarcely be pointed to as a safe model for young and aspiring batsmen, his peculiar and almost unique skill depending in large measure on extreme keenness of eye, combined with great power and flexibility of wrist. For any ordinary player to attempt to turn good-length balls off the middle stump would be futile and disastrous. To Ranjitsinhji on a fast wicket, however, everything seems possible, and if the somewhat too freely used word "genius" can with any propriety be employed in connection with cricket, it surely applies to the young Indian's batting.

Second Test

At Manchester, July 16, 17, 18, 1896. Australia won by three wickets.

This was in many ways one of the most remarkable matches of the season, for though England were defeated at the finish, the two best performances of the game were accomplished for them, Ranjitsinhji playing perhaps the greatest innings of his career, and Richardson bowling in a style he has seldom approached. The game at Manchester was awaited with unusual interest, owing mainly to the fact that the Australians from the time of their defeat at Lord's had been showing vastly improved form.

The match proved a great attraction on the first two days, and the attendance on the third only suffered from the fact that the Englishmen seemed in a hopeless position. As it turned out, however, the last day's cricket was the most remarkable of all, and those who had the good fortune to be present are never likely to forget it.

With the ground in such excellent condition for run-getting it was a fortunate circumstance for Trott to win the toss, and his team made admirable use of their opportunity. Richardson often puzzled the batsmen, and was many times unlucky in just failing to hit the wicket, but on the whole the bowling looked anything but deadly, and the Australians started so well that they seemed, in the first three hours, to have rendered themselves practically secure against defeat. Iredale played a beautiful innings of 108, and so excellent was the assistance afforded him by Giffen, Trott and Darling that at one time the score stood at 294 with only three men out. At this point the prospects of the Englishmen were particularly gloomy, but Richardson came with a fine effort, and before the call of time, eight wickets were down for 366.

On the following morning, thanks to a useful stand by Kelly and McKibbin, the total was carried to 412. With the conditions still most favourable and the wicket practically as good as ever, it seemed quite possible that the Englishmen would get very near to their opponents' total, but with a few exceptions the batting was particularly feeble and the whole side were out for 231. Trott changed his bowling with remarkable skill and judgment, and it was quite a stroke of genius to go on first himself with Jones. He easily got rid of Grace and Stoddart, thus giving his side the good start they so needed. Ranjitsinhji and Lilley played exceedingly well, but the other batting was certainly unworthy of the picked representatives of the old country.

England had to follow on against a majority of 181, and the start of their second innings was disappointing, as four of the best wickets fell before the drawing of stumps for 109. At the close of the second day, therefore, the Englishmen with six wickets to go down were still 72 behind, and nothing seemed less likely than that they would, before the end of the game, hold practically a winning position. Such however proved to be the case, the Englishmen playing a wonderful uphill game and struggling hard.

Much depended upon Ranjitsinhji, and the famous young Indian fairly rose to the occasion, playing an innings that could, without exaggeration, be fairly described as marvellous. He very quickly got set again, and punished the bowlers in a style that, up to that period of the season, no other batsman had approached. He repeatedly brought off his wonderful strokes on the leg side, and for a while had the bowlers quite at his mercy. Could the other batsmen have rendered him any material assistance, there is no saying to what extent the total might have been increased, but as it was, there was no other score higher than 19. Ranjitsinhji's remarkable batting, and the prospect of England after all running their opponents close, worked the spectators up to a high pitch of excitement, and the scene of enthusiasm was something to be remembered when the Indian cricketer completed the first hundred hit against the tourists.

MacLaren, Lilley and Hearne all tried hard to keep up their wickets for Ranjitsinhji, but Briggs after making 16 could not resist the temptation of jumping out to try and drive a slow ball from McKibbin. The innings came to an end for 305, Ranjitsinhji carrying his bat for 154. It is safe to say that a finer or more finished display had never been seen on a great occasion, for he never gave anything like a chance, and during his long stay the worst that could be urged against him was that he made a couple of lucky snicks. He was at the wickets for three hours ten minutes, and among his hits were 23 fours, five threes and nine twos.

The Australians were left with 125 to get, and with the ground showing very few signs of wear, most people looked forward to seeing them hit off for the loss of perhaps three or four batsmen. As it turned out, the Australians had many very anxious moments, Richardson making a magnificent effort, which was quite worthy of comparison with Ranjitsinhji's batting earlier in the day. Almost before one could realise what was happening, four of the best wickets had fallen for 45, and with the prospect of a keenly exciting finish, the remainder of the game was watched with breathless interest.

Another failure for the Colonials might have had the most serious results, but Gregory and Donnan played with splendid nerve at the critical time, and the score reached 79 before Gregory was caught at short leg for an invaluable 33. Still the match was far from over. Donnan was out at 95 and Hill at 100, the position being that the Australians, with three wickets to fall, wanted 25 to win. With Richardson bowling in his finest form, and nearly all the best batsmen gone, the Englishmen at this point seemed to have actually the best of the game, and the excitement was intense.

Everything rested upon Trumble and Kelly, and it would be difficult to speak too highly of how they got through a terribly trying ordeal. The bowling was so good that they could only score at rare intervals, and generally by singles, but they surely and slowly placed their side on the high road to victory. When only nine were required to win, Lilley, who up to that time had kept wicket absolutely without a mistake, failed to take a chance from Kelly. Had this come off, there is no saying what might have happened, but as it was Trumble and Kelly hit off the remaining runs, and a splendid match ended in favour of the Australians. Some idea of the excellence of the bowling may be gathered from the fact that the last 25 runs took an hour to obtain.

There was a scene of great enthusiasm at the finish, the Australians being received with a heartiness that reflected great credit on the Manchester public. Richardson, who bowled for three hours without sending down one really loose ball, took six for 76, and conceding that the ground scarcely afforded him any assistance, it is safe to say he has never accomplished a finer performance. In the whole match he bowled 110 overs and three balls, and took 13 wickets at a cost of 244 runs.

Toss: Australia. **Australia 412** (F. A. Iredale 108, G. Giffen 80, G. H. S. Trott 53, T. Richardson 7-168)
and 125-7 (T. Richardson 6-76); **England 231** (K. S. Ranjitsinhji 62, A. F. A. Lilley 65*)
and 305 (K. S. Ranjitsinhji 154*).

CRICKETER OF THE YEAR – TOM RICHARDSON

Thomas Richardson was born at Byfleet on August 11, 1870. He first found a place in the Surrey XI in 1892, when Surrey wound up by beating Notts for the Championship. It cannot do Richardson any harm now to say that when he first came into important cricket, his delivery was, to say the least of it, dubious. The fact that he went through the tour of Australia in 1894-95 without, so far as we have heard, his action being even questioned, is the best proof of the alteration in his style. The 1893 season took him to the top of the tree and he has from that time been the first of English bowlers. Lohmann's enforced absence through illness gave him a great opportunity, and he emphatically made the most of it, taking 99 wickets in the County Championship for something over 14 runs each, and coming out in the first-class averages with a record of 174 wickets at an average of 15.70. Since then he has never looked back, his greatest season being that of 1895, when in first-class matches he took the almost unprecedented number of 290 wickets for less than 15 runs each. His greatest feats last summer were performed in the England matches at Lord's and Manchester. On the last day at Old Trafford he bowled unchanged for three hours, and nearly won a match in which England had followed on. It is generally agreed that no bowler with the same tremendous speed has ever possessed such a break from the off. No professional cricketer in England enjoys greater popularity with the general public and among his brother players.

Third Test

At The Oval, August 10, 11, 12, 1896. England won by 66 runs.

The third and conquering Test match was preceded by a regrettable incident which for a time caused intense excitement in the cricket world. The Surrey committee, after much deliberation, chose nine cricketers as certainties for the England XI, and four others amongst whom the last two places were to be filled. Early in the week previous to the match, however, they received a letter signed by Lohmann, Gunn, Abel, Richardson and Hayward, in which they demanded £20 each for their services. £10 per man had been paid to the professionals at Lord's and Manchester, and the Surrey committee, without going into the question of whether £20 was an excessive fee on an occasion of such importance, declined point-blank to be dictated to. It is betraying no secret to say that they felt greatly aggrieved, on the eve of the most important match of the season, at being placed in a difficulty by four of their own professionals. However, they did not hesitate as to the course to be pursued, at once taking steps to secure the best possible substitutes for the revolting players. Friendly counsels, however, were soon at work, and on the evening of August 8 Abel, Hayward, and Richardson withdrew from the position they had taken up. After a good deal of deliberation, it was agreed that they should play. Lohmann did not, but later made his peace with Surrey.

Happily the match passed off in the pleasantest fashion, and proved a complete success. Played on a wicket ruined by rain, it produced some startling cricket, and was in the end won by England, the old country thus securing the rubber. Rain on the first day delayed the start until five minutes to five, and with the ground by no means so difficult as it became on the following day, England profited to a considerable extent by having won the toss. They started well, and at the close had scored 69 for one.

The second day was fine, and up to a certain point, England did very well, but after having had 113 on the board with only three wickets down, they were all out for 145. Trumble, after crossing over to the Pavilion end, bowled nine overs for ten runs and five wickets. Darling and Iredale made a wonderful start for the Australians, and when, with a little luck, the score reached 70 without a wicket, they seemed to have more than made up for the disadvantage of losing the toss. However, a foolish attempt to get a fifth run for a hit of his partner's cost Iredale his wicket at 75, and then, thanks chiefly to Hearne's fine bowling, such an astonishing change came over the game that the innings was finished off for 119, or 26 runs behind. England had a terribly difficult pitch to bat on, and at the close of play, five wickets were down for 60.

It was anybody's game on the third morning, everything depending on the condition of the ground. It was freely predicted that the wicket would improve, but such was far from being the case, it being perhaps more difficult than ever. England's innings was finished off for 84, the Australians being left with 111 to get. This task they commenced shortly before half-past 12, the excitement being at a very high pitch. In the second over, before a run had been scored, Darling was bowled, and then things went from bad to worse, the climax being reached when the seventh wicket fell at 14. All this time, Hearne and Peel had bowled in wonderful form. The ninth wicket was lost at 25, and England had the game in their hands, but McKibbin, by some plucky hitting, delayed the end, the total having reached 44 when Abel caught him most brilliantly at slip with one hand. Thus, amidst great enthusiasm, England won the match and the rubber.

Toss: England. **England 145** (H. Trumble 6-59) **and 84** (H. Trumble 6-30);
Australia 119 (J. T. Hearne 6-41) **and 44** (J. T. Hearne 4-19, R. Peel 6-23).

CRICKETER OF THE YEAR – HUGH TRUMBLE
1897

Hugh Trumble was born on May 12, 1867, and paid his first visit to England with the team of 1890. It can scarcely be said that during that tour – the least successful the Australians have ever had – he made any very deep impression. His high-delivery medium-pace bowling struck English batsmen as lacking both sting and variety, and at the end of the trip he could only point to a modest record, being completely overshadowed by Turner and Ferris. Trumble made ample amends when he came here again in 1893. In every respect he was a vastly better man than he had been three years before. Dividing the bowling pretty equally with Turner and Giffen, he took 123 wickets with an average of 16.48. As a batsman his advance was just as remarkable. Still, it was not until his third visit that Trumble convinced Englishmen he was entitled to rank among the great bowlers of Australia. On paper he did not do very much better than in 1893, but there can be no doubt that he proved himself a far finer bowler. When the rain came in August his bowling was

Hugh Trumble: 141 wickets against England, including two hat-tricks – one of them in his final Test.

deadly, a fact of which England at The Oval had especially convincing evidence. His strength lay in the combination of spin and extreme accuracy of pitch. Always the same, whether on the winning or the losing side, he is one of the most popular of Australian cricketers.

AUSTRALIA V ENGLAND 1897–98

To speak the plain truth there has not for a very long time been anything so disappointing as the tour of Mr Stoddart's team in Australia. They left full of hope that the triumph of three years before would be repeated, but came home a thoroughly beaten side. Five Test matches were played against the full strength of Australia, and of these the Englishmen only won the first, severe defeats being suffered in the other four.

This was a poor record indeed for a team of which so much was expected, and on the admission of Mr Stoddart himself, it was due to the vastly better cricket shown by the Australians. The Colonial players were much more consistent in batting and far superior in bowling. While admitting this, however, one cannot believe that the Englishmen played up to their home form. MacLaren and Ranjitsinhji batted magnificently; Storer and Hayward played many fine innings; and J. T. Hearne bowled with a steadiness beyond all praise; but the men as an XI never got really to their best. Richardson was rarely in any way the Richardson of Kennington Oval or indeed of the previous tour.

It must be said that the team had some misfortunes to contend against. Ranjitsinhji, though he made many runs, suffered a great deal from bad health and Stoddart was utterly out of form. An attack of influenza, the anxieties of captaining a losing side, and the shock caused by the news of his mother's death combined to spoil his cricket. The one who had the best cause to look back upon the trip with satisfaction was MacLaren. No English batsman – not even Arthur Shrewsbury – has ever played more splendidly in the Colonies.

There was some little unpleasantness during the tour, Mr Stoddart complaining bitterly of the "barracking" by a section of the crowds, but on such points as these there is no need to dwell at any length. The financial success was immense, the Test matches attracting an extraordinary number of people, and the public were delighted with the cricket shown by their own players. Above all the others in batting stood out the two left-handers Hill and Darling, while in a group of fine bowlers Noble shone conspicuously. Almost unknown when the season began, he developed surprising skill and several times on perfect wickets quite puzzled the Englishmen, keeping a fine length with a little work on the ball and being curiously deceptive in flight.

James Phillips accompanied the team through the whole tour as umpire, and caused a great sensation by twice no-balling the Australian bowler Jones for throwing.

THROWING – A NOTE BY THE EDITOR   Sydney Pardon, 1898

In reviewing the tour of the Australian team of 1896, I ventured to condemn as unfair the bowling of both Jones and McKibbin. I had no wish to say anything disagreeable, but I was so struck by the deplorable change that had come over the methods of Australian bowlers that I did not see how the question could be ignored. The criticism has, I think, been more than justified by subsequent events. A letter condemning McKibbin's action in most uncompromising terms was addressed by Mr Spofforth to the *Sporting Life*, and at Adelaide, in the first match played in Australia by Mr Stoddart's team, Jones was no-balled by James Phillips for throwing.

It is certain that Mr Spofforth would not, unless he had felt very strongly indeed on the matter, have gone to the length of denouncing a brother Australian as an unfair bowler, and no one who knows James Phillips can think it possible that he would have no-balled Jones without adequate cause. If years ago any representative English umpire had shown the same courage many scandals would have been avoided. As regards both McKibbin and Jones the point to bear in mind is that the fault lies primarily with English bowlers and English umpires. Australian bowlers never threw in England till we had shown them over and over again that the Law could be broken with impunity.

First Test

At Sydney, December 13, 14, 15, 16, 17, 1897. England won by nine wickets.

A very unpleasant incident, which gave rise to almost endless discussion, preceded the First Test, the trustees of the Sydney ground taking it upon themselves to postpone the commencement of the game without consulting the two captains. Heavy rain had fallen, but it was not thought by the players on Thursday – the match being fixed to start the following morning – that any postponement would be necessary. As it happened, the ground on Saturday, after heavy rain for several hours, was under water, and it thus came about that the anxiously expected game did not begin until the Monday.

The delay had one happy result for the Englishmen, Ranjitsinhji, who had been very ill, recovering sufficiently to take his place in the team and playing finer cricket than on any other occasion during the trip. Considering his physical condition – he was quite exhausted after scoring 39 on the first evening – his innings of 175 was a marvellous piece of batting. Before resuming play on the second morning he was in the hands of the doctor. He hit 24 fours, and was batting in all three hours and 35 minutes. Scarcely inferior was the cricket shown by McLaren, who made a third hundred in succession on the Sydney ground.

On the second afternoon the Australians in face of a total of 551 lost five wickets for 86, and from these disasters, despite the superb play in the second innings by Darling and Hill, they never recovered. The Englishmen won the match by nine wickets. With this victory their good fortune in Australia came to an end.

Toss: England. **England 551** (A. C. MacLaren 109, T. W. Hayward 72, G. H. Hirst 62, K. S. Ranjitsinhji 175) and **96-1** (A. C. MacLaren 50*); **Australia 237** (H. Trumble 70, C. E. McLeod 50*, J. T. Hearne 5-42) and **408** (J. Darling 101, C. Hill 96, J. T. Hearne 4-99).

Second Test
At Melbourne, January 1, 3, 4, 5, 1898. Australia won by an innings and 55 runs.

The Australians found ample compensation for their defeat at Sydney, beating the Englishmen in decisive fashion by an innings. They richly deserved their victory, showing much finer form than their opponents, but they were fortunate in having first innings, the wicket – owing probably to the excessively hot weather – cracking during the later stages of the game in a fashion very unusual at Melbourne. Noble was substituted for Lyons in the Colonial team with the happiest results, his bowling being wonderfully effective in the last innings. The Australian batting was consistently good, Charles McLeod's innings of 112, though not attractive to look at, being invaluable to his side. He was at the wickets for four hours and five minutes. In this match Jones was for the second time no-balled by Phillips for throwing.

Toss: Australia. **Australia 520** (C. E. McLeod 112, C. Hill 58, S. E. Gregory 71, F. A. Iredale 89, G. H. S. Trott 79); **England 315** (K. S. Ranjitsinhji 71, W. Storer 51, H. Trumble 4-54) **and 150** (H. Trumble 4-53, M. A. Noble 6-49).

Third Test
At Adelaide, January 14, 15, 17, 18, 19, 1898. Australia won by an innings and 13 runs.

The Englishmen were almost as badly beaten as at Melbourne, the Australians again winning by an innings. The Australians outplayed their opponents at every point. Excepting the fact that they won the toss they had nothing to favour them, the wicket wearing perfectly all through the game. Very marked indeed, in the admission of the English players themselves, was the superiority of the Australian bowling. The best compliment to Howell, Noble and the rest was to be found in the fact that it took MacLaren, on an unimpaired wicket, five hours and a quarter to get 124. MacLaren, Ranjitsinhji, Hayward and Hirst all played well, but 278 and 282 were poor totals at Adelaide. Among the Australian batsmen Darling took the chief honours with a superb 178. He made all his runs on the first day, being out in the first over next morning. His innings lasted exactly four hours and three-quarters. Hill, who played very finely, helped Darling put on 148 for the second wicket, and Iredale was also seen at his best.

Toss: Australia. **Australia 573** (J. Darling 178, C. Hill 81, S. E. Gregory 52, F. A. Iredale 84, T. Richardson 4-164); **England 278** (T. W. Hayward 70, G. H. Hirst 85, W. P. Howell 4-70) **and 282** (A. C. MacLaren 124, K. S. Ranjitsinhji 77, M. A. Noble 5-84, C. E. McLeod 5-65).

Fourth Test
At Melbourne, January 29, 31, February 1, 2, 1898. Australia won by eight wickets.

Of the five Test matches this was perhaps the most eventful. The Englishmen started in wonderful form by getting six wickets down for 57 runs, but after that they were quite outplayed, the Australians gaining a brilliant victory. The turning-point of the Australians' first innings was the partnership of Hill and Trumble, 165 runs being put on for the seventh wicket. Never before had Hill given quite so fine a display as his 188. He was batting a little over five hours and all things considered his innings may be described as perhaps the best seen in the Colonies during the season. With only a total of 323 to face on a perfectly sound wicket, the Englishmen seemed to have very good prospects, but they failed miserably, their dismissal for 174 marking the lowest point reached by their batting during the whole trip. They did not do very much better when they followed on, and it is no more than the truth to say that they richly deserved to be beaten. The Australians played their winning game wonderfully well, the variety and excellence of their bowling calling forth a high compliment from Mr Stoddart when the match was over.

Toss: Australia. **Australia 323** (C. Hill 188, J. T. Hearne 6-98) **and 115-2** (C. E. McLeod 64*);
England 174 (E. Jones 4-56) **and 263** (K. S. Ranjitsinhji 55).

Fifth Test

At Sydney, February 26, 28, March 1, 2, 1898. Australia won by six wickets.

The Englishmen had a splendid chance of to some extent retrieving their reputation, Richardson's bowling being so good that on the first innings they secured a lead of 96 runs. This advantage, however, was quickly discounted when they went in for the second time, MacLaren, from the first ball of the innings, being caught in the slips. Other disasters followed, and at the end of the day nine wickets were down for 172. The next morning the innings closed for 178, the Australians being left with 275 to get to win. This task was accomplished in wonderful style, the Australians winning the match by six wickets. Darling played one of his finest innings, departing from his cautious methods and hitting with immense power. This fourth win in five Test matches removed the last remaining doubt as to the superiority of the Australians.

Toss: England. **England 335** (A. C. MacLaren 65, N. F. Druce 64, E. Jones 6-82) **and 178** (H. Trumble 4-37);
Australia 239 (C. E. McLeod 64, T. Richardson 8-94) **and 276-4** (J. Darling 160, J. Worrall 62).

CRICKETER OF THE YEAR – WILFRED RHODES   1899

Wilfred Rhodes's appearance for Yorkshire illustrated in a most striking way the truth of the proverb that the hour brings forth the man. Robert Peel's long and honourable connection with Yorkshire having terminated under rather painful circumstances in 1897 *[he was summarily dismissed after turning up drunk for a match – Ed.]*, the county's pressing need was a left-handed slow bowler to take his place, and in young Rhodes exactly the bowler required was forthcoming. He made the fullest use of his opportunities and even if his gifts had been backed up by experience he could scarcely have proved more effective. Naturally when the dry weather set in he was less successful, but the occasions were very few on which he was fairly collared. He bowls with a high, easy action, his pitch is wonderfully accurate, and whenever the ground gives him assistance he can get a lot of spin on the ball. On some days, notably when Yorkshire beat Surrey in a single innings at Bradford, he was irresistible, combining so much break with a perfect length that the batsmen could do nothing against him. His value is by no means restricted to his bowling, as he has already proved himself a dangerous run-getter. Only 21, it will be disappointing if he does not enjoy a brilliant career.

England v Australia 1899 Sydney Pardon

By common consent the tenth Australian team formed the strongest combination that had come from the Colonies since 1882. It might be argued that this is too high an estimate, but personally I regard it as not in any way beyond the truth.

In estimating the strength of this Australian XI great allowance must be made for the disadvantages under which they laboured. Hill was laid aside by illness after the end of June, while Worrall, from the start of the tour, was hampered by a badly damaged knee. Iredale was kept out for more than a fortnight in June by a sharp attack of measles. Hill's illness would in itself have been sufficient to ruin the trip if they had not been so exceptionally rich in run-getters. He had to undergo an operation for the removal of some growth in the nose, and the after-consequences proved far more serious than had been expected. He lost weight and strength to an alarming extent, and was not himself again till the last matches were being played.

The Australians met England five times and did not once suffer defeat. I am personally of the opinion that the plan adopted for the first time in this country of playing five Test matches had a somewhat prejudicial effect upon the tour as a whole, the players, as was almost inevitable under the circumstances, saving themselves more than in former trips for the big events.

Darling proved himself one of the very best captains that ever took a team into the field. He placed the field with the nicest skill according to the peculiarities of different batsmen, and he showed a perfect genius for changing his bowling, always seeing to put the right bowler on at the right time and at the proper end. The way in which he utilised Jones's pace was in itself sufficient to prove him a great leader.

Very few Australian batsmen coming to England for the first time have approached the form shown by Noble and Trumper. They were quite different in style and method, Noble developing an amount of caution for which his colleagues were in no way prepared, while Trumper by his free and attractive cricket made himself, for a time at least, the most popular member of the XI. It is possible that Trumper may have the more brilliant future, but at present Noble, by reason of his finer defence and inexhaustible patience, is the greater personality on a side. I am, of course, speaking just now of batting alone, for as an all-round man Noble has had no equal in Australia except George Giffen.

First Test

At Nottingham, June 1, 2, 3, 1899. Drawn.

In picking the England team the committee had rather a thankless task. Many of the matches in May had been played on wickets damaged by rain, so there had not been a really fair chance of discovering what men were in form. The great difficulty, however, lay in the question of fast bowling. Lockwood had broken down; Richardson was obviously not himself, and Mr Kortright, owing to a bad strain, was incapacitated. It was decided to let Hirst, for this one occasion, be the England fast bowler. It cannot be said that the experiment was in any way a success. Hirst worked hard, his fielding indeed being perfection, but as a bowler he did not cause the Australians any trouble.

The match ended in a draw, time alone saving the English XI from defeat. When stumps were finally pulled up they had only three wickets to go down. Ranjitsinhji saved the side with a superbly played 98 not out. Never probably did a batsman, in the endeavour to save a match against time, play such a free and attractive game as he did during the last 40 minutes. In one respect, however, he was, nearly all through his innings open to serious criticism, his judgment in running being sadly at fault. What should have possessed him to attempt short runs when there was nothing to gain and everything to lose one cannot pretend to explain. The Australians stoutly maintained that in one of these purposeless ventures he was run out, but the umpire ruled otherwise, and there, of course, was an end of the matter.

Up to a certain point during this last innings a crushing defeat for England seemed inevitable. The team went in after luncheon with nothing to hope for but a draw, and at the end of 55 minutes four wickets were down for 19. Grace and Jackson were bowled by Howell in one over with beautiful break-backs. Hayward was Ranjitsinhji's best helper in saving the game, staying in for an hour and 25 minutes, during which time 63 runs were put on. The Surrey batsman, however, when he had scored 12, was fortunate in being palpably missed by Darling at forward short leg.

Apart from Ranjitsinhji's batting, the Australian took all the honours, and yet up to a certain time on the Friday it was quite an even match. Indeed, there was one point when England had, on paper, distinctly the better of the position. The Australians' first innings had been finished off for 252, and Grace and Fry were together with England's score at 70 for no wicket. Just after this, however, Grace lost his wicket in his overeagerness to score from Noble on the off side, and from then on the Englishmen were completely outplayed. The Australian batting was in nearly every respect admirable, but in the first innings it was marked by extreme slowness, the whole of the opening day being occupied in scoring 238 for eight wickets. The pitch was perhaps rather slower than had been expected in such fine weather, and the bowling and fielding were maintained at a very high pitch of excellence, but all the same, the Australian batsmen played with a care that would not often lead to victory in matches restricted to three days.

The hero of the game from the Colonial point of view was Clement Hill, who followed up a capital 52 with a splendidly played 80, without giving the semblance of a chance, and was out at last to a most brilliant catch by Grace at point, close to the ground with the right hand.

Toss: Australia. **Australia 252** (C. Hill 52, W. Rhodes 4-58, J. T. Hearne 4-71) **and 230-8 dec.** (C. Hill 80); **England 193** (C. B. Fry 50, E. Jones 5-88) **and 155-7** (K. S. Ranjitsinhji 93*).

Second Test

At Lord's, June 15, 16, 17, 1899. Australia won by ten wickets.

The Second Test was the only one of the five brought to a definite conclusion, and its result was a heavy blow to English cricket, the Australians gaining a brilliant victory on the third afternoon. They played a winning game all the way through, fairly beating the Englishmen at every point. Without in any way attempting to make excuses for an overwhelming defeat, it must be said that the committee in picking the England XI laid themselves open to obvious criticism. They made no fewer than five changes in the side from the First Test. As regards batting, they were probably right to leave out Grace and Gunn, but having done that they ought assuredly to have invited Shrewsbury to play. He had given conclusive evidence that he was in form, and with Grace standing down there would have been no difficulty about his fielding at point.

A still more serious blunder, however, was committed in connection with the bowling. It was tempting providence to go into the field on a fine day with no other fast bowler than Jessop, and it was a dangerous experiment to give Walter Mead the preference over J. T. Hearne on the latter's favourite ground. There was, too, some risk in playing MacLaren, who had not so far taken part in any first-class cricket during the season. In this case however, the committee had reason to congratulate themselves, MacLaren playing a magnificent second innings and making a great, though fruitless, effort to save the game.

The Englishmen really lost the match during the first hour or so on the opening day. When they went in it was confidently expected they would stay for the whole of the afternoon. To the dismay of the crowd, however, six wickets went down for 66 runs – a deplorable start from which the team were never able to recover. Jackson and Jessop saved their side from complete collapse, but Jackson, who played a superb innings, might have been run out by several yards when the score stood at 70. It was felt when the innings ended – Jones's terrific bowling being the chief cause of the breakdown – that the Australians had an immense advantage, and so it proved. For a little time there seemed some chance of an even game, Worrall, Darling and Gregory being got rid of for 59, but thenceforward the Australians were always winning.

The turning-point was the partnership of Hill and Noble. They had carried the score from 59 to 156 at the drawing of stumps, and the following morning took the total to 189. Then came another good partnership, Hill and Trumper putting Australia well in front with six wickets in hand. At this point Hill was brilliantly caught by Fry in the deep field. In their different styles Hill and Trumper played magnificent cricket. Trumper's innings was by far the more brilliant of the two, but inasmuch as Hill went in while there was still a chance of an even game, and had to play the English bowling at its best, it is only right to say that he had the greater share in his side's ultimate success.

Going in for the second time against a balance of 215, the Englishmen had a very gloomy outlook, and the position was desperate when at 23 their third wicket went down. Hayward and Jackson made things look a little better, but just before the close Jackson was easily caught and bowled in playing forward at Trumble. Hayward batted well, but when he had made a single he was palpably missed by the wicket-keeper, standing back to Jones. On the third morning MacLaren joined Hayward, and so long as they stayed together there was still a chance of England making something like a fight. Indeed things were looking comparatively cheerful when 150 went up without further loss. However Hayward, Tyldesley and Jessop were caught in quick succession, and the match was as good as over. MacLaren hit in wonderful form, but despite his efforts England were all out for 240. Never has MacLaren played a greater innings.

Toss: England. **England 206** (Hon. F. S. Jackson 73, G. L. Jessop 51, E. Jones 7-88)
and 240 (T. W. Hayward 77, A. C. MacLaren 88*);
Australia 421 (C. Hill 135, M. A. Noble 54, V. T. Trumper 135*) **and 28-0.**

CRICKETER OF THE YEAR – C. HILL

1900

Clement Hill was born on March 28, 1877, and reached his present position among the great batsmen of the world at as early an age as almost any of our English players. His name first came prominently before the public during the tour in the Colonies in 1894–95. In the closing match of that memorable trip, Hill, being then a lad of just 18, caused a sensation by scoring 150 not out and 56 for South Australia. He has never looked back, each succeeding year having added to his reputation till at the present time he stands, at any rate on hard wickets, scarcely second as a batsman to anyone except Ranjitsinhji.

High as was the estimate formed of him, English cricketers were scarcely prepared for the extraordinary form he showed in 1897–98. Against the Englishmen he scored 829 runs in 12 innings and averaged 75, his record being appreciably better than either Ranjitsinhji or MacLaren for Stoddart's side. He made 200 for South Australia in the first match of the tour, but an incomparably finer innings was his 188 at Melbourne in the fourth of the five Test matches.

So long as he remained in good health he was beyond question the best bat in Darling's team. No left-handed player has ever depended so much upon skill and so little upon mere punishing power in front of the wicket. Of course, he can drive an over-pitched ball when he is so disposed, but for most of his runs he relies upon his wonderful facility in scoring on the leg side. The way in which on a hard wicket he can turn straight balls to leg must be seen to be believed. Of course, he runs great risks and is constantly in danger of being out lbw, but his bat is always in the right place at the right moment. Next to his play on the leg side the strength of his game, so far as run-getting is concerned, lies in his cutting, which is as safe as it is brilliant.

Third Test

At Leeds, June 29, 30, July 1, 1899. Drawn.

The Third Test was in some respects the most exciting of the five, and it was a thousand pities that rain, by preventing a ball being bowled on the third day, should have caused it to be left drawn. The position at the finish was that England, with nine wickets to go down – Briggs being incapacitated – required 158 runs to win. The general opinion of the English players was that, with a continuance of fine weather, they would have obtained the runs required, but the Australians dissented, thinking that with the ground as it was they had the best of the game. Heavy rain the night before the match began had seriously affected the pitch, and at no time during the two days were runs at all easy to get. This naturally made the cricket all the more interesting, and it is safe to say that during the whole season no harder fight between bat and ball was seen.

The selection of the English XI was the subject of much deliberation. The side that went into the field differed in no fewer than five instances from the XI so badly beaten at Lord's. The selection of Briggs had a disastrous result, the popular player being seized on the Thursday evening with illness of so serious a character as to prevent him playing any more during the season and rendering necessary his detention in the Cheadle Asylum. It was a sad end to a very brilliant career. On the form in which he had been bowling there was some reason for picking Briggs, but the committee made a bad mistake in not retaining Rhodes. After the rain on Wednesday night, he would have been invaluable. The match marked the finish of Hill's splendid work for the Australians. He had to place himself in the doctor's hands the following week, and though he afterwards took part in three county matches he could not do himself justice.

The match from first to last was full of exciting incidents, fortune inclining first to one side and then to the other in a way that kept the spectators at extreme tension. The Australians did not gain much by batting first. Indeed, but for Worrall's fearless hitting on the soft wicket they would have fared very badly. His driving was a marvel of power. He was batting just under an hour and a half and scored 76 out of 95, including 14 fours. Worrall and Hill put on 71 in an hour after three wickets had been lost for 24. The fact of his getting the last two wickets made Young's figures rather flattering, but he certainly looked more difficult than either Hearne or Briggs. At the close of the first day England had four wickets down for 119.

The Englishmen entered on the second day under very discouraging circumstances, the news of Briggs's seizure having naturally upset them. Quaife and Fry were bowled without adding to the overnight score, and with only three wickets to go down England were 53 runs behind. Hayward and Lilley, however, played up with great pluck, and by putting on 93 were mainly instrumental in gaining for England a lead of 48.

The sensation of the match came when the Australians went in again. Worrall and Darling opened the innings in such style that 34 runs were scored in 20 minutes. Then, however, came an astounding collapse. Worrall was well caught in the deep field and in the following over J. T. Hearne did the hat-trick. With the third ball he bowled Hill, from the fourth Gregory was caught at extra slip, and from the fifth, amid indescribable excitement, Noble was caught at slip by Ranjitsinhji. Misfortune for the Australians did not end here, for Darling, evidently disconcerted by the disasters that had overtaken his side, hit out wildly at a ball from Young and was caught at third man.

With five wickets down the Australians were still nine runs behind and the match looked to be practically in England's hands. A great change followed, however, the Australians batting with such pluck and stubbornness as to carry their score to 224. The turning-point was the partnership of Trumper and Kelly, who stayed together for nearly an hour and put on 58 runs. During this time Young bowled superbly but with provoking luck, beating the bat again and again but always missing the wicket – two or three times by the merest shave. Trumble played a fine innings, he and Laver taking the score from 140 to 218. During the latter half of the innings the Englishmen sadly felt the loss of Briggs's services, as after Hearne and Young had been overcome there was no one who looked in the least degree difficult.

England wanted 177 to win, and at the drawing of stumps, Brown and Quaife had scored 19 without being separated. Rain fell for hours during the night and on Saturday the match was abandoned.

Toss: Australia. **Australia 172** (J. Worrall 76, H. I. Young 4-30) **and 224** (H. Trumble 56, J. T. Hearne 4-50); **England 220** (A. F. A. Lilley 55, H. Trumble 5-60) **and 19-0.**

Fourth Test

At Manchester, July 17, 18, 19, 1899. Drawn.

The result was a draw, but inasmuch as the Australians for nearly two days were fighting their hardest to avoid defeat, the honours were largely with England. By dint of untiring patience the Australians were able to declare with seven wickets down and set the impossible task of making 171 runs in about 65 minutes. Worn out by over 11 hours' fielding the Englishmen did not in this closing stage of the match play serious cricket and lost three of their best wickets, but as a draw had become inevitable the score at the finish mattered nothing.

The game showed English batting in a far more favourable light than any of the previous Test matches, and against a team possessed of no more than ordinary tenacity there is little doubt that a brilliant victory would have been obtained. The Australians, however, as match-savers have never been equalled, and in this particular instance their stubbornness and defence were something to marvel at. While frankly admitting all this, it must be added that the follow-on rule pressed very heavily on the Englishmen. They held a lead of 176 runs, and if they could then have gone in to bat instead of turning out to field again *[The laws at the time obliged England to enforce the follow-on. – Ed.]* they would have been in a splendid position. As it was their bowling was fairly worn out. Three dropped catches seriously prejudiced them, but they must scarcely be blamed, for it is quite hopeless to expect a side to stay in the field for two days without making mistakes.

On the first day England stayed in until just after six o'clock, their total reaching 372. Nothing in the early cricket gave promise of such a score. Despite fine weather in the morning the ground kicked a good deal during the first hour, and after 50 minutes' play four wickets were down for 47. Things changed a little when Hayward joined Jackson, who put on 60. Jackson was caught at slip off a bumping ball at 107, and though Brockwell played a very bright innings, when he left England's position was a very bad one, the only dependable batsman left to help Hayward being Lilley. These two had saved the situation at Leeds and again they did brilliant work together, putting on 113. When Lilley was lbw a speedy end was expected, but the Australian bowling had now lost its keen edge and some rare hitting followed. Hayward and Young took the score to 324, and then Young and Bradley added 35 in as many minutes. Sadly disappointed at the turn the game had taken the Australians became a little demoralised. Hayward's 130 was in every way magnificent. He took an hour and a half to make 20 runs, but so completely did the character of his cricket change when things were going better for his side that he added 110 in rather less than two hours and three-quarters.

The Australians lost one wicket on Monday and thenceforward they were batting till shortly after five o'clock on Wednesday. In the first innings Bradley and Young bowled superbly, but the continuous work proved far too much for them. Noble clearly saved the Australians from defeat, his batting being a miracle of patience and self-restraint. He withstood the bowlers for eight hours and a half and scarcely made a mistake. At one time on Wednesday he did not score for three-quarters of an hour.

Lilley, standing back to Bradley, missed Worrall and Trumper on Tuesday afternoon and on the last day Jackson missed Darling at mid-off. The three batsmen scored between them 155 runs, but if the catches had been held Worrall would have made one, Trumper and Darling three.

Toss: England. **England 372** (T. W. Hayward 130, A. F. A. Lilley 58) **and 94-3; Australia 196** (M. A. Noble 60*, H. I. Young 4-79, W. M. Bradley 5-67) **and 346-7 dec.** (J. Worrall 53, M. A. Noble 89, V. T. Trumper 63).

Cricketer of the Year – M. A. Noble   1900

M. A. Noble was born on January 28, 1873, and was thus a little later than some other famous Australians in paying his first visit to England. Still, though he was not seen on our cricket grounds till last season, his name was familiar to all who follow cricket. Before he came here Australian critics did not hesitate to describe him as the best all-round player in the Colonies, and we knew that a cricketer of George Giffen's class was to be expected.

From start to finish Noble was consistently successful as a batsman, but as a bowler he fell off during the last few weeks, the strain of playing with scarcely a break probably affecting him. As a batsman Noble impressed English critics chiefly by his patience and defence, but at home he has the reputation of being much freer in style. He said himself that he could not play forward with the same degree of safety as in Australia, and that the necessity of watching the ball much more closely from the pitch than he had been accustomed to, involved a considerable change in his method. It speaks volumes for his ability that, while altering his game, he should still have achieved such brilliant results.

Easy and graceful in style, he seems like all great batsmen to have plenty of time when playing back. Though by no means deficient in driving power, he depends for most of his runs on cuts behind point and a variety of skilful strokes on the leg side. No Australian batsman has ever shown better cricket during a first visit to England. As a bowler he has plenty of spin and varies his pace well. A good deal had been said about his ability to make the ball swerve in the flight, and there can be no doubt that this peculiarity in his bowling puzzled many of our batsmen, especially during the early part of the tour. Over and above his batting and bowling Noble is a superb field at point – quick, agile and fearless.

Fifth Test
At The Oval, August 14, 15, 16, 1899. Drawn.

Though the Test match ended in a draw, it had one highly satisfactory result. So amazingly good was the batting on the opening day, that English cricketers were once more placed on good terms with themselves, the depression caused by the severe defeat at Lord's being to a very large extent removed. When stumps were drawn England's score stood at 435 for four, these figures being only inferior to the 363 for two obtained at The Oval by Australia in 1884. The two performances, indeed, admitted

Long-playing record: Syd Gregory played in 52 Ashes Tests between 1890 and 1912, and toured England eight times.

of an even closer comparison than the totals would suggest. In 1884 the Australians played the strict game all afternoon and gave nothing away, whereas the Englishmen, in order to give themselves a chance of actually winning the game, began to force the pace soon after the score had reached 300 with only one wicket down. MacLaren asked a good deal of his side in instructing them to play false cricket when success meant so much in the way of individual glory, but that he took the right course will scarcely be disputed.

If by any chance England could have won the game, a full revenge for the defeat at Lord's would have been obtained, and the honours of the season equally divided. The well-meant effort failed, the wicket at The Oval being too good to admit of the Australians being got rid of twice in the time available, but the attempt to win was certainly worth making. MacLaren showed that he cared nothing for his own chances of distinction, for in hitting up his 49 he lifted the ball in a style quite foreign to his ordinary methods.

Such a wonderful start was made that 185 runs were scored for the first wicket, this number beating by 15 the fine stand by Mr W. G. Grace and the late William Scotton on the same ground in 1886. Jackson, who was the first to leave, scored 118, his innings lasting two hours and 50 minutes. In many respects he played splendid cricket, his off-driving being especially fine, but he was a good deal at fault when facing McLeod, making several bad strokes and giving a palpable chance to Trumble at slip when his score stood at 70. On the original batting order Townsend was to go in first wicket down, but by a good piece of generalship – the situation demanded brilliancy and not steady cricket – MacLaren changed his plans and sent Ranjitsinhji in. Some splendid batting followed and when the innings had been in progress something over four hours 300 went up.

This was perhaps the happiest moment experienced by England in any of the Test matches last season, the only incident to compare with it being Hearne's hat-trick at Leeds. Hayward and Ranjitsinhji put on 131 in less than an hour and a half. From an English point of view Hayward's play in the Test matches was the feature of the whole season. For the first time he had the opportunity of starting his innings when the side were not in difficulties, and nothing could well have been finer than his batting. Watching the game with the utmost closeness, he only made three strokes that could be described as dangerous. After Hayward was out, Fry and MacLaren put on 110 runs in 65 minutes, MacLaren being caught in the long field at 428.

The Englishmen having made themselves safe against all possibility of defeat, the remainder of the match resolved itself into an effort on their part to snatch a victory in the time that remained and a struggle by the Australians to secure a draw. It cannot be said that there ever looked to be much hope of victory. England's innings ended on Tuesday for 576, this being the largest total ever obtained in a Test in this country. The Australians naturally set themselves to play a steady game, and at the drawing of stumps their score stood at 220 for five, Darling after playing most skilful cricket being out in the last over of the day.

On the Wednesday the Australians played up in splendid style and saved the match, with so much to spare that in the end they were 30 ahead with five wickets to fall. Gregory, in carrying his overnight score of 37 to 117, played finer cricket than on any other occasion during the tour. McLeod in both innings showed wonderful defence, and Noble gave one of his best displays. Nothing, however, on this last day was quite so fine as Lockwood's bowling. By taking, in an innings of 352, seven wickets for 71 runs, he showed what his absence had meant to England in the four previous matches.

Toss: England. **England 576** (Hon. F. S. Jackson 118, T. W. Hayward 137, K. S. Ranjitsinhji 54, C. B. Fry 60, E. Jones 4-164); **Australia 352** (J. Worrall 55, J. Darling 71, S. E. Gregory 117, W. H. Lockwood 7-71) and 254-5 (J. Worrall 75, C. E. McLeod 77, M. A. Noble 69⁴).

Suggested Reforms
A. G. Steel, 1900

Look at the result of the past season's first-class cricket. Of the five international fixtures only one was finished; of 150 county matches 60 were drawn; the University Match was drawn, as also the Eton and Harrow match. Surely cricketers can find some way of escape from these weird results.

Even should no change in the laws materially assisting the bowlers at the batsmen's expense be made before the visit of the next Australian team, I should deprecate very strongly playing five Test matches to a finish. Three representative matches are in my opinion ample to test the merits of the two sides. Different views have been expressed by competent critics on the question of whether these matches should be played to a finish or not. I am of opinion that three full days' play, from 11 a.m. to 7 p.m. should be given to these matches and no more. If they are to be played to a finish, it will foster the tedious and weary style of play that has become the bane of the game. We all know what happened in Australia some years ago – spectators absent, no interest in the game, and batsmen working slowly on for hours! Let us take a lesson and do everything to stimulate energy and quick action in the game. What a treat it was in the early days of the Australian teams in England to see but a few short minutes of Massie, McDonnell or Bonnor. "Better 20 runs from Massie than a century from Quaife."

Australia v England 1901–02

In connection with cricket, history has not often repeated itself so curiously as in the experiences of the last two English XIs taken out to the Colonies. Mr Stoddart's second team, which went to Australia in the winter of 1897–98, won the first of their five Test matches and lost the other four, and precisely the same fate befell Mr MacLaren's XI in the Australian summer of 1901–02.

There was a great deal of difference in the general character of the cricket. MacLaren's side made a much bolder bid for victory, for in every one of their four defeats, there was a time when they stood apparently in a winning position. They lacked the tenacity of their opponents, however, and, to borrow a racing expression, failed to stay home. It is only fair to them to say that in the fifth and last Test match, which they only lost by the narrow margin of 32 runs, the weather was very unkind to them, the wicket being seriously damaged by rain during the last innings.

In one respect they were desperately unlucky. Barnes, who was picked on the strength of one performance for Lancashire and a good record in league cricket, bowled so finely in the early matches that he promised to be the special success of the tour, but his knee gave way in the Test match at Adelaide in January and he played no more. After January 18 he gave the team no assistance, his absence quite crippling the bowling.

As regards the team's general play two points stood out above all else. MacLaren batted magnificently, proving himself, as on the previous tour, a veritable champion on the Sydney ground, and the fielding was pronounced on all hands to be the most brilliant that English cricketers had ever shown in Australia.

First Test

At Sydney, December 13, 14, 16, 1901. England won by an innings and 124 runs.

The First Test proved to be, from the English point of view, the event of the tour, MacLaren's team gaining a glorious and altogether unexpected victory. On winning the toss MacLaren went in himself with Hayward as a partner, and by dint of very good but unwontedly steady cricket the two batsmen scored 154 for the first wicket. This splendid start, however, was not by any means well followed up, and at the close of the first day six wickets had fallen for 272. The ground being in perfect order for run-getting, this was not considered nearly good enough, but happily for the Englishmen Lilley and Braund made a great stand on the Saturday morning, putting on 124. The last three men all did well, and in the end the total reached 464.

The Australians started by losing Trumper very cheaply, but thanks to Gregory and Hill the score at the drawing of stumps had reached 108 with three wickets down. This being the position there seemed every reason on the Monday to expect a protracted match. As things turned out, however, the English bowlers carried all before them, getting 17 wickets down in the course of the afternoon and finishing the game. Braund, Blythe and Barnes, though the last-named was freely punished in the second innings, bowled very finely indeed, and were backed up by fielding and wicket-keeping of the most brilliant character. There was a regular collapse during the first quarter of an hour in the morning, Hill, Howell, McLeod and Kelly being all out at 112, and from these disasters the Australians, despite strenuous efforts, could never recover. The result of the match caused a great sensation all over the Colonies. It is worthy of note that the Australian team was composed entirely of players who went to England in 1899.

Toss: England. **England 464** (A. C. MacLaren 116, T. W. Hayward 69, A. F. A. Lilley 84, L. C. Braund 58, C. E. McLeod 4-84); **Australia 168** (S. F. Barnes 5-65) **and 172** (L. C. Braund 5-61, C. Blythe 4-30).

Second Test

At Melbourne, January 1, 2, 3, 4, 1902. Australia won by 229 runs.

The Second Test was in some respects the most remarkable of the series. Owing to a lot of rain for two or three days the wicket was very difficult on the opening day, but, as is not uncommon in Australia, it had practically recovered on the second morning. MacLaren, on winning the toss, put Australia in, but his bowlers – Barnes and Blythe – did not serve him so well as he had hoped, and when an innings had been completed on each side the Englishmen found themselves 51 runs behind. When the Australians went in for the second time, Darling, rightly judging that the ground would improve, kept some of his best batsmen in reserve, and at the close of the day five wickets had fallen for 48.

On paper the position favoured the Englishmen, but on the second day the cricket changed entirely in character, and the game all the afternoon went in Australia's favour. Hill played a magnificent innings, and at the drawing of stumps the score stood at 300 for nine, Duff being not out 71, with Armstrong as his partner. These two players, who had taken the places filled in the match at Sydney by Charles McLeod and Laver, added 53 on the third morning, their partnership for the last wicket producing in all 120 runs. Duff, who was batting for three hours and a half, had the distinction of making a hundred in his first Test match. Moreover, he showed by far the best batting while the pitch was difficult.

The Englishmen wanted 405 to win, and the task proved far beyond their powers. Tyldesley at last showed his true form, but five wickets fell before the end of the afternoon, and on the fourth morning the end soon came, Australia winning by 229 runs. Noble had a big share in the success of his side, taking in all 13 wickets for 77 runs. Barnes also took 13 wickets. He bowled finely, but was overworked in the second innings.

Toss: England. **Australia 112** (S. F. Barnes 6-42, C. Blythe 4-64) **and 353** (C. Hill 99, R. A. Duff 104,
S. F. Barnes 7-121); **England 61** (M. A. Noble 7-17) **and 175** (J. T. Tyldesley 66,
M. A. Noble 6-60, H. Trumble 4-49).

Obituary – John Briggs

1903

John Briggs died on January 11, 1902. The last reports as to the condition of Briggs's health had been so discouraging that the news of his death did not cause much surprise. Though he rallied so wonderfully from his seizure at Leeds, during the Test match in 1899, as to bowl with nearly all his old skill and success throughout the season of 1900, it was known that his ailment – a form of epilepsy – admitted of no permanent cure, and was liable to recur at any time. He had another attack sooner than had been expected; was compelled to go back to Cheadle Asylum; and took no part in the cricket of 1901. Five or six weeks before his death it was announced that he had again rallied after a serious relapse, but this time the improvement was of very brief duration.

Briggs had a long career, but at the time of his death he was only a little over 39. Like so many other famous professional cricketers, he was a Nottingham man, being born at Sutton-in-Ashfield, on October 3, 1862. While still a child, however, he went to live in Lancashire, and all his cricket was learnt in the county for which, during more than 20 years, he did such brilliant work.

He paid six visits to the Colonies, going out with Shaw and Shrewsbury's teams in 1884–85, 1886–87, and 1887–88; with Lord Sheffield's team in 1891–92, and with Mr Stoddart's XIs in 1894–95, and 1897–98. As it happened, he went once too often, proving a sad failure for Stoddart's second team. In the other trips, however, he did himself full justice. Among all his Australian experiences the most remarkable was the famous ten-runs win at Sydney, in December, 1894, when Australia suffered defeat after playing a first innings of 586. The Australians only had to get 177 in the last innings, and at the close of the fifth day they had scored 113, with two men out. After drenching rain in the night, however, Peel and Briggs secured the eight outstanding wickets for 53 runs, gaining for Stoddart's side perhaps the most sensational victory in the history of cricket. Briggs, as a slow bowler, had nearly every good quality. His beautifully easy action enabled him to stand any amount of work; he had plenty of spin, and no one was more skilful in tempting batsmen to hit on the off side.

Third Test

At Adelaide, January 17, 18, 20, 21, 22, 23, 1902. Australia won by four wickets.

It was in this match – a protracted struggle that lasted into the sixth day – that Barnes's knee gave way. He broke down on the second afternoon and, as events turned out, took no further part in the tour. It is not unreasonable to assume that if he had kept sound, the Englishmen would have gained a second victory. As it was, the Australians, though set to get 315 in the last innings on a pitch somewhat worn at one end, won by four wickets. As in the First Test, MacLaren and Hayward gave their side a splendid start, scoring 149 before they were separated. Something in the nature of a collapse followed, but Quaife and Braund batted very finely, and on the second day the innings ended for 388. Braund, in his 103 not out, hit a five and 12 fours. After losing Darling for a single, the Australians showed brilliant form, and at the drawing of stumps on Saturday their score was up to 165 runs ahead with nine wickets in hand. Thanks to some admirable bowling by John Gunn the innings was finished off on Monday for 321, or 67 runs behind. As at Melbourne, Hill just missed his hundred after playing superb cricket. The Englishmen then scored 38 for the loss of MacLaren's wicket and left off for the day in a splendid position, being 165 ahead with nine wickets in hand.

Tuesday's play was brought to an abrupt conclusion by a dust storm, the English score being then 204 with five wickets down. Barnes could not bat, and on the fifth morning the innings soon ended, Trumble bowling in great form. Quaife took two hours and three-quarters to get his 44. The Australians wanted 315 to win and at the close of the day, they were well within sight of victory, having scored 201 for four wickets. Hill again got into the nineties and again played in his finest form. Blythe being handicapped by a damaged finger, the English bowling on the last morning was very weak, but nevertheless the batsmen found it hard work to get runs on the slightly worn pitch. Darling took three and a half to score his 69, he and Trumble making the result a certainty before they were separated. It was a fine victory gained by most tenacious cricket.

Toss: England. **England 388** (A. C. MacLaren 67, T. W. Hayward 90, W. G. Quaife 68, L. C. Braund 103*)
and 247 (H. Trumble 6-74); **Australia 321** (V. T. Trumper 65, C. Hill 98, S. E. Gregory 55, J. R. Gunn 5-76)
and 315-6 (C. Hill 97, J. Darling 69, H. Trumble 62*).

Fourth Test
At Sydney, February 14, 15, 17, 18, 1902. Australia won by seven wickets.

Of all the matches during the tour this was, from the Englishmen's point of view, the most disappointing. They made a wonderful start, their score standing at 179 with only one wicket down, but at the end of the first day they had lost six wickets for 266. MacLaren, quite invincible on the Sydney ground, played a very fine innings and Tyldesley was also at his best. The next day the England innings finished for 317 and the Australians lost five wickets for 148, MacLaren's side being thus still in a very flattering position. From this point, however, all the honours were with Australia. There was only a difference of 18 runs on the first innings, but the Englishmen, on going in for the second time, collapsed before the bowling of Noble and Saunders, never recovering from MacLaren's early downfall. The reports cabled to England said that the wicket was perfect, but it probably gave the bowlers some assistance. The innings ended on the fourth morning of the match, and the Australians, only set to get 118, gained a brilliant victory by seven wickets. Their third win in the series gave Australia the rubber.

Toss: England. **England 317** (A. C. MacLaren 92, J. T. Tyldesley 79, J. V. Saunders 4-119)
and 99 (J. V. Saunders 5-43, M. A. Noble 5-54); **Australia 299** (M. A. Noble 56, W. W. Armstrong 55,
L. C. Braund 4-118, G. L. Jessop 4-68) **and 121-3** (R. A. Duff 51*).

Fifth Test
At Melbourne, February 28, March 1, 3, 4, 1902. Australia won by 32 runs.

The fifth and last of the Test matches resulted in another defeat for MacLaren's side after a very keen fight. The Englishmen led by 45 on the first innings, the modest run-getting being due to the fact that recent rain had considerably affected the ground. At the close of the second day the Australians in their second innings had made 226 for six, Hill taking the chief honours with a splendidly played 87. On Monday, owing to frequent showers, very little could be done, only 116 runs being scored in the course of the afternoon. The Englishmen were left with 211 to get, and at the close they had scored 87 with three men out, all three wickets falling in the last few minutes. The prospects of victory would have been hopeful next morning if the ground had improved, but the pitch turned out very difficult, and no one except A. O. Jones could cope with Noble's bowling. The result was that the Australians won the game, and so left off with a record in the Test matches of four victories as against one defeat.

Toss: Australia. **Australia 144** (T. W. Hayward 4-22, J. R. Gunn 4-38) **and 255** (C. Hill 87, L. C. Braund 5-95);
England 189 (H. Trumble 5-62) **and 178** (M. A. Noble 6-98).

ENGLAND V AUSTRALIA 1902

Sydney Pardon

From a cricket point of view the Australians had a triumphant tour, and as regards material reward they got on quite as well as could have been expected in such a deplorable summer. In going through a programme of 39 fixtures with only two defeats, they beat the records of all their predecessors. They formed a splendid all-round combination, the players new to England having been picked with the nicest judgment, but the team would not, with all their ability, have been able to show such consistently fine form week after week throughout a long tour, if the men had not taken scrupulous care of themselves when off the field. I make no apology for insisting rather strongly upon this point. Everyone who is at all behind the scenes in cricket knows perfectly well that in the case, both of English XIs in Australia and Australian XIs in England, the brightest hopes have sometimes been wrecked through want of self-control on the part of players on whom the utmost dependence was placed. In this connection it is, of course, impossible to mention names, but the famous cricketers who have captained XIs of both countries will know perfectly well the cases I have in mind.

It may be, as one of the most famous of English batsmen stoutly contends, that the bowling was a good deal inferior to that of the 1882 XI, and the batting, apart from Trumper's marvellous play, may not have been quite so good as in some other tours, but on this latter point I should be chary of expressing a positive opinion. The side battled against abnormal weather and it is impossible to say what the run-getting power would have been if we had been favoured with such a summer as that of 1899.

The Australians won the rubber and I should be the last to depreciate their achievement or to attempt to rob them of any of the credit so justly their due. Still, looking at the three finished matches and the two draws as a whole, I think it may fairly be said that the general result did not prove any marked superiority on their part.

Coming to the individual work of the various players, one is struck first by the pre-eminence of Victor Trumper. He stood alone among the batsmen of the season, not only far surpassing his own colleagues, but also putting into the shade everyone who played for England. In the course of the tour he obtained, despite the wet weather, 2,570 runs, thus easily beating Darling's 1,941 in the glorious summer of 1899, which up to this year was a record aggregate for any Colonial batsman touring in this country.

CRICKETER OF THE YEAR – VICTOR TRUMPER

1903

Victor Trumper, at the present time, by general consent, the best batsman in the world, was born on November 2, 1877. He came out in Australia in the same season as Clement Hill – 1894–95 – but his powers ripened far more slowly, and for a year or two he did little to foreshadow the career that was in store for him. In 1898–99 he showed marked improvement, and with a score of 292 not out against Tasmania convinced good judges of the game in Sydney that a new star had risen. Still it was only as 14th man that he was picked to come to England in 1899, and not until the tour had been some little time in progress, and his success assured, was he placed on the same financial footing as the other members of the team. He made a magnificent 135 not out against England at Lord's; against Sussex he scored 300 not out – the highest score ever obtained by an Australian batsman in this country.

The whole team were delighted with him, and it is said that Noble predicted that he would become a greater batsman than Ranjitsinhji. On getting home he added to his reputation, scoring 436 runs in eight innings and helping New South Wales to win the Sheffield Shield. Against MacLaren's team in 1901–02, however, he did not do himself justice, his cricket being affected by the fact that he was engaged a great deal in office work at night-time. Of his performances in this country during the past season, it will be sufficient to say that he put into the shade everything that had ever before been done in England by Australian batsmen.

Apart from his batting, Trumper is one of the finest of outfields, and a very serviceable change bowler. Success has not in any way spoilt him, and alike on English and Australian cricket fields he is deservedly one of the most popular of players.

First Test

At Birmingham, May 29, 30, 31, 1902. Drawn.

In the first of the five Test matches England experienced a strange mixture of good and bad luck. Up to a certain point fortune, in the shape of dropped catches, and a heavy downpour of rain that spoiled the game after the first day, was all on their side, but at the crucial point there came a complete change, rain by drenching the ground on the last day saving the Australians from a defeat that under ordinary circumstances would have been inevitable.

A beautiful wicket had been prepared, and when MacLaren won the toss, it was almost taken for granted that England would make a big score. In the end expectation was realised, but success only came after a deplorable start, and after the Australians had discounted their chances by two or three palpable blunders in the field. Happily for England, Jackson and Tyldesley, to some extent, saved the situation. Jackson ended a beautiful innings by chopping a ball from Jones on to his wicket, and again England were in a bad way. Then came the dropped catches that had such a vital effect on the day's cricket, Tyldesley, with his score at 43, having three escapes. He was missed low down at mid-off by Jones and then, after Lilley had been taken from a skyer, he was missed by Darling at mid-on, and nearly caught and bowled by Armstrong.

So much rain fell during Thursday night that it was not until nearly three o'clock that the match was proceeded with. Some people expected that MacLaren would at once declare, but he decided to go on batting for a time, so that his bowlers might not have to start work on a slippery foothold. He declared when the score had been raised to 376, and then followed one of the chief sensations of the cricket season of 1902, the Australians being got rid of in less than an hour and a half for 36, Trumper, who played fine cricket for 70 minutes, alone making a stand. The light was bad, but in the opinion of the umpires the wicket was by no means so difficult as to excuse such an ignominious breakdown.

The Australians had of course to follow on. Had Friday night remained fine the

Englishmen would have had the match in their hands, but rain fell for 12 hours without cessation, reducing the Edgbaston ground to such a condition that on Saturday morning it was seen at once that cricket would for several hours be out of the question. The afternoon turned out delightfully fine, but nothing was done until a quarter past five, and but for the fact of thousands of people having been admitted to the ground after four o'clock, the match would no doubt have been abandoned without another ball being bowled. The Australians easily played out time.

Toss: England. **England 376-9 dec.** (Hon. F. S. Jackson 53, J. T. Tyldesley 138, W. H. Lockwood 52*);
Australia 36 (W. Rhodes 7-17) **and 46-2.**

Second Test

At Lord's, June 12, 13, 14, 1902. Drawn.

The Second Test was utterly ruined by rain, play being restricted to an hour and three-quarters on the opening day. Cricket on Friday was out of the question, and on Saturday morning, the ground being almost under water, the match was abandoned about a quarter past 11, it being seen at once that there was no possibility of going on.

The game, so far as it went, was eventful enough to satisfy the strongest appetite for sensational cricket, England, starting at a quarter to three, losing Fry and Ranjitsinhji without a run, and then being saved from collapse by MacLaren and Jackson.

In a bad light MacLaren and Jackson took the total to 102 without being separated. MacLaren, apart from a one-handed chance to Darling in the slips off Trumper's bowling, when he had made 34, showed perfect cricket. His back play was wonderfully strong, and twice he scored most cleverly on the on side from fast-rising balls.

Jackson was lucky in making two or three strokes that fell out of harm's way, and with his score at 45 he would have been caught at mid-off if Saunders instead of standing in his place and throwing himself forward had moved a yard to get to the ball. The two batsmen were enthusiastically cheered at the drawing of stumps, and people went home contented, a total of 102 for two promising great things for England on a pitch that was never likely to be easy. However, the rain dashed all hopes, and the Second Test like the First had to be abandoned.

Toss: England. **England 102-2** (Hon. F. S. Jackson 55*).

Third Test

At Bramall Lane, Sheffield, July 3, 4, 5, 1902. Australia won by 143 runs.

The Third *[the first and only one ever played at Sheffield – Ed.]* was brought to a definite conclusion and resulted in a severe disaster for England, the Australians winning at a quarter past one on the Saturday. They played the finer all-round cricket, and fully deserved their victory, but it is no more than the truth to say that all the luck went their way. Bad light towards the close of the first day and a pitch damaged by rain the following morning told against the Englishmen, and in the closing stage of the match the wicket showed unmistakable signs of wear. The match naturally proved a strong attraction, but a mistake was made in fixing it for the latter part of the week, Monday being always the best day for public cricket at Sheffield.

At one point on the first day the Englishmen had much the best of the match as, after getting rid of the Australians for 194, they had 60 on the board when their first wicket went down. When, however, a quarter of an hour before the time for drawing stumps the bad light was successfully appealed against, five wickets had fallen for 102. The cause of this startling change in the game was the bowling of Noble and Saunders, Noble, who had previously shown the best batting for his side, being in wonderful form. Sufficient rain fell in the night to affect the wicket for a time, and the Englishmen on resuming cut such an inglorious figure that by a quarter to 12 the innings was all over for 145, the last seven wickets having actually gone down for 44 runs. The batsmen on the second morning were quite at fault in dealing with Saunders' breakbacks.

The Australians went in for the second time, and ran up a total of 289. This was quite enough to make them pretty sure of the match, but at one time they seemed likely to do a great deal better, their score when the fourth wicket fell standing at 187. Rhodes finished off the innings with a wonderful piece of bowling, taking four wickets in 19 balls. At the start of the innings MacLaren made a mistake in not putting him on at the end from which Saunders had been so successful. Trumper in the course of the season made many bigger scores than his 62 but on no occasion did he play a more marvellous innings. He obtained his runs out of a total of 80 in 50 minutes, doing just what he liked with the English bowling.

England wanted 339 to win, and it was felt that the task would prove too heavy. However, a good start was made, the experiment of sending Jessop in first with Abel proving a great success. Without being in any way reckless the famous hitter played a brilliant game and, when bad light stopped cricket for the day, he was not out 53, the total being 73 for one wicket.

Any hopes that the Englishmen might have had were soon destroyed on Saturday morning, Jessop, Tyldesley and Fry being all dismissed in the first half-hour for the addition of 25 runs. MacLaren made a great effort to save a lost game, and found a valuable partner in Jackson, but it was all to no purpose. After Jackson's dismissal at 162 the end soon came, the last five wickets falling for 33 runs. In this closing part of the match Noble bowled magnificently, breaking back again and again in an unplayable way. In the whole match he took 11 wickets for 103 runs. Trumble who, owing to a blow on his thumb, did not bowl on Friday afternoon, did admirable work at the finish.

Toss: Australia. **Australia 194** (S. F. Barnes 6-49) **and 289** (V. T. Trumper 62, C. Hill 119, W. Rhodes 5-63); **England 145** (J. V. Saunders 5-50, M. A. Noble 5-51) **and 195** (G. L. Jessop 55, A. C. MacLaren 63, M. A. Noble 6-52, H. Trumble 4-49).

CRICKETER OF THE YEAR – WARWICK ARMSTRONG   1903

Warwick W. Armstrong was born on May 22, 1879. Few players coming to England for the first time with an Australian team have done better work. As an all-round man he was an invaluable member of Darling's splendid XI, scoring 1,075 with an average of

27, and taking 72 wickets for 18.90 runs each. For a cricketer of 23 who could do all this under strange conditions, when for the first time in his life playing two matches a week, it is not unreasonable to expect a great future.

His success was assured from the start of the tour, as in the second match his bowling enabled the Australians to beat Notts after a draw had seemed certain. His value to the side was even greater as a bowler than as a batsman, there being something in his leg-breaks – probably a deceptive flight of the ball – that made him curiously difficult to hit. Never in the course of a fairly long experience have we seen a bowler in any season deliver so many balls that went wide of the leg stump without being punished. No doubt his great height – he stands well over six feet – helped to make him difficult. He did not as a rule try to get on a big break, but in combination with a good length he made the ball do quite enough.

He did well against MacLaren's team in the Australian season of 1901–02 having, next to Duff, the chief share in winning the second of the five Test games, and in the previous season he batted with great success in Inter-State matches, materially helping Victoria to carry off the Sheffield Shield. At that time he was played almost entirely for his batting, his bowling being a later development. As a batsman he is not very attractive to look at, an ugly bend of the right knee rather spoiling his style, but he watches the ball well and drives with great power.

Fourth Test

At Manchester, July 24, 25, 26, 1902. Australia won by three runs.

The fourth of the Test games produced one of the most memorable matches in the whole history of cricket, the Australians, after some extraordinary fluctuations of fortune, winning by three runs. At the end of the first day they looked to have the game in their hands, and at the end of the second it seemed equally certain that they would be beaten. Superb bowling and fielding pulled them through at the finish, but they would probably be the first to admit that fortune was very kind to them, five or six hours' rain during Friday night making the task of the Englishmen in the last innings twice as difficult as it had promised to be. In the opinion of most people England ought, despite the damaged pitch, to have won, but defeat by three runs after such a tremendous struggle certainly carried with it no discredit.

Nothing that English cricketers did against the Australians last summer was more brilliant than the way in which they recovered themselves on the second day, turning an apparently hopeless position into one that suggested an easy win. The Selection Committee left out Fry and Jessop, restored Ranjitsinhji to the place he had not been able to take at Sheffield, and brought in Palairet and Tate. As Fry had failed in three matches it was only right to drop him, but it was a mistake not to play Jessop as his absence, apart from all question of run-getting, sadly weakened the fielding. On the morning of the match another blunder was committed, Tate being played in preference to Hirst. The condition of the ground – very soft and slow after a lot of rain – offered some excuse for the course adopted, but it meant playing a bowler pure and simple in preference to a first-rate all-rounder, and the result proved anything but happy.

The Australians derived great advantage from winning the toss as up to lunch-time the ball did nothing at all on the soft turf. Trumper, Duff and Hill made splendid use of their opportunities, but it must be said that the bowlers did very poor work, pitching so short that it was often an easy matter to pull them. By magnificent hitting Trumper and Duff scored 135 for the first wicket and when lunch-time came the total without further loss had reached 173, the Australians seeming already on the high road to victory. After the interval Rhodes got rid of Trumper, Noble and Gregory in quick succession, but Darling punished him tremendously. With only five men out for 256 the Australians seemed sure to make considerably over 300, but the last few batsmen could do nothing against Lockwood, and the innings ended for 299. The chief batting honours rested with Trumper, who scored his 104 without making a mistake of any kind. His pulling was a marvel of ease and certainty.

The wicket had been drying fast since luncheon and the Englishmen on going in to bat could do little or nothing against Trumble and Saunders, five wickets going down in three-quarters of an hour for 44. Jackson and Braund then played out time, the total at the drawing of stumps being 70.

Friday was England's day, the cricket shown by the home side, apart from one lamentable blunder in the field, being magnificent. To begin with Jackson and Braund pulled the game round into quite a respectable position, carrying the overnight score to 185 before they were separated. It was a splendid performance, for although the wicket had improved a great deal and was in good condition, runs were very hard to get, the Australian bowlers being always able to get break on the ball. Lunch-time had nearly arrived when Braund, in stepping out to drive Noble, turned on to his wicket a ball that would have missed the off stump. After luncheon Jackson did not get much support, but he played a great game himself, forcing the hitting in the most skilful way while the last two men were in with him. In fourth wicket down on Thursday, with the score at 30, he was the last man out, England finishing up only 37 runs behind.

Excitement was at its highest point when shortly after four o'clock the Australians entered upon their second innings, everyone feeling that the result of the match might depend on the next hour's play. As it happened Lockwood's bowling was even more remarkable than Jackson's batting had been, and the game went entirely in England's favour. Trumper, Hill and Duff were out for ten runs, Trumper being caught at slip by Braund at the second attempt, and the fourth wicket would have fallen at 16 if Darling had not been missed at square leg off Braund's bowling by Tate. If the catch had been held it is quite likely that the Australians would have been out for a total of 50 or 60. As it was, Darling and Gregory stayed together for an hour, their partnership producing 54 runs. Then Lockwood got rid of Hopkins and Noble, and when the time came for drawing stumps eight wickets were down for 85. The Australians were only 122 runs ahead with two wickets to fall, and it is only reasonable to assume that if the weather had kept fine during the night, England would have won the match comfortably enough. Rain poured down for five or six hours however, and on Saturday morning the position had completely changed. Nothing could be done until shortly after 12, and for the addition of a single run the Australian innings ended, England being left with 124 to get to win. For Lockwood, the match was nothing less than a triumph, his analysis for the two innings coming out at 11 wickets for 76 runs.

As no one could tell how the wicket would play, the Englishmen entered upon their task under very anxious circumstances. At first, however, everything went well, MacLaren and Palairet scoring 36 in 50 minutes, and being still together at lunch-time. Still, the

England v Australia 1902 — Fourth Test

At Manchester, July 24, 25, 26, 1902. Result: Australia won by three runs.

AUSTRALIA	First innings		Second innings	
V. T. Trumper c Lilley b Rhodes	104	– c Braund b Lockwood		4
R. A. Duff c Lilley b Lockwood	54	– b Lockwood		3
C. Hill c Rhodes b Lockwood	65	– b Lockwood		0
M. A. Noble c and b Rhodes	2	– (6) c Lilley b Lockwood		4
S. E. Gregory c Lilley b Rhodes	3	– lbw b Tate		24
*J. Darling c MacLaren b Rhodes	51	– (4) c Palairet b Rhodes		37
A. J. Y. Hopkins c Palairet b Lockwood	0	– c Tate b Lockwood		2
W. W. Armstrong b Lockwood	5	– b Rhodes		3
†J. J. Kelly not out	4	– not out		2
H. Trumble c Tate b Lockwood	0	– lbw b Tate		4
J. V. Saunders b Lockwood	3	– c Tyldesley b Rhodes		0
B 5, l-b 2, w 1	8	B 1, l-b 1, n-b 1		3

1-135 2-175 3-179 4-183 5-256 6-256   299

7-288 8-292 9-292 10-299

1-7 2-9 3-10 4-64 5-74 6-76   86

7-77 8-79 9-85 10-86

First innings – Rhodes 25–3–104–4; Jackson 11–0–58–0; Tate 11–1–44–0; Braund 9–0–37–0; Lockwood 20.1–5–48–6.

Second innings – Lockwood 17–5–28–5; Braund 11–3–22–0; Rhodes 14.4–5–26–3; Tate 5–3–7–2.

ENGLAND	First innings		Second innings	
L. C. H. Palairet c Noble b Saunders	6	– b Saunders		17
R. Abel c Armstrong b Saunders	6	– (5) b Trumble		21
J. T. Tyldesley c Hopkins b Saunders	22	– c Armstrong b Saunders		16
*A. C. MacLaren b Trumble	1	– (2) c Duff b Trumble		35
K. S. Ranjitsinhji lbw b Trumble	2	– (4) lbw b Trumble		4
Hon. F. S. Jackson c Duff b Trumble	128	– c Gregory b Saunders		7
L. C. Braund b Noble	65	– st Kelly b Trumble		3
†A. F. A. Lilley b Noble	7	– c Hill b Trumble		4
W. H. Lockwood run out	7	– b Trumble		0
W. Rhodes c and b Trumble	5	– not out		4
F. W. Tate not out	5	– b Saunders		4
B 6, l-b 2	8	B 5		5

1-12 2-13 3-14 4-30 5-44 6-185   262

7-203 8-214 9-235 10-262

1-44 2-68 3-72 4-92 5-97 6-107   120

7-109 8-109 9-116 10-120

First innings – Trumble 43–16–75–4; Saunders 34–5–104–3; Noble 24–8–47–2; Trumper 6–4–6–0; Armstrong 5–2–19–0; Hopkins 2–0–3–0.

Second innings – Trumble 25–9–53–6; Noble 5–3–10–0; Saunders 19.4–4–52–4.

Toss won by Australia   UMPIRES I. Moss and T. Mycroft

difficulty they experienced in playing the bowling made one apprehensive as to what would happen after the interval. Palairet was bowled at 44, and then with MacLaren and Tyldesley together runs for a few overs came so fast that England seemed likely to win hands down. However, at 68 or only 56 to win, Tyldesley was caught in the slips. Another misfortune quickly followed, MacLaren, after playing very fine cricket, hitting out rashly at a ball from Trumble and being caught in the long field at 72.

At this point Ranjitsinhji was joined by Abel, and after the latter had been missed by Saunders at mid-on, a slight shower stopped the game for a quarter of an hour. The weather looked very threatening and it was clear, on cricket being again proceeded with, that Abel had received strict injunctions to hit. He played a game quite foreign to his ordinary methods, and for a time got on very well. Ranjitsinhji, however, did not seem to have the least confidence in himself. He was always in front of the stumps in trying to play Trumble, and at 92 he was lbw to that bowler. With six wickets in hand and only 32 runs wanted, England still seemed sure of victory, but from this point everything changed, Trumble and Saunders, backed up by superb fielding, bowling so finely that in 50 minutes five more wickets went down for 24 runs.

With 15 required, Rhodes joined Lilley and in three hits, one of them a big drive over the ring by Rhodes, the score was carried to 116, or only eight to win. At this point, Lilley, from a fine hit, was splendidly caught at square leg, Hill just reaching the ball when running at full speed. Tate got a four on the leg side from the first ball he received from Saunders, but the fourth, which came a little with the bowler's arm and kept low, hit the wicket and the match was over, Australia winning by three runs. Trumble and Saunders bowled extraordinary well, combining a lot of break with almost perfect length, and the fielding that did so much to win the match was unsurpassable.

Fifth Test

At The Oval, August 11, 12, 13, 1902. England won by one wicket.

Australia having already won the rubber, the fifth and last of the Test matches had not the same importance that would under other circumstances have attached to it, but it produced a never-to-be-forgotten struggle and a more exciting finish, if that were possible, than the one at Manchester. In face of great difficulties and disadvantages England won by one wicket after the odds had been 50 to one on Australia. Some truly wonderful hitting by Jessop made victory possible after all hope had seemed gone, and Hirst and Rhodes got their side home at the close.

The wicket, though a trifle slow from the effects of recent rain, was in very good condition, and the Australians, staying in for the whole of the first day, made the highly satisfactory score of 324. At one time they did not seem likely to do nearly so well as this for, though Trumper and Duff scored 47 for the first partnership, there were four wickets down for 82 and five for 126. The change in the game was brought about by Hirst, who for a time bowled in quite his form of 1901. With seven wickets down for 175 the outlook was none too promising. However, the three remaining wickets added 149, an invaluable partnership by Hopkins and Trumble putting on 81. The batting was very painstaking, but an unlucky mistake by Lilley at the wicket when Trumble had made nine had, from England's point of view, a deplorable effect on the game.

If the weather had kept fine the Englishmen would not have been afraid of facing a score of 324, but the bad luck that had handicapped them at Sheffield and Manchester still pursued them, heavy rain during the early hours of Tuesday morning making a great difference in the pitch. Under the circumstances they did not do at all badly to score 183, but apart from some bright hitting by Tyldesley there was nothing remarkable in the efforts of the early batsmen. Thanks to a bad blunder by Hill, who palpably missed Lockwood at long-on when that batsman had made 11, the follow-on was saved, the innings ending for 183. Trumble bowled throughout the innings in splendid form and took eight wickets.

The Australians looked, when they went in for the second time, to have the match in their hands. They opened their innings with a great misfortune, Trumper throwing away his wicket in attempting a foolish run, and for the rest of the afternoon the batting was marked by such extreme care that at the drawing of stumps the score, with eight men out, had only reached 114, two hours and three-quarters being occupied in getting these runs. The wicket was still rather difficult and Lockwood bowled very finely. Hill was out to a magnificent catch low down in the slips in one hand by MacLaren, and Noble bowled off his pads by a ball that he did not attempt to play with his bat.

On Wednesday morning Lockwood quickly obtained the two outstanding wickets, and England needed 263 to win. Tuesday's cricket, while the turf was still soft after rain, had damaged the pitch to no small extent, and up to a certain point the batsmen were so helpless against Saunders and Trumble that the easiest of victories for Australia appeared in prospect. Three wickets fell to Saunders for ten runs and but for Gregory missing Hayward badly at short leg there would have been four wickets down for 16. Even as it was half the side were out for 48 and the match looked all over.

At this point Jackson was joined by Jessop and a stand was made which completely altered the game. At first, however, Jessop's cricket was far from suggesting the wonderful form he afterwards showed. When he had made 22 Kelly missed stumping him and at 27 he gave a rather awkward chance to Trumper at long-off. At lunch-time the two batsmen were still together, Jackson, who had played superb cricket, being 39 and Jessop 29. After the interval Jackson was far indeed from keeping up his previous form, being repeatedly in difficulties and giving a palpable chance to Armstrong at slip. Jessop, on the other hand, settled down, and hit as he only can. At one point he scored four fours and a single off successive balls from Saunders. The partnership had added 109 in 65 minutes when Jackson was easily caught and bowled. Jessop went on hitting for some little time longer, but at 187 he closed his extraordinary innings by placing a ball gently into short leg's hands. He scored, in just over an hour and a quarter, 104 runs out of 139, his hits being a five in the slips, 17 fours, two threes, four twos, and 17 singles. All things considered a more astonishing display has never been seen. What he did would have been scarcely possible under the same circumstances to any other batsmen.

The rest of the match was simply one crescendo of excitement. Hirst played a great game and, after Lockwood's dismissal at 214, received such help from Lilley that victory gradually came in sight. The score was advanced to 248, or only 15 to win, and then from a good hard drive Lilley was finely caught at deep mid-off. Rhodes as last man had a trying crisis to face, but his nerve did not fail him. Once, however, he nearly lost his wicket, Armstrong at slip getting a catch in his hand, but, being partly overbalanced, dropping the ball. Hirst went on imperturbably, scoring again and again by means of cleverly placed singles, and at last he had the extreme satisfaction of making the score a tie. Then Rhodes sent a ball from Trumble between the bowler and mid-on, and England won the match by one wicket. Hirst's innings was in its way almost as remarkable as Jessop's. So coolly did he play that of his last 14 hits that scored 13 were singles, whereas in the early part of his innings he had hit half-a-dozen fours.

England v Australia 1902

Fifth Test

At The Oval, August 11, 12, 13, 1902. Result: England won by one wicket.

AUSTRALIA	First innings		Second innings	
V. T. Trumper b Hirst	42	– run out		2
R. A. Duff c Lilley b Hirst	23	– b Lockwood		6
C. Hill b Hirst	11	– c MacLaren b Hirst		34
*J. Darling c Lilley b Hirst	3	– c MacLaren b Lockwood		15
M. A. Noble c and b Jackson	52	– b Braund		13
S. E. Gregory b Hirst	23	– b Braund		9
W. W. Armstrong b Jackson	17	– b Lockwood		21
A. J. Y. Hopkins c MacLaren b Lockwood	40	– c Lilley b Lockwood		3
H. Trumble not out	64	– (10) not out		7
†J. J. Kelly c Rhodes b Braund	39	– (11) lbw b Lockwood		0
J. V. Saunders lbw b Braund	0	– (9) c Tyldesley b Rhodes		2
B 5, l-b 3, n-b 2	10	B 7, l-b 2		9

1-47 2-63 3-69 4-82 5-126 6-174   324   1-6 2-9 3-31 4-71 5-75 6-91   121
7-175 8-256 9-324 10-324   7-99 8-114 9-115 10-121

First innings – Lockwood 24–2–85–1; Rhodes 28–9–46–0; Hirst 29–5–77–5; Braund 16.5–5–29–2; Jackson 20–4–66–2; Jessop 6–2–11–0.
Second innings – Lockwood 20–6–45–5; Rhodes 22–7–38–1; Hirst 5–1–7–1; Braund 9–1–15–2; Jackson 4–3–7–0.

ENGLAND	First innings		Second innings	
*A. C. MacLaren c Armstrong b Trumble	10	– b Saunders		2
L. C. H. Palairet b Trumble	20	– b Saunders		6
J. T. Tyldesley b Trumble	33	– b Saunders		0
T. W. Hayward b Trumble	0	– c Kelly b Saunders		7
Hon. F. S. Jackson c Armstrong b Saunders	2	– c and b Trumble		49
L. C. Braund c Hill b Trumble	22	– c Kelly b Trumble		2
G. L. Jessop b Trumble	13	– c Noble b Armstrong		104
G. H. Hirst c and b Trumble	43	– not out		58
W. H. Lockwood c Noble b Saunders	25	– lbw b Trumble		2
†A. F. A. Lilley c Trumper b Trumble	0	– c Darling b Trumble		16
W. Rhodes not out	0	– not out		6
B 13, l-b 2	15	B 5, l-b 6		11

1-31 2-36 3-62 4-67 5-67 6-83   183   1-5 2-5 3-10 4-31 5-48 6-157   (9 wkts) 263
7-137 8-179 9-183 10-183   7-187 8-214 9-248

First innings – Trumble 31–13–65–8; Saunders 23–7–79–2; Noble 7–3–24–0.
Second innings – Trumble 33.5–4–108–4; Saunders 24–3–105–4; Noble 5–0–11–0; Armstrong 4–0–28–1.

Toss won by Australia   UMPIRES C. E. Richardson and A. A. White

NOTES BY THE EDITOR

Sydney Pardon, 1903

At their meeting at Lord's on December 8, the captains of the first-class counties carried two proposals. One, that Test matches in England should in future be reduced from five to three, with a week set apart for each game, and the other that by using thicker stumps the wicket should be increased in width from eight to nine inches. Inasmuch as the Australians in all probability will not be here again till 1905 the first proposition is not a very urgent matter. There seems to be a strong feeling in favour of playing Test games in this country out to a finish, irrespective of the time they occupy, and if our leading players are at one with the Australians in wishing the plan to be adopted there is not much use in raising objections. Personally, however, I am very doubtful of the wisdom of making cricket altogether independent of a time limit. Desirable as it is to see one side or the other victorious, the result is not everything, and from what I have read of the long games in Australia, extending sometimes into the sixth day, they are not so interesting as our three-day matches, the advantage derived from avoiding risks leading batsmen, even on perfect wickets, to play with laborious care. Given a fine day and a lively pitch batting of the stonewalling kind is emphatically not the best of cricket, and when England and Australia meet one would always like, irrespective of the result, to see the game at its highest point of excellence.

AUSTRALIA V ENGLAND 1903–04

In every sense, except the financial one, the trip [the first selected and administered by MCC rather than privately raised – Ed.] was a brilliant success, the general result far exceeding even the most sanguine expectations. Success was badly needed, for not only had the two previous English teams – under Mr Stoddart in 1897–98, and Mr MacLaren in 1901–02 – been beaten by four to one in the Test matches, but the Australians had carried off the honours on the occasion of their last two visits to England, winning the only Test match that was played out in 1899 and two out of the three that were decided in 1902.

Prestige counts for a good deal in the cricket field, and the victories last winter had a most beneficial effect in again putting English cricketers on thoroughly good terms with themselves. The fact of the MCC team winning the rubber by three matches to two so dwarfed everything else in the public mind that the players received less credit than was their due for their fine work outside the Test games.

The strong point was the variety of the bowling, and to this more than to any other cause may be attributed the success in the Test matches, Rhodes, Arnold, Hirst, Braund, and Bosanquet forming a splendid combination. Rhodes was the most effective bowler, but Bosanquet turned the scale in England's favour, the victory at Sydney in the Fourth Test being clearly due to his efforts. Rhodes quite confuted those who prophesied that he would be a failure in Australia, his figures being exceptionally fine. By taking 15 wickets at Melbourne he set up a new record in Test matches.

As regards batting, the Australians thought Tyldesley on all wickets much the best man. He played magnificently in the Second Test, scoring 97 and 62, in the second innings surmounting the difficulties of a wicket on which the others could do nothing. However, he had a long spell of bad luck and his record did not come out so well as at one time seemed likely. R. E. Foster, with his wonderful score of 287 at Sydney, established a record in Test matches that may not be beaten in this generation, and it was most unfortunate that he should have been checked by illness when he was at the top of his form.

First Test

At Sydney, December 11, 12, 14, 15, 16, 17, 1903. England won by five wickets.

The first of the five Test matches was in many ways the best of the series. Indeed a finer game has rarely been seen in Australia. It lasted into the sixth day, and attracted in all about 95,000 people. The Australians, on winning the toss, lost Trumper, Duff and Hill for a dozen runs, Trumper being out to a wonderful catch at slip. Thanks to Noble these disasters were retrieved, but when at the end of the day the score stood at 259 for six, the Australians did not seem to have done anything out of the common. However, rain in the night made their total look far more formidable.

Next day the Englishmen went in under very anxious conditions, as no one could tell how the wicket would play. Tyldesley, batting with the utmost skill, saved his side from a breakdown before lunch, and by four o'clock the wicket had practically recovered. At the drawing of stumps the total had reached 243 for four, Foster being not out 73. Noble was at the wickets four hours and three-quarters for his 133, and hardly made a mistake. The third day was marked by the most brilliant and sensational cricket seen during the tour, R. E. Foster, with a magnificent innings of 287, beating all records in Test matches. Altogether he was batting for seven hours, among his hits being 38 fours. The latter part of his innings was described on all hands as something never surpassed. Foster and Braund added 192 runs together, but with eight men out the Englishmen were only 47 ahead.

Then came the startling play, Relf and Rhodes helping Foster to put on respectively 115 and 130 runs for the ninth and tenth wickets. The last-wicket partnership set up a new record in Test games. Foster's triumph was the more remarkable as he had never before played in an England and Australia match. He did not begin at all well, and ought to have been caught when he had made 51, but his batting on the third day was beyond criticism. Going in against a balance of 292 runs, Australia had scored 17 without loss when stumps were pulled up.

Next day they did great things, carrying their score to 367 and only losing five wickets. There was a very regrettable and indeed disgraceful demonstration on the part of a large section of the crowd when Hill was given run out, a storm of hooting and booing going on for a long time. On the fifth day the Australian innings ended for 485, Trumper carrying out his bat for a faultless 185. His hits included 25 fours, and during a stay of three hours and 50 minutes he gave no chance. Rhodes bowled with the utmost steadiness on the hard ground, and in writing home Mr Warner said he did not know what the side would have done without him.

England wanted 194 to win, and found the task a very heavy one. They won on the sixth day by five wickets, but they would very probably have been beaten if, after four wickets had fallen for 83, Laver at short leg had not missed Hirst before he had scored a run. As it was Hayward and Hirst made a great stand, and almost won the game together. Hayward was batting just over four hours for his beautifully played 91.

Toss: Australia. **Australia 285** (M. A. Noble 133, E. G. Arnold 4-76) **and 485** (R. A. Duff 84, C. Hill 51, V. T. Trumper 185*, W. Rhodes 5-94); **England 577** (J. T. Tyldesley 53, R. E. Foster 287, L. C. Braund 102) **and 194-5** (T. W. Hayward 91, G. H. Hirst 60*).

Second Test

At Melbourne, January 1, 2, 4, 5, 1904. England won by 185 runs.

The significance of England's win was altogether discounted by the fact that before the Australians had any chance of batting, rain had ruined the pitch. England won the toss, and, by dint of over-careful batting against fine bowling and fielding, scored 221 on the first day for two wickets. Foster was then not out 49, but a severe chill prevented him taking any further part in the game. Little cricket was practicable on the Saturday, and it was not until the third day that England's innings ended for 315, the last three wickets falling for nine runs. Apart from one chance Tyldesley played superbly, being seen at his very best on the second afternoon when the wicket was difficult. In the Australians' first innings. Trumper gave a wonderful display and got his side within the 200 runs which would have involved a follow-on. In first, he was the last man out, and though he had a liberal share of luck his innings was one which perhaps no other batsman could have played under similar conditions. When England went in for the second time, Tyldesley again played superbly, but five wickets were down for 74. Owing to more rain play could not be resumed on the Tuesday until nearly half-past three, but just before six o'clock the match was over. Australia's second innings would have produced a far smaller score than 111 if the Englishmen had not blundered so deplorably in the field, a lot of catches being missed. Rhodes bowled splendidly and by taking, in all, 15 wickets beat the record in Test matches. The last seven Australian wickets fell for 38 runs. Rhodes had eight catches missed off him.

Toss: England. **England 315** (P. F. Warner 68, T. W. Hayward 58, J. T. Tyldesley 97, H. Trumble 4-107, W. P. Howell 4-43) **and 103** (J. T. Tyldesley 62, H. Trumble 5-34); **Australia 122** (V. T. Trumper 74, W. Rhodes 7-56) **and 111** (W. Rhodes 8-68).

Third Test

At Adelaide, January 15, 16, 18, 19, 20, 1904. Australia won by 216 runs.

The Australians found some consolation for their defeats at Sydney and Melbourne. Holding a strong advantage all the way through, they won by 216 runs. And there can be no question that they showed much better cricket than the Englishmen at every point. They opened the game by scoring 365 for six wickets on the first day, Trumper batting very finely for over three hours. The innings ended abruptly next morning for 388 – by no means an excessive total on an Adelaide wicket in fine weather. The Englishmen hoped to equal it, but never mastered the bowling, and at the drawing of stumps there were eight wickets down for 199. Tyldesley fell to a wonderful catch by the wicket-keeper on the leg side. The innings ended for 245, and the Australians going in with a lead of 143 had the match well in hand. Gregory batted far better than on any other occasion against the Englishmen, hitting brilliantly for two hours and ten minutes, and when play ceased the score stood at 253 for four. Thanks to Bosanquet's fine bowling the innings was finished off for 351, and then England went in to get 495. This was an overwhelming task, but Warner and Hayward made a great start and nearly played out time. At last, however, Hayward was lbw, and Arnold did next to nothing, the score at the close being 150 for two wickets. Warner and Tyldesley were promptly got rid of next morning, Tyldesley being out to a marvellous catch at short square leg, and after that there was no hope, Hirst's efforts only delaying an inevitable end.

Toss: Australia. **Australia 388** (V. T. Trumper 113, R. A. Duff 79, C. Hill 88, M. A. Noble 59) **and 351** (V. T. Trumper 59, M. A. Noble 65, S. E. Gregory 112, B. J. T. Bosanquet 4-73); **England 245** (G. H. Hirst 58) **and 278** (P. F. Warner 79, T. W. Hayward 67, A. J. Y. Hopkins 4-81).

Fourth Test

At Sydney, February 26, 27, 29, March 1, 2, 3, 1904. England won by 157 runs.

The fourth Test match of the series decided the rubber, the Englishmen gaining their third victory. It was thought in this country that the Australians had to play the last innings on a sticky wicket, but this was so far from being the case that they felt confident of getting the 329 runs required. Three men were out for 59, and then Bosanquet settled the matter in wonderful style. Going on at 74 he took five wickets for 12 runs, Lilley helping him splendidly. The Australians died very hard, Noble finding such a useful partner in Cotter that the last wicket added 57 runs. This was one of the few matches in which Trumper failed in both innings. Perhaps the best batting in the game was shown by Hayward, who played his second innings when the wicket was very difficult. He withstood the bowling for two hours and 40 minutes. Another admirable innings was Knight's 70 not out, the result of nearly four and a half hours' cricket. The game lasted into the sixth day, rain causing a lot of delay. In Australia's first innings the last five wickets fell for 17 runs, Rhodes and Arnold bowling with startling effect. In England's second innings Warner and Rhodes on the final day put on 55 runs for the last wicket.

Toss: England. **England 249** (A. E. Knight 70*, M. A. Noble 7-100) **and 210** (T. W. Hayward 52); **Australia 131** (W. Rhodes 4-33, E. G. Arnold 4-28) **and 171** (M. A. Noble 53*, B. J. T. Bosanquet 6-51).

Fifth Test

At Melbourne, March 5, 7, 8, 1904. Australia won by 218 runs.

By an unfortunate arrangement of dates the Fifth Test came immediately after the Fourth, the players having to get as quickly as they could from Sydney to Melbourne. As in the previous match at Melbourne the weather decided the issue, but this time fortune favoured the Australians. They gained a great advantage by batting first, and had everything their own way from start to finish. The Englishmen had to bat on Monday afternoon after a lot of rain had fallen, and could do very little against Noble and Cotter. Indeed so difficult were the conditions that Foster's innings of 18 was regarded as quite an achievement. The Australians went in for the second time with a lead of 186, and set England the impossible task, on a sticky wicket, of getting 320 to win. In the last innings Trumble bowled in his finest form, and was practically unplayable. Hayward was kept away by an attack of tonsillitis, but his presence could not have affected the result. Trumper's 88 on the first day was one of his finest displays, and quite free from fault.

Toss: Australia. **Australia 247** (V. T. Trumper 88, L. C. Braund 8-81) **and 133** (G. H. Hirst 5-48);
England 61 (M. A. Noble 4-19, A. Cotter 6-40) **and 101** (H. Trumble 7-28).

IMPRESSIONS OF THE 1903–04 TOUR
B. J. T. Bosanquet, 1905

So much has been written about the tour that it is difficult to know what aspects to write upon at this distant date. I propose to deal chiefly with the incidents of the tour, with individual performances, and, especially with the conditions under which the matches were played, and the influence of weather on their results, concerning which there appears to have been much misapprehension. Even in Australia an enthusiastic lady was good enough to send our captain an urn, labelled "The Ashes of Australian Cricket. Won by Captain Warner; assisted by Captain Weather!" I hope to be able to show how unjust this was, and to give an idea of the wickets on which we played.

Before touching upon the events in Australia, I wish to refer briefly to the remarkable soil known as Bulli, of which the wickets at Sydney are composed. Without some knowledge of the extraordinary qualities of this soil, it would be impossible for anyone to follow with any intelligence the course of the matches we played at Sydney. This soil was imported from the Bulli Range, laid down to a depth of some six inches, and rolled into a solid mass. In this form it possesses the unique property of being absolutely impermeable to water, which can never penetrate further than half-an-inch from the surface, and can only affect it to this depth owing to the roots of the grass, which break it up to a certain degree, and enable the water to penetrate to this slight extent. Where there is no grass a lump of Bulli will remain entirely unaffected by any immersion, however long in water. This being so it is not difficult to understand that the period during which the Sydney wicket remains affected by rain is of the briefest. Once the wicket becomes fit for play, it dries with extraordinary rapidity. The difficulty is to get it fit, for the water, as will be easily understood, being unable to sink through, simply lies on the surface and has to be mopped up, or run off to one side.

The first match v New South Wales is a very good illustration. The day before the match there was a terrific thunderstorm, and at six o'clock in the evening the playing arena was a veritable lake. Next day at 12 o'clock one end was quite dry, and hard, while the other was only sticky up to lunch-time, and had perfectly recovered when we went in. Rhodes was innocuous at one end, and it was not till he changed over that he did any damage.

Newcastle produced another draw, and here George Hirst was insulted. Having adjourned for a drink, he was just in time to hear someone say, that Hirst is a ****** rotten player! Leaving his drink he retired, being with difficulty restrained from wreaking summary vengeance, and never knew a happy moment till, having persuaded Foster to send him in first, he had taken 50 of the very best in our second innings.

This brings us to the first Test match. Of this I will merely say that the luck was evenly distributed and, that we thoroughly deserved our win. It is unnecessary to discuss the two matches at Melbourne, which were robbed of all interest by the weather. In the first we had all the luck, and winning the toss meant the match. In the second the conditions were exactly reversed, and they won the toss, and with it the match. The real struggle was confined to the two matches at Sydney, and the match at Adelaide. It was, in fact, a series of three matches, in which we won the rubber. In these three matches I venture to say – in spite of many assertions to the contrary – that the luck was as evenly distributed as possible.

In the first match at Sydney rain fell on the Friday night, and the wicket did not recover till lunch-time on the second day. In this period (two hours) their last three wickets fell for an addition of 26, and we lost Warner and Hayward. Only a magnificent effort by Tyldesley saved us from further disaster, as the wicket was quite difficult. After lunch it was much easier, though not quite perfect till about four o'clock. No one, therefore, can possibly maintain that this rain was to our advantage, and it was the only rain that fell. The rest of the match was fought out under absolutely even conditions, unless the fact of having fourth innings be counted a disadvantage to us, which it was to a certain extent, as the wicket had worn appreciably. At Adelaide no rain fell

The man who rekindled the Ashes legend: Plum Warner, England's captain in 1903–04.

at all, and conditions were again even, except that again we had to bat last. In the other match at Sydney a great deal of rain fell at various times, and it is somewhat difficult to convey a true notion of how it affected the play.

There had been a good deal before the match started, and the wicket was a bit soft on the first day, though never exactly difficult. Our score of 207 for seven, therefore, was not a bad one, though nothing out of the way. The wicket was much better next day, our last three wickets added 42 runs, and they had 35 for one wicket, when a slight drizzle came on. After this they had two hours on a fast true wicket, in a slight drizzle, and we got five of them for 114, a good performance on this wicket. There was no more play till the Tuesday at four o'clock. The wicket then was quite hard underneath, with water standing on the top (remember the Bulli soil). Rhodes and Arnold, for some unaccountable reason, got the rest of them out for an addition of 17 runs. Not a ball turned an inch, and why they got out is one of those mysteries that make cricket the game it is. We had an hour on the drying wicket, though it never got difficult, and Hayward and Foster made about 50 without being parted. Next day more rain, and a wicket getting worse right up to the end, which found us with nine men out for 155. Next day a plumb, fast wicket, as was shown by the ease with which Warner and Rhodes added 55 runs. Our opponents thus had to get 329, a task which they were confident of accomplishing in the condition of the wicket.

Well, I don't think there is much in all this that was to our advantage. Personally, I think things were about even. Now how was it we managed to win? Of course, as was only to be expected, we are informed that Australia is weaker at the present time than for years past. That is an assertion which I think it is unnecessary to refute, and its fallacy will be sufficiently demonstrated when they are over here next. I am inclined to think that it was the greater variety we possessed in bowling that carried the day. There was little to choose between the teams as far as batting was concerned. Trumper was far the best bat on either side, though Noble and Duff have improved enormously since they were seen over here in 1902. They had plenty of bowling, but it was all too much of a kind – nearly all right-hand medium – and it was this lack of variety that let them down.

In future tours one would like to see the up-country matches omitted. They do more harm than good, and in future a team would do far better either to play only first-class matches or, if that would be too great a strain, take six weeks' holiday in the middle of the tour, and visit New Zealand and Tasmania, playing a few matches, which would pay well – *pecunia omnia vincit* – and be of far more interest than those matches in Australia. The trip would be a most enjoyable one, and be a nice rest in the middle of what must always be an arduous undertaking.

It has been a great pleasure to go over the tour once more, if only in recollection. We had the very best of games, and the Goddess of Victory smiled on us. *Finis coronat opus*, and the tour may be written as successful in every way – except financially.

ENGLAND V AUSTRALIA 1905 Sydney Pardon

The general feeling of the Australians with regard to the tour of 1905 was one of disappointment. The reason for this is not far to seek. The plan, which in this country only dates from 1899, of having five Test matches makes the cricket success dependent to a far greater degree than was the case in the early tours upon the result of the meetings with England, and the fact of Darling's side losing the rubber without winning one of the five matches outweighed everything that was done in the other fixtures. There is no need to go over familiar ground and insist upon Jackson's extraordinary luck in winning the toss upon all five occasions. Even making the most liberal allowance for this good fortune, the play pointed to the superiority of England, and this, I believe, the Australians themselves admitted, though they naturally thought they would have got on far better if they had once or twice had the advantage of batting first.

It must be remembered that the Englishmen were only twice in a position of danger in the five games – on the first day at Nottingham and the last morning at The Oval. They won two matches, and in the three left unfinished they had much the best of the position. Still, even the most patriotic of English cricketers would hardly contend that there was so much difference between the sides. It so happened that the English batsmen, with Jackson easily first, did themselves full justice on these all-important occasions, whereas the best of the Australians were for the most part curiously unsuccessful. Trumper furnished the most striking example of failure where a big innings meant so much, his highest score in the five matches being only 31.

Darling is one of the best of captains, but in the light of subsequent events I cannot help thinking that his policy with regard to Armstrong's bowling was a mistaken one. The motive was clear enough, being to avoid at all costs the risk of losing the rubber while there remained a chance of winning it. It was, however, contrary to all the traditions of Australian bowling to play simply for safety, and the prestige of the team unquestionably suffered. To bowl as Armstrong did at Nottingham and Leeds was frankly a confession of weakness. For hours at a stretch he kept the ball outside the leg stump, trusting that sheer impatience would lead the batsmen to their destruction. Occasionally he succeeded, but the expenditure of time was so great as to make the cricket very flat and tedious. As a display of stamina and steady skill it was astonishing, but nothing more could be said for it. Untrammelled by this policy of run-saving, Armstrong, as the cricket in August proved, is a remarkable bowler. No one in our time has combined a leg-break with anything like such accuracy of pitch.

If asked to sum up the Australian batting in a phrase, I should say it was a little too brilliant. More attractive play from the spectators' point of view has perhaps never been shown by a travelling XI, but the extreme freedom of style involved some loss of stability, and it so happened that this lack of steadiness, though it did not matter in the ordinary games, told against the side in the two Test matches that were lost. A great change has come over Australian batting since the splendid team of 1899 laid themselves open to the charge of being too careful on perfect wickets. The fault is now just the other way, and it was especially noticeable in the cases of Trumper and Hill.

The great batsman of the side was Armstrong. He struck the happy medium, being brilliant without recklessness, and safe without over-caution. In point of style he has improved out of knowledge since he was here in 1902, all the clumsiness which then marred his fine natural powers having disappeared.

NOTES BY THE EDITOR Sydney Pardon, 1906

The Laws of Cricket were allowed to remain undisturbed in 1905, the desire for change, so much in evidence during recent years, having apparently lost its force. The proposition brought forward at the MCC meeting in May, to make the last sentence of Law 1 read "the choice of innings shall be decided by tossing, unless otherwise arranged" was beaten on a show of hands by such an overwhelming majority that no purpose would have been served by taking a vote. It was certainly curious that this effort to minimise the effect of luck should have been followed by F. S. Jackson's extraordinarily good fortune in winning the toss in every one of the five Test matches. Still, though Darling's unhappy experience strengthened the case for a modification of the existing rule as regards a series of games between the same sides, I hold strongly to the opinion that the toss, as an essential feature of cricket, should not be tampered with. Apart from all other considerations – such as the delightful uncertainty before a match begins as to which side will bat first – the toss for innings affords the best guarantee that wickets will in all cases be fairly and properly prepared. I would not for a moment suggest that in county matches the knowledge that the opposing team were going in first would in the ordinary way lead to any wrongdoing on the part of the ground-keepers. All the same there would be a danger which the law in its present shape prevents.

First Test

At Nottingham, May 29, 30, 31, 1905. England won by 213 runs.

When England won the toss a total of over 300 was regarded as almost a certainty, but to the consternation of the crowd four wickets went down for 47 runs. Tyldesley and Bosanquet did something to make up for this disastrous start, but by a quarter to four the innings was all over for 196, the advantage of the toss being entirely discounted. There was a little moisture in the ground before lunch, but the chief cause of the failure could be found in the demoralising effect of Cotter's bowling. Pitching little more than halfway at a terrific pace he made the ball get up more than shoulder-high, and there can be no doubt that the fear of being hit on the head upset the batsmen considerably. Laver, following up some splendid recent work, took seven wickets.

When the hundred went up with only one man out the Australians stood in a most flattering position. It was just after this that Jackson bowled his now famous over. Noble was out to the first ball, Hill to the fourth, and Darling to the last, the game undergoing a change that can only be described as astonishing. Still the Australians left off for the day with much the best of the game, their score standing at 158 for four wickets.

The second day brought with it an extraordinary change in fortunes. For a little while the Australians got on remarkably well, and when without further loss their overnight score had been carried to 200, they had every reason to feel satisfied. There was such a sudden collapse, however, that the last five wickets fell in less than 40 minutes, the innings being finished off for 221. The English fielding while these wickets were going down was amazingly brilliant. Indeed, nothing better could be imagined. The best piece of individual work was done by A. O. Jones, who, in getting rid of Laver, brought off a marvellous catch in the slips, throwing himself forward and taking the ball with the left hand close to the ground. Jessop's fielding on the off side was beyond praise. He stopped everything that came within reasonable distance of him, and such was the moral effect of his presence that a short run was never attempted when the ball went in his direction.

Standing in a far better position than they could possibly have expected after their paltry first innings, the Englishmen at the drawing of stumps had scored 318 for five. Under ordinary circumstances they would in the same space of time have made a bigger score, but at about three o'clock Armstrong was put on to keep down the runs. He took the ball at 110 and was not changed till the total had reached 301, delivering 35 overs for 50 runs. It was something quite new to see the Australians on the second afternoon of a Test match playing for a draw rather than a win, and the innovation gave rise to endless discussion. Armstrong's method of keeping the ball wide of the leg stump for over after over irritated the crowd who, quite forgetting their manners, became rather noisy.

MacLaren was out second at 222, being finely caught low down at mid-off from a hard drive. His 140 was for the most part magnificent. Just after lunch he was inclined to be reckless, but luckily for him the ball always fell out of harm's way, and he soon returned to safer methods. He scarcely cut at all, but drove and pulled with tremendous power, and nothing could have been more skilful than the way in which he turned the ball on the leg side. Jackson and Rhodes gave a splendid display, without being parted carrying the score to 426, Jackson then declaring.

The Australians wanted 402 to win, and when they went in four hours and a half remained. It was not to be supposed, especially with Trumper disabled, that the runs could be obtained, and the only question was whether the Australians would be able to avoid defeat. In the end, Bosanquet beat them. Darling opened the innings himself with Duff, and everything pointed to a draw when the total reached 60 with the two batsmen still together, but at 62 Duff was easily caught and bowled, and this proved the turning-point. Forty minutes later there were four wickets down. Hill was out to a remarkable catch. He hit a ball back to Bosanquet so high that only a man standing fully six feet could have got near it. Bosanquet jumped up, got the ball with one hand and kept his hold of it, though he stumbled backwards and fell to the ground.

It was a great change from 62 for no wicket to 93 for four, and a little later Armstrong was easily caught at cover point. Bosanquet had taken all five wickets. Gregory and Cotter added 39, but at the tea interval seven wickets had fallen for 173. The players were only away ten minutes but during that time the light became very faulty. Gregory, who had played splendid cricket for an hour, was out at 175 – caught at mid-on at the third attempt – and the last man Kelly joined McLeod. The light grew worse and worse with every sign of oncoming rain, and the Englishmen had reason to fear that all their efforts would be thrown away and the match left drawn. For a quarter of an hour play went on in deep gloom, and then McLeod was out lbw.

In bringing off the victory that MacLaren's hitting had first made possible, the Englishmen owed everything to Bosanquet. He took eight of the nine wickets that fell, completely demoralising the batsmen with his leg-breaks. He gained nothing from the condition of the ground, the pitch remaining firm and true to the end. In the first flush of his triumph his place seemed secure for the whole season, but he never reproduced his form, and dropped out of the XI after the match at Leeds.

Toss: England. **England 196** (J. T. Tyldesley 56, F. J. Laver 7-64) **and 426-5 dec.** (A. C. MacLaren 140, J. T. Tyldesley 61, Hon. F. S. Jackson 82*); **Australia 221** (C. Hill 54, M. A. Noble 50, Hon. F. S. Jackson 5-52) **and 188** (S. E. Gregory 51, B. J. T. Bosanquet 8-107).

Second Test

At Lord's, June 15, 16, 17, 1905. Drawn.

A deluge of rain in the previous week had reduced Lord's ground to the condition of a mud-heap, and though, as the result of bright weather during the Whitsuntide holidays, the turf recovered wonderfully, no one could tell when Jackson won the toss how the pitch would play. England, staying in for the whole of the first day, scored 258 for eight, and the following morning reached 282. Never perhaps has any performance in a big match given rise to such divergent opinions. In some quarters the Englishmen were denounced for their lifeless batting, and even Darling expressed the opinion that with the ground as it was the side ought to have made many more runs. Personally, we took a different view. Watching the game closely, we did not think that the wicket was ever very easy, and in our judgment a total of 282 was quite equal to 400 on a true run-getting ground.

One cause of the slow scoring could be found in the fact that Armstrong bowled for three hours at a stretch, keeping the ball wide of the leg stump, with seven men fielding on the on side. The fact that it took Jackson nearly an hour and a half to score 29, furnishes strong evidence that the conditions were not easy. Perhaps the best batting was that of MacLaren. For more than two hours he played very skilful cricket, rarely missing a fair chance of scoring.

Heavy rain for an hour or so on Thursday night was followed by bright sunshine on Friday, and the Englishmen felt confident that on the treacherous wicket they could get the Australians out for about a hundred, and make them follow on. These expectations, however, were far from being realised. The Australians hit with splendid power, and ran up a total of 181, or only 101 runs behind. Under the circumstances this was a very fine performance, and Darling himself thought that his team did wonders. Trumper and Duff, by dint of some astounding hitting, made 57 together in 35 minutes for the first wicket, and the moral effect of their fearless play could not be over-estimated.

England went in for the second time at four o'clock, and though a very smart catch in the slips sent Hayward back at 18, MacLaren hit with such brilliancy that in 40 minutes the score was up to 60. After Tyldesley – in a most unlucky way – had played on at 63, the character of the game changed, Fry being at the wickets 25 minutes for two runs. However, at six o'clock the total was up to 127, with only two wickets down, and the Englishmen looked to have the game in their hands. Then came a startling alteration, three wickets falling in the last half-hour to Armstrong's bowling. MacLaren lost his wicket through sheer impatience; Jackson was bowled first ball, and Jones was caught at point, apparently off the wicket-keeper's foot. Time was called with the total at 151 for five, and as events turned out nothing could be done on the third day, the conditions being so hopeless that the game was given up before half-past one.

Toss: England. **England 282** (A. C. MacLaren 56, C. B. Fry 73) **and 151-5** (A. C. MacLaren 79); **Australia 181** (Hon. F. S. Jackson 4-50).

Third Test

At Leeds, July 3, 4, 5, 1905. Drawn.

The Third Test ended in a draw, the Englishmen at the finish holding an overwhelming advantage. But for a couple of dropped catches in the last innings, they would, in all probability, have won the game, but the stubborn batting by means of which the Australians warded off defeat could scarcely be over-praised.

On a pitch that had not entirely recovered from recent rain the Englishmen were batting for the whole of the first day, their innings ending just before half-past six for 301. Up to a certain point there seemed little chance of such a score as this, for though Fry and Hayward made an excellent start four wickets were down for 64. As on many previous occasions Jackson saved his side, giving a magnificent display. He withstood the bowling for four hours and 20 minutes and took out his bat for 144. Running no risks he was at the wickets 100 minutes for his first 50 runs and completed his hundred in three hours and a half. His cutting on the rather slow wicket was a model of timing, and he made a number of hard drives. So safe was the game he played that during his long stay he only lifted the ball three or four times. With his score at 45 he had a narrow escape of being caught at slip, but his only palpable mistake was an easy chance of stumping when he had made 130. Among his hits were 18 fours.

After a dry night the wicket was faster than before, but though better than had been expected it was never exactly easy. The Australians were batting rather less than three hours and scored 195. It was a very uneven innings, eight batsmen failing to reach double figures. Thanks chiefly to Warren's great pace Trumper, Hill and Noble were all out in little more than half an hour for 36, but with only five wickets down the score was up to 161. Armstrong played superb cricket for more than two hours, driving with great power, and except for one lucky stroke at the start he never made a mistake.

The Englishmen put themselves in practically a safe position, scoring 169 before the drawing of stumps and only losing two wickets. Inasmuch, however, as over three hours were occupied it cannot be said that the best use was made of the time available. Armstrong bowled unchanged and so cramped Fry that that batsman took 100 minutes to make 30 runs. Hayward batted admirably, but also found it very difficult to get the ball away and the first liberty he took cost him his wicket. Tyldesley, very quick on his legs, played a much more vigorous and effective game. Towards the end of the day when firmly set he drew away from the wicket and managed to hit Armstrong on the off side. Armstrong's leg-theory bowling tried the patience of the crowd severely and at times there was a great deal of ironical applause.

On the third morning it was essential that England should score fast, but with Armstrong bowling outside the leg stump and McLeod wide of the off, the batsmen had a difficult task. Denton was out at 170, and at 202 Jackson was caught on the leg side. After this Tyldesley and Hirst hit very hard, but Armstrong missed them at slip off successive balls from Noble. At length Tyldesley was stumped, and when Hirst and Bosanquet had put on 37 the innings was declared at a quarter to one. Curiously enough the declaration was made at exactly the same time as in the match at Nottingham, and the Australians were set the same task – 402 to get in four hours and a half.

With no chance of winning the Australians set themselves sternly to work to save the game. They lost Trumper – easily caught in the slips – in the second over, and if Hayward at second slip had managed to catch Hill two wickets would have been down for six runs. As it was Hill stayed till the score had reached 64. Noble played with untiring patience, but by 20 minutes past four five wickets were down for 121. England might have won if Blythe had held a straight return from Noble, more than an hour still remaining for play. Profiting by his escape Noble stayed in till a quarter to six. Then losing his self-control for the first time he jumped out to drive Bosanquet and was easily stumped. Gregory and McLeod played steadily for half an hour, and ten minutes before time an appeal against the light caused the match to be left drawn.

Toss: England. **England 301** (Hon. F. S. Jackson 144*) **and 295-5 dec.** (T. W. Hayward 60, J. T. Tyldesley 100, W. W. Armstrong 5-122); **Australia 195** (W. W. Armstrong 66, A. Warren 5-57) **and 224-7** (M. A. Noble 62).

Fourth Test

At Manchester, July 24, 25, 26, 1905. England won by an innings and 80 runs.

The Fourth Test decided the rubber. Brilliant all-round cricket brought about the result, but luck was clearly all on England's side, the Australians having for the most part to bat under very trying conditions. As at Nottingham the result was arrived at only just in time, rain setting in immediately after the last wicket had fallen. Without proving quite such an attraction as had been expected, the match drew big crowds, nearly 20,000 people being present on the first day, and over 22,000 on the second.

Again fortunate in winning the toss, the Englishmen did so well on the Monday as to make their position almost secure, scoring 352 for six. On a pitch that had not completely recovered from recent rain, this was an extremely fine performance, but it was generally agreed that under the same conditions such a score could not have been obtained against the best Australian bowlers of former days.

At lunch-time the score stood at 97 for two, and when Fry was bowled it had reached 136. It was at this point – just before three o'clock – that Jackson went in, and once more rose to the occasion, playing his fifth three-figure innings in England v Australia matches. As usual he was at great pains to get set, never attempting to hit till he had really got the pace of the ground. Hayward, who had so far played superb cricket, suddenly fell off in his form. He gave a chance at slip, he might have been stumped, and a breaking ball that beat him just missed the wicket. However, he did not profit by his luck, an easy catch at third man bringing his innings to a close at 176. Jackson found a brilliant partner in Spooner, and in the course of an hour and three-quarters the score was carried from 176 to 301.

Rain fell heavily during the early hours of Tuesday morning, but the sun was shining when the game was continued, and during part of the day the wicket proved very treacherous. At first, however, it was rather too slow to be difficult, and in an hour and a half England increased their score to 446. Jackson only added ten runs and then sent a ball straight into mid-off's hands. As is always the case when he makes runs he scored well all round the wicket, his cutting being especially good.

The Australians looked to be in almost a hopeless position as when they went in the sun had been shining long enough to make the turf treacherous. The wicket seemed made for Rhodes, but Jackson decided to start with Hirst and Brearley. In a little over half an hour the Australians lost three of their best wickets for 27 runs. Brearley took two, getting Trumper easily caught in the slips and clean-bowling Noble. Duff was caught in the slips, from a ball that kicked up very awkwardly, and with four wickets down for 51 the position seemed desperate indeed. However, Darling – nearly always at his best when something big is asked of him – played a wonderful innings, and put quite a respectable appearance on the score. Fortune favoured him, but his driving was magnificent. McLeod patiently kept up his end while Darling hit. The English bowling became a little demoralised, and the fielding for a time went all to pieces.

Darling scored 73 out of 105 in less than an hour and a half and hit 13 fours, all but one of them being drives. Laver and Kelly hit freely for a few overs, but at half-past four the innings ended for 197. Splendidly as Darling hit and well as he was backed up, the Australians ought not, with the ground as it was, to have made so many runs. Bad fielding had much to answer for and Jackson was clearly at fault in the management of his bowling, leaning too heavily on Brearley and showing a curious want of faith in Rhodes. He only sent down 35 balls in the innings, but each time he went on he took a wicket in his first over.

The Australians had to follow on, but, luckily for them, the pitch rolled out much better than anyone had expected. At the drawing of stumps the score had reached 118 with only Trumper out. The Australians had pulled the game round in a remarkable way, being only 131 behind with nine wickets in hand. There seemed every likelihood that they would make a hard fight on the third day, but rain ruined all their hopes. There was a steady downpour between eight o'clock and ten on Wednesday morning, and the start of play had to be delayed till ten minutes past 12. In view of the rubber a draw was no use to the Australians, and they made up their minds to play a forcing game on the off-chance of hitting off something more than the balance of runs and putting England in at the end on a bad wicket.

The chance was of course a very remote one, and as it happened the attempt resulted in overwhelming disaster, fine bowling, and still finer fielding, giving England the match, and with it the rubber. In an hour and 20 minutes the innings was finished off, the game coming to an end just before lunch-time. If the last two batsmen could have stayed till after the interval the game would have ended in a draw, as rain fell for the rest of the day.

Toss: England. **England 446** (T. W. Hayward 82, Hon. F. S. Jackson 113, R. H. Spooner 52, C. E. McLeod 5-125); **Australia 197** (J. Darling 73, W. Brearley 4-72) **and 169** (R. A. Duff 60, W. Brearley 4-54).

Fifth Test
At The Oval, August 14, 15, 16, 1905. Drawn.

The fact of the rubber having already been decided did not to any appreciable extent affect the attendance at the final Test match, nearly 50,000 people visiting The Oval during the three days. Delightful weather favoured the game and the wicket from first to last was in capital order. The match ended in a draw, England, after going through a very anxious time on the third morning, leaving off with much the best of the position.

Winning the toss for the fifth time in succession, the Englishmen were batting for the whole of the first day, scoring 381 for seven wickets. At one point a much finer performance seemed in prospect, the score when the fourth wicket fell being up to 283. A very bad start was made, MacLaren being out at 12 and Tyldesley at 32, but after this the batting for a long time was superb, Hayward and Fry putting on 100 runs and Fry and Jackson 151. Fry's innings dwarfed everything else. For the first time in a Test match, the famous batsman did himself full justice. As a good deal had been said about his inability to play the Australian bowling, his success must have afforded him the keenest satisfaction. He drove very hard and was as skilful as ever in forcing the ball away on the leg side, but perhaps the most remarkable feature was his fine cutting. As a rule he does not cut much, but those who imagined that the stroke was outside his range found themselves quite in the wrong. His hits included 23 fours.

On the second morning England's innings was finished off in 25 minutes, but during that time the score was increased to 430. The Australians lost Trumper in the second over and Hill at 44, but at lunch-time the score had reached 123 for two. Just before the interval a blunder was committed which caused England a lot of trouble. Duff, when 78, put up a skyer in the slips and would have been out 19 times out of 20. MacLaren, however, thinking Hirst had lost sight of the ball, ran against him and the catch was dropped. Duff went on hitting in splendid form and was not got rid of till the score had reached 237, his being the fifth wicket to fall. He was missed by Hayward at long-on when he had made 134, but with all his luck he played a great innings, his driving being a marvel of power and cleanness. He hit 20 fours and had the satisfaction of making the highest score in the five Test matches. The total reached 363, or only 67 behind. The performance was a fine one but the English fielding was much at fault, four palpable catches being missed and two or three possible ones. Just after the Australians had made 200 Lilley split one of his fingers so badly that he had to leave the field. A. O. Jones, the twelfth man, was permitted by Darling to keep wicket, but such a concession should not have been asked for. Though there is no rule on the subject it is quite contrary to general practice and tradition for a substitute to act as wicket-keeper.

On the Wednesday morning the cricket up to a certain point was exciting in an extreme, the Englishmen for the first time in the Test matches since the opening day at Nottingham finding themselves in a position of real danger. In less than half an hour two wickets fell to Armstrong's bowling, MacLaren being beautifully caught by Kelly and Hayward out lbw. Three wickets were down for 13, and England were only 80 runs ahead. Tyldesley and Fry stayed together for nearly 40 minutes, but at 48 Fry was splendidly caught with one hand by Armstrong at deep mid-off from a hard drive. After this Tyldesley and Jackson had to face a crisis, and for fully half an hour no one could tell what would happen. Armstrong was bowling with extraordinary accuracy, and Cotter, keeping quite a good length, sent the ball down at a tremendous pace. Jackson was beaten more than once and nearly bowled by Cotter, but these dangers over he played a great game. He and Tyldesley took the score from 48 to 103, and it is safe to say they have never had to work harder for 55 runs. At last Jackson was bowled by Cotter, but when he left he had the satisfaction of knowing that all real danger of defeat was over.

Toss: England. **England 430** (T. W. Hayward 59, C. B. Fry 144, Hon. F. S. Jackson 76, A. Cotter 7-148)
and 261-6 dec. (J. T. Tyldesley 112*, R. H. Spooner 79); **Australia 363** (R. A. Duff 146, J. Darling 57,
W. Brearley 5-110) **and 124-4.**

AUSTRALIA V ENGLAND 1907–08

Inasmuch as the England team lost four of the five Test matches, their tour cannot be regarded as other than a failure. From that conclusion there is no getting away, but it is equally true that the side only just missed a triumph almost unexampled since the Australians more than 30 years ago began to play us on even terms. In three of the four Test matches in which they were beaten, the Englishmen at some time stood in such a position that it seemed long odds they would win. In the third match an unhappy blunder in the field completely turned their fortunes, and in the fourth fate dealt them a cruel blow, a downfall of rain compelling them to bat on a ruined wicket after they had, by dint of splendid bowling, got rid of Australia on a true firm pitch for a modest 214. It seemed to be the general opinion, even among the Australians themselves, that the Englishmen had rather more than their fair share of bad luck.

The president of the Melbourne Club expressed the opinion that a margin of three to two in Australia's favour would have expressed more accurately the difference in merit between the two XIs. In one respect the Englishmen were very unfortunate indeed, a severe attack of illness, which nearly developed into pneumonia, keeping A. O. Jones, their captain, out of the first three Tests. It is no disparagement to F. L. Fane to say that he lacks Jones's gifts as a leader, and still more his inspiring influence in the field.

George Gunn was not in the first instance chosen but, as he was going to Australia for his health, an arrangement was made by which he would be at Jones's command if required. He was not called upon until the First Test, but played so splendidly, scoring 119 and 74, that he was utilised in all the important games that followed. He proved himself the best bat in the XI, getting 462 runs in the five Tests, with an average of 51. His 119 at Sydney was compared by competent critics with the best innings played for previous teams by Arthur Shrewsbury and A. C. MacLaren, and in the last Test he kept up his form, scoring 122 not out. The other batsmen, with the exceptions of Hardstaff and Hobbs, were more or less disappointing in the Test games.

The strength of the team lay in the bowling of Crawford, Fielder and Barnes. Their figures do not look very much on paper, but with little or no support they did splendid work. It was said of Crawford that even on the most perfect wickets he could at times make the ball break back.

First Test

At Sydney, December 13, 14, 16, 17, 18, 19, 1907. Australia won by two wickets.

A. O. Jones being in hospital at Brisbane, the captaincy devolved upon Fane. George Gunn was called upon for the first time and with the idea of strengthening the batting, R. A. Young was picked as wicket-keeper, in preference to Humphries. The match proved a great attraction, the takings amounting to £3,000. On the second day the crowd numbered 32,000.

Winning the toss, the Englishmen stayed in for four hours and ten minutes for a total of 273. At one time they seemed likely to make a far bigger score, but some of the batsmen found Cotter's pace too much for them. George Gunn's batting was as nearly as possible faultless. Making his runs in two hours and a half, he hit 20 fours and his only mistake was a hard chance at third man, when 108. At the end of the afternoon the Australians had scored 50 for one wicket and on the Saturday they exceeded the English total by 27 runs. Hill played a splendid innings never, being at fault till Gunn caught him at third man.

In England's second innings all the honours went to the two Notts players, Gunn and Hardstaff putting on 113 for the fourth wicket. At one point a big total seemed in prospect but after the tea interval six wickets fell for 34 runs. The innings ended early on the fourth morning. The Australians were left with 274 to get. They lost Trumper, Hill and Macartney for 27 and when at five o'clock rain caused stumps to be drawn, the score stood at 63 for three. On the Wednesday the state of the ground made play impossible, and the following morning everything pointed to a win for England. The wicket recovered surprisingly well, but it was the general opinion that the bowlers ought to have done better during the first hour. The finish of the match was exciting to a degree. When their seventh wicket fell the Australians still required 89 to win. Carter, who played a fine innings, was out at 218 and then Cotter and Hazlitt amid great enthusiasm hit off the remaining 56 runs in less than 40 minutes, Australia gaining a glorious victory by two wickets.

Toss: England. **England 273** (G. Gunn 119, A. Cotter 6-101) **and 300** (G. Gunn 74, J. Hardstaff 63, J. V. Saunders 4-68); **Australia 300** (C. Hill 87, A. Fielder 6-82) **and 275-8** (H. Carter 61).

Second Test

At Melbourne, January 1, 2, 3, 4, 6, 7, 1908. England won by one wicket.

In the week previous to the Second Test, five inches of rain had been registered in Melbourne, but the weather cleared up and no fault could be found with the wicket. In fact the ground had dried so rapidly that it was not thought necessary to include Blythe in the England XI. The mistake of playing Young instead of Humphries was of course not repeated. On the first innings the Englishmen gained a lead of 116 and at one time they looked to have the match in their hands, but in the end they only scrambled home by one wicket, the Australians playing a splendid uphill game. Though intensely interesting the cricket was for the most part very slow, the Australians taking the whole of the first afternoon to score 255 for seven. It must be said, however, that Crawford and Fielder bowled extremely well. In England's first innings Hobbs and Hutchings were seen at their best. Hobbs, who had never before taken part in a Test match, scored 83 out of 160 in a trifle over three hours, his defence being very strong. Hutchings, after beginning quietly, hit in great form, his 126 including a six and 25 fours.

At the end of the third day Trumper and Noble scored 96 together without being parted. Next morning Trumper was lbw at 126, and when the fourth wicket fell the total was only 162. The position looked very serious, but Armstrong and Macartney added 106. Carter afterwards hit finely and the innings did not close until the total had reached 397. The batting all through was admirable, Armstrong showing the best form.

England wanted 282 to win, and at the drawing of stumps the score stood at 159 for four. On the sixth and last day they began badly and when their eighth wicket fell with 73 still required, the match looked all over. However, Humphries and Barnes put on 34 together and then, to the astonishment of everyone concerned, Barnes and Fielder hit off the remaining 39 runs, and won the match. Barnes played with great judgment and coolness for his 38 not out. The last run was a desperately short one and if Hazlitt, throwing in from cover point, had managed to hit the wicket, the result would have been a tie.

Australia v England 1907–08 — Second Test

At Melbourne, January 1, 2, 3, 4, 6, 7, 1908. Result: England won by one wicket.

AUSTRALIA

	First innings		Second innings	
V. T. Trumper c Humphries b Crawford	49	–	(2) lbw b Crawford	63
C. G. Macartney b Crawford	37	–	(6) c Humphries b Barnes	54
C. Hill b Fielder	16	–	b Fielder	3
*M. A. Noble c Braund b Rhodes	61	–	(1) b Crawford	64
W. W. Armstrong c Hutchings b Crawford	31	–	b Barnes	77
P. A. McAlister run out	10	–	(4) run out	15
V. S. Ransford run out	27	–	c Hutchings b Barnes	18
A. Cotter b Crawford	17	–	(9) lbw b Crawford	27
†H. Carter not out	15	–	(8) c Fane b Barnes	53
G. R. Hazlitt b Crawford	1	–	b Barnes	3
J. V. Saunders b Fielder	0	–	not out	0
L-b 1, w 1	2		B 12, l-b 8	20

1-84 2-93 3-111 4-168 5-197 6-214   266   1-126 2-131 3-135 4-162 5-268 6-303   397
7-240 8-261 9-265 10-266   7-312 8-361 9-392 10-397

First innings – Fielder 27.5–4–77–2; Barnes 17–7–30–0; Rhodes 11–0–37–1; Braund 16–5–41–0; Crawford 29–1–79–5.
Second innings – Fielder 27–6–74–1; Crawford 33–6–125–3; Barnes 27.4–4–71–5; Braund 18–1–68–0; Rhodes 16–6–38–0.

ENGLAND

	First innings		Second innings	
*F. L. Fane b Armstrong	13	–	(2) b Armstrong	50
J. B. Hobbs b Cotter	83	–	(1) b Noble	28
G. Gunn lbw b Cotter	15	–	lbw b Noble	0
K. L. Hutchings b Cotter	126	–	c Cotter b Macartney	39
L. C. Braund b Cotter	49	–	b Armstrong	30
J. Hardstaff snr b Saunders	12	–	c Ransford b Cotter	19
W. Rhodes b Saunders	32	–	run out	15
J. N. Crawford c Ransford b Saunders	16	–	c Armstrong b Saunders	10
S. F. Barnes c Hill b Armstrong	14	–	not out	38
†J. Humphries b Cotter	6	–	lbw b Armstrong	16
A. Fielder not out	6	–	not out	18
B 3, l-b 3, w 1, n-b 3	10		B 9, l-b 7, w 1, n-b 2	19

1-27 2-61 3-160 4-268 5-287 6-325   382   1-54 2-54 3-121 4-131 5-162 6-196   (9 wkts) 282
7-353 8-360 9-369 10-382   7-198 8-209 9-243

First innings – Cotter 33–4–142–5; Saunders 34–7–100–3; Noble 9–3–26–0; Armstrong 34.2–15–36–2; Hazlitt 13–1–34–0; Macartney 12–2–34–0.
Second innings – Cotter 28–3–82–1; Saunders 30–9–58–1; Armstrong 30.4–10–53–3; Noble 22–7–41–2; Hazlitt 2–1–8–0; Macartney 9–3–21–1.

Toss won by Australia   UMPIRES P. Argall and R. M. Crockett

CRICKETER OF THE YEAR – J. B. HOBBS

Few batsmen in recent years have jumped into fame more quickly than John Berry Hobbs. In his case there was no waiting for recognition, and no failure to show the skill he was known to possess. Like Hayward he was born in Cambridge, his birthday being December 16, 1882, and it was upon Hayward's advice that he determined to qualify for Surrey. He joined the staff at The Oval in 1903 and, two years later, having completed the necessary period of qualification, he was tried in the Easter Monday match against a Gentlemen of England team got together by W. G. Grace.

Given a place in MCC's team for Australia in the winter of 1907–08, he did not at first find the wickets at all to his liking, but before long he found his form, and finished up as one of the most successful batsmen in a good but unlucky side.

From the first he was very strong on the on side and though with increased experience he has naturally gained in variety of strokes, his skill in scoring off his legs remains perhaps the most striking feature of his play. The one defect in his on-side play is a tendency to be out lbw, but this he is gradually conquering.

Very keen on the game and ambitious to reach the highest rank, he is the most likely man among the younger professional batsmen to play for England in Test matches at home in the immediate future.

Third Test

At Adelaide, January 10, 11, 13, 14, 15, 16, 1908. Australia won by 245 runs.

The Englishmen lost the Third Test, allowing the game to slip out of their hands after it had seemed 20 to one on them. They played the same XI as at Melbourne, but the Australians made two changes, Hartigan and O'Connor taking the places of Hazlitt and Cotter, the last-named being kept away by a bad strain. Hill, suffering from influenza, was too unwell to field, but fighting against his illness he played a wonderful innings. Winning the toss the Australians scored 285, runs coming at the rate of just under one a minute. Macartney batted finely for two hours and a quarter, and Hartigan's first appearance was a great success. The innings ended on the second morning, the English bowling, despite the intense heat, having been maintained at a high standard.

The Englishmen batted very consistently and when play ceased they were only 26 behind with five wickets in hand. The Australians missed Cotter on the fast wicket. Crawford played finely the next morning, and the innings closed for 363, or 78 ahead. On Australia going in for a second time Barnes soon got rid of Trumper and Macartney, and at the drawing of stumps the Australians, with four wickets down, were 55 runs to the good. Noble, who played splendidly, left with two runs added next morning, and though Ransford and O'Connor put on 44 together the seventh wicket fell at 180. The Englishmen were in a tremendously strong position, but as events turned out a couple of dropped catches destroyed their chance. Hartigan, when 32, should have been caught by Fielder at point, and Hill, when 22, was badly missed by Barnes at mid-off.

Making the most of their luck the two batsmen played superbly and at the close of the afternoon they were still together, the score having been raised to 397. In all the partnership added 243 runs, Hartigan being out on the fifth morning at 423. In his 116 he hit a dozen fours. Hartigan's success in making a hundred in his first Test match was much appreciated. Hill was batting for five hours and 20 minutes for his 160 – a great effort considering his illness. He hit 18 fours.

The innings ended for 506, the Englishmen being left with 429 to get to win. There never seemed the least chance of this enormous task being accomplished. Hardstaff played very finely, but five wickets were down for 139 and on the following morning the match was finished off in less than an hour.

Toss: Australia. **Australia 285** (C. G. Macartney 75, A. Fielder 4-80) **and 506** (M. A. Noble 65, M. J. Hartigan 116, C. Hill 160); **England 363** (G. Gunn 65, J. Hardstaff 61, J. N. Crawford 62) **and 183** (J. Hardstaff 72, J. D. A. O'Connor 5-40, J. V. Saunders 5-65).

Fourth Test

At Melbourne, February 7, 8, 10, 11, 1908. Australia won by 308 runs.

The Fourth Test decided the rubber, Australia winning by 308 runs. Fortune was dead against the Englishmen. By means of splendid bowling – Crawford mixing up his pace with remarkable skill – and very fine fielding they got the Australians out on a perfect wicket for 214, and then had to bat themselves on a pitch ruined by heavy rain. From this disaster they never recovered. Hobbs, seizing every chance, hit up 57 in 70 minutes before the wicket got to its worst, but no one else could look at Saunders and Noble. Leading by 109 the Australians had an hour's batting before stumps on the second day. They lost Trumper, Noble, and McAlister for 28, Trumper for the second time failing to get a run, but Gregory and Hill played out time, carrying the score to 49.

On the intervening Sunday the ground dried, and on Monday the Australians had quite a good wicket to bat on. They rose to the occasion and although their fifth wicket fell at 77 they had at the drawing of stumps scored 358 with two wickets still in hand. Armstrong was the hero of the day, playing with perfect judgment for 114 not out. Up to a point he was very cautious, but when he had mastered the bowling he hit with great power. He was out next morning for 133, his innings having lasted nearly four hours and 50 minutes. The Australian total reached 385. The Englishmen wanted 495 to win. It was not to be expected that they would make such a number but, with the wicket still in good order, they ought to have made many more than 186. Probably the hopelessness of the position affected them, and they had to play some fine bowling from Saunders.

Toss: Australia. **Australia 214** (V. S. Ransford 51, A. Fielder 4-54, J. N. Crawford 5-48) **and 385** (W. W. Armstrong 133*, V. S. Ransford 54, H. Carter 66, A. Fielder 4-91); **England 105** (J. B. Hobbs 57, J. V. Saunders 5-28) **and 186** (J. V. Saunders 4-76).

Fifth Test

At Sydney, February 21, 22, 24, 25, 26, 27, 1908. Australia won by 49 runs.

Although Australia had already won the rubber the last Test match was contested with the utmost keenness. It produced a tremendous fight, the Australians, as in the previous games, showing an extraordinary power of recovery from a bad position, and winning after being 144 behind on the first innings. A lot of rain had fallen in Sydney, and Jones put Australia in to bat. Up to a certain point his policy was abundantly justified. Thanks to some fine bowling by Barnes, Australia's first innings was finished off in a little over two hours and a half for 137, and then, on an improving pitch, England before the drawing of stumps scored 116 for one.

On the second day there was very little cricket, a heavy downpour after lunch causing play to be abandoned at half-past four. The Englishmen lost two more wickets and added 71 runs. More rain fell on Sunday, and on Monday nothing could be done until half-past three. Feeling sure that the pitch would become very difficult before the end of the day, Jones gave instructions to have the innings finished off without loss of time, and the last few wickets were thrown away. Gunn, in scoring his 122 not out, played beautiful cricket for nearly five hours. The Australians had 40 minutes' batting and scored 18 without loss, Noble and O'Connor showing most skilful defence. The Englishmen, however, were greatly dissatisfied that Noble was not given out caught at the wicket in the first over.

On the fourth day, Trumper, making ample amends for some previous failures, played a magnificent innings. After scoring a single he might have been caught by Rhodes at short mid-on, but the chance was not an easy one. Thenceforward he was always at his best. Hitting 18 fours, he scored his 166 in four hours and five minutes, the number of runs put on during his stay being 317. He pulled the game right round and at the end of the afternoon Australia were 213 ahead with four wickets in hand.

Owing to more heavy rain play on the fifth day did not begin until one o'clock. The Australian innings closed for 422, the Englishmen being left with 279 to get to win. This was a terribly heavy task on the damaged pitch, and before the end of the afternoon the game was as good as over, six wickets being down with 162 still required. The wicket rolled out well on the last morning and during the partnership of Rhodes and Jones for the eighth wicket it seemed quite possible that England might win. However, when the two batsmen had put on 53 together Jones was bowled. The ninth wicket added 22 runs, and the tenth 31, the side fighting hard to the end.

Toss: England. **Australia 137** (S. F. Barnes 7-60) **and 422** (V. T. Trumper 166, S. E. Gregory 56, J. N. Crawford 5-141, W. Rhodes 4-102); **England 281** (J. B. Hobbs 72, G. Gunn 122*) **and 229** (W. Rhodes 69, J. V. Saunders 5-82).

ENGLAND v AUSTRALIA 1909
Sydney Pardon

Inasmuch as they beat England in decisive fashion – not only winning two of the three Test matches that were played out, but having all the best of the drawn games – the Australians can look back on the tour of 1909 with keen satisfaction. More and more in these days the interest centres in the matches with England, all the other fixtures being strictly subservient to the great games. This state of things became almost inevitable when in 1899 it was determined to have five Test matches instead of three.

Coming to the merits of the Australians, I am convinced that never before has a fine side been so under-rated. So grudging was the praise, and so many were the excuses urged on behalf of the beaten team, that it was not surprising to find the English press accused in the Australian papers of being one-sided. In expressing my personal belief that the Australians were estimated at far below their proper worth, I know that I am, if I may use the expression, rowing in the same boat as Mr C. B. Fry. The turning-point of the tour came with the victory over England at Lord's. Thenceforward the Australians enjoyed a career of uninterrupted success until Lord Londesborough's team beat them at Scarborough. I think the fact that they were unbeaten for more than three months should in itself be enough to give their detractors pause.

I freely admit that the bowling did not, as regards individual excellence, come up to the level of the batting. No one, taking the season as a whole, approached the excellence of such giants of the past as Spofforth, Palmer and Turner, but in the Test matches great things were done, Armstrong at Lord's and Birmingham, Macartney and Cotter at Leeds and Laver at Manchester, equalling the best performances of the old bowlers.

As regards the batting, one could write a column without exhausting the subject. Bardsley and Ransford were the heroes of the trip. Never have two Australian batsmen, coming to England for the first time, met with such extraordinary success. They proved themselves legitimate successors to Hill and Darling. Nothing in recent cricket has been more remarkable than the fact of Australia losing two champion left-handers and at once finding two others to take their places. Trumper was overshadowed, but nevertheless finished up with a record that for anyone but him would have been considered excellent. That he is still a very great batsman was proved at The Oval.

Macartney, as an all-round cricketer, took the honours. Although his batting record does not look much on paper he often played well; his bowling was mainly instrumental in winning the Test match at Leeds, and his fielding on the off side all through the tour was magnificent.

McAlister proved himself a good batsman, but he should have come here ten years ago. I think there was some feeling about his being made vice-captain over the heads of Trumper and Armstrong.

First Test

At Birmingham, May 27, 28, 29, 1909. England won by ten wickets.

There was on the part of the selection committee a curious indecision as to the choice of the England side, no fewer than 15 players having been asked to be in readiness at Edgbaston. The final choice was determined in a great measure by the condition of the ground. A lot of rain had fallen the previous day and during the night, and a drenching shower shortly before 11 involved a long delay in starting the game. There was a heavy downpour about half past 12, and not until five o'clock was cricket considered practicable. Hayward's knee was not sound, and the pitch was considered too soft to suit either Relf or Brearley.

Winning the toss the Australians seemed to have gained a considerable advantage, the wicket at the start being so soft and wet that a good deal of sawdust had to be used. However, the batsmen did not take advantage of their opportunities. In the little time available two wickets fell for 22 runs. The second day's play was full of interest. For the most part the wicket was slow and difficult but it improved during the afternoon, and towards the close the batting asserted itself. In the morning the Australians could never master Blythe and Hirst, who bowled unchanged, and in little more than an hour and a half the innings was finished off for 74. Armstrong and Noble were both batting for an hour, Noble's defence while Hirst was making the ball swerve in his most puzzling fashion being masterly.

Going in against such a moderate total of 74, England had a great chance, but the advantage was soon lost, three wickets going down before lunch for 17. Tyldesley and Jones made up for these disasters, putting on 41 together in rather less than an hour, but with five wickets down the total was only 61. Jessop hit up 22 in 20 minutes, but after he left no one could get the ball away and the innings ended for 121. Armstrong bowled wonderfully well. He kept a perfect length to his leg-breaks and was very difficult to play.

Forty-seven runs to the bad the Australians opened their second innings at five o'clock. In the fourth over with only four runs scored Macartney was lbw, and at 16 Noble fell to a magnificent catch at forward short leg, Jones taking the ball low down with one hand. Ransford and Gregory pulled the game round, and when bad light brought the day's play to a close the score had, without further loss, reached 67.

The third day's cricket proved quite sensational. In the end England won by ten wickets, but up to a certain point nothing seemed less likely than such a victory. So well did Ransford and Gregory bat that in half an hour the total reached 97, the Australians being 50 runs ahead with eight wickets in hand. Then came an astounding change, five wickets going down in the next half-hour for nine runs. The turning point was the dismissal of Gregory. Rendered over-confident by hitting a couple of fours the batsman tried to pull a breaking ball from Blythe and was out to a beautifully judged catch by Thompson, who ran from mid-on to short leg. Trumper, after an escape from being caught and bowled, was neatly taken at short leg, Ransford was bowled off his pads, Armstrong made a feeble hit into Jessop's hands at forward cover point and Carter was caught at long leg. Seldom has Armstrong thrown away his wicket so palpably, hitting out at Blythe before he had given himself any time to get the pace of the ground.

England wanted 105 to win, and as it happened, Hobbs and Fry hit off the runs in an hour and a half, without being separated. Hobbs from the first played superbly, but Fry seemed strangely anxious and had only just settled down when the match ended. The cricket at the finish was dazzling, Hobbs pulling Macartney round to square leg for three fours, and Fry making the winning hit – a four to square leg, all run.

Toss: Australia. **Australia 74** (G. H. Hirst 4-28, C. Blythe 6-44) **and 151** (G. H. Hirst 5-58, C. Blythe 5-58); **England 121** (W. W. Armstrong 5-27) **and 105-0** (J. B. Hobbs 62*).

NOTES BY THE EDITOR   Sydney Pardon, 1910

Never, I should think, in the last five-and-20 years have English cricketers felt more dissatisfied and disappointed with a season's play than in 1909. It was not merely that we lost the rubber. Such an experience is no new thing for us even at home, as in 1899 the Australians won the only Test match that was played out, and in 1902 two out of the three finished matches. In both those years, however, there was a good deal to compensate for defeat – a record score at The Oval in 1899 and in 1902 a glorious win at The Oval, after England in the series had had to battle against about the worst luck ever experienced in international cricket. Last summer things were very different. Allowing that fortune in the shape of Hayward's lameness, Blythe's uncertain health, and G. L. Jessop's accident told against us, there was an angry feeling that our downfall was courted by mismanagement. Complaint has been made that the selection committee came in for unfair attack, but I do not think the complaint can be justified.

To this day the extraordinary blundering in connection with the team for the Test match at Lord's – the game that was the beginning of England's troubles – remains unexplained. As regards the omission of one indispensable player, G. L. Jessop has assured me positively that he was not asked to play at Lord's.

In the columns of *Country Life* MacLaren, in reviewing the Test games, stated – a fact that had previously leaked out – that on the morning of the match he asked Walter Brearley to play. He did not, however, explain how it was that in the original list of players Jayes was picked as the fast bowler and Brearley left out. A good many people, including P. F. Warner, thought that even though his invitation was delayed till the last moment, Brearley ought to have played. Perhaps he should have thrown personal considerations on one side, but it is easy to understand his refusal. At that period of the season he was at the top of his form and he felt that in leaving him out the selection committee had deliberately slighted him. The mistakes over the match at Lord's did not end with the omission of Jessop and Brearley. By a sad error of judgment George Gunn was given the preference over Rhodes, the result being that England's bowling depended wholly upon Relf, Hirst, Haigh and King. If the catches had been held, the bowling, as things turned out, might have proved equal to the occasion, but that does not alter the fact that a great risk was run. After a tremendous rainfall the weather had improved and, failing Brearley, Jayes ought clearly to have played, a right-handed fast bowler being, according to nearly all expert opinion, an absolute necessity at Lord's.

If I have gone at rather undue length into this old story it is because the match at Lord's proved the turning-point of the season. I may be wrong, but I cannot help thinking that the selection committee, like the general public, were inclined at that time to under-rate the Australians, and thought that they would not require much beating. Cricket, like whist, does not forgive, and a very high price had to be paid for the mistake. In the matches at Leeds and Manchester the selection committee made the best use of the material at their command, but at The Oval a fatal blunder was committed in leaving out Buckenham – a blunder for which it was generally understood that MacLaren was responsible. Experts occasionally do strange things and this was one of the strangest. The idea of letting England go into the field in fine weather, on a typical Oval wicket, with no fast bowler except Sharp touched the confines of lunacy. The despised man in the street could not have been guilty of such folly. I must not be understood as wishing to take away in the smallest degree from the credit due to the Australians. Even when they lost three matches in a fortnight I personally felt no doubt that they would prove themselves a very fine side. All I contend is that with a wiser choice of players England would not have fared so badly.

Second Test

At Lord's, June 14, 15, 16, 1909. Australia won by nine wickets.

The Second Test marked the turning-point in the Australians' fortunes. Faced as they were with a possibility of the tour being a failure they were on the eve of the game much depressed, the extreme difficulty they had experienced in beating Somerset having greatly shaken their confidence. However, they beat England in most brilliant fashion and only once more – after an interval of over three months – did they suffer defeat.

Never in the history of Test matches in England has there been such blundering in the selection of an England XI. On no other occasion has there been such a storm of protest, nearly every newspaper in England condemning the action taken. As the ground had been under water on the previous Saturday it was decided to leave out Jayes, and so it came about that England went into the field at Lord's without a right-handed fast bowler – a deplorable error of judgment.

Rightly judging that the wicket in the absence of further rain would improve, Noble decided to put England in. All things considered England gave a very creditable display of batting, staying in until just upon six o'clock for a total of 269. The highest and best innings was played by King, who not only showed the value of left-handed batting, but did much to justify his selection. He played a good strong game, hitting cleanly on the off side and placing the ball well to leg. He and Tyldesley put on 79 for the fourth wicket, taking the score to 123, but they had to work very hard for their runs. Out at last to a smart catch at point, King was batting two hours and 40 minutes, his hits including half a dozen fours. By far the most vigorous hitting for England was shown by Lilley, who after a quiet start punished Cotter in front of the wicket in a style to which fast bowlers in these days are unaccustomed.

On the second day the match went all in favour of the Australians. The wicket rolled out very well and not until a quarter to six did the innings end, the total reaching 350 or 81 runs ahead. Then in the last 25 minutes England lost Hobbs's wicket for 16 runs. In gaining their big advantage the Australians owed nearly everything to Ransford, who had the satisfaction of making a hundred in his first Test match at Lord's. Going in with the score at 90 he withstood the England bowling for a little over four hours and took out his bat for 143. For the most part he played wonderfully well but fortune was kind to him. When 13 he was missed by MacLaren at slip, when 56 he might have been caught at the wicket and with his score 61 he gave a chance at second slip to Jones. Had any one of these three chances been taken the whole course of the game might have been different. Ransford was strong on the leg side, but the feature of his innings was his brilliant hitting past cover point. His great innings included 21 fours. He found valuable partners in Trumper and Noble, the fifth wicket putting on 79 and the sixth 71. King at one point bowled extremely well, but he never got over the disappointment of seeing Ransford and Trumper missed off him in one over.

The last day was a triumph for Australia and nothing less than humiliating for England. As the wicket had quite recovered from its drenching on Saturday most people thought that England would have little difficulty in saving the game, but in less than half an hour all hopes of this kind were destroyed. Tyldesley and Gunn were out in one over from Armstrong at 22, with one run added Hayward was run out; and then Armstrong, who was in wonderful form, clean-bowled King and Hirst with splendid balls, six wickets being down for 41. Jones and MacLaren doubled the score, putting on 41 together in 50 minutes. MacLaren, beaten at last by a fine break-back, played well, but Jones never inspired confidence. Lilley again hit freely, but the innings was all over for 121.

Never perhaps has Armstrong bowled quite so finely. More than once he varied his leg-breaks by making the ball turn a little the other way, and his length was a marvel of accuracy. At one point he had taken five wickets for eight runs. The match proved an enormous attraction, 50,166 people paying for admission during the three days.

Toss: Australia. **England 269** (J. H. King 60, A. Cotter 4-80) **and 121** (W. W. Armstrong 6-35);
Australia 350 (V. S. Ransford 143*, A. E. Relf 5-85) **and 41-1**.

Third Test

At Leeds, July 1, 2, 3, 1909. Australia won by 126 runs.

For two days the struggle was one of the sternest ever seen in Test match cricket, but on the Saturday England's batting went all to pieces, no one being able to cope with the fine bowling of Cotter and Macartney. The Australians fully deserved their victory, but England suffered an irreparable blow, Jessop, when the game had been in progress about 70 minutes on the first day, straining the muscles of the back so badly that he could not play again during the season. The loss of such a player and the fact of having to bat one man short in both innings had of course a most depressing effect.

During the previous week rain had been falling almost continuously at Leeds, but on the Tuesday before the match, the weather underwent a pleasant change and the ground made a wonderful recovery, the wicket never being half as difficult as had been expected. Apart from Jessop's deplorable accident the Englishmen had no reason to feel dissatisfied with the first day's cricket. They got the Australians out by half past four for 188, and then scored 88 for the loss of Hobbs and Fry's wickets. The Australian innings was a curiously uneven one. The total at lunch-time was up to 89 for two, and so well did Bardsley and Armstrong play that it reached 140 before the fifth wicket went down. Then came a remarkable change, Rhodes taking the next four wickets at a cost of seven runs. There were nine men out for 171, and after Trumper had hit Rhodes for four fours in one over the innings ended. The English bowling was very good, Barnes's figures of one for 37 by no means representing the value of his work.

England began badly, Fry being lbw with the score at eight and Hobbs bowled at 31. Just before being out Hobbs was appealed against for hit wicket, but the umpire gave him not out on the ground that he had completed his stroke before his foot touched the stumps. On the second day about 16,000 people watched a tremendous fight. Some of them found the stubborn defence of Armstrong and Noble too slow to please them, but others thought the keen struggle quite absorbing. So long as Tyldesley and Sharp stayed together in the morning England seemed certain of a substantial lead. The score was up to 130 for two, but at this point Noble made a change of bowling that, as it happened, completely turned the fortunes of the game. Macartney went on and bowled with astonishing success, sending down 13 overs and three balls for 31 runs and six wickets. He kept a fine length, and again and again did quite enough to beat the bat. The batsmen were freely blamed for feeble play, but it struck one that Macartney bowled wonderfully well. England's last six wickets fell in 70 minutes for 45 runs.

The Australians' second innings opened in sensational fashion. The first ball from Hirst – a real swerver – clean-bowled Gregory, and at 14 McAlister was caught at short leg. Then came some very stern cricket, Ransford and Armstrong playing the fine bowling of Hirst and Barnes with the utmost care. When 50 went up the innings had been in progress nearly 80 minutes. Then at 52 Ransford was out lbw for an invaluable 24. Not often has a harder struggle between bat and ball been seen. The pitch suddenly became difficult, and thanks chiefly to some splendid bowling by Barnes, the game underwent such a change that seven wickets were down for 127. Armstrong, bowled at last by Rhodes, was at the wickets for fully two hours and a half. The game was very much in England's favour, but Macartney kept up his end while Cotter and Carter hit, and at half past six the total was 175 for eight.

There seemed every promise of a fine finish on Saturday, but England's batting failed lamentably in the last innings. The Australians took their score to 207, Macartney playing with infinite patience. The task of getting 214 was not thought likely to be beyond England's powers, but the early play was far from encouraging. With the score at 17 Fry played a ball from Cotter on to his foot and into his wicket and, at 26, Tyldesley was caught and bowled from a hard return. Hobbs and Sharp raised the total to 56 before lunch, but Hobbs was never in the least degree comfortable.

After the interval there came a doleful collapse. Cotter and Macartney bowled in great form, the last seven wickets falling in less than an hour for 31 runs. To Macartney belonged the chief honours of the Australian victory. In the whole match he took 11 wickets, and only 85 runs were hit from him. Even the greatest bowlers of the early Australian teams could in the circumstances have done no better.

Toss: Australia. **Australia 188** (W. Rhodes 4-38) **and 207** (S. F. Barnes 6-63); **England 182** (J. T. Tyldesley 55, J. Sharp 61, C. G. Macartney 7-58) **and 87** (A. Cotter 5-38, C. G. Macartney 4-27).

CRICKETER OF THE YEAR – S. F. BARNES   1910

Sidney F. Barnes was born at Smethwick on April 19, 1876. Few bowlers have sprung into fame more suddenly. He played in two matches for Lancashire in 1899 without attracting much notice, and the general public knew nothing about him when in 1901 he reappeared in the Lancashire XI and took six for 70 against Leicestershire. This performance would not in itself have aroused much attention, but just afterwards the announcement was made that Mr A. C. MacLaren, unable to secure Hirst or Rhodes, had engaged Barnes for the team he was to take to Australia. The selection caused a great deal of surprise, but MacLaren knew perfectly well what he was doing. He had found a first-rate bowler and was not in the least afraid to trust his own judgment.

Barnes started the tour in astonishing form, and was, up to a certain point, the success of the team. Unfortunately his knee gave way during the third of the five Test matches, and he played no more. In the half-dozen 11-a-side matches in which he appeared he took 41 wickets for just under 16? runs apiece. The Australian batsmen were never in doubt as to his class. Indeed, some of them did not hesitate to say that a better hard-wicket bowler had never been sent from England. Returning home Barnes was associated with Lancashire for two years and added greatly to his reputation.

His connection with the county ended with the season of 1903. The disagreement that caused him to drop out of the XI was an even greater misfortune to Lancashire than to the player himself. There is no need at this distance of time to go into the merits of the quarrel. Barnes's own statement is that he wanted to be sure of a situation which would yield him a certain income when his days of first-class cricket were over, and this the Lancashire committee either could not or would not find him.

After leaving Lancashire Barnes for a time dropped out of first-class cricket, but his extraordinary success for Staffordshire – his native county – kept his name before the public. He began to play for them in 1904, and has ever since been the mainstay of the XI. In 1906 he took 119 wickets for less than eight runs each, and during the last three seasons his figures have come out at 79 wickets for less than six-and-a-half runs, 92 for just under nine, and 76 for under seven. His splendid form for Staffordshire led to his return to first-class cricket, the MCC offering him a place in the XI they sent to Australia in 1907–08.

As on the occasion of his previous visit he won golden opinions in Australia, M. A. Noble describing him as the best bowler in the world. Last season he ought to have taken part in all the Test matches against the Australians, but only played in the last three. Still he was clearly the best bowler we had, his work at Leeds and in the first innings at Manchester being up to his highest standard. Moreover, he had a genuine triumph against the Gentlemen at Lord's, being largely instrumental in winning the game for the Players by 200 runs. After this match P. F. Warner, who scored 58 in the Gentlemen's second innings, paid him some very handsome compliments in the *Westminster Gazette*: "Barnes certainly did not bowl one really bad ball during the two innings of the Gentlemen, and a finer bowler I have never played."

Fourth Test

At Manchester, July 26, 27, 28, 1909. Drawn.

Having already won two matches out of three the Australians at Old Trafford were more intent upon avoiding defeat than adding to their victories. At any rate, when in a very strong position on the third afternoon, they delayed the closure so long that England had no great difficulty in drawing the game. The match was considerably interfered with by rain, cricket on the second day being restricted to less than an hour and a half.

A good deal of rain had fallen in Manchester on the Sunday and on the first day, the wicket being always slow and rather difficult, the ball beat the bat to such an extent that an innings was completed on each side, Australians scoring 147 and England 119. The game opened in a way that gave England's supporters ground for great hope. For the fourth time in succession Noble won the toss, but so finely did Blythe and Barnes bowl that at lunch five wickets were down for 64. The sixth wicket fell at 66, but the last three batsmen hit with such determination that 81 runs were added. The Australians owed much to Armstrong who played with untiring patience. As he took an hour and 50 minutes to score his 32 not out, his play presented little attraction to the spectators, but his defence was invaluable.

Going in against such a moderate total as 147 England looked to have a splendid chance. For a time everything went well, Warner and Spooner staying together for 50 minutes. They only scored 24 runs, however, and it was thought they might have been more enterprising. From this point the batting fell to pieces, Laver bowling with astonishing success and carrying everything before him. In all he took eight wickets, and only 31 runs were hit from him, his performance being on the face of it one of the best ever accomplished in Test matches. Still without depreciating what he did, it must be said that his bowling was not so excessively difficult as to account for the failure of the batsmen. By general consent he was flattered by a great deal of feeble play. Probably the high wind helped him. He did not seem to break very much but his length was excellent and there was a good deal of variety in the pace and flight of the ball. Needless to say England's collapse caused bitter disappointment. No batsman was more at fault than Hirst, who with a wide space in front of him for a straight drive, pulled a half-volley and sent it right into the hands of Hopkins at long-on.

Of the little time available for cricket on the second day the Australians made excellent use. Going in with a lead of 28 they soon lost Gregory, but Bardsley and Macartney took the score from 16 to 77 before rain set in and nothing more could be done that day. Thanks to a dry night and a fair amount of sunshine the ground recovered to such an extent that the match was continued at a quarter past 12. The start, however, might well have been delayed for a little longer, the turf being so greasy that the English bowlers could not at first get a proper foothold.

The Australians gave a splendid display of batting, playing quite the right game. Rhodes alone bowled well. At lunch-time the score was up to 186, the Australians being 214 ahead with half their wickets in hand. It was thought that Noble would declare at about three o'clock, but he would not take the slightest risk and not until 20 minutes to four was the innings closed. There was, of course, nothing to play for but a draw, it being obviously impossible to get 308 runs in two hours and a half.

Toss: Australia. **Australia 147** (S. F. Barnes 5-56, C. Blythe 5-63) **and 279-9 dec.** (C. G. Macartney 51, V. S. Ransford 54*, W. Rhodes 5-83); **England 119** (F. J. Laver 8-31) **and 108-3** (R. H. Spooner 58).

CRICKETER OF THE YEAR – W. BARDSLEY   1910

Warren Bardsley was born at Warren, New South Wales, on December 7, 1884. Nothing in recent cricket has been so remarkable as the rise of this latest Australian star. On his form in this country last summer he may, without exaggeration, be described as the most dangerous batsman in the world, and yet it is less than two years since he was seen for the first time in a big match.

His chance came in February 1908, in the return match at Sydney between New South Wales and MCC. Bardsley failed in his first innings, but in his second he played splendidly for 108. This performance he followed up a month later with scores of 34 and 67 in Noble's Testimonial match, and his reputation was made.

However, though his claims were overwhelmingly strong, he was not one of the first men chosen for the English tour. Another left-hander, Ransford, had an even more astonishing record for the season and a great deal was expected of them both. Bardsley found his form in the opening match at Trent Bridge and never fell off. His successes culminated with his two separate hundreds in the Test match at The Oval.

In point of style Bardsley compares favourably with any left-handed batsman of this generation. The straightness of his bat and the upright position he adopts at the wicket lend a peculiar charm to his play. He uses his feet to perfection, and he is master of many strokes. In cutting behind point he is less brilliant, perhaps, than Clem Hill, but he is stronger in hitting past cover point and just as wonderful on the leg side. Moreover, he has at his command a very powerful straight drive. Indeed, no left-handed batsman in my time has possessed greater skill in scoring all round the wicket.

Fifth Test

At The Oval, August 9, 10, 11, 1909. Drawn.

Unlike the four previous fixtures the final Test match, favoured with delightful weather, was played on a perfect wicket, and to such an extent did the batting assert itself that there never seemed to be much chance of arriving at a positive result in three days. Had the result of the rubber depended on the game play would if necessary have gone on until the end of the week. As at Manchester the Australians were chiefly concerned in avoiding defeat, victory, in the happy position in which they stood, being quite a secondary consideration. Enormous interest was taken in the game, over 53,000 people paying for admission during the three days.

Thirteen players had been retained for England, among the number for the first time being D. W. Carr, the Kent bowler. The wicket being so hard and fast the selection committee could hardly have played Blythe as well as Carr, but the omission of Buckenham, for which MacLaren was understood to be responsible, was so grave a blunder that it is difficult to find words in which to speak of it. Old cricketers in the pavilion were astounded when they learned what had been determined on, the policy of letting England go into the field in fine weather at The Oval without a good fast bowler being condemned in uncompromising terms. Equalling F. S. Jackson's luck in 1905, Noble won the toss for the fifth time in succession and of course took first innings.

Staying in until half past five the Australians scored 325. On such a pitch this was quite an ordinary total, but considering that the first four wickets fell for 58 the performance was a fine one. At the start of the game Carr bowled with startling success, breaking through Gregory's defence at nine and getting Noble and Armstrong out lbw at 27 and 55 respectively. When at 58 Barnes, with a ball that came off the ground at lightning speed, clean-bowled Ransford the spectators were in a high state of excitement. However, with Ransford's downfall England's run of success came to an end. Bardsley, who from the first had played in magnificent form, was joined by Trumper and the two batsmen put on 118.

MacLaren was sadly at fault in his management of the bowling. He kept Carr on unchanged for over an hour and a half and for some inexplicable reason he put Sharp on in place of Barnes when the score stood at nine for one wicket. Trumper gave a chance to Barnes at mid-off when 48, but otherwise his 73 was a perfect innings. At no time did he seem troubled by Carr's deceptive breaks. At 259 Bardsley brought his great innings to a close by playing a ball from Sharp on to his stumps after batting three hours and three-quarters for his 136, his hits including one six (four from an overthrow) and a dozen fours. He hit finely all round the wicket, being especially strong past cover point and in front of short leg. When 30 he might have been caught at the wicket by Lilley and at 77 he was palpably let off by MacLaren at second slip, but these were the only blemishes in a truly splendid display. Carr's five wickets cost 146, but he would have got on much better had he been given a rest early in the day.

In the 40 minutes that remained for cricket England lost two wickets to Cotter for 40 runs, Spooner being beaten by a fast yorker and MacLaren lbw to a full pitch. On the second day the Englishmen were batting from 11 o'clock till about quarter past five, and by scoring 352 secured a lead of 27. At one point they seemed certain to obtain a far more substantial advantage, the total at the tea interval standing at 344 for six. Sharp was then 102 and Hutchings 58, having so far put on 138 together. Unfortunately for England they did not on starting afresh give themselves time to settle down again. Both were caught at 348 and England's four wickets fell after the tea interval for eight runs. In getting his 105 – the only hundred for England in the Test matches – Sharp was at the wickets for two hours and 50 minutes, hitting seven fours. With his score at 93 he gave a chance to the wicket-keeper, but this was his only mistake. He played a very fine game, hitting hard and well all round the wicket. The Australians were placed at a great disadvantage by losing Laver, who strained the muscles in his left thigh so badly that he could take no further part in the game.

The Australians had an hour's batting at the end of the afternoon and by beautiful cricket Gregory and Bardsley scored 76 without being parted. On the third day interest in the match declined, as a draw seemed inevitable. Noble did not attempt to force a win, delaying the closure until four o'clock when the Australian score stood 339 for five. Presumably he thought the pitch too good to give his bowlers any chance of getting England out before half past six. Still, though void of excitement, the day's cricket was memorable, Bardsley following up his 136 with 130 and thus performing the unprecedented feat in Test matches of getting two separate hundreds. Up to the time he reached his hundred his cricket was delightful to look at, but after that, perhaps from fatigue, he became strangely slow, taking 80 minutes to score his last 30 runs. He and Gregory put on 180 in two hours and a quarter for the first wicket. So complete was their command of the bowling that the partnership might have been indefinitely prolonged. In his eagerness to see Bardsley get a second hundred, however, Gregory lost his wicket, Hutchings and Rhodes running him out.

With two hours and 20 minutes left for cricket, England went in for a second time. Spooner and Hayes were soon dismissed, but on Fry joining Rhodes steady batting made England quite safe, 61 runs being added for the third wicket in 50 minutes. Rhodes, as in the first innings, batted admirably.

Toss: Australia. **Australia 325** (W. Bardsley 136, V. T. Trumper 73, C. G. Macartney 50, D. W. Carr 5-146) **and 339-5 dec.** (S. E. Gregory 74, W. Bardsley 130, M. A. Noble 55); **England 352** (W. Rhodes 66, C. B. Fry 62, J. Sharp 105, K. L. Hutchings 59, A. Cotter 6-95) **and 104-3** (W. Rhodes 54).

AUSTRALIA V ENGLAND 1911–12

The tour of the MCC's team in Australia was, in a cricket sense, a triumphant success. The Englishmen won the rubber of five Test matches by four to one. Mr P. F. Warner was chosen to captain the side, but after scoring 151 in the opening game he had a serious illness, and could take no further part in the tour, the leadership devolving on Mr Douglas, who, after the first Test match, proved himself an excellent captain.

Mr Warner wrote in the *Westminster Gazette*: "The team had some rare batting triumphs, but the batting never struck me as being relatively so good as the bowling and general out-cricket. Of our bowlers, Foster and Barnes achieved wonders. Finer bowling than theirs I have never seen on hard, true wickets. In the Test matches they took 66 wickets (Barnes 34, Foster 32) out of the 95 that fell.

"I have long since exhausted my vocabulary of praise in favour of Rhodes and Hobbs, and thanks in a very large degree to their superlative work, our batting was eminently successful. In innings after innings they gave us a wonderful start. Gunn batted most consistently, while Woolley played a great innings in the final Test, and is a beautiful batsman. I would as soon see him bat as anyone in the world.

"Every man was animated by one thought – the honour of English cricket – and we are proud and happy to have returned victorious. The knockdown blow I suffered has been to a large extent compensated for by the success of my men, for it is something to have taken two teams to Australia which returned unconquered."

First Test

At Sydney, December 15, 16, 18, 19, 20, 21, 1911. Australia won by 146 runs.

Outplayed from the start, the Englishmen lost the First Test, which lasted into the sixth day, by 146 runs. Fine batting put Australia in a commanding position, and Hordern did the rest, the googly bowler taking 12 wickets for 175 runs. The English batsmen mastered him in subsequent matches, but on this occasion they found him very difficult. On the first day Australia scored 315 for five, their batting being distinguished by caution rather than brilliancy. Trumper played well, but in a style quite foreign to his usual methods. Not out 95 at the end of the first day, he took in all three hours and three-quarters to score his 113. Minnett, who hit 14 fours, was far more vigorous and attractive. When stumps were drawn on Saturday, England had scored 142 for four, but, despite some fine play by Hearne and Foster, they finished up 129 behind on the first innings. Going in with this majority, Australia scored 119 for the loss of Bardsley's wicket before the call of time. Foster and Douglas bowled very finely on the fourth day, but the Englishmen could never make up the ground they had lost. Douglas made a great mistake in not letting Barnes start the bowling in either innings. Though his injured wrist still troubled him, George Gunn played an excellent second innings.

Toss: Australia. **Australia 447** (W. W. Armstrong 60, V. T. Trumper 113, R. B. Minnett 90) **and 308** (C. Kelleway 70, C. Hill 65, F. R. Foster 5-92, J. W. H. T. Douglas 4-50); **England 318** (J. B. Hobbs 63, J. W. Hearne 76, F. R. Foster 56, H. V. Hordern 5-85) **and 291** (G. Gunn 62, H. V. Hordern 7-90).

Second Test

At Melbourne, December 30, 1911, January 1, 2, 3, 1912. England won by eight wickets.

It was in the Second Test that the Englishmen first revealed their full strength. Up to this point they had not impressed the critics that they were anything more than an ordinarily good side, and few people in Australia thought they were at all likely to win the rubber. The match was won at the start, some marvellous bowling by Barnes giving England an advantage which, though seriously discounted at one point by weak batting, was never wholly lost. On Australia winning the toss and going in, Barnes led off by bowling five overs, four maidens, for one run and four wickets. Bardsley played a ball on to his wicket, Kelleway was out lbw, Hill clean-bowled, and Armstrong caught at the wicket. In this way, four of the best Australian wickets went down for 11 runs.

With six men out for 38, the Australians were in a desperate plight, but Ransford saved the situation by his fine defence, and thanks chiefly to a capital stand by Hordern and Carter, the total in the end reached 184. At the close of play England had scored 38 runs and lost Hobbs's wicket.

On Monday there was a big attendance, over 31,000 people being present. The Englishmen were batting all day. Rhodes and Hearne took the score to 137 before the second wicket fell, but at a quarter to six the innings was all over for 265. Out fifth at 224, Hearne made his 114 without a mistake of any kind. He hit 11 fours and was at the wickets three hours and three-quarters. Apart from him and Rhodes, the batting was very disappointing.

Going in on Tuesday against a balance of 81, the Australians made a very bad start, losing four wickets for 38 runs. Armstrong, however, played finely, and received such good support that, at the end of the day, the total, with eight wickets down, had reached 269. Armstrong hit 14 fours and gave no chance.

On the fourth day England won the match in most brilliant style. The Australians added 30 runs, leaving England 219 to get. Rhodes left at 57, and then Hobbs and Gunn practically won the match, carrying the score to 169 before Gunn was caught by the wicket-keeper. On Hearne going in the remaining runs were hit off without further loss. Hobbs played one of the finest innings of his life. He scored his 126 not out in just under three hours and a half, and did not give a chance of any kind.

Toss: Australia. **Australia 184** (S. F. Barnes 5-44) **and 299** (W. W. Armstrong 90, F. R. Foster 6-91); **England 265** (W. Rhodes 61, J. W. Hearne 114, A. Cotter 4-73, H. V. Hordern 4-66) **and 219-2** (J. B. Hobbs 126*).

CRICKETER OF THE YEAR – J. W. HEARNE   Sydney Pardon, 1912

John William Hearne was born at Harlington, Middlesex, on February 11, 1891. He first went to Lord's as a ground boy in 1906. He practically learned his cricket as a member of the Cross Arrows Club, which he joined during his first year at Lord's. In 1909 he was given his first trial for the county, playing in eight of the matches. A lad of little more than 18, and quite new to first-class cricket, he did not do much to suggest the success that was in store for him.

In 1910 he made a great advance, and convinced the Middlesex authorities that they had found a prize. Twice he scored over a hundred – against Somerset at Lord's and Sussex at Eastbourne – and though his bowling figures – 48 wickets for something under 25 runs apiece – did not look much on paper, he had some days of startling success.

At first there was a difficulty about Hearne going to Australia. Some members of the Middlesex committee thought he was too young for such a heavy tour, but in the end they yielded to Mr Warner's urgent request that he might be allowed to join the team. Up to the time I write he has done nothing as a bowler in Australia, but as a batsman he has met with wonderful success, making scores in the first two Test matches of 79, 43 and 114. As he has done so much before completing his 21st year, Hearne's future as a cricketer, given a continuance of good health, seems assured.

Third Test

At Adelaide, January 12, 13, 15, 16, 17, 1912. England won by seven wickets.

England won the Third Test, the game being, in some respects, the most remarkable in the whole tour. To an even greater degree than at Melbourne, the Australians discounted their chances by a disastrous start. Batting first on a perfect wicket, they failed so badly against Foster's bowling that in about three hours and a quarter they were all out for 133. Ransford, with his own score at six and the total at 17, received such a severe blow on the thumb that he had to retire, and did not bat again until the ninth wicket had fallen. This was a piece of very bad luck for Australia. Foster was in his deadliest form. He began by bowling 11 overs, six maidens, for eight runs and one wicket and finished up with the remarkable figures of five for 36.

Hobbs and Rhodes opened England's innings by scoring 147 together, and this time the batting was maintained at a very high standard. Only four wickets fell on Saturday, the score reaching 327, and on the third day the total was carried to 501. Hobbs took the honours with 187. He gave some chances in the latter half of his innings, but for the most part he played splendidly. He hit 16 fours and was at the wickets rather more than five hours and a half.

Though they had to face a balance of 368, the Australians made a great fight. Luck was all against them. Trumper, owing to an injured knee, had to go in last, and Ransford, though he made 38, was much hampered by his damaged thumb. Still, the innings, which began on Monday afternoon, did not end until Wednesday, the total reaching 476. The batting was consistently fine, Hill, who gave no chance during a stay of two hours and three-quarters, perhaps showing the best cricket. Barnes's bowling was wonderfully steady. Wanting 109 to win, England lost Hobbs with only five runs on the board, but Rhodes and Gunn by carrying the score to 102 settled the matter.

Toss: Australia. **Australia 133** (F. R. Foster 5-36) **and 476** (W. Bardsley 63, H. Carter 72, C. Hill 98, T. J. Matthews 53, S. F. Barnes 5-105); **England 501** (J. B. Hobbs 187, W. Rhodes 59, F. R. Foster 71, A. Cotter 4-125) **and 112-3** (W. Rhodes 57*).

CRICKETER OF THE YEAR – F. R. FOSTER
Sydney Pardon, 1912

Mr Frank Rowbotham Foster was born at Small Heath on January 31, 1889. There are some cricketers whose natural aptitude for the game is so great that directly the opportunity comes they jump into the front rank. In this select band Mr Foster may clearly be given a place. Nothing was known of him outside local cricket till 1908, when he took 23 wickets in five matches for Warwickshire, but two years later he bowled in such form for the Gentlemen against the Players that the best judges did not hesitate to describe him as an England cricketer of the future. Last summer he improved out of all knowledge as a batsman, and was, by general consent, the best all-round player of the year. The season was one long triumph for him, and, as a matter of course, he was asked to go to Australia, where his bowling was one of the main factors in winning a Test match at Melbourne.

What the future may have in store for Foster it is of course impossible to say, but he has already done enough for fame. From what I have seen of him, I should be inclined to say that he is a higher-class bowler than batsman. Though very brilliant and blessed with great confidence, he does not play quite straight and takes too many risks to be ranked yet awhile amongst the masters.

His bowling is another matter altogether. It is quite distinctive and individual. With an easy natural action, he has a decided swerve, and he possesses the sovereign merit of making speed from the pitch. His pace in the air is quite ordinary, but he comes off the ground with a rare spin, and in that lies his chief virtue. While Foster was making so many runs last season I feared his bowling would suffer, but so far he has with impunity done the work of two men. Everything is possible at three-and-twenty. Cricket at its brightest, is a young man's game, and Foster is the very personification of youthful energy.

Fourth Test

At Melbourne, February 9, 10, 12, 13, 1912. England won by an innings and 225 runs.

In the Fourth Test the Englishmen put the seal on their reputation, giving a most brilliant and convincing display of all-round cricket, and winning by an innings. As they had already won two matches, the victory gave them the rubber. The first day's play went far towards determining the result. Heavy rain had made the ground soft, and Douglas put Australia in. At first his policy did not seem likely to answer, the score reaching 53 before the first wicket fell, but Barnes and Foster afterwards bowled splendidly and, despite Minnett's hitting, the innings ended for 191. Hobbs and Rhodes saw out the first day, and on Saturday they set up a Test match record, scoring 323 for the first wicket. They were together for just upon four hours and a half. Hobbs, who was first to leave, hit 22 fours in his superb 178. At the drawing of stumps, the total was 370 for one wicket. On Monday, the Englishmen took their total to 589. Rhodes beat Hobbs's score by a single run, and was then caught at the wicket. Though not by any means free from fault, his innings, which lasted nearly seven hours, was a remarkable display of careful batting. The Australians went in for a few minutes at the end of the afternoon, and on Tuesday they failed, being all out just after the tea interval for 173. Douglas bowled in great form. At one point he had sent down 15 overs for 21 runs and four wickets.

Toss: England. **Australia 191** (R. B. Minnett 56, F. R. Foster 4-77, S. F. Barnes 5-74) **and 173** (J. W. H. T. Douglas 5-46); **England 589** (J. B. Hobbs 178, W. Rhodes 179, G. Gunn 75, F. R. Foster 50, F. E. Woolley 56).

Fifth Test

At Sydney, February 23, 24, 26, 27, 28, 29, March 1, 1912. England won by 70 runs.

Though England had won the rubber there was no lack of interest in the last of the Test matches. Monday and Thursday being blank through rain, the match went into the seventh day, England winning in the end by 70 runs. Owing to his repeated failures, Bardsley was left out of the Australian XI, Macartney being at last given a chance. It must be admitted that the Australians had the worst of the luck. Left with 363 to get in the last innings, they had, at the close of Wednesday's play, scored 193 for three, so that they had quite a reasonable chance of winning. Drenching rain on Thursday, however, damaged the wicket to a great extent and upset all calculations. Play did not begin on Friday until just after one o'clock. The batsmen did their best, but the task was too heavy for them. Armstrong was out at 209, Ransford was bowled at 220, and at 231 Minnett fell to a wonderful catch by Woolley at second slip. After that, the result was only a question of time. Finishing the tour in fine form, Foster took four wickets for 43 runs. Woolley, Gunn, and Hobbs shared the batting honours for England; Woolley's 133 not out – a beautiful innings – included a dozen fours.

Toss: England. **England 324** (G. Gunn 52, F. E. Woolley 133*, H. V. Hordern 5 95)
and 214 (G. Gunn 61, H. V. Hordern 5-66);
Australia 176 and 292 (V. T. Trumper 50, R. B. Minnett 61, F. R. Foster 4-43, S. F. Barnes 4-106).

England v Australia 1912

Inasmuch as the Australians won only nine matches, lost eight, and left 20 unfinished, their tour in England in 1912 cannot be regarded as much of a success. It was unfortunate that, in view of the Triangular Tournament, the Australians did not sink all personal differences and send us over their best team, but it is useless now to indulge in laments on this score. No doubt the members of the Board of Control knew, as well as anyone else, that the great players left behind could not be adequately replaced.

Ten of the 15 players had never been here before, and it was certainly bad luck for them that they should have had their first experience of England in such an appalling summer. The team, as time went on, leaned more and more heavily on Bardsley, Macartney and Kelleway. Bardsley, to our thinking, was an even greater batsman than in 1909. Increased responsibility seemed to bring out all that was best in him.

Macartney also had a great season, but he was not so consistent as Bardsley. He started in wonderful form, and before May was over people were beginning to compare him with Trumper. He did not quite live up to this reputation, but he, perhaps, played the innings of the year against England at Lord's. A marked characteristic of his play on his many good days was the quickness with which he settled down. He had nearly every scoring stroke at his command, cutting, driving to the off, and turning the ball to leg with equal facility. His power to turn straight balls to the boundary sometimes cost him his wicket, but it earned him heaps of runs. He had improved out of knowledge as a batsman since 1909, and watching his dazzling play it was difficult to understand why he had only been picked in one Test match out of five the previous winter.

The tour did not pass off without unpleasantness. Mr G. S. Crouch, the manager, on getting back to Australia, lodged a scathing complaint with the board, stating that some of the players had conducted themselves so badly as to lead to the team being socially ostracised. He urged that in the selection of future teams something more than the ability to play cricket should be taken into consideration. It may be added here that some of the players were not at all satisfied with Mr Crouch as manager.

THE TRIANGULAR TOURNAMENT
1913

The Triangular Tournament between England, Australia and South Africa – so long expected and so much discussed – duly came off last season. Of the nine matches three were played at Lord's, two at The Oval, two at Manchester, and one each at Leeds and Nottingham. The result was a victory for England, who won four matches out of six – beating the South Africans three times and the Australians once – and did not suffer a single defeat. From the first the South Africans were obviously outclassed. Owing to rain the matches between England and Australia at Lord's and Manchester had to be left drawn, but in a game which lasted four days England gained a decisive victory at The Oval, and so won the competition.

Bad weather interfered sadly with the success of the tournament. In the England and Australia match at Lord's play on the second day was only practicable for 20 minutes, and when the teams met five weeks later in Manchester rain caused great delay and not a ball could be bowled on the third day.

First Test
At Lord's, June 24, 25, 26, 1912. Drawn.

Under happier circumstances, the England and Australia match at Lord's might well have been the event of the season. Unfortunately, the weather ruined everything. Play on the first day was limited to about three hours, and on the second to little more than 20 minutes. A delightful Wednesday came too late to save the situation, and the match had, perforce, to be left drawn. Despite all disadvantages, over 35,000 people paid for admission during the three days. The Prince of Wales was present on the third day.

England did so well during the time available on the first day as to secure, on the damaged pitch, what looked like a winning position. Their score at the drawing of stumps, stood at 211 with only four wickets down. In doing this they owed nearly everything to Hobbs and Rhodes, who opened the innings by getting 112 together. After rain the players were out again just before half-past four, and for a time the wicket was too wet to be difficult. Hobbs took full advantage, hitting all-round with delightful skill. At 112, Rhodes, from a quick-rising ball, was caught at the wicket. His fine innings of 59 was marked by the strangest contrasts, the latter portion being as cautious as the first part was brilliant. The pitch had become very treacherous when Spooner went in, and he never looked at all comfortable. With Fry as his next partner, Hobbs hit away splendidly, completing his hundred soon after six o'clock. However, at 197, he was bowled. Very rarely has he shown finer cricket on a difficult wicket. Without being at all rash, he seemed to seize every opportunity of scoring. Batting for two hours and three-quarters, he hit 15 fours, one three, and eight twos. The Australians did a lot of smart work in the field and, generally speaking, their bowling was good. During the afternoon Hazlitt's delivery gave rise to a great deal of discussion, two famous cricketers, who were in the pavilion, condemning it in no measured terms.

On Tuesday, a sharp shower delayed the start until nearly half-past 11. Fry and Woolley added 30 runs, and then rain drove the players from the field. At first little more than a drizzle, the downpour became much heavier, and not another ball could be bowled during the day.

Wednesday produced some remarkable play. Being quite secure against any risk of defeat, the Englishmen made a desperate effort to force a win, but the Australian batting was too good for them, and, moreover, the wicket rolled out a great deal easier than expected. There was a great deal of excitement when, soon after 12 o'clock, the Australians went in to bat. It soon became evident that England had little hope of winning. Kelleway set himself to play an absolutely defensive game, being at the wickets more than half an hour before he made a run. There was no lack of interest in the cricket after luncheon, Macartney playing, perhaps, the finest innings seen at Lord's during the season. He showed himself master of nearly every scoring stroke, and though playing rather a daring game he never made a false hit. He missed his hundred by a single run, a catch on the leg side by the wicket keeper, standing back to Foster's bowling, getting rid of him at 173. He hit 13 fours.

Toss: England. **England 310-7 dec.** (J. B. Hobbs 107, W. Rhodes 59);
Australia 282-7 (C. Kelleway 61, C. G. Macartney 99).

Second Test
At Manchester, July 29, 30, 31, 1912. Drawn.

This proved an even greater disappointment than the First Test, rain spoiling everything. Play on the first day did not begin until close upon three o'clock; cricket on Tuesday was impossible until five o'clock and on the third day not a ball could be bowled.

In getting 203 – by no means a bad total on a dreadfully soft wicket – England owed nearly everything to Rhodes, who played with great skill and self-restraint. Before he had made a run he gave a chance to Hazlitt at point off Whitty's bowling – cutting a long-hop rather hard, but straight to the fieldsman – and when 70 he might have been caught at slip by Jennings, but these were the only real blemishes in a remarkable innings. Rhodes was 92 at the close of Monday's play, and everyone hoped when at last cricket became practicable on Tuesday he would reach his hundred. As it happened, however, he was out without making another run.

Hearne was badly missed by Whitty at mid-on when he had made a single. For this blunder the Australians had to pay rather dearly, as though Hearne did not personally profit much by his escape, he remained in with Rhodes while the total was being carried from 83 to 140.

England lost six wickets for 185 on Monday afternoon, but on the muddy pitch on Tuesday no one could get the ball away, Hazlitt bowling six overs and five balls for 18 runs and three wickets, and Whitty six overs for no runs and one wicket. The weather kept fine during Tuesday night, and though a little rain fell in the morning there was hope of play at half-past 11, the wicket being rolled, and the bell rung. However, rain set in again. At first it was only a drizzle, but such a heavy downfall followed that at quarter-past one the match was abandoned.

Toss: England. **England 203** (W. Rhodes 92, G. R. Hazlitt 4-77, W. J. Whitty 4-43); **Australia 14-0.**

Third Test

At The Oval, August 19, 20, 21, 22, 1912. England won by 244 runs.

Whatever might be said about last season's cricket as a whole, the closing Test match afforded convincing evidence of the enduring popularity of cricket. The match had much to contend against in the way of unseasonable weather, but in the course of the four days 44,717 paid for admission at the turnstiles.

No definite pronouncement had been made at the beginning of the season as to the method of deciding the Triangular Tournament, but almost at the last moment it was stated that the side successful at The Oval would be the winners, the match being played out to a finish even if it lasted a week. This involved some disadvantage to the Englishmen, who had beaten the South Africans three times whereas the Australians had gained two victories and played a rather unfavourable draw. Thus, if England had been beaten at The Oval, they would have been placed second in the Tournament with the same number of wins as Australia.

However, as it turned out no question arose, England gaining an easy victory at the finish. They had the best of luck as regards the condition of the ground, but their victory was gained by splendid all-round cricket. On the morning of the match a change had to be made in the England XI, Hayes, who was suffering from a cold, giving way to J. W. H. T. Douglas. No place had been found for Douglas in any of the previous Tests, but he is by temperament so much the man for a big occasion, that he might well have been picked for the whole series. That the public shared this view was proved when he went in to bat, the crowd giving him an overwhelming welcome.

Heavy rain on Sunday night had affected The Oval to such an extent that the start had to be delayed until 12 o'clock. At that time the sun was shining, but Fry had no hesitation in taking first innings. His policy met with brilliant success, England gaining an advantage that was never wholly lost. At the drawing of stumps England's score stood at 233 for eight – in the circumstances a wonderfully good start.

Hobbs and Rhodes once more proved an incomparable pair to open the innings in a big match. They scored 107 for the first wicket. This, on a pitch of varying pace and against superb fielding, was a great achievement. Hobbs made 60 before being caught at the wicket. Though never rash he seized every chance of getting runs, pulling the short balls with absolute certainty. Spooner was out to a wonderful catch at short leg, Hazlitt throwing himself forward and taking a hard hit close to the ground with his left hand, and then things went so badly that at the tea interval five wickets were down for 144. Rhodes was batting for three hours, his watchful defence being invaluable. After tea Woolley, with excellent help from Douglas and Foster, more than made up England's lost ground, the sixth and seventh wickets adding 33 runs each. Woolley, who was out just on the call of time, showed the finest hitting of the day, his splendid innings of 62 including 11 fours.

Cricket on Tuesday was restricted to little more than an hour and a half. England's innings was quickly finished off for 245, and the Australians scored 51 for two, Kelleway and Bardsley playing with great judgment after Gregory and Macartney had failed.

On the third day the weather was again very unfavourable. An extraordinary change came over the game from the moment Kelleway and Bardsley were separated. The pitch had become extremely treacherous and the last seven wickets actually went down for 21. The turning-point came with a change of bowling, Woolley going on at the pavilion wicket and Barnes crossing to the other end. Kelleway was lbw in Woolley's second over, and thenceforward the batsmen were helpless. Kelleway was in nearly two hours, his defence all that time being impregnable. Bardsley was bowled by a remarkable ball from Barnes. As it pitched well outside his leg stump he let it alone, but he failed to cover the whole of the wicket, and the ball turning very sharply hit the leg stump. After the eventful change Woolley took five wickets for 22 runs, and Barnes three wickets for ten runs.

Holding a lead of 134, England went in after luncheon. The wicket was very treacherous, the light bad, and rain evidently near at hand. A disastrous start was made, Rhodes being bowled with the score at seven, and Spooner caught at slip from the next ball. Had play gone on without interruption the bowlers would probably have had everything their own way, but when two runs had been added down came the rain. When at four o'clock the players came out again the pitch was considerably easier than before. So steady was the bowling, however, that at one point eight overs produced only one hit – a snick for three by Fry. Then the pace of the run-getting improved again, though Hobbs, spraining a muscle in his thigh, became rather lame. Hobbs fell to a smart catch at point at 51, having as in his first innings played splendid cricket. Woolley was bowled at 56, and when, on a second appeal against the light, play ceased for the day the score was 64 for four. Fry's defence, under trying conditions, was beyond all praise.

As there was no likelihood of the pitch ever being good the Englishmen – leading by 198 and having six wickets in hand – entered upon the fourth day's play without much anxiety. To all intents and purposes they had the game in their hands. At first the wicket was easy enough and by free hitting the score was carried from 64 to 91. Then Hazlitt went on and from the first ball he bowled Hearne was caught at short leg. However, Fry found another excellent partner in Douglas, and though the pitch, as it dried, naturally became difficult, the total at lunch-time had reached 149. Had the match been limited to four days Fry would have declared at once, but with two more days before him there seemed no need to run the slightest risk. As it happened the innings was quickly finished off for 175, Hazlitt going on in place of Whitty at 167, and taking the last five wickets at the cost of a single run. Subsequent events proved that his astounding success was for England a blessing in disguise, as it led to victory before the end of the day. For once in the Test matches Fry was his true self, his innings of 79 being a masterpiece of skilful defence.

The Australians wanted 310 to win – practically an impossible task on such a damaged wicket. In the second over, before a run had been scored, Kelleway was caught at a sort of backward point, Douglas managing to hold the ball at about the sixth attempt. Then came some startling cricket. Jennings punished Barnes for two fours to leg and Macartney hit so brilliantly that, though Woolley bowled in place of Barnes, runs were put on at an alarming pace. Everyone felt, however, that the pace could not last. At 46 Jennings was caught at extra cover point from a skyer, and at the same total Dean, with a fine ball, clean-bowled Macartney.

A disaster that followed took all the heart out of the Australians. Bardsley, starting for a short run, seemed to take things easily, and had his wicket thrown down from cover point – an amazing piece of work by Hobbs. There was a lot of discussion about the decision, several famous cricketers in the pavilion expressing a positive opinion that Bardsley was not out. However, Moss, the umpire, said that he had no doubt whatever on the point.

Bardsley's downfall meant the end of the game. Though very difficult, the pitch was not so bad as to excuse the utter feebleness of the subsequent batting. Three more wickets fell with the score at 51, and the innings was over for 65, England winning the match by 244 runs. If it had not been finished on the fourth day the match must have ended in a draw, as rain fell incessantly on the Friday and Saturday.

Toss: England. **England 245** (J. B. Hobbs 66, F. E. Woolley 62, W. J. Whitty 4-69, R. B. Minnett 4-34) **and 175** (C. B. Fry 79, G. R. Hazlitt 7-25); **Australia 111** (S. F. Barnes 5-30, F. E. Woolley 5-29) **and 65** (H. Dean 4-19, F. E. Woolley 5-20).

NOTES BY THE EDITOR Sydney Pardon, 1913

The Fates fought against the Triangular Tournament. Such a combination of adverse conditions could hardly have been imagined. To begin with, the Australians, who had been allowed to have everything their own way in choosing the time for the first trial of Sir Abe Bailey's ambitious scheme, quarrelled so bitterly among themselves that half their best players were left at home. In the second place the South Africans fell a good way below their form of 1907 and, to crown everything, we had one of the most appalling summers ever known, even in England.

In the circumstances it was not surprising that the Tournament, as a public attraction, failed to realise the expectations of its supporters. The result is that the experiment is not likely to be repeated for many years to come – perhaps not in this generation. Personally I could never get up any real enthusiasm for the Triangular scheme. To my mind there always seemed a great danger in crowding so much first-class cricket into a season of little more than four months. Still I am bound to admit that, if we had had a fine summer and the Australians had sent over their best team, the Test matches themselves, despite the weakness of the South Africans, would have proved a substantial success.

It is no business of mine to go into details with regard to the squabbles and quarrels in Australia. In the special circumstances I think all personal considerations should have been put aside and made subordinate to the prime need of sending over Australia's best men. However, all attempts at compromise failed. The personal differences went too deep to admit of adjustment. The Board of Control carried its point, but as regards the prestige of Australian cricket the victory was dearly won. It says much for the strength of Australia at the present time that with half a dozen crack players left behind such a good team could be sent to England, but there was no way of making up for the absence of Trumper, Armstrong, Ransford, Cotter and Hill. Even Australia cannot manufacture champion players at five minutes' notice. I venture to predict that when the Australians pay us their next visit they will send over their strongest team. In saying this, I am thinking far less of patriotic considerations than of the stern force of money.

Following the triumph in Australia during the winter, victory in the Triangular Tournament left England unquestionably at the top of the tree. Success did not mean so much as it would have done if Australia had been fully represented, but for that there was no help.

Obituary – Victor Trumper

Sydney Pardon, 1916

Victor Trumper died at Sydney on June 28, 1915. Of all the great Australian batsmen he was by general consent the best and most brilliant. No one else among the famous group, from Charles Bannerman 39 years ago to Bardsley and Macartney at the present time, had quite such remarkable powers. Trumper at the zenith of his fame challenged comparison with Ranjitsinhji. He was great under all conditions of weather and ground. He could play quite an orthodox game when he wished to, but it was his ability to make big scores when orthodox methods were unavailing that lifted him above his fellows.

For this reason Trumper was, in proportion, more to be feared on treacherous wickets than on fast, true ones. No matter how bad the pitch might be from the combined effects of rain and sunshine, he was quite likely to get 50 runs, his skill in pulling good-length balls amounting to genius. Of this fact our English bowlers had convincing evidence day after day during the season of 1902. Trumper paid four visits to this country – in 1899, 1902, 1905 and 1909 – but it was in 1902 that he reached his highest point. In that summer of wretched weather he scored 2,570 runs in 35 matches for the Australian team, with the wonderful average, in the circumstances, of 48. He was as consistent as he was brilliant, and did not owe his average to a few exceptional scores. Of 11 innings of over a hundred, the biggest was 128. Trumper did not again touch the same level in this country.

Trumper was the most popular Australian cricketer of his time. A match played for his benefit – between New South Wales and the Rest of Australia – at Sydney in February, 1913, produced gate-money and donations of nearly £3,000. Trumper was in his 38th year. He had been in bad health for some little time, and the latest accounts of his condition received in this country were so discouraging as to prepare his friends for the worst. He died of Bright's Disease. Trumper was never spoilt by success in the cricket field. When his name was in everyone's mouth he remained as modest and unaffected as on the day he first set foot in England.

The Roaring Twenties:
1920–21 to 1928–29

When cricket picked up the threads after the 1914–18 War, the Australian Board was keen to demonstrate a return to normality and renew the battle for the Ashes. The English authorities were less sure, thinking that their players were not yet ready for such a battle, but eventually agreed to send a team Down Under in 1920–21.

MCC's fears were justified, as England were hammered 5–0, the only Ashes "white-wash" until 2006–07. It was something of a patchwork England side, but nonetheless they were unfortunate to run up against one of the great Australian combinations, uncompromisingly led by Warwick Armstrong, the hulking pre-war veteran (he now weighed in at more than 20 stone). Armstrong also had at his disposal arguably Test cricket's first pair of shock fast bowlers, Jack Gregory and Ted McDonald, backed up by a whimsical leg-spinner in Arthur Mailey and a battery of very fine batsmen. Their fielding, led by Clarence "Nip" Pellew, was also a cut above the previous norm.

Unluckily for England, they also had to host those same Australians in the home summer of 1921, and the losing streak extended to eight Tests before that old reliable, bad weather at Old Trafford, helped stop the rot. Gregory and McDonald were among the stars of the season – both of them were chosen as *Wisden* Cricketers of the Year, as was their team-mate Charles Macartney, the pick of the batsmen – while England vainly tried a cast of thousands (well, 30, a record for any series) in the five Tests.

It seemed as if England were a million miles away from winning the Ashes, a feeling backed up when largely the same Australian team (minus Armstrong, who had finally retired) outgunned Arthur Gilligan's 1924–25 tourists 4–1 in a high-scoring series. But it wasn't all doom and gloom for England: they had an opening pair, in Jack Hobbs and Herbert Sutcliffe, to rank with the best of them all, while the lion-hearted efforts of Maurice Tate, who took 38 wickets and got through 316 eight-ball overs at a lively fast-medium, were another feature of the series that augured well for the future.

The 1926 series saw a sea-change. Some of the Australians who had kick-started the post-war era were now past their best: Gregory, for example, struggled for fitness and made almost no impact. It was a wet summer, and the teams went to the final Test at The Oval all square at 0–0. England changed their captain, bringing in the dashing Kent amateur Percy Chapman, and included the 48-year-old Wilfred Rhodes, who had made his debut in W. G. Grace's last Test in 1899, and was now a selector himself. In accordance with all the finest fairytales, Rhodes took six wickets, four of them as Australia collapsed in their second innings. England sailed home by 289 runs, and reclaimed the Ashes.

So England were in the ascendancy, and by the next series in 1928–29 they were boosted by the arrival of Walter Hammond, who made a case to be considered the best batsman in the world with 905 runs in the series (a short-lived record) including success-ive innings of 251 and 200, followed by twin centuries in the Adelaide Test. With Sutcliffe and the ageless Hobbs still producing the goods at the top of the order, it was England's turn to man the steamroller, and they won the first three Tests by wide margins. The fourth was closer – England won it by just 12 runs – and Australia won the last one, but England still won the series 4–1, and looked set for a period of Ashes dominance.

But appearances can be deceptive. There was a cloud on the English horizon. In the First Test of 1928–29, Australia had given a first cap to a promising 20-year-old batsman from up-country New South Wales. He only scored 18 and 1 in a massive defeat, and was left out of the next Test. It was the only time Donald Bradman was dropped from any cricket team, anywhere, and he made sure it wouldn't happen again with 79 and 112 when he was swiftly recalled for the Third Test at Melbourne. The man who would dominate Test cricket for the next 20 years had arrived.   S. L.

AUSTRALIA V ENGLAND 1920–21

The tour of MCC's team in the winter of 1920–21 resulted in disaster, all the Test matches being easily won by Australia. Never before in the history of English or Australian trips since Test matches were first played had one side shown such an overwhelming superiority. As the news came to hand of defeat after defeat people thought the Englishmen must be playing very badly. Not till the Australians came here in the summer and beat us three times in succession on our own grounds did we fully realise the strength of the combination that had set up such a record. MCC were very doubtful as to the wisdom of renewing the interchange of visits so soon, feeling that English cricket had not had time to regain its pre-war standard, and it will be remembered that they declined a pressing invitation to send out a team in the winter of 1919–20. However, in face of Australia's keen desire, they could not insist on further delay. That the Australian authorities had judged the situation rightly was proved by results. In a financial sense the tour was an immense success, the Test matches attracting bigger crowds than ever.

The general feeling when the team left home was one of full confidence in the batting – quite justified by the form shown in 1920 – but grave doubt as to the bowling on Australian wickets. It was clear, moreover, that the side would be short of first-rate outfields. On this point MCC were at fault, but otherwise they chose wisely from the players available. The chief cause of failure was the bowling, the worst fears as to its lack of quality being borne out. Parkin was the man on whom we most depended, and once or twice he did good work, but his 16 Test wickets cost him nearly 42 runs apiece. Fender, who played in three of the matches, came out best with 12 wickets for some-thing over 34 each. It must be said, however, that in a summer of continuous sunshine – remarkable even for Australia – the bowlers received no help.

The broad fact remains that the Australians had a vast superiority in bowling – a superiority that made the difference in batting seem greater than it really was. Still, our batting on the big occasions fell far short of what might reasonably have been expected. Hobbs and Douglas alone were up to their form at home. No doubt the finest display was Hobbs's 122 at Melbourne in the New Year match when rain had for the time being spoilt the wicket.

The tour on the whole passed off very smoothly, but a good deal of friction was caused by cable messages sent home to the *Daily Express* by Mr E. R. Wilson. This led to a resolution passed at the annual meeting of the Marylebone Club in May deprecating the reporting of matches by the players concerned in them.

First Test

At Sydney, December 17, 18, 20, 21, 22, 1920. Australia won by 377 runs.

Though the First Test ended in disaster for them, the Englishmen started uncommonly well, bowling and fielding so finely that the Australians took the whole of the first afternoon to score 250 for eight. The great chance for England came the next day, but it was hopelessly missed. In facing a modest total of 267 the team were in a far better position than they could have expected, and when 140 went up with only three men out the prospect was very hopeful. So dismally did the batting collapse, however, that the innings was all over for 190. Hobbs and Woolley alone showed much ability to deal with the skilful bowling, Hendren, in scoring his 28, being let off in the slips when he had made a single. For the failure in batting there was no forgiveness. Going in again with a lead of 77 the Australians before the drawing of stumps on the second day scored 46 without loss, and on Monday they carried their total to 332 for five. Following up his 70 in the first innings Collins gave a splendid display, hitting ten fours and completing his hundred in just over three hours and a half. Macartney, after a curiously slow start, was very brilliant. The most remarkable cricket of the match came on the fourth day, Armstrong playing a magnificent innings. Getting runs at the rate of 45 an hour, he scored 158 in less than three hours and a half out of the 246 put on while he was in. His hits included 17 fours, most of them splendid drives. The Englishmen were left with the impossible task of getting 659 to win and, considering their hopeless position, they did not do badly to score 281.

Toss: Australia. **Australia 267** (H. L. Collins 70) **and 581** (H. L. Collins 104, W. Bardsley 57, C. G. Macartney 69, J. M. Taylor 51, C. Kelleway 78, W. W. Armstrong 158); **England 190** (F. E. Woolley 52) **and 281** (J. B. Hobbs 59, J. W. Hearne 57, E. H. Hendren 56).

CRICKETER OF THE YEAR – J. M. GREGORY   Sydney Pardon, 1922

J. M. Gregory, the greatest match-winning force among the cricketers now before the public, was literally discovered during the tour of the Australian Imperial Forces team in this country in 1919. Though a member of a famous cricket family, he did nothing in his young days to foreshadow the fame that has come to him. In fact, he was not seen at all in matches of public interest. However, the tour of 1919 quickly revealed him as an all-round player of limitless possibilities. He took 131 wickets for just over 16 runs each, and scored 942 runs with an average of 29. English cricketers were impressed at once with the exceptional pace of his bowling. He was certainly faster than anyone else that season, and with his great height and long run he intimidated batsmen to an extent not seen in this country since Knox was at his deadliest in 1906.

As a right-handed bowler and left-handed batsman he was rather an unusual combination. He wound up the tour with some remarkable bowling at Scarborough and made such an impression that one member of C. I. Thornton's XI described him as probably a Test match-winner. This opinion has been verified up to the hilt. He more than confirmed his form when he got back to Australia, scoring 122 and 102 for the Imperial Forces team against New South Wales, and bowling with great effect.

Second Test

At Melbourne, December 31, 1920, January 1, 3, 4, 1921. Australia won by an innings and 91 runs.

In the Second Test the Englishmen suffered defeat by an innings. It is not at all likely that in any circumstances they would have won the game in face of a total of 499, but they had dreadful luck in having to bat on a wicket more or less ruined by rain. Hearne was taken ill after the first day, and no more was seen of him during the tour. Macartney was kept out of the match by gastritis. The Australians scored 282 for six on Friday, and were batting about seven hours and a half, the second afternoon being far advanced when their innings ended. Bardsley and Collins gave their side a capital start by scoring 116 together for the first wicket, but the chief batting honours were divided by Pellew and Gregory.

Not out 33 on the first day, Pellew scored his 116 in just over three hours, his play being in every way admirable. He and Gregory put on 173 in less than two hours for the eighth wicket. Gregory was very brilliant, hitting 12 fours. England began badly, two wickets being down for 32, but Hendren stayed with Hobbs, and at the drawing of stumps the score was 93. Drenching rain set in soon after midnight, and early on Sunday the wicket was under water. However, play was quite practicable on Monday, and in scoring his 122 under the altered conditions Hobbs played, from the English point of view, the finest innings of the tour. He was batting, in all, for three hours and a half. Hendren, playing with extreme care, helped Hobbs to put on 142, but no one else did much against Gregory's bowling. Following on, the Englishmen lost five wickets before time was called, and on the fourth day the match was soon over.

Toss: Australia. **Australia 499** (H. L. Collins 64, W. Bardsley 51, J. M. Taylor 68, C. E. Pellew 116, J. M. Gregory 100); **England 251** (J. B. Hobbs 122, E. H. Hendren 67, J. M. Gregory 7-69) **and 157** (F. E. Woolley 50, W. W. Armstrong 4-26).

Third Test

At Adelaide, January 14, 15, 17, 18, 19, 20, 1921. Australia won by 119 runs.

In an extraordinary game which lasted six days and produced an aggregate of 1,753 runs, England suffered defeat by a margin of 119, but inasmuch as they ran up totals of 447 and 370 the result, though it settled the question of the rubber, said a great deal for the batting strength of the side. On the first day the Australians scored 313 for seven but they would no doubt have been all out if some chances after lunch had been accepted. Four wickets were down for 96, but thenceforward the batting asserted itself. In first and out seventh, Collins obtained his 162 in something over four hours and a quarter. He played finely and hit 19 fours but he had quite his share of good fortune.

Saturday was a very good day for the Englishmen as after Parkin, by capital bowling, had finished off Australia's innings, they scored 233 for the loss of four wickets. Woolley played the best and most attractive cricket. On the following day he was hurt by a ball from Gregory and soon fell to a catch in the slips. Russell played wonderfully well, and with Douglas's help secured a useful lead on the first innings. In getting his 135 not out, he was at the wickets four hours and ten minutes, hitting a six and 12 fours. Three Australian wickets went down for 71 before the drawing of stumps, England finishing the third day in a very flattering position. Kelleway, not out 19, was missed at slip by Fender off Howell's bowling before he had made a run and for this blunder, as events turned out, a terribly high price had to be paid.

On the fourth day the Australians carried their score to 364 and lost only two more wickets. The batting of Kelleway and Armstrong presented a marked contrast. Kelleway, still in at the end of the afternoon with 115 to his credit, played a stonewall game, but Armstrong was superb, scoring 121 out of 194 runs made while he was at the wickets.

On Wednesday the English bowling was again completely mastered. Pellew hit brilliantly for over two hours, his 104 including 13 fours, and Gregory was almost as vigorous. Kelleway's innings lasted just upon seven hours. England required 490 to win and, as the wicket remained sound, the task was not quite impossible. However, as might have been expected, it proved too heavy. Hobbs was not out 50 at the close, and so long as he stayed in on the following day there was just a chance. He was bowled by Gregory soon after luncheon, being out third wicket down at 183. His innings, which extended over two hours and a half, was one of the finest he played during the tour. Woolley failed and after that the result, despite some excellent batting, always looked a certainty.

Toss: Australia. **Australia 354** (H. L. Collins 162, W. A. S. Oldfield 50, C. H. Parkin 5-60) **and 582** (C. Kelleway 147, W. W. Armstrong 121, C. E. Pellew 104, J. M. Gregory 78*, H. Howell 4-115); **England 447** (J. W. H. Makepeace 60, F. E. Woolley 79, C. A. G. Russell 135*, J. W. H. T. Douglas 60, A. A. Mailey 5-160) **and 370** (J. B. Hobbs 123, E. H. Hendren 51, C. A. G. Russell 59, A. A. Mailey 5-142).

Fourth Test

At Melbourne, February 11, 12, 14, 15, 16, 1921. Australia won by eight wickets.

The fact of the rubber having already been won by Australia did not seem to affect the interest taken in the Fourth Test. Owing to an injured thumb Russell could not play, but the loss of his batting was far outweighed by the absence, through illness, of Macartney from the Australian XI. For the first time in the series Douglas won the toss, but his side did not make the most of their good fortune in batting first on a perfect pitch. They took the whole of the first day to score 270 for six, and on Saturday the innings was quickly finished off. Makepeace, who played wonderfully well and did not give a chance in his 117, had a good deal to say when he returned to England about the difficulty he experienced in getting runs against the excellent bowling and matchless fielding.

On a Melbourne wicket in fine weather a total of 284 was obviously not good enough. Collins and Bardsley gave Australia a good start by scoring 117 together, but when six wickets had fallen for 153 the position suggested a great fight. It was mainly due to Armstrong that a lead of 105 was obtained. Though suffering from a recurrence of malaria he played a great innings, being in for nearly three hours and a half. He and Gregory added a hundred runs during their partnership.

On going in for the second time the Englishmen gave a good display, but in order to have a real chance of winning they would have required at least another 150 runs. The task of getting 211 was easily accomplished, Ryder and Gregory hitting off the last 130 runs together. It was not one of Gregory's matches as a bowler, but by scoring 77 and 76 not out he had a big share in the victory. Mailey, though at times freely punished, had a triumph, taking 13 wickets – nine in the second innings.

Toss: England. **England 284** (J. W. H. Makepeace 117, J. W. H. T. Douglas 50, A. A. Mailey 4-115) **and 315** (W. Rhodes 73, J. W. H. Makepeace 54, J. W. H. T. Douglas 60, P. G. H. Fender 59, A. A. Mailey 9-121); **Australia 389** (H. L. Collins 59, W. Bardsley 56, J. M. Gregory 77, W. W. Armstrong 123*, P. G. H. Fender 5 122) **and 211-2** (J. Ryder 52*, J. M. Gregory 76*).

Fifth Test

At Sydney, February 25, 26, 28, March 1, 1921. Australia won by nine wickets.

Australia won the last Test match by nine wickets, completely outplaying their opponents, and with their fifth victory in one season set up a record that may never be beaten. Whatever remote chance the Englishmen might have had was gone when on batting first they were got rid of for 204. From such a start – on the Sydney ground in fine weather – there was little hope of recovery. Hobbs ought not to have played, his injured thigh still causing him a great deal of trouble, and in the circumstances he did well to score 40 and 34.

The Australians began by losing Collins and Bardsley for 22 runs, but at the end of the first day they had carried their score to 70 and thenceforward they were always winning. Macartney played a magnificent innings – his first hundred in Test cricket against England. He was batting for just over four hours, hitting 20 fours in his 170. Gregory also played very finely, his partnership with Macartney for the fourth wicket putting on 198 and going far towards deciding the result of the match.

Two wickets – those of Woolley and Makepeace – fell for 24 runs in England's second innings before the drawing of stumps on Saturday, and six were down for 91. The game seemed all over, but Douglas withstood the bowling for nearly two hours and three-quarters and it was not till early on the fourth day that the end was reached. Making amends for failure in the first innings, Bardsley and Collins put on 91 together when the Australians went in to get 93. Taking seven wickets Mailey brought his number in the five Test matches up to 36. This beat Barnes's 34 in the tour of MCC's team in 1911-12.

Toss: England. **England 204** (F. E. Woolley 53, C. Kelleway 4-27) **and 280** (J. W. H. T. Douglas 68 A. A. Mailey 5-119); **Australia 392** (C. G. Macartney 170, J. M. Gregory 93, P. G. H. Fender 5-90) **and 93-1** (W. Bardsley 50*).

ENGLAND v AUSTRALIA 1921   Sydney Pardon

The Australians had a wonderful tour. One need not hesitate to say that Armstrong had a great side. One critic – usually the soundest of judges – went so far as to say that their bowling was weaker than that of almost any previous team from Australia. This, in face of the repeated failures of our batting, was rather an astonishing pronouncement. I am

The Big Ship: Warwick Armstrong (left), captain in the Ashes whitewash of 1920–21, with Victor Trumper.

inclined, personally, to take perhaps too flattering a view of them. They seemed to me to be fully equipped at every point for matches on fast wickets, and even if English cricket had been up to its pre-war standard I think they would have been terribly hard to beat. It was, of course, a strong testimony in their favour that they had won all the Test matches at home against MCC's team. That remarkable series of victories told us plainly what we should have to face.

Given fine weather the Australians as a side had not a weak point of any kind. They could all get runs; their fielding was magnificent; and above all they possessed in Gregory and McDonald two very fast bowlers of the highest class. Never before have English batsmen been so demoralised by great pace. The Test matches at Nottingham and Lord's were both practically lost in the first half-hour. I am sure that some of our batsmen, knowing they would have to face Gregory, were out before they went in. Since Knox bowled his fastest in 1906 I have never seen batsmen so obviously intimidated. McDonald struck one as being really the finer bowler of the two, but Gregory was by far the more alarming.

As to the collective excellence of the Australian batting the figures speak for themselves. Of the 15 players all but two could show an average for the whole tour of over 20, ranging from Macartney's 58 to Carter's 21. Bardsley hit up nine hundreds and Macartney eight, the latter's 345 against Nottingham being the highest score of the season and the highest ever obtained by an Australian batsman in this country.

People might argue that the Australian bowling and batting were not really quite so good as the figures make them out to be, but as to the fielding there could not be two opinions. Never day after day on hard wickets has one seen such run-saving. Within my experience there has never been a combination so perfect. Pellew was generally the most conspicuous figure, his speed in chasing the ball being exceptional.

First Test

At Nottingham, May 28, 30, 1921. Australia won by ten wickets.

Never in the history of Test matches in this country has English cricket been made to look quite so poor as in the first game of the series. We were not merely beaten but overwhelmed, the Australians showing a complete superiority at every point except wicket-keeping. The match ended on the second afternoon.

Whatever chance England might have had was lost at the start. Douglas won the toss, but any advantage that might have been accrued by batting first in the unsettled weather was soon discounted, three wickets falling for 18 to Gregory's very fast and rather intimidating bowling. Knight was caught by the wicket-keeper in nibbling at a ball on the off side, Ernest Tyldesley was out first ball, chopping an extra-quick one on to the stumps, and Hendren was beaten by a fine ball that broke far too quickly for him. From this dreadful beginning there was no recovery. After Hendren left England were always playing a losing game. They had one piece of bad luck, Woolley when nicely set being out to a marvellous catch by Hendry at second slip. The innings was all over for a paltry 112, the fast bowlers always looking masters of the situation. Gregory was the main cause of the downfall, but McDonald bowled just as well.

Cricket of a very different character was seen when the Australians went in. There had been some showers, but the pitch dried gradually under the influence of the wind.

Howell, keeping up a good pace, could not make the ball get up sufficiently high to cause the batsmen trouble, but the England bowling as a whole, though far from deadly, left little room for fault-finding, Richmond's googlies having to be very carefully watched. Bardsley played in something like his best form for two hours and a half, and at the call of time the Australians, with four wickets in hand, held the comfortable lead of 55.

A lot of rain fell during Saturday night, and no one could tell what would happen when on Monday the match was resumed. Douglas very properly put on Rhodes and Woolley, but the left-handed bowlers did not make the most of the conditions. With every run of value they sent down too many balls that asked to be hit, and Carter was quick to punish them. The result was that the Australian score reached 232, or 120 ahead. This was a formidable balance to face, and at no time did England look like making anything of a fight. Holmes was caught at short mid-on at 23, and after lunch at 41 Ernest Tyldesley was out in a desperately unlucky way. In trying to score from a fast long-hop he received a severe blow in the face, and the ball dribbled on to the wicket. Tyldesley was helped off, but the injury happily proved less serious than was feared. Another tragedy for England occurred at 60, Knight being run out – so far as one could tell through no fault of his own. Knight's 38 was perhaps the best display of batting given for England in a lamentable match. On no other occasion did he play the Australian bowling half so well.

The arrears were hit off with four wickets in hand, but the innings ended for 147. Woolley played finely, but the keen bowling and fielding kept him so quiet that he took an hour and three-quarters to get his 34. It struck one that with his advantages of height and reach he might well have ventured on a bolder game against Armstrong. He once drove him to the boundary, but in a long series of overs that was all.

Toss: England. **England 112** (J. M. Gregory 6-58) **and 147** (E. A. McDonald 5-32); **Australia 232** (W. Bardsley 66) **and 30-0**.

CRICKETER OF THE YEAR – E. A. McDONALD   Sydney Pardon, 1922

E. A. McDonald, whose doings in England last season earned him a place among the great Australian bowlers, was born in Tasmania on January 6, 1892. He played no cricket in his schooldays. He first became associated with the game when playing for West Launceston and was always a bowler. His powers were perhaps rather slow to ripen and, being still very young, he had not taken anything like a high position when the MCC's team visited Australia in 1911–12.

He jumped into fame some years later by means of an extraordinary performance for Victoria at Sydney in January 1919. In the first innings of New South Wales, when there was nothing in the condition of the ground to help him, he took eight wickets – six of them bowled down – for 42. Still, he was not on the winning side. In the second innings the batsmen mastered him, NSW, with 386 to get, gaining an astonishing victory by six wickets. In the following season he bowled very well without doing anything out of the common, and though he played in three of the Test matches in 1920–21 there was nothing to prepare the English public for his brilliant success in this country.

In England, however, his position was assured from the start. He revealed his pace at the nets, and there was no doubt as to his exceptional class. It is scarcely an exaggeration to describe him as the best bowler of his type since Lockwood, combining as he does great speed with a fine command of length and very pronounced spin. The English batsmen who had to face him were unanimous in his praise. He is that greatest asset any team can have – a bowler difficult to play on the most perfect wickets.

Second Test

At Lord's, June 11, 13, 14, 1921. Australia won by eight wickets.

The Englishmen were not disgraced as at Nottingham, putting up indeed a more creditable fight in face of tremendous odds, but again suffered a heavy defeat, the Australians winning easily on the third afternoon. The match proved an enormous attraction, but on the Saturday the arrangements for dealing with the crowd proved inadequate, many ticket-holders being greatly delayed and inconvenienced in getting through the gates. MCC came in for some sharp criticism.

In choosing the England XI the selection committee made drastic changes from the side that did so badly at Trent Bridge. They were disappointed with regard to C. B. Fry, who begged off on the ground that he did not feel satisfied with his form. Up to the last moment the exact constitution of the team was uncertain, and on the Saturday morning a surprise was sprung by bringing in Tennyson, who had not even been mentioned as a candidate. Dipper, one of the reserves, was chosen in preference to Holmes, who had been retained as twelfth man. A. J. Evans was played on the strength of his fine batting with MCC, but he did not prove a success, the occasion being perhaps rather too big for him. As a whole the selection did not turn out well, the fielding being indeed far below the Test match standard. To be quite candid, an England side so slow and generally inefficient had never previously been seen against Australia. The King honoured the match with his presence on the first day.

As at Nottingham, England won the toss, and again practically lost the match at the start, three wickets being down for 25 runs. Dipper was bowled in trying to turn McDonald; Knight from a ball very wide of the off stump gave the simplest of catches at slip, and Hendren was quite lost with one of McDonald's fastest. The result of these disasters was that the Englishmen at the end of half an hour found themselves playing an uphill game. Woolley and Douglas made a great effort, and as long as they stayed together there was hope of the position being retrieved. Things went well till at 108 Douglas mistimed a palpable long-hop that he tried to pull and was clean bowled. After Douglas left Woolley continued to play superb cricket, but he could get no one to help him. He was the last man to go, England being all out for 187. Nothing finer in English batting was seen last season than Woolley's 95. His innings lasted three hours and included ten fours.

The Australians went in with extreme confidence, and in little more than two hours scored 191 for three, thus leaving off with an overwhelming advantage. The English bowling had neither length nor spin, and from the first the batsmen made very light of it. Bardsley was at his best, and Macartney and Pellew hit away as they liked. The second day opened well for England, Bardsley being caught at slip with the score unaltered, and Armstrong bowled at 192. Here, however, our success ended, the

Australians hitting freely and cleanly to carry their score to 342. The bowling was up to a point far better than it had been on the Saturday, Parkin in particular sending down some splendid overs.

England had to go in against a balance of 155, and it was felt that the position was almost hopeless. Still, thanks chiefly to Woolley and Dipper, who put on 94, the arrears were cleared off soon after the tea interval with seven wickets in hand. Hopes were rising, but at 165 Woolley was out to a wonderful catch by Hendry at forward short leg. Woolley again missed his hundred, but his second innings was no less admirable than his first. His only mistake was a chance in the slips when 36. With Woolley out the bowlers soon re-asserted themselves. Tennyson hit vigorously after being missed by the wicket-keeper, and at the drawing of stumps England's score stood at 243 with eight wickets down.

Next morning Tennyson made a gallant effort, seizing every chance to score, but the innings was all over for 283. Tennyson hit ten fours, most of them powerful drives, and showed that he, at any rate, was not afraid of the fast bowlers. The Australians only required 129 to win – a trifling task for such a side on a pitch that showed scarcely any signs of wear. Bardsley and Andrews settled the matter by sending up 101 together.

Toss: England. **England 187** (F. E. Woolley 95, E. A. McDonald 4-58, A. A. Mailey 4-55) **and 283** (F. E. Woolley 93, L. H. Tennyson 74*, J. M. Gregory 4-76, E. A. McDonald 4-89); **Australia 342** (W. Bardsley 88, J. M. Gregory 52, F. J. Durston 4-102) **and 131-2** (W. Bardsley 63*).

Third Test

At Leeds, July 2, 4, 5, 1921. Australia won by 219 runs.

The Third Test ended in defeat for England, and so Australia won the rubber straight-away. It is not at all likely that in any circumstances the Australians would have been beaten, but England had horrible luck. Hobbs had sufficiently recovered from his leg troubles to take his place in the team, but he felt unwell before the match and after fielding for the greater part of the first afternoon he had to retire. He was found to be suffering from appendicitis. As if this misfortune were not enough, Tennyson, who had been made captain, split his hand badly while fielding on the Saturday, and though, as events turned out, he scored 63 and 36, he batted under great difficulties. Nor did trouble end here, as Brown was more or less disabled by the recurrence of an old injury, and was obliged to have a man run for him in the second innings.

There was great doubt up to the last moment as to the constitution of the England team. Hardinge, Ducat and Durston journeyed to Leeds on the previous afternoon, but when the final choice came Durston was left out and Parkin kept in. It is not easy to understand why the selection committee gave a place to Ducat. No one, so it was said, felt more surprised than the Surrey batsman himself, and he failed rather dismally.

On the first day the Australians put themselves on the high road to victory, scoring 407, and getting the best two English wickets – Woolley and Hearne – for 22. The early cricket rather flattered England, Bardsley being caught at slip at 22, and Andrews falling to an astonishing catch in the same spot, low down with his right hand, also by Woolley, at 45. After this, however, the Australians asserted themselves, Macartney and Pellew putting on 101 for the third wicket, and Macartney and Taylor 109 for the fourth.

The first of these long partnerships had only been in progress a few minutes when Tennyson met with his accident in trying to stop a terrific hit at extra cover point. Douglas took over the duties of captaincy. Gregory, Macartney and Hendry were out in quick succession, and with seven wickets down for 271 the Australians had done nothing exceptional. Macartney's 115 – the only hundred hit for Australia in the Test matches – was in many ways an excellent innings, but by no means a characteristic one. Macartney was often in trouble, and he had to play such a restrained game that he was at the wickets for three hours and ten minutes. Still, he was at times very brilliant, his hits including 13 fours. Any hope the Englishmen might have had of getting Australia out for 300 or so was soon destroyed, the eighth wicket adding 62 runs and the ninth 55. Armstrong at last played in something like his best form, driving with great power. Among the hits in his 77 were a six and ten fours.

England started on Monday under the most depressing conditions, it being known in the morning that Hobbs could take no further part in the match and had to undergo an immediate operation. In the circumstances it was quite a good performance to carry the overnight score to 259. When the fifth wicket fell at 57 the outlook seemed hopeless, but Douglas and Brown played a great game together and put on 97. After Brown left White was soon bowled by a yorker, but Tennyson, despite his bad hand, did wonders, seizing every chance and hitting so hard that he scored 50 in an hour. He and Douglas put on 87, and the last wicket saved the follow-on. Douglas played, perhaps, the innings of his life. He withstood the fine bowling for nearly four hours and was never at fault till Armstrong beat him.

Going in for the second time, the Australians found run-getting quite an easy matter, and at the drawing of stumps their score stood at 143 for two. On the third day Douglas could not field owing to the serious illness of his wife – suddenly attacked, like Hobbs, by appendicitis – but he was able to take his second innings. Armstrong declared at 273 for seven, leaving England to get 422 to win in four hours and 20 minutes. Andrews, who had played very finely, was bowled when only eight runs short of his hundred. There never seemed any hope of England escaping defeat, and in the end Australia won with an hour to spare. Brown played admirably and Tennyson hit again with great pluck, but it was all to no purpose.

Toss: Australia. **Australia 407** (C. G. Macartney 115, C. E. Pellew 52, J. M. Taylor 50, W. W. Armstrong 77, C. H. Parkin 4-106) **and 273-7 dec.** (T. J. E. Andrews 92); **England 259** (J. W. H. T. Douglas 75, G. Brown 57, L. H. Tennyson 63, E. A. McDonald 4-105) **and 202.**

Fourth Test

At Manchester, July 23, 25, 26, 1921. Drawn.

The Fourth Test brought with it a welcome change in the fortunes of the English team. They did not have the luck to win, but at least they had the satisfaction of getting all the best of a draw. This after the dismal experiences at Nottingham, Lord's and Leeds was no small consolation. The match had to be restricted to two days, a persistent drizzle making cricket impossible on the Saturday.

The selection committee had 15 men in readiness, and in the England team as finally decided on, there were various changes from the previous XIs, P. G. H. Fender,

Mead, Russell, Hallows and Parker coming in for the first time. Tennyson had the good fortune to win the toss and on a wicket that was far too soft and slow to be at all difficult England's batting at last asserted itself. Under the conditions that prevailed Gregory and McDonald held no terrors, and when Monday's play came to an end the score stood at 362 with only four men out.

An unfortunate and rather lamentable incident occurred during the afternoon. At ten minutes to six, with the total at 341, Tennyson came out on to the field and declared the innings closed, being quite forgetful of the fact that under Law 55, as amended by MCC in 1914, he had no power to do so. The first day having been a blank, the fixture became a two-day match and the declaration could not be made later than an hour and 40 minutes before time, so Tennyson was just an hour too late. It was strange that no one in the pavilion remembered the existing law sufficiently well to save him such a blunder. Armstrong signalled to his men to remain on the field, but eventually they as well as the umpires followed Tyldesley and Fender to the pavilion. A little argument soon put the matter right, play continuing after an interval of a little more than 20 minutes. The general confusion led to another breach of the laws, for on a fresh start being made Armstrong, who had bowled the last over, sent down the next.

England got off the mark very well in the morning, Brown and Russell sending up 65 for the first wicket, and there were no failures. Russell had the extreme satisfaction of getting a hundred and played for the most part exceedingly well. He was favoured by fortune, however, being missed in the slips when he had made six, and again when 85, Armstrong in both cases being the offending fieldsman. Apart from these chances Russell's innings, which extended over four hours, left no room for fault-finding. It was stated that 81 of his 101 runs were scored on the on side. Woolley played beautifully, but Mead, with his side in a very strong position, carried caution to an extreme. By far the most attractive batting was that of Tyldesley, who up to the time of the mistaken declaration gave a dazzling display.

Heavy rain fell during Monday night, but there was nothing to prevent play starting on time, and of course, Tennyson at once declared. The chance of England being able to force a win was remote, and as it happened the wicket, in weather that was cloudy after a brief spell of sunshine, never became really treacherous. Quite early in the afternoon a draw was seen to be inevitable. In warding off the danger of defeat the Australians were mainly indebted to Collins, who played with masterly skill and inexhaustible patience. For his innings of 40 he was batting four hours and 50 minutes.

Toss: England. **England 362-4 dec.** (C. A. G. Russell 101, G. E. Tyldesley 78*) **and 44-1;**
Australia 175 (C. H. Parkin 5-38).

Fifth Test

At The Oval, August 13, 15, 16, 1921. Drawn.

In the Fifth and last Test match Sandham and Hitch for the first time found places in the England XI. Their inclusion brought the number of players tried in the Test games up to 30. This fact in itself shows the extreme disadvantages under which we laboured. Instead of a real English XI we had a series of more or less experimental sides.

The Oval match, like the one at Manchester, was a good deal curtailed by rain. On the Saturday play could not be started till 20 minutes past 12, and in the afternoon the ground was so flooded as to cause a delay of nearly two hours and three-quarters. The loss of time could never be made up, and the match ended in a draw. The long interruption led to trouble, a large section of the crowd gathering in front of the pavilion and indulging in some unseemly barracking.

The match, like the one at Old Trafford, did something to restore our self-respect, English batting once more asserting itself. Tennyson won the toss, and in the time available on the Saturday 129 runs were scored and four wickets went down. When the rain came on Tyldesley and Woolley were together with the total at 83 for two. Just after resuming Woolley, who had played beautifully, was run out in an extraordinary way. He hesitated over a second run and paid the penalty, a wonderful return by Bardsley from deep third man hitting the wicket. Brown played the fast bowling very pluckily.

Monday was up to a point one of the best days for English cricket last season. For once the Australian bowling was more or less mastered, and when at ten minutes to four Tennyson put the closure in force the score stood at 403 for eight. The innings extended over six hours and a half, run-getting against the Australian bowling and fielding being very hard work. The chief honours rested with Mead, who had the satisfaction of making the highest score ever obtained for England in Test matches in this country. His 182 not out was a great achievement – a remarkable combination of untiring defence and well-controlled hitting. He ought to have been caught high up in the slips when he had made 75, but for the most part his play was beyond reproach. He hit 20 fours, and was batting for about five hours. His best support came from Tennyson, 121 being put on for the sixth wicket. Tennyson has never played better. As at Lord's and Leeds he attacked the fast bowling boldly, getting most of his runs by means of hard driving. When 21 he received a dreadful crack over the heart, and was nearly knocked out, but after a few minutes' delay he went on batting as if nothing had happened.

During the latter part of the afternoon the Australians scored 162 for three wickets, but the game might easily have taken a different course. Hitch bowled with all the fire and pace of his best seasons, but at the critical moment fortune played him false. He was lucky in getting Collins out lbw, but he beat Bardsley, and then Macartney, who had not made a run, was missed off him by Woolley at slip – quite an ordinary catch. For this blunder there was no forgiveness, Macartney and Andrews hitting away brilliantly till, just on the call of time, Macartney was bowled.

The last day's play need not be described at any great length. In some respects it was very unsatisfactory. Any remote possibility of England winning disappeared in the first half-hour, and the Australians went on getting runs so easily that when at last their innings came to an end the total stood at 389. Andrews, unlucky as at Leeds in missing his hundred, played a flawless innings, and for once on a big occasion Taylor was quite up to the high reputation he enjoys at home.

When England went in for the second time the Australians were not without hope of rattling them out and snatching a victory, but when half a dozen overs or so had been sent down without result Armstrong took a course that exposed him to severe criticism. Going out to the long field and only using Mailey of his serious bowlers he showed that he had no further interest in the proceedings, and so reduced the rest of the match to an exhibition. In the circumstances it was rather unfortunate that Russell made a hundred. His innings must, of course, take its place in Test match records.

Toss: England. **England 403-8 dec.** (C. P. Mead 182*, L. H. Tennyson 51, E. A. McDonald 5-143) **and 244-2** (C. A. G. Russell 102*, G. Brown 84, J. W. Hitch 51*); **Australia 389** (C. G. Macartney 61, T. J. E. Andrews 94, J. M. Taylor 75).

Test Match Accounts   1922

The statement of accounts for the Test matches between England and Australia, issued by MCC, shows the enormous interest that was taken in the five games. The receipts amounted to no less than £37,210 15s, of which the Australians took £11,375 3s 11d for their half-share of the gate, the total for the five grounds being: Trent Bridge, £5,925 12s 6d; Lord's, £9,173 15s; Leeds, £6,769 5s 6d; Manchester, £6,060 12s 3d; Oval, £9,270 9s 6d. After deducting all expenses, including £6,082 19s for entertainment tax and £1,330 for players and reserve men, £16,248 2s 9d was left for appropriation. Of this 60% was divided between 17 first-class counties and MCC, each one receiving £526 10s; 30% between the five grounds on which the matches were played (£947 14s each), and 10% between 15 second-class counties (£105 6s each).

Notes by the Editor   Sydney Pardon, 1922

During all the years I have edited *Wisden* there has never been a season so disheartening as that of 1921. England was not merely beaten but overwhelmed. The drawn games at Manchester and The Oval did something to restore our self-respect, but at best they afforded small consolation for the crushing defeats at Nottingham, Lord's, and Leeds. We had, of course, wretched luck in having to play without Hobbs – when at last he took the field he was suddenly attacked by serious illness – but the loss of his invaluable batting, though a tremendous handicap, did not wholly account for our failure. We had no Test-match bowlers of the pre-war standard, Parkin being by far the best of the various men tried, and our fielding compared with the brilliant work of the Australians was very second rate. At Lord's the contrast was humiliating. Never before was an England side so slow and slovenly.

The fact that 30 players appeared for England in the Test matches is in itself proof that we had not a real XI, but a series of scratch sides. Even at The Oval, when our fielding as a whole was better than in the previous matches, we could not boast a cover-point worthy of the name. In saying all this I have no wish or intention to deprecate the Australians. Far from that, I was among those who regarded them, at any rate on hard wickets, as one of the finest all-round teams that ever went into the field.

The members of the selection committee had a difficult task and it would be ungracious to find fault with them. Still I have a feeling amounting to conviction that they lacked a settled policy. They were inclined to catch at straws, and allowed themselves to be influenced too much by the latest form.

The great experiment the committee ventured on – the choice of Tennyson to play at Lord's – turned out, by happy chance, a triumph. If early in his second innings Tennyson had not been missed by the wicket-keeper – quite an ordinary catch – we should have seen no more of him in the Tests. As it was he scored 74 not out and made himself indispensable. His success at Lord's, Leeds and The Oval was a severe indictment of modern methods of batting. He played the fast bowlers in the old-fashioned way, trusting to honest driving and not trying to pull balls that came along at 60 miles an hour. Modern batting is far from being the tame unaggressive thing that some critics represent it – the huge scores prove that – but the experience of last summer revealed it as dismally ineffective against bowling of great pace.

While watching the feeble efforts to play Gregory and McDonald, my thoughts often went back to the Gentlemen and Players match at Lord's in 1895. I recalled the way in which W. G. Grace and Stoddart, on a rather fiery wicket, treated Tom Richardson and Mold.

AUSTRALIA V ENGLAND 1924-25

Setting forth in September 1924 with great hopes of recovering the mythical Ashes, the MCC team, under the leadership of Arthur Gilligan, failed in their quest, Australia winning the first three games and altogether four out of the five matches. The disappointment to everybody in this country was, of course, very great but, in these depressing days, some consolation could be found in the fact that the reputation of English cricket suffered no such damaging blow as on the occasion of the tour of 1920–21.

Finer and more consistent batting than that of Hobbs and Sutcliffe in the first four Tests could not well be conceived. Going in at Sydney against a total of 450, they put on 157 before being separated, and in the second innings when England had 605 to make to win, they raised the score to 110. An even greater achievement followed immediately at Melbourne where, after an innings of 600 by Australia, they started with a partnership of 283. Four times they participated in a first-wicket partnership of over 100. Sutcliffe enjoyed the distinction of making four separate hundreds in the Test matches – an unprecedented feat.

In its way quite as remarkable a performance as that of either of the crack batsmen was the bowling of Tate who, in taking 38 wickets for 23 runs apiece, beat the record of Barnes in 1911–12. Towards the close of a tour in which no one on either side except Tate had accomplished anything out of the way in bowling came the extraordinary success of Grimmett in the final Test of taking 11 wickets for 82 runs.

The first three Test matches each ran into seven days and the two others into five days apiece. No fewer than 514,084 people paid for admission to the five great contests, the total attendance being 687,134, and the takings amounted to £65,784. Eight balls to the over were allowed in all matches, whereas in 1920–21 the players had adhered to the law in vogue in this country, restricting the over to six balls.

First Test

At Sydney, December 19, 20, 22, 23, 24, 26, 27, 1924. Australia won by 193 runs.

After a prolonged struggle which established a record by lasting into the seventh day, Australia won the First Test by 193 runs. Their batting proved far more consistent than that of England and this difference mainly accounted for the result. Australia began well in each innings and their batsmen offered a stout resistance until the very last. Collins and Ponsford, by putting on 190, placed Australia in a happy position and though times came when England's batsmen obtained a mastery, there never seemed any likelihood of Australia being really hard-pressed.

Hobbs and Sutcliffe distinguished themselves greatly by starting each innings with a three-figure partnership. When they made 157 together, Australia's total of 450 did not appear unbeatable, but of the other batsmen only Hendren played up to form. The next-best stand was 33, and though 200 went up with only four men out, the last five wickets fell for 63 runs. Kilner did not play and late in the innings the want of such a capable left-handed batsman was severely felt.

Arthur Richardson and Taylor were the great batsmen in Australia's second innings. Richardson this time went in first with Bardsley while Taylor was No. 8 on the list. Mailey helped to put on 127 for the last wicket and, though England had got eight men out for 286, they were set the overwhelming task of making 605 in the last innings. Only once before had a side been asked to do so much, and it was not surprising that England failed after a gallant effort. Hobbs and Sutcliffe gave their side another fine lead, their partnership this time producing 110 runs. Woolley played a great innings which brought the aggregate of individual hundreds in the match up to six – three for each side. Freeman helped his Kent colleague to add 128, but this stand came too late to retrieve the situation. Woolley played the most attractive innings of the match. Although troubled by a weak knee, he scored his 123 in two hours and a half, hitting a six and 15 fours.

Gregory and Mailey bowled too well for most of the England batsmen, but they were surpassed by Tate, who did superb work in taking 11 wickets for 228 runs and had exasperating luck in often just missing the stumps. Hobbs scored his seventh hundred, beating MacLaren's record, and Taylor enjoyed this success for the first time in a match of this kind. Never before had 400 runs been scored in the last innings of a Test match.

England fielded most brilliantly and Strudwick showed his best form behind the wicket. Oldfield was extremely good for Australia.

The match aroused enormous interest, over 47,000 witnessing the first day's play.

Toss: Australia. **Australia 450** (H. L. Collins 114, W. H. Ponsford 110, M. W. Tate 6-130)
and 452 (A. J. Richardson 98, H. L. Collins 60, J. M. Taylor 108, M. W. Tate 5-98);
England 298 (J. B. Hobbs 115, H. Sutcliffe 59, E. H. Hendren 74*, J. M. Gregory 5-111, A. A. Mailey 4-129)
and 411 (J. B. Hobbs 57, H. Sutcliffe 115, F. E. Woolley 123, A. P. Freeman 50*).

Second Test

At Melbourne, January 1, 2, 3, 5, 6, 7, 8, 1925. Australia won by 82 runs.

Collins again won the toss and Australia gained a second victory. The wonderful strength of their batting stood out even more emphatically than before. They lost Collins, Bardsley and Arthur Richardson for 47 runs, and yet built up a record total of 600. Douglas and Richard Tyldesley were included in the England side instead of Sandham and Freeman, but again Kilner was left out. The changes did not strengthen the side, Douglas taking but one wicket and Tyldesley proving quite ineffective.

The same weakness in the batting after the first few men was as apparent as it had been at Sydney. The bowling of Tate all through the match and that of Hearne in the second innings contrasted more than favourably with anything in Australia's attack. England excelled in fielding, Gilligan doing grand work at mid-off. Strudwick, too, maintained his form behind the wicket, but, despite untiring perseverance, England took two days to dismiss their opponents. Ponsford and Taylor turned the fortunes of the game by adding 161. The sixth wicket put on 123 and the ninth 100, Oldfield playing a useful innings. What figure Australia would have reached if the two Richardsons and Taylor had not been run out can scarcely be conceived.

In answer to Australia's huge score Hobbs and Sutcliffe stayed together for a whole day and scored 283 in their third consecutive big partnership. After this superb start came the failure of Woolley and Hearne. Indeed so poor was the resistance offered that the second-best stand was that which produced 68 for the fourth wicket. When Bardsley, Arthur Richardson and Ponsford fell to Tate for 27 runs at the start of the second innings, something sensational seemed in store, but another sound display by Taylor altered the aspect of affairs. However, Australia were all out for 250, and England, after their great fight at Sydney, did not seem hopelessly placed in being asked to make 372.

Had Hobbs come off again all might have been well, but he left at 36, and, despite a superb display by Sutcliffe, England could never quite gain the upper hand. They had 200 up with three men out, but after Sutcliffe and Woolley left there was a sorry collapse. The last six wickets indeed fell for 79 runs. Sutcliffe, in scoring 176 and 127, equalled the achievement of Warren Bardsley in scoring two hundreds in a Test match between England and Australia, and he distinguished himself further by getting three successive hundreds in these matches. Beyond question, England had the worst of the wicket and the fight they made up to a point left a lasting impression.

Toss: Australia. **Australia 600** (W. H. Ponsford 128, J. M. Taylor 72, V. Y. Richardson 138, A. E. V. Hartkopf 80) **and 250** (J. M. Taylor 90, M. W. Tate 6-99, J. W. Hearne 4-84); **England 479** (J. B. Hobbs 154, H. Sutcliffe 176) **and 290** (H. Sutcliffe 127, F. E. Woolley 50, J. M. Gregory 4-87, A. A. Mailey 5-92).

Test Match Contretemps
A. E. R. Gilligan, 1939

In the Second Test at Melbourne in 1925, after only 15 runs were on the board – I was bowling at the time – I noticed that a great piece of leather had come off the ball. I immediately showed it to umpire Bob Crockett, who consulted his colleague, and a brand-new ball was brought out. Before lunch that day we had no fewer than four new balls with the total no more than 87! When we adjourned, we discovered that, by mistake, a wrong packet of balls had been delivered to the ground and that we had No. 3 grade cricket balls instead of No. 1. It was agreed between Herby Collins and myself to play out the first innings with both sides using the No. 3 grade variety, and it is interesting to note that we used eight new balls before the score reached 200 and Australia had seven. It came as quite a relief when we embarked on the second innings.

Third Test

At Adelaide, January 16, 17, 19, 20, 21, 22, 23, 1925. Australia won by 11 runs.

Having suffered two defeats, England needed to win to have a chance of success in the rubber. They made a glorious fight, but lost by 11 runs. Fortune proved very unkind or the result must have been different. The luck of winning the toss again was neutralised when Australia lost Collins, Gregory and Taylor for 22 runs and could Tate and Gilligan have gone on bowling, there is no telling what might have happened. Unhappily a sore toe compelled Tate to leave the field and Gilligan strained his left thigh. Tate managed to bowl a little more, but Gilligan did not return to the field, Chapman taking over the duties of captain. Arthur Richardson, who had opened the innings in the absence of Bardsley, played finely, but though Ponsford helped to add 92, six wickets were down for 119. Then, at the crisis, Andrews and Ryder came together and put on 136, while in all the last four wickets realised no fewer than 370 runs. Ryder carried out his bat after showing remarkable defence and sound hitting for six hours and a half, with the distinction of being the one batsman to play an innings of 200 in this series.

How well the Englishmen worked under their disadvantages is shown by the length of Australia's innings – it lasted eight hours and three-quarters. Going in late on the second day, England changed their batting order and lost Whysall and Strudwick while 36 runs were scored. Hobbs and Hendren alone became thoroughly set on the third day. Hobbs and Sutcliffe were together for two hours, and on the fourth day Hobbs completed his ninth hundred in Test cricket, but after he lost Hendren, the Surrey batsman received little help. Freeman had been off the field during part of Australia's first innings, but he was able to give Kilner and Woolley some help in the endeavour to dismiss Australia for a moderate total in the second. Ryder going in first wicket down again made the highest score for the home country.

Torrents of rain in the night altered the conditions so completely that Woolley and Kilner obtained the last seven Australian wickets for 39 runs in an hour. To that extent, England were helped, but they did not have a perfect pitch on which to play the last innings. They required 375 for victory and, reverting to their proper batting order, they struggled to the bitter end, failing to accomplish their task by a matter of 12 runs.

Hobbs and Sutcliffe put on 63, and Whysall was partner with the Yorkshireman on the fourth evening when the score was 133 for three. Chapman made another stand with Whysall, 89 runs coming at the rate of one a minute. So the struggle went on until play ceased on the Thursday evening with the game in a most exciting position, England wanting 27 to win with two wickets to fall. Gilligan and Freeman were partners and, with nine runs added, the England captain left. He had batted an hour and 50 minutes for 31 runs – a remarkable display of patience for a player of his temperament. Freeman also played well, but when he and Strudwick had added six, a catch at the wicket off Mailey brought the innings and match to a close and the honours remained with Australia. There was a scene of tremendous enthusiasm at the finish.

Toss: Australia. **Australia 489** (A. J. Richardson 69, J. Ryder 201*, T. J. E. Andrews 72, R. Kilner 4-127) **and 250** (J. Ryder 88, R. Kilner 4-51, F. E. Woolley 4-77); **England 365** (J. B. Hobbs 119, E. H. Hendren 92) **and 363** (H. Sutcliffe 59, W. W. Whysall 75, A. P. F. Chapman 58).

Fourth Test

At Melbourne, February 13, 14, 16, 17, 18, 1925. England won by an innings and 29 runs.

The rubber having been decided by Australia winning three matches off the reel, the Fourth Test naturally lacked something of the enormous interest taken in the previous engagements, but the players showed no slackening of endeavour. England had the satisfaction of gaining a great victory. Gilligan at last called correctly, and the difference that batting first made to the Englishmen could scarcely be overestimated.

Hobbs and Sutcliffe opened with a three-figure partnership for the fourth time in the series. The first day produced 282 runs for two wickets, Sutcliffe claiming just half the total, but he was out first thing in the morning. Batting four hours and 55 minutes without serious fault, Sutcliffe hit 14 fours in a great innings of 143 – his fourth hundred in the series. At the wickets for two full days, England put together their highest score. Not one of the leading batsmen failed; indeed all showed to advantage. Sutcliffe and Hearne put on 106, and Whysall and Kilner added 133, the best stand of the match.

Showers interfered with play on the Monday, handicapping the bowlers, and the impatient crowd by invading the ground did more damage to the pitch than was caused by the slight rain. Getting down five wickets for 109, England gained a big advantage, and, though Taylor and Andrews raised the score to 168, they were separated in the morning and the last four wickets fell for 96 runs. Tate, Hearne and Kilner bowled best on a pitch that dried fairly easily in the absence of much sunshine. Australia after batting nearly four hours at their first attempt followed on and lost four men for 175 before the third day ended with six wickets to fall and arrears still amounting to 104.

The pitch seemed perfect in the morning but Tate was irresistible, dismissing four men for 21 runs. Indeed the innings was finished off for an additional 75 in an hour and a half. The Englishmen were congratulated on all hands and cheered enthusiastically for gaining what was the first victory over Australia since August 1912.

Toss: England. **England 548** (J. B. Hobbs 66, H. Sutcliffe 143, E. H. Hendren 65, W. W. Whysall 76, R. Kilner 74, A. A. Mailey 4-186); **Australia 269** (J. M. Taylor 86) **and 250** (J. M. Taylor 68, M. W. Tate 5-75).

Fifth Test

At Sydney, February 27, 28, March 2, 3, 4, 1925. Australia won by 307 runs.

So far from realising the hope that they might gain a second victory, England were completely outplayed and lost the last Test match by 307 runs. It seemed a good performance to dismiss seven of the Australians for 239 on the first day, but the batting improvement that came after half the home side had fallen for 103 was continued to the end. Ponsford and Kippax – the latter playing in his first Test match – put on 105 and so turned the fortunes of the game, but the Englishmen could feel satisfied that on a Sydney wicket only that one long stand was made against them. However, well as Tate and Kilner had bowled, Grimmett, the slow right-hander, came out with a far finer performance, his phenomenal success on first being chosen for Australia standing out as the great achievement in the Test cricket of the tour.

Grimmett in the match took 11 wickets for 82 runs, his individual triumph being so pronounced that practically nothing was needed from Mailey. Sutcliffe in scoring

22 raised his aggregate to 734 and so gained a record in one series of Tests by beating G. A. Faulkner's 732 when South Africa visited Australia in 1910–11. Oldfield by catching Hobbs wide on the leg side greatly influenced the course of the match. The immediate fall of their great batsman affected the whole England team. Then, going for a short run, Sandham lost his wicket through wonderful fielding by Grimmett and Gregory. The fast bowler took a hot return from cover point and dislocated a finger of his right hand in putting down the wicket, but was able to resume. From these disasters England did not recover. When Australia by steady batting added 325 to their lead of 128 England were required to play the best last innings of the Test matches.

Failure to accomplish this caused no wonder. The surprise was that the task should have been so heavy. Australia had seven men out for 207, but Kelleway and Oldfield put on 128 and the fall of the last three wickets at one total did not matter – the mischief was done. England faced their more than formidable task on a pitch which had enabled Tate to beat the record of Barnes by bringing up his aggregate of wickets in a Test-match series to 38. As in the first innings a heavy blow came at once. Sutcliffe was beaten in Gregory's second over with three on the board and Grimmett got Hobbs stumped at 15. Bad light added to England's discomfiture and after a night's rain the last five wickets went down for 58 runs.

Toss: Australia. **Australia 295** (W. H. Ponsford 80, M. W. Tate 4-92, R. Kilner 4-97) **and 325** (T. J. E. Andrews 80, C. Kelleway 73, W. A. S. Oldfield 65*, M. W. Tate 5-115); **England 167** (C. V. Grimmett 5-45) **and 146** (C. V. Grimmett 6-37).

NOTES BY THE EDITOR
C. Stewart Caine, 1926

In view of the near approach of yet another visit of Australian cricketers to this country, it is interesting to note that there prevails a much more hopeful tone in relation to English cricket than has existed for several years. On the face of things, the record of the MCC team in Australia last winter – one win and four defeats – is not a very substantial basis upon which to build expectations of success. The narrowness of the margin by which on two occasions the Englishmen lost, coupled with the bad luck experienced in tossing for choice of innings appears, however, to have persuaded many people that the actual difference between the two sides was small, and that better times are in store for England. The enthusiasts may have forgotten the lack of solidity in the English batting displayed in several matches last winter, and may fail to realise the tremendous run-getting possibilities of the men Australia is sending over, yet there is no gainsaying the fact that a strong belief is widely entertained that the dark days are coming to an end. This spirit of optimism will possibly receive a rude shock during the next few months, but at the moment it is all to the good.

England's chances of recovering the Ashes will, of course, depend largely upon an intelligent choice of players to take part in the Test matches, so it is to be hoped that the authorities may be happily inspired in picking the members of the selection committee. Not only did this most important body work unsatisfactorily five years ago, but, further back, there were other selection committees which made strange blunders.

Indeed, it is scarcely too much to say that since the practice of appointing special selectors began there have been more palpable mistakes than in the days when, with the programme of Test games restricted to three, the teams were picked by the committees of Marylebone, Lancashire and Surrey in turn.

A further point the authorities may well take into consideration is the provision of accommodation for the England players on the occasions of Test matches. Five years ago in a northern town a leading cricketer on the eve of one of these games was seen wandering about late in the evening in the search for a bed.

ENGLAND V AUSTRALIA 1926

No such triumphal progress through the land as Armstrong's side had enjoyed in 1921 attended the efforts of the 16th Australian team to visit this country. Only one defeat, it is true, was suffered as against two sustained five years earlier, but that reverse occurred in the solitary Test match brought to a definite issue. In these days success in Test games outweighs everything else so the men of 1926 must be said to have failed.

For a team heralded as a band of supermen, this was a sorry record. Certainly fortune was not kind to the side. Such wretchedly wet weather prevailed that little or no practice was possible before the opening of the tour and right up to the middle of June practically every one of their matches suffered interference from rain. Further, there occurred three cases of illness. Seized with indisposition which turned out to be scarlet fever, Hendry played no cricket from the early days of May until the first week in August. Collins, owing to an attack of neuritis, was kept out of the field all through July, and Ponsford, suffering from tonsillitis, had to rest for three weeks in June.

A more serious matter was the misfortune which overtook Gregory. Scarcely had the tour commenced when he found himself suffering from leg trouble, and was compelled to stand out of several contests and at no time could he undertake a long spell of bowling. The loss his side suffered through his inability to go all out could scarcely be over-estimated. While in 1921 he had taken 120 wickets for 16 runs each, his aggregate for last summer was only 38 wickets, at 31 apiece.

The weight of the bowling fell upon Mailey and Grimmett. Wonderfully well as a rule did these two men – the one depending chiefly upon the googly, and the other upon his leg-break – acquit themselves day after day, but they were a strange pair to take the places which Gregory and McDonald had filled in 1921. A steadier bowler than Mailey, Grimmett had good reason to be gratified with his first visit to this country. With remarkable accuracy of pitch he proved no mean successor to Warwick Armstrong. He was rather under middle height and appeared somewhat slight in physique, while a low delivery suggested that he must be easy to see, yet the average English batsman certainly found him difficult to score from.

The Australians had to find what consolation they could in the doings of their batsmen. Here certainly was matter for gratification. Woodfull, seeing that he was without previous experience of English wickets, achieved an exceptional triumph, making hundreds in the Test matches at Leeds and Manchester. He lacks grace of style, but, possessing unlimited patience, he watches the ball most carefully, plays with a very straight bat and gets remarkable power into the strokes he makes so late.

The outstanding figure of the team was Macartney who, on the occasion of his third visit to this country, showed himself a truly glorious artist. His footwork was as remarkable as ever and the variety and brilliancy of his strokes gave unqualified joy to the spectator. Bardsley, doing comparatively little in the early games, ran into splendid form, and excelled himself at Lord's, carrying his bat for 193.

First Test

At Nottingham, June 12, 14, 15, 1926. Drawn.

Completely ruined by rain, the first of the five Test matches was restricted to 50 minutes' cricket on Saturday. The weather turned wet in the early morning and, although matters improved towards noon, the outlook was always unpromising. Still the game began shortly after midday, Carr having won the toss. The wicket upon which much labour had been expended was found impracticable and another pitch was utilised.

On a gloomy day Hobbs and Sutcliffe found themselves somewhat handicapped by the absence of sight-screens at either end, but on the other hand Gregory, to obtain a foothold, had to use a lot of sawdust and a slight intermittent drizzle kept the ball wet. The batsmen scored chiefly by neat strokes on the leg side and well placed shots for smartly run singles, but each player hit a no-ball from Macartney for four, and Sutcliffe sent a full-pitch from Gregory to the ring. The score had reached 32 when a heavy rainstorm burst over the ground, bringing play for the day to a close. Soon the water, despite the coverings at each end, lay in pools where a good-length ball would pitch, and the umpires decided that further cricket was impossible.

Delightful weather prevailed on Sunday, but on Monday alternations of downpour and drizzle led to all idea of play being abandoned shortly after two o'clock, and on Tuesday conditions were so hopeless that by half-past 11 the captains agreed to abandon the match.

Toss: England. **England 32-0.**

Second Test

At Lord's, June 26, 28, 29, 1926. Drawn.

In marked contrast to the dismal experience at Nottingham, the Test match at Lord's was favoured with splendid weather on all three days, while, so great was the public interest in the struggle, that even with the gates closed on Saturday when several more thousand people could have been safely admitted, the ticket-holders and those passing through the turnstiles numbered 72,976 in all.

The game, although drawn, produced a great batting triumph for England who, going in against a total of 383, headed that score by 92 runs and lost only three wickets. Australia, indeed, were only saved from disaster by a masterly display on the part of Bardsley, who, carrying his bat right through the tourists' innings, put together a score of 193 – the highest individual total ever registered in a Test match at Lord's. Compelled, owing to the failure of so many of his colleagues, to exercise great restraint, Bardsley did not really attempt anything in the nature of a drive until after three o'clock in the afternoon and he took nearly two hours to make his first 50, but even if he did not begin too well his skill in timing and glancing the ball on the leg side and in cutting square and late was most marked.

Collins made a sad mistake at the start of Australia's innings in dealing with a ball from Root, but Macartney, while beginning and finishing quietly, batted brilliantly at one period and helped Bardsley to add 73. There were six men out for 208 and, had Strudwick taken the chance Bardsley offered, there would have been seven wickets down for 215. Bardsley escaping, Richardson, without becoming really master of the situation, helped to put on 74 and then Ryder remained to assist in adding 56 during the last hour of the day. The England attack, if never deadly, came through a severe ordeal with distinct credit, for its quality was well maintained. The fielding, while sound, rather lacked dash in some instances but no one could have worked more brilliantly than Hendren. The King was present for two or three hours in the afternoon and all the players enjoyed the honour of being presented to His Majesty.

Early on Monday it was discovered that, someone having connected the hose with the water supply, water had saturated a considerable area of the ground and had wetted a narrow piece of turf in the middle of the pitch. This happening might have been very serious, but it did not delay the game by more than ten minutes.

Facing a total of nearly 400, England had a formidable task in front of them but Hobbs and Sutcliffe rose to the occasion in masterly fashion, raising the total to 182. The two batsmen brought the score up to 77 in 70 minutes before lunch. Afterwards matters still went so well with England that 150 was on the board in about two hours, but subsequently Hobbs held himself back in such strange fashion that he took an hour to raise his score from 90 to 100. Admittedly the leg-theory bowling was very accurate and the fielding keen, yet it is difficult to think that, whatever the nature of the attack on a good wicket, Hobbs could not have pushed along more vigorously. Overshadowed at first, Sutcliffe afterwards carried off the honours in an admirable 82 which included 11 fours. Hobbs at 219 fell to a brilliant running catch.

During the last hour on Monday Woolley and Hendren hit up 78, and England left off with 297 on the board and two men out. Next day England before lunch added 178 runs and lost only Woolley's wicket. Woolley and Hendren increased the total to 359, their partnership producing 140, and then Hendren and Chapman without being separated put on 116 more. Woolley played a delightful innings which was quite free from fault, and had 13 fours as its chief strokes. Hendren, making his first three-figure score in a Test match against Australia, batted splendidly. Playing himself in carefully, he afterwards missed no chance of punishing a loose ball and hit 18 fours.

England at lunch-time with the wicket in good order were only 92 runs ahead but, to the general surprise, Carr declared. What idea the England captain entertained was difficult to discover. The course he took merely gave the Australians batting practice. Happily for the spectators what threatened to be a very dull finish was redeemed by a delightful display of batting on the part of Macartney who scored all round the wicket, gave no chance and hit 12 fours. In the course of the three days only 18 wickets went down and 1,052 runs were obtained.

Toss: Australia. **Australia 383** (W. Bardsley 193*, R. Kilner 4-70) **and 194-5** (C. G. Macartney 133*);
England 475-3 dec. (J. B. Hobbs 119, H. Sutcliffe 82, F. E. Woolley 87, E. H. Hendren 127*,
A. P. F. Chapman 50*).

Third Test

At Leeds, July 10, 12, 13, 1926. Drawn.

Outplayed on the first day when Australia scored 366 for three wickets and finishing on the second evening 291 behind with eight men out, England on Tuesday retrieved their lost ground so handsomely that in the end they led by 54 runs and had seven wickets to fall in their second innings. Still the fact remained that the home side passed through a desperately anxious time and the conclusion could scarcely be avoided that, if the visitors' bowling had been up to the standard of most teams from Australia, England would have found themselves very hard put to escape defeat. The galling thing about the struggle was the way in which England courted trouble.

Carr won the toss and so could have taken first innings on a pitch which, while somewhat soft, was never difficult. He decided, however, to send Australia in. In excuse for the unhappy course taken it is only fair to England's captain to state that the ground had been practically under water on the previous evening and that for some hours prior to the start of the match the sun shone – if not with great power. The risk taken might have been justified by results had the day continued bright. As it happened the sky soon clouded over, and at no time did the ball really bite.

Played upon a different pitch from that originally intended, the game had a truly dramatic opening, Bardsley being caught at slip off the first ball sent down and Macartney off the fifth ball of Tate's over giving a chance in the slips to Carr. Thus the second wicket ought to have gone down with only two runs on the board. It did not fall until the score had been raised to 235. The occasion was seized upon by Macartney to give one of the most glorious displays of his great career. Going for the bowling at once, he was soon complete master of the situation generally and of Macaulay in particular. Driving, cutting and placing to leg superbly, he accomplished the remarkable feat of scoring a hundred before lunch – a performance previously achieved in a Test match only by Victor Trumper. His footwork was perfect and his off-driving magnificent. To such an extent did he overshadow Woodfull that he made 51 out of 64 and 100 out of 131 with never a false stroke – bar that at the start – until he skyed a short-pitched ball to mid-off. Included in his 151 – an innings it was a privilege to witness – were 21 fours.

Monday brought about such a change in the character of the cricket that Australia's seven wickets fell for 128 runs. England, indeed, bowling more skilfully and fielding more smartly than on Saturday, accomplished quite a good performance. Tate, very fittingly, had most to do with finishing off the innings. Curiously enough Woodfull – fourth out at 378 – after playing with a beautifully straight bat for nearly five hours, hit across at the ball which bowled him. His 141, if not particularly attractive to watch, was a triumph of sound, skilful batting. Richardson as well as Woodfull enjoyed the satisfaction of making his first hundred in a Test match. Using his power to hit in front of the wicket, Richardson played a strong game for three hours with ten fours as his chief strokes.

Perfect partners: Jack Hobbs (left), who made the last of his 12 Ashes centuries at the age of 46, with Herbert Sutcliffe.

Faced with the formidable task of making 345 to avoid a follow-on England went in to bat after lunch. For a time all went well, Hobbs and Sutcliffe playing so steadily that they remained together for 80 minutes and raised the score to 59. However, just when the famous pair seemed thoroughly set Sutcliffe played too soon at one of Grimmett's slows and gave that bowler a simple catch. The 100 was reached with one wicket down, but then came such a change that the score with four men out was only 112. Hobbs, after playing extremely well, put a ball up to Andrews in attempting a forcing stroke, Hendren from a hard skimming stroke was taken by the same fieldsman, and Woolley ran himself out. Carr and Chapman, batting doggedly, stayed some time but both were out by the time the total reached 140, and although Kilner made some fine hits, including four fours in one over from Mailey, the drawing of stumps found England with eight wickets down for 203 – a doleful position indeed.

England wanted 142 more runs to escape a follow-on, and had only two wickets to fall so the prospects of making that number were remote in the extreme. Curiously enough, where so many leading batsmen had failed, Macaulay and Geary achieved pronounced success. They had come together with the total at 182 and were not separated until it stood at 290, the partnership for the ninth wicket lasting nearly two hours. Macaulay, in scoring 76, hit ten fours, played fine resolute cricket and might have done still better had he not received a blow on the hand from Gregory.

Although England's arrears amounted to 200 runs, Hobbs and Sutcliffe in the follow-on batted with refreshing confidence as well as success, some worn places on the pitch notwithstanding. For nearly two hours and a half they remained masters of Australia's attack and had raised the total to 156 when Hobbs brought a faultless innings to a close by playing a ball from Grimmett on to the stumps. Sutcliffe, who also played splendid cricket, helped to bring the score to 210. Woolley, exercising great restraint, shared in a partnership of 52 and to wind up with Chapman hit away in very bright fashion, making his first 40 runs in a quarter of an hour.

Toss: England. **Australia 494** (W. M. Woodfull 141, C. G. Macartney 151, A. J. Richardson 100, M. W. Tate 4-99); **England 294** (G. G. Macaulay 76, C. V. Grimmett 5-88) **and 254-3** (J. B. Hobbs 88, H. Sutcliffe 94).

CRICKETER OF THE YEAR – W. M. WOODFULL

1927

William Maldon Woodfull, the most dependable and consistent run-getter of the last Australian team, was born at Maldon, Victoria, on August 22, 1897. As a boy he played cricket at home under the tuition of his father. The conditions were rather primitive, but from the very first Woodfull had impressed upon him the necessity and importance of the straight bat. The effect of this early coaching and the lessons then inculcated could plainly be seen in his style and methods in England last summer. In 1922 he first appeared in important cricket for Victoria against South Australia at Adelaide, and innings of 23 and 117 against New South Wales in the following summer made his position secure. During that season he averaged 85 in Sheffield Shield matches, and 74 two years later, when against South Australia his scores were 97 and 236. Probably the performance in Australia upon which he looks back with greatest personal satisfaction is that of 1924–25 when after New South Wales had made 614 in the first innings he, with innings of 81 and 120 not out, had a lot to do with Victoria gaining a great victory.

On his form during 1925–26 Woodfull was, of course, certain to be picked as a member of the combination under H. L. Collins. He more than justified his inclusion, heading the batting in all first-class matches and being third in the Test-match figures. He failed at Lord's, but was at his best at Leeds and Manchester with scores of 141 and 117. It is no exaggeration to say that Woodfull was probably the most difficult man in the Australian team to bowl out. He had no pretensions to grace of style – indeed, at first sight he gave the impression of being rather clumsy – but as to his ability there could be no two opinions. He watched the ball more closely than any of his colleagues, and kept his bat beautifully straight. His action seemed a little laboured by reason of the fact that he never lifted the bat any noticeable distance from the ground, but, blessed with strong forearms, he could drive with great power.

Fourth Test

At Manchester, July 24, 26, 27, 1926. Drawn.

Its opening stage restricted to ten balls, the Fourth Test, like the three preceding, resulted in a draw. No real progress being made with the game on Saturday, the shadow of a tame finish hung over all the rest of play, and robbed the struggle of real excitement. Macartney and Woodfull, it is true, shared in another splendid partnership, but there was nothing else outstanding in Australia's batting, and England, with no special object to achieve, were quite content to make runs steadily during the concluding hours of the contest.

The match proved a very unhappy affair for Carr who, after leading his men into the field on Saturday, found himself on Monday morning suffering from an attack of tonsillitis, and consequently unable to take any further part in the game. In the absence of the England captain, the leadership of the home team devolved upon Hobbs. Collins being still indisposed, Bardsley, as at Leeds, captained the Australian XI.

Not until the first bell had been rung did the weather turn wet, but light rain then was followed by a series of heavy showers, and it was nearly a quarter to three when the players entered the field. Bardsley, who had won the toss, took Woodfull in with him, but after an over from Tate, and four balls from Root, there came such a down-pour that everybody had to dash for shelter.

Showers on Sunday prevented the turf recovering from the drenching to which it had been subjected, but the weather being pleasant on Monday morning, conditions allowed of the game being proceeded with, half an hour after the appointed time. The score had only been increased to 29 when Stevens got rid of Bardsley with his second ball – a long-hop placed into the hands of short square leg. No other success attended England for three hours, and during that time, Macartney and Woodfull put on 192. Macartney accomplished the remarkable feat of registering his third hundred in three consecutive Test match innings. He was not so audacious or brilliant as at Leeds, but his footwork had all its exceptional quickness, and altogether he gave a delightful display, which, marked throughout by high skill and determination, was marred by very few false strokes and was certainly free from any actual chance. His hits included 14 fours. Woodfull began in his usual cautious style, taking nearly two hours and a half to make his first 50 runs, but he played a highly meritorious innings, which extended over four hours and 20 minutes. Only six times during his long stay did he send the ball to the boundary. A glorious catch by Chapman disposed of Andrews, and when the sixth wicket fell, the total had only reached 266. Ponsford showed sound defence, while Gregory, after making a few drives, settled down in strangely restrained fashion. For all that, eight wickets had fallen at the drawing of stumps for 322.

On Tuesday morning, Bardsley – rather to the general surprise – did not declare, but Tate soon finished off the innings for 335, the last eight wickets having gone down for 114. Under the conditions which prevailed, this was no mean achievement on the part of the England bowlers.

Hobbs and Sutcliffe gave England quite a useful start by raising the score to 58, before Sutcliffe was taken at the wicket. They had nothing to gain by forcing the pace, and their batting was – for them – undistinguished. Still, it served its purpose. Sutcliffe confined himself almost entirely to defence, and Hobbs, if playing most of the bowling easily enough, never seemed comfortable with Mailey, who like Grimmett made the ball turn a good deal and quickly. Tyldesley began very shakily, and after some good hits, had two narrow escapes from being caught off Grimmett. As it was, the second wicket produced 77 runs, the total being up to 135, when a catch at mid-off disposed of Hobbs. Joined by Woolley, Tyldesley, while batting in attractive fashion, enjoyed further luck, Oldfield missing a chance of stumping him off Grimmett. Woolley showed more freedom than any of his colleagues, making his 58 in an hour and a half. Stevens hit hard, but Hendren was strangely quiet until the last few minutes. At the close, England, with nominally five wickets in hand, had got to within 30 of their opponents' total.

Toss: Australia. **Australia 335** (W. M. Woodfull 117, C. G. Macartney 109, C. F. Root 4-84); **England 305-5** (J. B. Hobbs 74, G. E. Tyldesley 81, F. E. Woolley 58).

Fifth Test

At The Oval, August 14, 16, 17, 18, 1926. England won by 289 runs.

After a wonderfully interesting struggle, the Fifth Test– arranged, however long it might last, to be played to a finish – ended shortly after six o'clock on the fourth day in a splendid victory for England. Winning in this handsome fashion, the only one of the five Test games in which a definite issue was reached, the old country regained possession of the mythical Ashes that Australia had held since the wholesale triumph during the winter of 1920–21.

Looked forward to with extraordinary interest, the contest underwent some truly dramatic changes. England, on the opening day, appeared to have jeopardised their chances by some strangely reckless batting, and yet left off on the first evening in distinctly the stronger position. On Monday, Australia played an uphill game to such good purpose that they gained a slight lead. Tuesday brought with it some superb batting on a difficult wicket by Hobbs and Sutcliffe, and to wind up, came the collapse of Australia, who, set 415 to win, failed so completely that they were all out for 125.

England's XI underwent no fewer than four changes from that which had met Australia three weeks earlier at Manchester. Chapman succeeded Carr in the captaincy, and Geary, Larwood and Rhodes displaced Tyldesley, Kilner and Root. The inclusion of Rhodes, a man nearly 49 years of age, naturally occasioned a good deal of surprise, but it was crowned with complete success, the bowling of the veteran Yorkshireman proving no small factor in determining the issue of the struggle.

Chapman secured first innings for England on a wicket which varied in pace at times, but otherwise played well. The start was full of hope, Hobbs and Sutcliffe settling down in excellent style, and in rather less than an hour, putting on 53. Then, to the general amazement, Hobbs, who appeared to be in particularly fine form, was bowled by a full-pitch. Chapman hit out in vigorous fashion. Possibly he considered the position called for an endeavour to knock Mailey off his length. At any rate, he made 49 out of 87, but, following his departure, Mailey and Grimmett met with such poor resistance that the last six wickets went down in an hour for the addition of 91 runs. Sutcliffe batted admirably, his clean off-driving and the certainty of his strokes on the leg side being the chief features of his play. Tate hit up 23 out of 35, but the innings was all over in four hours and a quarter for 280. In a match un-limited as to time, the lack of restraint shown by several of the batsmen was difficult to understand.

Having disappointed so considerably in batting, the England team proceeded to atone for their shortcomings in that department by the excellence of their out-cricket. Australia's score was only nine when a catch behind the wicket sent back Bardsley, and Macartney played on in attempting to hit a long-hop to leg. Shortly afterwards, Ponsford, starting for a foolish run, could not regain his crease before a smart gather, and return by Larwood had enabled Strudwick to whip off the bails, while at 59, a fine break-back knocked Andrews' off stump out of the ground.

While on Saturday the attendance did not exceed that of a popular county match – the public having been frightened away by prophecies of overcrowding and tales of all-night vigils outside the ground – the crowd on Monday was so large that the gates had to be closed shortly after noon. Australia's captain proceeded to make a great effort for his side, but he lost his partner at 90. Only once previously had Woodfull faced Rhodes and on that occasion the second ball from the left-hander brought about his dismissal. Now he encountered Rhodes a second time, and the veteran, after sending down two maidens, led Woodfull to play on and so ended a watchful innings of more than two hours.

Australia, with six men out, were 158 runs behind, but Collins then found a splendid partner in Gregory. While his captain continued to bat with extreme caution, Gregory hit up 73 out of 107, with ten fours as his chief strokes. The stand completely altered the aspect of the game. Collins, who left directly after Gregory, withstood the England attack for three hours and 40 minutes. It was gratifying to notice that the excellence of the skill he displayed in trying to save his side was thoroughly appre-ciated by the crowd. Following Collins's departure came some capital batting by Oldfield and Grimmett, who added 67 for the ninth wicket. Out at last for 302, Australia, at the wickets two hours longer than England, secured a lead of 22. Tate bowled with remarkable steadiness; indeed, except just before the tea interval, when Oldfield and Grimmett were together, the English attack always looked as though it wanted a lot of playing.

Exactly an hour remained when Hobbs and Sutcliffe entered upon England's second innings. As no object was to be served by forcing the runs, they proceeded quietly and if Hobbs took a little time to settle down, at the close they had raised the total to 49. This hour's steady cricket had, unquestionably, a big influence upon the later stages of the struggle.

The crux of the match came before lunch on Tuesday, when Hobbs and Sutcliffe excelled themselves. A thunderstorm, accompanied by a good deal of rain, had broken over south London on Monday evening, rendering the pitch slow and dead to begin with, and afterwards very difficult. The two batsmen, it is true, enjoyed the advantage of playing themselves in before conditions became distinctly awkward, but, admitting this, their performance was an achievement of the highest order. They added 112 in rather less than two hours and a half before lunch, but directly afterwards Hobbs was at 172 bowled by a ball that came back a little and touched the top of the off stump.

His hundred was his 11th against Australia, while the stand was the seventh of three figures he and Sutcliffe had made in Test matches with Australia.

Sutcliffe withstood the bowling for rather more than seven hours and then in the last over of the day was bowled by a fine ball from Mailey. He gave no real chance, and hit 15 fours. England left off 353 ahead with four wickets to fall, and thus in a very strong position. On this day the Prince of Wales was present, and on the concluding afternoon the visitors included Prince Arthur of Connaught and the Prime Minister.

On Wednesday there was a slight shower before play started, and further rain setting in at a quarter-past one, there was no more cricket until ten minutes past three. While never heavy, the rain, being followed by sunshine, of course affected the pitch, but it is doubtful whether the conditions when Australia batted were ever as difficult as during the hour before lunch on Tuesday. To begin with, on the last day 65 minutes of actual cricket sufficed to finish off England's innings for the addition of 61 runs. Rhodes – missed when 12 by Gregory at slip – helped in a partnership of 43 for the eighth wicket, but the best batting was that of Tate, who hit up his 33 in 50 minutes.

Under the conditions which obtained, there never existed the slightest likelihood of Australia making the 415 runs required for victory, but no one could have been prepared to see a famous batting side collapse so badly. As matters went, an easy win for England was assured in 50 minutes, the first four wickets falling for 35. The heavy roller brought up little moisture, but Larwood made the ball fly, and Rhodes, directly he was tried, made it turn. Woodfull putting a ball up in the slips, Chapman brought Rhodes up from deep fine leg to the gully, and moved Geary to third slip. The effect was instantaneous, Woodfull, with only one run registered, edging the next ball straight into Geary's hands. The score was carried to 31 before Macartney also gave a catch to Geary, and then in quick succession, Rhodes got Ponsford taken low down at second slip, and Collins – cheered all the way to the wicket – at first slip.

At 63, Andrews, hitting too soon at a long-hop, was finely caught one hand at short leg by Tate. Twenty runs later, Bardsley gave the simplest of catches to slip, and Gregory, lashing out at Tate, placed the ball in the hands of mid-off. Eight wickets were down for 87, and the side were all out for 125. Rhodes, with four wickets for 44, and Larwood with three for 34, had the chief share in the cheap dismissal of Australia, but all round, the bowling was excellent. Moreover, not a catch was missed nor was a run given away, the whole side rising gallantly to the occasion. Naturally a scene of tremendous enthusiasm occurred at the end, the crowd swarming in thousands in front of the pavilion, and loudly cheering the players, both English and Australian.

Toss: England. **England 280** (H. Sutcliffe 76, A. A. Mailey 6-138) **and 436** (J. B. Hobbs 100, H. Sutcliffe 161); **Australia 302** (H. L. Collins 61, J. M. Gregory 73) **and 125** (W. Rhodes 4-44).

CRICKETER OF THE YEAR – H. LARWOOD 1927

Harold Larwood, than whom few fast bowlers have jumped to the top of the tree more quickly, was born on November 19, 1904, at Nuncargate, a Notts colliery village. Practically unknown in 1924 – he appeared once for Notts in that season – he received only two years later the honour of playing twice for England against Australia. Larwood became a member of the Trent Bridge groundstaff when 18, and for Notts Second Eleven against Lancashire at Kirkby in 1925 he obtained eight wickets for 44 runs. That performance secured him a place in the county XI almost immediately afterwards, and he soon became the leading bowler of the side. He did not come into the team until the middle of June yet he took 73 wickets – 11 of them for 41 runs against Worcestershire. Last season in all matches his record was 137 wickets.

England's resources in the matter of fast bowlers of real class being so limited, it was obvious that if Larwood kept his form in 1926 he was bound to be seriously considered for the Tests and he played at Lord's and The Oval. Bowling splendidly in the second innings of the last Test match he began Australia's collapse, getting Woodfull caught in the slips before a run had been scored, dismissing Macartney in similar fashion at 31, and Andrews at 63. In addition he caught Ponsford low down in the slips. Standing only 5 ft 7½ in high, and weighing ten stone eight pounds, Larwood – who began life as a miner – is, despite a somewhat frail appearance, very strong physically. He gets great pace off the ground, probably because he has a perfect run-up to the wicket, and at times makes the ball come back so much that he is almost unplayable. Except that he drags his right foot and is inclined to stoop slightly at the moment of delivery his action is all that a fast bowler's should be. Only 22 years of age he should have a big future.

NOTES BY THE EDITOR

C. Stewart Caine, 1927

Inasmuch as the one Test match brought to a definite issue last season resulted in a handsome victory for England, there is occasion for much thankfulness. The period of depression, started by the sorry failure of John Douglas's team in Australia in 1920–21, deepened by the triumph of Armstrong's side in this country the following summer, and only mildly relieved by the play of Arthur Gilligan's band in 1924–25, is – for the moment at least – at the end.

There is one recent development of cricket life that may, I fear, militate against the prospects of England against Australia. That is the ever-increasing tendency to undertake winter tours in different parts of the world. These trips are obviously very agreeable or they would not prove so popular, and in so far as participation in them is confined to amateurs and to professionals outside the foremost rank, there can be no objection to them. It is a different matter when, as happens at the present moment, our leading bowlers, after a season's heavy work and that of another in front of them, are subjected to a further call upon their powers during the intervening months. For a time, no doubt, men at the height of their physical strength may appear to undergo this additional strain without any deterioration in skill, yet the lack of rest must tell in the long run, and so tend to shorten a brilliant career. In the case of tours in Australia that danger has to be risked, and naturally men earning their living by the game cannot be expected to refuse opportunities of making money, but in the best interests of English cricket it would be well if matters could be so arranged that great bowlers, without loss of income, were enabled to conserve their energies for the summer.

The return home of the Australians was followed by announcements that two of the team – Ponsford and Arthur Richardson – were coming back to England to play for Lancashire League clubs. In the case of Ponsford steps have since been taken to retain his services in Australia. There is to most of us something objectionable in the idea of a man battling for Australia in Test matches one season, and a year later figuring as a paid player for an English local club.

AUSTRALIA v ENGLAND 1928–29 Sydney Southerton

Opinions may differ as to the exact place in the relative table of merit of visiting teams occupied by the combination which, for the first time since the war, won in Australia the rubber for England. Having had the good fortune to see all their matches, I have no hesitation in allotting to them a very high position. There may have been a team which included players more brilliant and skilful individually but rarely has a side gone to Australia and played from beginning to end of a strenuous tour with the team spirit so admirably maintained in every engagement. They set out with high hopes and a subdued confidence in their ability to retain the Ashes, and returned full of honours with the record of four victories in the Test matches and only one defeat.

It is proper to observe that the Australians found themselves in much the same position as existed in England in 1921. Many of their great players of preceding years had dropped out and it was quite obvious they would experience considerable difficulty in filling the places left vacant. Far be it for me to strike a jarring note in this respect by suggesting England had little to beat. On mature reflection I still think England would have won the rubber even if Australia could have produced a fast bowler to take Gregory's place. England were stronger in batting, more reliable and consistent in bowling and very definitely superior in fielding.

Beyond question, the batting success of the tour was Hammond. He made 251 at Sydney, following that with 200 at Melbourne in the next Test and finally enjoying the distinction of scoring two separate hundreds at Adelaide. In five consecutive Test innings he totalled no fewer than 779 runs, a truly phenomenal performance. Hammond exercised a certain restraint without, however, ever becoming a plodder. Like many other English batsmen he found it hard to get the ball away on the off side but, even with the field placed to meet his favourite shots, he discovered means of placing the ball through the covers in masterly style.

White may justly be described as one of the great successes and, without disparagement to him, the surprise of the team. Who would have imagined when the side left England that on the hard wickets of Australia he would, with his slow left-hand bowling, have been able to subdue all Australia's best batsmen? He owed triumphs to his deceptive flight and accuracy of length; and if he was not always taking wickets nobody mastered him. Moreover, his stamina was extraordinary. Of Tate, it would be hard to speak in terms of too high praise. He sent down over after over with scarcely a ball that could be hit with any approach to safety.

As everyone expected, Jardine was also a success. He impressed everybody with his great strength in defensive strokes no less than by his power in forcing the ball away when going back on to his right leg. One of his best innings was his 98 at Adelaide when all except Hammond and Tate failed. The manner in which he dealt with Grimmett on that occasion was masterly.

First Test

At Exhibition Ground, Brisbane, November 30, December 1, 3, 4, 5, 1928. England won by 675 runs.

Having by now run into first-rate all-round form, England entered upon the opening Test match with feelings of confidence, but not even the most sanguine member of the team could have anticipated that they would gain a victory by such an astounding margin as that of 675 runs – easily the most pronounced success by runs in the history of Test matches. The attack was limited to four bowlers, Larwood, Tate, White and Hammond, but aided by the weather, the breakdown of Gregory and the illness of Kelleway, England triumphed in such a startling manner as to cause real consternation in Australian cricket circles.

Chapman did his side a good turn winning the toss, Hobbs and Sutcliffe beginning so well as to score 85 between 12 o'clock and lunch-time. Then, in the last over before the interval, Sutcliffe was tempted to hit a short-pitched ball from Gregory round to leg and fell to a very fine running catch by Ponsford. Soon after lunch, Hobbs was run out, this being largely his own fault for not running a second quickly enough. A fine return by Bradman, supplemented by brilliant work from Oldfield, did the rest.

Hammond should have gone at 155, Oldfield missing a chance of stumping. England, with five wickets down for 217, had not made such a good start as expected. Ryder frequently changed his bowling and soon after Chapman went in there had been no fewer than 14 alterations in the attack. Hendren and Chapman raised the score to 272 before an appeal against the light was upheld. Next morning the score was carried to 291, and then Tate went in and hit up 26 out of the next 28.

Even then, England, with seven men out, did not seem to have made enough runs, but Larwood gave Hendren such magnificent assistance that the eighth partnership realised 124 in less than two hours, Larwood hitting a six, a five and seven fours in an invaluable innings. All this time, Hendren had been batting superbly, running no risk, and driving, cutting and hooking with the utmost certainty. Hendren was the last to leave. He batted nearly five hours, made no mistake and hit 16 fours.

England, with a total of 521, had effected a great recovery. Before this day ended, great things were to happen, for Australia lost four wickets for 44 runs. Woodfull, off the fourth ball of Larwood's first over, fell to a magnificent left-handed catch by Chapman standing rather fine in the gully. It is safe to say that few other men could have made the ground and held the ball. With the second ball of his third over Larwood bowled Ponsford with a yorker and, Tate changing ends, Kippax was caught and bowled, while Larwood, coming on again at 29, bowled down Kelleway's off stump at 40. Larwood's three wickets to this point cost nine runs. Next morning, Hendry and Ryder carried the score to 71, but nobody else did anything and on the fall of the ninth wicket the innings ended, Gregory being unable to go in. Australia batted less than two hours and a half, Larwood earning great fame by taking six wickets for just over five runs apiece.

England found themselves 399 ahead and Chapman took no risk but went in again. By tea-time both Hobbs and Sutcliffe were out and there were only 74 runs on the board. Next morning Hammond was out to a brilliant catch by Thompson, while Mead left at 165. Hendren, when six, was missed by Bradman at long-on, but then proceeded to hook and drive so well as to make 45 out of 63 in less than an hour, hitting two sixes, one of them a huge drive on to the top of the stand. Jardine, batting splendidly, received further valuable help from Chapman, Tate and Larwood, the Australian attack, so considerably weakened by the absence of Gregory and Kelleway, being thoroughly mastered. On the fall of Larwood's wicket, Chapman declared in order to get Australia in at a very anxious time.

Australia were thus set the tremendous task of getting 742 runs to win. With only six scored, Ponsford was caught by Duckworth. Australia's wretched position was made hopeless by heavy rain during the night, followed in the morning by bright sunshine. Kippax left at 33 and then, White going on at 43 and Tate changing ends, the issue was quickly settled. The last six wickets – the two invalids being still unable to bat – went down in 50 minutes, Australia being all out for 66. Woodfull, batting splendidly, received no support at all, nearly everyone who joined him hitting out wildly immediately on going in. The English fielding was again magnificent, and White had the astounding record of four wickets for seven runs.

Toss: England. **England 521** (E. H. Hendren 169, A. P. F. Chapman 50, H. Larwood 70)
and 342-8 dec. (C. P. Mead 73, D. R. Jardine 65*, C. V. Grimmett 6-131);
Australia 122 (H. Larwood 6-32) **and 66** (J. C. White 4-7).

Second Test

At Sydney, December 14, 15, 17, 18, 19, 20, 1928. England won by eight wickets.

England won the Second Test by eight wickets and they were, to all intents and purposes, definitely on top the whole way through. Happy as the result of the First Test had been, it was obvious that the risk of such a limited attack could not again be taken, so Geary was brought in instead of Mead. Australia were now in rather a desperate position and found themselves handicapped by having to go into the field without a fast bowler. Victor Richardson, Dr Nothling, and Don Blackie were substituted for Bradman, Gregory and Kelleway, but these changes made little difference to the effectiveness of the XI.

The match proved a great triumph for English batting, every man reaching double figures while Hammond carried off chief honours by playing the second-highest individual innings in Tests matches between England and Australia. When within reasonable distance of equalling or beating R. E. Foster's 287 on the same ground almost to a day 23 years before, Hammond got his feet mixed up and was bowled in playing back. His greatest innings was a wonderful test of his physical condition. He went in at 20 minutes past two on the second afternoon and was not dismissed until after one o'clock on the fourth. When 19, he was nearly run out; at 148, he gave a tremendously hard return chance to Ryder, and at 185, walked right in to Blackie but had the good fortune to deflect the ball with his leg – too wide for Oldfield to get at it. These were the only errors of judgment or execution during the whole of a very remarkable display characterised by watchful defence and extraordinarily fine hitting on the off side.

Ryder sent Richardson instead of Ponsford in with Woodfull, but before lunch two wickets fell for 69 runs. Richardson was bowled at 51 and Kippax off his pad at 65. The dismissal of the latter, now known as the Kippax incident, caused endless discussion, and at the time no small amount of feeling between the English team and Kippax himself. Happily, however, the good relations which existed throughout the tour were quickly restored. Soon after lunch Australia were again the victims of ill-fortune in the matter of injuries, Ponsford holding out his bat somewhat tentatively to a fast ball from

Larwood which rose a little but not unduly and receiving a blow on his left hand which broke a bone. Ponsford retired and played no more cricket during the season. At the close eight wickets had fallen for 251 runs. Geary had taken five of them for 35; he bowled very well, especially the ball which came with his arm a little, but did not, from the ring, appear to be anything like so difficult to play as his figures would suggest.

England's start was none too promising, Sutcliffe being out soon after lunch at 37 and Hobbs at 65. Grimmett was bowling a length which made him difficult to score from, only 52 runs having come from 29 overs, but he was mastered by Hammond and Jardine who raised the score next morning to 148. There followed a fine partnership by Hammond and Hendren, 145 runs coming in just over two hours. Hendren cut, hooked and drove with fine power and certainty. Hammond's chief hits were 30 fours. England's total of 636 was the highest ever made in any Test match.

Australia went in a second time 383 runs behind and after Richardson had been dismissed without a run on the board, Woodfull and Hendry made a great stand, carrying the score to 215. Hendry, after a somewhat uncertain start, played fine cricket and Woodfull batted in his usual sound style, but early in his innings he was nearly bowled by Geary, while with his score at 10 he played a ball from Tate hard on to the ground, whence it rebounded on to the top of the bails without removing them. Otherwise his batting was masterly. In the second over after lunch, however, bad judgment in running cost him his wicket, and although Ryder played a great captain's innings, the back of the batting was broken. Ryder, driving with splendid power, obtained his runs in 85 minutes and, with Nothling, added 101 in rather more than an hour.

Ryder was out early on the last morning, caught on the on side from a mistimed stroke, and the innings closed for 397. Tate bowled magnificently, having only 99 runs hit off 46 overs. England had to get only 15 runs to win, but Tate and Geary lost their wickets before these were obtained.

Toss: Australia. **Australia 253** (W. M. Woodfull 68, G. Geary 5-35) **and 397** (W. M. Woodfull 111, H. S. T. L. Hendry 112, J. Ryder 79, M. W. Tate 4-99); **England 636** (W. R. Hammond 251, E. H. Hendren 74, G. Geary 66, D. D. Blackie 4-148) **and 16-2**.

Third Test

At Melbourne, December 29, 31, 1928, January 1, 2, 3, 4, 5, 1929. England won by three wickets.

England, successful in the two previous Test games, naturally approached the third with a certain amount of confidence. In the end they won by three wickets, this victory giving them the rubber and the retention of the Ashes. There were many changes of fortune in the course of a great struggle but scarcely anything in the whole tour approached the long, drawn-out tension of the last innings before the winning hit was made. As at The Oval in 1926, the judgment and skill of Hobbs and the stubbornness of Sutcliffe really carried England to victory, but in awarding great praise to them for wonderful batting under difficult conditions, it must not be forgotten the part that Hammond, with his innings of 200, the bowling of Larwood, Tate, Geary and White, and the high standard of the fielding played in the success.

England had the same XI as at Sydney, but Australia made further changes, bringing in Bradman, a'Beckett and Oxenham for Ponsford, Nothling and Ironmonger. These alterations undoubtedly made Australia a better combination, for Bradman, with two fine displays of batting, showed what a mistake had been made in leaving him out of the second match.

Australia made such a poor start as to lose the first three wickets for 57 runs but then came a great stand by Kippax and Ryder, who added 161. Kippax had played well for an hour before lunch and directly afterwards he hit four fours to leg off Larwood, three of them in one over. Ultimately he was caught at long leg in repeating this profitable stroke. Bradman next helped Ryder to put on 64 in less than an hour, then Bradman and a'Beckett added 86, but nobody else did much. Bowled by a yorker at 373, Bradman scored well in front of the wicket, hitting nine fours during his stay of over three hours. Although he took only one wicket, White bowled with wonderful steadiness while Tate's work was beyond praise. On the second day 62,259 people witnessed the play, a record attendance for one afternoon.

England headed their opponents by 20 runs. The batting honours went to Hammond who, going in first wicket down, was fifth to leave at 364, brilliantly caught behind the bowler. Hammond, in a masterly display, hit only 17 fours, but he had to face a lot of steady bowling and accurate fielding. As at Sydney, he made great use of his favourite stroke through the covers, with an occasional square-drive. Sutcliffe, very restrained, helped him to add 133 and after the fall of the fourth wicket Hammond and Jardine put on 126. Following Hammond's dismissal, however, the last five wickets fell for 53. Blackie came out with the fine record of six wickets for 94.

When Australia went in a second time, Richardson again failed and although Woodfull batted uncommonly well and Kippax helped to add 78, there were four wickets down for 143. England then stood in a good position, but Bradman – nearly bowled by White when seven – proceeded to make his first hundred in a Test match. Woodfull, fifth out at 201, hit only seven fours during his stay of four hours and a half. His defence all through was wonderful. Bradman's innings closed at 345. He batted over four hours, hit 11 fours and brought off many splendid drives. Australia had two wickets to fall on the sixth day when, owing to rain during the night, play could not be resumed until nearly one o'clock, and it was noticed that Ryder did not have the wicket rolled.

England, wanting 332 to win, had to go in for five minutes before lunch. This period was safely tided over, but on resuming Hobbs was given a life by Hendry at slip. For that blunder a heavy price had to be paid. The ball was turning and at other times getting up almost straight, but Hobbs and Sutcliffe contented themselves for the most part in playing it, realising that the longer they stayed the better was England's chance of making the runs. Only 75 were obtained between lunch and tea, but altogether the two batsmen made 105 before Hobbs was lbw. He hit only one four in his 49, but the value of his innings could not be measured by the mere runs he made.

England were still a long way from victory, but Sutcliffe and Jardine, with the wicket steadily becoming less awkward, added 94. Incidentally, Jardine had been sent in next on the advice of Hobbs, who, signalling for a new bat, took the opportunity of suggesting this to Chapman. Jardine, before getting out next morning, played his part with the utmost fidelity. Sutcliffe and Hammond put on 58 and Hendren, missed when 21 at long-on by Bradman, helped in a stand which produced an invaluable 61, before Sutcliffe was lbw for 135, in the circumstances a great innings. England then had the match in their hands, but just before tea Hendren was bowled and afterwards Chapman and Tate lost their wickets before Geary made the winning hit at half-past four.

Toss: Australia. **Australia 397** (A. F. Kippax 100, J. Ryder 112, D. G. Bradman 79) **and 351** (W. M. Woodfull 107, D. G. Bradman 112, J. C. White 5-107); **England 417** (H. Sutcliffe 58, W. R. Hammond 200, D. R. Jardine 62, D. D. Blackie 6-94) **and 332-7** (H. Sutcliffe 135).

NOTES BY THE EDITOR   C. Stewart Caine, 1929

Not for 17 years has the reputation of English cricket stood as high as at the present moment. Away back in 1912, of the three games England played against Australia in the ill-starred Triangular Tournament, the only one brought to a definite issue was, it is true, won by the Old Country, and in 1926 the programme of five Test matches yielded a similar result, but for anything approaching the triumphal progress so far enjoyed by Mr A. P. F. Chapman and his men we have to go back to 1911 12, when the team proceeded, after losing the first of the representative encounters, to win the other four.

Then followed that deplorable post-war period during which three consecutive tours – two in Australia and one in this country   resulted in 12 defeats for England, only one victory and two drawn games.

Well may it thus be that the triumphs of our players – I am writing prior to the Fourth Test – have aroused a measure of enthusiasm unprecedented in the history of the game. The pronounced success is the more refreshing as, when the selection was made, not only did much doubt exist as to whether Larwood would stand the strain of six- and seven-day cricket on the hard wickets of Australia, but the inclusion of Geary, whose bowling arm had been operated upon during the summer, appeared to many people to be courting disaster. MCC, however, had obviously been well-advised as to the condition of the two men in question and, if possibly they took something of a risk, the course adopted has been convincingly justified.

Fourth Test
At Adelaide, February 1, 2, 4, 5, 6, 7, 8, 1929. England won by 12 runs.

The rubber having been won, the English team had no cause for anxiety beyond the desire to preserve their unbeaten record. Still they did not exhibit any lack of keenness in the Fourth Test which, characterised by very even scoring throughout, had a most exciting finish. England had no reason for changing their XI, but Australia brought in Jackson for Richardson, the young New South Wales batsman enjoying the distinction of playing a three-figure innings in his first Test match.

Before going further, it is only right to pay a great tribute to his performance. Accomplished in circumstances calculated to daunt a player of mature experience, it was, in point of style and beauty of execution and strokeplay, the best innings played against the Englishmen during the whole tour. Other achievements made the match memorable. Hammond followed his 251 and 200 by making two separate hundreds; Hobbs and Sutcliffe once more gave the side a good start; Jardine played an invaluable innings; and, above all, White, sending down over 124 overs, obtained 13 wickets for 256 runs, eight of them in the second innings. Well as he had bowled in all his previous games, White was really wonderful in his stamina, clever flighting and remarkable accuracy of pitch.

There existed reason for anticipating when Hobbs and Sutcliffe had made 143 in two hours and three-quarters that England's final score would be considerably higher. Both left at the same total, Grimmett going on when Hobbs was out and getting Sutcliffe second ball. Hammond saw Jardine and Hendren quickly dismissed, and although Chapman helped to add 67, nobody else did anything. Taking out his bat, Hammond scored 72 of the last 88 runs, his driving all through being splendid. Grimmett in this innings bowled better than in any other match against the Englishmen.

Australia made a deplorable start, three wickets falling for 19 runs. Off the fourth ball from Tate, Woodfull was magnificently caught at the wicket on the leg side, Hendry left at six and White bowled Kippax. It was then that Jackson revealed his great powers. The position did not seem to trouble him in the slightest, and he drove, cut and hit to leg with the utmost certainty and confidence. His superb innings ended at 287. Jackson batted for five hours and 20 minutes, gave no chance, and hit 15 fours. In the end Australia led by 35 runs. A word of praise is due to Tate for some fine bowling.

Going in on the fourth day just before half-past 12, England lost Hobbs and Sutcliffe for 21, Hobbs, like Woodfull, being splendidly caught on the leg side at the wicket with only one run scored. The position was serious, but Hammond and Jardine rose to the occasion in wonderful style. Both men forced the ball to the on side with clever strokes, and were not separated until Wednesday afternoon, and by adding 262 runs established a record for the third-wicket partnership in Test matches. Jardine, when he looked certain to reach his hundred, was caught at silly mid-off.

England had pulled the game round, but they proceeded to throw away their advantage, Hendren, Chapman and Larwood all leaving while the score was being raised to 302. Hammond was at length seventh out at 327. He hit 17 fours and this was probably his best innings of the tour. He was master of the bowling all the time. After tea Tate, hitting a six and five fours, played an invaluable innings and England set their opponents 349. Before play ceased 24 runs were scored without loss, and on Thursday and Friday there came a fight which will long be remembered by those who saw it. The first wicket fell at 65, and soon after lunch on the Thursday three men were out for 74. A little later occurred an incident which looked like losing the game for England, Ryder, with his score at 26, offering the simplest of catches to White who, to everyone's surprise and his own obvious annoyance, dropped the ball. Kippax and Ryder added 137, Australia then being on top, but soon afterwards White made amends for his previous blunder by holding a hard return from Ryder high up with the left hand.

A'Beckett stayed for 35 minutes, Hammond making a sensational catch at second slip to dismiss him, and when play ceased for the day Australia, with six men out for 260, required 89 to win. When, next morning, Bradman and Oxenham carried the score to 308, victory for Australia appeared more than likely. At 320, with Bradman run out, fortunes changed again. Oldfield hit a ball to cover point, both batsmen dashing for the run, but Hobbs returned like lightning for Duckworth to put down the wicket. Grimmett stayed for half an hour, but left at 336, Tate at short leg knocking up the ball from a hard hit and bringing off a great catch. Blackie went in amid tense excitement and carefully played four balls from White. Then came one pitched just a little shorter;

Blackie hooked it high into the long field in front of square leg where Larwood, running a few yards, brought off a fine catch and finished a wonderful struggle.

Toss: England. **England 334** (J. B. Hobbs 74, H. Sutcliffe 64, W. R. Hammond 119*, C. V. Grimmett 5-102) **and 383** (W. R. Hammond 177, D. R. Jardine 98, R. K. Oxenham 4-67); **Australia 369** (A. Jackson 164, J. Ryder 63, M. W. Tate 4-77, J. C. White 5-130) **and 336** (A. F. Kippax 51, J. Ryder 87, D. G. Bradman 58, J. C. White 8-126).

Fifth Test

At Sydney, March 8, 9, 11, 12, 13, 14, 15, 16, 1929. Australia won by five wickets.

Lasting eight days – the greatest duration of any Test match – the concluding representative engagement saw Australia successful by five wickets. Up to a point, England fared very well indeed. They batted into the third day in making 519, and subsequently obtained a lead of 28. They failed, however, at their second attempt, to reproduce their real form and Australia, left with 286 to get, always seemed likely to win. By this time, the visitors were tired and probably a little stale.

Sutcliffe's arm, which had been troubling him for some time, was too painful to warrant his inclusion and Ames, who would have been played for his batting, had broken a finger. Chapman himself stood down. He had scarcely recovered from an attack of influenza, but might possibly have turned out; the loss of his brilliant fielding was undoubtedly reflected in the general work of the side. Although not widely known, White was also handicapped by the effects of electrical treatment for muscular trouble. While this did not prevent him bowling, it undoubtedly affected his delivery.

Judged from the English standpoint, the cricket all through proved dreadfully slow, but such keenness characterised the spectators – every ball being closely followed – that the rate of scoring was not noticed. The first wicket produced 64 runs, the second 82 and the third 89, the score being up to 235 before Hobbs was out. In a careful, but very sound and skilful display, Hobbs hit 11 fours. At the close, England had 240 on the board with four men out, and the next afternoon saw a fine stand between Hendren and Leyland, who added 141. Hendren hit ten fours, chiefly drives and hooks. Leyland, making his first appearance against Australia, went on, with White the last man in, to complete his hundred. Missed when 13 by Fairfax in the gully, he did not make another mistake until he got out. He played with rare judgment for five hours and, driving beautifully through the covers, hit 17 fours. When he had reached 99 he remained there for a quarter of an hour, the Australian bowlers sending down not a single ball which could safely be hit.

Australia did well to reply with 491. Their batting was very sound throughout, the honours being carried off by Woodfull and Bradman. Kippax helped to add 89 for the second wicket, but on the third day when three wickets went down only 186 runs were scored altogether. Then followed the stand which put Australia almost on terms, Bradman and Fairfax scoring 183 for the fifth wicket. Bradman put together a delightful innings, his strokeplay being remarkable, and his driving very powerful, well kept down and nicely placed. He hit eight fours. The ninth wicket fell at 432, but Hornibrook and Grimmett added 59 for the last partnership. Geary, who bowled 81 overs – a record for a Test match – had a fine game, and on the fifth day actually obtained his five wickets for 51 runs. When the Australian innings ceased, play had lasted 18 hours and 27 minutes for 1,010 runs.

England had to go in a second time in a poor light with nearly 40 minutes left, and with one scored Jardine was out. Hobbs next day batted splendidly to make 65 out of 119 before being fourth out, but of the rest only Leyland and Tate accomplished anything. Wall, who bowled with plenty of life, not only making the ball swerve but get up sharply, accomplished a fine performance in his first Test match.

Left with 286 to win, Australia batted for ten minutes before defective light, as on the previous afternoon, stopped cricket at quarter to six. Next morning Oldfield was missed in the slips when eight. That proved a bad blunder, for he and Hornibrook, who had been sent in to play out time, shared in a stand which produced 51. Oldfield left at 80, Woodfull at 129 and Jackson at 158, every run having to be struggled for. Hammond, who took three of the four wickets, had one inspired spell when he made the ball break and come off the pitch at a rare pace. Next day Kippax, going for a fourth run, lost his wicket thanks to Leyland's pick-up and return from the long field, and then two incidents occurred which probably affected the result. In the first case, Bradman, when five, gave a chance of stumping while Ryder, at 27, had his wicket thrown down by Leyland, who had run behind the bowler from mid-off. It was the general opinion that Ryder was at least a yard out, but to the obvious surprise and chagrin of the Englishmen, Jones, the umpire, gave the batsman in. The score at lunch was 248 and afterwards the remaining runs were hit off without further loss. Both Bradman and Ryder batted very well.

Toss: England. **England 519** (J. B. Hobbs 142, E. H. Hendren 95, M. Leyland 137) **and 257** (J. B. Hobbs 65, M. Leyland 53*, M. W. Tate 54, T. W. Wall 5-66); **Australia 491** (W. M. Woodfull 102, D. G. Bradman 123, A. G. Fairfax 65, G. Geary 5-105) **and 287-5** (J. Ryder 57*).

AUSTRALIAN TOURS AND THEIR MANAGEMENT Sir Frederick Toone, 1930

I have from the very outset regarded these tours primarily as imperial enterprises, tending to cement friendship between the Mother Country and her Dominions. Players selected to take part in them – and this has always been borne in mind by the MCC – should not be chosen for their cricket qualities alone. They must be men of good character, high principle, easy of address, and in every personal sense worthy of representing their country, in all circumstances, irrespective of their work on the field.

The tours it has been my privilege to manage were those of 1920–21, 1924–25 and 1928–29. The three captains who have shared the responsibilities of the visits are Mr J. W. H. T. Douglas, Mr A. E. R. Gilligan and Mr A. P. F. Chapman. And here let me say that with all three I had the most happy relations. Nothing but absolutely good sportsmanship was the keynote of all our proceedings. Not a wrong word was spoken on any of the tours; nothing but the greatest good feeling prevailed among all the players.

Sunshine is lovely in Australia but it was never more lovely than the feeling which prevailed in defeat as well as in victory. Australia is a happy country and the cricketers privileged to visit and to play there are assured of five and a half happy months. They make very many friends whom they leave with regret.

The travelling arrangements for these tours, including the selection of the hotels at which the team will stay, have to be ratified by MCC. The carrying-out of these arrangements, of course, devolves upon the manager, who makes it his first duty to see that the comfort of the players is properly provided for.

An expert masseur always accompanies the team, and is constant in his attentions. The need of such services can be judged when it is said that, apart from the strains of continuous match-play, we had on the last tour to spend between 20 and 30 nights in the train, the longest journeys being from Perth to Adelaide, which occupied about four days – i.e. three nights on the train – and, after the last Test, from Melbourne to Perth. The whole tour means a round journey of between 40,000 and 50,000 miles.

Bradman, Bodyline and Bradman Again: 1930 to 1948

Before the Australians landed in England in 1930, several pundits – notably Surrey's captain, the former England all-rounder Percy Fender – predicted that Don Bradman would struggle on English pitches. His technique wasn't up to it, they said. He plays too many cross-bat strokes, they said. Maurice Tate will find him out, they said.

Bradman, who by then had annexed the world record for the highest first-class score (452 not out), obviously wasn't listening. He started the tour with 236 against Worcestershire, added 185 not out in the next match, and scooted past 1,000 runs before the end of May on his way to 191 against Hampshire.

And, demonstrating the remorselessness that was to become a feature of his batting, The Don went on and on... and on. His 131 in the First Test was followed by 254 at Lord's in the Second, the innings he personally rated as his best: "Practically without exception every ball went where it was intended to go, even the one from which I was dismissed, but the latter went slightly up in the air and Percy Chapman with a miraculous piece of work held the catch." Then came a colossal 334 in the Third Test at Headingley. Bradman finished the series with 974 runs, breaking Walter Hammond's 1928–29 mark (Bradman's record remained unbeaten into the 21st century) and he finished the whole tour with 2,960 runs at 98.66 – the sort of stratospheric average which few had ever approached before, but which became commonplace for Australia's new hero.

Stopping Bradman became a priority for opposing bowlers and captains, and the spectre of his batting inspired one of cricket's murkier episodes. The 1932–33 Ashes series has gone down in history not because England won it 4–1 but because of *how* they won it. A new, inflexible captain was appointed: Douglas Jardine had done well in 1928–29, but had not been enamoured of Australia and Australians. He fancied he had spotted a flaw in Bradman's technique against fast bowling when he was briefly caught on a wet wicket at The Oval in 1930, and based his whole strategy around it, packing his side with fast bowlers. Chief among them was Harold Larwood, not the tallest of men but one of the fastest bowlers cricket has ever seen. It was Larwood's speed and accuracy that enabled the plan to be carried through.

Bodyline entailed bowling short and fast to a packed leg-side field, with an inner ring of close catchers backed up by more fielders in the deep to snare aerial hooks and pulls. With almost no fielders on the off side, the attack had be zeroed in on the body, even the head, of the batsman. It was relentless, and although occasionally a batsman went on the attack and got away with it – as in Stan McCabe's superb 187 not out in the First Test – the percentages were against them. Bradman, who missed the First Test through illness, partially conquered Bodyline by drawing away and hitting through the untenanted off side, but this was a high-risk strategy, involving as it did a moving batsman and a horizontal bat.

Bradman's average was reduced to a more mortal 56, and England won the series, but the repercussions were huge. The Australian Cricket Board called the tactic "unsporting", and an affronted MCC threatened to recall their side. There was even high-level diplomatic activity. From this distance Bodyline sounds much like the tactics adopted by the West Indian fast bowlers in the 1980s, or Dennis Lillee and Jeff Thomson in 1974–75, but they at least were not backed up by the predatory fields, as the main measure to curb Bodyline was a restriction on the number of leg-side fielders.

The ripples of Bodyline took a long time to settle down, and the Australians were apprehensive about how they would be received in England in 1934. But, with Jardine diplomatically unavailable and Larwood not selected (indeed, he never played another Test after the Bodyline series), normal service was resumed – by Australia, who regained the Ashes, and by Bradman, who scored another Test triple-century at Headingley.

By 1936–37 Bradman was Australia's captain, and although he lost his first two Tests in charge after his side were caught on wet wickets he inspired them to win the last three – the only time in Test history that a series has been won from 2–0 down. With no Bodyline in sight Bradman made 270, 212 and 169 in those three Tests.

After the Second World War it was touch and go whether Bradman would continue. He had played little during the break, had also been ill, and was now 38. Australia suggested an Ashes series at home in 1946–47: as after the First World War, England correctly thought they were not ready for such a test, but felt obliged to go through with it. After much soul-searching Bradman was persuaded to play, and had made a scratchy 28 in the First Test when England were convinced they had had him caught: however, the umpire kept the finger down. The Don went on to 187, decided he could still hack it after all, and won another series. Then he hatched a plan for a triumphant farewell tour of England.

Bradman's 1948 team has gone down in history as "The Invincibles". They never looked like losing a Test, and went through the whole tour unbeaten too. Apart from Bradman himself the team included names which have lit up Ashes history, such as batsmen Arthur Morris, Neil Harvey and the pre-war survivors Lindsay Hassett and Bill Brown. The bowling was spearheaded by the magnificent opening partnership of Ray Lindwall and Keith Miller, backed up by the under-rated Bill Johnston and helped by an experimental rule that gave them a new ball after 55 overs, instead of the more usual 85, which meant that Bradman hardly needed a spinner (Bill O'Reilly, probably the greatest leg-spinner of the inter-war years, had not long retired).

After the Bodyline tour, Australia regained the Ashes in 1934 and rarely looked like relinquishing them during Don Bradman's career. Bradman's retirement gave England slight hope for the future, although Australia's 4–0 win in that 1948 series suggested they weren't ready to move over just yet.   S. L.

ENGLAND V AUSTRALIA 1930   Sydney Southerton

Coming to England while the experience of four consecutive defeats in their own land was still fresh in their memories, the 17th Australian team to visit this country accomplished a very fine performance. They not only achieved the great object of the tour by regaining the Ashes but, in the course of 31 engagements against first-class sides, they were beaten but once – in the opening Test match at Nottingham.

This particular tour will always be remembered for the amazing batting successes which attended the efforts of Bradman. It is not too much to say that he took both England and the whole cricket world by storm. Those who had seen him play in Australia were fully prepared for something out of the common, but little did we dream that his progress would be of such a triumphal nature. He lost no time in demonstrating that he was a most remarkable young cricketer, leading off with 236 against Worcestershire. For Test matches alone, without a not-out to help him, he had an average of rather more than 139 with an aggregate of 974 runs. He was also first in batting in first-class matches with an aggregate of 2,960 and an average of over 98.

There were several features about his batting with which one could not fail to be struck. To an eye almost uncanny in its power to gauge the length of a ball was allied really beautiful footwork. Bradman seldom played forward as a means of defence; he nearly always stepped back to meet the ball with a vertical bat. And this is where he had his limitations, for the tour proved that when he met a bowler who could make the ball just go away he never seemed quite such a master as against off-break or straight fast bowling. A glorious driver, he hit the ball very hard, while his placing was almost invariably perfect. He scored most of his runs by driving but he could cut, hook, or turn the ball to leg with nearly the same certainty. And only on rare occasions did he lift it.

While the Australians undoubtedly owed much of their success to Bradman's batting, an almost equally potent factor was the bowling of Grimmett. Curiously enough, he did not in the victory at The Oval bear anything like the great part that he had done in the previous encounters, but long before that he had established over most of the England batsmen an ascendancy which they never really overcame. He took 29 wickets in the Tests, but his average of nearly 32 does not convey a real idea of his effectiveness. Practically every time he went on he at once brought about a diminution in the rate of run-getting. To begin with he obtained most of his wickets with leg-breaks, but as the season advanced he bowled the googly more often and he got plenty of batsmen lbw with a well-disguised top-spinner.

First Test

At Nottingham, June 13, 14, 16, 17, 1930. England won by 93 runs.

England won the First Test shortly after half-past five on the fourth day. This was a satisfactory start, but they were helped to no inconsiderable extent by the weather, Australia, on the second afternoon, having to bat on a pitch made difficult by hot sunshine following heavy rain during the night. As an offset to this, however, England were greatly handicapped by being without Larwood, owing to an attack of gastritis, for the whole of the concluding day. Australia, set to get 429 runs to win, had scored 60 for the loss of Woodfull overnight, and, with the England attack thus weakened made, thanks to Bradman, a very fine fight of it. Indeed, when they had 229 on the board and only three men out, they possessed, with the wicket probably in better condition than at any previous time during the game, a reasonable chance of winning.

Bradman was well set and McCabe playing a bold and successful innings, but at that point McCabe fell to a splendid catch very low down at mid-on by Copley, a member of the groundstaff at Trent Bridge fielding as substitute for Larwood. Copley made a lot of ground, took the ball at full length and, although rolling over, retained possession. This catch turned the game in England's favour, for nobody, after Bradman's dismissal at 267, offered any real resistance.

Thus England won all right but it cannot be said that their form and particularly the batting inspired real confidence. The failure of Hammond and Woolley in both innings and of Hendren on the opening day was very disturbing and in no subsequent match did England's batting prove really sound.

At no time on the first day did the pitch play quite as well as had been expected. Even to begin with, there seemed to be just a little moisture in it. Still, Hobbs and Sutcliffe gave their side a fairly good start by scoring 53 before Sutcliffe was caught at slip off a rising ball. Hammond opened with a glorious off-drive but then came three dreadful disasters. At 63 Hammond was lbw and Woolley stumped first ball, while Hendren, before playing on at 71, gave a most inglorious display of feeble and hesitant batting. All the advantage of winning the toss had been discounted. At that point Grimmett had sent down 17 overs, taking three wickets for 33 runs. Happily for England Chapman rose to the occasion with a very fine display. He devoted himself to the task of knocking Grimmett off. He hit him for five fours – nearly all drives – and when at length he was caught wide at long-off he had made 52 out of 82 runs added in 65 minutes, with ten fours. Hobbs's fine innings ended when he was caught low down at second slip. The position had been such that he could take no risks but he batted throughout with marked skill.

Play ceased with the score at 241 for eight and the turf was so wet next day that not a ball could be bowled until quarter-past two. Grimmett bowled wonderfully well but England's 270 was not a particularly satisfactory performance. By the time the Australians went in, the sun had come out and in less than an hour they lost Ponsford, Woodfull and Bradman for only 16 runs. Woodfull was out to a brilliant catch in the gully and Bradman completely beaten by a break-back. Kippax then played very nearly his best innings of the tour. Certainly he was favoured by some bad-length bowling, but he brought off many fine hits to leg. Then Richardson, very uncomfortable to begin with, hooked and drove so brilliantly that he sent the ball seven times to the boundary while scoring 37 out of the next 44. There was not much resistance afterwards. At the close Australia were 140 for eight and on the Monday only four more runs were added.

So England led by 126 runs and very finely did Hobbs and Sutcliffe proceed to consolidate this advantage. In less than two hours they put on 125, Hobbs, who hit ten fours, batting superbly. He had to play a lot of good bowling but was always master, scoring by a wide variety of delightful strokes. He rather threw away his wicket for, having jumped in and hit Grimmett straight, he attempted the same stroke immediately afterwards to a shorter-pitched ball and was easily stumped. Nine runs after Hobbs left, Sutcliffe was hit on the thumb of the right hand and had to retire. Shortly after tea Hendren, who had played in his best style for nearly two hours, was caught at second slip. His 72 was a most valuable innings.

Fifty minutes remained for play when Australia entered upon their task of getting 429 runs to win. With only 12 scored, Woodfull was again caught in the gully, but Ponsford and Bradman played out time, carrying the score to 60. Next morning Ponsford, playing back to a half-volley, was bowled at 93, but England without Larwood had to work tremendously hard for the rest of the day. Bradman who had been quite brilliant overnight played such an entirely different game that not until a quarter to three did he hit another four. Bradman and McCabe soon played themselves in after lunch and it was quickly obvious that they might rob England of victory, but then at 229 came the catch by the substitute Copley.

Bradman's fine innings ended at 267, Robins bowling him with a googly which he made no attempt to play. Bradman hit ten fours in scoring his hundred in his first Test match in England. Off the first ball he received he made a lucky snick over slip's head and when 60 he again snicked a ball which went off Duckworth's glove to Hammond's left hand and then on to the ground, while at 75 he was nearly bowled by a leg-break. Thus his display, if in the circumstances very remarkable, was not free from fault. Richardson hit six fours in making 29 but latterly nobody else did anything and the match was over with less than an hour to spare.

Toss: England. **England 270** (J. B. Hobbs 78, A. P. F. Chapman 52, R. W. V. Robins 50*, C. V. Grimmett 5-107) **and 302** (J. B. Hobbs 74, H. Sutcliffe 58*, E. H. Hendren 72, C. V. Grimmett 5-94); **Australia 144** (A. F. Kippax 64*, R. W. V. Robins 4-51) **and 335** (D. G. Bradman 131).

Second Test .

At Lord's, June 27, 28, 30, July 1, 1930. Australia won by seven wickets.

After a memorable struggle, Australia took an ample revenge for their overthrow at Trent Bridge. The batting, particularly that of Bradman, will assuredly live long in the minds of those who saw it but, while giving the visitors the fullest praise for winning so handsomely after having to face a first-innings total of 425, it is only proper to observe that to a large extent England played right into the hands of their opponents. Briefly, England lost a match which, with a little discretion on the last day, they could probably have saved.

Chapman again won the toss and England scored 405 for nine on the first day. This, seeing that despite some delightful driving by Woolley and Hammond three wickets were down for 105, was a distinctly fine performance. Duleepsinhji and Hendren obtained the first real mastery over the attack, adding 104. The batting after lunch was delightful, Duleepsinhji driving with fine power and Hendren scoring by cleverly executed strokes to the on. Chapman and Allen failing, the game took a strong turn in favour of Australia and, while the 200 had gone up with only three wickets down, six men were out for 239. Duleepsinhji, however, found a valuable partner in Tate who hit so hard as to make 54 out of 98. Duleepsinhji seemed certain to play out time, but at quarter-past six, with the score at 387, he was caught at long-off. It seems ungracious to say it, but Duleepsinhji was guilty of a bad error of judgment. He had twice driven Grimmett to the boundary in glorious fashion and in the same over lashed out wildly. Had he been patient and stayed in until the close of play there is no telling what would have been the subsequent course of events.

Next day Tate bowled with great pluck but, generally, the England attack was indifferent, Allen especially being innocuous and expensive. The Australians batted to a set plan, Woodfull and Ponsford steadily wearing down the bowling for Bradman later on to flog it. Nearly three hours were occupied over the first 162 runs, but in another two hours and three-quarters no fewer than 242 came. Curiously enough the opening partnership terminated almost directly after both teams were presented to the King in front of the pavilion, Ponsford, who had batted very soundly, being caught at slip. Woodfull, always restrained but showing rare judgment, withstood the attack for five hours and a half. His defence was remarkable and he scarcely ever lifted the ball but he enjoyed one great stroke of fortune. Just before the King arrived, Woodfull, playing forward to Robins, dragged his foot over the crease. Duckworth gathered the ball and swept it back to the stumps but omitted to remove the bails. That little error cost England dear. Bradman, who went in when Ponsford was out and the bowling had been mastered, seized his opportunity in rare style and, hitting all round the wicket with power and accuracy, had scored 155 runs the close.

On the Monday, Australia added 325 runs for the loss of four more batsmen before declaring at the tea interval. The partnership between Bradman and Kippax, which did not end until Bradman was caught at extra mid-off, produced 192 in less than three hours. In obtaining his 254, the famous Australian gave nothing approaching a chance. He nearly played on at 111 and, at 191, in trying to turn the ball to leg he edged it deep into the slips but, apart from those trifling errors, no real fault could be found with his display.

England thus required 304 to escape an innings defeat. The score was up to 129 the next morning before Hammond left, but when the fifth wicket fell at 147 England looked like losing in an innings. Indeed, but for an unaccountable misunderstanding between Richardson and Ponsford, this would probably have happened. Chapman, before he had scored, mis-hit a ball and the two fieldsmen stood and watched it fall between them. Eventually settling down, Chapman hit in rare style, being especially severe on Grimmett. Allen, too, batted with marked skill and aggression. It was about this time that, with a little care and thoughtfulness, England might have saved the game for, at the luncheon interval, with five men out, they had cleared off all but 42 of the arrears. So far from devoting their energies to defence they continued hitting away, adding another 113 in an hour and a quarter afterwards but losing their last five wickets. Chapman, eighth to leave at 354, obtained his runs in just over two hours and a half. Four sixes and 12 fours were among his strokes. He drove and pulled with tremendous power in a very wonderful display. A foolish call by Robins cost a valuable wicket when White was run out, and the innings closed for 375.

Australia thus had to make only 72 to win, but in 20 minutes there was much excitement. Ponsford was bowled at 16, Bradman caught low down at backward point at 17, and Kippax taken at the wicket at 22. Visions of a remarkable collapse arose but Woodfull, exercising sound generalship by taking most of Robins's bowling himself, tided over an anxious period and he and McCabe hit the required runs.

England v Australia 1930   Second Test

At Lord's, June 27, 28, 30, July 1, 1930. Result: Australia won by seven wickets.

ENGLAND

	First innings		Second innings	
J. B. Hobbs c Oldfield b Fairfax	1	– b Grimmett	19
F. E. Woolley c Wall b Fairfax	41	– hit wicket b Grimmett	28
W. R. Hammond b Grimmett	38	– c Fairfax b Grimmett	32
K. S. Duleepsinhji c Bradman b Grimmett	173	– c Oldfield b Hornibrook	48
E. H. Hendren c McCabe b Fairfax	48	– c Richardson b Grimmett	9
*A. P. F. Chapman c Oldfield b Wall	11	– c Oldfield b Fairfax	121
G. O. B. Allen b Fairfax	3	– lbw b Grimmett	57
M. W. Tate c McCabe b Wall	54	– c Ponsford b Grimmett	10
R. W. V. Robins c Oldfield b Hornibrook	5	– not out	11
J. C. White not out	23	– run out	10
†G. Duckworth c Oldfield b Wall	18	– lbw b Fairfax	0
B 2, l-b 7, n-b 1	10	B 16, l-b 13, w 1	30

1-13 2-53 3-105 4-209 5-236 6-239   425   1-45 2-58 3-129 4-141 5-147 6-272   375
7-337 8-363 9-387 10-425   7-329 8-354 9-372 10-375

First innings – Wall 29.4–2–118–3; Fairfax 31–6–101–4; Grimmett 33–4–105–2; Hornibrook 26–6–62–1; McCabe 9–1–29–0.
Second innings – Wall 25–2–80–0; Fairfax 12.4–2–37–2; Grimmett 53–13–167–6; Hornibrook 22–6–49–1; McCabe 3–1–11–0; Bradman 1–0–1–0.

AUSTRALIA

	First innings		Second innings	
*W. M. Woodfull st Duckworth b Robins	155	– not out	26
W. H. Ponsford c Hammond b White	81	– b Robins	14
D. G. Bradman c Chapman b White	254	– c Chapman b Tate	1
A. F. Kippax b White	83	– c Duckworth b Robins	3
S. J. McCabe c Woolley b Hammond	44	– not out	25
V. Y. Richardson c Hobbs b Tate	30		
†W. A. S. Oldfield not out	43		
A. G. Fairfax not out	20		
C. V. Grimmett			
P. M. Hornibrook			
T. W. Wall			
B 6, l-b 8, w 5	19	B 1, l-b 2	3

1-162 2-393 3-585 4-588 5-643   (6 wkts dec.) 729   1-16 2-17 3-22   (3 wkts) 72
6-672

First innings – Allen 34–7–115–0; Tate 64–16–148–1; White 51–7–158–3; Robins 42–1–172–1; Hammond 35–8–82–1; Woolley 6–0–35–0.
Second innings – Tate 13–6–21–1; White 2–0–8–0; Robins 9–1–34–2; Hammond 4.2–1–6–0.

Toss won by England   UMPIRES F. Chester and T. W. Oates

CRICKETER OF THE YEAR – D. G. BRADMAN   Sydney Southerton, 1931

Donald George Bradman who, coming to England for the first time met with greater success as a batsman than any other Australian cricketer who has visited this country, was born at Cootamundra, a small up-country township in New South Wales, on August 27, 1908. Opinions differ as to the merit of Bradman's abilities, judged purely from the standpoint of the highest batsmanship. Certain good judges aver that his footwork is correct; others contend the reverse is the case. Both are right. For a fast, true wicket his footwork is wonderfully good. When the ball is turning, however, there are limitations to Bradman's skill. As was observed by those who saw him on a turning wicket at Brisbane and on one nothing like so vicious at Old Trafford last summer, this young batsman still has something to learn in the matter of playing a correct offensive or defensive stroke with the conditions in favour of the bowler.

Still, as a run-getter, he stands alone. He does not favour the forward method of defence, much preferring to go half-way or entirely back. His scoring strokes are many and varied. He can turn to leg and cut with delightful accuracy, but above all he is a superb driver. One very pronounced feature of his batting is that he rarely lifts the ball and as he showed English spectators so frequently last season, and particularly at Lord's, he will send two consecutive and similar deliveries in different directions. In grace of style he may not be a Trumper or a Macartney but his performances speak for themselves. Not yet 23, Bradman should have years of cricket ahead and, judging by what he has already accomplished, there would seem to be no limit to his possibilities.

Third Test
At Leeds, July 11, 12, 14, 15, 1930. Drawn.

The Third Test, while it afforded that remarkable young batsman, Bradman, the opportunity of leaving all individual batting records in representative matches far behind, was in many respects an unsatisfactory affair. England had the worst of it from start to finish but escaped with a draw, a heavy storm on Sunday night followed by further rain restricting the third day's play to 45 minutes while, on the Tuesday, further delay occurred owing to defective light.

The game will go down to history on account of the wonderful batting performance accomplished by Bradman who, with an innings of 334, beat the previous-highest score in England and Australia matches – 287 by R. E. Foster for England at Sydney – which had stood since December 1903. Bradman achieved fame in other directions. Like C. G. Macartney on the same ground four years previously, he reached three figures before lunch-time on the first day, and was not out 309 at the close. In playing two consecutive innings of over 200 in Test matches he equalled the performance of Hammond during the previous tour in Australia. Truly could it be called Bradman's Match. Bigger though it was and characterised by splendid strokeplay, Bradman's innings did not quite approach his 254 at Lord's in freedom from fault, but as to its extraordinary merit there could be no doubt. As usual, he rarely lifted the ball. His footwork was admirable, as was the way he played his defensive strokes to balls just short of a length.

Woodfull won the toss and Australia led off so brilliantly that, when the first day's play ended, they had 458 runs on the board with only three wickets down. The pitch, like those at Nottingham and Lord's, was, on the first day at any rate, lacking in life and pace and all in favour of batsmen. Jackson off the fifth ball of the second over was caught at forward short leg, but England had to wait until five minutes past three before they took another wicket, Woodfull and Bradman, in the meantime, putting on 192. This was very largely the work of Bradman who, quick to settle down, completed 102 out of the first 127. After Woodfull left, bowled trying to hook a shortish ball, Bradman found another admirable partner in Kippax who, if overshadowed by his colleague, played uncommonly well in helping to add 229. The next day McCabe stayed until 63 runs had been put on, but nothing of any consequence was accomplished by the rest. Bradman, sixth out at 508, obtained his 334 in six hours and a quarter, his score being made up of 46 fours, six threes, 26 twos, and 80 singles. When he had made 141 he put up a ball towards mid-wicket and at 202 he skyed a ball over Tate's head at mid-on – indeed, a man a little quicker than Tate might have caught it. But, Bradman gave only one chance, being missed at the wicket off Geary at 273.

The total was only 53 when Hobbs was out in a manner which provoked considerable discussion. A'Beckett, fielding very close in on the on side to Grimmett's bowling, took the ball from a gentle stroke very low down, turning a complete somersault but retaining possession. Hobbs was about to walk away but stepped back into his crease on overhearing a remark by Oldfield and an appeal from other members of the side. An appeal having been made, Hobbs was perfectly justified in waiting for the decision. Oates, the umpire at the bowler's end, was unable to give one, a'Beckett in falling over obscuring his view, so he referred to Bestwick at square leg. Unhappily, Bestwick hesitated before holding up his finger, and the great majority of the crowd took the view that a'Beckett had not properly made the catch.

Hammond and Duleepsinhji added 59 and then Leyland helped to put on 83, Hammond, when 52, having just previously been missed by Oldfield standing back to Wall. Geary was run out at 206 and England at the close of play found themselves 354 behind and requiring 205 to save the follow-on. On the Monday the weather following a storm in the night, which resulted in water lying in patches on the ground, was very bad. So long a delay occurred that not until half-past five was play proceeded with. Thirty runs were scored before an appeal against the light was upheld.

On Tuesday morning Duckworth batted so well that the score was up to 289 before he was caught at the wicket, 83 runs having been added in rather more than two hours. Hammond stayed until the score was 319 after resisting the bowling for five hours and 20 minutes. He hit only 14 fours but gave a splendid display of skilful batting, neglecting very few opportunities of scoring off anything in the nature of a punishable ball.

England followed on 179 behind and, as over three hours remained, there was always a possibility of them losing. Hobbs and Sutcliffe opened the innings in a very poor light. After a quarter of an hour, they appealed against it and the players went in. For some extraordinary reason the crowd took this in very bad part, booing the batsmen and cheering the Australians, while on the game being resumed there was a continuance of this unseemly behaviour. With 24 scored, Hobbs was brilliantly thrown out by Bradman from deep mid-off, but Sutcliffe and Hammond stayed nearly an hour to add 50. After Duleepsinhji had been caught at point off a ball which he did not see, another appeal against the light was made and no further cricket took place.

Toss: Australia. **Australia 566** (W. M. Woodfull 50, D. G. Bradman 334, A. F. Kippax 77, M. W. Tate 5-124); **England 391** (W. R. Hammond 113, C. V. Grimmett 5-135) **and 95-3.**

Fourth Test
At Manchester, July 25, 26, 28, 29, 1930. Drawn.

Interfered with by rain to a much greater extent than was the case in the game at Leeds, the Fourth Test had also to be left drawn. Cricket went on without interruption on the first two days, but play lasted only 45 minutes on the third afternoon and not a ball was bowled on the last day.

Under conditions which were expected to confer an advantage on them, England again had the worst of matters. For the fourth time the batting proved inconsistent, a promising start being discounted by certain failures which were only partially retrieved, while the bowling, apart from that of Peebles, did not really inspire confidence or achieve the success anticipated on a soft wicket. So soft was the turf that the start had to be delayed for half an hour and the foothold proved so uncertain that Chapman, fielding at silly mid-off, had to put down a lot of sawdust to prevent himself slipping.

Woodfull and Ponsford gave their side another fine start, putting on 106 for the first wicket. Ponsford batted admirably, in the circumstances better probably than on any other occasion during the tour. His footwork was first-class, his defence nearly perfect and his scoring strokes, especially in forcing the ball away on the on side, brought off with power and certainty. Woodfull also played extremely well, but for a long time before lunch he was definitely uncomfortable and uncertain in dealing with Peebles. The Middlesex amateur caused Ponsford little trouble; he constantly made Woodfull play false strokes. Indeed, Woodfull had made only ten when a googly, at which he did not play, went only just over the middle and leg stumps.

Bradman had a most unhappy experience. He was nearly bowled first ball by Peebles and, when ten, gave a chance low down in the slips. He hit one four off a full-toss and then, trying to cut a leg-break, was nicely caught at second slip. Just about this time, Peebles was bowling extremely well, Kippax being appealed against for lbw to the first three balls he received. On for an hour before lunch and an hour and a quarter afterwards, Peebles took only one wicket during this time but he bowled well enough to have obtained five or six. Ponsford and Kippax added 46 before Hammond, with an off-break – a very good ball – clean-bowled Ponsford at 184. England were on top, but Kippax suddenly found his best form and hit two fours in each of three overs from Peebles, his driving being delightful. Caught low down in the gully at 239, off a ball which got up quickly, Kippax hit eight fours during his stay of nearly two hours.

Next morning Grimmett, driving particularly well, made his highest score in a Test match by excellent batting. His experience in this match was curious, for he did not take a wicket. Peebles, whose three wickets cost 150 runs, was, by general consent, the best bowler on the England side and deserved a much better record. If one fault could be urged against him it was that he relied far too much on the googly.

Hobbs and Sutcliffe scored 29 runs before lunch, Hobbs receiving a nasty blow in the groin. It is more than likely that this affected his batting for he made only 31 out of the 108 put on for the opening partnership. Sutcliffe, on the other hand, gave a brilliant display of driving, pulling and hooking. He might have been caught directly after lunch if Hornibrook, fielding in the slips, had not baulked Richardson, but that was the only mistake in a dashing exhibition of strong forcing cricket. He was out to a remarkable catch at long leg off a big hit, Bradman taking the ball high up and then falling among the spectators. Scoring 74 out of 115, Sutcliffe hit a six and ten fours. Hammond playing on, England although the 100 had gone up with no wicket down, had three men out for 119 and, at the drawing of stumps, they were still 124 runs behind.

The next day it rained. The downpour was not continuous but rather in the shape of heavy squalls and not until half-past five could the game be resumed. England lost three wickets for 30, McCabe taking them all. Two appeals were made against the light, the second and successful one just after a quarter-past six, and soon after the players had gone in rain fell in torrents. The downpour continued throughout the night and so saturated did the already wet turf become that on Tuesday morning, an hour before the game should have been resumed, it was decided that play was out of the question.

Toss: Australia. **Australia 345** (W. M. Woodfull 54, W. H. Ponsford 83, A. F. Kippax 51, C. V. Grimmett 50);
England 251-8 (H. Sutcliffe 74, K. S. Duleepsinhji 54, S. J. McCabe 4-41).

Obituary – Charles Bannerman

1931

Charles Bannerman died in Sydney on August 20, 1930, aged 79. He was one of the three survivors of the 22 players who took part in the first Test match. Only those whose memories go back many years can recall this very fine batsman. In his day he was the best in Australia. He had a splendid style, standing well up to the ball, and was master of nearly every stroke; indeed his batting was essentially skilful and polished. He drove finely to the off, and could hit with power and accuracy to leg.

The match in which he really made his name took place in Melbourne in the middle of March, 1877. James Lillywhite's team was then touring Australia, and so much had the standard of cricket there improved since the previous visit of an English side that the challenge was made to play an 11-a-side match. The faith the Australians had in themselves was justified for, with England lacking the assistance of a recognised wicket-keeper, Australia won by 45 runs. Bannerman had the distinction of playing an innings of 165, and not one of his companions was able to reach 20. During the first day he scored 126 of his side's 166 for six wickets. Never before had an Australian batsman scored a century against an English XI.

Fifth Test

At The Oval, August 16, 18, 19, 20, 21, 22, 1930. Australia won by an innings and 39 runs.

Beating England in an innings with 39 runs to spare, Australia won the rubber and so regained possession of the Ashes they had lost four years previously on the same ground. The concluding match had to be played to a finish. Including the Thursday when, owing to rain, not a ball could be bowled, the encounter was spread over six days – a longer time than had ever before been occupied by a Test match in England.

Australia won fairly and squarely, replying to England's first innings of 405 with a total of 695, and then getting the Englishmen out for 251, but just as rain had assisted England in the First Test, so it operated against them at The Oval. They had to play their second innings on a pitch so entirely suited to bowlers that in the circumstances they actually accomplished a good performance in scoring as many runs as they did. Admitting the weather bore hardly upon the losers, it is but proper to observe that England contributed to their undoing by faulty work in the field. To stress the mistakes of any particular individual is never a congenial task, but as a matter of history it must be set down that Duckworth, usually so dependable a wicket-keeper, failed badly. At the very outset he missed Woodfull, let off Ponsford twice before he had made 50 and, on the Tuesday, failed to catch Bradman at the wicket. Between them these three made 396 runs, so it can easily be realised what a tremendous difference these blunders made to England's chances.

Once more Australia owed a great deal to Bradman, who followed up his previous successes with 232. As usual he scored well in front of the wicket but he obtained a large number of runs on the leg side, while from start to finish his defence was altogether remarkable. All the same he did not play in anything like the attractive style he had shown at Lord's; indeed, there were periods when he became monotonous.

The passing-over of Chapman, in whose stead Wyatt captained the side, raised a storm of protest. There can be no question that the absence of Chapman's inspiring influence in the field was felt. A much greater mistake was made in bringing in Whysall, who not only failed as a batsman but was obviously much too slow as a fieldsman for a Test match. As in all the other games, the England batting, despite the fine total put together, was inconsistent, weakness being developed where strength should have existed. The bowling, too, apart from that of Peebles, never looked really good enough to get Australia out at reasonable cost.

England stayed in for the whole of the first day and scored 316 for five, but at one point they were in a bad way, the fifth man leaving when the total was only 197. To begin with, Hobbs and Sutcliffe put on 68, Hobbs being caught at short leg just before lunch, while at 97 Whysall left. There came some delightful batting by Duleepsinhji who, driving, hooking and cutting in dazzling style, scored 50 out of the next 65 runs in 50 minutes. After tea, Sutcliffe batted beautifully and was 138 when play ceased. He and Wyatt had added 119 and before Sutcliffe was out on Monday morning the stand had realised 170.

Sutcliffe made exactly the same score as he had done in the corresponding match four years previously. He brought off some splendid hits to square leg and to the on, while his off-driving was admirable. As far as was seen he did not give a chance. Eighth to leave at 379, Wyatt was in for three hours for a most valuable 64, in which he hit hard in front of the wicket. On the Monday morning, five England wickets fell for 89.

Before lunch, both Woodfull and Ponsford should have been out, Woodfull being missed at the wicket when six and Ponsford at 23 giving a chance of stumping. Later on Ponsford, at 45, was let off again and for these mistakes England had to pay a heavy price. Altogether the two men put on 159 before Ponsford was bowled third ball after tea. He batted extremely well, if not perhaps quite so skilfully as at Manchester, the manner in which he dealt with Larwood clearly disproving the idea that he could not face him. Scoring at the start chiefly on the leg side, he cut and drove beautifully afterwards. With the score up to 190, Woodfull was out, his stay having extended over

The Don: the greatest batsman of all, pictured during his 232 at The Oval in 1930. Bradman made a record 974 runs in that series, and finished with 5,028 runs in 37 Tests against England.

three hours and a quarter. He hit only three fours but played a most valuable innings. When play ceased, Australia, with two men out for 215, were only 190 runs behind.

Then came the big stand of the innings, Bradman and Jackson not being separated until one o'clock on Wednesday, by which time they had put on 243. Jackson was nearly run out before he had scored and almost bowled when five, while Bradman, at 82, gave a chance at the wicket. Rain came on during lunch on the Tuesday, the score then standing at 371 for three, and a further break occurred with the score at 402.

On the Wednesday morning the ball flew about a good deal, both batsmen frequently being hit on the body. The partnership might have ended at 458 had Leyland returned the ball to the right end and on more than one occasion each player cocked the ball up dangerously but always just wide of the fieldsmen. Caught at length at extra cover-point, Jackson played nothing like as well as those who saw him in Australia knew he could. Bradman had gone steadily on but when joined by McCabe was overshadowed, the latter driving brilliantly. Another 64 were added and then Bradman was caught by Duckworth standing back. In seven hours he made 232 out of 411 with 16 fours. McCabe left at 594, but the tired England bowlers came in for further punishment, Oldfield and Fairfax putting on 76. In the end Australia were all out just before half-past five. Bowling 71 overs, Peebles took six wickets but had 204 runs hit from him.

England, 290 behind, went in again at a quarter to six. The Australians gathered round Hobbs and gave three cheers as a tribute to the great batsman, playing presumably his last innings for England. Sutcliffe had scored only six out of the eight runs on the board when he was missed at the wicket off Fairfax. This was indeed a great piece of luck for England, but when the score reached 17 Hobbs played on.

No play took place on the Thursday owing to rain. On Friday the sun shone and everyone realised that only a miracle could save England. Sutcliffe again batted well and Duleepsinhji gave another fine display. These two added 81 before Sutcliffe was caught at second slip from a ball which popped up and went off the shoulder of his bat. Hammond went for the bowling in rare style, hitting five fours in three overs off Hornibrook, and 54 runs were added in 40 minutes before Leyland left. With his dismissal, England's hope of saving the innings defeat disappeared. With the last man in Hammond was missed at long-off by Bradman, but three runs later he fell to a catch in the slips and the match was all over.

The bowling honours went entirely to Hornibrook who, on a pitch suited to his bowling, obtained seven wickets. Given a second spell when England were 106 for two, he sent down 24 overs and two balls – eight of which were maidens – for 72 runs and seven wickets.

Very appropriately, the day on which Australia regained the Ashes with this victory coincided with the birthday of Woodfull, their captain, who was then 33.

Toss. England. **England 405** (H. Sutcliffe 161, K. S. Duleepsinhji 50, R. E. S. Wyatt 64, C. V. Grimmett 4-135) and 251 (H. Sutcliffe 54, W. R. Hammond 60, P. M. Hornibrook 7-92); **Australia 695** (W. M. Woodfull 54, W. H. Ponsford 110, D. G. Bradman 232, A. Jackson 73, S. J. McCabe 54, A. G. Fairfax 53*, I. A. R. Peebles 6-204).

CRICKETER OF THE YEAR – C. V. GRIMMETT
Sydney Southerton, 1931

Clarence Victor Grimmett, the famous Australian slow bowler, was born on December 25, 1892, at Dunedin, New Zealand. Something of a wanderer until his real merit was appreciated by the South Australian Cricket Association, Grimmett first jumped into fame by his performances against the MCC team in 1924–25. Picked for the first time for Australia in the final Test match, he met with phenomenal success, taking 11 wickets for 82 runs and having the biggest individual share in England's defeat. From that time he never looked back, although on coming to England in 1926 his 13 wickets in the five Test matches cost nearly 32 runs apiece. Against the next MCC side in Australia he obtained 23 wickets in the Tests but was again expensive.

Last season he shared with Bradman the chief honours of the tour. At Nottingham he took ten wickets for 201 runs, at Lord's eight for 272, and at Leeds – in which match he bowled probably better than in any other – six for 168. Altogether he dismissed 29 England batsmen for just under 32 runs apiece, while in all first-class engagements he took 144 wickets.

In style Grimmett recalled memories of the days of the old round-arm bowlers but, owing to a pronounced bend over the left hip when he delivered the ball, his right arm was not so low as it appeared to be. Like all first-class slow leg-breakers he did not make the ball turn too much. He bowled the googly with a clever disguise of intention, and one of his most successful deliveries was the top-spinner with which he got so many men leg-before. Above everything else, however, he kept a practically perfect length. Only on rare occasions did he send down a loose ball.

NOTES BY THE EDITOR C. Stewart Caine, 1931

A big disappointment for everybody interested in the success of English cricket proved to be in store last summer. So little time having elapsed since A. P. F. Chapman's team won four Test matches out of five in Australia, there existed a general feeling of confidence that the side chosen by the Australian authorities to come to England in pursuit of the mythical Ashes would fail in the object of their endeavours. Not only had England apparently a big advantage in the call they possessed upon a considerable number of men of experience as well as ability, but there seemed to exist strong doubts as to whether the attack at the command of the tourists would prove strong enough.

Even after the Australians had been here some time and had clearly shown that they would always be hard to beat, I don't think many people regarded them as likely to win the rubber. That extraordinary young cricketer, Bradman, meeting with truly phenomenal success, put together scores of 334, 254, 232 and 131 in the Tests and the Australians' totals, after the first innings at Nottingham, were 335, 729 for six, 566, 345 and 695. Those figures speak only too eloquently for the run-getting powers of our visitors.

I trust that we have seen the last of playing a match to a finish, however many days may be required for that purpose. Given normal circumstances, four days are quite sufficient for the decision of a game contested in a reasonably enterprising spirit – the real cricket spirit. Over and above that question, the idea of a rubber in which in the deciding game the conditions are changed from those obtaining in the earlier encounters cannot logically be defended.

AUSTRALIA v ENGLAND 1932–33 Sydney Southerton

While in some of the early tours strong differences of opinion arose to cause trouble, it is very doubtful if ever a team from England met with such openly expressed hostility as that visiting Australia in the winter of 1932–33. The members of it were successful in their mission, and, winning four of the five Test matches, recovered the Ashes which had been lost at The Oval in 1930.

One must always be a little chary of comparisons, but it would be idle to pretend that anything like the same cordial feelings between our players and those of Australia existed during the more recent tour as they did on the occasion of the preceding visit. It is all past history now. Suffice it to say that a method of bowling was evolved – mainly with the idea of curbing the scoring propensities of Bradman – which met with almost general condemnation among Australian cricketers and spectators and which, when something of the real truth was ultimately known in this country, caused people at home to wonder if the winning of the rubber was, after all, worth this strife.

Jardine, while nothing like the batsman of four years earlier, captained the side superbly. Fortunate in having four fast bowlers in Larwood, Allen, Voce and Bowes, he rang the changes in most astute fashion; placed his field very judiciously and generally, despite the rancour he aroused by the manner in which he exploited fast leg-theory bowling, earned unstinted praise for his able management of the team in the field.

The tour having to be described largely from cabled reports and hearsay evidence, it may appear presumptuous, seeing that the team won the Ashes, to criticise the batting methods. One cannot resist a feeling that, having regard to the limitations of the Australian attack, the batting of the Englishmen was rather too often of a negative quality. In effect, too great attention seemed to be paid to what is known as digging in rather than to going for the bowling. Altogether Hammond had a very good tour, but if often brilliant was not quite the dominating personality of four years previously. Sutcliffe again acquitted himself with distinction, his highest score, 194, being made in the First Test at Sydney. To Paynter the trip must on the whole have been enjoyable, for, coming into the team in the Third Test, he played a great part in enabling England, after a truly deplorable start, to put together a good total, while the Fourth Test will always be associated with his name. Suffering with trouble to his throat, he got up from a bed of sickness to score a noble innings of 83 and then enjoyed the felicity of making the winning hit to give England the Ashes.

It was the opinion on all hands that to Larwood belonged chief credit for England winning the rubber. Sharply divergent views will probably always be held as to the desirability of the method of attack he employed. This, however, is not the place to discuss that somewhat thorny subject. Suffice it to say that his fast leg-theory bowling, with three or four fieldsmen close in and others deeper on the leg side, enabled him to establish an ascendancy over practically all the leading Australian batsmen. Whatever may be thought of this type of bowling, no possible doubt existed that Larwood proved himself the ideal exponent of it. Stronger probably than on his previous visit to Australia, and very judiciously nursed by Jardine, he not only maintained an extraordinarily accurate length necessary for this form of attack but kept up a tremendous pace. In his own way Larwood obviously must have bowled magnificently. His record of wickets and the standing of his victims proves this, and in match after match the batsmen clearly gave the impression of being overawed.

First Test

At Sydney, December 2, 3, 5, 6, 7, 1932. England won by ten wickets.

Leading off in fine style, England won early on the fifth day by ten wickets. The bowling of Larwood, who in the two innings dismissed ten men at a cost of 124 runs, and the batting of Sutcliffe, Hammond and Pataudi stood out as the prominent successes of the match from the English point of view.

At the same time the encounter brought great fame to McCabe who, with an innings of 187, obtained his first century in Test matches and scored off Larwood's bowling in a style which for daring and brilliance was not approached by any other Australian during the tour. Later in the game the displays of the three Englishmen discounted considerably the fine work done by McCabe. Sutcliffe gave a typical exhibition, being wonderfully sure in defence and certain in his off-driving; Hammond was eminently good, but Pataudi was, for the most part, plodding and rather wearisome to watch. He did not show the Sydney public anything like the great array of strokes of which he is known to be capable and seemed on the whole disinclined to take the slightest risk with balls which apparently were quite safe to hit. Still, it was a great performance on England's part that their first three wickets should each have produced over 100 and for Sutcliffe to have taken part in all three stands.

Before lunch on the first day, Australia scored 63 for the loss of Woodfull, their captain. Following the interval Larwood, bowling at a great pace, met with astonishing success, sending back Ponsford, Fingleton and Kippax as the score advanced only to 87. Then came another dramatic change, McCabe finding a valuable partner in Richardson, who helped to add 129. Both men took chances against the high-rising balls delivered at them, but everything came off, McCabe's hitting on the on side being marvellous.

Australia finished up with six men out for 290. They had no great reason to be dissatisfied, but England next day polished off the innings and proceeded to place themselves in a strong position. McCabe took out his bat, scoring 60 of the 70 runs added by the last four wickets. He and Grimmett put on 68, and when Wall was in 55 came in about half an hour. Except that he was nearly caught by Larwood at 159, McCabe gave a faultless display; in just over four hours he hit no fewer than 25 fours.

England batted for the rest of the day, scoring 252 for one. Sutcliffe and Wyatt made 112 together and then Hammond stayed with Sutcliffe for the rest of the afternoon, both men batting gloriously. England remained at the wickets the whole of Monday and, adding 227 for the loss of five more wickets, wound up 119 ahead with four men to be disposed of. The bowling, especially that of O'Reilly, remained very steady, but the Englishmen did not attempt to force the pace, being more concerned in consolidating a sound position. Hammond was second out at 300 after helping to add 188, but he did not quite approach the brilliance he had shown on Saturday. Still, his innings was a very fine one and then, shortly after tea, Sutcliffe was third to leave at 423. In his highest Test innings against Australia Sutcliffe hit only 13 fours. He had one great piece of luck when he was 43, playing a ball on to his wicket without, however, removing the bails. Otherwise his defensive strokes were perfect. For the rest of the time Pataudi dominated the proceedings and when on the fourth day the innings closed for 524, or 164 ahead, he was last out. He scored chiefly by leg-glances and strokes on the off side, but hit only six fours.

Going in a second time, Australia collapsed badly. Larwood, again bowling at a great pace, and well backed up by Voce, carried everything before him and when play ceased Australia had lost nine wickets for 164. Thus they had exactly cleared off the arrears. Larwood's speed was tremendous and nobody faced him with any confidence, but after eight men were out for 113 there came unexpected resistance from Nagel and Wall. Of the previous batsmen only Fingleton and McCabe stayed any time. The match being as good as over, there were less than 100 present to see the finish next morning.

Reference to the fact that Bradman, owing to illness, was unable to play must not be omitted, although in view of subsequent events it is, to say the least, questionable, if his presence would have staved off disaster.

Toss: Australia. **Australia 360** (S. J. McCabe 187*, H. Larwood 5-96, W. Voce 4-110) **and 164** (H. Larwood 5-28); **England 524** (H. Sutcliffe 194, W. R. Hammond 112, Nawab of Pataudi 102) **and 1-0**.

Second Test

At Melbourne, December 30, 31, 1932, January 2, 3, 1933. Australia won by 111 runs.

Jardine again lost the toss, but England started even better than at Sydney and, at the end of the first day, Australia had seven men out for 194. This splendid work was not followed up at all well when it came England's turn to bat and the match – over in four days – resulted in a victory for Australia by 111 runs.

Having recovered from his indisposition, Bradman was able to play for Australia, whose bowling was strengthened by the inclusion of Ironmonger. Bradman, dismissed for nought on the opening day, afterwards scored a brilliant 103 not out, but O'Reilly had most to do with the success of Australia by getting rid of ten of the Englishmen.

For a Test match in Australia, this was a game of small scores, and it can be said at once that the pitch proved quite different from any experienced in former tours. It lacked the usual firmness associated with wickets at Melbourne and Jardine, playing all his pace bowlers by including Bowes for Verity, was completely misled in his assumption that fast bowling would be likely to win the match. Apart from Wall, spin bowlers carried off the honours and of these England had only Hammond in their team.

Fingleton made 83 out of 156 before being fifth to leave. His defence throughout was wonderfully sound and his patience unlimited. At times he made poor strokes, but generally he timed those on the leg side well and his cutting was excellent. Australia had their worst shock when Bradman was out first ball to Bowes. He tried to hook it, but edged it down on to the stumps. At times the ball bounced a good deal, Woodfull on one occasion being struck over the heart.

On the second day the last three wickets went down for another 34 runs, but then England gave such a poor display against O'Reilly and Wall that at stumps nine wickets were down for 161. Sutcliffe scored 52, but enjoyed unusual luck in getting them. Although the score at tea was 91 for three, six men were got rid of afterwards for 70 runs.

On the third day there was a record crowd of nearly 70,000. England were finished off for 169, conceding a lead of 59. At their second attempt Australia, thanks almost entirely to Bradman, made 191 and at the end of the day England, left to get 251, had 45 minutes' batting. Jardine changed the order, sending in Leyland with Sutcliffe, and so well did this move turn out that they scored 43 together without being separated.

The day's cricket really was dominated by Bradman who, after a succession of failures, simply took his courage in both hands and played a wonderful innings. In a way his batting was masterly. He went in when two wickets had fallen for 27 and resisted a lot of good bowling for over three hours and a half to complete his hundred when Ironmonger, the last man, was in. While Wall and O'Reilly were his partners he sacrificed many runs to keep the bowling. To few other Australian batsmen could such an innings as Bradman played have been possible.

On the last day England required 208, but O'Reilly and Ironmonger proved too much on a pitch which by this time took spin to a pronounced degree. Sutcliffe and Leyland were soon separated and of the rest only Wyatt, Hammond and Allen stayed any time. For Australia the victory was a triumph of teamwork and they were to be congratulated on pulling the match out of the fire after their poor show on the first day. O'Reilly, bowling into the wind, made the ball float, while Ironmonger found a spot on the wicket and caused the ball to lift and at times turn abruptly. The fact that in fine weather 40 wickets went down in four days for an aggregate of 727 runs clearly suggested that at no time was the pitch all that it should have been.

Toss: Australia. **Australia 228** (J. H. W. Fingleton 83) **and 191** (D. G. Bradman 103*);
England 169 (H. Sutcliffe 52, T. W. Wall 4-52, W. J. O'Reilly 5-63)
and 139 (W. J. O'Reilly 5-66, H. Ironmonger 4-26).

Third Test

At Adelaide, January 13, 14, 16, 17, 18, 19, 1933. England won by 338 runs.

The Third Test will go down to history as probably the most unpleasant ever played. So hostile was the feeling of the Australian public against Jardine that on the days before the game started people were excluded from the ground when the Englishmen were practising. As England batted first nothing out of the common occurred to begin with, but later on, when Australia went in and Woodfull was hit over the heart again while Oldfield had to retire owing to a blow on the head, the majority of the spectators completely lost all hold on their feelings. Insulting remarks were hurled at Jardine, and when Larwood started to bowl his leg theory he came in for his share of abuse. Not to put too fine a point on it, pandemonium reigned.

A passage of words between Pelham Warner *[England's joint manager – Ed.]* and Woodfull in the dressing-room increased the bitter feeling prevalent in the crowd, and the dispatch of the cablegram protesting against Bodyline bowling served no purpose in whatever endeavours were made to appease tempers already badly frayed. Altogether the whole atmosphere was a disgrace to cricket. One must pay tribute to Jardine. He did not shrink from the line of action he had taken up; he showed great pluck in often fielding near to the boundary where he became an easy target for offensive and sometimes filthy remarks; and above all he captained his team in this particular match like a genius. Much as they disliked the method of attack he controlled, all the leading Australian critics were unanimous in their praise of his skill as a leader.

England made a dreadful start, four wickets going down in an hour for 30 runs and the score being 37 at lunch, but then came a stand which turned the course of the game and put England on the road to ultimate success. Leyland and Wyatt, if enjoying a certain amount of luck, batted, uncommonly well while adding 156. Leyland, who in the end played on, hit 13 fours in an innings which included many fine off-drives. Wyatt, whose hitting to square leg brought him three sixes, left soon afterwards, but Paynter – included in the side for Pataudi – and Allen added 32 useful runs, so that at the end of the day England had 236 for seven on the board. On the next morning Paynter continued to bat marvellously well, and Verity defended so manfully that the stand for the eighth wicket realised 96. Paynter pulled and drove well, while his cutting and leg-glancing were almost as good.

England were all out soon after three o'clock for 341 and followed this up by getting down the first four wickets for 51. It was during this time that Woodfull, ducking to avoid what he thought would be a rising ball, was hit on the body. Ponsford and Richardson added 58 in the last 70 minutes, but Australia wound up 232 behind with six wickets to fall. Ponsford played a fine fighting innings, cutting very well and meeting the leg-theory attack in able style. Next day he and Richardson put on 80, then Oldfield

Bodyline: the tactic dreamed up to keep Bradman quiet, in which fast, short-pitched balls were delivered to a packed leg-side field. Here Bill Woodfull, Australia's captain, drops his bat after being hit by Harold Larwood, the chief Bodyline exponent, during the Adelaide Test.

stayed for just over two hours before his participation in the match was closed by a blow on the head by a ball from Larwood.

Australia finished 119 behind, and although England lost Sutcliffe cheaply they were 204 runs ahead at the close. On the fourth day, England placed themselves in such a position that they could not very well lose, and realising that their team was going to be beaten the Adelaide public were not nearly so noisy and insulting. Leyland and Wyatt made useful scores, Verity supplemented his 45 in the first innings with 40, while Jardine, Hammond and Ames all played important parts in carrying England towards victory. As the wicket showed definite signs of wear, the outlook for Australia was very gloomy. Jardine did great work in wearing down the bowling. Altogether it was a very good day for the Englishmen. In the end Australia were left to get 532 to win.

Before the fifth day's play ended, the home side lost four of their best batsmen for 120 and to all intents and purposes the game was as good as over. Fingleton and Ponsford were out with only 12 on the board, but then came an excellent stand of 88 by Woodfull and Bradman, who was in first-rate form, hitting a six and ten fours, but just when he was becoming dangerous Verity caught him from a hard return.

On the last day Richardson and Woodfull defended stubbornly for a time, but they were separated at 171, and then Allen and Larwood quickly finished off the innings. The greatest praise is due to Woodfull, who carried his bat for the second time in a Test match. He was in for nearly four hours, making most of his runs on the leg side. The Englishmen fielded well throughout, while Allen bowled splendidly.

Toss: England. **England 341** (M. Leyland 83, R. E. S. Wyatt 78, E. Paynter 77, T. W. Wall 5-72)
and 412 (D. R. Jardine 56, W. R. Hammond 85, L. E. G. Ames 69, W. J. O'Reilly 4-79);
Australia 222 (W. H. Ponsford 85, G. O. B. Allen 4-71) **and 193** (W. M. Woodfull 73*, D. G. Bradman 66,
H. Larwood 4-71, G. O. B. Allen 4-50).

NOTES BY THE EDITOR
C. Stewart Caine, 1933

At the moment of writing the Third Test has just ended in a handsome victory for England, but while followers of cricket in this country rejoice the public in Australia appear to be getting very excited about the fast bowling of some of the Englishmen and what is variously known as leg theory, shock tactics and Bodyline methods.

Leg theory, as we have understood it, usually consisted in the delivery of a slow ball, with an off-break, pitched on the leg stump or well outside it, with three or four men fielding close in at leg and to the on. Given a ball of this description and the space nearby packed with fieldsmen, the batsman was called upon for the exercise of much judgment. Occasionally leg theory proved extremely effective but, as a rule, it tried the patience of both batsman and spectator and, if that of the batsman held out, slowed the play down to a most depressing extent.

The ball to which such strong exception is being taken in Australia is not slow or slow-medium but fast. It is dropped short and is alleged in certain quarters to be aimed at the batsman rather than at the wicket. It may at once be said that, if the intention is to hit the batsman and so demoralise him, the practice is altogether wrong – calculated, as it must be, to introduce an element of pronounced danger and altogether against the spirit of the game of cricket. Upon this point practically everybody will agree. No one wants such an element introduced. That English bowlers, to dispose of their opponents, would of themselves pursue such methods or that Jardine would acquiesce in such a course is inconceivable.

What exactly has been happening, it is difficult to realise. The shock bowlers, as they are being called, pitch apparently on the leg stump, rather short of a length and so place their field that the leg glance, the hook and the carefully guided stroke between short leg and mid-on become not only risky but, to a large extent, ineffective. Players pursuing the two-eyed stance and the ensuing movement of the right foot backwards lose largely the possibilities of run-getting in front on the off side, and an attack which shuts out practically all possibilities of scoring by well-controlled placing to leg leave the average batsman with very restricted possibilities. In these circumstances annoyance on the part of the batsman must be very easily generated, but that consequence of shock tactics is, if anything, rather an argument in favour of such methods.

Naturally such a plan, coupled with the inability of batsmen to change their game sufficiently to meet the situation, must inevitably render play rather tiresome and extend the feeling of annoyance to the spectators. Surely, however, the blame rests with the batsman rather than with the bowler. The batsman, in stepping in front of the wicket and using his pads as a second line of defence, may be within the letter of the law, but he is pursuing a mode of play which was certainly never contemplated by those who drafted the regulations. So long as that system prevails, so long will bowlers need to find something else than the good-length cleverly flighted off-break which, after beating the bat, is not allowed to hit the stumps. Two generations back, or even less, it was largely the practice of the batsman to stand clear of the leg stump and, if he stepped in front, that movement was made not in defence of his wicket but to give him power in bringing off a hit. Thus there could, in those times, be no such objection as prevails today to the lbw law.

To the abuse of this law may fairly be traced the trouble which has arisen. In suggesting that such bowling has become a menace to the best interests of the game, is causing bitter feelings between players and, unless stopped at once, is likely to upset the friendly relations between England and Australia, the Australian Board seem to have lost their sense of proportion. The idea that a method to which, while often practised in the past by Australian as well as English bowlers, no exception had been taken in public could jeopardise the relations of the two countries, appears really too absurd. At the same time all this acrimony, generated, I fear, partly through the papers demanding a news story daily, will not have been entirely purposeless should it, in the long run, bring about a return to the old rule as to lbw: "If the striker puts his leg before the wicket with a design to stop the ball and actually prevent the ball from hitting his wicket by it, the striker is out."

Fourth Test

At Brisbane, February 10, 11, 13, 14, 15, 16, 1933. England won by six wickets.

England won the Fourth Test by six wickets, so being successful in the rubber and regaining the Ashes. Once more Jardine captained his side with remarkable skill, his management of his bowlers and his placing of the field being worthy of great praise. In this respect he certainly outshone Woodfull, who had under his command three new men, while for England Voce, who was unwell, stood down for Mitchell.

The Australians at times seemed to have a reasonable chance, but they failed to drive home a temporary advantage, and generally they did not appear to be a well-balanced side, while there is no doubt that nearly all of them were overawed by Larwood. The match will always be memorable for the great part played in the victory by Paynter. Suffering from an affection of the throat, he left a sickbed and put together a splendid innings of 83, while he enjoyed the additional satisfaction later on of making the winning hit with a six.

Woodfull again won the toss, and this time took Richardson in with him. This proved highly successful, for both left the balls on the leg side severely alone and, thanks to their partnership of 133, Australia made 251 for three on the first day. The English fielding was not so smart as in former matches, but Jardine made a fine catch to dismiss McCabe, while Mitchell justified his inclusion by bowling Woodfull late in the day. Richardson after lunch made some splendid hits and Bradman carried on the good work, being 71 when stumps were pulled up. Verity kept an uncommonly good length while having only 32 runs hit off 22 overs.

On the second day, the innings closed a little after lunch for 340, the last seven wickets thus falling for 89. Larwood did great work in taking four wickets, bowling Bradman at 264 and Ponsford at 267. Bradman did not play at all well in the closing stages, drawing away more than once from Larwood's bowling. Darling and Bromley each made a few runs, the latter hitting out in rather carefree style. For the rest of the afternoon, Jardine and Sutcliffe occupied themselves in scoring 99 runs together.

The third day did not go quite so well for England, for at the close they had 271 for eight. Everyone reached double figures, but the batting generally was timorous and many balls which looked to be perfectly safe to hit were allowed to escape. This negative kind of batting, following the opening partnership of 114, was disappointing. Paynter, ill and weak, could not force matters, but he was 24 at the close, and next morning gave a superb exhibition. He scored by a variety of splendid strokes while Verity kept up his end in manly fashion. Paynter was not dismissed until England were in front, and in the end they gained a lead of 16 runs.

At Adelaide, Paynter and Verity put on 96 at a critical period; at Brisbane they added 92. Paynter's display of patient and skilful batting was certainly one of the greatest examples of pluck and fortitude in the history of Test cricket. He was in for nearly four hours, and sent the ball ten times to the boundary. As near as possible England were batting ten hours for their total of 356, which on the face of it seemed absurd.

They atoned for this by some splendid bowling and fielding, so that Australia lost four wickets for 108 and wound up only 92 in front by the close. Richardson led off in rare style, and Bradman batted brightly before falling once more to Larwood at 79. For the second time in the match Mitchell dismissed Woodfull. Apart from Darling, who at a very critical point lost his wicket through a misunderstanding with Bromley, nobody did anything of consequence on the fifth day and soon after lunch Australia were all out for 175. Once more, they showed what a long tail they had, the last five men scoring only 16 between them.

England were thus left only 160 to get, but Sutcliffe was soon out. Leyland then joined Jardine and the two men stolidly played themselves in. There was one period of over an hour when Jardine did not score, playing in this time no fewer than 82 deliveries. Altogether he and Leyland added 73, and play ended for the day with the score at 107 for two.

On the last day the flags all round the ground were at half-mast owing to the death that morning of Archie Jackson. Hammond left at 118 and Leyland 20 runs later, but then Paynter and Ames hit off the balance and soon after the match was won rain came on and poured steadily for 12 hours. Nothing could have been finer than Leyland's batting. He only hit when it was safe to do so and by his strong defence and watchful methods prevented the bowlers from getting on top at a crucial period.

Toss: Australia. **Australia 340** (V. Y. Richardson 83, W. M. Woodfull 67, D. G. Bradman 76, H. Larwood 4-101) **and 175; England 356** (H. Sutcliffe 86, E. Paynter 83, W. J. O'Reilly 4-120) **and 162-4** (M. Leyland 86).

OBITUARY – ARCHIE JACKSON 1934

Archibald Jackson died in Brisbane on February 16, 1933, the day that England defeated Australia and regained the Ashes, at the early age of 23. His passing was not only a very sad loss to Australian cricket but to the cricket world in general. Born in Scotland on September 5, 1909, he was hailed as a second Victor Trumper – a comparison made alike for his youthful success, elegant style and superb strokeplay. Well set up, very active on his feet, and not afraid to jump in to the slow bowlers and hit the ball hard, he accomplished far more in big cricket than Trumper had done at his age. Given a place in the Australian team when England toured in 1928–29, Jackson, on his first appearance in Test cricket, made 164 – at 19, the youngest player to score a hundred in a Test match. For sheer brilliance of execution his strokes during this delightful display could scarcely have been exceeded. He reached 100 with a glorious square-drive off Larwood. Jackson had a splendid return from the deep field and, if not so fast a runner as Bradman, covered ground very quickly. His later years were marred by continued ill-health and his untimely end *[he died of tuberculosis – Ed.]* was not unexpected. While lying in hospital on what was to prove his death-bed he was married.

Fifth Test

At Sydney, January 23, 24, 25, 27, 28, 1933. England won by eight wickets.

The rubber having been won by England, the batting of both sides in their first innings was generally much brighter than previously. The strain was lifted from both sides, but Australia gave a poor display in the second innings and England demonstrated their superiority in no uncertain fashion.

For Richardson in particular the match must have proved a dismal memory, for he was dismissed without scoring in each innings. On the other hand, Verity had joyful recollections, bowling so well as to take eight wickets for 95 runs, while Larwood, although damaging his foot when bowling, came out as a batsman with a splendid innings of 98. What a pity he could not have capped his great bowling successes by obtaining a hundred in a Test match!

For the fourth time Jardine lost the toss, and in the first over Richardson was out. Woodfull and Bradman carried the score to 59, but then Woodfull played on and in the next over Bradman left. Thenceforward, matters went well for Australia. O'Brien and McCabe played finely, although O'Brien was twice missed in the slips. Altogether they added 99 at about one a minute. At tea Australia had 183 on the board, and then Darling also played a very bright innings, so when play ceased for the day the score stood at 296 for five, this being the highest number of runs scored on the first day of any of the Tests. Darling, Oldfield and Lee all batting well on the second day, Australia added another 139 to their overnight score, the total of 435 being better than anything they had previously accomplished.

The success of their younger players was, from the Australian point of view, very gratifying. It was, however, estimated that England missed no fewer than 14 catches. Australia were also at fault, Jardine giving two chances before leaving at 31, but then came some brilliant batting. Sutcliffe played well, but was overshadowed by Hammond, who drove and turned the ball to leg in wonderful style, although he was also let off. When the partnership ended Larwood was sent in to play out time, England, with 159 on the board and two men out, finishing up 276 behind. During the afternoon, protests were made by the Englishmen about Alexander scratching up the pitch after he had delivered the ball.

On the Saturday, England batted all day and finished up only 17 behind with two wickets to fall. Hammond did not play in quite the same style, and most of the applause was earned by Larwood, who drove in glorious fashion and treated the spectators to a great display. They put on 92 before Hammond was dismissed just before lunch. Larwood and Leyland, after playing themselves in, added 65 in as many minutes. Then Larwood, trying to place the ball to the on for a two to reach three figures, did not time his stroke properly and was caught by Ironmonger, a notoriously bad fieldsman. Larwood treated the bowling as no other of the Englishmen had previously done. He made his runs in two hours and a quarter, hitting a six, a five and nine fours, and was loudly cheered.

Monday was full of sensation. England in increasing their score to 454 gained a lead of 19, Allen having a lot to do with this towards the end. Australia's first wicket once more fell before a run had been scored, but then Woodfull and Bradman put on 115. Bradman was in his most daring mood, often stepping back to the leg-theory bowling of Voce and Larwood and forcing the ball to the off. Verity, however, bowled Bradman when he misjudged the flight, and with his dismissal a breakdown occurred. At tea-time the score was 139 for four, and Woodfull's fine innings came to an end at 177 when he was seventh out, playing on to Allen. He batted just over three hours in his usual watchful style. Verity dismissed O'Reilly and Alexander with consecutive balls and as Ironmonger was next in had a good chance of doing the hat-trick. But Lee, who had swung the bat a good deal, was dismissed by Allen and the innings closed for 182.

England thus needed 164 to win, half an hour remaining for play. Jardine complained about Alexander running down the pitch, and the crowd booed and hooted. Alexander then bumped several balls down to Jardine, and when he was struck on the thigh sections of the crowd cheered. A disgraceful exhibition.

On the last day Ironmonger was making the ball turn off the scratched-up turf, and Hammond and Wyatt took some pains to play themselves in. Steadily the bowling was worn down and then Hammond surprised everyone by on-driving O'Reilly for six – one of the biggest hits ever seen on the Sydney ground. After that Hammond played in brilliant fashion and finished the match in dramatic style with another big six.

Toss: Australia. **Australia 435** (L. P. J. O'Brien 61, S. J. McCabe 73, L. S. Darling 85, W. A. S. Oldfield 52, H. Larwood 4-98) **and 182** (W. M. Woodfull 67, D. G. Bradman 71, H. Verity 5-33); **England 454** (H. Sutcliffe 56, W. R. Hammond 101, H. Larwood 98, R. E. S. Wyatt 51, P. K. Lee 4-111) **and 168-2** (R. E. S. Wyatt 61*, W. R. Hammond 75*).

THE BOWLING CONTROVERSY   Sydney Southerton, 1934

Cricketers can gather from the various cables between MCC and the Australian board the whole course of the disturbance over the question of fast leg-theory bowling. I have purposely omitted to use the expression "Bodyline bowling". It may have conveyed to those to whom it was presented at the outset the meaning the inventor of it wished to infer, but to my mind it was an objectionable term, utterly foreign to cricket, and calculated to stir up strife.

Happily the controversy is now at an end, and little reason exists to flog what we can regard as a "dead horse". But, obviously from the historical point of view, something on the subject must be said. I hope and believe that the ventilation of their grievances by the Australians, and the placatory replies of MCC, will have done much towards imparting a better spirit to Test matches which, of recent years, have become battles rather than pleasurable struggles.

There is no need to enter into some of the reasons for the hostility with which Jardine in particular and certain of his team were received by the huge crowds in Australia. Animosity existed and was fanned into flame largely by the use of the term "Bodyline" when Larwood and others met with such success. To such an extent had real bitterness grown that the storm burst during the Third Test at Adelaide. The dispatch of a petulant cablegram by the Australian Board even put the completion of the tour in jeopardy. Saner counsels prevailed, and MCC never lost their grip of the situation and, what was more important, refused to be stampeded into any panic legislation.

And now, what of this fast leg-theory method of bowling to which not only the Australian players themselves but the vast majority of the Australian public took such grave exception? With the dictum of MCC that any form of bowling which constitutes a direct attack on the batsman is contrary to the spirit of the game everyone must unquestionably concur. Jardine stated in his book that the bowling against which the Australians demurred was not of this description, and Larwood, the chief exponent of it, said with equal directness that he had never bowled at a man. On the other hand, there are numerous statements by responsible Australians to the effect that the bowling was calculated to intimidate, pitched as the ball was so short as to cause it to fly shoulder and head high and make batsmen, with the leg side studded with fieldsmen, use the bat as protection rather than in defence of the wicket or to make a scoring stroke.

Victor Richardson has said that when he took his ordinary stance he found the ball coming in to his body; when he took guard slightly more to the leg side he still had the ball coming at him; and with a still wider guard the ball continued to follow him. I hold no brief either for Jardine or Larwood or for Richardson, Woodfull or Bradman; but while some of the Australians may have exaggerated the supposed danger of this form of bowling I cling to the opinion that they cannot all be wrong. When the first mutterings of the storm were heard many people in this country were inclined to the belief that the Australians, seeing themselves in danger of losing the rubber, were not taking defeat in the proper spirit. I will confess that I thought they did not relish what seemed to me at that stage to be a continuous good length bombardment by our fast bowlers on to their leg stump. This idea I afterwards found was not quite correct.

There is nothing new in leg-theory bowling. The most notable exponent of it in recent years was Root, of Worcestershire; and to delve deeper into the past an Australian – no less than the famous Spofforth himself – would at times bowl on the leg stump with two fieldsmen close in on the leg side. Root was, however, medium-paced, while Spofforth, even if he had a very destructive fast ball, could not truthfully be classified as a fast bowler consistent in the pace of Larwood. Moreover, Root and Spofforth almost invariably bowled a good length, so the ball could be played either in a defensive manner or with the idea of turning it to leg, and when the batsman made a mistake in timing or in placing he usually paid the penalty by being caught.

That type of bowling is very different from the kind sent down at top speed with the ball flying past the shoulders or head of a batsman who has only a split-second in which to make up his mind whether he will duck, move away, or attempt to play it with the bat high in the air. Against one sort a perfectly legitimate and reasonable stroke could be played without any apprehension of physical damage; against the other it seems to me that by touching the ball in defence of the upper part of his body or his head a batsman would almost be bound to be out. We saw at Old Trafford *[in a Test between England and West Indies in 1933 – Ed.]* what I should conceive to be a somewhat pale – but no less disturbing – imitation of Larwood in Australia, when Martindale and Constantine on the one hand, and Clark on the other, were giving a demonstration of fast leg-theory bowling. Not one of the three had the pace, accuracy of pitch, or deadliness of Larwood, but what they did was sufficient to convince many people with open minds that it was a noxious form of attack not to be encouraged in any way.

Fast bowlers of all periods have delivered the ball short of a length on occasions – sometimes by accident, and sometimes by intention to keep batsmen on the *qui vive* – but in modern days some of our bowlers of pace have become obsessed with the idea that it is necessary do this three or four times in an over. I like to see fast bowling, the faster the better, but I do like to see it of good length and directed at the stumps.

The Australians without a doubt thought that during the last tour they were being bowled at, and small wonder that, edging away as some of them unquestionably did, they found themselves bowled when, instead of the expected bouncer, occasional straight good-length balls came along. It is significant that G. O. Allen, whom nobody would place quite in the same class as Larwood, enjoyed many successes and for the most part obtained his wickets by bowling with which we in England are familiar. Surely, with his extra pace, Larwood could have done as well as Allen and so have prevented that bitter ill-feeling which led a good many people in this country to the belief that the winning of the Ashes had been gained at too great a cost.

For myself, I hope that we never see fast leg-theory bowling exploited in this country. I think that (1) it is definitely dangerous; (2) it creates ill-feeling between the rival teams; (3) it invites reprisals; (4) it has a bad influence on our great game of cricket; and (5) it eliminates practically all the best strokes in batting. Mainly because it makes cricket a battle instead of a game I deplore its introduction and pray for its abolition, not by any legislative measures, but by the influence which our captains can bring to bear and by avoiding use of the objectionable form of attack take a great part in wiping away a blot.

ENGLAND V AUSTRALIA 1934

Sydney Southerton

The Australian team of 1934 arrived with the knowledge that during the previous series in Australia they had been beaten four times and successful only once and to the majority of people at home the idea of England losing the rubber was as remote as it had been in 1930. Australia, however, won two Test matches to England's one and, by a remarkable coincidence, Woodfull, again as in 1930, led his side at The Oval to the victory which regained the Ashes, on the anniversary of his birthday – August 22.

Australia, when the wickets were hard, bowled better, batted better and fielded better than England. That they won the rubber was, therefore, not surprising. The fact of England's only success being gained at Lord's after rain ruined the wicket, and gave Verity the opportunity of showing how effective he can be under these conditions, was indeed a sad commentary on the supposed and expected predominance of our own men. The England batting suffered atrociously from a pronounced weakness after the opening pair had been separated. A Jardine was sadly needed, but an unofficial cable from him and the fact that he had been engaged to write the Test matches in the press put his inclusion out of the question. In the same way the attitude of Larwood on a certain matter precluded the selectors from choosing him and so England were deprived of the services of two men who might easily have turned the scale.

The fame of O'Reilly as a bowler had preceded him. Like Grimmett, he had a fine command of length and even if, after a somewhat lumbering run-up, he sacrificed a little of the advantage of his great height by a pronounced stoop as he delivered the ball, this did not detract from his effectiveness. He wrapped his fingers round the ball with his wrist bent so that the ball almost touched the lower part of the inside of his forearm. He probably bowled no better ball the whole season than the one which dismissed Wyatt in a sensational over on the first day at Manchester.

The batting was tremendously strong. Ponsford enjoyed his best season in England. His style was much the same as before but in its important essentials his strokeplay had greatly improved; he seemed to hit the ball harder and he always looked sounder than in 1926 or 1930. Bradman had a curious season. It was noticeable that in many innings he lifted the ball to a far greater extent than when he came here first and there were many occasions on which he was out to wild strokes. To those, however, who watched him closely in his big innings it was obvious that in the course of four years he had improved his technique almost out of knowledge. He was much more interesting to look at because of the wider range of his scoring strokes.

First Test

At Nottingham, June 8, 9, 11, 12, 1934. Australia won by 238 runs.

Australia began the series with a splendid victory. On the first three days, at any rate, the fortunes of the game changed sufficiently to keep interest at its highest pitch, while on the last afternoon everyone was on the tiptoe of excitement in watching England's desperate but unavailing effort to stave off defeat – the decision was not determined until only ten more minutes remained. For a long time before this, however, the impression generally existed that England were engaged in a somewhat hopeless task. It is very easy to be wise after the event, but one could not resist the feeling that with 380 runs required to win, with rather less than five hours left for cricket, the England batsmen, having made up their minds to strive for a draw rather than go for the runs, played into the hands of bowlers like O'Reilly and Grimmett.

Before the match, England were in difficulties about the captaincy, Wyatt having had his thumb fractured in the Test trial just previously. The leadership of the XI devolved upon Walters – appearing for the first time in a Test match against Australia.

England up to a point fared quite satisfactorily, for, after Woodfull and Ponsford had made 77, two wickets fell before lunch, and shortly before quarter to four Australia had five men out for 153 and, up to then, had scarcely made sufficient use of their opportunity of batting first on a nice easy wicket. As it happened, no further wicket fell during the afternoon, McCabe, who played a bold confident game, and Chipperfield carrying the score to 207 when rain and bad light ended the day at quarter to six. On Saturday McCabe was out at 234, having made 65 out of 81, but unexpected assistance was given by Oldfield and Grimmett, and the innings did not end until 374. Chipperfield, in his first Test match, just missed the distinction of making a hundred. He was 99 at lunch-time, and out third ball afterwards. Chipperfield obtained his runs largely by cutting, his innings, while eminently useful, being nothing like so attractive as that of McCabe. England fared well for a time, despite the loss of Walters at 45, for Sutcliffe was in his best form, cutting and off-driving so finely as to score 62 out of 102.

Then the game turned. Hammond was out four runs later, and Leyland left at 114, and these three quick reverses caused Pataudi and Hendren to adopt such cautious methods that in 40 minutes before the end only 14 runs came, and England at the close found themselves 246 behind with six wickets to fall. Matters on Monday again went badly before the one real stand of the innings, Geary giving Hendren such valuable assistance that 101 were added. England, however, were all out 106 runs behind.

Still, Australia lost three wickets for 69 before the game turned once more. Brown, when 33 and the total 102, gave a chance of stumping and that probably had a big effect upon the subsequent course of events, for he and McCabe added 112, McCabe hitting a six and 15 fours in a very fine display. Brown, although playing with a very straight bat, did not approach his colleague in brilliance, but his cricket was always high class. Seventh out at 244, he was in nearly four hours and hit only three fours.

On the last day the other batsmen went for runs to give Woodfull the chance of declaring at the earliest possible moment. He did not do this until half-past 12, when 114 had been added to the overnight score. By this time the wicket was showing signs of wear, and when England went in Grimmett and O'Reilly were seen to be turning the ball. Sutcliffe and Walters put on 51, but after Sutcliffe had been caught at slip for the second time in the match the batting broke down, and by tea five men were out for 115. Leyland and Ames stayed for 70 minutes, but wickets fell at regular intervals and with O'Reilly taking the last three very quickly the innings closed at 20 past six for 141. O'Reilly took seven for 54 and bowled superbly. Clever variation in flight and pace combined with spin off the worn turf made him very difficult, and he deserved all the congratulations showered upon him at the close by his delighted colleagues.

Toss: Australia. **Australia 374** (W. H. Ponsford 53, S. J. McCabe 65, A. G. Chipperfield 99, K. Farnes 5-102)
and 273-8 dec. (W. A. Brown 73, S. J. McCabe 88, K. Farnes 5-77); **England 268** (H. Sutcliffe 62,
E. H. Hendren 79, G. Geary 53, C. V. Grimmett 5-81, W. J. O'Reilly 4-75) **and 141** (W. J. O'Reilly 7-54).

CRICKETER OF THE YEAR – W. J. O'REILLY   Sydney Southerton, 1935

William Joseph O'Reilly, the New South Wales schoolteacher whose rise to fame has been meteoric, was born on December 20, 1905. There is not the slightest question that O'Reilly and Grimmett did as much as any two others in the Australian team to win back the Ashes in England in 1934, and of the two O'Reilly probably caused more trepidation than even Grimmett. O'Reilly's career so far is remarkably short. He played for New South Wales in 1927–28, meeting with no pronounced success, and nothing more was heard of him until 1931–32 when the South Africans were touring Australia. In that season he played in the last five Sheffield Shield matches, taking 25 wickets at an average cost of 21, and so much was thought of him that he appeared in the Fourth and Fifth Test matches. When the MCC team went to Australia in 1932–33, O'Reilly jumped right into the front rank of Test-match cricketers. He finished with 27 wickets in the Tests, and it was the general opinion of the MCC team that he was the most difficult man they had met. Indeed, old judges of the game in Australia went so far as to say that of his type he was the best to play for them since George Giffen and Hugh Trumble.

Second Test

At Lord's, June 22, 23, 25, 1934. England won by an innings and 38 runs.

England took ample revenge at Lord's, winning in three days, their first success against Australia at Lord's since 1896 *[and their last to date – Ed.]*. While everyone in England naturally was jubilant over the triumph it could not be denied that they were helped in a pronounced degree by the weather.

Winning the toss England put together a total of 440, but before the end of the second day Australia had 192 on the board with only two men out. In view of this splendid start there existed no sound reason why they should not have closely approached if not have passed England's total, but they suffered the cruellest luck, rain falling during the weekend and rendering their chances almost hopeless. Fortunately England had a bowler capable of taking full advantage of the conditions, and Verity, obtaining seven wickets in the first innings for 61 runs, followed this up with eight for 43, to be the chief factor in such a pronounced success. With his full record for the match he excelled Rhodes's performance at Melbourne in 1903–04 when that even more famous left-hander took 15 wickets for 124. By a singular coincidence Rhodes was present at Lord's to see his brother Yorkshireman accomplish his wonderful performance.

Verity had taken one of the wickets which fell on Saturday, and on the Monday he dismissed 14 men for 80 runs, six of them after tea at a cost of 15. This amazing achievement would probably have been only possible to a man possessed of such length and finger-spin as Verity, because although the wicket certainly helped him considerably it could scarcely be described as genuinely sticky except for one period after lunch. Verity's length was impeccable and he made the ball come back and lift so abruptly that most of the Australians were helpless. The majority of them had had no experience of such a pitch, and they showed no ability or skill in dealing with bowling like that of Verity under these conditions. Those who tried to play forward did not get far enough, and their efforts at playing back were, to say the least, immature.

Earlier, Walters and Sutcliffe made 70 for the opening wicket, but then came that series of dreadful failures which characterised England's batting throughout the series. Hammond was out at 78, Hendren at 99, and Walters at 130. Leyland and Wyatt put on 52 to effect a partial recovery, which was consolidated by Leyland and Ames. By the time stumps were drawn these two had raised the score to 293, and next morning they carried it to 311, their partnership realising 129 runs. Leyland drove superbly in his great innings of 109, hitting a six and 14 fours. In the end he was bowled by what is known in Yorkshire as a long half-volley, hitting a little too late and over the ball. Ames, missed by Oldfield standing back at 96, was eighth out at 409. He hit 14 fours during his stay, powerful driving being the outstanding feature of an inspiring display.

Woodfull scored 22 out of the first 68, then Bradman, with seven fours, hit 36 of the next 73, but actually he never looked like staying very long, making many of his strokes without restraint. The England bowlers met with no further success that day, Brown and McCabe adding 51. McCabe brought off some wonderful hooks, while Brown, with admirable drives and cuts, completed 100 out of 184.

On the Monday, the light was very bad, an appeal being made directly the batsmen reached the wickets, but soon after the resumption Brown was out, after batting in first-rate style and hitting 14 fours. His dismissal was the beginning of the end. Darling left at 204, McCabe one run later, and Bromley at 218. Soon afterwards came a short break while the players were presented to His Majesty the King. Chipperfield and Oldfield put on 40, but by half-past two Australia were all out for 284, the last eight wickets having gone down for 92 runs. Verity took six of them for 37.

The visitors had to follow on, and with only ten on the board Brown was out to a fine catch at long leg, the ball travelling downwind at terrific speed. Verity quickly got to work again, dismissing McCabe and Bradman at 43 and 57, while Woodfull, who defended stubbornly for two hours, was fourth to leave at 94. The rest of the innings was a mere procession, for by this time the wicket had become even more difficult. Verity, who was supported by brilliant close fielding, took the last six wickets, and at ten to six the match was all over, seven men having left in an hour for 44 runs.

Toss: England. **England 440** (C. F. Walters 82, M. Leyland 109, L. E. G. Ames 120, T. W. Wall 4-108); **Australia 284** (W. A. Brown 105, H. Verity 7-61) **and 118** (H. Verity 8-43).

Third Test
At Manchester, July 6, 7, 9, 10, 1934. Drawn.

The Third Test had to be left drawn, the scoring being so heavy that in the course of the four days 1,307 runs were obtained and only 20 wickets fell. Seldom can an international engagement in this country have been played throughout under such wonderful conditions. From first to last the sun blazed down, the heat being at times almost unbearable. The Australians played the greater part of the game under a very serious handicap, an affection of the throat seizing Bradman, Chipperfield and Kippax in particular and others in a lesser degree, so that at one period it was feared that an attack of diphtheria had overtaken the visitors.

In these circumstances, therefore, the Australians – kept in the field until nearly four o'clock on the Saturday while England were scoring 627 for nine – naturally played in rather a depressed spirit, but they did not allow this to affect them and, replying with a score of 491, practically made certain of avoiding defeat.

While England, despite a series of staggering setbacks at the usually disastrous period of their innings, had cause for great satisfaction at making so many runs, it cannot be said that they could look back with any pronounced degree of complacency. For the third time they did not have a well-balanced XI and while on paper the batting was very strong, the bowling never looked good enough to get Australia out for anything like a reasonable total on an extraordinarily easy wicket.

Wyatt having won the toss, Walters and Sutcliffe opened so confidently that in 65 minutes 68 runs were on the board, Walters, who made 52 of these, driving so well as to hit eight fours. Then came an astonishing, and, for England, a humiliating, change. The ball, having gone out of shape, was given up for another as nearly as possible identical in wear and O'Reilly took three wickets in one over. With the first delivery he got Walters caught at forward short leg; with his next he bowled Wyatt middle stump and, after Hammond had scored four from a leg glance, O'Reilly bowled him with the fourth ball of the over. So, in ten minutes, England's position was transformed from no wicket for 68 runs to three for 72, and all the advantage of the splendid opening partnership had vanished. Hendren and Sutcliffe exercised a steadying effect, adding 77 in just over an hour, then Leyland and Hendren added 191. Hendren batted four hours for his 132 and hit 22 fours. He was severe in his leg-side strokes off Wall, while he drove O'Reilly and Grimmett with accuracy and power.

Next morning there came further great batting by Leyland and Ames, who were not separated until the score stood at 482, their stand realising 142. Leyland, who drove magnificently, hit a five and 19 fours in his second consecutive Test hundred. Allen, missed at long leg when two by Wall, played a fine forcing innings. He lost Ames at 510, but added 95 with Verity in 80 minutes before the declaration. O'Reilly was highly tried, but in taking the first six wickets off the reel, he accomplished most effective work.

In the time remaining Australia did well, for after Ponsford had been caught at slip at 34, Brown and McCabe put on 102. On Monday McCabe went along at a fine pace, and they were not separated until the stand reached 196. Then came a blunder, Woodfull being missed first ball from Clark at second slip by Hendren. Later on he gave a stumping chance but meanwhile McCabe had been got rid of by a slip catch at 242. He gave a fine exhibition of hard hitting and sent the ball 22 times to the boundary. Woodfull and Darling added 78 and just about this time Hopwood and Verity kept the batsmen quiet, but it cannot be said that Hopwood ever looked like getting a wicket. Woodfull and Bradman put on 58 in 65 minutes, but Bradman, when 26, gave Hammond a sharp return chance. Then at 409 Woodfull's watchful display came to an end when, thanks to Hammond's smart return from a cut by Oldfield, he was run out. He resisted the bowling for three hours and 50 minutes, but hit only seven fours. When play ceased with eight men out for 423, the Australians still wanted 55 to avoid having to follow on.

However, on the last morning, O'Reilly slashed about and Chipperfield, obviously unwell, batted steadily. They added 35 and the follow-on was saved before the innings ended with a delightful piece of fielding by Keeton, who, acting as substitute for Leyland, ran in from long leg, picked up smartly and threw out Wall. All out for 491, Australia were 136 behind, but they had kept England in the field for over ten hours.

Toss: England. **England 627-9 dec.** (C. F. Walters 52, H. Sutcliffe 63, E. H. Hendren 132, M. Leyland 153, L. E. G. Ames 72, G. O. B. Allen 61, H. Verity 60*, W. J. O'Reilly 7-189)
and 123-0 dec. (C. F. Walters 50*, H. Sutcliffe 69*); **Australia 491** (W. A. Brown 72, S. J. McCabe 137, W. M. Woodfull 73, H. Verity 4-78) **and 66-1.**

CRICKETER OF THE YEAR – S. J. McCABE

Sydney Southerton, 1935

Stanley Joseph McCabe was born on July 16, 1910. McCabe was first chosen for New South Wales in 1928 as a country cricketer – a rather unusual honour. Watching him last summer one could not fail to be struck with the immense strides he had made in the technique of batting. In 1930 he gave the impression of still having a good deal to learn; he was inclined to be somewhat slapdash. The intervening years had clearly made a great difference in him. Losing nothing of his power, he displayed a wider and safer range of strokes. He was third in the Test averages, with 483 runs for over 60 per innings, and he put together 137 in the Third Test at Manchester. Short and stockily built, McCabe possesses a pair of very strong arms with flexible wrists and in 1934 was a typical representative of the modern Australian batsman. He showed excellent footwork to supplement a good eye and the outstanding characteristic of his batting – whether driving, cutting or hooking – was the power with which he invested all his strokes. In this respect he almost bore comparison with Bradman; indeed, taking the summer all through it is scarcely too much to say that he instilled nearly as much fear into English bowlers as did his more famous colleague.

Fourth Test

At Leeds, July 20, 21, 23, 24, 1934. Drawn.

One of the shortest but heaviest rainstorms seen at a cricket match for years arrived just in time to enable England to draw a game in which they were completely outplayed. Escaping defeat in the luckiest manner possible, the England team accomplished nothing in the match on which they could congratulate themselves.

For the third consecutive game England enjoyed the advantage of batting first. Wyatt himself described the wicket as being like a featherbed, whatever that may have meant. The assumption at the time was that it would be slow and easy. There was nothing in the way it played during the first day to suggest that it was otherwise, yet England, giving one of the worst displays of batting probably ever seen under similar conditions, were dismissed for a paltry total of 200. It can be said that O'Reilly, Grimmett and Chipperfield bowled very well, but nothing they accomplished was quite sufficient to account for the shocking exhibition of weak and hesitant batting. Although Hammond and Hendren put on 50 in an hour none of the rest, equally with those who had gone before, played in form worthy of the occasion.

Further surprises were in store. Ponsford and Brown played the bowling so easily that there seemed no reason to expect any pronounced success for the England attack. Bowes, however, changed ends and, coming on again from the Pavilion wicket, bowled Brown at 37 and two runs later sent back Oldfield and Woodfull in one over. Stumps were then pulled up, Bowes having sent down ten balls from the Pavilion end and dismissed three batsmen without conceding a run. Australia, therefore, finished the day 161 behind with seven wickets left, and the situation had thus completely changed.

Those, however, were the last crumbs of comfort England were destined to enjoy. Bradman joined Ponsford next morning and not until ten to six on Saturday evening did another wicket fall. Giving a great display, the two famous Australian run-getters beat all previous partnership records in Test matches. They carried the score to 427 before Ponsford, hooking a short ball from Verity, trod on his wicket and knocked the leg bail off. Altogether their stand realised no fewer than 388 runs. They always scored at a good rate but pushed along very quickly after tea when, in an hour, 98 runs were put on. Each batsman gave a chance, for Ponsford when 70 should have been caught by Mitchell at cover-point while Bradman at 71 was let off by Hopwood. Ponsford obtained many of his runs by late cuts and turning to leg, and all through his innings, which included 19 fours, he hit the ball hard and placed it well. Moreover, his defence was rock-like. For the greater part of the day Bradman, who unlike Ponsford obtained most of his runs in front of the stumps, batted with the utmost certainty but during the last 35 minutes he played in a more light-hearted spirit. Twice he lifted the ball over the ring for six, and hit Hopwood for 15 runs in one over.

Australia, therefore, began the third day in a most comfortable position, being 294 runs on with six wickets to fall. Bradman and McCabe added 90 in an hour, but thanks to some most effective bowling by Bowes the innings was finished off, the last six wickets falling for only 90 runs. Bradman, sixth out at 550, made his 304 in six hours and 55 minutes. Not out with 271 overnight, he was perhaps lucky in reaching 300 because at 280 he was missed at third slip by Verity. He did not play so well on Monday morning, but all the same his innings was a masterly affair. He hit the ball very hard and placed his strokes beautifully, while until joined by McCabe he rarely sent the ball into the air. He hit two sixes and 43 fours.

England went in again 384 behind, so the most they could hope for was a draw. Keeton fell just before lunch and afterwards Hammond played better than in any other Test match during the season. He was seeing the ball well, hitting it hard and accurately and seemed likely to put together an innings in his best style. With the total 70, however, a dreadful disaster occurred, for Hammond, responding to the call of Walters for a foolish run and then checking himself, lost his wicket. Walters left at 87 but by dint of very hard work and much watchful batting Hendren and Wyatt added 65.

Hendren and Leyland, both entirely on the defensive, stayed together for the last 55 minutes. Coupled with the rain which fell on Tuesday this stand saved England, who began the last day with only 188 on the board, still wanting 196 to save the innings defeat. Heavy rain fell in the night and the wicket was very wet, while a further shower soon caused a delay. Hendren was out at 190 and when Ames left the end seemed very near. Just before one o'clock a thunderstorm broke over the ground and, although it lasted only ten minutes, the downpour was so severe that no further cricket was possible.

Toss: England. **England 200** (C. V. Grimmett 4-57) **and 229-6;**
Australia 584 (W. H. Ponsford 181, D. G. Bradman 304, W. E. Bowes 6-142).

Fifth Test
At The Oval, August 18, 20, 21, 22, 1934. Australia won by 562 runs.

Each side having won once, the concluding Test match was played without any restrictions as to the time involved in reaching a result. As it happened four days proved sufficient for Australia to win by 562 runs. Thus they regained The Ashes. The result was a fitting tribute to superior all-round skill. They batted, bowled and fielded better than England and thoroughly deserved what was, after all, a notable achievement.

Woolley was brought in on the strength of his wonderful batting for Kent, but as events proved it was a sad error of judgment to fall back on a man who had not played against Australia for four years and who, moreover, was 47. Dismissed for four and nought, Woolley failed in both innings at the very part of the order which previous experience during the summer had proved to be England's most vulnerable point.

The law of averages suggested that it was Woodfull's turn to win the toss. This he did and when Clark bowled Brown at 21 with the best ball sent down all day, it seemed as though the England attack on a hard wicket was about to come into its own. Never were hopeful anticipations more rudely dispelled. Ponsford and Bradman gave another glorious display of batting, engaging in a partnership which left that of Leeds far behind and produced 451 runs. This time Bradman was the first to leave, hitting over his head at a bouncing ball and being caught behind at 472. McCabe went in and played out time, Australia finishing the day with 475 on the board and only two men out. It would be hard to speak in too high terms of praise of the magnificent displays given by Ponsford and Bradman. Ponsford had shown an inclination to draw away from the bowling of Bowes, but he received inspiration from the example of his partner, who from the very moment he took up his stance was coolness and mastery personified.

The pitch did not help bowlers at all. Clark tried leg theory with a packed leg-side field but as, for the most part, he maintained a good length, his bowling, even if he now and again dropped short, scarcely came under the category of what is known as Bodyline. Clark and the others tried all sort of theories but they had no effect on Bradman who, as the afternoon wore on, invested his batting with increasing daring. He drove and cut with the utmost certainty and power, and when the ball did bounce he just stepped back and hooked it. He hit a six and 32 fours and a better display has rarely been seen. Ponsford was not quite so sure, and frequently turned his back to the ball to receive blows on the thigh. All the same, he drove with great power and was clever in getting the ball away between the fieldsmen. As during the day about 80 runs an hour were obtained it can be realised that too many long-hops and half-volleys were sent down. Ponsford offered three very difficult chances and one when 115 comparatively easy; Bradman, as far as was seen, was flawless.

On Monday England had further trouble before the innings closed at 701 – the second-highest in the history of Test matches between England and Australia. Of the fast bowlers Clark was the best from the point of sustained effort and real class but he had no luck. Allen was faster and more virile and Bowes had an inspired period when, going on at 605, he took three wickets for 19 runs. McCabe was out early at 488 and Ponsford gave another chance before once more hitting his wicket in drawing back to Allen. Fourth out at 574, he batted seven hours and 35 minutes for his workmanlike innings of 266 and he hit a five and 27 fours. It was curious that six of the Australians were clean bowled and in this connection it is proper to observe that Bowes, who started the day trying to bounce the ball, met with success directly he bowled normally.

An hour and a half remained when England went in, and Walters and Sutcliffe, scoring at a fine pace, made 90 without being separated. Still, England were 611 runs behind at the end of the day.

Tuesday was a black day for England: except for a superbly aggressive display by Leyland the batting proved deplorable. The openers were separated at 104, Sutcliffe being out to a good catch at the wicket on the leg side, and then followed a series of disasters. Walters and Woolley left in one over; Wyatt playing on gave Grimmett his 100th wicket in Test cricket and Hammond went at 142. Leyland and Ames put a better appearance on affairs but when they had added 85 Ames retired with a strained back. After that Leyland dominated the proceedings. He drove splendidly and when at length bowled at 321 he had made 110 out of 185. He hit a six and 15 fours, nearly all drives. The innings closed with Leyland's dismissal, the last three wickets having put on 179.

Australia, 380 ahead, scored 186 for two before the end of the day. Bradman and McCabe scored at a fine pace, making 144 in 90 minutes. Light rain fell during the night but the wicket next morning was not greatly affected. Ames was still away but Bowes soon dismissed Bradman, who had added 150 with McCabe, and then for the first time England's bowling got really on top so that, although the last partnership produced 55, Australia were all out for 327. Clark and Bowes shared the wickets, both bowling extremely well. Woolley kept wicket and made a catch standing back.

England were thus left with no fewer than 708 to get – only 34 short of what they had set Australia at Brisbane in 1928–29. They made a shocking start, Walters leaving at one and Woolley at three, but Sutcliffe and Hammond added 64. Hammond was fourth to leave after tea, and following that it became a question of whether the match would be over before half-past six. Leyland left at 109 and Wyatt at 122, and shortly before six o'clock the innings was all over for 145. As was the case four years previously Australia won the rubber on the anniversary of Woodfull's birthday.

Toss: Australia. **Australia 701** (W. H. Ponsford 266, D. G. Bradman 244,

W. E. Bowes 4-164, G. O. B. Allen 4-170) **and 327** (D. G. Bradman 77, S. J. McCabe 70, extras 50,

E. W. Clark 5 98, W. E. Bowes 5 55); **England 321** (C. F. Walters 64, M. Leyland 110)

and 145 (C. V. Grimmett 5-64).

Australian Cricket – Barracking
H. V. Evatt, 1935

When English critics speak of Australian barracking, they are apt to overlook the crowds' very generous treatment of most of our English visitors. Hobbs's reception from the Sydney crowd, first in December 1924 when he beat Victor Trumper's record of six Test centuries, and later in December 1928, when he was given a presentation, was quite wonderful. Players like Hobbs, Douglas, Gilligan, Kilner, Chapman, Parkin, Hendren and Tate were idols of Australian crowds. It is a great mistake to judge the Australian spectators by the reaction of some of them when many of their players were repeatedly hit in 1932–33 as a result of an entirely novel method of fast bowling. Unfortunately a section of the press exaggerates every trifle. It becomes an incident, then a dispute, and it ends in an international episode. In February 1920, for instance, at Sydney, Hobbs, who had a bad leg, was fielding at cover when Macartney drove a ball for four. Hobbs was allowed by two other English players (at mid-off and extra-cover) to limp to the boundary in order to return the ball. Some of the crowd chaffed, not Hobbs, but his two, apparently, inconsiderate colleagues. One or two English papers misunderstood what had happened and asserted that Hobbs himself had been barracked about his injury. It is all very well to counsel silence, but nothing in the world will prevent occasional comment by some of the spectators.

"Doc" Evatt was Australia's Attorney-General from 1941 to 1949, and then leader of the Australian Labor Party from 1951 to 1960.

THE SETTLEMENT OF THE BOWLING CONTROVERSY

The following communication was issued from Lord's Cricket Ground on November 21, 1934: "In 1933 the MCC Committee passed the following resolution: 'That any form of bowling which is obviously a direct attack by the bowler upon the batsman would be an offence against the spirit of the game.'

"On November 23, 1933, at a meeting at which 14 of the 17 captains of the first-class counties were present and the remaining three represented, this resolution was accepted and an understanding was arrived at to the effect that the captains would not permit or countenance bowling of such type. This principle was also affirmed by the Imperial Cricket Conference on July 25, 1934, and it was urged that the controlling bodies of cricket should not permit or countenance such form of bowling.

"As a result of their own observations and from the reports received the MCC Committee consider that there is evidence that cases of the bowler making a direct attack upon the batsman have on occasions taken place during the past cricket season. Bowling of this kind was not unknown in the past, but has developed and may continue to develop if left unchecked. In order to eliminate this type of bowling from the game and to ensure in future that there shall be no misunderstanding as to what exactly constitutes a direct attack by the bowler upon the batsman, the MCC Committee have ruled that the type of bowling regarded as a direct attack by the bowler upon the batsman and therefore unfair consists in persistent and systematic bowling of fast short-pitched balls at the batsman standing clear of his wicket."

NOTES BY THE EDITOR

Sydney Southerton, 1935

No matter the angle from which it may be viewed it is next to impossible to regard the cricket season of 1934 as other than unpleasant. I am not referring to the fact that England lost the rubber with Australia. That, after we had won four matches out of five in Australia in 1932–33, was a hard enough blow to our self-esteem; but the whole atmosphere was utterly foreign to the great traditions of the game. As a journalist, born and bred in cricket and in mature years coming under the influence of that great lover and writer of the game, Sydney Pardon, I deplored the attitude of a certain section of the press in what seemed to me an insane desire constantly to stir up strife.

One can only assume that the modern idea of being always in search of a stunt – horrible word – was the dominating influence which caused them to see trouble where none existed and, as the Hon. Mr Justice Evatt says, to magnify an incident into a dispute and subsequently into an international episode. All sense of proportion was lost and we constantly read not so much how the game was going or how certain players acquitted themselves, but rather tittle-tattle of a mischievous character which, in the long run, prompted the inevitable question: are Test matches really worthwhile? One outcome was that the Australians themselves, who had come here hoping to go through the season without any bother or recurrence of the arguments surging around direct-attack bowling, were constantly on the lookout for something which might give them just cause for complaint. Happily the season was nearing its close before anything happened to rouse their feelings, but at Nottingham in August they were subjected to a form of attack which not only they themselves, but the majority of people in England, fondly imagined had been scotched.

The county captains had come to an understanding that they would not permit any form of bowling which was obviously a direct attack on the batsman. Mr A. W. Carr, the Nottinghamshire captain, stated that not only was he opposed to direct-attack bowling but that neither Larwood nor Voce practised it. Consequently it was not surprising that, influenced by his opinions, so often freely and openly expressed, Voce and Larwood felt that they were justified in continuing to bowl fast bumping leg-theory deliveries with the leg side packed. Larwood escaped censure; Voce, on the evidence of the umpires, exploited direct-attack methods against the Australians at Trent Bridge and Middlesex at Lord's, but it is important to note that Carr did not play in either of these games. In each case complaint was made; the allegation was found proved and the Nottinghamshire committee, as they were bound to do, apologised.

AUSTRALIA V ENGLAND 1936–37

Although the MCC team which toured Australia under G. O. Allen failed in their quest to regain the mythical Ashes, it is probable that they would have achieved their object had not some wonderful batting by Bradman turned the scale. After winning two Tests, England were beaten in the remaining three and so for the first time *[and still, by 2009, the only time – Ed.]* a side which lost the first two games of a series came out on top.

To weakness in batting, more than any other cause, must be attributed the failure to return victorious. The deficiencies in run-getting threw a double onus on the bowlers, but Voce did some magnificent work with the ball and took 22 wickets in the first three Tests; he was definitely the outstanding bowler of the tour.

Seldom has a touring side been so dogged by injuries and illness. As many as seven of the team were out of action for long periods. The troubles began in the first week when Robins had the second finger of his right hand broken. Throughout the tour he could neither spin the ball nor get his injured finger round the bat, but despite his handicap he often fielded magnificently. Wyatt fractured his left arm and missed the first three Tests. Ames, who had played little during the summer in England owing to back trouble, fell ill almost as soon as he reached Perth and did not play until mid-November. Though Allen was extended great sympathy in failing to bring back the Ashes, the fact remains that his team was not quite good enough.

The weather played an important part, for only in the Fourth Test was there no interruption through rain. In the first two matches England benefited, but in the third and fifth matches the luck favoured Australia. Had England won the toss in the deciding Test, it is quite possible that they would have registered as decisive a victory as did Australia. This last Test, however, was not a happy one for England. Disastrous errors in the field were followed by weak batting for which there appeared to be no excuse.

Bradman emerges as the star player of the Tests. After a disappointing start, he had an aggregate of 810 runs, in which were included scores of 82, 270, 212 and 169, and an average of 90. Though McCabe was next with an aggregate of 491 runs, Hammond had rather the better average – 58 as against 54. The fluctuating nature of the struggles gripped the Australian public and financially the tour broke all records. The number of people who watched the five games was over 900,000 and the receipts amounted to £90,909. The experimental lbw rule and the eight-ball over were in force in all the matches.

First Test

At Brisbane, December 4, 5, 7, 8, 9, 1936. England won by 322 runs.

England gained a totally unexpected but wholly meritorious victory before lunch on the fifth day. Prior to this match, the team's record had been so poor that on form it was impossible to concede them more than an outside chance of making a good show. That England became transformed in a single night into a great and victorious side was entirely due to the example and enthusiasm of the captain; and this match will go down in history as "Allen's Test". Allen sprang surprises in his make-up of the XI, and his choices succeeded. He followed this up by winning the toss. Bradman will have reason to remember his first essay as captain of Australia, for he lost the toss, was in some quarters criticised for his captaincy, and failed with the bat.

A thunderstorm threatened when play began, but actually no rain fell until the night between the fourth and fifth days. The Brisbane wicket is always lively for an hour and a half or so on the first day and, though it later became easy, McCormick was able to make the ball lift during that spell. He had three batsmen in the pavilion with only 20 on the board: Worthington was caught behind off the first ball of the match.

The loss of Hammond, also out first ball, was a severe blow to English hopes. Happily, Leyland again proved himself reliable, so that the fourth wicket added 99 and Leyland, batting over four hours, made a hundred. The first day ended with England 263 for six, Hardstaff having justified his unexpected selection with 27 not out. On the second day Hardstaff and Robins gave one of the brightest batting displays of the match. Allen, too, batted splendidly and England reached 358. Bradman had been seriously handicapped on the Saturday by the inability to bowl of McCormick, who was attacked by lumbago and made only fitful appearances for the remainder of the game.

At the end of the second day England's worst fears looked like being justified, for Australia were 151 for two. It is true that Bradman had been dismissed, caught in the gully off Voce, but the third-wicket pair looked formidable and seemed capable of a huge partnership on such a good pitch. But on Monday the game swung round completely. England showed fight before lunch and Voce ran through the Australian team afterwards. That period between lunch and tea was the vital point of the match. Despite a calm innings by Fingleton, whose defence over five hours was admirable, Australia were dismissed for 234, leaving England with a lead of 124. Voce's ability to make the ball run away was mainly responsible for the collapse.

England's batting, particularly in regard to the vexed problem of finding an opening pair, again disappointed. At the close they were two down for 75. On the fourth day there came a further improvement, led by the captain, who figured in valuable partnerships with Hardstaff and Verity. The way Allen played O'Reilly was a revelation of concentration and masterly batting; he has rarely played a better innings. Again it was after lunch that England turned the tables, so that, with half an hour left, Australia opened their last innings wanting 381 to win. In a poor light, against which five appeals were made, Fingleton, the hero of the first innings, was bowled first ball by Voce.

The last shower before the fifth day's play occurred about 6 a.m., and the wicket, already worn, assumed the properties of a "sticky dog". In former days, fast bowlers would not have been able to get a foothold, but with the run-ups protected, Voce and Allen were able to bowl from first to last. The Australian batting was deplorable. Badcock was out to Allen's second ball of the day, and he dismissed Sievers and Bradman with the fourth and sixth balls of his second over. With Bradman's departure Australia's last hope disappeared. Half the side were dismissed with only 16 on the board, and they were all out for the paltry total of 58. Voce came out of the match with ten wickets for 57 runs, one of the finest Test feats imaginable.

Toss: England. **England 358** (C. J. Barnett 69, M. Leyland 126, W. J. O'Reilly 5-102) **and 256** (G. O. B. Allen 68, F. A. Ward 6-102); **Australia 234** (J. H. W. Fingleton 100, S. J. McCabe 51, W. Voce 6-41) **and 58** (W. Voce 4-16, G. O. B. Allen 5-36).

Second Test

At Sydney, December 18, 19, 21, 22, 1936. England won by an innings and 22 runs.

Possibly even more than in the First Test, the winning of the toss was of paramount importance. Owing to the long drought, the groundsman feared the wicket would not last as well as is usual at Sydney. The prospect of unsettled weather contributed to uncertainty about the way the wicket would play after the first day or two.

England occupied the wicket for the whole of the first day but scored no more than 279 for the loss of three wickets. Again England quickly suffered a reverse, but Hammond came in and graced the match with a hundred. A much-discussed feature of play before lunch concerned five overs sent down by McCormick, who was not only erratic but pitched short so that the ball flew all over the place. It should be made clear, however, that suggestions of Bodyline bowling were uncalled-for. McCormick merely used the recognised methods of the fast bowler and did not set an exaggerated leg field. Batsmen experienced little trouble in playing him later on; he had not fully recovered from lumbago and never again attained any real speed.

Barnett lost his wicket when he played outside a ball that came through faster than anticipated. Then Leyland came in to dash Australian hopes. He was criticised even more than Hammond for his slow play by Australian experts who neglected to give their own bowlers and captain credit for limiting the batsmen's scoring scope. Nevertheless O'Reilly rather wasted time with leg theory while Ward bowled on or just outside the leg stump, and so prevented Leyland from going all out for a shot without taking a risk.

At tea England were 209 for two, a much different state of things from some of the previous matches. Between lunch and tea the Australian fielding was surprisingly ragged, returns to the wicket-keeper being very loose. It improved afterwards when the batsmen, instead of putting on runs fast against a tired attack, proceeded even more slowly. The idea was for Hammond and Leyland to play for the close, but this they failed to do for Leyland was given out lbw under the new rule after a stand of 129.

Hammond was unbeaten with 147 and batted throughout the second day, curtailed by rain by 90 minutes, for an addition of 84. He batted 460 minutes and hit 27 fours. There was a curious incident when Hardstaff had 11. Robinson, the twelfth man, was fielding behind the square-leg umpire and Hardstaff hit a ball from O'Reilly hard into his hands. A shower had rendered the ball as slippery as a wet soap, and the catch was missed. Apparently both umpires were watching the fieldsman, but Bradman pointed out that Hardstaff had stepped on to his wicket sufficiently to dislodge a bail. Hardstaff was given the benefit of the doubt.

Heavy rain in the night created a problem for Allen, and as events proved, he was right in declaring straight away. Australia, as at Brisbane, were caught on a wet wicket, and figured in an inglorious collapse – all out for 80. Nothing more sensational can be imagined than their first dreadful quarter of an hour, when O'Brien, Bradman and McCabe were all out without scoring. Voce dismissed them with his seventh, eighth and tenth balls and equalled the feats of F. S. Jackson (at Nottingham in 1905) and O'Reilly (Manchester, 1934) in taking three wickets in four balls. Seven wickets were down for 31, but with lunch-time approaching, O'Reilly played a desperate innings and hit three sixes. Allen decided to put Australia in again. Already the wicket had shown signs of recovery, and it rolled out a perfect batting wicket, so he took a risk.

The general opinion was that Australia's batsmen had exaggerated the dangers of the wicket, which was damp not sticky. They did much better on going in again, and at the close of the third day Fingleton and Bradman were together with the score 145 for one wicket. But at five to one on the fourth day, Bradman was bowled by Verity for 82. McCabe alone refused to be unnerved. He proceeded to give the brightest batting exhibition of the whole match and mastered all the bowling, which was made to look suspiciously weak. Fortunately, Hammond kept the attack together with his perfect length and his speed off the pitch. Tea-time came with the score 309 for five, and odds-on England having to bat again. The interval gave the bowlers fresh heart; Voce once more found top form, and he and Hammond, bringing about another sensational collapse, won the match. McCabe tried to hit a ball from Voce to leg but it kept low and he was out lbw – the only ball that beat him in an heroic innings of 93.

Toss: England. **England 426-6 dec.** (C. J. Barnett 57, W. R. Hammond 231*);
Australia 80 (W. Voce 4-10) **and 324** (J. H. W. Fingleton 73, D. G. Bradman 82, S. J. McCabe 93).

Third Test

At Melbourne, January 1, 2, 4, 5, 6, 7, 1937. Australia won by 365 runs.

England were not disgraced even though the margin was a large one: outside influences had much to do with the result. The faith of Australians that their side would atone for the two previous disappointments was reflected in the attendances. All records for a cricket match were broken. On the third day alone there were 87,798 people present – the takings were £7,405 – and the aggregate attendance for the match was 350,534 and the full receipts £30,124.

As things turned out Bradman won the match when he won the toss, and his tactics influenced the result. On the second day he took the unusual step in a played-to-a-finish match of declaring his first innings, and sent England in on a pitch from which the ball often reared up almost straight and at other times kept low. It is important to mention that on the first day the wicket was lifeless and unhelpful to spin bowling, yet England got down six wickets for 130 and would probably have done still better had not rain set in and led to the bowlers being handicapped by the wet ball. Next day rain held up play until after lunch. The difficulties of the wicket quickly became apparent, and batsmen experienced such an unhappy time that in about three hours 13 wickets fell. England, after losing nine wickets for 76, also declared, so that for the first time in Test cricket each side closed its first innings.

It is possible England would have done better had Allen declared earlier but, as one authority put it, he could not be expected to possess second sight. At the close on the second day, one Australian – O'Reilly – had been dismissed for three runs and a Sunday without rain enabled the wicket to recover so that when Australia resumed the conditions were more favourable for batting than at any previous time.

Following the dismissal of Fingleton from a weak stroke after he had promised great things, McCabe was Australia's hero on the first day. Towards the end of the afternoon, with six wickets down, McCabe suddenly found his best form and revelled in a hectic ten minutes of big hitting, in which he was joined enthusiastically by Oldfield. The England bowlers were steady all day and the field gave nothing away.

Play on the second day was sensational throughout. On the "glue pot" wicket Australia's apparently feeble total of 200 assumed formidable proportions. Leyland was the one real success for England. Hammond scored more runs, and made some daring if desperate shots with a ring of fieldsmen almost within touch of his bat; Leyland never seemed in difficulties. Both were out to extraordinary catches by Darling at short leg, just as Rigg had fallen to Verity on the first day – catches that would have been missed 99 times out of 100.

Australia batted all the third day. It was inevitable that Bradman should find his form soon, and he chose the moment of his country's greatest need to do so. Rain fell in the afternoon and between – and during – the showers the bowlers were handicapped by a wet ball which they wiped with a towel between each delivery. Bradman took full advantage and, though not quite his old scintillating self, and eschewing the off-drive, he thrilled the crowd and subdued the bowlers. His 270 was his highest against England in Australia. Not until the evening was it revealed that he was suffering from a severe chill, which explained his sedateness. Rigg, reputed a poor starter, showed none of this failing, and the free use of his arms and wrists proved his class.

The fact that, on the fourth day, Bradman and Fingleton put up a sixth-wicket record of 346 – actually the highest stand for any wicket in a Test in Australia – was due to Bradman sending in his tail-end batsmen first. The pitch had become as perfect as any batsman could wish, and though the bowlers remained steady they had little chance of beating Bradman or Fingleton. One admired the brilliant fielding of the Englishmen all day. Hammond, Worthington, Allen and others were top class, while Robins was magnificent, constantly winning applause from the huge crowd.

Bradman, still suffering from mild influenza, was quickly dismissed on the fifth day, and after lunch England opened their second innings wanting 689 to win. Such a task had never been achieved in Test history, but the wicket was still very easy and a dour fight was anticipated. However, Leyland alone of the earlier batsmen, and Robins, towards the end of the day, batted really well. Hammond made a splendid 50 and then was out to a rather careless stroke. The scoring was certainly fast and delighted the spectators, but this was not quite the type of cricket the situation demanded.

On the sixth morning Leyland and Robins rose to their greatest heights. Previously, Leyland had carried such responsibility that he had repressed many of his most spectacular shots, but this time he exploited them all, his hitting through the covers being reminiscent of his finest innings in England. With Robins out England virtually were all out, and Leyland remained undefeated with a noteworthy 111.

Toss: Australia. **Australia 200-9 dec.** (S. J. McCabe 63) **and 564** (J. H. W. Fingleton 136, D. G. Bradman 270); **England 76-9 dec.** (M. W. Sievers 5-21) **and 323** (W. R. Hammond 51, M. Leyland 111*, R. W. V. Robins 61, L. O. Fleetwood-Smith 5-124).

Fourth Test
At Adelaide, January 29, 30, February 1, 2, 3, 4, 1937. Australia won by 148 runs.

Two factors lost England the match, which might have been won despite Bradman winning the toss. One was their batting collapse on the Monday, when the immense advantage gained by getting Australia out for the small total of 288 was frittered away by a deplorable display after Barnett and Leyland had put them in a splendid position. The other was Bradman's 212. The wicket was perfect throughout the match, and for the only time in the series no rain came to interfere with play. The batting failures, therefore, were inexplicable. Australia's win roused cricket enthusiasm in the country to a high pitch because it meant the final Test would decide the rubber.

The first day's play was witnessed by 39,000 people. Australia scored 267 for seven, a good day's work by England. Fingleton was run out at 26, a foolish sacrifice that had been foreshadowed by faulty running, but Brown and Rigg stayed together until the first over after lunch when Farnes dismissed both. McCabe came to the rescue and played a grand innings, but Bradman, who, unusually restrained, took 68 minutes to score 26, was clean-bowled by Allen when trying one of his favourite hook shots. Gregory, making his Test debut at the age of 20, showed promise, and McCabe indulged in an exhilarating burst of scoring immediately after the tea interval, and played Verity more confidently than anyone else had done during the tour. When in trying to hook Robins he was magnificently caught by Allen at deep square leg, McCabe had hit nine fours. Chipperfield played a resolute innings and was not out at the close with 45.

On the second day Australia were out for 288 and by the close England had 174 for two. They appeared to be in a very strong position, and Barnett's first Test century was completed early on the third day but, prior to that, in the same over from Fleetwood-Smith, Leyland had been taken in the slips. Then the game swung Australia's way. Wyatt failed, immediately after lunch Barnett left, and five England wickets were lost for 259 with Australia still 29 runs on – not as comfortable a position as had been promised.

Ames also batted well but a long tail meant England finished only 42 ahead. By the close Australia were 21 on with nine wickets in hand and Bradman in his most dangerous mood. The fourth day virtually settled the issue; a stubborn stand between Bradman and McCabe realised 109, and a big fifth-wicket partnership ensued between Bradman and Gregory. This, producing 135, was not broken until the fifth day when Bradman showed signs of tiredness. This was not one of his most brilliant efforts but he has never looked more sure of himself. He seemed to go in with the fixed determination of winning the match, and though England bowled with any amount of skill and heart he hit 212 in 437 minutes. There were only 14 fours – an indication of the dourness of the fight. On his dismissal the four remaining wickets went down for 11 runs.

At the close of the fifth day there was still a ray of hope for England, because Hammond and Leyland were together with 148 of the 392 runs required already scored and seven wickets in hand. The wicket, considering the amount of play on it, was in wonderful order. Fleetwood-Smith, however, was in an inspired mood and utilised the pitch as no bowler on the English side could have done. Neither of the overnight batsmen survived long and it was left to Wyatt to carry on while others failed. Wyatt, on reaching an excellent 50, gave up defensive tactics and fell to a catch at the wicket. That was the end of a match in which Bradman's batting and the skilful spin bowling of Fleetwood-Smith confounded England's prospects.

Toss: Australia. **Australia 288** (S. J. McCabe 88, A. G. Chipperfield 57*) **and 433** (D. G. Bradman 212, S. J. McCabe 55, R. G. Gregory 50, W. R. Hammond 5-57); England 330 (C. J. Barnett 129, L. E. G. Ames 52, L. O. Fleetwood-Smith 4-129, W. J. O'Reilly 4-51) **and 243** (R. E. S. Wyatt 50, L. O. Fleetwood-Smith 6-110).

Fifth Test

At Melbourne, February 26, 27, March 1, 2, 3, 1937. Australia won by an innings and 200 runs.

The weather was glorious for the first two days but less settled on the third, and a thunderstorm during the early hours of the fourth day denied England the chance of making a closer match of it, though by then their position was precarious to say the least. Again Bradman showed the way, after winning the toss for the third successive time, and his brilliant display made it easy for his colleagues to help build up the mammoth total of 604, the highest Australia have ever amassed against England in their own country.

All the bright, attacking, strokemaking batting came from Australia. On the first day Bradman and McCabe broke another record by putting on 249 for the third wicket, and Bradman, reaching three figures, equalled Hobbs's record of 12 hundreds in England-Australia Tests. At the close Australia were 342 for three, a total that should never have been achieved, as four important catches were dropped, all at short leg behind the umpire. Allen, who had been taking far harder catches during the tour, dropped two, and Farnes was the other delinquent. The bowlers stuck to their gruelling task in a humid temperature of 99°F with notable courage and stamina. Farnes was the best bowler: indeed throughout the match he bowled in his finest form.

This first day's play was a tragic one for England. Fingleton was dropped twice when one and two, while McCabe was missed early and again when 86. The fillip the fast bowlers would have gained had all the catches been taken was incalculable. McCabe gave a classic display, with delightful crisp cutting the feature of aggressive hitting all round the wicket. Bradman did not once put the ball into the air; nor did he give the semblance of a chance. The heat had its effect, and next morning he seemed unable to concentrate; he added only four more runs. Bradman hit 15 fours.

The Englishmen were on their toes for fresh successes, but the wicket was a batsman's paradise – it was not fast even on the first morning – and Gregory joined

Badcock in another great stand that realised 161. Badcock hit with great power and scored fluently in the manner of Hendren. His 118, his first Test century, took 205 minutes and contained 15 fours. Australia were 593 for nine at the close and raised the total to 604 on the third morning. Farnes came out with the magnificent figures of six wickets for 96 runs.

As the pitch was still perfect, giving no assistance to any bowler, England had a wonderful chance to make a telling reply, but after a dazzling start by Barnett and Worthington there was a disastrous collapse. In the first 17 minutes, 33 runs were scored, and then Barnett fell, caught at the wicket high up in trying to cut a ball. Had he not been seeing the ball perfectly from the start Barnett would not have tried such a stroke so early. Worthington was also in an aggressive mood but he had bad luck all through the series and his ill-fortune still pursued him. Soon after lunch when Worthington made a hook shot, he caught his heel against his wicket and knocked a bail off before completing his stroke. Hardstaff went on to play his best innings of the tour, but Hammond was pegged down by O'Reilly's leg theory and never looked like making progress. Trying a wristy flick at a leg ball from O'Reilly that had proved his undoing in the Adelaide Test, Hammond was caught at short leg. Leyland also failed, so England had four wickets down for 140 and the game looked as good as over. Wyatt played out time with Hardstaff, the score being increased to 184 at the close of the third day.

The fourth day clinched matters, for England had to bat on a wet wicket that O'Reilly was able to exploit. Faulty timing was the cause of Hardstaff's early dismissal and accounted for the failure of most of the other batsmen, but Wyatt met a ball from O'Reilly that turned and popped up suddenly. The last four wickets fell for three runs and England were all out and had to follow on 365 behind. O'Reilly was the chief agent of destruction while Nash, whose inclusion came as a surprise, bowled fast and well in his first Test. Though Barnett and Hammond added 60, England that night had lost eight second-innings wickets for 165, and two balls by Fleetwood-Smith on the following morning accounted for Voce and Farnes.

Toss: Australia. **Australia 604** (D. G. Bradman 169, S. J. McCabe 112, C. L. Badcock 118, R. G. Gregory 80, K. Farnes 6-96); **England 239** (J. Hardstaff 83, L. J. Nash 4-70, W. J. O'Reilly 5-51) **and 165** (W. R. Hammond 56).

NOTES BY THE EDITOR

Wilfrid H. Brookes, 1938

A warning note is also sounded concerning the effect on the counties generally of any serious decline in the popularity of Test cricket. Consequently the news that, for the Test matches of 1938, agreement has been reached again to restrict the games to four days apiece and to *reduce* the hours of play by one and a half hours in each match, came as a surprise. A reason advanced for the change is that neither Australian nor English cricketers relish a period of two and a half hours before lunch after the first day. To my mind, it is a retrograde step. There is no gainsaying the assertion that the long pre-lunch spell imposes a severe test upon bowlers, but the policy is directly opposed to the movement in England to revive the interest of the public. Are we to have another run of purposeless drawn games with the possibility of one play-to-a-finish Test deciding the rubber? Not since 1905 has an England–Australia match at Old Trafford produced a definite result, and the last three encounters at Leeds were drawn. Who can argue with conviction that a reduction of the time in which a Test match has to be decided is on all fours with the urgent need to enlist more support for the game generally by getting more definite results? It has been encouraging to note the growth of favourable opinion upon the idea of allocating more than four days to all Test matches between England and Australia in this country, and events during the series of 1938 may bring further support for the suggestion.

England v Australia 1938 Wilfrid H. Brookes

The visit of the Australian team coincided with a marked revival in English cricket, several young players of high merit coming to the front. Yet the Australians, although having the atrocious luck of losing the toss in each of the four Test matches played, drew the rubber and thereby retained the Ashes. That this was a most creditable performance is not likely to be questioned even by the severest critics of the team.

The strength of the team lay in batting and fielding, the weakness in bowling. There were more individual failures than usually occur in an Australian touring side and had a serious accident happened to either Bradman or O'Reilly early on the record must have been much less imposing. The very appearance of Bradman in the field was sufficient to inspire confidence in his colleagues. In every Test in which he batted, Bradman made a century. When in the Fifth Test he damaged his right ankle and was carried off, England were already in a position which made success a foregone conclusion, but there is no doubt that the moral effect of the loss of their captain accounted, to a very large extent, for the complete rout that followed.

The bowling was much less satisfactory. It is a moot point whether Grimmett would have improved it as much as those who criticised his omission declared. Nevertheless, it is reasonable to assume that he would have been of infinite value to O'Reilly, who carried heavy responsibilities and yet mined unapproached among leg-break bowlers for accuracy of length. Whenever O'Reilly was not getting wickets, the attacking limitations of the team were, more often than not, shown up vividly. Bearing these things in mind, one must extend hearty congratulations to the Australians in sharing the important spoils.

Next to Bradman, the big batting successes were Brown and Hassett. Hassett, adding together the runs he made and the runs he saved, was one of the most useful men on the side. He appeared to make his strokes very late and, although adopting almost a two-eyed stance, had, so far as could be seen, no technical faults.

Before McCormick came to England, he was acclaimed as the fastest bowler in Australia. Further, one of the party stated that he was the fastest Australian bowler ever sent to England. That, of course, was exaggeration and after seeing a good deal of his bowling one was inclined to the opinion that McCormick was the most over-rated bowler ever to come here. Most emphatically, he was the greatest disappointment of the tour.

First Test

At Nottingham, June 10, 11, 13, 14, 1938. Drawn.

England put together the highest total ever hit against Australia. Not until half-past three on the second day did Australia have an opportunity of batting, and with 151 scored half their wickets had fallen. McCabe then played an innings the equal of which has probably never been seen in Test cricket; for the best part of four hours he maintained a merciless punishment of the bowling. Although his phenomenal effort did not save his side from the indignity of having to follow on, it broke the control which England had held from the outset and by concentrating upon defence in their second innings Australia saved the game.

Australia put their faith in spin, but hardly ever did a ball turn and the bowlers came in for harsh treatment. On the opening day Barnett and Hutton shared a first-wicket partnership of 219, the best against Australia in England. For the first time in a Test, four individual hundreds were registered in one innings, while Paynter made the highest score against Australia in England and also shared a record fifth-wicket partnership of 206.

Barnett drove and cut in magnificent style and was particularly severe on Fleetwood-Smith. The satisfaction of a hundred before lunch was denied him, but off the first ball bowled after the interval he completed three figures and altogether made 126, hitting 18 fours. Hutton placed his strokes particularly well and his late-cutting was admirably done. He hit 14 fours. The next ball after his hundred ended Hutton's innings. Australia made better progress for a while, but England finished the day with 422 for four, the last hour and a half producing 141 runs from Paynter and Compton, whose stylish and confident play created a big impression. When on Saturday Compton was fifth out, England had 487. He hit finely on the leg side, also excelling with the drive and square cut, and in scoring 102, with 15 fours, he batted without a mistake.

When Hammond declared and Paynter left the crease on Saturday, 30,000 spectators rose to their feet, cheering him all the way to the pavilion. He hit Ward for a six and also had a five and 26 fours.

No such inspiring start was enjoyed by Australia. Going on at 29, Wright, with his fourth ball in a Test match, dismissed Fingleton, who played a long-hop on to his wickets. Brown and Bradman raised the score to 111 and then Bradman, deceived in the flight of a ball, played it against his pads from which it glanced into the wicket-keeper's hands. Before time Australia also lost Brown, who batted extremely well.

Monday began with Australia 138 for three, McCabe 19, made in 35 minutes. A record of these facts is a necessary preliminary to a description of the amazing batting which followed and gave such an epic turn to the game. Six wickets were down for 194 and then McCabe altered the whole aspect of affairs. In a little less than four hours, he scored 232 out of 300. His driving was tremendously hard, he hooked short balls with certainty and power, one off Farnes yielding a six, and showed real genius in battling efforts to keep him away from the bowling. While McCabe was running riot, Hammond delayed the new ball and took other measures in the hope of keeping down runs, but McCabe, having completed his first hundred, proceeded to score fours much more readily. Wright was hit for 44 off three overs. McCabe did not offer a real chance, but Edrich made a plucky effort to hold a ball hooked with terrific power. In the last ten overs McCabe hit 16 of his 34 fours, and in a last-wicket stand of 77 with Fleetwood-Smith scored 72 in

28 minutes. His glorious innings ended in a fitting way, for in attempting a big hit off Verity he skyed the ball to cover.

When Australia followed on, batting of a much different character was seen. Brown and Fingleton adopted stonewalling tactics which called forth mild barracking from some spectators, and Fingleton followed the extraordinary procedure of stepping away from his wicket, taking off his gloves and laying down his bat. A good left-hand slip catch by Hammond disposed of Fingleton after an opening partnership of 89, and Tuesday's play was notable for dour resistance by Brown and Bradman who, making a hundred apiece, batted with grim patience and admirable skill.

In view of the position they were of course justified in playing this type of game, and by adding 170 they robbed England of practically all chance of winning. Troubled by a leg strain, Bradman was never seen as an attacking batsman, but he amazed everyone by the power of his concentration while batting the whole day. There were only five fours in his not-out 144 which, being his 13th hundred in England-Australia matches, allowed him to take the record from Jack Hobbs. Verity bowled with precision and Wright sometimes made a ball turn, but the pitch was too good for England to force a win. Shortly after the interval Australia stood only 114 ahead with half their wickets gone, but they saved the match. Annoyed by the wearisome cricket, spectators late in the day indulged in ironical cheering, whereupon Bradman showed disapproval by standing clear of his wickets until the noise subsided.

Toss: England. **England 658-8 dec.** (C. J. Barnett 126, L. Hutton 100, E. Paynter 216*, D. C. S. Compton 102, L. O. Fleetwood-Smith 4-153); **Australia 411** (D. G. Bradman 51, S. J. McCabe 232, K. Farnes 4-106, D. V. P. Wright 4-153) **and 427-6 dec.** (W. A. Brown 133, D. G. Bradman 144*).

CRICKETER OF THE YEAR – DENIS COMPTON 1939

Denis Charles Scott Compton, of Middlesex, one of the youngest cricketers ever to play for England against Australia, was born on May 23, 1918. At the age of ten he showed form far above that of most lads of the same age. His outstanding ability did not long escape recognition. He was selected to play for London Elementary Schools at Lord's, and his brilliant batting in scoring 112 so impressed those who saw it, among them Sir Pelham Warner, that Compton was induced to join the Lord's staff as soon as he left school. His achievements were not solely confined to cricket for in the same year (1932) he joined Arsenal Football Club. Compton made rapid progress, and in 1936 gained a place in the Middlesex side, amply justifying the faith shown in him by completing 1,000 runs before the season ended. The following summer, he exceeded all expectations by scoring 1,980 runs at an average of 47. Although only 19, he was chosen to play against New Zealand at The Oval. The authorities at once realised that they had a ready-made England batsman for years to come. Chosen in all the Tests in 1938, Compton accomplished the feat of scoring a hundred in his first Test against Australia. An adaptable player with a touch of genius, he possesses a sound defence, a wonderful eye and the right stroke for every ball. He is particularly strong on the leg side and his confidence, coolness and resource are remarkable for so young a player.

Second Test

At Lord's, June 24, 25, 27, 28, 1938. Drawn.

A match of many fluctuations ended with Australia needing 111 to win with four wickets to fall. At Nottingham, the scoring of a double-hundred on each side had been unprecedented, and yet in the very next Test the same thing was done again. Hammond played an innings of 240 – the highest in England against Australia. Brown batted through the whole of Australia's first innings, scoring 206 and equalling the performances of Dr J. E. Barrett, Warren Bardsley and W. M. Woodfull by carrying his bat.

The danger of losing faced England on Tuesday when, on a rain-affected pitch, they led by no more than 148 with half the side out. Then Compton again met the bowling with admirable nerve and coolness for so young a player. From the inspiration of his effort and that of Paynter England recovered their grip and set Australia a task of 315 in two and three-quarter hours. On the last day Bradman, as in each of his four previous Tests against England, hit a century and in doing so exceeded the highest individual aggregate in the series – the 3,636 runs made by Hobbs.

After England's wonderful start in the previous Test, the events that followed success in the toss came as a rude shock. McCormick made the ball swing in and caused it to lift awkwardly; in half an hour he had Hutton and Barnett caught at short leg and in between Edrich played on in trying to hook. Actually, excluding no-balls, McCormick in 25 deliveries took three wickets for 15 runs, bowling more accurately than at any previous time during the tour. But now Paynter's resolute cricket gave Hammond confidence to play his natural game, and this fourth-wicket pair set up a new record by adding 222.

Hammond went to his hundred after some masterly batting and gradually Paynter scored more freely. It was his misfortune to miss a century by one run, but his competent display was made at a very opportune time. Besides a six off Fleetwood-Smith, he hit 13 fours. Compton was soon out but that was Australia's last success before stumps were drawn with a total of 409 for five showing a very fine recovery. So large was the crowd that the gates were closed before noon. Part of the partnership between Hammond and Paynter was watched by His Majesty the King.

On Saturday, the cricket was seen by the largest crowd ever to assemble at Lord's: the official attendance was 33,800. The gates were closed before the start and, after hurried consultations, spectators were permitted to retain positions they had taken up on the grass, the boundary ropes being moved forward a few yards. England gained the upper hand before the close. First, Hammond and Ames put on 186 before Hammond, playing late to a good-length inswinger, was bowled leg stump. Making the highest score for England in any home Test match, and hitting 32 fours, he batted over six hours. His driving was magnificent; he moved to meet the ball with the ease of a master.

By the close, Australia had lost half their wickets, but a fine fighting innings by Brown checked England's progress. Bradman played on and when McCabe's audacious hooks and hard cuts threatened another punishing effort Verity dismissed him with a brilliant catch in the gully. A longer partnership followed, Hassett batting with style and confidence, but Wellard disposed of Hassett and Badcock in one over. Brown left off with his score 140, and that of Australia 299 for five.

On Monday, England lost little time in strengthening their grip. Verity disposed of Barnett and Chipperfield in eight deliveries and when O'Reilly went in Australia needed 37 more to avoid a follow-on. O'Reilly promptly hit out and a serious mistake occurred in the field. It is not too much to say that had Paynter held the ball O'Reilly skyed to long-on, England would have been in a position to make Australia follow on. Paynter, however, misjudged the flight and came too far forward so that although he leapt up he could not complete a catch. Australia at this point required 17 more to save the follow-on and O'Reilly, pulling two successive deliveries from Verity for six and taking 16 off the over, soon settled that question.

After three hours had been lost to rain Brown, at 184, was also missed by Paynter, this time at mid-on, and with Fleetwood-Smith showing surprisingly good defence, Brown was able to complete a double-hundred before the innings ended. Australia's fine fight was almost entirely the work of Brown, who from start to finish played with a beautifully straight bat, kept an almost impregnable defence and, without ever appearing to make real effort to punish the bowling, hit a five and 22 fours.

The rain transformed an easy wicket into one soft on top and hard underneath, and England's opening pair fell for 28 so that when the last day started the match was fairly even. After dismissing Edrich in his first over, McCormick bowled Verity, who had been sent in overnight, and half the side were out for 76 when Hammond, who had a runner, tried a one-hand stroke at a ball outside his leg stump and skyed it. In the hour of great need, however, Compton batted superbly, playing fast rising balls from McCormick very coolly, driving grandly on either side of the wickets and relishing short-pitched balls. The eighth partnership realised 74, including a mighty pull by Wellard which sent a ball from McCabe on to the Grand Stand balcony.

Hammond declared, and left Australia an impossible task in the time available. Any thought of failure was soon dispelled by Bradman. After the tea interval he batted in brisk style, short bowling by Farnes receiving instant punishment. It had long since become evident that the Test would be another case of stalemate and Bradman kept life in the cricket by hitting his 14th hundred against England; his 102 included 15 fours.

Toss: England. **England 494** (W. R. Hammond 240, E. Paynter 99, L. E. G. Ames 83, E. L. McCormick 4-101, W. J. O'Reilly 4-93) **and 242-8 dec.** (D. C. S. Compton 76*); **Australia 422** (W. A. Brown 206*, A. L. Hassett 56, H. Verity 4-103) **and 204-6** (D. G. Bradman 102*).

Third Test

At Manchester, July 8, 9, 11, 12, 1938. Abandoned.

The Third Test was to have been played at Old Trafford, but owing to the persistent bad weather the game had to be abandoned without a ball being bowled. The captains did not toss and neither team was announced.

Fourth Test

At Leeds, July 22, 23, 25, 1938. Australia won by five wickets.

Australia's success enabled them to retain the Ashes. By general consent it was the most interesting of all the season's Tests. A fine test of skill had many glorious moments, and the cricket was often thrilling to watch. At no time was the wicket easy for batting and Australia won largely because they possessed better spin bowling. Exactly why the pitch, even during the early stages, played so queerly was hard to understand. A likely explanation was that it was kept on the damp side through moisture being drawn to the surface in the humid weather prevailing. At any rate bowlers were able to turn the ball and as the match progressed spin acted more quickly; by Monday the wicket had worn and O'Reilly took full advantage.

To see England's batsmen struggling for runs after Hammond, for the third successive match, won the toss was at once unexpected and perplexing. In the course of five hours, and despite a splendid effort by Hammond, the innings was over. The Australian bowling had far more accuracy about it than in the two previous Tests and from his first over O'Reilly puzzled the batsmen. Barnett, after offering two chances, was entirely responsible for Hardstaff being run out and although he batted through to lunch, during which only 62 runs were scored, he looked strangely uncertain. Not until after the interval did Hammond attempt to change the character of the cricket and then, having hit a no-ball from McCormick for six, he lost Barnett to a fine one-hand catch at the wicket. Paynter batted steadily, but how much Hammond dominated can be gathered from the fact that he scored 76 out of 108 and hit ten fours. A clever piece of wicket-keeping began a minor collapse after Paynter, losing his balance, was stumped. Some brave hitting by Wright and Verity brought 41 for the eighth wicket, but an effort by Farnes to follow suit was quickly stopped by Fingleton, who ran fully 20 yards to hold a skyer, and England, after batting five hours, were out for 223.

When Wright, with the first ball he bowled, got rid of Brown, Ben Barnett was sent in to play out time and the outcome of this far exceeded expectations. He played a most valuable innings and England bowled for nearly an hour and a half next morning before gaining further reward. The second-wicket partnership yielded 59 and Fingleton batted in dogged style for over two hours; Barnett, who made his highest score in Test cricket, was in ten minutes longer. Then McCabe and Badcock were bowled and Australia's first five wickets fell for 145. The light at this time was none too good but Bradman, as in each of the two previous Tests, made another three-figure score. Shielding his successive partners, Bradman astutely nursed the bowling. Bowes, who rarely pitched short and made the ball swerve, had a great moment when he knocked Bradman's middle stump out of the ground.

Barnett and Edrich survived an awkward 50 minutes prior to the close and they put on 60 before being separated next morning. This in fact was the most productive stand of the whole match. For the collapse which afterwards set in no one could have been prepared. O'Reilly, on a worn pitch, and ably supported by Fleetwood-Smith, finished off the innings before lunch, England's full ten wickets actually going down for the addition of 74 to the overnight score. Successive balls accounted for Hardstaff and Hammond, who was finely caught at short square leg, and Compton had the ill-luck to be caught off his wrist. Paynter made a gallant effort, but the sixth, seventh and eighth wickets all fell at 116, Fleetwood-Smith dismissing Verity and Wright with consecutive balls, a feat which O'Reilly performed at the expense of Farnes and Bowes. Except when he changed ends, O'Reilly bowled 15 overs without a rest and took five wickets. With six men on the leg side close to the bat, and with no one in the long field, he demoralised the majority of the batsmen. Paynter's innings was the one example of resolution and no one was bold enough to attempt to wrest the initiative from the spin bowlers. England's 123 was their lowest against Australia for 17 years.

Left to get 105, Australia had to struggle hard for success. Farnes kept up a splendid attack, but misfielding gave Australia valuable runs. Intense excitement came when Wright quickly sent back Bradman and McCabe. With the first four batsmen out, Australia had to contend with atrocious light, but the batsmen refrained from appealing and, as Hassett began to drive and pull in easy, confident style, England's chance of turning the tables gradually slipped away. A storm threatened and Hassett, no doubt anxious to settle the match before the rain came, tried to drive a leg-break and skyed the ball to point. His brave innings, however, had carried his side to within 14 of victory and there were five wickets to fall. Rain interrupted play with nine runs needed, but Australia got home without further loss. Wright puzzled the batsmen so much that he might have been a match-winner had the fourth-innings task exceeded 150.

Toss: England. **England 223** (W. R. Hammond 76, W. J. O'Reilly 5-66) **and 123** (W. J. O'Reilly 5-56, L. O. Fleetwood-Smith 4-34); **Australia 242** (B. A. Barnett 57, D. G. Bradman 103, K. Farnes 4-77) **and 107-5**.

Duration of Test Matches   Donald Bradman, 1939

One of the most debated subjects at the moment is whether Test matches should be limited or played out. Considerable colour has been lent to this particular aspect of cricket because of the remarkable happenings at The Oval last August. I have always held the opinion that it is futile to expect Australian teams to travel many thousands of miles to compete in a series of matches for the Ashes, and yet play under conditions which allow quite a big possibility of one match deciding the rubber, especially when that result may depend entirely on the weather and be inconsistent with the degree of skill otherwise displayed. But I rather doubt whether the big issue is limited or played-out Tests. I think the first consideration is the mental outlook of the individual who can, if he chooses, spoil any game by his interpretation of its character. And secondly, would it not be a better game if the possibility of a match extending beyond three or four days became extremely improbable?

A prominent English international, writing in the daily press, declared: "Give me another half-hour of Leeds and let me forget The Oval." He probably conveys the innermost thoughts of the majority of the players and the public. I agree with him, if I may add 1934 and 1938 after The Oval. I do that to ensure that my concurrence will not be misconstrued. At The Oval in 1934 we Australians accomplished approximately what England did in 1938, so I have experienced both winning and losing under those conditions. People left The Oval tired of watching the unequal fight. They did it when Ponsford and I were batting in 1934. They did it when Hutton and Hardstaff were batting in 1938. Not so at Leeds. The match was one succession of thrills. People fought to get into the ground, not out of it. Their hearts beat frantically with excitement, mine along with the rest of them. Did anyone think of that curse of modern cricket – batting averages? No! It was the game which mattered. Australia won. She nearly lost and if she had it would have been a greater game still. It was stirring, exhilarating cricket. There wasn't time to think of timeless Tests at Leeds.

Fifth Test
At The Oval, August 20, 22, 23, 24, 1938. England won by an innings and 579 runs.

No more remarkable exhibition of concentration and endurance has ever been seen on the cricket field than that of Leonard Hutton, the Yorkshire opening batsman, in a match which culminated in the defeat of Australia by a record margin. Record after record went by the board as Hutton mastered the bowling in calm, methodical fashion for the best part of two and a half days. At the end of an innings which extended over 13 hours 20 minutes, this batsman of only 22 years had placed the highest score in Test cricket to his name, and shared in two partnerships which surpassed previous figures. He added 382 with Leyland, a record for any wicket for England, and his stand of 215 with Hardstaff established a new record for their sixth wicket. As a boy of 14, Hutton at Leeds in 1930 had seen Bradman hit 334 – the record score in Tests between England and Australia. Now, on his third appearance in the series he left that figure behind with an innings of 364.

This Test will also be remembered for the calamity which befell Australia while their opponents were putting together a mammoth total of 903. Fingleton strained a muscle and Bradman injured his ankle so badly that he retired from the match and did not play again during the tour. Hammond probably would not have closed the innings at tea on the third day but for the mishap to the opposing captain. The moral effect of the loss upon the other Australians was, of course, very great. Several of them batted – to all appearances – with very poor heart, but Brown, going in first, was last man out before a follow-on 702 runs in arrears. He played an heroic innings under the shadow of impending defeat and Barnes, in his first Test, well justified his choice, but there was no real recovery.

Hammond's fourth consecutive success in the toss was, of course, one factor influencing the result. Another was the way in which the Australian team was chosen. The risks taken by Bradman in going into the match with only O'Reilly, Fleetwood-Smith and Waite to bowl seemed to be inviting trouble. Neuritis was given as the reason for the omission of McCormick, who in any case had done nothing to suggest he was likely to trouble England's batsmen on a good Oval wicket. Whether Bradman, as was suggested, gambled upon winning the toss after three failures and so being in a position to call upon his spinners when the pitch had become worn will probably never be known. Although deprived through injuries of Ames and Wright, England were able to include six recognised bowlers.

The first day's cricket brought about the overwhelming success of batsmen which, with the wickets easy-paced and true, it was natural to expect. Waite and McCabe, the opening bowlers, were innocuous and although O'Reilly soon got rid of Edrich – his 100th wicket against England – that was the one success before stumps were drawn with 347 scored. Coming together at 29, Hutton and Leyland settled down to a partnership which surpassed all previous records for England. Each of them enjoyed one escape. Hutton, when 40, jumping in to Fleetwood-Smith, missed the ball which, with the batsmen well out of his ground, Barnett failed to gather. Leyland, at 140, would have been run out had not Waite, the bowler, after a fast throw-in by Badcock, knocked the bails off before the ball was in his hands. A curiosity of the day was that four times a no-ball led either to the wicket being hit or the ball being caught.

Following the same steady lines as before, Hutton and Leyland carried on until

Len Hutton, on his way to 364 at The Oval in 1938 – the highest score in Ashes Tests – is congratulated by Don Bradman after passing his old record.

the stand ended through a wonderful piece of fielding. Hutton drove a ball from O'Reilly to the off side, and Hassett fumbled it. Then he slung in a fast return to the bowler's end and Bradman, sizing up the situation in an instant, dashed in from mid-on, caught the ball and broke the wickets before Leyland could complete a second run.

Out for 187 – his highest of seven centuries against Australia – Leyland hit 17 fours.

Hammond was at the wicket to see his personal record of highest score for England in a home Test surpassed by Hutton. It was a remarkable feature of the season's Tests that Philip Mead's 182 not out at The Oval in 1921, the record for England against Australia at home, was beaten four times during this series. Paynter's dismissal with one run scored after Hammond left was a surprise. Misjudgment of a leg-break was the reason. Rain extended the tea interval and Compton left immediately afterwards. By this time Hutton had entered upon the tenth hour of his innings, and he remained full of confidence even if becoming a little monotonous by reason of his grim, determined dominance. Hardstaff batted very surely and after an ovation to Hutton when he passed R. E. Foster's 287 at Sydney in 1903–04 – the highest innings against Australia – an appeal against the light led to stumps being drawn early. England after two days had 634 and only half their wickets had fallen.

Hutton claimed exactly 300 of the runs scored at this point and the 30,000 people who assembled at The Oval on Tuesday saw history made. The bowling and fielding looked more formidable than at any other time and as Hutton carried his score nearer to the record Test innings, Bradman, the holder of it, brought several fieldsmen close in for O'Reilly. As might be supposed, Hutton showed an occasional sign of strain and he completely missed the ball when with his total 331 he had an opportunity of beating the record by hitting a no-ball from O'Reilly. However, with a perfect cut off Fleetwood-Smith, Hutton duly reached his objective and the scene at the ground, with the whole assembly rising to its feet, and every Australian player congratulating Hutton will be remembered for a long time by those who saw it.

Finally Hutton lifted a stroke towards cover and Hassett held the ball easily low down. So a phenomenal innings, lasting from half-past 11 on Saturday until half-past two on Tuesday – the longest ever in first-class cricket – came to an end. In addition to 35 fours, Hutton hit 15 threes, 18 twos and 143 singles.

England's total had reached 770 for six and some spirited hitting by Wood came as a refreshing contrast to the stern batting which had gone before. Another three-figure stand resulted, Wood adding 106 with Hardstaff. Shortly after they were separated there occurred the tragic accident to Bradman, who when bowling caught his foot in a worn foothole, fell prone and was carried off. During tea, England's innings – the longest on record, the highest for any Test and the highest for any first-class match in England – was declared closed. It was said that O'Reilly, who bowled 85 overs, wore the skin off a finger.

Before Australia scored a run, Badcock fell to a catch at short leg, and McCabe left at 19. Hassett made some excellent strokes on the leg side; afterwards Barnes and Brown raised the total from 70 to 117 before stumps were drawn and altogether added 75. Bowes twice took two wickets in an over, but neither pace nor spin could disturb Brown. An unusual incident happened during the eighth and last stand. When Brown cut the last ball of an over, intending to run a single, Hutton, with the idea of trying to give the less-experienced batsman the strike, kicked the ball to the boundary. Instructions to umpires, however, provide for four runs to be added to those already made should a fieldsman wilfully cause the ball to reach the boundary, and as this meant the award to Brown of five runs he kept the bowling. In the end, Brown missed the distinction of carrying his bat, for Hammond, running from slip, knocked up the ball and caught it at the second attempt.

England v Australia 1938 — Fifth Test

At The Oval, August 20, 22, 23, 24, 1938. Result: England won by an innings and 579 runs.

ENGLAND	First innings	
L. Hutton c Hassett b O'Reilly		364
W. J. Edrich lbw b O'Reilly		12
M. Leyland run out		187
*W. R. Hammond lbw b Fleetwood-Smith		59
E. Paynter lbw b O'Reilly		0
D. C. S. Compton b Waite		1
J. Hardstaff jnr not out		169
†A. Wood c and b Barnes		53
H. Verity not out		8
K. Farnes		
W. E. Bowes		
B 22, l-b 19, w 1, n-b 8		50

1-29 2-411 3-546 4-547 5-555   (7 wkts dec.) 903
6-770 7-876

First innings – Waite 72–16–150–1; McCabe 38–8–85–0; O'Reilly 85–26–178–3; Fleetwood-Smith 87–11–298–1; Barnes 38–3–84–1; Hassett 13–2–52–0; Bradman 2.2–1–6–0.

AUSTRALIA	First innings		Second innings	
W. A. Brown c Hammond b Leyland		69	– c Edrich b Farnes	15
C. L. Badcock c Hardstaff b Bowes		0	– b Bowes	9
S. J. McCabe c Edrich b Farnes		14	– c Wood b Farnes	2
A. L. Hassett c Compton b Edrich		42	– lbw b Bowes	10
S. G. Barnes b Bowes		41	– lbw b Verity	33
†B. A. Barnett c Wood b Bowes		2	– b Farnes	46
M. G. Waite b Bowes		8	– c Edrich b Verity	0
W. J. O'Reilly c Wood b Bowes		0	– not out	7
L. O'B. Fleetwood-Smith not out		16	– c Leyland b Farnes	0
*D. G. Bradman absent hurt		–	– absent hurt	–
J. H. W. Fingleton absent hurt		–	– absent hurt	–
B 4, l-b 2, n-b 3		9	B 1	1

1-0 2-19 3-70 4-145 5-147   201   1-15 2-18 3-35 4-41 5-115   123
6-160 7-160 8-201   6-115 7-117 8-123

First innings – Farnes 13–2–54–1; Bowes 19–3–49–5; Edrich 10–2–55–1; Verity 5–1–15–0; Leyland 3.1–0–11–1; Hammond 2–0–8–0.
Second innings – Farnes 12.1–1–63–4; Bowes 10–3–25–2; Verity 7–3–15–2; Leyland 5–0–19–0.

Toss won by England   Umpires F. Chester and F. I. Walden

In the follow-on Brown again revealed better defence than any of his colleagues. Barnes and Barnett made some capital strokes while putting on 74, but Verity dismissed Barnes and Waite with the last two balls of an over, and although Barnett stayed for an hour and hooked and drove Farnes with certainty Australia were out for 123. They were actually dismissed twice in four and three-quarter hours.

AUSTRALIA V ENGLAND 1946-47 Norman Preston

The MCC tour to Australia in 1946–47 resembled that of 1920–21, not a Test being won by England. In both cases English cricket had not recovered from the effects of world war. MCC were most reluctant to send out a team so soon after the cessation of hostilities, but so pressing was the invitation from the Australian Board that they gave way. To my mind MCC took the proper course. The presence of the English side not only revived cricket enthusiasm throughout Australia but, thanks to the great publicity given to the tour, cricket throughout the marvellous summer which followed in England received bigger public support than ever before. After all, the game is the thing, and this MCC tour has ensured support for many years to come.

Weakness in bowling was the main cause of England's failure, coupled with poor catching which affected the side in spasms. Hammond's inability to make large scores and the time taken by Hutton and Compton to produce their true form were contributory factors. That the side did not fare as badly as the men of 1920–21 and lose all five Tests was due to the fact that these matches, instead of being played to a finish, were limited to six days of five hours each, England in turn agreeing to allot five days of six hours for the 1948 Tests.

Hammond was not the same inspiring leader as at home in 1938. I believe his own batting failure upset him. In the past he had been the merciless killer of slow bowlers, but now he became their prey. Although Hutton came out top of the England batting, he did not enjoy good health. More than once he was laid up before tonsillitis drove him to hospital during the final Test. Yet there were days when he batted splendidly. In the last three innings Hutton and Washbrook began with three-figure stands, equalling the feat of Hobbs and Sutcliffe in 1924–25. The fast bowlers tried to unsettle Hutton by persistently bumping the ball short at him, but, by ducking, he usually avoided trouble. I felt that Hutton was subjected to this barrage because there was no fast bowler in the England side to retaliate.

Australian pitches do not encourage the fast-medium bowler as they did in the days of Maurice Tate, otherwise Bedser would have fared better. Still, he served his side splendidly. He got through twice the amount of bowling done by the Australian opening pair, Lindwall and Miller, and if only there had been someone of really high speed to help, his burden would have been lightened. Bradman, whom Bedser bowled for a duck at Adelaide, considered he was one of the best of his type England have sent.

Australia produced one of the best teams ever to represent them. For this happy state of affairs I am sure they were largely indebted to Bradman. Early in the season he looked far from well, but long days in the sun soon restored him to almost his old self. At first his batting, for Bradman, was uncertain. He has set such a high standard that one could not help being surprised at seeing him in difficulties; but, as in the past, his mammoth scores put Australia on top.

England suffered from the lack of all-rounders compared with the number at Bradman's disposal. Three of their leading bowlers, Miller, McCool and Lindwall, hit hundreds; McCool also scored 95 on his debut, and Tallon, the wicket-keeper, claimed 92 as his top score.

First Test

At Brisbane, November 29, 30, December 2, 3, 4, 1946. Australia won by an innings and 332 runs.

Whereas England had twice caught Australia on a sticky wicket at Brisbane, this time the tables were turned and England in each innings batted after a violent thunderstorm. Many factors contributed to their downfall. First, there was the choice of team, particularly Gibb as wicket-keeper. Next, England took so long to dismiss their opponents. Had they got them out in reasonable time they might have had a chance to bowl on the drying turf. From the England point of view the whole course of the match balanced on an incident which occurred when Bradman was 28 and the total 74 for two. Facing Voce, he chopped the ball to second slip, where Ikin thought he made a perfectly good catch. Bradman survived the appeal, and not only went on to hit his first century against England at Brisbane but, with Hassett, added 276 and established a new third-wicket record stand for these matches as the Australians set up the highest Test total in their own country.

England began the match well enough after Bradman won the toss. From the third ball of Bedser's second over Morris was caught at first slip. Bradman entered, and immediately was in trouble against Bedser, edging the fifth ball of the same over to the slips and popping up the seventh to square leg. Barnes, hooking brilliantly, did his best to shield Bradman from the bowling until at 46 he was splendidly caught at square leg off a short ball. Bedser, like a goalkeeper, knocked the ball up and caught it at the second attempt. At this point Bradman had made only seven in 40 minutes very shakily. There followed the Ikin incident. After lunch Bradman and Hassett gradually wore down the bowling in the relentless heat. Bedser bowled nobly for long spells, but could not return after tea owing to stomach trouble – a legacy of his war service in Italy. Bradman found his true form, and the first day ended with Australia 292 for two.

Edrich broke the long stand next day by clean-bowling Bradman, who hit 19 fours, with his fourth ball. Then Miller joined Hassett in another long stand, during which the fielding deteriorated. The total reached 428 before Hassett was caught at mid-on: altogether he was dropped three times. Even at this early stage the bowlers had been no-balled 20 times, but even worse was the failure of Gibb to catch McCool who, when only one, offered a chance off Bedser. After tea, McCool and Johnson hammered the bowling freely, taking the total to 595 for five by Saturday evening. Rain and bad light limited cricket on Monday to 99 minutes. Bradman did not have the pitch mown and Australia lost their five remaining wickets for 50 runs. Playing back, McCool was lbw when wanting only five for a century. In an enterprising innings he hit 14 fours and his stand with Johnson produced 131.

England now faced Lindwall and Miller; both occasionally pitched short. During lunch the sky became overcast and thunder was heard when, with the second ball afterwards, Lindwall bowled Hutton playing back. Bad light and showers caused many stoppages, and the day ended with England 21 for one. Late that evening a violent thunderstorm broke, and next day England on a nightmare pitch reached 117 for five before another storm flooded the ground. During this shortened day England fought valiantly. Lindwall, Miller and even Toshack made the ball lift alarmingly. Compton batted bravely, Edrich was struck repeatedly, and when Hammond came in nearly every ball from Lindwall rose head-high. When taken at first slip, Edrich had withstood the bowling for one and three-quarter hours. He scored only 16, but his was one of the most skilful batting displays I have ever seen. Half the side were out for 56, but Hammond, at his best, and Yardley raised the score to 117 when, following several appeals against the light, the players left the field. Then came the second storm, with hailstones as big as golf balls.

Contrary to expectations, the ground made a remarkable recovery next day in the brilliant sunshine, but the pitch proved more treacherous than ever, and, though England never gave up the unequal struggle, 15 wickets fell and Australia won at ten minutes to five. The big shock was the fall of Hutton to the first ball of the second innings, to one of three catches by Barnes at short leg. The only real stand in the follow-on was between Ikin and Gibb, who put on 47. Miller achieved a fine all-round performance by making 79 and taking nine wickets for 77. Except for the respite given by the rain, the heat was always stifling.

Toss: Australia. **Australia 645** (D. G. Bradman 187, A. L. Hassett 128, K. R. Miller 79, C. L. McCool 95, D. V. P. Wright 5-167); **England 141** (K. R. Miller 7-60) **and 172** (E. R. H. Toshack 6-82).

Second Test

At Sydney, December 13, 14, 16, 17, 18, 19, 1946. Australia won by an innings and 33 runs.

When Hammond won the toss in ideal conditions, most people expected a big score. But England's troubles commenced in the second over, when Freer bowled Washbrook, who caught his glove against the inside of his pad as he went forward. Miller, rather erratic, caused the ball to lift, but Freer was steady and accurate. Hutton and Edrich set out to repair the damage, but the appearance of Johnson at 88 upset the stand. With his third delivery Johnson had Hutton taken on the leg side by Tallon, and in the next 25 minutes Australia virtually won the match when Tallon took two more catches off McCool which accounted for Compton and Hammond.

Once again the England batsmen had failed against the spinners. There followed a desperate stand by Edrich and Ikin. Johnson bowled his off-breaks so magnificently that at the end of 70 minutes, when given a well-earned rest, his analysis read 11–8–3–1. The score crept to 148, when Edrich was lbw. Yardley provided that vigilant wicket-keeper Tallon with his fourth catch, and Johnson completed a notable day by removing Smith and Evans. He might have claimed Ikin also before stumps were drawn at 219 for eight, for at 36 he was dropped by Barnes at silly mid-off.

Bradman, who limped badly the first day, did not field on Saturday, Hassett taking over the leadership. England were soon all out, Ikin being caught at mid-off after a stay of three hours. Johnson came out with six wickets for 42 runs. The Australian innings had been in progress only nine minutes when bad light, followed by an almost torrential downpour, held up the cricket for over three hours. On resuming, Edrich made the ball kick viciously, sometimes from a very short length, and at 24 Morris, turning his back, was bowled off his legs. Bradman preferred to rest his injured leg, and as soon as Johnson appeared Barnes repeatedly appealed against the light. At the fifth appeal the umpires gave way, and play ended with the Australians 27 for one. All told, only 93 minutes' cricket was possible on this second day.

Brilliant sunshine on Sunday transformed the pitch, which rolled out perfectly on Monday when cricket took place in glorious weather. The biggest crowd of the match,

51,459, saw Barnes bat all day. Wright bowled splendidly, and the batsmen were never really comfortable in face of his mixture of leg-breaks and googlies. Bedser and Edrich also bowled well. Only three wickets fell this day, all to Edrich, as after Miller left at ten to four, Bradman, without a runner, stayed with Barnes until stumps were drawn at 252 for four. Not until 20 to six the following day did England break this stand. Then, in successive overs, Bradman, who batted superbly despite a pronounced limp, and Barnes were dismissed at the same total. Each hit 234, and they established a new fifth-wicket Test-partnership record of 405. Bradman batted for six and a half hours and hit 24 fours; Barnes took ten hours 40 minutes over his runs and hit 17 fours.

On the fifth day Australia forced the pace, and at last Wright gained reward for his excellent bowling when in his 45th over he held a return catch from Tallon. In the next quarter of an hour Freer and Tribe put on 42 before Bradman declared, Australia again having made their highest total at home. Some 24 minutes remained before lunch, and in that time Hutton launched a fierce attack against Miller and Freer. Facing a closely set field, Hutton drove with such freedom into the open spaces that he made 37 out of 49 before he unluckily hit his wicket when facing the last ball before lunch. Actually Hutton struck the ball hard, but as the bat swung over his shoulders his glove slipped and he could not retain his grip. Edrich batted for the rest of the day and with Compton took part in their side's first century stand of the Tests.

The last day began with England 247 for three, and Edrich went on to complete his first century against Australia. Meanwhile England lost Hammond, who, mistiming McCool, was caught behind the bowler. Apart from Yardley, Australia encountered little more opposition and the match was all over by 3.15 p.m. Only once before had England been defeated by an innings in successive matches, in 1897–98.

Toss: England. **England 255** (W. J. Edrich 71, J. T. Ikin 60, I. W. Johnson 6-42) **and 371** (W. J. Edrich 119, D. C. S. Compton 54, C. L. McCool 5-109); **Australia 659-8 dec.** (S. G. Barnes 234, D. G. Bradman 234).

Third Test

At Melbourne, January 1, 2, 3, 4, 6, 7, 1947. Drawn.

England put up a much better show, but experienced astonishing ill-luck, suffering two tremendous handicaps. Early on Edrich, at short leg, received a frightful blow on the shin from a fierce hook by Barnes, and he retired for the rest of the day. Soon after lunch Voce left the field with a pulled groin muscle. In the face of these setbacks Bedser and Wright bowled superbly, and Yardley surpassed himself. Maintaining accurate length and direction, he moved the ball consistently from the off to a packed leg-side field.

Despite the comparatively cheap dismissals of Barnes, Morris and Hassett, things looked bad for England when the total reached 188 for three, Bradman again having lifted Australia out of trouble. Then with successive balls Yardley dismissed Bradman and Johnson. Bradman, feeling for an off-break, chopped the ball on. So restrained was he that he hit only two fours, a true indication of England's magnificent bowling. The next ball removed Johnson, lbw, and with only four runs added Miller was smartly taken by the wicket-keeper. So in 17 minutes the position changed to 192 for six.

Here McCool and Tallon gave an indication of Australia's immense all-round strength. Unperturbed by the state of the game, they played the bowling so confidently during the last 55 minutes that they added 63. On the second day Voce was still absent, but Edrich, although slightly lame, took a share in the bowling. In fact he sent down the first over of the day and, without addition, got Tallon caught behind. McCool punished the bowling unmercifully, hooking and driving with absolute confidence, and completing his first Test century before Dooland left after helping to put on 83. McCool, who took out his bat, hit eight fours, his stay having lasted three hours. Again Evans did not concede a bye. He kept magnificently.

England began their innings just before three o'clock, and received an early shock when Hutton touched a beautiful ball from Lindwall which swung away into the hands of McCool, who made a very fine catch at first slip. Washbrook and Edrich then played out the remaining time. Such was Washbrook's patience that he hit only one boundary, but Edrich, again in his best form, batted perfectly while scoring 85, including ten fours. So England finished a notable day in a fighting position, at 147 for one.

The third morning was the most vital of the match, and, to their bitter disappointment, England lost Edrich when he appeared to hit a ball from Lindwall hard on to his pads. Worse followed; Compton, believing the ball was outside leg, preferred to leave it alone because of Toshack's thickly set leg trap and also was lbw. This seemed to upset Hammond; he failed to treat the bowling with sufficient respect and gave a sharp return to Dooland. Then Washbrook, having defended solidly for nearly four hours, was caught at the wicket, making half the side out for 179. Ikin and Yardley set about retrieving England's fortunes, and in a gallant stand they added 113. A keen fight developed for the lead, 42 being required when the last man Wright came in, but he could not resist running in to a full-toss which bowled him, so Australia led by 14.

On the fourth day England captured only four wickets, Voce still being off the field. The day brought new honours to Yardley, who in 19 overs dismissed Barnes, Bradman and Miller. It was the third successive time that Yardley had removed Bradman. Morris batted all day while reaching 132, his first Test hundred. Voce bowled for the first time since the opening day, and England put forward a special effort. Morris, after batting for six hours, during which time he hit only eight fours, was fifth out at 333; and when the seventh wicket fell at 341 England still stood a chance, but Tallon and Lindwall completely changed the situation. The onslaught was violent, and in 87 minutes they put on 154. Tallon spent only one and three-quarter hours over his 92. His clean driving, like that of Lindwall, was masterly and the bowling went to pieces. For some time Hammond made no attempt to close the empty spaces in the field. Bedser, for instance, was bowling to three slips while the batsmen were punching him hard in front of the wicket. Lindwall completed a magnificent century by going down the pitch and driving Bedser with tremendous power all along the ground to the sightscreen, a majestic stroke worthy of such a grand display.

England wanted 551 in seven hours, and Hutton and Washbrook made a steady start by scoring 91 before the close. Hutton refused to be disturbed by short bumping deliveries from Lindwall and Miller, but lost his wicket after batting for three hours, when, attempting one of his few big hits during a painstaking innings, he gave a catch to long-off. On the final day rain caused four brief interruptions. At times the light was extremely bad, but England never appealed, not even when Yardley and Bedser were struggling hard to save the game and rain was falling steadily. Twice Bradman suggested that they should go in before the players left the field. Yardley played a great part by staying for the final 90 minutes. In the match he scored 114 for once out and took four wickets, including Bradman's twice. This was the first drawn Test in Australia for 65 years, but England's failure to win meant that Australia retained the Ashes.

The match proved a tremendous attraction. The official attendance aggregate was 343,675 and the receipts of £44,063 made a world record for a cricket match. At the time much was said and written about the umpires' decisions on the third day, but the crowd itself was very generous to England.

Toss: Australia. **Australia 365** (D. G. Bradman 79, C. L. McCool 104*) **and 536** (A. R. Morris 155, D. Tallon 92, R. R. Lindwall 100); **England 351** (C. Washbrook 62, W. J. Edrich 89, N. W. D. Yardley 61, B. Dooland 4-69) **and 310-7** (C. Washbrook 112, N. W. D. Yardley 53*).

Fourth Test

At Adelaide, January 31, February 1, 3, 4, 5, 6, 1947. Drawn.

There were four extraordinary features about this Test. It was played in perpetual heat and dense humidity, with the temperature sometimes 105°F; Lindwall finished the England first innings by taking three wickets, all bowled, in four balls; and both Compton and Morris achieved the rare feat of hitting two separate hundreds. England put up another brave struggle, but once again Hammond accomplished little with the bat and the bowling was not good enough.

In both innings Hutton and Washbrook gave England a splendid send-off with a three-figure stand, but after tea on the opening day Edrich, Hutton and Hammond were dismissed in a disastrous 35 minutes. Again England were upset by the slower bowlers, and it was not surprising that Bradman did not take the new ball at 200. Third out, Hutton batted without mistake for four hours.

The second day provided plenty of thrills. Hardstaff remained with Compton until after lunch and then, trying to hook Miller, he played on, the stand having put on 118. Ikin stayed while 61 were added, and, with Compton in complete control, Yardley helped put on 74 for the seventh wicket before Compton's great innings ended. Lindwall, after a rest and still using the old ball, held a sharp return catch from his first delivery. This was Compton's finest display so far during the tour; at the wicket four and three-quarter hours, he did not offer any kind of chance. His main scoring strokes were 15 fours and the feature of his play was powerful driving. Lindwall then took the new ball, and next over bowled both Bedser and Evans off stump with successive deliveries; the next just missed the wicket and the fourth bowled Wright. Some 25 minutes remained, and Bedser served England splendidly by causing Harvey to play on and then producing an almost unplayable ball that bowled Bradman for nought. Australia finished at 24 for two.

During the third day Australia made a complete recovery by adding 269 while losing only Morris – who hit his second Test century – and Hassett, who helped to put on 189 for the third wicket in nearly four hours. Bedser alone bowled well this day, as Wright, uncertain in his run, delivered many no-balls. Showing more freedom than previously, Morris drove delightfully and hit two sixes and 12 fours. Miller and Johnson carried the score to 293 for four before the close.

The heat was again almost overwhelming on the fourth day, when the fifth-wicket pair carried their stand to 150 before Johnson was lbw. The high temperature was too much for Bedser, who had to rest for a period in the pavilion. Again Yardley bowled his leg theory splendidly and quietened the batsmen, but Miller became the seventh Australian to hit a century in this series. When Lindwall left, Australia were 37 behind, and at this point Bedser returned; but without further loss Australia went ahead. The innings closed when Edrich brilliantly ran out Toshack. Miller, who offered three chances after passing three figures, remained unbeaten. No sooner had Hutton and Washbrook begun England's second innings than a sharp thunderstorm accompanied by vivid flashes of lightning held up the game for 23 minutes. Lindwall and Miller each bounced the ball freely, but Hutton and Washbrook seldom missed a scoring opportunity. Their praiseworthy stand reached 96 at the close.

On the fifth day Hutton and Washbrook soon completed their second three-figure opening stand of the match; then disaster occurred. Tallon, standing well back, held a snick from Washbrook. Some people thought the ball was scooped off the ground. For a time Edrich shaped well, but Johnson bowled Hutton, and Toshack caused such a collapse that by 5.15 eight wickets were down for 255. Compton alone of the recognised batsmen remained and, shielding Evans from the bowling, he defied all Bradman's devices to remove him. At the close England were 274 for eight; Evans had not scored.

Evans again produced a splendid defence on the rare occasions Compton could not face the bowling, but within a quarter of an hour of the resumption, when Compton was 60 and the total 282, Tallon failed to stump Evans off Dooland. Had this chance been accepted, Australia must have won, but, instead, England made such an excellent recovery that Hammond was able to declare. Evans was at the wicket 95 minutes before he got his first runs by placing Lindwall to leg for two. With the last scoring stroke before lunch Compton hit Dooland through the covers for four, so completing his second hundred. He hit ten fours, and his gallant stand with Evans realised 85.

When one ball had been sent down after lunch Hammond declared, setting Australia to make 314. Considering England's poor bowling resources and the experienced hitters at Australia's command, this was not an impossible task, but from the outset Bradman declined to accept the challenge. Up to a point Morris was enterprising, but Harvey, in his first Test, naturally declined to take risks. Morris and Bradman calmly played out time, and Morris became the second Australian to hit two centuries in a Test against England, the first being Warren Bardsley, another left-hander, at The Oval in 1909.

Toss: England. **England 460** (L. Hutton 94, C. Washbrook 65, D. C. S. Compton 147,
J. Hardstaff 67, R. R. Lindwall 4-52) **and 340-8 dec.** (L. Hutton 76, D. C. S. Compton 103*,
E. R. H. Toshack 4-76); **Australia 487** (A. R. Morris 122, A. L. Hassett 78, K. R. Miller 141*,
I. W. Johnson 52) **and 215-1** (A. R. Morris 124*, D. G. Bradman 56*).

Fifth Test

At Sydney, February 28, March 1, 3, 4, 5, 1947. Australia won by five wickets.

So much rain fell before and during this final Test that it produced the best cricket of the whole series, because the pitch, without ever becoming treacherous, always encouraged bowlers. England could fairly claim that they experienced wretched luck. Hutton, after batting splendidly throughout the opening day while making his first Test century in Australia, was stricken with tonsillitis. Rain prevented any play on the second day;

but Sunday was gloriously fine and the pitch, which had been under water – mushrooms sprang up in the outfield – dried quite firm. Despite the loss of Hutton, England, thanks to magnificent bowling by Wright and Bedser, were always challenging. Indeed, for the first time in the series they led on first innings, but on the final day, at a crucial point, Edrich dropped an easy catch off Wright offered by Bradman when only two and the total 47. Had that been accepted, victory might well have gone to England, for Bradman alone seemed able to establish any mastery over Wright and Bedser.

Hammond, unable to trust his fibrositis, stood down, and Yardley became captain for the first time in a Test. He led his men courageously, and that England did not win was certainly not his fault.

The feature of the Australian bowling throughout the match was the number of short bouncing balls delivered by Lindwall and Miller, although it was a very fine good-length delivery which bowled Washbrook in the first over. Nearly three hours passed before another wicket fell, while Hutton and Edrich added 150. Progress was never easy. From the outset Tribe was able to turn his left-arm slows, and Toshack, operating to a closely set leg trap, compelled respect. By tea the total was 162 for two, but Fishlock left at 188 and Lindwall, taking the second new ball at 207, immediately upset the batsmen with a mixture of intimidating bumpers and an occasional unplayable good-length ball. In five overs he removed Compton, Yardley and Ikin. Compton steered a very short ball away from his face but in so doing trod on his wicket. The day finished with England 237 for six, Hutton having batted for five hours.

Following the blank Saturday, Hutton was taken ill, and on Monday morning he went to hospital with a temperature of 103°. Some bold hitting by Evans was mainly responsible for the first innings realising 280. Lindwall achieved a remarkable performance in taking seven wickets. Undismayed by their moderate total, England bowled splendidly. The thermometer reached 102°, yet Bedser and Wright never spared themselves, and the fielding, with Evans, Compton and Fishlock in brilliant form, was also high-class. Barnes and Morris gave Australia a fine start. They began before lunch, and not until after tea did Bedser separate them, when Barnes, attempting to cut, was caught by Evans. Soon afterwards Bedser also accounted for Morris, and then Wright came into his own by bowling Bradman and getting Miller taken at second slip. Bradman ran down the wicket and, misjudging the spin, missed the ball. Wright bowled unchanged after tea. Next day, while Bedser in 11 overs conceded only 15 runs and completely shut up his end, Wright carried all before him. In 11 overs he dismissed five men for 42 runs.

Batting a second time, England also broke down. With the first ball Lindwall beat Fishlock by sheer pace and dismissed him lbw. There followed such skilful slow bowling by McCool that the day ended with six men out for 144. Even Edrich was greatly troubled by McCool, and Compton alone proved equal to the occasion, making 51 not out. To such an extent did the bowlers hold the mastery that 12 wickets fell for 208.

The fifth day sufficed to bring about a finish. Lindwall, with the wind behind him, was very aggressive and soon dismissed Smith, but Compton gave another brave display until he was caught in Toshack's leg trap for 76. On a pitch so helpful to bowlers, Australia's task of making 214 did not appear easy.

Yardley looked to Bedser and Wright for another great effort, and again they responded magnificently. Edrich sent down only one over before Wright appeared with three slips and a short leg. Barnes and Morris decided to get as many runs as possible while the effects of the roller remained good. Their progress was comparatively speedy,

Barnes using the square cut effectively against Wright, but at 45 Morris was run out going for a third. Compton mishandled the ball at long leg, but, recovering, he made a smart return and Evans did the rest. Bradman scored two and then offered the shoulder-high catch which passed between Edrich's hands. In the next over Barnes was well caught by Evans off Bedser, and then Bradman and Hassett, with almost a day and a half before them, decided to tire out the bowlers. During their first 50 minutes together they made only 13, but when Wright and Bedser had to be rested Bradman promptly appreciated the change. Smith sent down only two overs and back came Wright. By the tea interval the total reached 110 for two, and Australia were almost safe.

Wright did not find the pitch so responsive as on the previous day when he caused the ball to lift and turn awkwardly, and by sound batsmanship the total reached 149 before Bradman lifted a drive into the hands of Compton at extra cover. His stand with Hassett, which produced 98, turned the issue in Australia's favour. Hassett defended nobly, and on his dismissal Miller took charge. Showing excellent judgment in choosing the best ball to punish, he claimed six fours, mainly from superb drives. So Australia won by five wickets just before six o'clock with a whole day to spare.

Toss: England. **England 280** (L. Hutton 122*, W. J. Edrich 60, R. R. Lindwall 7-63) **and 186** (D. C. S. Compton 76, C. L. McCool 5-44); **Australia 253** (S. G. Barnes 71, A. R. Morris 57, D. V. P. Wright 7-105) **and 214-5** (D. G. Bradman 63).

ENGLAND v AUSTRALIA 1948   Reg Hayter

When, announcing his retirement, D. G. Bradman claimed that the 1948 side bore comparison with any of its predecessors, he accurately reflected the majority of opinion. In retaining the Ashes held by Australia since 1934, this side enjoyed almost uninterrupted success, becoming the first to go unbeaten through an English tour: certainly they achieved all that could be expected of a combination entitled to the description *great*. Yet they gave cause for reservation of such sweeping judgment, as the Tests were by no means so one-sided as results suggested. Still, for the most part, victory followed victory so inevitably that at times opponents took on an air of defeat almost before the match had been in progress more than an hour or two. Once or twice that impression extended even to the Tests.

In reaping full reward for superiority at all points the Australians were flattered by the margin of their Test victories. Several factors contributed to the accentuation of England's weaknesses. To counteract Yardley's presumed good luck in winning the toss, the weather mostly favoured Australia; England batted in appalling light at Nottingham, in bad light at Lord's and for a time at The Oval, but Australia did not once face such a handicap. Moreover, England stood in a fine position at the end of the third day at Manchester: it seemed fair to think that only rain robbed England of victory, but when they gained an equally strong advantage at Leeds and then suffered defeat the first opinion about Manchester required revision.

To complete England's disadvantages was the aid given Australia by the experimental rule of a new ball after 55 overs. Such good use did the visitors make of their frequent opportunities with the new ball that Bradman faced few bowling problems.

The Invincibles: the Australian tourists of 1948, arguably the strongest of all Test sides. They won the Ashes 4–0, and did not lose once during the whole tour. Standing (left to right): Neil Harvey, Don Tallon, Doug Ring, Ian Johnson, Ray Lindwall, Ron Saggers, Bill Johnston, Sam Loxton, Keith Miller, Ernie Toshack. Seated: Arthur Morris, Colin McCool, Lindsay Hassett, Don Bradman (captain), Bill Brown, Sid Barnes, Ron Hamence.

To put it briefly, the more powerful team enjoyed the larger share of good fortune and they missed few chances of capitalising on their strength.

The speed bowling of Lindwall, ably backed by Miller and Johnston, constituted the biggest single weapon on either side. Undoubtedly, Lindwall bore a major part in England's defeats. Not only did he combine controlled pace and accuracy, which allowed few moments of respite, but he helped the other bowlers to their triumphs because, worried by Lindwall, batsmen often took undue risks in their efforts to score from his colleagues. Lindwall introduced an additional source of concern to batsmen by the employment of the extra-fast bumper.

Compared with the Australians' sustained hostility England suffered from the absence of a genuine fast bowler. Hard as Bedser worked, he lacked adequate support. To him fell the distinction of dismissing Bradman in the first four Test innings. On the first three occasions Bradman sent a catch to Hutton at short fine leg, but after the Second Test he could not again be lured into the trap when facing a late inswinger pitched on the middle stump.

For Bradman the tour provided the most fitting climax possible to an illustrious career. Apart from leading Australia to continued Test dominance, he made more hundreds than anyone in the country. In addition to this supreme batting ability, Bradman demonstrated his knowledge of the game in captaincy and generalship.

First Test

At Nottingham, June 10, 11, 12, 14, 15, 1948. Australia won by eight wickets.

Reg Hayter

Bravely as England fought back, the result became nearly a foregone conclusion by the end of the first day after their disastrous batting against a fast attack of exceptionally high standard. Although only 20 minutes' play was possible before lunch on Thursday, Miller struck a vital blow by bowling Hutton and, on a pitch affected sufficiently by a heavy downpour to make the ball skid through, England lost eight wickets before tea for 74. True, the light never became good and the bowling reached a high level, but England played poorly and there could be no criticism of Yardley's decision to bat first.

When Laker and Bedser came together, there seemed every likelihood that England would be out for less than the lowest Test score at Nottingham – England's 112 in 1921 – but the pair batted confidently and more than doubled the total, adding 89. Laker hooked firmly and made many fine off-drives, and Bedser mixed good defence with clean driving. A dazzling slip catch by Miller set the keynote on Australia's excellent fielding, but Australia suffered a handicap when Lindwall pulled a groin muscle midway through the innings and could not bowl again in the match.

Although a good spell by Laker gave great encouragement on the second day Australia recovered and pressed home their advantage, but England deserved equal praise for limiting the batsmen to 276. Yardley mostly set defensive fields and, though lacking penetration, his bowlers concentrated on and just outside leg stump. At one period Laker's off-breaks put the Australians into a position where they struggled for runs. He owed a great deal to Evans for disposing of Barnes, who cut a ball hard on to the wicket-keeper's thigh whence it bounced into the air; Evans whirled round and diving full length held the ball with one hand inches from the ground.

Yardley caused surprise by taking off Laker in order to use the new ball against Brown, normally an opening batsman accustomed to swing. The change provided Bradman with an opportunity to hit his first four after 83 minutes, but again he relapsed into long periods of defence and, as Brown followed suit, scoring became very slow. Australia passed England's total without further loss, but at 184 Yardley once again showed his usefulness as a change bowler by getting Brown lbw with his fourth delivery. Seldom had Bradman been so subdued as he was over his 28th Test century. He did not welcome Yardley's tactics in asking his bowlers to work to a packed leg-side field, and he spent over three hours and a half in reaching his hundred.

In the third over on Saturday Hutton at short fine leg held the first of his series of catches given by Bradman off Bedser's late inswinger. Johnson fell to Laker's fifth ball and Young took a brilliant return catch from Tallon during a remarkable spell, before Hassett found an able partner in the hard-driving Lindwall, who did not require a runner in spite of his groin trouble. In one period Young sent down 11 overs without conceding a run and his figures for that complete spell were 26–16–14–1. In all he gave away only 79 runs in 60 overs.

The eighth wicket added 107 before Bedser knocked back Hassett's off stump. Though Hassett pursued his policy of defence for five hours 50 minutes he hit hard whenever the opportunity arose and hit a six and 20 fours. England's difficulties were increased immediately they batted again 344 behind: in Miller's second over Washbrook attempted to hook and edged a catch behind. Misjudgment cost Edrich his wicket at 39, but Hutton showed sparkling form and Compton overcame an anxious start. In a delightful display Hutton reached 50 with successive fours off Miller. At this period Miller bowled medium-paced off-breaks, but he turned again to fast deliveries and incurred the noisy displeasure of sections of the crowd when he bowled five bumpers to Hutton in his last eight balls, one of which struck him high on the left arm.

Before play began on Monday the Nottinghamshire secretary broadcast an appeal to the crowd to leave the conduct of the game to the umpires, and he deplored the barracking of Miller. The not-out batsmen continued their good work, but the light became even worse then play was held up when the ground caught the edge of a thunderstorm. Almost immediately on resumption Miller produced a fast break-back which beat Hutton completely in the still-gathering gloom. Rarely can a Test match have been played under such appalling conditions as on this day. Great credit was due to Compton and Hardstaff, even in the absence of Lindwall, for their resolution. Compton batted in masterly fashion during his third century in successive Tests at Trent Bridge, and Yardley gave sound aid till Johnston took a return catch smartly.

England began the last day only one run ahead with four wickets left, but hope remained as long as Compton was undefeated. He and Evans held out till shortly before lunch when Miller released a lightning bumper at Compton. The ball reared shoulder-high, Compton shaped to hook then changed his mind and tried to get his head out of the way. As he ducked he lost his balance on the muddy turf and tumbled into his wicket. This tragic end to one of his best innings sealed England's fate. Compton defied a first-class attack for six hours 50 minutes and hit 19 fours. Evans completed a gallant fifty, but Australia wanted only 98 to win.

Bedser added interest by bowling Morris and dismissing Bradman for his first duck in a Test in England, caught in exactly the same manner as in the first innings; but Barnes and Hassett quickly hit off the runs, Barnes showing tremendous power in square-cutting. The match ended humorously. After hitting a boundary Barnes thought the game was over when the scores were level, and he snatched a stump before racing towards the pavilion. He was halfway up the steps when the shouts of the crowd made him realise the error and he returned to the crease. When Hassett did make the winning hit another scramble for souvenirs took place; and in this Barnes was unlucky.

Toss: England. **England 165** (J. C. Laker 63, W. A. Johnston 5-36) **and 441** (L. Hutton 74, D. C. S. Compton 184, T. G. Evans 50, K. R. Miller 4-125, W. A. Johnston 4-147); **Australia 509** (S. G. Barnes 62, D. G. Bradman 138, A. L. Hassett 137, J. C. Laker 4-138) **and 98-2** (S. G. Barnes 64*).

Second Test

Reg Hayter

At Lord's, June 24, 25, 26, 28, 29, 1948. Australia won by 409 runs.

This convincing victory confirmed Australia's clear superiority. Only on the first day did England provide comparable opposition, and the selectors must have been very disappointed at the lack of determination by some of the batsmen against an attack again below full strength, this time because Miller was unable to bowl. Australia were the better team in batting, bowling, fielding and tactics, but England could not complain of lack of opportunities to wrest the initiative.

Although the heavy atmosphere aided swing in the early stages, that did not detract from the merit of England's performance in dismissing seven batsmen for 258 after Bradman won the toss for the only time in the series. The day began with excitement, Coxon in his second over of Test cricket dismissing Barnes, whose poor stroke to a short ball enabled Hutton at short fine leg to bring off the first of three successive catches there. His next victim was Bradman, who fell to the Hutton-Bedser combination again. Bradman, curiously uncertain and uncomfortable, might have been out in similar fashion when 13.

Morris showed far more confidence than Bradman against England's purposeful bowling, and after a quiet start he scored briskly in making 105 out of 166 before he gave gully a hard catch. Miller offered no stroke to a fast break-back from England's best bowler, the persistent and accurate Bedser, and Yardley finished a stubborn and defensive partnership between Hassett and Brown by getting rid of both in quick time. Helped by three lives, Hassett spent 175 minutes getting 47 runs. When Evans caught Johnson and seven wickets were down, England, despite the missed chances, could feel pleased with their efforts.

Subsequent events gave them little cause for satisfaction. The first change of fortune occurred early on the second day when, Tallon playing the leading role, Australia's last three wickets added 92. Then followed a magnificent speed attack by Lindwall. Unfortunately for England the light was not good, but that did not wholly account for a collapse redeemed only partially by a defiant stand between Compton and Yardley. Lindwall began by getting Washbrook caught at the wicket in his fourth over, and, after Hutton played outside a good ball from Johnson, Lindwall deepened England's gloom by clean-bowling Edrich and Dollery, both beaten by sheer pace, in three balls. Compton and Yardley aroused thoughts of a recovery before Lindwall and Johnston, refreshed by tea, returned with the new ball. A typically fine slip catch by Miller, close to the turf, disposed of Compton, and the first ball of the next over took Yardley's off stump. At the close of a one-sided day England stood 143 behind with one wicket to fall.

Except for one thrilling over by Yardley on Saturday Australia's batsmen revelled in the perfect pitch and glorious weather. Barnes, who should have been stumped when 18, and Morris consolidated Australia's lead with a first-wicket stand of 122. Morris eventually deflected a leg-side ball on to his stumps, but then Barnes and Bradman put on 174. At first Barnes was content to leave most of the scoring to Bradman, but he quickened after reaching 50, and upon the completion of his big ambition of a Test century at Lord's he went over to vigorous attack. He took 21, including two successive sixes, in one over from Laker and fell to a catch on the boundary. Yardley, the successful bowler, penetrated Hassett's defence first ball, and only a hurried jab by Miller prevented a hat-trick. Bradman looked destined to celebrate his farewell Test at Lord's with a century, but an acrobatic one-handed diving catch by Edrich brought about his dismissal 11 short. This was the first ball of a new spell by Bedser, who had thus disposed of Bradman in five consecutive Test innings, including the last of the 1946–47 series. At the close Australia were 478 ahead with six wickets left.

A break in the weather during the weekend aggravated England's plight. Rainclouds were again about when Australia resumed and three stoppages occurred while 117 runs were added before Bradman declared. Miller drove gloriously, and Lindwall was scarcely less entertaining. Soon after England started batting with nine hours in which to get 596 for victory, rain caused the fourth hold-up of the day. Frequent showers put sufficient life into the pitch to enable Lindwall and Johnston to make the ball rear awkwardly, and the batsmen were soon in trouble. In contrast to Washbrook, who showed a welcome return to form, Hutton looked plainly uncomfortable. He was missed at slip before scoring and several times flashed at rising balls before he gave slip an easy catch. Both Edrich and Washbrook had to face a number of fast short-pitched balls, Washbrook receiving blows on the knuckles, hip and elbows. When Toshack accounted for both in rapid succession three wickets were down for 65, but Compton and Dollery added 41 in the last half-hour.

England entered the last day with seven wickets left, but the slender chance of saving the game practically disappeared with the morning's second ball. Compton struck his toe in trying to drive and the edged stroke which resulted provided Miller with another opportunity to make a lightning low catch at second slip. That was virtually the end of the resistance, and the innings closed for the addition of 80 runs, of which the last two stands made 45. Well as Toshack bowled, Lindwall was the match-winner. His very fast ball and his bumper presented problems which few of the batsmen could answer, and he was even more devastating than his figures of eight for 131 indicate.

Toss: Australia. **Australia 350** (A. R. Morris 105, D. Tallon 53, A. V. Bedser 4-100) **and 460-7 dec.**
(S. G. Barnes 141, A. R. Morris 62, D. G. Bradman 89, K. R. Miller 74),
England 215 (D. C. S. Compton 53, R. R. Lindwall 5-70) **and 186** (E. R. H. Toshack 5-40).

CRICKETER OF THE YEAR – RAY LINDWALL   1949

By whatever standard he is judged, Raymond Russell Lindwall must be placed permanently in the gallery of great fast bowlers. The fact that in England his uncommon speed gave him an advantage over many batsmen meeting bowling of such pace for the first time did not detract from his superb control of length and direction, his change of pace and general skill. Even though his 27 wickets in the Tests equalled the highest by any Australian fast bowler in England and was only two short of C. V. Grimmett's total in 1930, Lindwall's effect could not be measured alone in terms of wickets. More important was that England gained the encouragement of a good opening stand in only one Test, at Leeds.

Lindwall, born on October 3, 1921, began by playing in the paddocks near his home at Mascot in Sydney, where often the wicket consisted of chalk markings on the fence. At 16 he first appeared for the St George club, whose captain, W. J. O'Reilly, took a hand in his development.

Putting power, rhythm and purpose into every stride of a 16-paced approach, this magnificent fair-haired athlete, 5ft 11in tall and weighing nearly 12 stone, from the moment of starting his run-up indicates a fine bowler, and, though his arm does not go over as high as the purists wish, he has preferred to retain his action and body swing rather than trying to bowl with an altered delivery. Previously Lindwall dragged his back foot nearly a yard before releasing the ball and was the subject of much controversy, but after seeing a film showing this drag Lindwall increased his run-up by a pace and in consequence rarely was no-balled in England. Constant practice during his early days enabled him to maintain remarkable accuracy for a man of his pace and he seldom allowed a batsman to leave a ball alone.

Uniquely, all five of Wisden's *Cricketers of the Year for 1949 came from the Australian touring team – the others were Arthur Morris, Lindsay Hassett, Bill Johnston and Don Tallon.*

Third Test

Reg Hayter

At Manchester, July 8, 9, 10, 12, 13, 1948. Drawn.

Fate dealt its sharpest blow of the series to England by the breaking of the weather over the weekend at a time when defeat for Australia appeared more than a possibility. By the end of the third day England had recovered so well from another disastrous start that they stood 316 runs on with only three wickets down in the second innings, but visions of Australia struggling to avoid being beaten were dispelled by rain which made further play impossible till after lunch on the last day.

The England selectors aroused intense discussion by their omission of Hutton. His replacement Emmett's mettle was soon tested, for Bradman, in his 50th Test, again lost the toss and England batted on a pitch lively for the first few overs. Probably upset by narrowly escaping a run-out first ball, the new opening pair did not look comfortable and Johnston began an early collapse by yorking Washbrook. Then Emmett pushed out his bat with one hand after losing sight of a short-pitched ball which lifted: Barnes, at short leg, took an easy catch. Lindwall began a number of bouncers, one of which led to an accident to Compton. After being struck on the arm he took a big hit at a bumper, but the ball flew off the edge of his bat on to his forehead. Compton staggered around and was led off with a cut head. Stitches were inserted and though he wanted to go back at the fall of the next wicket he was ordered to rest.

The situation called for the relentless defence which Edrich and Crapp adopted. At one point they scored only one run in 25 minutes and by lunch the total was 57. Crapp afterwards began to reveal his scoring strokes before Lindwall and Johnston returned with the new ball. Then in brief time Crapp was lbw, Dollery hit over a yorker and Edrich touched a rising flyer. Edrich deserved more credit for staying three hours while Compton was able to rest than criticism for scoring only 32 in that period. After a short knock in the nets, Compton resumed at 119 for five. At once he introduced an air of confidence into the batting and he found a fine partner in Evans, whose bold hitting helped bring 75 runs. At the close England were 231 for seven.

Though the new ball was in use at the start of the second day Australia could not retain their grip, for Compton received splendid support from Bedser, who shared in a stand of 121. Bedser used his height and feet well in dealing with the pace attack and looked capable of going on for a long time; unfortunately he was run out through an error of judgment by Compton. Soon after Bedser's dismissal occurred a second distressing accident. Barnes, fielding in his usual position about five yards from the bat at short leg, received a fierce blow under the ribs from a full-blooded pull by Pollard. Compton, who remained undefeated, might have been caught at the wicket four times – three chances were very difficult – but he gave a grand display of skill and courage. Nothing earned more admiration than the manner in which he withstood some lightning overs of extreme hostility by Lindwall. Compton hit 16 fours.

Pollard unwittingly struck a big blow when he hit Barnes, because Australia, having dropped Brown, possessed only one recognised opening batsman. The necessary rearrangement no doubt played its part in Australia's only batting failure of the Tests, but Bedser and Pollard deserved full credit for their share in gaining a lead of 142. A fine catch by Evans sent back Johnson, the emergency partner to Morris, and soon Bradman was lbw to the persistent Pollard. This was a great start for England on a slow, easy pitch and when Hassett misjudged Young's flight three men were out for 82. During these setbacks Morris batted cautiously, but he and Miller left early on the third morning to the new ball. So began a day when again everything went in England's favour. Barnes, who had practised in the nets where he collapsed after a few minutes, surprisingly went out to bat, but he was obviously in great pain and, after staying half an hour for a single, he sank to the ground and had to be assisted off. He was taken to hospital again and kept under observation for ten days. Loxton, Tallon and Lindwall drove hard in helping to avoid the follow-on, but Bedser and Pollard maintained their grip and altogether on Monday the last six wickets fell for 95.

Australia naturally flung everything into attack in the effort to recover lost ground. A dazzling right-hand catch by Tallon dismissed Emmett off his first ball from Lindwall, but Washbrook and Edrich stood firm while Miller and Lindwall bowled at great speed. The batsmen, helped by unusually poor fielding, strengthened England's position in a second-wicket stand of 124. Washbrook was twice dropped at long leg and once at slip, but Edrich did not offer a chance. Immediately after reaching 50 with a six he was run out, a fast throw from cover by Morris knocking two stumps out of the ground. Edrich played one of his best and most confident innings, and was not affected by a succession of bumpers from Miller which annoyed sections of the crowd. Crapp gave solid support to Washbrook through a new ball period and the partnership was unbroken at the close.

Then the weather intervened. No play took place on Monday and play was not resumed till after lunch on Tuesday. Yardley declared first thing, but more showers lessened the hope of victory. Although Young caused brief excitement when he got rid of Johnson with his second ball, the pitch was too lifeless to give bowlers help and Morris and Bradman contented themselves with dead-bat tactics, each remaining at one end. In one spell of 100 minutes they did not change ends.

Toss: England. **England 363** (D. C. S. Compton 145*, R. R. Lindwall 4-99) **and 174-3 dec.** (C. Washbrook 85*, W. J. Edrich 53); **Australia 221** (A. R. Morris 51, A. V. Bedser 4-81) **and 92-1** (A. R. Morris 54*).

Fourth Test

At Leeds, July 22, 23, 24, 26, 27, 1948. Australia won by seven wickets.

Leslie Smith

By the astonishing feat of scoring 404 for three on the fifth day when the pitch took spin, Australia won the rubber. Until that fatal last stage England were on top, but a succession of blunders prevented them gaining full reward for good work on the first four days. The biggest mistake occurred before the game started, for the selectors decided to leave out Young, the slow left-armer. Consequently England took the field with an unbalanced attack. Having only one slow bowler available, Yardley did not know what to do for the best on the last day, and he was forced to make Compton the spearhead. Even then England should have won. Evans, behind the wicket, fell a long way below his best form, and three catches were dropped in the field.

England v Australia 1948

Fourth Test

At Leeds, on July 22, 23, 24, 26, 1948. Result: Australia won by seven wickets.

ENGLAND

	First innings		*Second innings*
L. Hutton b Lindwall	81	– c Bradman b Johnson	57
C. Washbrook c Lindwall b Johnston	143	– c Harvey b Johnston	65
W. J. Edrich c Morris b Johnson	111	– lbw b Lindwall	54
A. V. Bedser c and b Johnson	79	– (9) c Hassett b Miller	17
D. C. S. Compton c Saggers b Lindwall	23	– (4) c Miller b Johnston	66
J. F. Crapp b Toshack	5	– (5) b Lindwall	18
*N. W. D. Yardley b Miller	25	– (6) c Harvey b Johnston	7
K. Cranston b Loxton	10	– (7) c Saggers b Johnston	0
†T. G. Evans c Hassett b Loxton	3	– (8) not out	47
J. C. Laker c Saggers b Loxton	4	– not out	15
R. Pollard not out	0		
B 2, l-b 8, w 1, n-b 1	12	B 4, l-b 12, n-b 3	19

1-168 2-268 3-423 4-426 5-447   496   1-129 2-129 3-232 4-260   (8 wkts dec.) 365
6-473 7-486 8-490 9-496 10-496   5-277 6-278 7-293 8-330

First innings – Lindwall 38–10–79–2; Miller 17.1–2–43–1; Johnston 38–12–86–1; Toshack 35–6–112–1;
Loxton 26–4–55–3; Johnson 33–9–89–2; Morris 5–0–20–0.
Second innings – Lindwall 26–6–84–2; Miller 21–5–53–1; Johnston 29–5–95–4; Loxton 10–2–29–0;
Johnson 21–2–85–1.

AUSTRALIA

	First innings		*Second innings*
A. R. Morris c Cranston b Bedser	6	– c Pollard b Yardley	182
A. L. Hassett c Crapp b Pollard	13	– c and b Compton	17
*D. G. Bradman b Pollard	33	– not out	173
K. R. Miller c Edrich b Yardley	58	– lbw b Cranston	12
R. N. Harvey b Laker	112	– not out	4
S. J. E. Loxton b Yardley	93		
I. W. Johnson c Cranston b Laker	10		
R. R. Lindwall c Crapp b Bedser	77		
†R. A. Saggers st Evans b Laker	5		
W. A. Johnston c Edrich b Bedser	13		
E. R. H. Toshack not out	12		
B 9, l-b 14, n-b 3	26	B 6, l-b 9, n-b 1	16

1-13 2-65 3-68 4-189 5-294 6-329   458   1-57 2-358 3-396   (3 wkts) 404
7-344 8-355 9-403 10-458

First innings – Bedser 31.2–4–92–3; Pollard 38–6–104–2; Cranston 14–1–51–0; Edrich 3–0–19–0;
Laker 30–8–113–3; Yardley 17–6–38–2; Compton 3–0–15–0.
Second innings – Bedser 21–2–56–0; Pollard 22–6–55–0; Laker 32–11–93–0; Compton 15–3–82–1;
Hutton 4–1–30–0; Yardley 13–1–44–1; Cranston 7.1–0–28–1.

Toss won by England   UMPIRES H. G. Baldwin and F. Chester

Yardley won the toss, gaining first use of a perfect pitch. After their disappointing starts in the earlier games, the openers gave England a great sendoff with a stand of 168. Hutton completely justified his recall and Washbrook successfully eliminated the dangerous high hook which often caused his downfall in earlier Tests. He completed an almost faultless hundred out of 189 and fell in the last over of the day.

Bedser, sent in overnight, proved such an efficient stopgap that a third successive century partnership resulted. Again the bowlers met with no success before lunch, and the third wicket realised 155 before Bedser, who made his highest Test score, gave a return catch. Edrich left three runs later. These quick wickets revitalised the Australians, and the batting broke down badly. From 423 for two, they were all out for 496.

Hassett and Morris opened for Australia, but did not shape confidently. Morris left at 13, and next morning Pollard, in his first over, sent back Hassett and Bradman in three balls, making Australia 68 for three. Then 19-year-old Neil Harvey joined Miller, and they put on 121 by glorious strokeplay. Loxton carried on the big hitting. Harvey hit 17 fours in making 112, while Loxton's terrific driving brought five sixes and nine fours. Despite this punishment England held the upper hand, for with eight wickets down Australia were 141 behind. As at Lord's, though, Australia's tail could not be dislodged. Johnston and Toshack, who batted with the aid of a runner, helped Lindwall with such success that the lead was restricted to 38.

Hutton and Washbrook opened with a century stand for the second time in the match, creating a new Test record in accomplishing the feat twice. Both left at 129, but Edrich and Compton put on 103 at more than one a minute and, although a slight collapse followed, Evans, with help from Bedser and Laker, punished the bowling. At the close of the fourth day England led by 400 with two wickets left.

Yardley's decision to continue next day came as a surprise and the reason for it aroused plenty of comment. The main idea was to break up the pitch by the use of the heavy roller. Three runs were added in two overs, and then Yardley declared, leaving Australia to score 404 in 345 minutes. The pitch took spin and the ball lifted and turned sharply. Unfortunately, Laker was erratic in length. Compton, bowling his left-hand off-breaks and googlies, baffled the batsmen several times, but without luck. Evans should have stumped Morris when 32. Compton held a return catch from Hassett at 57, but he ought to have dismissed Bradman, Crapp dropping a catch at first slip.

In half an hour before lunch Morris and Bradman put on 64, and after the interval, against a succession of full-tosses and long-hops, runs continued to flow. When 59 Bradman had another escape off Compton, and Yardley, in despair, called for the new ball even though the pitch favoured spin. Evans should have stumped Bradman when 108, and Laker at square leg dropped Morris when 126. Not until 301 had been put on did England break the stand, and by that time the match was as good as won. Miller did not last long, but Harvey made the winning stroke within 15 minutes of time. No fewer than 66 fours were hit in the innings, 33 by Morris and 29 by Bradman.

CRICKETER OF THE YEAR – ARTHUR MORRIS   1949

Whatever relief English bowlers may have felt knowing they were pitting their wits against D. G. Bradman for the last time must have been largely counterbalanced by the realisation that another record-breaking Australian batsman had arisen in Arthur Robert Morris, the New South Wales left-hander whose Test performances during the series surpassed even those of his captain. Morris hit three centuries in successive Test innings in 1946–47, and his feats in England led to his assessment as one of the world's best left-hand batsmen. Yet Morris made his entry into Australian grade cricket as a slow bowler whose batting ability was so little regarded that he went in last.

Before reaching his 19th birthday Morris set the cricket world talking when he scored a century in each innings of his first match for NSW against Queensland at Christmas 1940, a feat without parallel. Morris is at once imposing to opponents and impressive to spectators by his air of complete composure at the wicket. Possessed of an ideal temperament, he combines unusual defensive qualities with the ability to decide early in the ball's flight what his stroke shall be. Often he may walk right in front of the stumps to get well behind the ball when making a defensive stroke and looks likely to be out lbw, but rarely errs as he watches the ball off the pitch on to the bat. He compares well with Bradman in placing his strokes clear of fieldsmen and in keeping the ball along the ground. Seldom does the hittable ball find him unprepared and rarely is it allowed to go without full punishment. Like most left-handers, Morris is specially good at driving through the covers, hitting to leg and in powerful square-cutting, and few excel him in on-driving.

Fifth Test

Hubert Preston

At The Oval, August 14, 16, 17, 18, 1948. Australia won by an innings and 149 runs.

Australia met with little hindrance on the road to their most emphatic victory in this series of Tests, completing their triumph with four victories and one draw.

Extraordinary cricket marked the opening day. So saturated was the ground by copious rain during the week that the groundsmen could not get the pitch into a reasonable state for a punctual start. Play began at 12, and Yardley chose to bat – an inevitable decision with conditions uncertain and the possibility of more rain. As it happened, the weather proved fine until England fared badly for the second time. All things considered, the Australians found everything favourable for them, as was the case at Lord's. This does not explain the lamentable collapse of England for the lowest score by either side in a Test at The Oval, apart from the 44 for which Australia fell in 1896, the last occasion on which W. G. Grace led England to victory.

The sodden state of the pitch, with sawdust covering large patches of turf nearby, made one doubt its fitness for cricket. Bowlers and batsmen found much sawdust necessary for a foothold. This did not seem to trouble the Australians, and reasons for the downfall of England for such a meagre score were the splendid attack maintained by Lindwall, Miller and Johnston in a humid atmosphere against batsmen whose first error proved fatal. Hutton, the one exception to complete failure, batted in his customary stylish, masterful manner, being last out from a leg glance which Tallon held with the left hand close to the ground. Lindwall, with his varied pace and occasional very fast ball, excelled. Always bowling at the stumps, he made the ball rise at different heights. Four times he clean-bowled a hesitant opponent. Except that Watkins received a blow on the shoulder, the batsmen escaped injury during a most pitiful display. After lunch Lindwall bowled 8.1 overs, four maidens, and took five wickets at a cost of eight runs!

Everything became different when Australia batted. Barnes and Morris, with controlled assurance and perfect strokeplay, made 117, and shortly before six o'clock Bradman walked to the wicket amid continued applause from the standing crowd. Yardley shook hands and called on his team for three cheers, in which the crowd joined. Evidently deeply touched by the enthusiastic reception, Bradman survived one ball from Hollies, but, playing forward to the next, was clean-bowled by a sharply turning break-back – possibly a googly.

Morris missed the special distinction of making 200 through his own ill-judged call for a sharp run, Simpson, fielding substitute for Watkins, with a good return from third man causing his dismissal for 196. Morris hit 16 fours. His strokes past cover-point were typical of the highest-class left-handed batsman. His drives and hooks beat the speediest fieldsmen, and he showed marked skill in turning the ball to leg.

Facing arrears of 337, England lost Dewes at 20, but Hutton and Edrich raised the total to 54 before bad light stopped play. The conditions remained anything but good on Tuesday, when the early fall of Edrich to Lindwall preceded the only stand of consequence, Compton and Hutton putting on 61 before Lindwall, with his left hand at second slip, held a hard cut from Compton. Hutton maintained his sound form until a bumper from Miller struck Crapp on the head, soon after which Hutton gave Tallon a catch. Batting four hours and a quarter for 64 out of 153, Hutton was always restrained but admirable in defence.

After he left three wickets fell in deepening gloom for 25. Evans, from the way he shaped, obviously could not see the ball which bowled him, Lindwall, with the pavilion behind him, sending down something like a yorker at express speed. The players came off for bad light, and rain delayed the finish until Wednesday morning, when the remaining three wickets realised only ten runs in a sad spectacle for England.

Toss: England. **England 52** (R. R. Lindwall 6-20) **and 188** (L. Hutton 64, W. A. Johnston 4-40); **Australia 389** (S. G. Barnes 61, A. R. Morris 196, W. E. Hollies 5-131).

A Miracle Has Been Moved from Among Us   R. C. Robertson-Glasgow, 1949

Don Bradman will bat no more against England, and two contrary feelings dispute within us: relief, that our bowlers will no longer be oppressed by this phenomenon; regret, that a miracle has been removed from among us. So must ancient Italy have felt when she heard of the death of Hannibal.

For sheer fame, Dr W. G. Grace and Don Bradman stand apart from all other cricketers – apart, indeed, from all other games-players. The villagers used to crowd to their doors when W.G. and his beard drove through their little main street. Bradman, on his visits to England, could never live the life of a private citizen. He couldn't stroll from his hotel to post a letter or buy a collar-stud. The mob wouldn't let him. There had to be a car waiting with engine running, and he would plunge into it, like a cork from a bottle. When cricket was on, Bradman had no private life. He paid for his greatness, and the payment left some mark. The informal occasion, the casual conversation, the chance and happy acquaintance, these were very rarely for him, and his life was that of something between an Emperor and an Ambassador. Yet, for all that, there remained something of that boy who, 30 years before, had knocked a ball about in the back yard of a small house in New South Wales. He never lost a certain primitive and elemental cheekiness, and mingled, as it were, with his exact and scientific calculations, there was the immortal impudence of the *gamin*.

But, above all, Bradman was a business-cricketer. About his batting there was to be no style for style's sake. If there was to be any charm, that was for the spectator to find or miss. It was not Bradman's concern. His aim was the making of runs, and he made them in staggering and ceaseless profusion. He seemed to have eliminated error, to have perfected the mechanism of stroke. Others before him had come near to doing this; but Bradman did it without abating the temperature of his attack. No other batsman, surely, has ever been able to score so fast while at the same time avoiding risk. He was, as near as a man batting may be, the flawless engine. There were critics who found surfeit in watching him. Man, by his nature, cannot bear perfection in his fellow. The very fact that something is being done which had been believed to be impossible goads and irritates. It is but a short step from annoyance to envy, and Bradman has never been free from envy's attacks. So, when, first in 1930, he reeled off the centuries, single, double and treble, there were those who compared him unfavourably with other great ones – Trumper, Ranjitsinhji, Hobbs, Macartney. And Bradman's answer was more runs. Others, perhaps, *could* have made them, but they didn't. No one before had ever been quite so fit, quite so ruthless.

In 1948 he made his last visit as a Test cricketer to England. As a batsman he no longer flamed high above his fellows. He was now no more than a very fine player, and arguably both Barnes and Morris were stronger factors in the quelling of bowlers. But Bradman's fame, if possible, increased. Next to Winston Churchill, he was the most celebrated man in England during the summer of 1948. His appearances were like one continuous farewell matinée. At last his batting showed human fallibility. Often, especially at the start of the innings, he played where the ball wasn't, and spectators rubbed their eyes. But such a treasury of skill could spare some gold and still be rich. He scored 138 against England at Nottingham, and, when it much mattered, 173 not out at Leeds.

Most important of all, he steered Australia through some troubled waters and never grounded on the rocks. Returning home, he received the first knighthood ever given to a playing cricketer.

Bradman's place as a batsman is among the few who have been blessed with genius. He was the most wonderful run-scorer that the game has yet known, and no batsman in our own time has so highly excited expectation and so rarely disappointed it.

The Fifties and Sixties:
1950–51 to 1968

It was inevitable, perhaps, that there would be anticlimax in the cricket world AB (After Bradman). With the game's dominant personality slipping into well-earned retirement, cricket was less exciting to the casual observer. And, as the 1950s unfolded, Test cricket was not helped as pitch-preparation technology improved, leading to more batsman-friendly flat pitches that often made it easier to draw a game than win it (for example, between November 1952 and February 1961 India and Pakistan met each other in 13 Tests, and all of them were drawn).

The main exception to the rule in the '50s, though, were Ashes series, which were interesting throughout. The survivors of Bradman's Invincibles carried Australia through the 1950–51 series against an oddly selected England team, who cheered themselves up by winning the final Test.

Then, in 1953, England enlivened the Coronation summer by winning the final Test at The Oval to grab back the Ashes, for the first time since Bradman's second tour in 1934. In what became one of the most-familiar pieces of TV footage – mainly because for years it was used on test transmissions – Denis Compton swept the winning boundary to the fence, and an avalanche of spectators swept on to the outfield. It was the longest England have ever been without the Ashes, and the national elation was comparable to that of 2005, when the urn was regained after 16 years.

England were developing into the decade's dominant team. As early as 1950–51 *Wisden* shrewdly observed that even though they had lost the Ashes series England had the best batsman (Len Hutton), bowler (Alec Bedser) and wicket-keeper (Godfrey Evans) on view. By 1954–55 this trio had been joined by a top all-rounder (Trevor Bailey), a fine off-spinner (Jim Laker, although in a muddle-headed piece of selection he missed that Ashes tour), and a formidable array of fast bowlers. The longest-lasting of these pacemen were Fred Trueman (also surplus to requirements in 1954–55) and Brian Statham – but the fastest of them all was Frank Tyson.

"The Typhoon" stamped his mark on Ashes history by dominating the 1954–55 series, after cutting down his previously lengthy run-up (a move he knew would curtail his career as it increased the strain on his back). After collecting a nasty bang on the head in the Second Test, Tyson bounced back to take six wickets as Australia slumped to a defeat which squared the series. Tyson was at it again in the Third Test, in which the Melbourne pitch was illegally watered, polishing off Australia's second innings with an irresistible 7 for 27.

Tyson was a back number by 1956, but on a series of spin-friendly pitches that irked the Australians the executioner was of an altogether gentler sort. Off-spinner Jim Laker took 46 wickets in the series, an Ashes record, including 19 in the Fourth Test at Old

Trafford – a record which one can safely say will never be beaten – each one marked by a hitch of the trousers, a perfunctory handshake or two, and a walk back to his mark.

England continued to lord it over the other countries, especially at home: the time had not yet arrived when overseas cricketers played regularly in the County Championship, so touring teams usually had several players new to English conditions. Between 1950 and 1959 England played 47 Tests at home and won 26. They lost only eight, three of them to West Indies in 1950, the only home series lost in that time.

It was therefore a surprise when England toured Australia in 1958–59, with the likes of May, Bailey, Cowdrey, Evans, Laker, Trueman, Statham and Tyson on board... and lost heavily. There was a lot of grumbling about the bowling actions of some of the Australian bowlers, but, as *Wisden* observed, several of those England stalwarts had "turned the corner" – bluntly, they were past it. They were also up against a resurgent Australian side, shrewdly led by Richie Benaud – a marginal choice as captain, but an inspired one.

It was Benaud, later to become a peerless TV commentator, who led Australia to England in 1961. They regained the Ashes, and played attractive cricket throughout. Hopes were therefore high when Benaud's rival captain for the 1962–63 Ashes encounter was Ted Dexter, on the face of it an equally free spirit given to attack rather than defence.

Oddly, the mix didn't work. The 1962–63 series was one of the dullest on record, and it was matched by an equally colourless 1964 rubber, the best-remembered part of which remains the Old Trafford Test, when the pitch won to the extent that the first innings of both sides were only just completed by the end of the fifth day.

Some thought the concept of the Ashes, with its built-in advantage to the team holding them (convention had long dictated that if a series was drawn, the holders would retain the urn) was to blame for all this boring stuff. Mike Smith, who captained England in the 1965–66 series, was one who called for the Ashes to be abolished: ironically, he then presided over probably the most exciting rubber of the decade, lit up by the attacking play of Bob Barber.

The days when cricket was Britain's unrivalled summer sport were coming to an end. Falling interest in three-day cricket had already led to the introduction of limited-overs competitions in England, although few foresaw just how prevalent the international version of one-day cricket would become in the near future.

At least cricket was now being televised in colour, although few people yet had the requisite sets to see it. And colour was one of the themes of the 1968 Ashes series in England: Basil D'Oliveira, a non-white South African who had been forced to come to Britain to pursue his dream of playing first-class cricket, had broken into the England side, and he scored an unforgettable 158 at The Oval in the final Test. His innings changed the cosy face of cricket: it indirectly led to sporting ties with South Africa being severed after their Apartheid government intimated that D'Oliveira was not an acceptable tourist.

After all this, cricket needed a shot in the arm. It was soon to get it.   S. L.

AUSTRALIA v ENGLAND 1950–51   Reg Hayter

On February 28, 1951, Australia's record of 26 post-war Tests without defeat came to an end. That was a day for F. R. Brown and his colleagues to rejoice. Australia had not been beaten since the Oval Test of 1938, and rightly the victory was acclaimed as a fillip to English cricket. In a match played under equal conditions, the better side triumphed and Australia, as a whole, applauded the victors generously. Yet, in the midst of their jubilation, many of the team must have experienced pangs of regret at opportunities wasted. In slightly changed circumstances the final Test could easily have opened with the countries level at two each. That it did not was only partly the outcome of England's undue proportion of bad luck. They could not complain of lack of chances, but the way these were squandered was most disappointing.

On the first day at Brisbane England surprised even themselves by dismissing Australia for 228 on a good pitch. That evening, as the team sat in a theatre, they heard that a storm had broken. Virtually the news proclaimed that all their fine work had been fruitless. They were caught on a Brisbane sticky and, in spite of a masterly innings by Hutton, suffered the fate of many previous teams plagued by a Brisbane storm.

One of the most ironic features of the series was that England possessed the best batsman in Hutton, the best bowler in Bedser, and the better wicket-keeper in Evans. Hutton stood head and shoulders above every other batsman and, taking all factors into consideration, worthily earned the description of the finest present-day batsman in the world. At a distance of several months my most vivid tour memory is of Hutton thrashing Miller and Lindwall through the covers on the last day at Brisbane.

By no stretch of imagination could Australia be described as being as strong as in England in 1948. The retirement of Bradman and the temporary disappearance of Barnes left spacious gaps. Whereas their fielding seldom fell below the customary high standard and the variety of their attack brought the desired ends, the batting lacked solidity. Australia owed most to their captain, Hassett, and to vivacious Miller. Good as they were, figures could not indicate Miller's worth. The matches he turned with vital wickets or dazzling slip catches were too many to enumerate.

England discovered that the skill of Iverson had not been exaggerated. This 6ft 1in 16-stone bowler who doubles back his middle finger under the ball and imparts sharp spin, mostly off-break, maintained a precise length. His flight and pace were not such as to allow batsmen to leap out to him easily and his direction, at the leg stump, and carefully planned field-setting permitted few liberties.

First Test

At Brisbane, December 1, 2, 4, 5, 1950. Australia won by 70 runs.

How much the events of this Test influenced the remainder of the series could be only a matter of conjecture, but certainly England were entitled to feel that their misfortune here added to their subsequent tasks. Most Australians agreed with the general view that the intervention of a typical Brisbane storm brought in its train defeat for the side which batted better, bowled better and fielded better than the winners. Virtually the game was won and lost at the toss of the coin. When Brown called incorrectly, he allowed Australia first use of a good pitch more suited to batting, even though its slow pace did not encourage forcing strokes. Yet the first day belonged to England. They surprised everybody by dismissing Australia for such a meagre total in the conditions.

Australia v England 1950–51   First Test

At Woolloongabba, Brisbane, on December 1, 2 (*no play*), 4, 5, 1950. Result: Australia won by 70 runs.

AUSTRALIA	*First innings*		*Second innings*	
J. Moroney c Hutton b Bailey	0	– lbw b Bailey		0
A. R. Morris lbw b Bedser	25	– c Bailey b Bedser		0
R. N. Harvey c Evans b Bedser	74	– (6) c Simpson b Bedser		12
K. R. Miller c McIntyre b Wright	15	– (7) c Simpson b Bailey		8
*A. L. Hassett b Bedser	8	– lbw b Bailey		3
S. J. E. Loxton c Evans b Brown	24	– (4) c Bailey b Bedser		0
R. R. Lindwall c Bedser b Bailey	41	– (8) not out		0
†D. Tallon c Simpson b Brown	5			
I. W. Johnson c Simpson b Bailey	23	– (3) lbw b Bailey		8
W. A. Johnston c Hutton b Bedser	1			
J. B. Iverson not out	1			
B 5, l-b 3, n-b 3	11	N-b 1		1
	228		(7 wkts dec.)	32

1-0 2-69 3-116 4-118 5-129 6-156   228   1-0 2-0 3-0 4-12 5-19   (7 wkts dec.) 32
7-172 8-219 9-226 10-228   6-31 7-32

First innings – Bailey 12–4–28–3; Bedser 16.5–4–45–4; Wright 16–0–81–1; Brown 11–0–63–2.
Second innings – Bailey 7–2–22–4; Bedser 6.5–2–9–3.

ENGLAND	*First innings*		*Second innings*	
R. T. Simpson b Johnston	12	– b Lindwall		0
C. Washbrook c Hassett b Johnston	19	– c Loxton b Lindwall		6
†T. G. Evans c Iverson b Johnston	16	– (6) c Loxton b Johnston		5
D. C. S. Compton c Lindwall b Johnston	3	– (9) c Loxton b Johnston		0
J. G. Dewes c Loxton b Miller	1	– (3) b Miller		9
L. Hutton not out	8	– (8) not out		62
A. J. W. McIntyre b Johnston	1	– run out		7
*F. R. Brown c Tallon b Miller	4	– (10) c Loxton b Iverson		17
T. E. Bailey not out	1	– (4) c Johnston b Iverson		7
A. V. Bedser		– (5) c Harvey b Iverson		0
D. V. P. Wright		– c Lindwall b Iverson		2
L-b 2, n-b 1	3	B 6, n-b 1		7

1-28 2-49 3-52 4-52 5-56   (7 wkts dec.) 68   1-0 2-16 3-22 4-23 5-23   122
6-57 7-67   6-30 7-46 8-46 9-46 10-77 10-122

First innings – Lindwall 1–0–1–0; Johnston 11–2–35–5; Miller 10–1–29–2.
Second innings – Lindwall 7–3–21–2; Johnston 11–2–30–2; Miller 7–3–21–1; Iverson 13–3–43–4.

Toss won by Australia   UMPIRES A. N. Barlow and H. Elphinston

From the fourth ball of the day Hutton, at backward short leg, smartly held Moroney. That was just the tonic needed. For the rest of the innings the fielding touched the highest class and Evans was inspired. No better catches were seen in the Tests than those by which he dismissed Harvey and Loxton. Bedser rarely bowled a ball which did not compel the batsman's closest vigilance and he cut either way with marked nip and variation. Bailey attacked each batsman to a pre-arranged plan and his life with

Mystery spinner: Jack Iverson (left) shows the former Australian wicket-keeper Bert Oldfield the strange grip that perplexed England's batsmen in 1950-51.

the new ball enabled England to follow up their previous successes. Wright's figures told anything but the worth of his bowling. He had received injections to relieve fibrositis, but he produced many fine balls, several of which beat the bat and missed the wicket only because of their high bounce.

Well as England bowled and fielded, the batting was not convincing. Apart from Harvey, few of the batsmen gave the impression of being at ease. Harvey put his usual vigour into his strokes before being caught behind when glancing Bedser off the middle of the bat. His 74, made out of 118, contained ten sparkling fours.

To the end of the Australian innings the cricket was exciting enough. It became more so. A successful appeal against the light by England's new opening pair – Brown decided to put Hutton at No. 5 to give strength to the middle – was the final act on that dramatic Friday. Inside a few hours the storm broke, and cricket could not be resumed until shortly before lunch on Monday. For 30 minutes Washbrook and Simpson provided skill and courage so far unsurpassed in the match. In that time they scored 28 on a pitch just as treacherous as it played through the remainder of the day, in which 20 wickets went down for 102.

True to tradition, the pitch was the game's villain. Medium-paced bowling of good length presented a well-nigh-insoluble problem. Sometimes the ball reared head-high, at other times it kept horribly low. Both captains placed nearly all their fieldsmen a few yards from the bat, and 12 of the wickets resulted from close catches. When the back of England's innings had been broken, Brown declared. His one hope was to force Australia in again as soon as possible. Moroney, who experienced the disaster of a pair,

Morris and Loxton were out before a run was scored, and wickets continued to go down so quickly that Hassett retaliated by a declaration which gave England 70 minutes to bat before the close. They required 193 to win. If only two or three men had been lost then their prospects might have been bright. It was not to be.

A lightning yorker by Lindwall wrecked Simpson's wicket with the first ball of the innings. There followed half an hour of sound defence by Washbrook and Dewes. Each left within a few minutes of the other, but England's most crushing blow that evening occurred in the last ten minutes when three wickets were lost. Anxiety caused at least two of these dismissals, McIntyre, for example, being run out trying a fourth run when preservation of wickets was of paramount importance.

So England entered the last day wanting 163 to win with only four wickets left. The task was hard but not hopeless, because although still difficult, the pitch had lost some venom. Evans helped Hutton add 16 before he and Compton pushed successive balls from Johnston into the hands of forward short leg. Australia were within sight of victory, but it was not theirs until Hutton had given yet another exhibition of his wonderful batsmanship on tricky turf. He thrashed the fast bowlers majestically and played the turning or lifting ball with the ease of a master craftsman. When assisted by Wright in a last-wicket stand of 45, Hutton even looked capable of carrying England through, but Wright succumbed to temptation to hook the last ball before lunch. Hutton's was an innings to remember.

Second Test

At Melbourne, December 22, 23, 26, 27, 1950. Australia won by 28 runs.

One of the most exciting Tests in recent years finished with Australia two ahead in the rubber, but England again gave them a much harder fight than expected. As it was, lack of nerve and experience at a critical time cost England the match. This time Brown could not have been sorry to lose the toss. Complete covering to keep off heavy rain had contributed to making the pitch green and fast. An atmosphere which remained heavy most of the day and a grassy outfield provided other incentives to swing bowlers, and Bedser and Bailey gave of their best. Uplifted by the swift removal of Morris, Bedser, who moved the ball through the air and cut it either way, opened with a spell of sustained hostility lasting two and a half hours. Twice more he returned to hurl himself into the attack with life, lift and swing. No batsman played him with anything approaching relish and, for once, the adjective great carried no exaggeration. When shooting out his massive right hand at second slip and catching Archer, Bedser also helped Bailey to one of his four wickets.

Bedser and Bailey received support from Brown and Close, but Wright could not strike a length. Subsequent events emphasised the costliness of his eight overs. Australia owed much to Hassett and Loxton, who put on 84, the highest stand of the innings. Archer's first Test innings was notable for his self-discipline and concentration, but Harvey, with whom he added 61, could not look back with much satisfaction. Bedser beat him five times in two overs and to the end he was fortune's darling. Four wickets in the last ten minutes brought the innings to a close and the day to a dramatic end.

Undoubtedly conditions favoured England on the first day, but on the second the air was clear and the turf less helpful. At times the ball kept low, but generally batsmen should have held the advantage. Yet England crumpled. They were without Compton (swollen knee), but weak batting combined with accurate and zestful bowling caused six wickets to tumble for 61. Courage and determination followed: with a straight bat in defence, Bailey stayed while 65 were scored, mostly by Brown, who drove and cut with all his power. One huge hit off Johnson went for six and he proved conclusively that the Australian bowling could be punished. Evans, restrained at first, followed his captain's example and the lead was gained with the last pair together.

By taking 14 from Bailey's opening over, Australia more than wiped off the arrears. Then the game was held up for Sunday and Christmas Day. Scorching sunshine throughout those two days enlarged the cracks which had appeared in the turf, and when Australia resumed the tendency of the ball to keep low increased. Again Bedser, Bailey and Brown bowled excellently, and the last nine wickets fell for 99. Brown, the chief wicket-taker, relied on length and slight movement either way from the pitch.

England looked to have a golden chance when they began their second innings wanting 179 to win. Instead they provided the fourth batting failure of a Test in which, for the first time in Australia since 1888, a total of 200 was not reached in the four completed innings. All seemed to depend on Hutton, and he batted correctly for 40 out of 70 until mis-hitting Johnston to mid-wicket. Some of the other batsmen offered an excess of caution which played into Australia's hands. Possibly they were overawed by thoughts of breaking Australia's long run without defeat. Bedser, the No. 10, looked so much at ease that the failures of some of his colleagues received greater emphasis. At the end the impression could not be avoided that if England had been left with three or four hours to make the runs instead of three whole days they would have adopted different, and probably more successful, methods.

Toss: Australia. **Australia 194** (A. L. Hassett 52, T. E. Bailey 4-40, A. V. Bedser 4-37)
and 181 (F. R. Brown 4-26); **England 197** (F. R. Brown 62, J. B. Iverson 4-37) **and 150** (W. A. Johnston 4-26).

Third Test
At Sydney, January 5, 6, 8, 9, 1951. Australia won by an innings and 13 runs.

The scoreboard alone could not show how big a part Miller played in Australia's third successive win, which ensured their retention of the Ashes. After Brown won the toss for the only time, England survived so easily on a perfect pitch that the way looked clear for a huge total. Then Washbrook slashed at Johnson. Miller, at second slip, made ground as he anticipated the stroke and threw himself to his right. With both feet off the ground, he made a gorgeous one-hand catch. For a time Simpson could not fathom Iverson, but eventually he settled his problems, and when the score reached 128 he and the classical Hutton were still together.

With only ten minutes left before tea and the new ball available soon afterwards, Hassett unexpectedly summoned Miller. At once the scene changed. Miller bowled at his fastest. Hutton parried two balls. To the third he so hurried his stroke that he struck his pad, missed the ball, and was lbw. Compton dragged his third ball on to his wicket. A few minutes after tea Miller struck again, Simpson giving backward short leg a catch. Thus 128 for one had become 137 for four, Miller taking three for five in 3.7 overs.

As at Melbourne, Brown came to the rescue. He drove the new ball with a full swing of the bat, cut and hit to leg with fine weighty blows. The spirit of his batting aroused genuine admiration. Most of his nine fours were from thudding strokes which flashed past the fieldsman. Parkhouse helped in a stand of 50, and Bailey stayed while 71 were added for the sixth wicket. A burst of speed by Lindwall then did considerable damage. Besides clean-bowling Brown and Bedser, he delivered a very fast ball which rose and fractured Bailey's right thumb. Bailey twice resumed, the second time with his hand in plaster, but he was able to do little and the injury prevented him from bowling in the match.

England were also without Wright, who tore a groin muscle in a desperate but unavailing effort at a run. This meant that the burden of the attack fell on Bedser, Warr and Brown. All three responded gallantly. Apart from six overs by Compton, they took turns with the ball from 3.30 on Saturday until lunch-time on Tuesday. Through scorching heat, between them they bowled 123 eight-ball overs with scarcely a sign of flagging, although Brown was limping painfully long before the end. Moreover, at one stage they had so staggered Australia that at the fall of the sixth wicket they were 38 behind, Bedser having dismissed Morris cheaply for the fourth time in five Test innings. England stood on level terms and the swift capture of another wicket might well have changed the course of the match. Instead Miller found an apt partner in Johnson, who shared in a stand of 150, which made England's position almost hopeless. After losing Johnson, Miller batted with something approaching his usual freedom, but for the most part he was caution itself. The policy of attacking his leg stump with slightly short-of-length bowling also contributed to his slow scoring. Miller's 145 took exactly six hours and contained one six, late in the innings, and six fours. On the fourth morning Brown reverted to leg-breaks, and the amount of turn he gained foretold ensuing events.

Hassett soon called on his spinners. Iverson rapped Hutton four times on the pad and Washbrook could make little of him. The end was in sight. Iverson flicked his off-breaks and occasional straight-through ball to an unvarying length. His spin was sharp, he made speed from the turf and bounced high. In his first seven overs he sent back Hutton (to a remarkable juggling act between Tallon and Johnson), Simpson and Washbrook for two runs and later bowled Brown, Bedser and Warr in ten balls. Compton battled skilfully for nearly an hour in his highest innings of the series before mis-hitting a half-volley.

Toss: England. **England 290** (L. Hutton 62, F. R. Brown 79, K. R. Miller 4-37) **and 123** (J. B. Iverson 6-27); **Australia 426** (A. L. Hassett 70, K. R. Miller 145*, I. W. Johnson 77, A. V. Bedser 4-107, F. R. Brown 4-153).

NOTES BY THE EDITOR

Hubert Preston, 1951

I am writing just after the Third Test at Sydney, where injuries to Bailey and Wright seriously reduced our strength and England lost far more heavily than in the hard-fought struggles at Brisbane and Melbourne. So Australia hold the Ashes, as they have done since 1934. In recent years England bowlers have shouldered a lot of blame for our constant setbacks, but I have always felt that the batting has been the worst weakness. Since the war England have relied too much on Hutton, Washbrook, Edrich and

Compton to make runs. Fortunately, Hutton has maintained his brilliance, but the other three have shed much of their excellence, largely through injury or illness, and no young batsmen have come along to challenge them. I thoroughly agree with the selection committee in their desire to introduce young men, but although many have been tried none has shown the ability expected of cricketers elevated to Test status.

Yet for this tour the selectors gambled on five or six young men who had accomplished nothing in Test cricket. Close had spent the whole summer in the Army. Certainly he showed great promise in 1949, but constant match practice is necessary for youth to develop, and on the few occasions Close appeared in 1950 it was obvious he had gone back. His selection for Australia caused tremendous surprise. From the reports of reliable judges one could realise that instead of losing the first two Tests, England with two or three of the capable professional batsmen who were left behind might well have won both matches. I am afraid our selectors pay too much heed to the weekly averages which can be so misleading. For my part I would ignore all batting performances on those innocuous pitches at Cambridge and Nottingham.

Fourth Test

At Adelaide, February 2, 3, 5, 6, 7, 8, 1951. Australia won by 274 runs.

More than any other factor, inconsistent and occasionally injudicious batting brought England to their seventh successive Test defeat. From this criticism Hutton earned complete, and Sheppard and Simpson partial, exemption. When the gallant Bedser forced Archer into a leg-trap catch from the third ball of the game, he looked to have neutralised much of England's disadvantage in losing the toss. Nothing else occurred, however, on the opening day to disturb Australia's serenity on a slow, easy-paced pitch.

Hassett protected Morris from his *bête noir*, Bedser, during the first hour, and gradually Morris settled down to a long innings. By ordinary standards Morris played well, but not until the later stages did he produce his most scintillating form. His innings, generally, was that of a man fighting to regain confidence, and in his first hundred he scored seven runs from 51 balls Bedser bowled to him. In breaking his sequence of low scores Morris made his seventh century against England and first double-hundred in international cricket. Four years earlier he hit a century in each innings on the same ground. This time Morris batted with the utmost watchfulness and with scarcely a false stroke. Most of his 23 fours came in his second hundred.

When Miller began the second day by smiting Bedser for four from each of the first three balls, carrying Australia to 266 for three, most of the 32,000 spectators must have forecast a mammoth total, but so well did England hit back that the last seven wickets went down for 105. Bedser recovered so rapidly that his figures for the day were 7–1–26–2; Wright (11–1–33–3) found his rhythm and a nagging length, and Tattersall (11.3–4–49–3) amply justified his selection.

The poverty of England's reply only served to illuminate Hutton. The bowling held no terrors for him, and for the second time in six months he carried his bat through a Test innings, a feat not accomplished against Australia since R. Abel made 132 not out at Sydney in 1891-92. Hutton should have been stumped when 34 and gave a hard chance to mid-off when 135, but these were small blemishes in an innings that transcended all else in the match. His only worthwhile support came from Simpson, who stayed while 73 were added for the second wicket, and from Wright in a last-wicket stand of 53. Hutton batted ten minutes over six hours and hit 11 fours. Against Hutton the bowling looked almost mediocre, but most of the other batsmen made it appear lethal. Washbrook and Compton were again the two biggest disappointments. Both fell to Lindwall, Washbrook in his second over and Compton when leg-glancing the fourth ball of the fourth morning.

A century on debut by 20-year-old Burke, another sedate innings by Miller, who simultaneously hit his wicket and was bowled when trying to obtain a single for his century, and a flirtation with the fates which brought Harvey 68 runs, added concrete to Australia's already solid foundations, and England were set 503 to win. Burke, mainly a back player, revealed sound defence and an ideal temperament.

Washbrook and Hutton began with the biggest opening stand by either side in the series before Loxton, the substitute for Iverson (injured ankle at practice before the start of the third day), held a fierce hook from Hutton. Even when Johnston sent back Washbrook and Compton in three balls shortly before the close of the fifth day the pitch was playing so well that the issue was by no means certain. Simpson and Sheppard bore out this contention with a timely stand which continued until the last over before lunch on the final day. At that point Australia were showing unmistakable signs of flagging. Then Simpson's concentration lapsed.

Australia returned for a final assault and the batting broke down again, the last five wickets falling in half an hour. Miller took three for three in three overs of slow off-spinners, Evans and Bedser being out to his first two balls. Some of the strokes were not in keeping with the situation. If he had considered any possibility existed of saving the game Brown, who was injured in a car accident after the fourth day's play, would have batted, but the cause was lost.

Toss: Australia. **Australia 371** (A. R. Morris 206, D. V. P. Wright 4-99)
and 403-8 dec. (R. N. Harvey 68, K. R. Miller 99, J. W. Burke 101*);
England 272 (L. Hutton 156*) **and 228** (R. T. Simpson 61, W. A. Johnston 4-73).

Fifth Test

At Melbourne, February 23, 24, 26, 27, 28, 1951. England won by eight wickets.

At last promise turned to fulfilment. By a victory as worthily achieved as it was earned, England broke Australia's post-war run of 26 Tests without defeat. Australia strove to the end to preserve their record, but England won deservedly. Even so, their success was more a triumph of individuals than of teamwork. Hutton and Simpson with the bat, and Bedser, Brown and Wright in bowling practically carried the rest of the side. Many moments of anxiety and suspense occurred before the final scenes of elation.

The first-day honours went to the rival captains. Such good use did Australia make of Hassett's fourth success in the toss that, despite the early loss of Burke, shortly before tea they were 111 for one. Then Brown went on for his second spell. With the tendons of his shoulders not recovered from the car accident he had hoped not to be compelled to bowl, but when Bailey twisted an ankle the plan needed revision. Brown immediately changed the course of the innings. In 17 balls he accounted for Morris, Harvey and Miller without conceding a run. Hole's first duty on Test debut was to avert a hat-trick. This he accomplished, and he showed skill and grace before Bedser beat him with the new ball. Hassett remained Australia's hope and, with wickets falling fast at the other end, he emerged from defensive care. A flow of delicately timed drives and cuts carried him to within sight of a century before Hutton at slip took a catch wide to his right. Bedser and Brown encountered little other opposition. On a pitch much more in favour of batsmen they merited the fullest praise for dismissing Australia so cheaply. At the close of the first day, on which eight wickets fell for 206, Brown was limping and his shoulder gave him considerable discomfort.

Heavy rain prevented play on Saturday and, after a swift end to Australia's innings, England opened with a flourish on Monday. Forty runs came in half an hour before Washbrook edged a fast outswinger. Helped by unusual lapses in the slips, Hutton and Simpson carried England into a strong position. Their stand of 131 was broken by Hole, who beat and bowled Hutton with a flighted off-spinner. Worse followed when Lindwall and Miller took the new ball. In the most dynamic spell of the series they tore away the middle of the innings, and the total veered from 204 for two to 213 for six. Compton was beaten by an extra-good ball, Sheppard, Brown and Evans by sheer pace. The day ended with England only one run ahead and four wickets left. Simpson was then 80. Next day Simpson leapt into his finest form. Bedser, Bailey and Wright went almost at once, and when Tattersall joined him Simpson was eight short of a century. In the next hour he scored 64 to Tattersall's ten, and England led by 103. Simpson flayed fast and slow bowling to all parts. Six of his 12 fours came in his last 56 runs. His innings first held England together when collapse threatened, then gave his side the initiative. His first century against Australia was reached on his 31st birthday. Few onlookers could reconcile that this was the same player the off-spinners, particularly Iverson, had tied down in previous matches.

Once again Bedser broke through quickly. Morris and Archer were both victims of his late swerve and speed from the pitch. With Harvey hitting over a ball which kept low and Brown repeating his first-innings dismissal of Miller, Australia lost four of their best batsmen before the arrears were wiped off. A fifth-wicket stand by Hassett and Hole carried distinct menace until Wright delivered the knockout blow by dismissing Hassett and Johnson in one splendid over. The ball which bowled Hassett might have beaten anyone. A beautifully flighted leg-break pitched on the blind side, curled round the bat, and hit middle and off.

Hole again showed his class, but in two hours on the fourth morning England captured the last six wickets for 68 and needed only 95 to win. Bedser brought his match analysis to ten wickets for 105 and his Test aggregate to 30 – grand bowling in every way. If Hutton had failed, Australia might still have turned the game, and, indeed, they made England fight strenuously to the last, but Hutton's presence provided comfort and, fittingly, he crowned his own triumphant tour by making the winning stroke.

Toss: Australia. **Australia 217** (A. R. Morris 50, A. L. Hassett 92, A. V. Bedser 5-46, F. R. Brown 5-49)
and 197 (R. N. Harvey 52, G. B. Hole 63, A. V. Bedser 5-59);
England 320 (L. Hutton 79, R. T. Simpson 156*, K. R. Miller 4-76) **and 95-2** (L. Hutton 60*).

F. R. Brown – Leader of Men
Vivian Jenkins, 1952

Freddie Brown's experiences in Australia under D. R. Jardine, when the all-speed attack policy meant his exclusion from all the Tests, might have daunted one whose love for the game was less abiding. But even in the prison camps during the war he managed to fit in some cricket.

One story he tells, illustrating his inborn sense of fun – not the least of his attractions – is bound up with another great figure in England cricket of recent years, Bill Bowes, the Yorkshire speed merchant. At one time they were in the same PoW camp together in Italy. It was only natural that they should start a game of cricket, even though the pads were made of cardboard from Red Cross parcels stuffed with paper, and the pitch the road which went through the middle of the camp. It appears that the Italian guards thought there was something highly suspicious about these unfamiliar proceedings, with possibly an escape tunnel via the batsman's blockhole in contemplation. When Bowes was halfway through an over, they marched firmly down to a position midway between the wickets. Bowes, about to commence his run, hesitated. Said Brown, at mid-off: "Well, what are you waiting for, Bill? Why not let one go?" To which Bowes, with the twinkling eye that belies his otherwise inscrutable appearance, replied in the accent of his native Yorkshire: "Ah would, but tha never knows, ah might kill b*****." Perhaps it was just as well that discretion prevailed, and that Brown's injunction went unheeded!

All of which may help to explain the character of the man who, for a spell, at least, brought England cricket out of the post-war slough into which it had sunk, and which impelled the famous remark of the quayside vendor in Sydney. Anxious to promote a quicker sale of his wares, he produced his last trump: "Lovely lettuces," he cried, "only a shilling and 'earts as big as Freddie Brown's." It was worth the journey just to be able to transmit that particular remark to England.

England v Australia 1953
Norman Preston

After having held the Ashes for 19 years, the longest period on record, Australia surrendered them at The Oval where, after four drawn Tests, England won the last in convincing fashion.

If the winning of Test matches were the only thing that mattered, then Lindsay Hassett's team did not carry out its mission. But rarely has any series of matches produced such interesting and exciting cricket. Day after day and sometimes hour after hour the pendulum swung first towards Australia and then towards England. Time and again it seemed that one side had established absolute mastery only for it to be taken away. No other series of Tests captured such public attention. What with day-by-day front-page newspaper articles and radio and television broadcasts there were times when industry almost stood still while the man in the street followed the tense battle. Above everything else was the true spirit of cricket which existed between the England and Australian players both on and off the field.

The main difference between the sides was in batting. Since 1926 until the last tour all Australian sides in England had enjoyed the services of Bradman, who broke almost every individual batting record. Hutton has said he considered Bradman was worth three men to any team. By making his colossal scores at a colossal pace Bradman lightened the responsibility as well as the task of his colleagues. The gap his retirement left can be seen in the batting figures: for the first time in 50 years not a single Australian batsman could show an average of 40 in the Tests.

Turning to the bowling there was an appreciable weakness due to the absence of top-class spin to support the thrust of Lindwall, Miller and Johnston. Hassett must have regretted the decision to leave behind Johnson, the off-break bowler. None of the three leg-spinners, Ring, Hill and Benaud, was seen to advantage in the Tests. But one man England feared more than any other was Lindwall. Truly one of the world's finest fast bowlers of all time, he may have shed some of his fire. Yet he remained at the top of his form, taking 26 wickets at 18.84 in the Tests, compared with 27 at 19.62 in 1948. Whenever Lindwall took the new ball there was the possibility of a collapse; and when the shine had gone England breathed again.

First Test

Reg Hayter

At Nottingham, June 11, 12, 13, 15, 16, 1953. Drawn.

So stirring was the cricket of the first three days that the anticlimax brought about by prolonged bad weather aroused bitter disappointment. Chiefly through the magnificent bowling of Bedser, England finished on Saturday needing 187 to win with nine wickets left. The position promised a tremendous struggle, but heavy rain washed out any play on Monday and a resumption was impossible until half-past four on the last day. The consequences of the weather must have been particularly galling to Bedser, England's hero, with 14 wickets for 99. Only Wilfred Rhodes and Hedley Verity, who took 15 apiece, had dismissed more batsmen in the previous 159 Tests between England and Australia. Bedser deserved to join them, but he did pass the English record of 189 wickets held by S. F. Barnes, who, at 80 years of age, saw his own figures overtaken.

Bedser put Australia on the defensive by uprooting Hole's middle stump with the first ball of his second over. Hassett and Morris countered with extreme care, but Bedser was always menacing, and, when he took the new ball, he promptly broke the century stand and followed by trapping Harvey into giving a catch. When bad light brought the day to a close, Bedser's figures told of his toil: 25-12-26-3.

Australia resumed confidently against bowlers using a towel and sawdust on a ball saturated by grass still wet from rain. Although the soggy ball would not swing, the possibilities of a new ball doing so, should the rain abate and the grass dry, were unmistakable. Bailey kept the batsmen tied down, but Wardle was erratic at first: Hassett gratefully punished two short balls to complete his ninth Test century. Wardle eventually broke the big stand, Bailey at mid-wicket taking a fine catch from Miller over his shoulder as he ran backwards. At lunch Australia were 243 for four.

The game moved so swiftly afterwards that by the close most of the spectators felt exhausted through the sustained excitement. The outfield had dried but the atmosphere remained favourable to swing bowling, and Bedser and Bailey swept away the rest of the batting, six wickets crashing for six runs. From Bailey's first delivery with the new ball Evans took a superb left-hand catch off Benaud's leg glance. Evans made several feet before hurling himself sideways. Bedser ended Hassett's long innings with a ball which pitched on the leg stump and hit the top of off.

The Australian collapse, however, was but a prelude to a series of England failures caused by Lindwall's skill in exploiting the conditions. In his fourth over Kenyon edged an inswinger to short fine leg. Another inswinger dismissed Simpson second ball, and a lovely swooping catch in the gully sent back Compton. These three wickets fell in eight balls at the same total, 17. Hutton and Graveney checked the collapse, but, in worsening light, England's batting slumped again. Benaud made excellent catches from Graveney and Hutton, from a forcing stroke to gully, and then May edged to the wicket-keeper. Immediately afterwards the umpires decided the gloom was too much. England finished with six men out for 92, requiring eight to avoid the follow-on. Between lunch and the close 12 wickets fell for 98 runs.

Conditions for the third day were almost identical. Before lunch bowlers had to use a wet ball, but afterwards the grass had dried and the new ball moved considerably. Once more the cricket moved at breathtaking pace, 15 wickets going down for 217. First, England saved the follow-on and Australia's lead was restricted to 105. Bailey performed the first of his many defensive acts in the series by staying an hour and 40 minutes for ten runs. Australia opened their innings just before lunch and afterwards Morris began a fierce assault. Bedser, however, soon penetrated Hole's defence, and when a good-length ball stood up and struck Hassett on the glove before lobbing to short leg, two wickets were down for 44.

Australia never recovered, their batting indicating that they distrusted the pitch. Yet several batsmen were out attempting strokes bordering on the reckless. Bedser, who took the first five wickets for 22, was again in his most dynamic form and, when he took a rest, Tattersall maintained England's grip. Morris, who batted freely for 60 out of 81, was his first victim, bowled round his legs. More spectacular catches accounted for Davidson and Tallon, and Bedser swiftly closed the innings.

After a short break for bad light England began their task of making 229 to win. Against a close encircling field, Hutton and Kenyon played safely through the new ball, and Kenyon looked to be going well until he lifted a full toss to mid-on. Simpson might have been caught at slip second ball, but, that apart, the batting was more than adequate. Bad light again brought play to an early closure and left the match in the intriguing situation, the development of which was ruined by the heavy rain over the weekend.

Toss: Australia. **Australia 249** (A. R. Morris 67, A. L. Hassett 115, K. R. Miller 55, A. V. Bedser 7-55) **and 123** (A. R. Morris 60, A. V. Bedser 7-44); **England 144** (R. R. Lindwall 5-57) **and 120-1** (L. Hutton 60*).

Second Test

Reg Hayter

At Lord's, June 25, 26, 27, 29, 30, 1953. Drawn.

In its swift changes of fortune the cricket followed a pattern similar to that of the First Test, except that here the suspense continued to the last over of the fifth day. First one side, then the other, built up an apparently commanding position, only for a series of dramatic incidents to swing the balance again. Yet everything in the first four days paled before England's last-ditch stand which brought them a draw as stirring as the majority of victories. The three England changes included the recall of the chairman of selectors, F. R. Brown, at the age of 42, presumably on the theory that the Lord's pitch often favoured a leg-break bowler.

The first day was the least eventful of the five. Hassett again won the toss and opened with Morris. The packed crowd soon realised that the work facing the bowlers would be far from easy. Worried by a strained arm, Hassett at first did not reproduce his form of the First Test. A lightning stumping by Evans broke the opening stand, but not until after tea did another wicket fall. By then Harvey and Hassett had added 125 with solid, unspectacular batting. Although missed at slip when 55, Hassett shook off his early uncertainties, but after completing another century he retired with cramp. In his absence the bowlers found fresh heart, and in ten deliveries Wardle sent back Hole, Benaud and Miller, who hooked the previous ball for six. Australia finished the day 263 for five.

Apart from fielding errors, England felt thoroughly satisfied at the end of the second day. Australia lost their last five wickets, including Hassett, for 83. Davidson excelled with drives and cuts of exceptional power, and his 76 contained a six and 13 fours. Twice, however, he was let off. Hutton, who missed three chances, was England's unhappiest fieldsman. The errors, from one of which he bruised a thumb, did not upset Hutton's batting. He lost Kenyon in Lindwall's second over, but by stumps his stand with Graveney had reached 168, but even more important than the numerical value was the supreme confidence and freedom of the batsmen. The Australians tried everything, but Hutton and Graveney were masters. The sight of England batsmen giving free rein to their strokes brought undisguised delight to many who had bemoaned the lack of aggression in so much Test cricket. The spectacle was glorious to behold.

England resumed 170 behind, and on the third successive day of brilliant sunshine their chances of securing a substantial advantage looked high. So much for optimism. Not a run had been added when Lindwall, warming up for the new ball, hit Graveney's middle and off stumps with a yorker. Compton, anxious to redeem a long sequence of failures against Australia, faced the new ball immediately, and he and Hutton were called upon to combat Lindwall and Miller at their best and most hostile. The battle between the four provided one of the season's highlights. Hutton, as classical as ever, and Compton, who gained assurance and freedom with almost every over, were the victors. When Hutton hit Johnston to the square-leg boundary and took his score to 145, he reached 2,000 runs against Australia and sent the partnership into its second hundred, but that 16th four was his last scoring stroke. At lunch England, with three wickets down, stood only 59 behind. Then Australia hit back. The last seven wickets toppled for 93, giving England a lead of no more than 26. Watson was unlucky in being stumped off the wicket-keeper's pads and Compton misjudged the width of Benaud's leg-break.

The early departure of Hassett in Australia's second innings brought together Morris and Miller, and they remained until the close, when Australia stood 70 ahead. Thus, once more, the initiative had changed hands. Before lunch on Monday, Miller and Morris swung the game still further. In the first two hours 113 were added for the loss of Morris, who revelled in the chance to play all his strokes on a pitch of eminently easy pace. Compton, going on for a short spell before the new ball, broke the stand of 165, Statham holding a dazzling catch, running backwards at speed and tumbling head over heels as he took the ball. Miller subjugated his natural inclinations, but his was an equally valuable contribution. This was emphasised after lunch, when England hopes rose again through the capture of five wickets for 96.

One hour remained when England batted again, needing 343 to win. That was an hour to make Australia happy and England miserable. Lindwall struck two shattering blows, getting Kenyon caught at mid-on and Hutton at slip, and when Langley made a thrilling diving catch off Graveney three men were out for 12. Although Watson stayed with Compton to the close, he might have been caught off Ring at short leg in the last over. The costliness of that miss was to be seen on the last day.

Compton held out for 95 minutes next morning before being lbw to a ball that kept low. This brought in Bailey, the last of the recognised batsmen. Nearly five hours remained for play. The odds on Australia winning were high. At first Australia did not appear unduly worried, but, as Bailey settled down to his sternest defence, the bowlers produced all they knew. Still Bailey went on playing a dead-bat pendulum stroke to every ball on his wicket. Watson, too, met the ball with the full face of the bat. The most testing period came midway through the afternoon when Lindwall and Miller took the new ball. Three times Bailey was struck by a bouncer, but after each he paused only to wring his hand. When Australia's fast bowlers went off the total had risen by only 12 runs. As a result any visions of England snatching a sensational win had disappeared, but by now Australia showed their anxiety.

At the end of five and three-quarter hours Watson's vigil came to an end. Soon afterwards Bailey shook off his self-imposed shackles and essayed a cover-drive which resulted in a fairly easy catch. His annoyance was plain for all to see. Still 35 minutes were left, and the way the ball turned gave rise to thoughts that, after all, Australia might finish England's resistance in time, but, riding his luck, Brown struck out boldly. Even so, when he was out in the last over the prospects of Benaud taking three wickets in the last four balls to win the match were discussed seriously. Wardle soon brought speculation to an end.

So finished a Test of wonderful character. Without detracting from the merit of Watson, Bailey or Compton, the Australian slow bowlers did not make the best use of a pitch from which the ball could be turned sharply. No doubt Hassett would have preferred to give his spinners longer spells, but, in view of their lapses in length and direction, he had to think of the possibility of England accelerating sufficiently to knock off the runs. As it was, at the end they wanted 61 to win with three wickets left.

Toss: Australia. **Australia 346** (A. L. Hassett 104, R. N. Harvey 59, A. K. Davidson 76, A. V. Bedser 5-105, J. H. Wardle 4-77) **and 368** (A. R. Morris 89, K. R. Miller 109, R. R. Lindwall 50, F. R. Brown 4-82); **England 372** (L. Hutton 145, T. W. Graveney 78, D. C. S. Compton 57, R. R. Lindwall 5-66) **and 282-7** (W. Watson 109, T. E. Bailey 71).

CRICKETER OF THE YEAR – KEITH MILLER
Reg Hayter, 1954

Even the Golden Age of cricket would have been enriched by a character so colourful as Keith Ross Miller, proclaimed by many as Australia's finest all-rounder since the retirement of M. A. Noble some 40 years ago. Little quarrel could be found with this description. In the 1953 Test series, Miller emulated the hitherto unique achievement of Wilfred Rhodes with 2,000 runs and 100 wickets in international cricket. Yet figures are the last thing by which this unpredictable personality, a man with the instinctive flair for turning a crowd's annoyance into instant delight, should be assessed. Miller has always placed the fun of the game above every consideration. A true guide to the estimation of his fellow cricketers is that nearly every captain of a country defeated by Australia in her magnificent post-war run believed that, with Miller on his side, the issue would have been far closer, or have gone the other way.

The youngest of four children, he was born at Sunshine, Melbourne, on November 28, 1919, at a time when Sir Keith Smith and Sir Ross Smith were creating world history with the first flight from England to Australia. It took 27 days 20 hours. His parents gave him the Christian names of the two famous airmen. Years later his own exploits in the air, as a night-fighter pilot, earned for him a reputation as a dashing, devil-may-care fellow which his subsequent approach to big cricket confirmed.

Third Test

Norman Preston

At Manchester, July 9, 10, 11, 13, 14, 1953. Drawn.

For the ninth successive time since 1905 England and Australia could not reach a definite conclusion at Old Trafford. Again the weather was mostly to blame, rain restricting the cricket to less than 14 hours out of a possible 30. Nevertheless, the struggle proved absorbing, with a thrilling final hour when Australia lost eight wickets for 35 runs.

England suffered two early disappointments. First Hutton lost the toss again, then after only ten minutes Laker, in trying to prevent Morris's solitary scoring stroke, slipped on the rain-sodden turf and injured a muscle in his left leg. Yet England began well enough. Bedser bowled the first ball at 2.50 p.m. and soon three wickets were down for 48. Morris had the misfortune to divert the ball gently against his stumps, just removing a bail; Hassett was bowled, and Miller went the same way as Morris. Any luck England had enjoyed earlier was offset when Harvey touched an easy catch off Bailey to Evans. The ball travelled direct into his gloves, but in his excitement Evans put it on the ground. As events turned out this may well have deprived England of victory, for not until 12.30 on Saturday did they see the back of Harvey. Instead of leaving at 52 he saw the total reach 256. Hole gave Harvey valuable help in restoring Australia's fortunes. It was no easy task, for often the ball bounced higher than usual.

Despite heavy rain early next morning, play started at 11.55, but the weather was so bad that cricket was limited to 90 minutes in four separate attempts. Harvey played extremely well, and with Hole continuing his support the total was raised to 221 for three. The England players slithered about, yet their ground fielding was alert. There was no encouragement for the bowlers, and by 5 p.m. the ground was flooded.

The third day brought sunshine. Play began at noon, and Bedser dismissed Hole with his first ball after a stand of 173. Now came de Courcy, brim-full of confidence, and if some of his strokes, like Harvey's, flew perilously over the fielders, he pushed the score along. Harvey had reached 122 when Evans, atoning for his earlier error, caught him splendidly on the leg side. Yet he immediately committed another blunder, dropping an easy chance off Laker before Davidson had scored: it took 45 valuable minutes to remove him. At lunch, Australia were 290 for six, and the remaining four wickets went in half an hour for another 28 runs. The last seven actually fell on Saturday for 97, and of these 41 went to de Courcy. Bedser bowled magnificently into the strong south-west wind, and Laker offered little respite. Both made the ball lift spitefully.

When England batted Edrich was surprised by Hill turning a leg-break. Miller bowled off-spin round the wicket and tempted Graveney to make a poor stroke at a half-volley. There followed a superb partnership by Hutton and Compton. Both produced magnificent drives, specially through the covers, and Hutton also indulged in some glorious late cuts. Compton hooked Davidson for six. When it seemed that the two batsmen would survive over the weekend their partnership of 94 ended at 6.15 when Compton, playing for safety, gave a catch to the wicket-keeper. Without addition Lindwall beat Hutton by sheer pace. So England finished the third day at 126 for four, knowing that after one more over Australia could claim the new ball and 43 were still needed to avert the follow-on. As it happened, not a ball could be bowled on Monday.

More rain shortened the fifth day. Play could not be resumed until after lunch, and the only matter of interest seemed to be whether England could stay long enough to make Australia bat again. Lindwall and Miller took the new ball for the vital attack on Watson and Wardle, but in 85 minutes England obtained those 43 runs. Hill acquired unexpected life, but Simpson and Bailey put on 60 for the seventh wicket. Then came some breezy hitting by Evans and Bedser before Morris finished the innings by bowling his great rival. So the Australians gave Morris the honour of leading them off.

Whereas the Australian spinners erred in pitching short, Laker and Wardle soon showed the way to utilise the treacherous pitch. They kept the ball right up to the batsmen. Hutton opened with Bedser and Laker, and when Hassett took two boundaries in the opening over a placid finish was indicated. But Laker quickly revealed the pitch's true character by spinning the ball viciously and getting it to stand up sharply. Morris was caught off his gloves at slip, and after Bailey in the gully dived to hold a brilliant catch from Hassett, Miller, jumping yards out of his crease, was stumped by Evans. Without addition Bedser removed Hole. Hutton took him Bedser off and introduced Wardle, who in the remaining half-hour obtained four wickets in five overs for only seven runs. Several Australians preferred attack to defence, but none of them gave their wickets away. They simply could not master the turning ball, and so England after all emerged for the third time with an honourable draw.

Toss: Australia. **Australia 318** (R. N. Harvey 122, G. B. Hole 66, A. V. Bedser 5-115) and **35-8** (J. H. Wardle 4-7); **England 276** (L. Hutton 66).

Fourth Test

At Leeds, July 23, 24, 25, 27, 28, 1953. Drawn.

Norman Preston

Australia were always on top in this match and only by steadfast defence did England escape defeat. The game produced some excellent fast bowling by Lindwall and Miller, another grand effort by Bedser, and on the last day when England were in dire distress Bailey withstood the full brunt of the Australian attack for four hours 20 minutes, being last out for 38. Runs did not matter then, time alone counted, and by staying so long Bailey deprived Australia of victory.

Neither side was keen to bat when not only was the pitch recovering from a drenching but rain had seeped under the covers at the football end. When Hassett called correctly for the fourth time, Hutton threw away the coin in contemptuous disgust, but Hassett was not bluffed. He told Hutton to bat. Australia had not sent in England since 1909 at Lord's. England immediately suffered a blow from which they never properly recovered. Lindwall's second ball sent Hutton's middle stump flying, a bitter moment for England and also for the Yorkshire crowd of 30,000 who watched in silence their hero return to the pavilion.

England concentrated solely on defence. On this first day only 142 runs were scored for the loss of seven men. Yet it was not dull cricket. Every ball seemed vital. England were indebted to Graveney, the top-scorer with 55. Watson was struck on the ankle by a full toss: an lbw appeal was disallowed but the ball rolled against the leg stump and a bail fell. Evans played Lindwall to Hassett at mid-on and started for a quick single. Then he sent Bailey back, but he could not get home in time. In the scramble Bailey twisted a knee and England now had three casualties.

Next morning Australia maintained their stranglehold, the remaining three wickets falling for 25. Lindwall gave another outstanding exhibition of the art of fast bowling. Always in supreme control of length and direction, he varied his pace, conserving his energy for occasional bursts of full speed.

Facing a modest total, Australia showed a different approach and for the first time the batting became enterprising. The pitch was firmer, but Bailey, still limping, bowled only three overs. The value of Lock as a fielder was soon seen, for he held a sharp catch from Morris at short fine leg. He gained another wicket by catching Hassett splendidly at square leg, and then Bedser took a well-earned rest. Bailey succeeded him off a short-ened run and induced Miller to edge to slip. England were faring better than expected, but Harvey and Hole took Australia ahead without further loss. Bailey broke the stand by getting Harvey lbw. In just over an hour fortunes completely changed, the score moving from 165 for four to 218 for nine. Hole was the third man to be brilliantly caught by Lock. Again the lion-hearted Bedser had retrieved the position for England. By taking six wickets, he surpassed C. V. Grimmett's world record of 216 in all Tests.

Australia held a lead of 99 and with three days left a definite result seemed most probable, but on Saturday rain permitted less than two hours' play. Hutton and Edrich revealed a welcome change of attitude and their 57 was England's best opening stand of the series. When light rain was removing the shine, Hassett wanted to go off, but Hutton declined and was supported by the umpires. Possibly the stoppage disturbed Hutton's concentration, for he deflected the very next ball into Langley's gloves. Soon afterwards the game was stopped, and nothing more could be done until Monday, when England became involved in a tremendous battle for preservation on a rain-affected pitch.

More showers cut the cricket by two hours, but the deficit was cleared for the loss of only one more wicket. Then Compton and Edrich faced some very hostile bowling. They were subjected to several bumpers but added 77. The stand was broken in Lindwall's third over with the new ball, Edrich after four hours falling to a fine catch in the gully. Compton, having completed 50, received a damaging blow on the back of the left hand from Lindwall. He continued, but suddenly England again found themselves in trouble. Watson was splendidly caught off his glove by Davidson in the gully, and next ball Simpson was taken at second slip.

Miller had given Australia a great chance. Half the wickets were now down for 171, representing a lead of only 72, but Bailey not only averted a hat-trick but proceeded to play the most vital innings of the match. England obviously were not finished, but before the game continued next day Compton's left hand had become useless. He received treatment but could not grip the bat. Evans carried on the battle, but Miller soon caused him to give a catch at square leg. With only four wickets left and Compton doubtful, England's position was precarious, but once more the hour of crisis produced the unexpected, for Laker scored 48 out of 57 added with Bailey. Upright in stance, Laker thrilled the crowd by his fearless driving, notably when Lindwall and Miller took the third new ball. Compton resumed after lunch, but plainly could not overcome the handicap of his bruised hand. Lock lasted 40 minutes and Bedser 45 before Bailey's match-saving display ended in a catch to slip

Australia now faced a race with the clock. They wanted 177 in 115 minutes, but Hutton was not without hope, and began the bowling with Bedser and Lock. Australia went for the runs and, with Lock uncertain in length, the first 20 came in nine minutes. Morris pulled and cut freely, but having made 38 in as many minutes he was stumped. The excited crowd cheered everything, and Hole and Harvey treated them to a feast of sparkling strokes. In half an hour they added 57, and when Davidson came in 66 were needed in 45 minutes. It looked a walkover, but Hutton called on Bailey to use his long run and bowl outside leg stump with no slip.

The turning-point came when Hole swept and Graveney held the ball high above his head on the boundary. If he had missed it, it would have been six. Australia finished 30 short: only 12 overs were bowled in the last 45 minutes. Thus England escaped defeat and the way was left clear for a straight contest for the Ashes at The Oval, to which an extra day was added in the hope of reaching a definite conclusion.

Toss: Australia. **England 167** (T. W. Graveney 55, R. R. Lindwall 5-54)
and 275 (W. J. Edrich 64, D. C. S. Compton 61, K. R. Miller 4-63);
Australia 266 (R. N. Harvey 71, G. B. Hole 53, A. V. Bedser 6-95) **and 147-4**.

Fifth Test

Norman Preston

At The Oval, August 15, 17, 18, 19, 1953. England won by eight wickets.

England won by eight wickets and so won the Ashes for the first time since 1932–33. It was a most welcome victory in Coronation year and a triumph for Len Hutton, the first modern professional to be entrusted with the captaincy of England. This was the first time England had won the rubber at home since 1926. The absence of a genuine spin bowler proved a severe handicap to Australia. The issue was virtually decided on the third afternoon when Australia, 31 behind on first innings, lost half their side to Laker and Lock for 61.

As in 1926, stories of long all-night queues frightened away many would-be spectators on the first day when the ground was comfortable with 26,300 present. The news that Hassett had again won the toss was received gloomily, but by mid-afternoon, when seven Australian wickets were down for 160, pessimism changed to optimism. At first matters took the expected course. With six days at their disposal, there was no need for Australia to hurry, but they never ignored the loose ball. For example, the second ball of the day, a full-toss from Bedser, was hit truly by Hassett to the long-leg boundary.

Bedser broke the opening stand when his swerve deceived Morris. The Surrey giant had now dismissed Morris five times in this series and altogether 18 times in 20 Tests.

Within ten minutes Bailey claimed the dangerous Miller, who, padding up, was also lbw. Light rain during lunch seemed to enliven the pitch, and suddenly Bedser and Trueman drilled a big hole in the Australian batting. Half the side was out for 118, but while Archer defended Hole played a splendid innings. He pulled and drove until Trueman beat him by pace and Evans seized his third catch. Without addition, Archer, having stayed nearly an hour, lifted the first ball on Bedser's return back to the bowler. This turned out to be Bedser's final wicket, but it was an historic one. It gave him his 39th of the series and so he beat M. W. Tate's 38 in 1924–25, the previous-best in England–Australia matches.

Lindwall indulged in a magnificent display of clean hitting. His drives were of the highest class. The new ball did not halt him and he hit eight sparkling fours before he was last out. By adding 157 the last five wickets more than doubled the score. Before bad light stopped the struggle England might well have lost Hutton in Lindwall's tear-away first over. The fourth and fifth balls were bouncers. The fifth flew off the bat-handle and five slips surged forward for the catch which unexpectedly never arrived. The ball dropped short because it lost its pace through striking Hutton's cap, which it removed. The cap just missed the stumps.

If Saturday belonged to England, Monday went to Australia, for the close found England 235 for seven – 40 behind with only three wickets left. The conditions were not in their favour, but the Australians bowled and fielded as if their very lives were at stake. They dropped only one catch compared with five by England, and restricted the scoring-rate to less than 40 an hour. For a time England prospered. An early setback occurred when Edrich, having batted splendidly, left at 37, but there followed a grand partnership between Hutton and May. When that was broken England went through a very bad time. Hutton was bowled by a well-pitched-up ball from Johnston which moved from leg and hit middle.

When the interval arrived at 165 for three, Compton had spent an hour over 16. On a day made for batting, Lindwall and Miller were only warming up when Compton's disappointing exhibition ended in a spectacular flying catch by Langley well wide of the leg stump. Not until the 78th over did Australia take the new ball, and it brought immediate success. The second ball was enough for Graveney, who fell to a brilliant first slip catch by Miller. That meant half the England wickets down for 170. England stopped the slump, but the position was still precarious, particularly when Evans slipped on being sent back and Langley swept Davidson's lightning return into the stumps. Bailey had begun slowly, but he changed his methods and brilliant strokes to the off gave him 11 in an over from Johnston. Laker soon went, but Lock closed an end for the last 40 minutes of a dramatic day, England finishing at 235 for seven.

The way England pulled the game round on the third day was scarcely believable. Again Bailey foiled the bowlers. Dazzling fielding saved many runs, but not even the odd bouncer troubled Bailey, and only 13 separated the totals when the last man, Bedser, walked to the crease. England took 20 minutes to get those runs. Every ball seemed vital until Bedser lifted one from Johnston over mid-off and the batsmen ran four. Bailey drove and hooked beautifully until, going forward to Archer, he was bowled on the stroke of lunch by a fine ball which hit the top of the stumps.

To Hutton must be given the credit for bringing about Australia's subsequent collapse. He realised that the batsmen would thrive on pace bowling on this somewhat lifeless pitch, and soon introduced the Surrey spinners, Laker and Lock. That was the move that brought home the Ashes. The batsmen had not settled down before they were confronted by spin, and vulnerability to the turning ball led to their undoing. Suddenly a day which began so gloomily for England swung completely their way. Laker started the procession. Bowling round the wicket, he twice beat Hassett, then with the last ball of his first over got him lbw. An hour later half the batsmen were out for 61. In one astonishing spell of 14 minutes four wickets fell while only two runs were scored. Hole threatened danger, but again Hutton countered, placing a deep extra cover as well as a long-on, and Laker with his very next ball got Hole lbw.

Lock never erred in length or direction, and as Harvey shaped to drive he knocked back his off stump. Next over Trueman at short square leg hugged a sharp catch from Miller, and then Morris, playing back, was lbw. The only possible escape was a repetition of Lindwall's method. Archer began the offensive, but at 85 de Courcy was brilliantly run out by Bailey from mid-wicket. Archer and Davidson still hit at will, and at tea Australia were 131 for six. Afterwards, though, the four remaining wickets fell for 31.

England needed 132 to win, with ample time at their disposal. Fifty minutes remained on Tuesday, but at 24 Hutton brought about his own dismissal. He hit Miller firmly to square leg and took the obvious single, but when de Courcy fumbled he tried to steal a second run and failed to get home. May stayed with Edrich for the last 15 minutes and England finished at 38 for one.

They now needed 94, and only rain and a sticky pitch were likely to deprive them. But how those Australians fought to hold the Ashes! Johnston bowled tantalising slows without relief till 2.45, when, with only nine more wanted, Hassett ended the struggle by going on with Morris. Compton made the winning hit at seven minutes to three when he swept Morris to the boundary.

At once the crowd swarmed across the ground while the players fought their way to the pavilion. In a memorable scene both captains addressed the crowd, stressing the excellent spirit in which all the matches had been contested both on and off the field.

Toss: Australia. **Australia 275** (A. L. Hassett 53, R. R. Lindwall 62, F. S. Trueman 4-86)
and 162 (J. C. Laker 4-75, G. A. R. Lock 5-45); **England 306** (L. Hutton 82, T. E. Bailey 64,
R. R. Lindwall 4-70) **and 132-2** (W. J. Edrich 55*).

NOTES BY THE EDITOR

Norman Preston, 1954

It is a great pleasure to record the return of the Ashes to England during the Coronation year of our Queen.

To my mind not sufficient credit was given to Hutton for his part in lifting England out of the long period of depression which began when Australia took the Ashes in 1934. The first professional to captain England since the days of Shaw and Lillywhite, Hutton led his men conscientiously and also shouldered the main responsibility of the batting. He scored nearly 100 runs more than any other player on either side. True, he had one unfortunate period in the field at Lord's when he missed four catches, but not until afterwards did we discover that he was troubled with fibrositis. His 145 in that match was easily the finest innings of the whole series.

The bowlers, for once, were the dominant personalities. Bedser and Lindwall performed admirably and left no doubt as to their fitness to rank with the giants of all time. In the end England's victory was clear-cut, but all those who followed the Tests will long remember how close Australia went towards success at Lord's and Leeds.

The Tests aroused tremendous public interest not only in England but in all parts of the world where cricket is played. Modern publicity in the shape of television, sound radio and the press, which brought even Sir Donald Bradman across the high seas again, gave the game a new impetus by introducing it into the homes of countless thousands of strangers. If their newly won affection for cricket is to be retained the players must always strive to provide the public with something worth seeing.

The way history has repeated itself in cricket following two wars is remarkable. As in 1926, England conquered Australia eight years after the end of hostilities but, as on that former occasion, we may have found only the nucleus of the next team to do duty in the Antipodes.

Australia v England 1954–55

Norman Preston

Under the zealous and skilful captaincy of Len Hutton, England won the rubber in Australia for the first time for 22 years and so retained the Ashes. On paper the success appears most convincing and rather suggests a comfortable tour against indifferent opposition. That was far from the case. It was a hard tour with its days of triumph and regret, but in the end superb fast bowling by Tyson and Statham turned the scales so that finally the Australian batsmen were humbled.

Only twice did a team exceed 300. Australia reached 601 at Brisbane and England 371 at Sydney. While credit must be given to the bowlers the fact remains that no longer did the batsmen find themselves on shirt-front or even easy-paced pitches. As in England, the modern Australian groundsmen leave some grass and the pitches do not undergo so much rolling as when Sir Jack Hobbs and Sir Donald Bradman were in their prime.

For May, the tour brought enhanced reputation, for not only did it reveal his qualities of leadership when Hutton rested, but it put beyond doubt his ability as a batsman. Compton, after his wretched experiences of the previous tour, quickly found his form, but a fielding mishap accounted for his low scores in the First Test and not until late in the tour did he look his real self again. Against these batting disappointments was the success of Cowdrey, the Oxford captain of the previous English season.

Before the party was chosen the decision was reached to assail Australia with a battery of fast bowlers. The accent on speed turned out far more successful than anyone dared to hope. Moreover it was accomplished without much assistance from Bedser. He fell ill with shingles soon after the team landed in Perth. He was scarcely fit for the First Test and, let down by fielders who missed seven catches, he finished with one wicket for 131. Hutton included Bedser among the 12 for Sydney, but on the morning of the match he made the dramatic announcement that he would be omitted. This must have been a very hard decision, but there were many factors including the difficulty of hiding him in the field.

Events alone justified Hutton, but above everything else the transformation of Tyson between the First and Second Tests saved the captain from adverse criticism.

After taking only one wicket for 160 at Brisbane, Tyson shortened his run and gained complete control over length and direction without losing any of his fire. In the next three Tests he took 26 wickets and, with 15 falling to Statham, a devastating alliance was formed.

First Test

At Brisbane, November 26, 27, 29, 30, December 1, 1954. Australia won by an innings and 154 runs.

Australia won by an innings at ten past four on the fifth day with a day to spare. Nothing went right for the Englishmen. Before the match Evans fell ill with sunstroke and on the first morning Compton, when fielding, ran into the wooden palings, breaking a bone in the back of his left hand. Above everything else the whole course of the game probably turned on the decision of Hutton to give Australia first innings. Never before had an England captain taken such a gamble in Australia and certainly never before in a Test had a side replied with a total of 601 after being sent in.

Hutton may have made up his mind some time earlier that he would take this course. England had banked on an all-speed attack. He inspected the pitch most carefully: it looked a beauty, but he carried out his plan and although he could be condemned, the fact remains that besides the loss of Compton England allowed about 12 chances to go astray, including one from Morris to Andrew off Bedser before he had scored. If the fielding had approached any decent standard Hutton might well have achieved his objective.

Australia, captained for the first time by Johnson, averaged just over 40 runs an hour on the first day, when they lost two wickets. A splendid catch near his boots by Cowdrey at square leg removed Favell and then Miller charmed the crowd of 20,000 for 85 minutes before he chopped a harmless-looking ball into his stumps. Then the two left-handers, Morris and Harvey, entered on a long partnership. Both flicked at balls outside the off stump and never did they establish complete mastery. Immediately after tea Bailey at deep long leg gave Morris a life when he was 55: that mistake alone cost England dearly.

With the new ball available first thing on Saturday there was still hope, but now Morris and Harvey took absolute control. Australia added 295 that day for the loss of four more wickets. Considering the length of time the fast bowlers occupied completing an over this was extremely fast scoring in present-day Test matches. Hutton placed his men to save runs and Tyson cut yards off his run in order to gain accuracy: but not until mid-afternoon did Cowdrey, the only slip, hold a waist-high catch from Morris who batted seven hours for his 153. The stand produced 202.

England had to wait another two hours and 131 runs for their next wicket, when a fine throw by Tyson from long leg ran out Hole. Then Harvey fell to a brilliant catch at backward square leg, Bailey rolling over as he held a hard pull. Harvey's 162, his first century against England in Australia, included one five and 17 fours. More trouble came from Lindwall and Benaud, who both hit with great power, and Australia kept England in the field until lunch-time on Monday.

After his spell with the bat, Lindwall came out fresh and bowled superbly for an hour, during which time the first four England wickets crashed for 25. Not until Bailey arrived was there any sign of stability, but then he added 82 with Cowdrey who, in his first Test match, gave a foretaste of the great innings he was to play later in the series. The end of the third day found England 107 for five and defeat was obviously only a matter of time unless rain came to the rescue. Bailey continued the fight. Statham kept up his end for 35 minutes and when he left Bailey had reached 81. Against medical advice Compton decided to bat, but he was almost helpless and so Bailey hit out and was bowled. He batted for four hours 20 minutes. When he drove Johnson over the fence, Bailey won a prize of £100 offered by a local businessman for the first English six.

England followed on 411 behind and in the first hour lost Simpson and Hutton, but Edrich and May shared a defiant stand. They took the total to 130 at the close, but next day Australia were on top again. May, playing at a short ball, was lbw when the partnership had added 124, and next Edrich, having shaped splendidly, especially against Lindwall, also fell to a short ball. Edrich hit one six and 13 fours. Subsequently only Bailey and Tyson gave any trouble. In less than half an hour after tea the last four wickets fell to the spin of Benaud and Johnson, the match ending with a glorious running catch in the deep by Harvey.

Toss: England. **Australia 601-8 dec.** (A. R. Morris 153, R. N. Harvey 162, G. B. Hole 57, R. R. Lindwall 64*),
England 190 (T. E. Bailey 88) and **257** (W. J. Edrich 88).

Second Test

At Sydney, December 17, 18, 20, 21, 22, 1954. England won by 38 runs.

Victory seemed beyond any possibility when England – who were put in – lost eight wickets for 88, but among a crop of batting failures in both teams the tailenders made their presence felt. The match was a triumph for pace bowlers, in particular for Tyson and Statham. Many people feared that Tyson had been seriously hurt when, batting just before lunch on the fourth day, he turned his back on a bouncer from Lindwall and it struck him on the back of the head. Temporarily, Tyson was knocked out but not only did he resume his innings but next day he knocked out Australia, taking six wickets for 85.

Tyson won the match for England because he kept his head. After his painful experience he might well have been tempted to hurl down bouncers, particularly at Lindwall, but he never did so. Possibly Lindwall expected retaliation, for Tyson yorked him, as he had Burke and Hole. The cricket at this vital stage emphasised that, above everything else in bowling, perfect length and direction win matches.

The omission of Bedser on the morning of the match created a controversy, but subsequent events justified the introduction of Appleyard and Wardle, who brought variety to the attack. Yet the seam bowlers of both teams controlled the play; in fact Morris (captain in place of the injured Johnson) achieved what Hutton failed to accomplish at Brisbane, England being dismissed cheaply.

Lindwall, rarely bowling short and swinging the ball either way, kept the hesitant opposition on tenterhooks. The loss of Bailey and May for 19 put Hutton completely on the defensive and in 90 minutes before lunch England mustered only 34 runs. Between lunch and tea came a dreadful collapse, five wickets falling for 60, and as Cowdrey and Appleyard soon went on resuming, nine were out for 111. Then Wardle and Statham struck heartily: their stand of 43 was the best of the innings.

The only enjoyable moment that day for England came with the last ball, when Hutton at leg slip caught Morris. Next day the bowlers recovered much of the ground lost by the batsmen. At first Favell and Burke made speedy progress, paying little respect to Bailey and Statham, but on Bailey changing ends and sharing the attack with Tyson the tempo changed. Graveney held Favell at second slip, so that at lunch Australia were 88 for two – and quite comfortable. Bailey continued to bowl splendidly and with Tyson causing much trouble Australia were not only put on the defensive but between lunch and tea lost four more men for the addition of 70. A daring and lucky effort by Archer, who put on 52 with Davidson, saved Australia.

England, having restricted the deficit to 74, went in again first thing on Monday, but at lunch, with Hutton, Bailey and Graveney gone for 58, it seemed that Australia might win without any serious challenge. Happily, May found a worthy partner in Cowdrey and their stand of 116 altered the structure of the match. It was most heartening to see these two young amateurs master the bowling by their sureness in defence and their willingness to hit the half-volley or any loose ball. There was no semblance of a chance until Cowdrey, trying to hit himself out of a quiet spell, attempted to drive Benaud for six when there were two men waiting in the deep. Powerful cover-drives and hard hits to leg brought Cowdrey most of his runs. May used a wide range of strokes and compelled Morris to remove his array of leg fielders behind the wicket.

Edrich and May took the total to 204 for five by the close, but the new ball was due first thing in the morning. Because of the wet outfield Morris delayed claiming it, but May, having completed his century from the second ball of the day, added only three more runs in the next 50 minutes. Then Lindwall and Archer went into action with the new ball and immediately took charge, and the position changed to 250 for nine. The last pair, Appleyard and Statham, faced the situation calmly and, unafraid to play forward to the well-pitched-up ball, they added 46 – another invaluable late stand.

Australia wanted 223, not an unreasonable task, but at once Statham and Tyson, with more pace than Lindwall, made the ball fly nastily. Statham gave Morris a terrible time, beating him four times in the last over before tea and removing him lbw with the seventh ball. The interval came after 25 minutes, giving the two England bowlers time to rest. On resuming Tyson, with his sixth ball, beat Favell by sheer pace, Edrich taking a nice catch in front of his chest, and both openers were out for 34. That was a great start, but Harvey, after a shaky beginning, settled down. Burke did not score for nearly an hour and the pair played through the last 78 minutes, seeing the total to 72 for two at nightfall.

Australia now needed 151 more runs, and first thing the odds were in their favour. Though much rain fell during the night, the protected pitch played with less fire than at any stage of the match, but it was never slow. Tyson struck in the second over when he yorked both Burke and Hole. Hutton did not overtax either Tyson or Statham at this stage, and in Appleyard's second over, Benaud hooked a skyer which Tyson held.

At lunch the total stood at 118 for five and no one cared to hazard a guess as to the ultimate result. But in the next 50 minutes Statham and Tyson virtually clinched the issue, removing four wickets for only 27. For some time Harvey had played a lone hand and as his partners disappeared the more brilliant he became. When Johnston arrived it was obviously agreed that Harvey should have most of the strike. He hit boldly, but never chanced anything when a defensive stroke was imperative. Johnston made some queer strokes but lasted 37 minutes, playing only 16 of 80 balls sent down in a stand of 39. He hit runs to long leg off the backhand until finally he flicked a catch to Evans. Harvey remained unbeaten, after one of his finest innings.

While justice must be done to Tyson who bowled without relief for over 90 minutes downwind in that vital spell in which his figures were 7.4–1–41–3, England could not have won without the valuable work Statham accomplished bowling into the wind for 85 minutes. With ten wickets for 130 in the match, Tyson was England's hero, and Hutton's party faced Christmas and the New Year in a new frame of mind.

Toss: Australia. **England 154 and 296** (P. B. H. May 104, M. C. Cowdrey 54);
Australia 228 (T. E. Bailey 4-59, F. H. Tyson 4-45) **and 184** (R. N. Harvey 92*, F. H. Tyson 6-85).

CRICKETER OF THE YEAR – FRANK TYSON

Eb Eden, 1956

Not for a long time has a star burst upon the cricket firmament with such startling suddenness as has been the case with Frank Holmes Tyson, the Northamptonshire and England fast bowler. Born at Farnworth, Bolton, on June 6, 1930, Tyson played his first cricket on the rough backs near his home at about the age of four, progressing to school cricket of a more serious nature some six years later. Even in those days he cherished the idea of becoming a fast bowler of class. By 1952 he was acknowledged as the fastest modern bowler if not of all time, a view to which F. R. Brown, the Northants captain, fully subscribed.

In the First Test in Australia, Tyson took only one wicket and that at a cost of 160, and it looked as though the selectors had made a mistake in choosing him. Then he shortened his run by three or four yards with remarkable results. In the Second Test he took four wickets for 45 and six for 85, and in the Third at Melbourne achieved his best performance by dismissing seven men for 27 in the second innings. Such was his pace that Australian journalists gave him the pseudonym of "Typhoon" Tyson.

Essentially a quiet and modest man, whose thinning hair makes him look older than his 25 years, Tyson owes his triumphs to perseverance. Whether in League cricket or when playing in the Army he went on learning all the time. He discovered that fast bowling was a question not so much of strength as of rhythm. When finding himself engaged in three-day matches, he considered a longer run would help to conserve energy; yet in Australia he owed his success to the fact that he returned to the methods he employed earlier in his career. The career of a fast bowler is often notoriously short. Hence Tyson's concentration upon studies, for he always wanted to become a teacher.

Third Test

At Melbourne, December 31, 1954, January 1, 3, 4, 5, 1955. England won by 128 runs.

Once more the speed of Tyson and Statham proved too much, and again Cowdrey and May carried the England batting on a sporting pitch which was said to have been doctored on the Sunday. Certainly large cracks were evident on Saturday, yet on Monday these had closed and for a time the surface behaved more kindly to batsmen. An inquiry issued the following statement: "It is emphatically denied that the pitch or any part of the ground has been watered since the commencement of the match."

This time Hutton decided to bat, but apart from Cowdrey, Evans and Bailey England made a sorry show. Cowdrey went in when Edrich and May had fallen and soon he saw Hutton and Compton follow, these four wickets going down for 41. Then he and another defiant amateur, Bailey, checked the bowlers for two hours, adding 74, following which Cowdrey and Evans put on 54, before the last four wickets fell for 22. For four hours Cowdrey batted without mistake, getting in behind short rising balls which Lindwall and Miller were able to bowl almost at will. Cowdrey specialised in perfectly timed drives, and he forced the ball skilfully off his legs. Miller bowled magnificently throughout the 90 minutes before lunch, when his figures were 9–8–5–3, but as his knee was still suspect Johnson later preferred to conserve his energy for batting. Hutton, troubled by a heavy cold, decided only at the last minute to play.

So England faced the second day knowing that yet again the bowlers must rescue them from a crisis, and they did: the first eight wickets fell for 151. Hutton used his bowlers in short spells, for the heat was stifling. Maddocks, who had kept wicket neatly and efficiently, rallied Australia. Arriving when six men had gone for 115 he saw the total to 188 for eight at the close. He and Johnson added 54 in all, and Australia gained a lead of 40, their last four wickets adding 116 to England's 22.

The arrears were cleared before Edrich was bowled. May joined Hutton and proceeded to play masterly cricket in which the straight-drive predominated. There was always the possibility that he might be trapped by a creeper, but May watched the ball intently. At 96 Hutton fell to one which moved fast and low from outside off stump. Cowdrey soon played on, England being 159 for three at the close, May 83.

May soon left on the fourth day, but Bailey defended stoutly, and after Wardle hit 38 out of 46 in 40 minutes, Australia were left 240 to win. A superb right-hand catch by Cowdrey at forward short leg off Morris brought England their first success at 23, but in order to keep Miller fresh, Benaud came next and both he and Favell exercised great care until Appleyard yorked Favell.

By the close it was 79 for two, which meant Australia still required 165, a task that seemed far from impossible. The pitch was worn and the experts predicted that England must look to Appleyard – but Tyson and Statham took them home without Hutton having to look elsewhere. Sheer speed through the air coupled with the chance of a shooter at any moment left the batsmen nonplussed. Tyson blazed through them like a bush fire. In 79 minutes the match was all over, the eight remaining wickets crashing for 36. Tyson's figures that morning were 6.3–0–16–6, Statham's 6–1–19-2.

A wonderful leg-side catch by Evans when Harvey glanced the seventh ball of the day heralded the collapse. The loss of Harvey was a terrible blow, and with Benaud hooking too soon and Edrich catching Miller at slip from a ball which lifted, Tyson claimed three wickets in 21 balls in the first half-hour. Statham accounted for Hole; Maddocks played on to Tyson and in the same over Lindwall went to drive a half-volley which shot under his bat. Next Statham bowled Archer with a fast full toss and finally Evans took his third catch, this time from Johnston high with the left hand. Australia were all out in three hours and five minutes.

Toss: England. **England 191** (M. C. Cowdrey 102, R. G. Archer 4-33) **and 279** (P. B. H. May 91, W. A. Johnston 5-85); **Australia 231** (J. B. Statham 5-60) **and 111** (F. H. Tyson 7-27).

Fourth Test

At Adelaide, January 28, 29, 31, February 1, 2, 1955. England won by five wickets.

This victory gave England the rubber for the first time in Australia since 1932-33, and again the fast bowlers, Tyson and Statham, well supported by Bailey and Appleyard, played a major part. It was the only match of the series won by the side batting last.

With the temperature hovering near 100°F both sides wanted to win the toss; Johnson was the lucky man and when lunch arrived with Australia 51 for nought trouble seemed likely for England. In each session Hutton used Tyson and Statham in short spells. When 12 Morris offered a low chance off Statham to Hutton, otherwise there was no encouragement for the bowlers on this placid pitch until after the interval. Then Tyson made one rise and it touched Morris's glove in transit to Evans.

McDonald (43) received a life off Statham from Compton at mid-on but next over, trying to hit himself out of a negative spell, he was taken by May. Back came Tyson and he trapped Burke at short leg. After tea, Bailey put in a very fine effort while Tyson and Statham attacked in turn from the Torrens River end. Harvey edged Bailey to slip, but Benaud and Miller, avoiding all risks, remained together for the last 75 minutes taking the score to 161 for four – a very fine first day for England.

With the new ball coming later Hutton gave Tyson and Statham only two overs each next morning and switching to Appleyard he made an unsuspected and wise change. He took the wickets of Benaud and Miller in the course of only three overs. Archer greeted Wardle by pulling him for six first ball, but the new ball soon accounted for both Archer and Davidson, making Australia 229 for eight on a perfect pitch. Johnson and Maddocks by sensible batsmanship added 92 in as many minutes, though the stand should have ended at 270 when with both batsmen at the same end Appleyard at square leg shied the ball high over Evans.

England wilted in the heat, Evans notably missing chances, and Statham was handicapped with a sore foot caused by the removal of a toenail a few days before. Hutton and Edrich relieved the tension by making the best opening stand of the series. England waged a hard fight on the third day and reached 230 for three at the close. Australia struck two swift blows, dismissing Edrich and May. Already the pitch was favouring spin, but by cultured batting Hutton and Cowdrey added 99 before Hutton also fell to an amazing catch after four and a half hours. He unerringly hooked a long-hop and Davidson, only a few yards from the bat at forward short-leg, turned his back, shot out his hands to protect himself and the ball stayed. Although the new ball became due 40 minutes before the close Johnson preferred to rely on his spinners.

On the fourth day Miller and Davidson struck with the new ball, Cowdrey and Compton falling for the addition of only two runs. Cowdrey batted five hours and Compton two, but Evans hit cleanly and impudently and some steady efforts by Wardle and as usual Bailey led to a first-innings advantage of 18 by mid-afternoon.

On Australia batting a second time, Hutton gave only two overs to Statham before introducing Appleyard and this move, hailed as a touch of genius, gave England the upper hand. Exploiting worn patches caused by bowlers' footmarks, Appleyard removed Morris, Burke and Harvey in his first six overs at a personal cost of six runs. On this evidence alone, most people reckoned Appleyard would be unplayable next day, yet again those two demon fast bowlers, Tyson and Statham, denied him his chance. Statham staggered Australia by removing McDonald, Miller and Maddocks in his first three overs, between which Tyson yorked Benaud. Subsequently, Tyson accounted for Archer and Johnston so that at lunch Australia were 103 for nine. Bowling unchanged for 90 minutes, Tyson and Statham had caused six wickets to fall for 34.

Finally Wardle dismissed Davidson, who alone offered any resistance. One would emphasise that Tyson and Statham broke down the opposition without delivering one bouncer and as in the other successful Tests they were forced to rely on an orthodox field as England could not afford to give away runs.

England wanted only 94 and though no one sensed any real danger Miller provided shocks when in the course of 20 balls he disposed of Edrich, Hutton and Cowdrey. Next he caught May brilliantly at cover, but Compton and Bailey were equal to the situation and saw England within four runs of their objective before Bailey was lbw. So those two old campaigners, Compton and Evans, were there at the finish.

Toss: Australia. **Australia 323** (L. V. Maddocks 69) **and 111;**
England 341 (L. Hutton 80, M. C. Cowdrey 79, R. Benaud 4-120) **and 97-5.**

CRICKETER OF THE YEAR – COLIN COWDREY

Norman Preston, 1956

From the moment he was born in Southern India on Christmas Eve 1932, Michael Colin Cowdrey was destined for cricket. In naming him, his father gave him his initial start – MCC. Some sons disappoint their fathers by not adhering to their appointed course, but happily for the Cowdrey family, Colin always possessed cricket ability and a few days after celebrating his 22nd birthday he hit his first Test hundred for England.

It was on August 19, 1950, that Cowdrey began his first-class career for Kent at Derby. His side were overwhelmed but he scored 15 and 26, and *Wisden* commented: "Cowdrey, the Tonbridge School captain, made a promising debut for Kent." The season of 1954 saw him captain of Oxford and he left no doubts as to his flair for leadership. It was a wet summer and for various reasons he did not quite approach his best form. Both his aggregate and average fell. Happily for England the selectors had not lost faith in him. They gave him a place in Len Hutton's team for Australia and soon the wisdom of this decision became manifest.

Cowdrey realised this was his great opportunity. If he did well, a life of cricket was at hand and throughout the tour he proved to be one of only two dependable batsmen in the side. The other was Peter May, with whom he shared a cabin on the ship and with whom he was usually seen in company both off the field and at the crease. Hutton considered May and Cowdrey the two best batsmen in the world under 25.

Fifth Test
At Sydney, February 25, 26, 28, March 1, 2, 3, 1955. Drawn.

Abnormal downpours, the worst in New South Wales for 50 years, caused loss of life and costly damage in the Hunter Valley, and also held up play in this final Test until two o'clock on the fourth day. The delay gave time for Bailey (fractured finger), Cowdrey (tonsillitis), Tyson (strained leg) and Maddocks (bruised finger) to recover.

Instead of 30 hours, playing time was reduced to little more than 13. Johnson won the toss and preferred not to risk batting on a rain-affected pitch, for the covers had been of little use in the deluge. As it happened the pitch gave not the slightest help to the bowlers. Hutton left fourth ball, Burge catching him at the second attempt at leg slip, but Graveney and May played glorious cricket, their stand realising 182 before Graveney fell to a grand return catch. Magnificent drives were the feature of his superb innings. His first Test hundred against Australia contained 14 fours.

Cowdrey went first ball and in the last over May was taken at slip. Next day, Compton exercised much care with Bailey, but after lunch he treated the bowling with less respect, his last 62 runs coming in 80 minutes. The partnership yielded 134 and finally Evans and Bailey both fell to Lindwall, who thus reached 100 wickets in Australia–England Tests, a unique feat for a fast bowler. Bailey actually allowed himself to be bowled and then went down the pitch, being the first to congratulate Lindwall. Very slow and tedious early in the day, Bailey hit only four fours in his 72.

The pitch was livelier than on the previous day and Australia were pleased to see their opening pair, McDonald and Watson, survive the first onslaught of Statham and Tyson, but Watson played on in Wardle's fourth over and Favell soon went in Tyson's second spell. McDonald and Harvey took the total to 82 for two at nightfall, but on the last day only McDonald and Maddocks played with much confidence. When Compton ran out Johnson, Australia failed by one run to avoid the follow on. It was the first time since Hutton's 364 at The Oval in 1938 that England had made Australia follow on. As less than two hours remained, a definite result was unlikely, but Hutton offered no respite, and although Tyson cut down his run to six yards he employed five slips and two short legs and still looked very fast.

Hutton again used Wardle for long periods and again Australia broke down, leaving no doubt that besides being vulnerable to pace they were just as unsafe against the turning ball. England, so often criticised for loose fielding, gave almost nothing away. Watson, Favell and Harvey were out for 29, but McDonald again showed determination, so the outside chance of an unexpected victory vanished. During the day 14 wickets fell for 257 runs and Wardle claimed seven of them for 115 in 29 overs. One could excuse him amusing the crowd by bowling his final over almost on his knees!

Toss: Australia. **England 371-7 dec.** (T. W. Graveney 111, P. B. H. May 79, D. C. S. Compton 84, T. E. Bailey 72); **Australia 221** (C. C. McDonald 72, J. H. Wardle 5-79) **and 118-6.**

LEN HUTTON: THE MASTER

Neville Cardus, 1956

Len Hutton was the only batsman of his period to whom we could apply the term Old Master, referring in his case not to his number of years but to the style and vintage of his cricket. He followed in the succession of the classic professional batsmen who each went in first for his county and for England: Shrewsbury, Hayward, Hobbs and Sutcliffe – though Sutcliffe wore his classicism with a subtly Sutcliffian difference.

As Old Masters go, Hutton was young enough; the sadness is that physical disability put an end to his career in its prime. He had all the classic points of style when, not much more than 19, he came to Lord's in 1936 and scored 55. I then wrote of him in this strain of Cassandrian prophecy: "Here is a young cricketer who is already old in the head and destined to enliven many a Lancashire and Yorkshire match of the future."

Whether or not he was putting into practice his wide repertoire of strokes, he was the stylist always; rarely was he discovered in an awkward position at the crease, rarely was he bustled or hurried. Once at The Oval, Lindwall knocked Hutton's cap off. Such an outrage could be equalled in a cricketer's imagination only by supposing that Alfred Mynn's tall hat was ever likewise rudely removed.

On a bowler's wicket, when the ball's spin was angular and waspish in turn, he could maintain his premeditated technical responses, often using a dead bat, the handle held so loosely that when the ball came into contact with the blade's middle it was as though against a drugged cushion: the spin was anaesthetised into harmlessness. But Hutton was, when grace descended upon him, a versatile and handsome strokeplayer. He drove Lindwall with Spooneresque charm and panache at Brisbane in December 1950; at Lord's in the 1953, he played one of the most regal and most highly pedigreed innings ever seen in an England and Australia Test match on the hallowed ground.

If Hutton had lived and played in the Lord Hawke epoch, when even Test cricketers in England had somehow to adapt themselves and their skill to matches limited to three days, he would have been a different batsman in his tempo and mental approach. But he could not possibly have been greater.

NOTES BY THE EDITOR

Norman Preston, 1955

After waiting for 22 years, England have again won a rubber in Australia and retained the Ashes they retrieved in 1953. This is a great thing for English cricket. At last England are on top again and with so many excellent young players in the counties, the team should be even stronger when Australia renew the challenge in England next year.

Twelve months ago I drew attention to the way history has repeated itself in cricket following two wars. Now the circle has been completed. After the Second World War, as after the First, Australia overwhelmed England, winning the first three Test rubbers. In each case Australia won 11 times before England broke the monopoly. Then, as now, England won back the Ashes at The Oval in the fourth series and retained them in convincing fashion when touring Australia.

In 1954-55 Statham and Tyson routed Australia. Excluding the last Test – these Notes were written immediately after the rubber was clinched at Adelaide – they took 43 wickets at 22.65 apiece. In five innings Australia made only 228, 184, 231, 111 and 111.

Tyson is a very conscientious young man. From the time the England team sailed he kept himself in condition running many laps round the decks of the *Orsova* before breakfast and throughout the tour he made sure he was always physically fit for the big occasion. He is the fastest bowler in cricket today and gives every promise of being a telling force in England's fortunes for some years to come. It seems unbelievable that Lancashire turned him down on account of doubtful physique.

The giants of cricket come and go. The rise of Tyson has apparently hastened the end of Alec Bedser's glorious career in Test cricket. One Test failure sufficed to put Bedser on the shelf. Unfortunate to be stricken down with an attack of shingles at the beginning of his third tour of Australia, Bedser took only one for 131 at Brisbane and out he went – a vastly different experience from that of some batsmen who fail but still receive another chance. Bedser belongs to the truly great. One of four England bowlers who have obtained 100 wickets against Australia, he holds the record for the number of wickets taken in one series, 39, and he has dismissed more batsmen than any other bowler in Test history.

ENGLAND V AUSTRALIA 1956   Norman Preston

Australia's gradual decline since the retirement of Sir Donald Bradman was not halted by the team led by Ian Johnson in 1956. Although they lost the rubber by the bare margin of two wins against one they were more or less outplayed in four of the five Tests. Their confidence was shaken by the wettest of all summers in memory and in batting, bowling and fielding they were inferior to England.

The Australian is mainly a Saturday-afternoon cricketer, brought up on hard, true pitches, blazing sunshine and a clear light. In these conditions his keen eyesight will generally compensate for minor flaws in technique; yet we saw in 1954–55 that, when batsmen were faced by bowlers of genuine pace like Statham and Tyson, those without natural gifts and sound coaching behind them could not survive. Similarly these men had no answer in England when day after day the pitches favoured spin. Whenever they faced Laker they feared his off-spin. In seven matches, including two for Surrey, Laker claimed 63 wickets against them.

The Australians, realising the suspect nature of their batting, intended to use Miller mainly as a batsman, but the plan had to be revised when Davidson chipped an ankle and Lindwall pulled a leg muscle in the First Test. In the Second Test, thanks almost entirely to some magnificent bowling by Miller, who took five wickets in each innings, Australia won by 185 runs and went ahead. The turning-point in their fortunes came in the Third Test. Davidson was still on the injured list, and although Lindwall was fit, Miller complained of a sore knee which prevented him taking any part in the attack.

Most of the bowling fell upon Miller and Archer, but owing probably to the soft pitches, neither was consistently deadly, nor had England any fear of the old combination of Lindwall and Miller. Lindwall had shed much of his pace, though his action was as smooth as ever and his ability to swing the new ball remained. The team possessed three slow bowlers of repute, Johnson, Benaud and Wilson. Between them they claimed only 14 wickets in the five Tests compared with 61 obtained by Laker and Lock.

First Test

Norman Preston

At Nottingham, June 7, 8, 9, 11, 12, 1956. Drawn.

Although England declared twice, the loss of more than 12 hours to rain made a definite result impossible. From England's point of view there was much satisfaction in the batting of Richardson and Cowdrey. Both played admirably, putting on 151 in the second innings, England's first century opening partnership against Australia since Hutton and Washbrook made 168 and 129 at Headingley in 1948.

Tyson, Trueman and Statham were all ruled out by injury, and three more pace bowlers broke down during the game. On the first day Australia lost Lindwall, with a pulled thigh muscle, and Davidson, who fell when bowling and was carried off with a chipped ankle bone. Then on the third day, when Australia were 19 for two, England lost Moss, who pulled a stomach muscle while brilliantly fielding a hard drive at cover.

No sooner had May won the toss than a shower occurred. After a short delay, Richardson was preparing to take strike from Lindwall when another shower intervened and not until 12.25 did the game commence. At once England enjoyed a slice of luck; with only seven scored either batsman could have been run out. Unperturbed, both batsmen settled down to a confident display, but just after lunch Cowdrey edged a lifting ball to slip. Graveney, tied down by Johnson's high flight, was splendidly caught low by Archer at slip, but Richardson and May took England to 134 for two by the close.

Australia turned to Miller who, despite doubts as to his fitness, bowled with all his old enthusiasm. A deluge flooded the ground on Thursday evening and continuous thunderstorms prevented play on the second day. The conditions threatened to be very bad on Saturday, but before breakfast the groundstaff removed 80 gallons of water from the pitch, and to the agreeable surprise of most the game was resumed at 1.10.

Richardson and May produced attractive strokes in a stand of 108, and though the ball travelled slowly, they took every possible run by smart running. Even when Miller and Archer took the new ball they had only one slip. Richardson was shaping for a century on Test debut when, trying to hook, he was caught by Langley. England continued to sacrifice wickets in the quest for runs and May declared at tea.

Just under two hours remained, and with only nine scored May called on Laker and Lock. Neither found any help from the pitch, but May set a close, menacing field. McDonald swept too soon at Lock and was lbw; next Lock at leg slip, diving forward, held a neat catch from Burke before the rain returned.

The pitch still gave little assistance to Laker and Lock, although the occasional ball lifted slightly. Miller was lbw playing back second ball, four wickets being down for 36, but Harvey and Archer faced the crisis defiantly and their stand of 54 checked the collapse.

When England, leading by 69, batted again, Richardson was dropped in Miller's first over and experienced more uncertain moments, notably against the leg-spin of Benaud. Johnson's main concern was to keep down runs and he set his field deep, but the batsmen in a fine display took the total to 129 by the close.

More rain caused more delay next morning. Once play started the big stand ended on the stroke of one o'clock when Cowdrey fell attempting a forcing stroke. Richardson, who hit ten fours, skyed Archer above the wicket-keeper and next Watson went to a fine catch by Langley far out on the leg side.

May set Australia a sporting proposition of 260 in four hours, but their sole aim was to save the game although the pitch, true to Trent Bridge tradition, never became sticky. May allowed Bailey and Appleyard only seven overs before he sent Laker and Lock into action and soon McDonald was taken in the leg trap. A closely set field exaggerated the conditions, but Australia made only 18 in the first hour. Again Miller was lbw, but Burke remained a sheet anchor, applying the dead bat with genuine skill. Still, with three wickets down for 41 and Davidson unlikely to bat, the position was still open at four o'clock. Then Burge joined Burke, and they stayed till the finish.

Toss: England. **England 217-8 dec.** (P. E. Richardson 81, P. B. H. May 73, K. R. Miller 4-69)
and 188-3 dec. (P. E. Richardson 73, M. C. Cowdrey 81);
Australia 148 (R. N. Harvey 64, J. C. Laker 4-58) **and 120-3** (J. W. Burke 58*).

Second Test

Leslie Smith

At Lord's, June 21, 22, 23, 25, 26, 1956. Australia won by 185 runs.

Australia gained their first Test victory in England since 1948 at The Oval. The team took a firm grip on the game and never relaxed. There were several splendid individual performances, notably by Miller, Benaud and Langley, but it was really a triumph of teamwork. England, well served in bowling and fielding, twice failed with the bat.

After nearly three weeks of intermittent rain the weather improved and the pitch rolled out firm and easy-paced, but throughout the game the faster bowlers were able to make the ball move appreciably off the ground and this resulted in many snicks.

McDonald and Burke did Australia a great service when, after Johnson won the toss, they put on 137, the best start for Australia against England since 1930. Although they had one or two anxious moments later, Australia never really looked back. Finally Bailey, in the course of four balls, sent back McDonald and Harvey and eased England's anxieties. Trueman, at second slip, hampered somewhat by Cowdrey at first, held an excellent catch low with his left hand to dismiss McDonald. Soon after tea, Burke was drawn forward by Laker and stumped.

Australia finished with 180 for three, but next day lost their last seven wickets for 105. England fought back splendidly, only Mackay and Archer, who put on 53 for the sixth wicket, checking them for long. Mackay relied on dead-bat tactics and rarely attempted a scoring stroke. He stayed two hours 40 minutes for 38.

As in the First Test, Australia were soon plagued by injury. After sending down only 29 balls at the start of his Test career, Crawford pulled a muscle at the back of his thigh and could not bowl again. This threw a heavy strain on Miller and Archer, who again responded magnificently.

Richardson, repeatedly sparring, eventually touched one to the wicket-keeper, and Graveney was soon bowled. England looked to be recovering from these two early disasters, but the first of three really brilliant catches in the match ended the stand. Cowdrey hit a ball with tremendous power, but Benaud, in the gully, flung up his hands and held on to it with everyone looking towards the boundary. The force of the ball knocked Benaud backwards.

At the close England were 211 behind, only 179 having been scored throughout the six hours. Saturday provided a most exciting day's cricket as first one side then the other gained the upper hand. May made 63 and Bailey gave a typically defiant display, but the others failed and England were all out 114 behind. Miller, bowling for long spells and moving the ball either way at varying pace, took half the wickets for 72.

Australia's long lead looked like being decisive, but great-hearted bowling by Trueman and fine fielding put England back in the game. First Cowdrey in the gully held a fine low right-handed catch, almost as good as that by Benaud, to break the opening stand. Harvey took ten off the first three balls he received but was out to the fourth, brilliantly taken at short fine leg by Bailey, who dived full length and held a genuine leg-glide with his right arm outstretched. These two great efforts inspired the

Englishmen, particularly Trueman, who put every ounce of energy into his work and bowled really fast. He had Burke caught at first slip, yorked Burge and, after Bailey had dismissed Archer, returned for a final spell and sent back Miller. Australia finished the third day with six men out for 115, only 229 ahead.

At that point the game looked evenly balanced, but from Monday morning Australia took control. Benaud set about the bowling so wholeheartedly that England's chances soon waned. With Mackay a passive partner Benaud made 97, including one six and 14 fours, out of 117 for the seventh wicket. Finally, trying a big hit to complete his century, Benaud skyed a catch behind the stumps. Mackay, even more stubborn than in the first innings, spent 265 minutes over 31, one of the slowest Test innings on record.

England were set the formidable task of 372 to win or eight hours 40 minutes to bat. They soon ran into trouble, Richardson again being caught at the wicket. The final day began with England 72 for two, and again they were forced to struggle. Their lack of enterprise enabled the Australians to throw all their efforts into winning without worrying about the possibilities of England getting the runs. Watson was bowled when hitting across a full toss and Cowdrey, after just over three hours for 27, was lbw at 91.

Johnson set a close, attacking field, particularly to Cowdrey, and Burge stood astonishingly close at forward short leg, barely two yards from the bat. At one point May, after a word with Cowdrey, spoke to Johnson, but apart from moving round a little squarer, Burge remained almost in touching distance. While May and Bailey were together there seemed a faint chance that England might save the game, but the end was in sight when Bailey fell just before lunch.

May had just passed his third fifty in successive innings against Australia when he edged a catch behind. The remaining three wickets went down for six runs and shortly before three the match was over. Miller took five more wickets, making ten in the match for 152, a great performance for a 36-year-old fast-medium bowler.

No fewer than 21 wickets fell to catches behind the batsman. Evans did well for England, with six catches and one stumping, but Langley established a new Test record by helping to dismiss nine men in the match.

Toss: Australia. **Australia 285** (C. C. McDonald 78, J. W. Burke 65) **and 257** (R. Benaud 97, F. S. Trueman 5-90, T. E. Bailey 4-64); **England 171** (P. B. H. May 63, K. R. Miller 5-72) **and 186** (P. B. H. May 53, K. R. Miller 5-80, R. G. Archer 4-71).

Third Test
Norman Preston

At Leeds, July 12, 13, 14, 16, 17, 1956. England won by an innings and 42 runs.

Fortunate to win the toss, England looked bound for defeat at the end of the first hour when their first three wickets had fallen to Archer for 17 runs, but a century by May and a fine innings of 98 by Washbrook brought about a recovery. Later, Laker and Lock exploited a pitch which favoured slow bowling as early as the second day and victory was achieved with nearly four hours to spare. It was the first time England had beaten Australia at Headingley.

The England selectors were severely criticised for choosing Washbrook, one of their own members, who had not appeared in a Test since 1950–51, but after his long rest Washbrook returned refreshed and his experience was invaluable. Unfortunately for

Australia, Miller had a sore knee and was unable to bowl. He was greatly missed, for he would most probably have proved devastating in conjunction with Archer, who used the new ball to such effect that he dismissed Cowdrey, Oakman and Richardson in nine overs while conceding only three runs. Though Richardson managed to stay 65 minutes he fell to his 12th ball from Archer.

May and Washbrook were not separated until five minutes before stumps were drawn, when May, after hitting 12 fours, hit a high full toss to fine leg where Lindwall held a brilliant catch near his boots. The partnership of 187 was the best for England against Australia since the war. The Australian fielding fell below their usual standard. Superb driving was a feature of the displays by these two England batsmen.

Next morning Washbrook, exercising great care, fell lbw when hooking at a short ball, leaving when two short of a hundred. With Lock who came as night-watchman and Insole also falling to Benaud's leg-spin, seven wickets were down for 248, but while Bailey showed his usual safe defence Evans made 40 of the next 53 runs. Lindwall developed almost his full pace on the second day and took the last three wickets.

Trueman, aiming at off stump and pitching the ball up to lure the batsmen forward, showed the value of these methods when with the last ball of his first over he had McDonald caught behind. Burke batted splendidly. He was sure in defence and scored consistently with a fine variety of strokes, but as soon as Laker came on he turned his off-breaks on a dry dusty pitch that broke up at an astonishingly early stage.

Shortly after tea Lock joined Laker and in the following hour the two Surrey bowlers struck deep into the batting: soon six wickets were down for 69. Lock, with the last ball of his first over, tempted Harvey to glance to short leg. Burge and Mackay were too inexperienced to deal with Laker, and Burke, having made 41 out of 59, fell to a ball that came low. Archer made one high straight-drive only to play on, and although Benaud twice hit Laker to the off boundary, he and Miller were thankful that an appeal against the light was upheld at 6.15 when Australia were 81 for six. With three days left and 95 required to save the follow-on their position looked hopeless, but rain set in on Friday evening and continued for the next 48 hours so that not a ball was bowled on Saturday.

The game was resumed at 12.45 on Monday. At first, the sodden turf gave no help to Laker and Lock. Sawdust was needed for the batsmen as well as the bowlers to maintain a foothold. Miller showed the value of hitting with the spin, and he and Benaud increased the total to 112. Gradually the pitch became difficult, though it never became sticky. Australia's main objective was to avoid the follow-on, but no sooner did the sun appear than Benaud was caught off Laker on the boundary. He had helped put on 73, but 34 were still wanted, and the innings produced only one more run. Maddocks was taken at backward point and with the position desperate Miller discarded caution only to be bowled round his legs. Finally, Johnson drove a catch to Richardson at long-off.

So Australia followed on, 182 behind, and this time Trueman yorked McDonald, but Harvey proceeded to give his best display on a difficult pitch. With Burke also playing well, Australia's hopes of saving the game rose, but, after 80 minutes, he chose the wrong ball to attempt to punish and lost his off stump. May menaced the batsmen throughout the day with a close field, but Australia survived without further loss, the total being 93 for two when stumps were drawn.

Laker bowled from the pavilion end from 11.30 on the last day until the match ended at 2.20. He conceded one run in his first eight overs and in his ninth a sharp rising off-break struck Miller's gloves for Trueman to make a fine catch in the leg trap. Burge, Benaud and Johnson fell to Laker, but Lock captured the big prize by throwing himself almost halfway down the pitch and seizing a return catch from Harvey as he rolled over and over again. Seventh out at 138, Harvey had made a valiant but unsuccessful effort to save his side. Only five minutes remained before lunch, but Archer skyed to Washbrook at cover so that Australia had only two wickets left. They did not add another run after lunch: Maddocks failed to score for the second time in the match and Laker yorked Mackay. Apart from four overs by Trueman, first thing, Laker and Lock bowled unchanged on the last day when England captured eight wickets for 47 runs.

Toss: England. **England 325** (P. B. H. May 101, C. Washbrook 98);
Australia 143 (J. C. Laker 5-58, G. A. R. Lock 4-41) **and 140** (R. N. Harvey 69, J. C. Laker 6-55).

Fourth Test

Leslie Smith

At Manchester, July 26, 27, 28, 30, 31, 1956. England won by an innings and 170 runs.

England won by an innings with just over an hour to spare and so retained the Ashes. This memorable game will always be known as Laker's Match because of the remarkable performance by the Surrey off-break bowler in taking nine wickets for 37 runs in the first innings and ten for 53 in the second. Laker broke all the more important bowling records in the history of cricket. His main achievements were:

- Nineteen wickets in the match, the most in any first-class game. The previous-best was 17, achieved 20 times. The most in a Test match was 17 for 159 by S. F. Barnes for England v South Africa in 1913–14.
- Ten wickets in an innings for the first time in Test cricket.
- Ten wickets in an innings twice in one season for the first time. Laker previously took ten for 88 for Surrey, also against the Australians, at The Oval in May.

Those are bare facts, interesting in themselves, but they fail to capture the drama of one of the most exciting and controversial matches for a long time. The excitement came towards the last day, first when England were trying hard to make up for the time lost by rain to gain the victory which would settle the destination of the Ashes, and later as Laker drew nearer and nearer to his ten wickets in the innings. The controversy arose over the preparation of the pitch and for days cricketers, officials, critics and the general cricketing public could talk of little else.

The selectors continued their policy of relying on a four-man attack and Trueman was omitted. For Australia Langley, the wicket-keeper, was intended to play, but an unusual mishap kept him out: during the night he slept on his hand and damaged it.

May gave England a big advantage by winning the toss. The pitch was completely useless to fast and fast-medium bowlers and Richardson and Cowdrey, as at Nottingham, gave delightful displays. They took command from the first over and scored 174 for the opening stand. Cowdrey, strong in driving, was first to leave, but Richardson, who made his first Test century, did not survive much longer.

Sheppard and May continued, but towards tea-time, puffs of dust became noticeable when the ball landed and it seemed that the pitch was breaking up unusually early. Johnson and Benaud, the Australian spin bowlers, were unable to exploit the conditions and England finished with 307 for three. A curiosity was that the first five batsmen were all amateurs, something that had last happened against Australia in 1899.

Mutterings about the pitch could be heard that evening, but they rose to full fury next day. England went gaily on, adding 152 before being all out for 459. Sheppard completed a chanceless century. He drove delightfully and hit one six and 15 fours in all. Evans hit lustily and scored 47 out of 62 in 29 minutes. England made their runs in 491 minutes, an unusually rapid rate for Test cricket in recent years.

Australia began their reply just after half past two, and before play ended they had lost 11 wickets. McDonald and Burke began steadily, but had to fight hard against Laker and Lock, who were brought on early. Laker did not start his devastating work

Jim Laker took 19 of the 20 Australian wickets to fall in the 1956 Old Trafford Test, a record unlikely ever to be equalled.

until switched to the Stretford end, from where he took each of his 19 wickets. McDonald and Harvey fell at the same total and after tea the last eight wickets went in 35 minutes for 22 runs. Lock took his only wicket with the first ball after the interval and Laker did the rest, his after-tea spell being seven for eight in 22 balls. While admitting that Laker spun his off-breaks appreciably, the Australian batsmen gave a sorry display and appeared to give up too easily.

Following on 375 behind, Australia were unfortunate to lose McDonald, who retired with a knee injury after scoring 11. Harvey replaced him and was out first ball, hitting a full toss to short mid-on. The controversial storm broke that night. Accusations were made that the pitch had been prepared specially for England's spin bowlers, but these were denied by the authorities. The Australians were said to be extremely bitter, but their captain declined to comment. The arguments continued over the weekend and not until Laker's wonderful bowling on the last day overshadowed everything did they abate.

The weather changed completely on Saturday, when rain allowed only 45 minutes of play: Australia added six runs and lost Burke. Sunday was an atrocious day and Monday was almost as bad. In two spells Australia took their score to 84 without further loss. Conditions were terrible, a fierce wind making batting and bowling extremely difficult. Lignum bails were used and were most successful, not once being blown off.

England looked like being robbed of victory by the weather, but it improved considerably on the last day and play began only ten minutes late. The soaking left the pitch slow and easy-paced and by fighting cricket, McDonald and Craig remained together until lunch when the score was 112 for two with four hours left.

England v Australia 1956 · Fourth Test

At Manchester, on July 26, 27, 28, 30, 31. Result: England won by an innings and 170 runs.

ENGLAND · *First innings*

P. E. Richardson c Maddocks b Benaud	104
M. C. Cowdrey c Maddocks b Lindwall	80
Rev. D. S. Sheppard b Archer	113
*P. B. H. May c Archer b Benaud	43
T. E. Bailey b Johnson	20
C. Washbrook lbw b Johnson	6
A. S. M. Oakman c Archer b Johnson	10
†T. G. Evans st Maddocks b Johnson	47
J. C. Laker run out	3
G. A. R. Lock not out	25
J. B. Statham c Maddocks b Lindwall	0
B 2, l-b 5, w 1	8

1-174 2-195 3-288 4-321 5-327 6-339   459
7-401 8-417 9-458 10-459

First innings – Lindwall 21.3–6–63–2; Miller 21–6–41–0; Archer 22–6–73–1; Johnson 47–10–151–4; Benaud 47–17–123–2.

AUSTRALIA

	First innings		*Second innings (following on)*
C. C. McDonald c Lock b Laker	32	– c Oakman b Laker	89
J. W. Burke c Cowdrey b Lock	22	– c Lock b Laker	33
R. N. Harvey b Laker	0	– c Cowdrey b Laker	0
I. D. Craig lbw b Laker	8	– lbw b Laker	38
K. R. Miller c Oakman b Laker	6	– (6) b Laker	0
K. D. Mackay c Oakman b Laker	0	– (5) c Oakman b Laker	0
R. G. Archer st Evans b Laker	6	– c Oakman b Laker	0
R. Benaud c Statham b Laker	0	– b Laker	18
R. R. Lindwall not out	6	– c Lock b Laker	8
†L. V. Maddocks b Laker	4	– (11) lbw b Laker	2
*I. W. Johnson b Laker	0	– (10) not out	1
		B 12, l-b 4	16

1-48 2-48 3-62 4-62 5-62 6-73   84   1-28 2-55 3-114 4-124 5-130 6-130   205
7-73 8-78 9-84 10-84   7-181 8-198 9-203 10-205

First innings – Statham 6–3–6–0; Bailey 4–3–4–0; Laker 16.4–4–37–9; Lock 14–3–37–1.
Second innings – Statham 16–10–15–0; Bailey 20–8–31–0; Laker 51.2–23–53–10; Lock 55–30–69–0; Oakman 8–3–21–0.

Toss won by England   UMPIRES D. E. Davies and F. S. Lee

Shortly before the interval the sun appeared, and the ball began to spin quickly. Afterwards Laker began another devastating spell, sending back Craig, Mackay, Miller and Archer in nine overs for three runs. Craig, who helped McDonald add 59, gave a fine, courageous display for four hours 20 minutes; the other three failed to score,

Mackay, like Harvey, for the second time in the match. Benaud stayed to tea when, with an hour and 55 minutes left, England needed to capture four wickets.

Occasionally Laker changed ends, but only when he returned to the Stretford end did he continue his success. After tea the ball spun quicker than at any time in the match and Australia's last hope vanished when McDonald fell to the second ball. His 89 showed that the bowling could be played by determined concentration and he deserved the highest praise for his great effort.

The tension mounted as Laker captured his eighth and ninth wickets. There was never a question of giving him his tenth wicket, for England's only thought was victory. Lock repeatedly beat the bat, but at 27 past five a great cheer went up as Laker successfully appealed for lbw against Maddocks. The match was over and Laker had taken all ten wickets. He earned his triumph by remarkable control of length and spin and it is doubtful whether he bowled more than six bad-length balls throughout. As Johnson said afterwards: "When the controversy and side issues of the match are forgotten, Laker's wonderful bowling will remain."

LAKER'S WONDERFUL YEAR
Neville Cardus, 1957

Against the Australians in 1956, J. C. Laker bowled himself to a prominence which might seem legendary if there were no statistics to prove that his skill did indeed perform results and deeds hitherto not considered within the range of any cricketer, living or dead.

No writer of boys' fiction would so strain romantic credulity as to make his hero, playing for England against Australia, capture nine first-innings wickets, then help himself to all ten in the second innings. Altogether, 19 for 90 in a Test match. If any author expected us to believe that his hero was not only capable in one chapter of a marvel as fantastic as all this, but also in another chapter bowled a whole Australian XI out again – ten for 88 for Surrey – the most gullible of his readers would, not without reason, throw the book away and wonder what the author was taking him for.

Yet as far back as 1950 Laker was hinting that he possessed gifts which on occasion were at any moment likely to be visited by plenary inspiration and accomplish things not only unexpected but wondrous. At Bradford, five miles from his birthplace, Laker, playing for England v The Rest, took eight wickets for two runs in 14 overs. Against Nottinghamshire at The Oval in 1955, Laker took six for five.

Laker's actual finger-spin probably has seldom been surpassed on a sticky or dusty wicket, in point of velocity and viciousness after pitching. I can think only of Ted Wainwright, Cecil Parkin and Tom Goddard who shared Laker's ability to fizz the ball right-handed from the off side. There was more temper in Macaulay's attack than there is in Laker's, more vehemence of character. But for sheer technical potentiality, often for sheer actual spitefulness, Laker's off-spin must be regarded as entirely out of the ordinary, and very much his own.

His bowling is as unassuming as the man himself and on the face of it as modest. That's where the fun comes in; for it is fun indeed to see the leisurely way Laker sends his victims one after another, as though by some influence which has not only put the batsmen under a spell, but himself at the same time. Somebody has written that all genius goes to work partly in a somnambulistic way. Jim Laker is certainly more than a talented spinner.

Fifth Test

At The Oval, August 23, 24, 25, 27, 28, 1956. Drawn.

Norman Preston

Australia needed to win this match to save the rubber – the Ashes already belonged to England – but with more than 12 hours lost through rain, a definite result could not be reached. In any case, England generally dominated the struggle, and Australia, who in both of their innings lost half their wickets for less than 50, were fighting a rearguard action after tea on the last day.

The match began with some entertaining cricket which held the attention of everyone until immediately after lunch on Saturday. Then, when England had made 76 for the loss of Cowdrey in their second innings, a series of rainstorms left the ground in such a swamp that nothing could be done for three days, the game being resumed at ten past two on Tuesday with only four hours remaining for play.

The selectors, after their successes in picking Washbrook for the Third Test and Sheppard for the Fourth, enjoyed yet another triumph on this occasion when they brought back Compton, who top-scored with 94.

After May won the toss for the fourth time, Cowdrey fell to the fifth ball of the opening over, the first he received. Playing forward, he touched an outswinger. Lindwall and Miller, both employing five slips and two short legs, bowled admirably, but an early shower not only caused a brief stoppage but left the outfield so wet that the shine soon disappeared from the ball. The second pair had raised the score to 53 when Sheppard, who excelled in cutting and turning to leg, was taken at first slip.

Miller soon earned another success when Richardson, shaping for his favourite square cut, yet again became a victim of Langley behind the stumps. The crowd gave Compton a great welcome and he led a revival with his captain. They put on 156 before a remarkable change: Archer took three wickets in seven balls and, with Miller disposing of Evans, England slumped from 222 for three to 223 for seven at the close.

For his first ball, Compton faced his old friend and foe Miller, who gave him one of the fastest balls sent down on this easy-paced pitch. Compton let it go through and a quarter of an hour passed before he relieved anxiety by opening his score. Gradually, Compton unfolded all the familiar strokes of his golden days. The special leg-sweeps of his own brand and the most delicate of late cuts, as well as peerless cover-drives, took him and England to prosperity. May, too, produced some superb strokes, and by tea England were 159 for three. Then Australia put forward a great effort: between five and six o'clock England could add only 30 runs and finally lost Compton.

Heavy night rain followed by sunshine left Australia a fearful prospect on the second day. Laker bowled splendidly. His length was perfect and he obtained some spin, but Lock, in his keenness, sacrificed flight for pace. Each gained an early wicket for encouragement and Laker passed Bedser's record of 39 wickets in an England–Australia series when he induced Craig to make a rash stroke. The loss of three men for 30 prompted Johnson to promote himself while the pitch was in its most hostile, but when half the side had fallen for 47, Australia were in danger of the follow-on.

Johnson lasted 45 minutes, but the man who really saved the side was Harvey.

He made it his business to tackle Laker, but in the end a vicious off-break caused him to be caught at forward short leg. Archer fell to a spectacular catch by Tyson, but already Miller had established himself and the time was ripe for bold hitting when Benaud joined him. Both Laker and Lock received some ill-treatment, and Australia finished only 49 behind with two wickets still to fall – a remarkable recovery.

More night rain left the pitch soft and Australia added only four more, Miller being ninth out after three and a half hours. When England began their second innings on a drying pitch one had visions of Australia taking revenge for their collapses in the two previous Tests. Every time the ball pitched it left its mark. Laker and Lock would have been almost unplayable, but Australia possessed no spinner capable of taking advantage of the conditions. After half an hour of Lindwall and Miller with the new ball Johnson resorted to spin, calling on Davidson and Archer, who reduced his pace and tried off-cutters. In his first over Davidson produced a kicker which Cowdrey could not avoid and gave a simple catch in the gully.

Australia were handicapped when Langley received a cut on the forehead from a vicious ball from Archer. Harvey went behind the stumps while Langley was taken to hospital. Johnson and Burke tried a spell of off-breaks, but were ineffective. Indeed, Sheppard treated Burke with scant respect, putting Benaud in peril at short fine leg.

After lunch, only 11 balls were bowled before another storm broke and soon the whole ground was under water, the game being held up until ten past two on Tuesday. May might have essayed an early declaration, but not wishing to risk sacrificing the rubber, he waited until tea. This left his bowlers only two hours to dismiss Australia, who faced the impossible task of making 228 on a soft pitch and dead outfield.

Preservation of their wickets was Australia's main concern. Only one over was bowled by Statham before May brought on Lock, who rubbed the ball on the ground to remove the shine, and Laker. In the first hour England captured four wickets, only to meet stubborn resistance by Miller and Johnson, and when ten minutes remained bad light followed by rain finally ended the proceedings.

Toss: England. **England 247** (P. B. H. May 83*, D. C. S. Compton 94, K. R. Miller 4-91, R. G. Archer 5-53) **and 182-3 dec.** (D. S. Sheppard 62); **Australia 202** (K. R. Miller 61, J. C. Laker 4-80) **and 27-5**.

Notes by the Editor Norman Preston, 1957

The fine achievements England accomplished under Leonard Hutton received royal recognition when the Queen conferred on him a knighthood in the Birthday Honours last June. Hutton began England's resuscitation and Peter May has succeeded to the captaincy in the manner of a born leader. Quiet and unassuming, May has shouldered his responsibilities with tact and ability. To face Australia without Hutton might well have meant a series of collapses, but England were able to rebuild around May and, if the reconstruction of the batting has yet to be completed, the success of Richardson and Cowdrey, and the happy reappearance of Washbrook, Sheppard and Compton, kept the ship on an even keel.

I admit that I was among the critics who thought that the recall of Washbrook, after England had lost at Lord's, was a retrograde step, but with Hutton and Compton unavailable the selectors wanted a man of experience and Washbrook played a wonderful innings of 98 that turned England's fortunes. Then, at Manchester, Sheppard, having snatched a few days away from his curacy at Islington, hit a charming century which showed clearly that any young batsman with a degree of initiative allied to skill need not be tied to the crease for hours on end, strokeless and moribund. Finally, came Compton to The Oval, emphasising that cricket is a game to be enjoyed and he reaped the reward for his indomitable courage after so many operations on his troublesome knee.

Still, whatever deeds the batsmen accomplished, all were utterly dwarfed by Laker and his off-spin. It is said that all records are made to be beaten, but I never expect to see again one bowler take 19 wickets in any match, let alone all ten twice in the same season against the Australians. And will Laker's 46 wickets in an England-Australia rubber ever be surpassed?

AUSTRALIA V ENGLAND 1958-59

Harry Gee

Australia, under Richie Benaud, their new captain, won the Test series so convincingly by four victories to none that English enthusiasts were left wondering how their favourites came to lose the Ashes which they had held since 1953. England, captained by Peter May, certainly had a number of injuries, but neither this nor complaints about umpiring and the doubtful actions of several bowlers could gainsay the fact that the tourists were not good enough. This was the basic reason for their disappointing displays against a side which, though excellent as a team, was far from brilliant in individual achievement. On paper, the established players seemed to have justified selection, but long before this tour was over it became apparent that several had turned the corner. Tyson, who achieved such wonderful deeds four years previously, could not produce his bewildering speed; Bailey was not a match-winning quantity either as batsman or bowler, and Lock, for all his enthusiasm, rarely constituted a danger in the Tests. Evans was another stalwart who gave evidence of a decline.

Most of the batsmen were ill at ease against the ball moving from leg to off – the main form of attack by the left-arm fast-medium bowlers, Davidson and Meckiff, and the stock delivery of Benaud. The dominating part these men played is shown by the fact that, between them, they took 72 of the 94 wickets credited to Australian bowlers.

Negative cricket led to much dull and unenterprising play. The first four days at Brisbane typified this trend. In successive days of five hours the runs scored were 142, 148, 122 and 106. On the second day England, in the field all the time, bowled only 57 [eight-ball] overs. This was quite a gallop compared with the second day at Adelaide, when, with Lock the only spinner, only 51 overs were managed. Australia were not blameless in respect of wasting time by the slow walk of their bowlers back to their marks.

Still, the most regrettable aspect of the tour concerned the umpiring and the way decisions were received. There were errors – notably the giving-out of Cowdrey in the First Test, when, in my opinion, the ball bounced in front of Kline, and the run-out decision, afterwards altered, against McDonald in the Fourth Test when his runner was completely out of view of umpire McInnes, who gave the verdict.

On this very controversial tour, perhaps the most vexed question was related to the delivery action of some Australian bowlers. Not once in Tests or in other first-class matches did the umpires no-ball a man for throwing or jerking. Had they, as I saw things, strictly carried out the Law they should have called on many occasions Burke, Meckiff, Rorke and Slater, of the Test bowlers, and several others of lesser reputation.

First Test

At Brisbane, December 5, 6, 8, 9, 10, 1958. Australia won by eight wickets.

England, contrary to expectations, were beaten. Their batting sadly disappointed and O'Neill, in his first Test match, gave his rivals an object lesson in hitting the ball. The match was notable for a less admirable reason: a marathon batting performance by Bailey, who took seven hours 38 minutes over his second-innings 68.

The turning-point came on the fourth day when Graveney was run out and Cowdrey given caught by Kline though many present were convinced that a catch had not been made. England, who had been gaining a grip after a first-innings breakdown, lost their hold and surrendered the initiative to Australia.

May, who set a Test record by captaining England for the 26th time, won the toss and though the pitch showed some traces of green he decided to bat. Davidson and Meckiff, both left arm medium-fast, supported by Benaud, Australia's new captain, dismissed England in just over four and a half hours. The breakdown, in humid weather, began early with Milton yorked and Richardson taken low at third slip. Graveney, given a life when one, managed to stay during a critical period before edging to the alert Grout at wicket, and May kept up his end for two hours before Grout, moving to the off, brilliantly anticipated a catch which came high to him. Cowdrey, after a promising start, fell to a fine low catch at short square leg and the only other protracted resistance came from Bailey.

On the second day the England bowlers, in a shade temperature of 90°F, stuck determinedly to their task. Loader and Bailey, backed by smart fielding, took the honours. With the pitch having eased under hot sunshine, England had to wait until the last ball before lunch for a wicket, which came when Burke, who had been dazed by ducking into a Loader bouncer, was caught behind. McDonald gave a fairly confident display, but Harvey and Burge were soon out, and when Mackay was taken at the wicket, half the Australian wickets were down. May, using his bowlers in short spells to conserve their energies, saw a major obstacle in O'Neill removed when Graveney leapt to his right and brilliantly held a slashed stroke, and Australia at the close were 156 for six.

They lost their remaining wickets on Monday for 30. Loader and Statham again bowled in lively style and Laker finished the innings immediately he was brought on. England once again made an unimpressive start. A smart one-handed return catch disposed of Richardson. Bailey, promoted as insurance against another breakdown, quickly lost Milton, but he and Graveney defied the bowlers for the rest of the afternoon in adding 58. They could have hit harder, for the bowling, though steady, was far from dangerous on an easy paced pitch. The day's play produced only 122 runs in five hours while 63.1 overs were bowled.

Bailey, at stumps, had been at the crease nearly two and three-quarter hours for 27 out of 92 for two, and next day the crowd of about 8,000 – half the attendance of the previous day – endured even slower scoring before England were out for 198 a few minutes before time. So in practically a day's play of just under five hours only 106 runs were scored. Bailey batted in the most determined but unenterprising manner and lost opportunities of forcing the game against ordinary bowling through his insistence on dead-bat defence. Graveney proved equally strokeless and in the first hour and a half England added only 19. Eventually Graveney was run out by Harvey from cover, and May, after one on-side boundary, fell to Benaud's googly.

Then followed the controversial dismissal of Cowdrey, who was just seeing the ball well when Kline dived for a deflection. McInnes gave Cowdrey out after receiving confirmation from his colleague at square leg that in his opinion a fair catch had been made, but many onlookers were just as certain that the ball had bounced in front of Kline. The incident doubtless caused Bailey to concentrate even more on defence. Ten minutes from the close Bailey, to everyone's surprise, dashed out to hit Mackay, missed, and was bowled for 68. He scored off only 40 of the 426 balls he received.

Kline the bowler caused far less bother than Benaud, who brought the innings to an end three minutes from the close by luring Statham into lofting a catch to long-off. Australia, with two days left, needed only 147.

The pitch on the fifth day showed little signs of wear. Australia's strategy depended on Burke keeping up an end while his freer colleagues pushed the score along, but only 20 runs had come in 50 minutes when McDonald fell to a well-judged running catch at deep square leg. Harvey took over the role of strokemaker and the score was raised to 58 before he mistimed a forward-defensive to forward short leg.

With refreshing willingness to hit, O'Neill then played a delightful innings. He square-cut fiercely and drove off the back foot with tremendous strength and only smart fielding prevented many more boundaries. Australia were 96 for two at tea, and afterwards O'Neill, with a storm reported to be approaching Brisbane, hit even harder. He took ten in an over off Bailey, and helped his side to win by 5.20. O'Neill, who gave a chanceless display, made his 71 out of 89 in seven minutes under two hours – a gallop in comparison with earlier proceedings – and hit seven fours. The crowd gave him a great ovation as he walked off. His aggression was timely, for a thunderstorm with a heavy downpour, which saturated the outfield, followed.

Toss: England. **England 134 and 198** (T. E. Bailey 68, R. Benaud 4-66);
Australia 186 (P. J. Loader 4-56) **and 147-2** (N. C. O'Neill 71*).

Second Test

At Melbourne, December 31, 1958, January 1, 2, 3, 5, 1959. Australia won by eight wickets.

England were set back on their heels from the start when Davidson took three wickets in a sensational over on the first morning and although Statham also bowled finely the tourists never really recovered. The match produced a hostile bowling effort by the left-armer Meckiff, whose jerky action brought much criticism. The pitch, faster than at Brisbane, allowed batsmen to make strokes and also enabled the quick bowlers to show their paces. Before big crowds totalling over 230,000 England once more were found wanting in batting.

May, winning the toss on a fairly well-grassed pitch, again decided to bat. The start was amazing, for in the third Davidson sent back Richardson, Watson and Graveney with the first, fifth and sixth deliveries. Bailey and May fought back gallantly. Though instructed to keep up an end and give the strike to freer strokemakers, Bailey realised that the situation demanded aggressiveness and he brought off many forceful drives and cuts. Off-driving stylishly, May mastered pace and spin, and he and Cowdrey were still together at the close with the total 173 for four. May had been fortunate to receive a life when 20 for Benaud, diving to take a return catch, missed the ball when his knee knocked against his hand.

The second day produced exciting fluctuations of fortune. In the first eight overs 33 runs came, then the new ball, taken at 206, brought about a second collapse. May fell to a ball which moved in quickly, Evans was caught at backward short leg, and Cowdrey snicked to the wicket-keeper. May hit 11 fours in a meritorious display which lasted five and a quarter hours.

Burke left to a deadly ball which came back and left him offering no stroke, but McDonald and Harvey, who hit ten fours in his 60, defied England till the close while taking the score to 96. On the third day, when the attendance reached 71,295, England fought back in determined fashion after two century partnerships had made the outlook dismal. Harvey, forced to struggle for his hundred, scored 20 singles and only two more fours while adding the necessary runs, but on passing 100 he drove and cut more freely.

McDonald fell at slip just after lunch, then O'Neill stayed with Harvey till tea. At five o'clock it was 255 for two, but in five dramatic overs O'Neill, Harvey, Simpson and Benaud were out for seven more runs, wholehearted fast bowling by Statham and Loader earning justified reward. Australia finished the day 282 for six.

On the Saturday 15 wickets went down for 122, all to the quick men with the exception of Evans who was run out. The day began with Australia losing their last four wickets for 26 before lunch. Statham disposed of Mackay, Davidson whose off stump went flying, and Meckiff in two overs without cost. England had a golden chance to wipe off their arrears and gain a grip on the game, for the pitch was still unhelpful to spin, but another breakdown ensued. Richardson, flashing outside off, was magnificently caught by Harvey diving at slip, and soon half the side were out for 44.

May resisted, but there was no recovery and at 87 Meckiff sent Loader's off stump cartwheeling. The total was England's lowest in Australia since 1903–04, when they were out on the same ground for 61. Meckiff took six for 38, and Davidson, who bowled with him practically unchanged, three for 41. Davidson also held three brilliant catches.

Australia needed only 39 to win and the winning hit – a straight-drive for four by Burke – came after about an hour on the fifth morning.

Toss: England. **England 259** (P. B. H. May 113, A. K. Davidson 6-64) **and 87** (I. Meckiff 6-38); **Australia 308** (R. N. Harvey 167, J. B. Statham 7-57) **and 42-2.**

Third Test

At Sydney, January 9, 10, 12, 13, 14, 15, 1959. Drawn.

England, knowing that defeat would mean the loss of the Ashes, fought with more spirit after another first-innings breakdown had put them in serious danger, and emerged with an honourable draw. Two factors swung the course of the game after England faced a first-innings deficit of 138. Meckiff broke down with tendon trouble in his heel and the resistance of May and Cowdrey – the latter showing by far his best form of the tour – tipped the scales. May was able to declare and challenge Australia to make 150 in 110 minutes for victory, but on a wearing pitch they did not attempt the task.

May had to decide whether first use of what promised to be a good batting wicket would be offset by the expected movement of the ball through moisture due to late covering because of rain and swinging caused by humidity. He chose to bat, but both openers failed. With two wickets down for 23, Graveney and May survived a critical time before England were once more in trouble with the dismissal of May, Graveney and Dexter in two overs from Slater, the Australian newcomer, and one from Benaud. Cowdrey, realising the necessity for aggression, hit boldly in company with Swetman, who overcame early uncertainties and made a good impression by the manner in which he used his feet to the spin bowlers.

Slater began with medium-pace but changed after five balls of his second over to off-spin. His first two wickets in Test cricket cost him only four runs in four overs. The catching of Cowdrey at slip left England with six men out for 190 at the close, and the four other wickets added only 29 next day. The crowd had an unfortunate experience, for after morning rain they had to kick their heels outside while the staff took steps to dry an exposed pitch adjoining the covered Test strip. The game was not resumed until 4.15. Then several thousand spectators were let in free.

They saw England out in 50 minutes, the last three wickets falling to Benaud, who turned the ball appreciably, in nine deliveries for eight runs. Trueman pulled Benaud for six, but England were out soon after half-past five. They started well on the third day, disposing of Burke, Harvey and McDonald for 87 runs, but they lost their grip as O'Neill and Favell gained the upper hand in an unfinished stand of 97. May placed almost entire reliance on Laker and Lock, who bowled 27 overs each out of 68 sent down. They often turned the ball appreciably, but not sharply enough to cause a collapse. The day began hopefully for England when Burke, unhappy against spin, glanced to backward short leg where Lock swooped. Harvey, also uncertain against the turning ball, was beaten by Laker, and McDonald was splendidly caught at silly mid-off by a diving Graveney.

England met with early and late success on the fourth day, but they yielded ground during an excellent seventh-wicket partnership. May's faith in spin was justified when Favell, taken at slip, O'Neill, caught cutting, and Benaud, bowled in dashing out to drive, were dismissed for 11 runs. Favoured by luck, Davidson and Mackay restored the position for Australia in a stand of three hours before Trueman, who had been given little to do, flattened Mackay's off stump.

On the Wednesday, Australia suffered a big blow when Meckiff, in his second over, had to go off with a bruised heel and pulled Achilles tendon. Australia overcame the disadvantage with three cheap wickets, but May and Cowdrey, aided by fortune, took a grip on affairs. By strong driving and cutting they put on 52 in their first hour together and despite exaggerated defensive field-placings by Benaud, who dispensed with even one slip to Davidson, they added 114 by the end of the day. Davidson shouldered the burden of the pace attack, manfully conceding only 33 runs in 22 overs.

England, 40 ahead with seven wickets in hand, were reasonably well placed for the last day. May's strategy was to go for runs hoping that they would come quickly enough to permit a declaration. Benaud, in retaliation, once again set a defensive field even for the new ball, taken by Davidson and Slater who changed back to medium-fast. Cowdrey, twice driving him for four, soon saw him off, and in 90 minutes to lunch England added 53. Afterwards May, driving gloriously, gave evidence that he was bent on forcing a declaring position, and Benaud in desperation turned to the off-spin of Burke, who did the trick in his second over when May tried to force the ball off the back foot. May, who hit ten fours, missed a century by eight runs after a stand of 182 with Cowdrey.

Lock hit valiantly and after more than an hour in the nineties Cowdrey, with a scampered off-side single, completed his hundred, after just over seven hours. At the end of the over May declared.

After four overs, May brought on the spinners. Two successes fell to Laker, but time was all against England and O'Neill and Harvey safely played out the last half-hour. McDonald's dismissal occurred in curious circumstances. Running the first run, he stumbled and fell. Though limping he resumed for a while before asking for a runner, but when Slater came out McDonald, shaping up to Laker, was immediately bowled.

Toss: England. **England 219** (R. Benaud 5-83) **and 287-7 dec.** (P. B. H. May 92, M. C. Cowdrey 100*, R. Benaud 4-94); **Australia 357** (N. C. O'Neill 77, L. E. Favell 54, K. D. Mackay 57, A. K. Davidson 71, G. A. R. Lock 4-130, J. C. Laker 5-107) **and 54-2.**

Fourth Test

At Adelaide, January 30, 31, February 2, 3, 4, 5, 1959. Australia won by ten wickets.

Australia won by ten wickets and regained the Ashes. Their success was well deserved, being even more decisive than those at Brisbane and Melbourne. May, knowing that he had to win, took the bold course of sending Australia in, but his hopes were not realised. He had been faced with a predicament when just before the game Laker, after a test in the nets, decided that his finger would not stand up to the strain.

England showed more spirit in their second innings when the game was slipping away, but were not good enough. An important reason for Australia's victory was the fast bowling of Rorke, who, with Meckiff out through injury, made his first Test appearance, but his jerky delivery and habit of dragging detracted from the merit of his performance. Lindwall, recalled by Australia, bowled admirably and took three wickets.

The pitch soon lost its early liveliness and Statham, Trueman and Tyson toiled without reward. McDonald drove, cut and glanced in capital fashion, while Burke defended. Australia were 58 for no wicket at lunch and with the temperature nearing 90°F England faced a gruelling afternoon. Not until seven minutes past five was the opening stand broken, when Burke snicked Bailey to slip. Burke's passiveness was shown by the fact that he hit only two fours in his 66 out of the partnership of 171.

McDonald, 98 when Burke was out, struggled for another 25 minutes before obtaining the two runs he wanted for his first Test hundred against England. Australia were 200 for one at the close, and they consolidated their position on Saturday when, despite sweltering heat of nearly 100°F, they moved to 403 for six. Yet England met with fair success largely through the wholehearted fast bowling of Statham, who in one spell of three overs disposed of Favell and Mackay for two runs.

England's heavy task was not lightened until McDonald retired with a torn thigh muscle after adding 97 with Harvey. England took fresh heart, and in an hour three wickets fell for 26. Then Benaud went trying to pull, but Grout and Davidson stayed together for the last half-hour. Lock, in the role of stock bowler in the intense heat, did well to keep down runs as the pitch did not yield him the slightest assistance.

Evans kept wicket excellently after injuring his little finger again, and although an X-ray disclosed a fracture he decided to carry on – but changed his mind on medical advice next day, when Graveney kept wicket. Australia consolidated their position by adding 73 for the last four wickets, then getting three wickets for 115 before the close.

Trueman began by bringing fresh hope to England by fine fast bowling which brought him three wickets for 22 – including that of McDonald, who returned with Burke as runner and added 21. McDonald, having survived a controversial run-out incident when McInnes, the umpire, was positioned wrongly as Burke ran behind him, altogether defied England for over eight hours and hit 12 fours in his 170.

England started badly, quickly losing Richardson and Bailey, but May, who hit Lindwall for 11 in an over, and Cowdrey remedied things for a while. On the fourth day Cowdrey and Graveney ably resisted till lunch-time, when the total was 170 for three, but afterwards reverses came rapidly. Cowdrey's valuable innings, lasting nearly four hours, ended when he dragged the ball on. Next, Graveney deflected Rorke straight to Benaud at backward short leg. Benaud rubbed salt into the wounds with four wickets, but Statham, driving and cutting vigorously, and Watson stood firm in a last-wicket stand of 52.

Davidson twisted his right ankle late on, and Benaud was without his services when England followed on. At last, Richardson found something like his best form, and by the close he and Watson had made 43. On the fifth day, though finding scoring difficult, they managed to stay together till lunch, but their partnership was broken soon afterwards when Favell, running from mid-wicket, brilliantly caught Watson. Richardson eventually offered no stroke to a ball which moved in sharply. Benaud brought back Lindwall to attack Cowdrey, with success, but May and Graveney repelled the wiles of Benaud and the speed of Rorke. After tea English spirits rose when May made an onslaught on Benaud, pulling, square-cutting and on-driving perfectly timed boundaries off three successive balls, but in Rorke's next over a shooter completely beat him. With May went England's chances, though Graveney remained unbeaten at the close, which came with the unexpected dismissal of Bailey, who had batted stubbornly for an hour, caught behind on the leg side.

On the last day England, with five wickets left, still needed 38 to avoid an innings defeat. Spirited resistance made English supporters feel a little better. Lock and Tyson defied the new ball with Graveney, who took out his bat after a stay of just over five hours. Benaud appropriately ended the innings by catching Evans, who batted with his injured finger in splints. So Australia, with two hours remaining, found themselves needing only 35 to regain the Ashes.

Toss: England. **Australia 476** (C. C. McDonald 170, J. W. Burke 66, N. C. O'Neill 56, F. S. Trueman 4-90) **and 36-0; England 240** (M. C. Cowdrey 84, R. Benaud 5-91) **and 270** (P. B. H. May 59, T. W. Graveney 53*, R. Benaud 4-82).

Fifth Test

At Melbourne, February 13, 14, 16, 17, 18, 1959. Australia won by nine wickets.

England virtually lost before play began for a car accident in which Loader and Statham were hurt ruled them out of consideration. Benaud, with four fast bowlers, put England in and his policy was fully justified – the first occasion victory had attended a captain who put his rivals in since J. W. H. T. Douglas did so in 1911-12. Lindwall broke Grimmett's long-standing Australian record of 216 Test wickets, and wicket-keeper Grout equalled Don Tallon's record of 20 victims in an England–Australia series.

Bailey was out in Lindwall's first over and May fell at 13. Both fell to balls which kicked, Bailey at slip and May at gully. Fortunately for England, Richardson was at his best. Getting well behind the ball he met the fast bowlers firmly and by lunch he and Cowdrey had taken the score to 53. A good low slip catch sent back Cowdrey but another breakdown put heavy responsibility on Mortimore. When he lost Richardson, who batted well for three and a half hours, Mortimore, after surviving early mistakes, drove and pulled confidently and put on 63 with Trueman before the close at 191 for seven.

England's expectations of a reasonable total were soon dashed next day when Trueman skyed a return catch second ball, which lifted from the pitch that had sweated again through late uncovering after showers. England were out for the addition of 14.

Australia were given another useful start by McDonald and Burke. Both had uneasy moments against Trueman and Tyson, and McDonald received the benefit of the doubt when, after he had glanced Trueman to the fine-leg boundary, his leg bail was noticed to be on the ground. Wright, the bowler's umpire, referred the matter to Townsend, the umpire who had replaced the retired McInnes, and a not out decision was given.

The openers were together for nearly 80 minutes before Burke fell at short square leg and fortunes changed dramatically when Trueman, with the third and fourth balls of his eighth over, had Harvey caught at wicket and O'Neill at gully. McDonald and Mackay struggled against Trueman, but after tea May, to general surprise, reopened with Laker, whose fitness had been in doubt because of a fever and sore throat, and Bailey. With their chief menace removed, the Australians settled down and gained a grip which Trueman, recalled 20 minutes before the close, failed to shake off despite a series of bumpers.

The third day began with Graveney diving at forward short leg and brilliantly catching Mackay, but McDonald, after reaching his century, was let off behind the wicket off Laker when 103. He went on to make another 30 runs and bring his stay to five hours and 40 minutes before he chopped a catch to slip. Instead of the new ball bringing England gains, it suffered severe punishment from Benaud and Grout, who used the hook as his main scoring stroke. England's groundwork during this partnership was often slack and Grout made the most of field-placings which allowed him to exploit his favourite stroke with impunity. Trueman sent back Lindwall and Meckiff in one over, but Benaud, with Rorke last man in, monopolised the strike and Australia reached 351.

England needed 146 to avoid an innings defeat and when Lindwall, without a run on the board, yorked Bailey and beat Grimmett's record the enthusiasm of the Australians and their supporters overflowed. The scenes were repeated when Lindwall had May caught at slip and England, outplayed during one of their worst days of the tour, finished 124 behind with eight wickets standing.

With defeat staring them in the face, England made a great effort on the fourth day. Cowdrey trounced Davidson and hit seven fours before he was run out from a swift throw by O'Neill from point. Benaud, who because of a torn muscle had not intended to bowl before lunch, put himself on just before the interval and beat the painstaking Richardson. Graveney averted the innings defeat, and defended soundly, and with stylish drives and glances passed his previous-best score of the series before Harvey smartly caught him low at slip. Trueman brought the crowd to their feet by taking 14, including three fours, in a Davidson over and by hitting Benaud and Rorke for boundaries. but then Rorke beat him to end the innings.

Australia wanted only 69 to win, and the end of the series soon came on the fifth morning. The light-hearted and jubilant crowd, most of them admitted at half-price, swarmed on to the pitch.

Toss: Australia. **England 205** (P. E. Richardson 68, R. Benaud 4-43) **and 214** (T. W. Graveney 54);
Australia 351 (C. C. McDonald 133, R. Benaud 64, A. T. W. Grout 74, F. S. Trueman 4-92, J. C. Laker 4-93) **and 69-1** (C. C. McDonald 51*).

NOTES BY THE EDITOR
Norman Preston, 1959

The fight for the Ashes held the attention of the cricketing world, and not for the first time it produced a good deal of controversy. England went to Australia with the unofficial title of "world champions". At the time no one could deny that they ranked above all their rivals; yet when they went into action their standard of play bore no relation to their exalted position and they were toppled off their pedestal.

So, after an interval of six years, Australia regained the Ashes and England can look forward to a hard struggle when they attempt to turn the tables in 1961. To the millions of enthusiasts who got up early in the morning to listen to the news from Australia, England's failure came as a bitter disappointment. Defeat can be as honourable as victory when a side has gone down after giving of their best; but during those cold winter months we at home felt that England had been badly let down by the batting and fielding. The bowlers performed admirably, particularly Statham, Trueman and Laker, but apart from May and Cowdrey all the specialist batsmen failed.

Lately, the dice have been loaded far too heavily against the batsmen in England. Consequently the bowlers have not been compelled to toil for their wickets. No wonder things go wrong when our men go abroad. We have destroyed our breed of professional batsmen and at the same time extinguished the leg-spin and googly bowlers, besides producing a generation of fielders who show up poorly in the deep. Moreover, all-rounders like R. Benaud, Australia's new and inspiring captain, and A. K. Davidson are non-existent because of the modern fetish to rely solely on specialists. So England carry a long tail these days.

ENGLAND V AUSTRALIA 1961
Norman Preston

Adapting an almost carefree policy throughout, the 23rd Australian team to visit this country returned home with their main object achieved. They had won the rubber by

Morning, everyone: Richie Benaud, later a leading commentator, captained Australia to victory in 1961. The non-striker is the great England fast bowler Fred Trueman.

victories at Lord's and Old Trafford against one defeat at Headingley, and therefore retained the Ashes. Thirteen years had passed since Australia previously proved victorious in a Test series in England.

The tour was a personal triumph for Richie Benaud, possibly the most popular captain of any overseas team to come to Great Britain. As soon as he arrived Benaud emphasised that he and his men wanted to play attractive cricket wherever they went. Moreover, he stressed that, no matter what their opponents did, his side would not deviate from striving for the type of cricket which would please the onlookers.

At first sight it might appear that Australia won comfortably, but that was not the case. Winning the toss again proved a mixed blessing, as England found when facing South Africa the previous year. Indeed, only once did the side that won the toss win the Test – at Old Trafford where England more or less threw the match away twice on the last day. Since the decision was reached to cover the pitch when play is not in progress in England, there seems to be extra liveliness on the first day to the benefit of pace bowlers. In each of the five Tests, the side which fielded first led on the first innings.

In one respect this was not a happy tour for Benaud. With their refashioned attack which included five bowlers new to English conditions, it was clear that the Australians would rely on two key bowlers, Davidson and Benaud. During the first match at Worcester, Benaud broke down with an inflamed tendon in his right shoulder. For many weeks he underwent specialist treatment and though he did bowl with effect at Old Trafford and the latter stages of the tour, he suffered much pain which prevented him exploiting the leg-break or his most deadly delivery, the googly. At Old Trafford he bowled round the wicket, and relied on the worn bowlers' footholds to turn the ball. Even then, after only a few overs, the pain returned.

While the Australians were severely handicapped through the inability of Benaud to bowl in his normal style, they found batting strength from an unexpected source in Lawry. A tall, lean left-hander, Lawry possessed an extremely sound defence and he not only drove hard but scored freely on the leg side. No one who saw his long innings in the Lord's Test on a difficult pitch will forget his courage. He deserved all the luck which came his way. His value to Australia in the two Tests they won was immense, for he scored 130 and 1 at Lord's and 74 and 102 at Old Trafford.

First Test

At Birmingham, June 8, 9, 10, 12, 13, 1961. Drawn.

Norman Preston

Australia held the initiative for most of the match, but both sides proved weak in bowling and on the last day England, having faced a first-innings deficit of 321, effected a recovery. Personal honours went to Subba Row, who saved England by making 59 and 112 on his debut against Australia, and to Dexter, whose 180 on the last day was a superb innings of stylish, forceful strokes.

This was the first time since 1909 that the sides had met at Edgbaston. Unfortunately, the weather was disappointing. Biting winds and frequent showers spoiled the first and fourth days; play proceeded in light drizzle throughout Saturday and only on Friday and Tuesday did batsmen really enjoy themselves in sunshine. The time lost was seven hours 40 minutes, otherwise a definite result might have been possible.

England, having won the toss in every game of their two previous Test series, were successful for the 11th consecutive time. It was a green pitch and Benaud did not seem to be worried. The game had been in progress only 15 minutes when the first interruption occurred. It proved to be a day of shocks, for between the showers eight wickets fell for 180. Mackay, whose main virtues as a bowler were steadiness in length and direction, dismissed Barrington, Smith and Subba Row in the course of four deliveries split between overs. Between half-past four and the close Mackay bowled without relief for 19–8–32–3. Next day, Cowdrey did not have the pitch rolled, and Australia needed only 20 minutes to capture the two remaining wickets. While the rain-affected pitch encouraged the bowlers, much of the England batting was careless.

Australia, having dismissed England in 85 overs, proceeded to take the lead in only 59, thanks mainly to a fine stand between Harvey and O'Neill. Throughout the long innings, which extended till half-past five on Saturday, Statham alone did justice to his reputation.

Lawry and McDonald gave Australia a steady start and nearly an hour had passed before Illingworth held McDonald low in the gully. After lunch, Lawry was caught by Murray at the second attempt very wide of the off stump. A short ball from Trueman struck O'Neill in the ribs before he had scored, and during his first hour he dealt carefully with some accurate bowling by Statham and Illingworth. Some of the fielding was slow and untidy, but Dexter and Barrington did dazzling work in the covers.

England took the second new ball without unduly troubling the batsmen until at 242 O'Neill chopped the ball on when he intended to late cut. O'Neill took less than two hours making 82 out of the stand of 146, and hit 11 fours. Harvey's only mistake occurred when at 97 he lay back to punish a short-length ball from Statham and was dropped at cover. In the end Harvey was lbw playing back rather casually. He batted splendidly and hit 15 fours. At the close, Australia were 359 for five.

On a miserable cold and wet third day a record Edgbaston crowd of 25,000 saw the Australian batsmen again on top. The pitch remained easy-paced: Simpson, Mackay and Benaud scored freely. Australia's 516 was their highest total in England since 1934.

The weather interfered again on Monday. Persistent rain set in at half-past two when England were 106 for one. Only five minutes remained before lunch when Misson sent a loose ball down the leg side and a poor stroke by Pullar provided a catch for Grout. Subba Row repeated his fighting display of the first day, but just before the rain came Dexter twice edged Davidson to second slip, where Mackay lost sight of the ball against the dark background of the terraced stand.

The sun shone on Tuesday, but the bowlers never received the help they expected from the turf, which played easily all day. England cleared their deficit of 321 for the loss of only three men and stood 80 ahead with six wickets left when the struggle was given up. Dexter gave a glorious exhibition. He excelled with the drive, hitting 31 fours. Australia did not see the back of him until the total stood at 400 and only eight more minutes were left for play. Subba Row stayed just over four hours, hitting 14 fours. His stand with Dexter yielded 109 in under two hours, then Barrington, in a stand of 161, was content to let Dexter push the score along. When all danger had passed Dexter hit with complete abandon and was yards down the pitch when Grout stumped him. So England maintained their record of never having lost a Test at Edgbaston.

Toss: England. **England 195** (R. Subba Row 59, K. D. Mackay 4-57) **and 401-4** (R. Subba Row 112, E. R. Dexter 180); **Australia 516-9 dec.** (W. M. Lawry 57, R. N. Harvey 114, N. C. O'Neill 82, R. B. Simpson 76, K. D. Mackay 64).

Second Test

Leslie Smith

At Lord's, June 22, 23, 24, 26, 1961. Australia won by five wickets.

Australia were well on top until a startling collapse occurred when they went in to get 69 for victory. Even so, the game was over a day and a half early. Almost throughout, batsmen were worried by the fast bowlers on a lively pitch and there were several knocks and bruises, although fortunately none serious. There was talk from the first day of a ridge at the Nursery end, and immediately the match ended MCC called in experts to survey the pitch. They discovered several depressions and MCC stated that they would make an attempt to put things right.

The Australians were without Benaud, because of his damaged shoulder, and Harvey led the side for the first time. As it happened Benaud's slow bowling was hardly missed, for the pacemen controlled the game, taking 33 of the 35 wickets that fell.

Cowdrey retained the captaincy, despite the return of May, and yet again he won the toss. Once more, this did not help England, for they were soon in difficulties. Davidson made the ball rear around the batsmen's ribs when pitching just short of a length, and even off a length at times. Dropped catches looked like being costly. Pullar, when five, offered a simple chance to Burge in the gully, but he added only six. Lawry, at short leg, missed a sharp catch from Dexter, while Subba Row was dropped by Grout.

England appeared to have made the most of these escapes, but in the last five minutes before lunch both men were out at 87. The players were presented to the Queen before the resumption. Five more wickets fell before tea for only 80 runs. May received a fine ovation on his return to Test cricket, but after producing a few delightful strokes he was a victim of one of the many balls which lifted awkwardly. Murray stayed almost an hour, Illingworth fought hard for 70 minutes and Trueman and Statham added 39 for the last wicket, but even so England's total of 206 was disappointing.

In the last hour Australia lost McDonald and Simpson cheaply, but Lawry and Harvey prevented further disaster. When bowling McDonald, Statham took his 200th Test wicket, a feat previously accomplished for England only by Alec Bedser. The second day belonged to Lawry, the tall 24-year-old left-hander from Victoria, who gave a magnificent display of tenacity. Harvey helped Lawry add 75 before being caught at first slip after receiving two successive blows in the body.

Dexter captured the valuable wicket of O'Neill without any undue help from the pitch and with four wickets down for 88 Australia were struggling. Then Burge joined Lawry and they added 95. Lawry, extremely strong on the leg side and solid in defence, completed his maiden Test century in four and three-quarter hours. He was still there when Australia went ahead with four wickets to fall, but was out at 238. He hit 18 fours and did not give a chance, although he was occasionally beaten by Statham.

The last two wickets added 102 and practically ended England's chances of victory. Mackay played another of his stubborn innings, and McKenzie, celebrating his 20th birthday on the Saturday, and Misson showed remarkably good style and skill.

England, 134 behind, made a lively start, scoring 31 in 25 minutes before lunch. Then their troubles began. Subba Row was quickly out, Dexter was bowled off his body, Pullar gave a catch at the wicket and Cowdrey presented an easy catch to cover. They were then 84 for four. May and Barrington improved matters, adding 47 before Grout held a brilliant one-handed catch when May received another rising ball. The arrears were cleared with five wickets left, but practically everything depended on Barrington, who settled down to a determined effort. Murray provided good support and at the close England were 44 on with four wickets left.

These soon went. Barrington added only seven more, and McKenzie ended the innings with three wickets in 12 balls, finishing with five for 37 off 29 overs. Grout held five catches, including his 100th Test victim.

Australia needed only 69 for victory, but suddenly ran into trouble against Statham and Trueman, who made the most of the still-lively pitch. McDonald and Lawry both went at 15 and two more wickets fell at 19. With their leading batsmen gone Australia unexpectedly found themselves on the run. Had Lock held a difficult chance offered by Burge from the last ball before lunch Australia would have been 35 for five.

Burge ended England's faint hopes with a confident display, and although Simpson left with 11 still needed the result was never again in doubt. Burge finished the match with two successive fours off Statham. This was England's first Test defeat against anyone since 1958–59, after 18 matches without a reverse, the most in their history.

Toss: England. **England 206** (A. K. Davidson 5-42) **and 202** (K. F. Barrington 66, G. D. McKenzie 5-37); **Australia 340** (W. M. Lawry 130, K. D. Mackay 54, F. S. Trueman 4-118) **and 71-5**.

CRICKETER OF THE YEAR – BILL LAWRY

Tom Goodman, 1962

A comparatively unknown 24-year-old who came to England with Richie Benaud's 1961 team made the strongest impact of any post-war Australian batsman on his initial tour. He was William Morris Lawry, from Victoria, who as a left-handed opener established himself as successor to Arthur Morris.

Presenting a really straight bat, Lawry combined a well-organised defence with a satisfying, if not very wide, range of strokes, showing readiness to hit the loose ball and extraordinary facility in placing it. He was stout-hearted, stubborn or pugnacious as circumstances prescribed, and had the temperament to carry on unruffled by error.

Lawry was Australia's spinal column in the Second Test at Lord's. This was an indomitable effort of sheer graft under severe pressure with the ball flying about and he was tenacious, painstaking and wonderfully cool. He took bruising blows. True, he made some passes at Trueman and Statham, but he stuck it out for six hours, hitting the loose ball cleanly and placing it well. After the Old Trafford Test W. E. Bowes, a former England pace bowler, wrote that Lawry was one of the best players against fast bowling he had ever seen.

Third Test

Norman Preston

At Leeds, July 6, 7, 8, 1961. England won by eight wickets.

This will be remembered as Trueman's Match: two devastating spells by him caused Australia to collapse. The first occurred immediately after tea on the first day when Australia had reached 183 for two – in the course of six overs, he dismissed five men for 16 runs. His figures were even more remarkable when he came on at 3.40 on Saturday with Australia 98 for two. At once he conceded a single to O'Neill before he again claimed five wickets, this time in 24 deliveries, for no runs. Trueman finished the match with 11 wickets for 88, easily his best in Test cricket.

The game will also be remembered for the controversy over the state of the pitch. In the previous Test the Lord's ridge loaded the dice in favour of the bowlers. This time the batsmen were at the mercy of the bowlers on a whitish-green piebald surface. It had been chemically treated only a few weeks before the contest and never played true, although it did not carry the same physical danger to the batsmen as the one at Lord's. The main trouble was that no one could judge how the ball would behave. Sometimes it came through fast and low; at other times it would check in the broken soft places and stand up so that the batsmen had almost completed their strokes before establishing contact.

Compared with Lord's, both sides were under new management. May took over the England captaincy from Cowdrey, while Benaud considered himself fit enough to return. England were without Statham, suffering from a strain. That appeared to be a crippling blow, but not for the first time the selectors sought a player of experience to face Australia and so they sent for Jackson, the 40-year-old Derbyshire opening bowler.

Benaud was presumed to have gained a big advantage when he won the toss, breaking England's sequence of 12. Jackson soon proved he was worthy of his place.

He bowled throughout the first hour, while Lawry and McDonald scored 33 from 20 overs. England broke the opening stand ten minutes before lunch when Lawry was lbw to Lock. At the interval Australia had every reason to be satisfied with 77 for one.

McDonald had been at the crease for three hours when Lock bowled for the first time at the Kirkstall Lane end and produced a leg-break which left him stranded. Meanwhile, Harvey had become firmly settled. Quick on his feet, he drove cleanly and anything short was pulled vigorously. By tea Australia were 183 for two off 87 overs. Then came the new ball and the transformation. O'Neill faced Trueman, and first ball he was splendidly caught low in the gully by Cowdrey, the stand having yielded 74 in 70 minutes. Harvey also left, beautifully caught off Trueman by Lock at backward short leg. Jackson snapped up Burge and Mackay, and in successive overs Trueman, bowling with his long run and at his fastest through the air, removed Simpson, Benaud (first ball) and Grout before Allen finished the innings by taking McKenzie's off stump. Undoubtedly it was this inspired spell by Trueman which really decided the match. In 90 minutes after tea England had captured the remaining eight wickets for the addition of only 54 runs.

Friday belonged to the England batsmen. The openers took their stand to 54 before Davidson, coming on at the pavilion end with a shortened run, dismissed Subba Row lbw. There followed the biggest stand of this low-scoring match. Cowdrey, at his best for the only time in this series, and Pullar added 86 before Pullar fell to the first ball sent down by Benaud in his second spell.

Whereas most of the Australians had been playing too soon, the England batsmen, until Dexter arrived, effectively used the dead bat. Most of them avoided the drive, which was fatal, but May signalled his arrival with a beauty off McKenzie past extra cover. At one period when Davidson and Benaud shared the attack Cowdrey and May did not score for 20 minutes. Still England were 176 for two at tea. Afterwards Davidson induced a return catch from May who had spent 89 minutes over 26 – clear evidence of the troubles which beset the batsmen.

Cowdrey's was the innings of a master. He hit 11 fours and was trying to sweep a loose ball when it rose and touched his glove. Thereupon Dexter and Barrington survived the remaining half-hour, Barrington giving England the lead by hitting Benaud to the fine-leg boundary. They resumed on Saturday morning four runs ahead with six wickets standing. Dexter, Barrington and Murray rather overdid their caution on this third day. The first half-hour yielded only a single. Davidson (leg-cutters) and Benaud sent down 11 successive maiden overs, but for all his patience Dexter was bowled, having occupied over two hours for 28.

Trueman tried to take the offensive, but after one powerful drive was caught on the boundary. Australia were on top, but Lock launched a severe attack on Benaud. In 17 glorious minutes Lock smote him seven times to the boundary, scoring 30 in three overs before McKenzie returned and trapped him lbw with his second ball. Australia had exceeded expectations in taking the last six England wickets for the addition of only 61 to the overnight total. Davidson's analysis during this period was 14–11–9–3.

England appeared to have missed their chance; their lead was no more than 62 and they had to bat last. Jackson brought fresh hope, for his fifth ball flattened McDonald's leg stump. Harvey again played superbly. Like Cowdrey, he showed his class by keeping his head down and never committing himself too soon. May varied the bowling, but dropped Harvey in the gully off Trueman when he had ten.

Allen's first ball proved a winner. It whipped across for Lawry to edge into Murray's gloves, but Australia progressed satisfactorily when O'Neill joined Harvey. The arrears were cleared without further loss and then at 98 Trueman returned. He began with his full run and his third ball found Harvey playing too soon. That was the beginning of the procession. The secret of Trueman's success was that, after Harvey left, May advised him to bowl off-cutters off his shorter run to a tight leg trap. By this method Trueman compelled the batsmen to play at every ball. He bowled Benaud for a pair, and in 35 minutes the score changed to 109 for eight. After tea, Cowdrey gained Trueman his sixth wicket by diving to his left and holding Davidson at second slip, another brilliant catch. Trueman's exact analysis from the moment he went on at 98 read 7.5–4–5–6.

Already 16 wickets had fallen during this amazing day's cricket when just after five o'clock Pullar and Subba Row began the task of knocking off the 59 runs England needed for victory. They took no liberties. Davidson upset Subba Row's leg stump at 14, but Pullar and Cowdrey shaped confidently. With 40 minutes left England were within 20 of their objective when Cowdrey drove Benaud straight for the only six of the match. Cowdrey was then out but May, whose inspiring captaincy had done so much, was at the crease when Pullar off-drove Benaud for the winning hit.

Toss: Australia. **Australia 237** (C. C. McDonald 54, R. N. Harvey 73, F. S. Trueman 5-58) and 120 (R. N. Harvey 53, F. S. Trueman 6-30), **England 299** (G. Pullar 53, M. C. Cowdrey 93, A. K. Davidson 5-63) and **62-2.**

CRICKETER OF THE YEAR – ALAN DAVIDSON
Richie Benaud, 1962

When a cricketer can make 50 runs in a Test match he immediately becomes a valuable commodity to his side. When he has the ability to add to that five wickets and a brace of catches he is beyond price to his associates and skipper. Such a cricketer is Alan Davidson, born on June 14, 1929. Davidson is a dynamic cricketer! A superb left-hander with both bat and ball. Many of his exploits are legendary among his fellow modern-day players. New Zealand tourists tell of the match at Wairarapa where he took all ten wickets for 29 and then made a brilliant 160 not out to complete the day. The following game he relaxed by merely throwing out a scuttling batsman from the boundary with one stump at which to aim.

Davo played most of his early cricket in the Gosford district of New South Wales. In those far-off days fast bowling was far from his mind. He was one of the unorthodox Fleetwood-Smith variety that seem to appear regularly in Australia. Not until the year after leaving school did he turn to fast-medium bowling, and with such success that he was selected the following season, 1949-50, for the State side.

Who could care for statistics where there is concerned a player of the calibre of Davidson? Team-mates and spectators prefer to recall some of his paralysing bursts with the new ball for Australia and the sight of his batting in full cry, preferably to some slow bowler. "When you see that big right foot coming down the wicket, brother, you duck," is an accurate and revealing recommendation given by an Australian bowler one day when asked how he felt about the carving just administered.

One of his greatest moments in Test cricket was when he bowled Brian Statham to win the Ashes at Manchester in that fantastic Test of 1961. That day the big right foot was well in evidence.

This is thought to be the only case in Wisden *of one of the Five Cricketers of the Year being profiled by another of that year's Five (see below).*

Fourth Test

Leslie Smith

At Manchester, July 27, 28, 29, 31, August 1, 1961. Australia won by 54 runs.

Australia won by 54 runs and made certain of retaining the Ashes. They deserved great credit for fighting back three times when in difficulties, but England, on top for much of the match, disappointed, particularly on the last day. Dropped catches proved costly to England and had an important bearing on the result. The game was intensely keen throughout, and was the best of the series.

Benaud won the toss and batted on a green pitch which helped the faster bowlers appreciably on the first day. Simpson fell in Statham's first over and, switching ends, he also dismissed Harvey at 51. O'Neill, never happy, was struck frequently on the thigh and body when facing Flavell, and the game had to be held up occasionally while he recovered. Once he vomited when at the bowler's end. O'Neill was out when he fell into his wicket in trying a hook.

Flavell took his first Test wicket when he bowled Burge shortly after lunch and Australia, despite the sound batting of Lawry, were 106 for four. A little later rain ended play for the day. Next morning the remaining six wickets fell for 66, Statham and Dexter each claiming three. Lawry's splendid 74 took three hours. Statham thoroughly deserved his five wickets, frequently beating the batsmen with his swing and movement.

England lost Subba Row and Dexter cheaply, but gained the upper hand with a stand of 111 between Pullar and May. By the end of the second day England, with seven wickets left, were only three runs behind, but they ran into trouble first thing on Saturday, losing May and Close with 25 added. May, who hit 14 fours, was caught at first slip when Grout dived and scooped the ball up for Simpson. Barrington and Murray carefully put England back on top by adding 60, then Barrington and Allen put on 86 for the seventh wicket before Simpson restricted England's lead to 177.

Lawry and Simpson knocked off 63 of the arrears before the close, but England should have ended the stand at 38, Subba Row, at second slip, missing Lawry off Trueman. This proved an expensive mistake, for Lawry went on to his second century of the series. Another lapse occurred when Harvey was dropped in the slips by Close when two and he was missed again in the slips, this time by Barrington off Flavell, when 26.

Australia cleared their deficit for the loss of two wickets, but a fine catch by Trueman at backward short leg ended Lawry's stay. Firm drives, powerful hooks and leg-side deflections, brought him most of his 13 fours. Although O'Neill again received a painful blow on the thigh, he fought hard, but England steadily captured wickets. On the last morning Australia lost three men while the total went from 331 for six to 334 for nine. Allen took all three without cost in 15 balls. At that point Australia were only 157 on and England looked to have the game comfortably won, but there developed a splendid last-wicket stand between Davidson and McKenzie. Davidson took 20 in an over off Allen and removed his menace on a pitch taking a fair amount of spin. The other bowlers could make no impression, and 98 were added before the innings closed. This not only made England's task harder in terms of runs, but it took valuable time away from them: they were set 256 in three hours, 50 minutes.

Pullar and Subba Row began with a brisk partnership of 40. Then came a glorious display of controlled hitting by Dexter, which put England right up with the clock. Driving with tremendous power and cutting and hooking splendidly, he took only 84 minutes to score 76, which included one six and 14 fours. His stand with Subba Row produced 110 in that time.

Suddenly the position changed completely. Benaud, bowling round the wicket and pitching into the rough of Trueman's footholds, brought such a collapse that in 20 minutes to tea England virtually lost the game. After getting Dexter caught at the wicket, Benaud bowled May round his legs, had Close, following one drive for six, caught at backward square leg, and bowled the solid Subba Row.

England resumed needing 93 in 85 minutes with only Barrington of their leading batsmen left. When he and Murray fell for the addition of eight all thoughts of an England victory had gone, and it became only a question of whether Australia could finish the match in time. They did so with 20 minutes to spare, gaining their first Test win at Old Trafford since 1902. Benaud claimed his best figures against England. Owing to his shoulder trouble he attempted little spin, content to let the ball do its work on dropping into the rough.

Toss: Australia. **Australia 190** (W. M. Lawry 74, J. B. Statham 5-53)
and 432 (W. M. Lawry 102, R. B. Simpson 51, N. C. O'Neill 67, A. K. Davidson 77*,
D. A. Allen 4-58); **England 367** (G. Pullar 63, P. B. H. May 95, K. F. Barrington 78, R. B. Simpson 4-23)
and 201 (E. R. Dexter 76, R. Benaud 6-70).

AN ENJOYABLE VISIT TO BRITAIN Jack Fingleton, 1962

" – and, departing, leave behind us footprints on the sands of time."

Henry Longfellow himself departed long before Old Trafford became famous. He died in 1882 but the poet's lines had some significance in 1961, when, in the last tumultuous hour of an exciting Test, Richie Benaud pitched to Trueman's footprints and bowled Australia to the telling victory in the series. It was a famous victory for Australia; on the evidence, it was an infamous defeat for England.

Twice, on that last day, England had merely to close its collective fingers on victory. However, in sheer technique and command of a tight situation, there was not in the whole series a better partnership than the last-wicket one that followed between Davidson and McKenzie. Last-wicket partnerships, if of any duration, are generally good for a laugh, but there was nothing like that about this one: no chances; no mis-hits; no struggling to cope. Had Davidson, in his long Test career, not had to spend toiling hours as a fast bowler he would, I am sure, have revived batting memories of Frank Woolley. This is not sacrilege. He drives as Woolley drove – clean, full-blooded strokes of artistry and challenge that cleave the fieldsmen and singe the grass – but long stretches of fast bowling will dim the batting ardour of most.

Davidson, this day, came fresh to his batting task. In one over from Allen, he hit two prodigious sixes and two fours that surged to the boundary. At the other end was McKenzie, turned 20 only a few weeks before yet playing with the cool head of a veteran. For a period the partnership lost character in its indecisiveness and it was fortuitous that McKenzie should have fallen when he did, just on one o'clock. The partnership was 98. England thus wanted 256 runs in 230 minutes. In mid-afternoon, the game was as good as over. England, 150 for one, needed only 106 runs in as many minutes. Back in Australia, with the hour around midnight, most turned off their radios and went to bed, accepting the seemingly inevitable.

Come weal, come woe, no Test side in such a position should ever have lost this game. Dexter, in one of the great attacking innings of the century, was 76. Benaud didn't seem to have a card to play. All that England wanted was just ten more minutes of Dexter but, hereabouts, Benaud played absolutely his last card in the pack. He came around the stumps to pitch on Trueman's marks at the other end. He had to bowl around the stumps to hit the marks at such an angle that the batsmen were forced to play at the ball. Had he bowled over the stumps, the batsmen need not have played with the bat the ball off the roughage.

Dexter went and May came. Usually so reliable and capable, the English captain immediately perpetrated two palpable errors. A swing to fine leg is always risky. It is doubly risky to a ball coming in off the roughage but the biggest error May made was in attempting such a stroke without covering up his line of retreat. His legs didn't protect his stumps – he could not have been lbw at such an angle – and over they went. May hadn't scored. Close came to turn himself and everybody else inside out with some vainglorious swishes to fine leg. He hit Benaud almost straight for six but he swished fine again and was out and then Subba Row fell also. A pall fell over the ground. A game virtually won 20 minutes before tea was lost by tea and all because Benaud bowled round the stumps to Trueman's marks.

So, then, did Trueman's footprints on the Old Trafford pitch leave their imprint on the sands of cricket time. Thus is history made. A little but an important thing with a man like Benaud about.

CRICKETER OF THE YEAR – RICHIE BENAUD

Harry Gee, 1962

If one player, more than any other, has deserved well of cricket for lifting the game out of the doldrums, that man is Richard Benaud. Captain of Australia in four successive and triumphant series to the end of 1961, he has demonstrated to enthusiasts all over the world that the intention to make cricket, particularly Test cricket, attractive and absorbing is every bit as important as skilled technique in batting, bowling and fielding. He has succeeded in his aim to recreate interest in cricket because he loves playing it.

Richie, born at Penrith, 30-odd miles from Sydney, on October 6, 1930, showed a fondness for cricket at an early age. He had his father, a first-grade player for 20 years with the unique feat to his credit of 20 wickets in a match, as instructor and mentor. Benaud senior, a third-generation Australian of Huguenot extraction, bowled legbreaks and so it was natural that he imparted the art of delivering them with the appropriate variations the googly and top-spinner to his son.

The leg-break, the googly and the top-spinner have been used most often, and lately Benaud has added the flipper to his armoury. This is a ball, spun out of the finger-tips, which flashes across from off to leg – in effect an off-spinning top-spinner. The urge to trick the batsman has developed in Benaud the ability to evolve many more ways of getting a man out than his four basic deliveries. Changes of pace and flight, with the ball released from different heights, angles and lengths, have combined to make Benaud a perplexing rival for the best of batsmen. He really likes bowling as it affords him more chance than batting to keep in the thick of a fight he relishes.

Fifth Test

At The Oval, August 17, 18, 19, 21, 22, 1961. Drawn.

Norman Preston

Although the destination of the Ashes had already been decided, victory would have enabled England to draw the rubber. Instead, they made such a poor start they always seemed to be fighting against adversity. Three Australians, O'Neill, Burge and Booth, carried off the main honours, the first two making their first centuries against England. Barrington played two sound innings, and Subba Row, who had announced his retirement, stayed 400 minutes for 137 in ensuring England immunity from defeat.

May won the toss and decided to bat, although he was well aware of the danger of taking first innings at The Oval, where conditions always favour the pace bowlers in the early stages. Within 50 minutes Davidson and Gaunt had three wickets down for 20. Then May and Dexter played soundly until in the last over before lunch Dexter tried to cut a high ball and gave a catch to Grout. There followed the only real stand of a dismal innings, May and Barrington by cautious methods adding 80. The running between the wickets was sluggish. Murray alone showed the same sense of urgency to get the first single quickly as did all the Australians later.

There was a rare duel between the rival captains. May appeared to be the master and produced some superb strokes, lifting Benaud straight into the vacant deep until trying to force him over mid-on he skyed to deep point. May occupied just over three hours for his excellent 71 and hit 11 fours. Australia took the new ball in the 87th over and proceeded to remove Barrington, Murray and Lock, so that the end of the first day found England 210 for eight, having averaged only 35 an hour. Next day Australia passed England's 256 in four hours 20 minutes, having taken two and a half hours less.

Statham trapped Lawry second ball, Murray holding a fine catch as he leapt towards the slips. Then Flavell yorked Harvey and both bowlers looked menacing while the score rose to 49 at lunch. No sooner had the game been resumed than, with O'Neill only 19, Barrington dropped him at slip off Statham and, as in the previous Test, this proved a costly mistake. O'Neill went on to give a dazzling display while Burge played the sheet anchor. Such was O'Neill's brilliance in the next hour that he made 67 from 74 balls while Burge confined himself to 13 runs. During the whole of this scintillating partnership of 123, O'Neill claimed 83 from 110 balls compared with Burge's 40 off 126.

Finally, O'Neill hit at everything until M. J. Stewart, fielding for Cowdrey, intercepted a fierce cover-drive. O'Neill's excellent 117 included 14 fours. A sheer joy to watch, O'Neill pointed his left shoulder to the bowler and time and again danced down the pitch to drive. Now Burge seized the initiative. He excelled with the hook and sweep and was particularly severe on Allen. May did not take the new ball at 200 but waited an hour until Australia reached 265 before he recalled Statham and Flavell and by that time Booth was also established, Australia finishing the second day with 290 for four.

Despite two breaks for showers, Australia continued to score freely on the third day. Booth, a stylist, drove beautifully, hitting 12 fours. England now paid the penalty for not having used the new ball earlier. The crowd cheered Benaud all the way to the wicket and Burge maintained his onslaught until he was ninth to leave, having hit 22 fours in 181. Australia held a lead of 238 and England were thankful that their openers survived the final 50 minutes on Saturday.

Rain reduced play on Monday to three hours. The loss of Pullar and Dexter first thing for only a single seemed to have destroyed England's chance of survival, but Subba Row, although handicapped by a groin injury, saw them through the crisis. By adopting a more venturesome policy and giving the loose ball the punishment it deserved, both Subba Row and May set a good example. Despite a severe drenching the pitch never became treacherous and May drove superbly, treating Mackay with disdain until a lofted drive was well taken by O'Neill at deep mid-off despite colliding with Benaud. Mackay bowled craftily for two hours.

With Barrington hooking and cutting well England were 155 for four on Monday evening. Still 83 behind, they faced another hard struggle on the last day and that defeat was avoided was due mainly to Subba Row and Barrington, who took the score to 245 for four by lunch, a lead of seven. Their vigilant partnership yielded 172 before Subba Row presented a return catch to Benaud who had missed him off Davidson at silly mid-on when he was 100. Subba Row hooked Mackay for six and also hit 15 fours.

England became anxious again when Benaud accounted for Barrington, O'Neill taking a running catch at mid-on, and Mackay had Lock caught at short leg. England, with three wickets left, were only 45 in front. Murray and Allen again showed their ability as batsmen and their stand of 72 removed all danger. England finished 132 ahead with two wickets in hand. Barrington was so restrained in the later stages that his innings occupied four and three-quarter hours. Grout, by taking six catches finished the series with 21 victims, a record for a wicket-keeper in an England–Australia rubber.

Toss: England. **England 256** (P. B. H. May 71, K. F. Barrington 53, A. K. Davidson 4-83)
and 370-8 (R. Subba Row 137, K. F. Barrington 83, K. D. Mackay 5-121);
Australia 494 (N. C. O'Neill 117, P. J. P. Burge 181, B. C. Booth 71, D. A. Allen 4-133).

AUSTRALIA v ENGLAND 1962–63   Leslie Smith

England went to Australia under the captaincy of E. R. Dexter – and with the Duke of Norfolk as manager – with two main objectives: to regain the Ashes, and to provide cricket capable of recapturing public enthusiasm, as West Indies did two years earlier. They achieved neither, but in each case the margin between success and failure was so narrow that the tour could well have gone down as one of the most interesting for many years. Unfortunately, when everything seemed set for a thrilling climax, things began to go wrong, and in the end everyone felt there had been a big let-down which tended to obscure all that had gone before.

The situation could have been saved had the last Test been fought out in a bold, imaginative way. The position could not have been better for a great game of cricket. England were expected to go all out for the victory which would have given them the rubber; it was not anticipated that Australia would be satisfied with a drawn series, even though it enabled them to retain the Ashes. As it happened the final game turned out to be the dullest and by far the worst of the five. The Sydney ground must be held responsible to a large extent. The pitch was too slow; the square, devoid of grass in many places, tended to check the ball immediately it hit the ground, and until late in the match the outfield was not cropped closely enough. All this led to extremely slow scoring, but the players must also take a fair proportion of the blame.

The general opinion before the Tests began was that the batting would be far too strong for the bowling. This turned out to be incorrect. Except for occasional inspired bowling spells, neither attack looked formidable, but the batsmen rarely established a mastery and only one total of 400 was recorded in the series. It was difficult to separate the sides in batting and bowling, but once more Australia held the advantage in fielding, and this might well have cost England the rubber.

Barrington showed his remarkable consistency abroad. He again hit three centuries in the Tests, and played in the same solid way, rarely producing anything exciting, but showing an excellent temperament and the ability to take runs off any attack. Without his steadiness, the team might well have been in trouble on a number of occasions. Titmus rivalled Barrington as the success of the tour. Allen was originally regarded as the No. 1 spinner, but Titmus took over that role, and as the tour progressed he became a real personality whether bowling his cleverly controlled off-breaks, showing his fighting qualities as a batsman or revealing his keenness in the field.

First Test

At Brisbane, November 30, December 1, 3, 4, 5, 1962. Drawn.

For the first time, an England–Australia Test at Brisbane failed to produce a definite result. Australia eventually went close to winning, but England deserved to draw for their good fighting performance.

Benaud won the toss, but with some moisture in the pitch Australia began badly against Trueman, who, in his 50th Test, bowled with sustained hostility. He took three wickets and also held two catches, having a hand in five of the first six wickets to fall. Booth and Mackay led the recovery. By the close of the first day Australia were 321 for seven, the seventh wicket producing 103. With the pitch easing Booth played a lovely fluent innings, full of neat drives, cuts and glides. His 112 included 14 fours. Next morning, Mackay and Benaud took their partnership to 91, as the last four wickets added 210.

Pullar and Sheppard, both missed early, gave England a useful start with 62, but the appearance of Benaud changed the situation. He dismissed both, and although Dexter played a fine innings of 70, including ten fours, he also bowled him before the close when England were 169 for four. England made a good fight for the lead on the third day. Smith, sent in as an overnight stopgap, helped add 51, then Barrington and Parfitt put on 77. Further resistance came from Parfitt and Titmus, but England finished 15 behind. Despite their care most of the time several were out to rash strokes. Benaud finished with six wickets.

The pitch became extremely slow and Australia were never able to score as quickly as they hoped in the second innings. Simpson and Lawry occupied three hours over an opening stand of 136, but brisk fifties came from O'Neill and Harvey. Lawry's 98 took four hours 20 minutes. Benaud declared first thing on the last morning, setting England 378 to win in six hours. They never stayed with the clock, but did well up to a point. Pullar, missed at the wicket when 13, helped Sheppard put on 114, the first opening three-figure stand by England in Australia since 1946–47.

Dexter, not quite so dominant at first, later hit fiercely and missed a century by one run. He hit 13 fours. He and Barrington put on 66 at a run a minute, but the new ball curbed them, and when Dexter, Barrington and Parfitt left in quick succession Australia had a chance of winning. Benaud crowded nine men round the bat in the hope of taking the last four wickets in 27 minutes, but Titmus and Knight held out.

Toss: Australia. **Australia 404** (R. B. Simpson 50, B. C. Booth 112, K. D. Mackay 86*, R. Benaud 51) **and 362-4 dec.** (R. B. Simpson 71, W. M. Lawry 98, N. C. O'Neill 56, R. N. Harvey 57); **England 389** (E. R. Dexter 70, K. F. Barrington 78, P. H. Parfitt 80, R. Benaud 6-115) **and 278-6** (G. Pullar 56, D. S. Sheppard 53, E. R. Dexter 99).

Second Test

At Melbourne, December 29, 31, 1962, January 1, 2, 3, 1963. England won by seven wickets.

England won with an hour and a quarter to spare after a thrilling struggle throughout. Only on the last day did one side take command. The rest of the match was a tremendous battle for supremacy with each side gaining and losing the initiative several times.

Australia batted badly on the first day, losing their first six wickets for 164 on a good pitch, including O'Neill, Harvey and Lawry in the course of 15 balls. In hot, humid conditions, the bowlers could not follow up their success, but England were well satisfied with a score of 263 for seven. Next morning the last three wickets went for 53.

When Sheppard fell to the fourth ball and Pullar was out at 19, England looked in trouble, but Cowdrey and Dexter shared an excellent stand of 175. Dexter, for the second innings running, was out in the nineties. Cowdrey, missed off a hard chance at slip when 56, had 94 at the close. He and Barrington carried their stand to 60 next day, but both were out in successive overs. England's last six wickets fell for 77, and the lead was restricted to 13, with Davidson proving too much for the later batsmen.

Australia's hopes of making a big second-innings total were soon shattered by Trueman. Bowling extremely fast, in a fine fourth over he dismissed Simpson and O'Neill with successive balls. When Harvey was run out and Burge bowled, Australia were 69 for four. Lawry and Booth took the score to 105 by the close and stayed together until the last ball before lunch next day. They were extremely slow and added only 92 in three hours. Lawry batted just over six hours for 57, rarely trying an attacking stroke. The pitch was slow, but this did not excuse the refusal to make shots. Dexter showed wise tactics in holding back Trueman for the tailenders and with the new ball he caused another breakdown. Booth completed his second century in successive Tests with the last man in and batted six hours 48 minutes for 103.

England, needing 234 to win, lost Pullar overnight to a wonderful catch by Jarman, who held a leg glide at full stretch. Next morning, England gained full control. Sheppard and Dexter shared a fine stand of 124, then Sheppard and Cowdrey added 104. Sheppard, thrown out when going for the winning run, amply redeemed some indifferent fielding and his failure to score in the first innings. He drove exceptionally well for five hours. The Australian bowlers failed to take a wicket on the last day, but Sheppard was dropped at the wicket when 78 and Cowdrey missed at slip when seven.

England thoroughly deserved their first victory in Australia since 1954-55, showing better tactics and more aggression. Only in ground fielding did Australia match them. The attendance reached 247,831, with almost 70,000 present on the first day. The receipts of £A68,018 were a record for any match in Australia.

Toss: Australia. **Australia 316** (W. M. Lawry 52, F. J. Titmus 4-43) **and 248** (W. M. Lawry 57, B. C. Booth 103, F. S. Trueman 5-62); **England 331** (E. R. Dexter 93, M. C. Cowdrey 113, A. K. Davidson 6-75) **and 237-3** (D. S. Sheppard 113, E. R. Dexter 52, M. C. Cowdrey 58*).

Third Test

At Sydney, January 11, 12, 14, 15, 1963. Australia won by eight wickets.

Australia won with more than a day and a half remaining. Until England collapsed badly at the start of their second innings the game was fought out evenly and a fine struggle seemed in prospect.

Dexter won the toss for the first time, and after Sheppard left at four, England batted carefully. Pullar added 61 with Dexter, then 67 with Cowdrey. Pullar, on a slow pitch and outfield, found it difficult to get the ball away but stayed almost three and a half hours. The brightest batting came from Cowdrey and Barrington, who put on 69, taking the total to 201 for three. England looked well placed, but Davidson and Simpson caused a collapse with four quick wickets. Titmus and Trueman took the total to 256 by the close and next morning increased their partnership to 51. Simpson finished with easily his best Test figures.

A fine diving leg-side catch by Murray quickly accounted for Lawry, but he hurt his shoulder while falling and a little later left the field. Parfitt went behind the stumps for the rest of the match. Simpson and Harvey put Australia well on top with a stand of 160, although Harvey was never comfortable and gave chances when two and 32. Titmus ended the partnership and put England back in the game with a remarkable spell of four wickets for five runs in 58 deliveries. He turned the ball only a little, but baffled the batsmen by clever variation of pace, flight and length.

Australia ended the second day at 212 for five, Simpson having batted four hours. Titmus remained menacing after the weekend, and Australia were only one ahead when the ninth wicket fell. They turned the tables with a stand of 39 between Shepherd and Guest, and never again lost control. Titmus's figures were the best by an England slow bowler in Australia since J. C. White's eight for 126 at Adelaide in 1928-29.

Australia, 40 ahead, virtually won the game when Davidson, in a magnificent spell with the new ball, dismissed Pullar, Dexter and Sheppard in 25 balls. Cowdrey fell to Benaud's first delivery, which lifted, and England were still three behind with four wickets gone. Simpson, who had a fine all-round match, helped by holding three successive catches at first slip. Nobody could stop the rot and at the end of the third day England were 86 for six. Murray, handicapped by his damaged shoulder, made no attempt to score and batted 74 minutes before obtaining his first run. He stayed 100 minutes in all and took out his bat for three. The four remaining wickets went for 18.

Australia needed only 65 to win, and, despite a short delay through rain, the game was over 36 minutes after lunch. When the total was 63 hundreds of youngsters, thinking the match had ended, swarmed over the ground chasing souvenirs and had to be sent back by the police and the umpires. Three hours later persistent rain set in and continued for most of the night and next morning. Benaud's two wickets enabled him to become the leading Australian wicket-taker, beating Lindwall's 228.

Toss: England. **England 279** (G. Pullar 53, M. C. Cowdrey 85, A. K. Davidson 4-54, R. B. Simpson 5-57) **and 104** (A. K. Davidson 5-25); **Australia 319** (R. B. Simpson 91, R. N. Harvey 64, B. K. Shepherd 71*, F. J. Titmus 7-79) **and 67-2.**

Fourth Test
At Adelaide, January 25, 26, 28, 29, 30, 1963. Drawn.

Several factors contributed to the stalemate in this match, but to some extent it was due to a fear by either side of losing. In bringing back Mackay, who had not taken a wicket, and leaving out a specialist bowler, the Australian selectors appeared to be defensive-minded even before the start, probably banking everything on winning – or at least not losing – the last Test at Sydney, where England had played badly.

In hot, partly humid weather, Australia began by losing Simpson and Lawry for 16. A third wicket should have fallen at 21, Harvey being missed off successive balls from Illingworth at slip and backward square leg. He was dropped at slip again off Dexter when 26, and these errors may well have cost England victory. Harvey went on to an excellent 154, hitting one five and 18 fours with a lovely array of strokes. O'Neill at last struck his best form, taking only two hours 50 minutes over his century (13 fours). He and Harvey added 194 at faster than one a minute. Dexter dismissed both near the close of the first day, when Australia finished at 322 for five.

The temperature was in the nineties next day when the last four wickets fell for 71. When dismissing Shepherd, Statham took his 237th wicket, the most by any Test bowler, beating A. V. Bedser's 236. England soon lost Pullar. Barrington, going in No. 3 instead of Dexter, made a shaky start against Davidson. He took four fours off successive balls from him, but three were snicks which might have gone anywhere.

Australia's chance of victory virtually disappeared when Davidson broke down with a pulled muscle in his fourth over and could not bowl again. Sheppard and Barrington added 67 for the second wicket, but with McKenzie bowling splendidly England struggled. The fourth wicket fell at 119, but Dexter rallied the side with powerful hitting which brought him two sixes and six fours in 50 by the end of the second day. Rain prevented play before lunch next morning. Dexter fell early, but Titmus played a sound innings and Trueman hit 38 out of 52 added for the ninth wicket. Bad light ended play 45 minutes early with England 328 for nine. Three were added next morning and Australia led by 62.

They again began badly, but Simpson and Booth added 133. Dexter dismissed both in one over and a little later disposed of Shepherd. At the end of the fourth day Australia, with four wickets left, led by 287, and Benaud, without Davidson and on a still-perfect pitch, concentrated on saving the game. He declined a declaration, and when the innings ended just on lunch-time England needed 356 at 89 an hour.

Sheppard, who, like Illingworth, had developed throat trouble and was a doubtful starter, opened but failed, and when Pullar left at four there were visions of a collapse. Barrington and Cowdrey removed this with a fine partnership of 94, and although Dexter soon fell, Barrington and Graveney shared an unbroken stand of 101. Barrington, in fine form, batted three and three-quarter hours, hitting two sixes and 16 fours.

Toss: Australia. **Australia 393** (R. N. Harvey 154, N. C. O'Neill 100) **and 293** (R. B. Simpson 71, B. C. Booth 77, F. S. Trueman 4-60); **England 331** (K. F. Barrington 63, E. R. Dexter 61, F. J. Titmus 59*, G. D. McKenzie 5-89) **and 223-4** (K. F. Barrington 132*).

CRICKETER OF THE YEAR – FRED TITMUS

Harry Gee, 1963

Frederick John Titmus, the Middlesex batsman and off-spin bowler, earned his trip to Australia last winter after many seasons of success as one of the most consistent all-rounders in English cricket. His achievement in 1962 of completing the double of 1,000 runs and 100 wickets for the seventh time gave him high place in the modern records of such performances.

Titmus was born on November 24, 1932, in Kentish Town, almost on the doorstep of Lord's. Originally, he preferred batting, but he had learned to bowl an off-break fairly well by the time he left school at 16. Sport was uppermost in his mind. He wrote to Lord's for a trial, received an invitation to attend and, after bowling a dozen balls, he was taken on the MCC groundstaff.

Concentrating almost entirely on off-breaks in recent years, Titmus has acquired a reputation as a very skilful bowler who does not have to rely upon power of spin for unsettling rivals. He knows how to bowl short of a length to discourage quick scoring, but he far prefers to pit his wits against opponents by keeping the ball up to them and introducing subtle changes of pace and flight for their discomfiture.

Fifth Test

At Sydney, February 15, 16, 18, 19, 20, 1963. Drawn.

The deciding match of the series, far from being the exciting contest expected, turned out to be a dull, lifeless game which did immense harm to cricket, particularly in Australia. Much of the blame can be traced to the ground, but the players must be held responsible to a fair extent. Little effort was made to overcome the conditions. On most of the days there was a good deal of barracking and the game ended with booing and slow hand-clapping.

Dexter won the toss, but Cowdrey failed. Sheppard provided the medium-paced Hawke with his first Test wicket, but Barrington and Dexter prevented a collapse, adding 90. Extremely slow batting marked the opening day, England scoring only 195 for five. Barrington's soundness proved valuable. He batted five hours 20 minutes for 101, his second successive Test century, but hit only four fours.

England's later batsmen did well on the second day. Trueman, promoted, stayed 110 minutes without hitting a boundary. The slow square and matted outfield plus the dead pitch made forcing strokes extremely difficult. Australia finished the day at 74 for three. Only three fours were hit all day. With the pitch taking some spin, they were expected to struggle. Instead, O'Neill and Burge showed some of the best batting of the match and added 109 for the fourth wicket. O'Neill used his strength to force the ball away until Graveney, at short mid-on, held a great falling catch. Burge, missed at the wicket when 63, batted solidly. Rain and bad light cut 70 minutes off the playing time.

Australia, 285 for six at the close, added another 64, mainly through Benaud, and finished 28 ahead. Burge made 103 in five and a half hours and hit nine fours. Titmus again showed his liking for the Sydney pitch, taking five wickets. Illingworth opened the second innings instead of Cowdrey, and he and Sheppard began with 40, England's best opening stand since the First Test. Barrington again showed sound form and with Sheppard put on 97. By the close England were 137 ahead with seven wickets left, and on the last morning they tried hard to make up for time lost. Barrington fell when six short of his second century of the match, but he hit only two fours. Cowdrey, happier in the middle order, helped him add 94.

Dexter declared at lunch, setting Australia 241, but under the conditions it was a massive task. Trueman dismissed Simpson in his first over then left the field with muscle trouble. When Allen sent back O'Neill and Booth in one over, Australia gave up any slight hopes of victory and played to save the game. Lawry carried caution to the extreme and, despite jeers, kept going four hours for 45. Burge did better, and their unbroken stand produced 82. Harvey, in his last Test, did not do well with the bat, but equalled the Test record with six catches. Davidson, also playing his final Test, had the distinction of taking a wicket with his last ball.

For the first time three matches between the countries in Australia were drawn, and never before, when five games had been played, was the series undecided. During the match Trueman and Benaud equalled Bedser's 236 Test wickets, only Statham being ahead of them.

Toss: England. **England 321** (K. F. Barrington 101) **and 268-8 dec.** (D. S. Sheppard 68, K. F. Barrington 94, M. C. Cowdrey 53); **Australia 349** (N. C. O'Neill 73, P. J. P. Burge 103, R. Benaud 57, F. J. Titmus 5-103) **and 152-4** (P. J. P. Burge 52*).

NOTES BY THE EDITOR
Norman Preston, 1963

How pleasant it would have been for me, as an Englishman, had I been able in this 100th edition of *Wisden* to congratulate E. R. Dexter's team upon bringing back the Ashes and to praise both sides for giving the Australian public the same exciting type of cricket as was played by the West Indies team there in 1960-61.

Instead, the situation is entirely different. England have not regained the Ashes and much of the cricket fell below expectations. Too much emphasis was put on avoiding defeat in preference to thinking in terms of victory from the very first ball.

England, in sharing the rubber, did better than many of the experts predicted. Unreliable fielding, more than anything else, let the side down, far too many vital catches being dropped. After the overthrow of Peter May's team in 1958–59, the selectors stated that special consideration would be given to first-rate fielders. On this count, one wonders why Stewart, Lock and Sharpe were left at home. These are three of the best close catchers in present-day cricket and all were on the short list for the tour.

The selectors did not have a simple task. Since the days of Sir Leonard Hutton and Cyril Washbrook, England have not possessed a pair of consistently reliable opening batsmen and very seldom has the side received a good start to an innings. More recently there has been a dearth of genuine fast bowlers to support Statham and Trueman, and the leg-break and googly trundler of the Richie Benaud type seems to have no place in modern English cricket under the existing lbw law.

ENGLAND V AUSTRALIA 1964

Norman Preston

Opinions differed considerably concerning the quality of the 24th Australian team to visit the United Kingdom, but the fact remained that R. B. Simpson and his men achieved their objective in that they and returned home with the Ashes, which their country had held since 1958-59. The retirement of Benaud, Harvey and Davidson had certainly left the Australian ranks rather bare and, indeed, it could be said they arrived in England with an experimental side, eight of the 17 being in a land strange to them.

That the side fared as well as they did was due mainly to Simpson. He proved a shrewd captain as well as an outstanding all-round cricketer. Although he began the tour by opening the batting with Lawry, he soon realised that he was deficient in spin bowling. Consequently, he dropped himself to No. 6 for the first two Tests, but as Redpath accomplished little Simpson was compelled to go in first again.

Potentially, this Australian team was well equipped with batsmen, but there was a general lack of certainty when they came to the Tests. This was partly due to the wet weather as well as to the stubbornness of Lawry and Redpath, who surrendered the initiative to the England bowlers. The three most attractive batsmen were Booth, the vice-captain Burge and O'Neill. A true stylist, Booth gave some glorious displays without distinguishing himself in the Tests apart from his 98 at Manchester.

McKenzie, by taking 29 wickets in the five Tests, equalled the record number by an Australian in England – Clarrie Grimmett in 1930. Hawke virtually denied England any chance of drawing the rubber when on the first day of the Oval Test he played the main part in dismissing England for 182 by taking six wickets.

First Test

Norman Preston

At Nottingham, June 4, 5, 6, 8, 9, 1964. Drawn.

To the disappointment of thousands of people, this match was spoilt by rain. Nearly half the playing time, including the whole of Saturday when the crowd numbered 25,000, was lost to the weather. The match began badly for England. An hour before the start Edrich was pronounced unfit with a twisted ankle after treading on a ball at practice the previous afternoon. As no reserve batsman had been chosen, England were left with five specialist bowlers and Titmus was deputed to open.

The first shower of the day held up play for 22 minutes. Then Boycott, appearing in his first Test, faced McKenzie, who bowled downwind from the pavilion end throughout the shortened morning session. Rain intervened ten minutes before lunch and put an end to cricket for the day. Corling, also in his first Test, and Hawke shared the harder task of maintaining a lively pace against the wind. Titmus stayed with Boycott for an hour, surviving the occasional short lifting ball from Corling.

Just before the Duke of Edinburgh piloted his helicopter round the ground, the Australians raised the biggest cheer of this brief day's cricket for a genuine act of sportsmanship. Grout could have run out Titmus when Boycott placed Hawke towards midon and both batsmen dashed for a quick single. Hawke dived for the ball and in the process knocked Titmus over from behind. Titmus was far from home when the ball landed in the wicket-keeper's gloves, but Grout let him reach the crease and England were credited with a single. Justice promptly asserted itself, for in the same over Titmus was caught low by Redpath at second slip. No sooner had Dexter arrived than more rain terminated cricket for the day.

On Friday, when the rain returned after tea, England gave a tenacious and gallant display on treacherous turf while reaching 216 for eight. Boycott took the honours with 48 and Cowdrey, Barrington, Sharpe, Parks and Allen all played well in preventing Australia achieving an absolute breakthrough. The rain which ruined the opening day was responsible for a most absorbing struggle in conditions made for the bowlers.

Saturday was most exasperating. The sun shone warmly until breakfast and it was like the old days of Larwood and Voce to see the people of Nottingham wildly excited at the prospect of a really grand tussle. The ground was filled, but at 11 o'clock rain set in and not a ball could be bowled until Monday.

Timid batsmanship led Australia into trouble on the fourth day, when no time was lost to the weather. Although England were inclined to bowl loosely and missed vital catches, they gained a lead of 48. Dexter declared first thing in the morning and by lunch four Australian wickets had fallen for 85. Simpson saved his side by staying two and a quarter hours, showing marked skill in dealing with Allen's off-spin.

As Boycott cracked a finger in his left hand while fielding, Dexter opened the second innings with Titmus. He hit so fearlessly that by the close he made 56, including nine fours, of an unbroken stand of 71. Different conditions prevailed early on the last day. For the first time in the match the sun shone with real warmth and the outfield, freshly mown, was quite fast, so that for a change the batsmen gained full value for every forcing stroke. Simpson employed a defensive field and with Dexter falling early to a brilliant low catch by O'Neill at cover, England failed to push the score along. Cowdrey spent two hours over 33.

Finally, Dexter set Australia 242 in three and a quarter hours. Coldwell soon ran out Lawry, but Trueman, who employed five slips, preferred to test O'Neill with a series of harmless bouncers. O'Neill hooked each of the first four balls of Trueman's second over for four. Later, O'Neill retired with a bruised hand, but just as the match reached a most interesting stage, rain returned and again swamped the ground.

Toss: England. **England 216-8 dec. and 193-9 dec.** (E. R. Dexter 68, G. D. McKenzie 5-53); **Australia 168** (R. B. Simpson 50) **and 40-2.**

Second Test

At Lord's, June 18, 19, 20, 22, 23, 1964. Drawn.

Leslie Smith

Again, roughly half the game was lost because of the weather and although at one stage there seemed a slight chance of a result, the rain finally won. Not a ball could be bowled on either the first or second days and it ended the match just before 2.30 on the fifth day. Although no rain fell on the second day, the pitch had received such a drenching that play was impossible.

Cricket began on time on Saturday when Dexter won the toss and put Australia in. They struggled all day and were dismissed for 176, England replying with 26 for one. The pitch was never really difficult, but the faster bowlers were able to get some movement through the air and off the ground. Redpath and O'Neill looked like making a stand for the second wicket, but Dexter had O'Neill caught at long leg off a long-hop and followed by dismissing Burge. The only reasonable innings came from Veivers, who made his first Test fifty and showed that conditions were not as bad as some of the other batsmen suggested. Trueman bowled with much more control than at Nottingham and, although below his former pace, he was never mastered.

With Boycott unfit, Dexter offered to go in first as a temporary measure, but the move failed. He was yorked second ball. The fourth day belonged to Edrich, who had the satisfaction of scoring his first Test century, completing it shortly after the Queen and Prince Philip arrived just before tea. Without Edrich, England would have been in serious trouble, for only two other men reached 20. Cowdrey and Barrington fell early and England were 42 for three. Parfitt, who had earlier held two magnificent catches, helped Edrich add 41 and Sharpe, who hit seven fours in 35, shared a stand of 55. Edrich received more useful support from Titmus during a seventh-wicket partnership of 57. Eventually eighth out, Edrich batted just over six and a quarter hours and his 120 included two sixes off Simpson and nine fours. England gained a lead of 70.

Australia lost Lawry while scoring 49 overnight and when their fourth wicket fell at 148 with nearly four hours left they were in some danger, especially with the spinners getting a little help from the pitch. Dexter surprisingly kept Trueman on for 65 minutes and Coldwell for 100 despite the fact that conditions were against fast bowling. When he eventually turned to spin the Australians were worried. Gifford, slow left-arm, did reasonably well on his Test debut, although his habit of bowling from wide out cost him a few no-balls for stepping outside the crease. Burge hit forcefully for 59, once lifting Coldwell over long-on for six, but Redpath scarcely made an aggressive stroke. He stayed over three hours for 36 and did not add a run during his last 53 minutes.

The rain returned shortly after lunch and although it stopped late in the day bad light prevented a resumption.

Toss: England. **Australia 176** (T. R. Veivers 54, F. S. Trueman 5-48) **and 168-4** (P. J. P. Burge 59);
England 246 (J. H. Edrich 120, G. E. Corling 4-60).

Third Test

Norman Preston

At Leeds, July 2, 3, 4, 6, 1964. Australia won by seven wickets.

Australia won with more than a day to spare. At last the weather was fine throughout and, despite a period of tremendous anxiety, they finished easy winners of a contest which will always be known as Burge's Match. Many considered that England lost their chance after tea on Friday when Titmus was bowling superbly and seven wickets were down for 187. Dexter took the second new ball and relied on Trueman and Flavell to demolish the tail. At that stage, Burge was 38, but Trueman fed him with a generous supply of long-hops and not only did Burge finish with 160, but the last three wickets put on 211. Australia gained a valuable lead of 121 and never looked back.

The honours went to Australia on the opening day after Dexter had won the toss for the third time running. Prospects seemed bright for England when before lunch they scored 112 for the loss of their opening pair. Dexter set England a splendid example by his daring strokeplay, but Simpson handled his attack astutely and the fielding reached the highest Australian standards. Eight catches – some quite brilliant – were held and none was missed. The bowling honours went to Hawke and McKenzie, who attained steady pace and accuracy and were never found wanting in stamina. Australia achieved their most deadly work in the 70 minutes after lunch, when they disposed of Dexter, Barrington and Taylor. Hawke's round-the-wicket attack perplexed several batsmen, an exception being Parks who never looked in difficulty and drove especially well, but after tea Hawke ran through the tail with the new ball.

Next day, Trueman and Flavell were unable to make any impression and with Simpson and Lawry making their best start so far with a stand of 50 it seemed almost certain that England's 268 would be passed without much difficulty. Timid batsmanship by Redpath led Australia into trouble, and although the pitch did not encourage spin at this stage Titmus and Gifford managed to gain control. Titmus proved such a model of accuracy that he bowled from 1.20 until 5.50, his figures being 29–17–27–3, and while he operated Australia's fortunes swayed from 95 for one to 187 for seven.

Lawry served Australia splendidly for three hours. He hit ten fours before Redpath called him for a sharp single and Boycott returned the ball in a flash from third man to the bowler's end. It was on Lawry's departure that Burge began his valuable display. At this stage Titmus's figures were 10–8–3–0 and Australia had mustered only four runs in half an hour.

Even Burge needed 20 minutes to open his score. He broke free with a powerful straight-drive at the end of a spell by Gifford during which he conceded only 16 runs in 11 overs. Booth, Cowper (in his first Test), Veivers and McKenzie all failed and so at 187 Trueman took the new ball. Australia were on their knees, but in the next seven overs Burge and Hawke helped themselves to 42 runs, and proceeded to add 105. At the end of the second day, Australia's had 283 for eight with Burge 100, having excelled with the cut, hook and drive.

Grout is no stranger to helping Australia through a crisis and on Saturday morning he promptly showed Trueman that he could punish the long-hop as effectively as his partner. Three of these he despatched to the boundary when Trueman's first two overs cost 14. The Burge-Grout partnership produced 89 and England needed a third new ball before a very fine catch by the substitute Alan Rees (Glamorgan) at mid-wicket ended Burge's great innings. Burge, whose display was reminiscent of S. J. McCabe's 232 at Trent Bridge in 1938, batted five and a quarter hours and hit 24 fours.

Little went right for England in their second innings. Boycott for the third time in his three Test knocks was caught by Simpson at first slip (a very fine catch) off Corling. Parfitt had a knuckle broken first ball, whereupon Edrich and Barrington battled bravely until tea when England were 88 for one. A careless stroke to the first ball afterwards resulted in Edrich being taken on the leg side, but Barrington carried on with commendable enterprise. Dexter, strangely subdued, contributed only 17 in 75 minutes and on his departure Barrington, too, decided to concentrate solely on defence. With six minutes left he was lbw, so England finished with 157 for four – 36 runs ahead. They had plenty of time during the weekend to dwell on where they went wrong and plan a recovery. It was reckoned they needed a lead of about 200, but they added no more than 72 on Monday, so Australia needed only 109 for victory.

Lawry soon went, but time was on Australia's side and they had no need to hurry. Apart from a break of two overs which allowed him to switch ends, Titmus bowled through the innings and at tea, when Australia wanted only 18, his figures read 24–18–12–2. Redpath, almost passive at one period, settled the issue with his tenth four.

Toss: England. **England 268** (E. R. Dexter 66, J. M. Parks 68, G. D. McKenzie 4-74, N. J. N. Hawke 5-75)

and 229 (K. F. Barrington 85); **Australia 389** (W. M. Lawry 78, P. J. P. Burge 160, F. J. Titmus 4-69)

and 111-3 (I. R. Redpath 58*).

Fourth Test

Harry Gee

At Manchester, July 23, 24, 25, 27, 28, 1964. Drawn.

For all the remarkable personal achievements in the match, a bad taste was left in the mouth of the cricket enthusiasts who saw Australia retain the Ashes. Simpson's strategy was to make certain that Australia did not lose. Dexter, with England kept in the field until the third morning, had no hope of winning and so a boring situation resulted in which more than 28 hours were needed to produce a decision on the first innings!

Both sides were to blame for frequent periods of needlessly tiresome batting on a perfect firm pitch of placid pace which gave no bowler the slightest help. The intention to win was never once apparent after Simpson won the toss, and only rarely were the justifiable expectations of the spectators for entertainment realised.

The match yielded these records:

- Lawry and Simpson made 201 for the first wicket, an Australian record against England.
- Simpson's 311 was the highest ever made at Old Trafford.
- His innings, lasting 12 and three-quarter hours, was the longest ever played against England.
- Both sides' totals were their highest at Old Trafford.
- Barrington's 256 was England's highest at Old Trafford.
- Simpson scored his first Test century, in 30 matches.
- Barrington made his first Test century in England after hitting nine abroad.

- Veivers bowled 95.1 overs, only 17 balls short of the record number of 588 bowled in a Test innings by S. Ramadhin for West Indies against England at Birmingham, in 1957.

On the easy-paced turf Australia, setting themselves to build a formidable total, scored 253 for two on the first day. There was no encouragement to bowlers from the opening delivery, and although Cartwright, by control of length at medium-pace with some movement off the pitch, occasionally worried the batsmen – he had Simpson when 33 missed at the wicket – the attack posed no real danger. Lawry took a six apiece off Price, Cartwright and Rumsey before hitting his first four, but the strokeplay generally was far from forceful.

Methodically, the batsmen wore down the toiling bowlers. Titmus had a long spell, but Lawry reached his third hundred against England out of 179 in five minutes under four hours. His sound but unenterprising innings ended when he was run out for the third time in the series. Dexter crowded the batsmen when Redpath arrived, but Simpson, after five and a half hours with only six fours, completed his century. Cartwright gained reward for his steadiness when beating Redpath off the pitch for lbw.

On the second day, the Australians maintained their dominance yet seldom became free-scoring. Simpson again batted in subdued, if almost faultless, fashion and was barracked before displaying some of his characteristic cuts and drives. O'Neill had given promise of brightening proceedings before a ball swung and knocked back his leg stump. Burge did not settle down before Price caught him at backward square leg at 382.

Simpson, who had reached 160 at rather less than 20 an hour, at last decided to open his shoulders. He took 11 in an over off Price with the new ball, but soon reverted to his sedate mood. When 203, Simpson could have been run out backing up if Titmus had not been chivalrously inclined, and the bowler inappropriately suffered when Simpson, bestirring himself again, hit 14 in an over. At the end of another hot day Simpson had been in 12 hours for 265 out of 570 for four, and Booth had 82 in a partnership of 188. Cartwright had sent down 77 overs for 118 runs and two wickets.

Simpson continued next morning. Had he declared the previous evening and managed to snatch a couple of wickets victory might have been possible, but that is mere surmise. In the event, he made sure that Australia would not lose by extending the total to 656 before declaring. Simpson made no attempt to play safe and after straight-driving Mortimore for six paid the penalty for a slash off Price after a stand of 219 with Booth. The crowd, having overlooked the dull spells, generously gave him an ovation for his 311 out of 646 for six. He defied England for 12 hours 42 minutes, and in addition to his six hit 23 fours. Price took three for 183. He, like his team-mates, had his edge blunted by the unresponsive pitch.

When England began batting Edrich edged McKenzie to second slip with the score 15. Then came a renewal of hope with Boycott and Dexter driving and cutting excellently. The second wicket brought 111 before Boycott played too soon at a slower ball from McKenzie. A shaky start sent Barrington into his shell and Dexter, too, became so restrained that slow hand-clapping broke out. At one stage Barrington's disinclination to make a forcing stroke encouraged Simpson to employ four short legs for Veivers. Bad light stopped play 50 minutes early – a disappointing end for a crowd of 30,000.

Wanting 295 more to make Australia bat again, England had far their best day on Monday when Dexter carried his score to 174 and Barrington reached 153 not out.

Dexter was missed twice by McKenzie at backward short leg when 74 and 97, and narrowly escaped at 108 when Burge said he did not really know whether he had made a catch low down at cover, but the later part of Dexter's innings – his eighth Test hundred – provided much pleasure for the onlookers. From lunch, the batsmen were masters, forcing the game with drives, square cuts, late cuts and full-blooded leg-side strokes which punished quick and slow bowlers alike. Barrington was fortunate, when 99, that McKenzie at short slip failed to hold a cut. He had played 44 Test innings in England without making more than 87.

At tea, with 111 having come since lunch, England wanted 99 more to save the follow-on. Afterwards, they received an unexpected setback at 372. Hawke and Veivers, doing sufficient to keep the batsmen watchful, made runs scarce enough to set impatient onlookers slow hand-clapping, and whether or not Dexter had his concentration disturbed he eventually played across a ball pitched well up to him and was bowled. His fine innings, which included 22 fours, kept the Australians at bay for eight hours.

Barrington suffered a painful blow from a bouncer by Corling, but recovered and remained unbeaten at the close when England, 411 for three, needed 46 more to make Australia go in again. The fifth and last day proved the most disappointing for England supporters. Barrington pushed and deflected when he could have driven powerfully, and the opportunity to encourage his partners and discourage his rivals was lost. When Barrington was finally lbw he had been at the crease for 11 hours 25 minutes. He hit 26 fours in his 256.

With McKenzie enlivened and Veivers still pitching a length, the innings was soon settled after Barrington's departure on the stroke of tea, and England finished 45 behind. McKenzie's late successes, achieved by change of pace and deceptive movement, gave him a fine analysis in such a huge total, but the endurance of Veivers, who sent down 46.1 overs unchanged on the last day and 95.1 in all, was just as remarkable.

The Australians had to bat a second time for five minutes. Simpson, who square-cut Barrington for the four runs obtained, was on the field for all but a quarter of an hour of the match.

Toss: Australia. **Australia 656-8 dec**, (W. M. Lawry 106, R. B. Simpson 311, B. C. Booth 98) **and 4-0;**
England 611 (G. Boycott 58, E. R. Dexter 174, K. F. Barrington 256, J. M. Parks 60, G. D. McKenzie 7-153).

CRICKETER OF THE YEAR – BOBBY SIMPSON Harry Gee, 1965

Robert Baddeley Simpson was born in Sydney on February 3, 1936, of Scottish descent. His father – a professional soccer player with Stenhousemuir in the Scottish League – and mother hailed from Stirlingshire, whence they emigrated to Australia.

Simpson, who in his grade days fielded round the boundary, recalls that Keith Miller was responsible for turning his attention to slip fielding. Simpson was twelfth man for NSW in 1953-54, and when he came out as substitute he asked Miller where he should go. "Try the slips," was the reply. Simpson made two brilliant catches there and from that time found that he was quite at home with the ball coming fast at him.

Simpson also tells of another fortuitous occurrence which assisted him to find his batting *métier*. In 1959, after J. W. Burke had retired, Neil Harvey said: "Why don't you open? Opening is going to be a problem for Australia." Simpson took the hint with staggering effect. In 1959–60, in five first-class matches before going to New Zealand, he scored 902 runs in six innings, three times not out, averaging 300.66. He had many great performances to his name outside Tests, including 359 against Queensland, but all this time a Test century had eluded him. At Old Trafford in the Fourth Test – his 30th – he surprised himself and startled the cricket world by amassing 311.

Simpson's stance is easy and his style attractive, the result of a change of technique in the late 1950s when he turned from playing too square-on to side-on. Simpson found that it made all the difference in dealing effectively with the in-dipper and going-away balls, as he describes them. The flashing straight-drive and devastating square cut shows him at his best and these strokes, as well as the on-drive perfectly taken off his toes, are examples of power and elegance which never fail to evoke admiration.

Fifth Test

Leslie Smith

At The Oval, August 13, 14, 15, 17, 18, 1964. Drawn.

Rain prevented any play on the last day and ruined the faint chance England possessed of sharing the rubber, but once more the cricket only rarely rose above moderate. The batting of Boycott and Cowdrey, the bowling of Hawke and the slip fielding of Simpson stood out in an otherwise ordinary match, the fourth draw of the series.

Dexter won the toss for the fourth time, but England failed to capitalise. They found the pitch far from easy, but it was never difficult enough to justify their dismissal for 182. The first five each reached 20, but not one went on to 50: the innings in general was a dismal affair. Hawke deserved credit for a splendid bowling effort. Dexter had the unusual experience of seeing his bat break in halves over its full length when attempting a drive. Half the bat flew to cover, farther than the ball reached.

Bad light delayed the Australian reply, and next day they batted slowly, being happy to build a good position without worrying about time. Lawry stayed five and a quarter hours for 94. Cartwright and Titmus bowled with commendable steadiness and kept the batsmen tied down. Australia forged ahead with seven wickets in hand and finished the second day at 245 for five. They went on to a lead of 197, but the drama of the third day came right on lunch-time. Trueman, previously ineffective, suddenly bowled Redpath middle stump and had McKenzie caught at slip off successive balls.

There was no time for another delivery before the interval, and the crowd hurried back to their places to see whether Trueman could complete his hat-trick. He also needed one more wicket to become the only bowler to take 300 wickets in Test matches. Hawke survived the first ball, but eventually provided Trueman with his 300th victim. Trueman also dismissed Corling, but could not disturb Veivers, whose aggressive 67 included a six off Titmus.

England, as they have often done in the past, made a good recovery after a poor first effort, and scored 132 for two before the close. Boycott and Barber again provided a valuable start with a stand of 80. Dexter did his best to score quickly, but was well caught at slip. Titmus went in as night-watchman and next day gave further stubborn resistance, although more enterprise would have been valuable. Boycott proved that he had arrived as an England opening batsman with a fine innings lasting five hours. His maiden Test century was full of splendid strokes, particularly drives and square cuts.

When the fourth wicket fell at 255 England were only 58 on, but Cowdrey and Barrington put them on top. They proceeded carefully for a time, opening up after tea. England finished the fourth day 184 ahead, and fast scoring with an early declaration was expected. Unfortunately any chance of a good finish was ruined by the weather, and so this far-from-attractive series ended on a dismal note.

Toss: England. **England 182** (N. J. N. Hawke 6-47) **and 381-4** (G. Boycott 113, F. J. Titmus 56, M. C. Cowdrey 93*, K. F. Barrington 54*); **Australia 379** (W. M. Lawry 94, B. C. Booth 74, T. R. Veivers 67*, F. S. Trueman 4-87).

CRICKETER OF THE YEAR – GEOFFREY BOYCOTT

Bill Bowes, 1965

In 1963, his first season of county cricket, Geoffrey Boycott scored 1,778 runs at an average of 41.34 and was elected the best young cricketer of the year. Less than 12 months after becoming a professional cricketer he was chosen to open for England against Australia. He finished second in the averages with 291 runs at 48.50, and scored his first Test century at The Oval.

At a very early stage in his career he showed the ability to fashion an innings to suit the occasion and the state of the game. He is ruthlessly dedicated to the job of scoring runs, analyses his own game, and takes the trouble to learn about others'. Cricket for him is an all-absorbing occupation and in Yorkshire, where they expect 100% effort, he caused an uplift of eyebrows before the 1964 season, when he gave up his job as a wages clerk earlier than the county demanded, attended the Yorkshire schoolboys' practices in the mornings, stayed for the Colts and the senior coaching classes in the afternoon, and then left for Headingley to join evening practices with the Leeds club. He had four sessions of net practice each day, and regretted he could not get more.

As an opening batsman, he has one telling shot that he plays better than anyone else in the game. He can hit the just-short-of-a-length ball, coming close to his body, as well as most batsmen can play a square cut to a ball wide of the off stump. He moves into a defensive position right behind the ball; then, with the stroke, pulls his body away to take runs anywhere in the arc from cover point to third man. Most opening bowlers are accustomed to seeing this delivery played with a dead bat. Although he seldom hooks, Boycott has most of the shots. He shows no limitation because he wears spectacles. His limitations are self-imposed and these are designed to give the least encouragement to the opposing bowler.

Temperament and ability stamp him as a fine player. Experience and careful application may make him a very successful one for Yorkshire and England.

NOTES BY THE EDITOR

Norman Preston, 1965

I suppose that if England had won back the Ashes many of their supporters would have considered that all was well with first-class cricket. The issue was settled by the barest of margins and perhaps by E. R. Dexter's decision to take the new ball in mid-afternoon on the second day of the Headingley Test. Frankly, much of the cricket was commonplace, with too much emphasis once again placed on the determination not to lose. Cricket is a game to be enjoyed by the players. If they enjoy themselves they entertain the spectators who provide the wherewithal which enables the leading cricketers of all countries to travel around the world and experience a life of luxury, though how many of them really appreciate their good fortune?

To me, the season was one of missed opportunities. It fell flat by comparison with the exhilarating displays of West Indies in 1963. For the most part West Indies did not score their runs any faster, but they certainly conveyed the impression of enjoying themselves. In contrast, too many England and Australian cricketers appeared to be governed first by commercial interests and cricket suffered accordingly.

Where did England go wrong? Firstly, in not finding a settled team and possibly in the choice of captain. Australia possessed one of her finest leaders in Simpson and they chose the same XI for all five Tests, although O'Neill had to stand down a few minutes before play began at Headingley. England were always an experimental combination. The uncertainty began at Trent Bridge where Edrich twisted an ankle at practice on the eve of the match and there was no reserve batsman to take his place. So England played five bowlers and relied on Titmus to open the batting.

Dexter is a grand natural cricketer; indeed, a fine all-round sportsman, but has he managed to get the best out of his men? He has now led England in losing rubbers against India, Australia and West Indies. One has to admit that he has been far from blessed with a galaxy of stars. No one who knows him could suggest that Dexter has shirked his duties. He gives a tremendous amount of thought to the game, including tactics, bowling changes and field placings. He prefers to act alone and is usually reluctant to take advice.

AUSTRALIA v ENGLAND 1965–66
E. M. Wellings

MCC had two objectives when they began their tour of Australia. The winning of the Ashes is the ostensible purpose of all such tours. The other objective, which many considered more important, was, by playing with aggressive enterprise, to correct the impression left by the previous two teams that Englishmen now play their cricket only negatively on the defensive. When their venture ended they could claim a considerable measure of success. Had it ended three weeks earlier the impression left behind would have been even more favourable. And the Test series would have been won.

M. J. K. Smith and his followers were widely acclaimed as an enterprising side. Only one other post-war MCC side, that of 1954–55, enjoyed such respectful kindness from the Australian press. They established their reputation by their batting. Barber played exclusively attacking cricket from start to finish and his 185 off only 255 balls in the Sydney Test was the superlative achievement of the whole tour. When he succeeded, the runs gushed like oil from a new strike. Even when he was out early, the policy was based on taking the initiative by going for scoring strokes: even batsmen with reputations for treating big occasions with solemnity, notably Boycott and Barrington, played Test innings of splendid dash.

When the team was chosen, the batting was expected to be strong enough, and so it proved. The fears expressed concerned the bowling. A period of good fast bowling in English cricket had ended, and successors to Statham, Tyson and Trueman were far from obvious. England also suffered from a dearth of spin bowlers, quite simply because they had too long been discouraged in county cricket. Titmus and Allen, the off-spinners, were the only two regular slow bowlers in the side. Unfortunately Titmus was much less effective in the big matches than he had been three years earlier. As the tour progressed, and as he made more and more runs, his bowling became more and more defensive, his trajectory flatter and flatter. Allen was the better attacking spinner, but he was not handled to the best advantage.

The Australian batting was very powerful. Lawry failed only once, and Simpson scored heavily after recovering from injury. That Booth and Burge slipped back hardly mattered, for Cowper had come to the front along with Walters, who at 19 was a remarkably mature cricketer. He made a century in his first Test when four wickets had gone for 125, another in the second when he and Burge saved the match, and in the third he alone was able to fight long on a turning pitch.

First Test

At Brisbane, December 10, 11, 13, 14, 15, 1965. Drawn.

Back trouble kept McKenzie out of Australia's side and England were without Cowdrey. Russell was fit to play, but he split his right hand while fielding, and Boycott, who had been kept out of all but two of the first-class games by stomach trouble and sciatica, moved up from his intended position at No. 6 to open with Barber. He seized the chance to re-establish himself in that position for the series with two sound innings.

Rain cut the first day's play to two and three-quarter hours and washed out the second. Except briefly midway through the England first innings, a definite result was always out of the question, for Australia batted nearly nine and a half hours in the first innings, which ran into the fourth day.

Fine, lively bowling by Brown, who took the first three wickets for 45 in 12.6 overs, reduced Australia to 125 for four. Lawry and Walters then added 187 in even time. Lawry, obdurate as ever, batted seven hours, his stubborn defence punctuated by outbreaks of leg-side hitting and drives through extra cover, which brought him 20 fours. Walters, who became the ninth Australian to score a century in his first Test, and that in particularly testing circumstances, confirmed his class. With his quick footwork he played Barber's leg-breaks particularly well. In one over he hit him for four fours and later hooked him for six. He also drove Titmus over mid-off for six and, in addition, hit 11 fours all told.

England, unsettled by the leg-spin of Philpott and the pace of Hawke and Allan, lost four wickets for 115, but Parks, who drove Veivers straight and to the off for three sixes, played such a fine attacking innings that his side afterwards was not in serious danger. Parks hit 52 in a stand of 76 with Barrington, who batted over three hours for 53, and Titmus played so resolutely and well that England did not follow on until mid-afternoon on the last day.

In the final innings Boycott, batting throughout, supplied the solidity while Barber, Edrich and Barrington, each of whom hit one six, attacked successfully.

Barber made his 34 off 37 balls, and Barrington, by contrast with his first innings, batted only 54 minutes for 38.

Toss: Australia. **Australia 443-6 dec.** (W. M. Lawry 166, K. D. Walters 155, T. R. Veivers 56*);
England 280 (K. F. Barrington 53, J. M. Parks 52, F. J. Titmus 60, P. I. Philpott 5-90)
and 186-3 (G. Boycott 63*).

Second Test

At Melbourne, December 30, 31, 1965, January 1, 3, 4, 1966. Drawn.

Illness and injury kept Brown and Higgs out of the England side, and they were replaced by Jones and Knight. Hawke was omitted by Australia, but Simpson had recovered from the broken wrist which kept him out of the First Test. He and Lawry made 93 stodgily for the first wicket, but afterwards only a stubborn innings by Cowper, which lasted three hours 20 minutes, seriously held up England's substitute opening bowlers, who were well supported by Allen.

England scored very fast at the start of their innings. Barber and Boycott hit 98 before Boycott, who had the major share of the bowling and was badly missed in the slips in McKenzie's first over, was out in the 16th over. Edrich, who batted more than five hours, cemented the fine start during stands of 118 with Barrington and 105 with Cowdrey. Yet, despite the large total of 558, the most was not made of the inspiring start. Only Cowdrey, who made his third Test century in Melbourne and his fourth against Australia, scored briskly, making his 104 in three and a quarter hours.

On the fourth day 70 minutes were spent adding 42 for the last three wickets. At the close of that day Australia were 131 for one. Simpson, playing much more fluently than in the first innings, made 67 of an opening partnership of 120. In the first 80 minutes of the final day three more wickets fell for 45, and, if Parks had not missed a simple chance of stumping Burge off Barber when he was 34, England would surely have won the match. Burge did not finally yield his wicket until he and Walters had assured their side of a draw. They put on 198 in just over three hours, and both played supremely well.

Burge stayed four and a quarter hours and Walters a little longer. Burge tamed the English attack, while Walters was content to play soundly in his support until the time came for him also to attack.

Toss: Australia. **Australia 358** (R. B. Simpson 59, W. M. Lawry 88, R. M. Cowper 99, B. R. Knight 4-84)
and 426 (R. B. Simpson 67, W. M. Lawry 78, P. J. P. Burge 120, K. D. Walters 115);
England 558 (G. Boycott 51, J. H. Edrich 109, K. F. Barrington 63,
M. C. Cowdrey 104, J. M. Parks 71, F. J. Titmus 56*, G. D. McKenzie 5-134) **and 5-0.**

Third Test

At Sydney, January 7, 8, 10, 11, 1966. England won by an innings and 93 runs.

Illness kept Simpson out again, and Booth, as in Brisbane, was the captain. On a pitch which turned more and more the toss was the decisive event. Barber's greatest innings of the tour and the opening stand of 234 made certain that England would not lose the advantage of batting first. Again Australia paid a heavy price for dropping Boycott early. He was missed at backward short leg off the luckless McKenzie when 12. In two hours before lunch he and Barber made 93 off 36 overs, then in the next two hours, before Boycott at last fell to Philpott's leg-spin, they added 141. When Barber was second out at 303 he had batted four minutes under five hours and hit 19 fours in an innings of magnificent aggression, a match-winning innings.

His wicket started Hawke on a splendid new-ball spell which swept aside the middle order. In eight overs he took three for 14, and with his first ball on the second morning he also dismissed Brown. Despite his fine bowling in conditions which did not materially help pace England made an unassailable total, for Edrich scored a second successive Test century in almost four and a quarter hours. Finally Allen, who made his not-out 50 in 88 minutes, and Jones put on 55 for the last wicket.

On a wearing pitch Australia were always struggling after a second-wicket stand of 81 by Thomas and Cowper. Thomas revealed his wide range of beautiful strokes while making 51 of those runs with seven fours. Cowper by contrast batted four hours ten minutes for 60 and meekly played his side into the hands of the English fast bowlers. On his return to the side Brown took three wickets in his first over with the new ball, and finished with five for 63.

In the follow on the off-spin of Allen and Titmus was decisive on a broken pitch. The longest stand was 46 for the first wicket by Thomas and Lawry, but Walters was again responsible for the best batting. For two hours he played the turning ball with rare skill, and so for the third time running he came off splendidly when his side were in difficulties. Sincock, the left-arm spinner brought in to increase Australia's attacking options on the Sydney pitch, had an unfortunate match as a bowler, but in both innings he batted with admirable determination.

Toss: England. **England 488** (G. Boycott 84, R. W. Barber 185, J. H. Edrich 103, D. A. Allen 50*, N. J. N. Hawke 7-105); **Australia 221** (G. Thomas 51, R. M. Cowper 60, D. J. Brown 5-63) and **174** (F. J. Titmus 4-40, D. A. Allen 4-47).

CRICKETER OF THE YEAR – BOB BARBER
William Wanklyn, 1967

Lancashire coaches are not given to overstatement. It was thus high praise indeed when Stan Worthington first saw a tall, powerfully built young left-hander at the Old Trafford nets and said "That one needs no help from me." His assessment of Robert William Barber, who was born in Manchester on September 26, 1935, was to prove remarkably accurate. As a batsman he remains to this day virtually uncoached. Even as a bowler he had only an hour or two in the hands of that Australian back-of-the-hand specialist, George Tribe, whose maxim was "Spin first, length afterwards. Don't worry about the odd bad ball. They get wickets, too."

Barber, now the supreme individualist, scorns the orthodox routine that is so much a part of the contemporary game, and is one of the few English batsmen who can still draw the Australian crowds. Worthington could have had only one real regret: all Barber's best cricket came after he had switched allegiance to Warwickshire.

He was top-scorer on this tour in Australia with 1,001 first-class runs, all scored with the same commanding approach which did so much to help restore the tarnished image of English Test cricket. The crowds loved him as a player. The Australians respected him as an opponent. But other factors were emerging. As an executive in the group of companies of which his father is a director, and by now a family man, Barber felt he could no longer devote six days a week to county cricket.

Fourth Test

At Adelaide, January 28, 29, 31, February 1, 1966. Australia won by an innings and nine runs.

The roles were completely reversed in this match. England went into it soft after two weeks of holiday cricket. Australia were revitalised. They outfielded, outbatted and outbowled the victors of the previous Test. Simpson was fit to resume in charge of Australia and returned in buoyant mood and form. The side had four changes. Booth, Cowper, Philpott and Sincock were dropped for Simpson, Veivers and two young players, Chappell and Stackpole. A fifth change also discarded McKenzie, but a late injury to Allan caused his recall, with happy consequences. The changes cleared away the cobwebs and stirred the survivors to keener effort.

The reprieved McKenzie turned in the match-winning performance on the first day. While there was some early life in the pitch he and Hawke took the first three English wickets for 33, and Australia never relaxed their grip. Only during a third-wicket stand of 72 was there a suggestion of English recovery. The batsmen were playing well when Cowdrey mistook a call, as Barrington played the ball straight to mid-on, and rushed down the pitch to be run out. Though Barrington stayed more than three hours, followed by 90 minutes of fluent cricket by Parks and the usual stout resistance of Titmus, McKenzie strode on strongly to the finest bowling performance of the series.

England's 241 was exceeded by three before the first-wicket partnership of Simpson and Lawry was broken four and a quarter hours later. This great stand was Australia's highest for the first wicket in Test cricket. It was cemented by 75 minutes of fine stroke-play by Thomas, and Simpson went on until he had batted in commanding manner for just over nine hours, scoring his 225 out of 480 with a six and 18 fours. Stackpole also batted admirably in his first Test and bowled effectively when England went in again 275 behind.

Again McKenzie and Hawke broke the early batting by taking the first three wickets for 32, and England were decisively defeated with more than a day to spare. On the fourth day they mistakenly used defensive tactics when only bold methods might have prised loose Australia's hold. Titmus alone appreciated that fact and hit eight fours in his 53. Barrington stayed five and half hours for a century that contained only four boundaries. Cowdrey, his partner while 82 were added, hit only two fours in a pawky innings of over two and a half hours. This time Hawke was the outstanding bowler: together McKenzie and Hawke formed a match-winning combination.

Toss: England. **England 241** (K. F. Barrington 60, G. D. McKenzie 6-48)
and 266 (K. F. Barrington 102, F. J. Titmus 53, N. J. N. Hawke 5-54);
Australia 516 (R. B. Simpson 225, W. M. Lawry 119, G. Thomas 52, I. J. Jones 6-118).

Fifth Test

At Melbourne, February 11, 12, 13, 14, 15, 16, 1966. Drawn.

The final Test, on which the series depended, was anticlimax and doomed to be indecisive before rain washed out all play on the fourth day. England increased their seam bowling by including Knight at the expense of Allen. Australia recalled Cowper in place of Burge.

Up to a point England played with the necessary enterprise after a bad start. Boycott, though out of touch, took 60 of the first 80 balls bowled, then ridiculously ran out Barber and himself fell 20 minutes later. However, Barrington played his most aggressive Test innings; indeed he hit the fastest century of the series, for he needed only 122 balls. He hit two sixes and eight fours. By contrast Edrich needed 160 balls for his first 50. Though Cowdrey and Parks batted well, putting on 138, the pace slackened, and finally Titmus needed over two hours for 42.

Thoughts of victory gave way to the urge to ensure against defeat, and in the field England averaged only 96 balls an hour. Such time-wasting allowed Australia little chance of striking for a win, and they were content to play quietly. Lawry's 108, his sixth century against England, lasted over six hours. During the season he batted over 41 hours against the touring team and averaged under 24 runs an hour. He was an avid, but tedious, accumulator of runs. When he and Cowper had added 212 and batted together almost five and a half hours, the match was already half dead.

Cowper matched Lawry's patience. His first hundred occupied five hours ten minutes, his second three and three-quarter hours, and altogether he batted seven minutes over 12 hours for 307, a monumental innings in which were 20 fours. Fear of losing frustrated the good intentions with which both sides doubtless entered this disappointing and quickly-to-be-forgotten match. It was a sour ending to a generally appetising tour.

Toss: England. **England 485-9 dec.** (J. H. Edrich 85, K. F. Barrington 115, M. C. Cowdrey 79, J. M. Parks 89, K. D. Walters 4-53) **and 69-3; Australia 543-8 dec.** (W. M. Lawry 108, R. M. Cowper 307, K. D. Walters 60).

England v Australia 1968
Norman Preston

Of all the 25 Australian teams that have visited the United Kingdom the combination under W. M. Lawry was perhaps one of the most disappointing. Nevertheless, they succeeded in their main objective, to retain the Ashes, which Australia have now held for ten years.

The modern Australian batsman never plays on uncovered pitches in his own country, so that when he comes to England he needs the opportunity for plenty of match practice, especially in the early fixtures – but rain meant that 49 hours were lost from the scheduled 60 in the first two tour games. The 1968 party was the youngest in average age to go abroad, and no doubt the ten newcomers learned a great deal which will stand them in good stead in the future, but too often they failed when apparently having played themselves in.

Many Englishmen and even some Australians came to the conclusion that this was a very moderate side. They won only five of their county matches, while Yorkshire, captained by Fred Trueman, beat the Australians for the first time since 1902, and their colours were also lowered by Glamorgan. Yet for all their shortcomings Australia drew the rubber with England, possibly through the spin of the coin. Lawry won the toss in the First Test, Australia made 357 and went on to win comfortably. They had narrow escapes on the rain-affected pitches at Lord's and Edgbaston, but either side might have won at Headingley. The Oval Test went against Australia despite a valiant effort by Lawry, who scored Australia's only hundred in the series. Here England's bowling was clearly superior, even before the storm that nearly washed out the final proceedings.

Looking at the batsmen individually one felt that the best was not seen of Walters and Sheahan. Both had moments of brilliance, but in such a wet summer they failed to do themselves justice. The newcomer who really made his mark was Ian Chappell, grandson of the former Australian captain Victor Richardson. At the same time his young brother, Gregory, enjoyed a most successful first season in county cricket with Somerset.

First Test

At Manchester, June 6, 7, 8, 10, 11, 1968. Australia won by 159 runs.

Few people, except the Australians themselves, believed this success was possible before the match began, but in the event Lawry's men rose to the occasion and made the most of their opportunities whereas England generally offered feeble opposition.

Lawry gained a big advantage when he won the toss, but more important were the final team selections. Australia preferred a spinner in Gleeson to Inverarity, a batsman, but England omitted three bowlers, Brown, Cartwright and Underwood. It meant that the attack rested on Snow, Higgs and Pocock, plus Barber and D'Oliveira, the last pair having taken only seven wickets between them at that stage of the season. Undoubtedly, England's strength was sapped by the withdrawal of Barrington, who was replaced by Barber. Not for the first time the Old Trafford pitch came in for much adverse criticism, but it lasted the five days and D'Oliveira played well in the fourth innings.

England began well, Snow dismissing Redpath lbw and Cowper, who chopped a ball on, for 29. Lawry, resolute when necessary, later scored freely from Pocock. Walters showed his class in his first Test innings in England and hit 13 fours, but both fell to Barber, who was effective with mixed spin, though his length was erratic. Sheahan and Chappell took charge for the rest of the day, Australia finishing at 319 for four.

England made a surprising recovery on Friday when after ten fine days the weather broke and lopped off two hours' cricket. Australia soon collapsed in amazing fashion, their remaining six wickets going down for only 38 runs in the space of 90 minutes. It began when Sheahan played Snow towards Boycott at cover and surprisingly set off for a single; Chappell had no chance and although the return was wide, Knott gathered it and ran five yards to break the wicket. Sheahan never regained his composure after an impressive display.

Boycott and Edrich began quietly in the 25 remaining minutes before lunch, scoring only five; afterwards the weather deteriorated. Both batsmen survived difficult conditions including poor light before the umpires intervened at 5.15. So England resumed on the third morning, having extricated themselves from a poor position, but just as

Australia had collapsed following a run-out so did England. Boycott and Edrich had served their side splendidly by taking their stand to 86 but, going for a third run, Edrich reckoned without Walters's brilliance in the field and paid the penalty.

Thereupon the innings disintegrated and only a final stand by Snow and Pocock saved the follow-on. Australia spent a happy weekend; with two days left they led by 252 with eight wickets standing. They had lost Redpath and Lawry trying to force runs on an uncertain pitch, but Cowper and Walters settled to resolute defence. Altogether, Walters stayed three and a half hours for his second 80 of the match. Jarman consolidated a strong position by using the long handle when Pocock had taken charge and, using his feet to get to the ball, hit 41, including one six and five fours.

England wanted 413 to win. They had nine and a quarter hours at their disposal, but never had they accomplished such a task, their best being 332 for seven at Melbourne in 1928–29. Disasters soon overtook them as Boycott tried to seize the initiative from the start. Again McKenzie and Cowper caused most trouble, Cowdrey falling to a horrible ball which turned and lifted from a good length.

Five wickets fell for 105 before Barber and D'Oliveira saw the total to 152 at the close. The partnership realised 80, but on the last morning D'Oliveira alone worried the Australians. He demonstrated the value of the straight bat and drove cleanly, but with the issue a foregone conclusion the value of his belated effort was difficult to appraise. England needed him as an all rounder, and he had failed as a first-change bowler. By winning, Australia were already practically assured of retaining the Ashes, for never had England won the rubber in the past 70 years after being beaten in the opening match at home.

Toss: Australia. **Australia 357** (W. M. Lawry 81, K. D. Walters 81, A. P. Sheahan 88, I. M. Chappell 73, J. A. Snow 4-97) **and 220** (K. D. Walters 86, P. I. Pocock 6-79); **England 165** (R. M. Cowper 4-48) **and 253** (B. L. D'Oliveira 87*).

Second Test

At Lord's, June 20, 21, 22, 24, 25, 1968. Drawn.

The 200th Test between England and Australia had been eagerly awaited, but it was spoilt by the weather, rain reducing the playing time by half, 15 hours instead of 30. After their depressing performance at Old Trafford, England, with five changes, held a pronounced superiority and clearly shook the Australians' confidence, but the rain robbed them of valuable time and the much-sought victory.

The recall of Milburn exposed the frailty of the bowling, which he punished mercilessly, then Brown and Knight were responsible for Australia being put out for 78, their lowest Test total for over 30 years since G. O. Allen's team dismissed them for 58 on a sticky dog in Brisbane during the 1936–37 tour.

There were so many delays at Lord's that England's first innings occupied the first three days. On Thursday, when only 88 minutes were possible, England, having won the toss, made 53 for the loss of Edrich, caught off his gloves fending away a vicious bouncer. Boycott and Milburn batted admirably after a shower had enlivened the pitch. McKenzie was very awkward with his short-pitched bowling and Milburn, who made one glorious pull for six, took several painful blows.

It was on Friday that Milburn was seen at his very best. The pitch had recovered from the previous day's drenching. He began his onslaught in the first over with a superb cover-drive and a hook off McKenzie for four apiece. Cowper, who caused England so much trouble in the First Test, looked harmless enough. His first ball was short and Milburn hooked it with tremendous power high and far into the Grand Stand. The square cut, cover-drive and hook continued to flow until Milburn made his first mistake. He intended another mighty hit to leg only to present a catch to the ever-reliable Walters near the Tavern boundary. Altogether his memorable innings lasted two and a half hours and contained two sixes and 12 fours.

On his departure the tempo naturally dropped, though Cowdrey and Barrington batted soundly, but when Barrington retired at 61 with a damaged forefinger, Knight scored only eight in the last 70 minutes at a time when England should have been pressing for runs. So at the end of this second day England were 314 for five. Fewer than 14 overs were bowled on Saturday in three short spells; in the 53 minutes of play England reached 351 for seven, Barrington's 75 being his highest score of the season.

On Monday the England pace bowlers took charge. Cowdrey declared at the weekend total and on a greenish pitch Australia collapsed so utterly that only two men, Walters and Gleeson, managed to achieve double figures. A dull, heavy atmosphere made its contribution to the bowlers' hostility and Brown and Knight, who took three for 16, each finished with fine figures. Moreover, the close-set England fielders made few errors. Cowdrey, with three slip catches, passed Hammond's Test record of 110.

Jarman batted under a severe handicap. While keeping wicket his right forefinger had been chipped in two places and the first ball he received from Brown tore the nail and compelled him to retire. In mid-afternoon more rain caused a 50-minute break, and after the teams had been presented to the Queen at tea there was another delay of the same duration.

Australia needed 273 to avert an innings defeat and Lawry, brilliantly caught with the right hand on the leg side by Knott in the second over of the first innings, struggled to avoid a pair, but as conditions improved in the final session he and Redpath settled down and played well in taking the total to 50.

Given a full final day, England could well have won, but yet again the weather intervened and nothing could be done until 3.15. By tea, England could claim Lawry as their sole victim. Although Underwood, with change of pace, accounted for Redpath and Walters, each getting an inside edge, and Barrington induced an indiscreet stroke by Cowper, Australia, if worried at one period, were never in real danger. Indeed, Sheahan offered defiance for 50 minutes without scoring and looked quite safe.

Toss: England. **England 351-7 dec.** (C. Milburn 83, K. F. Barrington 75);
Australia 78 (D. J. Brown 5-42) **and 127-4** (I. R. Redpath 53).

Third Test

At Birmingham, July 11, 12, 13, 15, 16, 1968. Drawn.

This was another disappointing match left undecided, mainly due to the weather. No cricket was possible on the first day and only 90 minutes on the last when, as in the previous Test, England were doing their utmost to force a victory against the clock.

The match was notable for the personal performance of Colin Cowdrey. He became the first cricketer to complete a hundred Test appearances and he celebrated the occasion by making a century, his 21st in Test cricket. When he reached 60 he joined W. R. Hammond as the only batsman to make 7,000 runs in Test cricket. Sir Donald Bradman in 52 Tests and in 48 fewer innings than Cowdrey fell only four short of that total.

The Edgbaston outfield was so saturated by storms on Wednesday night that as early as 10 o'clock on Thursday morning the announcement came that play had been abandoned. The covered middle area was all right and the match proceeded without interruption on the next three days.

England began splendidly after Cowdrey won the toss. Edrich and Boycott managed only 65 runs in the two hours before lunch, but risks had to be avoided with only five specialist batsmen on duty and moreover McKenzie, Freeman and Connolly achieved plenty of movement. Gleeson later needed careful watching, for his deliveries were inclined to keep low. Boycott went, trying to sweep a half-volley from Gleeson, and then Cowdrey entered, cheered all the way to the crease by the 18,000 spectators as well as the Australian team.

Now the runs began to flow more freely. Cowdrey played beautifully, stroking the ball through the covers and continually beating the field on the leg side no matter where Lawry placed his men, and it must be emphasised that the agile Australians, notably Redpath, Sheahan and Walters, saved many runs. Taber, too, kept wicket admirably: he brought off a fine low leg-side catch off Freeman to get rid of Edrich, who had unhurriedly made 88. In his next over, Freeman produced a deadly break-back, giving Barrington no chance to settle. Meanwhile Cowdrey had gone lame with a badly pulled muscle in the back of the left leg (he had Boycott as runner for the last part of his superb innings) about the time he completed his 50, but with Graveney at his best England put on 67 in the last 70 minutes, finishing with 258 for three.

Next day Cowdrey spent half an hour getting the five singles to complete his century. Graveney maintained his masterly form until he tried to force Connolly, who had just changed to round the wicket, over mid-on, and was bowled leg stump for 96, made in nearly five hours. Apart from Snow and Underwood, who put on 33, the later England batsmen failed miserably.

Brown bowled with plenty of fire in the first assault and when Australia were deprived of Lawry (who had a finger broken by Snow) and Redpath so early the crowd of 25,000 grew really excited. By sound cricket Cowper, together with Chappell, made sure there were no more disasters before nightfall. In just over two hours they raised the score to 109 for one, and only two days remained: a draw seemed inevitable.

On Monday, England surprised most people by their positive cricket. At the end of the day they possessed a very good chance of victory and of levelling the series. Australia were set 330, and at the close Redpath and Cowper had scored nine from three overs. Early in the day Snow removed Cowper's middle stump, but Chappell went on to make 71, including nine fours. Knight made the breakthrough for England when he hit Chappell's leg stump. Australia were 193 for four at lunch. Afterwards, England's spin bowlers, Underwood and Illingworth, caused five wickets to go down while only nine runs were added, Australia only just saving the follow-on. England, 187 ahead with nine hours left, needed to push the score along. Boycott, Edrich and Graveney all displayed enterprise against keen bowling and grand fielding.

So to the last morning, when Redpath, Cowper and Chappell faced up nobly to the bowling. Snow trapped Redpath lbw, and that turned out to be England's final success. The left-handed Cowper took as much of Underwood as he could, while Chappell dealt with Illingworth. A light drizzle developed into steady rain, but the batsman put up with the inconvenience for 15 minutes. When they appealed, the umpires stopped play at 12.30, although the decision that no more play was possible did not come until three hours later.

Toss: England. **England 409** (J. H. Edrich 88, M. C. Cowdrey 104, T. W. Graveney 96, E. W. Freeman 4-78) and 142-3 dec. (J. H. Edrich 64); **Australia 222** (R. M. Cowper 57, I. M. Chappell 71) **and 68-1.**

Fourth Test
At Leeds, July 25, 26, 27, 29, 30, 1968. Drawn.

Australia, bent on retaining the Ashes, concentrated solely on avoiding defeat, and succeeded. Again England were let down by their middle batsmen. After so much rain the pitch was slow, with little bounce, and until late on the last day each side possessed a chance of victory, but neither had the courage to take it. By this time the pitch was responsive to spin, but Australia pinned their faith on their pacemen, which surprised the England players, who feared trouble from Gleeson, Cowper and Chappell.

Injuries prevented the two official captains taking part and the sides were led by Graveney and Jarman. A deep hand wound made Graveney doubtful until the last minute and England called up Sharpe as cover, but he was not needed. England recalled Dexter and introduced two new caps, Prideaux and Fletcher, who had the misfortune to begin at first slip where he made noble attempts to hold two or three hard chances before a Yorkshire crowd who reckoned that all would have been gathered by "Sharpie". Small wonder that Fletcher failed with the bat at the crucial moment, although he stayed 70 minutes at the bitter end of the match.

Jarman won the toss and Cowper took over Lawry's defensive role, contenting himself with 15 runs in two hours before lunch when the total reached 75 for one. Inverarity, in his first Test, soon fell to Snow, but Redpath batted extremely well, holding the innings together against some good bowling, but England missed difficult chances. When in sight of his century, Redpath attempted to sweep Illingworth and was bowled round his legs. Walters, Chappell and Sheahan played soundly for the most part, but Australia were perhaps fortunate to finish the first day at 258 for five, Knott having also missed one catch and a chance of stumping.

Next morning only Chappell and Freeman gave England much trouble and the remaining five wickets fell for 57. Underwood finished the innings by taking three for ten, finishing with four for 41 in 28 overs, a masterly performance.

England had one over to bat before lunch and for the next three hours, despite some fine fielding, the absence of Boycott and Cowdrey was not felt. Prideaux was the hero with Edrich shaping as well as he has ever done. Until Cowper bowled into the marks made by Snow, all went well for England. Prideaux drove and hooked in almost carefree fashion and Edrich excelled with the cover-drive. Then with 70 minutes left and 123 runs on the board – easily the highest opening stand of the series – Prideaux aimed for a mighty hit over square leg from Gleeson but the ball lifted from the rough, he checked his stroke, and Freeman running towards the players' pavilion held an amazing catch as the ball dropped over his shoulder with his arms outstretched. Jarman promptly brought back McKenzie, who put in a very good spell with Connolly. A large section of the crowd turned sour against Edrich and Dexter, who were pinned down, and in next to no time England lost both, the score being 163 for three at the close.

The manner in which England failed with the bat on the third day might have caused the disillusioned crowd of 25,000 to imagine that the bowlers were supermen. Fortunately Underwood, the last man, demonstrated the proper way to hit the ball by treating it on its merits. He began by taking ten from a Connolly over, and with Brown also confident and steady the last wicket put on 61 and cut down the lead to 13. One must emphasise that Underwood did not indulge in wild slogging but hit intelligently.

Redpath again batted splendidly for Australia, who before the end of the third day lost Cowper and Inverarity to Illingworth for 92. The cricket on Monday was very dull. In five hours only 191 runs were scored while the bowlers took four more wickets. Chappell stayed more than four hours for 81, a most valuable effort, and finally England faced the task of scoring 326 in five minutes under five hours. Illingworth and Underwood were never mastered and took the last five wickets for 39.

England needed to average 66 runs an hour and soon lost Prideaux who, cutting off the back foot, chopped the ball on. Edrich again played well and Dexter cut and drove in his best style until a break-back left him helpless. Connolly, the successful bowler, strove with unflagging energy, as did McKenzie. Graveney and Barrington displayed enterprise, but the runs never flowed freely enough and when Graveney went to a return catch in Cowper's first over Australia were already assured of the Ashes.

Toss: Australia. **Australia 315** (I. R. Redpath 92, I. M. Chappell 65, D. L. Underwood 4-41) **and 312** (K. D. Walters 56, I. M. Chappell 81, R. Illingworth 6-87); **England 302** (J. H. Edrich 62, R. M. Prideaux 64, A. N. Connolly 5-72) **and 230-4** (J. H. Edrich 65).

Fifth Test

Norman Preston

At The Oval, August 22, 23, 24, 26, 27, 1968. England won by 226 runs.

England won with six minutes to spare and squared the rubber, but the Ashes stayed with Australia. Down the years Kennington has generally proved a good place for England and now, after rain had robbed Cowdrey's men at Lord's and Edgbaston, even a storm that flooded the ground at lunch-time on the last day could not save Australia.

Just before lunch England's task appeared to be a mere formality with Australia toiling at 85 for five. In half an hour the ground was under water, but the sun reappeared at 2.15 and the groundsmen, ably assisted by volunteers from the crowd armed with brooms and blankets, mopped up to such purpose that by 4.45 the struggle was resumed. Only 75 minutes remained, and even then the deadened pitch gave the bowlers no encouragement. Inverarity and Jarman resisted nobly, no matter how Cowdrey switched his attack with a cordon of ten men close to the bat. Finally, he turned to D'Oliveira, who did the trick with the last ball of his second over; it moved in and hit the top of the off stump as Jarman reached forward.

Now 35 minutes were left to capture the four remaining wickets. Cowdrey promptly whisked D'Oliveira off and recalled Underwood, who finished the contest by taking those four wickets in 27 deliveries for six runs. He found the drying pitch ideal for this

Just in time: Derek Underwood claims the last Australian wicket (John Inverarity) with a few minutes to spare at The Oval in 1968. The whole England side celebrates (left to right): Ray Illingworth, Tom Graveney, John Edrich, Ted Dexter, Colin Cowdrey, Alan Knott, John Snow, David Brown, Colin Milburn and Basil D'Oliveira (who had earlier scored a memorable 158).

purpose, receiving just enough help to be well-nigh unplayable. The ball almost stopped on pitching and lifted to the consternation of the helpless batsmen. Underwood had Mallett and McKenzie held by Brown in the leg trap in the first over of his new spell, Gleeson stayed 12 minutes until his off stump was disturbed, and to everyone's surprise Inverarity, having defied England for four hours with rare skill, offered no stroke at a straight ball and was lbw.

So Underwood achieved his best bowling analysis in Test cricket. No praise could be too high for the way he seized his opportunity on this unforgettable day. In fact the match produced many heroes.

D'Oliveira was a late selection after Prideaux reluctantly withdrew, following illness. England left out Higgs, and Australia, who preferred not to include Cowper whose left thumb had been fractured the previous week, introduced Mallett to Test cricket. Cowdrey won the toss and on the first day England scored 272 for four, Edrich holding the innings together. The pitch was firmer than expected after heavy rain the previous weekend. In all Edrich batted seven and three-quarter hours, hitting 20 fours.

England had an anxious time on that first day until Graveney settled down and in his own graceful style put on 125 with Edrich. In the last hour D'Oliveira began his fine effort. He hooked superbly and next day drove magnificently. When 31, he offered a chance to the wicket-keeper, and after reaching his second Test century he was missed three more times when England needed to push the score along until hc was last out for 158. Apart from Knott, the later batsmen were singularly lacking in enterprise.

There remained 75 minutes for Australia to begin their reply and they lost Inverarity to a fine short-leg catch by Milburn while making 43. On Saturday, Lawry stood between England and a complete breakthrough, staying at the crease all day. At first Redpath batted well, and before lunch they added 77 to the overnight 43 before Redpath was held in the slips by Cowdrey. Four more wickets suddenly fell, and Australia were faced with the possibility of having to follow on. McKenzie defended stoutly after tea and Australia at the close were 264 for seven, having lost only McKenzie to the second new ball. Lawry was 135 not out.

The struggle went mostly England's way on Monday. Lawry fell without addition, being taken by Knott from an inside-edge off a rising ball. Lawry left no one in doubt that he disagreed with umpire Fagg's decision, and stopped to speak to him on his way off. His century was Australia's only one of the scries. Lawry batted seven and a half hours and hit 22 fours. For all his youth, Mallett defended with the skill of an experienced campaigner for just over three hours, but England held a valuable lead of 170.

Some of the best cricket came when England sought to score quickly in their second innings. Cowdrey alone stayed longer than an hour. The Australians fielded magnificently. Milburn set his side on the venturesome path. He hooked the first ball from McKenzie for four and pulled Connolly from outside off for six. In three hours England mustered 181, setting Australia 352 to win at 54 an hour.

Again Milburn began Australia's downfall with a fine low catch at short leg from Lawry, who thus was dismissed twice in the day. Then, facing the last ball before the close, Redpath padded Underwood away and was lbw. To remove these two stalwarts at the end of a momentous day was a great feat and put England in sight of victory.

Next morning, with the sun shining as it had done throughout the proceedings so far, England drove home their advantage, mainly through Underwood and Illingworth. Inverarity, who defied England for four hours, alone gave any cause for anxiety, and except for the thunderstorm, England would surely never have had to battle against the clock. To Australia's credit must be set their sportsmanship. They averaged 20 overs an hour when England were pressing for runs, and their batsmen passed each other on the way to the wicket even in that hectic final period, nor did they fritter time away by gardening.

Toss: England. **England 494** (J. H. Edrich 164, T. W. Graveney 63, B. L. D'Oliveira 158) **and 181** (A. N. Connolly 4-65); **Australia 324** (W. M. Lawry 135, I. R. Redpath 67) **and 125** (R. J. Inverarity 56, D. L. Underwood 7-50).

NOTES BY THE EDITOR   Norman Preston, 1969

The D'Oliveira controversy which shook the cricket and political worlds could only have been avoided if he had not succeeded on his recall to the England team for the final Test. I have seen all his Test innings in England and never have I seen him play better than he did at The Oval. He rose to the occasion, knowing it was his last chance to fulfil his ambition to play first-class cricket in his native country and before his own admirers. It must be remembered that D'Oliveira usually bats as low as sixth in the order and yet in 24 Test innings he has hit two hundreds and seven fifties and achieved an average of 50. This is something out of the ordinary by any standard.

I am sure that if the South African tour had taken place, D'Oliveira would have been a great success on the field, and off the field he would have behaved with the same dignity which has won him so many admirers over here. Cricket has been the loser with its name tarnished and MCC thrown into divided camps. MCC has always fostered cricket wherever the game is played and for all their faults in this imperfect world I was pleased that the majority of the members rallied to their support when the matter was thrashed out.

The Colour and the Money: 1970–71 to 1980

The 1970s was a tumultuous decade for cricket, especially in Australia. By 1976 Australia held the Ashes, and had walloped West Indies in a Test series too, so were undoubtedly the leading side in the world. After the monochrome 1950s and '60s, the Aussies had injected colour into the game: in the decade fashion forgot, Ian Chappell came into one of the early press conferences of his captaincy wearing a purple shell-suit, something Don Bradman never tried. And Bradman certainly didn't approve of sledging, the practice of trying to put the batsman off by abusing him (or "mental disintegration," as Steve Waugh later called it) which helped earned Chappell's side the tag of "ugly Australians".

Ugly or not, they were a great team, containing fine batsmen like Chappell himself and his brother Greg, the combative wicket-keeper Rod Marsh, and, crucially, the peerless paceman Dennis Lillee, later joined by Jeff Thomson, who might just have been the fastest bowler ever to tread the earth. Importantly, they were backed up by close catching of the very highest order.

But Australia's supremacy was interrupted by... an Australian. Kerry Packer, a well-heeled media mogul, had started taking an interest in cricket, which offered a lot of airtime (and Australian TV regulations at the time demanded a certain percentage of home-grown programming) at modest cost. Packer's Channel 9 put in a bid for the TV rights in Australia – but were turned down, even though the successful offer from the ABC (the no-ads state broadcaster which had screened cricket for years) was much lower.

Packer did not give up, and raised the stakes. He reckoned that if he could not show Test cricket then he could screen "Tests" of his own. He contracted many of the world's leading players for undreamed-of salaries – ironically, many of them signed on the dotted line during the showpiece match at Melbourne in March 1977 which was staged to mark the centenary of Test cricket. It was a glittering event, attended by the Queen and enlivened by Lillee's bowling for the home team and the batting of the unheralded Englishman Derek Randall. Remarkably, Australia won it by 45 runs, exactly the same result as the Test of 100 years earlier which it commemorated. We have included the details of this match in this book, even though the Ashes were not at stake in what was one-off game.

Australia were originally the favourites when the teams reassembled in England later in 1977, but then Lillee and Ian Chappell withdrew – in the words of *Wisden*, "leaving their flannels at the cleaners until the Packer fortunes became available" – and, once the details of World Series Cricket became public, the tourists' morale almost inevitably dipped. England, with Geoff Boycott making a triumphant return to the fold after three years' self-imposed exile, and a fresh-faced Ian Botham making his debut, won the series at a canter. Then they retained the Ashes with even more ease in 1978–79, when faced with a rag-tag Australian side lacking all the Packer players.

The public gave a huge thumbs-down to that one-sided Ashes battle, forcing the Australian board to parley with Packer – who was keen to talk anyway because his break-away "circus" was making large losses, too. The resultant peace treaty included another England tour of Australia, in 1979–80. Australia won all three Tests, although the Ashes technically stayed put, because the English authorities again declined to put them at stake.

A tumultuous decade ended with another centenary celebration, this time to mark 100 years of Test cricket in England (once again the Ashes were not at stake). But the match, played at Lord's (rather than The Oval, the venue of the 1880 game) was not a patch on the Melbourne one – it was dogged by bad weather, and is best remembered for some irate MCC members manhandling the officials after the umpires' umpteenth pitch inspection of a fractious Saturday.

It had all been rather different at the start of the decade. England kicked it off by regaining the Ashes in 1970–71 under Ray Illingworth, who was much indebted to the batting of Boycott and the pinpoint fast bowling of John Snow. The canny Illingworth kept hold of the urn at home in 1972, although there was not much doubt during a series eventually drawn 2–2 that his side was growing old together. Australia, now led by Ian Chappell, were the more vibrant team, with Lillee a fearsome sight as he hurtled in, long hair flowing.

Lillee was one of the stars of the time, his hair and moustache instantly recognis-able (and marketable) as TV exposure mushroomed. Long hair and moustaches, indeed, were a feature of Chappell's Australian team which, to no great surprise, dominated the 1974–75 Ashes series, mainly thanks to the terrifying fast-bowling partnership between Lillee (restored after injury) and Thomson. It was the first series from which colour pictures were beamed back to England, and sometimes it was harrowing viewing. Several England players were injured, including David Lloyd, now a garrulous TV commentator, who often recalls the time his protective box was turned inside out by a rocket from Thomson. It might not have been much fun for the players, but it was gripping for those looking on – like Kerry Packer, who soon determined that watching cricket on TV would never be quite the same again.   S. L.

AUSTRALIA V ENGLAND 1970–71   E. M. Wellings

No captain of a touring team since D. R. Jardine has had such a difficult task as Raymond Illingworth. Some English critics, who had championed M. C. Cowdrey, were against the skipper. The attitude of numerous Australians has never in my experience been so hostile to an English captain in advance of the tour. Before a ball was bowled Sir Donald Bradman was critical of Illingworth as a man who overdid leg-side field placing. Few, if any, of those critics had ever seen him lead a side, and for a country possessing W. M. Lawry as their captain to cavil at leg-side field-placings was to tread on dangerous ground.

Illingworth was put in an unfortunate position when the manager, Mr D. G. Clark, supported by two visiting MCC officials, agreed with the Australian officials to change the tour programme during the rain-ruined Third Test at Melbourne and play an extra Test. It meant a very heavy programme of big matches, four Tests in quick succession with only one-day fixtures separating them. The rearrangement gave Australia gates amounting in value to £70,000. English cricket received no share of the extra revenue.

Strangely the many difficulties which Illingworth had to overcome could be held as being partly responsible for the team's success. They produced a brand of team spirit which has been equalled during the post-war years only by sides led by M. J. K. Smith. Illingworth had his players solidly behind him, and Edrich and Boycott in the role of lieutenants were invaluable. Bolstered by that spirit, Illingworth and crew were able to ride the handicaps already mentioned and also the many injuries which crippled the team. The final triumph in Sydney was achieved with the top batsman, Boycott, and the top bowler, Snow, out of action.

England's success was based primarily on Snow's bowling, the batting of Boycott, Edrich and Luckhurst, and the wicket-keeping of Knott. Boycott put the seal of greatness on his batting, averaging 93.8 in the Tests. His finest and most dominating innings was not one of his hundreds, but his 77 in the Fourth Test, during which he revealed to the full his superb range of strokes. But it must not be supposed that this was other than a team triumph, to which the regular supporting players contributed handsomely as and when required. Prominent among them were the veterans, Illingworth and D'Oliveira, both of whom stood up to the most arduous tour of my experience remarkably well.

For Australia the series was a bitter disappointment. It was fortunate for them that the pitches were not as fast as usual, for their play of fast bowling was fraught with peril. Only Lawry was a well-organised batsman, and he was so defensive that he batted nearly 25 hours for his 324 runs, and Redpath was not much quicker. That Lawry should be relieved of the captaincy was not surprising. He was negatively unimaginative, but to drop him from the side for the vital last match was generous to England.

First Test

At Brisbane, November 27, 28, 29, December 1, 2, 1970. Drawn.

England fought back remarkably to finish on top. At one time on the second day Australia were 372 for two and apparently impregnably placed. Yet on the final day they had to fight to save the game. Stackpole by his aggression gave Australia their early advantage. He was fortunate to receive a favourable run-out decision when 18, after which he dominated the play, and the two sharp chances he gave off Underwood did not detract from his performance. His square-cutting and hooking contributed largely to his abundance of boundaries, one six and 22 fours.

Chappell was his sound partner in a stand of 151, and he put on 209 with Walters, whose innings again contained sparkling strokes and yet overall was streaky. After Snow, who at last reached top gear, had dismissed Stackpole, the vulnerable middle batting crumbled. Underwood dismissed Redpath, Sheahan and Walters in seven balls without conceding a run, and Snow raged through the tail: seven wickets fell in 47 minutes while 15 runs were scored.

England also slipped after reaching 245 before the third wicket fell. Luckhurst, Knott, who further improved his magnificent batting record in overseas Tests, and

Edrich all entered the 70s. The innings of Luckhurst, who seemed set for a century until run out by Knott's lapse of judgment, was the best, and he prepared the way for something faster than the succeeding batsmen managed. England slowly accumulated their lead of 31, D'Oliveira taking three and a quarter hours to score 57.

Australia also struggled. Lawry's obstinate batting, five and a half hours for 84, prevented an English win. Yet the servile nature of his play, it could be argued, upset the other batsmen and contributed to their failures. Early on the last day three were out for 64, and there followed a tedious stand of 73 between Lawry and Redpath, who batted more than two hours for 28. Shuttleworth, who had bowled as well as some of the more successful bowlers in the first innings, used the second new ball to take four wickets in his last five overs and finished deservedly with five for 47. Only an hour remained for England's second innings. They might consider that, if their bowlers had averaged 110 balls an hour, which is not much to expect, instead of 101, they would have saved 75 minutes and have had time to attempt a win.

Toss: Australia. **Australia 433** (K. R. Stackpole 207, I. M. Chappell 59, K. D. Walters 112, J. A. Snow 6-114) **and 214** (W. M. Lawry 84, K. Shuttleworth 5-47); **England 464** (B. W. Luckhurst 74, A. P. E. Knott 73, J. H. Edrich 79, B. L. D'Oliveira 57) **and 39-1.**

Second Test
At Perth, December 11, 12, 13, 15, 16, 1970. Drawn.

Perth's first Test match was an outstandingly successful promotion. It was perfectly organised, and nearly 85,000 spectators saw it. That number was nearly twice that at Brisbane, and gate receipts were almost three times as large. If not all the cricket was worthy of the enthusiastic people of Western Australia, the match was in the balance until the last afternoon. After Lawry had put them in, England again slipped from a position of strength, and once more Australia's batting was revealed as fragile.

Boycott and Luckhurst, with stands of 171 and 60, carried their total in ten opening partnerships to 994. Boycott's stolid 70 contained only three fours. Though the Perth boundaries are long Luckhurst managed nine in that time, and when bowled by McKenzie's break-back after 78 overs he had 13. Edrich also batted well and England were 257 for two at the close of the first day.

On the second Edrich ran himself out, and the middle batting failed. McKenzie bowled particularly well, but he was eclipsed by Snow. On a pitch which was not nearly so fast as it can be on this ground, Snow had appreciably more life than any other quick bowler in the match. In his first 18 balls he took two for one, and early on the third day Australia were desperately placed at 107 for five. They were magnificently rescued by Redpath and Greg Chappell, who was playing in his first Test. Redpath played thoroughly well, but by no means so surely as his less-experienced partner. Redpath was disconcerted by pace; Chappell never was. Slowly but surely they pulled their side round. At tea the total was 240, and afterwards Chappell cut loose. He mauled Snow, Lever and Shuttleworth so severely that 74 were added in ten overs. When Chappell went three overs later, he had hit his last 60 in 13 overs while Redpath collected 25.

Another indifferent batting performance, which Edrich redeemed with the aid of Illingworth and Knott, put England in peril. Though Boycott played his best innings of the series to date they were 152 for five, only 109 ahead and sorely puzzled by Gleeson's varied and accurate spin, and more than five and a half hours remained. Illingworth, however, batted well while 57 were added, and finally he declared to allow Australia two hours 25 minutes. To score 245 in that time would have required exceptional batting, but Lawry could have been expected at least to make a token attempt. Only Ian Chappell made a gesture. Lawry's batting was craven. His second run completed his 5,000 in Test cricket, his third his 2,000 against England. With that he seemed content. After 68 minutes he had made only six, and Australia spent 21 overs reaching 50. There was not a spark of enterprise about the batting of Lawry or Redpath until Fletcher and Cowdrey bowled their inaccurate leg-breaks.

Toss: Australia. **England 397** (G. Boycott 70, B. W. Luckhurst 131, G. D. McKenzie 4-66) **and 287-6 dec.** (G. Boycott 50, J. H. Edrich 115*); **Australia 440** (I. M. Chappell 50, I. R. Redpath 171, G. S. Chappell 108, J. A. Snow 4-143) **and 100-3.**

Third Test
At Melbourne, December 31, 1970, January 1, 2, 4, 5, 1971. Abandoned.

This match was abandoned on the third day after almost continuous rain had prevented any play. The captains tossed on the first day and Illingworth put Australia in. The abandonment was ordered by a conference of members of the Australian Board, led by Sir Donald Bradman, and the MCC manager with two visiting officials, Sir Cyril Hawker and G. O. Allen. It was later announced that a 40-over match would be played on the last day of the Test [*this is now recognised as being the first official one-day international – Ed.*], and that an additional Test would be inserted into the programme.

Fourth Test
At Sydney, January 9, 10, 11, 13, 14, 1971. England won by 299 runs.

Great batting by Boycott and superb fast bowling by Snow on a pitch taking spin, which was too slow for other pace bowlers, were too much for Australia. The latter were conclusively outplayed after the first day, on which their spin caused an English collapse helped by bad strokes. Boycott made 77 out of a first-wicket stand of 116 off 31 overs. Brilliant strokeplay brought him 11 fours. Though he fell to a catch on the boundary when hooking a long-hop, England passed 200 with only two wickets down. In 33 minutes they lost four wickets while 18 were scored, and Mallett had remarkable success with his off-breaks. In his first eight overs after tea he took three for six.

England's later batsmen, however, hit back bravely, the last four wickets adding 119, and the rally was continued by the bowlers, Underwood being mainly responsible for the last six Australian wickets going on the third morning for 47. The only stand for Australia in the match was one of 99, in which Redpath played much more soundly than Walters, who was dropped at first slip when three. Redpath also gave a slip catch, though a much more difficult one, when he was six. Lever was the unfortunate bowler on both occasions.

In the second innings England lost their first three wickets for 48, during which time Boycott ran out Edrich. He made amends during stands of 133 with D'Oliveira and 95 with Illingworth. Both partners played excellently while Boycott ruthlessly broke the attack. He played to a schedule which allowed Illingworth to leave over nine hours for Australia's second innings, staying six hours 50 minutes and hitting 12 fours. The England bowlers needed less than half that time, and only Lawry, who stayed throughout an innings of four hours and a quarter of stern defence, could live against Snow. And he faced few of Snow's deliveries on the final day, when he took five for 20 in eight overs. The pitch was without pace, but on occasions Snow made the ball kick viciously from a worn patch and had his opponents apprehensive from first to last.

Toss: England. **England 332** (G. Boycott 77, J. H. Edrich 55, J. W. Gleeson 4-83, A. A. Mallett 4-40) **and 319-5 dec.** (G. Boycott 142*, B. L. D'Oliveira 56, R. Illingworth 53); **Australia 236** (I. R. Redpath 64, K. D. Walters 55, D. L. Underwood 4-66) **and 116** (W. M. Lawry 60*, J. A. Snow 7-40).

Fifth Test

At Melbourne, January 21, 22, 23, 25, 26, 1971. Drawn.

Australia recovered some of their poise when England dropped eight catches in the first innings of a match marred by bad crowd behaviour. A stampede on the first day, when Ian Chappell reached 100, left its mark on the pitch. Fully 2,000 spectators rushed the pitch, stealing Chappell's cap, Cowdrey's white hat and a stump. Their offensive attitude towards the visitors culminated in an unsavoury demonstration in the final 40 minutes, when Boycott and Edrich batted against a continuous background of booing, hand-clapping in unison and the banging of empty beer cans. At one time the umpires conferred but allowed play to continue.

Cowdrey returned because Fletcher was injured, and disastrously, for his four missed slip catches in the first innings cost England their chance. He missed Ian Chappell off Snow before he scored and again off D'Oliveira when he was 14. Altogether he missed five in the match.

Australia's 493 was a remarkable innings, for all the main scorers were missed at least once and some of the batting was remarkably faulty. Walters scored a high proportion of his runs off the edge, as he did again in the second innings. After settling down Ian Chappell played strongly, hitting 12 fours in just over four hours, and Redpath again batted well in a stand of 180 after Lawry had been struck on the hand and retired. The most robust batting was by Marsh, who thumped the ball hard, hitting 12 fours. He gave two chances in the sixties, but otherwise played sterling cricket for his side.

Lawry long delayed his declaration into the evening of the second day and then astonishingly deprived Marsh of the chance to become the first Australian wicket-keeper to score a Test century. Lawry's captaincy indeed gave his side little chance of squaring the series. When he had a lead of 101 his second innings was geared so low that it lasted four and a quarter hours. He could not have expected England to attempt the task of making 102 more in 15 minutes less time on a slow pitch taking spin, particularly as Luckhurst could not bat and D'Oliveira, who had a badly bruised toe, could have done so only with a runner.

Luckhurst broke the little finger of his left hand quite early in a grand fighting innings, which pulled England round after Thomson, in helpful conditions, had them reeling at 88 for three. Despite his handicap Luckhurst stayed nearly five and a half hours for his second century of the series. D'Oliveira, his partner while 140 were scored, and Illingworth again played fine parts in rallying the side.

In Australia's second innings Snow was warned about his use of the bouncer by the new Test umpire, O'Connell, although he bowled considerably fewer than Thomson. In the final innings Boycott and Edrich, with only a draw to play for, scored 161 in the four hours. After 45 overs they had 133, but when the crowd made concentration difficult they inevitably fell back on defence.

This match attracted 184,503 people and the third day produced world-record receipts of £25,070. Altogether the series was watched by 678,486 spectators who paid £248,354.

Toss: Australia. **Australia 493-9 dec.** (W. M. Lawry 56, I. M. Chappell 111, I. R. Redpath 72, K. D. Walters 55, R. W. Marsh 92*) **and 169-4 dec.; England 392** (B. W. Luckhurst 109, B. L. D'Oliveira 117) **and 161-0** (G. Boycott 76*, J. H. Edrich 74*).

Sixth Test
At Adelaide, January 29, 30, February 1, 2, 3, 1971. Drawn.

Late on the third day England led by 235 and did not enforce the follow-on. Whether a different decision would have given England a win is open to question. Illingworth's key pace bowlers were tiring, and he had to think about the final Test in terms of bowlers tackling an unprecedented string of international matches in quick succession.

Luckhurst could not play, which allowed Boycott and Edrich to resume their long-established partnership. They did so successfully with 107 before Boycott was run out, though both had given chances early in the innings. Edrich, who batted with customary solidity for nearly six hours, during which he hit 14 fours, and Fletcher cemented the fine start, and England finished the first day with 276 for two. Fletcher played his best Test innings, despite the handicap of a damaged right hand.

Early on the second day Knott and Fletcher fell at the same total, but D'Oliveira and Hampshire, who was missed twice off Lillee, added 96, and Snow drove weightily. Lillee fully deserved his five wickets on his first Test appearance. Though Stackpole played a vigorous strokemaking innings, Australian wickets fell steadily to English pace. Stackpole struck 11 of the 12 fours hit before he was second out at 117 after just over three hours. The rest of the innings was little more than a procession. Lever, who had now adapted his bowling to Australian conditions, did his best work of the tour.

In the second innings Boycott and Edrich again topped 100 for the first wicket, scoring at nearly five an over, and Boycott reached 100 out of 169 with 11 fours in three and a quarter hours. Subsequently, Illingworth took up the running and raced to 48 off 88 balls, with eight fours, before declaring.

Australia were left 500 minutes to make 469. They were never in the hunt for victory, but also were never in danger of defeat. Stackpole and Ian Chappell made sure of that by adding 202. Stackpole, hooking impressively, hit 16 fours. Redpath brought the game to a dreary end by plodding nearly two hours for 21. A slow-paced pitch becoming easier for batsmen did not cater for a definite result. In such conditions it was remarkable that England dismissed Australia for only 235 in the first innings.

Toss: England. **England 470** (G. Boycott 58, J. H. Edrich 130, K. W. R. Fletcher 80, J. H. Hampshire 55,
D. K. Lillee 5-84) **and 233-4 dec.** (G. Boycott 119*); **Australia 235** (K. R. Stackpole 87, P. Lever 4-49)
and 328-3 (K. R. Stackpole 136, I. M. Chappell 104).

Seventh Test

At Sydney, February 12, 13, 14, 16, 17, 1971. England won by 62 runs.

A very different pitch from that on which bowlers toiled in Adelaide made sure that
the final match would reach a definite result. It did so early on the fifth day, the extra
day allowed on this occasion not being necessary. On the first day 12 wickets fell. Ian
Chappell, Australia's new captain, sent England in and the batsmen fell to spin, despite
another resolute innings by Illingworth. There was time for Lever and Snow to shoot
out Eastwood and Stackpole for 13.

Australia slumped to 66 for four, but England let their strong position slip, largely
because Walters was missed three times. He and the stubborn Redpath put on 81, and
Greg Chappell's three-hour innings carried Australia to a lead of 80. During the closing
stages of the innings Jenner ducked into a ball from Snow and was hit on the face.
Snow was warned by umpire Rowan against the use of persistent bumpers, which led
to a protest by Illingworth. The crowd demonstrated against Snow, and Illingworth led
his side off the field, but returned after being warned by the umpires that the match
would otherwise be awarded to Australia.

Edrich and Luckhurst more than countered the lead with an opening stand of 94,
and a series of useful scores finally set Australia 223, with the pitch helpful to spinners and not unfriendly to pace bowlers. Snow bowled Eastwood with his sixth ball,
but in the fifth over, going for a high catch at long leg, he broke his right hand on
the boundary fencing and was put out of action. Nevertheless, the other bowlers, with
Illingworth himself playing a notable part, had half the side out for 96. Only Stackpole
prospered, though he seemed fortunate not to be given out caught by Knott off Lever
when 13.

On the final day Greg Chappell was Australia's last hope, and he was winkled out
by Illingworth, who pulled out his best to compensate for Underwood being disappointing in conditions expected to make him the match-winner. For England to win
without Boycott, their top batsman, and then without Snow at the climax of the game
was a great achievement. Australia had recast their side, dropping Lawry, whose batting
was sorely missed. The 35-year-old Eastwood, who was not even in the Victoria side at
the start of the season, was no adequate replacement.

Toss: Australia. **England 184 and 302** (B. W. Luckhurst 59, J. H. Edrich 57);
Australia 264 (I. R. Redpath 59, G. S. Chappell 65) **and 160** (K. R. Stackpole 67).

WELCOME AUSTRALIA   Ted Dexter, 1972

I have on occasions taken a quite unreasonable dislike to Australians. Sorry, but it is
the truth. And if I blush at the thought, let alone the telling of it publicly, I derive a

Flashpoint: John Snow, England's bowling hero in 1970–71, is manhandled at Sydney. Shortly afterwards, the England team walked off.

certain amount of comfort from the knowledge that I am not alone among England's cricketers in my feelings, highly reprehensible though they of course are. Given suitable circumstances – and there can be few so absolutely right for a spot of disliking than a Test match between us Pommies and our most respected foes, the opposition from Down Under. Whether players, partisan spectators or mere uncommitted natives of that distant continent can without much effort it seems either on their part or ours, change radically from the affable earthy folk they most times are into creatures every bit as dreadful as the Hydra; as multi-headed and indestructible now as the day when Hercules received a helping hand from Iolaus to despatch the brute.

The story goes that Iolaus stopped new heads from growing by applying a burning iron to the wound as each neck was severed – Oh! Would that in moments of severe temptation I had had such an iron readily to hand and coals to heat it! Entirely irrational, I know. But I take further comfort from having long ago learned that this barbaric level of response is not entirely directed from us to them.

Under provocation no greater certainly than is needed to stimulate our own aggression Australians can, and do, quite readily and often in my experience, throw off all their 180 years of civilised nationhood; they gaily revive every prejudice they ever knew, whether to do with accent, class consciousness or even the original convict complex, and sally forth into battle with a dedication which would not disgrace the most committed of the world's political agitators. To try to give adequate reasons for this intensity of reaction, as quick, positive and predictable a process as when photographic paper is first exposed to light, would be to attempt the arduous, if not the impossible. Psychology, history, politics, sport, religion and many factors besides would need thorough investigation.

However, I cannot help feeling that an almost complete lack of guilt on both sides is a primary cause. Like puppies from the same litter we feel perfectly entitled to knock hell out of one another for as long as we like, until passions burn themselves low and we continue once more, for a limited period, to display outward signs of peaceful co-existence.

The indisputable fact is that we come from the same stock and can therefore indulge ourselves rather splendidly in an orgy of superficial hate which neither our consciences, nor *Panorama* (whichever of them it was that came first), can possibly allow in relation to any of the other cricketing nations with whom we consort.

ENGLAND V AUSTRALIA 1972 Norman Preston

In many respects the Australians surpassed themselves even if they did not regain the Ashes. It must be remembered that for three years Australian cricket had been at a low level. They surrendered the Ashes in 1970–71 and the previous season had been overwhelmed in all four Tests in South Africa. The odds were something like 3–1 against them winning. That they acquitted themselves so well was due to the intelligent work done by the selectors. They decided to give youth a chance: many were almost dumbfounded when the chosen 17 excluded Lawry, Redpath and McKenzie. Only seven of the team who toured England in 1968 were retained.

Dennis Lillee was the real find of the tour. He established a record for an Australian bowler in England with 31 wickets in the Test series, beating 29 by Clarrie Grimmett in 1930 and Graham McKenzie in 1964. Lillee surprised the England batsmen in the First Test, but Australia were put out for 142 and 152 and the England players dispersed happy in the thought that they were the masters. Then came the Lord's Test, where Lillee unloosened the top-notchers and Bob Massie, on his debut, swept through the rest with the staggering analysis of 16 wickets for 137.

Although outplayed, England managed to escape with a draw at Trent Bridge, then a freak storm turned the Headingley pitch into a slow bowler's paradise that Underwood and Illingworth exploited to the full. England thus retained the Ashes, but this did not spoil the attraction of the final Test. On three days the gates at The Oval were closed and the crowds enjoyed an enthralling struggle, which went Australia's way with the luck this time going against England. So honours were even, but perhaps most satisfaction for those who have the welfare of cricket at heart was the fact that four of the five Tests produced definite results and the outcome of the rubber remained undecided until the very last moment.

First Test

Norman Preston

At Manchester, June 8, 9, 10, 12, 13, 1972. England won by 89 runs.

England won with two and a half hours to spare. The majority of people preferred to stay at home and watch an exciting contest on TV; no one could blame them, for the wind was bitterly cold. England generally held the upper hand thanks to more reliable batting and accurate bowling, but the slip fielders of both teams dropped many vital catches. Stackpole alone of the Australian front-line batsmen really caused England anxiety, but when all seemed lost Marsh gave a Jessopian display and struck 91 in two hours.

Contrary to expert predictions, the pitch proved to be hard, and with some dampness always rising to the surface, it had life and bounce until the last day when it was more amiable after a downpour. Illingworth faced an awkward decision when he won the toss on his 40th birthday. Wisely he preferred to bat, and when play began at one o'clock, Boycott received a nasty blow from Lillee in the third over, and did not return after lunch. Edrich played confidently, but finally ran himself out trying for his fifty.

Greig joined D'Oliveira, but lived perilously. Still, he survived, whereas D'Oliveira's first wayward stroke brought about his downfall: England wound up the first day at 147 for five. Australia had scarcely made the best use of the lively pitch. Next day Greig and Knott, in poor light, added 63 valuable runs, and there was some admirable slow bowling by Gleeson.

A glorious first-ball hook by Stackpole off his old rival Snow raised false hopes in the touring team's camp, for although Snow was not at his best on another dreary day Arnold reached near-perfection in length, line and late swing either way. In his second over he had Stackpole missed off successive balls by Greig and Snow in the slips, and Francis should have been taken low by Snow off the next. These disappointments left Arnold unperturbed and he continued to bowl superbly. At length D'Oliveira broke the opening stand, and immediately afterwards England gained their biggest prize. Greig baited a long-hop; Ian Chappell hooked it high and as it was sailing for six the tall Smith, on the long-leg boundary, held it high above his head.

Arnold finally had his reward with a fast ball that trapped Stackpole, and Australia were 99 for four. Next morning, Snow and Arnold swept through the six remaining wickets for 39 runs, and England gained a valuable lead of 107. The recovered Boycott straight-drove Lillee's first ball to the sightscreen, and went on gathering runs in his own immaculate style. Although Edrich had his share of the strike he was content with nine in 90 minutes before tea against Boycott's 43. Surprisingly Boycott tried to sweep a straight ball from Gleeson and was lbw, and when Edrich mis-hit a loose ball from Watson three wickets had gone for 81.

With D'Oliveira offering bold strokes in a drizzle which seriously inconvenienced Smith, wearing glasses, this pair did well to take the total to 136 for three. The sun shone on Monday morning, and Lillee revealed his true potential as a fine young fast bowler. He took six of the remaining seven wickets, including the last three in four balls, and Marsh equalled the Australian record with five catches. For England, Greig was the man of the moment with 62 out of 94.

Australia wanted 342 in nine and a quarter hours, but rain reduced that by an hour. Again Australia were let down by their early batsmen, Stackpole excepted. Chappell fell attempting a similar hook to the first innings and at the close – 57 for two – it seemed that England could be foiled only by rain.

Stackpole and Greg Chappell resumed confidently, but careless strokes cost Chappell and Watson their wickets. An hour's cricket yielded 58 runs, but when Walters played on England were romping home. Stackpole was seventh to leave after a fine display. Then came the match's solitary three-figure stand, between Marsh and Gleeson. Illingworth tried to tempt Marsh by bringing on Gifford for the first time, but Marsh struck him for four mighty sixes. Finally Greig accounted for Marsh, and picked up Gleeson with the new ball. Forty-two years had passed since England had won the first Test of a home series against Australia – they humbled the old foe at Trent Bridge in 1930.

Toss: England. **England 249** (A. W. Greig 57) **and 234** (A. W. Greig 62, D. K. Lillee 6-66); **Australia 142** (K. R. Stackpole 53, J. A. Snow 4-41, G. G. Arnold 4-62) **and 252** (K. R. Stackpole 67, R. W. Marsh 91, J. A. Snow 4-87, A. W. Greig 4-53).

Second Test

Norman Preston

At Lord's, June 22, 23, 24, 26, 1972. Australia won by eight wickets.

Australia avenged their defeat at Manchester in a contest which will be remembered as Massie's Match. The 25-year-old fast bowler surpassed all Australian records by taking 16 wickets for 137 runs; in all Tests only J. C. Laker, 19 for 90 for England v Australia in 1956, and S. F. Barnes, 17 for 179 for England v South Africa in 1913–14, stand above him. Moreover, Massie performed this wonderful feat on his Test debut.

England were badly let down by their specialist batsmen, who failed lamentably in all respects. From the start they allowed the bowlers to take the initiative, and their excessive caution met with fatal results. Illingworth won the toss for the seventh consecutive time and one must admit that the hard fast pitch was ideal for men of pace. The atmosphere was also heavy and ideally suited to swing. Massie maintained excellent length and direction, and his late swing either way always troubled the batsmen. The conditions would also have suited Arnold, but England's best bowler at Manchester was suffering from hamstring trouble and was replaced on the morning of the match by Price, who proved rather disappointing.

One must also stress the important part Lillee played in the victory. Perhaps he was inspired by his six wickets in the second innings at Manchester. Anyhow, although this time his reward was confined to two wickets in each innings he looked a far better bowler. He had tidied his long, fast approach of 22 strides, he was truly fast and he sent down far fewer loose deliveries. Massie capitalised on the hostility of his partner.

A light drizzle delayed the start for 25 minutes. Australia lost little time in taking the initiative, Boycott, Luckhurst and Edrich being removed for 28 before any substantial resistance was offered. At times Massie bowled round the wicket, but Smith and D'Oliveira raised the score to 54 at lunch. Afterwards, D'Oliveira struck three fine boundaries only to be lbw to Massie's slower ball, whereupon Greig proceeded to hit his third successive fifty. Greig and Knott enabled England to make a satisfactory recovery in their stand of 96, but immediately after tea Knott spooned Gleeson gently to mid-wicket, where to everyone's amazement Francis dropped the catch. In the end both batsmen fell to casual strokes, but Illingworth and Snow played well so that at the close of a momentous and exciting first day England were 249 for seven.

Next morning the new ball was due after two overs: Massie snatched the remaining three wickets and led his team back to the pavilion. A superb century by Greg Chappell made the second day memorable after Australia had received early shocks in the loss of both openers for seven runs. Ian Chappell set a noble example, leading the recovery with an aggressive display. He used his favourite hook to some purpose while his brother remained strictly defensive. Ian struck one six near Smith before he fell to a fine running-in catch that Smith held rolling over near his ankles.

Snow, if not so fast as Lillee, bowled splendidly and soon induced a catch from Walters, but Greg Chappell, in for three hours before he hit his first boundary, now took charge, excelling with the off-drive. Chappell duly completed his hundred on the stroke of time and Australia wound up 71 behind with half their wickets intact. On Saturday Chappell lasted another hour and a half, and in his splendid upright style hit 14 fours overall. Australia went ahead through another gallant display of powerful hitting by Marsh. He struck two sixes and six fours, and his side gained a useful lead of 36. Snow alone of the England bowlers excelled.

Only the most optimistic Australian could have anticipated the success which so soon attended the efforts of Lillee and Massie. The England collapse – half the side were out for 31 – began when a fast, shortish ball from Lillee lifted and Boycott, instead of dodging, preferred to let it strike his body. It bounced off his padded front left ribs over his shoulder and dropped behind on to the off bail. The Australians now bowled and fielded like men inspired. Luckhurst had no positive answer to Lillee's pace, and was followed by Edrich, who was compelled to flick at a late outswinger that would have taken his off stump. Smith, again getting right behind the ball, kept up his end, but the remainder were bemused by Massie's accuracy and late swing. At the end of a miserable Saturday for England they stood only 50 ahead with nine wickets down.

It remained only for the weather to stay fine on Monday for Australia to gain their just reward. Gifford and Price put on 35 in the best stand of the innings, but Australia needed only 81 to win.

England v Australia 1972

Second Test

At Lord's, on June 22, 23, 24, 26. Result: Australia won by eight wickets.

ENGLAND

	First innings		Second innings	
G. Boycott b Massie	11	– b Lillee	6
J. H. Edrich lbw b Lillee	10	– c Marsh b Massie	6
B. W. Luckhurst b Lillee	1	– c Marsh b Lillee	4
M. J. K. Smith b Massie	34	– c Edwards b Massie	30
B. L. D'Oliveira lbw b Massie	32	– c G. S. Chappell b Massie	3
A. W. Greig c Marsh b Massie	54	– c I. M. Chappell b Massie	3
†A. P. E. Knott c Colley b Massie	43	– c G. S. Chappell b Massie	12
*R. Illingworth lbw b Massie	30	– c Stackpole b Massie	12
J. A. Snow b Massie	37	– c Marsh b Massie	0
N. Gifford c Marsh b Massie	3	– not out	16
J. S. E. Price not out	4	– c G. S. Chappell b Massie	19
L-b 6, w 1, n-b 6	13	W 1, n-b 4	5

1-22 2-23 3-28 4-84 5-97 6-193   272
7-200 8-260 9-265 10-272

1-12 2-16 3-18 4-25 5-31 6-52   116
7-74 8-74 9-81 10-116

First innings – Lillee 28–3–90–2; Massie 32.5–7–84–8; Colley 16–2–42–0; G. S. Chappell 6–1–18–0;
Gleeson 9–1–25–0.
Second innings – Lillee 21–6–50–2; Massie 27.2–9–53–8; Colley 7–1–8–0.

AUSTRALIA

	First innings		Second innings	
K. R. Stackpole c Gifford b Price	5	– not out	57
B. C. Francis b Snow	0	– c Knott b Price	9
*I. M. Chappell c Smith b Snow	56	– c Luckhurst b D'Oliveira	6
G. S. Chappell b D'Oliveira	131	– not out	7
K. D. Walters c Illingworth b Snow	1		
R. Edwards c Smith b Illingworth	28		
J. W. Gleeson c Knott b Greig	1		
†R. W. Marsh c Greig b Snow	50		
D. J. Colley c Greig b Price	25		
R. A. L. Massie c Knott b Snow	0		
D. K. Lillee not out	2		
L-b 7, n-b 2	9	L-b 2	2

1-1 2-7 3-82 4-84 5-190 6-212   308
7-250 8-290 9-290 10-308

1-20 2-51   (2 wkts) 81

First innings – Snow 32–13–57–5; Price 26.1–5–87–2; Greig 29–6–74–1; D'Oliveira 17–5–48–1;
Gifford 11–4–20–0; Illingworth 7–2–13–1.
Second innings – Snow 8–2–15–0; Price 7–0–28–1; Greig 3–0–17–0; D'Oliveira 8–3–14–1;
Luckhurst 0.5–0–5–0.

Toss won by England   UMPIRES D. J. Constant and A. E. Fagg

CRICKETER OF THE YEAR – BOB MASSIE

Richie Benaud, 1973

It needed no crystal ball to deduce that the greatest match in Bob Massie's life was the Lord's Test in 1972, when his own personal contribution of 16 wickets gave Australia a magnificent victory and squared the series. Two or three years before, Massie had been rejected by Northamptonshire after he had been offered a trial while he was playing in the Scottish League. Who knows? Had Northants recognised the talent and taken him on, Australia might well have been two down after that Lord's Test.

In the Massie family, Christian names are the vogue – Bob's father is Arnold Joseph George William. A Perth chiropodist, he and his wife Barbara called their son, born on April 14, 1947, Robert Arnold Lockyer Massie. To his team mates he is known as "Fergie", a shortening of Massey-Ferguson, the tractor people.

Massie rolled over the England batsmen in that Lord's Test almost as though he was using a tractor rather than a sphere of hard red leather. Although that game rates definitely as the most memorable in which he has ever played – his first Test – he doesn't list it as necessarily his best bowling. Rather he inclines to the game between Australia and the Rest of the World in Sydney in 1971–72, when he believes he got himself a trip to England by taking seven for 76 in 20.6 overs, including the wicket of Garry Sobers, who had pounded a remarkable 254 in the previous match.

Success, in fact, has come very quickly for Massie, and it would be unwise, apart from applauding, to pay too much attention to his one sensational performance at Lord's. He is basically a good young bowler, who will get better and better as he gains in experience, and the most important part of his tour of England was not that he took 16 wickets in a Test but that he fulfilled the selectors' hopes in that he improved steadily and went back to Australia a better bowler.

Bob Massie played only two more Tests after this series, and took just 15 further wickets.

Third Test

At Nottingham, July 13, 14, 15, 17, 18, 1972. Drawn.

Again England were let down by their batsmen and fielders, who put down five chances after Illingworth had caused a sensation by sending Australia in. He could not be blamed that his plan misfired. The weather experts predicted a fine period, and he received sound advice from his old Yorkshire colleague Brian Bolus, Nottinghamshire's captain, that the pitch would not only last but become easier and slower. Some reckoned also that Illingworth did not trust his batsmen against Lillee and Massie when the pitch would be at its fastest, but it was really placid, although after lunch, when the atmosphere become somewhat heavy, the seam bowlers were able to move the ball.

Although Australia did not force a win, because they had no genuine wrist-spinner to exploit the bowlers' footmarks, the match must have boosted their confidence. Stackpole made his first Test hundred in England and in the second innings, with Francis off colour, Edwards, promoted to open, gave a great display in hitting 170 not out. Just as important was the continued mastery of Lillee and Massie over the England batsmen, the only blemish being the dreadful slowness of the over-rate.

By the end of the first day Australia had 249 for six, but Stackpole when 46 was missed twice off Greig, by Knott and by Parfitt, a sitter at second slip. Greig missed Ian Chappell twice off D'Oliveira, yet later Parfitt brought off four excellent slip catches to compensate, partially, for his expensive error. Stackpole stayed over five and a half hours, and next morning the tail added 66, thanks to a steady display by Marsh and daring strokes by Colley. Snow alone of England's bowlers lived up to his reputation.

In recent years one has become accustomed to the negative methods of England batsmen, but there has been nothing more abysmal than the way Lillee and Massie were played here. Time and again Luckhurst, never attempting to get across and behind the ball, sparred at Lillee and missed. He took two hours to reach double figures, and to the close England averaged only 28 an hour off 56 overs, reaching 117 for four.

Australia pressed home their superiority on the third morning, Marsh again claiming five victims behind the stumps. Even if Lillee's length and direction were often wayward and his use of the bouncer overdone, he nevertheless accomplished a fine job. Massie, bowling round the wicket, swung the ball awkwardly and never looked easy to play. The timid England batsmen needed six and a half hours for their 189 runs.

Australia enjoyed a lead of 126, and although Luckhurst soon held Stackpole at first slip off the belligerent Snow, Edwards thrived on the long-hops provided by some loose bowling. Ian Chappell preferred to adopt a supporting role while Edwards with his neat upright style progressed steadily. Near the end of the third day, Illingworth at last decided to bowl and soon deceived his rival captain, whose stand with Edwards had yielded 124. Australia were 157 for two at the close on Saturday, and Chappell's only problem was when he should declare.

Edwards continued to give a chanceless exhibition with a fine array of off-side strokes, mainly off the back foot. Greg Chappell was equally free and Snow conceded 62 in 12 overs. The stand produced 146 before Chappell played on. Ian Chappell declared soon after lunch. Edwards took out his bat for 170, containing one five and 13 fours.

England had nine and a half hours to get 451, which was certainly not impossible, but after their inglorious first innings it seemed only a question of whether they could save the match. This time Luckhurst offered much better resistance, but soon after tea Massie, coming round the wicket, penetrated Edrich's defence with a prodigious late dipping inswinger. There followed a momentous struggle by Luckhurst and Parfitt, and England finished the day at 111 for one.

Six hours remained for Australia to complete their task, but the batsmen continued to resist. Luckhurst and Parfitt altogether held out for three and three-quarter hours before Luckhurst tried to sweep Ian Chappell against the spin and was out for a gallant 96. All the Australian bowlers exploited the rough patches and England suffered further setbacks when the new ball was taken. Lillee disposed of Parfitt and Smith, whereupon D'Oliveira and Greig came together with three hours remaining. They not only saw the shine off the new ball but remained together until Chappell declined the last half-hour. So a Test which was played for the most part in glorious sunshine and was watched by over 68,000 people ended disappointingly.

Toss: England. **Australia 315** (K. R. Stackpole 114, D. J. Colley 54, J. A. Snow 5-92) **and 324-4 dec.** (R. Edwards 170*, I. M. Chappell 50, G. S. Chappell 72); **England 189** (D. K. Lillee 4-35, R. A. L. Massie 4-43) **and 290-4** (B. W. Luckhurst 96, B. L. D'Oliveira 50*).

CRICKETER OF THE YEAR – GREG CHAPPELL

Richie Benaud, 1973

The Chappell brothers, Ian and Greg, are destined always to live with the shadow of their famous grandfather, the former Australian captain, Victor Richardson. The key words are "live with" rather than "live in", as happens with so many sportsmen who follow on from famous forebears. Ian and Greg are splendid Test cricketers in their own right and Greg Chappell, on the 1972 tour of England, confirmed his place as Australia's No. 1 batsman.

He played two superb innings, the first at Lord's in the Second Test where he made a magnificent 131, and the other at The Oval where, after two wickets had fallen for 34, he joined his brother in a wonderful 200-run partnership. The innings at Lord's can be rated alongside Bob Massie's bowling as the most vital performance in the whole game – a superbly judged piece of batting that, technically, was beyond reproach. Eighteen months before, Greg had made a century in his first Test match against England, the Second Test of the series in Perth. Most critics, however, would say that Chappell's outstanding performance was his batting at Lord's, and he would agree that, from the technical and concentration point of view, it was perhaps the innings he has most enjoyed in his cricket career. He makes an interesting point about the Test series in saying that he thinks a drawn series was probably a fair result, for although Australia played well in three of the Tests, they showed a lack of knowledge of how to win games in the light of the Trent Bridge result.

Gregory Stephen Chappell was born on August 7, 1948, at Unley in South Australia, the second son of Martin and Jeanne Chappell – the latter the daughter of Victor Richardson. His first Sheffield Shield match was in 1966–67, and he had an important two-year stretch with Somerset.

Fourth Test

Bill Bowes

At Leeds, July 27, 28, 29, 1972. England won by nine wickets.

England won at three minutes past five on the third day, to take a 2-1 lead in the series and so retain the Ashes. A pitch that afforded considerable help to the spinners found batsmen in both teams unable to cope and the Australians – the less practised against a turning ball – were completely outplayed, as they were on the same ground in 1956 and again in 1961. Not for a moment would one suggest that conditions had been deliberately engineered to produce such a result, but the fact remained that they were conditions least likely to help the tourists. The pitch was not up to Test standard, even allowing for the fact that Underwood is the most skilful bowler in the world when there is help for finger-spin. It was without pace, took spin from the first day, and grew progressively helpful.

Both teams made three changes, influenced by a quite evident distrust of the pitch which had been flooded by a freak thunderstorm over the weekend. That flood had restricted the use of the heavy roller, and the pitch was obviously damp on the first morning and quite grassless. Australia, on winning the toss, were no doubt pleased to bat first. Stackpole made an excellent start with a leg-glance and a drive for two boundaries in the first over from Arnold. Snow also made a great start, getting Edwards – who opened after his century at Nottingham – caught at the wicket when he touched a late outswinger in the first over. Snow bowled well. Time and again he beat the bat and when he was rested he had sent down seven overs for six runs and one wicket. Arnold, with the score at 32, had Stackpole (21) dropped by Fletcher in the slips.

Illingworth came on and, after he had delivered three overs, Underwood bowled. Spinners on the first morning of a Test? Illingworth had obviously read the signs aright. Although there was no indication of the havoc to be caused by spin when Australia lunched at 79 for one, things began to happen straight afterwards. Underwood shouted for lbw against Stackpole second ball and then, fifth ball, Stackpole played forward and edged a second catch to Knott. Greg Chappell joined his brother. Illingworth took over from Snow and Australia's troubles increased most seriously. Ian Chappell, after he had batted 46 overs, had scored only 26; Greg Chappell seemed to express the feelings of the tourists when he hit a ball rather uppishly from Underwood towards mid-off which he had intended to go along the ground. He moved down the pitch and gave the spot where the ball had dropped a sledgehammer blow with the bat. He left at 93 when he missed a straight one from Underwood and was lbw. In the next over Ian Chappell went out to drive Illingworth and hit a low return catch, then Walters, trying to cut, was bowled by Illingworth, making it 97 for five.

Sheahan fell to a spectacular one-handed catch by Illingworth at point off Underwood without scoring, and the England captain made a third catch when Marsh skyed Underwood and cross-batted to mid-on. Sensationally, Australia had slumped to 98 for seven, and the 19,000 crowd almost ironically applauded the 100, in the 62nd over. Inverarity and Mallett kept England waiting 80 minutes for the next success, adding 47 valuable runs, but Massie and Lillee both failed to score and Australia totalled only 146. In an hour's batting at the end of the day Edrich and Luckhurst made 43 without loss.

On the second day the off-spinner Mallett bowled at Underwood's pace and the left-armer Inverarity at Illingworth's pace. They returned some of the spin-bowling problems to England. By lunch England had lost six wickets for 112. Seven went with the fall of Greig at 128, and only an eighth-wicket stand of 104 by Illingworth and Snow swung the game again in favour of England. Illingworth played a real captain's part by scoring 54 not out in England's 252 for nine by Friday evening.

As expected, the Australian second innings disintegrated before the bowling of Underwood. After the initial opening of the fast bowlers (in which Arnold dismissed Edwards for a pair), Underwood took five for 18 in 13 overs and ripped through the heart of the batting. It seemed that the game would be over by tea, but fortunately for the crowd of 20,000 Sheahan and Massie were mostly instrumental in continuing the innings until that time, though England needed no more than 20 runs to win.

Toss: Australia. **Australia 146** (K. R. Stackpole 52, D. L. Underwood 4-37) **and 136** (D. L. Underwood 6-45); **England 263** (R. Illingworth 57, A. A. Mallett 5-114) **and 21-1**.

Fifth Test

Norman Preston

At The Oval, August 10, 11, 12, 14, 15, 16, 1972. Australia won by five wickets.

This was a splendid match with fortune swaying first to one side and then to the other. Among the several notable personal performances that of Lillee, Australia's demon fast bowler, was the keynote to his side's success. From the moment Illingworth won the toss again and chose to bat on an excellent pitch which lasted well throughout the six days, Lillee, by his sheer pace coupled with the occasional shock-telling bouncer, was the man England feared most. He took five wickets in each innings, bringing his number of victims for the series to 31, a record for an Australian bowler in England.

England were always fighting an uphill battle, for yet again their specialist batsmen let them down, and soon after tea on the first day eight wickets had fallen for 181, by which time Lillee had well-nigh exhausted himself as Knott came to the rescue. Earlier Wood, on his first appearance for England, gave a staunch exhibition after being struck a painful blow by Lillee on his upper left arm in the first over from an ugly bouncer.

England made 50 for the loss of Edrich and Wood before lunch. Then Parfitt and Hampshire settled down to a confident stand until just after the ball had been changed for the umpteenth time in the series, when Hampshire cut a high bouncer to short third man. Then came a landslide, only relieved on the appearance of Knott who, ably assisted by Arnold, took the total to 267 for nine at the close. Besides Lillee's pace, which brought him three wickets in four balls for the second time in the rubber, England had also been troubled by Mallett, who turned the ball quite a lot early on this first day to take three for 80. Knott continued to thrash away next morning, but when Lillee flung a bouncer at Underwood, possibly England's ace bowler in a six-day match, and struck his arm, Knott called it a day, having hit 17 fours in a grand knock.

Arnold and Snow soon disposed of the opening pair for 34, and then began the highest stand of the rubber, between the Chappells, who put on 201 – each reached three figures, the first time two brothers had hit a hundred in the same innings of a Test. Ian played the captain's part, paying strict attention to defence – he had a rare duel with Underwood and Illingworth. Eventually, Greg hit too soon at a shorter ball from Illingworth and was well caught at mid-on, having struck 17 fours. Australia were within ten of England and still had seven wickets intact to start the third day.

On Saturday, the game veered England's way, as Snow and Underwood, ably backed by Arnold and Greig, bowled splendidly. For the spectators, the day was spoilt by light rain, which prevented play for two hours after lunch, and at the end another half-hour was lost to bad light. The sun shone powerfully during the first session when Snow and Arnold fed Ian Chappell with the odd short ball, until his favourite uppish hook again brought about his undoing after he had hit 20 fours.

Underwood showed his class with some immaculate bowling on a firm true surface with four men close to the bat. Underwood undid Edwards, who hit nine fours in his 79, and then had three more quick strikes, taking four wickets in 13 overs for 29 runs – a masterly effort. So, at the weekend Australia were 394 for eight.

With the game equally poised at the halfway stage, England continued their strong challenge to win the rubber. They soon captured the two outstanding wickets for the addition of five runs, and the lead was restricted to 115. A stupendous effort was required from the batsmen, and considering that all the first nine proceeded to acquire double figures, this was forthcoming – but really only Wood, and later Knott again, answered the call as their supporters hoped. True, for the first time in the summer, England mustered 300, but in the process of clearing their deficit they lost Edrich, Parfitt and Hampshire, and throughout a praiseworthy struggle Australia's pace bowlers were dominant opponents. At first, Lillee harried Wood and Edrich with bouncers: Edrich played on first ball after lunch. D'Oliveira, refusing to be tempted while the bowlers persisted well outside his stumps, showed something of his best form in a stand of 80 with Wood, who stayed 275 minutes and hit 15 fours. After such a grand effort, he was unfortunate to miss a hundred on his Test debut by ten runs. It was good to see again someone present a straight bat to Lillee and Massie, and someone who was not afraid to get behind the line of the ball, ready to hook the bouncer. At the end of the fourth day England stood only 112 runs in front with half their wickets standing.

Next day Lillee soon removed both Illingworth and Greig, but Snow kept up his end sensibly while Knott plundered freely for a memorable hour as he helped himself to nine fours, being last out. So at three o'clock on the fifth day Australia began the task of making 242 to win. Arnold soon dismissed Watson lbw, whereupon Ian Chappell joined Stackpole in what was really the deciding partnership. For 50 minutes Snow and Arnold bowled admirably, but by tea, Australia were 56 for one. Then a rare tussle ensued, despite some aggression by Stackpole against Underwood who once more bowled superbly, as indeed did Illingworth round the wicket until he slipped on delivering and sprained his right ankle an hour before the close.

At stumps Australia were 116 for one. The loss of Illingworth, coupled with an injury to D'Oliveira, proved the death knell for England, well as Underwood and his colleagues maintained the challenge. Snow, too, took no part, having received a severe blow on his left arm when facing Lillee. Nevertheless, within half an hour of resuming on the last morning England accounted for Stackpole, Ian Chappell and Edwards for five runs. Australia still wanted 71. Sheahan, so often disappointing, was the man of the moment with his straight bat and upright stance. Marsh began carefully until the new ball was taken at 210, when he sensed victory at hand and unleashed many exciting leg hits which sent Australia – for the first time in their history without a single player from New South Wales in their team – hurrying to square the rubber.

Toss: England. **England 284** (P. H. Parfitt 51, A. P. E. Knott 92, D. K. Lillee 5-58) **and 356** (B. Wood 90, A. P. E. Knott 63, D. K. Lillee 5-123); **Australia 399** (I. M. Chappell 118, G. S. Chappell 113, R. Edwards 79, D. L. Underwood 4-90) **and 242-5** (K. R. Stackpole 79).

CRICKETER OF THE YEAR – DENNIS LILLEE   Richie Benaud, 1973

The Haslingden Club in the Lancashire League has a lot to answer for in the emergence of Dennis Lillee as Australia's trump card. Lillee, who is not yet at his peak, gives full credit to the season he had in the league: "I think it was probably one of the real turning-points in my career. It certainly forced me to become more accurate and learn a little bit about bowling. Quite often footholds would be too slippery to bowl really fast, and accuracy and movement off the pitch would be the prime requirements. Now this couldn't have come at a better time as, up to that stage, I'd been concentrating solely on pace."

Lillee definitely adds excitement to the game of cricket, if one can excuse the problem of perhaps too long a run to the crease. But, in keeping with other great fast bowlers like Lindwall, Tyson and Hall, the long run is inclined to add to the excitement. The dull thing is to watch a medium-pacer take too long a run – to see the players named above, scorching their way into the bowling crease, is a matter of apprehension for the batsman and excitement for the spectator.

Dennis Keith Lillee was born in Perth, on July 18, 1949, and began playing with the Perth club when 15 years of age. Australia had been looking for a fast bowler ever since the retirement of Alan Davidson, and, although Graham McKenzie had shouldered much of the burden, there was a tremendous need for someone with extra pace. In 1970-71 the selectors decided to make changes for the sixth Ashes Test at Adelaide. They put in Lillee and he repaid them by taking five wickets in the first innings and another three in the final Test.

When the 1971-72 South African tour of Australia was cancelled, a series against a World XI was put on in its place. When the second representative game came along in Perth Australians were able to welcome a new fast-bowling star. The match was scheduled for five days but lasted only three. The World XI made just 59, Lillee taking eight for 29, and then he chipped in with four more wickets in the second innings. Lillee marks this down as his most memorable game. "I felt shocking when I got to the ground – some sort of virus was going around – and, after bowling a couple of overs for the wickets of Gavaskar and Engineer, I felt terribly tired and asked Ian Chappell if I could possibly have a rest. He talked me into having one more over and things suddenly began to happen after McKenzie dismissed Kanhai and Zaheer was run out. I think that was the most memorable match I've played in from a personal performance point of view, but the best bowling experience I've had was in the final Test at The Oval, where we just had to win to square the series. It was a really hard grind on a beautiful batting pitch that gave a little bit of assistance to the pace bowlers if they were prepared to put a bit into it, and I finished up bowling 56 overs."

Australia v England 1974-75

John Thicknesse

An unpleasant surprise was in store for MCC on their eighth post-war tour of Australia. Having been selected on the assumption that after Dennis Lillee's back injury early in 1973 Australia were unlikely to call upon a genuinely fast bowler, Denness's side in fact found themselves confronting two – Lillee and a youngster from Sydney, Jeff Thomson, who up to that time had made a bigger name for himself by what he had said about hurting batsmen than by anything he had done on the field.

Thomson, six feet tall and 24 years old, took 33 wickets in four and a half Tests and looked sure to break Arthur Mailey's long-standing record of 36 in 1920-21 when he hurt himself playing tennis on the rest day in Adelaide and was unable to bowl again in the series. Lillee bowled with a hostility that bordered on savagery throughout the series, steadily gaining pace as he gained confidence in his back. And his pace was comparable to Thomson's so that England had no respite. Watching the two in action, it was easy to believe they were the fastest pair ever to have coincided in a cricket team. They would have been too good for better batting sides than Denness's even without the superb standard of catching, or without the help they got from the pitches. The catching reached its zenith at Perth, where the Chappell brothers, Mallett and Redpath shared 13 in the slips and gully, compared to one by Marsh, the wicket-keeper.

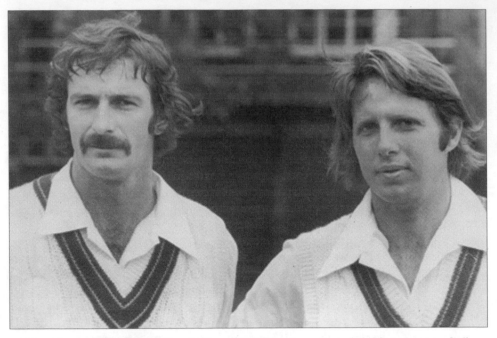

Double trouble: Dennis Lillee (left) and Jeff Thomson, Australia's blistering new-ball
pairing of the mid-1970s.

On top of those advantages, the umpires gave Thomson and Lillee considerable
freedom in respect of short-pitched bowling. Thomson's tremendous strength – or
perhaps some feature of his perfectly fair but "hurling" action – enabled him to get
the ball up from a fuller length that any fast bowler I had seen. But even from him
there were often two unmistakable bouncers an over, while Lillee sometimes bowled
three or even four.

England's batting, arguably their weakest in Australia since the war, had little experience against fast bowling and was painfully at sea against it, broadly because of an
inability or reluctance to get in line. They were without Boycott, who withdrew a month
before the team left England because "he couldn't do justice to himself"; saw their
other linchpin, Amiss, reduced to mediocrity, and to cap everything ran into a sequence
of injuries and illness. The most serious were to Edrich, the vice-captain, Amiss and
Lloyd, who all broke bones. Denness's adjustment to Australian conditions was hampered
by a virus that affected his back, while Willis, the fastest bowler, was troubled by sore
knees. Cowdrey joined the team in Perth, having hastily been summoned from an
English winter in the hope that 20 years after his first tour he could shore up the
batting. In making his sixth tour of Australia, Cowdrey equalled the record of J. Briggs,
the Lancashire slow left-arm bowler.

Denness made 188 in the Sixth Test, where England won by an innings. That was
at tribute to his determination, for it was not until his 13th tour innings that he even
managed a fifty, and his lack of form and technical deficiencies were such that he felt
obliged to leave himself out of the side for the Fourth Test.

First Test

At Brisbane, November 29, 30, December 1, 3, 4, 1974. Australia won by 166 runs.

Australia's victory – their fifth in eight post-war Tests at Brisbane – was achieved with 80 minutes to spare after a hard-fought match that had run narrowly their way from the second morning. It was played on a pitch of uneven bounce after hasty preparation by the Lord Mayor of Brisbane, Alderman Clem Jones, following storms that flooded the ground two nights before the start. (Mr Jones had dismissed the curator ten days earlier.) The bounce was especially unreliable at the southern end, where England lost 16 of their 20 wickets and Australia eight out of 15.

Australia's advantage lay in the possession of the one bowler strong and fast enough to profit from the conditions, Thomson's second Test bringing him nine wickets, including six for 46 in the second innings. Lillee, sparing his back at this stage, was aggressive but not as fast as in England in the previous series. He took two wickets in each innings on his return to Test cricket. So Thomson emerged as the key figure. He revealed himself as a pure slinger who changed feet two strides out, pulling back his right shoulder to get into position for a long swing of his arm, showing batsmen the studs of his left boot and a large area of his back in his delivery stride. His erratic control was shown by three wides and 13 no-balls, but his very inaccuracy had merit in that batsmen never knew what to expect. He broke Amiss's thumb in the first innings and his great speed, which often enabled him to explode the ball waist- or chest-high from almost a full length, made him an awesome opponent.

Despite uncertainty about the pitch, Ian Chappell chose to bat, and the decision was justified when after the quick loss of their opening batsmen Australia reached the midway point of the final session with only three men out. Chappell held the innings together with successive stands of 100 with his brother Greg and 87 with Ross Edwards, who provided Knott with his 200th Test dismissal. Three wickets in four overs, two of them taken with bouncers by Willis, reduced Australia to 219 for six at stumps, giving England the advantage. This was increased in the first 20 minutes of the second day when Jenner, hooking, and Marsh succumbed to the new ball. Then, on a pitch that appeared to have lost pace, England were unable to dislodge Walker and Australia regained control, adding 80 for the last two wickets.

England began disastrously, losing Amiss to a brutal ball from Thomson that cut in chest-high off a length and flew to gully off the gloves. But Edrich, dropped at one off Lillee, and Greig batted through to stumps, when England were 114 for four. Edrich was out early on the third morning, caught at slip off Lillee an over after being rapped hard on the top hand – the ball that caused the break. His 48 won England much-needed breathing space. Knott and Lever followed, but Greig found a determined partner in Underwood and England cut the lead to 44. Greig's hundred was a memorable mixture of brilliant off-side strokes, wild passes, and continual attempts to rattle Lillee by shadow-boxing underneath the bouncers. He batted five hours and hit 15 fours. His hundred was only the second for England at the Woolloongabba ground.

Australia's second innings began two and a half hours from stumps, but again they soon lost Wally Edwards, and when Underwood had Ian Chappell caught at slip, losing no more wickets became the top priority. This suited England and Underwood had a spell of 7–5–3–1. Two more consolidating sessions followed on the fourth day,

Australia advancing from 51 for two to 211 for five by tea. They made their push afterwards, Walters and Marsh extending their stand to 98 in even time before Chappell declared. Denness set England a tireless example in the inner ring and the fielding never wilted.

England needed to bat six hours 40 minutes to save the match, or make 333 to win. Only two overs were possible on the fourth evening, and at stumps England were ten for no wicket. They had a good chance of saving the match with a successful first session, but in mid-morning Thomson dismissed Edrich and Amiss in successive overs – Amiss, batting with a broken thumb, with another explosive ball that was edged to third slip – and from then on Australia were in command. After lunch England collapsed from 80 for three to 94 for six, Thomson again striking with wickets in successive overs, one of them when he yorked Greig with one of the fastest balls of the match. Knott, who batted two hours, and Underwood, who helped him to add 47 for the eighth wicket, resisted with determination as Thomson tired in great heat, but when Underwood mis-hit Jenner to mid-on the end came swiftly.

Toss: Australia. **Australia 309** (I. M. Chappell 90, G. S. Chappell 58, R. G. D. Willis 4-56)
and 288-5 dec. (G. S. Chappell 71, R. Edwards 53, K. D. Walters 62*);
England 265 (A. W. Greig 110, M. H. N. Walker 4-73) **and 166** (J. R. Thomson 6-46).

Second Test

At Perth, December 13, 14, 15, 17, 1974. Australia won by nine wickets.

The match was virtually decided on the first day when England, put in, collapsed from 99 for one to 208 all out. Australia built a lead of 273 by mid-afternoon on the third day, bowled England out for 293, and won late on the fourth day to go two up in the series. England were handicapped by the absence of Amiss and Edrich, but poor batting against Thomson and Lillee was again at the root of their defeat. Thomson added seven wickets to his nine at Brisbane, generating great speed on a pitch that gained pace after the first day, and Lillee again had four – a bag that would have been bigger if the luck had run for him.

England's troubles were accentuated by Australia's brilliant catching in the slips and gully. Greg Chappell established a Test record with seven catches in the match, all but two of them at second slip. On the second day England were briefly in contention when Australia were 192 for four, but a spectacular 103 by Walters, who made exactly 100 between tea and stumps, reversed the situation. Ross Edwards also played an important part, batting five hours 20 minutes and helping add 170 for the fifth wicket.

Four of England's five changes were caused by injury or illness. Lloyd, Cowdrey – pressed into service only four days after his arrival – came in for Amiss and Edrich, while Old, Arnold and Titmus replaced Lever (back trouble), Hendrick (throat infection) and Underwood, who was left out on the morning of the match when cloudy weather persuaded Denness to gamble on winning the toss and putting Australia in.

Thomson needed only five balls to inflict his first injury, hitting Luckhurst on the top hand off a good length. Luckhurst was able to bat on, but the hand swelled overnight, preventing him from fielding, and in the second innings he batted at No. 7. He and Lloyd were lucky to survive Lillee's new-ball spell, but Thomson was wildly erratic and the opening stand lasted 80 minutes before Luckhurst slashed Walker hard into the gully where Mallett held the first of Australia's fine catches.

Cowdrey stepped out for his 188th Test innings (first for 3½ years) to as warm an ovation as he is accustomed to at Canterbury, and having narrowly survived his first three balls gave a demonstration of defensive technique against fast bowling that was subsequently equalled only by Knott and Titmus, who was playing his first Test since February 1968. Only these three consistently observed the principle of moving their bodies into line, thus minimising the danger of being caught in the slips.

Lloyd and Cowdrey laid the foundation of a competitive score, but finally Lloyd dabbed Thomson to second slip and the innings collapsed. Four overs later Cowdrey moved too far across and was bowled behind his legs, and within 70 minutes of Lloyd's departure England were 132 for six. Knott and Titmus added 62 for the seventh wicket, but the damage was irreparable. To make matters worse, Fletcher could not hold a difficult slip catch offered by Redpath in Willis's single over.

On the second day Australia added 351 off 76 overs, Walters highlighting the performance with a vicious exhibition of pulling. In the hour after tea he made 67, including the majority of his 11 fours; but he lost the strike for lengthy periods against the second new ball and faced the last ball of the day at 97, needing a six to complete a hundred in a session for the second time in his Test career. Willis delivered a fast long-hop and Walters exultantly hooked it into the crowd at square leg.

On the third day Edwards went on to the first Test hundred by a Western Australian at Perth. But Walters was caught at slip off Willis's second ball of the day, and the threatened massacre did not materialise. Old polished off the tail and the last six wickets fell for 129. So just before the Test's halfway point Lloyd and Cowdrey opened England's second innings. Thomson ended a staunch partnership of 52 when a good-length ball cut back to hit Lloyd in the abdomen, causing him to retire hurt, but in 36 overs before stumps England lost only Cowdrey and began the fourth day at 102 for one, needing 171 to make Australia bat again.

Their slim hopes of making a close match vanished in Thomson's first three overs, when Greig and Denness were caught in the slips playing a long way from their bodies, and Fletcher touched his first ball, a lifting outswinger, to Marsh. Lloyd and Luckhurst held on well despite their injuries, but it was left to Titmus, playing his 50th Test, to underline the technical deficiencies of his more exalted team-mates with a nearly flawless 61 in three hours 20 minutes. When he was last out, brilliantly caught on the run by Greg Chappell at wide long-off, Australia needed only 21 to win.

Toss: Australia. **England 208** (A. P. E. Knott 51) **and 293** (F. J. Titmus 61, J. R. Thomson 5-93); **Australia 481** (G. S. Chappell 62, R. Edwards 115, K. D. Walters 103) **and 23-1.**

Third Test
At Melbourne, December 26, 27, 28, 30, 31, 1974. Drawn.

At the end of five tense days, Australia finished a low-scoring match eight short of victory with two wickets standing, much to the credit and relief of an England side reduced to four bowlers through an injury to Hendrick. Australia began their second innings late on the fourth evening needing 246, the highest total of the match, to win.

The pitch, though never true, played as easily as at any stage, and England were also worried that Titmus would be unable to bowl after a blow on the right knee from Thomson. In the event, however, a limping Titmus overcame his problems to the extent of bowling 29 overs for 64, and with determined help from his three fellow bowlers prevented Australia from taking control even after Redpath and Greg Chappell had played them into a winning position with a third-wicket stand of 101.

Walters kept Australia well within striking range with 20 in 15 minutes after tea; but when he was sixth out, with 75 needed in 45 minutes plus the mandatory last 15 overs, Marsh and Walker had to guard against a further quick loss and the last hour began with Australia still 55 from their goal. It was then that their tactics defied explanation, for they added only seven runs from seven overs from Titmus and Underwood, satisfying Denness that they had settled for a draw and that it was therefore safe to make a last attempt to win the match by taking the new ball. Instead, it had precisely the opposite effect. Marsh opened his shoulders to club a high four over mid-on in Willis's first over, which cost nine, and though Marsh was out next over, Walker and Lillee attacked so effectively that Australia reached the 13th over only 16 short of victory with three wickets in hand. Then, with the match apparently theirs and 42,827 spectators poised to shout them home, their tactics unaccountably changed again, only two runs coming from Greig's next over and a subdued Lillee making little effort to disturb a maiden by Underwood. Lillee's dismissal from the fourth ball of the last over virtually ended their chance and the match was left drawn.

An extraordinary Test had begun on Boxing Day in front of a crowd of 77,165 (the third-largest for any day's Test cricket: total attendance was 250,721) with Ian Chappell putting England in for the second time running. Moisture in the pitch gave some help to bowlers, but Cowdrey and Edrich were playing England into a promising position when they were out in successive overs shortly before tea. Edrich was much the more fluent, but when he was out, controversially judged caught down the leg side when Marsh was appealing for a stumping, the familiar collapse developed and England reached stumps at 176 for seven.

On the second morning a sturdy 52 by Knott, who passed 3,000 runs in Tests, enabled the last three wickets to add 66. Redpath and Wally Edwards gave Australia their best start in five innings, but their chance of taking advantage was lessened by the loss of two and a quarter hours to the weather on the second day and the fall of three wickets in the first four overs of the third, including Greg Chappell's to the type of rearing ball from Willis that England's batsmen had grown used to receiving from Thomson and Lillee. Australia were 126 for five when Redpath, after four hours, was a victim of the varied bounce when attempting to square-cut Greig; but Ian Chappell, Marsh and Walker – who was proving a batsman to be reckoned with at No. 8 – consolidated, and Australia were set for an important lead when in 20 minutes their last four wickets fell for four runs, Marsh becoming Titmus's 150th Test victim. Willis, deprived of Hendrick's help from the second morning through a pulled hamstring, bowled with sustained hostility to take five wickets.

On the fourth morning a beautiful innings by Amiss seemed to put England out of danger. With some luck, Lloyd helped him to put on 115 for the first wicket; but as though to disprove the belief that from such a start collapse was impossible, the middle batting yet again disintegrated and eight wickets crashed for 67. Greig's massive confidence and showmanship saved the situation and with studious help from Willis he added 56 for the ninth wicket to set the match up for its astonishing finale. Thomson, with eight wickets, increased his series bag to 24.

Toss: Australia. **England 242** (A. P. E. Knott 52, J. R. Thomson 4-72) **and 244** (D. L. Amiss 90, A. W. Greig 60, J. R. Thomson 4-71, A. A. Mallett 4-60); **Australia 241** (I. R. Redpath 55, R. G. D. Willis 5-61) **and 238-8** (G. S. Chappell 61, A. W. Greig 4-56).

Fourth Test

At Sydney, January 4, 5, 6, 8, 9, 1975. Australia won by 171 runs.

Australia recaptured the Ashes lost on the same ground four years earlier. This third victory was achieved with only 5.3 overs to spare, but Australia dominated from the time McCosker and Redpath put on 96 for the first wicket after Ian Chappell had, against expectations, chosen to bat on a humid morning and an unevenly grassed pitch. It proved the right decision, for Arnold got less movement with the new ball than England were hoping, while Willis looked jaded after his efforts at Melbourne.

Another factor was that Edrich, captaining because Denness stood down through lack of form, put insufficient pressure on McCosker, who had been brought in for Wally Edwards and was opening for the first time in a first class match. McCosker had plenty to remember from his Test debut because, apart from scoring 80, while fielding at forward short leg he was hit on the head during the first innings and forced to go off, and in the groin in the second, and obliged to take refuge in the slips.

McCosker played extremely well, as did Redpath. But for a player who had shown his strength off his legs during the NSW game, life was made easier than it should have been. Neither Willis nor Arnold was given a short leg in front of square and McCosker was able, with complete safety, to find his confidence with a succession of ones and twos to square and long leg. Australia had two escapes during the opening stand, the first at 36 when Redpath was given the benefit of the doubt when Fletcher's underarm return hit the bowler's stumps from extra cover, and at 69 when McCosker was missed in the gully from a low, fast slice off Willis.

The Chappell brothers consolidated, but when Walters was lbw to the second new ball early on the second morning, Australia were 255 for five and England had a chance of holding them. Another came at 310 for seven, when Greig held a brilliant left-handed catch at second slip to dispose of Greg Chappell. But Greig was overbowled to the exclusion of Titmus, and Australia added a priceless 95 for their last three wickets.

Lillee then bowled his best opening spell so far, but Walker made the breakthrough with the help of a wonderful left-handed gully catch by Mallett to get rid of Amiss. At 123 for five England were in danger of following on, but Edrich held an end for three and three-quarter hours and on the third day Knott rode his luck for a rollicking 82, lashing drives through the covers and past the bowler. In an hour after lunch he made 56, adding 92 with Titmus and Underwood. Then over-excitement got him out when he swung across Thomson and lost his leg stump. So midway through the day Australia were batting again, 110 ahead. They received an early setback when Lloyd brought off one of the best catches of a series remarkable for its number of great ones, when he dived low to his right at leg slip to pick up Ian Chappell. In now-perfect batting conditions, Greg Chappell imperiously took control, taking Australia to 123 for one at stumps.

On the fourth day defensive bowling of machine-like accuracy by Arnold prevented Australia from thrusting home their advantage as quickly as planned. Greg Chappell never looked likely to be denied his first hundred of the series, and he and Redpath steadily took their stand to 220, a record for Australia's second wicket against England at home.

England needed to bat eight and a half hours to save the match – their target of 400 was 105 more than they had scored in seven starts – but respite came in the form of a violent thunderstorm before the innings could begin. This trimmed 95 minutes from the day and when Amiss and Lloyd luckily survived 11 overs in the evening a draw should have been within their powers. Yet on the last day the demoralising effect of Thomson and Lillee was never more apparent. From 68 for no wicket in the 16th over, the score became 74 for three in the 22nd with Edrich on his way to hospital after being hit below the rib-cage first ball by a Lillee skidder. Though the pitch was playing true the match was virtually decided when he came back strapped and sedated at 156 for six, but with Willis and Arnold he showed how comfortably it might have been saved by blocking for over two and a half hours to make 33 not out. Willis stayed in 88 minutes and Arnold 35, performances that put the early batting in perspective.

Only Amiss, caught off his gloves off a bouncer that cut back, and Fletcher, shaken by a deflection on to his forehead two balls before his dismissal by Thomson, were exempt from blame, though Greig made a flashy 54 and Knott may have been unlucky to be given out caught at short leg.

Toss: Australia. **Australia 405** (R. B. McCosker 80, I. M. Chappell 53, G. S. Chappell 84, G. G. Arnold 5-86, A. W. Greig 4-104) **and 289-4 dec.** (I. R. Redpath 105, G. S. Chappell 144); **England 295** (J. H. Edrich 50, A. P. E. Knott 82, J. R. Thomson 4-74) **and 228** (A. W. Greig 54, A. A. Mallett 4-21).

Fifth Test

At Adelaide, January 25, 26, 27, 29, 30, 1975. Australia won by 163 runs.

England's fourth defeat was in many ways the most discouraging of the series because for the first time they had the makings of a winning position only to throw the advantage away. In addition to there being no play on the first day, in the second innings Australia were handicapped by the absence of Thomson, who sprained his right shoulder playing tennis on the rest day. Despite these setbacks Australia, cut down to 84 for five by Underwood in their first innings, took little more than three and a half days to win, underlining the huge gulf between the teams. On this occasion Lillee, with four wickets in each innings, was their match-winning bowler: a belated reward for his consistently dangerous bowling throughout the series.

The night before the match one of the covers blew loose, and play was abandoned at lunch. The pitch was still wet on the second morning, and when England won the toss (for the first time) Denness sent Australia in. With a hundred in Tasmania and 99 against NSW Denness had made certain of reclaiming his place even before Edrich was found to have two fractured ribs from his blow from Lillee in the Fourth Test.

Denness brought Underwood into the attack after three overs from Arnold, and with the ball turning and stopping gave him two slips, a gully and a forward short leg. Redpath and McCosker did a valuable job by resisting Underwood for 50 minutes.

Then in his sixth over he had McCosker caught at second slip, whereupon in 40 minutes up to lunch Australia lapsed from 52 for one to 77 for four.

England appeared to be lucky with the decisions that accounted for Redpath and Greg Chappell, but on a pitch palpably favouring finger-spin Denness invited criticism by using Titmus only for the over before lunch. In the afternoon he stuck to bowling Arnold and Greig in partnership with Underwood, who added Marsh to his bag with the help of a fine catch on the square-leg boundary. Walters and Jenner launched an aggressive recovery that added 220 in even time for the last five wickets.

By mid-afternoon the pitch had lost its bite, but this was brilliant opportunist cricket by Australia and psychologically the turning-point of the match. Underwood suffered his share of punishment and finished with seven for 113. (By taking four wickets in the second innings he became the first England bowler to take 11 in a Test in Australia since J. C. White in 1928–29.) By contrast Titmus had nought for 27 in seven overs, having come on too late in his second spell to take advantage of the drying pitch.

Amiss and Lloyd survived two overs before stumps, but by tea on the third day a dispirited England had been dismissed for 172 although the pitch had rolled out plumb. Only Denness and Fletcher played with freedom. Once again both were out trying to cut Thomson, and from 130 for four the last six wickets fell for 42. Thomson, with three wickets, took his aggregate to 33; but Lillee bowled faster and straighter for his four for 49, while Mallett profited from indisciplined batting to take three late wickets.

In two hours Australia extended their lead to 243 before stumps for the loss of McCosker and Ian Chappell. They were held up on the fourth morning when Underwood removed Redpath and Greg Chappell, and by a tight defensive spell by Arnold. Walters and Marsh added 112 in even time and the declaration came 80 minutes after lunch, leaving England 405 to make in eight and a half hours. Without Willis, who had aggravated his knee condition in the nets, England had made a satisfactory job of limiting their survival time, but their chance of a draw virtually disappeared when they lost wickets in each of the first three overs.

Amiss, caught at the wicket off Lillee's fourth ball, became the first of three batsmen to collect a pair; Lloyd was caught at third slip off Walker; and Cowdrey was fantastically picked up low and left-handed by Mallett in the gully, giving Lillee two for nought. When Denness and Greig also fell, making England 94 for five at stumps, there could be no recovery.

On the last day, however, Knott took some of the sting out of the inevitable defeat with his first hundred against Australia. Fletcher and Titmus lent him determined support in successive stands of 68, but the match was over 80 minutes after lunch. Willis, coming in with Knott 15 off his hundred, held an end until he reached it with an uppercut boundary off Lillee. Knott's 106 not out was only the second century by a wicket-keeper in the 219 Tests between the two countries: Kent and England also claimed the first one in 1934, when Leslie Ames scored 120 at Lord's.

Toss: England. **Australia 304** (K. D. Walters 55, T. J. Jenner 74, D. L. Underwood 7-113)
and 272-5 dec. (I. R. Redpath 52, K. D. Walters 71*, R. W. Marsh 55, D. L. Underwood 4-102);
England 172 (M. H. Denness 51, D. K. Lillee 4-49) **and 241** (K. W. R. Fletcher 63,
A. P. E. Knott 106*, D. K. Lillee 4-69).

Sixth Test

At Melbourne, February 8, 9, 10, 12, 13, 1975. England won by an innings and four runs.

England's big victory, impossible to foresee before the match even though Australia were without the injured Thomson, had its roots in Lever's excellent bowling on the first morning, when in six overs he took four wickets for five runs. Ian Chappell had a difficult decision when he won the toss, for a hot, oppressive morning made it likely the ball would swing, and to complicate matters there was a damp patch in line with the stumps at the southern end where water had splashed off the covers as ground-staff were removing them following a rainy night. The patch was a yard or so short of a good length for Lever, who replaced the injured Willis, and none of his wickets was taken with a ball that pitched on it. One that did, however, climbed viciously to hit Greg Chappell on the jaw, and there was no doubt that from then on its existence weighed on the batsmen's minds.

Without going out of his way to avoid him, Ian Chappell saw less of Lever than his team-mates. But with Australia in trouble, he produced his best innings of the series and it did not look beyond him to rescue them when he was given out caught at the wicket attempting to glide. This was the first of several arguable decisions in the match, the majority arising from rejected lbw appeals by England; though in Australia's second innings Chappell again seemed to be unlucky with another catch by Knott. By tea Australia were out for 152, Lever finishing with six for 38, great figures stemming from sustained speed, accuracy, and movement away from the bat to a field.

Rain delayed England's reply, and then Lillee dismissed Amiss fourth ball, his third duck running. Lillee followed two big outswingers and a wild delivery down the leg side with a fast break-back that Amiss not surprisingly played outside. Australia seemed to have a real chance of recovering lost ground when in the first over of the second day Walker got one to lift to Cowdrey's gloves, bringing in Denness with the ball still shiny. Lillee briefly troubled him, but after two overs he left the field, suffering from a bruise on the ball of his right foot – and England became free. Never was the value of two men more obvious than in their absence, for without Lillee and Thomson to worry about England's next three wickets added 149, 192 and 148. . . compared to a lone three-figure stand in the previous ten innings of the series!

On a pitch now dry and slow Walker and Dymock, a nippy left-hander, posed few problems, and though Denness was badly dropped at 36 by McCosker at square leg off Walters, the bat was in control. England were ahead by the time Edrich, cutting hard, was superbly dragged down by Ian Chappell at first slip, but with Denness lancing the off side off both feet with lovely timing, the lead at stumps was 121. Denness had offered two more chances, sharp ones to Marsh at 98 and Ian Chappell at 121, in his first hundred against Australia; but on the third morning neither he nor Fletcher made a relevant mistake as England extended their advantage. Denness was on the verge of a double-century when a mistimed forcing stroke gave Walker a sprawling caught and bowled, but he did record his highest innings in first-class cricket and the highest by an England captain in Australia, beating 173 by A. E. Stoddart at Melbourne in 1894–95.

At 359 for three the position was set up for Greig, and he hammered 89, including 13 fours. Fletcher opened up after passing his first Test hundred in Australia, and England were approaching a declaration when shortly after tea Greig and Fletcher fell to mis-hits in the same over, whereupon with the ball occasionally seaming on an overcast evening Walker completed a spell of five for 17 as six wickets crashed in 36 minutes. Walker's eight for 143, his best in Test cricket, was a fitting reward for the willingness with which he shouldered extra work in Lillee's absence. But without their fearsome warhead Australia's attack lacked penetration in the slow conditions.

Australia, 377 behind with 13 hours to play, faced a big task to save the match. Redpath and McCosker got over the first hurdle by staying till stumps, and on the fourth morning completed Australia's first three-figure opening stand of the series against an attack lacking Lever, who had flu. Arnold surprised McCosker with a ball that hurried off the pitch, but Redpath and Ian Chappell batted through the afternoon and Australia were still in control when Chappell was out. England's hopes revived when Redpath, after six hours' dogged occupation, hooked Greig and was splendidly caught at the second attempt by Amiss at leg slip. No more wickets fell before stumps when, with Greg Chappell and Edwards together and the new ball four overs old, Australia were 103 behind at 274 for three.

The match was effectively decided in the opening hour of the last day when Arnold removed Edwards and Walters – the latter to a fine ball that pitched middle and off and hit the top of off stump – and Marsh went to a recovered Lever. Walker stayed with Chappell for 75 minutes, but soon after lunch lost his concentration against Greig (bowling off-breaks). Three overs later Chappell, having completed a flawless hundred, misjudged Lever's length and was bowled, and soon the match was over.

Toss: Australia. **Australia 152** (I. M. Chappell 65, P. Lever 6-38) **and 373** (I. R. Redpath 83, R. B. McCosker 76, I. M. Chappell 50, G. S. Chappell 102, A. W. Greig 4 88); **England 529** (J. H. Edrich 70, M. H. Denness 188, K. W. R. Fletcher 146, A. W. Greig 89, M. H. N. Walker 8-143).

ENGLAND v AUSTRALIA 1975

Norman Preston

The Australians rendered a great service to English cricket by staying in the country after the inaugural World Cup and playing four Test matches, for the tour was not in the original calendar. It was arranged a few months earlier while England were in Australia and losing heavily. The presence of the two controversial and hostile fast bowlers Lillee and Thomson ensured the attendance of large crowds.

Australia's main objective was to retain the Ashes, which they had deservedly won back earlier in the year. That they did was due to two factors, their luck in catching England on a rain-affected wicket at Edgbaston and the loss of the fifth day at Headingley where England had a good chance of winning had not vandals ruined the pitch.

I doubt whether any previous Australian side has brought together such a galaxy of genuine pace bowlers. Many other captains would have envied Ian Chappell's problem of whom to leave out. Even such a superb all-rounder as the left-handed Gilmour appeared in only one Test. Of the 16 players, nine were newcomers to Britain, six under 25 and the oldest 28. The new batsmen, strangers to English conditions, usually acquitted themselves well, notably McCosker, but the fast bowlers laboured on very different surfaces than the rocklike ones at home. Nevertheless, one enjoyed the beautiful rhythm of Lillee as he moved along his approach to the crease and his perfect delivery. No longer did he nearly tear himself to pieces as three years earlier. Now he had absolute control of length and direction as well as the ability to move the ball either way off the seam. His was a great feat to take 21 wickets in the four Tests. Thomson, in his quest for lightning speed, had some very wild spells.

Looking at the batting, Australia owed most to Ian Chappell and McCosker. Most disappointing was the lack of success of Greg Chappell. Whereas in five Tests in 1972 he hit 437 runs, now in four matches he made only 106, average 21.20. Walters, too, seldom did himself justice in the Tests. The steadiness of Ross Edwards saved some critical situations, notably in the First Test.

The Australians were brilliant in the field. Sometimes there was an array of six in the slips including Mallett, a superb gully, the two Chappells, McCosker and Walters, all splendid in holding hot catches, with Turner and Gilmour close on the leg side and Edwards himself at cover. And far away behind the stumps was the ever-reliable Marsh, leaping hither and thither when the pacemen were wide of the mark.

First Test

Norman Preston

At Birmingham, July 10, 11, 12, 14, 1975. Australia won by an innings and 85 runs.

Australia won with a day and a half to spare after Denness had sent them in. It was a gamble which the majority of the England team supported on a dull grey morning, but the weather forecast for the next days predicted rain, so Denness took the risk of his batsmen being caught on a wet wicket – and this was exactly what happened. The general opinion was that the England batsmen were not anxious to face Lillee and Thomson, preferring to postpone the evil hour.

This was the tenth time in 215 Tests that England had put Australia in, and only once had they won – at Melbourne in 1911–12 when heavy rain had left the ground soft. Obviously, England hoped that the ball would move about under a cloudy sky, but the seamers found no response either through the air or off a lifeless pitch. Occasionally, McCosker and Turner (in his first Test) looked in difficulty, but they batted safely through the first two hours, scoring 77. After lunch the bowlers obtained some movement, but the ball never rose awkwardly, yet by five o'clock England were happier with five wickets down for 186. Then Edwards held firm while Marsh hit 47 out of 57 added before rain stopped play with Australia 243 for five.

The second day also went in Australia's favour. Edwards led a charmed life when Snow and Arnold took the second new ball, and altogether he stayed four hours for his 56, but the main value of his great effort was that 197 were put on while he was at the crease. Marsh made 61, and showed much displeasure at his dismissal which followed a delay of five minutes when the ball had lost its shape within eight overs of first coming into use. Thomson swung his bat until at last England remembered Underwood, and in his only over for 24 hours he promptly ended Thomson's frolics.

No sooner England's reply begun than a thunderstorm drenched the ground. The hold-up lasted one hour 40 minutes, but with the late extra hour now added in such circumstances there remained enough time for Australia to capture seven wickets for a paltry 83 runs. Thomson was so erratic that Chappell allowed him only two overs before turning to the more reliable Walker. Lillee, in great form, caused the ball to lift awkwardly, but while Edrich defended gallantly until just before the close, his partners were helpless against two splendid bowlers whose analyses at the end of the day read Lillee 12–6–13–3, Walker 15–5–35–4.

Australia never released their tight grip on the game. They took the last three wickets in 25 minutes on Saturday morning. The match must have been completed that day but for two more hold-ups through rain. This time, Thomson found proper length and direction to add to England's problems. The first setback in the follow-on came in Lillee's third over. Amiss turned his back on a short ball and it struck him a painful blow just below the left elbow that made him quite ill. Fletcher alone managed to survive, his runs coming mainly through skilful leg strokes and square-cutting over the slips, until Walters at third slip juggled and held a difficult catch. Gooch, in his first Test, survived only three balls in the first innings and seven in the second when he received a horrible lifter from Thomson, but he was only one failure among so many in a nightmare situation. England had lost five wickets on Saturday night for 93 runs.

A thunderstorm in the early hours of Monday delayed the resumption, and further hindrance soon occurred, but only 45 minutes were lost before lunch and by three o'clock England had suffered their first defeat in 17 Tests at Edgbaston. Amiss, now recovered, soon fell, caught off the glove from a lifting ball, but there was resistance from Knott and Snow, who once drove Mallett over mid-off for six. Thomson took the second-innings bowling honours, and true to their reputation for splendid fielding the Australians brought off many remarkable catches in a victory they so thoroughly deserved.

Toss: England Australia 359 (R. B. McCosker 59, I. M. Chappell 52, R. Edwards 56, R. W. Marsh 61); England 101 (D. K. Lillee 5-15, M. H. N. Walker 5-48) and 173 (K. W. R. Fletcher 51, J. R. Thomson 5-38).

Second Test

At Lord's, July 31, August 1, 2, 4, 5, 1975. Drawn.

Norman Preston

Graced on the first day by the Queen, to whom the players were introduced at tea, this match produced much splendid cricket while the fortunes of both sides ebbed and flowed. As Denness had indicated during England's unhappy time in the First Test that he was willing to resign, the captaincy now passed to Greig, and after another disastrous start he lifted England's morale with a dashing 96, including nine fours.

Before Greig arrived at the crease after winning the toss, Lillee had begun with another telling spell of four for 33, and throughout the match he was always menacing, varying his pace and sometimes reducing his run-up. Thomson, on the other hand, was so erratic on the first day that he was no-balled 22 times for overstepping and he also delivered four wides, but his occasional ball was fast and deadly.

A surprise choice by England was David Steele, the bespectacled grey-haired 33-year-old Northants batsman. He entered when Wood was the first of five men lbw. Three times Steele hooked Lillee, and he also cut effectively, but above all he showed the value of playing forward in a calm and calculated manner. With Knott in his most perky form and Woolmer playing soundly in his first Test, England eventually reached 315.

The second day provided some extraordinary cricket during which England were completely on top for a long time. Snow, bowling within himself and keeping splendid length and line, made the breakthrough by removing Turner and the Chappell brothers, and he was well supported by Lever, who accounted for McCosker, with a fine return catch, and Walters. Soon after lunch seven wickets had fallen for 81, and it seemed that England would enjoy a substantial lead, yet in the end it amounted to only 47. Australia were indebted first to Edwards, who punished the bowlers for 15 fours before he hit across a yorker from Woolmer and was lbw for 99. In a confident display Lillee, whose previous-highest score was 46, played calmly until Edwards left at 199, and then with three massive sixes and eight fours he reduced the bowlers to threads while scoring 73 not out. The last three wickets piled on 187 runs.

On Saturday England, not daring to take risks, were content to score 272 off 95 overs for the loss of Wood and Steele, while Edrich made his seventh hundred against Australia. With the total at 230 for two, England entered the fourth day needing a more enterprising approach. The pitch was still easy-paced but, as throughout, of somewhat uneven bounce. Edrich remained the anchor man and one felt that Greig might promote himself, but he stuck to his batting order and consequently the acceleration was delayed.

Lillee, who soon dropped to a short run, bowled splendidly through the morning session in company with Walker, who toiled in the heat for 90 minutes. At length, Edrich was held at long-on, having defied the bowlers for nine hours. His 175 contained 21 fours and was surpassed for England against Australia at Lord's only by Hammond's 240 in 1938. Greig waited until twenty to four before declaring and setting Australia 484 to win.

They replied with 97 for one by the end of the fourth day. It was evident then that a stalemate was certain unless a thunderstorm intervened. It arrived an hour before play was due to restart, but the wholly covered pitch remained intact. An hour's cricket was lost while the outfield improved. McCosker stayed four hours 20 minutes and Ian Chappell nearly as long for his valuable 86, which included 13 boundaries, as he rarely missed an opportunity to punish the loose ball. Played mostly in stifling heat, the match attracted vast crowds, the gates being closed on the first three days with 27,000 attending.

Toss: England. **England 315** (D. S. Steele 50, A. W. Greig 96, A. P. E. Knott 69, D. K. Lillee 4-84)
and 436-7 dec. (B. Wood 52, J. H. Edrich 175); **Australia 268** (R. Edwards 99, D. K. Lillee 73*,
J. A. Snow 4-66) **and 329-3** (R. B. McCosker 79, I. M. Chappell 86, G. S. Chappell 73*, R. Edwards 52*).

CRICKETER OF THE YEAR – DAVID STEELE

Alex Bannister, 1976

Few events in the heady summer of 1975 occasioned greater public delight than the part played by David Stanley Steele in rousing England from fast-fading faith to the dignity of a fighting force at least able to match Australia on equal terms. Test cricket has not enjoyed such a romantic story for decades. In the space of three matches, and at the age of 33, after 12 seasons on the county circuit, Steele emerged as the much-needed national hero with the skill, nerve and character to stand up and offer fair fight to Lillee, Thomson and Co. His selection in the shake-up following the disaster at Edgbaston was inspired.

He applied a refreshingly new outlook, confidence and patriotism to a daunting task, and perfectly complemented the drive of the new captain, Tony Greig. At the end of the series Greig said that Steele's inclusion was the best thing that had happened to England – and none challenged the opinion as exaggerated praise. Steele, born at Stoke-on-Trent on September 29, 1941, did more than accumulate 365 runs and bat almost without fault for 19 hours in six innings. He showed how a sensible technique, concentration and courage could be an effective shield to the brilliant aggression of Lillee, at least on English pitches. Here was a batsman, not in mourning for the recent past or overawed by occasions, but cocking a snook at bowlers who had carried all before them for so long.

Perhaps unfairly he was branded as almost exclusively a front-foot batsman. Steele protests that he is neither front nor back, but a close watcher of the ball which is then played strictly on its merits. What better technique can there be? What the selectors did not know until it was put to the test was his incredible temperament and superb response to a challenge.

Third Test

Norman Preston

At Leeds, August 14, 15, 16, 18, 19, 1975. Drawn

This match was abandoned as a draw after vandals sabotaged the pitch in the early hours of Tuesday, the fifth day. The perpetrators got under the covers at the pavilion end and dug out holes with knives near the popping crease, and poured a gallon of crude oil in the region where a good-length ball would have pitched. They made certain that millions of people in England and in Australia would be deprived of the enjoyment of what promised to be a truly great day's cricket. As it happened, rain set in at midday and would have washed out the proceedings in any case.

There had been a night guard of one solitary policeman, and following this outrage it was obvious that much greater vigilance would be necessary to ensure that grounds should receive better protection. The captains, Greig and Ian Chappell, looked at other parts of the square but could not find a suitable alternative pitch on which to continue.

During the four days when cricket did take place there were many exciting moments and much splendid play. Early on the third day England held a lead of 153, and eventually Greig set Australia 445 in ten and a quarter hours. Never had a Test side made so many in the fourth innings and won, but Australia faced the fifth day favourably poised, having already knocked off 220 runs for the loss of only three wickets.

After Greig had won the toss on what turned out to be a slow, easy-paced pitch which lasted much better than most of the experts expected, England scored 251 for five on the first day, when the gates were closed with at least 21,000 present. Edrich shaped well for 62 out of 137. He hit nine fours and his stand of 112 with Steele placed the innings on a sound foundation. Steele repeated his competent display at Lord's: now he was top-scorer in both innings with 73 and 92.

Except when he delivered two overs at the end of the day, Ian Chappell relied solely on his four quick bowlers, who were quite content to bowl off the wicket. Sometimes the batsmen were compelled to play only one or two balls an over, and one gained the impression that the tourists would be satisfied to go away with the draw which would suffice for them to retain the Ashes.

Anyhow, next day England collapsed, their five remaining wickets all falling to Gilmour for the addition of only 37 runs. First Gilmour, at short leg, ran out Greig, and in 10.1 overs he claimed four wickets for 14, giving him six wickets on debut against England, a most impressive performance.

Facing a modest total, Australia soon lost McCosker, held low at second slip by Hampshire. Ian Chappell settled down and Marsh defended nobly until Snow, coming back for a second spell, removed his off stump as he played back. Suddenly the situation changed completely, for in the last 70 minutes Australia lost six wickets for 29 and slumped to 107 for eight. England's hero was Edmonds, the tall left-arm spinner, who in his first 12 overs in Test cricket took five for 17 from the pavilion end.

The sight of Edmonds turning two balls in his first over clearly disturbed the Australians, and in his second over, Ian Chappell, with the intent probably of knocking him off his length, pulled heartily over a shortish ball which kept low and upset his middle stump. Edwards, who injured an ankle while fielding, arrived with a runner only to pad away a straight ball and was lbw. Greig placed eight men round Walters, who prevented a hat-trick, but the procession continued. Next morning, Edmonds bowled eight more overs without effect and so Snow came back and promptly removed Lillee and Thomson. For all their success in the field, England put down three catches, whereas throughout the game the Australians excelled in this department.

When England batted a second time a grim struggle ensued while the batsmen endeavoured to consolidate the advantage. In five hours they squeezed out 184 runs from 72 overs for the loss of Edrich, Wood and Fletcher. Again Steele kept his end firmly closed, making 59 in the last 200 minutes. The seamers gave little away and Mallett sent down 12 overs of off-spin, but the ball turned only slightly and slowly.

On the fourth day the tempo changed, 327 runs being scored while ten wickets fell. The remaining seven England wickets were sacrificed in 95 minutes for 107. Even Steele came out of his shell. He straight-drove Mallett for six and there were also seven fours in his 92, which occupied four hours 26 minutes.

To McCosker and Ian Chappell went the main honours in the final innings. It began with odds of 9-1 against Australia making 445, but at the end of the day these were halved to 9-2. Marsh stayed to see the opening stand to 55, then Chappell put on 116 with McCosker before being lbw when hitting across Old. It was soon evident that Edmonds was not getting the same response from the pitch as in the first innings, and moreover his direction strayed too often to the leg side. Ian Chappell hit Greig over mid-wicket for six and also struck 11 fours, clearly showing that he was all out to win.

Greg Chappell began with three priceless boundaries only to edge Edmonds to slip. That opened the door for England, but McCosker, who dealt faithfully with the loose ball and hit 12 fours, found a valuable assistant in the experienced Walters.

Toss: England. **England 288** (J. H. Edrich 62, D. S. Steele 73, A. W. Greig 51, G. J. Gilmour 6-85) **and 291** (D. S. Steele 92); **Australia 135** (P. H. Edmonds 5-28) **and 220-3** (R. B. McCosker 95*, I. M. Chappell 62).

NOTES BY THE EDITOR
Norman Preston, 1976

Few bowlers have enjoyed such a successful Test debut as did Phil Edmonds, of Middlesex and Cambridge University, on the second day at Headingley when at the age of 24 he took five wickets for 17 in his first 12 overs. Taller and different in method from Underwood, Edmonds, born in Northern Rhodesia, with an English father and Belgian mother, learned most of his cricket at Skinners' School, Cranbrook, and Cambridge. Edmonds did not fare so well when Australia batted a second time, nor did he cause them much bother in the final Test at The Oval, but he has arrived on the scene and with more experience, especially in the art of setting his field, he should prove an asset to England.

Fourth Test

Geoffrey Wheeler

At The Oval, August 28, 29, 30, September 1, 2, 3, 1975. Drawn.

By the end of the first day of this six-day match, England had lost nearly all hope of winning the game to square the series. The Australian score then stood at 280 for one and subsequently England faced an uphill struggle to save the match. That they did so was due to a fine second-innings recovery to which all the batsmen contributed, Woolmer justifying his promotion to No. 5 with a marathon effort which brought him his maiden Test century as he stayed eight hours 19 minutes for 149.

Another factor in England's favour was the slowness of the pitch, which even at the end of the six days showed little signs of wear, confounding both captains' predictions that it would help the slow bowlers before the end. After such a fine summer it was strange that it was so lacking in pace.

Ian Chappell, in his 30th and last match as Australia's captain, won the toss for the first time in the series. Turner was soon dismissed, but thereafter England did not take a wicket until Friday morning. On his way to his maiden Test century McCosker offered one chance at 57 when he was missed at slip by Roope off Underwood. Ian Chappell gave Snow a caught-and-bowled opportunity in the last over of the day shortly after England had taken the new ball. Otherwise seven bowlers toiled in vain. From 66 for one at lunch Australia accelerated to 185 at tea, and consolidated in the final session.

England had a relatively successful second day, taking eight wickets for 252 before Chappell declared. Old gave them a flying start by dismissing McCosker for 127 and Greg Chappell for nought with his 12th and 13th balls of the day. McCosker's downfall brought to an end a partnership of 277 with Ian Chappell, who went on to make 192 before swatting a short ball from Woolmer to Greig at square leg. There were 17 boundaries in Chappell's innings which was always aggressive in intent.

Apart from a bright 32 by Marsh, the rest of the Australian batsmen were content to let the runs come in their own time. Walters at last had a success with his highest Test score in England since the match at Old Trafford which began the 1968 series. Even so he needed nearly three hours for 65, the high spot being three boundaries in an over from Greig. Old was the pick of the England bowlers, Edmonds bowling too many balls down the leg side. His was a disappointing performance after an impressive debut at Leeds.

Edrich and Wood played out time on Friday, but found that weather conditions had changed ominously on Saturday morning. Whereas Australia had batted in two days of unbroken sunshine, England had to contend with bad light and an atmosphere particularly helpful to Walker's brand of swing. The light and drizzle delayed the start until 12.45, and the openers were still together at lunch. Wood's dismissal soon afterwards was the prelude to a collapse. Further stoppages tested the batsmen's concentration and helped to keep the bowlers fresh. Only Steele stayed for long and England finished the day perilously placed at 169 for eight.

Thomson soon took the last two wickets on Monday before England followed on 341 behind and began to fight back. In much brighter weather Walker could slant the ball but not swing it. Lillee and Thomson obtained little bounce and Mallett spun in vain. Wood scored only 22, but he stayed nearly three hours while he and Edrich made 77, which provided a sound foundation for the big total England had to make. Edrich and Steele took the score to 179 by the close of the fourth day, and rarely looked in trouble. The rearguard action carried on throughout the next day and when bad light stopped play 65 minutes early the score had climbed slowly to 333 for four, only eight being needed to make Australia bat again.

All three wickets that fell went to Lillee, who had a fine morning spell with the new ball. He broke the second-wicket partnership of 125 by knocking out Edrich's middle stump when he was within four of his eighth century against Australia. He had been in for just over six hours. Steele lasted three hours 40 minutes for his faultless 66 before, for once, he played a loose stroke outside the off stump. The rally was carried on by Roope and Woolmer, first-innings failures, who stayed from 12.40 until 5.20, Roope making his best Test score of 77 as 122 were made for the fourth wicket. Woolmer, who began tentatively and needed some luck to survive, had 37 at the end of the day.

England were still in peril when Greig went early on the last day, for they then led by no more than 30 with five hours and only five wickets remaining. Woolmer was equal to the challenge. Three times edged strokes off Lillee flew through the slips, but he survived and gradually wore down the fast bowler, who made a great last effort to win the match for his country. Lillee bowled 52 overs and was always dangerous. Knott was a perfect foil for his county colleague, and by lunch England, at 427 for five, were nearly safe.

Woolmer's 11th four, a drive off Mallett, took him to his century in six hours 36 minutes, the slowest by an Englishman against Australia. With the game drifting towards a draw Walters took four wickets in the afternoon. Knott was caught behind after making 64 of a partnership of 151, and Woolmer was last out on the stroke of tea when Australia needed 198 in roughly 85 minutes. They lost two wickets before the end. One of these was Edwards, warmly received by the England players and the spectators on his farewell to Test cricket.

Toss: Australia. **Australia 532-9 dec.** (R. B. McCosker 127, I. M. Chappell 192, K. D. Walters 65) **and 40-2; England 191** (J. R. Thomson 4-50, M. H. N. Walker 4-63) **and 538** (J. H. Edrich 96, D. S. Steele 66, G. R. J. Roope 77, R. A. Woolmer 149, A. P. E. Knott 64, D. K. Lillee 4-91, K. D. Walters 4-34).

CRICKETER OF THE YEAR – IAN CHAPPELL
Richie Benaud, 1976

Australian cricket was going through a disastrous period when Ian Michael Chappell was thrust into the captaincy in the final Test of the 1970–71 series against England. He lost his first Test by 62 runs, his second by 89... and then was never beaten in a Test series against any country. When Chappell took over, the national team had not won a Test in the previous nine times of asking. To make room for him at the top, the selectors removed Bill Lawry in a step that had about as much subtlety as the guillotine in the French Revolution. Not only was Lawry dropped from the captaincy but from the team as well. Chappell captained Australia 30 times, won 15 of those games and lost only five, two of the latter being his first two efforts. By the time he retired from the leadership he had lifted Australia right back to the top in world cricket.

Ian left him a legacy of a very good cricket team with a wonderful team spirit and a burning ambition to stay on top. He did more than that however for his players. Chappell is and was very definitely a players' man. He has had more brushes with officialdom than anyone since Keith Miller and Sid Barnes just after the end of the war, and most of those brushes have been because of his unwillingness to compromise. Nothing is a shade of grey to Chappell and, although his candid speech and honesty can be refreshing, the same attributes also have landed him in trouble with administrators on several occasions.

He has been a most reliable No. 3 for his country – never backward in taking on the fast bowlers with the hook shot, though in recent times he has been more careful to pull in front of square leg rather than hook in the area behind the umpire.

Australia v England 1976–77
Gordon Ross, 1976

On March 15, 1977, the greatest event in cricket history will be celebrated – the 100th anniversary of the first Australia v England Test match, which began in Melbourne on March 15, 1877, the start of a rivalry which has become a piece of history, and has survived the ravages of one war after another, to stand the passage of time unchallenged in national affection. The green caps of Australia (even the actual cap seems different in physical shape from any other cricketing cap!) have had a special magic about them; tradition has not tarnished a golden image; the cricket has mellowed through the years; it has lost nothing of its bouquet.

The Ashes were not at stake during this one-off match.

Centenary Test
Reg Hayter

At Melbourne, March 12, 13, 14, 16, 17, 1977. Australia won by 45 runs.

An occasion of warmest reunion and nostalgia, the cricket continuously compelling, a result straining credulity. Hans Ebeling, former Australian Test bowler and the inspiration of it all, should have been christened Hans Andersen Ebeling.

From Ebeling, a vice-president of the Melbourne Cricket Club, originated the suggestion to signalise 100 years of Test cricket by a match between England and Australia on the same ground – in 1877 the Richmond Police Paddock – on which David Gregory's team beat James Lillywhite's England side. The Victorian Cricket Association and the Melbourne Club co-operated to bring this about and a masterpiece of organisation resulted in an event which none fortunate enough to be present could forget. Unlucky were those who missed it.

Arrangements were made for the England team visiting India to extend their tour to play an official Test in the same month as the 1877 Test, and invitations were sent to the 244 living cricketers who had played for Australia or England in the series. All but 26 were able to accept for an event unique in history. The oldest Australian Test player present was the 87-year-old Jack Ryder. Even though suffering from near-blindness, the 84-year-old Percy Fender made the enervating air journey from Britain as the oldest English representative. He was accompanied by his grandson, Jeremy, who became his cricketing eyes.

Of those who went to Melbourne many told unusual stories. Colin McCool was marooned in his Queensland home by floods and had to be hauled up from his front lawn by helicopter to the airport. Jack Rutherford's train broke down and he finished the journey to the airport by taxi. Denis Compton – who else? – left his passport in a Cardiff hotel and, but for the early start to the pre-flight champagne party at London Airport which enabled a good friend to test the speed limits on the M4, would have missed the plane.

Some ex-England players – Harold Larwood, Peter Loader, Tony Lock, Barry Knight, Frank Tyson – already lived in Australia, while the Australian Neil Hawke flew home from England. The gradual gathering of all at the Hilton Hotel, 200 yards across Jolimont Park from the ground, brought meetings and greetings of unabated happiness. Not a hitch, not one.

Fittingly, this was also Melbourne's Mardi Gras, a week called "Moomba", the Aboriginal word for "Let's get together and have fun". After a champagne (much was drunk between London and Melbourne and back) breakfast and an opening ceremony on which ex-Test captains accompanied the teams on to the field, the crowd were also given the opportunity of a special welcome to all the former Test players.

Greig called correctly to Greg Chappell's spin of the specially minted gold coin and chose to field first. Probably he felt apprehension about his batsmen facing Lillee while moisture remained in the pitch. The resolute fast-medium bowling of Willis, Old and Lever, helped by Underwood's customary left-handed accuracy and breathtakingly supported in the field, appeared to justify Greig's decision in Australia's dismissal for 138 in front of a crowd of over 61,000.

Australia, handicapped by the early departure of McCosker, who fractured his jaw when a ball from Willis flew off his hand into his face, were always on the defensive. England's batting buckled even more swiftly against Lillee, at the zenith of his form and speed, and Walker – Australia's fielding being no whit inferior to that of England.

That was the last of the bowling mastery. Over the next three days Australia increased their lead of 43 so much that their declaration left England 463 to win at 40 an hour. Marsh, who had already beaten Wally Grout's record of 187 Test victims, added to his triumph by his first Test century against England, and Walters joyfully rode his fortune. Yet the spotlight centred on 21-year-old David Hookes, who played an innings straight from the fount of youth. This powerful left-handed batsman, who had scored five centuries in 1976–77 Sheffield Shield cricket, strode to the crease with a confidence even more apparent when he struck Greig for five fours in an over – off, pull, cover, mid-wicket, cover.

Australia v England 1976–77   The Centenary Test

At Melbourne, March 12, 13, 14, 16, 17, 1977. Result: Australia won by 45 runs.

AUSTRALIA	First innings			Second innings	
I. C. Davis lbw b Lever	5	–	c Knott b Greig		68
R. B. McCosker b Willis	4	–	(10) c Greig b Old		25
G. J. Cosier c Fletcher b Lever	10	–	(4) c Knott b Lever		4
*G. S. Chappell b Underwood	40	–	(3) b Old		2
D. W. Hookes c Greig b Old	17	–	(6) c Fletcher b Underwood		56
K. D. Walters c Greig b Willis	4	–	(5) c Knott b Greig		66
†R. W. Marsh c Knott b Old	28	–	not out		110
G. J. Gilmour c Greig b Old	4	–	b Lever		16
K. J. O'Keeffe c Brearley b Underwood	0	–	(2) c Willis b Old		14
D. K. Lillee not out	10	–	(9) c Amiss b Old		25
M. H. N. Walker b Underwood	2	–	not out		8
B 4, l-b 2, n-b 8	14		L-b 10, n-b 15		25

1-11 2-13 3-23 4-45 5-51   138   1-33 2-40 3-53 4-132 5-187   (9 wkts dec.) 419
6-102 7-114 8-117 9-136 10-138   6-244 7-277 8-353 9-407

First innings – Lever 12–1–36–2; Willis 8–0–33–2; Old 12–4–39–3; Underwood 11.6–2–16–3.
Second innings – Lever 21–1–95–2; Willis 22–0–91–0; Old 27.6–2–104–4; Underwood 12–2–38–1; Greig 14–3–66–2.

ENGLAND	First innings			Second innings	
R. A. Woolmer c Chappell b Lillee	9	–	lbw b Walker		12
J. M. Brearley c Hookes b Lillee	12	–	lbw b Lillee		43
D. L. Underwood c Chappell b Walker	7	–	(10) b Lillee		7
D. W. Randall c Marsh b Lillee	4	–	(3) c Cosier b O'Keeffe		174
D. L. Amiss c O'Keeffe b Walker	4	–	(4) b Chappell		64
K. W. R. Fletcher c Marsh b Walker	4	–	(5) c Marsh b Lillee		1
*A. W. Greig b Walker	18	–	(6) c Cosier b O'Keeffe		41
†A. P. E. Knott lbw b Lillee	15	–	(7) lbw b Lillee		42
C. M. Old c Marsh b Lillee	3	–	(8) c Chappell b Lillee		2
J. K. Lever c Marsh b Lillee	11	–	(9) lbw b O'Keeffe		4
R. G. D. Willis not out	1	–	not out		5
B 2, l-b 2, w 1, n-b 2	7		B 8, l-b 4, w 3, n-b 7		22

1-19 2-30 3-34 4-40 5-40   95   1-28 2-113 3-279 4-290 5-346   417
6-61 7-65 8-78 9-86 10-95   6-369 7-380 8-385 9-410 10-417

First innings – Lillee 13.3–2–26–6; Walker 15–3–54–4; O'Keeffe 1–0–4–0; Gilmour 5–3–4–0.
Second innings – Lillee 34.4–7–139–5; Walker 22–4–83–1; O'Keeffe 33–6–108–3; Gilmour 4–0–29–0; Chappell 16–7–29–1; Walters 3–2–7–0.

Toss won by England   UMPIRES T. F. Brooks and M. G. O'Connell

Then it was England's turn. And, in the presence of the Queen and the Duke of Edinburgh – during an interval they drove round the ground and were hugely acclaimed – royally did they apply themselves. Well as Amiss, Greig, Knott and Brearley batted, however, the innings to remember was played by Randall, a jaunty, restless, bubbling character, whose 174 took England to the doorstep of victory. The Australian spectators enjoyed his approach. Once, when Lillee tested him with a bouncer, he tennis-batted it to the mid-wicket fence with a speed and power that made many a rheumy eye turn to the master of the stroke, the watching Sir Donald Bradman. Words cannot recapture the joy of that moment. Another time, when Lillee bowled short, Randall ducked, rose, drew himself to his full five foot eight, doffed his cap and bowed politely. Then, felled by another bouncer, he gaily performed a reverse-roll. This helped to maintain a friendly atmosphere in what, at all times, was a serious and fully competitive match.

The Australians responded. When Randall was 161, umpire Brooks gave him out, caught at the wicket. Immediately Marsh intimated that he had not completed the catch before dropping the ball. Would that this spirit was always so! At the end of the game Randall was awarded the first prize of $A1,600 as the Man of the Match. To be chosen ahead of the superb Lillee, whose colleagues chaired him from the field when he finished the match with an analysis of 11 for 165, was a feat indeed.

Some time after it was over someone discovered that the result of the 226th Test between the two countries – victory by 45 runs – was identical, to the same side and to the very run, with that of the 1877 Test on the same ground. Hans Andersen Ebeling had even scripted the final curtain.

ENGLAND v AUSTRALIA 1977
Harold Abel

Although the day should never come when an Australian cricket team is described as colourless, the 1977 party took on a very light shade of grey. The players had none of the air of their predecessors and the longer the tour went on the more one's mind drifted back to the billowing green caps which had fallen out of fashion. A bad start with the weather did not help. But still, a side no more than a good average was allowed to beat Australia, with some comfort, in three Tests in England for the first time since 1886, so winning back the Ashes at home for only the third time this century.

The focal point of the tour was TV. Though it was kept secret until the second week in May, plans had long since been set in motion by one of the media's main manipulators in Australia, Kerry Packer, to milk the game of its stars in order to set them before his own audience. This has to be seen as an integral part of this tour. Thirteen of the 17 Australians flew into London with Packer contracts in their pockets. They had already inflicted the initial wound in those who sent them 11,000 miles to represent an organisation not long since celebrating something of 100 years' duration. Looked at in retrospect, there was a good deal of heresy in what the players were doing, and it was too much to expect the side to go through an arduous tour without some reaction. It would have been a major surprise had the cricket not been affected.

This was never going to be one of the stronger Australian sides. With Ian Chappell, Lillee and Edwards leaving their flannels at the cleaners until the Packer fortunes became available, the powerhouse of the 1975 side had been removed. Thomson could not be the same force without Lillee, and the switching from the extrovert Ian to his more introvert brother, Greg, as captain, had its effect on the drive behind the effort.

For Australia to dispose of Boycott for a duck when they played Yorkshire must have looked fine at the time. Clearly it was likely to rebound, as it did with a century in the second innings. Then for McCosker to drop Boycott when 20, after three hours' painful acclimatisation at Trent Bridge on his return to Test cricket, was courting utter disaster. Instead of 87 for six England remained 87 for five, and with the assistance of Knott, Boycott ensured that another 210 were added before the next wicket went down. Boycott's influence on the series did not end there. He chose his own Headingley ground for his 100th century, and went on to 191. The balance of power had been shifted by this one player who came from a three-year self-imposed exile to average 147.33 in five innings. Before his return there was little between the sides man for man.

First Test

Norman Preston

At Lord's, June 16, 17, 18, 20, 21, 1977. Drawn.

In many ways this was a splendid match with the initiative passing from one side to the other and even when a draw seemed certain there was an exciting finish. Personal honours over the five days went to Woolmer, Willis, whose hostile speed gained him his best Test return, Greig and Randall. For Australia, most prominent was Serjeant, who threatened to equal the feat of his fellow countryman, Harry Graham, the only player to hit a century on his Test debut at Lord's (in 1893).

The solitary disappointment occurred on the second day when bad light and intermittent rain permitted only one and three-quarter hours' play. Over 20,000 people were present and the pitch was not covered until the evening, which meant that Australia faced the prospect of batting on a rain-affected wicket, but in the event the surface remained unharmed.

Brearley, captain of England for the first time [Greig had been sacked for his involvement with World Series Cricket, although he remained in the side – Ed.], won the toss, but apart from Woolmer and Randall, the batsmen fared badly, and the whole side were out for 216. Thomson was in grand form, as was Walker. Both kept a pretty full length and moved the ball off the pitch just sufficiently to be extremely difficult to play. Pascoe, too, maintained genuine speed coupled with accurate length and direction.

By removing Amiss and Brearley in the early overs, Australia promptly gained the upper hand, but Woolmer was sure in defence while Randall produced some glorious strokes. In two hours their stand yielded 98 before Randall paid the penalty for trying a Sunday-afternoon cut. From that moment Woolmer fought a lone battle. He stayed four and a half hours and in the end was smartly run out by Walters, dashing in from cover and hitting the stumps.

McCosker and Robinson began confidently in a bitter north wind on Friday morning, until in the sixth over Lever bowled Robinson with a fine ball that straightened off the wicket. Underwood delivered four successive maidens, and Old was equally economical, but when Willis returned and sent down a bouncer to McCosker, the umpires went off for bad light. They came back later, but for only four overs and Australia finished the day 51 for one.

Batting with great care on the third day under heavy grey skies, Australia, who lost McCosker without addition, gained the lead with only three wickets down, but Willis and Old restored the position for England, and Australia at the close were no more than 62 ahead with three wickets left. Two prolonged stands were the main feature of their display. Serjeant occupied 40 minutes before getting his first run, but kept his head down, as did Chappell who spent three hours before he hit his first boundary. They added 84 and then Serjeant and Walters put on 103. Willis and Old shared the six Australian wickets which fell that day and on Monday morning Willis captured the last three that added only 18.

When Amiss played on to Thomson fourth ball, England made another dreadful start, which was remedied by Brearley and Woolmer in a valuable partnership of 132. Brearley led a perilous life, but gallantly defied the pace trio. Woolmer showed his class with a sure defence by virtue of his perfectly straight bat. He produced some superb cover-drives, and cut and forced off his pads to leg. Eventually Brearley fell to a smart low catch by Robinson at short square leg off O'Keeffe, and then Greig stayed with Woolmer to the close, taking the score to 189 for two.

Woolmer lasted 50 minutes more on Monday and was then neatly held at first slip, having batted for five hours and hitting 13 fours in his 120. Subsequently, Greig alone caused Australia any difficulty and even he committed uncertain strokes for an hour before finding better form until he lofted Pascoe to O'Keeffe at cover. With Knott and Old also caught in the same place, England collapsed so completely that the last six wickets fell for 19.

Australia required 226 in two and three-quarter hours, and at first they set busily about the task on another cloudy day on a pitch that was still in good order. But England gained immediate encouragement by removing Robinson and McCosker for five runs. Chappell played Willis well and Hookes hooked him for six. The search for runs proved fatal and Chappell, Walters and Serjeant all left to leg-side catches. In fact with 21 overs remaining, England needed to take the last five wickets, then in the 11th over of the final 20, Hookes mis-hooked a return catch to Willis.

Marsh and O'Keeffe defended solidly against some tantalising bowling by Underwood until the light deteriorated. Five overs remained when the umpires offered relief to the batsmen and neither hesitated to race into the pavilion. Between them, Willis, Old and Underwood had given Australia a real fright. The receipts £220,384, were a record for any cricket match in Britain, the full attendance being 101,050.

Toss: England. **England 216** (R. A. Woolmer 79, D. W. Randall 53, J. R. Thomson 4-41) **and 305** (R. A. Woolmer 120, A. W. Greig 91, J. R. Thomson 4-86); **Australia 296** (G. S. Chappell 66, C. S. Serjeant 81, K. D. Walters 53, R. G. D. Willis 7-78) **and 114-6** (D. W. Hookes 50).

Second Test

At Manchester, July 7, 8, 9, 11, 12, 1977. England won by nine wickets.

Geoffrey Wheeler

A splendid all-round performance by England combined with Australian batting frailties brought victory after 95 minutes on the fifth day. England bowled tightly and held their catches to overcome the disadvantage of losing the toss, then batted consistently to build a first-innings lead of 140. Despite a magnificent 112 by Chappell, Australia in their second innings never appeared likely to produce enough runs to worry England. Underwood took six wickets and Brearley's side needed only 79 to win.

Lancashire had been without a regular groundsman for a month, and some doubts were expressed about the lasting qualities of the pitch. In the event it played very well, although helping the slower bowlers to some extent after the weekend. Both sides included an extra spinner. England brought in the off-break bowler Miller, who played an important part on the first day when Walters came within 12 of his first Test century in England. Apart from a classic 44 by Chappell the early batting was insecure, and when the captain was dismissed by a fine ball from Greig they fell away to 140 for five, Lever having removed both Serjeant and Hookes in a sterling afternoon spell.

Then Walters, on the ground where he scored 81 and 86 in his first Test in England in 1968, found an obdurate partner in Marsh and together they wore down the pace attack. Half an hour from the close a complete recovery seemed possible, so well were they playing. Then Miller was called on. In his third over he broke the stand of 98 when Marsh, tempted into a big hit, was caught at cover. Seven balls later Walters, who had hit 15 fours, drove a full toss to Greig at extra cover and England were back on top.

On the second morning the last three wickets added 50. England soon lost their openers, but Woolmer and Randall regained the initiative in a partnership of 142 which was full of good strokes, especially by Randall, who hit 12 fours in a bubbling display. He scored 79 before falling lbw to a full-pitch from Bright. Woolmer gave another solid performance, although he had one fortunate escape at 43 when he edged Thomson straight to second slip, where McCosker missed what proved to be a vital chance.

On Saturday, when only 230 runs were scored, Woolmer moved to 137, his third century against Australia. He took nearly an hour at the start to get the 18 required to become the first Englishman since Ken Barrington in 1965–66 to score centuries in successive innings against Australia. He allowed Greig to make most of the running in a partnership of 160 which ensured a sizeable advantage. This pair prevented Thomson and Walker breaking through with the new ball, and it was the wrist-spinner O'Keeffe who finally removed Woolmer when he had batted six hours 20 minutes to confirm himself as England's natural No. 3.

Greig was caught brilliantly, one-handed by Walker, for 76, while Knott, after some telling blows, managed to hole out to third man, cutting at Thomson. The four main Australian bowlers performed heroically, but Pascoe was sadly missed. England's last wicket fell first thing on Monday, a day notable for a century by Chappell as brilliant as it was defiant. Australia cleared the arrears of 140 for the loss of four batsmen, but the dismissal of Hookes, Marsh and Bright in the space of 20 balls in mid-afternoon left Chappell to play a lone hand. When he was eighth out at 202 the cause was lost.

Before lunch Chappell, impervious to the disasters at the other end, made 54 with eight fours. His timing was majestic and his placing of the ball almost flawless. McCosker and Davis both fell to mistimed hooks; Serjeant was Underwood's first victim and Walters fell in the last over of the morning when Brearley called Greig up for a single over. Hookes stayed while 54 were added before being caught at slip driving at Miller, and the game turned into a struggle for supremacy between Chappell and Underwood, who took the last five wickets, removing Marsh and Bright in the same over.

At tea Chappell was 92. A straight-drive off Willis brought him to his sixth century against England, his 14th in all Tests. It was generously received by the England players as well as the crowd. It was a masterpiece of skill and concentration. Chappell finally fell playing Underwood into his stumps as he made room to cut. O'Keeffe, who had kept an end going while 55 were added, watched helplessly as Underwood prised out Walker and Thomson before leading England off the field after one of his greatest days.

Eight of the 79 needed were safely made on Monday evening, and spectators were admitted for 40p on the last morning. Thomson was fast and frightening, but Brearley and Amiss, although kept busy ducking and weaving, were in no mood to be intimidated. England were within four runs of their target before Brearley was caught at cover. Coming off the field he learned that he had been appointed captain for the rest of the series, a deserved reward for skilled and unflappable leadership.

Toss: Australia. **Australia 297** (K. D. Walters 88) **and 218** (G. S. Chappell 112, D. L. Underwood 6-66); **England 437** (R. A. Woolmer 137, D. W. Randall 79, A. W. Greig 76) **and 82-1.**

Third Test

Norman Preston

At Nottingham, July 28, 29, 30, August 1, 2, 1977. England won by seven wickets.

England won ten minutes after tea on the last day. It was their first victory against Australia at Trent Bridge since 1930, when Bradman made his first Test appearance in England and was on the losing side the only time after scoring a century. Blessed with fine weather, the ground was packed on the first four days and made a wonderful sight.

Memorable mostly from a cricket point of view was the return of Boycott to the England team after three years of self-imposed absence. Naturally, Boycott hoped for success and he exceeded all expectations by scoring 107 and 80 not out. He had the unusual experience of batting on all five days of the match and altogether spent over 12 hours at the crease.

Botham distinguished his Test debut by taking five wickets for 74. He moved the ball each way and at one time took four for 13 in 34 balls. It was this feat which put England in the ascendancy on the first day after Chappell had won the toss and gained first use of a fast, hard pitch. Again England supported their bowlers brilliantly in the field, especially in the slips, where Hendrick held three catches. Outstanding was the way he dived to his left and held one-handed a slash by Hookes.

McCosker and Davis gave Australia a sound start, and although McCosker edged Botham's second ball through a gap where third slip had been, Botham strayed too much on the leg side during his first spell. The opening stand had produced 79 when Underwood offered a slower ball to Davis, who lifted it to mid-on.

After lunch, when Australia were 101 for one, Hendrick and Willis renewed their attack and soon McCosker touched a ball that left him, for Brearley at first slip to snap up a low catch. For a time Chappell and Hookes looked safe, but then came Botham's devastating spell. His first ball was short and Chappell, intending a fierce drive, played on, and with Walters, Marsh and Walker also falling to Botham's varied swing, Australia were reduced to 155 for eight. Then O'Keeffe stood firm, playing the major part while the last two wickets put on 88. At the end of the day Brearley and Boycott negotiated three overs and scored nine runs.

Australia fought back on the second day, and had England reeling thanks to some splendid pace bowling by Pascoe and Thomson, well supported by Walker. Boycott kept his end shut but no sooner had he been joined by Knott, after batting three hours for

20, than he was dropped off Pascoe by McCosker at second slip, which would have made the position 87 for six.

Earlier, Brearley had been caught brilliantly in the gully and Woolmer went lbw to his third ball. Randall began in great style but was run out when Boycott went for an impossible single after stroking the ball down the pitch. In the end Randall sacrificed his wicket to save Boycott, who stood dejected covering his face with his hands. Boycott freely admitted that he was to blame, and continued to defend with the utmost resolution. With Australia now on top, Knott rose to the occasion in his own impudent style. When bad light ended the contest that evening the Boycott-Knott stand had yielded 160 and left England only one behind with half their wickets in hand.

On Saturday, Australia were able to claim the new ball first thing, and Knott was first to his hundred. The pair had just equalled the previous sixth-wicket record of 215 by Hutton and Hardstaff at The Oval in 1938 when Boycott was caught at slip, having batted seven hours and hit 11 fours. Knott went on to make the highest score by an England wicket-keeper against Australia, beating the 120 of Les Ames at Lord's in 1934. He hit one five and 18 fours.

By mid-afternoon Australia were batting again, 121 behind. Willis soon disposed of Davis, held at second slip, but McCosker played confidently only to see his captain fall to a very fine ball by Hendrick which he edged as it came back rather low. Hookes then stayed with McCosker till the close, when Australia were 112 for two. The pair continued their solid resistance on Monday, but having stayed over three hours while 94 runs were added Hookes left lbw to Hendrick. Walters lasted an hour before he lofted a half-volley to cover.

Underwood sent down 16 overs for only 18 runs, and then the new ball was taken, whereupon McCosker completed his excellent hundred. Willis, fast and accurate, immediately had him taken at first slip. There was further resistance by Robinson and O'Keeffe, but Willis would not be denied and finished with five wickets.

England needed 189 to go two up, and before the close Brearley and Boycott made 17 from seven overs. On the last day, with the pitch true but slow, the only problem was the weather, as thunder-showers had been forecast. With much of the bowling outside off and ignored by the batsmen, progress was still slow. Eventually Brearley accelerated, until trying to force Walker off the back foot he played on. As England now needed to hurry, Knott and Greig went in. Both failed, as Walker claimed three wickets in six balls. Finally, Randall took charge and made the winning hit. He walked off arm in arm with Boycott, the run-out completely forgotten.

Toss: Australia. **Australia 243** (R. B. McCosker 51, I. T. Botham 5-74) **and 309** (R. B. McCosker 107, R. G. D. Willis 5-88); **England 364** (G. Boycott 107, A. P. E. Knott 135, L. S. Pascoe 4-80) **and 189-3** (J. M. Brearley 81, G. Boycott 80*).

CRICKETER OF THE YEAR – IAN BOTHAM
Eric Hill, 1978

Ian Terence Botham, aged 21, took five Australian wickets on his first day of Test cricket.

Two Sunday matches in 1973 gave him his first taste of county cricket and by 1976 he was learning to harness his glorious straight hitting and square-cutting, and beginning to vary his bowling techniques under the guidance of that doyen of medium-pacers, Tom Cartwright. Bouncers of different paces, and a brisk inswinging yorker added spice and batting danger to his outswinger.

The 1977 season was marred only by a foot injury which ruined the end of the season and probably robbed him of a rare double. He finished with 88 wickets and 738 runs. He found the England team spirit magnificent, with everyone working for each other as he took five wickets in the first innings of each of his first two Tests, and the birth of his son in August crowned a marvellous year.

Botham (pronounced as in "both" by the family, although colleagues sound it as in "moth") was on his way. A determined, straightforward, pleasant character, who knows where he is aiming, and who, in the best old-fashioned sense, has a good conceit of himself, Ian will, quite naturally and fiercely, be addressing himself to an interesting view, held by several knowledgeable cricketers. It is that before his Test-match triumphs he was under-rated, but that after them he was over-rated.

Botham has the tenacity, courage and exciting ability to prove them wrong. After all, when he joined the Lord's groundstaff his father gave him two aims: "Play for your county at 18 and your country before 25." He achieved one and handsomely surpassed the other – a remarkable start to a very stiff programme.

Fourth Test
Geoffrey Wheeler

At Leeds, August 11, 12, 13, 15, 1977. England won by an innings and 85 runs.

The completeness of England's triumph, following wins at Manchester and Nottingham, left no room for doubt as to which was the superior side. It was the first year since 1886 that England had won three Tests in a home series against Australia. A historic game was made more memorable by Boycott who, on the opening day, became the first player to score his 100th century in a Test. The Yorkshire crowd seemed to regard the achievements of this landmark as inevitable, and Boycott batted with such ease and assurance that he gave his loyal supporters few qualms and the bowlers scant hope.

His was a remarkable feat, for he was only the 18th cricketer to reach this goal. Two of the others, Herbert Sutcliffe and Sir Leonard Hutton, were present for at least part of the match. By the time Boycott was finally out for 191, Australia had lost any hope of saving the series.

A strong local conviction that history was about to be made helped to fill the ground close to overflowing on the first two days when the gates were shut well before the start. England won the toss, and although Brearley was caught at the wicket off Thomson's third ball, Boycott soon took the measure of the attack and apart from one edge off Walker, which nearly carried to Marsh, looked well-nigh invincible.

Partners came and went, Woolmer, Randall and Greig contributing briskly, while Boycott proceeded as his own measured pace. Thirty-four runs before lunch, another 35 by tea. He had been in for five hours 20 minutes when a full-throated roar from the crowd told those for miles around that the local hero had done it. An on-driven boundary off Chappell, his 14th four from the 232nd ball he had received, took the Yorkshire captain to three figures and brought the inevitable invasion of the middle. Happily this did not cause a lengthy hold-up or cost Boycott his cap, which was sheepishly returned by a would-be souvenir hunter.

England finished the first day already strongly placed at 252 for four. The match was virtually settled on the Friday, truly a Glorious Twelfth for England, who carried their score to 436 and then captured five wickets for 67. Boycott succeeded in his objective of batting England into an invincible position, and when he was last out he had hit 23 fours. As at Trent Bridge, Knott was again his best partner: they put on 123.

After their long stint in the field, the Australians batted like men in a state of shock after bowling at Boycott for 22½ hours since his return to the England side. With the ball swinging under evening cloud the batting was taxed beyond its resources. Hendrick claimed victims with his second and 13th balls and McCosker, who was making a staunch fight, was brilliantly run out by Randall when backing up a shade too eagerly.

Hendrick and Botham combined to complete the destruction of the first innings on Saturday morning. The last five wickets went for 36, and Australia's 103 was their lowest against England since Lord's in 1968 when they were put out for 78, but were saved by rain after following on. Botham, who took five for 21 to follow his successful debut at Trent Bridge, soon removed Marsh and the rest went quietly.

When two wickets in the second innings had been captured by lunch England had high hopes of repeating a three day win on the same ground as in 1961 and 1972. Greig made the breakthrough, Knott catching Davis down the leg side for his 250th Test success before diving in front of first slip to send back McCosker with a marvellously athletic effort. An object lesson on how to play the swinging ball was provided by Chappell throughout Saturday afternoon when the light was often dim. Brearley, with five bowlers of medium-pace or above, allowed the batsmen little respite and more wickets would have fallen had some of the seamers bowled a more attacking line. Nevertheless despite the loss of almost all the final session through rain and bad light Australia at 120 for four were in a dreadful plight.

Monday dawned wet but play started at two o'clock. Chappell, having added but seven runs, prodded forward at Willis to be caught at second slip. Marsh hit fiercely and put on 65 with Walker. With Botham injured and Hendrick resting, England struggled for a wicket for the only time in the match. The new ball, taken at 243 for seven, brought a speedy end. Willis wrecked the stumps first of Walker and then Thomson, his 100th Test wicket. The honour of taking the final wicket went deservedly to Hendrick, who had done so much to undermine the opposition. Marsh skyed him to wide mid-off where Randall wheeled to get under an awkward catch. Most of the England players set off for the dressing-rooms, and Randall did not let them down. The catch safely completed, he threw the ball high in the air and did a joyous victory cartwheel before joining his colleagues on the players' balcony to acknowledge the cheers of thousands.

Toss: England. **England 436** (G. Boycott 191, A. P. E. Knott 57, J. R. Thomson 4-113, L. S. Pascoe 4-91); **Australia 103** (M. Hendrick 4-41, I. T. Botham 5-21) **and 248** (R. W. Marsh 63, M. Hendrick 4-54).

THE CENTURIONS – GEOFFREY BOYCOTT

Terry Brindle, 1978

Geoffrey Boycott's place in cricket folklore was assured long before that warm Headingley evening when he succeeded where only would-be bombers and the infernal weather had succeeded before and stopped an English Test match in its tracks for almost ten

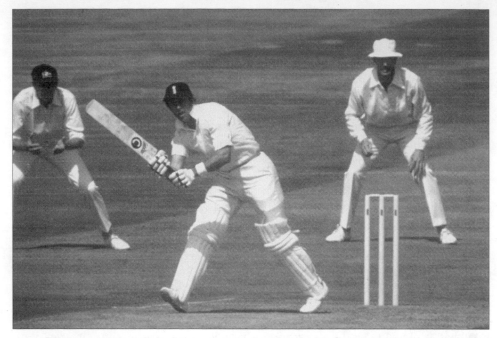

Geoff Boycott on the way to his 100th first-class hundred, at home at Headingley during the 1977 Ashes series.

minutes. Boycott's 100th century – in a Test match, before his Yorkshire public – was indeed the stuff that dreams are made of. There was hardly a dry contact lens in the house.

But the abiding significance of his 100th century was not simply statistical; Boycott himself conceded that one century was much the same as the one before or the one to follow. It was the realisation, vitally important to Boycott himself, that the public were prepared to accept his peace offering after a controversial absence from Test cricket.

Boycott and controversy have shared the longest opening partnership in the game. The owlish, introverted young man who broke into county cricket in 1962 and who was regarded as a dedicated technician rather than a talented strokemaker developed his skills to prove the unbelievers wrong and neglected his personality to convince his critics they were right. The trauma of Trent Bridge and the Headingley homecoming which followed combined, as never before, Boycott the public man with Boycott the private person. To his unconcealed delight, the public showed themselves ready to accept both.

His welcome back into Test cricket and the warmth of his receptions tapped a fund of popular sympathy and admiration which Boycott never knew existed. Rather like a clip from an old film in which a reclusive Queen Victoria returns from a triumphal jubilee procession and confides with some surprise, "Y'know, I really think they like me after all . . ." Corny, perhaps, but Boycott was never more sincere.

At 5.49 p.m. on August 11 Geoffrey Boycott reached 100 hundreds and realised he could count on the support, understanding and even friendship of 1,000 thousand. It would not be easy to decide which he values more. And he achieved the feat in his 645th first-class innings. Only Sir Don Bradman (295), Denis Compton (552) and Sir Leonard Hutton (619) did it more quickly.

Fifth Test

At The Oval, August 25, 26, 27, 29, 30, 1977. Drawn.

Geoffrey Wheeler

The Australians ended a rain-ruined game with a clear advantage, but there was little hope of a result once the first day had been lost because sections of the square and outfield were waterlogged. Chappell's team did their best to make up for lost time by dismissing nine England batsmen for 181 on Friday, before the surrender of another four and three-quarter hours to the weather on Saturday ended their hopes of salvaging a win from a disastrous summer.

An atmosphere of anticlimax hung over the match because the series was already decided, and there was also an air of sadness that this might be the last meeting between full-strength sides of the two countries for a number of years.

The key player for Australia proved to be Malone, the swing bowler who had previously achieved little on the tour. He entered his first Test because of a doubt about Pascoe's fitness. England played Lever for the unfit Botham as their only change, although there had been a strong lobby to omit the Packer signatories in the cause of experiment. Brearley's arguments for the strongest available side won the day. However, there was no denying that the fine edge had gone from England's form. The close catching, all but faultless previously, was of a poor standard and the batting lacked concentration.

Yet this was not a charge that could be levelled against Boycott and Brearley who, after England had been put in, launched the innings with a partnership of 86 before Walker broke through. The breach was well exploited by the tall, powerful Malone, who after an innocuous first few overs caused everyone trouble by his movement away from the bat. At the close Malone had bowled 43 overs and taken five for 53, showing a splendid appetite for work. His only break was for two overs just before lunch. Other than the opening batsmen only Roope looked comfortable before he was nonplussed by Thomson's speed with the new ball.

In Saturday's brief spell of play Willis and Hendrick added 33, taking England to a more respectable 214. Hendrick had the distinction of striking the only boundary off Malone in his 47 overs. The last pair hit seven of the 16 boundaries in the innings.

Australia, who began in indifferent light, were 11 for one when a mid-afternoon storm washed out play for the day. While the pitch still showed traces of damp on Monday, Australia struggled and might have been put out cheaply yet again had McCosker been caught at slip by Hendrick when he was two. He stayed for three and a quarter hours until the pitch became a typically slow Oval surface. Hookes then entertained a large Bank Holiday crowd in an innings of 85 which compensated for Underwood's dismissal of Chappell when he seemed set to play a major farewell innings. Hookes needed some luck on and around the off stump, but so sweetly timed were his off-side strokes that he was always good to watch.

Using the same weathered bat with which he scored five centuries in six Sheffield Shield innings Hookes, in company with Marsh, rescued his side from 104 for five.

When Hookes was sixth out for 184, having hit 12 fours, Australia were in sight of a first-innings lead for only the second time in the series. Yet with an advantage of only 12 on the final morning with four wickets in hand they had little chance of forcing a win. Malone, surviving a slip chance to Greig before he had scored, and Walker, badly missed by Brearley at 19, put on exactly 100, mainly by reputable strokemaking. Malone did not fall until the last ball before lunch while Walker finished unbeaten with his highest score. Willis's five wickets brought his tally for the five Tests to 27, easily a record for an England fast bowler in a home series with Australia.

There were fewer than three hours remaining when England went in again. In a final burst of speed, before limping off with a damaged ankle, Thomson removed Brearley. Malone rounded off an auspicious debut by dismissing Woolmer, but Boycott, who when two completed 5,000 runs in Tests (the eighth Englishman to do so) was still batting solidly when the game was given up soon after a stoppage for bad light at 4.50.

Toss: Australia. **England 214** (J. R. Thomson 4-87, M. F. Malone 5-63) **and 57-2;**
Australia 385 (D. W. Hookes 85, R. W. Marsh 57, M. H. N. Walker 78*, R. G. D. Willis 5-102).

CRICKETER OF THE YEAR – BOB WILLIS
Alex Bannister, 1978

If Geoff Boycott's timely return made all the difference to the batting, the new-ball firepower of Bob Willis, which yielded 27 wickets, was of special significance in England's high summer of success. No England bowler of authentic speed can boast a comparable record in a home series against Australia – only Jim Laker (46) and Alec Bedser (39) of different styles have done better – and, fittingly, in the final euphoric moments at Headingley when the Ashes were recaptured Willis took his 100th Test wicket.

It was singularly appropriate that team and personal triumph should go hand in hand, for few players have given such loyal and unstinted service to England as the wholehearted Willis. And he has had more than his fair share of the other side of fortune. As late as May 1975, his career was imperilled by major operations to both knees, and while in hospital he suffered a blood clot and spent several unpleasant hours. Until the middle of that season he was on crutches.

In Willis's own words the operations were similar to a 50,000-mile service, but his comeback would not have been complete without his own determination and a fortuitous meeting with Dr Arthur Jackson, an Australian disciple of the German Van Aaken's theory of the value of slow long-distance running to build stamina. Willis first met Dr Jackson during the 1974–75 tour of Australia, and formed a close friendship which has continued with phone and letter exchanges.

NOTES BY THE EDITOR
Norman Preston, 1978

The summer of 1977 will be remembered by most people for the Queen's Silver Jubilee. For lovers of cricket there were two other important topics. First, England won back the Ashes and secondly, there came the announcement in May that Kerry Packer, the

Australian newspaper and TV magnate, had secretly signed up at fabulous fees 35 Test stars from England, Australia, the West Indies, South Africa and Pakistan.

Earlier in the year at Melbourne, Australia and England had celebrated the centenary of the first Test match in that city in 1877. It was a wonderful occasion with 200 former Test players present and it produced some splendid cricket. Many Australians had by then made up their minds to break with tradition to earn as much as they could from the game whatever the consequences. Mr Packer's eyes may have opened wider to the amount which big cricket itself could attract by the happenings at Melbourne, but this could not be put forward as the reason for his determination to skim the game of its cream. The lack of response from the Australian Cricket Board to his overtures for TV rights for his Channel 9 commercial station was clearly at the root of the trouble, and this was further illustrated both during Mr Packer's visit to Lord's to meet the International Cricket Conference and the protracted High Court case in London in which Mr Justice Slade came down heavily against the cricket authorities. By then the world of cricket outside Australia had been drawn into an intricate and complicated web of other people's making.

No one can be positive for the time being about the success or failure of Mr Packer's venture. It is said that he would be willing to spend as much as $A9million to put his World Series Cricket on the map, but in the end it will be the public who will pronounce the verdict, mainly by their attendance at his matches and the time they devote to his TV presentations. The big test will come at the end of the year when England visit Australia for cricket of the traditional kind in another struggle for the Ashes.

AUSTRALIA V ENGLAND 1978–79

Alex Bannister

A lone trumpeter on the sparsely filled Hill at Sydney grimly symbolised Australia's embarrassing defeats, domestic confusions and divided loyalties, by sounding the Last Post as England won the Sixth Test inside four days and the series 5–1. For Brearley it was a continuation of his triumphant progress since he took over the captaincy from Greig. In the space of 20 months he defeated Australia eight times in 11 Tests, and it is not uncharitable to say that his one defeat might have been avoided if he had not lost an important toss.

Brearley's critics will no doubt argue that Australia, drained by defections to World Series Cricket, have never been weaker in the 102 years of struggle between the two countries. In another era Brearley might not have succeeded as he did, but he had disposed of an Australian team full of Packer players by 3–0 in 1977. He was expected to win in Australia, and, to his credit, he did all that was expected of him.

The competition from World Series Cricket put heavy demands on the Australian authorities, and the game at large suffered from an over-heavy programme and too much exposure on TV. The well-oiled and professional WSC publicity machine often distracted attention from the Ashes series, and the public grew tired of supporting a losing team.

They longed for better results and new heroes. One emerged in Rodney Hogg, the 27-year-old fast bowler, whose 41 wickets passed the record of 36 by Arthur Mailey in 1920–21. Fittingly Hogg broke the old record in front of his home crowd at Adelaide.

From the drama of the opening morning at steamy Brisbane when the first six

Australian batsmen were out for 26 it was a series for bowlers. Runs were hard to come by. Both sides bowled well, often brilliantly, but there was a marked change in the character of the pitches. Often damp at the start, they were seldom friendly to batsmen.

At 21, and in just his second season for England, Gower was the only batsman on either side to exceed 400 runs and an average above 40. At the end of the series Brearley described him as a minor genius who may become a major genius. Even this tribute might be considered a guarded judgment on a player already inviting comparison with Frank Woolley and Graeme Pollock. Technically he was left with some faults to iron out but, after many halting starts by England, it looked a different game when Gower, with his priceless sense of timing, stroked his runs.

First Test

At Brisbane, December 1, 2, 3, 5, 6, 1978. England won by seven wickets.

Fifty years of Test cricket at Brisbane was fittingly celebrated by an arresting match of fluctuations, changing moods, and a determined fightback by Australia after a catastrophic start. Yallop, leading Australia for the first time, had a difficult choice to make and opted to bat in humidity and under a thick cloud cover.

Disaster swiftly overtook Australia. Starting with the unlucky run-out of Cosier by Gower fourth ball, six wickets went down for 26 to Willis – suffering from skinned toes and blistered feet – Old and Botham. They revelled in the conditions with devastating swing and cut off the wicket. Although Old was off with a dislocated finger for 45 minutes, and not every chance was accepted, Australia were in sad disarray. Not one of the first six reached double figures.

Total calamity was avoided by the lower half scoring a brave 90. Maclean and Hogg, in their Test baptism, fought valiantly and helped by Yardley set a standard of resilience and resistance for the remainder of the match. Willis, Botham and Old had given England the key to victory, but Hogg, with an impressive six wickets, and Hurst, only fractionally less hostile, made it anything but a walkover.

Randall played the first of two innings which won him the match award, and when batting was far from easy Gower and Botham hit cleanly to make 95. Before that Randall and night-watchman Taylor had scored 73. Taylor held out for two hours 50 minutes for his 20, and with Miller and Old adding useful runs, England gained a solid lead of 170. A clue to the conditions was that the wicket-keepers, Maclean and Taylor, shared ten catches in the first innings.

In their second innings, Australia again made the worst of starts. Cosier was bowled first ball by an inswinger from Willis, and Toohey fell to Botham's fourth delivery. The total was two for two, and at 49 Wood was out. The likelihood of England having to bat again seemed remote, but Yallop and Hughes refused to be intimidated and produced a third-wicket stand of 170. Before a brilliant reflex catch by Willis ended his innings, Yallop had become the second Australian to hit a century in his maiden Test as captain, repeating the feat of Greg Chappell against West Indies in 1975–76. He set the best of examples, which Hughes was not slow to follow. Last out, Hughes batted for just on eight hours; he faced 409 balls and hit two sixes and eight fours. The next-highest contribution from the bat was 16. Even if they could not prevent the inevitable, Yallop and Hughes at least brought dignity to Australia's depression.

England had nearly seven hours to reach 170, but there were some uneasy moments before victory arrived in mid-afternoon on the fifth day. Toohey provided a nasty shock by running out Boycott from cover, but Randall and Gower gradually overcame keen bowling and tigerish fielding to get the last 96 runs. As Brearley said afterwards, Australia should not have been too disappointed at the way they were defeated.

Toss: Australia. **Australia 116** (R. G. D. Willis 4-44) **and 339** (G. N. Yallop 102, K. J. Hughes 129); **England 286** (D. W. Randall 75, A. G. Hurst 4-93, R. M. Hogg 6-74) **and 170-3** (D. W. Randall 74*).

Second Test
At Perth, December 15, 16, 17, 19, 20, 1978. England won by 166 runs.

The foundation for England's success was laid on the opening day by Boycott, in his most obdurate mood, and Gower, whose youthful genius was again revealed in his maiden century against Australia. In their contrasting but complementary styles they repaired the damage of a dismal start (41 for three) and proceeded to bat out a difficult day at 190 for three.

When Hogg dismissed Gooch and Randall for only three, it looked as if Yallop's decision to put in England in overcast conditions with a swirling wind was justified. Not only did Boycott and Gower end the collapse, but they survived a fierce new-ball attack 40 minutes from the close. Their fourth-wicket stand of 158 was soon broken on the second morning, but England had established a measure of control which was never seriously relaxed. Gower hit nine fours on a slow outfield, but Boycott's only four – in a marathon seven and a half hours in which he faced 340 deliveries – was all-run and included two overthrows. Nevertheless, it was an invaluable effort for his side.

Despite the splendid fast bowling of Hogg in both innings, which won him the match award, England were able to extend their total to 309. Miller, who played an important all-round role, made 40. The worth of Gower and Boycott was immediately apparent when, in 20 overs, Australia slumped to 60 for four. Once again Willis, this time with Lever's support, struck early and decisive blows.

England had a formidable attack for a seaming pitch, though generally Australia batted under the sun and England under cloud cover. Australia's plight worsened when Darling was run out by a marvellously quick pick-up and throw by Botham off the seventh ball of the last over. Only Toohey stood firm, and he was unlucky to run out of partners as he approached a century. Without his fine skill the innings would have been a disaster.

As it was, England led by 119, an advantage increased by 58 as Gooch and Boycott saw through the last 23 overs. England's policy, with a lead of 177 and two days left, was to go for the runs and leave as much time as possible for their bowlers to attack Australia who, with the pitch losing much of its pace, were becoming confident of a draw. As so often happens, however, it was easier said than done, particularly as Hogg maintained his impressive form. Used in short spells he again took five wickets, and dismissed any suggestion that Australia's bowling could be treated with contempt. Dymock, Hurst and Yardley backed him up creditably and England, sacrificing wickets in the cause of quick runs, were all out for 208. This left Australia 328 to win. All ten

413

England wickets went in four hours for 150, and Hogg's haul in his first two Tests was 17 out of 33 to fall – as good a start as any new bowler could hope to make.

Australia's never-strong hopes of winning virtually disappeared with the loss of 88 minutes to an unseasonal downpour. With Darling already out to a venomous kicker from Lever, they needed 317 on the final day with nine wickets in hand. The pitch was none the worse for the deluge, and England attacked with a ring of eager slips and gullies. They were rewarded in the seventh over when Gooch, at fourth slip, held a fierce cut from Hughes off Willis, then Yallop and Toohey were dismissed in successive deliveries by Hendrick. Although England went through a bad patch of missed chances and half-chances – including two offered by Wood to Boycott at mid-wicket off Botham – and despite the Wood-Cosier fifth-wicket stand of 83, the end was quick. Australia's last six wickets fell in 66 balls and 46 minutes to Miller (three for nought in 23 balls) and Lever. The spirit of England was epitomised by Botham's last flying left-handed catch at slip – a stunning example of athleticism and reflex action.

Toss: Australia. **England 309** (G. Boycott 77, D. I. Gower 102, R. M. Hogg 5-65) **and 208** (R. M. Hogg 5-57); **Australia 190** (P. M. Toohey 81*, R. G. D. Willis 5-44) **and 161** (G. M. Wood 64, J. K. Lever 4-28).

Third Test

At Melbourne, December 29, 30, 1978, January 1, 2, 3, 1979. Australia won by 103 runs.

Australia threw off the depression of two defeats to rekindle interest in the series with an emphatic victory founded on a century by Wood and the dynamic fast bowling of Hogg. The pitch provoked criticism for its variable and unpredictable bounce, which began as early as the second day. Thus winning the toss – Yallop's third success in a row – gave Australia a considerable advantage which they seized avidly.

Two opening stands of 65 and 55 by Darling and Wood – whose century took nearly six and a half hours – were essential elements in Australia's triumph. In contrast, England suffered badly with the loss of the first two wickets for three runs in the first innings, and two for only six in the second when they needed 283 to win with no time worries. In both innings the early breakthrough was achieved by Hogg, whose ten wickets took his series tally to 27, and the left-armer Dymock was always in steady support. England never recovered, laboured under a deficit of 115 in the first innings, and finally were comprehensively beaten by a team given little chance before the match.

There can be little argument that victory was set up on the first day when the pitch was at its best and Australia reached 243 for four. Incredibly, the last six wickets went to Hendrick (three for 11 in seven overs), Miller and Botham for a pittance of 15 runs before the bounce became erratic. By the end of the second day 14 wickets had gone for 122 runs.

Although Brearley was justified in describing the pitch as curious and one which gave the winner of the toss an inordinate advantage, the conditions did not fully explain England's poor first-innings total of 143. The tactical mistake was the tendency to play back against a ball occasionally keeping low. Hogg dismissed both Boycott and Brearley, restored as opener, and amid tremendous crowd enthusiasm – the aggregate attendance was 128,758 – he ended with five wickets again. Dymock took three for 38.

Australia's growing control was extended with 48 from Hughes, despite some excellent bowling. The target of 283 always looked beyond England after Brearley tried to drive Dymock's slanted ball which could have been left alone. When Randall was out at six to Hogg, a huge responsibility rested on Boycott, Gooch and Gower. Well as they responded, Australia remained in firm control. Again Hogg was the key bowler with five for 36: in contrast, Willis failed to take a wicket in the match. With eight wickets down and still needing 112, England lasted 24 minutes on the final morning when the crowd were admitted free to savour Australia's glowing moment of triumph.

Although the resurgence proved all too fleeting, it reflected credit on the much-criticised Yallop and his young team. It might have been different if the toss had gone the other way, but England could not rise above their difficulties.

Toss: Australia. **Australia 258** (G. M. Wood 100) **and 167;**
England 143 (R. M. Hogg 5-30) **and 179** (R. M. Hogg 5-36).

Fourth Test
At Sydney, January 6, 7, 8, 10, 11, 1979. England won by 93 runs.

Swiftly recovering from the shock of Melbourne, England, with a team weakened by a virus infection and heat exhaustion, retained the Ashes after staging one of Test cricket's most astonishing recoveries. At lunch on the second day Australia seemed to have taken a giant stride towards victory and squaring the series. Hurst had played a large part in dismissing England for paltry 152, and Australia were 126 for one. No side could have been better placed. Hughes, however, drove the first ball of the afternoon session straight to mid-off to end his second-wicket stand of 125 with Darling.

England's position worsened with the departure of the sick Willis after two overs – and only five in all – but Australia's control began to decline against the determination and ability of Hendrick and Botham. Because of the heat and the absence of Willis, Brearley was obliged to manipulate his resources with a fine balance and skill. Consequently, although the much-improved Darling and Border – unbeaten in both innings – batted well, the lead was restricted to 142; large enough but manageable. When Boycott was lbw to Hogg off the first ball of the second innings, however, Australia's prospects again soared. It was Boycott's first duck in 67 Test innings since 1969.

An enormous responsibility fell on the out-of-form Brearley and Randall, and they were not found wanting. With intense concentration they put on 111 for the second wicket, and at the end of the third day England were only nine runs in arrears with eight wickets left. Slowly but surely Randall pulled England round and the match away from Australia in the longest innings of his career. Missed at 113, 117 and 124, he batted in all for 11 minutes under ten hours and hit 13 boundaries, three of which came in four deliveries when Hogg took the new ball. It was Randall's first century in Tests since his 174 in the Centenary Test in March 1977.

Randall's discipline and stamina in the heat were considerable, and ultimately his innings was the match-winning effort. Gower, with a fever, and Botham, also unwell, lent valuable support. Higgs's leg-spin proved too much for the tail, however, and Australia were left to score 205 in 205 minutes plus the mandatory 15 eight-ball overs.

From an early stage Brearley had contended that around 200 to 220 would be difficult to score in the last innings. It was a sound prediction. Darling and Wood started splendidly, clearly aiming to unsettle an attack deprived of Willis for all but two overs, and to deny Brearley a close-set field. Again Hendrick bowled with consummate skill, and once Darling fell to a good falling catch by Gooch at second slip, and Wood went for a single that was never safe, the trap was set. Wood drove to Botham's right hand at cover and set off. Hughes refused to accept the call and, with both batsmen at the same end, all Botham needed to do was return the ball to Taylor. Only the left-handed Border, who batted well in both innings, escaped the spinning web of Emburey and Miller (three for 38). Sure in defence and quick to punish the loose ball, he was in a lonely class of his own as Brearley applied all the pressure needed with his field on top of the batsmen.

When Australia were all out for 111, Brearley could justifiably claim he had led the greatest comeback of his career – perhaps in the long history of the Ashes. Moreover he was the first England captain to retain the Ashes since Len Hutton in 1954–55. It was a triumph of astute captaincy, individual resolution and highly professional team-work. For Australia, it was a singularly disconcerting experience coming so closely after the Melbourne success. Having led on points they were knocked out in the final round.

Toss: England. **England 152** (I. T. Botham 59, A. G. Hurst 5-28) **and 346** (J. M. Brearley 53, D. W. Randall 150, R. M. Hogg 4-67, J. D. Higgs 5-148); **Australia 294** (W. M. Darling 91, A. R. Border 60*) **and 111** (J. E. Emburey 4-46).

Fifth Test

At Adelaide, January 27, 28, 29, 31, February 1, 1979. England won by 205 runs.

Brearley added to his triumphs by taking the series, and he became the first England captain since Jardine in 1932–33 to win four Tests in a series in Australia. For Yallop it was a profoundly disappointing experience. England, put in to bat on a green and lively pitch, were twice in serious trouble, but Australia, set to make 366 in nine and a quarter hours, experienced the worst batting collapse and this cost them the match.

With England at 27 for five Yallop had cause for great expectations. A crowd of 25,004 celebrated Hogg's record in passing Mailey's 36 wickets against England in 1920–21, and with Hurst also displaying controlled aggression, it was left to Botham to halt the slide to total disaster. He did so with a brilliant 74, including two sixes and six fours, and went on to demonstrate once again his considerable all-round flair with four wickets for 42. Australia, looking for a substantial lead to justify the gamble of conceding first innings, could do not better than England and finished five runs behind.

Hurst again bowled well and effectively in England's second innings, and when, despite a careful effort of over three hours by Boycott, they were down to 132 for six, Australia's revived hopes were justifiably high. Miller, who made a big advance on the tour, and Taylor represented England's last chance, and they could not have better served the needs of their side. Batting with rare skill and application – certainly it was Taylor's innings of his life – they more than doubled the total. When Miller was out 13 minutes from the close they had put on 135 and put England in a position of strength, Another stand of 69 with Emburey meant Taylor had stayed while 204 runs were scored, and there were many regrets when he was caught at the wicket well down the leg side off the last ball before lunch on the fourth day. With 97 he equalled his best score, and, as in the first innings, the Australians were frustrated by the resolution of batsmen in the lower half of the order. Taylor batted for six hours and hit six fours.

With the pitch eased and well behaved, Australia, for whom Hogg bowled only nine overs on the crucial third day because of muscle soreness, were still in with a chance. However, Wood made it that much harder by running himself out again – Boycott made a direct hit at one stump from mid on – and Darling left his leg stump exposed as he tried to whip Botham to leg.

On the final day the target was slimmed down to 284 with eight wickets left. England's hopes were largely pinned on the spin of Miller and Emburey, but Hughes and Yallop batted with such fluency that Brearley was obliged to call on Willis and Hendrick to control the scoring-rate. At once the situation changed dramatically. Hendrick dismissed Yallop with an exceptional delivery, then Gower, at square cover, made a brilliant diving catch to dismiss Hughes. Willis, who had not bowled with his customary fire since the Second Test, suddenly regained his fire and rhythm. The rot set in with a vengeance and six wickets crashed for 15. Miller also struck, and in 100 astonishing minutes Australia's last eight wickets had gone.

Once again experience, strength in depth, and a sharply developed team spirit had prevailed. Nevertheless, England were honest enough to admit they had never expected such a headlong rush to victory, and Brearley was apt to describe it as freakish.

Toss: Australia. **England 169** (I. T. Botham 74, R. M. Hogg 4-26) **and 360** (G. Miller 64, R. W. Taylor 97, A. G. Hurst 4-97); **Australia 164** (I. T. Botham 4-42) **and 160**.

Sixth Test

At Sydney, February 10, 11, 12, 14, 1979. England won by nine wickets.

Brearley completed his conquests with the winning hit in mid-afternoon on the fourth day. In many aspects it was the most humiliating of Australia's five defeats, for they should have made much better use of the advantage of batting first. A total of 198 on a blameless pitch was a bad letdown and inexcusable. They paid the inevitable penalty when the pitch took early and increasing spin, and finally Miller and Emburey won the Test for England. Australia's failure was redeemed only by Yallop's 121, his runs coming out of 179 while he was at the wicket and including 13 fours. It must have been particularly galling for the Australian captain to bat so magnificently and see wickets tumble at the other end.

The almost inevitable first-wicket run-out began the slide. This time the victim was Hilditch, playing his first Test innings, and the fielder was Gooch. One run later Hughes was spectacularly caught by Botham diving to his right, arm fully extended, at second slip. Botham went on to take four cheap wickets, including the last two with successive balls. Hendrick was as deadly as ever.

The pattern of the match soon emerged as Brearley, Gooch – with by far his best innings of the tour – Gower, and finally Taylor took England to a lead of 110. By now it was evident that Australia were in deep trouble. England's significant stands were between Brearley and Gooch – 69 for the third wicket – and Gower and Gooch – 67 in 49 minutes for the fourth. Gooch, refusing to be tied down by spin, once off-drove Yardley for six and there were also seven fours in his fine attacking innings. Gower and

Botham were beginning to prosper when the last two hours were lost because of a thunderstorm. Higgs's leg-spin gained him four wickets; Hurst, an intelligent fast bowler, took three, but Hogg had to be satisfied with one.

Australia, soon began to totter, and when Wood, Toohey and Carlson went in nine balls from Emburey and Miller, any serious doubts about the outcome vanished. Yardley, using his feet well, bravely carried on the fight after Yallop was so comprehensively beaten by Miller that he was given out caught and stumped at both ends. The catch at the wicket took precedence. Miller ended with his best Test figures, and England were left with the formality of scoring 34 to win. The skilful bowling of Miller and Emburey was magnificently supported by Taylor, who made 18 catches and two stumpings in a brilliant series, and by Hendrick, Botham and Gooch in the leg-side trap.

Oddly, Australia were allowed to use an old ball from the start. Brearley's protests were overruled, even though Law 5 states that either captain may demand a new ball. No previous agreement had been made to the contrary by the captains, and the innings was delayed six minutes while Brearley argued his case.

Toss: Australia. **Australia 198** (G. N. Yallop 121, I. T. Botham 4-57) **and 143** (B. Yardley 61*, J. E. Emburey 4-52, G. Miller 5-44); **England 308** (G. A. Gooch 74, D. I. Gower 65, J. D. Higgs 4-69) **and 35-1**.

AUSTRALIA V ENGLAND 1979–80 Peter Smith

Forty-eight hours before England flew out of Melbourne for the last time, their manager Alec Bedser was asked to present his considered view of the experimental twin-tour programme, the first product of the marriage between the Australian Cricket Board and World Series Cricket which had taken place some nine months earlier. He gave it a definite thumbs-down. He received majority support from those who had the best interests of cricket at heart, particularly Australian cricket below Test level. This had been swamped by the accent on Test and one-day internationals, neatly parcelled for maximum exploitation on TV.

Privately, at least, the Australian players agreed with Bedser. With a programme of six Tests – three each against England and West Indies – plus a triangular one-day competition, the Australian players became very much a touring side inside their own country. So anxious was their captain Greg Chappell to rejoin a family he had hardly seen for two months that he was flying home to Brisbane within an hour of bringing the final Test against England in Melbourne to a swift and victorious conclusion.

It was not only the match programme but the whole atmosphere that the England players found disagreeable. Their captain, Brearley, was the subject of a disgraceful campaign wherever he went, and a large section of the Melbourne crowd was so abusive that the Australian team manager was moved to issue a statement in which he said they made him ashamed to be an Australian.

For the first time for three years, Australia had available their full complement of players, with Lillee and Thomson on hand to team up with Hogg, who had taken 41 Test wickets against England the previous winter. Greg Chappell was back to provide the leadership and batting expertise missing 12 months earlier, and there were half a dozen others rich in Test experience. The availability of these players promised to provide England with their toughest opposition since Brearley assumed the captaincy in 1977.

There were pockets of resistance in each Test, such as Boycott's unbeaten 99 in the First Test when trying to save the game, Gower's unbeaten 98 in the second innings of the Second Test, Gooch's 99 in the first innings of the final Test and Botham's 119 not out in the second innings to delay Australia's victory. Brearley, too, offered stern resistance in every Test; but Lillee proved that, at 30, he was still a match-winning bowler, even if he had lost that explosive edge. He took 23 wickets, 11 of them in the final Test when he cut his pace and produced a mixture of leg- and off-cutters which drew the highest praise from Brearley.

The English Board declined to put the Ashes at stake for this experimental three-match series.

First Test

At Perth, December 14, 15, 16, 18, 19, 1979 Australia won by 138 runs.

It was unfortunate that Australia's victory in an enthralling match was soured by Lillee's unsavoury behaviour in seeking to use an aluminium bat in the first innings despite objections from Brearley, the umpires and his own captain. He caused play to be held up for ten minutes before being persuaded by Chappell to exchange it for the traditional willow. The incident served only to blacken Lillee's reputation and damage the image of the game as well as, eventually, the reputation of the Australian authorities because of their reluctance to take effective disciplinary action. Lillee's behaviour also partly overshadowed other individual performances more in keeping with the spirit of the game, notably the bowling of Botham and Dymock, the batting of Hughes and Border, and Boycott's gallant attempt to save England on the final day.

Although only once before had an England captain won a Test in Australia when asking the opposition to bat first – at Melbourne in 1911–12 – Brearley opted for that course now to support the decision to go into the match with two off-spinning all-rounders, plus Underwood who was making his first Test appearance in Perth. Brearley must have been reasonably content with his decision when Australia's first innings closed at 244. It was built in the main around Hughes, who made 99 in almost four hours and defied the remarkable bowling effort of Botham, being used as both strike and stock bowler. In 35 overs he took six wickets. But any feelings of satisfaction Brearley held were soon swept away as Randall and Boycott went without scoring and the first six England wickets fell for only 90. Brearley rescued the situation himself, batting stubbornly for four hours ten minutes and producing one of his best innings for his country. Dilley, on his Test debut, gave him fine support, batting nearly three and a half hours for 38 not out, and Australia's lead was limited to 16.

By the end of the third day, however, Australia seemed to be in a strong position, 174 ahead with eight second-innings wickets in hand, after Wiener, with a half-century in his first Test, and Laird had opened with a stand of 91. But another marathon bowling stint by Botham, refreshed after the rest day, changed the situation dramatically, and Australia owed much to Border for their eventual lead of 353. He was repeatedly in trouble against Botham early on but survived to pass 1,000 runs in Tests in 11 days short of a year. Botham, with five wickets in the innings, ended with match figures of 11 for 176 from 80.5 overs.

Only 65 minutes remained when England started their second innings, but it was time enough for Randall's second failure before bad light stopped play. Worse was to follow on the final day, most of the wounds self-inflicted as England lost wickets regularly while Chappell switched attack intelligently and Dymock responded with accurate seam bowling. Only Boycott showed the technique and determination needed to survive and he was still unbeaten, one short of his century, when England's last man, Willis, became Dymock's sixth victim with 14.4 of the last 20 overs left.

Toss: England. **Australia 244** (K. J. Hughes 99, I. T. Botham 6-78) **and 337** (J. M. Wiener 58, A. R. Border 115, I. T. Botham 5-98); **England 228** (J. M. Brearley 64, D. K. Lillee 4-73) **and 215** (G. Boycott 99*, G. Dymock 6-34).

Second Test

At Sydney, January 4, 5, 6, 8, 1980. Australia won by six wickets.

Australia won by six wickets with a day to spare. A decision to give the Sydney ground-staff the day off to celebrate the New Year virtually decided the outcome of the Test and the three-match series. The pitch was left exposed to a violent thunderstorm, and further rain over the following two days resulted in it still being damp and patchy when the match began nearly four hours late.

Winning the toss almost guaranteed victory. Chappell, who protested that conditions were not fit, won it, and although the pitch was never as spiteful as many imagined, England were bundled out in 43 overs, a strange selection of strokes by the middle order helping their downfall. Even so, it is doubtful whether Australia would have matched England's 123 if England's bowlers had been given first use of the pitch.

Brearley wasted little time introducing Underwood on the second day – he was on after only four overs – but once again it was Botham who proved the more effective as Australia inched to a 22-run lead. For this modest advantage they were heavily indebted to Ian Chappell, recalled to Test cricket after a three-year absence who demonstrated his undoubted class during his 105-minute stay.

By the close on the second day England were in trouble once more, having lost three wickets for 59 and been forced to send in Underwood as night-watchman. He took this role so seriously that he turned it into a day-time occupation next day, surviving until after lunch and falling to a catch at short leg only two short of his highest Test score. Brearley and Randall proved effective partners before Gower took over to boost England's hopes of squaring the series. Gower lived dangerously during his first half-century, going for his strokes but missing as often as he connected. Once he reached 50, though, almost immediately everything clicked and for the last 100 minutes of his innings he again looked one of the most talented batsmen in the world. Like Boycott in Perth, Gower was denied his century, being marooned on 98 when Willis was last out.

Australia, requiring 216 to clinch the series, were 191 short with all ten wickets intact when the third day ended. England were convinced both Wiener and McCosker should have been given out during the last 35 minutes, and they suffered a further disappointment on the fourth day when Greg Chappell, then 32, survived a concerted appeal for a catch behind off Dilley. A wicket then and England would have been well in the hunt. Both openers, plus Ian Chappell, had fallen and Greg Chappell and Hughes were still struggling to impose their authority. The not-out verdict proved the turning-point, for the Australian captain and his vice-captain added 105 to put victory in sight. Chappell, having secured it, was offered a long-hop by Botham for the winning runs, and a chance to reach his century with a six, but he managed only a four.

Toss: Australia. **England 123** (D. K. Lillee 4-40, G. Dymock 4-42) **and 237** (D. I. Gower 98*);
Australia 145 (I. T. Botham 4-29) **and 219-4** (G. S. Chappell 98*).

THE PASSING OF WORLD SERIES CRICKET   John Woodcock, 1981

On the surface, the end of traditional cricket's acrimonious dispute with Mr Kerry Packer brought a reasonably harmonious return to normality. But at what cost to the game? Cricketers who were previously paid too little are now, in some cases, being paid more than the game can afford or they themselves are worth. Money has become the talk of the dressing-rooms, with the average county cricketer feeling that Test players are getting a disproportionately large slice of the cake.

In Australia, one worrying aspect of the settlement which led to the running-down of World Series Cricket is the new structure of the first-class game there, this now being devised to accommodate commercial television. When England were in Australia in 1979–80, a tour they shared with West Indies, such was the confusion of fixtures that attendances and authenticity both suffered. The public seemed not to know what to expect next, or indeed for what trophy any given match was being played. As for the players, they were given little chance to settle down to any one type of cricket, whether one-day, four-day or five-day, all of which call for different tactics and not necessarily the same skills. It is important that before England tour Australia next, in 1982–83, they should negotiate resolutely for the itinerary they consider to be in the best interests of both countries.

Third Test
At Melbourne, February 1, 2, 3, 5, 6, 1980. Australia won by eight wickets.

A fine innings of 99 by Gooch enabled England to start their first innings with a bang. And a remarkable century by Botham, with only the tail for support, allowed them to finish with a captivating flourish. In between, however, events were largely dictated by Lillee, bowling a mixture of leg- and off-cutters which presented Australia with a clean sweep in the series.

England looked to have every chance of ending the tour on a high note when Brearley won the toss and Gooch and Boycott produced England's highest opening partnership since they scored 111 together against New Zealand at Trent Bridge in 1978. When Boycott went at 116, Larkins, on his Test debut, helped Gooch take the score to 170 before the all-too-familiar middle-order collapse. Five wickets fell for just 22 runs, including Gooch who ran himself out in the final over before tea going for the single that would have brought him his maiden Test century. Once again England were indebted to a defiant innings from Brearley – he batted for close on four hours – while Lillee, with six wickets, caused the damage at the other end.

England's total of 306 was their best of the series, but Australia had little difficulty building a useful lead of 171. With the exception of Hughes, all their leading batsmen were among the runs. Laird, a gritty, determined opener, and Ian Chappell put on 127 for the second wicket; Greg Chappell and Border added 126 for the fifth, Chappell spending the rest day needing one run to complete his 16th Test century. The third delivery on the fourth morning saw him duly reach it after 254 minutes at the crease, during which time he suffered both a leg injury and a stomach upset. Lever, playing his first Test of the series, was England's most successful bowler, putting in one memorable stint when he bowled for more than two hours without a break.

Although the wicket was offering help to the bowler capable of cutting the ball, there seemed no reason why England, with sensible batting and application, should not make it tight for Australia. Yet within two and a half hours they were 88 for five and Australia appeared set for an innings victory. Botham's entrance changed the picture. He soon lost Brearley, but with the help of Taylor – 32 in an hour and a half – and Lever – 12 in 106 minutes – Botham showed the Australians how well he could bat by scoring a century in exactly 200 minutes.

Left to make 103 in just under two and a half hours, Australia set about their task cautiously, determined not to repeat England's mistakes. Even so they lost both their opening batsmen in the first hour and a half, and still required another 61 when Greg Chappell joined his elder brother. In another 53 minutes it was all over, Greg Chappell having helped himself to 40 of those runs as he batted with supreme arrogance.

Toss: England. **England 306** (G. A. Gooch 99, J. M. Brearley 60*, D. K. Lillee 6-60)
and 273 (G. A. Gooch 51, I. T. Botham 119*, D. K. Lillee 5-78, L. S. Pascoe 4-80);
Australia 477 (B. M. Laird 74, I. M. Chappell 75, A. R. Border 63, G. S. Chappell 114,
J. K. Lever 4-111) **and 103-2.**

ENGLAND V AUSTRALIA 1980

The reason for Australia's brief visit to England in August 1980 was to play a Centenary Test match. It was 100 years since the two countries had first met in England, and although the original match was played at The Oval in September 1880, this celebration was held at Lord's.

Australia's performance in the Centenary Test did them much credit. Whereas the occasion was memorable, the match itself was not; but for the disappointments on the field and the controversies which developed off it the Australian cricketers were blameless. They bowled, batted and fielded better than England, putting behind them the unconvincing form of their earlier matches.

Both Hughes and Wood scored Centenary hundreds, Hughes showing a flair that marked him as a new star in the Australian constellation, and the left-handed Wood batting with a doggedness that England first encountered when he scored 100 against them at Melbourne in 1978–79. As vice-captain of the party, Hughes had the look of Chappell's natural successor.

The Ashes were not at stake during this one-off match.

Centenary Test

Crawford White

At Lord's, August 28, 29, 30, September 1, 2, 1980. Drawn.

It had been hoped that England's Centenary Test – to mark the centenary of the first Test played in England, at The Oval in 1880 – might be played in late-summer sunshine with many a nostalgic reunion, some splendid fighting cricket and a finish to savour. Over 200 former England and Australian players assembled from all over the world; it was impossible to move anywhere without meeting the heroes of yesteryear. The welcoming parties, the dinners and the takeover by the sponsors of a London theatre for a night were all hugely successful. Sadly, however, the party in the middle was markedly less so.

After almost ten hours had been lost to rain in the first three days, the match ended in a tepid draw, with many disappointed that England did not make a bolder bid to meet a challenge to score 370 in 350 minutes.

As much as for the cricket, though, the game will be remembered for a regrettable incident, seen by millions on TV, in which angry MCC members were involved in a momentary scuffle with umpire Constant as the umpires and captains moved into the Long Room after their fifth pitch inspection of the third day. Ian Botham, the England captain, and Greg Chappell, his Australian counterpart, saw to it that matters got no worse. When play finally started at 3.45, police escorted the umpires through the Long Room and on to the field.

Fifty minutes were lost to rain on the first day and all but an hour and a quarter on the second. On the third, rain in the early morning left a soft area around two old uncovered pitches on the Tavern side. The groundstaff, however, thought play could have started by lunch, as did a crowd of some 20,000 who were growing increasingly impatient in sunshine and breeze. Umpires Bird and Constant were the sole judges of when play should start, with one captain noticeably keener to play than the other; Australia being in the stronger position, Chappell was the more eager. They conducted inspection after inspection, seemingly insensitive to the crowd's rising anger and the need for flexibility on such a special occasion. By the time the president of MCC, Mr S. C. Griffith, exerted pressure on the umpires to get the game started, the pavilion fracas had occurred.

On the field Australia were much the more convincing side. After Chappell won the toss Australia batted well through repeated interruptions before declaring on Saturday evening. Wood contributed a battling 112, before being brilliantly stumped by Bairstow off Emburey, and Hughes graced the occasion with a spirited 117, every stroke being played according to the fighting intentions of his side. Against such aggression England's bowling, with the exception of Old, looked very ordinary.

Lillee and Pascoe, with faster and more skilful bowling, routed England on the Monday with enough time left that evening for Australia to take their lead to 286. Boycott, Gower and Old were the only batsmen to pass 20. Lillee, superbly controlled, removed the first four batsmen, and Pascoe finished the innings with a spell of five for 15 in 32 balls. Both bowlers took all their wickets at the Nursery End, once so infamous for its ridge. Chappell insisted that the ridge was still plainly visible and very much in play, although the pitch had been shifted some four or five feet away from the Pavilion End in an effort to escape its influence.

England's first-innings collapse, in which they lost their last seven wickets for 68, had left Australia in a potentially winning position when the last day began. They hammered a further 83 runs in under an hour before Chappell's second declaration left England to score for almost six hours at over a run a minute. Chappell himself made a sound 59 and Hughes a brilliant 84. Moving into his shots with zest and certainty Hughes played the most spectacular stroke of the match when he danced down the pitch to hit the lively Old on to the top deck of the pavilion.

England did not attempt to meet Chappell's challenge. When Lillee trapped Gooch lbw for 16 and Pascoe removed Athey for one, survival became the priority. Boycott dropped anchor and Gower curbed his attacking instincts as they consolidated. When the score had reached 112 for two by three o'clock, with play possible until seven, many felt it would have been fitting if Botham had come in himself and had a fling. But England looked upon their first-innings collapse as good enough reason for not risking another. Amid more boos than cheers they moved unhurriedly towards a draw.

Toss: Australia. **Australia 385-5 dec.** (G. M. Wood 112, K. J. Hughes 117, A. R. Border 56*)
and 189-4 dec. (G. S. Chappell 59, K. J. Hughes 84); **England 205** (G. Boycott 62, D. K. Lillee 4-43, L. S. Pascoe 5-59) **and 244-3** (G. Boycott 128*, M. W. Gatting 51*).

CRICKETER OF THE YEAR – KIM HUGHES

Ian Brayshaw, 1981

The distinction of scoring the first hundred in Anglo-Australian Tests on English soil belonged, fittingly, to the legendary W. G. Grace. That of scoring the first in the second century of these games went to Graeme Wood with a fine 112, but it was Wood's Western Australian team-mate, Kimberley John Hughes, to whom the Centenary Test of 1980 at Lord's really belonged. In two innings of the highest quality, Hughes put his manifest talents on display on each of the five days of the game.

His 117 in the first innings was spread over the first three rain-hit days. He hurried to 47 late on the first day, advanced to 82 in the 75 minutes available on the second, and charged to 117 when play finally got under way on the third. This memorable century contained three sixes and 14 fours, all put together with an air of casual disregard for the importance of the occasion. As if such a smorgasbord of strokes was not sufficient for the connoisseur, he tickled the palate with a lot of new ones in the second innings with a breathtaking 84 in 114 minutes, which included two sixes and ten fours. One of his sixes, hit off paceman Chris Old on the run some three yards down the wicket, landed on the top deck of the pavilion, failing by only an extra erg or two to clear the building altogether. Another stroke, from even further down the pitch and also against a pace bowler, was slashed to the point boundary with such speed as to leave standing a fieldsman on the ropes only a yard or two from its scorching path.

The marvellous appeal of Hughes's batting lies in the repertoire of his strokes and his unashamed enthusiasm in playing them. Most are straight from the copybook and executed with the fine touch of the artist's brush; some, however, are of his own design and despatched with a grand flourish. The high backlift, the skipping footwork, the flashing blade and the full-blooded follow-through – all hallmarks of the great strokeplayers – are evident at their very best when Hughes is in full flight.

NOTES BY THE EDITOR
John Woodcock, 1981

This great jamboree, arranged to celebrate 100 years of Test cricket between England and Australia in England, had been eagerly awaited. Its counterpart, at Melbourne in 1977, had been a wonderful success. But last summer's match was ill-fated from the start.

Some would say that the hours from 11 o'clock until six on the Saturday were like a nightmare. So incensed were certain members of MCC by the middle of the after noon that play was not in progress, owing, as they thought, to the obstinacy of the umpires, that a scuffle took place on the steps of the pavilion, in which the umpires, one or two members, and the captains were involved. As a result of it, the umpires were shaken, the reputation of MCC was damaged and the occasion impaired.

If good is to come from a sorry affair, it will be to see that efforts are redoubled to provide the best possible covering on all first-class grounds, especially those where Tests are staged. As many have said, it seems laughable to be able to land a man on the moon yet to have discovered no adequate way of protecting the square at Lord's.

Botham and Beyond:
1981 to 2002–03

Until 2005, the Tests of the 1981 English summer remained a contender for the title of Best Ashes Series. It came alight in the Third Test at Headingley, when England, apparently certain to go two down when they were 135 for 7 in their follow-on, came from behind and pulled off a sensational victory that stopped the whole country in its tracks.

The lead role in the astonishing fightback was taken by Ian Botham, who had looked a hapless leader in the first two Tests before resigning, just ahead of the selectors' bullet. Mike Brearley, who had won the Ashes back in 1977, resumed the captaincy, and asked Botham whether he wanted to play in the Third Test. Luckily for England, he did – and turned the match around with a buccaneering century, which gave Bob Willis just enough scope to bowl Australia out. It was only the second time a Test had been won by the side following on (England also did it at Sydney in 1894–95, during another amazing series).

Lightning isn't supposed to strike twice, but Botham did, wrapping up another low-scoring thriller at Edgbaston by taking five wickets for one run. Suddenly England were ahead, and they made sure of the Ashes with another victory at Old Trafford, with Botham again starring with another forthright century.

Even Beefy couldn't repeat the magic in Australia in 1982–83, when Greg Chappell, in his final Ashes battle, emerged victorious, though England won the most memorable game of the series, at Melbourne, by just three runs. Chappell – and Dennis Lillee and Rod Marsh – had bowed out by 1985, and with Australia's bowling uncharacteristically toothless England sailed home with ease. Then, in 1986–87, Australia's side included some raw but unformed talent, while the Poms' professionalism won the day.

Little did England know that that would be their last taste of success against Australia in the 20th century. Australia returned under Allan Border in 1989, but this was a new Border: worried that he had ceded an advantage in 1985 by being too nice, now he hardly spoke to the opposition. And since the opposition was hit by injuries and defections to a rebel South African tour (Australia's own "rebels" were back in the fold for this tour) his task was eased. Australia won the series 4–0: England, who rarely competed, lost both their captain and chairman of selectors.

The 1990s were a decade of untrammelled Aussie dominance – so marked in the end that some leading writers Down Under started suggesting that England were not worth five-Test series any more. It was a depressing time to be an England fan. Tours to Australia were seemingly disaster areas, with player after player going down injured, often in bizarre circumstances. In 1990–91, Australia won 3–0, helped when England's captain Graham Gooch injured his hand badly and missed the first two Tests. In 1994–95 it was 3–1, with more English injuries. The series started with Australia's hyperactive opener Michael Slater belting the first two balls to the boundary, and England never recovered. In 1998–99, Australia won 3–1 again. And four years later, despite a fine performance from Michael Vaughan, Australia wrapped up the Ashes on December 1, after only 11 playing days, by winning the first three Tests.

Australia were developing into easily the most powerful team in world cricket. Border handed over to Mark Taylor in 1993–94, by which time the side had acquired two bowlers destined to give their captain control in most of the Tests for the next dozen years or so. Glenn McGrath, a gangling right-arm fast bowler from the far reaches of New South Wales, offered a metronomic line, and repeatedly hit an awkward length. Shane Warne, however, was a one-off, simply the most accurate leg-spinner cricket has ever seen. He was capable of sending down a big leg-break – such as the one which entered Ashes folklore when his first ball against England turned a mile and bowled a disbelieving Mike Gatting at Old Trafford in 1993 – but was equally unafraid to unveil the "zooter", a ball of his own invention which, according to its advance publicity, probably turned a cart-wheel, but actually went straight on.

Warne continued playing (and talking) a great game until 2006–07, by which time he was the leading wicket-taker in England–Australia Tests with 197 (McGrath is third with 157, behind Lillee's 167). It's easy to say that we will never see his like again – but I don't think we will. Warne was unique.

Things weren't much better for England when Australia came calling. In 1993 Australia were four up before they relaxed and lost at The Oval. The 1997 series promised something different when Australia dipped to 54 for 7 on the first morning of the First Test, and England pressed on to win comfortably. When the Second Test was a rain-affected draw, England had a whiff of the Ashes – but Australia won the next three matches to clinch the series, before England gained another consolation victory at The Oval, at last getting their selection right.

And, apart from one topsy-turvy day at Headingley, when Mark Butcher carried all before him, Australia were on top throughout 2001, eventually winning the series 4–1. Between 1989 and 2002–03 there were 43 Ashes Tests: Australia won 28 and England seven (and most of those were dead matches).

The lure of the Ashes was fading. Something special was needed to restore their lustre.   **S. L.**

ENGLAND V AUSTRALIA 1981   John Woodcock

Although from an English point of view the visit of Kim Hughes's Australian side was memorable, for the tourists themselves it must have been one of almost unbearable frustration. Having come, more than once, to within an ace of making sure of at least a share of the Test series, they lost it in the end by three matches to one. England thus retained the Ashes, which had not been officially contested when the two sides had last met – on an *ad hoc* basis in Australia in 1979-80.

Feeling in need of a rest from cricket, Greg Chappell did not make the tour. When Australia were losing the Third Test by 18 runs and the Fourth by 28, his absence made all the difference. The Australians were also deprived through injury, for the last three

Test matches, of the bowling of Lawson, whose support of Lillee and Alderman in the first three had been a telling factor. For all that, it was the brittleness of Australia's batting that let them down. Needing only 130 to win the Third Test, they were bowled out, on an admittedly awkward wicket, for 111. In the Fourth Test, when, on a much better wicket, they needed 151 to win, they could make only 121, in spite of having been at one time 105 for four. Next, at Old Trafford, they allowed themselves to be bowled out in their first innings for 130 in 30.2 overs.

The chief successes of the tour were Lillee and Alderman with the ball and Border with the bat. The first two took no fewer than 81 Test wickets between them. At 32, and having been far from well, Lillee was seldom anything like as fast as in the middle '70s. Such was his control, however, and his craftsmanship, that it was not until the later stages of the Fifth Test that he was played with any sort of comfort. If this was Lillee's last tour of England, as in all likelihood it was, it was one of great distinction.

Hughes had a difficult time. His public relations were pretty good, and on the field he was always prepared to take advice from Marsh, his more experienced deputy. He is a lovely fielder and a fine cricketer, and in most respects he stood up well to the severe pressures of a hard, close and, for him, disappointing series. He should, however, have made more runs. For someone who had batted so brilliantly in the Centenary Test of 1980, a tally of 300 runs from 12 Test innings, with a top score of 89, was something of an anticlimax.

First Test

Steve Whiting

At Nottingham, June 18, 19, 20, 21, 1981. Australia won by four wickets.

Australia, underdogs for the Tests, spent the fourth day, the longest of the year and the first Sunday of Test cricket in England, marking off the 132 runs they needed to win on a home-made scoreboard in their dressing-room. When Trevor Chappell, the youngest of the three grandsons of Victor Richardson, made the winning hit in his first Test, Australian joy was unbounded. The match ended in brilliant sunshine, a fact which no doubt eased Australia's path to victory, taking just a little of the life out of a pitch which had been green and too moist from the outset. The Trent Bridge featherbeds, bound hard by the marl from the river nearby, are a thing of the past.

Hughes put England in under a cloudy sky. England, who would have done the same given the opportunity, left Emburey out and, Australia having omitted Bright, we were left with a Test in which not a single over of spin was bowled. The cricket which ensued, however, was so enthralling and unpredictable that few had time to notice that the over-rates were as low as 14 an hour.

On the first day the ball rarely stopped moving around as England were put out for 185 in 56.4 overs. Woolmer, brought in to try to solve the problematical No. 3 position, received a typically nasty ball from Lillee to set him on his way to a pair in his comeback Test. Gatting, playing crisply and sensibly, reached 50 in 147 minutes but was out soon afterwards pulling at a ball from Hogg which was not quite short enough.

The feature of the innings was the emergence of Alderman, a 24-year-old teacher from Western Australia, who was destined to make a major impact on the series. He was never afraid to keep the ball up to the bat, counting the occasional driven four as a fair price to pay for the harvest of wickets he took in the summer. Now he took four for 68 in 24 overs, being helped by some brilliant close catching. That was the difference between the teams: Australia held their catches, England did not. At a conservative estimate, England missed six in the first innings, the most vital being Border, dropped behind the wicket when only ten. He went on to make 63 out of 179. Once again, the weather did not help on the second day, dark skies and rain causing 183 minutes to be lost, though 50 of those were made up under the rule which allowed play to continue in the event of an hour or more being lost earlier.

The difference was highlighted when England batted again. Once again the weather made matters thoroughly miserable. Only 12 runs had been scored when Yallop took off at full length in the gully to hold Gooch, who had presented the full meat of the blade to a back-foot square-drive off Lillee. By Saturday night England were 94 for six, only 100 ahead. Early next morning they were all out for 125, and Alderman had another five wickets to give him nine for 130 in his first Test.

Australia's progress towards the 132 they needed was neither sure nor certain. They owed much to opener Dyson, who made 38 out of their first 80 before being caught behind off Dilley, who also accounted for Hughes, Border and Marsh, but by then Australia needed only ten to win – a task duly accomplished by Chappell and Lawson.

Toss: Australia. **England 185** (M. W. Gatting 52, T. M. Alderman 4-68) **and 125** (D. K. Lillee 5-46, T. M. Alderman 5-62); **Australia 179** (A. R. Border 63) **and 132-6** (G. R. Dilley 4-24).

Second Test

Terry Cooper

At Lord's, July 2, 3, 4, 6, 7, 1981. Drawn.

Lord's and Test-match time in recent years have become synonymous with bad weather, controversy and abysmal public relations, redeemed only partially by isolated individual performances. This Test followed this morbid trend. At the end of a personally disappointing match, which concluded a fruitless year as captain, Botham resigned as leader.

On a pitch that was dry with an erratic bounce, Hughes put England in again, and Gooch played in his best thumping style for 75 minutes. It was only when he was out that things began to go wrong, both with the innings and the match. Boycott and Woolmer became bogged down and Woolmer's troubles were increased when Lawson struck him on the arm. He struggled passively for some time before going off. With Gower inactive and bad light removing more than half an hour's play, England added only 28 between Gooch's dismissal at 12.45 and 3.30. Gatting enlivened the second half of the day by cracking the loose ball for four, but unfortunately for England he was out for 59 shortly before the close, which came at 191 for four.

On the second day the combination of a protracted innings by night-watchman Emburey and the loss of over two hours from the first half of the day meant a lack of impetus, though the value of the Emburey-Willey stand was emphasised when the innings disintegrated after they were split. After Alderman had opened the way and Emburey had been carelessly run out, Lawson scythed through an assorted lower order, which included Woolmer, batting under handicap. Lawson's speed had proved sharp enough to defeat the top batsmen, and four quick wickets at the end sent him off with the best figures by an Australian in a Lord's Test, save for Bob Massie's in 1972.

Controversy came when the umpires took the players off for bad light during the extra hour of this second day. The sun reappeared, but Messrs Oslear and Palmer were under the false impression that no resumption could be allowed once play had stopped in the extra period. The crowd jeered and threw their cushions on to the ground in protest, and next day the TCCB issued a statement regretting the misunderstanding.

After the loss of 35 minutes at the start on Saturday, Australia took their score from ten for no wicket to 253 for six. England did not bowl a full enough length, and with no-balls frequent (Willis alone bowled 28) the 55 extras were a record for one innings in England-Australia Tests. Wood batted enterprisingly before Taylor, on his Test recall, took the first of two marvellous catches, the other being by Gatting at slip. With Australia at 81 for four, England had the chance of taking command, but they were denied by their own deficiencies and the cool control shown by Border in partnership first with Hughes and then Marsh.

It took England almost half the fourth day, at the cost of 92 more runs, to work their way through the last four wickets. Marsh and Lawson vanished to the new ball, but Bright and Lillee found plenty of loose deliveries. When England, batting again, lost Gooch and Woolmer for 55, Boycott and Gower had to repair matters in the final 105 minutes, and this they did effectively. But the necessary acceleration on the last day towards a declaration came too late. Boycott, who batted 279 minutes, seemed set on a century to mark his 100th Test, but England seemed not to appreciate that wickets in hand were a cushion against the hazards of attack. Still, an hour's batting after lunch brought 68 runs, and Australia were set 232 in 170 minutes. When they were 17 for three in the second over after tea, with the ball turning, England were hopeful, but Chappell dug in and when he was out, with 15 overs left, Wood remained unshakable.

Toss: Australia. **England 311** (M. W. Gatting 59, P. Willey 82, G. F. Lawson 7-81) **and 265-8 dec.** (G. Boycott 60, D. I. Gower 89); **Australia 345** (A. R. Border 64) **and 90-4** (G. M. Wood 62*).

Third Test

Alan Lee

At Leeds, July 16, 17, 18, 20, 21, 1981. England won by 18 runs.

A match which had initially produced all the wet and tedious traits of recent Leeds Tests finally ended in a way to stretch the bounds of logic and belief. England's victory, achieved under the gaze of a spellbound nation, was the first this century by a team following on, and only the second such result in Test history.

The transformation occurred in less than 24 hours, after England had appeared likely to suffer their second four-day defeat of the series. Wherever one looked, there were personal dramas: Brearley, returning as captain like England's saviour; Botham, who was named Man of the Match, brilliant once more in his first game back in the ranks; Willis, whose career has so often heard the distant drums, producing the most staggering bowling of his life when his place again seemed threatened.

Others, too, had good reason to remember this game. It was the first time in 19 Tests that Willey had been on the winning side, there were wicket-keeping records

Take that: Ian Botham pulls Geoff Lawson during the rollicking century that stood the 1981 Headingley Test – and the series – on its head.

for both Taylor (all first-class cricket) and Marsh (Tests), and Dyson made his maiden century. But if the statisticians revelled in such facts, they were, for most of us, submerged in the tension of a climax as near to miraculous as a Test ever can have been.

None of this had seemed remotely likely on the opening day when the familiar slate-grey clouds engulfed the chimneys which stretch away from the Kirkstall Lane End. England went in with four seamers and only Willey to provide a measure of spin. It was a policy which caused considerable discussion. Brearley later confessed he lost sleep on the first night for fear that it had been a mistake. As things transpired, however, it was largely irrelevant.

Australia ended a shortened first day in fine health at 203 for three. Dyson batted diligently for his century, playing chiefly off the back foot, and survived one chance, to Botham in the gully, when 57. Chappell, who supported Dyson staunchly in a stand of 94 for the second wicket, was twice reprieved – by Gower and Botham again – so England, not for the first time this summer, suffered for their ineptitude in the field.

It will come as a surprise when, in future years, people look back on a Test of such apparently outrageous drama, to know that the second day was pedestrian in the extreme. Botham, to some degree, salvaged English pride by taking five more wickets, all of them in an after-tea spell costing 35 runs. Australia still extended their score to 401. It was another day of patchy weather and patchy cricket, completed when Gooch and Boycott saw out an over apiece from Lillee and Alderman without mishap.

At this stage, the odds seemed in favour of a draw. An England win was on offer generously, though by no means as extravagantly as 24 hours later when Ladbrokes posted it at 500–1. The reason for their estimate was a truncated day on which England were dismissed for 174 and, following on 227 behind, lost Gooch without addition. Australia's seamers had shown what could be done by bowling straighter and to a fuller length than their counterparts. Other than Botham, who opted for all-out aggression, England at no stage commanded and were occasionally undone by deliveries performing contortions at speed. Botham fell victim to just such a ball from Lillee.

The third day ended with unhappy scenes similar to those at Lord's, when spectators hurled cushions and abuse at the umpires. On this occasion, Messrs Meyer and Evans had walked to the middle at five to six, after a lengthy stoppage for poor light. They consulted their meters and summoned the covers, abandoning play just before the hour. With cruel irony, the light improved instantly, the sun was soon breaking through and the large crowd was incited to wrathful demands for explanations as to why they were not watching the prescribed extra hour. Once more, it seems, confusion in interpretation of the playing regulations was the cause of the ill-feeling: they stated only that conditions must be fit for play at the scheduled time of finish and not, as the umpires thought, that play must actually be in motion. Whether it was, in fact, fit at six o'clock is open to doubt, but the ruling was soon adjusted to allow play to restart at any stage.

All this seemed likely to achieve nothing more than a stay of sentence for England, a view which appeared amply confirmed by late afternoon on the Monday. England were then 135 for seven, still 92 behind, the distant objective of avoiding an innings defeat surely their only available prize. Lillee and Alderman had continued where they were forced to leave off on Saturday, and for all Boycott's skilful resistance, the cause seemed lost. Boycott, who batted three and a half hours, was sixth out to an lbw decision he seemed not to relish, and when Taylor followed quickly, the England players' decision to check out of their hotel seemed a sound move. Three hours later, registration desks around Leeds were coping with a flood of re-bookings, Botham having destroyed the game's apparently set course with an astonishing unbeaten 145, ably and forcefully aided by Dilley. Together, they added 117 in 80 minutes for the eighth wicket. Both struck the ball so cleanly and vigorously that Hughes's men were temporarily in disarray; when Dilley departed after scoring 56 precious runs, Old arrived to add 67 more with Botham, who still had Willis as a partner at the close, with England 124 ahead.

Botham advanced his unforgettable innings to 149 next morning, but Australia, needing 130, still remained clear favourites. Then, at 56 for one, Willis, having changed ends to bowl with the wind, dismissed Chappell with a rearing delivery and the staggering turnabout was under way. Willis bowled as if inspired. It is not uncommon to see him perform for England as if his very life depended on it, but this was something unique. In all, he took eight for 43, the best of his career, as Australia's last nine wickets tumbled for 55 despite a stand of 35 in four overs between Bright and Lillee. Old bowled straight and aggressively and England rose to the need to produce an outstanding show in the field. Yet this was Willis's hour, watched or listened to by a vast invisible audience. At the end, the crowd gathered to wave their Union Jacks and chant patriotically, eight days in advance of the Royal Wedding.

England v Australia 1981 — Third Test

At Leeds, July 16, 17, 18, 20, 21. Result: England won by 18 runs.

AUSTRALIA	First innings		Second innings	
J. Dyson b Dilley		102	– c Taylor b Willis	34
G. M. Wood lbw b Botham		34	– c Taylor b Botham	10
T. M. Chappell c Taylor b Willey		27	– c Taylor b Willis	8
*K. J. Hughes c and b Botham		89	– c Botham b Willis	0
R. J. Bright b Dilley		7	– (8) b Willis	19
G. N. Yallop c Taylor b Botham		58	– (5) c Gatting b Willis	0
A. R. Border lbw b Botham		8	– (6) b Old	0
†R. W. Marsh b Botham		28	– (7) c Dilley b Willis	4
G. F. Lawson c Taylor b Botham		13	– c Taylor b Willis	1
D. K. Lillee not out		3	– c Gatting b Willis	17
T. M. Alderman not out		0	– not out	0
B 4, l-b 13, w 3, n-b 12		32	L-b 3, w 1, n-b 14	18

1-55 2-149 3-196 4-220 5-332 (9 wkts dec.) 401 1-13 2-56 3-58 4-58 5-65 111
6-354 7-357 8-396 9-401 6-68 7-74 8-75 9-110 10-111

First innings – Willis 30–8–72–0; Old 43–14–91–0; Dilley 27–4–78–2; Botham 39.2–11–95–6; Willey 13–2–31–1; Boycott 3–2–2–0.
Second innings – Botham 7–3–14–1; Dilley 2–0–11–0; Willis 15.1–3–43–8; Old 9–1–21–1; Willey 3–1–4–0.

ENGLAND	First innings		Second innings (following on)	
G. A. Gooch lbw b Alderman		2	– c Alderman b Lillee	0
G. Boycott b Lawson		12	– lbw b Alderman	46
*J. M. Brearley c Marsh b Alderman		10	– c Alderman b Lillee	14
D. I. Gower c Marsh b Lawson		24	– c Border b Alderman	9
M. W. Gatting lbw b Lillee		15	– lbw b Alderman	1
P. Willey b Lawson		8	– c Dyson b Lillee	33
I. T. Botham c Marsh b Lillee		50	– not out	149
†R. W. Taylor c Marsh b Lillee		5	– c Bright b Alderman	1
G. R. Dilley c and b Lillee		13	– b Alderman	56
C. M. Old c Border b Alderman		0	– b Lawson	29
R. G. D. Willis not out		1	– c Border b Alderman	2
B 6, l-b 11, w 6, n-b 11		34	B 5, l-b 3, w 3, n-b 5	16

1-12 2-40 3-42 4-84 5-87 6-112 174 1-0 2-18 3-37 4-41 5-105 6-133 356
7-148 8-166 9-167 10-174 7-135 8-252 9-319 10-356

First innings – Lillee 18.5–7–49–4; Alderman 19–4–59–3; Lawson 13–3–32–3.
Second innings – Lillee 25–6–94–3; Alderman 35.3–6–135–6; Lawson 23–4–96–1; Bright 4–0–15–0.

Toss won by Australia   UMPIRES D. G. L. Evans and B. J. Meyer

Fourth Test

Derek Hodgson

At Birmingham, July 30, 31, August 1, 2, 1981. England won by 29 runs.

A startling spell of bowling by Botham, which brought him five wickets for one run in 28 deliveries, ended an extraordinary match at 4.30 on a glorious Sunday afternoon.

And so, for a second successive Test, England contrived to win after appearing badly beaten. As at Leeds, a large crowd helped give the match an exciting and emotional finish and once again critics, commentators and writers were left looking foolish, a fact that the players of both teams were quick to point out afterwards.

For a third time in the series, the pitch was the centre of controversy, though when Brearley elected to bat on a fine sunny morning on what is traditionally thought one of the finest surfaces in England, it looked in superb condition. Hughes was reported to have said that it looked good for 800. The outfield was fast and the temperature acceptable to Melbourne. Certainly no one at Edgbaston could have dreamt that this would be the first Test anywhere since 1934 in which no batsman made a fifty.

Boycott and Brearley opened, a change in the order that had caused misgivings, and had reached 29 in 45 minutes when Alderman's late swing defeated Boycott and then, two overs later, provoked Gower, a reluctant No. 3, to try, unsuccessfully, to hit over mid-on. Alderman had figures then of 7–4–4–2, and although Brearley denied himself a run for an hour, surviving a vehement appeal for a slip catch by Wood, he and Gooch saw Alderman and Lillee off. It was Bright, making the spinner's now customary appearance just before the interval, who tempted Gooch into a rash pull that cost a third wicket at 60.

The afternoon was an English disaster. Bright used the rough outside leg stump while Alderman, with Lillee in the unusual role of deputy, and Hogg were straight and swift from the other. By 5.30 England had been dismissed for 189, of which Brearley had made 48 in just under four hours, four boundaries off Lillee promoting his innings from one of mere resistance. Alderman had taken five wickets before Old, from that same Pressbox End, then rattled the teaspoons in the Australian dressing-room by removing Dyson and Border, in five overs, for 19 runs by the close.

The pitch, declared England's players the following day, was untrustworthy. It was too dry, the surface was less than firm, the occasional ball kept low, and there was turn for the spinner. Shoulder to shoulder, Australia's batsmen were later to demonstrate their solidarity with their English colleagues.

Friday was cool and grey and England did well to restrict the lead to 69. Brearley was at his best, constantly varying pressure on each batsman by his bowling and fielding changes, never losing the initiative, while his men responded admirably, running out Wood and Hogg and causing enough apprehension to deter Australia from attempting up to a dozen further singles. Hughes, batting well through a stormy spell by Willis, whose five bouncers in two overs caused the umpires to confer, was unlucky to be lbw to a low bounce. Although Brearley fell to Lillee on a gloomy evening, England had narrowed the margin to 20 runs.

Blue sky and Saturday sunshine attracted 15,000 spectators, whose holiday mood was not jollied along by Boycott, who spent three hours raising his score to 29 – seven short of Colin Cowdrey's England aggregate record – before falling to Bright. So, too, did Gower, Gooch and Willey, and when Botham was caught behind off Lillee, England's lead was no more than 46, with four wickets standing. Fortunately for England their tailenders, urged on by the combative Gatting, batted bravely. Emburey, 37 not out, demonstrated that Bright's line allowed him to be swept profitably, while Old hit straight and hard before taking the ball to dismiss Wood in the evening haze. Yet Australia needed only another 142 to win, with two days to play. Miracles, wrote a distinguished correspondent, like lightning, do not strike twice.

England v Australia 1981 — Fourth Test

At Birmingham, July 30, 31, August 1, 2. Result: England won by 29 runs.

ENGLAND	First innings		Second innings	
G. Boycott c Marsh b Alderman	13	– c Marsh b Bright		29
*J. M. Brearley c Border b Lillee	48	– lbw b Lillee		13
D. I. Gower c Hogg b Alderman	0	– c Border b Bright		23
G. A. Gooch c Marsh b Bright	21	– b Bright		21
M. W. Gatting c Alderman b Lillee	21	– b Bright		39
P. Willey b Bright	16	– b Bright		5
I. T. Botham b Alderman	26	– c Marsh b Lillee		3
J. E. Emburey b Hogg	3	– (9) not out		37
†R. W. Taylor b Alderman	0	– (10) lbw b Alderman		8
C. M. Old not out	11	– (8) c Marsh b Alderman		23
R. G. D. Willis c Marsh b Alderman	13	– c Marsh b Alderman		2
B 1, l-b 5, w 1, n-b 10	17	L-b 6, w 1, n-b 9		16

1-29 2-29 3-60 4-101 5-126 6-145   189
7-161 8-161 9-165 10-189

1-18 2-52 3-89 4-98 5-110 6-115   219
7-154 8-167 9-217 10-219

First innings – Lillee 18–4–61–2; Alderman 23.1–8–42–5; Hogg 16–3–49–1; Bright 12–4–20–2.
Second innings – Lillee 26–9–51–2; Alderman 22–5–65–3; Hogg 10–3–19–0; Bright 34–17–68–5.

AUSTRALIA	First innings		Second innings	
G. M. Wood run out	38	– lbw b Old		2
J. Dyson b Old	1	– lbw b Willis		13
A. R. Border c Taylor b Old	2	– c Gatting b Emburey		40
R. J. Bright lbw b Botham	27	– (8) lbw b Botham		0
*K. J. Hughes lbw b Old	47	– (4) c Emburey b Willis		5
G. N. Yallop b Emburey	30	– (5) c Botham b Emburey		30
M. F. Kent c Willis b Emburey	46	– (6) b Botham		10
†R. W. Marsh b Emburey	2	– (7) b Botham		4
D. K. Lillee b Emburey	18	– c Taylor b Botham		3
R. M. Hogg run out	0	– not out		0
T. M. Alderman not out	3	– b Botham		0
B 4, l-b 19, n-b 21	44	B 1, l-b 2, n-b 11		14

1-5 2-14 3-62 4-115 5-166 6-203   258
7-220 8-253 9-253 10-258

1-2 2-19 3-29 4-87 5-105 6-114   121
7-114 8-120 9-121 10-121

First innings – Willis 19–3–63–0; Old 21–8–44–3; Emburey 26.5–12–43–4; Botham 20–1–64–1.
Second innings – Willis 20–6–37–2; Old 11–4–19–1; Emburey 22–10–40–2; Botham 14–9–11–5.

Toss won by England   Umpires H. D. Bird and D. O. Oslear

Willis, bowling again as if the devil were at his heels, removed Dyson and Hughes in the first 40 minutes on the fourth morning, but Border was his resolute self and at 105 for four, with only 46 more needed, Australia seemed to have the match won. However, Border was then desperately unlucky to be caught off his gloves, a ball from

Emburey suddenly lifting prodigiously. Brearley, who had ordered Willey to loosen up, changed his mind and called on a reluctant Botham.

Somerset's giant bowled quicker than for some time, was straight and pitched the ball up, and one after another five batsmen walked into the point of the lance. The crowd, dotted with green and gold, were beside themselves with agony and ecstasy as, only 12 days after Headingley, history amazingly repeated itself.

NOTES BY THE EDITOR

John Woodcock, 1982

In two unforgettable months, English cricket emerged from a period of much gloom to a wellbeing that was reflected even in the enthusiasm with which ordinary men and women set about their labours. After several weeks of dreadful weather, culminating in the loss of the First Test, the sun got the better of the rain and England gained two of the more dramatic victories in the history of the game. A third, soon afterwards, meant that the Ashes were retained.

The change in England's fortunes coincided with Michael Brearley's return as captain. This not only lifted the spirits of the side, it improved its direction and freed Ian Botham of a burden which was threatening to ruin his cricket. Botham's record speaks for itself. In his 12 matches as captain, between June 1980 and July 1981, he scored 276 runs at 13.80 (top score 57) and his 35 wickets cost 32 apiece. Yet by the end of last season he had made eight Test hundreds and taken five wickets in an innings 17 times – always when without the cares of captaincy.

The seventh of these hundreds, in the Third Test, snatched victory from the jaws of defeat; the eighth won the Fifth Test. With some wonderful hitting Botham reached three figures in 87 balls at Headingley and 86 at Old Trafford. At Edgbaston, between giving the bowlers two such unmerciful poundings, he finished off the Fourth Test by taking five for one when Australia needed only a handful of runs to win. Botham's catching, too, was back to its prehensile best. Small wonder that Australia's captain, Kim Hughes, said that the difference between the two sides was represented by one man and one man only.

No one, I believe, can ever have played a finer Test innings of its type than Botham's at Old Trafford. I have been told that Australia's attack was by no means one of their strongest, and that by the time Botham came in the best of their bowlers, Lillee and Alderman, were on their last legs. To which I will say only that you would never have known it from the way they were bowling. At Headingley and Old Trafford we witnessed the reincarnation of Gilbert Jessop. Those who saw Willis take eight for 43 at Headingley or watched Brearley's cool handling of each succeeding crisis also have a great story to tell – one to last them a lifetime.

Fifth Test

John Thicknesse

At Manchester, August 13, 14, 15, 16, 17, 1981. England won by 103 runs.

England regained the Ashes by going 3–1 up in the series. Like its two predecessors, the Fifth Test was a game of extraordinary fluctuations and drama, made unforgettable by yet another *tour de force* by Botham, who, with the pendulum starting to swing Australia's way, launched an attack on Lillee and Alderman which, for its ferocious yet effortless power and dazzling cleanness of stroke, can surely never have been bettered in a Test match, even by the legendary Jessop.

Striding in to join Tavaré in front of 20,000 spectators on the Saturday afternoon when England, 101 ahead on first innings, had surrendered the initiative so totally that in 69 overs they had collapsed to 104 for five, Botham plundered 118 in 123 minutes. His innings included six sixes – a record for Anglo-Australian Tests – and 13 fours, all but one of which, an inside edge that narrowly missed the off stump on its way to fine leg, exploded off as near the middle of the bat as makes no odds. Of the 102 balls he faced (86 to reach 100), 53 were used up in reconnaissance in his first 28 runs. Then Alderman and Lillee took the second new ball and Botham erupted, smashing 66 off eight overs by tea with three hooked sixes off Lillee and one off Alderman, a huge pull far back in the crowd to the left of the pavilion. He completed his hundred with his fifth six, a sweep, added the sixth with an immense, and perfectly struck blow over the sightscreen, also off Bright, and was caught at the wicket a few moments later off Whitney.

Unkindly, it was to the debutant Whitney, running back from deep mid-off, that Botham, at 32, offered the first of two chances – nearer quarter than half – a high, swirling mis-hit over Alderman's head. The other came at 91 when Dyson, sprinting off the third-man boundary, then sliding forward on his knees and elbows, made a heroic effort to get his hands underneath a sliced cut off Lillee. Of the 149 Botham and Tavaré added for the sixth wicket – after a morning in which England had lost three for 29 in 28 overs – Tavaré's share was 28. But his seven-hour 78 was the rock on which Knott and Emburey sustained the recovery as the last four wickets added 151.

With the pitch growing steadily easier, the full value of Tavaré's survival was seen on the fourth and fifth days when, thanks to Yallop's artistic century and a fighting 123 not out in six and three-quarter hours by Border, batting with a broken finger, Australia more than once seemed to be within reach of scoring 506 to win. Border's hundred, taking 373 minutes, was the slowest by an Australian in a Test, beating by four minutes Hughes's time against England in 1978-79.

Had Australia managed to win, it would have been in keeping with a bizarre series; but with Lillee buoyantly supporting Border for the eighth wicket, Brearley threw a smokescreen over proceedings by allowing both batsmen singles – and the Australians, suspecting some sinister motive, lost impetus and purpose. The end came with 85 minutes left for play, when Whitney was caught by Gatting at short leg.

Except that after Headingley and Edgbaston one was forewarned that the impossible was likely to become commonplace, there was no indication on the first day that the match would produce such captivating theatre. Allott, who was to play a vital role, was one of three England changes, winning his first cap on his home ground in place of the injured Old, while Tavaré came in for Willey and Knott for Taylor.

It was a toss Brearley would not have minded losing. But with Australia's fourth-innings collapses in mind, he chose to bat. On a slowish, seaming pitch and in often gloomy light, the pacemen reduced England to 175 for nine by close of play, with 40 minutes lost to rain. Boycott passed Colin Cowdrey's record of 7,624 runs for England, but the only innings of note was Tavaré's stoic 69 in four and three-quarter hours – the first half-century in 12 Tests by an England No. 3.

Next morning Hughes unaccountably used Whitney as Lillee's partner rather than Alderman, his most prolific bowler, and Allott and Willis added a priceless 56. Allott, displaying a technique and calmness well above his station, mingled some good strokes through the covers with a few lucky edges to make his highest first-class score.

Wood began with three hooked fours and a six off Willis and Allott, like a man working off an insult. But just as suddenly Australia were 24 for four and en route to their shortest innings since 1902, when Rhodes and Hirst bundled them out for 36 after rain. But on this occasion they had no such excuses to fall back on; indeed, they batted with a manic desperation wholly at odds with their need to win the match. The collapse began with three fine deliveries from Willis and one from Allott in the space of seven balls, a combination of disasters to shake the most confident of sides. In Willis's third over, Dyson and Yallop could not keep down rapid, rising balls, while Hughes was trapped lbw by a break-back; and the first ball of the next over, by Allott, came back to have Wood lbw. Kent counter-attacked strongly with 52 in 70 minutes, but the loss of Border, to a stupendous overhead catch by Gower at fourth slip, and Marsh, when he could not pull his bat away in time to avoid another lifting ball from Willis, wrecked Australia's chances of recovery.

Just under a day later, when England had slumped to 104 for five, Australia may have entertained the hope that their 130 would not be terminal. But then came Botham . . . and it was.

Toss: England. **England 231** (C. J. Tavaré 69, P. J. W. Allott 52*, D. K. Lillee 4-55, T. M. Alderman 4-88) **and 404** (C. J. Tavaré 78, I. T. Botham 118, A. P. E. Knott 59, J. E. Emburey 57, T. M. Alderman 5-109); **Australia 130** (M. F. Kent 52, R. G. D. Willis 4-63) **and 402** (G. N. Yallop 114, A. R. Border 123*).

Some Thoughts on Modern Captaincy   Michael Brearley, 1982

At Old Trafford in 1981, F. S. Trueman, broadcasting on the radio, was writing Bob Willis off in extreme terms; he did not know by what right Willis was drawing his money, he had never seen such inept bowling. (I wonder even whether Trueman had the decency to be abashed when Willis took three wickets in his next over.) And because current Test players are under far more scrutiny than ever before, the captain has to bear the brunt of it on behalf of his team. D. R. Jardine was able to toss up before the start of a Test, walk back into the dressing-room – where all 17 members of the party would be dressed in whites, opening batsmen padded up – and pin the teamsheet on the wall. He felt no need to tell the players in advance, let alone the two British pressmen, one an expert on lawn tennis, who accompanied the team on its sensational journey around Australia. Harold Larwood told me that if any journalist had dared to ask Jardine if he was considering standing down from the side, Jardine would have punched him on the jaw.

Today's press are more demanding and inquisitive. They expect answers, quotes and co-operation. Kim Hughes, speaking at a dinner shortly before last summer's final Test, agreed that his team had not batted well and deserved criticism. But, he went on, some of the things said about them were such that, if you were walking along the street and a fellow said that to you, if you had any go about you at all, you'd deck him!

Last summer, I found an England team more embittered by the press than I'd ever known. Ian Botham refused to speak to them after his century at Leeds, and Willis was outspoken on TV immediately after that match. I myself felt that rows were planted, cultivated and encouraged out of the most arid, unpromising soil by certain sections of the media. Of course there always has been some meanness in the relations between performer and critic, but the type of writing fostered by the modern craving for excitement and sensation puts today's public figures under a type of pressure unknown to their pre-war predecessors.

Sixth Test

At The Oval, August 27, 28, 29, 31, September 1, 1981. Drawn.

Graeme Wright

Although the Ashes had already been retained by England, there was still an air of expectancy among the capacity crowds who basked in the sunshine of the opening days. The previous Tests had prepared them for drama, but in the event this was more an occasion for the statistician.

Brearley gambled on putting Australia in, whereupon Wood and Kent showed handsome appreciation in compiling Australia's first century opening partnership since January 1977. Kent's promotion saw the omission of Dyson in favour of Wellham. It was again Botham who changed the pattern, in ten minutes removing Wood, unable to avoid contact with a rising delivery, and Kent. When, at third slip, he clutched from high above his head Yallop's flick at Willis, Australia had gone from 85 for no wicket at lunch to 169 for three at tea.

Hughes and Border displayed how fast and true the wicket was by the sureness of their timing until Hughes, pulling Botham, dislodged a bail in playing the stroke. Border gave no such sign of fallibility, a pulled four taking him to 50, and despite the new ball Australia ended the day without further loss. Wellham, solid in defence and deft of foot, looked ominously competent, but next morning Willis tore through his defences as he and Botham put England back in contention. Only Border thwarted them, going to his hundred with strokes classical and improvised while Whitney hung on. Border's century took 275 minutes and included 12 fours: the innings took his unbeaten occupancy of the crease to 11 hours 50 minutes.

England began their innings at 2.42 and by the close had lost Larkins, playing back and edging Lillee's leg-cutter at 61. With him went any impetus, for in the remaining 21 overs England crawled to 100. Saturday's full house saw Boycott go to a Test-record 61 half-centuries off the first ball of the morning, and then settled back to await his hundred, which took 328 minutes and included only three boundaries – a fair reflection of an innings built mainly on tucks and touches. In contrast, Gatting's half-century fairly bristled with aggression until, padding up once too often, he was beaten by the new ball. Brearley, promoting himself to protect Parker, got a nasty one from Alderman, and three balls later the unfortunate Parker followed the wrong ball.

Boycott, meanwhile, batted on, a flyer off Lillee passing through first slip's hands to bring up England's 250, and it took a brilliant catch by Yallop, high, wide and one-handed at gully, to end his innings. Knott brightened the post-tea period with his tiptoe driving and cutting, his 36 coming from 49 deliveries before he became Lillee's seventh victim. In 21 overs of the new ball, eight wickets had fallen for only 68 runs.

Australia had just under an hour to bat, during which time Brearley made seven changes in 14 overs and was rewarded with the wickets of Kent and Hughes. But on Bank Holiday Monday, the excellent wicket, an injury to Willis and a half-fit Botham dictated the course of the game as Border, Wellham and Marsh secured a commanding lead. Border, having batted for another three hours 12 minutes, finally yielded up his wicket, propping forward at Emburey; Marsh, given two lives by Knott, hit a typical 52 before Gatting's over-the-shoulder catch gave Botham his 200th Test wicket; and finally Wellham, after 25 minutes on 99, struck a four off Botham to become the first Australian since Harry Graham in 1893 to score a hundred in England on his Test debut. Dropped by mid-on at 18 and by mid-off at 99, he hit 12 fours.

Having held back until Wellham's hundred, Hughes declared overnight, giving England all day to score 383. But the only likelihood of a positive result was in Australia's bowling out England, and Lillee made this a possibility when he removed Boycott with his fourth delivery. In the eighth over Whitney persuaded Tavaré to jab uncharacteristically at a ball slanted away from him, but Gatting, with seven fours in his half-century, put the attack in truer perspective. Brearley, too, batted with distinction and determination for two and three-quarter hours, and later in the afternoon Knott again showed his appetite for the tiring bowlers, hitting 11 fours in his unbeaten 70 and seeing England safely through.

Lillee was Man of the Match, but Botham was indisputably the Man of the Series.

Toss: England. **Australia 352** (G. M. Wood 66, M. F. Kent 54, A. R. Border 106*, R. G. D. Willis 4-91, I. T. Botham 6-125) **and 344-9 dec.** (A. R. Border 84, D. M. Wellham 103, R. W. Marsh 52, I. T. Botham 4-128, M. Hendrick 4-82); **England 314** (G. Boycott 137, M. W. Gatting 53, D. K. Lillee 7-89) **and 261-7** (M. W. Gatting 56, J. M. Brearley 51, A. P. E. Knott 70*, D. K. Lillee 4-70).

AUSTRALIA V ENGLAND 1982–83 John Woodcock

England's tour of Australia had two redeeming features: one of the most exciting Test matches ever played, at Melbourne immediately after Christmas, resulted in victory, and despite some transparently poor umpiring England played the game in a good spirit. But the Ashes, which England had held since 1977, were surrendered, Australia winning the Test series 2–1.

With those players who had been to South Africa in the spring of 1982 being barred from Test cricket, England flew to Brisbane on October 13 some way below full strength. Of the outcasts none was missed more than Graham Gooch. Without him England were practically never given a good start to an innings. Against his inclinations, Tavaré was obliged to open in four of the five Test matches.

Once again fast bowling proved the decisive factor in the Test series. Although Lillee and Alderman were injured in the First Test, Australia were still able to field much the stronger pace attack, Lawson, Thomson and Hogg all being faster and more consistently hostile than anything England could muster. England lost the Second and Third Tests easily enough to go to Melbourne for the Fourth in some disarray. Victory there was a great tonic, not only for Bob Willis and his side but for everyone associated with English cricket. Had Dyson, one of Australia's opening batsmen, been given run out, as he palpably should have been, in the first over of the Fifth Test, the series might even have been saved and the Ashes retained, though had that happened it would not have reflected Australia's undoubted superiority.

First Test

At Perth, November 12, 13, 14, 16, 17, 1982. Drawn.

Ugly crowd scenes marred an otherwise good match, Alderman, on the second afternoon, becoming the first player to be badly hurt in Test cricket after a field invasion. In the fighting that followed 26 arrests were made.

A pitch that lasted better than expected helped foil the bowlers of both sides, though Lawson gave Australia a clear advantage with early wickets in the second innings. On the last day a hundred by Randall, a typical mixture of effervescence and resolution, was needed to put the match beyond Australia's reach.

Greg Chappell put England in, but Australia bowled with insufficient accuracy to take advantage of what early moisture the pitch held. Lillee became increasingly churlish as several raucous appeals were rejected. Tavaré, concentrating solely on survival, was the cornerstone of England's innings. At the end of the first day he had made 66 out of 242 for four. He survived chances at 31 and 41, to second slip off Lawson and to forward short leg off Yardley, but otherwise gave the bowlers little hope. Gower played in his best vein before falling to a brilliant diving catch at short square leg by Dyson.

Next day Tavaré and Randall were not separated until shortly before lunch, when Tavaré was brilliantly caught at leg slip trying to sweep. Tavaré batted seven and three-quarter hours, hitting nine fours. Randall became Yardley's 100th Test victim, caught at short leg, before the innings was usefully, if streakily, extended by Taylor and Willis. It was when these two took the total past 400 that about 15 spectators, some carrying Union Jacks, ran on to the field. One intruder, coming from behind, cuffed Alderman round the head. Alderman dislocated his right shoulder as he brought his man down with a rugby tackle, Lillee and Border joining in before the offender was led away in handcuffs and Alderman carried off on a stretcher. Although the shoulder was soon put back, the injury effectively ended Alderman's season. With the incident causing numerous fights to break out, Chappell led his side from the field. The game was resumed after 14 minutes, whereupon England's innings soon ended. Wood and Dyson came safely through the day's last 52 minutes.

Chappell and Hughes averted the threat of a collapse next day with some exhilarating batting. They added 141 in 34 overs, both driving and pulling splendidly against bowling which, Willis apart, looked very ordinary. Cowans, on his Test debut, bowled too short. Hughes, after two hours of delightful batting, was caught at deep mid-off, but Chappell went on to reach his 21st Test hundred, his eighth against England.

Willis was finally rewarded after taking the new ball, Chappell deflecting a rising ball high over the slips and Lamb holding a good low catch at deep third man. Chappell had hit two sixes and 11 fours. After the rest day Australia added a further 91, mainly through Hookes and Lawson, before declaring at lunch with a lead of 13. With Australia reduced to three front-line bowlers, the situation brought forth the best in Lawson and also Lillee, until he wrenched his troublesome right knee in a loose foothold and was reduced to a shortened run. These two alternated while Yardley, flighting well, bowled from the other end. With some loose strokes contributing to the loss of their first five wickets, England ended the penultimate day only 150 ahead and in danger of defeat.

Australia's victory hopes declined on the final morning when they were unable to dismiss Taylor, England's night-watchman, for a further 90 minutes. With Lawson looking tired and Lillee struggling the Australians were unable to summon the zest and penetration they had shown the previous day. Taylor was bowled off his pads after a vital 77 had been added in 25 overs; Miller failed, but Pringle hung on with Randall after Australia had taken a new ball just before lunch. Randall completed his third century against Australia, all made in Australia and when England had their backs to the wall. When at last he chopped Lawson into his stumps, he had been in for four and a half hours and hit 13 fours, mostly from sweeps and sparkling drives. England's lead at this point was 279, and with Pringle and Cowans lasting together for 65 minutes, Australia were left with the impossible task of scoring 346 in two hours.

Toss: Australia. **England 411** (C. J. Tavaré 89, D. I. Gower 72, D. W. Randall 78, B. Yardley 5-107) **and 358** (A. J. Lamb 56, D. W. Randall 115, G. F. Lawson 5-108); **Australia 424-9 dec.** (J. Dyson 52, G. S. Chappell 117, K. J. Hughes 62, D. W. Hookes 56, G. F. Lawson 50, G. Miller 4-70) **and 73-2.**

Second Test

At Brisbane, November 26, 27, 28, 30, December 1, 1982. Australia won by seven wickets.

Batting failures in their first innings, which could not be blamed on the pitch, coupled with some wayward fast bowling, always left England struggling in a match full of incident. Australia, in spite of dropping eight catches in the second innings, deserved their success, owing much to Wessels, who made a remarkable debut, and to Lawson, who took 11 wickets. Other features included a warning to Thomson for intimidatory bowling, and to Willis, Lawson and Cowans for running on the pitch. Crumbling footholds, especially at the Vulture Street end, were partially blamed for this, as they were for the match's 84 no-balls.

Chappell again put England in, but a greenish pitch seldom provided the early assistance expected. Lawson soon put Australia in control, helped by some brilliant catching. Fowler and Tavaré went cheaply and Gower, having survived one chance to backward short leg, was held in the same place just before lunch. Lamb and Botham added 78 in 13 overs before Botham sliced to deep backward point. With three more wickets falling before tea, England were in deep trouble. A spectacular left-handed leg-side catch ended Lamb's stay and gave Marsh his 300th catch in his 88th Test. When bad light brought play to a close 65 minutes early, England were 219 for nine, and Cowans was out first ball next morning.

Australia also made a poor start, but they were rescued by a solid innings from the left-handed Wessels, who was born in South Africa but took up residence in Australia in 1978. He gathered runs steadily in an arc between cover point and third man, with occasional hits to the leg side. One of his few mistakes came when he was 15, a hard chance being put down in the gully off Botham.

Australia were 130 for five after Chappell, when playing well, had badly misjudged a single to Miller at cover point and Hughes and Hookes both fell cheaply. Marsh lingered for 78 minutes and Yardley stayed with Wessels as he inched towards his century. At 97 Wessels might have been stumped off Hemmings – the ball bounced awkwardly for Taylor – and by the close Australia were 246 for six, Wessels having just become the 13th Australian to make a hundred in his first Test. The innings lasted until just before lunch on the third day, Wessels being last out after seven and three-quarter hours and hitting 17 fours. Towards the end of his innings he showed some freedom.

England, going in again 122 behind, were given a torrid time by the fast bowlers. Tavaré was dropped twice before being caught behind for 13, trying to leg glance, and at tea England were 65 for one with Fowler in all sorts of trouble. The light deteriorated during the interval, and, one ball afterwards, a bouncer from Thomson was enough to bring a stoppage. An hour later, when 15 more balls were bowled, Thomson was given an official warning for under-pitching and Gower survived a chance in the gully.

There was no let-up for England after the rest day when Thomson, bowling to a slightly fuller length and with fine control, swung the game Australia's way. Rackemann went off after half an hour with a groin strain, which meant that for the second Test running Australia had a depleted attack. But Yardley again kept one end tight, and Thomson, bowling with pace and lift, took five for 12 in 47 balls, spread over three spells, to wreck the innings. Fowler rode his luck outside off for almost six hours, but there was little other resistance until Miller and Hemmings held out against a tiring attack through the last 100 minutes.

England thus went into the final day 157 ahead, with three wickets standing. Lawson collected the remaining wickets at a personal cost of 21, leaving Australia 188 to win in five hours on a pitch with rough patches outside the left-handers' off stump. With the new-ball bowlers wayward and Wessels being badly missed at cover point before he had scored, Australia raced to 60 in an hour, despite losing Dyson, hit on the shoulder by Willis. There was some excitement in the afternoon when three quick wickets went down and Hemmings bowled well. But Hughes and Hookes batted carefully and, eventually, freely. The match ended in the second of the last 20 overs. The 19 catches Australia held in the match constituted a Test record.

Toss: Australia. **England 219** (A. J. Lamb 72, G. F. Lawson 6-47) **and 309** (G. Fowler 83, G. Miller 60, extras 52, G. F. Lawson 5-87, J. R. Thomson 5-73); **Australia 341** (K. C. Wessels 162, G. S. Chappell 53, B. Yardley 53, R. G. D. Willis 5-66) **and 190-3** (D. W. Hookes 66*).

Third Test

At Adelaide, December 10, 11, 12, 14, 15, 1982. Australia won by eight wickets.

For the second time in a fortnight England could find no adequate answer to the Australian fast bowling, which now included Hogg, playing his first Test for nearly 18 months. His speed and hostility, no less than Lawson's and Thomson's, came as a nasty shock to the batsmen. Between them these three took 17 wickets in the match, Lawson bringing his tally from the first three Tests to 26.

England took the major gamble of putting Australia in. The pitch, though damp the day before the match, looked a beauty by the time Willis chose to field. He was, he said, well aware of the disasters which had attended previous England captains who had done the same thing in Australia (eight defeats and only one victory) but felt the first morning provided his bowlers with the best chance of getting back into the series.

In the event, it was an hour before a ball got past the bat, and Australia, by the close of the first day, were 265 for three. Chappell's second hundred of the series, his 22nd in Tests and first in Adelaide, was smoothly and chancelessly compiled. It contained 19 fours and was ended only by a blinding catch in the gully by Gower.

England's one good day of the match was the second when, by accurate bowling and keen fielding, and with the pitch playing at its very best, they claimed Australia's last seven wickets for the addition of 173 runs. Gower held another brilliant catch, this time at cover point, and Botham two, one at second slip, the other at deep square leg. Hemmings, despite a sore shoulder, played an important part by pinning the batsmen down with his excellent control. With Lamb and Gower gaining confidence after two early wickets, England, in their first innings, were 66 for two at the end of the second day and 140 for two at lunch on the third.

Their collapse on the third afternoon was one of the worst they have ever suffered in Australia. When Gower was out in the first over after lunch, caught at the wicket off a ball of steep bounce, England needed only 99 to save the follow-on. It seemed they had nothing to worry about. Yet by tea they were padding up again, having lost their last seven wickets for 76, the last six of them for 35. If Lamb was unlucky to be given out, caught at the wicket down the leg side for a well-made 82, what happened owed no more than that to chance. Things only began to look really ominous for England when Randall and Miller went in quick succession, Randall yorked second ball. Botham was still there, playing carefully, but at 213 he was eighth out, caught at short mid-wicket off the first ball of a new spell by Thomson, who then finished off the innings, with England still 23 short of saving the follow-on. With the rest day to come, Chappell had no hesitation in enforcing it.

When, in the third over of England's second innings, Thomson had Tavaré caught at short leg, he had taken four wickets in 22 balls for six runs. No wicket had fallen in the morning of this third day, and none fell in the last 110 minutes, but between 1.42 and 4.10 nine went down. Until affected by the heat, in the last hour or so, Lawson, Thomson and Hogg made a fast and awkward trio.

England began the fourth day still 132 behind and knowing that they would need to bat for four full sessions, probably more, to save the match. Only when Gower and Botham were adding 118 for the fourth wicket did they look remotely like managing it. Gower was eventually fifth out at 247, and there were still 50 minutes of the fourth day left when Australia went in again, needing only 83 to win. Gower's splendidly staunch hundred was his fifth for England, though his first for 38 Test innings. The increasingly uneven bounce of the ball added to its merit. Australia cantered to victory on the last morning.

Toss: England. **Australia 438** (G. S. Chappell 115, K. J. Hughes 88, I. T. Botham 4-112) **and 83-2;**
England 216 (D. I. Gower 60, A. J. Lamb 82, G. F. Lawson 4-56) **and 304** (D. I. Gower 114,
I. T. Botham 58, G. F. Lawson 5-66).

Fourth Test

At Melbourne, December 26, 27, 28, 29, 30, 1982. England won by three runs.

A magnificent Test match, to be ranked among the best ever played, produced a finish of such protracted excitement that it had the whole of Australia by the ears. Needing

292 to win, Australia were 218 for nine when Border and Thomson embarked on a last-wicket partnership of epic proportions. At the end of the fourth day they had taken the score to 255 for nine, leaving another 37 runs to be found on the last morning for Australia to regain the Ashes.

Although, on this last day, the match could have been over within moments, 18,000 spectators, admitted free, went to the MCG in the hope of seeing Border and Thomson achieve their improbable goal. All things considered, among them a new ball taken at 259 for nine, Thomson was rarely in trouble; Border never was. By the time Botham began the 18th over of the morning Australia were within four runs of victory. His first ball was short of a length and wide of the off stump. Thomson, sparring at it, edged a none-too-difficult catch to Tavaré, the second of two slips. Tavaré managed only to parry it, the ball bouncing away behind him but within reach of Miller, fielding at first slip. With a couple of quick strides Miller reached the catch and completed it, the ball still some 18 inches off the ground.

No one who played in the game or watched it, or who saw it on TV, or who listened to it on the radio, could have been left unmoved. In terms of runs, the only closer Test ever played was the Brisbane tie between Australia and West Indies in 1960–61. In 1902 at Old Trafford the margin between England and Australia was also three runs, on that occasion in Australia's favour.

For the fourth time in the series the captain winning the toss chose to field. With the match being played on a pitch that had been laid only nine months before, Chappell took a calculated gamble when he committed Australia to batting last. In the event the pitch lasted surprisingly well and was, as Chappell expected, damp enough on the first day for England to be in early trouble. When Gower was out, immediately after lunch, they were 56 for three. The innings was saved by a brilliant fourth-wicket stand of 161 in only 32 overs by Tavaré and Lamb. With Cook and Fowler going in first, Tavaré was able to bat at No. 3, which he much prefers to opening. After his usual slow start he began to attack the bowling, especially Yardley's, with unaccustomed vigour. By the time he was very well caught in the gully, England had fairly galloped to 217. But Lamb soon followed Tavaré, a fine innings ending a little unworthily when he got himself out to Yardley, and by the close England, having fallen right away, were all out for 284.

Each of the first three days saw one full innings completed. On the second Australia were bowled out for 287, on the third England made 294. By taking the wickets of Dyson and Chappell with successive balls in the first innings, Cowans made his first impact on a match from which he was to emerge as a hero. Chappell hooked his first ball to deep square leg, where Lamb had just been carefully stationed. In the end Australia owed their narrow lead to Hughes's application, Hookes's good fortune laced with strokes of fine timing, and Marsh's belligerence. By now the umpiring of Rex Whitehead was becoming an irritant. On the second and third days England were in danger of allowing it to undermine their resolve. After the match it was forgotten, all else being dwarfed by the climax, but it was undoubtedly erratic.

At 45 for three in their second innings England faced their next crisis. This time, however, after Botham had made 46 in 46 balls, their last five wickets made a vital contribution. Pringle and Taylor added 61, every run of some concern to Australia, faced by the prospect of batting last. Fowler, too, until hit on the foot by Thomson and forced to have a runner, had played much his best innings of the tour. When Lawson found Pringle's edge Marsh claimed his 27th victim of the series, a new Test record.

Australia v England 1982–83

Fourth Test

At Melbourne, December 26, 27, 28, 29, 30, 1982. Result: England won by three runs.

ENGLAND	First innings		Second innings	
G. Cook c Chappell b Thomson		10	c Yardley b Thomson	26
G. Fowler c Chappell b Hogg		4	b Hogg	65
C. J. Tavaré c Yardley b Thomson		89	b Hogg	0
D. I. Gower c Marsh b Hogg		18	c Marsh b Lawson	3
A. J. Lamb c Dyson b Yardley		83	c Marsh b Hogg	26
I. T. Botham c Wessels b Yardley		27	c Chappell b Thomson	46
G. Miller c Border b Yardley		10	lbw b Lawson	14
D. R. Pringle c Wessels b Hogg		9	c Marsh b Lawson	42
†R. W. Taylor c Marsh b Yardley		1	lbw b Thomson	37
*R. G. D. Willis not out		6	not out	8
N. G. Cowans c Lawson b Hogg		3	b Lawson	10
B 3, l-b 6, w 3, n-b 12		24	B 2, l-b 9, n-b 6	17

1-11 2-25 3-56 4-217 5-227   284   1-40 2-41 3-45 4-128 5-129   294
6-259 7-262 8-268 9-278 10-284   6-160   7-201 8-262 9-280 10-294

First innings – Lawson 17–6–48–0; Hogg 23.3–6–69–4; Yardley 27–9–89–4; Thomson 13–2–49–2; Chappell 1–0–5–0.
Second innings – Lawson 21.4–6–66–4; Hogg 22–5–64–3; Yardley 15–2–67–0; Thomson 21–3–74–3; Chappell 1–0–6–0.

AUSTRALIA	First innings		Second innings	
K. C. Wessels b Willis		47	b Cowans	14
J. Dyson lbw b Cowans		21	c Tavaré b Botham	31
*G. S. Chappell c Lamb b Cowans		0	c sub (I. J. Gould) b Cowans	2
K. J. Hughes b Willis		66	c Taylor b Miller	48
A. R. Border b Botham		2	(6) not out	62
D. W. Hookes c Taylor b Pringle		53	(5) c Willis b Cowans	68
†R. W. Marsh b Willis		53	lbw b Cowans	13
B. Yardley b Miller		9	b Cowans	0
G. F. Lawson c Fowler b Miller		0	c Cowans b Pringle	7
R. M. Hogg not out		8	lbw b Cowans	4
J. R. Thomson b Miller		1	c Miller b Botham	21
L-b 8, n-b 19		27	B 5, l-b 9, w 1, n-b 3	18

1-55 2-55 3-83 4-89 5-180   287   1-37 2-39 3-71 4-171 5-173   288
6-261 7-276 8-276 9-278 10-287   6-190 7-190 8-202 9-218 10-288

First innings – Willis 15–2–38–3; Botham 18–3–69–1; Cowans 16–0–69–2; Pringle 15–2–40–1; Miller 15–5–44–3.
Second innings – Willis 17–0–57–0; Botham 25.1–4–80–2; Cowans 26–6–77–6; Pringle 12–4–26–1; Miller 16–6–30–1.

Toss won by Australia   UMPIRES A. R. Crafter and R. V. Whitehead

Although the occasional ball was keeping very low, Australia's target of 292, on an uncommonly fast Melbourne outfield (a prolonged drought had restricted watering), was eminently attainable. The equality of the four totals tells of the unyielding nature of the match, with first one side, then the other, holding the advantage. When Chappell again fell cheaply to Cowans, splendidly caught low down in the covers by Gould (fielding substitute for Fowler) off a hard slash, England were in front, Wessels having already been bowled off his pads by Cowans. When, at 71, Dyson was beautifully caught at slip by Tavaré, it remained that way. Hughes and Hookes then added 100, which gave Australia the initiative. Hughes's departure to a tumbling catch by Taylor off Miller, followed quickly by Hookes's, restored it to England. With Cowans, inspired by his successes over Chappell and generously encouraged by the crowd, claiming four wickets for 19 in seven overs, England had all but won when Thomson, his hair dyed platinum blond, joined Border.

As Thomson took root and Border switched to the attack, Willis adopted tactics which, though they brought final victory, were much criticised at the time. When Border had the strike Willis placed all his fielders in a far-flung ring, which meant that if England were to win they would almost certainly have to get Thomson out. Even for the last two overs of the fourth day, after a brief stoppage for rain, Border was allowed to bat unharassed by close fielders. It was the same next morning, even against the new ball. Thus flattered, Border, whose previous 15 Test innings had brought him only 245 runs, was now at his fighting best. Thomson, growing in confidence, occasionally pierced England's off-side field, his feet spread-eagled.

As Australia slowly closed the gap, every run was cheered to the echo. England showed understandable signs of panic. Cowans, though he continued to bowl well, failed to find quite his best rhythm; Willis, though admirably accurate, lacked his old pace. In the end, all hope for England almost gone, Botham produced the ball that not only won the match but revived the tour.

For the first time in a Test match, Melbourne's huge video scoreboard was in operation, the screen being used to show action replays and advertisements as well as the score and other sundry details. It was, on the whole, well received, although Willis remarked after the match that there had been occasions when, needing to know the score, he found himself looking instead at a picture of a motor car or a meat pie.

Fifth Test
At Sydney, January 2, 3, 4, 6, 7, 1983. Drawn.

Australia achieved, without too much trouble, a result which was enough to make sure they regained the Ashes, held by England since 1977. After the match Chappell produced a silver cup, presented by an Australian supporter, which he said contained the ashes of one of the bails used at Sydney and which, in future, would be kept in the Australian Board's offices. "Who said the Ashes never come back to Australia?" commented Chappell, a reference to the fact that the original urn is permanently housed at Lord's.

With the ball expected to turn appreciably later in the match, Chappell, on winning the toss, chose to bat. Off the last ball of the first over, without a run on the board, Willis, off his own bowling, looked to throw out Dyson, who had answered Wessels's call for a sharp single. Although shown on film to have been a good 18 inches short of his ground, Dyson was given not out by umpire Johnson, who said afterwards that he had given Dyson the benefit of the doubt, being unsure whether he was six inches in or six inches out. No one could do more than speculate as to the significance, not least from a psychological viewpoint, of this unhappy decision. England had to wait for another hour before they took a wicket; Dyson went on to make 79, and Australia, by the close on the first day, were 138 for two, nearly three hours having been lost to rain. For totalling 314 Australia had to thank Border, who, after a shaky start (he survived a difficult chance to silly point off Hemmings when 15), played very well. Botham held four splendid catches in the match, the first of them at slip in the first innings, when he clung to a flash from Hookes off Hemmings.

Left with two and a half hours' batting on the second evening England made their customary poor start, soon being 24 for three. Gower and Randall, continuing into the third morning, then added 122 with some rousing strokeplay. Until Gower was sixth out, brilliantly caught at slip by Chappell, diving to his left, it looked as though England might do better than the 237 with which they finished. In the end, though, only a partnership of 50 between Taylor and Hemmings enabled them to get even as far as that.

With the ball starting to turn, Australia were glad of a first-innings lead of 77. In the closing stages of the third day and for the first hour of the fourth, their batsmen were under pressure from England's spinners. Had Hughes been given out, caught at short leg off Hemmings, as England were convinced he was, Australia would have been 88 for four in their second innings, a lead of 165 with their last two specialist batsmen together. Instead, Miller and Hemmings, given every chance, took time to settle into a length, and with Hughes going on to make a superb 137, his third hundred against England and eighth for Australia, and Border, another fine player of spin, helping him to add 149 for the fifth wicket, England's chances of winning had virtually gone by the middle of the fourth afternoon.

With 460 needed in 375 minutes – scarcely more than an academic proposition – England's hopes for the last day were concentrated on putting up a spirited resistance, which, for the most part, they did. Led by Hemmings, who had gone in as a nightwatchman on the fourth evening and came within five runs of scoring an improbable hundred, England managed to save the game without boring the crowd. With an hour of the match left, and faced by a possible 11 overs of a new ball, England, at 293 for seven became finally safe from defeat only when Miller and Taylor dug their toes in.

Toss: Australia. **Australia 314** (J. Dyson 79, A. R. Border 89, I. T. Botham 4-75) **and 382** (K. C. Wessels 53, K. J. Hughes 137, A. R. Border 83); **England 237** (D. I. Gower 70, D. W. Randall 70, J. R. Thomson 5-50) **and 314-7** (E. E. Hemmings 95, B. Yardley 4-139).

ENGLAND V AUSTRALIA 1985

David Frith

The 1985 Australian touring team, the 30th to play Test cricket in England, disappointed its supporters. After four Tests, both sides had a victory apiece, and one further success by Australia in the remaining two matches would have ensured their retention of the Ashes. At this point, while England were felt to be the better side, it was beyond most objective pundits to foresee their two crushing victories, each by an innings, that unveiled a conclusive superiority.

That so many of Australia's shortcomings remained only half-revealed for so long was attributable to the determined and often daring batsmanship of Allan Border, the captain, who was always the batsman whose downfall meant most to both sides. The inconsistency of Australia's batting turned to downright fragility in the last two encounters as nerves snapped and technique was found wanting before the surging skill and confidence of a settled England team.

The bowling was even more disappointing. Lawson's bronchial problems reduced his effectiveness, and Holland's leg-spin, hailed as an aesthetic asset and triumphant in the Lord's Test, was used unadventurously. Thomson, who turned 35 during the Fifth Test, tried in vain to muster the speed and bite of bygone summers. The outstanding success was McDermott, fiery, strong and seemingly more mature than his 20 years. Though, understandably, he could not always sustain the pace and accuracy that earned him eight wickets at Old Trafford, he was a perpetual menace, and returned a worthy 30 wickets in the Test series.

The selection of the touring party was hampered by the unavailability of those who chose to sign up for a disapproved tour of South Africa, though Hughes and Yallop joined only after their surprising omission from the team for England. They and bowlers Alderman, Hogg, Maguire and Rackemann would unquestionably have strength-ened the side, almost to the same extent that the presence of Gooch, Emburey, Willey and Taylor – all newly liberated from three-year bans for similar defections to South Africa – fortified England.

First Test

Matthew Engel

At Leeds, June 13, 14, 15, 17, 18, 1985. England won by five wickets.

The match had to withstand inevitable comparisons with the epic Headingley Test of 1981, and to the end there was an outside chance that history would be reversed in an equally bizarre manner. Four years earlier, Australia, needing 130, had managed only 111. This time England, set 123, spluttered their way to victory with 13.2 overs left.

The game did not need the comparisons; it was a remarkable contest in its own right, effectively settled on a gloriously sunlit Saturday afternoon when the England batsmen seized the initiative spectacularly, led by Robinson, with 175 in his first home Test, and Botham. The bat outshone the ball throughout, helped by a fast outfield. The pitch was less eccentric than many on this ground, but was uneven in bounce, and if either side had bowled more accurately, the scores would have been far lower.

Part of the bat's domination was dictated by conservative selection policies. Determined not to lose the first match of a six-Test series, both sides played an extra batsman. On the opening day when Australia, having won the toss, batted first and immediately took advantage of some short, wide bowling by England. Hilditch found form, showing great skill, especially square of the wicket, scoring 119, his second century in three Tests since being recalled the previous December. At one stage Australia were 201 for two, but on a rain-affected second day England bounced back, taking the last four wickets in ten balls. Three of these fell in four balls to Botham, who narrowly missed a hat-trick when he whistled one past Lawson's defence.

On the Saturday, as the sun returned and all swing ceased, England took control. However defective the English bowling had appeared, the Australians were hopelessly exposed, and McDermott (in his third Test) and O'Donnell (in his first) were forced to carry the attack. This proved impossible when Botham launched one of his most brilliant assaults: 60 off 51 balls in a golden hour of explosive batsmanship. While Botham was in, Robinson (firmly keeping his helmet on at the non-striker's end because

Botham was a far greater danger than the bowling) was almost forgotten. But he surprised many people by the range and vigour of his strokeplay, especially off the back foot. His 175 took only 271 balls, good going for a supposed anchor-man.

The Australians reached exasperation on the Monday morning when Cowans and Downton put on 49 for the last wicket. Their old feeling that Headingley had something against Australians was heavily upon them, and they lost six wickets before wiping off the deficit of 202, despite another fine innings from Hilditch, well supported by Wessels. By now the bounce was becoming increasingly strange – Ritchie was bowled by a shooter – and England must have expected to wrap up the match early on the last day. However, Phillips caused a delay with an innings too handsome and free to look like a serious match-saving effort but enough to keep England fielding until after lunch. They then had three hours 20 minutes to score the 123 runs they needed. But wickets kept falling, and England finally crawled over the finishing line like exhausted marathon runners. Even then, Willey, one of the not-out batsmen, had given a simple chance off Thomson, which Border, at mid-wicket, put down.

However, this was quickly eclipsed as a talking point by the crowd's performance at the end. An invasion of the field in England's moment of triumph gave more than usual cause for concern. The mostly young spectators who rushed on prematurely – described by England's captain as a pack of mad dogs – almost certainly distracted Lawson as he tried to catch Lamb and prevent the winning runs.

Toss: Australia. **Australia 331** (A. M. J. Hilditch 119) **and 324** (A. M. J. Hilditch 80, K. C. Wessels 64, W. B. Phillips 91, I. T. Botham 4-107, J. E. Emburey 5-82); **England 533** (R. T. Robinson 175, M. W. Gatting 53, I. T. Botham 60, P. R. Downton 54, C. J. McDermott 4-134) **and 123-5**.

Second Test

Brian Scovell

At Lord's, June 27, 28, 29, July 1, 2, 1985. Australia won by four wickets.

This was Border's match. He scored 43% of his side's runs – 237 out of 552 – and led them superbly to maintain Australia's unbeaten run at Lord's since Verity bowled them to defeat in 1934. Border's 196 in the first innings was his highest Test score, and he displayed a command and range of shot which few contemporary players could equal. The only time he seemed at all disconcerted was when, with Australia needing ten to win but batting anxiously, a statement was read out asking spectators not to run on to the pitch at the finish.

A fine match was played in a good atmosphere. It was remarkable that play was able to start on time, for the afternoon before an MCC assistant secretary had worn Wellington boots to inspect the sodden outfield. However, the groundstaff worked through the night to remove surface water and, although the pitch was soft and the square still wet, the umpires allowed the game to begin at the appointed time. Border won the toss and asked England to bat. The pitch being too slow at that stage for his leg-spinner, the 38-year-old Holland, Border was gambling on his three pace bowlers to bowl England out, and he was not disappointed.

McDermott bowled magnificently. He had both openers, Gooch and Robinson, lbw, though Gooch's decision appeared a harsh one. Gower dominated with batting which persuaded the selectors to confirm him in the captaincy for the remaining four

Tests. Lawson, still not bowling as fast or aggressively as he is able to, took the crucial wicket of Botham, having him caught on the cover boundary, driving at a slower ball.

Play on the second day was interrupted five times and finally curtailed by bad light, to the annoyance of a capacity crowd. Loud disapproval was expressed when play was halted for the last time with the spinners in action. Border, then 92 out of 183 for four, might have gone at 87 when his pull off Edmonds struck Gatting's wrist at short leg. As the fielder strove to control the ball, he seemed, prematurely, to try to throw it up in celebration of what would have been a remarkable catch. The ball escaped Gatting's despairing lunge, and in response to a somewhat half-hearted appeal umpire Bird ruled that it had not been retained in such a way as to satisfy Law 32.

Border's fifth-wicket stand of 216 with Ritchie ended soon after lunch on the third day when Botham, kept out of the attack in the morning to protect a slightly strained ankle, upset Ritchie's equanimity with a couple of bouncers and followed them with a straight delivery which had him lbw. Botham bowled as fast as for some time and his five wickets prevented the Australians from running away with the match.

Trailing by 135, England needed a sound start to their second innings; but Gooch was caught behind, trying to leg glance McDermott, and Robinson's bat caught in his pad as he defended against Holland. Gower then took the controversial decision to send in not one but two nightwatchmen. The promotion of two tailenders meant that a major batsman was likely to be left stranded later in the innings, and so it proved. On the Monday morning Lawson reduced England to 98 for six when he removed the nightwatchmen Emburey and Allott, then Lamb, Gower having gone for a one-day-style 22. But Botham, suffering from a bruised toe sustained when he was hit by a golf ball at Wentworth the day before, added 131 with Gatting. They were on the way to turning likely defeat into possible victory when Holland went round the wicket at the Nursery End, aiming for the rough created outside leg stump by McDermott, who had been officially warned for running down the pitch. Botham's reply was to keep padding the ball away until, going for a big hit, he was caught just backward of point. Downton went next ball, caught at slip. Holland's five wickets on his first appearance in a Test in England were a splendid reward for accurate, intelligent bowling.

Australia faced 21 overs before the close, by when they were 46 for three, needing 127. Hilditch was caught hooking, Wood in the gully off a lifter, both off Botham, and Ritchie was bowled by the accurate Allott. Wood's wicket was Botham's 326th in Tests, making him England's most prolific wicket-taker. On the last morning Border's nerve held after Australia had declined to 65 to five, Wessels, the striker, being run out by a quick return from Gower at short leg and Boon bowled.

Toss: Australia. **England 290** (D. I. Gower 86, C. J. McDermott 6-70) **and 261** (M. W. Gatting 75*, I. T. Botham 85, R. G. Holland 5-68); **Australia 425** (A. R. Border 196, G. M. Ritchie 94, I. T. Botham 5-109) **and 127-6**.

Third Test

At Nottingham, July 11, 12, 13, 15, 16, 1985. Drawn.

Rod Nicholson

The match produced neither the excitement nor the outright result of the first two Tests, though it entertained with imposing individual performances, notably by Gower,

Wood and Ritchie, all of whom made substantial centuries. Gower won the toss with a ten-franc coin, thus breaking a losing sequence of six Tests, and decided to bat on a light-coloured pitch which promised and produced a feast of runs.

Robinson began at breakneck pace, England's first 50 coming in just 12 overs, but at 55 he edged a catch to Border off Lawson. This united Gower with the increasingly confident Gooch, and the partnership yielded 116 in 30 overs before Gooch lost concentration, guiding a cut to Wessels in the gully off Lawson. Gower's seemingly inevitable century, the tenth of his Test career, came with nine boundaries. Undefeated with 107 at the end of the first day, Gower divulged his hopes of a total of about 600 to enable his bowlers to place strong pressure on the tourists, and there seemed no reason to dispute the prospect when England reached 358 for two just before lunch on the second day. Inexplicably they then lost eight wickets while scoring 98, a decline triggered by a cruel run-out for Gatting after he had contributed 74 to a 187-run partnership with his captain. Gower hit a straight-drive off Holland's leg-spin, and the bowler's unintentional deflection found Gatting backing up too far. Just before tea Gower edged O'Donnell to the wicket-keeper. His 166, off 283 balls, was an innings full of drives and cuts of quality, and he hit 17 boundaries. Lawson and McDermott shared six wickets in 13 overs, and England fell substantially short of Gower's target.

Australia began confidently enough with Hilditch and Wood, who had been on the verge of being omitted from the Test following a string of low scores, opening with an 87-run partnership. Hilditch then fell to Allott, but Wood and the night-watchman, Holland, carried Australia to 94 for one by stumps. Sidebottom, making his Test debut following the withdrawal with a back injury of Foster, trapped Holland early next day. But Australia reached 205 before Wessels was caught at the wicket. Border, with a six and two fours in his 23 off 17 deliveries, was hinting at a repeat of his Lord's triumph when adjudged caught at slip off Edmonds, a controversial decision. When Boon then presented Emburey with a return catch for 15, Australia were vulnerable at 263 for five, no longer in danger of having to follow on but still 193 in arrears.

However, Wood, who reached his eighth Test century, found in Ritchie a partner prepared to attack the bowling, and a stand of 161 in 66 overs left Australia only 32 runs in arrears when Wood's marathon innings ended at 172, his highest in 51 Tests. After ten hours and 449 deliveries, Wood left the ground with his Test career revived and Australia's fighting qualities restored. Ritchie, who had missed a worthy century at Lord's by only six runs, confirmed his growing maturity with an innings of 146, and with O'Donnell making 46 Australia finished with a lead of 83. Botham, who was warned for running on the wicket and for intimidatory bowling by umpire Whitehead during an explosive over, in which he also had Ritchie caught off a no-ball, gave his all as usual, while Edmonds and Emburey bowled 121 overs between them for a return of five wickets. The unresponsive pitch, coupled with a toe injury to Sidebottom and Allott's stomach upset, eased the task for the Australians, but the batting of Wood and Ritchie was full of character.

England's second innings, held up by rain and bad light, was of little consequence, though Robinson boosted his average and standing with an unconquered 77.

Toss: England. **England 456** (G. A. Gooch 70, D. I. Gower 166, M. W. Gatting 74, G. F. Lawson 5-103) **and 196-2** (R. T. Robinson 77*); **Australia 539** (G. M. Wood 172, G. M. Ritchie 146).

Fourth Test

Terry Cooper

At Manchester, August 1, 2, 3, 5, 6, 1985. Drawn.

After the first session and until the final hour England made all the running, but a prolonged defensive effort by Australia's middle order, organised by Border, enabled them to draw the game. They were helped in this by breaks for rain and an impossibly sluggish pitch, although the groundstaff worked diligently to keep the match going between frequent showers. It seemed a pity, none the less, that they were protecting a pitch that had been inexplicably wet at the start. It offered no pace and a low bounce. Batsmen who attacked with profit on it and wicket-taking bowlers, especially McDermott, could feel more satisfaction than usual.

Gower put Australia in, but his bowlers did not immediately vindicate the move. Wessels was the only man dismissed before lunch. Edmonds turned the game permanently England's way in the afternoon with three wickets. The most important of these was that of Border, who reacted to being tied down by going headlong down the pitch for a speculative drive and being stumped. Ritchie gave Edmonds a return catch in the same over and, at 122 for four, Australia's innings needed extensive repairs. Boon mustered all his skill and Phillips settled in with him, but England struck again at the start of the evening session through Botham. Like England's other faster bowlers, Botham had not been at his best in the morning, but now he had both Boon and Phillips caught cutting. Matthews and Lawson followed, but the new ball was propelled fruitlessly before Edmonds ended the day by finishing off the innings.

Robinson was removed early in England's reply by McDermott, but Australia enjoyed only isolated encouragement after this, largely because McDermott was the only bowler taking wickets. Lawson was accurate enough, but unrecognisable in terms of penetration. O'Donnell had Gooch dropped, but seldom menaced the batsmen's survival. Boon spilled that chance and also missed Gower off McDermott. The task of the Australian spinners looked forlorn. Although 40 minutes were lost at the start of the second day, England had reached 233 for three by the close. Gooch and Gower, who went to a fine, tumbling catch on the square-leg boundary, made their exits within minutes of each other, but Gatting and Lamb became established in the final two hours.

Play could not resume until two o'clock on Saturday, whereupon the cricket settled into a pattern, with Gatting driving and hooking while Lamb thrust fiercely through mid-wicket. They had added 156 when Lamb was run out by a beautiful piece of fielding from Matthews in the covers. Gatting, whose responsibilities increased when Botham was caught on the long-leg boundary, completed his first home Test century shortly afterwards. He had batted for nigh on six hours (266 balls) and had nailed down his place as England's No. 4 when he was caught behind. On Monday morning, as England went for further quick runs, McDermott hit the stumps three times and so marched off as the third-youngest to take eight wickets in a Test. He had bowled 36 overs, defying the sponge-like pitch by obtaining occasional bounce.

Australia, 225 behind, were thus in by noon. Matthews had been asked to open, to allow Wessels to drop back to No. 3, and he helped Australia past the first hurdle by remaining until lunch. Immediately afterwards he became the first of four batsmen to be prised out by the spinners before the close. Border conceded that a last day of rain would not go amiss, and he was accommodated to the extent that only three overs could be bowled before lunch. England's dejection increased when play did start, Border soon surviving an awkward chance. Australia were 33 behind at the time, and they cleared the arrears after ten of the 50 overs to which the day was reduced had been bowled. Emburey had cheered England by bowling Ritchie, but Phillips was quite clear as to what his job was. He remained on nought for 50 balls. Border also gave England no more hope, seeing his side to safety in an innings of 334 balls and 346 minutes.

Toss: England. **Australia 257** (D. C. Boon 61, I. T. Botham 4-79, P. H. Edmonds 4-40) **and 340-5** (K. C. Wessels 50, A. R. Border 146*, J. E. Emburey 4-99); **England 482-9 dec.** (G. A. Gooch 74, M. W. Gatting 160, A. J. Lamb 67, C. J. McDermott 8-141).

Fifth Test

David Field

At Birmingham, August 15, 16, 17, 19, 20, 1985. England won by an innings and 118 runs.

Rain, rivalling Australia as England's greatest adversary, rolled away on the final afternoon to allow just enough time for Gower's side to force a thoroughly warranted victory. There was, however, a dark cloud of controversy waiting to shed its gloom. Australia's captain asserted that the crucial, quite freak dismissal of Phillips should not have been allowed, claiming that enough doubt existed for the umpires to have judged in the batsman's favour. Border insisted that the incident cost Australia the match. Phillips hit a ball from Edmonds hard on to the instep of Lamb, who was taking swift evasive action at silly point. The rebound gently stood up for Gower, a couple of yards away, to catch, and 48 minutes later England won when it had seemed that the weather-induced frustrations which prevailed at Manchester would deny them again.

It was a pity Border blamed defeat on this one incident, especially as England had forged their supremacy with a succession of outstanding individual performances, none more so than Ellison's. The Kent swing bowler fought off the debilitating effects of a heavy cold to capture ten for 79 in the match and announce his coming of age as a Test bowler. Gower, in addition to savouring the fruits of victory and being appointed ahead of schedule for England's winter tour of the West Indies, exquisitely unveiled his strokemaking talents with a career-best 215 on the ground where he had scored his previous double-hundred for England, against India in 1979. Helped by some badly directed bowling, the England captain remorselessly punished Australia in a sumptuous, high-speed partnership of 331 with Robinson. Then Gatting, almost clinically, added a top-quality hundred – resourceful, chanceless and occupying only 125 balls.

England's domination was triggered by Gower when he ran out Lawson for a fighting 53 off the first ball of the third day. The fifth delivery of the same over ended Australia's first innings for 335, the tourists being indebted to the obdurate Wessels for a dogged 83. With two days, both rain-interrupted, already gone, this was a position from which Australia should not have lost, but their wasteful bowling and an astonishing collapse early in their second innings cleared England's way.

By the third evening Gower and Robinson had already taken England into the lead with their respective centuries. Australia were rendered powerless as England amassed 355 for one, the only interruption being Thomson's dismissal of Gooch, his 200th Test wicket and 100th against England. England's huge second-wicket stand, when it concluded on Monday with Robinson playing on to Lawson, was the second-highest for this wicket against Australia, short only of Hutton and Leyland's 382 at The Oval in 1938. It was the seventh alliance of over 300 by an England pair and the best in England since John Edrich and Ken Barrington added 369 against New Zealand at Headingley in 1965. Gower, by that time, had gone past Denis Compton's record aggregate of 562 in a home series against Australia.

England's declaration at 595 for five, a lead of 260, was sped by Lamb and briefly by Botham, who struck his first and third balls from McDermott for straight sixes and his fourth for four. Ellison, bowling to a full length and achieving late swing, then ripped away the top layer of Australia's innings with a spell of four wickets for one run in 15 balls, including Border's. Australia, going into a desperate final day at 37 for five, had their prayers for rain initially answered. Thick drizzle promised to save the match for them, but at 2.30 Phillips and Ritchie were finally summoned to fight it out. Phillips, in particular, displayed a strong nerve in making 59 before his controversial departure. Umpire Shepherd, not having a clear view of the incident, asked Constant, standing at square leg, for his version, and the latter unhesitatingly confirmed that the ball had at no time hit the ground. Australia's last four wickets offered little resistance.

Toss: England. **Australia 335** (K. C. Wessels 83, G. F. Lawson 53, R. M. Ellison 6-77)
and 142 (W. B. Phillips 59, R. M. Ellison 4-27);
England 595-5 dec. (R. T. Robinson 148, D. I. Gower 215, M. W. Gatting 100*).

NOTES BY THE EDITOR

John Woodcock, 1986

In all the years since England and Australia first met, there is no remote precedent for either side averaging 60 runs per 100 balls throughout a series, as England did in 1985. In the original Test match, played at Melbourne in 1877, both sides averaged below 30. Even Bradman's Australians in 1948 were kept to 46.6. In 1930, when Bradman himself scored 974 runs at a rattling rate, Australia's overall average was 45.2. In 1928–29 in Australia, one of the best of all England batting sides (the first six were Hobbs, Sutcliffe, Hammond, Jardine, Hendren and Chapman) averaged only 38.53, albeit in a series of timeless Tests.

Only once in 25 years after the last war did England average more than 40. Yet here they were making their runs at 60.67 per 100 balls, or getting on for four an over, at once an indication of the range and belligerence of their own batting and the unfitness of some of the Australian bowling. Being covered the pitches, too, were immune from the vagaries of a wet, wretchedly grey summer; but that has applied for some years now.

Sixth Test

John Thicknesse

At The Oval, August 29, 30, 31, September 2, 1985. England won by an innings and 94 runs.

Australia's modest chance of salvaging the Ashes effectively vanished when Gower won an exceptionally good toss and was then blessed by a good deal of luck in the first hour of what blossomed into a match-winning stand of 351. Gooch, who had been rather overshadowed in the first five Tests by Robinson, his opening partner, made a chanceless 196 (27 fours, 423 minutes); but though Gower, too, went on to play brilliantly in scoring 157 (20 fours, 337 minutes), he had started loosely, lobbing the slips at two while attempting to kill a rising ball from McDermott, and surviving further narrow escapes at 31 and 35 during an over from Lawson. Given extra help by ill-directed bowling, much of it over-pitched and leg-side, England had sped to 100 for one off 25 overs by lunch, from which point Australia played like a losing side.

Several factors were involved in their demoralisation, among them the cumulative effect of so little cricket between Tests because of rain, and the tour-long battle for full fitness of Lawson, their most experienced bowler. But ill-judged selection also played a part. At The Oval, where they had to win the match to save the series, a bowler was omitted in favour of a batsman. Holland was dropped in conditions better suited to a leg-spinner than in any previous Test.

Australia's one moment of supremacy came after 37 minutes when McDermott yorked Robinson with a late inswinger. Had Gower's mis-hit gone to hand in his next over, England would have been 29 for two. Instead, Australia were outplayed on a pitch of pace and generous even bounce that shared its favours equally between bat and ball. Because of their sluggish over-rate of 13 an hour, Australia were already on overtime, in the hottest weather for weeks, when Gower lashed a cut to deep gully after a part-nership with Gooch in which the runs had come at 4.6 an over. Twenty-five minutes later Gatting was caught at the wicket off Bennett from a ball that turned – an ominous portent for Australia – but when England reached the end of the first day at 376 for three, with Gooch 179, it seemed certain they were heading for a total of at least 600.

In the event, after he and Emburey, the night-watchman, had added 27 in three overs off the new ball, Gooch mistimed a low full toss and McDermott checked in his follow-through to bring off a very good caught-and-bowled, wide to his right with his knuckle almost on the turf. Against long odds, the innings ended two hours later, improved fast bowling and over-confident batting accounting for most of the six wickets which fell for 61. But the early loss of Wood to a possibly unlucky decision, and the mortifying sight of Hilditch falling into Botham's hooking trap for the third time in the series, combined with their drubbing on the first day, knocked the fight out of Australia. With the exception of Ritchie they batted with little resolve or basic technique, even Border taking too little account of the extra pace in the pitch as he played on to Edmonds, attempting a forcing stroke against the spin. A brilliant over-head catch at second slip by Botham to remove Lawson hastened the end, and 15 minutes after lunch on the third day Australia followed on 223 behind.

After a lengthy stoppage through rain at 12 for no wicket, Hilditch and Wood picked up the second innings with an hour and three-quarters left before the revised time for drawing stumps. But the faults of the first innings were soon in evidence. With only one run added, Botham bowled Wood, and three overs later Hilditch, having resisted several temptations to hook Botham, drove a widish ball from Taylor to cover point. When Wessels chased an even wider one from Botham, Australia were 37 for three, Downton taking a fine catch full to his left. Wellham, out of his depth against Ellison's outswing, was lbw to a break-back, and at the close Australia were 62 for four, still 161 behind.

As on the previous three days, every seat had been sold in advance for the fourth day, a crowd of 15,000 assembling to see if Australia's captain had one more heroic saving innings in him. And as at Old Trafford, the day began ominously for England when in overcast conditions Downton missed Border in the first over before he had

That winning feeling: David Gower salutes the crowd after England clinch the 1985 Ashes series at The Oval, watched by his opposite number Allan Border, who turned the tables decisively on his next two visits to England.

added to his score, diving for a mistimed leg-glance off Ellison. However, Border's resolution struck no chord among his team-mates. Ritchie, driving at a wide one, and Phillips, making room to cut, were swept aside, and at eight minutes past noon Australia's last vestige of resistance disappeared when Border edged Ellison to second slip. There was time for Botham, leaping to his left to drag down a fast edge by McDermott, to add another to his galaxy of slip catches before Taylor caught and bowled Bennett to end the match and the series. In 96 minutes Australia had lost six for 67.

As in 1926 and 1953, when the Ashes were also regained at The Oval, several thousand spectators massed in front of the pavilion when the match was over, to hail the England captain and his team and to give Allan Border a heartfelt cheer.

Toss: England. **England 464** (G. A. Gooch 196, D. I. Gower 157, extras 50, G. F. Lawson 4-101, C. J. McDermott 4-108); **Australia 241** (G. M. Ritchie 64*) **and 129** (A. R. Border 58, R. M. Ellison 5-46).

AUSTRALIA v ENGLAND 1986–87   John Thicknesse

England's tour of Australia, under the captaincy of Mike Gatting, brought a timely and much-needed boost to English confidence after the tribulations of the previous months. Having flown from Heathrow carrying the prayers rather than the aspirations of their countrymen, following three lost series in succession – eight defeats in 11 Tests without a single win – they returned triumphantly not only with the Ashes safe till 1989 but also as winners of two one-day competitions in which West Indies were involved. It was an excellent performance, not least because at the outset England had given no sign of emerging from the pit. They lost to Queensland in the opening first-class fixture and were outplayed by Western Australia in the third on the eve of the First Test. Few, at that stage, would have given much for their retaining the Ashes.

One of the most pleasing aspects was the unity within the team and the way they dovetailed on the field. Broad, with the bat, and Dilley, Small and DeFreitas with the ball enjoyed outstanding personal success. But nearly everyone contributed and some, notably Emburey and Edmonds, the spinners, played a more important role than was suggested by their figures. Gower was fighting what looked to be a losing battle with his concentration early in the tour, a reaction possibly to being passed over as vice-captain. But a life at Brisbane proved his turning-point. Gatting batted as he captained, without frills. His team knew where they stood with him.

In the Second Test the left-handed Broad struck the prolific form that was to earn him the title of "International Player of the Season". His height, composure, concentration and sound technique were well suited to Australian pitches, and from the early matches he had batted impressively without taking full advantage of a series of good starts. All that changed at Perth, where his stylish 162 was the first of three hundreds in three successive Tests, an achievement equalled for England against Australia only by J. B. Hobbs, W. R. Hammond and R. A. Woolmer, the last-named in different series.

Batting was by far Australia's stronger wing. Marsh proved himself an adhesive opener of limitless endurance, and in Jones and Stephen Waugh Australia had two youngsters of obvious class, both well equipped with strokes and always on the lookout to take the battle to the bowlers.

First Test

At Brisbane, November 14, 15, 16, 18, 19, 1986. England won by seven wickets.

Following England's poor performance in their preceding tour match and the development of several of their own players on the recent tour of India, Australia were widely fancied to achieve what would have been their seventh victory in 11 post-war Tests against England at Woolloongabba. Lamb and Botham were the only England batsmen in form, while Slack's failures left the selectors little alternative but to entrust Athey with the task of opening against the type of bowling – fast-medium left-arm – which had caused such problems in the state games. Another handicap for England was that their fast bowling had been inconsistent and the slip-catching unreliable. It was understandable therefore that, when Border followed recent precedent by putting England in, only their most phlegmatic supporters received the news with an outward show of confidence.

England's emphatic victory, which was completed 35 minutes after lunch on the fifth day, was a salutary reminder of the dangers of reading too much into omens and too little into experience. The opening session was to have a decisive bearing on how the match developed. Though Reid moved one away to have Broad caught at the wicket after 35 minutes, the attack lacked the accuracy to put England under pressure, too many balls being bowled short or off the stumps. Gatting, taking the onus of batting at No. 3 after Gower's failure at Perth, had an edgy start, nearly playing on to Reid; but

Athey was composed, showing good judgment of the ball to leave alone. When England went to lunch at 65 for one, much of the advantage of the toss had disappeared.

Australia, ill served by their fast bowlers, at no stage promised to recover. Hughes ended a stand of 101 by bowling Gatting off his pads, but Lamb was soon into his stride. When rain and bad light took 80 minutes off the final session, England at 198 for two were nicely placed. On the second morning, however, the game changed rapidly. Lamb was out first ball, Athey three overs later with the score unaltered, and still at 198 Gower was missed by Craig Matthews at third slip, a sharp chance off a slash two-handed to his right. The match turned in that instant. While Gower took half an hour to settle, Botham played with much authority; he dominated their stand of 118. Australia had an opening when Craig Matthews dismissed Gower and Richards in successive overs, but Border surrendered the initiative by pushing seven and sometimes eight fielders on to the boundary to deprive Botham of the strike. The lessening of pressure had much to do with DeFreitas's confident contribution as they added 92 in not much more than an hour. Botham's 138, which included an assault on Hughes which brought 22 in the over of his century, was comparable to his 118 at Old Trafford in 1981 for power and control. He hit four sixes – straight drives – and 13 fours before Hughes sprinted in to catch him at long leg.

Australia lost Boon, pulling to mid-wicket, to close the second day at 33 for one. But on a pitch now free of moisture, there seemed little danger of their failing to score 257 to avoid the follow-on as Zoehrer, the night-watchman, was helping Marsh add 70. Dilley made the breakthrough with a highish lbw and Australia lost their grip as he maintained good line and pace to achieve his first five-wicket return in Tests. However, the critical dismissal was that of Border at 159. Tied down for an hour by Emburey, he made an ill-judged attempt to assert himself when Edmonds took over; the result was a skyed catch to cover. The spinners played a crucial role by restricting Australia to 191 off 85 overs, when the new ball came due.

Marsh's disciplined 110 – he batted in great heat for 392 minutes – was the corner-stone of Australia's resistance in the follow-on. But three wickets, including Border's, fell for 92, and only while Ritchie shared a fourth-wicket stand of 113 did Australia look to have a fair chance of survival. When DeFreitas ended that partnership with the new ball – a second debatable lbw decision – and Greg Matthews was caught and bowled off a front edge by Dilley 15 minutes from the close, Australia started the final day only 35 ahead at 243 for five, needing a lengthy stand between Marsh and Waugh to leave England a task against the clock.

They began with confidence, scoring 15 in two overs. Then, after 28 minutes, Marsh's gritty innings ended when he edged DeFreitas into his stumps, and in 31 minutes the last four wickets fell for 20. Emburey picked up three for two in 23 deliveries, belated reward for dismissing Border to a bat-pad catch in one of the best overs of the game. He finished with five for 80, claiming Waugh as his 100th Test victim in the process. England, needing 75, were certain winners from that point; but starting shakily they reminded their followers that the contest might have finished otherwise had Australia scored another 100 runs.

Toss: Australia. **England 456** (C. W. J. Athey 76, M. W. Gatting 61, D. I. Gower 51, I. T. Botham 138) **and 77-3; Australia 248** (G. R. Marsh 56, G. R. J. Matthews 56*, G. R. Dilley 5-68) **and 282** (G. R. Marsh 110, J. E. Emburey 5-80).

Second Test

At Perth, November 28, 29, 30, December 2, 3, 1986. Drawn.

After Border had lost the toss for the first time in nine Tests, Broad and Athey shared a stand of 223 – England's fifth-highest opening partnership against Australia – which gave their side control for much of the match, even if they were unable to turn their supremacy into victory. England were denied victory first by a resolute 125 in 372 minutes by Border, who saved the follow-on in the company of the No. 11; by an indecisive approach to their own second innings, which resulted in a delayed declaration; and by Australia's determined batting on the fifth day on a pitch which played truer than it had any right to on its appearance.

John Maley, who as travelling curator during World Series Cricket had produced a number of true pitches under hothouse conditions, set out to prepare a surface which would be good for batting on the opening day, in contrast to recent Tests at Perth, where not since 1977–78 had a captain chosen to bat first. This pitch started exceptionally dry by modern standards, with several cracks beginning to peep through, and finished resembling a giant jigsaw puzzle, split by a wavy crack (into which it was possible to slide a little finger) in line with the stumps at each end. Its appearance was alarming enough for Border to decline the use of a roller when the declaration left Australia to bat through the fifth day; but in the event the cracks proved an illusory advantage to England's bowlers, balls hitting them tending to deviate too much to create problems.

In the eighth over, Border missed Athey at second slip, but that apart the remodelled new-ball partnership never threatened to make inroads. Indeed, the new ball was wasted with more profligacy than at Brisbane. Broad played majestically throughout, never looking back after superb fours to mid-wicket and extra cover in Craig Matthews's second over. When, by tea, England were 187 for no wicket, with Broad two away from his first Test hundred, a huge total was assured. Reid, the steadiest of the bowlers, deprived Athey of a well-deserved maiden Test hundred by yorking him for 96, and next over had Lamb caught at the wicket.

Australia lost their faint chance of recovering lost ground on the second morning when, shortly after Gatting had cut Matthews to gully, Broad was dropped by Ritchie at third slip in Lawson's best spell of the innings. Broad added only 15 more before Reid had him caught behind, his innings having spanned 435 minutes and included 25 fours; but by then Gower, given the easiest of starts by Matthews with two loose balls on his legs, was in full stride with 35, pulling and off-driving with severity and perfect timing. After Botham had been caught off Reid at second slip, Richards in his second Test played with such assurance that Gower was content to let him dominate a sixth-wicket stand of 207. They had been together 212 minutes when Gower (19 fours) was caught at cover after completing his sixth hundred against Australia and his second at Perth. Half an hour later, with a declaration imminent, Richards (16 fours) was caught at mid-off, two short of the highest score by an England wicket-keeper against Australia – Alan Knott's 135 at Trent Bridge in 1977.

Australia, left with half an hour's batting on the second day, needed 393 to save the follow-on and were at once in trouble when Boon played on in the second over. Waugh, promoted four places, vindicated high opinions of his timing by making 71, which included the only six of the match, but England, helped by a brilliant catch by

Broad at backward short leg off a well-hit hook by Marsh, worked steadily through the top half of the order. When, shortly before tea, Ritchie was caught at slip off a ball that hit a crack, turned and lifted, the prospects of a second win were good, but Border's technique, patience and relish for a fight were never better illustrated than in the next two sessions. Content to remain in occupation, yet missing next to nothing overpitched, he nursed four partners so that when Reid came in at 385 for nine only eight were needed to make England bat again. Border himself made the decisive stroke three minutes before lunch on the third day, cutting Emburey for four and giving a little skip of joy as the ball crossed the line. When he was out ten minutes after the interval England, 191 ahead, had nine hours 40 minutes at their disposal to win the match.

Through good defensive bowling by Reid and Waugh, however, and concern that a start of 50 for three might lead to a collapse, England's second innings got going only while Gower was making 48 in 72 minutes. With Botham failing again, momentum was lost, and Gatting drew back from the declaration he had been aiming for before the close of play. Instead, he waited until the following morning.

Dilley made up lost time when, with the first ball of the last day, he had Boon caught by Botham at second slip, his 100th catch in Tests. But in Dilley's next over Botham missed a difficult low chance in the same position, and Marsh and Jones, both receiving the benefit on close lbw decisions, virtually made the game safe with a stand of 126. Soon after lunch, Botham tore a muscle in his left side delivering a bouncer, but when Edmonds had Border caught off bat and pad in the over after tea, England had another opening. However, the pitch remained true and slow with little turn, and despite many close calls against the spinners, Ritchie and Greg Matthews held out until Gatting gave them best midway through the final 20 overs.

Toss: England. **England 592-8 dec.** (B. C. Broad 162, C. W. J. Athey 96, D. I. Gower 136, C. J. Richards 133, B. A. Reid 4-115) **and 199-8 dec.** (M. W. Gatting 70, S. R. Waugh 5-69); **Australia 401** (S. R. Waugh 71, A. R. Border 125, G. R. Dilley 4-79) **and 197-4** (D. M. Jones 69).

Third Test

At Adelaide, December 12, 13, 14, 15, 16, 1986. Drawn.

A perfect batting pitch exposed the limitations of both sets of bowlers. Although late on the fourth evening there was an outside chance of a result when Australia lost two wickets for eight runs at the start of their second innings, after leading by 59 on the first, in the conditions a draw had looked the likely outcome from the time the captains tossed. In the event, only 20 wickets fell for 1,209 runs, and four men made hundreds.

When Zoehrer damaged a shoulder in practice, Dyer took his place behind the stumps. He had a tidy first Test, although he experienced occasional difficulties taking Sleep and missed a stumping chance, given by Emburey, which might have earned Australia a three-figure lead. In the second innings he suffered a broken nose when a ball from Sleep deflected off Broad's pads. Overall, however, he looked at least the equal of Australia's first choice.

The omission of Bright was regretted by Border in hindsight when, after winning a good toss, he was able to declare at 514 for five. Botham's rib muscle, which was proving slow to heal, obliged England to make their first change of the series, Whitaker winning his first cap on the ground where he had earlier scored 108. This left England a seam bowler short, a setback when Australia were in trouble early in their second innings, but as holders of the Ashes the tourists could be excused for consolidating their batting. Whitaker, as it happened, spent an uncomfortable 51 minutes scoring 11 in his only innings. He went some way towards making up for his failure with the bat through the zeal with which he fielded during the 11 hours of Australia's first innings. With Gower, whose cutting-off was brilliant, and DeFreitas, whose speed over the ground and fine throwing arm saved many runs in the elongated outfield, Whitaker shared the distinction of being a member of the first trio of Leicestershire players to play in the same England team.

Given the circumstances, a big Australian score was always on the cards, the more so when Dilley and DeFreitas, who was no-balled for over-stepping ten times in his first ten overs, made poor use of a new ball dampened by two showers. Marsh and Boon laid the foundations with Australia's first three-figure opening in a home Test against England since 1974–75, but Edmonds and Emburey exercised their usual tight control and there was no worthwhile acceleration until just before the declaration when Matthews and Waugh added 49 in four overs. Jones did his best, repeatedly going down the pitch at Edmonds, only to be thwarted by his subtleties of flight and the fielding of mid-off and mid-on set deep. Yet for all his aggression and swift running between the wickets, Jones batted 283 minutes for his 93 before being well caught, low on the leg side, by Richards off a mis-hit hook. Boon, finding his confidence early on with a square cut and some good stroke off his legs, needed five hours for his first hundred against England, a strong, compact innings which contained 14 fours and no chance. Border's range of strokes, and expert placing, enabled him to score 70 before becoming the only batsman to fall to a defensive stroke, a looping leg-side bat-pad to Richards; but it was not until Waugh's improvisation and crisp driving wrung a response from Matthews that Australia scored with freedom.

England were never in danger of being asked to follow on. On the contrary, after Broad and Athey had put on 112 for the first wicket, and Broad and Gatting 161 for the second, they had prospects of taking a sizeable lead until Lamb and Gower were out within an over of each other in the last ten minutes of the third day. Without matching the majesty of his 162 in Perth, Broad played with smooth assurance, hitting a six and 12 fours, while Gatting vigorously attacked the spin bowlers. Emburey held the innings together until after lunch on the fourth day, troubled only by Sleep, who turned and pitched his leg-breaks throughout.

Australia, left 160 minutes batting before the close, were forced to consolidate when Boon and Jones fell to the new ball, but showers on the final morning made the last day academic. Border made a token declaration at tea after completing his 21st Test hundred (seventh against England); he survived a stumping chance off Emburey at 85 and hit 11 fours. It was a disappointing match, played in mostly cool and cloudy weather, and crowds of 7,158 on the fourth day and 3,653 on the last reflected waning interest.

Toss: Australia. **Australia 514-5 dec.** (D. C. Boon 103, D. M. Jones 93, A. R. Border 70, G. R. J. Matthews 73*,
S. R. Waugh 79*) **and 201-3 dec.** (A. R. Border 100*); **England 455** (B. C. Broad 116, C. W. J. Athey 55,
M. W. Gatting 100, B. A. Reid 4-64, P. R. Sleep 4-132) **and 39-2.**

Fourth Test

At Melbourne, December 26, 27, 28, 1986. England won by an innings and 14 runs.

A combination of excellent outswing bowling by Small, in his first Test of the series, and an inept appraisal by Australia of their best means of success, effectively decided the match, and the destination of the Ashes, by tea on the first day. Australia, put in on a pitch not fully dry, were bowled out for 141 in 235 minutes, Small maintaining a high degree of accuracy to take five for 48 in 22.4 overs. A last-minute replacement for Dilley, who failed a fitness test on a jarred knee, Small amply justified his selection by dismissing five of the first seven batsmen. He added two more wickets in the second innings, including Border when he was showing signs of keeping Australia in the match, a valuable 21 not out at No. 11, and a good catch in the deep to finish the game.

Well as Small bowled, however, both he and more especially Botham were helped by Australia's ill-conceived approach. Botham, bowling off a shortened run, took five for 41, a disproportionate reward for 16 overs at medium-pace with faster variations. The loss of Boon in Small's third over did nothing for Australia's confidence. But it was hard to disassociate the way they set about their innings from a well-publicised comment by Border, in a pre-match interview, that to revive their chance of winning back the Ashes, Australia needed to play boldly.

On quite a lively pitch, with a stronger growth of grass than for some years following a transplant of couch grass from a local golf course, Australia should have been content to let runs come. The pitch was never a straightforward one to bat on, yielding extra and variable bounce for the faster bowlers when they bent their backs, but the home side should have known from experience that at Melbourne, with its huge, slow outfield, a total of 250 would have given them at least an even chance. Marsh, for one, looked to lose his wicket through eagerness to follow the assumed instructions of his captain. Anything but a regular player of the hook – in some 30 hours' batting against England on the tour, he had produced no more than half a dozen – he attempted to hook a rising ball from Botham which pitched well outside off stump; Richards took the first of five catches in the innings with a gymnastic upward leap.

That wicket made it 44 for two, and when, 40 minutes later, Richards took a second fine catch to dismiss Border, diving to his left, Australia were in trouble. Against the advice of Border and Bob Simpson, the cricket manager, the selectors had omitted Ritchie, a specialist batsman, in favour of an all-rounder, to give the side an extra option in the field. In practice, with Greg Matthews not called upon to bowl in an innings lasting 120 overs, the decision served only to weaken the batting.

Jones, who hit Emburey out of the attack with two lofted leg-side fours, was the one batsman to pass 20. He batted 154 minutes, hitting one glorious on-drive off DeFreitas, before being caught at mid-off off the leading edge, attempting to tuck Small to leg. A wonderful running catch by Richards, who sprinted 30 yards to square leg to take a mis-hit hook by McDermott, hastened Australia's downfall.

It was a lamentable piece of batting which was duly reflected in a second-day attendance more than 20,000 down on the 58,203 of Boxing Day. England had set themselves to bat for two days. But a mixture of over-attacking batting and Australia's best bowling and fielding of the series saw them out for 349 at stumps, despite at one time being 163 for one through a second-wicket stand of 105 by Broad and Gatting. Broad was the one batsman who played the bowling strictly on its merits, while making due allowance for the foibles of the pitch. He demonstrated the right combination of patience and sound method to produce a lengthy innings, showing the bowlers the full face of the bat and waiting for the ball to drive. His 112 took 328 minutes, although Sleep played a part in fanning the impatience of the batsmen by bowling most of his overs round the wicket into the rough outside leg stump.

Australia, starting their second innings on the third morning with a deficit of 208, were never on course for the score of 450 that would have made a match of it. Border's dismissal at 113 after 85 minutes' resistance, superbly caught by Emburey at third slip after driving at a widish ball from Small, wrecked their chances. Not until Marsh was run out by Edmonds in the covers, however, did England have prospects of an innings win. Unsettled by being given the benefit of the doubt by umpire French earlier that over, when a ball from Emburey bounced from his gloves to Athey at short leg, Marsh was sent back by Waugh after embarking on a risky single and never had a hope. He had batted determinedly for 213 minutes. On his departure Australia lost their will to battle on. The last six wickets fell for 41 in 80 minutes to the spin of Emburey and Edmonds; just 40 minutes after tea the game was over, leaving the Australian Board to rue attendance figures that were 125,000 down on those of 1982–83.

Toss: England. **Australia 141** (D. M. Jones 59, G. C. Small 5-48, I. T. Botham 5-41)
and 194 (G. R. Marsh 60); **England 349** (B. C. Broad 112, C. J. McDermott 4-83, B. A. Reid 4-78).

NOTES BY THE EDITOR

Graeme Wright, 1987

Has there ever been an Australian side as weak as that beaten by England this past winter? Yet there are players with the potential to be good. What is missing, it seems, is the tempering of that potential before it is exposed to international cricket. The place for that is not in the succession of airport terminals and one-day internationals through which the leading Australian cricketers pass each season. It is in a healthy domestic first-class competition. In 1985–86 the Australian selectors called 24 players to the colours. State sides once proud with great names are frequently bare of current Australian players caught up in the commercial whirlpool of international cricket, simply to satisfy the TV mogul and his marketing minions.

Fifth Test

At Sydney, January 10, 11, 12, 14, 15, 1987. Australia won by 55 runs.

When, with one over left, Sleep bowled Emburey to complete Australia's first Test win in more than a year, it was an unexpected as well as welcome victory. Indeed, at the start of the final 20 overs England appeared to have the better chance. Recovering from the loss of four wickets in eight overs, among them Botham first ball to Taylor in his maiden Test, they had been carried to within 90 of their target by the pugnacity of Gatting with determined help from Richards in a stand of 131. Only once before had England scored more than 300 to win – at Melbourne in 1928–29 when Hobbs and Sutcliffe shared one of their most celebrated partnerships, 105 on a rain-affected pitch.

However, at 230 for five, with Australia faltering, the odds had swung their way. Even when Gatting was caught and bowled by Waugh for 96, with only another three on England's total, it was not until Sleep dismissed Richards and Edmonds with successive balls in the 11th over of the final 20 that Australia scented victory.

Small defended resolutely through seven overs until, with only 14 balls remaining, Border at first slip, one of eight men round the bat, claimed a sharp, low catch off Reid. Then, with 12,684 spectators in a state of high excitement, Sleep penetrated Emburey's defence with a grubber to give Australia their first win in 15 Tests. Of Sleep's five for 72, his best Test figures, three were taken in his last five overs as England, through neither carelessness nor lack of fight, lost five for 31 in 70 tense minutes.

If their leg-spinner delivered Australia's *coup de grâce*, however, there was no question that their hero was the 30-year-old Peter Taylor, a sandy-haired off-spinner from Sydney's Northern District club who had played only six first-class matches in his life, and only one that season, restricted to few appearances for New South Wales by their three Test spinners. So little was known about him that when Australia announced a Twelve containing only one opening batsman, Marsh, there was speculation in some quarters that he owed selection to an error in transmission, confusing him with Mark Taylor, a dour left-handed opener who had been making runs for NSW.

There was no substance to the allegations, and in a saga that developed along the lines of a story in *Boy's Own*, the unassuming Taylor gloriously vindicated the selectors' judgment, not to say courage, with a performance of such merit that he was named Man of the Match. Figures of six for 78 in England's first innings and two for 76 in the second revealed him as a thoughtful bowler with more than average powers of spin. But well as he did in his specialist department, it was his batting – angular, left-handed and blessed with common sense – that made possible Australia's win. Going in at No. 9, he batted for 244 minutes in both innings while 142 runs were scored, enabling Jones to add 111 with his last three partners in the first innings and sharing a stand of 98 with Waugh in the second when Australia's needs were even greater.

Jones, whose 184 not out in 540 minutes was his first Test hundred on home soil, was Australia's other match-winner in a game that each day produced more runs than the bowlers should have allowed on a pitch which helped spin as well as seam. Faulty umpiring contributed to that, Jones, when five, being the fortunate recipient of a benefit-of-doubt decision when Richards dived to take a leg glance and Gower, when 62, surviving an lbw appeal when Taylor got through a back-foot defensive with a straight ball which kept low. Lack of confidence appeared to be at the root of the umpires' difficulties. It was to Jones's credit that he made the most of his luck while Gower failed to, driving a half-volley to extra cover early next morning.

That England trailed by no more than 68 on first innings, bowled Australia out for 251 in their second, and came within a whisker of saving the match after Sleep's removal of Richards and Edmonds was due in large measure to Emburey, who was in the thick of things with the ball and bat for more than 14 hours of the 30. Handicapped by a strained groin for most of his 210-minute 69, he went on to take seven for 78, his best Test figures, in the second innings and finally logged another 68 minutes' batting in the last session. Like Gatting, Small and Richards, he deserved better than to finish on the losing side.

Toss: Australia. **Australia 343** (D. M. Jones 184*, G. C. Small 5-75) **and 251** (S. R. Waugh 73,
J. E. Emburey 7-78); **England 275** (D. I. Gower 72, J. E. Emburey 69, P. L. Taylor 6-78)
and 264 (M. W. Gatting 96, P. R. Sleep 5-72).

AUSTRALIA v ENGLAND 1987–88

Alan Lee

After the explosive events on the pre-Christmas tour of Pakistan, peace might well have
been the first priority for this leg of the trip. It was not, however, worthily achieved,
for England's players again allowed their on-field behaviour to plunge to unacceptable
levels. During the Australian Bicentennial Test match in Sydney, a glittering event
attended by good crowds and played in a fine spirit, Chris Broad – after batting for
more than seven hours and scoring 139 – petulantly smashed the stumps with his bat
after playing on to Waugh. His action was the mark of a man who finds it difficult to
accept dismissal, whatever his score at the time. It was nothing new to see him look
disbelieving when out, as those who saw the Pakistan tour would agree. On this occasion the England management acted promptly to fine the player £500.

*The Ashes were not at stake during this one-off match to celebrate the bicentenary of white
settlement in Australia.*

Bicentennial Test

At Sydney, January 29, 30, 31, February 1, 2, 1988. Drawn.

This would not have qualified as a memorable Test under any circumstances; but for
it to be dismissed as tedious, because it paled in contrast to other events in Australia's
colourful bicentennial celebrations, was unfair. It was destined to be an attritional affair
once England had amassed 425 and inflicted the follow-on. Australia's pride was then
salvaged by an innings from Boon, rich in discipline and defiance, spanning more than
eight hours. For the connoisseur, the cricket was absorbing until midway though the
final day, when the draw became inevitable. But it must be said that it was not a match
of great distinction or quality play; nor, considering the two sides, was it likely to be.
Australia's loudly heralded renaissance was largely based on the evidence of limited-
over competitions and they remained some way short of being a powerful five-day
side. England, despite controlling this match for much of its duration, were a team of
no great flair, and the shortcomings of their bowling were exposed when the game was
there to be won.

Recent traditions dictated that the toss would be crucial, but as it transpired, the
pitch was not as helpful to spin as had been anticipated. Gatting was right to bat first.
Australia were unfortunate to go unrewarded through the first session, in which three
catches were missed and the bat was beaten on numerous occasions. McDermott was
especially unlucky. Sleep, the leg-spinner, broke the opening stand, but Robinson then
played with refreshing authority. Broad was past 100 by the close, his fourth hundred,
on separate grounds, in only six Tests in Australia. Only one other Englishman, John
Edrich, had made Test centuries on four Australian grounds.

Broad achieved rightful acclaim for his feat, yet sacrificed it early on the second day by reacting to his dismissal in a childish manner. Bowled off his body by Waugh, he flattened the leg stump with a violently swung bat. It was a petulant gesture quite without logic, for he had been fortunate to survive several torrid periods on the opening day and, in 434 minutes at the crease, had never played with complete conviction. The tour manager instantly applied the maximum available fine and Broad was warned that any future transgression would result in sterner punishment.

This incident detracted from another good day for England, who progressed to their formidable total through useful contributions right down the order. Six wickets fell to the spinners, which was more than England's pair of slow bowlers achieved in the subsequent three days. Australia lost Boon, Marsh and Border early on the third day, Capel taking two wickets with indifferent balls, and they were reduced to a defensive operation from then on. The pre-lunch session on the fourth day was the tensest of the game as Australia crept to within 12 runs of avoiding the follow-on before a marvellously acrobatic catch by Foster at mid-on denied them. With a little more than five sessions left, England should have expected to win. The pitch, however, was becoming slower and less co-operative by the hour. Australia seemed suddenly to remember they were playing Test and not one-day cricket, and, to frustrate England further, the weather again deteriorated.

Almost two hours had been lost to bad light on the third evening; another 90 minutes were sacrificed on the fourth when Gatting, unintelligently, recalled Dilley in failing light. With Boon and Marsh resuming in the same immovable mood, England's chance quickly disappeared on the final day. Boon, unrecognisable from the loose, diffident player who had failed so often a year earlier, hit his highest Test score, his sixth hundred for Australia, and remained unbeaten to the end, having faced 431 balls and hit 14 fours. England ended disappointed and, with both their strike bowlers, Foster and Dilley, off the field injured, in some disarray.

Toss: England. **England 425** (B. C. Broad 139, P. L. Taylor 4-84); **Australia 214** (D. M. Jones 56) **and 328-2** (D. C. Boon 184*, G. R. Marsh 56).

ENGLAND V AUSTRALIA – THE BRAND LEADER?   Matthew Engel, 1989

The first Australian team to visit England after the war was welcomed in the 1948 *Wisden* by Vivian Jenkins, who described Tests between the two nations as an ever-recurring wonder that stirs the blood of each succeeding generation as they see it come to light anew. Jenkins's generation had just suffered a conflict infinitely more important than any game, and there was indeed a sense of wonder about the renewal of cricket. The Editor's Notes that year, referring to the 1947 season, were headed "A Wonderful Season", and the sub-headings included "Bowlers of Many Types", "Batsmen Excel", "Close Finishes" and "Great Crowds". Despite the present Editor's best intentions, the 1989 edition is inevitably a little less upbeat.

This is, in part, the penalty for more than 40 years of peace. Sport has fallen into a routine. Every four years – immediately after leap year, the American presidential election and the quadrennial shellacking of English cricket by West Indies – the Australians arrive. Is that such a big deal any more?

Modern cricket, professional and problematical, cannot recapture the delight people felt in the late 1940s simply in being alive and, incidentally, involved in the game again. We have come to take the good things in life for granted. Players and journalists secretly rejoice when a tour is cancelled because it gives them a break. Meanwhile, cricket has become a competing brand name in the leisure industry; it has to be sponsored, marketed and packaged for TV.

England v Australia is a product. And if it remains the brand leader, it is hard to pretend that is anything to do with superior quality. It is highly improbable that the series this summer will be won by the world's best team. If *Which?* magazine was conducting a survey, it would probably rate India v New Zealand a better buy. And yet. Ad-men understand better than anybody the importance of mystique, and in cricket we are absolute suckers for it. Somehow this spring is a little different from last spring, the one before and the one before that. The first grass cuttings smell just a mite sweeter; the tang of anticipation is that tiny bit keener. The Ashes are at stake. In spite of everything, England v Australia is an ever-recurring wonder, even in 1989.

But if it is to stay that way, we perhaps ought to understand the phenomenon a little better. It is probably 28 years since the two teams met as the best cricket teams on earth. Even so, there have been a stack of series and individual games since then that have stirred the blood in a way no other contest could have.

Part of this is because, somehow, England and Australia understand each other's cricket. Thinking about this, I wondered whether this might be something to do with the unfashionable concept of kith'n'kin. But it is not. That rapport is never there with the New Zealanders. Lovely people, of course – but on a tour of New Zealand it soon becomes clear that everyone there would be far more interested if you were playing rugby or, worse, a best-of-50 one-day series. With England and Australia, there is a shared instinct. For more than a century, cricket's founder-nations have managed to rub along together. The relationship has often been terse, even gruff, because both countries prefer it that way. But when problems have arisen – Bodyline, the chuckers and drag artists of the '50s, even the Packer intervention – they have been settled in the end with a mutual regard and sympathy.

It happens that in the 1980s there has been a great deal of personal friendship between the dressing-rooms. This is partly a reaction to the sledging '70s, and partly due to the personal qualities of the leading players of the era, Allan Border in particular. We have grown used to the sight of Australia's captain playing for Essex, though it would have been inconceivable for his predecessors. On the whole, I am inclined to think that it is a precedent which ought not to be encouraged. This is nothing to do with the desperate theory that England's prospects of winning Tests are being ruined by the small number of overseas players now allowed to appear in county cricket. It is everything to do with the freshness that Australians still bring to every fourth English summer.

Dean Jones, who was established as one of the world's leading players until he lost form in 1988, is still only a rumour to most English cricket-watchers. Ditto Bruce Reid. One feels that the appeal of the West Indians, for instance, would have been infinitely greater through the 1980s if the sight of Richards and Marshall had been rationed, instead of being on offer seven days a week, summer after summer, to those who bothered to turn up at Taunton and Southampton.

Australian touring teams really do arrive still, unlike Indians and West Indians who sort of coalesce over the course of a few days from exotic winter quarters in places like Oldham. Even with the Aussies, it is not quite the same as in the old days, when the liner would dock at Tilbury, and Woodfull or Bradman would stand on a windswept quayside in a full-length mackintosh and make a brief but graceful speech (having had a month on board for preparation, with only formal dinners and deck quoits as distractions) about making friends, playing bright cricket and winning the series.

Nowadays, the players arrive at Heathrow, shortly after finishing their latest set of utterly forgettable one-dayers against somebody or other. They will be driven to a hotel in central London and troop into a function room, probably with chandeliers. The team will be green-blazered, bleary-eyed, unshaven; if precedent is followed exactly, one or two may be suffering from very severe hangovers indeed. The captain will then make a brief but graceful speech about making friends, playing bright cricket and winning the series.

It is not necessary for anyone to believe this, even the captain. After all, in the past 25 years, Australia have won only one series in Britain – on the hastily arranged tour of 1975. However, he is probably being utterly insincere only if he says he intends to win all the county matches as well. The Australian tour, alone of them all, still retains a sense of occasion outside the Tests; it remains an event when the team arrives in Northampton or Southampton. It would be an event in Hove or Canterbury, too, but this year Kent and Sussex are likely to get a fixture only by being knocked out of the NatWest Trophy before the semi-finals, which is not something they are going to contrive on purpose. Among spectators, the enthusiasm remains; but it represents the triumph of hope and folk-memory over recent experience. The 1977, 1981 and 1985 Australians played 42 first-class matches between them outside the Tests and drew 31 of them. The last two visiting teams were unbeaten in first-class matches outside the Tests, just as the 1953 team was. It would be nice to see this as a tribute to their strength. Unfortunately, it has more to do with a truncated fixture list, appalling weather and pathetic attitudes on the part of both touring teams and counties.

I hereby propose a minor amendment to either the Laws of the Game or the tour conditions, to apply to (a) any touring captain who says he would have declared but thought that so-and-so needed the batting practice, and (b) any county captain who, on the first morning of the tourists' game, suddenly discovers that all his adult fast bowlers and front-line batsmen happen to have hay fever or groin strains; viz., that they should be taken at once to the traditional beneficiary's barbecue and served up roasted whole with the jacket potatoes.

However, these are the 1980s. If something is to be done, it will probably require a form of sponsorship. An attempt was made a decade ago, with an improbable £100,000 jackpot offered to the touring team if they won every county match. The 1980 West Indians actually got almost halfway – five wins out of 11 – towards scooping the pool before being confounded by that very wet summer. It seems to me that something similar may have to be devised again, this time with an equally juicy bone for the counties to gnaw.

Occasionally, a classic match still happens. For the opening game of first-class cricket on the 1985 tour, the Australians went to Taunton and there were 507 runs on the first day, a marvellous duel between Botham and the visiting attack, and then a burst of fast bowling from Jeff Thomson which implied that he and his team were ready to storm through the summer. It was an illusion, in various ways; but the tour as a whole was unforgettable none the less. One way or another, it always is. Pray heaven it always will be.

ENGLAND V AUSTRALIA 1989

John Thicknesse

Allan Border could hardly have dared hope for a more triumphant fourth tour of England than the one that unfolded in 1989. Arriving with a record which, though markedly better than England's since 1985, was still far from satisfactory, Australia gained such confidence from winning the First Test that when the series ended they had a right to consideration as the next strongest to West Indies in the world.

Firm favourites to keep the Ashes when the series started, an England team dogged by injuries, and further weakened by the South African defections, would in my view have been hard-pressed to hold Australia at The Oval with 12 players. The single reservation is a suspicion that the bowler who played the biggest part in England's overthrow, Terry Alderman, received undue co-operation from the umpires in respect of lbw decisions. Of Alderman's 41 wickets, which made him the only bowler twice to take 40 or more in a series, 19 were lbw compared with six bowled. Disproportionate as those figures are historically in relation to other bowlers of his type – fast-medium with movement away from the right-handers – what was in question was not, in general, the credibility of the decisions in his favour as much as the impression that, in similar circumstances, England's bowlers not infrequently seemed to be denied.

Taylor scored a half-century or more in every Test, and at Trent Bridge he broke with Marsh the record opening stand in Tests between England and Australia, their 329 beating the 323 by Jack Hobbs and Wilfred Rhodes at Melbourne in 1911–12. Taylor made 219, and of Australians only Sir Donald Bradman, with 974 in 1930, has scored more runs in a series than Taylor's 839. It was at Headingley that Waugh broke the hundred barrier. His timing had marked him as a young batsman with a future from his debut as a 20-year-old against India in 1985–86. But though he had scored his share of runs, including consecutive 90s against West Indies, his 26 successive Tests had not included a hundred. At Leeds, and in the Second Test at Lord's with a mature 152 not out, he decisively made up for it.

Defeat was a disconcerting as well as a bitter experience for England, who used 29 different players in the Test series. After losing two series each to West Indies and Pakistan since 1985, and one each to India and New Zealand, they were counting on keeping the Ashes as proof that however low they had sunk, it was not to the bottom of the heap. But it was a sobering thought that, in spite of the longest losing run in England's cricket history, the penny had still not dropped for the selectors. The weaker the raw material, the more essential it became to get the optimum XI on the field.

First Test

John Callaghan

At Leeds, June 8, 9, 10, 12, 13, 1989. Australia won by 210 runs.

England's first match under the new management team headed by Ted Dexter (the new paid chairman of the "England Committee"), and with Gower restored as captain, fell sadly into the sorry pattern of so much that had gone before in that they contributed significantly to their own downfall. It was their fourth successive defeat at Headingley, where Australia had not won since 1964.

Very much the outsiders at the start, Australia outplayed England to an embarrassing extent. England's plans were thrown into confusion by injuries to Botham and Gatting (Smith and Barnett were the replacements), but it could not be argued realistically that this misfortune had a serious influence on the outcome. More important were two major errors of judgment by Gower and his advisers. In the first place they left out Emburey, so that the attack was desperately short of variety; and, ignoring the groundsman's advice, they then gave Australia first use of an excellent pitch. The Test strip had been relaid, and although lacking in bounce, so that the occasional delivery kept low, it hardly encouraged the quicker bowlers. The decision to field first was apparently based on the theory that a build-up of cloud might allow movement through the air. In fact it was much too cold and the ball behaved predictably in every way.

All the seamers persistently bowled short and wide, offering easy runs, and no matter how he juggled his resources, Gower could not change the bowling. This remained undemanding medium-pace so long as any of his specialists were in action. Equally neither Gooch nor Barnett, with his rather rusty leg-spin, challenged the batsmen's authority. Taylor laid the foundations for a massive Australian total with a solid, patient innings. Missed by Gower at slip off Defreitas when 89, he went on to occupy the crease for 393 minutes while hitting 16 boundaries. Border provided the necessary acceleration before Jones and Waugh shared in the decisive partnership, adding 138 in 31 overs and breaking the back of the England resistance.

Waugh, wearing a cap instead of the familiar helmet, reminded many spectators of a bygone age, despatching the ball stylishly through the gaps and timing his forcing strokes so well that he brought an effortless quality to the proceedings. His unbeaten 177 – like Taylor's, his first century in Tests – included 24 fours, many of them driven gloriously off the back foot through the off side in the textbook manner. Against this onslaught, only Foster came close to achieving the essential accuracy in terms of length and line. To complete England's misery, Hughes hit out cheerfully to score 71.

When England batted Alderman, bowling very much wicket to wicket, commanded respect with his nagging accuracy and subtle variations of pace. Barnett, always looking to get on the front foot, played positively for 80 after overcoming some initial uncertainty, and Lamb held the innings together with a typical effort in the course of which he savaged anything the least bit short. His 125 included 24 fours. However, there was a distinct warning note in the collapse which followed his departure. England's last six wickets fell for 107 in 31 overs and Australia, left with a lead of 171, now looked to put the match out of reach while at the same time giving their bowlers scope to bowl England out a second time. England needed to bowl tightly and field keenly to put them under pressure. Instead they again fell into error, allowing Australia to maintain a run-rate of four an over without recourse to the unorthodox. Border and Jones were particularly effective in an unfinished partnership of 101 in 56 minutes, and Border was able to declare next morning and set England a remote 402 for victory.

The more interesting part of the equation related to the 83 overs which were available to dismiss England. In theory, the bowlers' prospects of success should have been no brighter than the batsmen's of surviving, but so feeble was England's response that Australia had 27 overs to spare in completing their task. Only Gooch, battling through

176 minutes for 68, caused Border to worry. Barnett shared in a stand worth 50 and Gower in one which added 57, both in 12 overs, but England for the most part found the straight ball unplayable.

Broad fell lbw to one that kept very low, although he made matters worse by aiming across the line with an angled bat, and too many of his colleagues pushed and prodded with a worrying lack of conviction. Gower was guilty of a particularly careless act, being caught down the leg side, glancing, as the Australians set a very obvious trap. In many ways that one incident summed up the difference between the two teams. Australia had done their homework and knew exactly what they were trying to do, whereas England lived more in hope than expectation.

Toss: England. **Australia 601-7 dec.** (M. A. Taylor 136, A. R. Border 66, D. M. Jones 79, S. R. Waugh 177*, M. G. Hughes 71) **and 230-3 dec.** (M. A. Taylor 60, A. R. Border 60*); **England 430** (K. J. Barnett 80, A. J. Lamb 125, R. A. Smith 66, T. M. Alderman 5-107) **and 191** (G. A. Gooch 68, T. M. Alderman 5-44).

Second Test

David Norrie

At Lord's, June 22, 23, 24, 26, 27, 1989. Australia won by six wickets.

Victory not only gave Border's side a 2–0 lead, a position from which England had never come back to win or even draw an Ashes series, but continued the home side's dismal record at the game's headquarters this century against their oldest rivals. England's sole success remained 1934; 21 other contests had brought Australia nine victories.

The tourists confirmed their Headingley form, while England, again badly hit by injuries, took a different route to defeat. Gower's side struggled badly for three days before staging a spirited fightback which, with a little more help from the rain on Tuesday, would have earned them a reprieve. Gower, cast as the villain for rushing out of Saturday night's press conference to go to the theatre, was hailed as a hero on Monday after his 15th Test century. But character and courage were not enough to repair the earlier damage and, despite the threat of rain and then Foster's bowling, Waugh saw Australia through to a conclusive victory just after five o'clock on Tuesday.

When Gower won the toss, England were soon reduced to 58 for three, including the loss of Gatting first ball; but Gooch and Gower added 73 in 17 overs. Gooch went shortly after reaching his 19th fifty in his last 18 first-class games, and although England recovered to 180 for four, they slumped to 191 for seven. They had tried to blast their way out of trouble. Gower's 50 came off only 54 ball, while Waugh's first four overs cost 38, a statistic more in keeping with limited-overs cricket, but the batsmen paid the price for their aggression and indiscretion. Only a disciplined innings from Russell brought back a sense of normality and saved England from total disaster. Hughes, Australia's best bowler, was warned by umpire Bird for overdoing the bouncer at the tailenders, Foster's helmet grill having already been smashed.

Australia batted in a much more sedate manner on Friday, reaching 276 for six by the close. England started and finished the day well. Russell took a brilliant diving catch to dismiss Marsh first thing, then England evened up the contest by taking four wickets in the final session. In between Boon and Taylor had added 145 for the second wicket, Boon making his highest Test score in England. Australia were within 65 of the lead with seven wickets left, but England were given a glimpse of hope when Border top-edged an attempted sweep at Emburey.

Saturday, which dawned with hope of England levelling the series, turned out to be the day the Ashes went Australia's way. By the close, England – with Gooch, Broad and Barnett gone – needed another 184 runs to avoid an innings defeat. Waugh, the tormentor at Headingley, turned torturer with an undefeated 152 (17 fours). But the real agony as the last four wickets added 263 was Lawson's highest Test score; he and Waugh put on 130 in 108 minutes, a record for Australia's ninth wicket in England. Emburey's return to form was some consolation as he took three for 28 in his 16 overs on Saturday, but Dexter's pre-Test talk of using Gooch's bowling was not reflected in Gower's captaincy. Gooch came on in the 140th over with the score at 494 for eight; his inactivity was complete when he became Alderman's 100th Test victim in the opening over of the second innings. Soon England were 28 for three and it was all over bar the shouting.

That came at the press conference when Gower, looking agitated as he entered, gave little evidence of his laid-back style in dealing with routine questions – some from former Test cricketers turned journalists – about the day's tactics. Even less dignified was his early exit, explaining there was a taxi waiting to take him to the Prince Edward Theatre for a preview of Cole Porter's *Anything Goes*. It was not a good omen; the show had originally opened on Broadway in 1934, the year the Australian last regained the Ashes in England. Gower received a reprimand, although Dexter added that the skipper still had his full confidence.

Nobody complained about Gower's performance on Monday. He had hit the ball more sweetly, but never with such determination and purpose. His first Test century since Perth in November 1986, and his bravest knock since defying West Indies in Jamaica eight years previously, ended after 269 minutes when he tried to fend off a vicious, lifting delivery from Hughes, who had not received the same words of warning about his short-pitched deliveries from umpire Plews that Bird offered on Thursday. Gower's departure just before tea did at least allow time for a quick shower and brushdown before meeting the Queen, who had arrived early because of England's precarious position. Gower and Smith put on 139 for the fifth wicket after Gatting was lbw shouldering arms, not for the first time in a Test at Lord's. Smith's display over 270 minutes was every bit as encouraging as Gower's, especially as only injury had given him his chance in the First Test. It took the ball of the day from Alderman to deny Smith a maiden Test hundred. England had been 300 for six before that delivery, but Alderman ended realistic hopes of a worthwhile lead with three wickets in 16 balls.

England's innings lasted until just after midday on Tuesday, with Dilley and Emburey adding 45 for the final wicket to leave Australia 118 for victory, just 12 fewer than they needed at Headingley in 1981, with rain threatening. Marsh failed again and a violent thunderstorm held up play until 2.25. The 7,000 crowd that stayed saw Foster take three wickets and Australia tumble to 67 for four. Nor was Foster the only hero. Eighteen-year-old Robin Sims, from the Lord's groundstaff, was made England's twelfth man in the morning. That afternoon, because of Smith's damaged hamstring, Sims ended Border's brief stay with a confident catch at long leg. But Boon and Waugh ensured there was no further upset or Headingley repeat, Waugh taking his series aggregate to 350 without loss. For Gower this was an eighth successive defeat in two spells as England captain and, despite his brave batting and just two Tests back in charge, his and Dexter's honeymoon period was well and truly over.

Toss: England. **England 286** (G. A. Gooch 60, D. I. Gower 57, R. C. Russell 64*, M. G. Hughes 4-71)
and 359 (D. I. Gower 106, R. A. Smith 96, T. M. Alderman 6-128);
Australia 528 (M. A. Taylor 62, D. C. Boon 94, S. R. Waugh 152*, G. F. Lawson 74, J. E. Emburey 4-88)
and 119-4 (D. C. Boon 58*).

Third Test

At Birmingham, July 6, 7, 8, 10, 11, 1989. Drawn.

Graham Otway

While making allowances for the poor showing of their batsmen in the opening two Tests, there was no conceivable reason why England should not have arrested their losing run once wet weather caused the loss of ten hours' play on days two and three. Yet the final morning dawned with the home side in grave danger of being forced to follow on, and only spirited tailend resistance spared them further embarrassment.

If the Australians possessed any lingering doubts about their ability to protect their 2–0 lead, they were quickly dispelled after Border won the toss. With an unchanged and confident side, he was able to choose to bat first on a placid surface while England were still trying to regroup their resources. In the hours leading up to the match, England had to reshuffle after losing Lamb, Smith and Foster to injuries, and Gatting after a family bereavement. Eleventh-hour calls went out to Jarvis, Curtis and Tavaré, whose last Test appearance had been against Sri Lanka in 1984.

In sultry conditions Dilley struggled to find his rhythm, having undergone knee surgery just a month earlier, and Jarvis bowled without confidence as Marsh and Taylor saw off the new ball in an opening stand of 88. Emburey made the breakthrough, having Taylor stumped, and Botham marked his return to Test cricket after 23 months by trapping Marsh lbw in the 13th over of his comeback. When Border, having just passed 8,000 Test runs, was bowled around his legs by Emburey, Australia were in a rare spot of trouble at 105 for three.

England's hopes of working their way back into the series ended there as Jones and Boon added 96 for the fourth wicket, parted only when Jarvis deflected a drive from Jones on to the stumps and Boon, backing up, was unluckily run out. The first day ended with Edgbaston under water after a cloudburst. Despite the impressive pitch covering, only 59 minutes' play was available late on the second day, but it brought some consolation for England when they dismissed Waugh for the first time in the series, bowled by Fraser in an impressive and accurate spell. Fraser's first Test wicket ended Waugh's remarkable run of 393 runs in four Test innings, during which time he had successfully fended off 584 other deliveries.

The third day's play was equally badly hit by the weather, with no play possible before three o'clock and only 31 overs bowled. In this time Jones took his score to 141 with a complete range of strokes which frustrated each bowler in turn. He finally fell for 157 on Monday morning well caught at deep long leg by England's substitute, Folley, and when Australia's innings finally ended at 11.50, England should not have been stretched to bat out the game for a draw.

However, Alderman, with support from the other seamers, quickly reduced England to 75 for five. The situation called for a rescue act from Botham, and with intrepid help from Russell he rallied England. Curbing his natural aggression, Botham batted two and a half hours for 46 before his patience eventually gave way and he was bowled through the gate by the eager Hughes. Russell was out an over later to the leg-spinner Hohns, and England entered the final day still 40 short of avoiding the follow-on with only three wickets in hand. This immediately became two when Fraser was run out in the first over of the morning, but Dilley played responsibly, Emburey and Jarvis scored valuable runs in less orthodox but effective fashion, and the danger was averted.

With Australia's lead 182 and 72 overs left, there was some conjecture that Border would send his batsmen out for a quick thrash, declare and still find time to heap further misery on England. He ignored the temptation and opted instead for practice, content with a moral victory and the knowledge that England were in further disarray.

Toss: Australia. **Australia 424** (D. M. Jones 157, A. R. C. Fraser 4-63)
and **158-2** (M. A. Taylor 51); **England 242.**

Fourth Test

Don Mosey

At Manchester, July 27, 28, 29, 31, August 1, 1989. Australia won by nine wickets.

Australia's win gave them the series and the Ashes, and Border thus became the first captain since W. M. Woodfull in 1934 to win them back in England. It was a success which was all the more noteworthy because few people in this country had given the tourists much chance of victory when the party was first announced.

Paradoxically, England played more positively on the third and fifth days than they had at any stage of the series so far, and centuries were scored by Smith and Russell who, apart from keeping wicket immaculately and at times spectacularly, registered a maiden first-class hundred, the fourth Englishman to do so in a Test. It was a game played not only beneath the familiar Manchester clouds but also others of an even more threatening nature hovering over the England captain. Gower had been the object of an increasingly virulent campaign in some newspapers since the first defeat of the series, and even the more sober and responsible journals had expressed disquiet at what seemed to be a lack of positive leadership. Gower's resignation after four Tests appeared to be unavoidable before salvation came from an unexpected quarter. On the final morning came formal confirmation that 16 players had signed up for a disapproved tour of South Africa, thus effectively debarring themselves from international cricket for seven years.

Three of the players – Robinson, Emburey and Foster – were involved in this Test; a fourth, Dilley, had been selected but was unfit on the first morning. Five of the others had already played in this series. This, then, was the atmosphere in which the haunted Gower won *two* tosses of the coin half an hour before play began. One gave him the prerogative of batting first on a pitch which, like the previous three, had been prepared specifically to last five days and not much else. The other was to decide to use the Reader ball rather than the Duke, which was the Australians' preference. In the event, this seemed to have little effect on the game. The fallibility of England's leading batsmen was once again evident, and this time it was the quicker though less subtle bowling of Lawson which brought about the downfall. Smith, with noble help from Foster later on, scored his first hundred for England, and apart from one fiendishly difficult chance to gully, he rarely appeared to be in trouble in almost six hours at the crease. It was a fine innings by any standards; amid the fragility of so many more experienced players it was outstanding. Sadly, it was not destined to inspire his senior colleagues to more assertive efforts in the second innings.

Australia again approached their reply with the air of men with a specific sense of purpose. Border showed a keen eye for detail in his forward, long-term planning, as well as in the more immediate tasks of dealing with each opponent on his merits. All too clearly he had done his homework industriously – in the Bradman manner, dare one say? Field-placing was carried out with a certain knowledge of technical short-comings and weaknesses. His bowlers, not the most penetrative, potent or gifted to leave Australia's shores, did their work like honest craftsmen by bowling the right line and length. Little more but nothing less.

Throughout Saturday afternoon Border's intentions were very clear indeed: to pass England's total with wickets to spare, to achieve as big a lead as possible without heroics or exhibitionism, and to present the opposition with an impossibly uphill struggle. Border ground out his own 80 with an ominous inevitability, and Taylor played a similar role with 85 from 180 balls. That left Jones and Waugh (again!) to please the spectators, if not the chauvinists, with their panache. Australia achieved a lead of 187 on the fourth morning and before lunch had destroyed what last quivering remnants of morale might have remained in the English dressing-room. . . 10 for one, 25 for two, 27 for three, 28 for four. After the interval Botham went (38 for five) and then Gower, the cares of the world on his bowed shoulders, departed for 15 (59 for six).

Russell and Emburey were together when rain, it seemed, prevented a premature end to the decisive Test. Incredibly, they were still together through the following morning's session in sunlight, and they remained together in the afternoon until Emburey finally left for 64, having batted for 220 minutes in probably his last innings for England. Russell valiantly battled on to the end, forcing Australia to bat again in search of 78 to win. It was little short of tragic that Russell's 351 minutes' representation of English cricketing pride should be squeezed into far fewer column inches than it deserved, overshadowed instead by the announcement of the South African venture. But Australia, their own problems of banned tourists to South Africa behind them, could rejoice in the recovery of the Ashes. That so clearly meant more to Australia than the loss of them appeared to mean to England.

Toss: England. **England 260** (R. A. Smith 143, G. F. Lawson 6-72) **and 264** (R. C. Russell 128*, J. E. Emburey 64, T. M. Alderman 5-66); **Australia 447** (M. A. Taylor 85, A. R. Border 80, D. M. Jones 69, S. R. Waugh 92) **and 81-1**.

CRICKETER OF THE YEAR – JACK RUSSELL Colin Bateman, 1990

At the beginning of 1989, Jack Russell had played only one Test for England and was not considered a good enough batsman to merit a place in the one-day squad to face the Australians. By the end of the year he was the only Englishman who could justifi-ably expect a place in anyone's World XI.

In the course of a summer of England mediocrity on the field, and damaging South African recruitment off it, Russell sailed serenely through the storm, proving he could reproduce his supreme wicket-keeping performances for Gloucestershire in the intensity of Test cricket. He was one of only two ever-presents in the England side (the other was the captain, David Gower).

Robert Charles Russell was born in Stroud on August 15, 1963. Two days before his 14th birthday, he saw a catch on TV that changed his life. "McCosker. . . caught Knott. . . bowled Greig, Headingley '77." He reels it off as if it were yesterday. "Low down, one-handed, across first slip. Brilliant. I thought then that I would like to be able to do that. That's where it started, that was the inspiration."

Russell was soon a boy among men in Stroud's first team alongside his father, and within four years he was keeping wicket for Gloucestershire. Like Knott, Russell, in his floppy white hat and taped-up pads, looks as dishevelled as a truant schoolboy behind the stumps, but he is immaculate in his preparation and work. He has the fitness of a jump jockey and the finesse of a fencer. And like most wicket-keepers – as with goal-keepers in soccer – he is cheerfully self-contained: an independent spirit in a team game. He eats nothing but steak and chips on tour – not always easy in the likes of Nagpur and Gwalior – and when he wants to relax, it is not with the headphones and lager can to which most of his colleagues turn. Rather it is an adventure out into the local surroundings, whether that be the tranquil banks of the Severn in Worcester or the teeming shanty towns of Bombay, sketchbook, pencil and camera in hand. Russell had discovered a penchant for drawing, and the hobby he took up to pass the time on rain-affected English summer afternoons has become a second profession.

Fifth Test

Martin Johnson

At Nottingham, August 10, 11, 12, 14, 1989. Australia won by an innings and 180 runs.

The bad luck which seems to accompany a side guilty of bad play (or should it be the other way round?) struck again when Small withdrew on the eve of the match, thus preserving England's 100% record of being unable to choose from the originally selected squad in every Test in 1989. This left them with the inexperienced new-ball pairing of Fraser, playing in his third Test, and Malcolm, winning his first cap. Atherton was the only other debutant, the selectors having responded to calls for a major transfusion of new blood with little more than a smear.

On a flat, grassless pitch expected to assist the spinners as the match wore on, England named both Cook and Hemmings, and Cook it was who took the first Australian wicket. As it arrived at 12 minutes past 12 on the second day, this was not a matter for great rejoicing. Border won an important toss, and then spent the best part of four sessions joining in the applause as Marsh and Taylor went past numerous records in their opening partnership of 329. The milestones began just after lunch on the first day with the comparatively modest figure of 89 – Australia's previous-highest opening partnership at Trent Bridge – and ended at 323, the highest by any two opening batsmen in Ashes history, a record that had stood to Jack Hobbs and Wilfred Rhodes since 1911-12. Moreover, by stumps on Thursday, Marsh and Taylor had become the first pair to bat through a full day's play in a Test in England, and only the ninth in Test cricket anywhere.

Taylor continued his remarkable summer with a career-best 219 in 550 minutes (461 balls, 23 fours) to take his series aggregate to 720 runs at an average of 90. Only three Australian totals in Ashes history remained above that, all of them by Don Bradman. Despite the fact that Australia eventually put together 602 for six declared, their highest at Trent Bridge, England for once had not totally let themselves down. Malcolm bowled with genuine hostility when fresh, the batsmen's apprehension augmented by the fact that Malcolm's uncertainty as to where the ball was going led to several accidental beamers. Fraser's contrasting accuracy allowed him to bowl for a quarter of the innings at a cost of no more than two per over, and Cook rediscovered the flight and control that had deserted him in the previous Test. Nor did the fielding, as it had on previous occasions, disintegrate.

With the notable exception of Smith, however, there was not much consolation from the batting. The first wicket went down after four deliveries (740 fewer than England had required to remove the first Australian), and when Atherton made a second-ball debut duck, Smith arrived for the second over with the score one for two. His strokeplay, particularly around the off stump, was little short of ferocious. Hughes took a beating, and a pull off Hohns resulted in Boon, at short leg, literally having the helmet torn from his head. It was a miracle that he was helped off in need of nothing more than a couple of aspirin and a lie-down.

Smith's magnificent 150-ball century none the less stood alone amid another familiarly depressing tale. Such was England's gruesome technique that Australia had little more to do than bowl at the stumps, certain in the knowledge that sooner or later either a crooked bat would miss the ball or a front pad – planted not far enough down the pitch to confuse the umpire – would get in its way. England had suffered more bad luck when Botham dislocated a finger on his right hand, failing to take a sharp chance in the slips. Coming in at No. 9 he could bat more or less only one-handed, and having already been informed that the injury would prevent him from playing at The Oval, he did not bat in the second innings.

Following on 347 behind on Monday morning, England were bowled out for 167 soon after tea. Atherton, batting almost three hours for 47, was the one batsman to make a half-decent fist of it. Only once before, to Bradman's 1948 side, had England lost four home Tests in an Ashes series, and the final ignominy in the statistical avalanche was the fact that the margin of defeat was England's heaviest by Australia at home.

Toss: Australia. **Australia 602-6 dec.** (G. R. Marsh 138, M. A. Taylor 219, D. C. Boon 73, A. R. Border 65*, extras 61); **England 255** (R. A. Smith 101, T. M. Alderman 5-69) **and 167.**

CRICKETER OF THE YEAR – MARK TAYLOR   John Coomber, 1990

It was no coincidence that Australia's record sequence of first-innings totals of 400 or more in nine consecutive Test matches in 1989 began with Mark Taylor's arrival on the scene. The sturdily built left-hander from New South Wales was the missing link the selectors had been seeking, even though it meant breaking up the previously successful combination of Geoff Marsh and David Boon to accommodate him. The critical point in Taylor's favour was his left-handedness, which allowed a return to the left- and right-hand opening combination advocated by Australia's coach, Bob Simpson, whose own partnership with southpaw Bill Lawry in the 1960s had been so prolific.

Before his arrival in England, Taylor was virtually unknown outside Australia, apart perhaps from his unwitting role in the confusion that followed the selection of his off-spinning club and state team-mate, Peter Taylor, for the Sydney Test against England in January 1987. (Mark believed for three hours that he was in the Test team.) Born in Leeton on October 27, 1964, Mark Anthony Taylor learned the basics of batting while his father threw cork compo balls to him in the concrete garage of their home in Wagga Wagga, where the family had moved when Mark was eight. The family cricketing hero was Arthur Morris, the great NSW left-hand opener, whose 1948 aggregate of 696 runs Taylor passed in the Fifth Test at Trent Bridge. Morris wrote to congratulate him.

Sixth Test

David Field

At The Oval, August 24, 25, 26, 28, 29, 1989. Drawn.

An autumnal gloom descended on Kennington like a symbolic final curtain to close yet another English summer of despair and emphatic failure. The deteriorating visibility concluded the one-sided series with 20.5 overs remaining and spared England from an outside chance of another beating by an ultra-professional side seeking to embellish its regaining of the Ashes with a fifth victory. It was widely believed that Gower would resign the captaincy the new selection chairman, Ted Dexter, had conferred on him with great expectations 146 days earlier. Instead, Gower said he would ponder his position and then discuss his future with the selectors. Dexter himself amazed a defeat-saddened nation by insisting, during his post-match oratory, "I am not aware of any mistakes I've made."

Injury, which had disrupted every England selection during the series, reached a chaotic level and stretched the fast-bowling resources to their limit. Malcolm suffered a back spasm and was ruled out; his replacement, DeFreitas, pulled a hamstring; Fraser withdrew with the niggling effects of the knee he injured at Nottingham; and Thomas informed the selectors that he was joining the unofficial South African tour as the replacement for DeFreitas. Ultimately Igglesden, of Kent, was recruited for his Test debut 24 hours before the match, and Pringle was recalled. Stephenson, the Essex opening batsman, was included for the first time, and Small finally took the place pencilled in for him at Trent Bridge. This increased to 29 the number of players used by England in the series, second only to the 30 called upon in the five Tests of 1921.

Australia, meanwhile, were able to observe these problems from a distance and named an unchanged side for the fifth time in succession. They also won the toss, and took first use of a splendid, straw-coloured pitch. Well before the end of the first day, England were facing a depressingly familiar uphill climb. The indomitable Taylor rendered the new-look attack as impotent as its predecessors. A rare error brought his downfall for 71, and when Boon was taken at third slip by Atherton, England could feel relatively pleased with 149 for three. However, Border and Jones ruthlessly added 176 in an untroubled manner before the close, Border supplying measured solidity and the highly competitive Jones providing brilliance and aggression as he completed his sixth Test hundred in just 119 balls.

Having amassed two 600s, a 500 and two 400s in their previous first innings, Australia were again in a position to maximise their advantage. And Border, resuming with 66, seemed poised for a first hundred of the series to crown his Ashes triumph. It was not to be. England enjoyed one of their rare sustained periods of dominance and captured the last seven wickets for 143, Pringle claiming four of them. The decline was triggered by Border's uncharacteristic leg-side flick at Capel's first ball of the day, which lobbed gently to Russell. The stand had produced 196. Next Jones, having hit 17 fours, departed to an outstanding left-handed slip catch by Gower, and Waugh was bowled off the inside edge. Healy, undeterred, provided a bristling run-a-ball 44 to help Australia advance to the still-imposing total of 468. Bad light and rain halted play for the day at 3.05, but not before Gooch had been lbw to Alderman in the first over.

Stephenson and Atherton revived England's morale with 44 minutes of fighting cricket on the third morning, but Alderman returned to the field after taking oxygen to counter a bronchial complaint and removed the middle order either side of lunch. Gower, however, emerged from the wreckage, unbeaten with 43 when rain prevented any play after 3.25, his innings made with the air of a man shortly to be reprieved after a summer of unmitigating stress and struggle. At the start of the fourth day, England, with four wickets in hand, still needed 145 to avoid the follow-on. Gower charmed the big Bank Holiday crowd with an array of sumptuous strokes in his 79 before flashing unwisely at a leg-side ball and giving Alderman his sixth five-wicket analysis of the series. England owed their eventual survival to Small, who pluckily fought a successful rearguard action for two and a quarter hours and was rewarded with a best Test score of 59. Cook stayed with him while a vital 73 were added for the ninth wicket.

Australia led by 183 and still had sufficient time to embarrass England. With Taylor, the epitome of confidence, orchestrating affairs once more, their advantage was stretched to 270 by the close, prompting speculation on the timing of Border's declaration. In the event, he gave his bowlers four hours in which to win the match, closing at lunch with a lead of 402 when, arguably, he could have declared an hour earlier. Taylor's aggregate came to rest at 839, the second-highest by an Australian and third-best in Test history after Bradman's 974 and W. R. Hammond's 905. When, at tea, England were 67 for four in the 27th over, Border's strategy had high chances of succeeding. But Smith confirmed his status as England's premier batsman of the series with a fearless 77 not out, his fifty arriving in just 66 balls, before the bad light brought an early end to the summer's international programme.

Toss: Australia. **Australia 468** (M. A. Taylor 71, A. R. Border 76, D. M. Jones 122, D. R. Pringle 4-70) **and 219-4 dec.** (A. R. Border 51*, D. M. Jones 50); **England 285** (D. I. Gower 79, G. C. Small 59, T. M. Alderman 5-66) **and 143-5** (R. A. Smith 77*).

NOTES BY THE EDITOR
Graeme Wright, 1990

Last season, as England were handsomely and decisively beaten by a well-prepared Australian team, I could see no reason, other than wounded nationalism, for the hollering and head-hunting that followed each Test defeat. What was new? In the four years I have been writing these Notes, England have lost every home series, beaten by India,

New Zealand, Pakistan, West Indies and now Australia. Only victory in a one-off Test against Sri Lanka interrupts the sorry tale of England's failure to win a Test at home since 1985.

Nothing had changed to indicate it would be any different in 1989. All that happened was that the Australians were better than many had expected. And yet, man for man, were they that much better than England's cricketers at the start of the series? It was in their attitude and their approach that they were superior. They played with a purpose that was missing from England's players. As Allan Border once said of his own team, they had forgotten the reason for playing Test cricket: the feeling of national pride.

Not that David Gower, England's captain, would have said such a thing. It was not his style – and as Ted Dexter said when announcing that Gower would captain England, he was looking to him to set the tone and style for the team. For the man who, at the end of the series, said he was not aware of any errors that he made, this was probably his first mistake.

It is the call for tone and style which interests me, for in the context of England performances in recent seasons, character and not style was the requirement. The two are not synonymous, though it has often seemed to me that in England style is mistaken for character. By character I mean mettle: a combination of ability, mental toughness and judgment. Style is apparent; and it has its place in, among other things, the arts, in the art of batting, in fashion and in good manners. Nevertheless, when inner reserves are required, it is character and not style which sees one through. Gower has shown this in his batting; his leadership has never been so clear-cut. It has been said of him that the quality of life is important to him, but it has seemed sometimes that it is the quality of his own life which is important: his lifestyle. When defeat began to sour his life, Gower was not able to dig deep into his own character to make his players respond to the crisis. Instead, they were carried along by the air of despondency which enveloped him. It was not the tone and style Dexter had envisaged.

AUSTRALIA V ENGLAND 1990–91

John Thicknesse

England were badly beaten in Australia, and against a strong and well-knit team they might well have suffered the same fate even had luck been on their side. In the event, deprived of Graham Gooch, the captain, for a month spanning the First Test, Allan Lamb, another mainstay of the batting, for the Second and Third Tests, and Angus Fraser, the best bowler, for the Third and Fifth, they were never in contention.

It was apparent from the start that to recover the Ashes, won so convincingly by Australia in 1989, a minimum of six players had to strike their best form and maintain it. When that condition was not met, it was predictable that the upshot should be a series dominated by Australia. Admirably led by Allan Border, they won 3–0 on merit, England's one minor consolation being that, unlike in 1989, there were moments in each Test when the initiative was theirs. Contrary to expectation, batting was the chief weakness. Collapses developed from the unlikeliest positions early on, and became habitual long before the tour ended.

Using 14 players in the series, compared with England's 16, and reinforced by the return of Reid, the 6ft 8in fast left-armer, Australia were even more impressive than in the previous Ashes series, despite the fact that Taylor, Jones and Steve Waugh, the batting successes in England, scored only 458 runs between them in 21 innings. Waugh was dropped midway through the series after an unbroken run of 42 Tests since his first appearance. Mark Waugh, replacing his elder twin, gave 17,000 Adelaide spectators memories for life with a maiden hundred that, for balance, footwork, timing and variety of stroke, stood comparison with any century in a Test between the countries since the end of the Second World War.

Gooch's absence from November 10, when he had an operation on a poisoned hand, to mid-December was far and away the most damaging of England's many injuries: indeed, a blow from which they never recovered. It stemmed from what seemed an insignificant injury. Attempting a return catch in the opening practice game, Gooch gashed the fourth finger of his right hand below the lower knuckle. Though the cut was deep enough to expose the bone, the doctor who inspected it decided that stitches were unnecessary, and used butterfly tape to hold the skin together. All seemed well when Gooch suffered no reaction for more than a fortnight. In this time he played nine days of cricket, only to feel acute pain while batting in the nets during the South Australia match at Adelaide. The initial diagnosis then was that the finger had turned septic; but a second examination, carried out in hospital, revealed that the poison had spread dangerously to the palm of Gooch's hand, which was operated on that evening.

First Test

At Brisbane, November 23, 24, 25, 1990. Australia won by ten wickets.

A Test which looked evenly balanced after two days ended in an astonishingly easy win for Australia on the evening of the third, following a familiar England collapse in the face of Alderman. Outshone by Reid in the first innings, he bowled his outswing with excellent control to take six for 47, his best Test figures. Yet future generations will surely wonder how Marsh and Taylor scored 157 without being parted, a ground record against England, to complete Australia's win after the first three innings had yielded just 194, 152 and 114. The short answer is that England had no bowler to match Alderman or Reid, and that by the third day the pitch had belatedly turned in favour of the bat. Australia reached their target at 3.41 runs per over, the fastest scoring of the match by nearly one an over. In effect the game had begun a day too early.

In humid weather after a rainy night, which had turned the pitch green under its tarpaulin covers, there was enough moisture to make Border's decision to field a formality. Enough remained on the second day for England, bowling well and catching brilliantly, to find themselves with an unexpected lead, but the position was deceptive in that nearly every uppish stroke had gone to hand. Moreover, England's good fortune was to rebound on them. Batting again before the pitch was fully dry, they lost three wickets before the close.

Gooch's absence was a huge blow to England, both in psychological terms and the loss of the runs he might have scored. But with the ball swinging and seaming as it did, there was nothing to be ashamed of in their first-day batting, disappointing as it was to make only 194 after reaching 117 before the third wicket, that of Lamb, fell. The acting captain's 32 took him past 4,000 Test runs and 25,000 in first-class cricket. Had Gower not used up three innings' worth of luck in making 61, however, England's limit might well have been 150. Smith, yorked by a fast inducker from Reid, was the victim of the day's most fiendish ball, while Border took a lovely catch, right-handed at second slip, to see the back of Lewis.

Australia's troubles on the Saturday began in the second over when Fraser had Marsh lbw with a ball that straightened. Then, 39 minutes later, Lewis in the gully took a firmly hit square-cut by Taylor with sublime ease, and the pattern of the day was set. Of seven later chances, six were taken, among them outstanding efforts at mid-off by Small and at cover by Smith, and two very droppable ones by Atherton at second slip. Australia had every right to be dissatisfied with their batting. Only Matthews, back in favour after four years, and Healy played as the situation demanded, in a stand of 46. Nevertheless the ball did run badly for them.

Reid struck an immediate blow in the second innings when Larkins, who had fielded only in the later stages because of an infected tooth, went back to a full-length inswinger first ball and was lbw. Even so, England were in sight of finishing the day strongly placed until, in the last half-hour, Atherton lost his off stump to an unplayable late outswinger from Alderman, and Gower, in the next over, dragged a wide ball from Hughes into his stumps. It was the second time in the match that Gower had been out in the over after the loss of an important wicket, both times to strokes of poor conception. When next morning Lamb was lbw to the sixth ball of the first over, mistakenly on the back foot, England had lost three wickets for 18 runs. With the exception of the night watchman, Russell, who stayed for 116 minutes, they subsided without fight.

Toss: Australia. **England 194** (D. I. Gower 61, B. A. Reid 4-53) **and 114** (T. M. Alderman 6-47); **Australia 152 and 157-0** (M. A. Taylor 67*, G. R. Marsh 72*).

Second Test

At Melbourne, December 26, 27, 28, 29, 30, 1990. Australia won by eight wickets.

A hard-fought match of many fluctuations was won by Australia with surprising ease. They were apparently in difficulties at 28 for two at the start of the last day, but Marsh and Boon scored the remaining 169 in five hours without being parted. It was an excellent, singleminded piece of batting on a slow, low bouncing pitch, and showed what could be done by concentrating on strokes which could be played with a straight bat. Had England's batsmen followed the same principles, the best Australia could have hoped for would have been a draw; instead they indulged in what the manager Micky Stewart, in understandable irritation, described as 50 minutes of madness after tea on the fourth day, when Reid and Matthews shared six wickets in 12 overs while three runs were scored.

Reid, who had never taken more than four wickets in an innings in 19 Tests, came out of his 20th with six for 97 and seven for 51, without seeming to bowl any better than when he took two for 101 for Western Australia at the beginning of the tour. His height, deceptive changes of pace, left-arm-over angle and control made him a bowler any team would welcome. Yet there was little sign of the inswing that gave England such problems at Perth and in the First Test. At Melbourne he slanted the ball across the batsmen and waited for mistakes: nine of his wickets came from catches off the outside edge from balls missing the off stump. For England, Gower made his eighth hundred against Australia and 17th in all Tests, despite a badly bruised right wrist, and Fraser returned his best figures in Test cricket, six for 82, at the expense of a hip injury in a marathon of 39 overs. This was the first match played at the MCG since the demolition of the Southern Stand, which reduced capacity to 60,000 and opened up a view of leafy Yarra Park. The removal of this 200-yard windbreak may have added to the ball's reluctance to swing.

When Atherton and Gooch were dismissed in the first 40 minutes, the captain shouldering arms to an incoming ball from Alderman, England were in danger of wasting a good toss. But Larkins, who would have lost his place had Lamb been fit, spent three and three-quarter hours patiently building a platform for recovery before giving Healy the second of five first-innings catches, nibbling at Reid. Gower, taking painkillers, was smoothly in command, and added 122 with the impetuous but lucky Stewart before being caught off the splice, mistiming a leg-side turn two balls after completing his hundred. He had batted for 254 minutes. Though Stewart lasted another 100 minutes, surviving a fast and short-pitched spell from Hughes, the last five wickets added only 78.

Solid batting by Taylor (256 minutes) and Border (239), plus a cameo by Jones, whose pattering 44 from 57 balls was by far the fastest scoring of the game, looked to have given Australia control when they were 259 for four at tea on the third day. However, Fraser, armed with a new ball, straightened one to hit Waugh's off stump two overs afterwards. And spurred by a piece of luck 37 minutes later, when Border was caught off a leg glance, he bowled unchanged until the close to earn England a lead of 46. Wicket to wicket his spell was six for 23 in 13.4 overs, and on the day he took six for 34 off 26, a workload that stirred memories for the watching Alec Bedser.

Soon after lunch on the fourth day, with Gooch playing freely and Larkins on the way to his second patient fifty of the match, England's one problem on the slow, low pitch looked to be dismissing Australia a second time. They remained comfortably placed at tea – 147 for four, 193 ahead. But in the first over of the final session, an ambitious drive by Stewart against Reid's angle was brilliantly taken low to his right by Marsh at gully, and the innings fell to pieces. Two catches by Atherton at gully revived English hopes before the close, and they might still have had an outside chance if, in the fourth over next morning, Malcolm had won an lbw appeal against Boon, who had moved across the stumps to play a ball to leg. Otherwise neither batsman gave England another chance until Australia were within 31 runs of victory. Tufnell was unlucky to miss a first Test wicket when Boon, cutting, edged to Russell.

Toss: England. **England 352** (W. Larkins 64, D. I. Gower 100, A. J. Stewart 79, B. A. Reid 6-97) **and 150** (G. A. Gooch 58, W. Larkins 54, B. A. Reid 7-51); **Australia 306** (M. A. Taylor 61, A. R. Border 62, A. R. C. Fraser 6-82) **and 197-2** (G. R. Marsh 79*, D. C. Boon 94*).

Third Test

At Sydney, January 4, 5, 6, 7, 8, 1991. Drawn.

The enterprise of Gooch and the competitive response of his players kept alive until the final hour a game which had seemed Australia's after they had scored 518 in 652 minutes in the first innings. It was not until the fourth morning that England, anchored by Atherton's 105 in 451 minutes and embellished by Gower's cultured 123, saved the follow-on, but Gooch's declaration at 469 for eight, 49 behind, brought the game to life in a quite unexpected way. The ball was turning, and Gooch wasted no time in bringing on his spinners.

There was no mistaking the psychological effect of England's declaration. That evening Marsh and Taylor fell cheaply for the second time – in nine Tests against England, Taylor had never before failed to pass 50 – and Australia entered the final day without their usual buoyancy. In the event they survived until two and a quarter hours from the scheduled close, leaving England the almost impossible task of scoring 255 in 28 overs, a rate of 9.1 an over. They made a valiant stab at it, and Gooch's aggression could well have set up a brilliant win had the game followed only a slightly different pattern. The night-watchman, Healy, for example, who made 69 and lasted until 17 minutes after lunch, gave an awkward chance low to the left of Gower at square leg in Hemmings's first over of the day; while Rackemann, abetted by Gooch's pessimistic view that Malcolm's back strain prevented him bowling, held out for 32 overs against the spinners, a well-advanced left pad thwarting them as often as his bat.

Well as Tufnell bowled, turning the ball perceptibly more than Hemmings and giving full value for his figures, Gooch was over-committed to his spinners. When, after four hours in the field, Malcolm was finally handed an overdue new ball – the last pair had been together 25 minutes – he bowled Rackemann with his sixth delivery. Theoretically, England retained a chance while Gooch and Gower were scoring 84 at seven an over, before Gower, having passed 8,000 Test runs, was caught a few yards inside the long-off boundary. Realistically, hopes had ended during Rackemann's 112-minute occupation.

Consistency underlay Australia's batting on the first two days. Malcolm had made good use of the pitch's early pace, having Marsh caught at first slip and Taylor down the leg side, off his gloves, but from the start England tended to bowl too short. Boon, adding 147 with Border, scarcely missed a chance to cut, and his fourth successive Sydney Test hundred looked there for the taking when, having cut and driven Gooch for three fours in four balls to leap from 85 to 97, he sliced an off-side long-hop to deep gully. The selectiveness of Boon's attacking play is illustrated by his tally of 17 boundaries in an innings of 201 minutes. Border, Jones and Waugh consolidated, and Matthews, unsettling Hemmings by his darting footwork, made 128 in 242 minutes with 17 fours, his fourth hundred in 24 Tests. Only Malcolm's stamina and strength saved England from submersion.

The only rain in a sweltering match restricted England's reply that evening to one over, sparing them a testing hour. Gooch and Atherton turned their good fortune to good account with a stand of 95 that lasted until 20 minutes after lunch on the third day, when Reid had Gooch caught down the leg side. And after Larkins and Smith had gone cheaply, the former run out by Border's direct hit from mid-wicket, Gower and Atherton swept away the danger of the follow-on in a stand of 139. Atherton completed a dogged hundred, at 451 minutes the slowest in Ashes Tests, with a lovely cover-drive off Rackemann, one of only eight fours in his innings, before succumbing to his 349th ball, caught off Matthews at short leg. For the past hour he had been little more than a spectator of his partner's spectacular hitting. Gower went on to adorn the SCG with his first hundred there in any form of cricket (312 minutes, 15 fours). When he had added 99 with Stewart, who scored a crisp 91 from 146 balls, Gooch had the material for his declaration.

Toss: Australia. **Australia 518** (D. C. Boon 97, A. R. Border 78, D. M. Jones 60, G. R. J. Matthews 128,
D. E. Malcolm 4-128) **and 205** (I. A. Healy 69, P. C. R. Tufnell 5-61);
England 469-8 dec. (G. A. Gooch 59, M. A. Atherton 105, D. I. Gower 123, A. J. Stewart 91)
and 113-4 (G. A. Gooch 54).

Fourth Test
At Adelaide, January 25, 26, 27, 28, 29, 1991. Drawn.

For the second Test in succession, an engagingly irrational batting display by England on the final day transformed a routine draw into something that briefly promised more. History, as much as England's lack of depth, proclaimed that they had no chance of scoring 472 when Border declared three-quarters of an hour before the close of the fourth day. The scoreboard proved history and the formbook correct, but only after England had gone to tea on the fifth afternoon at 267 for two, thanks to an opening stand of 203 between Gooch and Atherton, and a cameo by Lamb. England had scored 152 in 30 overs since lunch, and Border was disconcerted enough to let the game drift to stalemate, rather than move on to the attack when England lost Lamb, Gower and Stewart within ten runs.

Australia made their one batting change of the series, bringing in Mark Waugh at the expense of his brother, Steve. For Mark, by four minutes the younger of the 25-year-old twins, it proved a glorious debut. He produced an innings which a batsman of any generation would have been overjoyed to play any time in his career, let alone on Test debut and in a situation which verged on crisis. When he came in 52 minutes after lunch, DeFreitas had dismissed Border and Jones in four balls, the former cramped by a quick break-back making extra height, which he played into his stumps. Boon followed 38 minutes later, caught at deep third man, to leave Australia 124 for five.

Waugh's shot off the mark, a flowing straight three off his second ball, was a portent of what was in store. In the evening his timing, range of strokes, and quick and confident footwork dazzled. He passed 50 in 74 balls, and needed only another 52 to reach his hundred, which came out of 148 in 176 minutes with his 15th four. Tufnell, unable to find either a trajectory or a length to hold him, was picked up over the on side from down the pitch or hit off the back foot through the covers with equal certainty and style. On the second day Waugh lost his touch, but Matthews, almost unnoticed in their stand of 171, stretched a valuable but tedious innings to five and a quarter hours, and with McDermott steered Australia to 386.

England made a bad start when, in McDermott's third over, Atherton was judged lbw, padding up well outside off stump, and Lamb was caught at the wicket, the first of five catches for Healy. However, Gooch and Smith added 126 in 200 minutes, but Gower, obligingly chipping the last ball of the morning to long leg, one of three men positioned for the stroke, ushered in a collapse that saw seven wickets fall for 69. McDermott could have no complaint with figures of five for 97 in his first Test since 1988-89. Australia, leading by 157 with seven sessions to go, lost momentum when Marsh, Taylor and Jones were out by the tenth over. But the immovable Boon more than atoned for running out Taylor, adding 66 with Hughes, the night-watchman, and 110 with Border. Nothing he played at passed the bat in 368 minutes until he swept clumsily at Tufnell and was bowled for 121, his second Adelaide hundred against England. Border added 74 more with Matthews before his declaration.

When, in the first over of the final day, Atherton and Gooch sprinted four from a stroke to third man, rather than jogging three, it was obvious that Gooch had more than survival on his mind. Atherton confirmed it with three hooked fours, hitting each so well it was a mystery he played the stroke so rarely. It was only at lunch, though, with England 115 for no wicket, that Gooch decided the distant goal was worth a try. His explosive driving, mainly off Matthews and McDermott, brought him another 58 in 57 minutes before Marsh, at gully, caught a full-blooded slash off Reid. His first Test hundred in Australia contained 12 fours. Atherton followed 36 minutes later, hitting Reid to cover, but Lamb, 46 at tea off 38 balls, kept the goal in sight until McDermott and Hughes forced England on to the defensive.

Toss: Australia. **Australia 386** (M. E. Waugh 138, G. R. J. Matthews 65, P. A. J. DeFreitas 4-56) **and 314-6 dec.** (D. C. Boon 121, A. R. Border 83*); **England 229** (G. A. Gooch 87, R. A. Smith 53, B. A. Reid 4-53, C. J. McDermott 5-97) **and 335-5** (G. A. Gooch 117, M. A. Atherton 87, A. J. Lamb 53).

Fifth Test

At Perth, February 1, 2, 3, 5, 1991. Australia won by nine wickets.

Australia took only ten sessions to improve their unbeaten run against England to eight victories and four draws since the Sydney Test of 1986–87, despite Reid's absence with a callus on his foot and the fact that at tea on the first day they were looking at an England scoreboard reading 212 for three. Dashing, attacking play from Lamb and Smith, combined with Australia's loosest bowling of the series on the fastest outfield, lifted England's hopes; a moment's over-confidence, a dubious lbw decision, the well-established temperamental and technical flaws of the lower-order batting, and fiery bowling by McDermott reversed the position in the twinkling of an eye.

Although McDermott disposed of Gooch, Atherton and later Smith in the first two sessions, his 18 overs had cost 80 runs. After tea he had five for 17 in 6.4 overs, giving him eight England wickets in an innings for the second time (he also took eight for 141 at Old Trafford in 1985). The critical dismissal came in the first over after the resumption when Lamb tried to pull a ball from clear of his off stump and was caught behind the bowler by Border, running from mid-on. If it was a dangerous stroke immediately after an interval, the under-pitched ball had proved highly profitable for both Lamb and Smith in a third-wicket stand of 141 at three an over. Lamb's highest Test score in Australia was crisply struck off 122 balls, and contained a straight six off Matthews and 13 fours. Smith, who was caught head-high at second slip off a fast-flying edged drive 25 minutes before tea, hit a six and nine fours off 120 balls.

On an ideal batting pitch, in perfect weather and with an outfield so quick that Atherton found the 95-yard boundary only just behind square leg when he jammed down on a yorker in the second over, a score of 400 was still possible. But in McDermott's next over after Lamb's dismissal, Stewart was given out lbw off a ball that seemed likely to miss the leg stump, and the innings folded. From 212 for three, England were all out for 244 in 70 minutes and 12.4 overs. Newport, borrowed from the England A team in Sri Lanka three days before the match, was out first ball, McDermott's seventh victim.

Australia's innings illustrated one of the essential differences between the teams – lower-order batting strength. Midway through the second day they were 168 for six, but for the third time Matthews became England's stumbling block, supervising the addition of 139 for the last four wickets in a typically adhesive, three-and-a-quarter-hour innings. He also displayed tactical flair, for the first time in the series exercising the right to continue batting after 6 p.m. if fewer than 90 overs had been bowled. With nine overs due, and Alderman looking untroubled, it was the right decision against a team flagging after six hours in a temperature of 82°. Ironically the No. 11 fell five balls later to DeFreitas.

Only 63 behind, England still had hopes of fighting back to win. In the event there was more movement for the fast bowlers than locals could recall on a third day at Perth. But for luck running against Hughes, and Newport's robust 38-run stand with Malcolm at the end, Australia could have finished the series as they started, with a three-day win. Hughes's line hardly wavered from off stump or just outside, and figures of four for 37 did not do him justice. They did, however, take him past 100 Test wickets; and when DeFreitas was caught behind, Alderman had his 100th wicket in Ashes Tests.

Australia, needing 120, lost Taylor in the final over of the day, but Marsh and Boon scored the remaining 81 in 87 minutes after the only rest day of the series. Fittingly, the winning runs, a sprinted two, came from a defensive stroke by Boon that rolled no further than the square-leg umpire, a range that, because of the speed of Australia's fielding, would have restricted England to a single.

Toss: England. **England 244** (A. J. Lamb 91, R. A. Smith 58, C. J. McDermott 8-97) **and 182** (M. G. Hughes 4-37); **Australia 307** (D. C. Boon 64, G. R. J. Matthews 60*) **and 120-1** (G. R. Marsh 63*).

ENGLAND v AUSTRALIA 1993   John Thicknesse

Australia's third overwhelming Ashes victory in succession was as well merited as its predecessors in a series that ended Graham Gooch's reign as England captain and Ted Dexter's as chairman of the England Committee. The course of the series stemmed even more than usual from confidence. In England's case, it was the lack of it, following a tour of India and Sri Lanka on which they lost all four Tests and five one-day internationals out of eight. It was no surprise, then, that when Mike Atherton, taking over the captaincy, led England to a big win at The Oval in his second match in charge, the change of fortune aroused relief as much as joy.

Annoying as it was for Australia to stumble at the final hurdle, defeat did no more than tarnish a fine all-round performance, in which 23-year-old leg-spinner Shane Warne played the starring role. Although Warne had two startling analyses to his credit in his 11 previous Tests, his reputation before the tour was more that of a beach-boy than a budding Test-winner. His shock of dyed blond hair, earring and blobs of white sun-block on the tip of his nose and lower lip lent his appearance a deceptive air of amiability, which an expression of wide-eyed innocence enhanced. However, his incessant niggling of umpires and truculent questioning of unfavourable decisions made it obvious that the sunny exterior hid a graceless streak, which stopped him earning his opponents' unqualified respect. In his hitherto unexplored method of attack, founded on ferociously spun leg-breaks, as often as not angled a foot or more outside the leg stump from round the wicket, he left no doubt that Australia had uncovered not only a match-winner of singular inventiveness but a cricketer crowds would flock to see.

Thanks to TV, Warne's first ball in Ashes cricket, which bowled Mike Gatting, may become the most famous ever bowled. Had Gatting been in half an hour longer, or ever faced Warne before, he might have got a pad to it. As it was the ball was unplayable and, by impressing the bowler's capacities on England, it had a profound impact on the series. Of Warne's subsequent 33 wickets, only two came from deliveries that seemed to turn as far – 18 inches or more – and in each case the spin was accentuated by the ball being delivered round the wicket. Gooch was the victim on both occasions.

Despite the promise of England's win at The Oval, the figures of the last three series were conclusive: England 1, Australia 11, drawn 5.

First Test

At Manchester, June 3, 4, 5, 6, 7, 1993. Australia won by 179 runs.

Patrick Murphy

An enthralling match of splendid individual achievements was won by Australia with 9.4 overs to spare. A rarity among modern Tests in England, it was shaped by slow bowling and finally decided by leg-spin. Warne returned match figures of eight for 137, the best by an Australian leg-spinner in England since Bill O'Reilly took ten for 122 at Leeds in 1938. One particular delivery from Warne set the tone for the series. His first ball in an Ashes contest pitched outside leg and hit the top of Gatting's off stump. Gatting looked understandably bewildered as he dragged himself off the field. Thereafter only Gooch played Warne with conviction: never, perhaps, has one delivery cast so long a shadow over a game, or a series. Warne also produced a stunning catch at backward square leg to dismiss Caddick in the tense final stages as England tried to salvage a draw.

No time was lost in the Test but a succession of wet days beforehand had hampered the preparations. The soft pitch was not planned but it allowed the spinners to hold unexpected sway on the first two days, and improved the cricket. It ought to have given England the advantage since they fielded two spinners to Australia's one. Such found himself bowling before Thursday lunch-time and shared the first day's honours with Taylor – who made another impressive start to an Ashes series – and Slater. The opening pair, both from the New South Wales town of Wagga Wagga, began with a stand of 128 but then Australia lost three wickets for 11 in the final hour, including Steve Waugh, who was bowled off stump trying to drive – a classic off-spinner's dismissal. On the second day, Such moved on to take six for 67 and his cool and control compared favourably with the palpable lack of confidence shown by Tufnell.

With Australia out for 289 and Gooch and Atherton resuming their sequence of reassuring opening partnerships England briefly looked like a team ready to compete for the Ashes. Then Atherton was out, Warne came on for the 28th over, bowled what became known as "The Ball from Hell", and the series really began. Gatting's departure

"The Ball from Hell": Mike Gatting is bamboozled by Shane Warne
at Old Trafford in 1993, to the delight of Ian Healy.

was followed by that of Smith, caught at slip, and Gooch, who hit a full toss to mid-on. By the close England had eight down and Keith Fletcher, the England manager, was saying he had never seen a Test pitch in England turn so much.

The third day began with another flurry of wickets. Such came on to bowl the ninth over of the Australian innings and with his fifth ball had Taylor lbw, sweeping. But Boon then batted with his customary pragmatism while Mark Waugh unleashed

490

a series of glittering strokes. The cricket was more attritional after Waugh was out but Australia were just as sure-footed: Steve Waugh and Healy batted England out of the match with an unbroken stand of 180 in 164 minutes. Healy became the first Australian to make his maiden first-class century in a Test since Harry Graham, exactly 100 years earlier. England looked depressingly pallid in the field during this partnership. With the pitch drying out and the spinners negated by the lack of bounce, there was little attempt to wrest the initiative.

The declaration came at three o'clock, and England were left to score 512 in a day and a half. Gooch and Atherton again batted securely, with the captain notably author-itative. Then Gatting played with freedom until he was bowled off his pads from the last ball of the day by the indefatigable Hughes, a due reward for his willingness to vary his line and length. Gooch was understandably more circumspect on the final morning and – although Smith was tormented and then bowled by Warne – he reached his 18th Test hundred and England had the chance of a draw. Yet half an hour after lunch Gooch became the fifth cricketer, and the first Englishman, to be dismissed handled the ball in a Test as he instinctively flicked out with a glove at a ball dropping on to his stumps. Umpire Bird had no hesitation in giving Gooch out, with the moral victory, if not the wicket, going to Hughes for extracting extra bounce on an increas-ingly lifeless pitch.

Although the first ten English batsmen all batted for at least half an hour in the second innings, none could match the technical skill and authority of Gooch. For a time Caddick and Such threatened an unlikely stalemate but brilliant catches by Warne and Border completed their downfall. The Australians embarked on some typically committed celebrations.

Toss: England. **Australia 289** (M. A. Taylor 124, M. J. Slater 58, P. M. Such 6-67)

and 432-5 dec. (D. C. Boon 93, M. E. Waugh 64, S. R. Waugh 78*, I. A. Healy 102*);

England 210 (G. A. Gooch 65, M. G. Hughes 4-59, S. K. Warne 4-51) **and 332** (G. A. Gooch 133,

M. G. Hughes 4-92, S. K. Warne 4-86).

CRICKETER OF THE YEAR – SHANE WARNE
Vic Marks, 1994

When Martin Crowe announced just before the 1993 Ashes series that Shane Warne was the best leg-spinner in the world, few alarm bells clanged in England. No Australian wrist-spinner had made a significant impact in an English Test series since the days of Grimmett and O'Reilly between the wars. England, it was assumed, had to quell McDermott and Hughes to have a chance of retrieving the Ashes.

Such a complacent misconception was dispelled at Old Trafford by Warne's first delivery in Test cricket in England. It was bowled to Mike Gatting, an acknowledged master of spin. Warne does not indulge in low-risk looseners, and that first ball was flicked vigorously out of the back of the hand. It set off on the line of Gatting's pads and then dipped in the air further towards the leg side until it was 18 inches adrift of the stumps; by this time Gatting was beginning to lose interest, until the ball bounced, turned and fizzed across his ample frame to clip the off bail. Gatting remained rooted at the crease for several seconds – in disbelief rather than dissent – before trudging off to the pavilion like a man betrayed. Now the Englishmen knew that Crowe's assessment was more than propaganda.

Throughout six Tests they could never master Warne. He bowled 439.5 overs in the series, took 34 wickets – surpassing Grimmett's 29 in the five Tests of 1930 – and also managed to concede under two runs per over, thereby flouting the tradition of profligate wrist-spinners buying their wickets. Some English batsmen were completely mesmerised; Robin Smith, England's banker in the middle order, was unable to detect any of his variations and had to be dropped. The admirable Gooch could obviously distinguish the googly from the leg-spinner, yet Warne still disposed of him five times in the series. Once Gooch carelessly clubbed a full toss to mid-on, but otherwise he was dismissed while playing the appropriate defensive stroke, the surest indication that Warne has a special talent.

On a broader scale he has triggered a mini-renaissance in the art of wrist-spin bowling. In the summer of 1993 young village cricketers could be spied on the outfield, no longer seeking to emulate Curtly Ambrose or Merv Hughes, but attempting to ape the more subtle skills of Warne. For that we should all be grateful.

Second Test

Vic Marks

At Lord's, June 17, 18, 19, 20, 21, 1993. Australia won by an innings and 62 runs.

England's lamentable record against Australia at Lord's – their last win was in 1934 – continued as the tourists romped to an innings victory. Of more immediate concern, this was England's seventh consecutive Test defeat, prompting a national outcry on a scale more familiar in football. For Australia the match offered reassuring confirmation of the stamina and resourcefulness of a bowling attack deprived of McDermott. He was rushed to hospital on the second day for an operation on a twisted bowel, which was to rule him out of the rest of the series.

Even before the game began there were signs of desperation in the England camp. After the defeat at Old Trafford Gooch, who had originally been appointed to lead the side for the first three Tests, was, perversely, entrusted with the captaincy for the rest of the series. Yet a throwaway remark by Gooch that he would stand down if performances did not improve only added to the disarray in the dressing-room. By the end of the third day, when another defeat was well-nigh inevitable, speculation about his position was rife.

England resisted wholesale changes, merely replacing DeFreitas with Foster, who thus played his first Test for four years. But on a docile pitch at Foster's least favourite Test ground his recall was not a success. Indeed, after only one more county game he retired. Australia replaced Julian with the off-spinner May, a more fruitful decision.

Border won the toss and settled back to watch his batsmen expertly dissect the English attack. But for an aberration by Mark Waugh against Tufnell on 99, the first four batsmen would have completed centuries. Taylor was anonymously effective, Boon was remorseless in the pursuit and achievement of his elusive first Test hundred on English soil, but Slater, in his second Test, was captivating. After an uncertain start against Caddick, his 152, punctuated by a series of immaculate straight drives and 18 fours, dominated the first day. His impromptu jig of delight when he reached his hundred was followed by a beaming smile and a kiss bestowed on the Australian badge on his helmet. This exuberant display of joy enchanted a capacity crowd as much as his fleet-footed strokeplay. It was nearly five hours before he became England's first wicket; by then Australia had 260.

Mark Waugh and then Border sustained the demolition of England's attack with such certainty that, when a ball eventually beat the bat, there was a spontaneous, if somewhat desperate, round of applause from the stands. By 11.45 on the third morning Border was able to declare at 632 for four.

On such a bland surface a draw should have been within England's capabilities, but May and Warne conjured more turn than the home spinners and Hughes, refusing to be daunted by the sluggishness of the pitch or the absence of McDermott – Mark Waugh shared the new ball – was not to be denied. Gooch and Gatting were dismissed in unfamiliar and humiliating ways; Gooch was caught at long leg, hooking, while Gatting, supposedly the master of spin, was bowled through the gate by a perfectly flighted off-break. But the most notable dismissal was that of Smith, who became the first victim in an English Test of trial by TV. Smith came down the wicket to May, the ball turned down the leg side and Healy whipped off the bails. Umpire Kitchen signalled to the third official, Chris Balderstone, at the top of the pavilion and, after 69 seconds, three TV replays and a brief walkie talkie conversation, raised his finger.

Only Atherton, who batted 253 minutes for 80, had a clear idea of how to blunt the attack as England were bundled out for 205. Atherton was also the cornerstone of the second innings, remaining for another 242 minutes until a moment of masochistic madness. After Gooch had succumbed to a perfect Warne leg-break, Atherton and a subdued Gatting had added 104 to offer hope of scrambling a draw. Atherton had reached 97, batting more fluently than in the first innings, when he clipped a ball to mid-wicket. Both batsmen were swayed by the impending landmark as they debated a third run. Atherton set off, stalled and then slipped as Hughes hurled the ball from the boundary; he was agonisingly stranded as Healy removed the bails. If he had been on seven or 87 a third run would not have been contemplated.

Despite resistance from Hick and Stewart on the fifth day England were unable to recover from this self-inflicted wound. The Australian spinners, who shared 15 wickets in the match, patiently removed the middle order. Warne then took the last two wickets in consecutive balls by bowling Such and Tufnell around their legs, a suitably humiliating end. For the Australians there was enough time to spruce themselves up before meeting the Queen who, optimistically, had maintained the tradition of visiting Lord's at tea-time on the Monday, even though, with Sunday play, it was now the final day.

Toss: Australia. **Australia 632-4 dec.** (M. A. Taylor 111, M. J. Slater 152, D. C. Boon 164*, M. E. Waugh 99, A. R. Border 77); **England 205** (M. A. Atherton 80, M. G. Hughes 4-52, S. K. Warne 4-57) **and 365** (M. A. Atherton 99, M. W. Gatting 59, G. A. Hick 64, A. J. Stewart 62, T. B. A. May 4-81, S. K. Warne 4-102).

Third Test

Greg Baum

At Nottingham, July 1, 2, 3, 5, 6, 1993. Drawn.

Rarely before can a draw have been welcomed with such rapture in England, for, after seven consecutive defeats, this was not only a moral victory but a victory for morale.

After three days, another loss looked almost certain. That evening, however, Australia were severely censured by the referee, Clive Lloyd, for their deportment on the field after complaints from both umpires. To what extent that influenced the change that overtook the match is problematic. Australian coach Bob Simpson said not at all: if his players were more subdued after the rest day it was just that England gave them nothing to become excited about.

What could be quantified were inspiring centuries from the patriarch Gooch and the initiate Thorpe, the first since Frank Hayes in 1973 to score a century on Test debut for England. By Tuesday evening, it was England who felt cheated out of victory. But this was a very different England team. At last recognising the stability they had sought for the stagnation it had become, England dropped Gatting, Hick, Foster, Lewis and Tufnell and brought into the squad Igglesden, McCague, Bicknell, Hussain, Thorpe and Lathwell to go along with the uncapped Ilott – seven men, with a total experience of four Tests, none gained in the previous three years.

The selection of McCague provoked a storm in both hemispheres, for although he was born in Ulster, he grew up in Port Hedland in Australia's dusty north-west, graduated from the Australian Cricket Academy, and played Sheffield Shield cricket. But when he was made twelfth man for the 1991-92 Shield final, he became disillusioned with Western Australia. He had already joined Kent, where his Irish birth conveniently made him an English player, and now an England player – a rat joining a sinking ship, said a Sydney paper.

Igglesden again had to withdraw through injury, and Bicknell was omitted. That left an attack whose total exposure to Test cricket was the four games Caddick and Such had played between them in this series, but a seven-men batting line-up, with Gooch dropping down to No. 5 so Lathwell could open, even though the Gooch-Atherton partnership had been just about England's only success of the first two Tests.

The pitch was predicted to be a spitting, seaming monster, but neither captain could see it and Gooch had no hesitation in batting first. The early portents were familiar. Smith, relieved to have escaped the purge and elevated to No. 3, made a roistering 86 until Julian, seeking only to stop a powerful drive, caught and bowled him with one outflung hand. Hussain, in his first Test for three years, batted elegantly for a maiden fifty, but Hughes and Warne were too good for the others and England were out early on Friday for 321. Hughes, now Australia's premier bowler, took five wickets in an innings for the first time against England.

McCague immediately entered into the affections of uncertain Englishmen by making the first breach in Australia's innings. But Boon and Mark Waugh ran up their third century partnership in successive Tests, 123 at more than five an over, until the brilliant and enigmatic Waugh again threw away a century, swiping at Such for McCague to take a catch in the outfield. Boon proceeded serenely and smoothly to another century; the elusive was now becoming a habit. Australia faltered slightly, but Border, batting laboriously at No. 8 because of illness, and Warne stretched the lead to 52.

Then came the acrimony. Atherton stood his ground after a low catch by Healy. While the Australians clustered around Atherton, umpire Meyer seemed to waver for a moment before giving him out. Warne cast a spell over Lathwell and deceived Smith with a beautiful leg-break. That left England 122 for four at the close and in familiar waters. However, on Monday, it took a chastened Australia more than an hour to remove the night-watchman Caddick, who had now batted nearly seven and a half hours in the series, and almost another four to claim the next wicket. Gooch repaid Australia's aggression with 11 boundaries in the first session, and though he was less cavalier later, he achieved his 19th Test century, his 11th as captain, and his 8,000th Test run. It was a masterful innings, and yet he could scarcely bring himself to make one celebratory flourish of his bat, for all the statistics would ring hollow if England were to lose another match.

Warne eventually turned out Gooch, but Thorpe remained and early on Tuesday reached his century with his patent whipped hook. The Surrey left-hander had batted with a poker-faced stoicism that enabled him to rise above the suspicion that, after four England A tours, he was not good enough for Test level, and the indignation of the public that he was not Gower.

Thorpe and Hussain had put on 113 when Gooch felt able to indulge himself in the rare luxury of a declaration, leaving Australia 371 to win in 77 overs. Slater went before lunch, charging impetuously at Such, and the batsmen suddenly seemed mortal and susceptible to pressure. Australia lost five wickets in a feverish middle session – more than they had lost in the entire Second Test – as Caddick began, without notice, to swing the ball disconcertingly. It was 115 for six at tea, but Australia need not have feared. Julian, seemingly oblivious to the gravity of the position, stroked his way to 47 and then hoisted Such's arm-ball into the stands at long-on to go to his maiden Test fifty. Steve Waugh also rose to Australia's two hours of need. The ball grew soft, the pitch remained firm, the bowlers became tired and, in the finish, Australia averted disaster comfortably.

Before the match, there had been another rash of reports that Gooch would resign if England lost. Asked to verify them afterwards, he answered: "We didn't lose, did we?" In a more emotional man, those words might have caught in his throat; it had been nearly a year since the last Test when he was able to utter them.

Toss: England. **England 321** (R. A. Smith 86, N. Hussain 71, M. G. Hughes 5-92)
and 422-6 dec. (R. A. Smith 50, G. A. Gooch 120, G. P. Thorpe 114*);
Australia 373 (D. C. Boon 101, M. E. Waugh 70, M. J. McCague 4-121) **and 202-6** (B. P. Julian 56*).

CRICKETER OF THE YEAR – MERV HUGHES   Bruce Wilson, 1994

At the end of the Ashes season, the England captain who failed to regain them, and resigned his job as a result, looked back in an interview on it all: the good, the bad, the indigestible. In the course of it, Graham Gooch spoke of "dear old Merv Hughes". What? No matter that Gooch is eight years Hughes's senior. It is not the old that might send the moustaches twirling; it is the dear old. Whoever spoke of dear old Joel Garner at the end of a series in which he had taken 31 wickets, or dear old Dennis Lillee?

Perhaps it is the action. When many of us saw Hughes for the first time in 1989, there was a mixture of mirth and disbelief: the mincing little steps leading to a stuttering run, the absurd stovepipe trousers, the pre-bowl calisthenics, the whiskers, the silent-movie bad-guy theatrics. The action is not much different today, although it might tend a little more towards outswing and the googly variation is not used quite so often. The eyes above the hooked nose still glare with the same passion. Insults fly, though if Gooch is to be believed not especially imaginative or distressing ones. Sometimes, too, a childlike smile appears, all perhaps indicating the man behind the moustache: pretty straightforward, not too gaudy.

Now Hughes has been involved in two Ashes tours, and in each he has taken key wickets at key times. Last summer, in the absence of the one man thought to separate the two sides in strikepower, Craig McDermott, Hughes showed that in fact it was he who was the difference in the seam-bowling department. If Warne bowled the ball which launched a thousand paragraphs, Hughes ground out the overs which gave Australia a decent front-line assault.

In the course of the summer, Hughes took his 200th Test wicket and passed the Test tallies of two Australian fast bowlers, Geoff Lawson and Jeff Thomson, the second legendary and the first deeply respected. In doing this, Hughes had a strike-rate roughly the equal of Thomson's and rather better than Lawson's. Yet, until recently, it was unthinkable that he would be mentioned as being in the same class as those two. He has paid a price for his eccentricities, not least not being taken seriously.

Fourth Test

Peter Johnson

At Leeds, July 22, 23, 24, 25, 26, 1993. Australia won by an innings and 148 runs.

England lost the Ashes and, within minutes, their captain too when Gooch honoured his promise to resign. His departure was inevitable. This was his 34th Test in charge and, though ten of those ended in victory, this was England's eighth defeat in their last nine. It was by far the most comprehensive and, six weeks earlier, Gooch had said he would go if there was no improvement.

Ironic, though, that it should all end so meekly at Headingley where, in the two previous summers, Gooch had made defiant, match-winning centuries against West Indies and Pakistan. But this was not the Headingley he knew and loved, the pitch which traditionally transforms the tidy English seam bowler into a monster. To Gooch's unconcealed disgust, that had been dug up after bad reports from the umpires the year before. The board denied that they had ordered the excavation but Yorkshire, fearful that another pitch scandal would cost them their place on the Test rota, felt obliged to do it anyway. The new strip, laid in 1988 and used for only one first-class match – in which Essex, without Gooch, lost to Yorkshire by an innings – was an unknown quantity and called for some shrewd guesswork from the captains.

Gooch guessed wrong. Having named an unchanged squad, England left out off-spinner Such, gave a Test debut to Bicknell and went into the match with four pace bowlers who had a combined experience of five Tests. By the end of the first hour – traditionally the bewitching hour at Headingley – it was clear that they were ill-equipped. Through an innings lasting nearly 14 dismaying hours, Bicknell, who trapped Taylor lbw with only his 17th delivery, was the pick of the attack. But that is not saying much. England had an unforeseen problem when, on the second day, McCague went off with an injury later diagnosed as a stress fracture of the back. Their bowling, however, was shorter and shoddier than at any time in the series; long before they adjusted their sights they had been, literally, cut out of the match.

Slater glided to 67 before he got too audacious and played across the line at Ilott. Boon, the rock on which so many Australian innings had been balanced, gratefully took everything on offer. His five-hour 107 was his third century in successive Tests. It was the second morning before Ilott got him lbw, the only wicket to fall on Gooch's 40th birthday. By then Boon had shared one punishing stand of 106 with Mark Waugh – their fourth century partnership of the series – and another cold-blooded affair of 105 with Border, whose first double-hundred in England was always intended to be psychologically brutal. He was not building an unassailable total so much as grinding down the will to resist. He batted for 569 minutes and shared an unbroken stand of 332 with Steve Waugh. This was the Waugh of 1989 when, it seemed, England were destined never to get him out. The pickings, it has to be said, were just as easy. Nearly half his 157 came from boundaries, hit with wrists of flexible steel. Only Bradman and Sidney Barnes had exceeded their fifth-wicket partnership in Tests – against England at Sydney in 1946–47. Border's declaration came on the third morning when he drove his 200th run and carried on running, fists pummelling the air, into the pavilion.

England simply shrank in awe from a total of 653 for four – the highest ever made at Leeds, but Australia's second over 600 in successive visits. When Lathwell chased Hughes's third ball into Healy's gloves, the pattern was set, the sense of futility rampant. Significantly it was Reiffel, the closest thing the Australians had to an English seamer, who did the damage. He began the series third in line behind McDermott, who departed, and Julian, now injured. Yet he took five for 65 and always looked quicker and better able to move the ball than the England quartet. Only Atherton and Gooch, with a fourth-wicket stand of 108, challenged the supremacy of the Australians, as well as the doubtful wisdom of dropping Gooch into the middle order. Atherton was widely believed – rightly so, it transpired a few days later – to be batting for the captaincy. He spoiled a solid half-century by shouldering arms to an inducker from Reiffel. But he returned next day, when England followed on 453 behind, to get another 63 and make it a long weekend by spending more than seven hours at the crease.

This time he fell to a stumping decision so hairline that even the TV umpire lingered over his verdict. Then Gooch was stumped, leaving only a few formalities to be completed on the final day. Stewart, formerly the favourite for the captaincy, aimed for an electioneering hundred but fell 22 short. Hughes took some punishment from him but became the seventh Australian to reach 200 Test wickets when he got Caddick. At 2.22 it was Border, fittingly, who accepted the skyer from Ilott which gave him victory, the Ashes, the series and the unwelcome distinction of costing his old mate Gooch his job. The crowd at the end was very subdued. But as in other recent Tests at Leeds and elsewhere, the chanting and swearing from the lager drinkers through the game, especially on the Western Terrace, caused great offence to other spectators.

Toss: Australia. **Australia 653-4 dec.** (M. J. Slater 67, D. C. Boon 107, M. E. Waugh 52, A. R. Border 200*, S. R. Waugh 157*); **England 200** (M. A. Atherton 55, G. A. Gooch 59, P. R. Reiffel 5-65) **and 305** (M. A. Atherton 63, A. J. Stewart 78, T. B. A. May 4-65).

Fifth Test

Chris Lander

At Birmingham, August 5, 6, 7, 8, 9, 1993. Australia won by eight wickets.

England stumbled from one crisis to another as the post mortem raged over Gooch's failure to wrest the Ashes from Australia. They began hopefully, as Atherton became his country's 71st captain and the sixth from Lancashire. But England were vanquished by another huge margin. Their downfall was overshadowed by Ted Dexter's resignation as chairman of selectors, six months before his five-year term officially ended, an announcement greeted with applause around the ground.

Maynard was summoned for his first Test since his debut against West Indies in 1988 and subsequent ban for touring South Africa. Then, 48 hours before the match and 17 days before his 41st birthday. Emburey was recalled, as an afterthought, when team manager Keith Fletcher realised the truth of warnings about a bare pitch likely to suit the spinners.

Atherton's initial strategy must have been to win the toss, bat first and score at least 450. The first two he pulled off, the last was wishful thinking. Atherton himself played with a calming assurance that suggested he would enjoy the mantle of captaincy. His 72, in 192 minutes, was England's biggest contribution in either innings and set the kind of example which had been Gooch's trademark, until he was scuttled by a shooter from Reiffel, leaving England 156 for five. Their unexpected rescuer was Emburey, perhaps Test cricket's most effective No. 8. He frayed Australian tempers for 160 minutes as he chiselled out 116 priceless runs with Thorpe, Bicknell, Such and Ilott. His unbeaten 55 demonstrated a burning desire to survive and a variety of improvised strokes hinting at a DIY batting kit rather than the MCC coaching manual.

However, when Ilott became Reiffel's sixth wicket on the second morning Atherton may have been regretting the decision to go for Emburey's bowling. England were left with the new-ball pairing of Bicknell and Ilott (joint Test record: eight for 468) and two off-spinners, one of whom thought his Test days were over. By the end of the day Australia were 258 for five, 18 behind. England were virtually out of the contest and heartily fed up with the Waugh twins. It could have been very different had Stewart stumped Steve off his second ball, from Such, when Australia were 80 for four. Reprieved, he united with his brother as never before in 13 Tests, adding 153 for the fifth wicket. It said much for the calibre of Mark's strokeplay that he batted with such fluency and dominance after Australia's most jittery start to date. He picked the ball off his toes and exhibited the strength in his wrists with a stream of whippy leg-side shots. His 137, including 18 fours, was Australia's tenth Test century of the summer, equalling the Ashes record and eclipsing the eight shared by Bradman's Invincibles in 1948.

Atherton shuffled his bowlers well, no easy task with such limited resources, and placed his field shrewdly. Nor was he shy of consulting Gooch and Stewart, his chief rival for the captaincy. Gooch responded with a warm hug when Mark Waugh was finally dismissed on Friday evening, lured into a trap at backward square leg which he and his successor had planned minutely. But on Saturday an exasperated England lost their grip in the face of rampant lower-order batting, led by Healy, and began to match earlier Australian dissent. When umpire Shepherd ignored raucous appeals for a bat-pad catch against Hughes, Thorpe was so peeved he chucked the ball to the ground in a sulk, while Stewart had already raced down the pitch to congratulate Such. Thorpe was officially rebuked by Fletcher, and referee Clive Lloyd noted Stewart's reactions. Atherton, without condoning these antics, felt that they stemmed from the team's new-found enthusiasm.

England entered the fourth day at 89 for one, trailing by 43. Gooch was still there but his early departure, bowled round his legs by Warne, must have sent more jitters through the dressing-room. Baffled by May's flight and sharp turn, Maynard looked as though he was batting in quicksand, and lasted just 24 balls in two innings. There was a glimmer of hope that the Australians might face a tricky run-chase, with the tenacious Thorpe and Emburey holding the fort on 216 for six at tea. Thorpe resisted the spinners without apparent stress for nearly four hours. But once Emburey – whose six hours of batting in the match represented far better value than his three wickets – was prised out the Australians sensed another runaway win. At 5.27 the innings ended in bizarre fashion, with Ilott bowled off his backside. England had been spun dry by May and Warne, who split the wickets evenly between them.

Australia did suffer a couple of hiccoughs on Monday morning, losing both openers on 12. But Mark Waugh played with such freedom and panache against Such and Emburey that they seemed to be bowling on a different pitch to the Australians, and Waugh and Boon extended their run of century partnerships to five in five Tests. By two o'clock Australia were 4–0 up, after their 12th success in 18 Tests against England, and looking to make it 5–0 for only the second time in Ashes history.

Toss: England. **England 276** (M. A. Atherton 72, J. E. Emburey 55*, P. R. Reiffel 6-71) **and 251** (G. P. Thorpe 60, T. B. A. May 5-89, S. K. Warne 5-82); **Australia 408** (M. E. Waugh 137, S. R. Waugh 59, I. A. Healy 80) **and 120-2** (M. E. Waugh 62*).

NOTES BY THE EDITOR

Matthew Engel, 1994

Shortly after lunch on the first day at Edgbaston, Shane Warne was bowling leg-breaks to Alec Stewart, who had discarded both his helmet and his faded baseball cap in favour of a real, old-fashioned, three lions of England version. As he pushed forward, he looked the image of his father at the crease. Behind the stumps, there was Ian Healy wearing his baggy cap and air of ageless Australian aggression. And there was Warne, bowling beautifully with a method thought to have been relegated to the museum.

For a moment the years seemed to roll away. The detail of the cricket was suspended; the game was overtaken by the timelessness of the scene. It was summer in England and all was well. Then, of course, Stewart got out and everything became secondary to the fact that we were being licked again.

In a number of respects cricket had a very good year in 1993. In England, India and Australia, crowds showed they would respond to the thrill of an exciting Test series, as well as to the gimcrack appeal of one-day cricket. Warne was the most talked-about player of the year and single-handedly did a huge amount to switch cricket back into a game where the batsman's fear is of mental torture rather than physical.

Sixth Test

Matthew Engel

At The Oval, August 19, 20, 21, 22, 23, 1993. England won by 161 runs.

To general astonishment, England reversed the form of the summer, outplayed Australia and won the final Test deservedly and decisively. The result came more than six and a half years or – as one paper recorded – 2,430 days, 11 hours and 49 minutes after England's last win over Australia, at Melbourne in December 1986. It brought about a halt, at least temporarily, in the mood of national teeth-gnashing that had accompanied England's previous failures. For Australia, who had enjoyed a triumphal progress round the British Isles with only trivial setbacks, the defeat came hours before they flew home; it was like having the perfect holiday and then being nabbed by customs.

The win was a particular triumph for the England captain Mike Atherton, in his second game in charge. It was a cause for quieter satisfaction for Ted Dexter, the much-vilified chairman of selectors who had announced his resignation two weeks earlier. This was the last team for which he was responsible.

It was a greatly changed team too, but if England finally found the right combination there was as much accident as design and, at last, a bit of luck. Smith was dropped, after 45 Tests, along with Ilott and Emburey. Back into the squad came Hick, Tufnell and Malcolm. But the selectors took what might have been a gamble by naming Fraser, whose brief but brilliant Test career had been halted two and a half years earlier by a serious hip injury, as cover for Bicknell, who had a dodgy knee. The evidence that Fraser was back to his best was based on only a couple of games but when Bicknell did pull out he had to play. It was a turning-point. The combination of Fraser, Malcolm and Watkin (who made it into the final XI this time, while Tufnell did not) on a pacy wicket transformed England. None had played a game before in the series; they shared the 20 wickets between them.

England had to make a fifth change less than an hour before the start when Thorpe was hit on the hand by a net bowler, broke his thumb and fainted; Ramprakash was summoned from Lord's. The short notice meant it had to be someone playing nearby; had Middlesex been at Swansea or Darlington, someone else might have got the change. As it was, Ramprakash – in his tenth Test – finally passed 30 and began to add a little achievement to his unquestioned promise.

The next bit of English luck came when Atherton won the toss. England made their familiar good start, racing to 143 for one. Australia were again unchanged, except that they were two weeks further along a hard tour and even someone as great-hearted as Hughes was beginning to show signs of weariness. The batsmen were right on top all day but, in familiar English fashion, they got themselves out, often for no good reason – Hick, in particular, was blazing away and hit a regal six to reach 80 two balls before being caught at third man off a thoroughly ill-judged cut.

In the field, Australia seemed more intent on getting mad than getting even, and the verbal battle appeared to reach new heights, or depths: the managers were called in for a quieter word by the referee after the first day. Next morning, England were all out for 380 and the consensus was that they had scored a hundred too few. But that assumed England's attack would live up to past form. Instead, Malcolm's speed, Watkin's resilience and Fraser's relentlessness completely transformed their prospects. The wicket was hard enough to favour strokeplay and to ensure that class bowlers could always make a batsman uncomfortable. England fielded tightly, with the young men darting everywhere and Gooch loyally putting on the short-leg helmet. Australia crumpled to 196 for eight. But England could not finish them off and the last two wickets took the score past 300.

Australia could have got back in the game but, again, the top three England batsmen tore into some jaded bowling and by the middle of Saturday afternoon already looked fireproof at 157 for one. The runs included an off-driven four off Reiffel by Gooch which took his total of Test runs to 8,235, more than Gower and every other

England player. The applause was unstinting, though the moment had a bittersweet touch: Gower might have scored many more if Gooch, as captain, had let him play.

The innings meandered later and England's prospects were hindered on the fourth day by the loss of two hours' play to the weather – only 41 minutes had been lost throughout the series while Australia had been on top. But the presence of the seventh specialist batsman, Ramprakash, enabled England to take the lead to 390 before they were bowled out to save Atherton having to decide whether to risk a declaration.

The rain effectively ruled out the remote chance of an Australian win. Could England do it? Again the luck was with them. The weather improved and umpire Meyer gave them two successive decisions that might have gone the other way: replays showed that Slater was given out caught off his armguard, and the first-ball lbw decision against Boon was not a certain one. Then Taylor played on and it was 30 for three. There was a stand between Mark Waugh and Border, who was caught behind – another decision that was not universally approved – straight after lunch and left an English cricket field for what was presumed to be the last time without once looking up. Mark Waugh and Healy were both out hooking and, though Steve Waugh dug in with Hughes, Malcolm was getting ready for another burst. His first ball back had Waugh lbw.

At 5.18, England won. The heroes of the hour were English but the heroes of the summer were Australian. What England had won, at the very last minute, was some self-respect.

Toss: England. **England 380** (G. A. Gooch 56, M. A. Atherton 50, G. A. Hick 80, A. J. Stewart 76) **and 313** (G. A. Gooch 79, M. R. Ramprakash 64); **Australia 303** (M. A. Taylor 70, I. A. Healy 83*, A. R. C. Fraser 5-87) **and 229** (S. L. Watkin 4-65).

WHY WE BEAT THE POMS

Ian Chappell, 1994

Why do Australia beat England? In general, because Australia play an aggressive brand of cricket and, when the talent is there, they get in position to seek victory more often. Notwithstanding that, Australia couldn't have lost the last three Ashes series even if they had bet heavily on the opposition. England played badly, often. In particular, the bowling was abysmal.

During 1993 I constantly heard the lament, "What is wrong with English cricket?" In part, the answer is the inability of people directing the English game to recognise the good that there is. For instance, one of the more common moans was "Where are all the England fast bowlers?" Answer: Devon Malcolm was playing for Derbyshire for the first five Tests. Or "What has happened to the old-fashioned English seamer?" Answer: Steve Watkin was playing for Glamorgan for the first five Tests. Or "Why were England 4–0 down after five Tests?" Answer: From the time of the second one-day international when Graham Gooch froze like a rabbit caught in the headlights, it was obvious he wasn't the man to lead England to an Ashes victory.

England's ability to over-theorise and complicate the game of cricket is legendary. Ever since I became involved in Ashes battles, I've felt that Australia could rely on some assistance from the England selectors. In 1993 they ran truer to form than many of the players they picked. Their magnanimity gave Australia a four-game start before the penny dropped. They then promoted Mike Atherton to the captaincy and, in no time, England picked a reasonably well-balanced side with an attack that bore some semblance of hostility.

Atherton had one piece of good fortune which every captain needs to be successful. Angus Fraser chose the appropriate moment to return to full form and fitness. But even before that Atherton had displayed considerable cricket wisdom. He said at Edgbaston after only three days in the job: "Our most important task is to identify the talent to win games. Then we must be prepared to stick with them."

Until the advent of Atherton, England's selections had often lacked rhyme or reason. A classic case was the predicament of 21-year-old Mark Lathwell in the one-day international series. At Lord's, Australia had an unbeatable 2–0 lead, so their selectors took the opportunity to play their talented 21-year-old, Damien Martyn. As he made mincemeat of the bowling on his way to a glorious half-century, an MCC member said to me, "How come you Australians always produce good young batsmen?" With Lathwell needlessly sitting in the pavilion watching his third match in a row, the answer wasn't difficult. "We play them," I replied.

AUSTRALIA v ENGLAND 1994–95 — John Thicknesse

England's tour of Australia resembled its predecessor in that a key player suffered severe damage to a finger within a week of arrival, in each case with far-reaching consequences. In 1990–91, Graham Gooch, the captain, was kept out of the First Test, which England duly lost inside three days. In 1994–95, vice-captain Alec Stewart's broken index finger mended in time for him to play at Brisbane. But when he broke it again in the Second Test, and sustained a further blow to it as soon as he was passed fit Mike Atherton was deprived of his regular opening partner in all the last three Tests.

In a series in which it was clear from the start that England needed luck to smile on them, the handicap of Stewart's absence might alone have ensured that Australia kept the Ashes. In the event, England's misfortune with illness and injuries was so uniformly foul that Stewart's was merely the first item on a list so long that six replacements were required. Granted Australia's known superiority, especially in bowling through Shane Warne's devastating leg-spin and Craig McDermott's fire and pace, it was no disgrace in the circumstances that, after being two down with three to play, England held the margin to 3–1.

It was a tribute to McDermott's strength that, at 29, he outlasted a spinner four years his junior, taking 32 wickets to Warne's 27. That eight supporting bowlers had to be content with 30 wickets, though, showed how much Australia relied on their big two. Glenn McGrath's sharp form in Perth suggested England were lucky he bowled so untidily in Brisbane – he was left out of the following three Tests.

Darren Gough, the find of the tour with 20 wickets in three Tests and some carefree batting, and Graeme Hick, who averaged 41.60, both missed the last two Tests. But the most damaging setback to morale probably came when the attacking spearhead, Devon Malcolm, went down with chicken-pox 48 hours before the First Test. Hollow laughter was afforded by the fact that the oldest players, 41-year-old Graham Gooch and 37-year-old Mike Gatting, were available for every match.

As Angus Fraser was to prove when he was eventually called up, he should have been an automatic choice. At 29, he had lost some of the explosiveness he possessed before his hip and back injuries on England's previous tour Down Under, but he was still by far the best and most accurate bowler of his type.

There was a brittleness about Australia's batting that England had not experienced in three series. The change was reflected by the average partnership: 33.94 per wicket, against 57.86 in 1989, 38.57 in 1990–91 and 51.28 in 1993. One thing, regrettably, was incontestable: neither England's batting, bowling, nor fielding, nor organisation was improving. Of the 22 Tests played over the four series, Australia won 14 compared with England's two – both of them achieved when the battle for the Ashes was already decided.

First Test

At Brisbane, November 25, 26, 27, 28, 29, 1994. Australia won by 184 runs.

Yet another display of exceptional all-round cricket took Australia to victory by the now-familiar crushing margin. Warne, who had held England's batsmen spellbound from the moment he bowled Gatting at Old Trafford in 1993, was again the executioner, taking three for 39 and eight for 71 – his best analysis in first-class cricket. It was not until the final innings, though, that he commandeered the spotlight. During the first three days, it was the combined efforts of Slater, Taylor, Mark Waugh, McDermott and Healy which forced the tourists into a position from which there was little prospect of escape.

England suffered a severe setback when Malcolm went down with chicken-pox three days before the game, and one of even greater significance when Atherton lost the toss on Brisbane's driest and most closely shaven pitch for an Ashes Test in more than 20 years. It was a formality that Australia would bat. Indeed, it was so obvious that there would be more help for spinners the longer the game lasted that Taylor chose to bat again with a lead of 259, rather than enforce the follow-on, after England, through pitiful batting against McDermott, were dismissed for 167 on the third day. It was a mistake because it allowed England the opportunity to regain a little self-respect, but it did no lasting damage.

The ball swung on the first morning. But when an erratic start by DeFreitas and McCague allowed Slater and Taylor to score 26 off four overs by doing nothing more than punish leg side balls and off-side long-hops, the initiative was won and lost in 20 minutes. In the 33rd over Slater was responsible for Taylor's run-out, failing to respond to a call for a sharp single to mid-off. But the mistake increased his resolution. He scored a dashing 112 out of 182 with Mark Waugh, and was on course to pass 200 in the day when, 36 minutes from the close, he failed to clear mid-off against Gooch. Slater faced 244 balls and scored a hundred in fours.

Australia lost six for 97 on the second day; Mark Waugh, who completed his third century against England, was ninth out when a ball from Gough inexplicably reared shoulder-high and carried to the covers from a fend-off. But then England's disintegration began. Stewart was caught at the wicket off a wide outswinger in what might otherwise have been the last over of McDermott's new-ball spell; Hick soon followed, caught behind, mis-hooking; only while Atherton and Thorpe were adding 47 did England briefly promise to recover. All that subsequently redeemed a supine effort were 234 minutes of orthodox defence by Atherton and a huge swept six by Gooch off Warne, during a calculated attempt to hit the spinners off their length. But Gooch perished after half an hour, another catch for Healy, off a soaring top edge when May's drift from round the wicket undermined a sweep.

Batting again before lunch on the third day, Australia began with a stand of 109 from Taylor and Slater. But frustrated by Tufnell's accuracy over the wicket, into the rough, they lost eight for 92 before Healy pushed the lead beyond 500. Taylor's declaration left his bowlers 11 hours to win the match.

There was a possibility of Australia winning inside four days when, in Warne's second and third overs, Stewart was bowled by an undetected flipper midway through a pull and Atherton played back to a full-length leg-break and was lbw. Hick and Thorpe spared England that embarrassment, doggedly adding 152 in four hours to the close. On the last day, however, Warne was irresistible. In action from the start with May and – in contrast to the fourth day – bowling mainly round the wicket, he pinned Thorpe to defence for half an hour before beating him with a yorker after a stand of 160, England's highest in eight Ashes Tests. Any chance of survival ended there, however: in Warne's next over, Hick was caught behind via pad, chest and back of bat. Gooch hit ten fours in scoring 56, but he became the last of Healy's nine victims (equalling the Australian Test record) and the first wicket of Warne's final spell, in which he captured the last four to bring his figures on the final day to six for 27 off 25.2 overs. They truly told the story of Warne's brilliance.

Toss: Australia. **Australia 426** (M. J. Slater 176, M. A. Taylor 59, M. E. Waugh 140, D. Gough 4-107) **and 248-8 dec.** (M. A. Taylor 58, P. C. R. Tufnell 4-79); **England 167** (M. A. Atherton 54, C. J. McDermott 6-53) **and 323** (G. A. Hick 80, G. P. Thorpe 67, G. A. Gooch 56, S. K. Warne 8-71).

Second Test

At Melbourne, December 24, 26, 27, 28, 29, 1994. Australia won by 295 runs.

The first ball of the third day, a full toss which Gooch drove back to McDermott, marked the moment when England lost their chance of cancelling out their defeat in Brisbane. From then until McDermott sealed Australia's victory, two days later, what was left of England's resolve and fighting spirit disappeared. It was almost a relief when a hat-trick by Warne, the first in an Ashes Test since 1903–04, hurried his side to within a wicket of a 2–0 lead on the final morning. Tufnell fell in McDermott's next over and Australia completed their 14th Ashes victory in 21 starts since the Fifth Test of 1986–87.

From Gooch's dismissal, which pulled England back to 148 for five from what had been a promising 119 for one, the only redeeming features of England's cricket were Atherton's determination, Gough's buoyancy and Tufnell's discipline in bowling defensively against his inclinations in the second innings.

Crushing as the defeat was, however, it was an unlucky match for England. If Australia's 279 was at least 80 more than Atherton would have hoped for, having let his bowlers loose on a damp first-day pitch, England might still have overtaken it with several wickets standing. But the first ball after lunch broke Stewart's right index finger, for the second time on the tour, and close decisions went against the other three top-four batsmen. England had scored ten when Stewart, defending a length ball from McDermott on the back foot, was unable to adjust to its lift. Though he returned next morning and batted at No. 7 in the second innings, his scores had no bearing on the match.

Forty minutes later, Hick was given out by umpire Randell after a break-back appeared to deflect to Healy off his thigh. Through sensible and watchful cricket, Atherton and Thorpe re-established the innings, adding 79 off 33 overs, only for both to fall to Warne, leaving England 124 for three. Atherton was lbw to a leg-break that turned at least an inch before hitting his pad; umpire Bucknor declined to give him the benefit of the doubt. Thorpe, like Atherton defending on the front foot, fell bat-pad to Mark Waugh at silly point. The appeal, from all four close fielders, was instantaneous, but Thorpe clearly believed the deflection came off pad alone. Taken in conjunction with Steve Waugh's narrow lbw escape off his first ball, from Gough, two crucial wickets in seven overs were a reverse England could not withstand.

Australia exploited the opening with the efficiency of a team who knew they had the edge. Handed Gatting's wicket 23 minutes later, when Steve Waugh, 30 yards from the bat behind square leg, acrobatically pulled down an ill-judged sweep, Warne and McDermott finished England off in 15.4 overs on the third morning, following Gooch's crestfallen departure.

Batting again with a lead of 67, Australia had Boon to thank for keeping them in control. Using every time-wasting device, Atherton saw to it that England bowled no more than 124 overs in 533 minutes – 13.95 per hour – despite Tufnell bowling 48 of them. Through the ICC's inflated allowances (four minutes per drinks break, two minutes per wicket), plus the fact that over-rates were being calculated over the whole match, no fine could be levied. But if, as some believed, the torpor induced in the players was a factor in their subsequent collapse, Atherton and England got what they deserved. Boon's patience was inexhaustible as he completed his first Test hundred at Melbourne, his 20th in all. On an uneven, two-paced pitch, he was sustained for 378 minutes by his on-drive and square-cut.

England's remote chance of holding out for 120 overs vanished when Fleming, in only his second Test, had Gooch caught behind and Hick bowled with textbook outswingers in his first two overs. When Thorpe succumbed to a loose stroke and Atherton, after an untroubled 73 minutes, received a second dubious decision from Bucknor, England closed at 79 for four. The remaining batsmen fell in 12.5 overs on the final day, McDermott and Warne – who had passed the milestones of 250 and 150 Test wickets respectively – taking three each. DeFreitas, Gough and Malcolm formed Warne's hat-trick, his first in any cricket. All were victims of leg-breaks, DeFreitas lbw on the back foot to one that skidded through, Gough well taken at the wicket off one that turned and bounced, and Malcolm brilliantly caught off his gloves by Boon, who dived two feet to his right to scoop up a fast low half-chance.

Toss: England. **Australia 279** (M. E. Waugh 71, S. R. Waugh 94*, D. Gough 4-60)
and 320-7 dec. (D. C. Boon 131); **England 212** (G. P. Thorpe 51, S. K. Warne 6-64)
and 92 (C. J. McDermott 5-42).

Third Test
At Sydney, January 1, 2, 3, 4, 5, 1995. Drawn.

An eighth-wicket stand between Warne and May, lasting 77 minutes, saved Australia from an astonishing defeat in a game that had seemed dead two and a half hours earlier.

Australia, who abandoned a bold pursuit of 449 only when rain intervened, were then 239 for two. An hour and a quarter later, however, they were 292 for seven; in three overs Fraser scythed down their middle order with a spell of four for four. With play continuing until 7.26, England were handicapped in their final thrust by fading light, which forced Atherton to stop using his pace bowlers. But, with up to eight fielders round the bat, it was a gritty achievement by the tailenders to survive, thus ensuring Australia would hold the Ashes for a fourth successive term.

It was a match of startling fluctuations and surprises, not least the fact that Warne bowled 52 overs for a solitary wicket – Malcolm's. On every day except the fourth, when only one wicket fell for 304 runs, as England constructed a cautious declaration and Taylor and Slater aggressively replied, the faster bowlers took charge. Of 29 wickets to fall, they claimed 27. The pitch had pace and regular bounce but, before Australia's brief first innings, sweated under its ground-level covers. In humid and frequently over-cast conditions, the ball often swung.

Atherton had to bat first. But, with McDermott and Fleming exploiting the humidity, England were 20 for three inside an hour; Gooch, opening in Stewart's absence, fell in the second over. Their luck turned when Bucknor denied Fleming a convincing lbw appeal against Atherton: reprieved, he put the innings on its feet, adding 174 with Crawley, who played with composure in his first Ashes Test. It looked like England's day, before McDermott darted an offcutter with the new ball between bat and pad to bowl Atherton for 88, and four balls later had a hapless Gatting caught behind. Before the close, Crawley edged Fleming to second slip and Rhodes was run out attempting one off a misfield; Australia had the initiative again.

It was recaptured, however, by Gough, with a jaunty innings of village-green inno-cence and charm. Throwing his bat at anything pitched up and hooking or pulling vigorously when it was short, he cracked 51 in 56 balls, before he mis-hooked McDermott to deep fine leg. Malcolm followed Gough's example, needing only 18 balls to make 29, his highest Test score. He was bowled whirling at a leg-break after straight-driving Warne for his second six. When Fraser, the night-watchman turned anchor man, was caught off a skyer, Gough's joyous thrash had inspired the addition of 111 runs in even time that morning.

Those extra runs completely changed the picture. For when rain allowed only 3.3 overs after lunch and a downpour next morning forced groundstaff to replace the covers before play restarted, Slater and Taylor found themselves resuming in ideal conditions for the seamers. Not helped by Boon and Steve Waugh, who shouldered arms to Gough and were bowled, Australia collapsed to 65 for eight, needing another 45 to save the follow-on. Though Taylor was still in, there might have been no escape had Malcolm, at mid-on, run to catch a mis-hit off Gough by McDermott, instead of leaving it to Gooch, more distant at mid-off. When Malcolm came on to bowl, Taylor and McDermott counter-attacked, taking 17 off his first three overs. Then, at 107 for eight, an inept Malcolm bouncer sailed high over Rhodes for four byes and the follow-on was saved. Almost immediately, Gough took a return catch from Taylor off his slower ball, and next ball yorked Fleming. But England's best chance of victory had gone.

Atherton's respect for Australia's batting was implicit in the tempo of England's second innings. Despite a lead of 193, they took 72 overs to make 255 for two, and it was not until Thorpe joined Hick that they stepped up to four an over. In what was thought to be the last-but-one over Hick, on 98, blocked three successive balls, and Atherton lost patience and ungenerously declared; he had batted far more slowly himself.

No team had ever made as much as 449 to win a Test. But Taylor and Slater set out with such a will that Australia might have had a real chance had the weather held. Overnight, they needed another 310 off 90 overs. Atherton was concerned enough to instruct Tufnell to bowl over the wicket to a five-man leg-side field. But though that held Australia to 67 off 31 overs up to lunch, the openers were still together, despite a run-out appeal which Taylor might not have survived had umpire Hair called for the replay. It was only when rain prolonged lunch long enough to embrace an early tea that Taylor decided that chasing 243, at 4.67 an over, was too risky. Officially, only seven overs were lost, because of the additional hour, but the conditions had also turned against Australia.

Both men reached hundreds. Slater was superbly caught by Tufnell, running diagonally backwards at deep square leg, and at 239 Taylor was bowled by Malcolm with the new ball. But it was not until Gough and Fraser swept aside five wickets in nine overs that England – too late – began running between overs. Thanks to the earlier slow rate, it was 6.25 when the umpires signalled the start of the last hour. Seven wickets were down, but Fraser and Gough managed only three more overs before the darkness impelled Atherton to take them off. Warne and May handled what followed so calmly that when Warne was put down at mid-off by Malcolm off Gooch, off the final ball of the minimum 15 overs, there was very little chance that it affected the result. In the event, a great Test ended bizarrely when, with the batsmen almost through the players' gate and tractors circling the infield, Atherton pointed out that the clock indicated 7.24, leaving time for a 16th over. May negotiated four balls from Tufnell safely.

Toss: England. **England 309** (M. A. Atherton 88, J. P. Crawley 72, D. Gough 51, C. J. McDermott 5-101) **and 255-2 dec.** (M. A. Atherton 67, G. A. Hick 98*); **Australia 116** (D. Gough 6-49) **and 344-7** (M. A. Taylor 113, M. J. Slater 103, A. R. C. Fraser 5-73).

CRICKETER OF THE YEAR – ANGUS FRASER

Mike Selvey, 1996

It is a sight as familiar now as once was Trueman's surge, Botham's bull-charge or Willis's manic flapping. Angus Fraser's trundle begins with a shuffle, and gathers momentum as he picks up his size 13s and leans forward like a trawlerman breasting a brisk nor'easter. It is all rather inelegant and unathletic: a man trampling through a nettle-bed pursued by a swarm of bees.

This is only the prelude, though. He hits the crease with the minimum of elevation, and his delivery stride – short by any standard, let alone a man approaching six and a half feet – scarcely spans the width of the crease. There is no resistance in his action and he bowls through his run rather than setting himself. Nor does he bend his back. Not much for the purist so far. But now something happens. His front arm reaches out and inscribes an imaginary line to a point just outside the batsman's off stump, tugging his bowling arm after it in a replica arc so high that his knuckles could snag on the clouds and pull them down. Unencumbered by being yanked out of plane, the ball can only follow the line. The geometry of it all is simple, and the result predictable, but it is a gift given to few.

Angus Fraser deals in parsimony and red-faced effort. He is perennially grumpy, kicks savage lumps from the turf at a conceded leg-bye, and could murder a misfielder: the opposite to the millionaire spendthrifts who buy their wickets with boundaries. Somewhere, he believes, he can always get a cheaper deal. Runs are a commodity to be hoarded, not frittered away on the undeserving. This is Scrooge in flannels. Batsmen? Bah! Humbug!

The fates have conspired against him almost as much as his expression suggests. From his debut until the end of the 1995 season, England played a total of 65 Tests but Fraser took the field in just 29. Injury has played a large part, not least the debilitating hip ailment that manifested itself in Melbourne over Christmas of 1990, and which took two frustrating years from his cricket life. He missed 24 consecutive Tests, although when he did return for the final match of the 1993 Ashes series his match figures of eight for 131 helped bring England a consolation win at the end of a trying summer.

More mystifying, however, has been the reluctance of selectors to recognise his virtues as a thoroughbred Test match bowler, mistaking his downcast demeanour – Eeyore without the *joie de vivre* – for lack of spark.

Fourth Test

At Adelaide, January 26, 27, 28, 29, 30, 1995. England won by 106 runs.

An over-confident and ill-paced attempt by Australia to score 263 in 67 overs led to England's first Test win in Australia for eight years, a further example of the ability of Atherton's England to win occasional Tests when the odds were most stacked against them. Handicapped by injury and illness as England had been in Brisbane and Sydney, here they were reduced to five fit batsmen, injuries to Hick, Stewart (index finger – for the third time) and Fairbrother having forced them out of the tour. Additionally, Gough had flown home with a foot in plaster. Lewis, who had been playing club cricket in Melbourne, joined the party.

In keeping with this disordered background, Gatting, who thought he had played his final game on tour, made the top score: a laborious 410-minute 117 which ensured England did not wholly waste an opening stand of 93 after winning a useful toss. It was Gatting's first Test hundred since 1987, tenth in all, and one he will never forget. Taylor made him fight for every run, with Warne and McDermott helping to hold him for 77 minutes in the nineties – an agonising 31 minutes on 99. It was almost as much a relief to the 16,000 crowd as it was to Gatting when, in the 11th over of McDermott's mighty spell, a crooked throw by Steve Waugh enabled DeFreitas to complete a jumpy single after a stop-go in mid-pitch. Gatting was last out, caught at short third man mistiming a leg-break from Peter McIntyre, one of two new caps. The other, 23-year-old Greg Blewett, became the 16th Australian to score a hundred on Test debut.

Slater and Taylor opened with a commanding 128 on an even-bouncing pitch with no extra pace. Some rebuilding was needed when Taylor was removed by a question-able lbw and Mark Waugh was beaten by Fraser's late movement. But Blewett and Healy advanced to 394 for five by the close and a match-winning lead seemed likely. Instead, the five outstanding wickets fell in 50 minutes, Blewett needing the support of McIntyre at No. 10 to see him past his hundred – just as last man McDermott returned from hospital after suffering stomach cramps. More used to opening for South Australia, Blewett, lightly and athletically built, gave no chance in 261 minutes, handsomely cover-driving boundaries off balls most would have pushed for ones and twos.

England resumed only 66 adrift, and Thorpe scored a dashing 83 after lunch on the fourth day. Despite Warne's waning influence, however, England appeared to be heading for a third defeat when Lewis was bowled at 181 for six. Crawley and DeFreitas steadied the ship, but the lead was only 154, with four wickets standing, at the close. Next day, however, with nine overs to bowl before the new ball, no established third seamer, and Fleming troubled by a hamstring, Taylor chose to open with McDermott. The move misfired. From the moment the new ball was taken DeFreitas saw it like a football – and a flagging McDermott was hammered for 41 in three overs. Mark Waugh, *en route* to a Test-best five for 40, ended a run-a-minute stand of 89 with a return catch off Crawley. DeFreitas, though, hitting classically through the off side, proceeded to plunder 22 off McDermott's third over – four fours and a six. He was deprived of a deserved maiden Test hundred when he was caught behind pulling Waugh. Orthodox but aggressive, without a single ugly stroke, he scored 68 of England's 108 in 18.5 overs on the final morning.

On a pitch still favouring the bat, it was hard to see beyond a draw or a third home win when Australia were 16 for no wicket at lunch. But just afterwards, Taylor was caught at first slip, whereupon three more fell in 16 balls. Steve Waugh was beaten by Malcolm's pace and bowled between bat and pad, but Boon and Slater – mis-hooking – made presents of their wickets. Australia were unlucky when a deflection from Gatting's toecap at short leg bounced into his hands, dislodging Mark Waugh who was batting easily. But the damage was done: when Lewis dismissed Warne and McDermott in the over spanning tea, Australia were 83 for eight. Fleming stayed with Healy nearly two hours but, with eight overs to go, a short ball from Lewis stayed down, trapping him lbw as he tried to pull. Finally Malcolm, replacing Tufnell, won an unconvincing lbw against McIntyre with his range-finder. England won with 35 balls remaining. Healy, with a second disciplined fifty, showed how easily the match could have been saved.

Toss: England. **England** 353 (M. A. Atherton 80, M. W. Gatting 117) and **328** (G. P. Thorpe 83, J. P. Crawley 71, P. A. J. DeFreitas 88, M. E. Waugh 5-40); **Australia** 419 (M. J. Slater 67, M. A. Taylor 90, G. S. Blewett 102*, I. A. Healy 74) and **156** (I. A. Healy 51*, D. E. Malcolm 4-39, C. C. Lewis 4-24).

Fifth Test

At Perth, February 3, 4, 5, 6, 7, 1995. Australia won by 329 runs.

Chastened by losing in Adelaide, Australia hit back with their biggest win of the rubber. Blewett became their third player, after Bill Ponsford (1924-25) and Doug Walters (1965-66), to score hundreds in his first two Tests; Slater made his fourth in 11 Tests against England, and McDermott ended proceedings before lunch on the last day by taking six England wickets for 38 runs. A vigorous hundred by Thorpe and two calm innings from Ramprakash, who displaced Tufnell from the winning team of Adelaide, were England's only gains.

Things started going wrong from the moment Gooch, at third slip, missed Slater off Malcolm's fourth ball – the first of seven missed catches in the innings, and ten by England in the match. Gooch had announced that his 118th Test, breaking David Gower's England record, would be his last, and Gatting followed suit. Though Gooch finished with 8,900 Test runs, scores of 37 and four for him, and nought and eight for Gatting, were an inappropriate end to distinguished Test careers.

Winning a good toss and scoring 402, Australia lost command only while Thorpe and Ramprakash were adding 158 in England's first innings. Thrown together at 77 for four on the second evening, they were still there 40 minutes into the third afternoon. Then, at 235, Thorpe jumped down the pitch to off-drive Warne, and was expertly stumped by Healy off a top-spinner that reached him shoulder-high.

England might have seized the initiative. After Lewis, in a fast spell, dismissed Taylor and Boon in successive overs, he had Mark Waugh dropped at 18 by Crawley in the gully. Then Malcolm missed Slater at 59 off an undemanding caught and bowled and gave him a third life, at 87, when he misjudged a hook off DeFreitas. After Slater and Waugh had added 183, Lewis and DeFreitas traded catches off each other's bowling to remove them at last. England made a lucky start to the second day when Blewett was given out caught from a deflection off his thigh, but their catching soon redressed the balance. The most expensive miss came when Steve Waugh, on 35, slashed DeFreitas shoulder-high between two motionless slips, Thorpe and Atherton. Angel, who helped Waugh add 58, was also dropped, twice, by Rhodes and Atherton. Waugh was finally stranded on 99 when his twin Mark, McDermott's runner, attempted an improbable single and was thrown out at the bowler's end by Gooch. Steve, frequently beaten in his first 50, had dug in for 289 minutes, sealing Australia's advantage.

The temporary absence of McDermott, who had strained his back, provided little relief. After three Tests as twelfth man, McGrath, in his first over, had Atherton caught down the leg side off a glove and next ball bowled Gatting via an inside edge. Ninety minutes later, Mark Waugh's first over saw off Gooch and Crawley.

Thorpe, hitting confidently through the line of his off- and straight-drives, needed only 218 balls to score 123 and struck 19 fours. Most of Ramprakash's 11 fours were sturdily driven between mid-off and mid-on, but his encouraging innings ended when he attempted to ward off a huge leg-break from Warne. Lewis, missed off a sharp caught-and-bowled chance by Angel before scoring, hit eight fours in an hour. Nevertheless, from Thorpe's dismissal, England lost six for 60 to be 107 behind.

Despite having his right thumb broken in Malcolm's third over, Slater made a flying start, scoring 45 off 55 balls before Atherton took a lovely diving catch at second slip. Australia were forced to consolidate when they slipped to 123 for five. But Blewett, off-driving as handsomely as in Adelaide and scoring as smoothly off his legs, removed all danger of defeat. Outscoring Waugh by 114 to 77 in a stand of 203, he hit 19 fours.

Left 104 overs to hold out for a draw after Taylor's declaration – a target of 453 was well out of range – England's hopes were shattered when McDermott and McGrath ripped five out for 27 in 14 overs before the close. Menacingly as they bowled to a catching ring of seven, it was feeble batting on a pitch still full of runs. Atherton's dismissal to the 12th ball of the final morning, again caught down the leg side off McGrath, made Australia's third win a certainty. Ramprakash and Rhodes, adding 68, threatened to take the game into the afternoon, until Mark Waugh cramped Ramprakash with unexpected bounce; unable to get on top of it, he cut to gully. McDermott saw the tail off in four overs, claiming his 32nd wicket of the series by cartwheeling Malcolm's middle stump with a dramatic yorker.

Toss: Australia. **Australia 402** (M. J. Slater 124, M. E. Waugh 88, S. R. Waugh 99*)
and 345-8 dec. (M. A. Taylor 52, S. R. Waugh 80, G. S. Blewett 115); **England 295** (G. P. Thorpe 123, M. R. Ramprakash 72) **and 123** (C. J. McDermott 6-38).

NOTES BY THE EDITOR   Matthew Engel, 1995

It is easy to see why England might fear an official Test World Championship: someone might eventually propose that the bottom country be relegated.

The consequences of the latest remarkable Ashes series cannot be ignored, as they provide yet more threads in the seamless story of cricket, and the ongoing saga of the adventures of England's raggle-taggle army. Despite their defeat in Adelaide, Australia's victories in Brisbane, Melbourne and Perth ensure that they retain the Ashes, which they have held since 1989, at least until 1997. On some reckonings this sequence is already the most one-sided ever.

Australia retain the Ashes theoretically, anyway. As every schoolboy used and ought to know, the urn and its contents rest permanently in the museum at Lord's. This is, of course, legally as it should be: they were given to MCC in 1927. But the Ashes is no longer a contest between a mother country and its colonial offshoot, far from it; it is a battle between two independent nations. Works of art are transported round the world. It would be in keeping with MCC's historic mission if it were to agree that the trophy should be displayed in the country that holds them.

Such a move would generate enormous public interest in both nations and give a huge emotional charge to the moment the Ashes changed hands. This would not just be an act of generosity. It would be terrific for English cricket's long-term wellbeing: children could then be taken to Lord's, forced to stare at the empty plinth and swear that they would help bring about the urn's return. There is no single reason why England lose so often at cricket, but it is easy to underestimate the power of symbolism and patriotism and passion.

ENGLAND V AUSTRALIA 1997   Tim de Lisle

The best skyline in English cricket is the one you see from the top of The Oval pavilion, encompassing the gasometer, Big Ben, the incongruous gaudiness of the MI5 head-quarters, and, on a clear day, half of London. In 1997, there was an extra attraction: "The World's First Tethered Balloon Ride", in the Harleyford Road. Every so often, a hot-air balloon would rise behind the sightscreen at the Vauxhall End, dangle for a few minutes, and return to earth.

It could have been put there to represent England's summer. They started so commandingly, in the one-day internationals and the First Test, that the nation became more excited about the team's performance than it had been at any time, arguably, since Headingley 1981. But the Australians dug deep into their reserves of skill and willpower. After having the better of a rainy stalemate at Lord's, they needed only three Test matches to draw level, pull ahead, and then secure both the Ashes and the series. At The Oval, England finished as they had begun, with a pulsating victory. It was too late. The balloon had been tethered all along.

For Australia, it was a third major victory in nine months, following the series against West Indies and South Africa, and a fifth consecutive series win over England – a sequence they had never achieved in 115 years of the Ashes. And they had overcome, if not the odds, then a powerful conspiracy of circumstances. Their captain, Mark Taylor, was so out of form that he dropped himself from the one-day team. Their acclimatisation was made harder still by the climate: if it was not actually raining, it was grey and dank. They were tired: leading players such as Ian Healy and the Waugh brothers had flown 70,000 miles since October 1996. And for once, steps were taken – unofficially, but unmistakably – to fix the pitches in England's favour. Only one Test out of six was played on a flat track.

Australia had won the previous four series with cruel ease: 4–0, 3–0, 4–1 and 3–1. In the context of 17–4, 3–2 wasn't bad. And although the victory was convincing, it was never insulting. There were two critical differences between the sides. The first, as widely predicted, was the Australian bowlers – though, as not predicted at all, it was the bowlers' batting that really stood out. In McGrath and Warne, Australia had far and away the best bowlers, yet the two top orders performed identically – each team's first five wickets raised, on average, 186 runs. The second half of the order was another story: England's remaining wickets added an average of 60, Australia's 117.

First Test

At Birmingham, June 5, 6, 7, 8, 1997. England won by nine wickets.

John Etheridge

The ripples of patriotic optimism which followed England's 3–0 victory in the one-day series had become a tidal wave of emotion and euphoria by the end of this extraordinary match. There were reasons to think England might perform well – their growing confidence in New Zealand, the whitewash in the one-day internationals, Taylor's personal purgatory, Australia's injuries and general lack of form – but nothing had prepared a disbelieving public for what actually happened.

The game had everything as far as England were concerned: Australia's collapse on the opening morning, magnificent innings by Hussain and Thorpe, a heroic century by Taylor and a suitably dramatic finale. England won at 6.52 on Sunday, when Stewart cracked Warne to the extra-cover boundary. They passed their target of 118 in just 21.3 overs and the crowd, close to a fourth successive full house, engulfed the field. "They're coming home, they're coming home, Ashes coming home," they sang, to the tune made famous in the Euro '96 soccer championships. Not even the most hard-bitten realists dared argue: the electric, jingoistic atmosphere was a feature of the grand occasion.

Taylor chose to bat and, by 12.36, Australia were 54 for eight from 20 overs. The sheer drama of it all scrambled the senses. Gough's first ball fizzed past Taylor's outside edge – by contrast, the opening delivery of the previous Ashes series was a long-hop from DeFreitas which Slater square-cut for four at Brisbane. Gough, bowling with pace, rhythm and confidence, made the initial thrusts, removing three of the top four, while

Malcolm persuaded Taylor to chase a wide one and disturbed Bevan with lift. Caddick then swept through the middle and lower order. Only a flurry from Warne took Australia beyond three figures.

Edgbaston's future as a Test venue was already threatened, because the matches of 1995 and 1996 finished well inside three and four days respectively. Ten wickets in two and a half hours scarcely calmed the demeanour of Dennis Amiss, Warwickshire's chief executive, or his groundsman. But Australia's collapse had little to do with demons in the pitch. There was some uneven bounce and lateral movement, certainly, but it was swing and self-destructive shots which undermined their batsmen.

Mutterings about the pitch continued as England's top three succumbed in an hour. But they were silenced when Hussain and Thorpe put on 288, England's highest fourth-wicket partnership against Australia. Here were two friends demoralising the ultimate foe and the best side in the world. Hussain was touched by genius during a truly great innings. When Warne dropped short, he cut with power and precision. When the quick bowlers overpitched, he drove with skill and certainty. In all, he batted for 440 minutes and 337 balls; 38 fours peppered his maiden double-hundred in any cricket, England's first against Australia since David Gower scored 215 on the same ground in 1985. Thorpe was Hussain's equal; indeed, he probably displayed superior range and execution of shot on the first day, when they added 150 in 169 minutes. Thorpe's cutting and sweeping of Warne were crucial in seizing the initiative.

Warne was ineffective, partly because his sore shoulder reduced the rip he could impart and partly because Hussain and Thorpe never allowed him to settle. McGrath bowled where he would do in Australia, rather than the fuller length required in England, and Gillespie retired with a hamstring strain. Kasprowicz, who had failed to take a wicket in his previous two Tests, sustained his hostility and was easily their best bowler. Healy took six catches, equalling the Australian Test record.

Facing a deficit of 360, Taylor knew failure could mean the end of his international career. He had not reached 50 in his previous 21 Test innings and he was being casti-gated, it seemed, by every old Test player with a platform. His batting was a monument to courage and determination – if not technique, because he was still susceptible around off stump. He reached his first century since November 1995 on Saturday evening, sharing stands of 133 with Elliott and 194 with Blewett, whose cover-driving on the up was dazzling: he became the first man to score centuries in his first three Ashes Tests. Shortly before lunch on the fourth day, Australia were 327 for one – just 33 adrift. But once Croft had winkled out the top three, Gough, in another inspired burst, removed the heart of their innings in seven overs. Ealham finished them off with three for nought in ten balls.

Suddenly, England knew they could win with a day to spare. They required 118 and had a possible 32 overs. They did it in style. Butcher set the tempo, striking 14 in ten balls, then Atherton and Stewart blazed away. "The adrenalin was flowing so much," said Atherton, "that I couldn't stop myself playing attacking shots." He scored 57 in 65 balls, passing 5,000 Test runs on the way. Victory brought an outpouring of elation, in front of the pavilion and across the country; people suddenly felt the little urn could, indeed, be recaptured.

Toss: Australia. **Australia 118** (A. R. Caddick 5-50) **and 477** (M. T. G. Elliott 66, M. A. Taylor 129, G. S. Blewett 125); **England 478-9 dec.** (N. Hussain 207, G. P. Thorpe 138, M. A. Ealham 53*, M. S. Kasprowicz 4-113) **and 119-1** (M. A. Atherton 57*).

Second Test

David Frith

At Lord's, June 19, 20, 21, 22, 23, 1997. Drawn.

Rain prevented a conclusive result, ending Australia's run of 18 Tests without a draw. But there was never a chance of England ending their melancholy sequence of failure against Australia at Lord's; their 1934 victory was confirmed as their only success in 24 Tests there in the 20th century. By the end, they were not remotely concerned about that; having been humiliated for 77, they were grateful that the weather enabled them to cling on to their series lead. Atherton lost an important toss on his 42nd appearance as England captain (surpassing Peter May's record of 41). This time, Taylor put England in, and bowled them out for even less than Australia had managed after choosing to bat in not dissimilar conditions at Edgbaston.

No play had been possible on the scheduled first day, and only an hour and a half on the second. In that time, England, fielding an unchanged XI for the first time in home Tests since June 1991, lost Butcher, Atherton and Stewart – who left an off-cutter – all to McGrath, on a pitch of uneven bounce. Thorpe almost went too, before he had scored, but Healy was uncertain about his catch and said so, prompting a burst of applause from umpire Shepherd.

At that stage, England's supporters were still more concerned about the ruin of the great occasion. On the Saturday, the cricket became more of a concern. The rest of England's wickets toppled before lunch next day while they scraped together just 39. The tall McGrath, continuing from the Pavilion End, adopted a fuller length than at Edgbaston and bowled with pace, lift, movement off the seam and unwavering accuracy to pick up five more wickets. The batsmen found no relief at the other end, for Reiffel bowled a tight line and moved the ball away dangerously. He found Thorpe's edge for a catch via the pad and later deceived Ealham into playing early. The rigid England batsmen could scarcely score a run an over off him. McGrath swept away the rest: Crawley played especially limply, probably with Stewart's fatal leave-alone in mind. When Caddick was lbw, McGrath had the best analysis in the 31 England-Australia Tests staged at Lord's, the second-best for Australia in England (behind Frank Laver's eight for 31 at Old Trafford in 1909), and the third-best by an Australian bowler in any Test (behind also Arthur Mailey's nine for 121 against England at Melbourne in 1920–21). England's 77 was their lowest in any Test on this ground since 1888; only nine times in 287 Tests against Australia had they fared worse. The national spirit of self-confidence which followed victory at Edgbaston had been both drenched and deflated.

The stunned atmosphere was relieved a touch by the early dismissal of Australia's captain when they began their reply. Gough bounded in and, in his third over, Taylor deflected a widish delivery into his stumps. Blewett soon saw a looping edge off Caddick fall safely, but settled to play some resonant strokes before edging Croft to slip. It was not the end of England's maladroitness, however. In a bizarre spell in the late-afternoon dankness, Elliott was missed three times as he reached 55 – twice by Butcher at slip and by Malcolm at long leg. Meanwhile, Mark Waugh gave a sharp chance to Hussain at slip and a difficult leg-side stumping opportunity to Crawley (deputising for Stewart, who had suffered a back spasm), both off Croft. England were suddenly unrecognisable from the competent unit of a fortnight earlier.

Impatient to level the series, Australia were frustrated again on the fourth day, when only 17.4 overs were bowled as shower after shower sprayed Lord's. From 131 for two they progressed to 213 for seven, the pace resembling that of a one-day match. Waugh slashed a catch to third man and brother Steve went back to his first ball and was lbw. In between, Warne, promoted to No. 5, had wafted a high off-side catch. And all this happened with the score 147. Undeterred, Elliott still sought to score from every delivery, and ran to his first Test century from his 171st ball. He fell soon afterwards to his favoured stroke, the hook, having loaded his 112 with 20 fours, an exceptional proportion.

Declaring overnight in the hope of cashing in a lead of 136, Australia were favoured with clearer weather at last, but the pitch had calmed. Prepared for a gruelling final day with their backs to the wall, England firmly reclaimed their poise, though only after Taylor, at slip, had spared Butcher when he was two. But at lunch England were 70 without loss, and they had eased to a lead of 26 before Atherton accidentally kicked his off stump as he played to leg. When light rain forced a slightly early tea at 169 for one, the only remaining interest was whether Butcher, seeming more and more comfortable, might reach a hundred. But his hopes were dashed by a well-flighted ball from Warne – looking more like his old self – that spun out of the rough. From there, England batted it out: chastened but still one up.

Toss: Australia. **England 77** (G. D. McGrath 8-38) **and 266-4 dec.** (M. A. Butcher 87, M. A. Atherton 77); **Australia 213-7 dec.** (M. T. G. Elliott 112, A. R. Caddick 4-71).

CRICKETER OF THE YEAR – GLENN MCGRATH   Bruce Wilson, 1998

Friends who were there recall a day, deep in the Queensland bush "out the back of Longreach", on a pig-shooting weekend with the man they call "Pigeon" and the cricketing world knows as Glenn McGrath. The tall fast bowler had spotted a large boar, and he disappeared into the bush in hot pursuit. Three shots were heard, and McGrath came loping back into view, reached into the four-wheel drive, said "Out of ammo," and loped off again, all, at the same relentless, steady pace. He got the pig. It is a story many who have played against him will recognise uneasily; wild boar or batsman, Glenn McGrath tends to get what he is hunting.

He was demonstrably the best quick bowler on either side in the Ashes series of 1997 and, but for the presence of one Shane Warne, could claim to be the best bowler of all; indeed, it is a claim he might make anyway, if he were a different kind of man. To do so, though would be big-noting and, where McGrath comes from, there are few greater sins.

Glenn Donald McGrath was born on February 9, 1970, in Dubbo, a wheat and sheep farming centre a couple of hundred miles north-west of Sydney – not quite the real bush, but McGrath's father farmed in a succession of tiny settlements outside Dubbo with names smelling of gum-leaves: Eumungerie, Galgandra, Narromine. It was at the last that the young Glenn went to school, and where he started to play cricket.

At 19, at Doug Walters's instigation, McGrath moved to Sydney and the Sutherland club. Odd jobs and living in a caravan followed, and four seasons of weekend cricket, until, in January 1993, he was selected for New South Wales. By November, he was playing his first Test, against New Zealand at Perth: three wickets for quite a lot. Since then, he has become Australia's strike bowler, with Warne. At the end of 1997, McGrath had 164 wickets at the remarkable average of 23.43 from 36 Tests. It is a figure very close to the man upon whom McGrath has based his career, Dennis Lillee, whose 355 Test wickets came at 23.92.

Third Test

Ken Casellas

At Manchester, July 3, 4, 5, 6, 7, 1997. Australia won by 268 runs.

The slumbering giant, aroused by the unaccustomed situation of trailing in a Test series, awoke, flexed its not inconsiderable muscle and demolished the opposition with brutal efficiency. Australia's emphatic triumph put them back on track after a stuttering start and weeks of depressing grey skies and rain. Suddenly, the weather resembled something vaguely like summer. The contest had high achievement and occasional drama, but, from the moment Steve Waugh put his stamp on it, the whip hand was held by Australia. Waugh became the first batsman to score twin Ashes hundreds for 50 years; backed up by Warne, who convincingly returned to his best form, he well and truly wrested the initiative.

Australia had reinforced McGrath's intimidating pace with Gillespie, who replaced Kasprowicz. England gave Dean Headley a historic debut: he was the third generation of his family to play Test cricket, following his grandfather George and his father Ron, who both represented West Indies. Headley was straight into the action, striking Taylor on the helmet as he ducked into a bouncer. England had hardly concealed their joy when Taylor chose to bat on a moist, green pitch with bare patches at either end. It seemed a foolish gamble; it proved a brave and calculated decision – one made easier for a captain with Warne's genius at his disposal. But Taylor was the first sufferer. Headley pressed home the advantage in his third over, squaring him up with a fiery delivery which was edged to first slip. Taylor's headache worsened as Australia declined to 42 for three. That was when Steve Waugh entered the fray, but he got little support from the middle order. The total was a miserable 160 for seven Reiffel joined him, just before tea.

Their luck changed, shortly after a break for bad light, when Reiffel was dropped on 13 by Stewart, off Headley. This could be construed as the turning-point of the entire season. Reiffel contributed 31 to a tremendously important stand of 70 before he finally fell next morning, to Gough's trademark inswinging yorker. By then, Waugh had completed a century of enormous skill and character. With his lucky red handkerchief poking from his trouser pocket like a matador's cap, he faced the charging attack for four hours, and later called it his finest Test innings. When he was ninth out, edging Gough on to his middle stump, he had seen Australia to 235, an admirable total in testing conditions. Headley ensured it went no higher with his fourth wicket, thanks to Stewart, whose sixth catch equalled England's record for an innings against Australia; later, he added two more to break the record for a match. His opposite number, Healy, soon retaliated. A brilliant leg-side stumping off a full toss from Bevan removed Butcher and provided Healy's 100th dismissal in 25 England–Australia Tests.

Healy's 99th victim had been Atherton, who, for the third time in three Tests went cheaply to McGrath. This time, he gloved a seemingly erratic leg-side delivery. But Butcher, possibly sensing his last chance to justify his place, and Stewart steered England serenely to 74. Then Warne made his first telling impact and sent shivers of apprehension through the home camp. Recalling his ball from hell to dismiss Mike Gatting here four years earlier, he bowled a sharply spinning leg-break; Stewart, nonplussed, jabbed desperately and jerked his head back to see Taylor fling himself sideways at slip and snaffle a superb low catch. Now Warne was ready to put Australia in charge, and he had just the pitch to encourage him. The green demon of the previous day had been transformed into a brown strip, already scarred by footmarks. Flighting the ball cleverly and getting some vicious spin, he dismissed Thorpe, Hussain and Crawley for one run in a magical spell of 26 balls, as the baffled Englishmen slumped to 111 for six with barely a whimper. He and McGrath mopped up the final two wickets in 22 balls of the third morning, and England were all out for 162. Warne finished with six for 48 from 30 overs, his first haul of five or more since November 1995.

Australia led by 73, but Headley and Croft removed their top three for 39 by the 14th over. Controversy enveloped the second wicket: Hussain, at slip, lunged forward as Blewett drove at Croft, and the ball bounced out of his right hand before he clasped it with his left. Umpire Venkataraghavan was unsure whether the edge had carried and consulted his colleague before giving Blewett out. But the Waughs combined to guide Australia into safer waters. Mark played a sublime two-hour 55, with seven fours and a six, while the flint-eyed Steve, often wincing in pain as he snatched a badly bruised right hand away from his bat, held firm for more than six hours. In that time, he became the third Australian to score a century in each innings against England, and the first right-hander, joining Warren Bardsley, at The Oval in 1909, and Arthur Morris, at Adelaide in 1946-47. Though Bevan failed again, the lower order did themselves proud. Taylor finally declared 20 minutes after Sunday lunch.

He left England a theoretical target of 469 in 141 overs – 63 more than anyone had ever made to win a Test. The pressure was overwhelming and England buckled. Butcher and Atherton opened aggressively, Atherton hooking Gillespie for six; the angry bowler struck back by trapping him lbw as he snapped up three for five in 19 balls. Warne and McGrath completed the rout. Warne became the third Australian bowler, after Dennis Lillee and Craig McDermott, to take 250 Test wickets, in his 55th match; his legend was further enhanced when Healy put on a helmet, complete with grille, to keep to him. Only Crawley resisted, but he emulated Atherton at Lord's by treading on his wicket when in sight of a century. England were all out for 200 at 12.30 on the final day. Australia's champagne celebrations were in stark contrast to the glum atmosphere in the home camp; the series was level at 1–1, but the momentum now was all one-way.

Toss: Australia. **Australia 235** (S. R. Waugh 108, D. W. Headley 4-72) **and 395-8 dec.** (M. E. Waugh 55, S. R. Waugh 116, S. K. Warne 53, D. W. Headley 4-104); **England 162** (M. A. Butcher 51, S. K. Warne 6-48) **and 200** (J. P. Crawley 83, G. D. McGrath 4-46).

Fourth Test

At Leeds, July 24, 25, 26, 27, 28, 1997. Australia won by an innings and 61 runs.

Mark Ray

Australia had levelled the series at Old Trafford through fine work from some of their senior players. The most notable aspect of their comprehensive win at Headingley, which gave them the lead, was that the protagonists were young players in their first

Ashes series. Elliott, 25, and Ponting, 22, scored centuries to lead them out of trouble and into an unbeatable position, after the 22-year-old Gillespie had destroyed England's first innings with the best figures by an Australian in a Headingley Test. England returned to their old ways, bowling and fielding poorly to concede a huge first-innings score, and batting with minimal application under sustained pressure.

Having won his fourth consecutive toss, Taylor chose to bowl on a green pitch. Rain restricted the first day's play to 36 overs, which Atherton survived unbeaten on 34, with England 106 for three. The apparent solidity of that start crumbled to dust the next day when Gillespie produced a spell of genuine speed and outstanding control. After he had caught Atherton at long leg, out to McGrath yet again, Gillespie took the last five wickets as England added just 18 in nine overs. They were all out for 172.

That fragility with the bat was to be mirrored by a sloppy performance in the field. Not for the first time, they made a fine start, on a pitch offering England's seam attack more than enough assistance. Australia were in some strife at 50 for four in the 18th over. That brought their two most inexperienced batsmen, Elliott and Ponting, together. They promptly accepted the challenge by counter-attacking with courage, common sense and, in Elliott's case, a little luck. As in his century at Lord's Elliott was dropped three times. Yet, in between those lapses, he drove, hooked and cut with impressive assurance and deceptive power. The first miss, when Elliott was on 29 and Australia still only 50, was a relatively easy chance to Thorpe at first slip off the bowling of Smith, the left-arm swing bowler who ended up wicketless in what turned out to be his only Test. It was deemed by many observers to be the sort of dropped catch that costs a Test series. Although that is too simplistic, Thorpe's lapse was typical of England's poor play. Elliott went on to bat for seven and a half hours and 351 balls, hitting three sixes and 23 fours, before being bowled, one short of a double-hundred, by a superb swinging yorker from England's best bowler, Gough. Meanwhile, Ponting's chanceless maiden Test century, on his Ashes debut, was as near perfection as could be expected from a young player returning to the team; he had missed the previous eight Tests through a selection decision that still seemed harsh some seven months later. From the start, he drove and pulled superbly, to gather 19 fours and a six. Together, Elliott and Ponting added 268 for the fifth wicket in 263 minutes, and Elliott shared further half-century partnerships with Healy and Reiffel.

When Taylor declared at lunch on the fourth day, Australia had a lead of 329. But England played well over the next two sessions: by stumps, they were 212 for four. Hussain had completed his second century of the series and had put on 123 with Crawley. Any hopes of a draw inspired by their stand were dashed early on the final morning, however, when Warne took his only wicket of the match (he bowled one solitary over in the first innings): he deceived Hussain in flight for a simple catch to Gillespie at mid-off. Crawley went on to 72, but the end came quickly enough. England were bowled out for 268 to lose by an innings, with Reiffel adding five more wickets to his 54 not out.

Gillespie had bowled down the hill from the Kirkstall Lane End to excellent effect, something none of the England bowlers seemed able to do. In hindsight, the decision to prefer Smith to Caddick looked a disaster: uneven bounce was more relevant than swing, and Caddick should have been able to exploit that far better.

Once again, there was tension between the fierce Headingley stewards and the sometimes raucous spectators in the Western Terrace, especially those keen on the fashion for attending Tests in fancy dress. Two men dressed in a pantomime-cow costume cavorted round the boundary, and were crash-tackled by officials after play: the man playing the rear end needed treatment in hospital. Brian Cheesman, a university lecturer dressed as a carrot, was frog-marched from the ground for drunken and abusive behaviour. He vehemently denied the allegations. Mr Cheesman had been attending Headingley Tests in fancy dress since 1982.

Toss: Australia. **England 172** (J. N. Gillespie 7-37) **and 268** (N. Hussain 105, J. P. Crawley 72, P. R. Reiffel 5-49); **Australia 501-9 dec.** (M. T. G. Elliott 199, R. T. Ponting 127, P. R. Reiffel 54*, D. Gough 5-149).

Fifth Test

At Nottingham, August 7, 8, 9, 10, 1997. Australia won by 264 runs.

Peter Johnson

Crushing defeat cost England the series and the Ashes but not, this time, their captain. Atherton withstood all the demands that he follow the example of his predecessor, Graham Gooch, who had fallen on his sword in similar circumstances four years earlier. But the public debate about his future did nothing to ease the pressure on Atherton.

There were times when England's out-cricket was impeccable – disciplined, athletic and enthusiastic. Yet it seemed only to incite the Australians to lift their game, to emphasise that the series had, since the upset at Edgbaston, been an unequal contest between honest endeavour and pure talent.

Accepting that, the England selectors revoked their vow after the Old Trafford defeat to stand by their men, left out those useful tradesmen Butcher, Ealham and Smith, and went instead for action heroes. Pace bowlers Malcolm and Caddick were restored and the brothers Adam and Ben Hollioake, left to bask in the public's adulation since their one-day heroics, were asked to give the side some of their Australian-bred self-confidence. Adam, seen by many as a serious candidate for the captaincy, needed to prove his ability as a Test batsman. Ben, at 19 years 269 days, was the youngest England Test debutant since Brian Close in 1949. The Hollioakes were only the fifth set of brothers to play a Test for England, and the first since Worcestershire's Peter and Dick Richardson in 1957.

The Hollioakes' inclusion was a gamble, but not the only one forced upon England. Conscious that Stewart's role as wicket-keeper-batsman was crucial, yet aware that he was desperately out of touch, the selectors tried some daring alternative medicine. Instead of keeping him back at No. 3, they asked him to open again. It was a temporary and seemingly unfair expedient – but it inspired his finest innings of the series. By the time Stewart made those spectacular runs, though, two unpredictable factors had given Australia a command they never relaxed. First Gough, England's most successful bowler, failed a fitness test on an inflamed knee. Then Atherton lost the toss for the fifth successive time.

Given first use of the only flawless pitch of the series, Australia used it entertainingly but mercilessly. Headley, Caddick and Malcolm bowled with speed, devotion and some accuracy under a relentless sun. England's ground fielding was superb. Yet, on that decisive opening day, the first four batsmen made half-centuries, each different in style but all tinged with an air of inevitability, as Australia advanced to 302 for three.

Headley eventually broke the opening stand of 117 when he had Elliott taken behind off a dubious inside edge. Taylor was bowled by Caddick after becoming the sixth Australian to pass 6,000 Test runs, and Ben Hollioake claimed his first Test wicket, Blewett, with his 38th ball. Hollioake minor was carefully nursed and allowed to bowl only eight overs of bland medium-pace. But it was a painful learning experience, as he went for five an over. He and Adam shared another moment of history by bowling in tandem – brothers against brothers – at the Waugh twins. Steve completed the fifth 50 of the innings next morning, but Australia lost their last seven for 116 as the bowlers were finally rewarded for their hard labour.

Australia's 427 left them virtually fireproof. Yet they were singed by Stewart's 87. He made the runs with his old, instinctive timing off only 107 balls, hitting 14 fours. He and Atherton had reached 106 in 27 overs and were promising England an honourable retreat when Warne turned in another of his hugely influential spells, removing both of them, plus Hussain, in 40 deliveries. England rallied again on the third day to reach 313, a deficit of 114. Thorpe reached his first Test 50 since Edgbaston, supported by Adam Hollioake in a stand of 102, and Ben hit a few fearless shots in his 28. But, by the close, Australia had stretched their lead to 281. And on the fourth day, England totally lost the plot.

Some wildly off-line bowling gave Healy the chance to show he is still the game's supreme and toughest wicket-keeper-batsman. Together with Ponting, he thrashed 105 in 104 minutes, and hit nine fours in his 63, as Australia went through one of their familiar spirit-crushing routines.

Left to get 451 or to survive for more than eight hours, England lasted just 48.5 overs. From the moment Atherton glanced a jaw-threatening bouncer from McGrath into Healy's gloves, it was an innings with no visible plan, a strange mix of strokeless submission and devil-may-care defiance. Only Thorpe looked sure of what he was doing and why. But even he could not stop the rampant Australian attack and their hawk-like fielders from picking off the stragglers. His last six companions contributed 14 as he scored 68.

Australia claimed the extra half-hour at 173 for eight and one of the more lifeless and misguided England innings of a dark decade passed quietly into history with seven balls to spare. Warne led Australia's cavortings in front of the pavilion as they claimed the Ashes for the fifth time in a row. Atherton resolutely declined journalists' invitations to resign at once.

Toss: Australia. **Australia 427** (M. T. G. Elliott 69, M. A. Taylor 76, G. S. Blewett 50, M. E. Waugh 68,
S. R. Waugh 75, D. W. Headley 4-87) **and 336** (G. S. Blewett 60, I. A. Healy 63);
England 313 (A. J. Stewart 87, G. P. Thorpe 53, G. D. McGrath 4-71, S. K. Warne 4-86)
and 186 (G. P. Thorpe 82*).

Sixth Test

Matthew Engel

At The Oval, August 21, 22, 23, 1997. England won by 19 runs.

Too late to rescue the Ashes, but not too late to rescue their self-respect, England won a sensational victory after a contest fit to rank with the great games of Ashes history. The match was over at 5.24 on the third day, but the cricket that did take place was amazing, and the climax utterly riveting. Australia, needing only 124 to win, were bowled out for just 104. The Oval crowd celebrated England's triumph in a manner not seen at least since the Edgbaston win, 11 weeks earlier – but that seemed like an awfully long time ago.

Australia's collapse maintained their reputation for vulnerability in a run-chase, and for flunking the Tests that matter least. It was the third time in 1997 they had lost the last match of a series they had already won. It did not much dent their reputation as one of the great Ashes teams. The result meant far more to England. In advance, they would have settled for losing 3–2, a result that suggested tangible progress after all the bleak years.

Like so many great matches, this came about thanks to what is conventionally known as a bad pitch. It was too dry, and by the second day it was crumbling. This came as a surprise to just about everyone. When England were all out on the first day, it was assumed to be yet another pathetic batting failure, and perhaps a terminal one for Atherton's captaincy. The first assumption was correct, because the pitch was still mild and there was no excuse at all for their collapse from 128 for three to 132 for seven. But for once the luck favoured England. After five successes in a row, Taylor's habit of shouting his nickname – tails – at the toss let him down. England were able to bat first and hoped to give Australia the runaround in steamy, Brisbane-like heat. They must have fancied 500; even afterwards, Atherton thought 350 was par; they made 180, a useful total only at darts.

England's final XI had four changes from Trent Bridge: Butcher was quickly recalled, along with the in-form Ramprakash and Martin, plus Tufnell, in the squad but not the team for the previous five Tests. Australia made two changes: Gillespie and Reiffel had flown home, so Kasprowicz came back in, along with Shaun Young, who had been making heaps of runs for Gloucestershire but seemed like a potential weak link in a four-man attack. At first it made no difference. After the openers were out cheaply, Stewart, Hussain and Thorpe gave England hope of a decent score. But McGrath once again was both insistent and persistent, and the middle order suddenly crumpled in a sort of cataleptic fit. Hussain, who had been unconvincing even against Young, drove to mid-on, and the flock followed. Caddick and Martin each hit a six, which was something, but England were all out before tea. McGrath finished with seven for 76, including England's top six; he did little more than bowl fast and straight.

Tufnell removed the openers in the evening session, but even so England's position looked dire, and direr still when Australia were 94 for two. But then the game changed. Over the years, Tufnell had displayed more than his share of the slow left-armer's traditional eccentricity; now he displayed the breed's quieter virtues. He kept his line and his patience and, in the afternoon, as the pitch began to wear visibly, he reaped his reward. Bowling unchanged for 35 overs, he worked his way through the Australian batting. He, too, finished with seven and, until Warne began slogging him, conceded hardly more than a run an over.

And so, after tea, England were in again, their hopes renewed. But the first three batsmen were gone before they had even wiped off their narrow deficit. And Saturday began with two blows. Firstly, Australia's lead was recalculated from 38 to 40 because a four hit by Blewett was ruled a six after the third umpire had pored over the TV evidence. And in this game every run mattered. Then, to the third ball of the morning, Hussain toe-ended a cut straight to Elliott. England were effectively 12 for four.

But the luck had turned. England supporters had long since assumed that injuries happened only to their side. However, Warne had been struggling on the second night, and now it was obvious he had a nasty groin strain. He was only able to lope in off three paces, and it seemed to curb his variety. That did not stop him turning the ball viciously out of the rough, and could not save the likes of Hussain, bent on doing something daft. But the next pair avoided the daft, and put on 79. Thorpe, not for the first time, failed to convert a fifty into a century but, since he scored the only half-century of the match, that was wholly forgivable. It was an innings of exceptional quality and tenacity. Ramprakash made 48, which was worth at least double.

At the time it still did not look enough. The England tail was useless yet again – the last four wickets fell for three – and Kasprowicz followed McGrath and Tufnell in taking seven in an innings; three bowlers had never before done this in the same Test. Australia needed just 124 to win. But there was a sense that the situation was not hopeless. The crowd roared Malcolm in as he took the new ball, and he responded by straightening his fourth delivery to dismiss Elliott.

Tufnell bowled over the wicket to turn the ball from the crumbling pitch rather than the footmarks, and applied enough pressure to help the bowler at the other end. The beneficiary was Caddick, who removed Taylor and Blewett, given out caught behind, though TV replays suggested this was a quaint decision – by no means his first – by umpire Barker. The Waughs soon followed. Australia were 54 for five and suddenly all England was agog, even if it was the first day of the football season.

Ponting and Healy battled back, with a stand of 34. But Tufnell finally trapped Ponting on the back pad, and Caddick took a return catch from Healy, juggled with it one-handed twice, and then clung on. Warne, batting with a runner, tried to lash out again. This time Martin got underneath his first big hit. Since Martin's fielding is willing rather than athletic, and he had dropped Warne badly 24 hours earlier, he seemed a plausible candidate to be the modern answer to Fred Tate. But he took it easily. England were confident now. The last act was Thorpe catching McGrath at mid-off – Tufnell's 11th victim – and his sunglasses falling off as he did so.

This was the first three-day Test at The Oval since 1957. On the Saturday evening Mark Taylor received a replica Ashes urn from the master of ceremonies David Gower, who had waved around a similar copy 12 years earlier. But this was greeted with only casual applause. It was a moment for England, and not just for the team. For the administrators, desperate to keep the game alive in the hearts of the public in difficult times, it was a priceless victory.

Toss: England. **England 180** (G. D. McGrath 7-76) **and 163** (G. P. Thorpe 62, M. S. Kasprowicz 7-36);
Australia 220 (P. C. R. Tufnell 7-66) **and 104** (P. C. R. Tufnell 4-27, A. R. Caddick 5-42).

AUSTRALIA v ENGLAND 1998–99
John Etheridge

England were once more overwhelmed by Australia, who won their sixth successive Ashes series. More than a century earlier, England won eight on the trot, but only one was a five-Test rubber; and the haphazard tours of the 1880s are hardly comparable to the intensity of modern Test cricket. To be realistic, Australia's success in 1998-99 continued a period of unrivalled dominance in Test cricket's most enduring conflict. Since 1989, they had won 20 Tests to England's five. After pushing closer in 1997, England's margin of defeat this time, 3–1, was the same as on their previous tour. So not much had changed. Indeed, rain probably saved them from defeat in the First Test, and an unexpected collapse, blamed by Australia's captain on complacency, allowed England a dramatic victory in the fourth. It could have been 5–0.

Alec Stewart and his team claimed some mitigation. For a start, he incorrectly called heads in every Test, the first time one captain has won every toss in a five-Test Ashes series in Australia. It meant Mark Taylor was able to bat first in the heat of Adelaide and on a deteriorating pitch in Sydney, decisions fundamental to the outcome of each match. England argued, too, that crucial third-umpire's verdicts unjustly went against them, notably the catch which dismissed Atherton in Adelaide and Slater's run-out escape in Sydney.

Yet such slices of ill-fortune were side issues in the general pattern of Australia's command. The truth is that England were inferior in every department. Their batting surrendered frequently and feebly, the single most important factor. The middle and later order rarely provided any resistance. England lost their last six wickets for 60 runs in their first innings in Brisbane, ten for 110 and five for 33 in Perth, seven for 40 and five for 16 in Adelaide, seven for 70 in the first innings at Melbourne, seven for 83 and eight for 78 in Sydney. England possessed neither the technical nous nor, apparently, the resolve to halt these collapses. The bowling was more encouraging, but still lacked Australia's variety and penetration, and they dropped at least 20 catches – about four times as many as Australia – in the series.

First Test

Steven Lynch

At Brisbane, November 20, 21, 22, 23, 24, 1998. Drawn.

A spectacular thunderstorm, which set in forcibly at tea on the final afternoon, prevented any further play and allowed England to escape with a draw. They had been set 348 to win by Taylor, in his 100th Test, and briefly threatened to worry Australia but reality soon set in. MacGill, the leg-spinner playing only because Warne had not fully recovered from a shoulder operation, bamboozled Butcher, and later Hussain and Ramprakash as well, by which time England had more than one eye on the darkly massing clouds.

A result might just have been obtained if the floodlights had been turned on in the gathering gloom before tea. But the England management had vetoed their use, saying that the case for using the lights was unproven. England were very satisfied to escape from Brisbane without suffering the deflating First-Test defeats which had shaped the previous two Ashes series in Australia.

Overall, England had only themselves to blame for sliding into trouble. On a good batting pitch, they reduced Australia to 178 for five on the first day, but then gave Steve Waugh and Healy two lives apiece. Late on the first day, Waugh, then 68, was dropped by Hussain at second slip, low to his right off Gough. Earlier, on 29, Waugh had escaped a run-out when Mullally, the bowler, stuck his hand in front of a wicket-bound throw from Stewart. Healy, cutting and carving characteristically on his home ground, had 36 when he mis-pulled Gough to third man, where Fraser grassed the chance. And early next morning, on 62, Healy played on – to the despairing Gough again – but the bails stayed put.

This experienced pair, both with more than a century of Tests behind them, needed no second – or third – invitations to make hay. Steve Waugh eventually completed his 16th Test century (easing himself ahead of his twin) and Healy his fourth. With Healy comfortably outscoring his obdurate senior partner ("It wasn't difficult, was it?" he joked afterwards), they added 187 for the sixth wicket, their sixth and highest century partnership together in Tests. On 112, Waugh edged Mullally to the diving Stewart, and Healy finally spooned Fraser to mid-on – but then Fleming flailed away, classic drives interspersed with comic swishes, for 71, his highest first-class score. Gough was unlucky and Mullally, in his first Test for 22 months, finished with five wickets, but the rest of the bowling was uninspiring.

England had chosen only five specialist batsmen plus jack-of-all-trades Stewart, whose indifferent form against Australia continued. Butcher led the way with an impressive 116, containing 16 fours, most of them well-thumped drives. His innings, his second century, was his best for England so far: he seemed so untroubled at times that he might have been plundering a second-rate county attack on a friendly track at The Oval. And this followed a troubled start to the tour, which saw him collect more facial stitches (ten) than runs (nine) in the warm-up matches. Butcher slowed down after reaching three figures, but then Thorpe and Ramprakash took up the cudgels. A draw looked the likeliest result after three days when England were 299 for four in reply to Australia's 485. But on the fourth morning, an incisive spell from McGrath, who took five for nine in 35 balls, reduced the tail to rabbit stew – a sight which was to become familiar as the series progressed. Ramprakash was left high and dry with 69 not out after four hours.

Australia lost no time in building on their lead of 110. England's bowlers looked toothless as Slater caned them to all parts. His ninth Test century – fifth against England – came up in 172 minutes, and in all he hit 13 fours, and a six off Croft into the Clem Jones Stand. Langer assured himself of a run in the side with 74, and Taylor's eventual declaration left England a probable 98 overs to reach their improbable target. Atherton led the early batting flourish, but McGrath was tight again, and MacGill turned the ball alarmingly at times. When Butcher was given lbw by umpire Hair he was on the back foot – and so were England, who were grateful that Cork and Croft hung on until the rains came.

Toss: Australia. **Australia 485** (S. R. Waugh 112, I. A. Healy 134, D. W. Fleming 71*, A. D. Mullally 5-105) **and 237-3 dec.** (M. J. Slater 113, J. L. Langer 74); **England 375** (M. A. Butcher 116, N. Hussain 59, G. P. Thorpe 77, M. R. Ramprakash 69*, G. D. McGrath 6-85) **and 179-6.**

Second Test

At Perth, November 28, 29, 30, 1998. Australia won by seven wickets.

Malcolm Knox

A Test match completed in two days and two sessions, 33 wickets falling for 607 runs, and an individual highest score of 68 combine to suggest a farcical encounter on a ticked-up or underprepared pitch. Yet the WACA strip produced an engrossing contest, ending in an Australian win by a flattering margin.

What constitutes a good cricket wicket depends on point of view: fast bowlers who have played at Perth would rate it among the best, certainly one of a kind in world cricket. Most importantly, although this one bounced steeply and engendered tremendous pace, it carried truly, and gave every batsman a fair chance. Few of them coped, which just indicated how seldom they see such a pitch. The destroyers were not so much the downwind fliers as the upwind shapers of the ball. Until Gillespie's withering burst in the second innings, the great majority of wickets in the match had gone to bowlers pushing against the Fremantle Doctor. Fleming gave a masterclass on the superiority of guile and sideways movement to sheer pace on even the quickest pitches. And England's debutant, 21-year-old Alex Tudor, who replaced Fraser, grabbed five wickets by beating batsmen with lateral deviation rather than straight speed.

Fleming started his work in his second over of the match, following a series of inswingers with one that slid across Butcher and drew the edge. By lunch on day one, England were 76 for six. Atherton and Hussain both edged McGrath to Healy, Crawley played a culpable waft to slip and Hick (standing in for the injured Thorpe) nicked his second ball of the tour. Only the captain, Stewart, found the centre of the bat, although his 38 (off 29 balls) had the vertiginous feel of a desperate, doomed counter-assault and eventually he dragged one on from McGrath, just after completing 1,000 Test runs in 1998. Ramprakash lasted 97 minutes before giving Taylor his 150th Test catch. With Fleming mopping up the tail (woeful except for the assured Tudor), England perished for 112, their lowest total in Perth, in three hours.

There followed perhaps the most crucial passage of the match. Taylor was able to guide Australia to a lead for the loss of only one wicket. He had survived longer than the entire England innings when he managed to nick a brute of an offcutter from Cork. In retrospect, this period was the easiest time for batting in the entire match, and Australia were to be grateful for their sound reply. By the second morning, the pitch had dried out and hardened, and was playing considerably faster, though with less movement, than on day one. Mark Waugh and night-watchman Gillespie laboured for an hour and a half over their 27-run partnership before the English pace attack triggered a collapse of seven for 75. Tudor's first two Test wickets were the Waugh brothers, Steve with an indipper and Mark with a late awayswinger. Gough chimed in with three, but Tudor's four for 89 propelled him from potential to reality. Unfortunately, injury and puzzling selection were to keep him out of the series until Sydney, where an unhelpful wicket restricted his opportunities.

Australia's 128-run lead looked even more formidable as England's top order failed again. Fleming removed Butcher, Hussain and Stewart in 16 balls, and added an unusually aggressive Atherton by the end of his first 11-over spell. When Crawley popped one up from Miller, a historic two-day Test loomed. Enter Hick. Ridiculed after his first-innings duck, he set about the bowlers with a flashing blade, twice pulling Gillespie over the mid-wicket boundary. Was this finally the Test-winning innings that Hick had promised all his life? Australia's collapse had given England real hope that they could steal the match – but only if they could establish a target of around 150 or more. While Hick was at the crease, supported by Ramprakash, anything seemed possible. On the third morning, they were still in occupation. As Hick passed his half-century, the Australians looked anxious. England were 30 ahead with five wickets in hand before Gillespie had his revenge. Humiliated the previous evening, he struck five times in seven overs. First to go was Hick, caught at third slip for 68, with eight fours and two sixes. Cork attempted to continue the rally with Ramprakash, but Gillespie picked up the final four wickets for one run in six balls, the last three going for ducks.

Only 64 were needed, but three wickets were enough to show England what might have been. The Waughs dispersed thoughts of a miracle, taking the home side to a deceptively comfortable victory. On this wicket, against good pace bowling, all batsmen proved vulnerable. England were left to regret their inability to set Australia a testing target.

Toss: Australia. **England 112** (D. W. Fleming 5-46) **and 191** (G. A. Hick 68, D. W. Fleming 4-45, J. N. Gillespie 5-88); **Australia 240** (M. A. Taylor 61, A. J. Tudor 4-89) **and 64-3**.

Third Test

At Adelaide, December 11, 12, 13, 14, 15, 1998. Australia won by 205 runs.

Matthew Engel

Australia secured the Ashes for the sixth successive series after another one-sided Test. Never before had the whole thing been settled before Christmas (the previous record was set when England won the Melbourne Test on December 28, 1986). The early conclusion was partly due to the scheduling, partly due to Australia's obvious superiority and partly – just partly – due to luck. The good fortune England had enjoyed in Brisbane was only temporary. Everyone knew this would be a horrible toss to lose, and Stewart lost it.

Adelaide Oval is normally a bat-first pitch, and the weather compounded the situation. The first day, at 40.2°C (104°F), was the hottest December day there since the 1980s, but the forecast was for cooler weather halfway through the second day: in other words, just in time for the change of innings. Australia were able to run England ragged in the heat, and then wait for the batting to collapse – which it duly did, twice.

The rest of the game was evenly contested. But when England were bad, they were horrid: it was men v lemmings. In the first innings, the last seven wickets went down for 40; and in the second the last five for 16. The madness lasted only 64 minutes the first time and 23 the second, but it decided the series.

Despite the blazing sun, both teams began the game in shadow: England because of their cricket; Australia because of the recent revelation that two of their stars, Shane Warne and Mark Waugh, had accepted money from an Indian bookmaker four years earlier, a fact that had been covered up by the Australian Board. The preliminaries were overshadowed by the recriminations; the injured Warne was flown in specially to face the media. Selection thus received less attention than usual. England appeared to be taking a risk by bringing in Such from the also-rans, though they were actually trying to play safe, picking seven batsmen and Headley rather than two spinners and the tearaway Tudor. The real risk-takers were Australia, who played only two quick bowlers, which could have led to disaster had they lost the toss. But Taylor's captaincy skills now seemed almost mystical, Brearley-esque even: he did not lose the toss.

In the heat England performed manfully, with Gough especially staunch and unlucky. The bowlers worked their way through the innings with great skill, but they kept being dashed against the rock of Langer, who scored almost half the runs. He batted 491 minutes – equal to four sessions – never taking control and never losing it either, his careful game nicely adapted to a ground which discourages flamboyant driving. The failures included Mark Waugh, who found himself being booed by a section of the crowd. But for a last-wicket stand of 37 between Langer and McGrath, England might have gone in very pleased with themselves.

Their position was still strong by the end of the second day. At 160 for three, 231 behind, England looked on course to get close to Australia, and their position would have been even better but for a terrible piece of judgment by Paul Angley, the inexperienced third umpire. He had only one decision to make all match, when Atherton, who had been batting superbly, was picked up low down by Taylor at first slip. It probably was a fair catch, but that was less than certain after countless replays. Angley sent Atherton on his way in five seconds; panic is the only explanation.

Next morning, at 187, Ramprakash edged to second slip to end a stand of 103 with Hussain. While Hussain remained unbeaten, the rest strode on and off again as fast as models on a catwalk. Since the failures began with Crawley and Hick, it was not merely the bowlers whose batting was to blame. It was a wretched performance which took all the tension out of the game and the series. By the fourth day, the anti-Pom banners round the ground became more contemptuous, and serious commentators began to mutter about allowing England only a three-Test series in future. Yet 14,000 were in the ground, suggesting that the Ashes still had something going for them.

Australia's progress towards a declaration was slow at first, but untroubled even before Slater began to play his most exuberant shots, including a six to the distant straight boundary, to reach one of the simpler Ashes centuries. England were set a notional 443 in 140 overs. Hussain, Stewart and Ramprakash all played in businesslike fashion, without ever really suggesting that the game might be saved, let alone won. MacGill offered them more bad deliveries than Warne ever did, but by now both he and Miller were beginning to give the ball serious rip, emphasising the difference with Such, who looked an essentially defensive operative at this level. The end came at 2.03 on the fifth day. One can always speculate on what might have happened if Stewart had changed his policy and called tails. It would certainly have been a very different game. But England could easily have lost anyway; the gap between the teams now looked like a chasm.

Toss: Australia. **Australia 391** (M. A. Taylor 59, J. L. Langer 179*, S. R. Waugh 59, D. W. Headley 4-97) **and 278-5 dec.** (M. J. Slater 103, J. L. Langer 52, M. E. Waugh 51*); **England 227** (N. Hussain 89*, M. R. Ramprakash 61, S. C. G. MacGill 4-53) **and 237** (M. R. Ramprakash 57, A. J. Stewart 63*, G. D. McGrath 4-50).

Fourth Test

Simon Briggs

At Melbourne, December 26, 27, 28, 29, 1998. England won by 12 runs.

After their limp showing at Adelaide and embarrassing defeat in a tour game at Hobart, England flew to Melbourne in low spirits. But English players are at their most dangerous when their pride and places are threatened, and at Melbourne they responded with the latest in a series of overseas wins against the run of play. It took them only three days, after the first was washed out. Thousands of travelling fans made the most of the moment, though in their hearts they knew that these touring triumphs are almost always one-offs.

The key to the sudden turnaround was the late withdrawal of Tudor, who had a sore hip. England had intended to use him as the fifth prong of an all-seam attack that would also include the recalled Fraser; now they had to rethink. The obvious replacement was Cork, the last pace bowler in the party, but he had bowled 12 wicketless overs for 76 in the Hobart debacle, so wicket-keeper Warren Hegg won one of the more unexpected debuts in Test history. Even on the morning of the game, he had no idea he might be playing.

Freed of the gauntlets, Stewart was able to move to his preferred position at the top of the order. But, although Taylor chose to field, it was some time before his opposite number could get into the action. Boxing Day, one of the highlights of the Australian sporting calendar, brought a crowd of 58,000 (on a fine day, there could have been a record attendance) and almost continuous rain. When play did begin, on Sunday, McGrath made the early running, dismissing England's two other specialist openers for ducks in the first 13 minutes. Stewart responded in characteristically belligerent fashion. After a streaky start, he dominated a partnership of 77 with Hussain, which was finally broken by Nicholson, the raw, debutant fast bowler. Ramprakash then took over as Stewart's sidekick, shepherding him to a 142-ball hundred – his first in 23 Tests against Australia – before both fell in the space of two overs. England were 202 for five and, with only Hick and the tail in reserve, they could do no better than 270 all out.

Despite some varied bounce, this was not an imposing total. The bowlers needed to work hard to keep Australia in range, and they did – especially Gough, who regularly rated over 140kph (87.5mph) on the radar gun, more than any of his opponents could manage. His five wickets left Australia chewing their fingernails at tea on the second day of play, 252 for eight with only MacGill and McGrath left to partner Steve Waugh.

A classic battle for the lead was in prospect, but in the event it wasn't even close. MacGill capitalised on Gough's tiredness, hacking the ball into the MCG's wide open spaces to reach 43, a career-best. At the other end, Steve Waugh's famous determination became cavalier improvisation – one minute he was charging the seamers, the next he was hooking airily to reach his 17th Test hundred (seventh against England), passing Bradman's 6,996 Test runs on the way. Australia took a lead of 70, and Stewart was widely castigated for giving Waugh singles in order to get at MacGill.

In an elongated final session (the hours of play had been extended by 30 minutes at each end to make up for the first day's rain), England lost two wickets – including Atherton, for his first Test pair – without quite wiping off the deficit. Butcher was particularly unlucky, when a full-blooded sweep lodged under the armpit of Slater, cowering at forward short leg.

The next day was believed to be the longest in Test history. First, Stewart, Hussain and Hick all reached 50 without being able to go much further. It took some MacGill-style heaves from Mullally to lift the target to 175, theoretically simple but the sort that has often turned Australia shaky. At 103 for two, those shakes were hardly visible; the bowlers weren't getting any change out of a hard-wearing pitch. But a remarkable piece of fielding from Ramprakash, who plucked a scorching pull from Langer out of the air, lifted England's spirits. Headley soon forced Mark Waugh to edge to second slip, then followed up brilliantly in a spell of four for four in 13 balls. Even with Steve Waugh still hanging on grimly, at 140 for seven Australia were suddenly in danger.

Australia v England 1998–99 — Fourth Test

At Melbourne, December 26 (*no play*), 27, 28, 29, 1998. Result: England won by 12 runs.

ENGLAND	First innings		Second innings	
M. A. Atherton c Healy b McGrath		0	b Fleming	0
*A. J. Stewart b MacGill		107	c Slater b MacGill	52
M. A. Butcher c Langer b McGrath		0	c Slater b MacGill	14
N. Hussain c Healy b Nicholson		19	(5) c Slater b Nicholson	50
M. R. Ramprakash c McGrath b S. R. Waugh		63	(6) b Nicholson	14
G. A. Hick c Fleming b MacGill		39	(7) b Fleming	60
†W. K. Hegg c Healy b S. R. Waugh		3	(8) c MacGill b Nicholson	9
D. W. Headley c Taylor b McGrath		14	(4) b McGrath	1
D. Gough b MacGill		11	c Slater b MacGill	4
A. R. C. Fraser not out		0	not out	7
A. D. Mullally lbw b MacGill		0	c and b McGrath	16
L-b 7, w 1, n-b 6		14	B 2, l-b 4, n-b 11	17

1-0 2-4 3-81 4-200 5-202 6-206   **270**   1-5 2-61 3-66 4-78 5-127 6-178   **244**
7-244 8-266 9-270 10-270   7-207 8 221 9 221 10 244

First innings – McGrath 22 5 64 3; Fleming 19 3 71–0; Nicholson 10–0–59–1; MacGill 19–2–61–4;
S. R. Waugh 6–2–8–2.
Second innings – McGrath 20.2–5–56–2; Fleming 17–4–45–2; Nicholson 15–4–56–3; MacGill 27–3–81–3;
M. E. Waugh 1–1–0–0.

AUSTRALIA	First innings		Second innings	
*M. A. Taylor c Hick b Gough		7	(2) c Headley b Mullally	19
M. J. Slater lbw b Gough		1	(1) lbw b Headley	18
J. L. Langer c Hussain b Gough		44	c Ramprakash b Mullally	30
M. E. Waugh lbw b Fraser		36	c Hick b Headley	43
S. R. Waugh not out		122	not out	30
D. S. Lehmann c Hegg b Gough		13	c Hegg b Headley	4
†I. A. Healy c Headley b Fraser		36	c Hick b Headley	0
D. W. Fleming c Hick b Mullally		12	lbw b Headley	0
M. J. Nicholson b Gough		5	c Hegg b Headley	9
S. C. G. MacGill c Hegg b Mullally		43	b Gough	0
G. D. McGrath b Mullally		0	lbw b Gough	0
B 4, l-b 6, n-b 11		21	B 4, l-b 1, n-b 4	9

1-13 2-26 3-98 4-127 5-151 6-209   **340**   1-31 2-41 3-103 4-130 5-140 6-140   **162**
7-235 8-252 9-340 10-340   7-140 8-161 9-162 10-162

First innings – Gough 28–7–96–5; Headley 25–3–86–0; Mullally 21.3–5–64–3; Ramprakash 2–0–6–0;
Fraser 22–0–78–2.
Second innings – Gough 15.4–2–54–2; Headley 17–5–60–6; Mullally 10–4–20–2; Fraser 4–0–23–0.

Toss won by Australia   UMPIRES S. A. Bucknor and D. J. Harper

Nicholson ratcheted the tension still higher, showing an assurance out of all proportion to his experience as he and Waugh took the score to 161 – 14 short of victory. At 7.22, Waugh claimed the extra half-hour, despite Stewart's appeals to the umpires to use their discretion. Because of an early tea, and the attempts to make up for lost time, England had already been on the field for three hours and 50 minutes.

Headley and Gough had more reason to object than anyone, having bowled the previous six overs. But, as shadows stretched across the ground, they just kept coming. Headley found Nicholson's edge, then Waugh took a single off the first ball of Gough's next over. Stewart, whose captaincy had clearly benefited from his lightened workload, was sticking to his policy of attacking the tailenders, and this time it came off: Gough fired his trademark inswinging yorker through MacGill's defences, and hit McGrath on the toe two balls later. Umpire Harper raised his finger, ending the day, after eight hours three minutes, and the match. England had won a superb Test, and the series was not merely vibrant again, but set for a tumultuous finale at Sydney.

CRICKETER OF THE YEAR – DARREN GOUGH

Matthew Engel, 1999

There are two different England teams these days. This is nothing to do with the increasingly disparate Test and one-day sides, because the difference affects them both. One lot is the downbeat, fatalistic crew who have become all too familiar: heads bowed, expecting the worst. The other is seen when Darren Gough is fit and firing.

Against New Zealand in 1994, Gough made one of the most sensational Test debuts of modern times. He took a wicket in his first over and had figures of four for 47. Earlier, he had gone out and hit a rousing 65, with ten fours. He was 23 years old. Everyone yelled "New Botham", which was not a Yorkshire mining village but already a cliché, and later a rather sad joke.

That winter, with England having been humiliated in the Melbourne Test, they went to Sydney looking hopeless. One young man took the game by the scruff. England 309 (Gough 51, and a thrilling 51 at that). Australia 116 all out (Gough six for 49). The Test was not quite won, but its hero was suddenly the hottest property in English sport. He was young, good-looking, an authentic Yorkshireman with that air of sleeves-up defiance which the nation adores. Vast wealth as well as glory looked a certainty.

But Gough had felt pain in his left foot even while the cheers were echoing. He ignored it. In a one-day international a few days later, he broke down and went home with his foot in plaster. It took four years to recapture that exuberance, in which time his career veered between wretched injuries and fated comebacks. And yet the omens of 1994 have been proved right. In 1998 he delivered. At Headingley, with his home crowd roaring him on, he ripped through South Africa's second innings to settle the series with six for 42, three of them in a dramatic opening burst. Then he was at the heart of England's epic win in Melbourne before starting 1999 with a hat-trick in the Sydney Test. In any case, Gough's contribution to the team cannot merely be computed. He is an inspirational cricketer in an uninspiring era. And his successes make the Tests he has missed even more poignant.

Fifth Test

Gideon Haigh

At Sydney, January 2, 3, 4, 5, 1999. Australia won by 98 runs.

Australia held the initiative throughout this eventful match from the moment Taylor became the first Australian captain to coinwash an Ashes rival since Lindsay Hassett in 1953, though England's brave attempts to wrest it back kept an aggregate crowd exceeding 142,000 intrigued almost throughout. It was a triumph for the 27-year-old leg-spinner MacGill, whose 12 for 107 were the best Test figures at the arena whose initials he bears since Charlie Turner's 12 for 87 at England's expense in February 1888.

Given Sydney's reputation as a spin haven, both sides prepared accordingly. Australia recalled both Miller and Warne, for his first Test since Bangalore in March 1998 and a subsequent operation on his shoulder; England included Crawley, as their best player of spin, and off-spinner Such. Croft was spurned; Fraser and Mullally were dropped. And, finally capitulating to his aching back, Atherton was a last-minute scratching.

Tickets for the first day were sold out and the 42,124 who got in – representing the biggest SCG Test crowd for 23 years – were rewarded by proceedings that sustained the tempo established in Melbourne. England started and finished memorably. Australia lost three for 52 in 68 minutes, including Taylor for two. They also lost an astounding five wickets for three in the day's last 15 deliveries, including a hat-trick by Gough, the first by an Englishman in an Ashes Test since Jack Hearne at Leeds in 1899. After getting Healy and MacGill, he completed the set with a swerving torpedo that robbed Miller of his off stump.

Between times, however, the Waughs put together a stand of 190 at close to a run a minute, encompassing Mark's 16th Test hundred – after two let-offs – and Steve's record ninth Test 90. It was their second-highest Test partnership together, beaten only by their 231 at Sabina Park in the crucial Test of 1994–95. It was also batting of the highest quality, enterprise without recklessness, power without force, and something England could not emulate on the second day. Faced by niggardly bowling, smart fielding and adroit captaincy, they interspersed long periods of inertia with foolhardy strokes, and could squeeze out only 41 singles in 80 overs. Warne trapped Butcher with his fourth delivery, to the acclaim of the second consecutive full house, but was generally outshone by the increasingly buoyant MacGill, who improved his Test-best figures. Further personal milestones included McGrath's 200th Test wicket (Stewart snared at slip) and Mark Waugh's 100th Test catch (Hussain at silly point).

England fought manfully on the third day, Such pursuing a more attacking line than in the first innings and bagging five for the first time since his baptismal Test in June 1993. But the tourists were checked by a contentious and crucial umpiring decision. Slater was 35 and Australia 60 for two then, returning for a second to long-on, he seemed to have been caught short by a direct hit from Headley on the non-striker's stumps. Slater penitentially sloughed off his gloves as umpire Dunne referred the arbitration to third umpire Taufel but, after a long delay, he received the benefit of video doubt. It transpired that the cameras on which Taufel relied were not perpendicular to the crease, and that the bowler, Such, had inadvertently obscured the precise instant of the stumps' disintegration.

After this intimation of mortality, Slater watched everything right on to the bat and abstained from extravagance until his score had doubled and the last recognised batsman, Steve Waugh (No. 7 because of a hamstring strain), had departed. He then cut loose with a starburst of boundaries, including a skimming drive past mid-off from the flagging Gough to register his 11th Test hundred – seventh against England. Responsible for 66.8% of Australia's 184, Slater almost disturbed the oldest Test record remaining: Charles Bannerman's 67.34% of Australia's total in the inaugural Test of March 1877.

By this stage, indeed, it was becoming difficult to keep pace with the profusion of landmarks. The completion of McGrath's pair equalled a 20-year-old Ashes record at the opposite end of the spectrum to Slater's: the 37th cipher of the series (22 to Englishmen, 15 to Australians). When both England's openers were stumped that evening after a promising start to their pursuit of 287, it was only the fourth such instance in Test cricket. Ramprakash's edge in the fifth over of the fourth day furnished Taylor with his 157th Test catch, passing Allan Border's 156 to reach the top of the fielding-honour roll.

Ramprakash's failure also undermined England's quest, and their remaining seven wickets could muster only 78 as MacGill mocked their immobility. Some abominable strokes were played against him – the most egregious being Hick's absent-minded sweep – but his third-day figures of six for 23 from 73 deliveries were just reward for intelligent exploitation of the conditions; only Hussain resisted for long. England's experiences were summed up by their final wicket: Such middled MacGill firmly, only to see it rebound from silly point Slater and arc gently back to the bowler for his seventh victim. Four weeks later, Taylor was to announce his retirement from international cricket after captaining Australia in 50 Tests. He had won 11 series out of 14. The contrast with England's travails was overwhelming.

Toss: Australia. **Australia 322** (M. E. Waugh 121, S. R. Waugh 96, D. W. Headley 4-62) and **184** (M. J. Slater 123, D. W. Headley 4-40, P. M. Such 5-81); **England 220** (S. C. G. MacGill 5-57) and **188** (N. Hussain 53, S. C. G. MacGill 7-50).

NOTES BY THE EDITOR

Matthew Engel, 1999

England went to Australia to face a team that would be without Warne, their nemesis in the three previous Ashes series, until the last Test. It was a curious series, in that England were highly competitive most of the time, only to revert to their old ways for short but decisive periods. These happened mostly against Warne's deputies: Stuart MacGill, a leg-spinner who had been temperamentally unsound in English league cricket, and Colin Miller, a happy-go-lucky journeyman seamer who had started experimenting late in life with off-breaks. Both would probably have been regarded as too oddball to make an England team.

Technically, England might have had bowlers to match them. But Miller and MacGill bowled with exuberance and panache, as though they would take a wicket any minute. England's spinners conveyed the air of men about to be straight-driven for four. There were gifted cricketers in the England team. But the players were numbed by inhibition, as though fear (of failure, of being dropped, of being insulted by the crowd or the press) had drained all their zest for the game. It was the same off the field, too: the team seemed to take little pleasure from the experience of touring – with some reason, since the slightest indiscretion can be picked on by one of the more sanctimonious papers. There are several aspects of Australian cricket that England ought to emulate, but the studied nonchalance of Mark Taylor's team was perhaps the least attainable.

ENGLAND V AUSTRALIA 2001

David Frith

Seldom has such high expectation before an Ashes series ended in such summary demolition. Peter May's 1958–59 England team, which had a truly formidable look about it, was crushed 4–0 by Richie Benaud's eager combination, yet it was 63 days into the series before the Ashes were relinquished. In 2001, with its compressed schedule (five Tests within 54 days), Steve Waugh's Australians made sure of retention in only 31, framing a mere 11 days of combat; Benaud's needed 22. After emphatic defeat in seven successive Ashes series, will deflated England ever be equipped to challenge the Baggy Green brigade seriously? Or will Australia be capable of introducing reliable talent after the likes of the Waughs, McGrath and even Warne are gone? This side's average age was 30, Australia's ripest since 1948.

They arrived in England as outstanding favourites, notwithstanding their reversals at Kolkata and Chennai and the revival in England's performances under Nasser Hussain and coach Duncan Fletcher. England had crushed Zimbabwe and West Indies the previous summer, and their winter tour had returned notable successes in Pakistan and Sri Lanka. At the outset, Steve Waugh knew England were stronger than in recent years, and acknowledged that forecasting was fraught with difficulties. But he did add ominously, "If we can get on top early, we can open up some old scars."

English optimists felt that the rubber might be decided by whoever benefited more from the luck that forever swirls about cricket. The toss, the weather, injuries, umpiring errors? As it transpired, these factors nearly all went against England from the start, the most serious being the absence through injury of three first-choice batsmen in Thorpe (for four Tests), captain Hussain (two) and Vaughan (all five), as well as the left-arm spinner Giles (four). When this ill-fortune was overtaken by some dismal cricket from England, particularly the inept catching at Lord's, the outcome was inescapable.

It remained for us to try to assess whether we had been watching the best cricket team of all time. Wasted though the exercise may be, the man in the traffic jam or the halted railway carriage was eager for debate about the relative qualities of the 1902, 1921, 1948 and 1975 Australians, the 1950s England sides, South Africa 1969–70, and the West Indies combination of 1984.

First Test

Graeme Wright

At Birmingham, July 5, 6, 7, 8, 2001. Australia won by an innings and 118 runs.

One session was all Australia needed to settle into their defence of the Ashes. When England were 106 for one with an over to lunch, pre-match fears for Hussain's reconstructed team looked overblown. Then Steve Waugh introduced Warne. Butcher pushed a pad at his second ball and gloved a catch to Ponting, diving forward from short cover. It was the beginning of the end. When, in the second innings, Gillespie broke Hussain's little finger with a startling delivery, England's whole campaign was threatened.

The opening day provided exhilarating cricket. The sun beat down on a full house and runs blazed off the bat: between them, the teams scored 427 at almost five an over, including 236 after tea. Century stands topped and tailed England's innings: Atherton and Butcher put on 104 after Trescothick had edged Gillespie's first ball to slip, and Stewart and Caddick whacked a merry 103 for the tenth wicket. Caddick struck seven fours and a six in his 49 not out, his best score in Tests and the second-best by an England No. 11 after John Snow's unbeaten 59 against West Indies in 1966. But in between it was an old story. After Atherton, rapped on the fingers by Gillespie, had edged his next ball to second slip, Hussain padded up to McGrath, who then had Ward playing on from a nothing defensive stroke. Warne, meanwhile, had been stock-bowling at the other end, but a trademark leg-break out of the rough – an off-break to the left-handed Afzaal – opened up the lower order. In seven overs either side of tea, four wickets fell for 21 as Warne claimed his 17th five-wicket return in Tests – his fifth against England.

Slater launched the reply by crashing Gough's first two deliveries (one a no-ball) behind point for four, then taking another two fours in an opening over that cost 18. Hayden caught his mood and they had put on 98 in 15 overs when White, twisting to his left in mid-air, intercepted Hayden's mid-wicket flick off Giles. Gough, albeit over-stepping, had Ponting lbw before the close, then bowled Slater with his first ball next morning. But if the game appeared nicely poised at 134 for three, Steve Waugh's 26th Test hundred, and some ill-judged England seam bowling in helpful conditions, tipped it Australia's way.

Waugh was unforgiving as he stamped his authority on England's ambitions, drilling fours through Hussain's attacking fields – 13 all told in 181 balls – and becoming the third, after Allan Border and Sunil Gavaskar to reach 9,000 Test runs. While he and twin Mark were adding 133, it seemed unimportant that Mark's form was sketchy. Giving Mark two lives mattered more to England psychologically, however, than it had meant to Australia when they missed two catches the previous morning. Australia simply rectified the fault; England's errors – up to half a dozen chances went begging – opened a confidence fault-line.

Martyn, often sublime, confirmed Australia's depth and shut the door on England. Had bad light and rain not limited Friday's final session to two balls, and taken the equivalent of a session out of Saturday, the match might not have entered the fourth day. Yet England had openings. Gough trapped Steve Waugh first thing Saturday with a ball that kept low and, immediately after a two-hour stoppage either side of lunch, had Martyn, then 65, dropped by Stewart as he dived in front of first slip. He and Gilchrist added another 109 after that. Martyn went to tea on 99; soon after he was caught at cover off Butcher as he tried to repeat the sumptuous cover drive with which he celebrated his maiden Test century.

For a brief moment, Butcher's part-time swing bowling seemed unplayable. He capped Martyn's wicket with three more in five balls. But it was an illusion. Gilchrist, 93 when joined by last man McGrath, reached his hundred in 118 balls by anticipating Caddick's bouncer, stooping and scooping it inventively over the wicket-keeper for four. Then he went into overdrive, upping his boundary tally to 20 fours and five sixes, including 22 runs off Butcher to equal the most expensive over in Ashes history. By the time Gilchrist was caught at long-on for 152, the last wicket had added 63. McGrath's contribution was a single; when he had Atherton prodding to second slip, dismissing him for the 14th time in 26 innings, his day was complete.

England resumed on Sunday 234 behind. Again Butcher was solid, adding 95 with Trescothick until Lee undid him with one that reared from just short of a length.

Gillespie found something more damaging for the hapless Hussain – trapping his left hand against the bat handle and forcing him to retire – then blew away the middle order with fast bowling of frightening intensity. He should also have had Giles first ball after lunch. Mark Waugh uncharacteristically dropped the slip chance but quickly helped Warne account for Trescothick and Giles, moving to within one catch of Mark Taylor's Test-record 157. For England, Trescothick's defiant 76, containing 11 fours and one six apiece off McGrath and Lee, offered a solitary silver lining.

Toss: Australia. **England 294** (M. A. Atherton 57, A. J. Stewart 65, S. K. Warne 5-71)
and **164** (M. E. Trescothick 76); **Australia 576** (M. J. Slater 77, S. R. Waugh 105, D. R. Martyn 105,
A. C. Gilchrist 152, M. A. Butcher 4-42).

CRICKETER OF THE YEAR – ADAM GILCHRIST

Stephen Fay, 2002

Adam Gilchrist had never been so nervous at the start of a Test as he was at Edgbaston last summer. This was his Ashes debut and he had always been keen to excel in England, where he had played as a young man and enjoyed himself. The nerves showed; he dropped two straightforward catches in the first session.

Gilchrist has an equable nature, but he felt he had let himself down and reparation was required. Two days later he came in to bat when Australia were 336 for five. It was a crucial moment. If England could get rid of the tail quickly, they might make a game of it. Gilchrist transformed that hope into fantasy. He put on 160 with Damien Martyn; his own hundred came up with an unorthodox flick over the keeper's head off glove and bat. When he was last out, having hit five sixes and 20 fours in his highest Test score, Australia had 576. He had humiliated the opposition, and set a pattern that was to repeat itself through the series, except at Headingley where Gilchrist, as stand-in captain, allowed the game to slip away. That was the only dark shadow over a memorable summer. England's fans, and no doubt their cricketers, felt contradictory sensations of fear and expectation each time he strode to the crease, but he soon became the Australian the crowd most enjoyed watching.

The significance of Gilchrist's batting is that, after the specialist batsmen have established a platform, he is capable of putting Australia's score out of reach of the opposition. He is a breaker of wills. Of course, he knows failure, having scored two runs in four consecutive innings against India in March 2001 after starting the series with a century. But at the end of the Ashes summer his average was 51.30 from 22 Tests; against England, he had just averaged 68.00. He had also taken 94 catches and made seven stumpings – more dismissals per game than Ian Healy, the record-holder.

Second Test

Hugh Chevallier

At Lord's, July 19, 20, 21, 22, 2001. Australia won by eight wickets.

Australia ended England's run of three Lord's victories with a display of all-round brilliance that approached perfection. For England, events had a depressing familiarity. Again the batting, notably the middle order, fractured – quite literally – under pressure. At

Edgbaston, Hussain broke a finger: at Lord's, Thorpe a bone in his right hand. Once again, only the weather dragged play into a fourth day. And so, for the fifth time in seven Ashes series, England found themselves 2–0 down after two Tests. Quite simply, Australia looked insuperable. To begin to compete, England needed more runs and, as importantly, quality support for Gough and Caddick.

Beforehand, though, England's quest was for a locum captain to replace the brittle-boned Hussain: Stewart declined the post after leading them to seven straight international defeats, while Butcher, dropped after his only foray into Test captaincy in 1999, ruled himself out. Gough optimistically volunteered his services, but Atherton, for a record 53rd time, was preferred.

Steve Waugh won Australia's 13th toss in 14 Ashes contests, England's ninth consecutive reversal since winning at Lahore the previous November. Play began 90 minutes late because of rain, whose return, abetted by intermittent bad light and an unreschedulable visit from the Queen, played merry hell with the timetable for the rest of the day, preventing batsman or bowler from finding rhythm. Given the conditions, England did well to pick their way to 121 for three. Atherton contributed a phlegmatic 37, Butcher a steady 21, and Thorpe and Ramprakash were constructing a useful stand. But before the weather closed in for the last time, Lee, disappointing hitherto, castled Ramprakash with a majestic ball that swung away then seamed up the slope between bat and pad. It gave Australia an initiative they never relinquished.

Under Friday's brighter skies, England withered in the face of a devastating McGrath onslaught. Immediately finding an exacting length, he took three for one in 20 pitch-perfect deliveries, starting with Stewart and ending with White, both for nought. Stewart's was his first Lord's duck in 29 Test innings, White's his fifth in eight international innings. The prize catch, though, came sandwiched between the two, Thorpe wafting his bat at one better ignored. Ward grittily hung on till the end which, despite an unconvincing hooked six by Cork, came – unlike Edgbaston – with a whimper.

A take-no-hostages opening salvo from Gough and Caddick briefly fostered hopes that 187 was not, after all, quite so feeble. But a diet of deliveries pitching on middle or leg – especially from Cork and White – fed Mark Waugh's insatiable appetite for on-side runs. In the most eloquent style, he revived Australia from a troubled 27 for two. Even so, had Gough held a sharp return catch from Steve Waugh, on 14, they would have been 136 for four. Instead, the Waughs powered on, adding 107 for the fourth wicket. Mark was eventually run out for a cultured 108. By the close, Martyn and Gilchrist had given Australia a lead of 68.

England were desperate for an early breakthrough, and their prayers seemed answered next morning when Gilchrist, 13, edged Gough's first ball straight to second slip, where it bounced out of Butcher's hands, leaving him a distraught, crumpled heap. It set an ugly trend. Atherton spilled the simplest of Gilchrist's four reprieves – all off Gough – allowing him to make a typically aggressive 90 before he swished at a short ball, by now the sole weapon in the English armoury. Australia, dismissed for 401, were 214 ahead.

With few signs of deterioration in the pitch, there were runs to be had, provided batsmen kept their heads. The Australians, however, were masters in exploiting the merest weaknesses. Every lapse cost an England wicket. Gillespie had Trescothick caught behind for the second time, Warne bowled Atherton round his legs, and Lee, having already broken Thorpe's right hand, had him lbw to leave England 50 for three at tea.

Butcher, combining patience and courage with good fortune, led an overdue fight-back with Ramprakash, whose 40 was his best score in 13 unhappy Test innings at Lord's. Together they added 96. Incorrigible optimists thought back to the derring-do of Botham and Willis, but these Australians were never going to buckle like their predecessors of 1981. On the fourth morning, McGrath, summoning an array of devastating deliveries with apparent ease, snuffed out the daydream with three for four in 11 balls. The *coup de grace* came when Mark Waugh held a record 158th catch to dismiss Gough. Many of the other 157 had been more difficult, but it was just the kind of chance England had grassed the previous morning. Australia made a pig's ear of reaching 14, but their overall performance was phenomenal.

Toss: Australia. **England 187** (G. D. McGrath 5-54) **and 227** (M. A. Butcher 83, J. N. Gillespie 5-53); **Australia 401** (M. E. Waugh 108, D. R. Martyn 52, A. C. Gilchrist 90, A. R. Caddick 5-101) **and 14-2**.

Third Test

At Nottingham, August 2, 3, 4, 2001. Australia won by seven wickets.

Gideon Haigh

Australia won their seventh consecutive Ashes series at 4 p.m. on August 4, their successful defence of the trophy having taken not quite 4,000 balls, or just over a week in actual playing time. Victory at Trent Bridge was a testament to their resourcefulness, for England at two stages held the upper hand. Australia trailed by 80 with three wickets remaining at the end of the first day, and England led by 110 with eight wickets left late on the second: the visitors regrouped on both occasions in dynamic fashion, led first by Gilchrist, then by Warne. England, meanwhile, experienced their usual quota of misfortune and miscellaneous acts of God.

First of these was the loss of their captain moments after he had won England's first toss in ten attempts. McGrath's second delivery looped from Atherton's forearm guard to second slip, and umpire Hampshire upheld the appeal for a catch, a decision greeted with hoots of dismay when the big screen replayed the contact. It went down as Atherton's 20th Test duck, an England record. The pitch, recently relaid, offered bowlers discomfiting bounce and sideways movement, and England might have been dismissed before lunch had it not been for the stoical Trescothick: he did not make a mistake for more than two hours, striking 13 emphatic boundaries, including three sumptuous pull shots from Lee. Otherwise, Stewart aside, McGrath encountered little resistance from batsmen frankly overawed by both his craft and his reputation. The narrow man from Narromine claimed five wickets in a Test innings for the 20th time, the fifth against England. The wider Warne snuck in to claim his 100th Ashes wicket, having Croft taken at silly point.

It appeared business as usual when Hayden and Slater steered Australia to 48 without loss in 55 minutes against some rather ragged new-ball bowling, but Tudor made it seem like two weeks since his last Test, rather than two years, as he trapped Hayden lbw for 33. A remarkable 93 minutes followed in which Australia lost seven for 54 in less than 20 overs, with Gough and Caddick also profiting from the conditions: Steve Waugh's snick to slip and out for 13 seemed to send a tremor through their dressing-room. Gilchrist, however, remained, by now perhaps a wicket more coveted than that of his captain.

The sun broke through on the second morning, but England, after removing Lee, did not. Gilchrist bolted to his half-century from 47 deliveries with ten boundaries, twice edging to fine leg within a breath of leg stump but otherwise unassailable. With the courageous Gillespie, he added 66 from 15 overs, sufficient to conjure an undreamt-of lead. Tudor, a doubtful starter because of a side strain, claimed five wickets for the first time, but England's bowling in general was spasmodic rather than systematic.

As the weather closed in after lunch, Atherton and Trescothick showed considerable composure in crafting their best opening stand of the series. For once, McGrath lacked penetration, and grew frustrated after Venkat declined an lbw appeal against Atherton – playing no shot as at Lord's – when he was 12. The breakthrough, against the tide of play, came by freakish means. Trescothick's well-struck sweep rebounded from short leg Hayden's ankle and Gilchrist leapt forward to collect the catch. In fact, Trescothick was trebly unfortunate: TV replays revealed that Warne had narrowly overstepped the front line, and immediately after his dismissal the players left the field because of rain.

The resumption brought a tense period of play, Lee touching his top speed in removing Butcher and hitting Atherton a glancing blow on the jaw at 91.8mph. But it was after a further break for bad light that Warne truly turned the Test on its head. Atherton may or may not have touched the ball he was judged to have edged to Gilchrist, but there was no doubt about the careless dismissals of Stewart and Ramprakash – who, charging down the wicket with nine overs of the day remaining, squandered more than an hour and a half of painstaking application. White became Warne's fourth victim for 11 in 36 deliveries from the day's final ball, and the advantage was consolidated when Gillespie claimed three for six from 14 balls on Saturday morning, including his 100th Test wicket (Caddick). Warne's figures were his best in Tests since November 1995, before the finger and shoulder operations that had imperilled his career.

Australia required 158, which they might have experienced some pangs about had Venkat upheld Gough's lbw shout against Hayden from his second ball. As it was, some punchy shots, judicious calling and a stream of boundaries to the untenanted third man set them on their way. The fifth and last fifty partnership of the match was the largest and fastest, an unbroken 69 in 11 overs as Mark Waugh and Martyn propelled Australia to victory. By then Steve Waugh had succumbed to a strained left calf, sustained while setting off for his first run. The scores were levelled by a stylish clip for four to mid-wicket by Mark Waugh, and the Ashes retained by a Caddick no-ball, an apt sequence of events for a series in which Australian style had been decisive but English ineptitude had played a part.

Toss: England. **England 185** (M. E. Trescothick 69, G. D. McGrath 5-49) **and 162** (M. A. Atherton 51, S. K. Warne 6-33); **Australia 190** (A. C. Gilchrist 54, A. J. Tudor 5-44) **and 158-3.**

Fourth Test

Jim Holden

At Leeds, August 16, 17, 18, 19, 20, 2001. England won by six wickets.

Few cricketers play a Test innings that will become an Ashes legend. Mark Butcher joined this elite when he struck an exhilarating 173 not out to ensure single-handedly that there would be no "greenwash", and show that, for a day at least, McGrath, Gillespie and Warne could be tamed.

Butcher's score matched that of Don Bradman in 1948, when Australia made 404 for three here on the last day to win against the odds. But the immediate comparison was with Ian Botham's 149 not out in 1981, when his hitting transformed not only a match but a whole summer, and a whole sport. Butcher's knock was not as important as that. A fairer parallel would be the fabled 1902 innings of Gilbert Jessop, whose attacking shots and endless verve inspired a remarkable Test victory no one thought possible. As here, it was England's only win of the series.

Butcher's innings, entirely out of character with the rest of a one-sided Ashes contest, was Jessopian in vein: he cut anything short of a length with exquisite power and timing, stepped forward to drive McGrath through the covers, and clipped sweet boundaries off his legs when the bowlers erred in line. The Australians could not contain him and, though it was the only such day of the summer, his innings will never be forgotten.

Australia's stand-in captain, Gilchrist, had not thought anything like it possible when he declared on the fourth evening with a lead of 314 and 110 overs still to play. Rain had seriously disrupted his game-plan, taking maybe two sessions of batting time. But Gilchrist's decision spoke volumes for the tourists' aura of invincibility, and their desire to win the series 5–0. Few in England gave the home side hope of victory either: only once, at Melbourne in 1928–29, had England scored as many in the fourth innings to win. Yet, by conventional cricketing logic, the target was attainable even after bad light and further rain removed 17.3 overs that Sunday evening, revising England's task to 311 from 90 overs.

When Atherton and Trescothick fell cheaply next morning, it seemed that a routine humbling of the English batting would occur. Butcher's early overs were spent evading a wonderful spell from McGrath – but, at 60 for two, the restored England captain Hussain hooked Gillespie out of the ground. Many thought this the turning-point, not for the bravura shot itself but for the fact that the ball was lost. Its replacement didn't help the bowlers as much and, on a pitch that was never the minefield predicted, batting became less of an ordeal.

Still, it needed a miraculous performance, and Butcher, whose technique had been modified the previous winter with help from his father, Alan, produced it. He was particularly severe just after lunch, when it dawned on the capacity crowd that they were witnessing an epic day. Butcher reached his hundred to a seemingly endless ovation, and when Hussain went, England's sole loss in a session worth 104, they had added 181. McGrath and Warne had one last attempt to turn the screw, bowling with economy and menace, but, thanks to the generous declaration, Butcher could afford to be patient.

After tea the outcome was not in doubt. Ramprakash succumbed in sight of the finishing line, leaving Butcher to complete the task. He carved Gillespie for a cracker-jack six behind point in an over that brought 19. Finally, he steered Warne away for three and England were home with 20 overs to spare. At their rate of scoring they could have chased 400 and still won, illustrating the extraordinary nature of Butcher's innings. He batted five and a quarter hours, faced 227 balls, and hit 23 fours as well as that six.

Gilchrist and all the Australian players shook the English hero's hand. Their sportsmanship was welcome, and genuine. Even though they had dominated the first four days and were superior in class and attitude, their smiles were not forced. On the first day, they had opted to bat after winning the toss and scorched to 288 for four. It may not sound much, but rain had delayed the start until 2.15. Hussain later lambasted his side's lackadaisical approach. Ponting batted with rare panache, his 144 from just 154 balls laced with three sixes and 20 fours, while Martyn had 18 fours when last out for 118 shortly after lunch next day. Katich, Australia's first debutant specialist batsman for over three years, compiled a nervous 15, but 447 looked a good score on a Headingley pitch with a worryingly dry top.

England responded with general competence, all the top-order batsmen starting well but failing to reach 50. Stewart, starting at No. 7 for the first time in 114 Tests, and unhappy at the demotion, responded with a bizarre innings, throwing the bat with daredevil irresponsibility. But his luck held, the follow-on was averted and, after a two-hour interruption either side of tea on Saturday, England reached 309, even making Australia take the second new ball for the first time in the series. McGrath's figures, which took him to 351 wickets, were those of a maestro and, in a normal Test, a match-winner. But this was no normal game.

When Ponting flew to 30 before the light deteriorated, and increased his momentum with wonderful batting next morning, everything pointed to Australia taking the game beyond England's reach. Instead, the weather permitted only 30 runs between lunch and Gilchrist's declaration at 5.35, as well as limiting the day's play to just 25 overs. It was frustrating for the big crowd, but many would be back on Monday, little realising that Sunday's conditions had provided the stage on which Butcher would storm into Ashes history.

Toss: Australia. **Australia 447** (R. T. Ponting 144, M. E. Waugh 72, D. R. Martyn 118, D. Gough 5-103) **and 176-4 dec.** (R. T. Ponting 72*); **England 309** (A. J. Stewart 76*, G. D. McGrath 7-76) **and 315-4** (M. A. Butcher 173*, N. Hussain 55).

Fifth Test

Matthew Engel

At The Oval, August 23, 24, 25, 26, 27, 2001. Australia won by an innings and 25 runs.

Normally, the glow from a sensational Test victory ought to last for weeks or months; in the case of Headingley '81 it has lasted 20 years. The last embers of English joy from Headingley '01 were snuffed out inside 72 hours, thanks to the first back-to-back Tests in England in 89 years, and a dramatic and total reversion to the familiar pattern of Australian mastery. This was only Australia's second win at The Oval since 1948, when Bradman led them to an innings victory despite a duck in his final Test. The other came in 1972, when the Chappell brothers both scored centuries: this time, the Waughs did the same.

Steve Waugh was not what anyone else would have called fit but, with awesome courage and determination, not to mention skill, he came back to ensure that Australia returned to business as usual with astounding rapidity. He started by winning the toss, yet again, and England sensed what lay in front of them. Before the opening day was gone, the only question was, yet again, whether they might save the game.

But there was more discussion about the subplots: whether Mike Atherton really was going to retire (he was) and whether Gough and Stewart would be allowed to cherry-pick which parts of the winter tour they wanted to go on (they were not). Monday's hero, Butcher, who had increased his standing with one innings in a way reminiscent of Derek Randall at the 1977 Centenary Test, was loudly applauded to the crease twice by his home crowd – and back again, without achieving anything much.

Katich, as expected, had to make way for Steve Waugh, but Australia also dumped Slater. Being dropped by Australia is always a more fearful and sometimes final blow than being dropped by England, and in this case Slater's replacement, Langer, seized his opportunity on day one. He was up against another makeshift England attack, with the retread Tufnell and debutant Jimmy Ormond replacing Mullally and Tudor, whose inability to stay fit remained a source of exasperation. Tufnell's triumph at The Oval four years earlier, however, seemed a lifetime away, and all the England bowlers had their hearts broken on the opening day. The pitch was benign, but the faster men might have been helped by a day of late-summer haze had even one of them struck up a rhythm. Instead, the new opening pair put on 158 and, after an understandably patchy start Langer scored his eighth Test century in his familiar, understated style. Four overs later, he retired hurt, having been hit on the helmet trying to hook Caddick, but there seemed no other way to remove him.

It got worse for England. On Friday, the sun shone and, in four hours 35 minutes, Australia raced from 324 for two to 641 for four, their highest score on the ground since 1934, when double-centuries from Ponsford and Bradman propelled them to 701. Mark Waugh's 20th Test century was a thing of beauty, as ever, and took him ahead of David Boon into fourth place on Australia's all-time run-list. But Steve's 27th showed that class is not the only determinant of quality. About 99% of cricketers would not have dreamt of turning out in his condition: he winced his way to 157 not out.

England began their response in something of the same spirit, with Trescothick racing to a run-a-ball 55 before the close. But by then Warne had turned one massively on to Atherton's leg stump. And, next morning, Trescothick lasted only two balls and Butcher, having briefly displayed his new-found dominance, pushed a catch to short leg. The main business, thereafter, seemed to have more to do with fringe players establishing themselves than saving the follow-on. Ramprakash and Afzaal achieved their personal objectives without quite doing what the team required. Afzaal showed spirit in his 54, and something of the judgment the selectors had sensed when they picked him: Ramprakash survived until the fourth morning, scoring 133, his second Test century. For the time being, it ended a decade of doubts about the gap between his ability and his temperament.

But no one ever truly mastered either McGrath or Warne, whose seven for 165, his best analysis overseas, made him the first Australian to reach 400 Test wickets. The landmark was not quite the moment of mellowness Warne deserved: Stewart was convinced he had not touched the ball on its way to Gilchrist, and made that clear enough to be fined 20% of his match fee. Gilchrist concluded the innings with his own record, his 100th dismissal in his 22nd Test. England missed the follow-on by ten.

They still had hopes of survival, even though Warne was getting ever more unplayable, because the Sunday was wet and only 21.3 overs were bowled. That was enough time for one last episode in the McGrath v Atherton saga, which ended in McGrath's 19th personal victory, a catch at first slip. Atherton, however, was determined to control what happened next: there would be no unseemly fuss, none of the show-bizzy demonstrations that accompanied the farewells to Curtly Ambrose and Courtney

Walsh here a year earlier. The only clue he gave that this really was goodbye was an extra wave of the bat. Thus ended the career of England's best batsman of the past decade. No flowers, please, by request. Cussed to the last, our Mike.

England as a whole were far less cussed. They lost four wickets to Warne and McGrath in the first hour on Monday, and the biggest stand of the innings was 58 for the ninth wicket between Ormond and Gough. It was over before tea. Australia had won the series 4–1 and, in case anyone had taken Headingley too seriously, had reiterated that their reign goes on – ad infinitum, England fear.

Toss: Australia. **Australia 641-4 dec.** (M. L. Hayden 68, J. L. Langer 102*, R. T. Ponting 62, M. E. Waugh 120, S. R. Waugh 157*, D. R. Martyn 64*); **England 432** (M. E. Trescothick 55, N. Hussain 52, M. R. Ramprakash 133, U. Afzaal 54, S. K. Warne 7-165) **and 184** (G. D. McGrath 5-43, S. K. Warne 4-64).

AUSTRALIA V ENGLAND 2002–03   Scyld Berry

As in 1989 and the six subsequent Ashes series, so it was in 2002–03. The standard of Australia's cricket was so superior that England never came close, and lost for the eighth time running. When the series was alive, in the first three Tests, Australia won by mountainous margins, and so swift was their despatch of England that only 11 days of play were necessary for the destiny of the Ashes to be decided.

In only two respects were the Australians anything less than magnificent. Strangely enough, it was not one of their better fielding sides. Adam Gilchrist tired as a wicket-keeper as the series went on, although his batting remained phenomenal until the end (his strike-rate was 102 runs per 100 balls). Before the series, Mark Waugh was dropped and announced his retirement from Test cricket; Ricky Ponting filled the vacancy at second slip to the pace bowlers, but there was no adequate replacement when Warne was bowling.

The second respect was behaviour. So long as Australia were winning, everything was fine, but as soon as England got on top in the final Test, the game got bad-tempered. Matthew Hayden, after a debated lbw, was fined 20% of his match fee for breaking the glass of a pavilion door, and Gilchrist received an official reprimand for swearing after his appeal for a catch was turned down. Throughout the series some of the sledging, led by Hayden and Justin Langer, was all too obvious. If Steve Waugh's team generated the same admiration as the Invincibles, they did not prompt quite the same public affection.

For the rest, Australia were superlative. Either their top three batsmen, led by Hayden, captured the initiative, with strokes of demoralising power, or their attack did. It was either intimidating batting or intimidating bowling which took England apart. But if one statistic summarised the difference between the two sides, it was that Australia's bowlers earned 91 wickets in the series, England's 63. Hussain was widely criticised, not least by himself, for sending Australia in at Brisbane rather than playing to the relative strength of England's batting. But it was hard to see how his depleted attack could have dismissed the home line-up twice at any time while the series was alive.

First Test

Trevor Marshallsea

At Brisbane, November 7, 8, 9, 10, 2002. Australia won by 384 runs.

It will go down as one of the costliest decisions in Test history. England captain Nasser Hussain had forecast in his newspaper column that "the worst nightmare" would be working out what to do if he won the toss. Despite the fact that opening batsmen Vaughan and Trescothick were clearly his side's most potent weapons, Hussain sent Australia in. At stumps on day one, Australia were 364 for two. There went the match and the momentum. Hussain's choice will rank up there with David Gower's invitation to the 1989 Australians to bat at Headingley, a gesture repaid by a score of 601 for seven. Australia went on to win that Ashes series 4–0, and have been winning them ever since.

Hussain later admitted his mistake, saying it had been based on a belief there would be enough early life in the green-tinged pitch to help his inexperienced seam attack. The pitch quickly dried out into the proverbial belter, and Hayden and Ponting feasted. They put on 272 for the second wicket in 253 minutes, Hayden marching imperiously to 186 not out at stumps, while Ponting fell in the final hour of the day for 123. By then, the young pace bowler Simon Jones had tumbled out of the attack – and the series – when he horribly ruptured knee ligaments in the field. He bowled only seven overs, and dismissed Langer with his ninth ball.

Both captains pointed out that, whatever a team does with the toss, they still have to execute their plans well. While Australia surged, England did not help their own chances. The tourists put down four catches on the opening day; Hayden survived on 40, when the luckless Jones held a catch on the fine-leg boundary but cancelled it by falling over the rope. Hayden, dropped also on 102, 138 and 149, moved to within three runs of a double-century early on the second morning before gloving a leg-side catch off Caddick. There began a substandard batting performance from the new-look middle order, now bereft of Mark Waugh, sacked after 107 consecutive Tests. They lost four for 37, with Martyn, Steve Waugh and Gilchrist all failing, and helping to reduce England's target from mammoth to merely daunting. Waugh, who was still on four after an hour at the crease, fell to a clever leg-gully trap set by Hussain, the first chapter of an intriguing battle between the captains over the series. It was left to Warne, with some lusty hitting, to scramble a total of 492.

England began well against an attack missing Lee, who had been sent back to state cricket to find form, a move which would pay off handsomely later. Vaughan showed glimpses of what lay ahead in the series with a quick 33, then Trescothick and Butcher took their side through to stumps at 158 for one. It was Australia's turn to underperform in the field, with each batsman dropped once and Butcher surviving a stumping chance. Both men were out in the same McGrath over next morning, but Hussain – dropped on 12 as the fielding mishaps continued – and Crawley continued to take the game to the feared Australian attack, adding 97. Once Hussain was out for 51, however, the familiar England collapse began – from 268 for three to 325.

Facing a deficit of 167, Hussain went on the attack, and his aggressive fields were rewarded when Australia quickly lost Langer and Ponting to Caddick. Normal order was soon restored, though, and the following day, the awe-inspiring Hayden cracked 60 off as many balls to reach his second hundred of the match, his seventh in ten Tests, and his sixth in seven Tests on home soil. He fell for 103, but with Martyn and the quick-scoring Gilchrist reaching half-centuries, Waugh was able to declare on 296 for five, scored in just 71 overs against an attack both undermanned and unimaginative.

In contrast with their first-innings resistance, now came the darkest hour for England. Needing to make a fanciful 464 to win or bat for 47 overs and a day to avert defeat, Hussain's men lost Vaughan, again to McGrath, off the third ball of the innings, and went on to capitulate pathetically for 79 in just 28.2 overs. That Butcher scored 40 of them says much about his colleagues. It was one of the worst England batting efforts since Tests began, with the last seven wickets (Jones was absent) falling inside 13 overs, and the innings lasting little more than two hours. The final result was their fourth-heaviest defeat by runs; it was also a 50th defeat in 123 Tests for Stewart, who completed his first Test pair. It would take a phenomenal effort for England to rebound from here.

Toss: England. **Australia 492** (M. L. Hayden 197, R. T. Ponting 123, S. K. Warne 57, A. F. Giles 4-101) **and 296-5 dec.** (M. L. Hayden 103, D. R. Martyn 64, A. C. Gilchrist 60*); **England 325** (M. E. Trescothick 72, M. A. Butcher 54, N. Hussain 51, J. P. Crawley 69*, G. D. McGrath 4-87) **and 79** (G. D. McGrath 4-36).

Second Test

John Etheridge

At Adelaide, November 21, 22, 23, 24, 2002. Australia won by an innings and 51 runs.

When England reached 295 for three with four balls of the first day remaining, they appeared for once to be offering a genuine challenge. Then, however, Vaughan's magnificent if controversial innings of 177 was ended and, in little more than seven further sessions, England descended to a crushing defeat. Australia's superiority in every facet was again obvious and, despite Hussain's insistence to the contrary, they dominated the touring team mentally as well as technically.

Vaughan's dismissal in the 90th over of the opening day was a microcosm of why Australia are so good. He had batted sublimely and, metaphorically at least, his head was touching the pillow after a full day's labour. Yet Australia never relent. Steve Waugh brought back Bichel, an honest toiler alongside three wonderful craftsmen, for a single over; he ran in as hard as if it was his first spell, nudged one away from Vaughan's bat and Warne held the catch at slip. It was the turning-point of the match.

Bichel did it again when Waugh turned to him for the final over of the third evening and he breached Hussain's defences. Equally revealing, and even more spectacular, was Vaughan's second-innings dismissal: a running, diving, stunning catch by McGrath at deep square leg. McGrath, who was in the middle of a spell at the time, is a six-and-a-half-foot quick bowler and as such meant to be a lumberer in the field. It is unlikely that any of England's bowlers would have even contemplated a catch, let alone possessed the athleticism actually to reach the ball.

England's preparation was even more chaotic than usual. Giles's left wrist was broken by Harmison in the nets two days before the game – just after he had been measured for a new, longer armguard – and he became the third player, following Jones and Gough, to fly home. When Vaughan tweaked his knee during pre-match fielding practice, England's problems had become almost comical. Hussain decided Vaughan had to play. In fact, he batted superbly, driving and pulling and punching his trademark back-foot shots behind square on the off side, often from good-length balls. When he had scored 19, the naked eye insisted he was caught by Langer at point and TV replays appeared to provide corroboration. But Vaughan, like most batsmen these days, stood his ground and Steve Davis, like most third umpires these days, judged him not out. Once more, debate raged about the efficacy of TV decisions for catches.

Vaughan gave two more chances, at 56 and 151, and Hussain was also reprieved twice as they put on 140. In the afternoon, Vaughan reached his fifth Test century of 2002, and went on to what was then England's highest innings in a Test in Australia since Mike Denness scored 188 at Melbourne in 1974–75. But once he was dismissed, the remainder of the batting subsided meekly; next morning, England lost their final six wickets for 47. Gillespie, operating with pace and intelligence, turned in a spell of four for ten in 32 balls.

Hayden and Langer responded with their seventh century opening stand in Tests, at nearly five and a half an over – Caddick's initial spell of seven overs cost 40 runs – and then Ponting made his second century of the series. Although he was not as commanding as at Brisbane, there was a feeling of inevitability as he cruised to three figures, with dazzling footwork, certainty of stroke and hard running between the wickets (he struck only nine fours). England suffered a gruelling time in the field. Caddick was restricted by a back problem and Harmison, fast enough to cause some unsettling moments, was so drained by the end that he struggled to reach the stumps. With Vaughan unable to field after being struck on the right shoulder by Gillespie, England used four different substitutes. Catches continued to go down – five, including Martyn, who was badly spilled by Stewart on 37 as he and Ponting added 242 for the third wicket. White collected four wickets, including his brother-in-law, Lehmann. Australia's lower order continued to plunder the weary attack, extending the lead to 210.

Tired and dejected by their toil in the field, England lost three wickets inside 12 overs on the third evening. Although Vaughan and Stewart added 74 next morning, Australia's march to victory was not long delayed. Stewart reached 8,000 Test runs when 52, and Dawson had the temerity to strike McGrath for three off-side boundaries in as many balls, but McGrath, as usual, had the final word, finishing with four wickets, plus his astonishing catch. By then it was occasionally spitting with rain; on what would have been the fifth day it poured, taunting a demoralised team.

Toss: England. **England 342** (M. P. Vaughan 177, J. N. Gillespie 4-78, S. K. Warne 4-93) and **159** (A. J. Stewart 57, G. D. McGrath 4-41); **Australia 552-9 dec.** (R. T. Ponting 154, D. R. Martyn 95, A. C. Gilchrist 54, C. White 4-106).

Third Test

Vic Marks

At Perth, November 29, 30, December 1, 2002. Australia won by an innings and 48 runs.

England's quest for the Ashes came to an end before those back home had opened a door on their Advent calendars. They were thrashed again, and there was barely a redeeming feature for the 4,000 diehard English supporters who swelled the crowd at the WACA to record proportions.

It had taken 11 days for the Australians to dismantle the English team; for the fundamentalists it took only six to make the world. By these standards alone England had been obdurate in this series. But it was difficult to regard this team as fundamentalist in approach. Hussain may have preached a "back to basics" doctrine, but no one in his ranks seemed to pay much attention. Indeed there were times when Hussain himself, through eccentric bowling plans or the odd wild hook shot, deserted his own philosophy.

By now the side was disorientated – by two thumping defeats at Brisbane and Adelaide and by a catalogue of injuries which had reached ridiculous proportions. For this game Caddick was absent, having failed to recover from his back spasms in Adelaide, and so was Crawley. Even so, a measure of desperation was evident in England's selection. They decided to drop Hoggard for Silverwood, who had flown out as a replacement when Jones was injured and had not bowled in the middle. He shared the new ball with another recent arrival, Tudor. Almost inevitably, Silverwood bowled only four overs before his ankle gave way. An ECB press release quickly pointed out: "This is a new injury and not related to the joint inflammation he experienced in the same ankle at the end of the English season." Which convinced nobody. The Ashes campaign had been a shambles.

There were plenty of examples of England's disintegration in Perth, but the most obvious were two run-outs, one scarring each innings. Both involved Vaughan and Butcher in dismissals which would have left primary-school coaches aghast; both times, the needless sacrifice of a wicket led to the rest of the batting subsiding.

England's ineptitude tended to mask Australia's ruthless efficiency. Apart from some fallibility in their close catching, the Australians were routinely brilliant here, but they were never put under any sort of pressure. Losing the toss for the third time running hardly inconvenienced them. Given recent history and a patchwork bowling attack, Hussain had to bat first but, on the paciest wicket seen even at Perth for years, batting would present unique challenges. When the WACA pitch is fast, it bears no relation to any other in the world – and Australia's fastest bowler, Lee, had returned in place of Bichel.

At 69 for one, England appeared to be competing well, but then came the first mix-up between Vaughan and Butcher. Waugh, from cover, unerringly hit the stumps at the non-striker's end with Butcher yards adrift, a self-inflicted blow from which England never recovered. Soon there were ill-judged pulls and hooks from Hussain, Vaughan and Stewart, all caught behind as they failed to come to terms with exceptional bounce and pace. Only Key, in a stout, mostly passive knock, resisted long, and he was duped by the introduction of Martyn's gentle medium-pacers just before tea.

Run-scoring was a more straightforward occupation for Australia. Silverwood soon limped off, though not before his throw from the leg-side boundary had accounted for Langer, seeking an ambitious third. Thereafter, all the Australians settled and sparkled briefly, though none of them managed a major innings. Ponting, in sublime form, looked set for his third century of the series until he played on to White. Martyn's measured 71 was the highest score. White snaffled five wickets, which flattered him, Harmison just one, which didn't. Harmison bowled with pace, usually short, and he often tested both the batsmen and a sprawling Stewart behind the stumps. He overcame a minor attack of the yips with impressive grit. On the second morning, he consistently lost his run-up, stuttering as he approached his delivery stride. Even so, he kept going and was still faster and more threatening than the other bowlers.

With a lead of 271, there was never much chance of Australia having to bat twice. Again, England folded after a masochistic run-out. This time Vaughan was the victim, but Butcher was so ruffled by a second running aberration that he missed his next ball, from McGrath, was patently lbw, and swiped the bails with his bat to earn a fine. Having started the third day on 33 for one, England should have been 34 for five when Warne dropped a straightforward catch at first slip from Hussain's first ball.

A battling innings from Hussain, another stubborn one from Key and a flighty, though futile, effort from Stewart enabled England to reach 223. Just before the end, Tudor received a sickening blow to the head as he ducked into a bouncer from Lee. He was stretchered off and for a moment thought he had lost an eye. Fortunately, he suffered just a nasty gash, which required stitches, and a terrible headache.

Lee justified his return by bowling with fierce pace throughout. He looked briefly concerned by the damage he had caused to Tudor, but it did not deter him from bowling a vicious bouncer at the hapless Harmison second ball. Soon after that, Lee splattered Harmison's stumps and it was all over. The Australians had retained the Ashes, even though the little urn, to their dismay, was still locked away in St John's Wood.

Toss: England. **England 185 and 223** (N. Hussain 61, A. J. Stewart 66*);
Australia 456 (R. T. Ponting 68, D. R. Martyn 71, S. R. Waugh 53, C. White 5-127).

Fourth Test

Steven Lynch

At Melbourne, December 26, 27, 28, 29, 30, 2002. Australia won by five wickets.

With the Ashes already surrendered yet again, England made a better fist of matters at the MCG – but still lost. On an exciting final day, Australia wobbled, showing signs of their old fallibility when chasing small targets, but finally made it 4–0 with five wickets to spare.

It might have been closer: after the on-song Harmison had grabbed two wickets in his sixth over, Waugh came in, suffering from a migraine, and somehow survived a manic over from Harmison, in which he was beaten, caught behind (but no one appealed because the racket from the Barmy Army drowned out the noise of the ball kissing the bat-face), then caught off a no-ball. Waugh hadn't heard the call, and was halfway to the dressing-room before he realised. The spell was broken with an emphatically driven four and, although Waugh really was out a few overs later, the moment had passed.

All this drama seemed unthinkable as Australia racked up another huge first-innings total. Langer and Hayden combined in an opening stand of 195, then a blitzkrieg from Waugh lifted Australia to 356 for three, the highest first-day score by one side in any Melbourne Test. Again, it might have been different: Hayden hooked his first ball from Caddick, which ballooned to long leg. But Hussain had brought Harmison in off the rope, and the ball sailed over his head for four. Hayden never looked back, clattering ten fours and three sixes – two off White into the stands over long-on – in his 12th Test hundred, his ninth in the last 14 months.

Langer rolled on to a massive 250, the highest of his 13 Test centuries. It took him 578 minutes and 407 balls, and included 30 fours; he reached his hundred with a six over long-on off Dawson. After Waugh celebrated the 17th anniversary of his Test debut with a staccato 77, studded with 15 fours – several cracked through the covers with a whipped follow-through as he sprinted to 50 in 49 balls – there was time for a mature innings from Martin Love. Fresh from two double-centuries against these tourists, for

Queensland and Australia A, Love had played an Australian-record 129 first-class matches before his first Test.

Warne was also absent, after dislocating his shoulder in a one-day international, prompting a recall for his understudy, MacGill. Injuries affected England too: they had to reshuffle their side, including only four bowlers, when Stewart dropped out with a bruised hand. Foster, his tidy replacement, did not concede a bye in Australia's big first innings, but he was quieter than Stewart might have been when that final-day catch skimmed through from Waugh.

Some spineless batting condemned England to follow on. McGrath, playing in his 54th consecutive Test to pass Courtney Walsh's record for a specialist fast bowler, removed Vaughan, then a Lee screamer accounted for Trescothick. Hussain, reprieved by the third umpire after seemingly being caught by Gillespie at mid-on when 14, added only ten more before MacGill had his revenge.

With Hussain's dismissal on the third morning, England slumped to 118 for six. But then White, playing his maiden first-class match on the ground where he cheered England on as a displaced Pommie schoolboy, collared the bowling. His 85 not out included nine fours and three sixes (all off MacGill), and almost doubled his previous aggregate against Australia – 86 in 11 completed innings. But it was a bittersweet knock: White batted in the painful knowledge that he had twanged an intercostal muscle while bowling. Apart from his second innings, he played no further part in the tour.

Following on 281 behind, England faced an unprecedented third successive innings defeat. They lost Trescothick for his second promising 37 of the match, one of five wickets for the persevering MacGill and one of several dubious decisions from umpire Tiffin. But Vaughan ploughed on, pulling imperiously and cover-driving as if he had been studying videos of Colin Cowdrey. He purred to 145, with 19 fours and three sixes, out of 236. On the way, he eclipsed Dennis Amiss's England record of 1,379 runs in a calendar year, and finished with 1,481, an annual tally exceeded only by Viv Richards (1,710 in 1976) and Sunil Gavaskar (1,555 in 1979). Vaughan's second century of the series, like Hayden's his sixth of 2002, stamped him as a player of the utmost class. The Australians paid him their highest compliment: they stopped sledging him.

A plucky maiden half-century from Key swelled the total, but a characteristic collapse, in which the last five tumbled for only 45, meant the target was a seemingly simple 107. But Langer seemed unable to time a thing, and Caddick – ineffective in the first innings, as so infuriatingly often – suddenly clicked into top gear. Hayden swung the last day's first ball to Tudor, the substitute, on the square-leg boundary. Later, Caddick had Waugh gloving into the slips, and wrung another dubious decision out of Tiffin to trap Langer lbw.

In between, Harmison worked up a head of steam, beating Ponting and Martyn for pace in the space of four balls. But Gilchrist stopped the rot, popping the winning four over point in the 24th over. The thrilling last morning was fine fare – and free – for a crowd of 18,666. The match total was an impressive 177,658, despite the loss of a chunk of the stands on the railway side of the ground as rebuilding rumbled on.

Toss: Australia. **Australia 551-6 dec.** (J. L. Langer 250, M. L. Hayden 102, S. R. Waugh 77, M. L. Love 62*) **and 107-5; England 270** (C. White 85*, J. N. Gillespie 4-25) **and 387** (M. P. Vaughan 145, R. W. T. Key 52, S. C. G. MacGill 5-152).

A Star is Vaughan

Tim de Lisle, 2003

In *Roget's Thesaurus*, cricket appears in the same section as dancing. Sport and dance aspire to the same beautiful aimlessness – light-footed, swivel-hipped, free-spirited. But you wouldn't know it from the recent history of English batsmanship.

For a decade the dominant influence has been Graham Gooch, a batsman admirable in almost every way but not noted for twinkling toes. Gooch's method disregarded the feet in favour of shifting his weight, and that of the boulder he used for a bat. It worked for him and seeped into the technique of a couple of his opening partners, Alec Stewart and Mike Atherton, who had a spring in their heels but edited it out as the arteries hardened. Stewart and Atherton in turn opened with Marcus Trescothick, who was Gooch in a mirror: tall, strong, and stiff as a toy soldier. Now Trescothick's partner is Michael Vaughan, who became, in 2002, both a top-class player and a one-man reversal of this trend. He pirouetted to pull respectable deliveries; he went right forward, with a high elbow and a mean look in his eye, to send the ball skimming past cover; he went back to late-cut as if in a sepia newsreel. He reminded John Woodcock of Len Hutton. Best of all, he went down the wicket to loft world-renowned spinners over mid-wicket. With his quick feet, hands and wits, he could not have been nimbler if he had been wearing white tie and tails.

Vaughan's hundreds at home came on flat pitches, against modest seam attacks, but then he did it all over again on his first Ashes tour, in cricket's hottest kitchen. Asked to name the best moment of his career, he said the Ashes – scoring his three centuries. Asked for the worst moment, he said the Ashes again – losing them 4-1. So he has balance as well as talent.

Fifth Test

Christian Ryan

At Sydney, January 2, 3, 4, 5, 6, 2003. England won by 225 runs.

England carried over their Melbourne momentum to inflict Australia's first home defeat in four years. It was tempting to blame it on dead-rubber syndrome, but this was a hard-fought, fair-dinkum English victory. Their two previous wins against Australia hinged on a miraculous spell by Dean Headley and an even more miraculous innings by Mark Butcher. This time, they played grinding cricket for five days. They did it under a hot sun and an unflinching leader. And maybe, just maybe, they exposed the first crack in a mighty empire.

The match was witnessed by the second-biggest Sydney crowd in history. A further 2.1 million TV viewers – one in nine Australians – tuned in for the gripping second evening. And yet, for all of them, this was about one man. Steve Waugh's 102 was not, contrary to local hyperbole, the greatest century in Ashes folklore; next day, Gilchrist and Vaughan produced a couple every bit as good. But few, if any, have hit hundreds with such a sense of inevitability.

The looming US invasion of Iraq dominated the New Year, but Australians were preoccupied with a different Waugh. Should he stay or should he go? Waugh entered the Test – his 156th, matching Allan Border's record – knowing it could be his last. He entered the final over of the second day needing five runs for 100. Then came the magical bit. Dawson's first three balls were dead-batted down the pitch. Waugh square-drove his fourth for three, but Gilchrist did the right thing and pushed a single. One ball left, two runs needed. Unflustered, Waugh leaned back and drilled a flattish delivery through extra cover for four, sparking a roar that the writer David Frith reckoned was the loudest he had heard in 52 years' watching at the SCG.

For the first time since November 1992, Australia started with neither McGrath (side strain) nor Warne (shoulder). Without those two, as many had long suspected, they were half the side. Still, a half-strength Australia is troublesome enough. After Hussain chose to bat on a true pitch, England were soon in a familiar fiddle. Lee swung the ball both ways at high speed, before Butcher and Hussain combined for what was briefly England's highest third-wicket stand at Sydney. They were dropped three times, underlining how much Australia missed Mark Waugh, who made a lunch-time lap of honour round his home ground. But few begrudged Hussain, in particular, his luck. Gone were the frazzled, manic starts of earlier innings. Instead, he seemed to smile more. Butcher's 124, peppered with delicious cover-drives and neat tucks off his body, was the performance he had hinted at all series. As with Headingley 2001, however, it was only once the Ashes were lost that he loosened up enough to produce it.

Steve Waugh eventually brought himself on, mesmerically trapping Key lbw with an innocuous half-volley. But it was another endangered old-timer who swung things England's way. Stewart had been restored after his Melbourne injury, only to be taken to Sydney's Clinic of Infectious Diseases before the match with a mysterious rash across his face. The rash proved undiagnosable and Stewart unflappable, swiping 15 boundaries. Though Bichel, standing in for McGrath, bowled him on 71, England stretched the total to 362.

The Australians went one better, thanks largely to Waugh's Bradman-equalling 29th Test hundred. This was not the methodical, crablike Waugh of recent years, but the footloose version of the late 1980s, thriving on crunching cover-drives and meaty slashes over the slips. He became the third man to scale 10,000 Test runs, after Gavaskar and Border, and took only 130 balls over his hundred. (The next morning was an anticlimax; Hoggard, recalled because of White's injury, removed him in his first over.) Yet Waugh looked almost pedestrian beside Gilchrist, who required only 94 balls for his century, despite barely hazarding an unconventional stroke. The exception was the shot that got him there: instead of ducking a Harmison bouncer, Gilchrist lifted his bat vertically above his head and swatted the ball tennis-style into the empty expanses of mid-on for three.

Even more praiseworthy, and only slightly more prosaic, was Vaughan's seventh hundred in eight months. This was his best yet. He erupted in the third over of the innings, swinging Gillespie for a glorious six off his hips, before settling into an almost flawless rhythm, which brought 27 fours from 278 balls. Trescothick became Lee's 100th victim, nudging an armpit rocket on to his stumps, but Vaughan, ever methodical but never monotonous, sailed on. He sat on MacGill's stock big-turner and feasted on his plentiful loose offerings. MacGill appeared over-anxious, too eager to impress, while Gillespie, always deadlier at the start of a series, conspicuously failed to lead the attack. Vaughan put on 189 with Hussain – an upgrade on the first day's record – before succumbing to a recklessly idiosyncratic lbw decision, one of several by umpire Tiffin. But as the bowlers wilted, the lower order, better late than never, took advantage; when Hussain declared on the fourth evening, Stewart and last man Harmison had added 43 unbeaten runs in seven overs.

That set Australia 452. Fat chance turned swiftly to no chance. Langer, Hayden and Ponting were despatched lbw on a tense fourth evening, Langer Tiffined by a ball pitching eight inches outside leg. Bichel was mystifyingly sent in 18 overs before stumps – a pinch-watchman, perhaps? – and swung sensibly before falling to Caddick, that other golden oldie rumoured to be past his use-by date, at the start of the final morning. Banging the ball in purposefully, Caddick made the most of some uneven bounce and undisciplined batting to collect ten wickets in a Test for the first time. Martyn and Love lingered briefly, but the rest went down swinging. Waugh's men have achieved many wondrous feats; they don't, however, do draws. Batting seven hours to save a match proved hopelessly beyond them.

Hussain, long-sleeved shirt buttoned to his throat and wrists, was his usual gloomy self at the post-match press conference. But he had glimpsed a new world, a brighter world, a world without McGrath and Warne. It was hard to shake the feeling that, after 14 years of ritual Ashes humiliation, the worst for England might finally be over.

Toss: England. **England 362** (M. A. Butcher 124, N. Hussain 75, A. J. Stewart 71)
and **452-9 dec.** (M. P. Vaughan 183, N. Hussain 72); **Australia 363** (S. R. Waugh 102, A. C. Gilchrist 133,
M. J. Hoggard 4-92) **and 226** (A. R. Caddick 7-94).

TRYING TO MELT THE ICEMAN
Nasser Hussain, 2004

Steve Waugh was not a cricketing god or a genius, like Tendulkar or Lara, nor even technically brilliant like Rahul Dravid. Like the rest of us, he was human. But a previously unremarkable household in suburban Sydney was definitely given more than its fair share of talent when the Waugh twins arrived on the scene. Their little games of backyard cricket eventually led to the pair of them playing nearly 300 Tests and scoring nearly 20,000 runs between them. Some would argue that one was given a little bit more talent than the other. As one member of the Barmy Army once said, as he dared to sledge the greatest sledger of them all, "Oy, Stephen, best batsman in the world? You ain't even the best batsman in your family!"

Well, for over a decade Stephen Waugh made himself into the best batsman in the world. He was given two useful cricketing skills at birth: incredible hand-eye co-ordination and the fastest pair of hands of any cricketer I have played against. The rest he has had to work for. He has proved one cricketing cliché during his career: that the higher the level you play, the more it is played in your head. And he was, mentally, the strongest player of his era.

He didn't deal with the short ball particularly well and he moved around the crease a lot as the bowler delivered, staying back and not really transferring all his weight on to the front foot when the ball was pitched up. But, hey, that is the game. Every batsman has weaknesses, and it is up to the player to overcome them and the opposition to exploit them. Waugh overcame his deficiencies because his hand-eye co-ordination meant he could keep the good ones out and put the bad ones away – and because his mental toughness helped him through every situation batting can throw up.

Sometimes, if we were doing really well and had reduced Australia to 300 for three, we would be pleased with ourselves. In comes Waugh, red handkerchief hanging out of pocket, pushes the ball (usually to someone like dopey Gough standing at mid-on) and scampers a single, smiles and stays off strike for a while. This would be followed by a few short balls (which Waugh finds uncomfortable, but never gets out to), and the bowlers begin thinking that they had better start pitching it up. They over-correct and these incredible hands start to caress the ball through the covers. Before you know it, you look up at the scoreboard and he's 30 not out, off and running. Groundhog Day! You've seen it all before, but there seems nothing you can do to stop it happening all over again.

As a player, Waugh was always at his most dangerous when confronted by a real challenge. All his great innings came in the face of adversity. Whether it was a poor wicket, or a poor calf, or a poor press hinting at the waning of his power, he felt most at home in difficult situations. It was as if he believed in his own reputation as the "Iceman" and was keen to enhance it. Nothing would give him more pleasure than reading the next day about another gutsy Steve Waugh innings.

There could not have been any more pressure on a cricketer than in January 2003 against England at the SCG. Waugh has since admitted that if he hadn't got runs in that Test it would have been his last. He was not particularly playing well in the series, and looked surprisingly nervous. He came in when Australia were 56 for three and I immediately thought "Dangerous". Everything I tried to do that day seemed almost pointless. It was as if the script had already been written.

That evening, with Waugh on 98 and the last ball of the day coming up, I ran up to Richard Dawson, told him I had no real cunning plan but to stall things, get Waugh nervous and hope he would make a mistake. Dawson bowled a perfectly good ball and those Waugh hands just flicked it away through the covers with complete disdain.

I have always found Waugh intriguing. How did he make himself so good? He told me that the most important aspect to him was body language. He liked to almost sprint to the crease to emphasise that he was relishing the battle ahead; he liked to give off an aura of aggression. Nothing emphasises this more than when, in Port-of-Spain nine years ago, Waugh stood face to face with one of the greatest fast bowlers of all time, Curtly Ambrose.

Now, here is a man who doesn't play the short ball particularly well, doesn't pull or hook, telling the man who has dismissed him the most in Test cricket to get back to his mark and bowl. Robert Craddock wrote in that year's *Wisden*: Waugh "stood his ground like John Wayne when Ambrose engaged him in a verbal exchange of fire from two metres; the bowler had to be tugged away. 'It's Test cricket,' the unrepentant Waugh said afterwards. 'If you want an easy game, go play netball'." Waugh made 63 not out in that innings and went on to make 200 in the next game, when Australia won by an innings and regained the Frank Worrell Trophy.

Throughout his career, Waugh, almost on purpose, maximised the challenge – whether it be a sore calf, a last-chance-saloon innings, or a fired-up Ambrose – to bring the best out of himself. Basically, for over 20 years he has been playing mind games with himself and the opposition.

The Greatest Series – and the Worst? 2005 to 2006-07

The final Test of the 2002–03 series at Sydney, which England won in the absence of both Shane Warne and Glenn McGrath, hinted at a shift in the balance of power, and an end to Australia's tight grip on the Ashes, which had been unthreatened since Allan Border's side regained them in 1989. But then in 2005, after a frenetic first day which initially gave England hope, Australia won at Lord's, as they usually do (England won only one Ashes Test there in the whole of the 20th century, and that only when the Aussies were caught on a wet wicket). Funnily enough, Australia's win probably harmed them more than England, as it allowed a group of players used to the Poms tamely rolling over to think that history was about to repeat itself.

The over-confidence stemming from the win at Lord's persuaded Ricky Ponting, when he won the toss in the Second Test, to put England in even though McGrath, his best fast bowler, had been ruled out just before the start after he trod on a practice ball and hurt his ankle. England again started strongly, but this time they kept going, and thanks to ferocious bursts with bat and ball from Andrew Flintoff – the undoubted man of the summer – they should have won easily. But Australia's tail turned an already absorbing match into even more of a classic, the last pair inching the total to within three runs of victory before the last wicket fell.

England's win set up the series, and the summer. As the correspondent lucky enough to be reporting the match for *Wisden*, I wrote: "It was the right decision for cricket: 2–0 to Australia would have been the signal for the football season to begin; 1–1 lit the blue touchpaper." A huge audience had been watching on (free-to-air) television, possibly from behind the sofa, as the Edgbaston game came to its heart-stopping climax, and they stayed watching as cricket grabbed the front pages of the newspapers and resolutely refused to retreat to the back (in one particular week, the front page of *The Times* newspaper was dominated by a cricket picture on every day). People also charged out into the garden, or down to the park, to re-enact what they had just seen: for the first time in years cricket was being played on open spaces around the country more often than football.

The momentum now was with England, who just failed to convert supremacy in the Third Test into victory, in the only match of the series which Australia never had a sniff of winning. Then Michael Vaughan's men went ahead with another gut-wrenching win in the Fourth Test, by just three wickets over an Australian side once again missing the injured McGrath, before the final encounter at The Oval swung this way and that. England were helped by the weather and a superb 158 from their new hero Kevin Pietersen – but, had KP not been dropped when only 15, England could well have lost and Australia would still have retained the Ashes. In one of those cruel twists in which cricket specialises, the culprit – dropping a relatively straightforward breastbone-high catch at first slip off Brett Lee – was Warne, who could hardly have done more in the series, taking 40 wickets in the five Tests.

England's recapture of the Ashes urn after 16 years launched an open-top bus parade, MBEs for all the players, a rush-issue DVD, and more than a dozen tour books. It also earned from *Wisden* the deserved accolade of the Greatest Test Series ever: few would argue with that, not even those weaned on Headingley '81 and the rest of "Botham's Ashes".

It all meant that the fevered hype which preceded the 2006–07 rematch Down Under dwarfed even that for 2005, which had been pretty spectacular in itself. But there was a significant difference between the two sides. Australia had spent most of the preceding 15 months licking their wounds and planning revenge – some time before the series started Lee signed a cricket ball for a friend of mine with the ominous prediction "Ashes 2006–07: 5–0 to Australia" – and had beaten all comers since. England's players, on the other hand, arguably let the Trafalgar Square celebrations (not to mention the audiences at Buckingham Palace and 10 Downing Street) go to their heads, and had had mixed results on the field.

At the end of November 2006, after the first morning of the First Test, Australia's regaining of the Ashes was almost never in doubt. Steve Harmison opened with the widest wide most people can remember – a year later Ian Healy was still calling big wides "Harmies" on TV – and England were never in contention in the First Test, then somehow managed to lose the second despite declaring their first innings at 551 for 6, after a wretchedly timid batting display on the last day at Adelaide. From then on it was only a question of whether Lee's prediction would be fulfilled.

It was, helped by the fact that after Warne and McGrath both announced that they would be retiring the Australians really had something to play for in the final Test, whereas in previous seasons they had often taken their feet off the pedals once a series was settled. And so 5–0 came to pass – just the second Ashes whitewash, after Australia beat a war-ravaged England in 1920–21 – but only the most rabid Aussie supporters enjoyed the series anything like as much as the classic 2005 one.

Which brings us back to the essence of a good rivalry: it has to be close, otherwise it's not really much fun. And over the years the Ashes really has been good fun, often much more than that, for generations of cricket lovers – not only those in England and Australia, but also almost anyone interested in cricket, anywhere. The hope for 2009 and beyond is that, whoever wins, the Ashes will continue to serve up magical, memorable, mesmerising moments to add to the legend.   S. L.

ENGLAND V AUSTRALIA 2005   Stephen Brenkley

If there has been a more compelling series, history forgot to record it. If there is a better one in the future, you would beg to be there. England regained the Ashes, after a gap of 16 years and 42 days, when bad light brought a formal end to the Fifth Test: a series full of extraordinary climaxes and reversals, in the end, just dwindling away in the more usual cricketing fashion to the point where an Australian victory became impossible, even in this summer.

It finished 2–1 to England, though but for a run here, a wicket there or a catch almost anywhere it could conceivably have been either 4–1 or 0–4. It is somehow soothing to relate the bare facts and the strangely prosaic conclusion. The contest was gripping from the beginning. As it reached the end, not just regular English cricket followers, but the whole country and the rest of the cricketing world were in its thrall. It was so intense and played with such purpose that it supplanted football on the back pages and much else on the front pages. TV viewing figures went through the roof.

The First Test was topsy-turvy, but eventually resulted in an easy Australian victory, leading most people – including, crucially, the Australians themselves – to assume their dominance would remain unchallenged. The Second ("The Greatest Test", many thought) produced the first sensational finish and a two-run England win. Australia just held out to save the Third. England clung on to edge the Fourth. And, though the Fifth reached a conclusion more bizarre than thrilling, everyone was so galvanised by the whole affair and, in England, by the impending return of the urn that no one minded. By the halfway mark, a debate had begun about whether it was the best Ashes series of all; it moved swiftly on to whether it was the best Test series ever, with a substantial body of informed opinion thinking it was. At various times, the matches entered that peculiar realm where you could not look away but found it unbearable to keep watching.

But there was another dimension too. The image of England's monumental all-rounder Andrew Flintoff consoling a distraught Brett Lee immediately after England had won the Second Test flashed round Planet Cricket. It seemed to show a world where forgotten virtues of honour, decency, respect and commiseration for your opponent still held sway. After years when every aspect of English cricket had been savaged or mocked, the game was now being reborn in the country where it had been conceived and nurtured, and looking like something with a great deal to teach rival sports and the rest of an often bad-tempered country.

First Test

David Frith

At Lord's, July 21, 22, 23, 24, 2005. Australia won by 239 runs.

The longest period of ambitious anticipation in living memory as far as England's Ashes hopes were concerned came to a juddering halt in the opening encounter. Australia's bowling champions, McGrath and Warne, proved as effective as ever in exploiting both the conditions and batsmen's nerves. Further swaying the outcome was England's failure to hold catches. Seven were grassed, one with dire consequences. The upshot was that Australia's 71-year unbeaten sequence in Lord's Tests would be extended to at least three-quarters of a century. And, misleadingly, it was assumed that business as had been usual since 1989 was being maintained.

There was a hectic start. Before the first drinks break, Harmison, from the Pavilion End, struck Langer painfully on the arm, dented Hayden's helmet grille as he tried to hook, and drew blood from Ponting's cheek when he too tried to punish a fiercely rising ball: three injury delays during which the Englishmen merely talked among themselves. By lunch, the jam-packed ground was buzzing after the pace foursome had the visitors half out for 97 on a responsive pitch. Many an innings has been turned around by Gilchrist, but he edged behind after slicing and slamming six fours. At this stage, England's misses mattered little when their biggest threat, Harmison, returned to bowl Warne and blow away the last four in 14 balls.

At tea, England were ten without loss, and Australia's 190 looked paltry. But McGrath's first delivery after the break brought him his 500th wicket in 110 Tests, and by the close they were 92 for seven. In an unforgettable spell from the Pavilion End that swung the match, McGrath landed the ball exactly where he desired, and with sufficient zing to beat Trescothick and Strauss, both caught at slip, then Vaughan, Bell and Flintoff, all bowled: five for two in 31 balls.

From 21 for five, defiance came with a stand of 58 by Pietersen, making what looked like a nerveless debut, and Geraint Jones, who needed runs to offset criticism of his keeping. There were sad cheers when he square-cut a four, but further relief came when Gillespie replaced Lee, who had bowled with awesome speed and accuracy, conceding only ten in his first eight overs, after 17 Tests out of the side. Driving and pulling, Pietersen and Jones remustered hope on a field now sunlit. But Lee returned and unseated first Jones and then Giles, who just escaped decapitation, then gallantly on-drove for four, before treading on his leg stump.

Next morning, under another low, grey sky, England dragged themselves towards Australia's total. Pietersen was the force. His treatment of McGrath was soul-stirring: in three deliveries he cross-batted him to the pavilion railings, lofted a slower ball into the seats, and cover-drove the next for four. It was a performance that reminded some of the arrival of another super-confident South African-born England batsman, Tony Greig, more than 30 years before.

Pietersen cracked Warne for six into the Grand Stand, and almost did it again, but this time the sprinting Martyn dived to hold a breathtaking catch. A stand of 33 by last pair Harmison and Simon Jones, the second-highest of the innings, took them to within 35 of Australia, and left England, after all, close enough to nurse hopes of overcoming McGrath's amazing opening spell. The pitch still belonged to the bowlers. It would be a matter of holding every catch offered.

The sky was thick with cloud again when Australia went in, and the top three were gone with the lead only 135. Harmison was England's McGrath, bowling 12 overs for 20 and a few near-misses, and Jones was the best of the support bowlers. He bowled probably the decisive ball of the match, just before tea, with Australia 139 for three. Clarke pushed it to cover, where Pietersen, moving to his right, fluffed the catch – his third drop. Clarke stroked 70 more runs, and the outcome was assured. For England this was a dark reprise of Lord's 2001, when Gilchrist was spared four times in reaching 90.

Clarke's was a handsome knock. After his spectacular introduction to Test cricket, he had sometimes struggled on English pitches, and this was no marble-top. With the under-praised Martyn, he set about gaining control, and did so with 91 off only 106 balls before frustration – by his own admission – got the better of him. A loose drive, an inside edge, and the glory of a century on Ashes debut was denied him.

Martyn departed next ball, and Gilchrist was bowled off an inside edge. But the lead was already past 300, and lengthening, as Katich batted on intelligently with the stubborn tail. England's frustration was evident. Keeper Jones missed a one-handed catch off Gillespie, then spilled McGrath, also missed by Flintoff at slip. England's hallucinatory target turned out to be 420.

They were half out by the close, three of the wickets to Warne, despite an encouraging start of 80 by Trescothick and Strauss. Although Pietersen continued to counter-attack, England were in ruins. Their only hope was really bad weather, and rain did delay play on the fourth day until 3.45. Australia needed just 61 balls. England went meekly, always excepting Pietersen, the first since Greig in 1972 to top-score in both innings on debut for England. For the first time in 51 Tests, England had been bowled out twice for under

200. Ponting expressed gratitude that Lord's had been chosen as the opening venue. It remained easily their favourite ground in the world.

Toss: Australia. **Australia 190** (S. J. Harmison 5-43) **and 384** (D. R. Martyn 65, M. J. Clarke 91, S. M. Katich 67); **England 155** (K. P. Pietersen 57, G. D. McGrath 5-53) **and 180** (K. P. Pietersen 64*, G. D. McGrath 4-29, S. K. Warne 4-64).

Second Test

At Birmingham, August 4, 5, 6, 7, 2005. England won by two runs.

Steven Lynch

If Australia had been rolled over in a couple of balls on the fourth morning, which was wholly possible, this would still be remembered as a great Test match: it produced exciting, fluctuating, often brilliant cricket from day one. But the crowd that turned up and filled Edgbaston on the Sunday seemed to sense they would be seeing something more worthwhile than three minutes' cricket and a victory singsong.

They still got the win they desperately wanted and expected, but in a manner that will never be forgotten. When the Third Test began four days later, *The Greatest Test* DVD was on sale. And no one was arguing with the description. On that sunlit fourth morning, England strode out on to the field with Australia 175 for eight, chasing 282. The main batsmen were all gone, and so was the swaggering confidence that had characterised Australia's Test performances for almost the whole of the previous 16 years.

But sometimes there is nothing quite as invigorating as a hopeless situation. Warne started brightly, Lee jumped solidly behind the ball, collecting bruises as well as runs, and the target ticked down. Warne trod on his stumps with 62 wanted, but still it wasn't over. The bowlers dug the ball in too short and too straight, aiming for catches off the splice rather than in the well-stocked slip cordon. England's confidence turned to concern to alarm to panic. And the last pair, Lee and Kasprowicz – with plenty of help from Extras – whittled the target down towards single figures.

With 15 required, Kasprowicz flicked Flintoff uppishly to third man, where Simon Jones failed to hold on to a difficult catch as he dived forward. England's last chance appeared to have gone. But finally, with just three wanted, Harmison banged one into the left glove of Kasprowicz, who hunched down horrified as the ball looped down the leg side and Geraint Jones plunged for the winning catch, the signal for tumultuous celebrations. A mournful Kasprowicz said afterwards. "It just got big quick, and I didn't see too much of it." Nor did umpire Bowden.

After umpteen TV replays, it was possible to conclude that Kasprowicz's left hand was off the bat at the moment of impact so, technically, he was not out. Bowden, however, would have needed superhuman vision to see this, and an armed escort involving several regiments to escape the crowd had he actually refused to give it out. It was also the right decision for cricket: 2–0 to Australia would have been the signal for the football season to begin; 1–1 lit the blue touchpaper. The Greatest Test became the Greatest Series, and the pyrotechnics illuminated the summer. The final margin was the closest in England–Australia Tests, edging the three-run thrillers at Old Trafford 1902 and Melbourne 1982–83 – and neither of those could match this one in its relentless unmissability.

The drama began before the toss, when McGrath trod on a ball during practice and tore his ankle ligaments. Despite losing his leading fast bowler, Ponting decided to field on a cloudy morning, influenced by some gloomy predictions about the pitch, which had been under water less than a week beforehand after Birmingham was struck by a mini-tornado. But, in keeping with Australia's flawed backroom work throughout the tour, Ponting's decision ignored well-informed local opinion on both the weather and the tendency of Edgbaston wickets to deteriorate.

Vaughan could hardly believe his luck, and Ponting rapidly got the sinking feeling of a captain who has made a very, very big mistake. Against a McGrathless attack, England shed their inhibitions and their vulnerability, and hurtled to 407 inside 80 overs, the most conceded by Australia on the first day of any Test since 1938. Trescothick led the way with a blazing 90, as the bowlers obligingly served the ball into the perfect groove for his crunching cover and off-drives. He hit 15 fours and two sixes, but was out shortly after lunch, in sight of his first Ashes century. Bell followed third ball, and Vaughan hooked straight to long leg, but that set up a crucial stand of 103 between the big-hitting pair of Pietersen and Flintoff.

Unsure at first against Warne, who wheeled down 25.2 overs, Flintoff hit his way out of trouble, carting him into the stands and once swatting a Lee bouncer over the rope despite taking his eye off the ball and trying to withdraw the bat. Few innings of such power and importance have conveyed so little authority: Flintoff was feeling his way uncertainly into the series but, once he got there, he commandeered it. After 45 overs, the official halfway mark, England were already 236 for four, a day's ration in the dour 1950s and '60s.

Flintoff had carved five sixes and six fours when he became Gillespie's 250th Test victim, just after tea. But then Pietersen, who had intelligently held back while Flintoff flailed, took over to score his third half-century in his first three Test innings, this time wafting a forthright 71 with a six and ten fours, several from a whipped forehand drive to mid-wicket reminiscent of the tennis court, more Borg than Border. The tail joined in too: Simon Jones was the fifth man to hit a six on a day which featured ten of them, as well as 54 fours, and the eventual scoring rate was a breathless 5.13 an over.

Australia started badly next day when Hayden drove his first ball straight to cover, his first Test duck for 40 months and 68 innings. Langer dug in after being hit on the head in Harmison's first over – he said his old coach always liked to see him get hit early on, as it sharpened him up. And he resisted for four and a half hours, lasting long after Ponting had gone for a pleasant 61. But the middle order misfired, and Gilchrist was stranded on 49 when Flintoff struck twice in two balls, leaving England with a handy lead of 99. That increased by another 25 on the second evening, for the loss of Strauss, who was fooled by Warne's second ball, a huge turner which fizzed across his body and crashed into the stumps. It made Warne the first overseas bowler to take 100 Test wickets in England, and brought – for England – unnerving comparisons with the Gatting ball of 1993.

Indeed, after an initial burst from Lee reduced England to 31 for four – Vaughan's off stump was sent flying by a 91mph nip-backer – Warne dominated the third day. He bowled unchanged from the City End, usually round the wicket into the rough, often turning the ball unfeasible distances. Bell and Pietersen might have been unlucky to be given out caught behind, but Pietersen, whose 20 included two huge sixes over mid-wicket off Warne, survived a confident caught-behind appeal from Lee first ball.

Warne's fifth wicket reduced England to 131 for nine, 230 ahead, but Flintoff then cut loose, slamming four more sixes to take his match total to nine, an Ashes record,

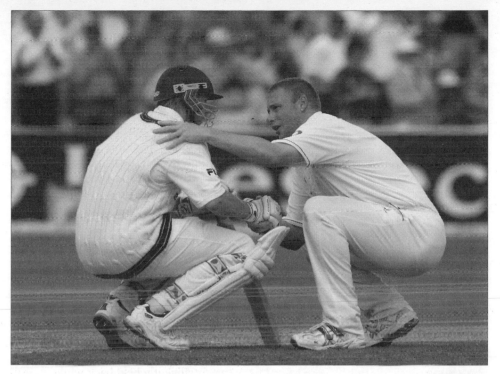

So close: Andrew Flintoff (right) consoles Brett Lee after England win the 2005 Edgbaston Test by just two runs, setting up the most memorable series of them all.

outbeefing Ian Botham's six at Manchester in 1981. Now, this was Flintoff in full command of both his shots and the situation. One Kasprowicz over went for 20, despite a ring of fielders on the boundary, then Lee disappeared for 18, with one of two sixes being fished out of the TV cables on the pavilion roof by Graham Gooch. Flintoff was finally bowled for 73 – Warne's tenth wicket of the match and 599th in Tests – but the last-gasp stand of 51 with Simon Jones had swelled the lead and given England's dressing-room the scent of victory.

The frenetic pace continued in a three-and-a-half-hour session on the third evening. Australia galloped to 47 in 12 overs before Flintoff, almost inevitably, shook things up. Langer dragged his second delivery into his stumps, and Ponting nicked the seventh (after a no-ball), a leg-cutter, having kept out some searing inswingers. Hayden grafted to 31 before being well caught by the tumbling Trescothick at slip, and three more went down before Flintoff, in his second spell, thudded a straight one into Gillespie's pads.

With the score at 140 for seven, England claimed the extra half-hour in a bid to polish the match off in three days. But Warne went on the offensive, lofting Giles for two sixes, and the only casualty of the extra period was Clarke, bamboozled by Harmison's rare slower ball after another easy-on-the-eye innings. That turned out to be the final ball of the day. At the time, it seemed slightly unfortunate that there would probably be so little left for a full house on the fourth day. But for the crowd the simple prospect of beating Australia was unmissable. Soon, their enthusiasm was to ripple out across the whole country.

England v Australia 2005

Second Test

At Birmingham, August 4, 5, 6, 7. Result: England won by two runs.

ENGLAND	*First innings*		*Second innings*	
M. E. Trescothick c Gilchrist b Kasprowicz		90	– c Gilchrist b Lee	21
A. J. Strauss b Warne		48	– b Warne	6
*M. P. Vaughan c Lee b Gillespie		24	– (4) b Lee	1
I. R. Bell c Gilchrist b Kasprowicz		6	– (5) c Gilchrist b Warne	21
K. P. Pietersen c Katich b Lee		71	– (6) c Gilchrist b Warne	20
A. Flintoff c Gilchrist b Gillespie		68	– (7) b Warne	73
†G. O. Jones c Gilchrist b Kasprowicz		1	– (8) c Ponting b Lee	9
A. F. Giles lbw b Warne		23	– (9) c Hayden b Warne	8
M. J. Hoggard lbw b Warne		16	– (3) c Hayden b Lee	1
S. J. Harmison b Warne		17	– c Ponting b Warne	0
S. P. Jones not out		19	– not out	12
L-b 9, w 1, n-b 14		24	L-b 1, n-b 9	10

1-112 2-164 3-170 4-187 5-290 6-293   **407**   1-25 2-27 3-29 4-31 5-72 6-75   **182**
7-342 8-348 9-375 10-407   7-101 8-131 9-131 10-182

First innings – Lee 17–1–111–1; Gillespie 22–3–91–2; Kasprowicz 15–3–80–3; Warne 25.2–4–116–4.
Second innings – Lee 18–1–82–4; Gillespie 8–0–24–0; Kasprowicz 3–0–29–0; Warne 23.1–7–46–6.

AUSTRALIA	*First innings*		*Second innings*	
J. L. Langer lbw b S. P. Jones		82	– b Flintoff	28
M. L. Hayden c Strauss b Hoggard		0	– c Trescothick b S. P. Jones	31
*R. T. Ponting c Vaughan b Giles		61	– c G. O. Jones b Flintoff	0
D. R. Martyn run out		20	– c Bell b Hoggard	28
M. J. Clarke c G. O. Jones b Giles		40	– b Harmison	30
S. M. Katich c G. O. Jones b Flintoff		4	– c Trescothick b Giles	16
†A. C. Gilchrist not out		49	– c Flintoff b Giles	1
S. K. Warne b Giles		8	– (9) hit wkt b Flintoff	42
B. Lee c Flintoff b S. P. Jones		6	– (10) not out	43
J. N. Gillespie lbw b Flintoff		7	– (8) lbw b Flintoff	0
M. S. Kasprowicz lbw b Flintoff		0	– c G. O. Jones b Harmison	20
B 13, l-b 7, w 1, n-b 10		31	B 13, l-b 8, w 1, n-b 18	40

1-0 2-88 3-118 4-194 5-208 6-262   **308**   1-47 2-48 3-82 4-107 5-134 6-136   **279**
7-273 8-282 9-308 10-308   7-137 8-175 9-220 10-279

First innings – Harmison 11–1–48–0; Hoggard 8–0–41–1; S. P. Jones 16–2–69–2; Flintoff 15–1–52–3;
Giles 26–2–78–3.
Second innings – Harmison 17.3–3–62–2; Hoggard 5–0–26–1; Giles 15–3–68–2; Flintoff 22–3–79–4;
S. P. Jones 5–1–23–1.

Toss won by Australia   UMPIRES B. F. Bowden and R. E. Koertzen

THE LEADING CRICKETER IN THE WORLD – ANDREW FLINTOFF

Simon Barnes, 2006

The old legend of Andrew Flintoff is The Man Who Changed: the man who belatedly came to the realisation that talent alone was not enough. So he added application and resolution to the mix and became one of the best cricketers in the world.

But the new legend is better. It tells of the man who changed again, and made a still more momentous leap. He had gone from jolly good to excellent – well, many others have done that. But during the Ashes series of 2005, Flintoff made the infinitely rarer transition – the quantum, the Beamon leap – from excellence to greatness.

How to explain the concept? Not by numbers, certainly. Great players always have great numbers: but so do many players of mere excellence. A great player is one who dominates – and wins – by means of his own performances, his own nature, his own force. Flintoff and the Ashes series of 2005 will always be regarded as a perfect demonstration of cricketing greatness.

He made the transition somewhere between the end of the First Test and the beginning of the second. He bowled well at Lord's. But his batting was meek and deferential, that of a man who knows he is second-best. Australia won, Flintoff made three runs in the match and was part of England's ghastly same-old-Poms collapse in the second innings.

So what happened? Like a cuckolded husband, Flintoff was the last to know. He just came out to bat on the first day of the Second Test and took over the series. He brought off the rare all-rounder's double of succeeding in both disciplines in the same match. His bowling had gone from useful-third-seamer to firecracker strike bowler. He had found pace, subtlety, and the psychological domination he had never before possessed. His batting became filled with a massive, easy confidence. There was no swagger: just a huge relish for the confrontation, and an inner certainty about his newly acquired greatness.

This was most perfectly demonstrated in his series-turning innings in the Fourth Test, when he compiled – rather than swatted or biffed or bludgeoned – a century of murderous purpose. It was an innings that did more than score runs: it brought the beginnings of despair to the opposition. Flintoff was exceptional in the final match too, when his last spell brought the Australians from dominance back to uncertainty.

Flintoff performed well in everything he did last season, but it was his personal epic of the Ashes summer – The Freddiad? – that was the real expression of his greatness. Everything else was peripheral. The subtle balance between the two sides was tipped by the performances of one man. With, if you must have it, 24 wickets and 402 runs.

The only possible rival for the title of the world's leading cricketer for 2005 is Shane Warne. Warne is one of the greatest cricketers that ever lived, and had the best year of any bowler in history, with 96 Test wickets. Statistically, he has the better claim. But in the brutal arithmetic of sport, the fact is that, in the greatest competition of them all, Warne's team lost and Flintoff's team won. It really is that simple. Had Kevin Pietersen not staged his innings of rescue, the result of the Test series and the destination of the title of leading cricketer would have been different. But then Pietersen was dropped on 15. Warne dropped him. This was England's summer: and, unarguably, if by the finest of margins, Flintoff's year.

Third Test

Chloe Saltau

At Manchester, August 11, 12, 13, 14, 15, 2005. Drawn.

Cricket had hardly caught its breath after Edgbaston; the superlatives had not even settled. But now 2005 had something else to give. A draw, of all things: the first in 17 Ashes Tests. Yes, five days passed and nobody won. But an estimated 10,000 had to be turned away from Old Trafford on the final morning, and thousands more were turned back before they could get close. Roads were clogged for miles around.

Those who failed to join the 22,000 in the ground had to join the estimated 7.7 million who watched the conclusion on TV. This involved Australia's last pair, Lee and McGrath, keeping out the last 24 balls to save the game. Two nations held their collective breath yet again. The end was only made possible by an inspirational innings from Ponting – the man who got the blame for Edgbaston this time deserving the credit. He batted nearly seven hours for 156 after England had set Australia 423 to win. It was the loneliest of hands on a wearing pitch: no one else even got close to 50; no one else could ease his misery if, as now seemed possible, he lost the Ashes. When he was ninth out, with four overs to go, he thought he had blown it. Ponting left the field, not with the satisfaction of having played a great innings, but in a fury. He went to the dressing-room and threw a private tantrum while his tailenders in the middle kept their cool.

The prologue had been tense, too. Hours before the toss, the Australians were still unsure who would be taking the new ball. Lee had begun the week wired up to a drip in a Birmingham hospital due to an infected knee, while McGrath was grumpily waiting for bar staff at the team hotel to bring a bucket of ice in which to sink his swollen ankle. McGrath's name was not on the scorecards. But in the end both played. Some said the gamble was a sign of Australian insecurities: they had no trust in their back-up bowling. And though the two wounded warriors eventually saved the game, the suspicion remained that McGrath, in particular, was nowhere near fit enough to lead the attack in such a vital match.

It was a Test in which human failings emerged on both sides. The simplest catches were dropped, the most straightforward stumpings missed. The very public decline of a once formidable fast bowler, in Gillespie, contrasted with the emergence of Simon Jones, whose reverse swing was quietly turning into a weapon Australia could neither counter nor equal. But it was also a captains' match: Ponting's 156 was preceded by 166 from Vaughan, which set the tone and made this the one contest of the series Australia never really contemplated winning.

Vaughan was under a different sort of pressure from Ponting: bowled three times in the first two Tests, he had found a way of making straight balls look unplayable. He was lucky this time, too: on 41, he was missed by Gilchrist, and it went for four; next ball he was bowled by a McGrath no-ball; and he was dropped again on 141. But he benefited from Gillespie's awful form, and attacked wayward length mercilessly with exquisite strokes off the back foot through cover point. During a particularly desperate over, Vaughan reached 150 with two successive fours, then rocked into a powerful pull to make it three in a row.

Vaughan shared the first-day headlines with Warne, who became the first to take 600 Test wickets when Trescothick tried to sweep and was caught by Gilchrist. Warne kissed a white wristband given to him by his daughter Brooke, who had urged him to "be strong", and continued to bowl tirelessly. McGrath, labouring on his dodgy ankle by the first evening, was luckless and wicketless in the first innings, but Lee bowled with enough fire to finish with four wickets, including Pietersen, who played a foolish shot within sight of the close. But Flintoff and Geraint Jones batted gamely next day, and England ended on 444.

There was no adequate response. Even Australia's brightest young hope was in trouble: Clarke's chronic back pain was triggered in the second over of the match. He spent two days in bed, tottered to the crease like an old man and batted like one. Perhaps only Katich would have felt worse: he failed to pick the direction of Flintoff's frighteningly fast reverse swing, and watched in horror as a ball he was leaving alone bent in and took off stump. This dismissal haunted him in the second innings, when he reached outside off and edged to the slips. Katich looked confused, and was not alone. Whether or not, as Ian Chappell suggested, the batsmen had allowed their egos to obscure the need to play more defensively against a talented, relentless attack, the highest scorer in the first innings was Warne. He blunted the reverse swing where his more highly regarded colleagues could not, saved the follow-on during the 14 overs that survived the rain on Saturday, and came within ten of a much-coveted maiden Test century. He finally succumbed to Jones, who snuffed out the innings on the fourth morning with a Test-best six for 53.

England were 142 ahead. Their second innings belonged to Strauss, who was struck by a Lee bouncer in the second over, and scored his first Ashes century with an undignified piece of white plaster stuck to his ear. The plaster did nothing for his street cred, but a fine 106 did everything for the reputation of a man who had made five hundreds in his first 11 Tests but until now struggled against this attack. Strauss and Bell helped build a lead of 422.

Ponting looked a worried man. At one stage, during the 127-run stand between Strauss and Bell, he stood near the pitch with his head bowed and Warne's arm slung around his shoulders. But Ponting reaffirmed his leadership in the way he knew best. He came to the crease in the second over of the final day, after Langer had edged to the keeper, and he saw Hayden worked over magnificently by Flintoff before being bowled behind his legs. Martyn got a dubious lbw decision from umpire Bucknor. The lucky ones who had got through the queues were going crazy, but Ponting kept calm, adapted his game and played positively throughout. As his innings grew, and steady partnerships with Clarke and Warne flourished, the tension mounted yet again.

Pietersen dropped a simple catch, his fifth of the series, to give Warne a life, and for a time it seemed he had presented Australia with the ultimate get-out clause. Then Geraint Jones pulled off a ripper of a catch to dismiss Warne after the ball bounced off Strauss's thigh in the slips. Lee joined Ponting at the crease, with only McGrath – the consummate No. 11 – to come. But Vaughan, too, lost an option when Simon Jones pulled up with cramp and limped off with seven overs to go.

A few balls later, Jones's substitute, Stephen Peters, nearly ran out Lee as Ponting took a quick single to keep the strike. And then Ponting thought all was lost. He tickled a catch down the leg side, hung his head and trudged off. "I had all sorts of different emotions and feelings going through me. I thought the game had slipped away from us," he admitted. "It was difficult enough for me batting out there against Flintoff and Harmison at the end, and having Glenn and Brett subjected to it for four overs – I didn't have a lot of faith in them."

Both Lee and McGrath, though, held up their ends. Harmison's last over lacked the lethal mixture of pace and bounce required, and when Lee fended his final full toss for four the Australian balcony went into raptures. Relief was written deep on their faces, for they knew what Vaughan said afterwards was true: "Three weeks ago we were written off, 5–0 I kept hearing. Now we're 1–1 with two to play and we're playing good cricket."

Toss: England. **England 444** (M. E. Trescothick 63, M. P. Vaughan 166, I. R. Bell 59, B. Lee 4-100, S. K. Warne 4-99) **and 280-6 dec.** (A. J. Strauss 106, I. R. Bell 65, G. D. McGrath 5-115); **Australia 302** (S. K. Warne 90, S. P. Jones 6-53) **and 371-9** (R. T. Ponting 156, A. Flintoff 4-71).

CRICKETER OF THE YEAR – RICKY PONTING

Bruce Wilson, 2006

After that most delirious of summers, now destined to bore countless thousands of unborn grandchildren, it might seem perverse-to-absurd to include in this annual salute to excellence a batsman whose Test average dipped, who made arguably the worst decision by an Australian captain in 30 years, who was fined for what might be called excessive surliness and who lost the Ashes.

Yet Ricky Ponting joins this roll-call for any number of reasons, some of which approach the abstract; not least, for example, is the one that it takes two to tango. Without Ponting's own particular persona combating Michael Vaughan's very different one, the chemical formulae that exploded into the 2005 Ashes would not have reacted as spectacularly as they did. Ponting's flaws and strengths were all part of the magic mix. His strengths included one of the great match-saving innings – by far the most consequential batting performance by an Australian all summer, the 156 at Old Trafford, when he stood between Australia and total Ashes melt-down. It was his 23rd Test century, made in circumstances far rougher than most of the others.

Ponting's greatness as a batsman has never been in dispute, nor his place in the *Wisden* pantheon. In 2004, he was the first recipient of the almanack's newest award, the Leading Cricketer in the World. That came after a 2003 when he led Australia to victory in the World Cup, scored 11 international centuries and unleashed successive double-centuries against India, the series that until last year stood as Australia's most eventful and competitive of recent times. In 2005, though, there was a strong argument that, as commanding officer, he was responsible for the warship losing its teeth. The questions over his tactical captaincy, the nuts-and-bolts everyday stuff of field placings and just when to turn the screw, persisted until the last day of the series. But Ponting's defenders went to The Oval noting that with just a couple of drops of luck Australia could have been leading the series 3–0. And the failure of so many of his team-mates to reach their normal heights was not his fault.

Back home, Ponting said that even as it all drifted away that last day in south London he was able to console himself. He was confident his position as captain was secure. "I just thought, well, they're only out on loan, the Ashes. It's less than 18 months away, and then we'll have them back."

Fourth Test

Lawrence Booth

At Nottingham, August 25, 26, 27, 28, 2005. England won by three wickets.

The law of averages demanded a dull draw after the showstoppers at Edgbaston and Old Trafford, but this was a series in which the usual laws did not apply. By the time Giles and Hoggard scampered the winning runs on a sun-kissed Sunday, both teams – both nations – had been put through the wringer once more.

But now England were ahead, a point not lost on the home supporters. "What's the score, Glenn McGrath, what's the score?" they chanted at the 5–0 predictor on the Australian balcony. He responded with another forecast, holding up two fingers on each hand, but the gesture seemed poignant. Not only was a 2–2 draw the best Australia could still hope for; McGrath himself had now missed two Tests in the series, both lost. This time, it was down to wear and tear to his right elbow. In his absence, and with Gillespie no longer trusted, Australia recalled Kasprowicz and awarded a first cap to Shaun Tait, a 22-year-old speed merchant whose slingy action prompted English observers to draw uneasy comparisons with Jeff Thomson.

England were unchanged for the fourth Test in a row, and their air of solidity was reinforced when Australia lost a crucial toss on a benign pitch. Ponting then watched in dismay as his bowlers made a mockery of what their coach John Buchanan described as a "zero-tolerance policy" on no-balls, overstepping 18 times in the 27 overs before lunch, which England took at 129 for one. The sole casualty was Strauss, who swept Warne to slip via his right boot – the only foot the openers put wrong all morning. Rain permitted only 20 deliveries (including another no-ball) between lunch and tea, after which Trescothick's fluent 65 was ended by a full inswinger from Tait, who quickly added a tentative-looking Bell, caught behind, Gilchrist's 300th Test dismissal. Vaughan repaired the damage, but he nibbled outside off to give Ponting his first Test wicket of the 21st century and, at 213 for four, England were in danger of conceding the initiative.

Pietersen went early next morning, but the game turned on a partnership between Flintoff and Geraint Jones that was a study in contrasts: the lumbering giant and the nifty urchin; the bully and the pickpocket; the front-foot driver and the back-foot cutter. What they shared was urgency, and they added 177 at high speed. Australia were convinced Jones had edged Lee on 34 first ball after lunch, but otherwise it was one-way traffic travelling in fifth gear. When Flintoff tucked Warne to leg for a single to complete his fifth Test hundred, from only 121 balls, Trent Bridge erupted. Moments later, he aimed across the line against Tait and the fun was over, but the stand had deflated the Australians and ushered England to a third successive first-innings score of 400 for the first time in nearly 19 years of Ashes cricket. Jones fell 15 short of three figures, and Australia were left with a session on the second evening in which to chip away at England's 477.

Instead, the breaches came from the bowlers. Hoggard located his awayswinger for the first time in the series in an 11-over burst of three for 32, and Harmison undid Clarke in the last over of the day, as he had at Edgbaston. Both Ponting and Martyn were given out lbw to balls they had edged, but the nicks were imperceptible to the naked eye and could not detract from the truth: Australia were being outplayed again. The sense that the force was with England was confirmed on the third morning, when Strauss dived full stretch at second slip to hold on to Gilchrist's edge, before Jones, hostile and incisive, cleaned up. Not even Lee's hard-hit 47 could prevent Australia from following on for the first time since Karachi in 1988-89.

Still, at 155 for two second time round, they were progressing smoothly. Then Martyn called Ponting for a single, only to see his captain beaten by a direct hit from the covers. Ponting's fury at losing his wicket at a crucial stage was compounded by the identity of the fielder: Gary Pratt, who had not played a first-class game for Durham all summer, was substituting for Simon Jones, who had limped off with an ankle injury. Pratt's presence on the field was thus legitimate, but the Australians had objected to England's constant use of subs, apparently to rest their bowlers, and Ponting vented his feelings towards the home balcony on his way to the pavilion. The outburst would cost him 75% of his match fee. More immediately, his side's momentum was checked. When Martyn feathered Flintoff two overs later, Australia were still 98 behind with six wickets left.

What followed was the most attritional passage of batting in the series yet, as Clarke and Katich added 100 – only Australia's second century stand in four games – in 48 overs to wipe out the lead. But Hoggard persuaded Clarke to nibble at the second new ball just before lunch on the fourth day, before becoming the first seamer to win an lbw appeal against Gilchrist in his 72 Tests. Harmison mopped up with three wickets, including Katich, who was furious when his 262-minute vigil was ended by a poor lbw decision from Aleem Dar. His all-too-obvious displeasure earned him a 50% fine, and England were eventually left needing an awkward 129.

At 32 without loss after five overs, they were coasting. But cricket has never had a scene-stealer – not even Ian Botham – who could match Warne. He removed Trescothick and Vaughan with the opening deliveries of his first two overs, then snared Strauss at leg slip in his fifth to make it 57 for three. When Bell hooked Lee to long leg without addition, the talk was of Australian revenge for Headingley '81. As on the Sunday morning at Edgbaston and Monday afternoon at Old Trafford, news from Trent Bridge began to savage the peace of a warm August English Sunday. Pietersen and Flintoff, against type, calmed everyone's nerves by adding 46, but Lee had Pietersen caught behind with the first ball of a new spell and in his next over bowled an incredulous Flintoff with a beauty that proved Australia *could* produce reverse swing. With 13 still needed, Jones spooned Warne to deep extra cover. England were down to the bowlers.

The anxiety was not confined to the spectators. As Hoggard trooped to the crease, Giles provided a cheerless assessment of Lee's bowling: "He's reversing it at 95mph." Somehow, though, the runs came in dribs and drabs: Giles kept out Warne, Hoggard handled Lee. Catharsis arrived when Hoggard drove a Lee full toss to the cover fence to take England within four runs of their target, and victory was secured in the next over when Giles clipped Warne through mid-wicket.

With more support for Lee and Warne – Kasprowicz and Tait bowled six wicket-less overs for 43 between them – Australia might have won. Instead, it was England who celebrated a result which ensured that, for the first time in nine Ashes series, they would not be on the losing side.

Toss: England. **England 477** (M. E. Trescothick 65, M. P. Vaughan 58, A. Flintoff 102, G. O. Jones 85, S. K. Warne 4-102) **and 129-7** (S. K. Warne 4-31); **Australia 218** (S. P. Jones 5-44) **and 387** (J. L. Langer 61, M. J. Clarke 56, S. M. Katich 59).

CRICKETER OF THE YEAR – KEVIN PIETERSEN

Paul Hayward, 2006

When talent announces itself these days we rush to buy tickets for the burnout. This modern scepticism attached itself to Kevin Pietersen long before his bludgeoning and decisive innings of 158 on the final day of the Ashes. The genre for Pietersen's rise as cricketer and celebrity is one known to David Beckham, Jenson Button of Formula One and the self-basting Gavin Henson, Welsh rugby's icon for the iPod generation. With all these ubiquitous idols we observe the billboard competing with the score-board. It's a truism of modern sport that many young athletes have the party before they have fully done the work.

Pietersen certainly did the work at The Oval, and he sure as hell had the party afterwards. But when Pietersen stopped the victory bus to dive into Starbucks to relieve himself, cynics expected him to come out clutching a deal establishing him as the new face of the caramel macchiato.

He wasted no time affirming his status as cricket's first rock star. "Get your hair cut, Pietersen!" one MCC member barked as Vaughan's men finally made it back to the Long Room after a long day of handshakes, hangovers and grins. The heckler was expressing the prejudices of those who regarded the lurching hero with suspicion.

The talent is the thing. Always the talent. If the gift is authentic it's easier to ignore the peripheral ringing of tills and the vacuous celebrity chatter. On that front, Pietersen struck 473 runs in five Tests against Australia. This, after he had averaged 73.09 in 23 one-day internationals. These are the figures of a resoundingly good cricketer. The ICC anointed him both Emerging Player and One-Day Player of the Year. His belligerent and fearless innings at The Oval lit the imagination's touchpaper way beyond cricket. His team-mate Ashley Giles observed: "It was real grandchildren stuff. 'Gather round and I'll tell you about that innings I played with Pietersen, with the white stripes and the earrings'." In the ensuing tide of euphoria it was swiftly forgotten that KP had been dropped three times, most calamitously by Shane Warne, his Hampshire colleague and friend. That simple error turned Pietersen into a household name and millionaire. Sport's soundtrack is the music of chance.

Geoff Boycott, and others, will cite the skunk hairdo, the £50,000 earrings, the Three Lions tattoo, the dates with Caprice and a former Big Brother contestant, and the Los Angeles celebrity party to which Pietersen gained access with help from the dissolute actor Mickey Rourke. There he was romantically linked with Paris Hilton – an heiress, incidentally, not somewhere nice to stay in France. The game has never seen anything like this. Pietersen is surely the first man in flannels who chose to be famous – who set out to be world-renowned. So now we stand back to find out whether he will be remembered as the cricketer who ate himself or a legend of the willow. Take your eyes off him if you can.

Fifth Test

At The Oval, September 8, 9, 10, 11, 12, 2005. Drawn.

Hugh Chevallier

The Ashes series ended in the sort of obscure anticlimax which baffled outsiders were inclined to associate with cricket before the summer of 2005. But this time it did not produce bewildered shakes of the head. It delivered one of the most exhilarating moments in the history of English sport, never mind cricket.

As England moved towards the draw that clinched the Ashes, the roads went quiet as the nation headed for the TV screens to concentrate on the moment. Next day, the noise was on the streets as England paraded the replica trophy from an open-top bus, and the game's new fans jumped into the Trafalgar Square fountains in delight as they awaited the team's arrival.

Could stuffy old cricket really have caused all this? The answer was yes. The euphoria released when England brought back the Ashes after an absence of 16 years 42 days confirmed that cricket's place in the country's soul had survived eight successive humiliating series against the Australians. But more than that, what was noticeable was how young those in Trafalgar Square were: many were unborn when Mike Gatting's team won in 1986–87. A new generation had been enticed to the game by this amazing summer. Cricket was unmissable; cricket was cool.

Perhaps it should have been no surprise. This was the climax of what was already being called the Greatest Series Ever. And despite that impossible billing, it matched expectations in all but its very end. It helped that the stage was perfectly set: with England 2–1 up, only defeat could prevent the triumphant restoration of the Ashes. It meant that tension suffused every move. And Ponting had two enemies to overcome: England were a known quantity, the September weather was not.

The buzz beforehand was so loud even the Arabic TV channel Al-Jazeera came to see what the fuss was about. Actually, it was about arms and legs. One of each was what it would cost to buy a ticket on the grey market. (Figures of £1,000 for a £66 seat were bandied around, though seldom substantiated.) The other limbs fascinating the media were Glenn McGrath's elbow and Simon Jones's ankle: each was suspect, each vital to the plot. Australia sighed with relief when the elbow passed a fitness test, England with dismay when the ankle failed. Forced into their only change of the series, the selectors overlooked poor Chris Tremlett, twelfth man since Lord's, and called up Collingwood to deepen the batting: not a positive statement. McGrath gently elbowed aside Kasprowicz.

The crowd were so partisan that even the toss was greeted with a bellow of delight: Vaughan had won it, and naturally batted. This had become the pattern of England's success, and in no time the openers were singing along at around five an over. A true pitch, lightning outfield and hot sun – belying the latest-ever start for a Test in England – made scoring look easy. At least it did for an hour, until Warne made an early entrance. Suddenly, the game wore a different face. By his 11th over, despite scant turn and little more bounce, Warne had single-handedly rescued Australia, doing something new in his 128th Test: never before had he taken the first four wickets in a first innings. The score lurched from 82 for nought to 131 for four.

It looked as though England had squandered the advantage. But if one thing was certain this summer, it was that nothing was certain. Strauss and Flintoff knuckled down, initially defending against Warne and attacking the others. Soon after tea, Flintoff opened his shoulders and hit Warne for three successive fours. As Strauss reached a hundred dripping with quality cuts and drives, England were smiling again. The pair added 143, but with both going before the close – Strauss for 129 and Flintoff for 72 – the Australians still narrowly shaded the first day. Next morning, the tail lifted England to 373, almost par on this pitch.

After a wretched series, Australia's opening partnership had to come good. Langer was all fight, lofting Giles for two sixes in his first over, and heavily outscored a hesitant, scratchy Hayden, traditionally the more fluent but now playing for his place. At least the runs were coming – until they weren't. To general disbelief, the batsmen took the light immediately after tea. The skies had filled in but, with the forecast iffy, it made no sense. Play eventually resumed 30 minutes late next morning, and it was a case of stop-start thereafter.

Australia were 185 when a wicket finally fell. In his 13th over, Harmison, largely anodyne till now, was riled by two bouncers being ruled wides and by two fours, the first bringing up Langer's century, the second his 7,000th Test run. Harmison instantly bit back, beating Langer for pace and fury. Rain interrupted again, though Hayden later found time to reach his first hundred for 14 months, more gritty than pretty. At 277 for two on the third evening, Australia looked impregnable. Impregnable, though, was no use; victory was Ponting's only currency, and the decision to go off for light again was unfathomable.

The murk on the fourth morning was similarly unfathomable, but now the batsmen did stay on, heralding a prodigious passage of play. Bowling unchanged from the Pavilion End from the start until six overs after lunch, Flintoff was awesome. Relentlessly hitting a length, he found seam, a hint of swing, four wickets and a place in Ashes legend. His spell of 14.2–3–30–4 could only hint at the intensity of the battle. Australia lost seven wickets for 44, their last five for 11. Hoggard, his late swing the perfect foil for Flintoff, contributed a sublime spell of four for four from 19 balls to finish things off.

Far from a commanding lead, Australia trailed by six, failing to make 400 in a series of four or more Tests for the first time since 1978–79. Ponting's only option was to blast England out double quick, but the light remained sepulchral. McGrath idiotically bowled a bouncer, and they were off – though not before Warne found extravagant, anxiety-inducing spin to remove Strauss. On their return, in marginally brighter conditions, all the Australians sported sunglasses. The pantomime caught on: with Warne a constant threat, some spectators theatrically unfurled umbrellas against non-existent rain. Nearby Aussies promptly stripped off their shirts and basked in illusory sunshine. The umbrellas won. To applause that might have been thunder, everyone trooped off. It meant no more cricket; the paying public, for once, didn't care.

The final day dawned brightly, with every result possible and tension upgraded from danger level to crisis point. England were 34 for one, but they had to get through a notional 98 overs without giving Australia a look-in. With the score on 67, McGrath struck twice with two exquisite deliveries. The hat-trick ball looped into the slips, sparking huge appeals and much queasiness. Somehow, umpire Bowden got it right. Not out: it had hit Pietersen's shoulder. Next over, he was dropped off Warne; had it stuck, England would have been 68 for four. They were nurturing the shoots of a recovery when Lee found Pietersen's edge. The ball flashed at head-height to Warne, safest of first slips. He parried it. As his despairing lunge failed to grab the rebound, the stands erupted.

The release of tension was short-lived. Warne snaffled Trescothick and Flintoff to give Australia the edge: at lunch, they were 133 behind, just five wickets to filch and more than 70 overs left. Some found it all too much. David Graveney, the chairman of selectors, headed for the car park to calm down, missing an epic shootout between Pietersen, oozing conviction, confidence and courage, and Lee, touching 95mph.

Supported by Collingwood, whose 72-minute ten justified his selection, and then Giles, Pietersen reeled off shots outrageous in any circumstances, unimaginable in these. By tea, he had pulled, punched and smashed his way to an extraordinary maiden Test hundred, applauded by Warne, 23,000 in the stands and millions in their living-rooms.

Even then, Australia – 227 behind, three batsmen to dislodge, nearly 50 overs available – had a chance of victory. Not for long. No one could say precisely when the draw and England's Ashes became inescapable: certainly before Pietersen fell for an unforgettable 158, including seven sixes. Giles consolidated his reputation for reliability with 59, his highest Test score, and Warne wheeled away for a lion-hearted six wickets – 12 in the match, a staggering 40 in the series.

Yet the denouement of this Test, unlike the previous three, was pure bathos. Even though there was nothing to be gained from Australia starting their second innings, ICC regulations dragged the players back out. Four meaningless balls later, they came off for the umpteenth and last time, in fading light. The game theoretically remained live for another 16 minutes, and then, to a roar audible in Sydney, the umpires, adding their own piece of theatre, removed the bails: the Ashes were England's.

Toss: England. **England 373** (A. J. Strauss 129, A. Flintoff 72, S. K. Warne 6-122) **and 335** (K. P. Pietersen 158, A. F. Giles 59, S. K. Warne 6-124); **Australia 367** (J. L. Langer 105, M. L. Hayden 138, M. J. Hoggard 4-97, A. Flintoff 5-78) **and 4-0.**

NOTES BY THE EDITOR
Matthew Engel, 2006

There they were in Trafalgar Square, the boys of summer, the men of the moment. Under the noonday sun, they were wearing blazers, dark glasses to hide their bloodshot eyes, and the broadest of grins. Thousands and thousands of people gazed up at them and hung on every syllable they spoke, however inane. Many of those present were so young they would be hard-put to say whether Mike Brearley came before or after the stegosaurus.

Questioned about the seven and a bit exhilarating weeks that had just concluded, the players revved up their favourite clichés and let them all rip. It had been a "nightmare" (really?); an "emotional rollercoaster" (whatever that might be); and, again and again, "fantastic". And it really did appear to be a fantasy. This was the England cricket team, for heaven's sake, being greeted on the streets of London as though they were pioneering astronauts getting a tickertape reception through New York. They were lauded on the front page of every newspaper. At one stage, they were simultaneously on BBC1, ITV and Channel 4. Alongside them were their counterparts, the England women's team who, by happy coincidence, had just won their own version of the Ashes. Stuffy old cricket suddenly looked inclusive: a game for everyone.

Journalists still tended to write that we had witnessed Probably The Greatest Test (Edgbaston), Probably The Greatest Series, and Probably The Greatest Crowd To Greet A Victorious England Team. There is no need for the nervous adverb. This was The Greatest. The 2005 Ashes surpassed every previous series in cricket history on just about any indicator you choose. There had been close contests before, and turnarounds, and tension (1894–95, 1936–37, 1956, Australia v West Indies 1960–61, 198. . .), but never had cricket been so taut for so long. And certainly, previous players had never enjoyed adulation like this.

In the summer of 1953, when England regained the Ashes after 19 years rather than a mere 16, there were indeed huge crowds on the streets. But they were there for the Queen, in her Coronation year. Len Hutton, the victorious Ashes captain 52 years earlier, had to be content with a reception at the Albert Hall. No, not *the* Albert Hall – the Albert Hall, Pudsey.

England's years of failure and ultimate victory were crucial to this glorious story. Had they held the Ashes a series or two back, there wouldn't have been the pent-up emotion and resentment that made the release so wonderful. Had their victory been obvious, there wouldn't have been the build-up of tension that drew in so many of the uncommitted. Had England failed, it would have been melodrama rather than drama; anticlimax not climax; repression not catharsis. The patriotism was essential to the plot.

But in the final analysis, this was not primarily a victory for England. It was a victory for Australia too. It was – and this cliché is for once the simple truth – a victory for cricket. This was the old game routing its enemies, including those inside the walls. The 2005 Ashes constituted cricket in its purest form. There was no artificial colouring, no artificial flavouring, no added sugar. Nothing had to be sexed up or dumbed down. Everything was already there.

The matches didn't need supersubs or powerplays; they didn't need to be so short that they didn't actually feel much like cricket. Cricket didn't have to talk down to its audience ("here's something we don't enjoy much ourselves but you lot might like it"). Exhilarating contests just unfolded before our eyes. For 22 days of play one hardly dared fetch a beer, have a pee, or sometimes even blink, because the situation could turn on its head in that instant.

It was a triumph for the real thing: five five-day Test matches between two gifted, well-matched teams playing fantastic cricket at high velocity and high pressure with the perfect mix of chivalry and venom. Here was the best game in the world, at its best. And now millions more people know about it.

AUSTRALIA v ENGLAND 2006–07

Simon Briggs

For just over 14 months, since England seized the Ashes from Australia, two great cricketing nations had been keyed up for a humdinger of a return contest – an epic page-turner, it was assumed, with all the plot twists and somersaults of 2005. But from the moment Steve Harmison opened the series with a wild embarrassing wide that went straight into the hands of Andrew Flintoff at second slip, reality took hold.

This time there were to be no twists, at least not during the Test series. The story of the first ball would essentially be the story right through to the last. If England won the 2005 series by a nose, they lost the rematch by the length of the Nullarbor Plain. They were defeated in every one of the five Tests – a fate previously reserved for one team in Ashes history. And J. W. H. T. Douglas's 1920–21 side represented a country still devastated by the effects of the Great War. Flintoff's team had no such excuse.

The nearest England came to a winning – or even drawing – position was in the

Second Test, where they declared at 551 for six and would have had Australia 78 for four if Ashley Giles had not dropped a straightforward chance. Although Australia regrouped from there, the match was heading towards stalemate until England caved in against Shane Warne on the final morning. The bewilderment that overcame England that day never left them. From then on, they rarely competed for more than a session at a time.

On December 18, England lost at Perth, and the Ashes formally changed hands. Nonetheless, the huge number of English tourists due to arrive for the Melbourne and Sydney Tests came out on schedule, and maintained their zest rather better than the players. They were able to see another great Australian team performing at the top of their ability. They saw three members of it – Warne, Glenn McGrath and Justin Langer – make an elaborate farewell at Sydney. They did not see England redeem themselves.

It was a bad time for them to fail so badly. The palaver surrounding this series was unprecedented. An estimated 40,000 England supporters attended at least one Test or another. Crowds everywhere threatened the records; in Perth, there were even 17,000 to watch a Legends match between Ashes alumni. And the chief topic of conversation for every Pom in Australia was "Why?"

Both on and off the field, Ricky Ponting, the Australian captain, outclassed Flintoff and won the Compton-Miller Medal for player of the series. Asked at Sydney whether he had been motivated by revenge, Ponting claimed: "I have never mentioned that word once, not even to myself." But such was his intensity, both at the crease and in the field, that it was hard to believe him. He fashioned a flawless hundred on the first day of the series, and went on to lead the run-scoring with 576 at 82.28. While the 2005 Ashes series had left him with a scar on his cheek, this one was a feather in his baggy green cap. For England, things fell apart; the centre could not hold. It might not have been revenge, but this was payback time.

First Test

Lawrence Booth

At Brisbane, November 23, 24, 25, 26, 27, 2006. Australia won by 277 runs.

Rarely can an Ashes defence have begun as bathetically as this. All the mouth-drying tension of the build-up seemed to be channelled into Harmison's opening delivery, which went straight to Flintoff at second slip and was signalled wide by umpire Bucknor. As a record Gabba crowd of nearly 40,000 roared with derision or disbelief, the two teams drew their own conclusions: Australia grinned quietly, England grimaced visibly.

The hostility of the first morning at Lord's 16 months earlier became a distant memory. By stumps, Australia were well on their way to victory in the opening match of an Ashes series for the eighth time out of ten. But just as none of the previous nine had been weighed down by the precedent of 2005, so none had descended quite as quickly into the realms of anticlimax.

Several England players explained they had been riddled with nerves, which was honest enough, but not the sort of honesty international sportsmen tend to indulge in; many outsiders felt England had simply chosen the wrong team. Most controversial was the choice of Giles, who had played only two warm-up games since a hip injury a year earlier, ahead of Panesar, the people's favourite. Anderson beat Mahmood to the fourth seamer's slot, thanks to his form in the warm-ups, while Jones was preferred to

Read as wicket-keeper. Australia went for the experienced seamer Stuart Clark instead of the promising swinger Mitchell Johnson, a decision that assumed the proportions of a masterstroke as the game unfurled.

The significance of Flintoff's incorrect call at the toss soon took second place to the symbolism of Harmison's looseper. Emboldened, Australia seized their moment on a true and bouncy pitch. Harmison was flayed out of the attack by Langer after two overs costing 17; after seven overs, the openers had carved out 40. Hayden nibbled Flintoff to second slip, but at lunch Langer – manic on adrenalin – had 68, and the horse had long since bolted up the Gold Coast. Australia kept their foot down between lunch and tea, adding 108 for the loss of Langer, who cut once too often, providing Pietersen with his first Ashes catch at the seventh attempt, and Martyn, who cut to slip off Giles.

But Ponting, in the form of his life, belied the pressure that had been mounting since he lost the Ashes at The Oval. He hit his ninth hundred in 12 Tests, equalling Steve Waugh's national record of 32, and added 209 with the unobtrusive Hussey. Apart from Flintoff, England's attack was on the fleshy side of toothless. Harmison bowled only 12 overs in the day, and started the second morning the same way as the first: with another off-side wide. Hoggard briefly demonstrated that a flat pitch need not preclude guile, trapping Ponting four short of a double-hundred then removing Gilchrist from round the wicket three balls later. But salt-in-the-wound merriment from Clark and Lee completed the rout and prompted a declaration, at 602, that allowed Australia 17 overs at England before the close. It was enough to decide the match.

Beforehand, McGrath – playing his first Test since January after taking time out to be with his sick wife – had predicted he would get Strauss on the pull and Cook from round the wicket. In the space of two balls, he was proved eerily correct. When Clark had Collingwood groping to the keeper, England were 42 for three.

The following morning, things got worse. Pietersen padded up to a ball from McGrath that would have missed off stump and, in the next over, Flintoff feathered Lee to the keeper. No matter that Bell, on his way to a 162-ball fifty, was legitimising his own place; suddenly, Australians were asking themselves how they had ever lost the Ashes to this lot in the first place. Wickets fell like confetti, and Giles's swipe to point meant six wickets for McGrath, whose affected hobble towards the pavilion made light of comments about his team resembling Dad's Army.

Australia luxuriated in a lead of 445, but Ponting decided not to enforce the follow-on, reasoning that his bowlers would enjoy a breather and the pitch would become harder to bat on. Some felt he had signposted England's only possible escape route, but Langer took advantage of some resigned bowling to hit his first Test hundred since the sides met at The Oval, and Ponting, driving and pulling peerlessly, became the seventh batsman to pass 9,000 Test runs. The upshot was that England needed to score 648 to win, or to survive 172 overs to draw. It was debatable which was the less likely.

They began poorly. Strauss went early, pulling, for the second time in the match; Bell regressed when he missed Warne's slider; and Cook prodded to short leg. At 91 for three, humiliation beckoned. But Collingwood overcame another shaky start to uppercut Lee for six, and Pietersen used his leverage and feet to take on Warne. Only the futility of the counter-attack detracted from its brilliance, and Collingwood eventually perished as he had prospered, on the charge to Warne: stumped for 96 to end an alliance of 153 in 34 overs. Flintoff slogged Warne to long-on, and England began the final day five wickets down and clinging on to optimistic forecasts of a tea-time thunderstorm.

The rain never arrived, but it would not have saved England even if it had, as they folded in 90 minutes. Pietersen whipped Lee's fourth ball of the day to short mid-wicket without adding to his overnight 92, and the only consolation of some late-order swipes was the highest fourth-innings total in 49 Tests at Brisbane. But if one statistic summed up the difference between the sides, it was the fact that Clark's match figures of seven for 93 embarrassed England's collective effort of ten for 804, one of them a run-out.

Competition in the stands never materialised either, thanks to the officious Gabba authorities, who banned the Barmy Army's official trumpeter Bill Cooper (or at any rate, banned the trumpet) and kept the England fans scattered until the fifth morning, when empty seats allowed them to congregate and find their voice. In all, 164,727 spectators attended the match, another ground record. It was just a shame England were unable to provide them with a more compelling contest.

Toss: Australia. **Australia 602-9 dec.** (J. L. Langer 82, R. T. Ponting 196, M. E. K. Hussey 86, M. J. Clarke 56,

A. Flintoff 4-99) **and 202-1 dec.** (J. L. Langer 100*, R. T. Ponting 60*); **England 157** (I. R. Bell 50,

G. D. McGrath 6-50) **and 370** (P. D. Collingwood 96, K. P. Pietersen 92, S. R. Clark 4-72, S. K. Warne 4-124).

Second Test

Matthew Engel

At Adelaide, December 1, 2, 3, 4, 5, 2006. Australia won by six wickets.

Great Man theory, originally associated with the philosopher Thomas Carlyle, holds that the whole of human history has been determined by a handful of people. In cricketing terms, it has always been hard to dispute, especially when you're sitting at Don Bradman's home ground.

For four days and 43 minutes of this Test match, there was plenty of time to think about such matters, and also whether it might be more amusing to spend the final afternoon hiring a pedalo on the River Torrens instead of watching this turgid contest dribble away to its inevitable draw. Then came the Great Man.

Shane Warne conjured up perhaps the most astounding victory of even his career. Here was a pitch that, all along, had offered the possibility to a batsman with sufficient stamina and perseverance of staying at the crease until the 2010–11 Ashes. Suddenly the placid earth began to crack and crumble and boil and bubble, as if the San Andreas Fault had opened directly underneath. But the fault was all England's. In the first innings, they had convinced themselves the Wizard of Oz was no great magician but just a cunning illusionist. Now they thought he could make the earth move. And so he did.

He was given a shove by the first bad umpiring decision of the match: Bucknor gifted Warne the wicket of Strauss, caught off his pad. From that moment, every demon that has haunted English cricket started to play inside the batsmen's heads. And the greatest of those demons was bowling at them.

From 69 for one, England withered to 129 all out. Australia's task – 168 in 36 overs – was no certainty. But the force was with them, and they won with 19 balls to spare. You could replay the final day a hundred times, and the game might be drawn every time. But it won't be replayed. Such a day could never happen quite like this again. To understand the drama of the turnaround, it is necessary to loll awhile amid the languor that came before. There was a shock at the start: both teams were unchanged, which meant England were defying public and pundits alike by again omitting Panesar and keeping Anderson and Giles. There was a second shock too, in the sense that English fatalists presumed such an important toss was bound to be won by Australia. In fact, Flintoff correctly called heads, and he did not attempt a third shock by fielding.

There have been better batting pitches – some England players said it was the slowest they had seen all year – but few more disheartening for bowlers. Warne did get some first-day turn, which was remarkable. But it was soon clear this was unlikely to be one of McGrath's Tests and, when the second new ball came, it was handed to the wholehearted Clark. The only good news for Australia was that the Adelaide weather was unusually cool and breezy.

It took a while for England to establish any kind of command. Though Bell and Collingwood dug in, Bell wrecked his good work by mis-hooking on 60. That brought in Pietersen, but even he could not assert himself. Collingwood reached his hundred off the eighth ball of the second day; Pietersen followed him before lunch. And though the stand easily surpassed the 153 they had put on in adversity at Brisbane, England still had trouble upping the rate. This was due partly to the pitch, partly to the batsmen's caution, and partly to Warne opting for negative round-the-wicket bowling, which Pietersen could only kick away. He later claimed this showed he had Warne beaten.

Relentlessly, though, both men kept climbing. Collingwood's determination had never been in doubt; but he also soared above his presumed limitations as a primarily leg-side player, cutting and cover driving, and then dancing down the track to straight-drive Warne to reach 150. Shortly before tea, he became the first England player to score a Test double-century in Australia since Wally Hammond 70 years earlier. Not Hutton, not May, not Boycott, not Gooch, not Atherton... Collingwood. Moments later, he wearily fell for 206, after 515 minutes, 392 balls and 16 fours. The stand was worth 310, England's fourth-wicket record against Australia. Pietersen, however, failed to reach the strange landmark he craved: 159. He was out for 158 for the third time in his 20 Tests. Since he was run out, going for a twitchy single trying to get off his own personal version of 99 or Nelson, we may assume this was no coincidence.

The runs kept coming afterwards, not as fast as England wanted, but quickly enough for Flintoff to declare once the total had hit 550. Some thought at the time he should have batted on longer; Australia lost here with 556 only three years earlier. As it was, England soon found out what Australia had learned the hard way: it was no fun bowling on this. But they did make inroads with the new ball, and worried an unusually scratchy Ponting, who flirted with the exit several times. The most notable was on 35: he hooked Hoggard to the deep square boundary where Giles, in from the rope, misjudged the trajectory, and (some said) dropped the Ashes.

Ponting left scratchiness far behind but settled for a mere 142, his tenth hundred in the last 13 Tests, and a stand with Hussey of 192. Hussey hustled impressively but narrowly missed his hundred; Clarke, only playing because Watson was injured, asserted squatter's rights and made his. Gilchrist returned to form, and there was 43 from Warne – important in lots of ways, not least in helping the England coach Duncan Fletcher justify retaining Giles as a decent No. 8. Hoggard finished with his third seven-for in

Test cricket, a remarkable performance, bearing in mind that Warne (the 13th wicket of the match on the stroke of fourth-day tea) was arguably the first batsman who had not been dismissed by either the new ball or his own impetuosity.

Australia were just 38 behind, and only the TV commentators – paid to make the cricket sound interesting – and the English gloompot Geoff Boycott even tried to pretend there was any prospect of anything happening on the final day. Still, 20,000 turned up, but the weather was warmer now, and the Adelaide Oval an agreeably summery place to sit. They got their money's worth.

From the start, England's cricket seemed suddenly tentative. After Strauss was given out (even the appeal sounded only threequarter-hearted), the doubts turned into blind panic. Warne was turning the ball, but mainly out of the footmarks. And Lee was getting reverse swing. A few good hits, though, would have made England safe. They hit three fours in four hours. Bell dithered disastrously over a single; Pietersen swept Warne and was bowled round his legs (the ball hit the outside of off stump). Mastery, eh? Then Flintoff swished aimlessly. Collingwood stood firm but was completely constricted and, though the tail did better than the body, England were gone by 3.42.

The gates were thrown open, and spectators began to arrive as they used to do when they heard Bradman was batting. Instead, it was his successors, Ponting and Hussey. There was a wobble when Ponting and Martyn went in quick succession; and Flintoff, leading the charge on his damaged ankle, nearly bowled what would have been the first maiden of the innings. But a wild Pietersen throw turned a last-ball three into a seven, and then for England there was only deflation.

Afterwards, the ageing Australian players galloped and danced with delight round the field before retreating into the evening shadows. Summed up the series, really.

Toss: England. **England 551-6 dec.** (I. R. Bell 60, P. D. Collingwood 206, K. P. Pietersen 158)
and 129 (S. K. Warne 4-49); **Australia 513** (R. T. Ponting 142, M. E. K. Hussey 91, M. J. Clarke 124,
A. C. Gilchrist 64, M. J. Hoggard 7-109) **and 168-4** (M. E. K. Hussey 61*).

Notes by the Editor Matthew Engel, 2007

On the day after England's disastrous defeat at Adelaide, the Ashes were resting in a glass case inside a darkened room at the South Australian Museum, just across from the collection of stuffed llamas and monkeys. A very steady stream of visitors came by to see the urn, which was supervised by a rather jolly security guard called Marie.

How do people react? "They mostly say 'Isn't it small?'" she replied. "Or they ask 'Is it the real one?' Or sometimes 'All this fighting over something so little!'" Marie's point was proved instantly. A smart-suited businessman, in jacket and tie despite the midsummer heat, strode towards the display. He stared for a few moments. "Is that it?" he asked incredulously.

The previous day's cricket had effectively ensured that the Ashes would, in the mythology of the game, return to Australia. But, in physical fact, the urn would shortly go in the other direction again. Mad, of course. But cricket is a perverse game, with moments of madness. And the previous day the nearest England had got to the Ashes was the fact that they batted like stuffed monkeys.

The notional Ashes usually reside in Australia. By 2009, England's next opportunity, it will be three-quarters of a century since Bill Woodfull took repossession after England's rather ignoble victory in the Bodyline series. In all that time England will have been holders for barely 20 years.

Yet the actual urn has only been allowed to visit Australia twice. Inevitably, this visit gave new life to the question: "Why?" It was unfortunate, however, that it required the intervention of the tycoon and self-publicist Sir Richard Branson to bring the argument to public attention. Branson did not help on an intellectual level, since he had no idea what he was talking about, and regularly referred to the urn's owners, MCC, as MMC.

But he did force MCC to address it. Why shouldn't the Ashes stay in the country that holds them? The traditional argument – that the urn is far too precious to withstand the travel involved – has been destroyed by its tour this winter. It made eight separate flights, and rather more car journeys. Had it been physically moved on every occasion it supposedly changed hands, it would only have made ten flights in the 75 years. So that's clearly nonsense. The second argument, advanced by an MCC spokeswoman after Branson had blathered, is "it's not a sporting trophy, it's a museum artefact". She will have to do better than that: it's obviously both – or why would anyone care? No sane person would suggest that the real urn should be presented and then booted round the winners' dressing-room. It is tiny. It is fragile. But museums lend their prize possessions to other museums all the time.

There is no need to dispute MCC's ultimate ownership or its right – indeed duty – to oversee the urn's safe keeping. Australia should be told that if they construct a suitable display in one city (no messing about between Sydney and Melbourne), then the Ashes would be loaned to them whenever appropriate.

This is only fair. It would also add yet another layer of magnificence to this already sumptuous rivalry by bringing in the potent concept of "the empty plinth" for the losing country. The case for this was first argued here a dozen years ago. It's an idea whose time will come.

Third Test

Gideon Haigh

At Perth, December 14, 15, 16, 17, 18, 2006. Australia won by 206 runs.

After doing without the Ashes for only three Tests and 462 days – the briefest custody in history – Australia regained them at 2.13 on December 18, when Warne bowled Panesar to secure an unbeatable 3–0 lead in the series. As at Adelaide, England had had their chances; as at Adelaide, they squandered them.

England were at their best on the first day when, having finally included Panesar, they found a way through Australia's top half without, for once, being inconvenienced by the bottom half. Harmison, aided by bounce and breeze, trapped an uneasy Ponting, and it was 69 for three at lunch when Langer played inside Panesar's seventh ball. Once again, England could not budge Hussey, who remained insuperable after four hours. But Harmison and Panesar made good progress in the afternoon against some reckless strokes, not least from Symonds, recalled after Martyn's sudden retirement; he top-edged Panesar soon after hitting him for two straight sixes. Panesar was only the fourth spinner to take a five-for in a Perth Test, a reward for bounce in more than one sense, and he belied his unathletic reputation with bounding celebrations of each dismissal.

The only batsman who could consider himself unfortunate was McGrath, given out caught by umpire Koertzen when the ball struck his shoulder. Obviously irked, McGrath began Australia's retaliation by tempting Cook into another indiscreet drive, while Lee had Bell caught behind and the impressive Clark tormented Collingwood before the close. Seemingly racked by the memory of Adelaide, a succession of English batsmen tilted at the bowling before they had the measure of the conditions. Koertzen claimed another victim, Strauss, giving him out caught behind when he missed an attempt to repeat a cover-driven four. Otherwise, the strokes were as impetuous as Australia's, and more inept.

Flintoff, having skipped the tour match against Western Australia, looked not only as though he had never batted at the WACA before, but almost as though he had never batted, floundering against Symonds's auxiliary medium-pace. Jones, after 51 innings before getting a Test duck (an England record), completed the first of a brace with a tame prod to gully.

After an anxious start, Pietersen opened out attractively: tall enough to cope with the bounce, strong enough to manhandle such loose deliveries as he received. However, he overestimated the need to attack once the tail joined him and misread the risks of hitting into the Fremantle Doctor; Symonds accepted a catch at deep mid-off from a hit of greater height than length. Harmison and Panesar then showed up the earlier batsmen by adding 40 in nine overs for the last wicket, without the semblance of risk. No better stroke was seen in the innings than Panesar's on-driven boundary off Clark.

When Langer was bowled through the gate by the first ball of Australia's second innings, an inswinger from Hoggard, 21 wickets had fallen in 812 deliveries – a rate of one every six and a half overs, hinting at some good bowling and profligate batting. Ponting and Hayden put a stop to this, exploiting Flintoff's lacklustre captaincy and some slovenly English outcricket to build on their team's modest lead. Australia were 148 to the good with nine second-innings wickets in reserve at stumps and, even though Ponting fell early the following morning, these were pivotal runs.

The third day was a jumbo pack of incident, featuring 427 runs and five wickets in temperatures of more than 40°C. Four of the wickets, but 408 of the runs, were Australian, including Hussey's first Ashes hundred, Clarke's second and Gilchrist's third. Hayden might have had his fifth had he not lost patience in sight of lunch and tried to force the persevering Panesar off the back foot. The fierce heat taxed everyone, even Hussey's concentration lapsing at times, and his 103 was probably his least accomplished innings of the series: Koertzen rejected a confident appeal for a catch at silly point when he was 15, Jones on the run towards long leg failed to reach a top edge at 48, and Strauss got only his right wrist to a snick at 78.

Clarke kept Hussey company in a stand of 151 at almost five an over. Pretty soon, however, Clarke stood back and let Gilchrist bludgeon England towards submission. After sauntering to 50 in 40 balls, he plunged headlong to 100 in another 17: only Viv Richards had scored a faster Test century, taking 56 balls against England at St John's in 1985–86. Gilchrist's innings eventually consumed 59 balls, studded with 12 fours and four sixes. Recently out of sorts, he benefited from some English hospitality. He did not face Flintoff after he was 11, nor Hoggard until he was 74, or Harmison until 81. Able to ease in against Pietersen's part-time off-breaks and Mahmood's mediocre mediums, he was also invited to hit Panesar with a stiff breeze towards the mid-wicket boundary. Some of his strokes, nonetheless, were majestic. The first ball of Panesar's 34th over was nudged into the off; 26646 followed, all in the direction of the Gloucester Park trotting track. After the over, Gilchrist, then 73, solicited advice from his captain: should he continue attacking in order to expedite a declaration? "We read the answer as a yes, apparently it was a no," Gilchrist explained. "At our boot camp, communications skills were one of the topics. Obviously we didn't pass." He and Clarke had ransacked 162 in 20 overs, and 59 in the next five, before they heard from Ponting again.

Set an academic 557 to win, England lost Strauss to the fourth ball of the innings, padding up to Lee and given out again by Koertzen, who was apparently oblivious to the height. But Cook and Bell kept Australia waiting more than three hours into the fourth day for the next wicket, with a mixture of sound defence and judicious strokes. Bell's highest score against Australia was ended by the hard-working Warne; Cook prolonged his calm maiden Ashes hundred into the evening, finally succumbing to McGrath and the second new ball. Night-watchman Hoggard was yorked in the same over, and only some lusty blows by Flintoff and untroubled defence by Pietersen, undefeated after four hours, delayed the recovery of the Ashes. It came two balls after lunch when Panesar attempted a primitive sweep and gave Warne his 699th Test wicket.

Toss: Australia. **Australia 244** (M. E. K. Hussey 74*, S. J. Harmison 4-48, M. S. Panesar 5-92) **and 527-5 dec.** (M. L. Hayden 92, R. T. Ponting 75, M. E. K. Hussey 103, M. J. Clarke 135*, A. C. Gilchrist 102*); **England 215** (K. P. Pietersen 70) **and 350** (A. N. Cook 116, I. R. Bell 87, K. P. Pietersen 60*, A. Flintoff 51, S. K. Warne 4-115).

Fourth Test

Greg Baum

At Melbourne, December 26, 27, 28, 2006. Australia won by an innings and 99 runs.

Shane Warne stole his own show. From the moment he announced his retirement a few days beforehand, this Test was always going to be about Melbourne's farewell to its favourite cricketing son. Glenn McGrath's decision to quit, too, sharpened the sense of a grand occasion. Already, record crowds had been forecast to flock to the refurbished MCG. Now the match would surely be five festive days of farewell.

Two forces of nature intervened. One was rain over Christmas – much needed in a parched state, but not here, not now. It was a cold rain too, and trimmed the crowd figure on Boxing Day to a mere 89,155 (an Ashes record, but 1,645 below the 46-year-old record for any properly audited day's Test cricket). It also meant the pitch spent a sweaty Christmas under covers, leaving it underprepared. Mike Gatting, one of the innumerable guest stars invited to speak at innumerable functions during this series, described it as a "slow shitheap".

The other force was Warne himself. His five first-day wickets thrilled the crowd, but put an end to the match before it had properly begun. It took Australia just two more days to complete victory, forcing the authorities not only to refund $A2.3m (more than £900,000) worth of tickets for day four, but to wring their hands at the thought of the takings lost on day five.

England brought in Read for Jones, and so at last fielded the side critics felt should have begun the series. Flintoff won the toss, prompting roars from both sets of fans:

the English because they would bat first, the Australians because Warne would bowl on Boxing Day, needing one wicket to become the first to 700 in Tests. But gloomy weather necessitated floodlights, rain delayed the start by half an hour, and squalls interrupted twice, apparently making it a propitious day for seamers, rather than spinners – or heat-seeking English spectators.

McGrath began with a cultured but luckless 14-over spell, prolonged by two rain-breaks, as Strauss burrowed in. Australia betrayed their own cause with two dropped catches, two missed run-outs and later a botched stumping. Midway through the day, England were 101 for two and glimpsing light beyond the pylons. Warne's introduction had the effect of a detonator. Extra security appeared inside the fence. Soon, Collingwood fell to Lee, then Strauss, so watchful for three and a half hours that he managed just one four, suddenly hit over and around a conventional leg-break and was bowled. Warne had his milestone wicket, the crowd its keepsake moment. England's resistance thereafter was minimal. Pietersen, again left with the tail, hit out and got out, and they finished up with 159. Warne took five in an innings for the 37th time in Tests, again transfixing England in conditions that should have put him at their mercy.

Australia lost Langer and night-watchman Lee to consecutive balls from Flintoff that evening, and were fortunate not to lose Hayden, too: twice he looked to be lbw to all except struggling umpire Koertzen. Nonetheless, an hour into the next day, Australia were 84 for five and cut off at the pass. Not for the first time, England, with the high ground, found their rifles were all jammed.

Symonds, still on probation, took 21 balls to break his duck, but his boon companion Hayden was at the other end to temper rushes of blood. Separately, they composed high-class innings, together a pivotal partnership. England, so menacing in the morning, again retreated too quickly, conceding singles to Symonds when mental pressure might have ruined him, and setting no close fieldsmen for Panesar. The pitch settled, the outfield sped up. Emboldened, Hayden and Symonds were soon rushing along at five an over. Hayden reached his fifth century in his last six MCG Tests, with lofted drives for six and four from Panesar; Symonds reached his maiden Test hundred by driving a six from Collingwood, bowling for the first time in the series. Symonds let out a primordial scream and leapt into Hayden's arms, but was speedily back at work, facing up to his next ball before the crowd had stopped applauding. His innings had been a revelation, probably even to himself.

Both men were using bats sporting pink grips, signifying a sponsor's promise to donate funds for breast-cancer research; together, they raised $A4,400 as their stand grew to 279, effectively winning it for Australia, after the 15 preceding wickets had totalled only 243. Hayden fell just before stumps, tired but exultant, seven hours of hawkish vigilance at last taking their toll. The evening was taken up by a farcically grave English investigation into how their bowling plans had found their way into the media, intimating that MCG security had not been all it should. Hoggard kept a sense of proportion, and humour, which was a good move because outsiders wondered whether England had any plans at all.

Australia were out summarily next morning for 419, with six catches for the impressive Read, though not before Warne had seized on some misguided short bowling from Mahmood to slather his way to 40 not out. As it transpired, only one Englishman beat that cameo – Strauss, in the first innings.

Mentally crushed, England collapsed so rapidly that for a moment it seemed Warne would not get a spell on his day of valediction. Once Pietersen, promoted to No. 4, had been removed by a surgically precise offcutter from Clark, only formalities remained. Lee sustained his improvement in this series by bowling Australia to victory, leaving Warne two tailenders as a bonus, including Mahmood from a rare flipper.

Warne had most enjoyed his cricket when Australia were in crisis and it was all up to him: in this match, England gave him no such challenge. The end came in an almost indecent rush. The last wicket fell at 5.44, and the news was scheduled for six o'clock. Warne waved, bowed deeply and rode from the ground on the unsteady shoulders of Hayden and Symonds, returned to receive a rather dubious match award, then was gone. The occasion called at least for a lap of honour, and the crowd had expected one. But TV schedules wait for no man.

Australia did not apologise for winning the match so quickly, nor at such an awkward time of day. Their idea of giving Warne and McGrath a decent sendoff was not to have gestures and ceremonies, but simply to win the series 5–0. But it did make Warne's exit from his Melbourne stage a flatter moment than had been envisaged. To Warne, the consummate cricketer, this was unimportant. But as a way for the instinctive showman to go, it was incongruous: a fading into the night.

Toss: England. **England 159** (A. J. Strauss 50, S. K. Warne 5-39) **and 161** (B. Lee 4-47); **Australia 419** (M. L. Hayden 153, A. Symonds 156, S. I. Mahmood 4-100).

Fifth Test

Matthew Engel

At Sydney, January 2, 3, 4, 5, 2007. Australia won by ten wickets.

After all the presentations were finally over, the Australian players were led by their three retiring heroes – Warne, McGrath and Langer – in an approximation of the traditional lap of honour. However, the exercise bore little relation to the theatrical farewell Steve Waugh had organised here precisely three years earlier. It was more of an amble of honour. The players promenaded around the boundary, several of them clutching a child with one hand and waving vaguely with the other. A stroll in the park, like the series itself.

The final Test fitted into the broad pattern of the entire 2006-07 Ashes. In a match curiously short of compelling individual achievements – no century, no four-fors, even – England were notionally competitive until just after lunch on the third day. Australia were then 325 for eight, only 34 ahead of England's 291. But yet again Australia's tailend batting had infinitely more conviction than England's bowling. And when the innings finally ended at 393, and the tailenders returned to the day job (for the last time in the case of Warne and McGrath), there was no contest, and no expectation of one. The whitewash was completed before lunch on the fourth day. England, lost in weary self-disgust, hardly distracted the Aussies from all their hugging.

Flintoff won the toss, which was one bit of luck. Against that, he was without his most reliable enforcer: Hoggard's side strain ended his sequence of 40 consecutive Tests, which meant an unexpected recall for Anderson. Batting first was not the overwhelmingly obvious decision, since there were showers around, which only cleared away for good on day three. The toss probably made little difference: the pitch was firm and fair throughout, offering a little encouragement to everyone without giving batsmen the

We'll never see their like again: four Aussie greats take their leave after the 2006–07 Ashes whitewash. Shane Warne, Glenn McGrath, Justin Langer and Adam Gilchrist.

suggestion of permanence. In any case, England came through the opening day in reasonable condition at 234 for four. Bell played one of his most mature innings yet, before being bowled by a classic McGrath nip-backer. He might have lasted longer had not McGrath just been gifted a retirement present from Pietersen, whose century stand with Bell ended with an impulsive down-the-pitch top-edged hook.

There was still Flintoff, who played his best innings of the series by far: there were glimpses of his old panache, and consistently good judgment. But his task was made impossible by the uselessness of England's late order: Nos 7–11 made four runs between them, and the last six wickets fell for 46 on the second morning. They could not even take advantage of three dropped catches by Langer.

"Thx Shane" and "Thx Glenn" had been painted, in text-message format, into the mobile-phone sponsor's logo on the outfield. With Langer making his announcement only on the eve of the match, "Thx Justin" had to be added hastily. And Langer, a man who uses the word "emotion" as often as Flintoff uses "fantastic", seemed to have a tear in his eye far more real than the mythical one credited with causing Don Bradman's final-innings duck. He was clearly more distracted than either Warne or McGrath. Could England exploit this? Could they heck! The three misses cost just ten runs.

Langer was able to bat competently enough. But England's weakened attack stuck to their task, with Harmison showing signs of potency on this bouncy wicket. They were helped by indifferent light, and a well-timed rain-break on the second evening. None of Australia's top six reached 50, not even Ponting, who had one of his run-out mishaps on 45 when Anderson scored a direct hit from mid-on.

If England reached 190 for five in this series, it was time for the groundstaff to start the roller. For Australia, it was just the beginning. Symonds rollicked along for a while, and Gilchrist and Warne were in blazing form: their fifty stand came up in 36 balls. It ended just after Anderson took the new ball, though the more relevant factor was umpire Bowden, who gave a caught-behind decision against Gilchrist bizarre enough for the crowd to boo the lone replay they were allowed.

Warne found another companion in Clark, and they put on a further 68 for the ninth wicket. The Warne magic is so pervasive that many spectators convinced themselves he would, at the very last attempt, reach the Test century that had so cruelly eluded him. It was a slash-and-burn innings that had pretty much everything, including some characteristically lippy exchanges with Collingwood. But there was no century: after Clark went, Warne had insufficient trust in McGrath, and was stumped for 71, made in 65 balls.

England, 102 behind, found trouble right away. Cook went quickly and, two balls later, Lee felled Strauss with a 93mph bouncer that hit him on the base of the helmet. He resumed groggily, but not for long enough. England were soon 98 for four. They inched into the lead shortly before the third-day close. Then, to a thunderous cheer, Warne returned to the attack. He had bowled an over before tea, possibly the worst of his life, including three full tosses which Bell smacked through the on side for four. The first over of his second spell was notably stiff. In the next, Flintoff reached right forward to stun a leg-break. He missed, wearily failed to get his back foot behind the line, and thus became Warne's 708th and last Test victim.

Next morning, the ground was still 80% full. But the insanely confusing practice of varying the starting time to make up for interruptions meant that most of the crowd missed the one moment that might have mattered: Pietersen was caught behind off the third ball of the day.

Thirteen minutes before lunch, the cricket was over, Hayden declining to mess about and give Langer the honour of hitting the winning run. There were still two hours of presentations, celebrations, perambulations and congratulations before the crowd dispersed to let the Australians perform their private rituals in the dressing-room.

There were two significant moments in the field: Warne was first to come back to shake hands with his vanquished opponents; and Flintoff went over to the Barmy Army and salaamed them. In contrast to 2005, few will have felt moved to salaam him back.

Toss: England. **England 291** (I. R. Bell 71, A. Flintoff 89) **and 147**;
Australia 393 (A. C. Gilchrist 62, S. K. Warne 71) **and 46-0**.

Notes by the Editor
Matthew Engel, 2007

We can see it clearly now: Australia would have regained the Ashes even if England had played up to their 2005 standards. Anyone who has ever seen a western knows that when a group of old compadres get together for one last, vital mission, it cannot end in failure. And these compadres were way too good, way too committed. Even the most embittered England supporter should take pleasure in the fact that they have seen Ricky Ponting and Adam Gilchrist bat and, above all, seen Shane Warne bowl.

England's one chance was essentially negative: that the intensity of the schedule would favour the younger team. But though England were younger, they weren't fitter. The fact of losing was no disgrace: it is 36 years now since England last won an away series against a full-strength Australian side. The manner of it was disgraceful. England were at once worn out but underprepared; complacent yet over-apprehensive; inward-looking yet dysfunctional as a unit; closeted yet distracted.

There were many reasons. The captaincy was not especially significant. Doubtless Michael Vaughan would have done the job better than Andrew Flintoff. So might Andrew Strauss. Indeed, any one of us who sensed that England should have batted on into the third morning at Adelaide would have averted the whitewash.

When the Flintoff v Strauss conundrum first arose last summer, it seemed to have the makings of one of those great English captaincy arguments which always pit a public school/university chap from the Home Counties against a working-class north-erner: Sheppard v Hutton; Cowdrey v Close; Cowdrey v Illingworth; Brearley v Boycott. Yet the debate never really took wing (the public got more passionate about the wicket-keeping, and later the spin bowling). My own feeling is that if your best player really, really wants the captaincy, there has to be an excellent reason to deny him – which there wasn't. And simply, the captaincy makes less difference these days.

Everywhere now (perhaps less in Australia than elsewhere), the power rests with the coach, and England's coach had become very powerful indeed. Duncan Fletcher took over the job in 1999, in a climate of despair after a World Cup performance that was not so much disastrous as farcical. A sympathetic ECB chairman, Lord MacLaurin, ensured that he had resources – central contracts, specialist assistance, luxury travel – that his predecessors could only fantasise about. Above all, he had authority: on tour, it became unbridled to an extent previously matched only, very briefly, by Ray Illingworth; at home Fletcher saw off a rival as intimidating as Rod Marsh, who found his views on wicket-keeping disregarded; even the chairman of selectors, David Graveney, was kept at arm's length. And Fletcher also made certain the contracted players played as little cricket as possible whether under his direct control or not – traditional warm-up and practice matches, difficult enough given the current schedule, were disdained.

Against this background, Fletcher was able to create a hermetically sealed world in which he believed his players could thrive. This was the "England bubble". And the players did thrive. The first five years of this millennium represented English cricket's most sustained period of success since the 1950s. England played some vibrant, thrilling cricket. Fletcher's professionalism, his seeming omniscience and his sense of certainty played a major role in making this happen. It all culminated in the summer of 2005.

But there are problems living inside a bubble: eventually the oxygen runs out. And if this one began as the Eden Project, it had turned by this winter into something like the Big Brother house. Accurate information rarely seeped out; it also stopped seeping in. In the nature of things, players came and went from the bubble, but Fletcher was ever-present, and in the rare downtime allowed by this demanding job, he disappeared to his home in Cape Town. He isn't a man given to cocktail-party chitchat either (to put it mildly). So he lost touch. Even experts have to keep listening and learning;

Fletcher, on the evidence of the 2006-07 Ashes, just stopped. One senior county coach, a man who should be in constant touch with the England management, told me recently that Fletcher had not spoken to him in more than two years.

English supporters at the Adelaide Test talked non-stop even to strangers about the team selection. The chairman of selectors was there on a private visit, yet Graveney was not party to the decisions. If one enquired about this, there was some piffle about "protocol", as though this were the Japanese imperial palace rather than a cricket tour.

The team was evidently picked by Fletcher and his tyro captain. There may have been some input from the "tour committee" (Strauss, Paul Collingwood and Geraint Jones) though it is hard to imagine what: "Who do you think should keep wicket, Geraint?" Afterwards, Fletcher hinted that the decision to play Anderson and Giles and not Panesar had been based on the evidence of a practice match, the sort of game he had spent his reign demolishing and decrying, and that he had wanted Panesar to play, anyway. "I am not the only selector," he said, which was a cowardly comment.

To survive in sports team management long-term, flexibility is paramount. The trick is to sense developing flaws and take action, well before they become obvious to the outside world. Instead, Fletcher foolishly failed to consider the consequences of Giles's long-term injury or to grasp that Panesar was the one weapon he had with even the possibility of surprising the Australians. Instead, he initially spurned him, then allowed (or encouraged) Flintoff to set defensive fields when Panesar did play, sending a message to the enemy that he was no threat – the very reverse of the psychology Warne had applied so effectively against all-comers over the past 14 years.

Records

	Captains						
Season	England	Australia	T	E	A	D	
1876–77	James Lillywhite	D. W. Gregory	2	1	1	0	
1878–79	Lord Harris	D. W. Gregory	1	0	1	0	
1880	Lord Harris	W. L. Murdoch	1	1	0	0	
1881–82	A. Shaw	W. L. Murdoch	4	0	2	2	
1882	A. N. Hornby	W. L. Murdoch	1	0	1	0	

The Ashes

	Captains						
Season	England	Australia	T	E	A	D	Held by
1882–83	Hon. Ivo Bligh	W. L. Murdoch	4*	2	2	0	E
1884	Lord Harris[1]	W. L. Murdoch	3	1	0	2	E
1884–85	A. Shrewsbury	T. P. Horan[2]	5	3	2	0	E
1886	A. G. Steel	H. J. H. Scott	3	3	0	0	E
1886–87	A. Shrewsbury	P. S. McDonnell	2	2	0	0	E
1887–88	W. W. Read	P. S. McDonnell	1	1	0	0	E
1888	W. G. Grace[3]	P. S. McDonnell	3	2	1	0	E
1890†	W. G. Grace	W. L. Murdoch	2	2	0	0	E
1891–92	W. G. Grace	J. M. Blackham	3	1	2	0	A
1893	W. G. Grace[4]	J. M. Blackham	3	1	0	2	E
1894–95	A. E. Stoddart	G. Giffen[5]	5	3	2	0	E
1896	W. G. Grace	G. H. S. Trott	3	2	1	0	E
1897–98	A. E. Stoddart[6]	G. H. S. Trott	5	1	4	0	A
1899	A. C. MacLaren[7]	J. Darling	5	0	1	4	A
1901–02	A. C. MacLaren	J. Darling[8]	5	1	4	0	A
1902	A. C. MacLaren	J. Darling	5	1	2	2	A
1903–04	P. F. Warner	M. A. Noble	5	3	2	0	E
1905	Hon. F. S. Jackson	J. Darling	5	2	0	3	E
1907–08	A. O. Jones[9]	M. A. Noble	5	1	4	0	A
1909	A. C. MacLaren	M. A. Noble	5	1	2	2	A
1911–12	J. W. H. T. Douglas	C. Hill	5	4	1	0	E
1912	C. B. Fry	S. E. Gregory	3	1	0	2	E
1920–21	J. W. H. T. Douglas	W. W. Armstrong	5	0	5	0	A
1921	Hon. L. H. Tennyson[10]	W. W. Armstrong	5	0	3	2	A
1924–25	A. E. R. Gilligan	H. L. Collins	5	1	4	0	A
1926	A. W. Carr[11]	H. L. Collins[12]	5	1	0	4	E
1928–29	A. P. F. Chapman[13]	J. Ryder	5	4	1	0	E
1930	A. P. F. Chapman[14]	W. M. Woodfull	5	1	2	2	A
1932–33	D. R. Jardine	W. M. Woodfull	5	4	1	0	E
1934	R. E. S. Wyatt[15]	W. M. Woodfull	5	1	2	2	A
1936–37	G. O. B. Allen	D. G. Bradman	5	2	3	0	A
1938†	W. R. Hammond	D. G. Bradman	4	1	1	2	A
1946–47	W. R. Hammond[16]	D. G. Bradman	5	0	3	2	A
1948	N. W. D. Yardley	D. G. Bradman	5	0	4	1	A
1950–51	F. R. Brown	A. L. Hassett	5	1	4	0	A
1953	L. Hutton	A. L. Hassett	5	1	0	4	E
1954–55	L. Hutton	I. W. Johnson[17]	5	3	1	1	E
1956	P. B. H. May	I. W. Johnson	5	2	1	2	E
1958–59	P. B. H. May	R. Benaud	5	0	4	1	A
1961	P. B. H. May[18]	R. Benaud[19]	5	1	2	2	A
1962–63	E. R. Dexter	R. Benaud	5	1	1	3	A
1964	E. R. Dexter	R. B. Simpson	5	0	1	4	A
1965–66	M. J. K. Smith	R. B. Simpson[20]	5	1	1	3	A
1968	M. C. Cowdrey[21]	W. M. Lawry[22]	5	1	1	3	A
1970–71†	R. Illingworth	W. M. Lawry[23]	6	2	0	4	E
1972	R. Illingworth	I. M. Chappell	5	2	2	1	E

1974–75	M. H. Denness[24]	I. M. Chappell	6	1	4	1	A
1975	A. W. Greig[25]	I. M. Chappell	4	0	1	3	A
1976–77‡	A. W. Greig	G. S. Chappell	1	0	1	0	—
1977	J. M. Brearley	G. S. Chappell	5	3	0	2	E
1978–79	J. M. Brearley	G. N. Yallop	6	5	1	0	E
1979–80‡	J. M. Brearley	G. S. Chappell	3	0	3	0	—
1980‡	I. T. Botham	G. S. Chappell	1	0	0	1	—
1981	J. M. Brearley[26]	K. J. Hughes	6	3	1	2	E
1982–83	R. G. D. Willis	G. S. Chappell	5	1	2	2	A
1985	D. I. Gower	A. R. Border	6	3	1	2	E
1986–87	M. W. Gatting	A. R. Border	5	2	1	2	E
1987–88‡	M. W. Gatting	A. R. Border	1	0	0	1	—
1989	D. I. Gower	A. R. Border	6	0	4	2	A
1990–91	G. A. Gooch[27]	A. R. Border	5	0	3	2	A
1993	G. A. Gooch[28]	A. R. Border	6	1	4	1	A
1994–95	M. A. Atherton	M. A. Taylor	5	1	3	1	A
1997	M. A. Atherton	M. A. Taylor	6	2	3	1	A
1998–99	A. J. Stewart	M. A. Taylor	5	1	3	1	A
2001	N. Hussain[29]	S. R. Waugh[30]	5	1	4	0	A
2002–03	N. Hussain	S. R. Waugh	5	1	4	0	A
2005	M. P. Vaughan	R. T. Ponting	5	2	1	2	E
2006–07	A. Flintoff	R. T. Ponting	5	0	5	0	A
	In Australia		.165	54	85	26	
	In England		.151	43	46	62	
	Totals		.316	97	131	88	

* The Ashes were awarded in 1882–83 after a series of three matches which England won 2–1. A fourth match was played and this was won by Australia.
† The matches at Manchester in 1890 and 1938 and at Melbourne (Third Test) in 1970–71 were abandoned without a ball being bowled and are excluded.
‡ The Ashes were not at stake in these series.

Notes: The following deputised for the official touring captain or were appointed by the home authority for only a minor proportion of the series:

[1]A. N. Hornby (First). [2]W. L. Murdoch (First), H. H. Massie (Third), J. McC. Blackham (Fourth). [3]A. G. Steel (First). [4]A. E. Stoddart (First). [5]J. M. Blackham (First). [6]A. C. MacLaren (First, Second and Fifth). [7]W. G. Grace (First). [8]H. Trumble (Fourth and Fifth). [9]F. L. Fane (First, Second and Third). [10]J. W. H. T. Douglas (First and Second). [11]A. P. F. Chapman (Fifth). [12]W. Bardsley (Third and Fourth). [13]J. C. White (Fifth). [14]R. E. S. Wyatt (Fifth). [15]C. F. Walters (First). [16]N. W. D. Yardley (Fifth). [17]A. R. Morris (Second). [18]M. C. Cowdrey (First and Second). [19]R. N. Harvey (Second). [20]B. C. Booth (First and Third). [21]T. W. Graveney (Fourth). [22]B. N. Jarman (Fourth). [23]I. M. Chappell (Seventh). [24]J. H. Edrich (Fourth). [25]M. H. Denness (First). [26]I. T. Botham (First and Second). [27]A. J. Lamb (First). [28]M. A. Atherton (Fifth and Sixth). [29]M. A. Atherton (Second and Third). [30]A. C. Gilchrist (Fourth).

Highest innings totals

For England in England: 903–7 dec. at The Oval 1938
    in Australia: 636 at Sydney 1928–29

For Australia in England: 729–6 dec. at Lord's 1930
    in Australia: 659–8 dec. at Sydney 1946–47

Lowest innings totals

For England in England: 52 at The Oval 1948
    in Australia: 45 at Sydney 1886–87

For Australia in England: 36 at Birmingham 1902
    in Australia: 42 at Sydney 1887–88

Double hundreds

For England (11)

364	L. Hutton at The Oval	1938
287	R. E. Foster at Sydney	1903–04
256	K. F. Barrington at Manchester	1964
251	W. R. Hammond at Sydney	1928–29
240	W. R. Hammond at Lord's	1938
231*	W. R. Hammond at Sydney	1936–37

216*	E. Paynter at Nottingham	1938
215	D. I. Gower at Birmingham	1985
207	N. Hussain at Birmingham	1997
206	P. D. Collingwood at Adelaide	2006–07
200	W. R. Hammond at Melbourne	1928–29

For Australia (23)

334	D. G. Bradman at Leeds	1930
311	R. B. Simpson at Manchester	1964
307	R. M. Cowper at Melbourne	1965–66
304	D. G. Bradman at Leeds	1934
270	D. G. Bradman at Melbourne	1936–37
266	W. H. Ponsford at The Oval	1934
254	D. G. Bradman at Lord's	1930
250	J. L. Langer at Melbourne	2002–03
244	D. G. Bradman at The Oval	1934
234	S. G. Barnes at Sydney	1946–47
234	D. G. Bradman at Sydney	1946–47
232	D. G. Bradman at The Oval	1930

232	S. J. McCabe at Nottingham	1938
225	R. B. Simpson at Adelaide	1965–66
219	M. A. Taylor at Nottingham	1989
212	D. G. Bradman at Adelaide	1936–37
211	W. L. Murdoch at The Oval	1884
207	K. R. Stackpole at Brisbane	1970–71
206*	W. A. Brown at Lord's	1938
206	A. R. Morris at Adelaide	1950–51
201*	J. Ryder at Adelaide	1924–25
201	S. E. Gregory at Sydney	1894–95
200*	A. R. Border at Leeds	1993

Individual hundreds

For England (220)

12: J. B. Hobbs.

9: D. I. Gower, W. R. Hammond.

8: H. Sutcliffe.

7: G. Boycott, J. H. Edrich, M. Leyland.

5: K. F. Barrington, D. C. S. Compton, M. C. Cowdrey, L. Hutton, F. S. Jackson, A. C. MacLaren.

4: I. T. Botham, B. C. Broad, M. W. Gatting, G. A. Gooch, M. P. Vaughan.

3: M. A. Butcher, E. H. Hendren, P. B. H. May, D. W. Randall, A. C. Russell, A. Shrewsbury, G. P. Thorpe, J. T. Tyldesley, R. A. Woolmer.

2: C. J. Barnett, L. C. Braund, E. R. Dexter, B. L. D'Oliveira, W. J. Edrich, W. G. Grace, G. Gunn, T. W. Hayward, N. Hussain, A. P. E. Knott, B. W. Luckhurst, K. P. Pietersen, K. S. Ranjitsinhji, R. T. Robinson, Rev. D. S. Sheppard, R. A. Smith, A. G. Steel, A. E. Stoddart, A. J. Strauss, R. Subba Row, C. Washbrook, F. E. Woolley.

1: R. Abel, L. E. G. Ames, M. A. Atherton, R. W. Barber, W. Barnes, J. Briggs, J. T. Brown, A. P. F. Chapman, P. D. Collingwood, A. N. Cook, M. H. Denness, K. S. Duleepsinhji, K. W. R. Fletcher, A. Flintoff, R. E. Foster, C. B. Fry, T. W. Graveney, A. W. Greig, W. Gunn, J. Hardstaff, jun., J. W. Hearne, K. L. Hutchings, G. L. Jessop, A. J. Lamb, J. W. H. Makepeace, C. P. Mead, Nawab of Pataudi, sen., E. Paynter, M. R. Ramprakash, W. W. Read, W. Rhodes, C. J. Richards, P. E. Richardson, R. C. Russell, J. Sharp, R. T. Simpson, A. J. Stewart, G. Ulyett, A. Ward, W. Watson.

For Australia (276)

19: D. G. Bradman.

10: S. R. Waugh.

9: G. S. Chappell.

8: A. R. Border, A. R. Morris.

7: D. C. Boon, W. M. Lawry, R. T. Ponting, M. J. Slater.

6: R. N. Harvey, M. A. Taylor, V. T. Trumper, M. E. Waugh, W. M. Woodfull.

5: M. L. Hayden, J. L. Langer, C. G. Macartney, W. H. Ponsford.

4: W. W. Armstrong, P. J. Burge, I. M. Chappell, S. E. Gregory, A. L. Hassett, C. Hill, S. J. McCabe, K. D. Walters.

3: W. Bardsley, G. S. Blewett, W. A. Brown, H. L. Collins, J. Darling, A. C. Gilchrist, K. J. Hughes, D. M. Jones, P. S. McDonnell, K. R. Miller, K. R. Stackpole, G. M. Wood, G. N. Yallop.

2: S. G. Barnes, B. C. Booth, M. J. Clarke, R. A. Duff, R. Edwards, M. T. G. Elliott, J. H. Fingleton, H. Graham, I. A. Healy, F. A. Iredale, R. B. McCosker, C. C. McDonald, G. R. Marsh, D. R. Martyn, W. L. Murdoch, N. C. O'Neill, C. E. Pellew, I. R. Redpath, J. Ryder, R. B. Simpson.

1: C. L. Badcock, C. Bannerman, G. J. Bonnor, J. W. Burke, R. M. Cowper, J. Dyson, G. Giffen, J. M. Gregory, R. J. Hartigan, H. L. Hendry, A. M. J. Hilditch, T. P. Horan, M. E. K. Hussey, A. A. Jackson, C. Kelleway, A. F. Kippax, R. R. Lindwall, J. J. Lyons, C. L. McCool, C. E. McLeod, R. W. Marsh, G. R. J. Matthews, M. A. Noble, V. S. Ransford, A. J. Richardson, V. Y. Richardson, G. M. Ritchie, H. J. H. Scott, A. Symonds, J. M. Taylor, G. H. S. Trott, D. M. Wellham, K. C. Wessels.

Record partnerships for each wicket

For England

323 for 1st	J. B. Hobbs and W. Rhodes at Melbourne	1911–12
382 for 2nd†	L. Hutton and M. Leyland at The Oval	1938
262 for 3rd	W. R. Hammond and D. R. Jardine at Adelaide	1928–29
310 for 4th	P. D. Collingwood and K. P. Pietersen at Adelaide	2006–07
206 for 5th	E. Paynter and D. C. S. Compton at Nottingham	1938
215 for 6th }	L. Hutton and J. Hardstaff jun. at The Oval	1938
	G. Boycott and A. P. E. Knott at Nottingham	1977
143 for 7th	F. E. Woolley and J. Vine at Sydney	1911–12
124 for 8th	E. H. Hendren and H. Larwood at Brisbane	1928–29
151 for 9th	W. H. Scotton and W. W. Read at The Oval	1884
130 for 10th†	R. E. Foster and W. Rhodes at Sydney	1903–04

For Australia

329 for 1st	G. R. Marsh and M. A. Taylor at Nottingham	1989
451 for 2nd†	W. H. Ponsford and D. G. Bradman at The Oval	1934
276 for 3rd	D. G. Bradman and A. L. Hassett at Brisbane	1946–47
388 for 4th†	W. H. Ponsford and D. G. Bradman at Leeds	1934
405 for 5th†	S. G. Barnes and D. G. Bradman at Sydney	1946–47
346 for 6th†	J. H. Fingleton and D. G. Bradman at Melbourne	1936–37
165 for 7th	C. Hill and H. Trumble at Melbourne	1897–98
243 for 8th†	R. J. Hartigan and C. Hill at Adelaide	1907–08
154 for 9th†	S. E. Gregory and J. McC. Blackham at Sydney	1894–95
127 for 10th†	J. M. Taylor and A. A. Mailey at Sydney	1924–25

† *Record partnership against all countries.*

Most runs in a series

England in England	732 (average 81.33)	D. I. Gower	1985
England in Australia	905 (average 113.12)	W. R. Hammond	1928–29
Australia in England	974 (average 139.14)	D. G. Bradman . .	1930
Australia in Australia	810 (average 90.00)	D. G. Bradman . .	1936 37

Ten wickets or more in a match

For England (38)

13–163 (6–42, 7–121)	S. F. Barnes, Melbourne	1901–02
14–102 (7 28, 7 74)	W. Bates, Melbourne	1882–83
10–105 (5–46, 5–59)	A. V. Bedser, Melbourne	1950–51
14–99 (7–55, 7–44)	A. V. Bedser, Nottingham	1953
11–102 (6–44, 5–58)	C. Blythe, Birmingham	1909
11–176 (6–78, 5–98)	I. T. Botham, Perth	1979–80
10–253 (6–125, 4–128)	I. T. Botham, The Oval	1981
11–74 (5–29, 6–45)	J. Briggs, Lord's	1886
12–136 (6 49, 6 87)	J. Briggs, Adelaide	1891–92
10–148 (5–34, 5–114)	J. Briggs, The Oval	1893
10–215 (3–121, 7–94)	A. R. Caddick, Sydney	2002–03
10–104 (6–77, 4–27)†	R. M. Ellison, Birmingham	1985
10–179 (5–102, 5–77)†	K. Farnes, Nottingham	1934
10–60 (6–41, 4–19)	J. T. Hearne, The Oval	1896
11–113 (5–58, 6–55)	J. C. Laker, Leeds	1956
19–90 (9–37, 10–53)	J. C. Laker, Manchester	1956
10–124 (5–96, 5–28)	H. Larwood, Sydney	1932–33
11–76 (6–48, 5–28)	W. H. Lockwood, Manchester	1902
12–104 (7–36, 5–68)	G. A. Lohmann, The Oval	1886
10–87 (8–35, 2–52)	G. A. Lohmann, Sydney	1886–87
10–142 (8–58, 2–84)	G. A. Lohmann, Sydney	1891–92
12–102 (6–50, 6–52)†	F. Martin, The Oval	1890
11–68 (7–31, 4–37)	R. Peel, Manchester	1888
15–124 (7–56, 8–68)	W. Rhodes, Melbourne	1903–04
10–156 (5–49, 5–107)†	T. Richardson, Manchester	1893
11–173 (6–39, 5–134)	T. Richardson, Lord's	1896
13–244 (7–168, 6–76)	T. Richardson, Manchester	1896
10–204 (8–94, 2–110)	T. Richardson, Sydney	1897–98
11–228 (6–130, 5–98)†	M. W. Tate, Sydney	1924–25

11–88 (5–58, 6–30)	F. S. Trueman, Leeds		1961
11–93 (7–66, 4–27)	P. C. R. Tufnell, The Oval		1997
10–130 (4–45, 6–85)	F. H. Tyson, Sydney		1954–55
10–82 (4–37, 6–45)	D. L. Underwood, Leeds		1972
11–215 (7–113, 4–102)	D. L. Underwood, Adelaide		1974–75
15–104 (7–61, 8–43)	H. Verity, Lord's		1934
10–57 (6–41, 4–16)	W. Voce, Brisbane		1936–37
13–256 (5–130, 8–126)	J. C. White, Adelaide		1928–29
10–49 (5–29, 5–20)	F. E. Woolley, The Oval		1912

For Australia (43)

10–151 (5–107, 5–44)	T. M. Alderman, Leeds		1989
10–239 (4–129, 6–110)	L. O'B. Fleetwood-Smith, Adelaide		1936–37
10–160 (4–88, 6–72)	G. Giffen, Sydney		1891–92
11–82 (5–45, 6–37)†	C. V. Grimmett, Sydney		1924–25
10–201 (5–107, 5–94)	C. V. Grimmett, Nottingham		1930
10–122 (5–65, 5–57)	R. M. Hogg, Perth		1978–79
10–66 (5–30, 5–36)	R. M. Hogg, Melbourne		1978–79
12–175 (5–85, 7–90)†	H. V. Hordern, Sydney		1911–12
10–161 (5–95, 5–66)	H. V. Hordern, Sydney		1911–12
10–164 (7–88, 3–76)	E. Jones, Lord's		1899
11–134 (6–47, 5–87)	G. F. Lawson, Brisbane		1982–83
10–181 (5–58, 5–123)	D. K. Lillee, The Oval		1972
11–165 (6–26, 5–139)	D. K. Lillee, Melbourne		1976–77
11–138 (6–60, 5–78)	D. K. Lillee, Melbourne		1979–80
11–159 (7–89, 4–70)	D. K. Lillee, The Oval		1981
11–85 (7–58, 4–27)	C. G. Macartney, Leeds		1909
11–157 (8–97, 3–60)	C. J. McDermott, Perth		1990–91
12–107 (5–57, 7–50)	S. C. G. MacGill, Sydney		1998–99
10–302 (5–160, 5–142)	A. A. Mailey, Adelaide		1920–21
13–236 (4–115, 9–121)	A. A. Mailey, Melbourne		1920–21
16–137 (8–84, 8–53)†	R. A. L. Massie, Lord's		1972
10–152 (5–72, 5–80)	K. R. Miller, Lord's		1956
13–77 (7–17, 6–60)	M. A. Noble, Melbourne		1901–02
11–103 (5–51, 6–52)	M. A. Noble, Sheffield		1902
10–129 (5–63, 5–66)	W. J. O'Reilly, Melbourne		1932–33
11–129 (4–75, 7–54)	W. J. O'Reilly, Nottingham		1934
10–122 (5–66, 5–56)	W. J. O'Reilly, Leeds		1938
11–165 (7–68, 4–97)	G. E. Palmer, Sydney		1881–82
10–126 (7–65, 3–61)	G. E. Palmer, Melbourne		1882–83
13–148 (6–97, 7–51)	B. A. Reid, Melbourne		1990–91
13–110 (6–48, 7–62)	F. R. Spofforth, Melbourne		1878–79
14–90 (7–46, 7–44)	F. R. Spofforth, The Oval		1882
11–117 (4–73, 7–44)	F. R. Spofforth, Sydney		1882–83
10–144 (4–54, 6–90)	F. R. Spofforth, Sydney		1884–85
12–89 (6–59, 6–30)	H. Trumble, The Oval		1896
10–128 (4–75, 6–53)	H. Trumble, Manchester		1902
12–173 (8–65, 4–108)	H. Trumble, The Oval		1902
12–87 (5–44, 7–43)	C. T. B. Turner, Sydney		1887–88
10–63 (5–27, 5–36)	C. T. B. Turner, Lord's		1888
11–110 (3–39, 8–71)	S. K. Warne, Brisbane		1994–95
11–229 (7–165, 4–64)	S. K. Warne, The Oval		2001
10–162 (4–116, 6–46)	S. K. Warne, Birmingham		2005
12–246 (6–122, 6–124)	S. K. Warne, The Oval		2005

† *On first appearance in England–Australia Tests.*

Note: A. V. Bedser, J. Briggs, J. C. Laker, T. Richardson in 1896, R. M. Hogg, A. A. Mailey, H. Trumble and C. T. B. Turner took ten wickets or more in successive Tests. J. Briggs was omitted, however, from the England team for the first Test match in 1893.

Seven wickets or more in an innings

In addition to those listed above, the following have taken seven wickets or more in an innings:

For England

7–40	R. G. Barlow, Sydney	1882–83	7–40	J. A. Snow, Sydney	1970–71
7–44	R. G. Barlow, Manchester	1886	7–57	J. B. Statham, Melbourne	1958–59
7–60	S. F. Barnes, Sydney	1907–08	7–79	F. J. Titmus, Sydney	1962–63
8–107	B. J. T. Bosanquet, Nottingham	1905	7–27	F. H. Tyson, Melbourne	1954–55
8–81	L. C. Braund, Melbourne	1903–04	7–36	G. Ulyett, Lord's	1884
7–78	J. E. Emburey, Sydney	1986–87	7–50	D. L. Underwood, The Oval	1968
7–68	T. Emmett, Melbourne	1878–79	7–78	R. G. D. Willis, Lord's	1977
7–109	M. J. Hoggard, Adelaide	2006–07	8–43	R. G. D. Willis, Leeds	1981
7–71	W. H. Lockwood, The Oval	1899	7–105	D. V. P. Wright, Sydney	1946–47
7–17	W. Rhodes, Birmingham	1902			

For Australia

7–148 A. Cotter, The Oval	1905	7–63 R. R. Lindwall, Sydney ...1946–47
7–117 G. Giffen, Sydney	1884–85	8–141 C. J. McDermott, Manchester 1985
7–128 G. Giffen, The Oval	1893	8–38 G. D. McGrath, Lord's 1997
7–37 J. N. Gillespie, Leeds	1997	7–76 G. D. McGrath, The Oval 1997
7–69 J. M. Gregory, Melbourne	1920–21	7–76 G. D. McGrath, Leeds 2001
7–105 N. J. N. Hawke, Sydney	1965–66	7–153 G. D. McKenzie, Manchester 1964
7–25 G. R. Hazlitt, The Oval	1912	7–60 K. R. Miller, Brisbane 1946–47
7–92 P. M. Hornibrook, The Oval	1930	7–100 M. A. Noble, Sydney 1903–04
7–36 M. S. Kasprowicz, The Oval	1997	7–189 W. J. O'Reilly, Manchester 1934
7–55 T. K. Kendall, Melbourne	1876–77	8–43 A. E. Trott, Adelaide 1894–95
7–64 F. J. Laver, Nottingham	1905	7–28 H. Trumble, Melbourne 1903–04
8–31 F. J. Laver, Manchester	1909	8–143 M. H. N. Walker, Melbourne 1974–75
7–81 G. F. Lawson, Lord's	1981	

Most wickets in a series

England in England	46 (average 9.60)	J. C. Laker (5 Tests)	1956
England in Australia	38 (average 23.18)	M. W. Tate (5 Tests)	1924–25
Australia in England	42 (average 21.26)	T. M. Alderman (6 Tests)	1981
Australia in Australia	41 (average 12.85)	R. M. Hogg (6 Tests)	1978–79

Wicket-keeping – most dismissals

	M	Ct	St	Total
†R. W. Marsh (Australia)	42	141	7	148
I. A. Healy (Australia)	33	123	12	135
A. P. E. Knott (England)	34	97	8	105
A. C. Gilchrist (Australia)	20	89	7	96
†W. A. Oldfield (Australia)	38	59	31	90
A. A. Lilley (England)	32	65	19	84
A. J. Stewart (England)	26	76	2	78
A. T. W. Grout (Australia)	22	69	7	76
T. G. Evans (England)	31	64	12	76

† The number of catches by R. W. Marsh (141) and stumpings by W. A. Oldfield (31) are respective records in England–Australia Tests.

Note: Stewart held a further 6 catches in 7 matches when not keeping wicket.

Scorers of over 2,000 runs

	T	I	NO	R	HS	100s	Avge
D. G. Bradman (Australia)	37	63	7	5,028	334	19	89.78
J. B. Hobbs (England)	41	71	4	3,636	187	12	54.26
A. R. Border (Australia)	47	82	19	3,548	200*	8	56.31
D. I. Gower (England)	42	77	4	3,269	215	9	44.78
S. R. Waugh (Australia)	46	73	18	3,200	177*	10	58.18
G. Boycott (England)	38	71	9	2,945	191	7	47.50
W. R. Hammond (England)	33	58	3	2,852	251	9	51.85
H. Sutcliffe (England)	27	46	5	2,741	194	8	66.85
C. Hill (Australia)	41	76	1	2,660	188	4	35.46
J. H. Edrich (England)	32	57	3	2,644	175	7	48.96
G. A. Gooch (England)	42	79	0	2,632	196	4	33.31
G. S. Chappell (Australia)	35	65	8	2,619	144	9	45.94
M. A. Taylor (Australia)	33	61	2	2,496	219	6	42.30
M. C. Cowdrey (England)	43	75	4	2,433	113	5	34.26
L. Hutton (England)	27	49	6	2,428	364	5	56.46
R. N. Harvey (Australia)	37	68	5	2,416	167	6	38.34
V. T. Trumper (Australia)	40	74	5	2,263	185*	6	32.79
D. C. Boon (Australia)	31	57	8	2,237	184*	7	45.65
W. M. Lawry (Australia)	29	51	5	2,233	166	7	48.54
M. E. Waugh (Australia)	29	51	7	2,204	140	6	50.09
S. E. Gregory (Australia)	52	92	7	2,193	201	4	25.80
W. W. Armstrong (Australia)	42	71	9	2,172	158	4	35.03
I. M. Chappell (Australia)	30	56	4	2,138	192	4	41.11
K. F. Barrington (England)	23	39	6	2,111	256	5	63.96
A. R. Morris (Australia)	24	43	2	2,080	206	8	50.73

Bowlers with 100 wickets

	T	Balls	R	W	5W/m	10W/m	Avge
S. K. Warne (Australia)	36	10,757	4,535	195	11	4	23.25
D. K. Lillee (Australia)	29	8,516	3,507	167	11	4	21.00
G. D. McGrath (Australia)	30	7,280	3,286	157	10	0	20.92
I. T. Botham (England)	36	8,479	4,093	148	9	2	27.65
H. Trumble (Australia)	31	7,895	2,945	141	9	3	20.88
R. G. D. Willis (England)	35	7,294	3,346	128	7	0	26.14
M. A. Noble (Australia)	39	6,845	2,860	115	9	2	24.86
R. R. Lindwall (Australia)	29	6,728	2,559	114	6	0	22.44
W. Rhodes (England)	41	5,791	2,616	109	6	1	24.00
S. F. Barnes (England)	20	5,749	2,288	106	12	1	21.58
C. V. Grimmett (Australia)	22	9,224	3,439	106	11	2	32.44
D. L. Underwood (England)	29	8,000	2,770	105	4	2	26.38
A. V. Bedser (England)	21	7,065	2,859	104	7	2	27.49
G. Giffen (Australia)	31	6,457	2,791	103	7	1	27.09
W. J. O'Reilly (Australia)	19	7,864	2,587	102	8	3	25.36
C. T. B. Turner (Australia)	17	5,195	1,670	101	11	2	16.53
R. Peel (England)	20	5,216	1,715	101	5	1	16.98
T. M. Alderman (Australia)	17	4,717	2,117	100	11	1	21.17
J. R. Thomson (Australia)	21	4,951	2,418	100	5	0	24.18

Results on each ground

In England

	Matches	England wins	Australia wins	Drawn
The Oval	34	15	6	13
Manchester	28	7	7	14†
Lord's	33	5‡	14	14
Nottingham	20	4	7	9
Leeds.	23	7	8	8
Birmingham.	12	5	3	4
Sheffield	1	0	1	0

† Excludes two matches abandoned without a ball being bowled.
‡ England have won only once (1934) since 1896.

In Australia

	Matches	England wins	Australia wins	Drawn
Melbourne	53	19	27	7†
Sydney	53	21	25	7
Adelaide	29	8	16	5
Brisbane				
Exhibition Ground	1	1	0	0
Woolloongabba . . .	18	4	10	4
Perth	11	1	7	3

† Excludes one match abandoned without a ball being bowled.

Index